UNCERTAINTY MODELS FOR KNOWLEDGE-BASED SYSTEMS

A Unified Approach to the Measurement of Uncertainty

UNCERTAINTY MODELS FOR KNOWLEDGE-BASED SYSTEMS

A Unified Approach to the Measurement of Uncertainty

Irwin R. GOODMAN
Naval Ocean Systems Center
San Diego, California
U.S.A.

and

Hung T. NGUYEN
New Mexico State University
Las Cruces, New Mexico
U.S.A.

N·H
P C

1985

NORTH-HOLLAND – AMSTERDAM • NEW YORK • OXFORD

ISBN: 0 444 87796 7

Publishers:
ELSEVIER SCIENCE PUBLISHERS B.V.
P.O. Box 1991
1000 BZ Amsterdam
The Netherlands

Sole distributors for the U.S.A. and Canada:
ELSEVIER SCIENCE PUBLISHING COMPANY, INC.
52 Vanderbilt Avenue
New York, N.Y. 10017
U.S.A.

Library of Congress Cataloging-in-Publication Data

Goodman, Irwin R.
Uncertainty models for knowledge-based systems.

Bibliography: p.
Includes indexes.
1. Uncertainity (Information theory) 2. Expert systems. I. Nguyen, Hung T., 1944- . II. Title.
Q375.G66 1985 001.53'9 85-10275
ISBN 0-444-87796-7 (U.S.)

PRINTED IN THE NETHERLANDS

To my mother and to the memory of my father,

H. T. Nguyen

To Mankind,

I. R. Goodman

FOREWORD

One of the major problems facing the decision makers and designers of knowledge-based expert systems is to develop a meaningful model of uncertainty associated with complex and difficult-to-understand subjective and objective real-world phenomena. Stimulated by the research in artificial intelligence and related areas, the field of knowledge-based expert systems blossomed in the mid-1970's and has enjoyed more than a decade of vigorous growth. Contributions to the growth have come from many theories of uncertainty including Bayes' Statistics, Zadeh's Possibility Theory and Belief Functions, etc., and have embodied many disciplines of mathematics and engineering such as statistics, mathematical logic, measure theory, communication theory, operations research, systems theory, psychology, linguistics and computer science. Readers who sample the literature in the field of knowledge-based systems will soon appreciate the color and vigor that make up the discipline.

This diversity in model-making, though healthy in developing phases, has posed some serious problems before the students, researchers, as well as users of the models. No single volume on model-making embraces all of these approaches.

This Research Monograph authored by Irwin R. Goodman and Hung T. Nguyen is a first attempt to present a general framework for the manipulation and explanation of uncertainty in the design of knowledge-based expert systems. It provides mathematical foundations and gives extension and applications of various theories of uncertainty, including Bayes' Statistics, Zadeh's Possibility Theory and Belief Functions.

Also, this monograph addresses topics such as knowledge representation, inference rules, and combination of evidence. The general framework is based upon the theory of formal languages and semantic evaluations from different systems of mathematical logic. The underlying processes of reasoning lead to decision analyses in various contexts of knowledge-based system theory. A general discussion is presented on topics such as generalized set theory from a viewpoint of multi-valued logic and its connection with Category Theory. In presenting these topics, the authors do an impressive job in introducing some basic concepts which provide a rigorous foundation for uncertainty analysis. This monograph also gives a survey of the state-of-the-art of research in the areas of fuzzy sets and Zadeh's Possibility Theory.

The authors' exposition in this present monograph is an outgrowth of their research involvement in the field over the last decade. Naturally, this serves to present a unified approach to uncertainty models and its applications in areas such as medical diagnosis, fault analysis, geological prospecting and other disciplines of expert systems and decision analysis. The authors deserve to be complimented for presenting such a coherent account of such a diversified field. It is a seminal work. This is a first major contribution which gives both theory and applications of uncertainty models and poses many open research problems and unresolved issues which may be of great interest to our future researchers.

Madan M. Gupta
University of Saskatchewan
Saskatoon
October, 1984

PREFACE

This monograph is an attempt at presenting a unified treatment of uncertainty modeling which has been developed by many researchers over the past two decades. Uncertainty modeling has been widely used in systems analysis, as , e.g., in expert systems treating medical diagnoses, fault determinations and geological prospecting.

The general inferential problem can be described as follows: Consider some real-world system of interest such as the disease condition of a given patient, the possible areas where oil may be found, and the relationships of reported targets in a military scenario. By a system, in general, we mean a collection of possible real-world situations or "states". A process is a system where the collection of possible states may also depend on time or other indices. Associated with any system is a collection of attributes used to describe the system. These attributes could be, e.g., position, temperature, sea state, blood pressure, degree of comfort, degree of happiness or any other description, linguistic or numerical, that could be applied to a system. At a given time t , often it is not known which state or states of a system are present. This is called the uncertainty of the system at time t . This leads to the establishment of an experiment in order to gather data or evidence concerning which states of the system are present at time t and to what degree. The design of the experiment will of course depend on the type of system considered. Thus, a medical situation requires asking a patient questions resulting in some linguistic (or natural language) data, while the problem of investigating the safety level of a particular street corner typically involves a statistical experiment with numerical data. The outcomes of the experiment may be sorted according to possible attributes associated with the system. Each attribute has a domain of possible values (numerical or linguistic, etc., and possibly time dependent) some of which are observed as data. Thus, in the medical situation mentioned above, some attributes could be: Patient's degree of comfort which could include the possible domain of outcomes "feeling badly," "can't breathe," "feel tired and thirsty," and temperature, which could range from 90 to 100 degrees fahrenheit. On the other hand, for the safety level problem, typical attributes might include: The number of accidents at that corner over a three year period, with domain being integer-valued and the traffic flow rate described by the number of vehicles passing the area per unit time.

Two types of uncertainties arise: The first involves only uncertainties in the outcomes of the experiment, the second involves, in addition, uncertainties in the meaning of the data. Examples of the first situation occur in any well-defined random experiment such as tossing a coin, observing queues, and recording observed signals. Examples of the second type include experiments involving linguistic outcomes, where for information processing purposes, it is necessary to exercise greater care in the modeling of meaning representation.

Depending on the nature of uncertainties present in a system and the data, different types of uncertainty models are appropriate. An uncertainty model may consist of a class of chosen measures or distributions together with a logical system or calculus of operators on these measures. On the other hand, uncertainty models may be completely heuristic, reflecting, e.g., the common knowledge of a group of individuals or "experts". Ideally, uncertainty models can be both rigorous and heuristic in the sense that the mathematical aspect of the model contains all necessary expert knowledge appropriately encoded. Three well-known examples of uncertainty models are the probabilistic model, Zadeh's possibilistic model, and the inexact reasoning model in medicine using certainty factors, as developed by Shortliffe, Buchanan and others.

Recently, expert systems have come to the forefront in the modeling of problems. The most important problems in designing expert systems are those of knowledge representation and combination of evidence. These problems are of a semantic/mathematical nature due to the subjective character of natural language. Zadeh's possibilistic model (also called PRUF) and related generalizations are attempts to deal with these important issues. Once a class of uncertainty measures has been chosen for analyzing a system at hand, the reasoning process can be implemented within an appropriate calculus.

Our general approach is through the concept of a "dispersion" or generalized set membership function. By a dispersion, we mean a distribution in the general sense, not just the probabilistic interpretation, nor necessarily the possibilistic meaning, i.e., fuzzy set membership function or possibility distribution. A dispersion ϕ_A of an attribute A having domain $D(A)$ is usually defined as a mapping $\phi_A : X \to [0,1]$, where $X \supseteq D(A)$ is some (base) space representing the universe of all possible elements (or objects or values) of interest relative to A which may be in numerical, linguistic or other forms. Then each element $x \in X$ is assigned the value $\phi_A(x)$ representing the degree of truth or uncertainty associated with x with respect to possessing attribute A or being "in" A considered as a general (or fuzzy) subset of X.

One example of a dispersion is derived from probability theory where $(\Omega, \mathcal{A}, Pr)$ is a probability space. In this case, $X = \mathcal{A}$ (not Ω !), A is an attribute whose domain of values $D(A)$ consists of the subsets of Ω constituting the σ-algebra $\mathcal{A}$ such that $\phi_A = Pr$. Note that the sum of ϕ_A over $\mathcal{A}$ in general exceeds unity or is divergent. (Of course, the sum of ϕ_A restricted to any disjoint collection of sets from $\mathcal{A}$ will not exceed unity, compatible with the usual requirement of Pr being a probability measure.) Another example is furnished by the attribute "tall" with X representing the range of heights of men in feet. Then ϕ_A is non-decreasing.

Sometimes dispersions may represent more general concepts of distributions with values lying in a lattice or a Heyting algebra, or dispersions may be understood in the sense of Manes as used in his "fuzzy theories". The modeling of uncertainty will be carried out within a rigorous framework called a general logical system.

By a general logical system we usually mean: (i) a triple of logical operators $(\complement, \times, +)$ representing the connectives "not", "and", "or", and (ii) a dispersion mapping $\mathcal{F}$: Set $\to$ Set, where Set is a collection of sets of interest and for any X in Set, $\mathcal{F}(X)$ is a class of dispersions over X. In practice, due to the complexity of the problem considered, a hybrid logical system consisting of a collection of logical operators may be more appropriate. A logical system may or may not be truth-functional, i.e., the operators may or may not be in functional composition form with respect to dispersions. For example, a generalized set system (extending Zadeh's fuzzy set theory) consists of the triple of operators ϕ_{not} , ϕ_{and} , ϕ_{or} , with $\phi_{not} : [0,1] \to [0,1]$ a negation, $\phi_{\&}$ and $\phi_{or} : [0,1]^2 \to [0,1]$ being a t-norm and a t-conorm, respectively, with $\mathcal{F} : \text{Set} \to \text{Set}$, usually chosen so that Set is some subcollection of well-formed sets and for any set X , $\mathcal{F}(X) = \mathcal{F}(X)$, the class of all attributes A (or fuzzy subsets) of X . Each A may be identified with its membership function $\phi_A : X \to [0,1]$ and more generally $\mathcal{F}(X)$ may be identified with $[0,1]^X$. For this system, $\times$ and $\dagger$ are defined by:

$$\phi_{A\times B}(x,y) = \phi_{\&}(\phi_A(x),\ \phi_B(y))$$

$$\phi_{A\dagger B}(x,y) = \phi_{or}(\phi_A(x),\ \phi_B(y))$$

for all $A \in \mathcal{F}(X)$, $B \in \mathcal{F}(Y)$, $x \in X$, $y \in Y$ and X , Y arbitrary sets.

Thus, the above important system which extends classical two-valued logic is a truth-functional one. On the other hand, consider the following system:

Let $\text{Set} = \{\mathcal{B}_1\}$,

$$\mathcal{F}(\mathcal{B}_1) = \left\{A_{Pr} \;\middle|\; (\mathbb{R}, \mathcal{B}_1, Pr) \text{ is any probability space}\right\} \subseteq \mathcal{F}(\mathcal{B}_1) ,$$

where $\mathcal{B}_1$ is the Borel σ-algebra of $\mathbb{R}$ and where $\phi_{A_{Pr}} = Pr$. Let $\phi_{\&}$ be any infinite copula. (This condition is equivalent to forcing the generator of the canonical representation of $\phi_{\&}$ to be any fixed completely monotone function.) Let ϕ_{or} be a modular (or equivalently a valuation or Frankian) cocopula with respect to $\phi_{\&}$, i.e., $\phi_{or}(x,y) = x + y - \phi_{\&}(x,y)$. Now let $A_{Pr_1},\ldots,A_{Pr_n} \in \mathcal{F}(\mathcal{B}_1)$, $n \geq 2$, be arbitrary. Also, let $a \in \mathbb{R}$ be arbitrary and define $I_a = (-\infty,a) \in \mathcal{B}_1$ and denote $F_j(a) = Pr_j((I_a)), j = i,\ldots,n$.

For these $A_{Pr_1},\ldots,A_{Pr_n} \in \mathcal{F}(\mathcal{B}_1)$ and $a_1,\ldots,a_n \in \mathbb{R}$, by Sklar's theorem we have (see also sections 2.3.6 and 2.3.9):

$$F_{1,\ldots,n}(a_1,\ldots,a_n) \stackrel{d}{=} \phi_{\&}(F_1(a_1),\ldots,F_n(a_n))$$

$$= Pr_{1,\ldots,n}\left[\mathop{\times}_{i=1}^{n} I_{a_j}\right] = \phi_{\&}(Pr_1(I_{a_1}),\ldots,Pr_n(I_{a_n})) ,$$

which yields $F_{1,\ldots,n}$ a joint probability distribution function for marginals $F_1,\ldots,F_n$, determining uniquely joint probability measure $Pr_{1,\ldots,n}$ for probability space $(\mathbb{R}^n, \mathcal{B}^n, Pr_{1,\ldots,n})$. In particular, note that we may rewrite

$$\phi_{A_{Pr_{1,\ldots,n}}}(I_{a_1},\ldots,I_{a_n}) = F_{1,\ldots,n}(a_1,\ldots,a_n)$$
$$= \phi_{\&}(\phi_{A_{Pr_1}}(I_{a_1}),\ldots,\phi_{A_{Pr_n}}(I_{a_n}))$$

which is a truth-functional form for the system relative to all "points" $I_a \in \mathfrak{B}_1$, $j = 1,\ldots,n$. If $\phi_{\&}$ = prod (ordinary product), the above equation may be extended to arbitrary "points" $C_j \in \mathfrak{B}_1$, $j = 1,\ldots,n$, and thus the logical system remains truth-functional. However, in general, if $\phi_{\&} \neq$ prod, there are many $C_j \in \mathfrak{B}_1$, $j = 1,\ldots,n$, such that

$$\phi_{A_{Pr_{1,\ldots,n}}}(C_1,\ldots,C_n) \neq \phi_{\&}(\phi_{A_{Pr_1}}(C_1),\ldots,\phi_{A_{Pr_n}}(C_n)) ,$$

i.e.,

$$Pr_{1,\ldots,n}(C_1\times\ldots\times C_n) \neq \phi_{\&}(Pr_1(C_1),\ldots,Pr_n(C_n)) ,$$

because of the additivity constraint of probability measures. Indeed, for $n = 2$, let $C_2 = \complement C_1$, for $C_1 \in \mathfrak{B}_1$ such that

$\frac{1}{4} \neq Pr_{1,2}(C_1 \times C_1) = Pr_{1,2}(C_2 \times C_2) \leq \frac{1}{2}$,

$Pr_{1,2}(C_2 \times C_1) = Pr_{1,2}(C_1 \times C_2) = \frac{1}{2} - Pr_{1,2}(C_1 \times C_1)$.

Thus, $Pr_1(C_1) = Pr_2(C_1) = Pr_1(C_2) = Pr_2(C_2) = \frac{1}{2}$.

Yet, $Pr_{1,2}(C_1 \times C_2) = \frac{1}{2} - Pr_{1,2}(C_1 \times C_1) \neq Pr_{1,2}(C_1 \times C_1)$.

Thus, $Pr_{1,2}(C_1 \times C_2)$ is not a function of $Pr_1(C_1)$, $Pr_2(C_2)$, for all $C_1, C_2 \in \mathfrak{B}_1$. Again, by use of Sklar's theorem, it can be shown that all joint probability measures are obtainable through use of some copula.

Associated with any general logical system is a class of propositions many of which are of the form <x is in A> for any $x \in X$ and any attribute A with domain $\mathrm{dom}(A) \subseteq X$, any set of interest. In addition, a class of compound propositions may be constructed as strings of propositions employing the basic connectives. Moreover, both conditional and quantified propositions may be defined.

All of the above may be considered as semantic or truth evaluations of appropriate generalized set membership predicates within a formal language.

Models of uncertainty can be used, in turn, in designing rule-based systems, leading to decision procedures such as estimation, hypotheses testing or confidence region construction.

The book deals with mathematical foundations, applications and extensions of previous attempts in treating uncertainty for knowledge representation, relating these whenever possible to semantic evaluations of well-formed formulas in the form of set membership relations, within a formal language structure. These approaches include: Classical objective and subjective probability theory; Zadeh's concepts of fuzziness and possibility and its generalizations; Dempster and Shafer's upper and lower probabilities and belief, doubt and other uncertainty measures; and other schools of thought such as Gaines' uncertainty logic and Watanabe's system, as well as various compound systems and briefly, other approaches such as Shackle's surprise theory and Cohen's inductive probabilities. Applications investigated include natural language symbolizations, semantic content evaluations and some specific rule-based type systems, including the target association problem.

Although many researchers have contributed to various aspects of uncertainty modeling (Zadeh, Manes, Gaines, Watanabe, Fu among others), little attention has been paid to developing a unified treatment which directly relates probability concepts with other uncertainty ideas. One of our main tools in presenting a unified approach in this monograph is random set theory (as developed originally by Kendall and Matheron). We are concerned here with the application of random set theory to uncertainty modeling rather than further development of random set theory by itself (an extensive area in its own right where much research remains to be done.). However, the connections established between the two areas could be useful in random set theory proper, such as the systematic study of coverage functions.

The book is designed to be primarily a reference book which can be utilized by both applied mathematicians interested in the foundations and connections between modern approaches to modeling of imprecise information, as well as by systems engineers and others interested in studying expert systems.

Lastly, apropos to the title, this monograph emphasizes the development and analysis of uncertainty models to be used in knowledge-based systems and other appropriate structures. Relatively little is presented here concerning the general theory of knowledge-based systems, the area being treated more appropriately within Cognition and Artificial Intelligence proper. (Gregg [98'] and Barr and Feigenbaum [12'] present good introductions to the subject and in Chapters 8 and 9 and section 2.3.5 some aspects of knowledge-based systems are considered.)

ACKNOWLEDGEMENTS

The authors wish to express their appreciation to Professor M. M. Gupta, University of Saskatchewan, for encouraging us to write this book and to Professor L. A. Zadeh, University of California at Berkeley, whose original work in the area inspired us to further investigations.

We would like to thank the Department of Mathematical Sciences of New Mexico State University, Las Cruces, for providing typing assistance and secretarial help, and Drenda Woodson for her excellent typing of the manuscript.

The first author, in particular, would like to express acknowledgements to: Dr. Eugene Cooper, Dr. Alan Gordon, and Dr. John Silva of the Naval Ocean Systems Center Independent Research and Independent Exploratory Development (IR/IED) Program, for multiple-year support of the related PACT (Possibilistic Approach to Correlation and Tracking) Project; to Michael Mudurian of the IOS (Integrated Ocean Surveillance) Program at NOSC, for his support and useful comments in implementing the PACT algorithm; to John Schuster and Dr. Paul Girard, Naval Electronics Systems Command, for partial support in the research aspects of PACT; and to Dr. Christopher Bowman of VERAC Corporation for many valuable discussions and suggestions.

The second author would like to thank Professor L. A. Zadeh for his constant support and overall generosity in allowing him to participate in the Berkeley Expert Systems Seminar during the summers of 1976-1983.

I. R. Goodman and H. T. Nguyen

San Diego, Winter 1984.

PROLOGUE

Although this monograph is concerned with various types of multi-valued logical systems, as usual, all descriptions of those systems and their proofs, i.e., the meta-level of this book, are in terms of ordinary two-valued logic and set theory. This is consistent with the philosophy that on one hand describes both subjective and objective real-world phenomena (and related models) within a multiple-truth-valued context, yet, at the same time, in order to prevent a possible infinite regress of nested multi-truth evaluations, the meta-level of description must be classical. Perhaps someday (the authors are unaware of any work in this direction), serious textbooks will be published which might typically include: "Pr(Theorem A) = 0.3" or "Pr(Pr(Theorem A) > x) = q(x) , for most x in B" , with all "proofs" developed through multi-valued or multi-multi-valued logic. However, until that time arrives, we must be content with this apparent paradoxical situation. As researchers in probability theory, information theory, possibility theory and multi-valued logical systems in general, we all seem to be collectively stating, to paraphrase the well-known adage: "Don't do as I do, do as I say!"

TABLE OF CONTENTS

CHAPTER 1

INTRODUCTION

1.1 Motivation and basic framework of analysis.

Many problems of common concern involve the gathering and processing of both statistical and linguistic-based information. For example, the outcome of a jury trial or police investigation may well hinge upon both expert witness testimony, and, to a lesser degree, upon other sources. In deciding the culpability of Oswald in the assassination attempt upon General Walker, an expert ballistics analysis group indicated "could have come, and even perhaps a little stronger, to say that it probably came from this ... [gun]", while the FBI investigating team, as a matter of policy, avoiding the category of "probable" identification, refused to come to a conclusion [256]. Other corroborative evidence included a written note, also requiring an expert verification of authenticity, and verbal testimony of witnesses. Based upon this combination of evidence, the Warren Commission concluded that the suspect was guilty.

The process involved in the above situation could be analyzed as involving:

(1) Observed data.
This included markings on recovered bullets from the assassination attempt and laboratory-fired ones from plausible gun sources and handwriting from the note and previously established characteristics of the suspect's handwriting.

(2) Error distributions or trends of occurances.
This was indicated by the reliability of the data in representing what was observed. Factors that had to be accounted for, included: quality of the note paper, bullet distortions, and reliability of witnesses.

(3) Inference rules which reflect the legal expertise and experience of the Commission in relating the matching of evidence with conclusions concerning final culpability.

Another problem of importance involving combination of evidence occurs in tracking and "correlation", i.e., data association of targets: Two target histories of interest are being considered by a sensor operator for possible correlation. He receives information labelled as A, B, C :

A: Two dimensional position observations with associated updated error ellipses of some prescribed confidence level.

B: Reports concerning tentative classification of targets, such as Filipino type Q4 or Liechtensteinian type R7.9.

C: Visual sightings, including partial identifications, clues, hull lengths, mast shapes, etc.

Clearly, if information categories B and C are ignored, statistical hypotheses testing theory may be applied to A to establish a standard weighted metric (Mahalanobis distance, see, e.g., Rao [212], Chapter 8) for testing for correlation and determining the level of correlation (statistically) between the two track histories of interest. Rough gating procedures could then be added to see if B and C confirm or perhaps contradict the crucial geolocation criterion results for A . (See, e.g., Goodman, et al. [87], Bar-Shalom [12], Reid [213] and Bowman [23] for descriptions of tracking/correlation systems utilizing the related procedures.) But, how should gates or their softer distributional analogues be systematically established for B and C and integrated with the results for A ? Furthermore, can we use human in-field operator experience to relate in some way information matches, mismatches, and everything in between, occurring for categories B , C and A , as well, for correlation? This problem will be treated in detail in Chapter 9. Certain aspects of this problem have been previously addressed through the establishment of the PACT (Possibilistic Approach to Correlation and Tracking) algorithm (see [80], [82], [83], [86]). In the above example, the parameter of interest is the true correlation level. The above example motivates us to formulate the following scheme for dealing with parameter estimation problems. We need to:

(1) Categorize the incoming information into subcategories as A, B, C, ... These categories should be carefully chosen for non-redundancy, if possible. Further analysis of taxonomy should prove useful (for general procedures, see, e.g., Jardine and Sibson [124'] or for specialization to social or psychological context, see Nowakowska [195']).

(2) Establish a rigorous and systematic framework for quantifying information. This may be identified with the problem of determining the natural domains of attributes A, B, C, ... For example, in the above example, A's domain consists of all ordered pairs of 2 by 1 vectors and ellipses, while for B, perhaps simplified labels such as Q4, R7.9, S6, ... will do.

(3) Derive matching level tables or equivalently error "distributions" (in a sense possibly extending the classical statistical ones) that can occur between what is reported, observed or predicted, depending on the context, and what the true values are for each attribute category.

(4) Determine relative weights of importance between the various attribute categories. For example, how much will we tolerate a total mismatch with respect to B , when a relatively good match occurs relative to A ? This weighting problem, to a certain extent, is addressed implicitly through the establishment of inference rules as discussed below.

(5) Establish logical connections - based on either physical considerations or human operator experience - between the various information categories. The connections could be either in the form of inference/modus ponens rules or posterior distributions constraining or delineating the unknown parameter of interest. (See

Goodman [82], [86] for earlier approaches to parameter estimation when some of the informational input is in a linguistic format.)

More generally, we might ask: How do we model uncertainty and conclusions concerning this within a general framework?

Obviously, once we remove ourselves from "hard" statistical information, subjectivity and personal interpretive variation play important roles. The logical connections mentioned in item (5) above are usually given in the form of modus ponens inference rules or posterior distributions. In the latter case, at least for the classical statistical situation, Bayes' theorem is usually invoked with respect to more basic conditional data and prior distributions. For the former case, predicates restricting or describing the unknown parameter of interest and other parameters or values determined through various attribute categories are related through an "if ( ) then ( ) " structure. Schematically, we have the restrictions on unknown parameter Q, say:

$$\phi(Q|Z) \quad \text{for} \quad \text{"If } P(Z) \text{ then } V(Q)\text{"}.$$

The left hand side represents the posterior distribution (possibilistic or ordinary, see Zadeh [281] for clarification and explanation of possibilistic distributions) of Q given data Z, while the right hand side represents the inference rule "If $P(Z)$ is true, then $V(Q)$ must also hold," where $P(Z)$ is some predicate describing Z and $V(Q)$ is some predicate describing Q. For example, let $Z = (Z^{(i)}, Z^{(j)})$, with $Z^{(i)} = (Z_1^{(i)}, Z_2^{(i)})$ and $Z^{(j)} = (Z_1^{(j)}, Z_2^{(j)})$, the superscript i referring to data for track history i and j for track history j, and the subscript 1 referring to attribute category A and 2 referring to attribute B. Then, we may let, for example,

$P(Z)$ = " $Z_1^{(i)}$ and $Z_1^{(j)}$ very mildly (or to a low level) match and $Z_2^{(i)}$ and $Z_2^{(j)}$ strongly match".

$V(Q)$ = "correlation level Q is high at least".

The words "very mildly", "strongly", "high at least" could, if sufficient information were present, be replaced by more quantitative values such as α_1, α_2, α_3, where each α_k is some number between 0 and 1 indicating the intensity of matching level. (Again, see, e.g., [80] or Chapter 9 for clarification and elaboration of this idea.) It should be noted that many posterior distributions and/or inference rules may be present which restrict the possible values of Q given Z.

With the problem modeled according to the above mentioned scheme, the next basic question concerns the actual mathematization or translation of the problem into symbols which can be manipulated according to some established calculus. How do we translate the problem into a consistent rigorous framework? What means do we use to translate the atomic or fundamental information parts? How are compound informational parts to be exhibited through appropriate choice of operators? Which parts of the problem are more amenable to ordinary statistical/probabilistic analysis and modeling, and which parts to possibilistic modeling? Certainly, natural language descriptions appear more easily put into possibilistic structure than classical probabilistic ones. (See Dubois and Prade [51] for a survey.) On the other hand, even concepts that may appear statistically describable may also be modeled via a dispersion theory. For example, classification often entails rather overlapping possible values or classes, based on various contributing factors. Indeed, some classes may actually be subsets of others. In addition, it is possible that the exact definitions of the classes themselves are vague, and moreover, the relations between the classes may not be clear. For example, B could contain E and F , which are defined by knowledge of frequencies, ship size, shape, and number of emitting energy sources on-board. Overlaps between E and F may abound. Thus, it is not appropriate to consider ordinary probability distributions over B since the elementary events E and F , among others for example, are not distinct or disjoint. Rather, because of the overlapping flavor of B , either random sets of B or, more generally, certain equivalent classes of random subsets of B should be used. (Equivalence, as used here, is in the sense of having the same one point coverage function, see Chapter 5.)

Analysis of uncertainty in its most general form requires modeling and measuring imprecise concepts expressed by natural language. By natural language we mean that medium through which all human ideas are formed, including classical set theory and two-valued logic, as well as more ambiguous concepts, such as probability distributions representing measurements, and the still more ambiguous terms occurring in ordinary speech descriptions such as "tall", "happy", "within 3 units of", "close to", "almost all", "there exists", "approximately a subset of K to degree 0.6", "member of set G", "approximately a member of H to degree 0.4".

The difficulty in using natural language modeling as a direct tool for analysis is emphasized by the lack of organization of the field. Despite the heavy influence of pioneer linguists Sapir, Bloomfield, Jespersen, Boas, Whorf (establishing the famous Whorf-Sapir Hypothesis on language restricting the thoughts of native speakers), and the later work of formal linguists Hiz, Harris, and Chomsky, among others (see [35], [107]), what is evident is that a unified theory of linguistics entailing both semantics (meaning) and syntactics (operations or form) is needed which is suitable for complete mathematization. (One candidate approach is due to Zadeh [290] using fuzzy set theory. See also the work of Grenander for a different perspective, [98]).

The basic analysis of uncertainty modeling revolves around a series of general topics:

a) <u>Internal vs external modeling</u>.

In the internal approach, explicit analytic relations are sought connecting one approach of uncertainty to another. For example, Negoita and Ralescu, through their representation theorem [184] tied up very neatly classical fuzzy set operations with "flou" (equivalently, level) set operations. As another example of the internal approach, Goodman, Orlov, Nguyen, and Höhle among others (see [90], [197], [190], [116]) demonstrated direct connections between random sets and fuzzy sets and certain of their operations.

In the external approach, unifying generalizations are sought which reduce to various approaches to uncertainty modeling. Here the work of Hirota [111], Schefe [224] and Gaines [68] may be cited for developing structures that simultaneously generalize probability and fuzzy set systems.

The most far reaching work in this area is due to Manes [169] who derived a collection of axioms which not only generalize probability theory and Zadeh's (min-max) fuzzy set theory [276'], but a whole host of other systems, including topological neighborhood theory and credibility theory. (However, see Chapter 7 for details on Manes' work, where it is shown certain restrictions must be imposed on general logical systems to satisfy Manes' axioms.)

b) Prelinguistic concepts and ideas obtained through natural language. Cognition.

This topic concerns itself with the ability of natural language to express ideas accurately and succinctly as well as the formalizing mathematizing of natural language for dealing with uncertainties. Comments were made previously on the lack of progress in this extremely difficult area. Ironically, we can express in a few words, ideas such as love, happiness, temporal vague concepts, ambiguous descriptions - which are perfectly understandable to another reasonably educated speaker, as well as various combinations and operations on these ideas - yet we cannot express these concepts easily within a rigorous frame-work in terms of all the component primitive or atomic parts. On the other hand, "complicated" mathematical terminology such as is typically found in category theory or algebraic topology or deductive logic studies, really express concepts far simpler in nature than what language can express. (Of course, we cannot discount the ability of language to represent - albeit, how awkward - pure mathematical concepts.)

c) Concept of dispersions.

It is the firm conviction of both authors, as well as others, (see Goodman [89], [90]) that because mathematical analysis has shown that fuzziness is a weak form of randomness, i.e., a looser type of randomness without the constraints of a probability distribution entailed, dispersions and their operations (see Chapter 2) are natural tools to express linguistic concepts rather than probability distributions. Thus, the fundamental idea of a point partially belonging to a set with degree specified as some number between 0 and 1 may well be taken as an intuitive concept representing the possibility that the point is in the set, rather than the probability that it is in the set (the set is now considered as a random set). See Chapter 5 for the development of explicit relations between dispersion and random sets. Essentially, a dispersion is equivalent mathematically to the class of all random sets, which have in common the same one point coverage function, namely the dispersion itself.

d) Development of general logical systems and problem of ambiguities.

This topic is basic in developing a unified approach to uncertainty modeling. Too often in the past (e.g., Dubois and Prade [51]) myriad distinct logical systems have been proposed for use in modeling uncertainties, without paying attention to the inherent ambiguity of definitions present. More specifically, consider the problem of defining an appropriate concept for the intersection of two generalized sets. Originally, Zadeh proposed that minimum as an operation on the respective membership functions was the most appropriate. Later, Bellman and Giertz [14] were among the first to justify on a rigorous basis the use of minimum as an intersection operation. (See also the survey of Klement [140] on rigorous characterizations of various fuzzy set operations, including intersection, union and complementation.) However, the justification required certain constraints (such as mutual distributivity) which are not realistically required within a general setting. Other definitions for intersection resulted, including the use of product, also justified, with again appropriate restrictions (again see Dubois and Prade [51] for a survey). Clearly, minimum and product, while both extending ordinary intersection (relative to zero-one type membership functions) are considerably different. Zadeh's original fuzzy set system and its many generalizations are all truth-functional systems, i.e., evaluations of logical relations depend on functional compositions as does intersection, in particular. Other non-truth-functional definitions for intersection could be used such as that for probabilistic logic. (See Chapter 2 for further details.) Which one to choose or not? The answer to this problem may well lie in defining an entire class of dispersion operations - not just a single operation - which in the most natural way abstracts the ordinary concept of intersection. At least for truth-functional systems, such a class has been proposed. (See, e.g., Klement [140], Goodman [88]). This class is called the t-norms, a term borrowed from a branch of probability theory totally independent of dispersion theory and developed by Schweizer and Sklar [226] based on an earlier proposal of Menger. These operators are symmetric, associative, usually assumed also continuous, obey certain boundary conditions for compatibility with ordinary intersection, are nondecreasing in their arguments, and numerically are bounded above by (the largest t-norm) the minimum operation. (See again, Schweizer and Sklar [226]. See also, Haack [101] and Rescher [214] for listings of multi-valued logical systems where special cases of t-norm and t-conorm operators are used for "and" and "or". The associativity and symmetry conditions above may be dropped, with some loss of structural properties in modeling conjunction. (See sections 2.3.5, 2.3.6.)

Similarly, other classes of definitions may be developed for union (t-conorms), complement (negations, often in the form of involutions), and in turn, these general definitions, through multi-valued logic, may be used to develop general compound dispersion operations and relations, including implication, the quantification "for all", and "there exists," as well as various intermediate quantifications such as "most", "few", and general subset and arithmetic relationships. In addition, this leads to the general concept of conditional dispersions or equivalently conditional attributes (analoguous to conditional probability distributions), a form of Bayes' theorem and in turn, a theory of sampling based on dispersions (Goodman [86]). (See also sections 8.2, 2.6 and the appendix at the end of Chapter 10.)

Even with the general unifying approach as described, problems of ambiguity of definition still arise. For example, the quantified expression "for all x in X, if x has property A then x has property B" is definable by the relation as expressed in English by the repeated form

" $<(x_1 \in A) \Rightarrow B>$ & $<(x_2 \in A) \Rightarrow B>$ &,...,& $<(x_n \in A) \Rightarrow B>$ " where $<(x_j \in A) \Rightarrow B>$ means "if x_j is in A then x_j is in B " or equivalently "if x_j has property A then x_j has property B ". The x_j vary over the entire universe of discourse X and A and B need not represent ordinary sets but some general attributes corresponding to dispersions. On the other hand, the same concept could conceivably be expressed directly by a unary operation on a properly chosen conditional form or, alternatively on the generalized cardinality $\frac{1}{n} \sum_{j=1}^{n} \phi_{(A \Rightarrow B)}(x_j)$, where $n = \mathrm{Card}(X)$. This unary operation is a generalization of "for all", i.e., a monotonically increasing function over the unit interval which rises sharply towards one near domain value one and which otherwise is zero before these values. Similarly, monotonic operations can be used in dispersion theory to define "almost all", "at least most", etc. It is easy to see that in general, though again two concepts extend the ordinary meaning in zero-one logic set theory of "for all," they represent two different approaches to the universal quantifier. It should be noted that the two approaches to defining the universal quantifier depend upon the logical system chosen. Thus, in a truth-functional context, the choices of t-norm or copulas representing conjunction, complement operators representing negation, and t-conorms and co-copulas representing disjunction all play a key role. Which ones to choose? Also, there is the fundamental problem in modeling dispersions corresponding to the original linguistic concept. What individual variation of response should be allowed? How specific should the universe of discourse be? For example, when considering the attribute "long", do we consider ships, cars or both? Is there some grand scale where "long" can be quantitatively established through a dispersion, other that the obvious fact that it is some monotone increasing dispersion? This problem is analogous to that of modeling an appropriate probability distribution: Parameterize the allowable family of dispersions and then choose the most appropriate value or values of the parameter (and hence, corresponding dispersion from the family through some estimation technique based on empirically obtained evidence). (See Lakoff [150], Hersh and Caramazza [109], Zimmermann [291], e.g., for various approaches to the modeling of such functions.) Finally, the functional extension problem should be mentioned, where ordinary functions or relations between sets are extended to (still ordinary) functions between generalized sets. Even if this ambiguity is resolved other problems arise in designing how dispersions should be logically combined. More specifically, in classical logic, any multiple-argument (with zero-one values) Boolean truth function f (polynomial) may be expressed as $f = g \circ (\phi_{not}, \phi_{and}, \phi_{or})$ where $\phi_{not}, \phi_{and}, \phi_{or}$ are the classical Boolean functions (by the completeness property of the above operations - see, e.g., Enderton [54]). Then f can be extended to have a domain and range where $\{0,1\}$ is replaced by $\mathcal{F}[0,1]$. In turn, f may be used as Manes [169] and Gaines [68] proposed to combine dispersions - on the other hand, the general logical operators for negation, conjunction and disjunction as discussed earlier, combine dispersions differently. (See Chapter 2.3.6 for details.)

e) **Relationships between dispersions and their operations and probabilistic concepts.**

The details of these relationships will be spelled out in Chapters 5 and 6. Recalling the last comments of subsection c), given a dispersion, it may be expeditious to choose one particular random set one point coverage equivalent to it. Which one to choose? How much information loss occurs when one random set is chosen as opposed to the entire equivalence class? Could some mathematical criterion be used to weed out this random set - such as maximum entropy? What about semantic content? For example, consider the simple attribute "tall". Clearly, this is represented by a monotone increasing dispersion, i.e., the membership function of the attribute "tall" must be monotonically increasing. However, it can be shown that among the equivalent random sets for any such monotone increasing dispersion, two considerably different random sets can be constructed: The S_U-type , which is a random interval with right end point fixed at the maximal element in the universe of discourse, and the T-type , which has a highly disconnected sturcture, not an interval. Clearly, the first is more compatible with the concept of "tall" - if one point is covered randomly by such a random set representing "tall", shouldn't all points to the right, representing larger heights also be covered? Similarly, there may be a most natural choice of random set representation for a given attribute, when the corresponding dispersion is of some prescribed type, such as unimodal, continuous, discrete, or is in the form of a step function?

In a related vein, we may pose the question as how should semantic-based information, and thus dispersions, be combined with independently derived statistical information concerning a common unknown parameter vector? Finally, it is of importance to ascertain, through the relationships mentioned above, if random set theory could be used to derive properties for dispersions.

1.2 Background and survey.

A key problem currently faced in AI (Artificial Intelligence) and related systems is the determination of the most appropriate way to model and integrate natural language information with numerical and statistical information. There is no question that the solution to this problem must - at the very least - draw upon the fields of cognitive learning processes and psychometric theory, formal linguistics, including an integrated view of semantics and syntactics, probability and generalized forms of measure theory, and both classical and multivalued logic. It is our belief here that an encompassing theory of uncertainty can be established employing all of the above mentioned disciplines which may successfully treat this basic problem in AI.

Some investigators in the field of cognitive rationality have come to the conclusion that rational decision making by humans is really unattainable [128]. Others, such as Cohen [38], hold the belief that intuition, properly systematized, can serve as a basis for the choice of a normative theory of decision making. In turn, the latter depends critically upon which fundamental theory or theories of uncertainties and belief to accept. Polemics aside, techniques will have to be developed which in some reasonable sense, model uncertainties as faithfully as possible so that applications to decision making - such as the reconciliation of incoherent data as discussed by Brown and Lindley [25] - may be carried out on both the basic intuitive level and normative/rigorous level. The philosophy of approach here is optimistic: It is the opinion of the authors that Cohen's remarks are valid, despite the temptation to present analogues (well-worn) with Heisenberg's uncertainty principle in quantum mechanics.

Until relatively recent times, little systematic effort was expended in developing a rigorous scientific approach to the analysis of natural language. This does not belittle the extremely important contributions of Whorf and Sapir (Whorf-Sapir Hypothesis) on language influencing logic (see [163]), Bloomfield's ground-breaking work [20] nor Carnap's attempts at formalizing language influencing logic [26], [27]. Nevertheless, it was not until the 1950's and 1960's, beginning with Chomsky [34], [35], Harris [107] and others, that a rigorous approach was taken to the analysis of syntactic transforms and relations in natural language. At present, many diverse viewpoints (see, e.g., [47]) mark the field of formal linguistics (see [173] for surveys illustrating several conflicting viewpoints). In the area of semantics, similar diverse viewpoints have sprung up. (See, e.g., Lyons [163] and Leech [153] as well as earlier interesting empirical studies of Osgood, et al., [198] and the independent recent theories of Grenander [98].) In addition, statistical techniques have been used in analyzing various linguistic problems such as message rates, speech patterns and comparisons of literary styles [108]. Nevertheless, relatively little effort within the large body of present day formal linguistics has been devoted to analyzing natural language from a multi-valued logic viewpoint.

It is our opinion that more emphasis must be placed upon integrating semantics with syntactics within a general logic viewpoint.

Beginning in the 1920's with the Polish school of multi-valued logic (see Rescher [214] for an excellent survey of the field), other related logics were developed, including modal logic [245], [28], intuitionistic logic [110] and temporal logic [215], [173']. (See Haack [100], [101] for a survey of various systems.) These logical systems (especially all of the variants of Lukasciewicz Logic) were developed because of the apparent inability of classical logic to model degrees of truth and uncertainty. It was not until Zadeh's pioneering work in 1965 [276'], and apparently independently, Klaua's similar (but not as well known) development in 1965 [139], that comprehensive models of sets based upon multi-valued logic were established. Earlier work in this area include: Black's "consistency profiles" [19]; Shirai's [234], and independently, Skolem's set theory [239] both based upon three-valued logic; Borel's ideas [22] - also discussed in Godal and Goodman [75]; Sheppard's quantification of linguistic concepts [233]; Watanabe's continuous set membership function applied to quantum mechanics [268]; Gilmore's partial sets [74]; Chang's infinite-valued set theory [31]; and Zinov'ev's [292] and Körner's contributions [145]. (See also Maydole's treatise on many-valued logic as a basis for set theory [172].)

Since Zadeh's first work, he and others have developed extensive theories and applications of fuzzy sets based upon infinite-valued logic - especially, with truth values in the unit interval, or more generally within some lattice-like structure. Particular emphasis has been on the development of fuzzy logic and the interpretation of natural language [280], [283], [286] - [290]. In addition, other schools of thought have arisen concerning modeling of sets and uncertainties, including Dempster-Shafer's belief theory [46], [230], Cohen's inductive probability theory [37], Shackle's degree of surprise concept [222] as well as many variants on classical and subjective probability theory. (See, e.g., Lindley, Tversky and Brown [157] for second order probabilities and Fine [58] for an extensive survey of approaches to probability models.) Freeling [64] has recently made some comparisons of these schools. The Dempster-Shafer theory is motivated to a large degree by Dempster's original theorem [46], [230] establishing "upper" and "lower" probability uncertainty measures bounding the actual induced probability measure by a functional transform of a random variable - when the transform is known only up to coverage set values (resulting in a random set). Somewhat analogous is the work of Bertsekas and Rhodes [16] and Schweppe [225] in using set estimates in filtering problems. The uncertainty measures (yielding all four Choquet capacity forms [90]) consist of equality-inequality extensions of the Poincaré expansion of the probability of the union of a collection sets in terms of the alternating sum of the probabilities of the intersections of all subclasses of the collection, and the dual expansion. The Choquet capacity theorem [36] - as demonstrated by Nguyen [187] (see also Goodman [90]) shows that upper and lower probability - as well as other associated measures from the Dempster-Shafer theory - may all be represented through subset and superset coverage and incidence functions for uniquely determined random sets associated with these measures. Indeed, there is a relatively simple simultaneous bijective correspondence between the class of all possible random subsets (distinct, relative to distributional considerations) of a given space and each of the four classes of uncertainty measures [90], [116]. (See also Chapter 3.) A list of various uncertainty measures is presented in Dubois and Prade [51]. (See again Chapter 3.) See also the recent interesting arguments between Bayesian and Dempster-Shafer proponents over Shafer's approach [231] to the Lindley "paradox" and in a connected vein, see Lindley's claim [158] that subjective probability theory is the only appropriate approach to uncertainty modeling. (However, see our discussions on Lindley's claim in Chapter 10.)

Random set theory and its modifications, (such as through equivalence classes of random sets), could well provide a key to a meaningful analysis of the many approaches to the modeling of uncertainties by the establishment of rigorous relationships between the theory of perception, natural language descriptions, multivalued truth and set theory, and other disciplines. The intuitive basis for the use of random sets appears only slightly more complicated than that for ordinary random variables. Indeed, as some results in this text show, there is a natural relationship between random sets and random variable representations of dispersions (Chapter 5.2).

If dispersion theory and associated calculus are to become a useful approach to knowledge-based systems, not only must feasibility of implementation be shown (as the many applications in literature indicate - see, e.g., Dubois and Prade for a listing [51]), but also a sound theoretical foundation must be established. Moreover, it is imperative to determine what direct relationships, if any, are there between dispersion theory and existing well-established theories such as probability theory and set theory.

Four steps toward the above-mentioned goals will be discussed in the text. In summary:

1. General logical systems can be constructed which contain

classical probability logic. (See section 2.3.5.) On the other hand, any attribute may be represented by the class of all random subsets of the attribute's domain space which have a common one point coverage function coinciding with the dispersion for the attribute. A related result holds with respect to random variables. In addition, isomorphic-like relations (i.e., isomorphic relations modified for equivalence in the one point coverage sense) exist between large classes of dispersion operations and ordinary corresponding operations on random sets. In general, each ordinary set operation on random sets has many isomorphic-like dispersions extensions. (See Chapter 6.)

2. Dispersions may be derived as truth function realizations within the unit interval of truth values of compound predicates involving basically memberships of points in sets. These compound predicates - before evaluation - are in the main, motivated by, and have the same forms as, those in classical two-valued logic. Alternatively, a topos (or topos-like) structure (Johnstone [127], Fourman and Scott [59]) encompassing dispersion theory can be established so that all classical concepts can be put into a formal language which is realizable through that structure and may be interpreted as generalizations of the classical concepts (Eytan [56], [57], Ponasse [204]). (See section 2.4.)

3. Natural language expressions may be symbolized, and subsequently analyzed, in an efficient manner by use of dispersion operations, often without the constraints posed by a probability formulation. Rather, more compatible with the often vague and non-numerical nature of language, an equivalence class of probabilistic models (more specifically, random sets) should be used, which in effect is the same as simply employing a dispersion description. A number of examples will be presented in section 2.6 showing how a variety of different sentence types may consequently be interpreted within a dispersion formulation. (See also the appendix in Chapter 10.)

4. By making use of the results presented in this monograph, a detailed application is given in Chapter 9, demonstrating how dispersion theory may be used as a vehicle in the symbolization and utilization of natural language information in conjunction with any probabilistic information present.

1.3 Organization of the monograph.

The book is composed of ten chapters. The bibliography of those works cited here is given at the end.

With respect to the mathematics involved, a standard knowledge of mathematical logic, measure theory, probability theory and mathematical statistics is required. In Chapter 2, some topos theory and algebraic logic background is necessary. Since the book is motivated and developed towards applications, familarity with systems concepts may also be useful.

Graduate students in applied mathematics, engineering science, and mathematical statistics should find no great difficulty in reading the treatise.

This chapter has presented some motivations for studying uncertainty models, as well as a framework of analysis, and a brief survey of the field. Chapter 2 deals with the concepts of natural and formal language, semantic evaluations, multiple-valued logic and set theory and general logical systems. General logical systems encompass both (i) truth-functional systems that extend Zadeh's and other concepts of fuzzy set theory and (ii) classical probability logic (a semi-truth functional system) and a natural extension (Lebesgue-Stieltjes Logic). Also in Chapter 2, examples of truth evaluation of natural language are shown. (Because of the number of topics treated, which are important for the development of the remaining portion of the text, Chapter 2 is of much greater length than the other chapters.) Chapter 3 treats useful classes of uncertainty and the concept of dispersions. Chapter 4 gives an introduction to the well-established (but relatively little known) theory of random sets needed for subsequent investigations. In Chapter 5, a systematic study of the connection between random sets and dispersions is carried out. Following this, Chapter 6 develops the isomorphic-like connections between general logical systems and random set models. Chapter 7 discusses some relevant theories of uncertainty, including the ideas of Manes, Watanabe and Gaines. Chapter 8 develops rules of inference based upon techniques of general logical systems investigated in preceeding chapters. These rules can be applied to the problems of knowledge representation, combination of evidence and decision making in knowledge-based systems. Chapter 9 is a detailed application of the techniques developed in this monograph to a specific problem, namely the target data association problem.

A summary of the chief results of the text is given in Chapter 10. This chapter also contains the discussion of research issues and future directions.

CHAPTER 2

SYMBOLIZATION AND EVALUATION OF LANGUAGE

2.1 Introduction

One of the most distinguishing features of mankind with respect to other life forms is the ability to develop and formalize abstract concepts and ideas (the recent chimpanzee-ape language controversy notwithstanding - see [68']). Natural language is the initial vehicle through which these ideas and concepts are expressed. The most complex mathematical expressions are meaningless unless they represent concepts at least theoretically expressable in natural language. Thus in summary, it is not unreasonable to state that all ideas may be posed within a natural language format. In many cases, vagueness or ambiguity of descriptions are not easily captured by rigid mathematical expressions, but are more conveniently represented in natural language.

In many real-world problems, information arrives in the form of natural language expressions such as "if the skin color is pink, jaundice may be present" or "most blue birds have feathered wings". Thus, natural language as interpreted here is capable of both expressing exact concepts as well as ambiguous or vague ideas.

In order to make such problems more precise and to establish rigorous solutions, a formal language for meaning-representation must be established, wherein all natural language concepts are carried over into semiotic forms, i.e., strings of symbols, appropriately formed. The semantic evaluation of these strings reflects the degrees of uncertainty associated with concepts represented by the strings. Ideas which are "absolutely true" or certain are evaluated as T or unity. On the other hand, concepts such as "John is quite tall" or "an orange is big" may have less than unity truth values associated with them, if the relevant logic is not just restricted to $\{0,1\}$.

This chapter establishes a unified framework connecting natural language, formal language, and semantic evaluations of expressions.

The following diagram in Figure I illustrates roughly the flow of knowledge from conception to evaluation:

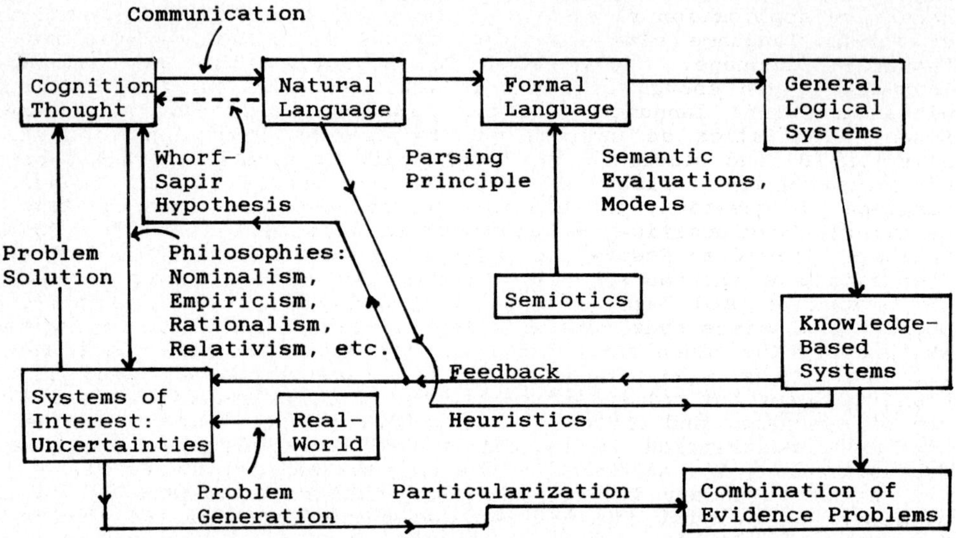

Figure I. Flow of knowledge from conception to evaluation.

2.2 Natural and formal languages

2.2.1 Preamble

As mentioned before, all thoughts of man are enunciated through natural language. Whether the particular language spoken by an individual restricts or otherwise channels his thoughts - as, e.g. color limitations of certain African tribes or expansion of subtlety as in German philosophy or Eskimo descriptions of snow conditions - is still a matter of controversy. (This goes back to the famous Whorf-Sapir hypothesis concerning natural languages influence upon thinking and the Berlin-Kay "universalistic" antithesis [271], [153].) These concepts include vague ideas such as "love", "hate", "much", "some", "above", as well as more arithmetic concepts "if two convex bodies in Hilbert space are disjoint, then a separating hyperplane may be found", " $\int_a^b \cos(x)\,dx = \sin(b) - \sin(a)$ ", etc. See Allerton [3] and Dingwall [47] for analytic surveys of natural languages. See Lenneberg [155] for a discussion of the biological basis of language. Leech [153] proposes that language can be roughly divided into three areas: pragmatics, syntactics and semantics.

The seminal paper of Lakoff [150'] on linguistics and natural logic is completely in accord with the spirit of the approach taken in this text: *to model how humans empirically perceive truth through natural language descriptions and associated reasoning*.

Formal language in its most general form can be described as a collection of (1) primitive symbols, (2) syntactic rules for combining symbols, and (3) compounds of strings of symbols produced by the recursive application of (2) to (1) and itself. An interpretation of formal language always exists, symbol by symbol, within some "natural" language. Conversely, it is assumed that any natural language, given enough time and patience, can be fully symbolized within a formal language setting. Indeed, the thrust of modern formal linguistics as carried out by Chomsky [35], Lyons [162], Allerton [3] and others is the development of formal language rules of syntax which reflect and explain the nature of the natural language in question, as opposed to the earlier structuralistic-behavioristic-classificatory approach to language. (See "On Noam Chomsky: "Critical Essays", pp. 2 - 32, by Searle [227] for further discussions of the two schools of thought as well as the entire book for summaries and implications of Chomsky's work.) Basically, Chomsky emphasises syntactic modeling via (1) phrase structure rules which carry the "deep structure" and determine therefore the semantic content and (2) transformational rules which act upon (1), changing forms but not semantic content, such as inversion of words, use of synonyms, and change of voice from active to passive. Even the above description is subject to many exceptions and changes. (See Dingwall [47], Allerton [3] for surveys and controversies.)

It is necessary to keep in mind that we are interested in a mathematically sound form of semantics rather than the "formal linguistic" approach as mentioned above. Thus, syntactic structures that will be developed will correspond approximately to formal linguistic phrase structure rules rather than to transformational rules.

Parsing principle

In applications we assume a mapping exists between any given natural language and its formal language representation.

For further details on the Parsing Principle and other related procedures interpreting natural language in terms of formal language, see section 2.6 and the appendix at the end of Chapter 10. For an excellent survey of cognitive processes and natural language see, e.g., Winograd [274']. See also Gregg [98'] for a compendium of papers on knowledge and cognition. For an extensive presentation of semiotics (the study of symbols used in language and codes), see Eco [53'].

2.2.2 Basic structure of a formal language

We present here the basic structure for a formal language. The metalanguage and metalogic of the following study is ordinary English within the two-valued classical predicate calculus setting. (See the remarks in the Introduction (Chapter 1).)

A many-sorted (possibly higher order) formal language $\mathcal{L}$ consists of a syntax part $\mathcal{L}_{syn}$, plus a possible additional theory $Th_K(\mathcal{L})$ and the results of that theory. In addition, $\mathcal{L}$ operates upon its alphabet or collection of symbols, symb($\mathcal{L}$), including parentheses ( ) , letters $\alpha, \beta, \gamma, \ldots$, a, b, c, ..., i, j, k, ..., braces { } , formal deduction $\vdash$, and specially designated symbols such as $\emptyset$, 1_a, Ω , $\forall$, etc. From now on, we will use Symb($\mathcal{L}$) , but not consider it as a formal entity. (Note, however, the cardinality of Symb($\mathcal{L}$) is needed, e.g., for the Lowenheim-Skolem property. See 2.3.3 (a) (xii).)

$\mathcal{L}_{syn}$ contains, firstly, a category of types of things, Core($\mathcal{L}$) . (See the appendices at the end of 2.4 for definitions and properties of categories and deduction categories.) The objects of category Core($\mathcal{L}$) are the actual types, including the subclass of sorts, consisting of Ob($\mathcal{L}$) , an index, referring formally to relevant universes of discourse, Ar($\mathcal{L}$) , an index, referring to arrows (generalizations of functions) between these universes of discourse, and an index Rel($\mathcal{L}$) , referring to relations upon the universes of discourse. The arrows of category Core($\mathcal{L}$) are the function symbols occurring between the types, each such symbol formally representing a function from one type to another. (Two given types may have an infinity of arrows between them.) The collection of all such arrows or function symbols for Core($\mathcal{L}$) contains several important subclasses, including: Cat($\mathcal{L}$) , the class of all function symbols representing category (and deduction category) theory concepts, such as arrow domain, codomain, composition, projection, identity, product, substitution, signature, used for sets, functions and relations (as later interpreted in the semantic evaluations in section 2.3); Foun($\mathcal{L}$) , the class of all function symbols representing set theory concepts, including membership, equality, class abstraction; Loc($\mathcal{L}$) , the class of all functional symbols representing logical connectors, including T , ⊥ , not , & , or , implication, etc.; and Quan($\mathcal{L}$) , the class of all function(al) symbols representing quantifications such as universal quantification and existential quantification, as well as including possibly various degrees of partial quantification ("much", "many", "about 3/4", etc.).

Secondly, $\mathcal{L}_{syn}$ contains a theory of syntax $Th_{syn}(\mathcal{L})$ consisting of axioms and rules described through sequents (or certain ordered pairs involving predicate symbols) which produce the class of deducts or theorems $De(Th(\mathcal{L}_{syn}))$, from which, in turn, one obtains $\tilde{V}ar(\mathcal{L})$.

$\tilde{V}ar(\mathcal{L})$ is a deduction category representing all basic variables for $\mathcal{L}$. The object part of $\tilde{V}ar(\mathcal{L})$, $Ob(\tilde{V}ar(\mathcal{L}))$ consists of the collection of all formal universes of discourse of interest, i, j, k, ...; the arrow part of $\tilde{V}ar(\mathcal{L})$, $Ar(\tilde{V}ar(\mathcal{L}))$, contains all arrows (or generalized functions) between the formal universes of discourse, $(f : i \to j)$, $(g : k \to j)$, $(h : j \times j \to k)$, $(f_1 : k \to i)$, including the subclass Wfv($\mathcal{L}$) of all projections here or individual variables such as $x^{(i)} = (proj_i(k \times i) : k \times i \to i)$, $y^{(k)} = (proj_k(k \times i \times j) : k \times i \times j \to k)$, etc., and the bigger subclass of all individual terms Wft($\mathcal{L}$) which is defined as the composition of all arrows of $\tilde{V}ar(\mathcal{L})$ with all elements (i.e., arrows) of Wfv($\mathcal{L}$) , where well-defined (by use of $Th_{syn}(\mathcal{L})$) , such as $f(x^{(i)}) \overset{d}{=} f \circ x^{(i)}$, $g(y^{(k)}) = g \circ y^{(k)}$, $h(f(x^{(i)}), g(y^{(k)})) = h \circ (\langle f \circ x^{(i)}, g \circ y^{(k)} \rangle)$, etc.

The relation part of $\tilde{V}ar(\mathcal{L})$, $Rel(\tilde{V}ar(\mathcal{L}))$ consists of all relation symbols (formally representing relations) upon the formal universes of interest, r_i, s_i, ..., $r_{j \times i}$, r_j, s_j, t_k, ... This includes the subclass $\mathrm{Wfat}(\mathcal{L})$, the atomic well-formed formulas, which is defined as the class resulting from the substitution operation (where well-defined) of individual terms into relation symbols such as $s_i[x^{(i)}]$, $r_{j\times i}[<f(x^{(i)}),\ f_1(y^{(k)})>]$, etc. In turn, $\mathrm{Wfat}(\mathcal{L})$ is included in a generally bigger class, $\mathrm{Wff}(\mathcal{L})$, of $\mathrm{Rel}(\tilde{\mathrm{V}}\mathrm{ar}(\mathcal{L}))$, the class of all well-defined formulas of $\mathcal{L}$, generated or spanned recursively, by applying $\mathrm{Loc}(\mathcal{L})$ and $\mathrm{Quan}(\mathcal{L})$ (where well-defined) to $\mathrm{Wfat}(\mathcal{L})$.

We define the class of all basic well-formed terms of $\mathcal{L}$ as $\mathrm{Wfter}(\mathcal{L}) \overset{d}{=} \mathrm{Ar}(\tilde{\mathrm{V}}\mathrm{ar}(\mathcal{L})) \cup \mathrm{Rel}(\tilde{\mathrm{V}}\mathrm{ar}(\mathcal{L}))$, which contains the class of all well-formed expressions of $\mathcal{L}$, $\mathrm{Wfex}(\mathcal{L}) \overset{d}{=} \mathrm{Wff}(\mathcal{L}) \cup \mathrm{Wft}(\mathcal{L})$.

Connected with $\mathrm{Wfex}(\mathcal{L})$ are the total, free, and bound individual variable maps which identify which individual variables occur in a given well-formed expression, which are bound or controlled by quantifiers, and which are free of control.

$\mathrm{Th}_K(\mathcal{L})$, analagous to $\mathrm{Th}_{syn}(\mathcal{L})$, consists of axioms and rules involving sequents, but in this case, the sequents are all of the form $(\Psi,\ \vdash_{\mathcal{L}}\ \theta)$, where $\Psi, \theta \in \mathrm{Wff}(\mathcal{L})$ and $\vdash_{\mathcal{L}}$ is the fixed predicate symbol representing formal or deductive implication and hence $(\Psi \vdash_{\mathcal{L}} \theta)$ may be interpreted as " Ψ deductively implies θ " , etc. The chief consequence of $\mathrm{Th}_K(\mathcal{L})$ is $\mathrm{De}(\mathrm{Th}_K(\mathcal{L}))$, the class of all sequents here obtained by (recursively) applying the rules to the axioms. Each such $(\Psi,\ \vdash_{\mathcal{L}}\ \theta) \in \mathrm{De}(\mathrm{Th}_K(\mathcal{L}))$ may be considered a theorem of $\mathrm{Th}_K(\mathcal{L})$ with hypothesis Ψ and conclusion θ . Depending on the choice of $\mathrm{Th}_K(\mathcal{L})$, $\mathrm{De}(\mathrm{Th}_K(\mathcal{L}))$ will reflect the various relationships between wff's relative to $\mathrm{FuncSymb}(\mathcal{L})$. The choice of $\mathrm{Th}_K(\mathcal{L})$ - as presented later in this part - usually emphasizes $\mathrm{Foun}(\mathcal{L})$, $\mathrm{Loc}(\mathcal{L})$, and $\mathrm{Quan}(\mathcal{L})$ - as opposed to $\mathrm{Th}_{syn_o}(\mathcal{L})$ which essentially refers only to $\mathrm{Cat}(\mathcal{L})$. Although, a specific theory will be chosen for $\mathrm{Th}_K(\mathcal{L})$ here, it is obvious that any other theory, say, $\mathrm{Th}_{K'}(\mathcal{L})$ could be appended in place of $\mathrm{Th}_K(\mathcal{L})$ and developed analogously. Indeed, it is in this sense that we define a formal language as used throughout the remainder of the text. Whenever $\mathrm{Th}_K(\mathcal{L})$ is actually used in $\mathcal{L}$, this will be so indicated (and called $\mathrm{Th}_K(\mathcal{L})$).

I. Basic syntax of $\mathcal{L}$

The basic syntax $\mathcal{L}_{syn}$ of $\mathcal{L}$ may be described as consisting of the core of $\mathcal{L}$, $\mathrm{Core}(\mathcal{L})$, the syntax theory $\mathrm{Th}_{syn_o}(\mathcal{L})$, the variable class $\tilde{\mathrm{V}}\mathrm{ar}(\mathcal{L})$, the well-formed term class $\mathrm{Wfter}_o(\mathcal{L})$, the well-formed expression class $\mathrm{Wfex}_o(\mathcal{L})$, and the free and bound individual variable maps $\mathrm{FV}_o(\mathcal{L})$, $\mathrm{BnV}_o(\mathcal{L})$, respectively.

Specifically, $\mathrm{Core}(\mathcal{L}) = (\mathrm{Obj}(\mathcal{L}),\mathrm{Arr}(\mathcal{L}))$ is a category of types, so that we may identify $\mathrm{Typ}(\mathcal{L}) = \mathrm{Obj}(\mathcal{L})$, the object class of Core($\mathcal{L}$) and FuncSymb($\mathcal{L}$) = Arr($\mathcal{L}$) , the arrow or functional symbol class of Core($\mathcal{L}$) . (For a review of category theory concepts, see appendices at the end of 2.4.) $\mathcal{L}$ is a higher order formal language, in general here, because Sort($\mathcal{L}$) , the class of basic types or kinds of things we are concerned with, is more than one in number. Here Sort($\mathcal{L}$) = (Ob($\mathcal{L}$),Ar($\mathcal{L}$),Rel($\mathcal{L}$)) , where: Ob($\mathcal{L}$) refers to objects which later (in the semantic evaluation) may be interpreted as generalized sets or members of such (generalized) sets; Ar($\mathcal{L}$) refers to things which later may be interpreted as functions or arrows between the objects or generalized sets; Rel($\mathcal{L}$) refers to things which may be interpreted as relations in, or on, the generalized sets. In turn, Typ($\mathcal{L}$) , the class of all types, can be considered as the class of all possible compound or mixtures of sorts, relative to the primitive operation $\otimes$, cartesian product, and possibly additionally $\textcircled{\Omega}$, exponentiation. Thus, we can write

$$\mathrm{Typ}(\mathcal{L}) = \mathrm{span}(\mathrm{Sort}(\mathcal{L}),\{\otimes, \textcircled{\Omega}\}) .$$

By the symbol span(A,Q) , we mean: A is a given collection of entities and $Q = \{Q_1,Q_2,...\}$ is a collection of operators or more generally, procedures, with appropriate mixed iterates $Q_{\omega_1}\cdots Q_{\omega_n}$ well-defined , $\{\omega_1,...\omega_n\} \subseteq \{1,2,...\}$ where in particular, we note $Q_\omega{}^n = Q_\omega\cdots Q_\omega$ and Q_ω^0 = Identity, such that

(1) $Q_{\omega_1}\cdots Q_{\omega_n} \circ \mathrm{span}(A,Q) \subseteq \mathrm{span}(A,Q)$; for all $\omega_1,...,\omega_n,\ n \geq 0$.

(2) span(A,Q) is the smallest such collection in (1) so constructed.

Another name for this procedure is the free algebra generated by Q over A or the strings generated by Q over A . (See Enderton [54], Chapter 1 for further elaborations and connections with homomorphic extensions, etc.)

Back to types: A typical example of a type here is

$$\mathrm{Ob}(\mathcal{L}) \times \mathrm{Ob}(\mathcal{L}) \times \Omega^{\mathrm{Rel}(\mathcal{L})\times\mathrm{Ar}(\mathcal{L})} , \text{ etc.}$$

(Note also, the symbols $\times$ and Ω as used in a later part of the development of $\mathcal{L}$ will have a different interpretation.)

The arrows or functional symbols making up Arr($\mathcal{L}$) are of the typical form (remember that Core($\mathcal{L}$) is assumed to be a legitimate category!) $(F : \alpha \to \beta)$ or equivalently $F \in \mathrm{Arr}_{\alpha,\beta}(\mathrm{Core}(\mathcal{L}))$, for any $\alpha,\beta \in \mathrm{Typ}(\mathcal{L})$. Thus, composition and identity are assumed well-defined here so that, if $\alpha,\beta,\gamma \in \mathrm{Typ}(\mathcal{L})$ and $F \in \mathrm{Arr}_{\alpha,\beta}(\mathrm{Core}(\mathcal{L}))$, $G \in \mathrm{Arr}_{\beta,\gamma}(\mathrm{Core}(\mathcal{L}))$, then $G\circ F \in \mathrm{Arr}_{\alpha,\gamma}(\mathrm{Core}(\mathcal{L}))$ and $\mathrm{Id}_\beta \circ F = F = F\circ \mathrm{Id}_\alpha$, etc. (Again, note that abuse of notation takes place here, since $\circ$, Id are used later for a different meaning.)

Arr($\mathcal{L}$) contains a number of specially designated function symbols, i.e.,

$$\mathrm{Arr}(\mathcal{L}) \supseteq \mathrm{Cat}(\mathcal{L}) \cup \mathrm{Foun}(\mathcal{L}) \cup \mathrm{Loc}(\mathcal{L}) \cup \mathrm{Quan}(\mathcal{L}),$$

where:

$$\mathrm{Cat}(\mathcal{L}) \supseteq \left\{ \begin{array}{llll}
S & = & (S : \mathrm{Ar}(\mathcal{L}) \to \mathrm{Ob}(\mathcal{L})) & \text{- domain map} \\
B & = & (B : \mathrm{Ar}(\mathcal{L}) \to \mathrm{Ob}(\mathcal{L})) & \text{- codomain map} \\
\circ & = & (\circ : \mathrm{Ar}(\mathcal{L}) \times \mathrm{Ar}(\mathcal{L}) \to \mathrm{Ar}(\mathcal{L})) & \text{- composition map} \\
\mathrm{Id} & = & (\mathrm{Id} : \mathrm{Ob}(\mathcal{L}) \to \mathrm{Ar}(\mathcal{L})) & \text{- identity map} \\
\mathrm{proj} & = & (\mathrm{proj} : \mathrm{Ob}(\mathcal{L}) \times \mathrm{Ob}(\mathcal{L}) \to \mathrm{Ar}(\mathcal{L})) & \text{- projection map} \\
\sigma & = & (\sigma : \mathrm{Rel}(\mathcal{L}) \to \mathrm{Ob}(\mathcal{L})) & \text{- signature map} \\
\cdot[\cdot\cdot] & = & (\cdot[\cdot\cdot] : \mathrm{Rel}(\mathcal{L}) \times \mathrm{Ar}(\mathcal{L}) \to \mathrm{Rel}(\mathcal{L})) & \text{- substitution map} \\
\times & = & (\times : \mathrm{Ob}(\mathcal{L})^n \to \mathrm{Ob}(\mathcal{L})) & \text{- (cartesian object) product map} \\
\dagger & = & (\dagger : \mathrm{Ob}(\mathcal{L})^n \to \mathrm{Ob}(\mathcal{L})) & \text{- (cartesian object) sum or coproduct map} \\
\langle , \rangle & = & (\langle , \rangle : \mathrm{Ob}(\mathcal{L}) \to \mathrm{Ar}(\mathcal{L}) \times \mathrm{Ar}(\mathcal{L})) & \text{- special arrow product map}
\end{array} \right.$$

$$\mathrm{Foun}(\mathcal{L}) \supseteq \left\{ \begin{array}{llll}
\Omega & = & (\Omega : \mathrm{Ob}(\mathcal{L}) \to \mathrm{Ob}(\mathcal{L})) & \text{- exponent map} \\
\in & = & (\in : \mathrm{Ob}(\mathcal{L}) \to \mathrm{Rel}(\mathcal{L})) & \text{- membership map} \\
\asymp & = & (\asymp : \mathrm{Ob}(\mathcal{L}) \to \mathrm{Rel}(\mathcal{L})) & \text{- equality map} \\
\mathrm{Ex} & = & (\mathrm{Ex} : \mathrm{Ob}(\mathcal{L}) \to \mathrm{Rel}(\mathcal{L})) & \text{- existence map} \\
\{\cdot|\cdot\cdot\} & = & (\{\cdot|\cdot\} : \mathrm{Ob}(\mathcal{L}) \times \mathrm{Ob}(\mathcal{L}) \times \mathrm{Rel}(\mathcal{L}) \to \mathrm{Ar}(\mathcal{L})) & \text{- class abstraction map} \\
\vdots & & \vdots \quad \vdots \quad \vdots &
\end{array} \right.$$

$$\mathrm{Loc}(\mathcal{L}) \supseteq \left\{ \begin{array}{llll}
T & = & (T : \mathrm{Ob}(\mathcal{L}) \to \mathrm{Rel}(\mathcal{L})) & \text{- truth map} \\
\bot & = & (\bot : \mathrm{Ob}(\mathcal{L}) \to \mathrm{Rel}(\mathcal{L})) & \text{- false map} \\
\mathrm{nt} & = & (\mathrm{nt} : \mathrm{Rel}(\mathcal{L}) \to \mathrm{Rel}(\mathcal{L})) & \text{- negative map} \\
\& & = & (\& : \mathrm{Rel}(\mathcal{L})^n \to \mathrm{Rel}(\mathcal{L})) & \text{- conjunction map} \\
\mathrm{or} & = & (\mathrm{or} : \mathrm{Rel}(\mathcal{L})^n \to \mathrm{Rel}(\mathcal{L})) & \text{- disjunction map} \\
\Rightarrow & = & (\Rightarrow : \mathrm{Rel}(\mathcal{L}) \times \mathrm{Rel}(\mathcal{L}) \to \mathrm{Rel}(\mathcal{L})) & \text{- implication map} \\
\mathrm{id} & = & (\mathrm{id} : \mathrm{Rel}(\mathcal{L}) \to \mathrm{Rel}(\mathcal{L})) & \text{- identity relation map} \\
\mathrm{maybe} & = & (\mathrm{maybe} : \mathrm{Rel}(\mathcal{L}) \to \mathrm{Rel}(\mathcal{L})) & \text{- doubt relation map} \\
\mathrm{poss} & = & (\mathrm{poss} : \mathrm{Rel}(\mathcal{L}) \to \mathrm{Rel}(\mathcal{L})) & \text{- possibility map} \\
\vdots & & \vdots \quad \vdots \quad \vdots \quad \vdots & \vdots
\end{array} \right.$$

$$\mathrm{Quan}(\mathcal{L}) \supseteq \left\{ \begin{array}{llll}
\forall & = & (\forall : \mathrm{Ob}(\mathcal{L}) \times \mathrm{Ob}(\mathcal{L}) \times \mathrm{Rel}(\mathcal{L}) \to \mathrm{Rel}(\mathcal{L})) & \text{- universal quantification} \\
\exists & = & (\exists : \mathrm{Ob}(\mathcal{L}) \times \mathrm{Ob}(\mathcal{L}) \times \mathrm{Rel}(\mathcal{L}) \to \mathrm{Rel}(\mathcal{L})) & \text{- existence quantification} \\
\mathrm{Mo} & = & (\mathrm{Mo} : \mathrm{Ob}(\mathcal{L}) \times \mathrm{Ob}(\mathcal{L}) \times \mathrm{Rel}(\mathcal{L}) \to \mathrm{Rel}(\mathcal{L})) & \text{- "most" map} \\
\mathrm{Abt}^3/4 & = & (\mathrm{Abt}^3/4 : \mathrm{Ob}(\mathcal{L}) \times \mathrm{Ob}(\mathcal{L}) \times \mathrm{Rel}(\mathcal{L}) \to \mathrm{Rel}(\mathcal{L})) & \text{- "about 3/4" map} \\
\vdots & \vdots & \vdots \quad \vdots \quad \vdots \quad \vdots & \vdots
\end{array} \right.$$

Note that we can classify the logical connective functional symbols as

$$\mathrm{Loc}(\mathcal{L}) = \bigcup_{n=1}^{\infty} \mathrm{Loc}_n(\mathcal{L}) ,$$

where $\mathrm{Loc}_n(\mathcal{L})$ represents the n-ary logical connectors of interest. Hence,

$$\mathrm{Loc}_1(\mathcal{L}) \supseteq \{nt, id, \ldots\}$$

$$\mathrm{Loc}_2(\mathcal{L}) \supseteq \{ \Rightarrow , \Leftrightarrow, \&, or, \ldots\} ,$$

etc.

Note that in the case of & and or , we may well wish to extend their domains to include any number of arguments. (One way of doing this is to formally assume symmetry and associativity, introduced by adding the appropriate axioms and rules. (See the later development for $\mathcal{L}$ in III and VI for basic theorems connected with theory $\mathrm{Th}_K(\mathcal{L})$, demonstrating symmetry and associativity of operators &(=∧ here) and or(=∨ here).)

In order to complete the syntax of $\mathcal{L}$ we need the concept of a theory for $\mathcal{L}$. In addition, we will also need this concept when we consider logical, set foundations and quantification properties for $\mathcal{L}$.

First, define the (Gentzen) sequent class.

Let Predsym($\mathcal{L}$) be a collection of predicate symbols. Then

$$\mathrm{Seq}_{\mathcal{A}}(\mathcal{L}) = \mathcal{A}(\mathcal{L}) \times \mathrm{Predsym}(\mathcal{L}) \times \mathcal{A}(\mathcal{L})$$

where $\mathcal{A}(\mathcal{L})$ is some class of elements, so that typically, if $\Psi,\theta \in \mathrm{Term}(\mathcal{L})$, $(\Psi \vdash_{\mathcal{L}} \theta) \in \mathrm{Seq}_{\mathrm{Term}(\mathcal{L})}(\mathcal{L})$, or if, further, $\Psi,\theta \in \mathrm{Var}(\mathrm{Ar}(\mathcal{L}))$, $(\Psi =_{\mathrm{Ar}(\mathcal{L})} \theta) \in \mathrm{Seq}_{\mathrm{Var}(\mathrm{Ar}(\mathcal{L}))}(\mathcal{L})$, etc.

Then any axiom collection Ax($\mathcal{L}$) for $\mathcal{L}$ and $\mathcal{A}(\mathcal{L})$ satisfies

$$\emptyset \neq \mathrm{Ax}(\mathcal{L}) \subseteq \mathrm{Seq}_{A(\mathcal{L})}(\mathcal{L})$$

and any rule collection Rul($\mathcal{L}$) for $\mathcal{L}$ and $\mathcal{A}(\mathcal{L})$ satisfies

$$\emptyset \neq \mathrm{Rul}(\mathcal{L}) \subseteq \mathrm{Seq}^{(\infty)}_{\mathcal{A}(\mathcal{L})}(\mathcal{L}) \overset{d}{=} \bigcup_{n=1}^{\infty} \underbrace{\mathrm{Seq}(\mathcal{L})\times\ldots\times\mathrm{Seq}(\mathcal{L})}_{n \text{ factors}} .$$

A corresponding theory Th($\mathcal{L}$) is then defined to consist of

$$\mathrm{Th}(\mathcal{L}) \overset{d}{=} (\mathrm{Ax}(\mathcal{L}), \mathrm{Rul}(\mathcal{L})) ,$$

with the class of deducts or theorems De(Th($\mathcal{L}$)) produced by Rul($\mathcal{L}$) acting upon (or more formally, as a relation or function product upon) Ax($\mathcal{L}$) . Thus, we write

$$\mathrm{De}(\mathrm{Th}(\mathcal{L})) = \mathrm{span}(\mathrm{Th}(\mathcal{L})) \subseteq \mathrm{Seq}_{\mathcal{A}(\mathcal{L})}(\mathcal{L}) .$$

In general, each element $R \in Rul(\mathcal{L})$ is in the form

$$if \quad (\Psi_1\gamma_1\theta_1), \ldots, (\Psi_n\gamma_n\theta_n) \quad then \quad (\Psi_{n+1}\gamma_{n+1}\theta_{n+1})$$

where "if" and "then" are in the usual 0 – 1 metalogic context and $(\Psi_\omega\gamma_\omega\theta_n) \in Seq_{\mathcal{A}(\mathcal{L})}(\mathcal{L})$.

Furthermore, we may be interested only in some subclass of deducts

$$Ser_{\mathcal{A}(\mathcal{L})}(\mathcal{L}) \subseteq De(Th(\mathcal{L})) .$$

For any $(\Psi\gamma\theta) \in Seq_{\mathcal{A}(\mathcal{L})}(\mathcal{L})$, we call Ψ the hypothesis and θ the *conclusion* or *inference*.

Next, the basic variables and constants of $\mathcal{L}$ will be considered. This is provided by a fixed basic variable mapping compatible with $\times$ and Ω

$$Var : Typ(\mathcal{L}) \to Ob(SET) ,$$

where SET = (Ob(SET), Ar(SET)) is the category of all ordinary sets and functions between them. (Again, see Appendix 1 at the end of 2.4) , so that in particular the basic variables are

$$Var(Ob(\mathcal{L})) \supseteq \{i, i_1, i_2, \ldots, j, j_1, j_2, \ldots, k, \ldots\}$$
individual object symbols

$$Var(Ar(\mathcal{L})) \supseteq \{f, f_1, f_2, \ldots, g, \ldots, h, \ldots\}$$
individual arrow or function symbols

$$Var(Rel(\mathcal{L})) \supseteq \{r, r_1, r_2, \ldots, s, s_1, \ldots, t, u, \ldots, w, \ldots\}$$
individual relation symbols

$$Var(Ob(\mathcal{L})\times Ob(\mathcal{L})) = Var(Ob(\mathcal{L}))\times Var(Ob(\mathcal{L})) ,$$

$$Var(Ar(\mathcal{L})\times\Omega^{Rel(\mathcal{L})}) = Var(Ar(\mathcal{L}))\times\Omega^{Var(Rel)(\mathcal{L}))} ,$$

etc., where the right-hand side symbols $\times$, Ω are ordinary cartesian product and exponentiation.

Note also that generally, basic variables include basic constants, denoted by $Cons(\cdot)$, so that

$$Var(Ob(\mathcal{L})) \supseteq Cons(Ob(\mathcal{L})) = \{1_a, 1_b, \ldots, \emptyset, \ldots\} ,$$

where $1_a, 1_b, \ldots$ represent individual constants or terminal objects in category theory notation and $\emptyset$ represents the null object or null set or the initial object (in category theory notation).

Other constants (or semi-constants, such as terminal arrows $f_{i,a} : i \to 1_a$) or initial arrows $(g_{\emptyset,j} : \emptyset \to j)$ can be designated as needed in $Cons(Ar(\mathcal{L})) \subseteq Var(Ar(\mathcal{L}))$, etc. (Again, abuse of notation here involves 1 and $\emptyset$.) We define the class of all basic variables as

$$\mathrm{Var}(\mathrm{Typ}(\mathcal{L})) \overset{d}{=} \bigcup_{\alpha \in \mathrm{Typ}(\mathcal{L})} \mathrm{Var}(\alpha)$$

and the ordered pair

$$\mathrm{Var}(\mathcal{L}) \overset{d}{=} (\mathrm{Var}(\mathrm{Ob}(\mathcal{L})),\ \mathrm{Var}(\mathrm{Ar}(\mathcal{L}))) \ .$$

Next, we consider the class of basic terms, $\mathrm{Term}(\mathcal{L})$, possibly quantified formulas $\mathrm{Form}(\mathcal{L})$, atomic formulas, $\mathrm{Atom}(\mathcal{L})$, individual terms, $\mathrm{Indterm}(\mathcal{L})$, and individual variables, $\mathrm{Indvar}(\mathcal{L})$, and individual constants, $\mathrm{Indconst}(\mathcal{L})$.

We first form the formal spans generating successively, these classes. But in order to restrict the classes to meaningful quantities, we must add the first-level syntax theory $\mathrm{Th}_{I,syn}(\mathcal{L}) = (\mathrm{Ax}_{I,syn}(\mathcal{L}),\ \mathrm{Rul}_{I,syn}(\mathcal{L}))$ giving $\mathrm{Var}(\mathcal{L})$ a category structure. (See later remarks.)

In turn, we also add the second-level syntax theory $\mathrm{Th}_{II,syn}(\mathcal{L}) = (\mathrm{Ax}_{II,syn}(\mathcal{L}),\ \mathrm{Rul}_{II,syn}(\mathcal{L}))$, to completely specify the well-formed terms $\mathrm{Wfter}_o(\mathcal{L})$ and well-formed expressions $\mathrm{Wfex}_o(\mathcal{L})$.

Thus, we have formally,

$$\begin{aligned}
\mathrm{Term}(\mathcal{L}) &\overset{d}{=} \mathrm{span}(\mathrm{Var}(\mathrm{Typ}(\mathcal{L})),\ \mathrm{Arr}(\mathcal{L})) \\
&\supseteq \mathrm{Form}(\mathcal{L}) \overset{d}{=} \mathrm{span}(\mathrm{Form}'(\mathcal{L}),\ \mathrm{Quan}(\mathcal{L})) \\
&\supseteq \mathrm{Form}'(\mathcal{L}) \overset{d}{=} \mathrm{span}(\mathrm{Atom}(\mathcal{L}),\ \mathrm{Loc}(\mathcal{L})) \\
&\supseteq \mathrm{Atom}(\mathcal{L}) \overset{d}{=} \mathrm{Var}(\mathrm{Rel}(\mathcal{L}))[\mathrm{Indterm}(\mathcal{L})] \\
&\qquad\qquad \overset{d}{=} (\cdot[\cdot\cdot])(\mathrm{Var}(\mathrm{Rel}(\mathcal{L})),\ \mathrm{Indterm}(\mathcal{L})) \ .
\end{aligned}$$

Also,

$$\begin{aligned}
\mathrm{Term}(\mathcal{L}) &\supseteq \mathrm{Indterm}(\mathcal{L}) \overset{d}{=} \mathrm{span}(\mathrm{Indvar}(\mathcal{L}),\ \mathrm{Var}(\mathrm{Ar}(\mathcal{L}))) \\
&\supseteq \mathrm{Indvar}(\mathcal{L}) \overset{d}{=} \mathrm{proj}(\mathrm{Var}(\mathrm{Ob}(\mathcal{L}))\times\mathrm{Var}(\mathrm{Ob}(\mathcal{L}))) \\
&\supseteq \mathrm{Indconst}(\mathcal{L}) \ ,
\end{aligned}$$

with the class of predicate symbols

$$\mathrm{Predsym}(\mathcal{L}) = \{=_{\mathrm{Ob}(\mathcal{L})},\ =_{\mathrm{Ar}(\mathcal{L})},\ =_{\mathrm{Rel}(\mathcal{L})},\ \vdash_{\mathcal{L}},\ \subseteq,\ \in,\ \ldots\}$$

used in the theories $\mathrm{Th}_{I,syn}(\mathcal{L})$, $\mathrm{Th}_{II,syn}(\mathcal{L})$.

Some selected *first-level syntax axioms and rules* from the 18 given in Appendix 2 on Deduction Categories and Formal Topoi (at the end of 2.4):

For all $i \in \mathrm{Var}(\mathrm{Ob}(\mathcal{L}))$,

$$R_{I,syn,1;i}: \quad (S(\mathrm{Id}(i)) =_{\mathrm{Ob}} B(\mathrm{Id}(i)) =_{\mathrm{Ob}} i)$$

For all $k \in \mathrm{Var}(\mathrm{Ar}(\mathcal{L})$,

$$R_{I,syn,2;k}: \quad (k\circ(\mathrm{Id}(S(k))) =_{\mathrm{Ar}} \mathrm{Id}(B(k))\circ k =_{\mathrm{Ar}} k)$$

and $(S(f) =_{Ob} B(g))$, $(S(g) =_{Ob} B(h))$.

$R_{I,syn,4;f,g,h}$: For all $f,g,h \in Var(Ar(\ell))$

then

$$((f\circ g)\circ h =_{Ar} f\circ(g\circ h)) .$$

For all $i,j \in Var(Ob(\ell))$,

$R_{I,syn,8;i,j}$: $(B(proj_{1(i)}(i\times j)) =_{Ob} i)$,

$(B(proj_{2(j)}(i\times j)) =_{Ob} j)$.

$R_{I,syn,17;f,a}$: For all $1_a \in Cons(Ob(\ell))$, all $f \in Var(Ar(\ell))$,

$(B(f) =_{Ob} 1_a)$ then $(f =_{Ar} p_a(S(f)))$ (p_a a terminal arrow map).

Remarks concerning individual variables.

Recall

$$Indvar(\ell) \overset{d}{=} proj(Var(Ob(\ell)) \times Var(Ob(\ell)))$$
$$= \bigcup_{i\in Var(Ob(\ell))} Indvar_i(\ell) .$$

If $i,j \in Var(Ob(\ell))$,

$$x^{(i)}_{i\times j} \overset{d}{=} proj((i\times j)\times i) \overset{d}{=} proj^{(i\times j)}_{1(i)} \in Indvar_i(\ell) ,$$

$$x^{(j)}_{i\times j} \overset{d}{=} proj((i\times j)\times j) \overset{d}{=} proj^{(i\times j)}_{2(j)} \in Indvar_j(\ell) ,$$

etc.

We usually drop the subscript $i \times j$ from the individual variables.

Note also the distinction, e.g.,

$$x^{(i)} \overset{d}{=} proj_3(k\times i\times i\times j\times i)$$

and

$$y^{(i)} \overset{d}{=} proj_2(k\times i\times i\times j\times i) .$$

Also, note the basic identification (which can be produced as a rule or theorem) for all $i,j \in Var(Ob(\ell))$,

$$proj_{1(i)}(i) = Id(i) \; ; \; Id(i\times j) = \langle proj_i(i\times j), proj_j(i\times j)\rangle$$
$$= \langle x^{(i)}, x^{(j)}\rangle , \text{ etc.}$$

Finally, note the individual constant maps:

$$\mathrm{Indconst}(\mathcal{L}) = \bigcup_{\substack{j \in \mathrm{Var}(\mathrm{Ob}(\mathcal{L})), \\ 1_a \in \mathrm{Cons}(\mathrm{Ob}(\mathcal{L}))}} \mathrm{Ar}_{j,1_a}(\mathrm{Var}(\mathcal{L})) ,$$

where category $\mathrm{Var}(\mathcal{L})$ is described later.

Analogously, *second-level syntax axioms and rules* may be obtained as abstracts of the corresponding ones in Appendix 2 at the end of 2.4. In the following development, all quantities may be interpreted as ordinary sets and elements and all predicate symbols such as $\subseteq$, $\in$, $=$, ... may be correspondingly interpreted as the usual set relations $\subseteq$, $\in$, $=$, ... with only a minor abuse of notation.

$R_{II,syn,1}$: $(\mathrm{Var}(\mathrm{Typ}(\mathcal{L})) \subseteq \mathrm{Term}(\mathcal{L}) = \bigcup_{\alpha \in \mathrm{Typ}(\mathcal{L})} \mathrm{Term}_\alpha(\mathcal{L})$.

For all α , β , F , g :

$R_{II,syn,2,\alpha,\beta,F,g}$: If $(\alpha,\beta \in \mathrm{Typ}(\mathcal{L}))$ and $(g \in \mathrm{Var}(\mathcal{L}))$,

$((F : \alpha \to \beta) \in \mathrm{Arr}(\mathcal{L}))$

then

$(F(g) \in \mathrm{Term}_\beta(\mathcal{L}))$.

For all i ,

$R_{II,syn,3;i}$: If $(i \in \mathrm{Var}(\mathrm{Ob}(\mathcal{L})))$,

then; $(\mathrm{Indvar}_i(\mathcal{L}) \subseteq \mathrm{Indterm}_i(\mathcal{L}))$.

For all $i,j,x^{(i)}, f$,

$R_{II,syn,4,i,j,x^{(i)},f}$: If $(i,j \in \mathrm{Var}(\mathrm{Ob}(\mathcal{L})))$, $(x^{(i)} \in \mathrm{Indvar}_i(\mathcal{L}))$,

$(f \in \mathrm{Var}(\mathrm{Ar}(\mathcal{L})))$, and

$(S(f) = i)$, $(B(f) = j)$,

[i.e., $f = (f : i \to j)$] ,

then $(f(x^{(i)}) \in \mathrm{Indterm}_j(\mathcal{L}))$,

where $f(x^{(i)}) \overset{d}{=} f \circ x^{(i)}$.

Note, using $f = (\mathrm{Id}(i) : i \to i)$, $R_{II,syn,3}$ becomes superfluous.

$R_{II,syn,5}$: $(\mathrm{Indterm}(\mathcal{L}) = \bigcup_{j \in \mathrm{Var}(\mathrm{Ob})(\mathcal{L}))} \mathrm{Indterm}_j(\mathcal{L}))$

For all $i, r, x^{(i)}$,

$R_{II,syn,6 \atop i,r,x^{(i)}}$: If $(i \in \mathrm{Var}(\mathrm{Ob}(\mathcal{L}))$, $(r \in \mathrm{Var}(\mathrm{Rel}(\mathcal{L})))$,

$(x^{(i)} \in \mathrm{Indvar}_i(\mathcal{L}))$, $(\sigma(r) = i)$,

then

$(r[x^{(i)}] \in \mathrm{Atomform}(\mathcal{L}))$

$R_{II,syn,7}$: $(\mathrm{Atomform}(\mathcal{L}) \subseteq \mathrm{Form}'(\mathcal{L}))$.

For all $\Psi_1, \ldots, \Psi_n$, γ, n ,

$R_{II,syn,8 \atop n,\Psi_1,\ldots,\Psi_n,\gamma}$: If $\Psi_1, \ldots, \Psi_n \in \mathrm{Form}'(\mathcal{L})$, $(\gamma \in \mathrm{Loc}_n(\mathcal{L}))$,

then

$(\gamma(\Psi_1, \ldots, \Psi_n) \in \mathrm{Form}'(\mathcal{L}))$.

$R_{II,syn,9}$: $(\mathrm{Form}'(\mathcal{L}) \subseteq \mathrm{Form}(\mathcal{L}))$.

For all $i, j, x_{i\times j}^{(i)}$, q , Ψ

$R_{II,syn,10 \atop i,j,x_{(i\times j)}^{(i)},q,\Psi}$: If

$(i, j \in \mathrm{Var}(\mathrm{Ob}(\mathcal{L}))$, $(x_{i\times j}^{(i)} \in \mathrm{Indvar}_i(\mathcal{L}))$,

$(q \in \mathrm{Quan}(\mathcal{L}))$,

$(\Psi \in \mathrm{Form}(\mathcal{L}))$, $(\sigma(\Psi) = i \times j)$,

then

$((q\ x_{i\times j}^{(i)})(\Psi) \in \mathrm{Form}(\mathcal{L}))$,

$(q\ x_{i\times j}^{(i)})(\Psi) \overset{d}{=} q(x_{i\times j}^{(i)}, \Psi)$.

For all i, j, $x_{i\times j}^{(i)}$, Ψ

$R_{II,syn,11, \atop i,j,x_{i\times j}^{(i)},\Psi}$: If $(i, j \in \mathrm{Var}(\mathrm{Ob}(\mathcal{L})))$, $(x_{i\times j}^{(i)} \in \mathrm{Var}(\mathrm{Ob}(\mathcal{L})))$,

$(\Psi \in \mathrm{Form}(\mathcal{L}))$, $(\sigma(\Psi) = i \times j)$

then

$$(\{x_{i\times j}^{(i)} \mid \Psi\} \in \text{Indterm}_{\Omega(i)}(\ell)) \;.$$

Again, see Appendix 2, end of 2.4 for all corresponding deduction rules and axioms concretized for deduction categories and formal topoi.

We summarize the axioms and rules previously introduced and connect them with $\text{Term}(\ell)$ in order to produce the class of well-formed expressions:

$$\text{Th}_{I,syn}(\ell) = (\text{Ax}_{I,syn}(\ell) \;,\; \text{Rul}_{I,syn}(\ell)) \;,$$

where, because axioms can usually be formed as deduction rules and vice-versa, we simply abuse notation and let

$$\begin{aligned}&\text{Ax}_{I,syn}(\ell) \cup \text{Rul}_{I,syn}(\ell)\\ &\quad \overset{d}{=} R_{I,syn,1} \cup \dots \cup R_{I,syn,17}\\ &\quad \subseteq \text{Seq}_{\text{Term}(\ell)}(\ell) = \text{Term}(\ell) \times \{=_{Ob}, =_{Ar}, =_{Rel}\} \times \text{Term}(\ell) \;.\end{aligned}$$

$$\text{Th}_{II,syn}(\ell) = (\text{Ax}_{II,syn}(\ell), \text{Rul}_{II,syn}(\ell)) \;,$$

$$\begin{aligned}&\text{Ax}_{II,syn}(\ell) \cup \text{Rul}_{II,syn}(\ell) \overset{d}{=} R_{II,syn,1} \cup \cdots \cup R_{II,syn,11}\\ &\quad \cup R_{I,Th,0} \cup R_{I,Th,1} \cup R_{I,Th,2}\\ &\quad \subseteq \text{Seq}_{A_{II}(\ell)}(\ell) = A_{II}(\ell) \times \{\in, \subseteq, =\} \times A_{II}(\ell) \;,\end{aligned}$$

where

$$\begin{aligned}A_{II}(\ell) \overset{d}{=} \{&\text{Term}(\ell), \text{Term}_{\alpha}(\ell), \text{Term}_{\beta}(\ell), \text{Indvar}_{i}(\ell),\\ &\text{Indterm}_{i}(\ell), \text{Atom}(\ell), \text{Form}'(\ell), \text{Form}(\ell), \dots\} \;,\end{aligned}$$

and where, e.g.,

$$R_{I,syn,1} \overset{d}{=} \{R_{I,syn,1,i} \mid \text{all} \quad i\}$$

$$R_{II,syn,11} \overset{d}{=} \{R_{II,syn,11;\, j,x_{(i\times j)}^{(i)},\Psi} \mid \text{all} \quad i,j,x_{(i\times j)}^{(i)},\Psi\} \;,$$

etc.

We combine the two theories together yielding

$$\text{Th}_{syn_o}(\ell) = (\text{Ax}_{syn_o}(\ell), \text{Rul}_{syn_o}(\ell)) \;,$$

$$\text{Ax}_{syn_o}(\ell) \cup \text{Rul}_{syn_o}(\ell)$$

$$= R_{I,syn,1} \cup \cdots \cup R_{I,syn,17}$$
$$\cup R_{II,syn,1} \cup \cdots \cup R_{II,syn,11}$$
$$\cup R_{I,Th,0} \cup \cdots \cup R_{I,Th,2}$$
$$\subseteq Seq_{Term(\ell)}(\ell) \cup Seq_{A_{II}(\ell)}(\ell) \ .$$

In turn, now form the class of deducts

$$De(Th_{syn_o}(\ell)) = span(Th_{syn_o}(\ell)) \ .$$

Next, project out the first component in all sequents of the form $(\Psi \in \theta)$ and intersect these with the appropriate subclass of $Term(\ell)$ to obtain the well-formed subclasses of $Term(\ell)$:

$$Wfter_o(\ell) \overset{d}{=} proj(\cdot\in\cdot\cdot)\ (De(Th_{syn_o}(\ell))) \ ,$$

the class of all well-formed terms (in, $Term(\ell)$) , which, by use of $Th_{syn_o}(\ell)$, may be identified with $Var(Ar(\ell)) \cup Var(Rel(\ell))$,

$$Wff_o(\ell) \overset{d}{=} Wfter_o(\ell) \cap Form(\ell) \ ,$$

the class of all well-formed formulas (wff's) ;

$$Wfat_o(\ell) \overset{d}{=} Wfter_o(\ell) \cap Atom(\ell) \ ,$$

the class of all well-formed atomic formulas;

$$Wft_o(\ell) \overset{d}{=} Wfter_o(\ell) \cap Indterm(\ell) \ ,$$

the class of all well-formed individual terms,

$$Wfv_o(\ell) \overset{d}{=} Wfter_o(\ell) \cap Indvar(\ell) \ ,$$

the class of all well-formed individual variables ,

$$Wfc_o(\ell) \overset{d}{=} Wfter_o(\ell) \cap Indconst(\ell) \ ,$$

the class of all well-formed individual constants.

Then define the well-formed expressions of ℓ as:

$$\begin{aligned} Wfex_o(\ell) &\overset{d}{=} Wff_o(\ell) \cup Wft_{(o)}(\ell) \\ &= Wfter_o(\ell) \\ &= Var(Ar(\ell)) \cup Var(Rel(\ell)) \ , \end{aligned}$$

since we can use $R_{I,syn,14}$ to identify any $r \in Var(Rel(\ell))$ with $r[Id(\sigma(r))] \in Wff_o(\ell)$, noting that $Id(\sigma(r)) \in Wfv_o(\ell)$, and where compatible with $Th_{syn_o}(\ell)$, we can identify the originally apparently smaller class $Var(Rel(\mathcal{L}))$ with $Wff_o(\mathcal{L})$!

$Th_{syn_o}(\mathcal{L})$, with the appropriate spans generating $Term(\mathcal{L})$, $Form(\mathcal{L})$, $Atom(\mathcal{L})$, $Indterm(\mathcal{L})$, etc., implies $Var(\mathcal{L})$ is a category and $\tilde{V}ar(\mathcal{L}) \overset{d}{=} (Var(\mathcal{L}), \mathcal{K}(\mathcal{L}))$ is a deduction category, where $\mathcal{K}(\mathcal{L})$ is specified below. (See the appendices at the end of section 2.4 for definitions and properties of deduction categories and formal topoi.)

First,

$Var(\mathcal{L}) = (Ob(Var(\mathcal{L})), Ar(Var(\mathcal{L})))$ is a category, where

$$Ob(Var(\mathcal{L})) \overset{d}{=} Var(Ob(\mathcal{L})) = \{i,\ldots,j,\ldots,k,\ldots\}$$

$$Ar(Var(\mathcal{L})) \overset{d}{=} Var(Ar(\mathcal{L})) = \{f,\ldots,g,\ldots,h,\ldots\} ,$$

where we note that (because of $Th_{syn_o}(\mathcal{L})$) we may identify

$f = (f : i \to j)$, for $i,j \in Var(Ob(\mathcal{L}))$, with $f \in Ar_{i,j}(Var(\mathcal{L}))$ and the identify arrow is $Id(i) = (Id(i) : i \to i)$ (having the usual category properties) and composition here (is derived from $\circ : Ar(\mathcal{L}) \times Ar(\mathcal{L}) \to Ar(\mathcal{L})$ as a function symbol) is the usual category composition: $(f : i \to j)$, $(g : j \to k)$, yields $(g \circ f : i \to k)$, etc.

In addition, $\mathcal{K}(\mathcal{L}) : Var(\mathcal{L}) \to Preord$ is a contravariant functor given as follows:

For all $i \in Var(Ob(\mathcal{L}))$,

$$\mathcal{K}(\mathcal{L})(i) \overset{d}{=} \{r \mid r \in Rel(\mathcal{L}) \text{ and } \sigma(r) = i\} .$$

We write

$$\mathcal{K}(\mathcal{L})(i) = \{r_i, S_i, t_i, \ldots\} .$$

The predicate symbol $\vdash_{\mathcal{L}}$ is an appropriate partial order on each $\mathcal{K}(\mathcal{L})(i)$ by use of axioms $R_{I,Th,0} - R_{I,Th,2}$ and $R_{I,syn,15}$ (see Appendix 2, at the end of 2.4). In turn, we can extend this order in a natural way, for any $r_i, s_i \in \mathcal{K}(\mathcal{L})(i)$:

Define $(r_i \vdash_{\mathcal{L}} s_i)$ iff $(r_i \vdash_{\mathcal{L}} s_i) \in De(Th_{syn_{b},b}(\mathcal{L}))$, for the appropriate case of b ($b = 0$, here, later extended to $b = K$) . For any $i,j \in Var(Ob(\mathcal{L}))$, and any $(f : i \to j)$ (i.e., any $f \in Ar_{i,j}(Var(\mathcal{L})))$,

$$\mathcal{K}(\mathcal{L})(f) \in Ar_{\mathcal{K}(\mathcal{L})(j),\ \mathcal{K}(\mathcal{L}))(i)}(Preord)$$

where for any $s_j \in \mathcal{K}(\mathcal{L})(j)$,

$$\mathcal{K}(\mathcal{L})(f)(S_j) \overset{d}{=} s_j[f] ,$$

and since $\sigma(s_j[f]) = i$ (see axiom $R_{I,syn,12}$ of Appendix 2) ,

$\mathcal{H}(\ell)(f)(s_j) \in \mathcal{H}(\ell)(i)$.

Note also $\mathcal{H}(\ell)$ is order preserving w.r.t. $\vdash_\ell$ by use of $R_{I,Th,O}$.

Finally, the basic syntax of ℓ will be completed with the addition of the free and bound individual variable mappings.

The free individual variable, total individual variable and bound individual variable maps are given by, respectively,

$$FV_o(\ell),\ TV_o(\ell),\ BnV_o(\ell)\ :\ Wfex_o(\ell) \to \mathcal{P}(Wfv_o(\ell))$$

given by $BnV_o(\ell) = TV_o(\ell) \dashv FV_o(\ell)$, where

(i) For all $x^{(i)} \in Wfv_i(f)$, $i \in Var(Ob(\ell))$,

$$TV_o(x^{(i)}) = FV_o(x^{(i)}) \overset{d}{=} \{x^{(i)}\}$$

and hence

$$BnV_o(x^{(i)}) = \emptyset$$

(ii) For all $i,j \in Var(Ob(\ell))$, $(f : i \to j) \in Var(Ar(\ell))$, $t^{(i)} \in Wft_o(\ell)$, $r = r_i$ $(i = \sigma(r)) \in Var(Rel(\ell))$,

$$TV_o(f(t^{(i)})) = FV_o(f(t^{(i)})))$$
$$= TV_o(r_i[t^{(i)}]) = FV_o(r_i[t^{(i)}])$$
$$= TV_o(t^{(i)}) = FV_o(t^{(i)}) .$$

Hence,

$$BnV_o(f[t^{(i)}]) = BnV_o(r_i[t^{(i)}]) = BnV_O(t^{(i)}) = \emptyset .$$

The class of all formal sentences of ℓ is

$$Sent_o(\ell) \overset{d}{=} \{\Psi \mid \Psi \in Wfex_o(\ell) \text{ and } FV_o(\Psi) = \emptyset\}$$
$$= \{\Psi \mid \Psi \in Wff_o(\ell) \text{ and } FV_o(\Psi) = \emptyset\}$$

where the class of all open expressions of ℓ is

$$Open_o(\ell) \overset{d}{=} \{\Psi \mid \Psi \in Wfex_o(\ell) \text{ and } BnV_o(\Psi) = \emptyset\}$$
$$\supseteq Wft_o(\ell) \cup Wfat_o(\ell) .$$

The sequent class for $Wff_o(\ell)$ relative to the special

predicate symbol $\vdash$ can now be formed. This class is the basis for investigating all additional theories:

$$\mathrm{Seq}_{\mathrm{Wff}_o(\mathcal{L})}(\mathcal{L}) \overset{d}{=} \mathrm{Wff}_o(\mathcal{L}) \times \{\vdash\} \times \mathrm{Wff}_o(\mathcal{L})$$

$$= \{(\Psi \vdash \theta) \mid \Psi, \theta \in \mathrm{Wff}_o(\mathcal{L})\} .$$

In summary, the basic syntax of $\mathcal{L}$ has been established and - this point - we may express $\mathcal{L}$ as

$$\mathcal{L}_{\mathrm{syn}_o} = (\mathrm{Core}(\mathcal{L}),\ \mathrm{Th}_{\mathrm{syn}_o}(\mathcal{L}),\ \tilde{\mathrm{V}}\mathrm{ar}(\mathcal{L})\ ;\ \mathrm{Wfex}_o(\mathcal{L}),\ \mathrm{FV}_o(\mathcal{L}),\ \mathrm{BnV}_o(\mathcal{L})) ,$$

with

$$\mathrm{Ser}_o(\mathcal{L}) \overset{d}{=} \mathrm{Seq}_{\mathrm{Wff}_o(\mathcal{L})}(\mathcal{L}) \cap \mathrm{De}(\mathrm{Th}_{\mathrm{syn}_o}(\mathcal{L}))$$

as the class of deducts or theorems of interest relating to $\vdash_{\mathcal{L}}$.

II. <u>**Expanded syntax of $\mathcal{L}$**</u>

In general, we may wish to add more structure (or in fact take away structure) to $\mathcal{L}$ in the form of an additional theory, say $\mathrm{Th}_K(\mathcal{L})$. However, this theory may well entail further operations and constraints on them. Hence, $\mathcal{L}_{\mathrm{syn}_o}$ must be expanded appropriately in order to serve as a basis for the extended language.

Specifically, let $\mathrm{Th}_K(\mathcal{L})$ be a theory concerning logic, set foundations and quantifications, which will be treated in the next section. Define

$$\mathrm{Ax}_{\mathrm{syn}_K}(\mathcal{L}) \cup \mathrm{Rul}_{\mathrm{syn}_K}(\mathcal{L})$$

$$\overset{d}{=} \mathrm{Ax}_{\mathrm{syn}_o}(\mathcal{L}) \cup \mathrm{Rul}_{\mathrm{syn}_o}(\mathcal{L})$$

$$\cup\ R_{I,\mathrm{syn},18} \cup \cdots \cup R_{I,\mathrm{syn},36} ,$$

where as before each $R_{I,\mathrm{syn},\omega}$ has a concrete counterpart in Appendix 2 at the end of 2.4.

Then analogous to the development in (I), we obtain for the expanded syntax theory $\mathrm{Th}_{\mathrm{syn}_K}(\mathcal{L}) = (\mathrm{Ax}_{\mathrm{syn}_K}(\mathcal{L}),\ \mathrm{Rul}_{\mathrm{syn}}(\mathcal{L}))$, $\mathrm{De}(\mathrm{Th}_{\mathrm{syn}_K}(\mathcal{L}))$. In particular, the free variable total variable and bound variable maps now extend to:

For any $n \geq 1$, $\Psi, \Psi_1, \ldots, \Psi_n \in \mathrm{Wff}_o(\mathcal{L})$, $q \in \mathrm{Quan}(\mathcal{L})$, $\gamma \in \mathrm{Loc}_n(\mathcal{L})$, $i \in \mathrm{Var}(\mathrm{Ob}(\mathcal{L}))$, $x^{(i)} \in \mathrm{Wfv}_i(\mathcal{L})$,

$$FV_K(\gamma(\Psi_1,\ldots,\Psi_n)) = \bigcup_{\omega=1}^{n} FV_K(\Psi_\omega) ,$$

$$TV_K(\gamma(\Psi_1,\ldots,\Psi_n)) = \bigcup_{\omega=1}^{n} TV_K(\Psi_\omega) ,$$

$$FV_K(\{x^{(i)} \mid \Psi\}) = FV_K(q\, x^{(i)})(\Psi))$$

$$= FV_K(\Psi) \dashv FV_K(x^{(i)})$$

$$BV_K(\{x^{(i)} \mid \Psi\}) = BV_K(qx^{(i)})(\Psi))$$

$$= \{x^{(i)}\} \cup BV_K(\Psi) .$$

$$TV_k(\{x^{(i)} | \Psi\}) = TV_k(qx^{(i)}(\Psi)) = TV_k(\Psi) \cup FV_k(x^{(i)}) .$$

We abuse notation somewhat:

$$\{x^{(i\times j)}\} = \{x^{(i)}, x^{(j)}\}, \text{ etc.}$$

Thus, we now can let the formal language be

$$\mathcal{L}_{syn_K} = (\mathrm{Core}(\mathcal{L}), \mathrm{Th}_{syn_K}(\mathcal{L}), \widetilde{\mathrm{Var}}(\mathcal{L}), \mathrm{Wfex}_K(\mathcal{L}), \mathrm{FV}_K(\mathcal{L}), \mathrm{BV}_K(\mathcal{L})) ,$$

with

$$\mathrm{Seq}_{\mathrm{Wff}_K(\mathcal{L})}(\mathcal{L}) \stackrel{d}{=} \mathrm{Wff}_K(\mathcal{L}) \times \{\vdash_{\mathcal{L}}\} \times \mathrm{Wff}_K(\mathcal{L}) ,$$

and

$$\mathrm{Ser}'_K(\mathcal{L}) = \mathrm{Seq}_{\mathrm{Wff}_K(\mathcal{L})}(\mathcal{L}) \cap \mathrm{De}(\mathrm{Th}_{syn_K}(\mathcal{L})) .$$

Note that it is assumed, without loss of generality, that all pertinent symbols, including function symbols constituting $\mathrm{FuncSymb}(\mathcal{L})$ (and its subclass of distinguished function symbols) and $\widetilde{\mathrm{Var}}(\mathcal{L})$, are given in the beginning of the construction of $\mathcal{L}$, although relations between them and their compounds and substitutive forms may or may not be present through $\mathrm{Th}_{syn_o}(\mathcal{L})$ or even $\mathrm{Th}_{syn_K}(\mathcal{L})$. In any case, not due to any structural changes, but rather to the class of well-formed expressions apparently shrinking, because of further identifications of forms through the added theory $\mathrm{Th}_K(\mathcal{L})$, we employ the subscript K in $\mathrm{Wfex}_K(\mathcal{L})$, $\mathrm{Wff}_K(\mathcal{L})$, $\mathrm{Wfat}_K(\mathcal{L})$, $\mathrm{Wfv}_{(K)}(\mathcal{L})$, etc. However, again abusing notation, we assume that we can identify all compound wff's with appropriate elements in $\mathrm{Var}(\mathrm{Rel}(\mathcal{L}))$ and all such wft's with these in $\mathrm{Var}(\mathrm{Ar}(\mathcal{L}))$.

III. Added theory for $\mathcal{L}$ for logic, set foundations and quantifications.

Define the added theory $\mathrm{Th}_K(\mathcal{L}) = (\mathrm{Ax}_K(\mathcal{L}), \mathrm{Rul}_K(\mathcal{L}))$ by

$$Ax_K(\ell) \cup Rul_K(\ell) \overset{d}{=} R_{I,Th,3} \cup \cdots \cup R_{I,Th,24} \subseteq Seq_{Wff_K(\ell)}(\ell) \ ,$$

where again each $R_{I,Th,\omega}$ has an obvious concrete counterpart given in Appendix 2 at the end of section 2.4.

We then define the full expanded theory for ℓ as

$$Th_{syn_K,K}(\ell) = (Ax_{syn_K,K}(\ell) \ , \ Rul_{syn_K,K}(\ell)) \ ,$$

where

$$Ax_{syn_K,K}(\ell) \cup Rul_{syn_K,K}(\ell) = Ax_{syn_K}(\ell) \cup Rul_{syn_K}(\ell)$$

$$\cup\ Ax_K(\ell) \cup Rul_{syn_K}(\ell) = R_{I,syn,1} \cup \cdots \cup R_{I,syn,36} \cup R_{II,syn,1} \cup \cdots \cup R_{II,syn,11} \cup R_{Th,0} \cup \cdots \cup R_{Th,24} \ .$$

Hence, finally, we define the full expanded formal language as

$$\ell_{syn_K,K} = (Core(\ell),\ Th_{syn_K,K}(\ell),\ \widetilde{V}ar(\ell),\ Wfex_K(\ell),\ FV_K(\ell),\ BV_K(\ell))$$

with the general deduct class and deduct-of-interest class given as

$$De(Th_{syn_K,K}(\ell)) = span(Th_{syn_K,K}(\ell))$$

and

$$Ser_K(\ell) = Seq_{Wff_K(\ell)}(\ell) \cap De(Th_{syn_K,K}(\ell)) \ .$$

With this additional structure (summed up by $Th_{syn_K,K}(\ell))$, the deduction category $\widetilde{V}ar(\ell)$ becomes now a formal topos. This is a basic algebraic structure for semantic evaluation. Furthermore, this structure can always be imbedded in a natural way into a topos which plays a key role in set theory. (See section 2.4.)

IV. Additional remarks

We may wish to consider additional concepts for ℓ . For example, we may wish to add, e.g., the concept of double implication $\Leftrightarrow$ or alternate denial or other quantifications or logical connectives, without defining them as primitive concepts (such as, elements of $Arr(\ell)$, here) which are described by additional axioms and rules added to $Th_{syn_K,K}(\ell)$. This can be done by *defining* these operations eliminatively through those already established through ℓ . For example, $(\Leftrightarrow : Rel(\ell) \times Rel(\ell) \to Rel(\ell))$ is defined most naturally as

$$\Leftrightarrow (\cdot,\cdot\cdot) \overset{d}{=} \&(\Rightarrow (\cdot,\cdot\cdot), \Rightarrow (\cdot\cdot,\cdot)) ,$$
(composition)

which through the category theory structure of Core(ℓ) is a legitamate member of Arr(ℓ) , as are & and $\Rightarrow$. (See for example, Coste [41], p. 10, where T , F , $\Rightarrow$, $\in$, $\forall$, $\exists$ can all be defined eliminatively through only $\vee$(=or) , $\wedge$(=&) , $\times$, Ω , $\{\cdot|\cdot\cdot\}$, $\cdot[\cdot\cdot]$, σ .) Note also that, compatible with the intuitionistic-like structure of $Th_{syn_K,K}(\ell)$, we can define negation nt directly through $\Rightarrow$ and $\perp$ formally as $nt(\cdot) = (\cdot) \Rightarrow \perp (\cdot)$. See also the Gödel-Intuitionistic Logic in section (C), 2.3.2 and the remarks on Fuz(H), etc. in section 2.4. (See also Maydole [172], p. 13 for other examples of eliminative definitions.)

An example illustrating the form of a well-formed formula and well-formed terms:

Let : $i,j,k \in Var(Ob(\ell))$; $(f : i \to j)$, $(g : j \times j \to k)$, $(h : j \to j) \in Var(Ar(\ell))$; $x^{(i)} \in Wfv_i(L)$, $x^{(j)}$, $z^{(j)} \in Wfv_j(\ell)$, $z^{(k)} \in Wfv_k(\ell)$, $y^{(i)} \in Wfv_i(\ell)$; r_k, t_k, $w_k \in Var(Rel(\ell))$ with $\sigma(r_k) = \sigma(t_k) = \sigma(w_k) = k$; and consider nt , & , and $\Rightarrow \in Loc(\ell)$. Assume throughout that $S(x^{(i)}) = S(x^{(j)}) = S(z^{(j)}) = S(z^{(k)}) = S(y^{(i)}) = \ell \overset{d}{=} i \times j \times j \times k \times i$, and hence, $x^{(i)} = x_\ell^{(i)} = proj_{1(i)}(\ell)$, $x^{(j)} = x_\ell^{(j)} = proj_{2(j)}(\ell)$, etc.

$$f\circ x^{(i)} = f(x^{(i)}), \quad h\circ f\circ y^{(i)} = h(f(y^{(i)})) \in Wft_j(\ell) ,$$

$$g(<f(x^{(i)}), h(f(y^{(i)}))>) \in Wft_k(\ell) ,$$

$$r_k[g(<f(x^{(i)}), h(f(y^{(i)}))>)] \in Wfat(\ell) ,$$

with signature ℓ

$$s_k[g(<z^{(j)}, x^{(j)}>)] \in Wfat(\ell) ,$$

with signature ℓ,

$$w_k[z^{(k)}] \in Wfat(\ell)$$

with signature ℓ . Then, in turn,

$\Psi \overset{d}{=} ((r_k[g(<f(x^{(i)}), h(f(y^{(i)}))>)] \;\&\; nt(s_k[g(<z^{(j)}, x^{(j)}>)])) \Rightarrow w_k[z^{(k)}]) \in Wff(\ell)$. Indeed, $\Psi \in Open(\ell)$, with $\sigma(\Psi) = \ell$.

Then note that

$$\theta \overset{d}{=} \forall(i, j\times j\times k\times i, \Psi) \overset{d}{=} (\forall x^{(i)})(\Psi) = (\forall x^{(i)})\Psi\,[Id_\ell]$$
$$= (\forall x^{(i)})\ \Psi[<x^{(i)}, x^{(j)}, z^{(j)}, z^{(k)}, y^{(i)}>] \in Wff(\ell) ,$$

with

$$FV(\theta) = \{x^{(j)}, z^{(j)}, z^{(k)}, y^{(i)}\} .$$

Also, note that

$$\kappa \overset{d}{\equiv} \forall(j, i\times k\times i, \exists(j, i\times j\times k\times i, nt(s_k[g(z^{(j)}, x^{(j)})])))$$

$$= (\forall x^{(j)})(\exists z^{(j)})(nt(s_k[g(z^{(j)}, x^{(j)})])) \in Sent(\ell) .$$

Also, note the use for $\sigma(s) = i \times j$,

$$w^{(i)} \overset{d}{\equiv} proj_i(k\times i\times j),\ w^{(j)} \overset{d}{\equiv} proj_j(k\times i\times j),\ w^{(k)} \overset{d}{\equiv} proj_k(k\times i\times j) ,$$

$$\lambda \overset{d}{\equiv} (\forall k)(i\times j, r[proj_{i\times j}(k\times i\times j)])$$

$$= (\forall w^{(k)})(r[<w^{(i)}, w^{(j)}>][Id_{k\times i\times j}])$$

$$= (\forall w^{(k)})(r[w^{(i)}, w^{(j)}>][<w^{(k)}, w^{(i)}, w^{(j)}>])$$

$$\overset{d}{\equiv} (\forall w^{(k)})(r(w^{(i)}, w^{(j)}, w^{(k)})) ,$$

etc.

(See Appendix 2 at the end of 2.4 for further details concerning the properties of $\forall$, $\exists$, Ω , $\in$, $\cdot[\cdot\cdot]$, $\{\cdot|\cdot\cdot\}$, etc.)

V. Summary of structure of ℓ

A formal language may be developed in two stages, stage 0, the syntactic level and stage K, the expanded level (or more generally, for $b \subseteq K$).

Let subscript $b = 0$ or K , with $b = 0$ referring to the basic level of development of ℓ and $b = K$ referring to the additional level of development. Then, denoting

$$\ell_{syn_o, 0} \overset{d}{\equiv} \ell_{syn_o} ,$$

$$Th_{syn_o, 0} \overset{d}{\equiv} Th_{syn_o} ,$$

$$Ax_{syn_o, 0} \overset{d}{\equiv} Ax_{syn_o} ,$$

$$Rul_{syn_o, 0} \overset{d}{\equiv} Rul_{syn_o} ,$$

we have:

$\mathcal{L}_{\mathrm{syn}_b,b} = (\mathrm{Core}(\mathcal{L}),\ \mathrm{Th}_{\mathrm{syn}_b,b}(\mathcal{L}),\ \widetilde{\mathrm{Var}}(\mathcal{L}),\ \mathrm{Wfex}_b(\mathcal{L}),\ \mathrm{FV}_b(\mathcal{L}),\ \mathrm{BnV}_b(\mathcal{L}))$,

$\mathrm{Sort}(\mathcal{L}) = \{\mathrm{Ob}(\mathcal{L}),\ \mathrm{Ar}(\mathcal{L}),\ \mathrm{Rel}(\mathcal{L})\}$,

$\mathrm{Core}(\mathcal{L}) = (\mathrm{Ob}(\mathrm{Core}(\mathcal{L})),\ \mathrm{Ar}(\mathrm{Core}(\mathcal{L}))$, the type-category,

$\mathrm{Obj}(\mathcal{L}) = \mathrm{Ob}(\mathrm{Core}(\mathcal{L})) = \mathrm{Typ}(\mathcal{L}) = \mathrm{span}(\mathrm{Sort}(\mathcal{L}),\ \times,\ \Omega)$,

$\mathrm{Arr}(\mathcal{L}) = \mathrm{Ar}(\mathrm{Core}(\mathcal{L})) = \mathrm{FuncSym}(\mathcal{L})$

$\supseteq \mathrm{Cat}(\mathcal{L}) \cup \mathrm{Foun}(\mathcal{L}) \cup \mathrm{Loc}(\mathcal{L}) \cup \mathrm{Quan}(\mathcal{L})$.

(See part I for a listing of special designated function symbols.)

$\mathrm{Var} : \mathrm{Typ}(\mathcal{L}) \to \mathrm{Ob}(\mathrm{SET})$,

$\mathrm{Var}(\mathcal{L}) \overset{d}{=} \bigcup_{\alpha \in \mathrm{Typ}(\mathcal{L})} \mathrm{Var}(\alpha)$, where in particular

$\mathrm{Var}(\mathrm{Ob}(\mathcal{L})) = \{i,\ldots,j,\ldots,k,\ldots\}$

$\mathrm{Var}(\mathrm{Ar}(\mathcal{L})) = \{f,\ldots,g,\ldots,h,\ldots\}$ with $f = (f : i \to j)$, etc.

$\mathrm{Var}(\mathrm{Rel}(\mathcal{L})) = \{r,\ldots,s,\ldots,t,\ldots\}$ with $r = r_i$, etc.

$\mathrm{Var}(\mathcal{L}) = (\mathrm{Ob}(\mathrm{Var}(\mathcal{L})),\ \mathrm{Ar}(\mathrm{Var}(\mathcal{L})))$, the variable object-arrow category,

$\mathrm{Ob}(\mathrm{Var}(\mathcal{L})) = \mathrm{Var}(\mathrm{Ob}(\mathcal{L}))$,

$\mathrm{Ar}(\mathrm{Var}(\mathcal{L})) = \mathrm{Var}(\mathrm{Ar}(\mathcal{L}))$,

$\widetilde{\mathrm{Var}}(\mathcal{L}) = (\mathrm{Var}(\mathcal{L}),\ \mathcal{K}(\mathcal{L}))$ the variable-deduction category,

$\mathcal{K}(\mathcal{L}) : \mathrm{Var}(\mathcal{L}) \to \mathrm{Preord}$, the variable-relation contravariant functor.

For all $i,j \in \mathrm{Var}(\mathrm{Ob}(\mathcal{L}))$, all $(f : i \to j) \in \mathrm{Var}(\mathrm{Ar}(\mathcal{L}))$,

$\mathcal{K}(\mathcal{L})(i) = \{r_i \mid r_i \in \mathrm{Var}(\mathrm{Rel}(\mathcal{L}))\ ,\ \sigma(r_i) = i\}$,

$\mathcal{K}(\mathcal{L})(f) \in \mathrm{Ar}_{\mathcal{K}(\mathcal{L})(j),\mathcal{K}(\mathcal{L})(i)}(\mathrm{Preord})$,

with for all $r_j \in \mathcal{R}(\mathcal{L})(j)$,,

$\mathcal{K}(\mathcal{L})(f)(r_j) = r_j[f] \in \mathcal{K}(\mathcal{L})(i)$,

$\mathrm{Predsymb}(\mathcal{L}) = \{=_{\mathrm{Ob}},\ =_{\mathrm{Ar}},\ =_{\mathrm{Rel}},\ \in,\ \subseteq,\ \vdash_{\mathcal{L}},\ \ldots\}$.

In a sense, span refers to suitably well-defined operations (determined by $\mathrm{Th}_{\mathrm{syn}_b,b}$) :

$\mathrm{Term}(\mathcal{L}) \supseteq \mathrm{Wfter}_b(\mathcal{L}) = \mathrm{span}(\mathrm{Var}(\mathcal{L}),\ \mathrm{FuncSym}(\mathcal{L}))$

$= \mathrm{Var}(\mathrm{Ar}(\mathcal{L})) \cup \mathrm{Var}(\mathrm{Rel}(\mathcal{L}))$

$$= \mathrm{Wfex}_b(\ell)$$

$$= \mathrm{Wff}_b(\ell) \cup \mathrm{Wft}_{(b)}(\ell) ,$$

$$\mathrm{Var}(\mathrm{Rel}(\ell)) \supseteq \mathrm{Wff}_b(\ell) = \mathrm{span}(\mathrm{Wfat}_b(\ell)\ ;\ \mathrm{Loc}(\ell),\ \mathrm{Quan}(\ell))$$

$$\supseteq \mathrm{Wfat}_b(\ell) = \mathrm{Var}(\mathrm{Rel}(\ell))[\mathrm{Wft}_{(b)}(\ell)]$$

$$\overset{d}{=} \cdot[\cdot\cdot](\mathrm{Var}(\mathrm{Rel}(\ell)),\ \mathrm{Wft}_{(b)}(\ell)) ,$$

$$\mathrm{Var}(\mathrm{Ar}(\ell)) \supseteq \mathrm{Wft}_{(b)}(\ell) = \mathrm{span}(\mathrm{Wfv}_{(b)}(\ell),\ \mathrm{Var}(\mathrm{Ar}(\ell)))$$

$$\supseteq \mathrm{Wfv}_{(b)}(\ell) = \mathrm{proj}(\mathrm{Var}(\mathrm{Ob}(\ell))\times\mathrm{Var}(\mathrm{Ob}(\ell)))$$

$$\supseteq \mathrm{Wfc}_{(b)}(\ell) = \mathrm{proj}(\mathrm{Cons}(\mathrm{Ob}(\ell))\times\mathrm{Cons}(\mathrm{Ob}(\ell))) ,$$

$$\mathrm{Sent}_b(\ell) = \mathrm{FV}_b^{-1}(\emptyset),\ \mathrm{Open}_b(\ell) = B_nV_b^{-1}(\ell)(\emptyset)$$

$$\mathrm{Th}_{\mathrm{syn}_b,b}(\ell) = (\mathrm{Ax}_{\mathrm{syn}_b,b}(\ell),\ \mathrm{Rul}_{\mathrm{syn}_b,b}(\ell)) ,$$

$$\mathrm{Ser}_b(\ell) = \mathrm{Seq}_{\mathrm{Wff}_b(\ell)}(\ell) \cap \mathrm{De}(\mathrm{Th}_{\mathrm{syn}_b,b}(\ell)) ,$$

$$\mathrm{Seq}_{\mathrm{Wff}_b(\ell)}(\ell) = \mathrm{Wff}_b(\ell) \times \{\vdash_\ell\} \times \mathrm{Wff}_b(\ell) .$$

A word of caution: Unfortunately, the word "sentence" is used universally in the literature of formal linguistics and the analysis of natural language to refer to any (compound) form, obeying natural language grammar/syntactics. By the Parsing Principle, this corresponds to some wfex (well-formed) expression in the formal language. However, the latter may or may not be a formal sentence. In addition, such wfex's usually have specific labels for their individual variables, such as, $x^{(i)}$ = "John" and $y^{(\Omega^i)}$ = "happy", etc., as in the natural language sentence "John is happy, but Sam likes to read". These labels indicate which individual variable assignment map values are to be given to the free variables, as part of the semantic evaluation of the wfex. (See 2.3.2.)

VI. Basic theorems of $\mathrm{Th}_{\mathrm{syn}_K,K}(\ell)$:

In the following, $a,b,c,d,\ldots \in \mathfrak{X}(i)$ for some $i \in \mathrm{Ob}(\mathcal{C})$, $(\mathcal{C},\mathfrak{X})$ a deduction category with all additional properties as required. Equality " = " really means " $=_{\mathfrak{X}(i)}$ " ; " $\le$ " means " $\le_{\mathfrak{X}(i)}$ " . We also use R_α for $R_{I,Th,\alpha}$, $\alpha = 0,1,\ldots,24$.

Theorem 1

(i) $a \wedge b \le a,b \le a \vee b$

(ii) $a \le b$ iff $a \wedge b = a$ iff $a \vee b = b$

(iii) $a = b$ iff $a \wedge b = a \vee b = a = b$

Proof: (i) : R_1 , R_4 , R_5 , R_9 , R_{10} .

(ii) : If $a \le b$, since $a \le a$ by R_1 , then $a \le a \wedge b$, by R_6 . But $a \wedge b \le a$ by (i) and hence $a = a \wedge b$. If $a = a \wedge b$, then since $a \wedge b \le b$, by (i) , R_2 implies $a \le b$. A similar proof holds for the remainder.

Theorem 2 Symmetry

$$a \wedge b = b \wedge a .$$

Proof: From Theorem 1 (i), and R_6 , $a \wedge b \le b \wedge a$ and by arbitrariness of a and b , $b \wedge a \le a \wedge b$ and hence, $a \wedge b = b \wedge a$.

Theorem 3 Idempotence

$$a \wedge a = a = a \vee a .$$

Proof: By Theorem 1 (i) , for $b = a$, $a \wedge a \le a$. But since $a \le a$, a , by R_6 , $a \le a \wedge a$. Similarly, use R_8 to obtain $a = a \vee a$, using Theorem 4.

Theorem 4 Marginal properties

$$a \wedge T = T \wedge a = a$$

$$a \vee T = T \vee a = T$$

$$a \wedge \bot = \bot \wedge a = \bot$$

$$a \vee \bot = \bot \vee a = a$$

Proof: Use R_3 , R_7 , etc.

Theorem 5 Associativity

$$a \wedge (b \wedge c) = (a \wedge b) \wedge c$$

$$a \vee (b \vee c) = (a \vee b) \vee c$$

Proof: By Theorem 1 and R_4 , $a \wedge b \le a$, $(a \wedge b) \wedge c \le a, c$. Then R_6 implies $(a \wedge b) \wedge c \le a \wedge c$. Similarly, $(a \wedge b) \wedge c \le b \wedge c$. Hence by Theorem 3, $(a \wedge b) \wedge c = (a \wedge b) \wedge c) \wedge (a \wedge b) \wedge c) \le (a \wedge c) \wedge (b \wedge c) \le a \wedge (b \wedge c)$. By arbitrariness of a,b,c, we can reverse inequality with a and c interchanged.

(iii) Use part (ii), applying R_{12} .

(iv) Note that (iii) above applied to Theorem 1 (i) yields

$$nt(a \vee a) \leq nt(a) \;,\; nt(b) \leq nt(a \wedge b) \;,$$

and hence by R_6 and R_8

$$nt(a \vee b) \leq nt(a) \wedge nt(b) \;,$$

$$nt(a \wedge b) \geq nt(a) \vee nt(b) \;.$$

Finally, note that by part (ii) above, assuming distributivity (see Theorem 8)

$$nt(a) \wedge nt(b) \wedge (a \vee b)$$

$$= (nt(a) \wedge nt(b) \wedge a) \vee (nt(a) \wedge nt(b) \wedge b)$$

$$\leq (nt(a) \wedge a) \vee (nt(b) \wedge b) = \bot \vee \bot = \bot \;.$$

Hence, applying R_{12} :

$$nt(a) \wedge nt(b) \wedge (a \vee b) \leq \bot$$

Hence,

$$nt(a) \wedge nt(b) \leq nt(a \vee b) \;.$$

Similarly by considering the above proof for $a \wedge b$ replacing $a \vee b$, R_{12} again yields the desired result.

Note: Since $\wedge$ and $\vee$ are associative and symmetric, they can be extended recursively in the obvious way, unambiguously, to an arbitrary finite number of arguments, and in turn, formally to any number of arguments.

(v) Consider $T = nt(\bot) = nt(a \wedge nt(a)) = nt\ a \vee nt(nt(a))$,

$$a = a \wedge T = a \wedge (nt(a) \vee nt(nt(a))$$

$$= (a \wedge nt(a) \vee (a \wedge nt(nt(a))) = a \wedge nt(nt(a)),$$

Theorem 6 Non-decreasing

If $a \leq b$, then $a \wedge c \leq b \wedge c$, $a \vee c \leq b \vee c$.

Proof: By Theorems 2, 5, 3,

$$(a \wedge c) \wedge (b \wedge c) = (a \wedge b) \wedge c = a \wedge c \;.$$

Then by Theorem 1 (ii), $a \wedge c \leq b \wedge c$.

Theorem 7 Negation properties

Define $nt(a) \overset{d}{=} a \Rightarrow \perp$.
Then

(i) $nt(T) = \perp$, $nt(\perp) = T$.

(ii) $nt(a) \wedge a = \perp$ (Law of Excluded Middle).
Hence, if $a \leq b$,
$nt(b) \wedge a = \perp$.

(iii) If $a \leq b$, then $nt(b) \leq nt(a)$ (Nonincreasing).

(iv) $nt(a \vee b) = nt(a) \wedge nt(b) \leq nt(a)$
$nt(a \wedge b) = nt(a) \vee nt(b)$ (DeMorgan's Laws)

(v) $nt(nt(a)) \neq a$, in general,
$nt(a) \vee a \neq T$, in general,

but:

$nt(a) \vee nt(nt(a)) = T$,
$a \leq nt(nt(a))$.

Proof: (i) Use R_{11} , etc.
(ii) Use R_{11} , noting $b \leq b$, $\perp \leq \perp$ and hence $b \wedge (b \Rightarrow \perp) \leq \perp$; then use, e.g., Theorem 6. Then by Theorem 1 (ii), $a \leq nt(nt(a))$.

Theorem 8 Distributivity

$$a \wedge (b \vee c) = (a \wedge b) \vee (a \wedge c) ,$$

$$a \vee (b \wedge c) = (a \vee b) \wedge (a \vee c) .$$

(**Proof**: Since $(a \wedge b) \leq (a \wedge b) \vee (a \wedge c)$ and $(a \wedge c) \leq (a \wedge b) \vee (a \wedge c)$, R_8 implies $a \wedge (b \vee c) \leq (a \wedge b) \vee (a \wedge c)$. The converse procedure is easily verified.)

Theorem 9

(i) $a \wedge (a \Rightarrow b) \leq b \leq (a \Rightarrow b)$.

(ii) If $a \geq b$, $(a \Rightarrow b) = T$.

(**Proof**: Use R_{11} and R_{12} .)

Remarks.

Thus, under $Th_{syn_K,K}(\mathcal{L})$, an intuitionistic-like theory, it follows that operators $\wedge$ and $\vee$ will have the properties of general t-norms and t-conorms, respectively, and nt is a general negation (see section 2.3.6) with the added structures of idempotency, DeMorgan and distributivity - all properties that ordinary minimum and maximum have.

It may be desirable to replace $Th_{syn_K,K}(\mathcal{L})$- for example by a less restricted theory-where $\wedge$ is replaced by & being a t-norm, $\vee$ by or, being a t-conorm, nt (and hence $\Rightarrow$) by a general negation (and hence implication) operator. However, in this case, the formal topos structure will no longer be valid.

2.3 Semantic evaluations.

2.3.1 Preamble.

Two schools of thought arise regarding the semantic or truth evaluation of a formal language. The platonistic approach interprets the semantic evaluation as a statement about the real world. On the other hand, the formalistic approach allows no such interpretation.

Despite the setbacks in platonism (the advent of non-Euclidean geometry, discovery of paradoxes in naive set theory, Gödel's uncertainty theorem, Heisenberg's uncertainty principle, etc.), the philosophy has a great deal of appeal. This is because of the continuing egocentric viewpoint that Man has with the rest of the universe. Hence, we continue to persue knowledge and "prove" theories (within possibly inconsistent systems) and attempt to relate these concepts to our surroundings.

2.3.2 Basic evaluations of formal language.

The structure of a formal language $\mathcal{L}$ has been given in the previous section (2.2). In this subsection, we present semantic evaluations of $\mathcal{L}$. These evaluations are all carried out within a deduction category framework. If $\mathcal{L}$ has enough structure, (such as in the form $\mathcal{L}_{syn_K,K}$ - see 2.2.2), then $\mathcal{L}$ may be further evaluated within a formal topos. Since a construction can be carried out showing any deduction category with some additional structure (in particular, a formal topos) can be imbedded within a corresponding category (or topos) (see Appendix 2 at the end of section 2.4), the above semantic evaluations of $\mathcal{L}$ may be naturally thought of as being within a category - or topos. (Compatible with this, we can identify any ordinary topos $\mathcal{C}$ as a formal topos $(\mathcal{C},\text{Sub})$.)

Since a semantic evaluation of $\mathcal{L}$ may be thought of as an interpretation of $\mathcal{L}$, there are (in fact, infinitely) many interpretations of $\mathcal{L}$, which, although certainly valid within the very general and encompassing structure of a deduction category (including essentially all systems of our interest), may not hold within the much more restrictive form of a formal topos (or topos), even if $\mathcal{L}$ has sufficient structure. For example, in a given situation, it may be more appropriate to interpret the logical connector " & " (in Loc($\mathcal{L}$)), not as a minimum operator but as a product or more generally as a t-norm operator. (See section 2.3.6) In particular, (see Appendix 2 at the end of 2.4) it follows that rule $R_{I,Th,6}$ is violated, in general, unless $\wedge$ is a minimum type operator. On the other hand, we may still wish to retain - at least formally - the same evaluation procedure, as if a formal topos were present. We will apply this principle to the important case of general logical systems (section 2.3.5), the cornerstone of the approach taken in this text to the analysis of uncertainty, and in particular, to the combination of evidence problem (see Chapter 8).

We can summarize the role of natural language, formal language and semantic evaluations in the analysis of uncertainty as follows:

Natural language can be used as the vehicle to express cognition explicitly, although, often somewhat vaguely. (But keep in mind that all "rigorous, mathematical" concepts are, by definition, expressable in natural language.) Through the Parsing Principle, all of this is translated into a formal language. Thus the problem of uncertainty or combination of evidence being considered concerning an unknown parameter - such as "How old is Charles?", through all the information supplied, including statistical data, linguistic information, and general inference rules that are applicable - may be modeled at first within a formal language structure. (See Chapters 8 and 9 for further details on how such problems may be treated.) Then a class of appropriate semantic evaluations must be chosen to determine the truth content of all of the information as a whole, and in particular, that for which projects to the unknown parameter. First, we choose the class of possible semantic evaluations upon the relevant formal logical connectors $Loc(\ell)$ - such as nt (not), & (and) , or, if ( ) then ( ), etc. - and relevant formal quantifiers $Quan(\ell)$ - such as $\forall$ (for all), $\exists$ (there is), Mo (most), etc. This is the *logic* for the problem, i.e., a collection of semantic evaluations having in common a particular evaluation upon $Loc(\ell) \cup Quan(\ell)$ is called a logic. (See 2.3.3.) Next, we consider also, in effect, a subclass of semantic evaluations upon $Foun(\ell)$, the *set theory connectors* $\in$ - membership, $\asymp$ - equivalence of sets, etc., which have common values and which are compatible with the logic chosen. (See 2.3.4.) In addition, we consider the class of semantic evaluations upon the basic "objects" involved, yielding the universes of discourse or semantical domains, such as the set of all men, the set of all ordered pairs of numbers, one representing heights of women in inches and the other weights in lbs. (See the development in this section for details.)

Also, in conjunction with the above, we must determine the appropriate class of semantic evaluations upon other basic relations (corresponding to predicates or verbs in natural language) and wff's (well-formed) formulas, formed as compounds (or strings or the spanning) of basic relations together with the substitution of various functions (or terms) within the relations. The semantic evaluation of relations yields dispersions or membership functions: in general, numerical-valued functions upon their signatures which become their corresponding universes of discourse through the semantic evaluation. If any universes of discourse have as elements, "events" or equivalently sets of more primitive elements - such as in the case of probability measures and Choquet capacity-type measures, where for the former, a given universe of discourse - corresponding to a given probability measure (there may be many probability measures for a given problem, and hence many universes of discourse) - consists of σ-algebra of subsets of a given set or equivalently a Boolean algebra of events, then we call the corresponding dispersions *uncertainty measures*.

Finally, we evaluate semantically all the relevant individual or particularized *variables* from the universes of discourse - such as "Charles", "age of" and, in turn, by appropriate substitution, obtain the desired numerical truth values.

I. Semantic evaluations within a deduction category.

Let $(\mathcal{C},\mathfrak{R})$ be a given deduction category, with finite products and having possibly additional properties when needed.

Define a typical *partial semantic evaluation* (or structure or assignment) map from $\mathrm{Core}(\mathcal{L}) \cup \mathrm{Term}(\mathcal{L}))$ into SET , denoted symbolically by $\| \ \|_{(\mathcal{C},\mathfrak{R})} : (\mathrm{Core}(\mathcal{L}), \mathrm{Term}(\mathcal{L})) \to \mathrm{SET}$ where $\| \ \|_{(\mathcal{C},\mathfrak{R})} : \mathrm{Core}(\mathcal{L}) \to \mathrm{SET}$ is made into a functor between categories $\mathrm{Core}(\mathcal{L})$ and SET . (Unless stated otherwise, both $\mathcal{L}$ and $(\mathcal{C},\mathfrak{R})$ are fixed, and consequently, we will drop the subscript $(\mathcal{C},\mathfrak{R})$ from the semantic evaluation map from our writing, but not from our thoughts! Later, another subscript ω will be used, but for a different purpose.)

Consider first the three distinguished objects $\mathrm{Ob}(\mathcal{L})$, $\mathrm{Ar}(\mathcal{L})$, $\mathrm{Rel}(\mathcal{L}) \in \mathrm{Ob}(\mathrm{Core}(\mathcal{L}))$:

The class of *universes of discourse* or *semantical domains* is:

$$\begin{aligned}\|\mathrm{Ob}(\mathcal{L})\| &\overset{d}{=} \|\mathrm{Var}(\mathrm{Ob}(\mathcal{L}))\| \\ &\overset{d}{=} \{\|i\|, \|i_1\|, \ldots, \|j\|, \ldots, \|k\|, \ldots\}\end{aligned}$$

where typically $\|i\| \in \mathrm{Ob}(\mathcal{C})$, and hence

$$\| \ \| : \mathrm{Var}(\mathrm{Ob}(\mathcal{L})) \to \mathrm{Ob}(\mathcal{C}) \text{ , with}$$

$$\|\mathrm{Var}(\mathrm{Ob}(\mathcal{L}))\| = \{\|i\| \mid i \in \mathrm{Var}(\mathrm{Ob}(\mathcal{L}))\} \subseteq \mathrm{Ob}(\mathcal{C}) \text{ .}$$

Similarly, the class of arrows between the universes of discourse is:

$$\begin{aligned}\|\mathrm{Ar}(\mathcal{L})\| &\overset{d}{=} \|\mathrm{Var}(\mathrm{Ar}(\mathcal{L}))\| \\ &\overset{d}{=} \{\|f\|, \ldots, \|g\|, \ldots, \|h\|, \ldots\} \\ &\subseteq \mathrm{Ar}(\mathcal{C})\end{aligned}$$

and the class of relations on the universes of discourse is:

$$\begin{aligned}\|\mathrm{Rel}(\mathcal{L})\| &\overset{d}{=} \|\mathrm{Var}(\mathrm{Rel}(\mathcal{L}))\| \\ &= \{\|r\|, \ldots, \|s\|, \ldots, \|t\|, \ldots\} \\ &\subseteq \mathrm{Rel}(\mathcal{C},\mathfrak{R}) \overset{d}{=} \bigcup_{a \in \mathrm{Ob}(\mathcal{C})} \mathfrak{R}(a) \text{ .}\end{aligned}$$

Furthermore, let

$$\|\mathrm{Sort}(\mathcal{L})\| \overset{d}{=} \{\|\mathrm{Ob}(\mathcal{L})\|, |\mathrm{Ar}(\mathcal{L})\|, \|\mathrm{Rel}(\mathcal{L})\|\} \text{ .}$$

In turn, for any $\alpha \in \mathrm{Typ}(\mathcal{L})$, define

$$\|\alpha\| = \|\mathrm{Var}(\alpha)\| = \{\|a\| \mid a \in \mathrm{Var}(\alpha)\} \text{ .}$$

$$\|Typ(\mathcal{L})\| = \{\|\alpha\| \mid \alpha \in Typ(\mathcal{L})\}$$

$$= span(\|Sort(\mathcal{L})\| \; ; \times \, , \Omega) \, ,$$

where $\times$ and Ω are cartesian product and exponentiation, if needed, for $\mathbb{C}$.

Thus, e.g., $Ob(\mathcal{L}) \times Rel(\mathcal{L}) \in Typ(\mathcal{L})$ and

$$\|Ob(\mathcal{L}) \times Rel(\mathcal{L})\| = \|Ob(\mathcal{L})\| \times \|Rel(\mathcal{L})\| \, , \text{ etc.}$$

Consider next the semantic evaluation on $FuncSymb(\mathcal{L})$ (the arrows of $Core(\mathcal{L})$) :

For any $\alpha,\beta \in Typ(\mathcal{L})$ and $F = (F : \alpha \rightarrow \beta) \in Ar_{\alpha,\beta}(Core(\mathcal{L}))$, choose some

$$\|F\| = (\|F\| : \|\alpha\| \rightarrow \|\beta\|) \in Ar_{\|\alpha\|,\|\beta\|}(SET) \, ,$$

i.e., $\|F\|$ is some ordinary function from the set $\|\alpha\|$ to the set $\|\beta\|$, where for any $a \in Var(\alpha)$ and hence $F(a) \in Term_{\beta}(\mathcal{L})$,

$$\|F(a)\| \stackrel{d}{=} \|F\|(\|a\|) \, , \text{ noting } \|a\| \in \|\alpha\| = \|Var(\alpha)\| \, .$$

Also, for any $(F : \alpha \rightarrow \beta)$, $(G : \beta \rightarrow \gamma) \in Ar(Core(\mathcal{L}))$, and $id_{\alpha} : \alpha \rightarrow \alpha$ in $Ar(Core(\mathcal{L}))$,

$$\|G \circ F\| = \|G\| \|\circ\| \|F\| \, ,$$

$$\|id_{\alpha}\| = id_{\|\alpha\|} \, ,$$

where the composition and identity, $\circ$, id , in $Core(\mathcal{L})$ become ordinary composition $\|\circ\|$ and ordinary identity id for SET . From now on, we abuse notation and let $\|\circ\| = \circ$, etc.

Obviously, the partial semantic evaluation maps of most interest are those which are compatible with $Th_{syn_o}(\mathcal{L})$. Specifically, we say $\| \;\|$ is a *model* of $Th_{syn_o}(\mathcal{L})$, iff by definition, for any $(\Psi \; \gamma \; \theta) \in Ax_{syn_o}(\mathcal{L}) \cup Rul_{syn_o}(\mathcal{L})$, $\|\Psi\| \; \|\gamma\| \; \|\theta\|$ holds, where, e.g., $\|\gamma\|$ is ordinary $=$, for $\gamma \in \{=_{Ob}, =_{Ar}, =_{Rel}\}$ and $\|\in\|$ is ordinary $\in$.

It follows that the same property holds for all $(\Psi \; \gamma \; \theta) \in De(Th_{syn_o}(\mathcal{L}))$. (This definition of a model extends to any given theory and formal language in the obvious way.)

We now assume that $\| \;\|$ *is a model of* $Th_{syn_o}(\mathcal{L})$ *within deduction category* $(\mathbb{C},\mathfrak{R})$.

Thus, we have:

For any $f \in Var(Ar(\mathcal{L}))$, we may write $f = (f : i \rightarrow j) \in Ar_{i,j}(Var(\mathcal{L}))$ for some $i,j \in Var(Ob(\mathcal{L}))$, and hence (from $Th_{syn_o}(\mathcal{L})$) , $S(f) = i$, $B(f) = j$, where $S = (S : Ar(\mathcal{L}) \rightarrow Ob(\mathcal{L}))$, $B = (B : Ar(\mathcal{L}) \rightarrow Ob(\mathcal{L}))$. Then

$$\|f\| = (\|f\| : \|i\| \to \|j\|) \in Ar_{\|i\|,\|j\|}(\mathcal{C}) ,$$

where

$$\|S\| = (\|S\| : \|Var(Ar(\ell))\| \to \|Var(Ob(\ell))\|) ,$$

$$\|B\| = (\|B\| : \|Var(Ar(\ell))\| \to \|Var(Ob(\ell))\|) ,$$

$$\|Id\| = (\|Id\| : \|Var(Ob(\ell))\| \to \|Var(Ar(\ell))\|) ,$$

$$\|proj\| = (\|proj\| : \|Var(Ob(\ell))\| \times \|Var(Ob(\ell))\| \to \|Var(Ob(\ell))\|)$$

are the source (or domain), codomain, identity-making, and projection-making maps for $\mathcal{C}$, respectively. Thus,

$$\|S(f)\| = \|S\|(\|f\|) = \|i\| ,$$

$$\|B(f)\| = \|B\|(\|f\|) = \|j\| .$$

For any $i,j \in Var(Ob(\ell))$,

$$\|Id(i)\| = Id_{\|i\|} ,$$

an identity arrow $Id_{\|i\|} : \|i\| \to \|i\|$ of $\mathcal{C}$, and for any $f,g \in Var(Ar(\ell))$ with $S(f) = S(g)$, i.e.,

$$f = (f : i \to j) \quad \text{and} \quad g = (g : i \to k) ,$$

say, then

$$\|proj_1(i,j)(f\times g)\|$$

$$= \|proj_1\|(\|i\| \times \|j\|)(\|f\| \times \|g\|)$$

$$= \|f\| .$$

Similarly, it follows that $\|\ \|$ is compatible with all axioms and rules (from $Th_{syn_o}(\ell)$) characterizing the functional symbols S , B , $\circ$, Id , $proj$, $\times$, $<\ >$, σ , and $\cdot[\cdot\cdot]$.

In particular, consider again $\|Rel(\ell)\|$:

For any $r \in Var(Rel(\ell))$, we may write $r = r_{\sigma(r)}$ or $r = r_i$, $i = \sigma(r) = \sigma(r_i)$

Now, the function symbol $\sigma = (\sigma : Rel(\ell) \to Ob(\ell))$ has the evaluation

$$\|\sigma\| : \|Var(Rel(\ell))\| \to \|Var(Ob(\ell))\|$$

the signature map for $(\mathcal{C},\mathfrak{R})$ and

$$\|\cdot[\cdot\cdot]\| : \|Var(Rel(\ell))\| \times \|Var(Ar(\ell))\| \to \|Var(Rel(\ell))\| ,$$

the substitution map for $(\mathcal{C},\mathfrak{R})$.

$$\|\sigma(r_i)\| = \|i\| = \|\sigma\|(\|r_i\|) .$$

For all $(f : j \to i)$, $(g : k \to j) \in Var(Ar(\ell))$, $\sigma(r_i) = i$,

$\sigma(r_i[f]) = j$,

$\sigma(r_i[f][g]) = \sigma(r_i[f\circ g]) = k$,

$\sigma(Id(\sigma(r_i))) = \sigma(Id(i)) = i$,

$\|j\| = \|\sigma(r_i[f])\| = \|\sigma\|(\|r_i[f]\|) = \|\sigma\|(\mathfrak{R}(\|f\|)(\|r_i\|))$,

$\|k\| = \|\sigma(r_i[f][g])\| = \|\sigma\|(\|r_i[f\circ g]\|) = \|\sigma\|(\mathfrak{R}(\|f\|\circ\|g\|))(\|r_i\|))$,

$\|i\| = \|\sigma(Id(\sigma(r_i)))\| = \|\sigma\|(Id_{\|\sigma\|(\|r_i\|)}) = \|\sigma\|(Id_{\|i\|})$,

noting

$$\|r_i[f]\| = \mathfrak{R}(\|f\|)(\|r_i\|) ,$$

$$\mathfrak{R}(\|f\|) : \mathfrak{R}(\|i\|) \to \mathfrak{R}(\|j\|) .$$

Clearly in establishing the functor $\|\ \| : Core(\ell) \to SET$, we have also established $\|\ \|$ as the functor $\|\ \| : Var(\ell) \to \mathcal{C}$.

Next, we consider the predicate symbol $\vdash_\ell$, representing (through $R_{I,Th,0} - R_{I,Th,2}$) a partial order over $Var(Rel(\ell))$.

Define

$$\|\vdash_\ell\| = \leq_{Preord} ,$$

where, for any $i \in Var(Ob(\ell))$, and hence $\|i\| \in Ob(\mathcal{C})$ and $\mathfrak{R}(\|i\|) \in Preord$,

$$(\|\vdash_\ell\| \mid \mathfrak{R}(\|i\|) = \leq_{\mathfrak{R}(\|i\|)} .$$

But from the properties of $\leq_{Preord}$ here, it follows that $R_{I,Th,0} - R_{I,Th,2}$ are all realized compatibly:

For any $i,j \in Var(Ob(\ell))$ and r_i , s_i , $t_i \in Var(Rel(\ell))$, with $\sigma(r_i) = \sigma(s_i) = \sigma(t_i) = i$, and $(f : j \to i) \in Var(Ar(\ell))$,

(i) If $(r_i \vdash_\ell s_i)$ (abstractly) then

$$\|r_i\| \leq_{\mathfrak{R}(\|i\|)} \|s_i\| ,$$

$$\|r_i[f]\| = \mathfrak{R}(\|f\|)(\|r_i\|) \leq_{\mathfrak{R}(\|j\|)} \|s_i[f]\| = \mathfrak{R}(\|f\|)(\|s_i\|) ,$$

(ii) $|r_i\| \leq_{\mathfrak{R}(\|i\|)} \|r_i\|$,

(iii) If $(r_i \vdash_{\mathcal{L}} s_i)$, $(s_i \vdash_{\mathcal{L}} t_i)$, then

$$\|r_i\| \leq_{\mathfrak{X}(i)} \|s_i\| \leq_{\mathfrak{X}(i)} \|t_i\|$$

and

$$r_i \vdash_{\mathcal{L}} t_i \; .$$

In turn, it follows that $(\|\ \|, \tau_{\|\ \|}) : \tilde{V}ar(\mathcal{L}) \to (\mathfrak{C},\mathfrak{X})$ is an arrow between the two deduction categories (see 2.3.3 (B)). Since $\|\ \| : Var(\mathcal{L}) \to \mathfrak{C}$ is already a functor and $\tau_{\|\ \|} : Ob(Var(\mathcal{L})) \to Ar(Preord)$, where for any $i \in Ob(Var(\mathcal{L})) = Var(Ob(\mathcal{L}))$,

$$\tau_{\|\ \|}(i) \in Ar_{\mathcal{H}(\mathcal{L})(i),\mathfrak{X}(\|i\|)}(Preord) \; ,$$

where for any $r_i \in \mathcal{H}(\mathcal{L})(i)$, $(\sigma(r_i) = i)$,

$$\tau_{\|\ \|}(i)(r_i) \overset{d}{=} \|r_i\|$$

is a natural transform

$$\tau_{\|\ \|} : \mathcal{H}(\mathcal{L}) \overset{\cdot}{\longrightarrow} \mathfrak{X}\circ\|\ \| \; ,$$

since for all $i,j \in Var(Ob(\mathcal{L}))$, $(f : j \to i) \in Var(Ar(\mathcal{L}))$, and hence

$$\|f\| : \|j\| \to \|i\| \; ,$$

$$\mathfrak{X}(\|f\|) : \mathfrak{X}(\|i\| \to \mathfrak{X}(\|j\|) \; ,$$

and therefore

$$(\mathfrak{X}\circ\|\ \|)(f)(\tau_{\|\ \|}(i)(r_i))$$

$$= \mathfrak{X}(\|f\|)(\|r_i\|)$$

$$= \|r_i[f]\|$$

$$= (\tau_{\|\ \|}(j))(\mathcal{H}(\mathcal{L})(f)) \; .$$

Next, consider $\|\ \|$ over $Wfex_o(\mathcal{L})$:

Again noting that (due to $Th_{syn_o}(\mathcal{L})$) $Wfex_o(\mathcal{L}) \subseteq Wfter_o(\mathcal{L})$, the evaluation of $\|\ \|$ over $Wfex_o(\mathcal{L})$, and hence over $Wff_o(\mathcal{L})$, $Wfat_o(\mathcal{L})$, $Wft_{(o)}(\mathcal{L})$, $Wfv_{(o)}(\mathcal{L})$ and $Wfc_{(o)}(\mathcal{L})$, become a special case of determining $\|\ \|$ over $Wfter_o(\mathcal{L})$.

Thus:

$$\|Wfc_{(o)}(\mathcal{L})\| = \{\ldots,\|1_a\|, \|1_b\|,\ldots\} \; ,$$

where $\|1_a\|$, $\|1_b\|$, ... are terminal objects in $\mathcal{C}$;

$$\|Wfv_{(\circ)}(\ell)\| = \{..,\|y^{(j)}\|, \|x^{(k)}\|,...\} ,$$

where typically

$$y^{(j)} = y^{(j)}_{i\times k\times j} = proj_j(i\times k\times j) ,$$

$$x^{(k)} = x^{(k)}_{i\times k} = proj_k(i\times k) \in Var(Ar(\ell)) ,$$

$$\|y^{(j)}\| = \|proj\|_{\|j\|}(\|i\|\times\|k\|\times\|j\|) \in Ar(\mathcal{C}) ,$$

$$\|x^{(k)}\| = \|proj\|_{\|k\|}(\|i\|\times\|k\|) \in Ar(\mathcal{C}) , ... ;$$

$$\|Wft_{(\circ)}(\ell)\| = \{...,\|f(y^{(j)})\| , \|g(h(z^{(k)}), x^{(i)})\|,...\} ,$$

where typically, $(f : j \to k)$, $(h : k \to \ell)$, $(g : \ell \times i \to j) \in Var(Ar(\ell))$, $y^{(i)} = y^{(j)}_{i\times k\times j} \in Wfv_j(\ell)$, $z^{(k)} = z^{(k)}_{i\times k} \in Wfv_k(\ell)$, $x^{(i)} = x^{(i)}_{i\times k} \in Wfv_i(\ell)$, $i,j,k,\ell \in Var(Ob(\ell))$ and

$$\|f\| \in Ar_{\|j\|,\|k\|}(\mathcal{C}) , \|h\| \in Ar_{\|k\|,\|\ell\|}(\mathcal{C}) , \|g\| \in Ar_{\|\ell\|\times\|i\|,\|j\|}(\mathcal{C}) ,$$

$$\|f(y^{(j)})\| = \|f\|\circ\|y^{(j)}\| \in Ar_{\|i\|\times\|k\|\times\|j\|,\|k\|}(\mathcal{C}) ,$$

$$\|g(\langle h(z^{(k)}), x^{(i)}\rangle)\|$$

$$= \|g\|(\langle\|h\|\circ\|z^{(k)}\|, \|x^{(i)}\|\rangle) \in Ar_{\|i\|\times\|k\|,\|j\|}(\mathcal{C}) ,$$

$$\|Wfat_\circ(\ell)\| = \{...,\|t_{j\times k}[g(\langle h(z^{(k)}), x^{(i)}\rangle) \times f(y^{(j)})]\|,...\}$$

where typically, g , h , $z^{(k)}$, $x^{(i)}$, $y^{(j)}$ are as above and $t_{j\times k} \in Var(Rel(\ell))$ $(\sigma(t_{j\times k}) = j \times k)$,

$$\|t_{j\times k}[g(\langle h(z^{(k)}), x^{(i)}\rangle) \times f(y^{(j)})]\|$$

$$= \mathfrak{R}(\|g(\langle h(z^{(k)}), x^{(i)}\rangle)\| \times \|f(y^{(j)})\|) (\|t_{j\times k}\|) \in Rel(\mathcal{C},\mathfrak{R}) .$$

This completes the specification of $\| \ \|$ over $Wfex_\circ(\ell)$, noting that because only $Th_{syn_\circ}(\ell)$ is present, $\| \ \|$ over $Wff_\circ(\ell) \dashv Wfat_\circ(\ell)$, in general, is arbitrary fixed so that for any $\Psi \in Wff_\circ(\ell) \vdash Wfat_\circ(\ell)$, $\|\Psi\| \in Rel(\mathcal{C},\mathfrak{R})$ with $\|\sigma\|(\|\Psi\|) = \|\sigma(\Psi)\|$, etc., as is compatible with $Th_{syn_\circ}(\ell)$ only.

We also obtain

$$\|FV_o\|, \|TV_o\|, \|BnV_o\| : \|Wfex_o(\mathcal{L})\| \to \mathcal{P}(\|Wfv_o(\mathcal{L})\|)$$

and in turn, $\|Sent_o(\mathcal{L})\|$, $\|Open_o(\mathcal{L})\|$ in the obvious ways.

Thus, in summary, we can write the typical partial semantic evaluation model symbolically as

$$\| \ \| : \mathcal{L}_{syn_o} \to SET ,$$

where

$\| \ \| : Core(\mathcal{L}) \to SET$ is a functor,

$(\| \ \|, \tau_{\| \ \|}) : \tilde{V}ar(\mathcal{L}) \to (\mathbb{C}, \mathfrak{R})$ is an arrow,

$\|\alpha\| = \|Var(\alpha)\|$, $\alpha \in Typ(\mathcal{L})$,

$\|Var(Ar(\mathcal{L}))\| \cup \|Var(Rel(\mathcal{L}))\| = Ar(\mathbb{C}) \cup Rel(\mathbb{C},\mathfrak{R})$

$= \|Wfter_o(\mathcal{L})\| = span(\|Var(Typ(\mathcal{L}))\|, \|FuncSym(\mathcal{L})\|)$

$\supseteq \|Wfex_o(\mathcal{L})\| = \|Wff_o(\mathcal{L})\| \cup \|Wft_{(o)}(\mathcal{L})\|$,

$\|Wfat_o(\mathcal{L})\| = span(\|Var(Rel(\mathcal{L}))\| \times \|Wft_{(b)}(\mathcal{L})\| \ ; \mathfrak{R}(\|\cdot\cdot\|)(\|\cdot\|))$,

$\|Wft_o(\mathcal{L})\| = span(\|Wfv_{(o)}(\mathcal{L})\|; \|Var(Ar(\mathcal{L}))\|)$

$\supseteq \|Wfv_o(\mathcal{L})\|$

$= proj(\|Var(Ob(\mathcal{L}))\| \times \|Var(Ob(\mathcal{L}))\|)$

$\supseteq proj(\|Cons(Ob(\mathcal{L}))\| \times \|Cons(Ob(\mathcal{L}))\|)$,

$\|Th_{syn_o}(\mathcal{L})\| = \{(\|\varphi\| \ \|\gamma\| \ \|\theta\|) \mid (\varphi \ \gamma \ \theta) \in Th_{syn_o}(\mathcal{L})\}$,

$\|De(Th_{syn}(\mathcal{L}))\| = \{(\|\varphi\| \ \|\gamma\| \ \|\theta\|) \mid (\varphi \ \gamma \ \theta) \in De(Th_{syn}(\mathcal{L}))\}$,

etc.

Note, that the evaluation of any $\varphi \in Wfex_o(\mathcal{L})$, depends on the evaluation of $TV_o(\varphi)$ - which is a collection of projections. Each such projection becomes a projection in the sense of category $\mathbb{C}$ (under the evaluation), in a natural corresponding sense. However, this is not enough to specify an actual realization. For example, let $r_i \in Var(Ob(\mathcal{L}))$ and

$x^{(i)} = x_{k\times i}{}^{(i)} = proj_i(k \times i) \in Wfv_i(\mathcal{L}) \subseteq Var(Ar(\mathcal{L}))$, yielding

$\varphi \overset{d}{=} r_i[x^{(i)}] \in Wfat_o(\mathcal{L})$ (with signature $\sigma(r_i[x^{(i)}]) = k \times i)$.

Then, as we have seen, $\|\Psi\| = \mathfrak{R}(\|x^{(i)}\|)(\|r_i\|)$, where $\|x^{(i)}\| = proj_{\|i\|}(\|k\| \times \|i\|) \in Ar(\mathcal{C})$ and $\|r_i\| \in Rel(\mathcal{C},\mathfrak{R})$ (with $\|\sigma\|(\|r_i\|) = \|i\|$, etc.). However, if we wish to further evaluate $\|\Psi\|$ for particular possible domain values of $\|x^{(i)}\|$ (relative to $\|r_i\|$, of course) , we must consider some kind of constant arrow in $\mathcal{C}$ which in some sense has its constant value in $\|i\| \in Ob(\mathcal{C})$.

To abstract the above need in a general setting, we will assume the following for deduction category $(\mathcal{C},\mathfrak{R})$:

(ω) For each $a \in Ob(\mathcal{C})$, there exists (possibly, many) terminal objects 1_a such that the arrow $(f_{1_a} : 1_a \to a) \in Ar(\mathcal{C})$ is a subobject of a (i.e., a monic - see Appendix 1 at the end of 2.4). Denote the class of all such arrows (as a runs over $Ob(\mathcal{L})$) as $\mathcal{T}(\mathcal{C})$. In turn, consider some collection of interest $\mathcal{A} \subseteq Wfex_o(\mathcal{L})$. Then define a mapping (again as for $\| \ \|$, in general, there are an infinite variety of choices) called the *individual variable assignment map*

$$\omega : FV_o(\mathcal{A}) \to \mathcal{T}(\mathcal{C}) ,$$

such that for any $x^{(i)} \in FV_o(\mathcal{A})$ $(x^{(i)} \in Wfv_i(\mathcal{L})$, etc.) ,

$$\omega(x^{(i)}) \stackrel{d}{=} f_{1_{\|i\|}} ,$$

for any choice of $f_{1_{\|i\|}}$.

Finally, the full semantic evaluation of $\mathcal{L}_{syn_o}$ together with the selected collection of well-formed expressions in $\mathcal{L}_{syn_o}$ is denoted as

$$\| \ \|_\omega : \mathcal{L}_{syn_o} \to (\mathcal{C},\mathfrak{R}) ,$$

or simply (where $\mathcal{L} = \mathcal{L}_{syn_o}$ is understood)

$$\| \ \|_\omega : \mathcal{L} \to (\mathcal{C},\mathfrak{R}) .$$

It should be noted that many semantic evaluations indeed satisfy condition (ω) . Using the previous example of $\Psi = r_i[x^{(i)}]$, we note the following interpretations for deduction category $(\mathcal{C},\mathfrak{R})$ (see Appendix 2 at the end of 2.4):

(i) $(\mathcal{C},\mathfrak{R})$ = (SET, Sub) .

Then, noting that $\|i\| \in Ob(SET)$ and here $1_{\|i\|} \in \|i\|$ may be arbitrary, $\|r_i\| \subseteq \|i\|$, and without loss of generality we have $f_{1_{\|i\|}} : 1_{\|i\|} \to 1_{\|i\|}$, a one-point map, so that

$$\|\Psi\|_\omega = Sub(f_{1_{\|i\|}})(\|r_i\|)$$

$$= f^{-1}_{1_{\| \|}}(\|r_i\|)$$

$$= \begin{cases} 1_{\| \|} & \text{iff } 1_{\| \|} \in \|r_i\| \\ \varnothing & \text{iff } 1_{\| \|} \notin \|r_i\| \end{cases},$$

establishing when a point $1_{\|i\|}$ is in the relation $\|r_i\|$ or not.

(ii) $(\mathcal{C}, \mathfrak{X}) = (SET, H^{\cdot})$, $H^{\cdot}$ being exponentation, where $H = [0,1]$. Again, $\|i\| \in Ob(SET)$ and $1_{\|i\|} \in \|i\|$, arbitrary, $f_{1_{\|i\|}}$ as before. But here $\|r_i\| \in H^{\|i\|}$ and

$$\|\Psi\|_\omega = H^{\cdot}(f_{1_{\|i\|}})(\|r_i\|)$$

$$= \|r_i\| \circ f_{1_{\|i\|}}$$

$$= \|r_i\|(1_{\|i\|}),$$

establishing, in a general sense, the degree to which assignment $1_{\|i\|}$ of $x^{(i)}$ is compatible (or is "in") with the evaluation $\|r_i\|$ of r_i.

Again, to reiterate, from now on through the remainder of the text, the semantic evaluation $\| \; \| : \mathcal{L}_{syn_o} \to (\mathcal{C}, \mathfrak{X})$ is always assumed to be a model of $Th_{syn_o}(\mathcal{L})$. When the structure $\mathcal{L} = \mathcal{L}_{syn_o}$ is understood, we simply write $\| \; \| : \mathcal{L} \to (\mathcal{C}, \mathfrak{X})$.

II. The canonical deduction category.

In part (I) of this section, a formal language $\mathcal{L}_{syn_o}$ was evaluated in a given deduction category, and, further, the concept of models within that deduction category was treated. But note the obvious partial converse: A deduction category, namely $\widetilde{Var}(\mathcal{L}) = (Var(\mathcal{L}), \mathcal{H}(\mathcal{L}))$, is always present within $\mathcal{L}_{syn_o}$ (see 2.2.2) so that $\| \ \|_{\widetilde{Var}(\mathcal{L})} : \mathcal{L}_{syn_o} \to \widetilde{Var}(\mathcal{L})$ is a canonical model - and $\widetilde{Var}(\mathcal{L})$ can be considered a canonical deduction category - defined as follows:

(i) For any $\alpha \in Typ(\mathcal{L})$,

$$\|\alpha\|_{\widetilde{Var}(\mathcal{L})} \stackrel{d}{=} \|Var(\alpha)\|_{\widetilde{Var}(\mathcal{L})} = Var(\alpha) \ ,$$

(ii) $\|Wfter_o(\mathcal{L})\| = Wfter_o(\mathcal{L})$, etc.,

(iii) Ordering is the same. We can let $(r \leq_{\mathfrak{R}} s) = (r \vdash_{\mathcal{L}} s)$, for all $r,s \in De(Th_{syn_b,b}(\mathcal{L}))$, $b = 0,K$, etc.

Thus, essentially $\| \ \|_{\widetilde{Var}(\mathcal{L})} : \mathcal{L} \to \widetilde{Var}(\mathcal{L})$ is an identity-like map.

III. Semantic evaluations within a formal topos.

In part (I) of this section, we developed a class of semantic evaluation procedures of $\mathcal{L}_{syn_o}$ with values within a given deduction category $(\mathfrak{C},\mathfrak{R})$. Some of the syntactic axioms and rules (the second level ones - $R_{II,syn,10}$ and $R_{II,syn,11}$) involved certain of the specially designated function symbols $(\Omega : Ob(\mathcal{L}) \to Ob(\mathcal{L}))$, $(\in : Ob(\mathcal{L}) \to Rel(\mathcal{L}))$, $(\& : Rel(\mathcal{L})^n \to Rel(\mathcal{L}))$, $(\forall : Ob(\mathcal{L}) \times Ob(\mathcal{L}) \times Rel(\mathcal{L}) \to Rel(\mathcal{L}))$, ...) only in a cursory way. However, it is often important to give these additional symbols meaning. $\mathcal{L}_{syn_K,K}$, certainly at the formal level, presents one approach to their interpretation. In turn, the semantic evaluation of this part of formal language must also be considered. That is, we need additional structure on $(\mathfrak{C},\mathfrak{R})$ in order to evaluate the important aspects of set-theoretic foundations, logical connectors and quantifiers.

The additional structure for $(\mathfrak{C},\mathfrak{R})$ we consider here is in the form of a formal topos. (See Appendix 2, end of section 2.4.)

We simply extend $\| \ \| : \mathcal{L}_{syn_o} \to (\mathfrak{C},\mathfrak{R})$ to $\| \ \| : \mathcal{L}_{syn_K,K} \to (\mathfrak{C},\mathfrak{R})$ (now a formal topos) over the set-theoretic foundation symbol class, $\mathrm{Foun}(\mathcal{L}) = \{\Omega, \in, \times, \{\cdot|\cdot\cdot\}, \ldots\}$, the class of logical connectors, $\mathrm{Loc}(\mathcal{L}) = \{\mathrm{nt}, \&, \mathrm{or}, \Rightarrow, \ldots\}$, and the class of quantifiers, $\mathrm{Quan}(\mathcal{L}) = \{\forall, \exists, \ldots\}$. In addition, we wish this extension to be compatible (analagous to that for $\mathcal{L}_{\mathrm{syn}_\circ}$ with $\mathrm{Th}_{\mathrm{syn}_\circ}(\mathcal{L})$) with $\mathrm{Th}_{\mathrm{syn}_K,K}(\mathcal{L})$, i.e., to be a model for $\mathcal{L}_{\mathrm{syn}_K,K}$. In particular,

$$\|\mathrm{Foun}(\mathcal{L})\| = \mathrm{Foun}(\mathfrak{C},\mathfrak{R}) ,$$

$$\|\mathrm{Loc}(\mathcal{L})\| = \mathrm{Loc}(\mathfrak{C},\mathfrak{R}) ,$$

$$\|\mathrm{Quan}(\mathcal{L})\| = \mathrm{Quan}(\mathfrak{C},\mathfrak{R}) ,$$

where again, see Appendix 2 for all characterizing properties.

Note also, that analagous to part (II),

$\|\ \|_{\tilde{\mathrm{V}}\mathrm{ar}(\mathcal{L})} : \mathcal{L}_{\mathrm{syn}_K,K} \to \tilde{\mathrm{V}}\mathrm{ar}(\mathcal{L})$ can be considered a canonical model for $\mathcal{L}_{\mathrm{syn}_K,K}$ in $\tilde{\mathrm{V}}\mathrm{ar}(\mathcal{L})$, having now a formal topos structure (à la $\mathrm{Th}_K(\mathcal{L})$).

In summary, we write for a semantic evaluation of $\mathcal{L}_{\mathrm{syn}_K,K}$ into formal topos $(\mathfrak{C},\mathfrak{R})$ as

$$\|\ \| : \mathcal{L}_{\mathrm{syn}_K,K} \to (\mathfrak{C},\mathfrak{R})$$

and if individual variable assignment map ω is also applied, we write

$$\|\ \|_\omega : \mathcal{L}_{\mathrm{syn}_K,K} \to (\mathfrak{C},\mathfrak{R}) .$$

Or, again for simplicity, when the structure of $\mathcal{L}_{\mathrm{syn}_K,K}$ is understood, we write simply

$$\|\ \|\ \mathcal{L} \to (\mathfrak{C},\mathfrak{R})$$

and

$$\|\ \|_\omega : \mathcal{L} \to (\mathfrak{C},\mathfrak{R}) ,$$

respectively.

IV. Semantic evaluations within a category or category with additional structure, or topos.

As (1) a consequence of the universal arrow and imbedding properties of deduction categories with possible additional structure within the generic $(\mathcal{S}(\mathfrak{C},\mathfrak{R}),\mathrm{Sub})$ as given in Appendix 3, section 2.4.2, (2) because of the characterizing result that include, e.g., $(\mathfrak{C},\mathrm{Sub})$ is a formal topos iff $\mathfrak{C}$ is a topos (see the beginning part of Appendix 3), and (3) compatible with the basic literature, denote the semantic evaluation $\| \; \| : \mathcal{L} \to (\mathcal{C}, \mathrm{Sub})$ as simply $\| \; \| : \mathcal{L} \to \mathcal{C}$. Similarly, $\| \; \| : \mathcal{L} \to \mathcal{C}$ is a model means $\| \; \| : \mathcal{L} \to (\mathcal{C}, \mathrm{Sub})$ is a model (for some theory $\mathrm{Th}(\mathcal{L})$). Similar remarks hold for $\| \; \|_\omega : \mathcal{L} \to \mathcal{C}$.

V. Summary

Why consider (deduction) categories and (formal) topoi for semantic evaluations of a formal language?

Firstly, deduction categories are the appropriate vehicles for the ranges of semantic evaluations of a formal language $\mathcal{L}$, since as seen in the constructions in this section, they contain all - and in general, require no more than - the structure necessary for certain of the semantic evaluations to be models of $\mathrm{Th}_{\mathrm{syn}_\circ}(\mathcal{L})$. If $\mathcal{L}$ has additional structure in the form of $\mathrm{Th}_K(\mathcal{L})$, an intuitionistic logic-set theory, then for $\| \; \| : \mathcal{L} \to (\mathcal{C}, \mathfrak{X})$ to be a model, $(\mathcal{C}, \mathfrak{X})$ must be a formal topos. In so many words: each topos has an internal intuitionistic logic-set theory, as displayed in Appendix 2, 2.4.2. In addition, the (generic) Bénabou and related constructions $(\mathcal{F}(\mathcal{C}, \mathfrak{X}), \mathrm{Sub}))$ show that without loss of generality, standardized and enriched formal topos forms may always be chosen for semantic evaluations of $\mathcal{L}$ when $\mathcal{L}$ includes $\mathrm{Th}_K(\mathcal{L})$. (See Appendix 3, section 2.4.) Moreover, $\mathrm{Th}_K(\mathcal{L})$ is sound and complete relative to topos evaluations. Similarly, fragments of $\mathrm{Th}_K(\mathcal{L})$ are sound and complete relative to deduction categories with appropriate corresponding additional structures. (See 2.3.3 (b) and Appendix 3, section 2.4.) Thus topoi (formal topoi) and deduction categories with certain additional structure represent generalized set theories in the above sense. But in addition, when $\mathrm{Th}_K(\mathcal{L})$ is modified and strengthened to $\mathrm{Th}_{\mathrm{zer}}(\mathcal{L})$, topoi (equivalently, formal topoi with contravariant functors being Sub) correspondingly strengthened with additional properties, including "well-pointedness", "partial transitivity", etc., are ranges of legitimate models of $\mathrm{Th}_{\mathrm{zer}}(\mathcal{L})$, in a minimal sense. (See section 2.4.2 (G).)

But again, a note of caution: Because many of the problems that all of us deal with are data-driven or "real-world" ones, it may not be appropriate to assume when modeling these problems at the formal language level that the restrictive form of $\mathrm{Th}_K(\mathcal{L})$ is correct. This leads to the relaxation of topos structures - but, not in general, category structures, for those sufficiently flexible! This is considered throughout sections 2.3.3 - 2.3.9. (See especially, section 2.3.5.)

2.3.3 Logics for a formal language.

In sections 2.2, 2.3.1, 2.3.2, we developed first a basic formal language $\mathcal{L}_{\mathrm{syn}_\circ}$ together with semantic evaluations $\| \; \|_\omega : \mathcal{L}_{\mathrm{syn}_\circ} \to (\mathcal{C}, \mathfrak{X})$, for a deduction category $(\mathcal{C}, \mathfrak{X})$. Then, we expanded $\mathcal{L}$ to include a more encompassing theory $\mathrm{Th}_{\mathrm{syn}_K, K}(\mathcal{L})$, yielding $\mathcal{L}_{\mathrm{syn}_K,K}$ and considered semantic evaluations $\| \ \|_\omega : \mathcal{L}_{\mathrm{syn}_K,K} \to (\mathcal{C},\mathfrak{X})$, where $(\mathcal{C},\mathfrak{X})$ was assumed to have additional properties, in particular, that of a formal topos. Indeed, this structure, when appropriate, leads to a most important property for any model: soundness and completeness. (This will be clarified later in this section.) $\mathrm{Th}_{\mathrm{syn}_K,K}$ as mentioned previously, may not be the appropriate theory for a given situation and hence should be replaced by some $\mathrm{Th}_{\mathrm{syn}_K,K'}(\mathcal{L})$. Furthermore, $(\mathcal{C},\mathfrak{X})$ need not have a formal topos structure. Indeed, it will often follow that in order for models $\| \ \| : \mathcal{L}_{\mathrm{syn}_K,K'} \to (\mathcal{C},\mathfrak{X})$ to exist, $(\mathcal{C},\mathfrak{X})$ may have to have a very different structure from a topos. (See, e.g., section 2.3.5 where general logical systems are considered as well as this subsection.)

Although in this section we first present some basic properties and results for formal languages and semantic evaluations in general - depending of course on the choices of $\mathrm{Foun}(\mathcal{L})$, $\mathrm{Loc}(\mathcal{L})$, $\mathrm{Quan}(\mathcal{L})$, and the corresponding theories - the emphasis will be upon logical theories and corresponding semantic evaluations, i.e., logics. That is, roughly speaking, a logic is a collection of semantic evaluations which have the *same* evaluations (or "trace" of evaluations) upon $\mathrm{Loc}(\mathcal{L}) \cup \mathrm{Quan}(\mathcal{L})$. Similarly, a set theory "system" (there being no term in vogue for the analogue of "logic") is a collection of semantic evaluations which have the same evaluations upon $\mathrm{Foun}(\mathcal{L})$ as well as usually upon an associated set theory and compatible logic. (See 2.3.4 for some set theory considerations.)

(a) Basic definitions

Let $\mathcal{L}$ be a fixed formal language. We denote generically $(\mathcal{C},\mathfrak{X})$ as any deduction category and $\| \ \|_\omega : \mathcal{L} \to (\mathcal{C},\mathfrak{X})$ as any semantic evaluation map. Using the notation of 2.3.2 - but omitting all unnecessary subscripts - we present a list of relevant basic definitions involving logical considerations:

For any $i \in \mathrm{Var}(\mathrm{Ob}(\mathcal{L}))$, define

$$\mathrm{Wff}_{(i)}(\mathcal{L}) \overset{\mathrm{d}}{=} \{\Psi \mid \Psi \in \mathrm{Wff}(\mathcal{L}) \text{ and } \sigma(\Psi) = i\} .$$

(i) For any $\| \ \|$ and any $\Sigma_1,\Sigma_2 \subseteq \mathrm{Wff}_{(i)}(\mathcal{L})$, we define $\Sigma_1 \models_{\| \ \|} \Sigma_2$ iff

$$\|\Sigma_1\| \overset{\mathrm{d}}{=} \{\|\Psi_1\| \mid \Psi_1 \in \Sigma_1\} \leq_{\mathfrak{X}(i)} \|\Sigma_2\| \overset{\mathrm{d}}{=} \{\|\Psi_2\| \mid \Psi_2 \in \Sigma_2\}$$

i.e., for all $\Psi_1 \in \Sigma_1$ and all $\Psi_2 \in \Sigma_2$,

$\|\Psi_1\| \leq_{\mathfrak{X}(\mathrm{Ob}(\mathcal{C}))} \|\Psi_2\|$, which is read "$\Sigma_1$ *logically* (or materially) *implies* Σ_2, relative to $\| \ \|$" or "Σ_2 is a *logical consequence* of Σ_1 for $\| \ \|$", or "the *sequent* $(\Sigma_1 \vdash \Sigma_2) \overset{\mathrm{d}}{=} \{(\Psi_1 \vdash \Psi_2) \mid \Psi_1 \in \Sigma_1,\ \Psi_2 \in \Sigma_2\}$ is *valid* for $\| \ \|$".

(ii) For $\Sigma \subseteq \mathrm{Wff}_{(i)}(\ell)$ and given $\| \ \|$, we say " Σ is *satisfiable* by $\| \ \|$ " iff

$$\|\Sigma\| = \|T(i)\| = \|T\|(\|i\|) .$$

Thus,

$$(T \ {}_{\| }\!\models_{\| } \ \Sigma) ,$$

and equivalently

$$(\Sigma_1 \ {}_{\| }\!\models_{\| } \ \Sigma) , \text{ for all } \Sigma_1 \subseteq \mathrm{Wff}(\ell) .$$

We define compatibly

$${}_{\| }\!\models_{\| }(\Sigma) \text{ iff } (T \ {}_{\| }\!\models_{\| } \ \Sigma) , \text{ i.e., } \Sigma \text{ is satisfiable by } \| \ \| .$$

Note that many authors (see, e.g., Maydole [172]) define validity in a weaker sense than here: $(\Psi_1 \vdash \Psi_2)$ is valid for $\| \ \|$ in the weak sense iff (Ψ_1 satisfiable for $\| \ \|$ implies Ψ_2 satisfiable for $\| \ \|$). Whenever we discuss validity and related definitions and results of such authors, the term "weak" will be appended. On the other hand, Zadeh's "fuzzy logic" (e.g., [280]) is a semantically based theory, where deduction and validity coincide with the concept discussed here. (See also section 2.5.)

(iii) For $\Sigma \subseteq \mathrm{Wff}_{(i)}(\ell)$ and $\mathcal{N}$, a class of $\| \ \|$'s , we say Σ is a *tautology* with respect to $\mathcal{N}$ iff for all $\| \ \| \in \mathcal{N}$, Σ is satisfiable by $\| \ \|$. We say $\Psi \in \mathrm{Wff}_{(i)}(\ell)$ is *contradictory* w.r.t. $\mathcal{N}$ iff $\|\Psi\| = \|\bot(i)\|$ for all $\| \ \| \in \mathcal{N}$.

(iv) Consider now $\mathcal{N}_1$ the class of all $\| \ \|$'s . Then $\mathcal{N}_1$ decomposes into a disjoint exhaustive partitioning (union) of equivalence classes L , such that for any such L and any $\| \ \|^{(1)}, \| \ \|^{(2)} \in L$, $\| \ \|^{(1)}$ and $\| \ \|^{(2)}$ coincide over $\mathrm{Loc}(\ell)$ and $\mathrm{Quan}(\ell)$, the latter, for also all individual variable assignments ω . Call each such class of $\| \ \|$'s a *logic* for ℓ . Specific examples of logics are given in part (C). We will alternatively use the notation $\mathrm{Logic}_{\| \ \|}(\ell)$ to indicate a particular logic.

(v) For any $\mathcal{N}$, a class of $\| \ \|$'s , and any $\Sigma_1, \Sigma_2 \subseteq \mathrm{Wff}_{(i)}(\ell)$, we write:

(α) $\Sigma_1 \underset{\mathcal{N}}{\models} \Sigma_2$ iff $(\Sigma_1 \vdash \Sigma_2)$ is *$\mathcal{N}$-valid*,

i.e., $(\Sigma_1 \vdash \Sigma_2)$ is valid for all $\| \ \| \in \mathcal{N}$, or equivalently Σ_1 *logically implies* Σ_2 relative to $\mathcal{N}$.

(β) $\Sigma_1 \models_{\mathcal{N}}\!\!\dashv \Sigma_2$ iff $(\Sigma_1 \models_{\mathcal{N}} \Sigma_2)$ and $(\Sigma_2 \models_{\mathcal{N}} \Sigma_1)$, which is read " Σ_1 and Σ_2 are *equivalent* (or *tautologically equivalent*)". Thus, if $\Sigma \subseteq \text{Wff}(\mathcal{L})$ is a collection of tautologies with respect to $\mathcal{N}$, then

$$\vDash_{\mathcal{N}}(\Sigma) \overset{d}{=} (T \vDash_{\mathcal{N}} \Sigma) \quad \text{is the same as} \quad (T \vDash\!\!\dashv_{\mathcal{N}} \Sigma) .$$

(γ) We also denote

$$\text{Val}(\mathcal{L}), \|\ \|) \overset{d}{=} \{(\Psi \vdash \theta) \mid (\Psi \vdash \theta) \text{ is a sequent valid for } \|\ \|\}$$

and

$$\text{Val}(\mathcal{L},\mathcal{N}) = \bigcap_{\|\ \| \in \mathcal{N}} \text{Val}(\mathcal{L},\|\ \|) ,$$

as the class of all sequents valid simultaneously for all $\|\ \| \in \mathcal{N}$.

Note the specialization of (α) , (β), (γ) when $\mathcal{N} = L$; in the case of (γ) , we use the term "logically equivalent with respect to L " , etc.

(vi) We say a logic L is *truth functional* iff for each $n \geq 1$, each $\gamma \in \text{Loc}_n(\mathcal{L})$, there is a function f_γ such that for all individual variable assignment functions ω , all $\|\ \| \in L$, all $\Psi_1, \ldots, \Psi_n \in \text{Wff}_{(i)}(\mathcal{L})$,

$$\|\gamma(\Psi_1,\ldots,\Psi_n)\|_\omega = f_\gamma(\|\Psi_1\|_\omega,\ldots,\|\Psi_n\|_\omega) .$$

The large class of truth functional logics L *generated* by negations, t-norms and t-conorms is treated in section 2.3.6. On the other hand, in Example 4 of part (C) of this section, the non-truth functional logic PL (Probability Logic) is briefly considered. (See also 2.3.9 (A) for more details.)

In particular, note the special case where for all $\|\ \|_\omega \in L$,

$$\|\text{Wff}(\mathcal{L})\|_\omega \overset{d}{=} \{\|\Psi\|_\omega \mid \Psi \in \text{Wff}(\mathcal{L})\} = H ,$$

a fixed lattice of some kind (such as $\{0,1\}$ for classical logic and $[0,1]$ for many multi-valued logics), and where for each $\gamma \in \text{Loc}_n(\mathcal{L})$, $f_\gamma : H^n \to H$; we call H the *truth space* for L .

We call the set of *all* possible $f : H^n \to H$, $\text{Bool}_n(H)$, the class of H-valued *Boolean* functions. We call the subset of Bool(H) used in L, the designated semantic truth functions for L . In part (C) of this section, many of the logics are described through the evaluations of their logical connections being Boolean functions.

(vii) Truth functional completeness. (See also Rescher [214], 62-66, Maydole [172], 140-141).

A truth functional logic is truth functionally complete iff all possible Boolean truth functions (relative to the appropriate truth space H) can be defined as functional combinations of the designated semantic truth functions (Boolean) for the logic. For example, classical logic (Lukasiewicz logic with $n = 2$) is complete with respect to NOT, AND, OR. In multi-valued logics, in general, this is not true. However, Postean n-valued logic is truth functionally complete, where indeed a single binary connective has been shown to generate all Boolean connectives (Rescher [214], p. 65). In particular, all Lukasiewicz n-logics, for $\aleph_o > n \geq 2$, are truth functionally complete. Finally, no infinite-valued logic which has a finite set of designated logical connectives can be truth functionally complete.

(viii) Briefly, we again define the following:

$$Th(\mathcal{L}) = (Ax(\mathcal{L}), Rul(\mathcal{L}))$$

is a theory for $\mathcal{L}$, when $Ax(\mathcal{L})$, the axioms, is a collection of relevant sequents from $Seq(\mathcal{L})$, the class of all possible sequents of wff's usually involving the order symbol $\vdash$. $Rul(\mathcal{L})$ is a class of deduction rules, i.e., relations among the axioms. In turn, the class of all theorems or deducts of $Th(\mathcal{L})$ is

$$De(Th(\mathcal{L})) = span(Th(\mathcal{L}))$$

(See also section 2.2.2.)

Note that axioms and deductive rules for theories may be presented in several different (and in general, non-equivalent) ways. (See section 2.2.2, for example, for the presentation of the theories $Th_{syn_o}(\mathcal{L})$ and $Th_K(\mathcal{L})$, in terms of sequents, as we have agreed tacitly to do throughout the text.) Within this structure, one may choose a number of ways that a given idea may be represented as an axiom or rule sequent. Consider for example the basic (Z) set theory Axiom of Extension (Z1) (see section 2.3.4.b), using simplified notation for all individual variables. (Z1) as formulated as a single wff Ψ:

$$\text{(Z1)} \qquad \Psi \overset{d}{=} (\forall x)(\forall y)(\forall z)(((x \in y) \Leftrightarrow (x \in Z)) \Rightarrow (y \asymp z)) .$$

Approach 1: $(T \vdash \Psi)$.
Equivalently: $(\theta \vdash \Psi)$, for all $\theta \in Wff(\mathcal{L})$

Approach 2: $(\big((\forall x)(\forall y)(\forall z)((x \in y) \Leftrightarrow (x \in z))\big) \vdash (y \asymp z))$,
etc.

We define analogous to that of tautologies:

$$\vdash(\Psi) \overset{d}{=} (T\vdash\Psi)$$

We define $Th(\mathcal{L})$ to be *consistent* iff

$$De(Th(\mathcal{L})) \subset Seq(\mathcal{L}) \quad \text{(proper)}$$

and to be *inconsistent* iff

$$De(Th(\mathcal{L})) = Seq(\mathcal{L}) .$$

(ix) We also recall that $\| \| : \mathcal{L} \to (\mathcal{C},\mathfrak{R})$ is called a *model* for some theory $Th(\mathcal{L})$ iff $Ax(\mathcal{L}) \subseteq Val(\mathcal{L},\| \|)$, which in general (assuming modus ponens, etc. holding - see, e.g., Appendix 2, end of section 2.4, rule $R_{I,Th,2}$), in which case $De(Th(\mathcal{L})) \subseteq Val(\mathcal{L}),\| \|)$, the (deductively) *soundness property* of $Th(\mathcal{L})$ for $\| \|$.

In addition, we define for a given logic L and theory $Th(\mathcal{L})$, the class of all models of $Th(\mathcal{L})$ relative to L as

$$Mod(Th(\mathcal{L}),L) \overset{d}{=} \{\| \| \mid \| \| \in L \ \& \ \| \| \text{ is a model for } Th(\mathcal{L})\} .$$

If $Mod(Th(\mathcal{L}),L) \neq \emptyset$, we say $Th(\mathcal{L})$ (or $Ax(\mathcal{L})$) is *model-consistent*.

More generally, for any $\Sigma \subseteq Seq(\mathcal{L}) = Wff(\mathcal{L}) \times \{\vdash\} \times Wff(\mathcal{L})$, we say Σ is *model-consistent* iff there exists a $\| \|$ such that $\Sigma \subseteq Val(\mathcal{L}, \| \|)$. For any collection $\mathcal{N}$ of $\| \|$'s, we say Σ is model-consistent w.r.t. $\mathcal{N}$ iff $\Sigma \subseteq Val(\mathcal{L},\mathcal{N})$. On the other hand, we say Σ is *model-inconsistent* for (or in) $\mathcal{N}$ it is not model-consistent w.r.t. $\mathcal{N}$. (In particular, we can consider the case $\Sigma = De(Th(\mathcal{L}))$.)

We also abuse notation somewhat and define the class of all models $\| \| : \mathcal{L} \to (\mathcal{C},\mathfrak{R})$ of $Th(\mathcal{L})$, for $(\mathcal{C},\mathfrak{R})$ fixed as $Mod(Th(\mathcal{L}), (\mathcal{C},\mathfrak{R}))$.

In turn, we say $Th(\mathcal{L})$ is a (deductively) sound theory for logic L iff

$$De(Th(\mathcal{L})) \subseteq Val(\mathcal{L},L) .$$

On the other hand, we say $Th(\mathcal{L})$ is a (deductively) *complete theory* for L iff

$$Val(\mathcal{L},L) \subseteq De(Th(\mathcal{L})) .$$

Similarly, we also use the notation, $Val(\mathcal{L},(\mathcal{C},\mathfrak{R}))$ and consider soundness and completeness relative to all $\| \|$'s having ranges in a fixed $(\mathcal{C},\mathfrak{R})$.

(x) Note that if $Mod(Th(\mathcal{L}),L)$ has non-degenerate members $\| \|_\omega$, then if $Th(\mathcal{L})$ is sound and model-consistent relative L, then $Th(\mathcal{L})$ is also consistent. (Proof: If Th(L) is sound, model-consistent, yet inconsistent, then there exists $\| \|_\omega$ (non-degenerate) such that $Seq(\mathcal{L}) = De(Th(\mathcal{L})) \subseteq Val(\mathcal{L},L) \subseteq Val(\mathcal{L}, \| \|) \subseteq Seq(\mathcal{L})$, whence equality holds throughout and $Seq(\mathcal{L}) = Val(\mathcal{L}, \| \|_\omega)$. Hence for all $\Psi,\theta \in Wff(\mathcal{L})$, $\|\Psi\| \leq_L \|\theta\|$ and $\|\Psi\| \leq_L \|\theta\|$, i.e., $\|\theta\| = \|\Psi\|$, for an appropriate choice of $\leq_L$.)

(xi) Let theory $Th(\mathcal{L})$ and logic L for $\mathcal{L}$ be given. Then:

$Th(\mathcal{L})$ is *logically complete* w.r.t. L iff for all $\Psi \in Wff(\mathcal{L})$, if $\vDash_L \Psi$, then $(\vdash\Psi) \in De(Th(\mathcal{L}))$.

$Th(\mathcal{L})$ is *logically sound* w.r.t L iff for all $\Psi \in Wff(\mathcal{L})$, if $(\vdash\Psi) \in De(Th(\mathcal{L}))$, then $\vDash_L \Psi$.

Note that if $Th(\mathcal{L})$ is (deductively) complete w.r.t. L then it is logically complete w.r.t. L . $Th(\mathcal{L})$ *axiomatizes* L iff $Th(\mathcal{L})$ is (deductively) sound and complete w.r.t. L and for any $\Sigma \subseteq Val(\mathcal{L},L)$, $\Psi \in Wff(\mathcal{L})$, if $\Sigma \models_L \Psi$, then $(\vdash\Psi) \in De(Th(\mathcal{L}))$ (the "capturing" property for $Th(\mathcal{L})$, w.r.t. L) .

(xii) Finally, note some miscellaneous definitions will be mentioned:

$Th(\mathcal{L})$ has the *compactness* property for logic L , iff for each finite set $\mathcal{A} \subseteq De(Th(\mathcal{L}))$, there is a $\| \ \|_{\mathcal{A}} \in L$ such that $\mathcal{A} \subseteq Val(\mathcal{L}, \| \ \|_{\mathcal{A}})$, implies that there is a $\| \ \| \in L$ such that $De(Th(\mathcal{L})) \subseteq Val(\mathcal{L}, \| \ \|)$. Obviously, if $Th(\mathcal{L})$ is sound for L then it is compact for L .

Let $\mathcal{L}$ be a countable language, i.e., $\mathcal{L}$ has at most a countable number of symbols and hence terms, etc. Then the *Löwenheim-Skolem* property holds for $Th(\mathcal{L})$ iff, when there exists $\| \ \|$ such that $De(Th(\mathcal{L})) \subseteq Val(\mathcal{L}, \| \ \|)$, then $\| \ \| : \mathcal{L} \to (\mathfrak{C},\mathfrak{R})$ may be chosen so that its semantic domain $(\|Var(Ob(\mathcal{L}))\| \subseteq Ob(\mathfrak{C}))$ is at most countable.

For the basic concepts of *negation-consistency* $((\theta \vdash \Psi)$ and $(\theta \vdash not\ \Psi)$ not occurring for $Th(\mathcal{L}))$ and the related *Law of Excluded Middle*, see Rescher [214], pp. 161-166, 148-154. For other definitions, including *decidability* and *recursion*, see, e.g., Enderton [54], Curry [44], and Rescher [214].

(b) Soundness and completeness.

In this subsection, we proceed to establish the soundness and completeness for certain theories relative to semantic evaluations in (deduction) categories, and in particular in (formal) topoi. The materials presented below are drawn from Coste [41], using however, our notations. Roughly speaking, soundness and completeness means that the deduction system, that is, the choice of theory $Th(\mathcal{L})$, and class of semantic evaluations, is "correct".

First, (F,α) is called an *arrow between two deduction categories* $(\mathfrak{C},\mathfrak{R})$ and $(\mathfrak{D},\mathcal{S})$ iff $F : \mathfrak{C} \to \mathfrak{D}$ is a functor and $\alpha : \mathfrak{R} \to \mathcal{S}\circ F$ is a natural transform. When these deduction categories are formal topoi, we continue to call (F,α) an arrow if, in addition, α preserves order and all the properties $Foun(\mathfrak{C})$, $Loc(\mathfrak{C})$, $Quan(\mathfrak{C})$, used to define a topos. (See Appendix 2, end of section 2.4.) It follows that $DeCat \overset{d}{=} (Ob(DeCat), Ar(DeCat))$ is a category where $(Ob(DeCat)$ = class of all deduction categories, and $Ar(DeCat)$ = class of all arrows as defined above.

Lemma 1 (See, e.g., Coste [41], p. 15.)

Let $\mathcal{L}$ be a formal language of the form $\mathcal{L}_{syn_b,b}$ for either $b = 0$ or K (or $b \subseteq K$ symbolically indicating that only a certain fraction of $Th_K(\mathcal{L})$ is assumed) as developed in section 2.2.2. Also, recall the canonical deduction category $\widetilde{Var}(\mathcal{L})$ (a formal topos for $b = K$) and the canonical model $\| \ \|_{\widetilde{Var}(\mathcal{L})} : \mathcal{L} \to \widetilde{Var}(\mathcal{L})$

(see 2.3.2 (II), e.g.) with

$$\mathrm{Val}(\mathcal{L}, \|\ \|_{\widetilde{\mathrm{Var}}(\mathcal{L})}) = \mathrm{De}(\mathrm{Th}_{\mathrm{syn}_b,b}(\mathcal{L})) .$$

Hence, $\mathrm{Th}_{\mathrm{syn}_b,b}(\mathcal{L})$ is model-consistent.

Then, in addition, it follows that for each deduction category $(\mathcal{C},\mathfrak{R})$ (formal topos, for $b = K$, and more generally, a deduction category with some additional structure corresponding to symbolically $b \subseteq K$ - see Appendix 3, section 2.4 for details on these intermediate forms) there is a bijection $\Psi_{(\mathcal{C},\mathfrak{R})}$,

$$\Psi_{(\mathcal{C},\mathfrak{R})} : \mathrm{Mod}(\mathrm{Th}_{\mathrm{syn}_b,b}(\mathcal{L}), (\mathcal{C},\mathfrak{R})) \to \mathrm{Ar}_{(\widetilde{\mathrm{Var}}(\mathcal{L}),(\mathcal{C},\mathfrak{R}))}(\mathrm{DeCat}) ,$$

the latter collection of arrows being order preserving, where for any $\|\ \| \in \mathrm{Mod}(\mathrm{Th}_{\mathrm{syn}_b,b}(\mathcal{C},\mathfrak{R}))$,

$$\Psi_{(\mathcal{C},\mathfrak{R})}(\|\ \|) \overset{\mathrm{d}}{=} (\|\ \|, \tau_{\|\ \|}) , \text{ where } \tau_{\|\ \|} \text{ is given in 2.3.2.}$$

Theorem 1 (See Coste [41], p. 15)

Let $\mathcal{L}$ and $(\mathcal{C},\mathfrak{R})$ be as in the last lemma. Then $\mathrm{Th}_{\mathrm{syn}_b,b}(\mathcal{L})$ is (deductively) sound and complete in $(\mathcal{C},\mathfrak{R})$ ($b = 0$ or $b = K$, or $b \subseteq K$), hence (by result (x) of part (a)) consistent.

(Proof: Note that for any $\|\ \| \in \mathrm{Mod}(\mathrm{Th}_{\mathrm{syn}_b,b}(\mathcal{L}), (\mathcal{C},\mathfrak{R}))$, the following diagram commutes (i.e., the obvious arrow compositions are equal):

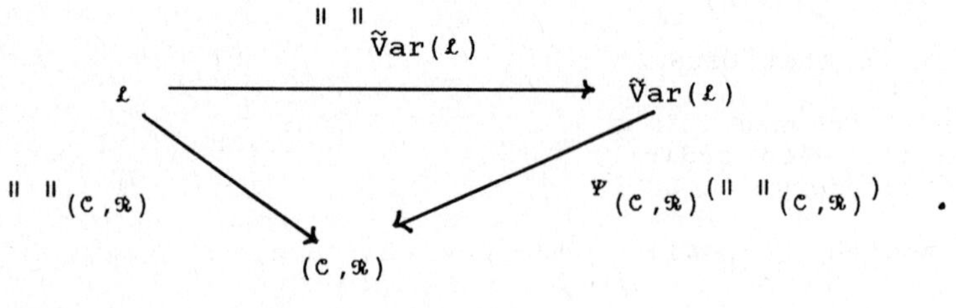

Hence,

$$\begin{aligned}\mathrm{Val}(\mathcal{L},(\mathcal{C},\mathfrak{R})) &= \mathrm{Var}(\mathcal{L}, \|\ \|_{\widetilde{\mathrm{Var}}(\mathcal{L})}) \\ &= \mathrm{De}(\mathrm{Th}_{\mathrm{syn}_b,b}(\mathcal{L})).)\end{aligned}$$

Remark.

Any tautology $\Psi_i (\in \mathrm{Wff}(\mathcal{L}))$ for any $\|\ \|_{(\mathcal{C},\mathfrak{R})}$, as above, can be written in the formal language as $(T_i \leq_{\mathcal{L}} \Psi_i)$, and hence by the rules $(T_i =_{\mathcal{L}} \Psi_i)$, yielding for any model, involving T , $\|T_i\| \leq_{\mathfrak{X}(\|i\|)} \|\Psi_i\|$, and by the maximality of $\|T_i\|$ (preserving T_i) , $\|T_i\| =_{\mathfrak{X}(\|i\|)} \|\Psi_i\|$. Thus, e.g. (by its very definition) T_i , itself is always a tautology (for any model) as will be (see 2.2.2, VI, Theorem 7) $\theta_i \overset{d}{=} nt(\Psi) \vee nt(nt(\Psi))$, for any $\Psi \in Wff(\mathcal{L})$; hence we can write in $\mathcal{L}$, $(T_i \leq_{\mathcal{L}} \theta_i)$. Moreover, by the soundness and completeness property of, e.g., $Th_{syn_K, K}(\mathcal{L})$, it follows that all tautologies $\phi_i \in Wff(\mathcal{L})$ may be identified as $(T_i \vdash_L \phi_i)$.

Next we obtain soundness and completeness of $Th_{syn_b, b}(\mathcal{L})$ relative to ordinary categories (corresponding to $b = 0$) , ordinary topoi (correspondding to $b = K$) , and intermediately, categories with additional structure (corresponding to $b \subseteq K$) . (See 2.3.2 IV for the definition of semantic evaluations in ordinary categories or topoi.)

Theorem 2

Let $\mathcal{L}_{syn_b, b}$ $(b = 0$ or K or $b \subseteq K)$ be given with $\mathcal{C}$ as in Lemma 1.

Then $Th_{syn_b, b}(\mathcal{L})$ is sound and complete in $\mathcal{C}$, i.e., in $(\mathcal{C}, Sub)$.

Proof:

The composite map

$$(G_{\widetilde{Var}(\mathcal{L})}, \beta_{\widetilde{Var}(\mathcal{L})}) \circ \| \|_{\widetilde{Var}(\mathcal{L})} : \mathcal{L} \to (\mathcal{S}_{II}(\widetilde{Var}(\mathcal{L})), Sub)$$

is a model so that because $(G_{\widetilde{Var}(\mathcal{L})}, \beta_{\widetilde{Var}(\mathcal{L})})$ is order preserving so is the entire map. In addition, analogous to Lemma 1, there is a bijection for each ordinary category $\mathcal{C}$ (or topos) expressed as deduction category $(\mathcal{C}, Sub)$

$$\Psi_{(\mathcal{C}, \mathfrak{X})} : Mod(Th_{syn_b, b}(\mathcal{L}), (\mathcal{C}, Sub)) \to Ar_{(\mathcal{S}_{II}(\widetilde{Var}(\mathcal{L})), Sub), (\mathcal{C}, Sub)}(DeCat) .$$

The following diagram commutes:

$$\begin{array}{ccc}
\mathcal{L} & \xrightarrow{\| \|_{\widetilde{Var}(\mathcal{L})}} & \widetilde{Var}(\mathcal{L}) \\
\Big\downarrow{\scriptstyle \| \|_{(\mathcal{C}, Sub)}} & & \Big\downarrow{\scriptstyle (G_{\widetilde{Var}(\mathcal{L})}, \beta_{\widetilde{Var}(\mathcal{L})})} \\
(\mathcal{C}, Sub) & \xleftarrow[\Psi_{(\mathcal{C}, Sub)}(\| \|_{(\mathcal{C}, Sub)})]{} & (\mathcal{S}_{II}(\widetilde{Var}(\mathcal{C})), Sub)
\end{array} .$$

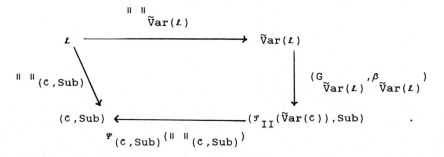

Thus, Theorem 1 applies completely here.

Remark.

The ideas developed through this subsection may be extended (or attempted to be extended) as follows, when category or topos structure is lacking:

Establish, for each structure $\mathfrak{D}$ to be considered, a bijection

$$\Psi : \mathrm{Mod}(\mathrm{Th}(\mathcal{L}),\mathfrak{D}) \to \mathrm{Map}(\widetilde{\mathrm{V}}\mathrm{ar}(\mathcal{L}),\mathfrak{D})$$

where "Map" in some natural sense replaces arrows and is an order preserving class. Then all we need consider (or we can define to be considered) is the identity-like model $\| \; \|_{\widetilde{\mathrm{V}}\mathrm{ar}(\mathcal{L})}$, for relating properties of $\mathcal{L}$ with properties of $\mathfrak{D}$.

(c) Examples of logics

In the following examples, we consider only semantic evaluations of the form $\| \; \| : \mathcal{L} \to (\mathrm{SET},H^{\cdot})$. Moreover, of the seven types of logics briefly considered, only one - Probability Logic - is a non-truth functional one. In any case, it follows that all of these logics involve relations and functions upon H in the determination of $\| \; \|$ restricted to $\mathrm{Loc}(\mathcal{L})$ and $\mathrm{Quan}(\mathcal{L})$. See Rescher [214] for a more comprehensive treatment of such logics.

1. $\mathrm{Logic}_{\| \; \|}(\mathcal{L})$ = Lukasiewicz Logic_n, $n = 2,3,4,\ldots,\aleph_0,\aleph_1$.

$Ł_n \overset{a}{=}$ Lukasiezicz Logic_n.

$Ł_2$ = Classical two-valued logic.

Define:

$$I_n \overset{d}{=} \begin{cases} [0,1] \text{ (unit interval)} \; ; & n = \aleph_0 , \\ \text{set of all rationals in } [0,1] \; ; & n = \aleph_0 , \\ \{0,1/(n-1),\ldots,1\} \; ; & n = 2,3,\ldots , \end{cases}$$

where $H = I_n$ = truth space of $Ł_n$

Now consider:

$$\mathcal{L} = Ł_2 ,$$

where $\mathrm{Loc}(\mathcal{L}_2) = \{\mathrm{nt}, \Rightarrow, \exists\}$

with compound/eliminative definitions:

$(\Psi_1 \vee \Psi_2)$	for	$(\Psi_1 \Rightarrow \Psi_2) \Rightarrow \Psi_2$,
$(\Psi_1 \wedge \Psi_2)$	for	$\mathrm{nt}(\mathrm{nt}\Psi_1 \vee \mathrm{nt}\Psi_2)$,
$(\Psi_1 \Leftrightarrow \Psi_2)$	for	$(\Psi_1 \Rightarrow \Psi_2)\wedge(\Psi_2 \Rightarrow \Psi_1)$,
$(\forall)(\Psi_1)$	for	$\mathrm{nt}(\exists(\mathrm{nt}\;\Psi_1))$,

for any $\Psi_1, \Psi_2 \in \mathrm{Wff}(Ł_2) \overset{d}{=} \mathrm{Wff}(\mathcal{L}_2)$, slightly abusing notation.

We do not consider $Ł_{\aleph_0}$ because of closure problems in truth evaluations.

Truth space $(Ł_2)$ = range of semantic truth functions of $Ł_2 = \{0,1\}$.

Semantic Truth Func$(Ł_2)$

$$= \{\|nt\|, \|\&\|, \|or\|, \|\Rightarrow\|, \|\Leftrightarrow\|, \|\exists\|, \|\forall\|\},$$

where for all $\theta, \Psi \in \mathrm{Wff}(Ł_2)$,

$$\|nt(\theta)\| = \|nt\|(\|\theta\|) \quad (\|\theta\| \in \{0,1\})$$
$$= 1 - \|\theta\|$$
$$\|\theta \wedge \Psi\| = \min(\|\theta\|, \|\Psi\|)$$
$$\|\theta \vee \Psi\| = \max\|\theta\|, \|\Psi\|)$$
$$\|\theta \Rightarrow \Psi\| = \|(nt\theta) \text{ or } \Psi\|$$
$$= \max(1-\|\theta\|, \|\Psi\|)$$
$$\|\theta \Leftrightarrow \Psi\| = \min(\max(1-\|\theta\|, \|\Psi\|), \max(1-\|\Psi\|, \|\theta\|),$$

pointwise.

$$\|(\exists\alpha)\Psi\|_\omega = \sup\{\|\Psi\|_{\omega'} \mid \omega' \in G(\alpha,\omega)(\Psi)\},$$
$$\|(\forall\alpha)\Psi\|_\omega = \inf\{\|\Psi\|_{\omega'} \mid \omega' \in G(\alpha,\omega)(\Psi)\},$$

where

$G(\alpha,\omega) \overset{d}{=} \{\omega' \mid \omega'$ individual variable assignment such that

$$\omega'(y) = \begin{cases} \omega(y), & y \in TV(\Psi) \dashv \{\alpha\} \\ \text{arbitrary}; & y = \alpha \end{cases}\}.$$

Note that validity and satisfaction in classical logic are directly connected because of the simple truth space $I_2 = \{0,1\}$:

For $\Sigma_1, \Sigma_2 \subseteq \mathrm{Wff}(Ł_2)$, $\Sigma_1 \vDash_{Ł_2} \Sigma_2$ iff whenever Σ_1 is satisfiable by any $\|\ \| \in Ł_2$, then so is Σ_2, etc.

Basic Theorems for $Ł_2$ (see also $Ł_n$)

For all $\phi, \Psi \in \mathrm{Wff}(Ł_2)$:

(i) $\|\phi\| \le \|\Psi\|$, iff $\phi \;{}_{\|}\!\vDash_{\|}\; \Psi$

iff $\|(\phi \Rightarrow \Psi)\| = 1$,

and

$\|\phi\| = \|\Psi\|$ iff $\phi \underset{\|\ \ \|}{\vDash\!\dashv} \Psi$

iff $\|\phi \Leftrightarrow \Psi\| = 1$,

for all $\|\ \| \in Ł_2$.

(ii) Ψ is contradictory iff Ψ is model-inconsistent.

(iii) Ψ is a tautology in $Ł_2$ iff $nt(\Psi)$ is contradictory in $Ł_2$.

(iv) When we add various basic theories $Th(Ł_2)$ to $Ł_2$ we can obtain (deductive) soundness, (deductive) completeness, logical completeness, logical soundness, consistency, and that $Th(Ł_2)$ axiomizes $Ł_2$. In particular, (see Maydole [172], pp. 50-54) Maydole's ${}_2\mathcal{T}_{QL_2}$ is such a theory, with five axioms (all in formal tautology form $(\vdash\Psi)$) and two deduction rules (modus ponens and universal quantification). (See also 2.3.4(b) for a listing of these axioms and rules A1 - A5, R1, R2.)

Note that for $Ł_2$, all weak and non-weak properties coincide, including validity and satisfaction, due to the simple truth space $\{0,1\}$.

An excellent treatment of $Ł_2$ may be found in Curry [44]. Enderton [54] and Lightstone [156] also present comprehensive studies of classical logic, together with set theory models, including - via the compactness property, in effect - Robinson's nonstandard numbers.

For $n = 2,3,4,\ldots$, (finite), $Ł_n$ is the same as $Ł_2$ except for truth space $(Ł_2) = \{0,1\}$ is replaced by truth space of $Ł_n = I_n$.

Basic Theorems on $Ł_n$, $n = 2,3,\ldots,\aleph_0, \aleph_1$.

(i) For all n: for all $\theta,\Psi \in Wff(Ł_n)$, (abusing notation slightly)

If $\models_{Ł_n} (\theta \Rightarrow \Psi)$, then θ implies Ψ relative to $Ł_n$.

Note that for all θ,Ψ,

$$\models_{Ł_n} (\theta \Rightarrow \Psi)$$

iff

$$\max(1-\|\theta\|, \|\Psi\|) = 1$$

iff

$$\|\Psi\| = 1 \text{ or } \|\theta\| = 0 .$$

(ii) For all n: for all $\Psi \in Wff(Ł_n)$, if Ψ is contradictory in $Ł_n$, then Ψ is model-inconsistent in $Ł_n$.

(iii) For all n: for all $\Psi \in Wff(Ł_n)$, if $\models_{Ł_{\aleph_1}} (\Psi)$ then $\models_{Ł_n} (\Psi)$, which in turn implies $\models_{Ł_n} \Psi$.

(iv) Weak compactness theorem holds for all $Ł_n$: i.e., $\forall\ \Sigma \subseteq Wff(Ł_n)$, Σ is satisfiable (for some model) iff $\forall\ \Sigma' \subseteq \Sigma$, Σ' finite, Σ' is satisfiable (for some model).

(v) The weak Löwenhem-Skolem property holds for all $Ł_n$, i.e., for any $\Sigma \subseteq Wff(Ł_n)$, if Σ is satisfiable then there is a countable semantical domain and a corresponding model which also makes Σ satisfiable (analogue of Lindelöf covering property).

(vi) $Ł_{\aleph_1}$ is not axiomiatizable and hence any $Th(Ł_{\aleph_1})$ cannot be both logically sound and logically complete for $Ł_{\aleph_1}$ (weak sense, here). Hence, if $Th(Ł_{\aleph_1})$ is logically sound for $Ł_{\aleph_1}$, it cannot be (deductively) complete for $Ł_{\aleph_1}$.

(vii) For any $\phi, \Psi \in Wff(Ł_n)$, define

$$(\phi \overset{n}{\Rightarrow} \Psi) \overset{d}{=} \phi \Rightarrow \underbrace{(\phi \Rightarrow (\Rightarrow \cdots (\phi \Rightarrow \Psi) \cdots))}_{n \text{ terms}} .$$

Then

$$\|\phi \overset{n}{\Rightarrow} \Psi\| = \min(1, n(1-\|\phi\|) + \|\Psi\|) ,$$

for all $\|\ \| \in Ł_2$.

(See Maydole [172], pp. 105-111, for further facts.)

See the paper of DeGlas [45'], where the Stone representation theorem is extended to provide a semantic basis for Lukasiewicz and Post logics, which in turn can be used as a basis for fuzzy set theory.

2. Logic($\mathcal{L}$) = Bochvarian Logic. $B_n \overset{d}{=} n = 2,3,4,\ldots$.

Syn($\mathcal{L}$) - same essentially as for $Ł_2$. Loc($\mathcal{L}$) = {nt, $\Rightarrow$, $\exists$, or, &, $\Leftrightarrow$} with $\forall$ a compound or eliminative definition.

$$H = \text{Truth Space}(B_n) = \{0, \frac{1}{n-1}, \frac{2}{n-1}, \ldots, \frac{n-2}{n-1}, 1\} .$$

Sem Truth Func(B_n) = $\{\|nt\|, \|\Rightarrow\|, \|\Leftrightarrow\|, \|\&\|, \|or\|, \|\exists\|, \|\forall\|\}$

$$\|nt(\theta)\| = 1 - \|\theta\|$$

$$\|\theta \Rightarrow \Psi\| = \begin{cases} \min(1, \|\theta\| + \|\Psi\|) , & \text{if } \|\theta\|, \|\Psi\| \in \{0,1\} \\ Z_n \overset{d}{=} \begin{cases} 1/2 , \text{ if } \|\theta\|, \|\Psi\| \text{ otherwise and } n \text{ odd,} \\ \dfrac{n-2}{n-1} , \text{ if } \|\theta\|, \|\Psi\| \text{ otherwise and } n \text{ even.} \end{cases} \end{cases}$$

$$\|\theta \ \&\ \Psi\| = \begin{cases} \|\theta\| \cdot \|\Psi\| & \text{iff } \|\theta\|, \|\Psi\| \in \{0,1\} , \\ Z_n & \text{if otherwise} \end{cases} .$$

For $B_{\aleph_1}$, everything is same as above, except Truth Space $(B_{\aleph_1}) = [0,1]$,etc. (See also Maydole [172], p. 125.)

3. $Log_{\| \|}(\mathcal{L})$ = Gödel-Intuitionistic logic G_n , n = 2,3,4,..., .

Sem truth func $(G_n) = \{\|nt\|, \|\Rightarrow\|, \|\&\|, \|or\|, \|\Leftrightarrow\|\}$; and $G_{\aleph_1}$ can be considered, also.

Note that here, the truth space is a Heyting algebra H . More specifically, H is a fixed *complete Heyting algebra*, i.e.,

(a) H is a *lattice* - a partially ordered set with order $\leq_H$, say, over $H \times H$, which is reflexive, autisymmetric and transitive, such that operations $\wedge$, $\vee$: $H \times H \to H$ exist, where for any $x,y \in H$, $x \wedge y$ is the meet (minimum or greatest lower bound) and $x \vee y$ is the join (maximum or least upper bound), having the unique properties

(i) $x \wedge y \leq_H x,y$.

(ii) For all $z \in H$, if $z \leq_H x,y$, then $z \leq_H x \wedge y$.

(iii) $x,y \leq_H x \vee y$.

(iv) For all $z \in H$, if $x,y \leq_H z$, then $x \vee y \leq z$.

It follows that $\wedge$ and $\vee$ are idempotent, commutative, associative (and hence extendable to any number of arguments recursively unambiguously) and absorptive.

(b) H has a greatest element, say, 1_H *or* T_H (or simply 1) relative to $\leq_H$ and a distinct least element, say 0_H or $\perp_H$ (or simply 0) relative to $\leq_H$, with

$$0_H < 1_H , x \wedge 0_H = 0_H , x \vee 0_H = x , x \vee 1_H = 1_H ;$$

all $x \in H$.

(c) H is a *complete lattice*, i.e. in addition to being a lattice, if $C \subseteq H$, then there exist x_C , $y_C \in H$ such that, abusing notation

(i) $x_C \leq_H C \leq_H y_C$.

(ii) If $z_1, z_2, \in H$ and $z_1 \leq_H C \leq z_2$, then
$z_1 \leq x_C \leq_H y_C \leq z_2$,

i.e., x_C and y_C are greatest lower bound and least upper bound elements, respectively, for C relative to H . (Of course, x_C , $y_C \notin C$, in general.)

(d) H has the *Heyting-Brouwer property*:
For any $u,v \in H$, define

$$C_{u,v} \overset{d}{=} \{z \mid z \in H \ \&\ u \wedge z \leq_H v\} .$$

Then, using the notation from (c)(ii), let $y_{C_{u,v}}$ be the least upper bound element in H for $C_{u,v}$. It is then assumed that $y_{C_{u,v}} \in C_{u,v}$, i.e., $C_{u,v}$ has a maximal element in it with respect to order $\leq_H$.

Define also

$$(u \Rightarrow v) \overset{d}{=} y_{C_{u,v}} = \vee(C_{u,v})$$

called the *pseudo-complement* of u relative to v or the *intuitionistic implication* "if u then v". We can also define the double implication $\Leftrightarrow$ in the obvious way:

$$u \Leftrightarrow v \quad \text{for} \quad (u \Rightarrow v) \wedge (v \Rightarrow u) .$$

It follows that H is also distributive for $\wedge$ over $\vee$ and vice-versa for *any* index set. In addition

(i) For all $x \in H$,
$(x \Rightarrow x) = 1_H$.

(ii) For all $x \in H$,
$nt(x) = (\sim x) \overset{d}{=} (x \Rightarrow 0_H)$

is the pseudo-complement of x relative to 0_H or the *intuitionist negation*.

Two basic examples of a complete Heyting algebra are:

Example 1. Any totally ordered complete chain H such as a closed interval in $\mathbb{R}$ - in particular, $H_0 = [0,1]$. In this example, for any $x,y \in H$,

$$(x \Rightarrow y) = \begin{cases} y, & \text{if } x >_H y \text{ (i.e. } x \nleq_H y) \\ 1_H, & \text{if } x \leq_H y , \end{cases}$$

and hence

$$nt(x) = (\sim x) = \begin{cases} 0_H, & \text{if } x >_H 0_H \text{ (including } x = 1_H) \\ 1_H, & \text{if } x =_H 0_H . \end{cases}$$

Example 2. Consider any Boolean algebra H - i.e., H has two binary operations, say $\wedge, \vee : H \times H \to H$ and a unary operation $C : H \to H$ such that $\vee$ and $\wedge$ are symmetric, associative, $\vee$

finitely distributive over $\wedge$ and vice-versa and contains 0_H and 1_H such that for all $x \in H$,

$$x \wedge 0_H = 0_H \; ; \; x \vee 0_H = x \, ,$$

$$x \wedge 1_H = x \; ; \; x \vee 1_H = 1_H \, ,$$

$$x \wedge Cx = 0_H \, , \; x \vee Cx = 1_H \; ; \; 0_H = C1_H \, .$$

Then define partial order $\leq_H$ by for any $x,y \in H$,

$$\begin{aligned}(x \leq_H y) \quad &\text{iff} \quad x \wedge y = x \\ &\text{iff} \quad x \vee y = y \, .\end{aligned}$$

Also define $\Rightarrow$ by, for any $x,y \in H$,

$$(x \Rightarrow y) \overset{d}{=} (Cx) \vee y \, .$$

Thus, H is also a Heyting algebra. Also, H may be a *Boolean σ-algebra*, i.e., H is also σ-complete - for any at *most countable* set $C = \{x_1,x_2,\ldots\} \subseteq H$, x_C, and equivalently, $y_C \in H$, and hence H is a σ-complete Heyting algebra, etc. Usually, H is interpreted as a collection of subsets x of a space X, where the null set $\emptyset$ is identified with 0_H, X with 1_H, $\cap$ with $\wedge$, $\cup$ (or symmetric set difference Δ) with $\vee$, and C with ordinary set complementation relative to X.

In addition, we can add an equivalence relation over $H \times H$ together with two other associated relations: Let $\theta : H \times H \to H$ be arbitrary such that $R_{I,Th,18}$ and $R_{I,Th,19}$, of Appendix 2, section 2.4 hold for θ replacing $\asymp$ there:

$$\theta(x,y) = \theta(y,x)$$

$$\theta(x,y) \wedge \theta(y,z) \leq \theta(x,z) \, ,$$

for all $x,y,x \in H$. Thus, e.g., we can choose $\theta = \delta_H$ or $\theta = \wedge_H$, etc.

Define

$$D(\theta) : H \to H \quad \text{by}$$

$$D(\theta)(x) \overset{d}{=} \theta(x,x) \; ; \; \text{all} \quad x \in H \, ,$$

and finally, in turn, define $e_\theta : H \times H \to H$ by

$$e_\theta(x,y) \overset{d}{=} (D(\theta)(x) \vee_H D(\theta)(y)) \Rightarrow \theta(x,y) \, ,$$

for all $x,y \in H$.

Some specific examples of θ, $D(\theta)$ and e_θ for H a complete chain:

(i) $\theta(x,y) \overset{d}{=} D(\theta)(x) \wedge D(\theta)(y)$, all $x,y \in H$

$$e_\theta(x,y) \overset{d}{=} \begin{cases} T_H & \text{iff } D(\theta)(x) = D(\theta)(y) \\ D(\theta)(x) \wedge D(\theta)(y) , & \text{iff } D(\theta)(x) \neq D(\theta)(y) \end{cases}$$

In particular, note the case $\theta = Id_{H\times H}$:

$$e_\theta(x,y) = \begin{cases} T_H & \text{iff } x =_H y \\ x \wedge_H y & \text{iff } x \neq_H y \text{ ; } x,y \in H . \end{cases}$$

(ii) $\theta(x,y) \overset{d}{=} T_H$; all $x,y \in H$

$$e_\theta(x,y) = T_H \text{ , all } x,y \in H .$$

(iii) $\theta(x,y) \overset{d}{=} \delta(H)_{(x,y)}$ (ordinary Krönecker)

$$= \begin{cases} T_H & \text{iff } x =_H y \\ \perp_H & \text{iff } x \neq_H y \text{ ; } x,y \in H \end{cases}$$

$$e_\theta(x,y) = \delta(H)_{(x,y)} \text{ , all } x,y \in H .$$

It can then be shown that e_θ is an equivalence (or equality) relation in the sense that $R_{I,Th,17} - R_{I,Th,21}$ of Appendix 2, section 2.4 all hold with $\asymp$ replaced by e_θ , $proj_1(i\times i) = (proj_{1(i)}(i\times i) = x^{(i)}_{(i\times i)})$ by x , $proj_2(i\times i)$ by y , etc.

For the basic properties of θ , $D(\theta)$ and e_θ , couched in terms of Higg's topos and related structures, see Appendix 3 (iv).

Indeed, all of the axioms and rules given in Appendix 2, section 2.4 for $\wedge$, $\vee$, $\Rightarrow$, $=$, etc., are all (generalized) intuitionistic logic ones and are compatible for the case considered here - H . (See also 2.2.2 (VI) for theorems one can derive for $\wedge$, $\vee$, $\Rightarrow$, $\asymp$, etc.)

4. Probability Logic(PL)

Probability logic (PL) is a non-truth functional logic over $\mathcal{L}$.

We present here a brief outline of PL. Additional properties for PL and related logics may be found in section 2.3.9 (A).

In this case, we choose $H = [0,1]$ (unit interval) as the truth space.

For each i , let $X_i \in Ob(SET)$ and $\|i\| \subseteq \mathcal{P}(X_i)$ be a sigma algebra. For each $(f : i \rightarrow j) \in Var(Ar(\mathcal{L}))$, $\|f\| : \|i\| \rightarrow \|j\|$ and for each $r_i \in Var(Rel(\mathcal{L}))$, with $\sigma(r_i) = i$, let $\|r_i\| \in [0,1]^{\|i\|}$ be such that $\|r_i\|$ is a probability measure and hence for any individual variable assignment function ω and, say, $\Psi = r_i[x^{(i)}]$, $\|\Psi\|_\omega = \|r_i\|(A_\omega) \in [0,1]$, where $A_\omega = \omega(x^{(i)}) \in \|i\|$, etc.

As usual, for any $\alpha,\beta \in \text{Typ}(\mathcal{L})$, and $(F : \alpha \to \beta) \in \text{FuncSymb}(\mathcal{L})$, $\|F\| : \|\alpha\| \to \|\beta\|$, with $\|\alpha\| = \|\text{Var}(\alpha)\|$, etc.

In particular, consider the logical and quantitative aspects of $\| \ \|$, noting here we let

$$\text{Rel}(\mathbb{C},\mathfrak{R}) = \bigcup_{i \in \text{Var}(\text{Ob}(\mathcal{L}))} [0,1]^{\|i\|} ,$$

$$\|\text{nt}\| : \text{Rel}(\mathbb{C},\mathfrak{R}) \to \text{Rel}(\mathbb{C},\mathfrak{R}) ,$$

so that for any $\Psi \in \text{Wff}_{(i)}(\mathcal{L})$

$$\|\text{nt}(\Psi)\| = \|\text{nt}\|(\|\Psi\|) \overset{d}{=} 1 - \|\Psi\| \in [0,1]^{\|i\|} .$$

Hence, for any $A \in \|i\|$, denoting $\complement A \overset{d}{=} X_i \dashv A$,

$$\begin{aligned}\|\text{nt}(\Psi)\|(A) &= \|\text{nt}\|(\|\Psi\|)(A) \\ &= 1 - \|\Psi\|(A) \\ &= \|\Psi\|(\complement A)\end{aligned}$$

Next, consider

$$\times : \text{Var}(\text{Rel}(\mathcal{L})) \times \text{Var}(\text{Rel}(\mathcal{L})) \to \text{Var}(\text{Rel}(\mathcal{L})) ,$$

where for any $r_i, s_j \in \text{Var}(\text{Rel}(\mathcal{L}))$, it is assumed $r_i \times s_j \in \text{Var}(\text{Rel}(\mathcal{L}))$ with $\sigma(r_i \times s_j) = i \times j$. Then

$$\|\times\| : \text{Rel}(\mathbb{C},\mathfrak{R}) \times \text{Rel}(\mathbb{C},\mathfrak{R}) \to \text{Rel}(\mathbb{C},\mathfrak{R})$$

is defined so that for any $\Psi,\theta \in \text{Wff}(\mathcal{L})$, $\|\Psi\times\theta\| \overset{d}{=} (\|\Psi\| \, \|\times\| \, \|\theta\|)$ is some choice for a joint probability measure, given the marginal probability measures $\|r_i\|$ and $\|s_j\|$.

Also define

$$\|\dagger\| : \text{Rel}(\mathbb{C},\mathfrak{R}) \times \text{Rel}(\mathbb{C},\mathfrak{R}) \to \text{Rel}(\mathbb{C},\mathfrak{R}) ,$$

so that for all $\Psi,\theta \in \text{Wff}(\mathcal{L})$,

$$\begin{aligned}\|\Psi\dagger\theta\| &\overset{d}{=} \|\Psi\| \, \|\dagger\| \, \|\theta\| \\ &\overset{d}{=} \|\Psi\| + \|\theta\| - \|\Psi\| \, \|\times\| \, \|\theta\| ,\end{aligned}$$

noting, because of the range of $\| \ \|$ being in $[0,1]$, all arithmetic operations as above are well-defined.

In particular, define

$$\|\&\|, \|or\| : Rel(\mathfrak{C},\mathfrak{R}) \times Rel(\mathfrak{C},\mathfrak{R}) \to Rel(\mathfrak{C},\mathfrak{R}),$$

for all $\Psi, \theta \in Wff_{(i)}(\ell)$, and all $A \in \|i\|$,

$$\|\Psi \;\&\; \theta\|(A) \overset{d}{=} (\|\Psi\| \;\|\&\|\; \|\theta\|)(A)$$

$$\overset{d}{=} (\|\Psi\| \;\|\times\|\; \|\theta\|)(A\times A) \; .$$

For any $\Psi, \theta \in Wff_{(i)}(\ell)$,

$$\|\Psi \text{ or } \theta\|(A) \overset{d}{=} (\|\Psi\| \;\|or\|\; \|\theta\|)(A)$$

$$\overset{d}{=} (\|\Psi\| \;\|\dagger\|\; \|\theta\|)(A\times A)$$

$$= \|\Psi\|(A) + \|\theta\|(A) - (\|\Psi\| \;\|\&\|\; \|\theta\|)(A) \; .$$

It also easily follows that for any

$\Psi \in Wff_{(i)}(\ell)$, $\theta \in Wff_{(i)}(\ell)$, any $A \in \|i\|$, $B \in \|j\|$,

$$(\|\Psi\| \;\|\times\|\; \|\theta\|)(A\dagger B) = (\|\Psi\| \;\|\dagger\|\; \|\theta\|)(A\times B) \; ,$$

where $A \dagger B \overset{d}{=} (A\times X_j) \cup (X_i\times B)$, etc.

In addition, one defines for any $\Psi, \theta \in Wff_{(i)}(\ell)$,

$$\|\Psi \Rightarrow \theta\| \overset{d}{=} (\|\Psi\| \;\|\Rightarrow\|\; \|\theta\|)$$

$$\overset{d}{=} \|((nt\Psi) \text{ or } \theta)\|$$

$$\overset{d}{=} \|nt\Psi\| \;\|or\|\; \|\theta\| \; ,$$

$$\|\Psi \Leftrightarrow \theta\| \overset{d}{=} \|(\Psi \Rightarrow \theta) \;\&\; (\theta \Rightarrow \Psi)\|$$

$$= (\|\Psi\| \;\|\Rightarrow\|\; \|\theta\|) \;\|\&\|\; (\|\theta\| \;\|\Rightarrow\|\; \|\Psi\|) \; ,$$

and the quantifiers are evaluated as for any $\Psi \in Wff_{(i\times j)}(\ell)$,

$x^{(i)}_{i\times j}$, as for classical logic

$$\|(\forall x^{(i)}_{i\times j})\Psi\|_\omega \overset{d}{=} \inf \{\|\Psi\|_{\omega'} \mid \text{all } \omega' \in G(x^{(i)},\omega)(\Psi)\}$$

$$\|(\exists x^{(i)}_{i\times j}\Psi)\|_\omega \overset{d}{=} \sup \{\|\Psi\|_{\omega'} \mid \text{all } \omega' \in G(x^{(i)},\omega)(\Psi)\}$$

where

$$G(x^{(i)},\omega) \overset{d}{=} \{\omega' \mid \omega' \text{ individual variable assignment such that}$$

$$\omega'(y) = \left\{ \begin{array}{ll} \omega(y) & ; \; y \in TV(\Psi) \dashv \{x^{(i)}\} \\ \text{arb} & ; \; y = x^{(i)} \end{array} \right\} \; .$$

It can be shown that for any $\Psi_1, \Psi_2 \in \mathrm{Wff}(\mathcal{L})$,

$$\|\Psi_1\| = \|\Psi_2\|$$

iff Ψ_1 and Ψ_2 are equivalent for L_2 .

Finally, note that PL is not truth-functional, since there is no function $f_{\|\times\|} : [0,1]^2 \to [0,1]$ such that for all individual variable assignment functions ω , and all $\Psi, \theta \in \mathrm{Wff}(\mathcal{L})$

$$\|\Psi\times\theta\|_\omega = (\|\Psi\| \; \|\times\| \; \|\theta\|)_\omega$$

$$= f_{\|\times\|}(\|\Psi\|_\omega, \|\theta\|_\omega) \quad -$$

or equivalently, for all $A \times B \in \|i\times j\|$,

$$\|\Psi\times\theta\|(A\times B) = f_{\|\times\|}(\|\Psi\|(A), \|\theta\|(B)) \ .$$

In particular, there is no $g_{\|\&\|} : [0,1] \to [0,1]$ such that for all Ψ , θ and ω ,

$$\|\Psi\&\theta\|_\omega = (\|\Psi\| \; \|\&\| \; \|\theta\|)_\omega$$
$$= g_{\|\&\|}(\|\Psi\|_\omega, \|\theta\|_\omega) \ .$$

See section 2.3.9 for connected results.

5. Standard Sequence Logics. (See Maydole [172], p. 130-132.)

6. Modal Logic. (Rescher [214], pp. 188-197).

Essentially, modal logic is characterized by a collection of unary logical connectives, for example, the three alethic modal operators: Necessity, Possibility, and Actuality/Assertion. The corresponding logic can be developed by specifying unary truth-functional tables. In addition, of course, other logical connectives are used such as not, and, or, $\Rightarrow$, etc., and in turn, compound or eliminative logical connectives can be defined in turns of these connectives. Also, theories have been established characterizing modal logic. All these logics are special cases of multi-valued logics. (See also [245].)

7. Generalization of truth functional logics using negation operators, t-norms, t-conorms. (See section 2.3.4 for a comprehensive presentation.)

2.3.4 Set theory for multi-valued logic

(a) Introduction

All mathematical concepts and reasoning may be based upon some form of set theory. (However, see, e.g., Von Neumann [257] for a primitive function approach, Lake [149] for a related procedure, or Gilmore [74], for a symbolic operator approach replacing set theory.) In the past, set theory has been mainly confined to the scope of classical two-valued logic. In modeling problems of the real world, two directions present themselves. First, one can attempt to make concepts - especially those couched in linguistic terms - conform more narrowly to classical 0 - 1 logic by "mathematizing" vague concepts. For example, "some apples are bad in that bunch," can be made more precise by perhaps artificially specifying "three-sevenths of the apples are bad in that bunch". (But is three-sevenths exact?) On the other hand - the view taken in this monograph - is to keep the ambiguity or vagueness of such descriptions, but consider the corresponding truth evaluation not necessary restricted to T (or 1) and ⊥ (or 0) , but rather to lie within the unit interval. Correspondingly, set theories for a given natural language, and, in turn, using the Parsing Principle, for a related formal language, may be established also within a multi-valued truth setting. An application of this is the establishment of knowledge-based systems from both experts and analytic considerations, from a multiple truth viewpoint. (See Chapter 8).

In the following development, $\mathcal{L}$ is any fixed formal language and $L = \text{Logic}(\mathcal{L})$ is some fixed logic, unless otherwise stated. Initially, a list of the most common axioms used to develop set theories will be presented, followed by a list of compatible logical axioms needed to develop the set theories for various logics. Then, in addition, deduction rules are added to the various axiom sets to complete the theories, eight of which are summarized below. Finally, a brief survey of basic relations, properties and problems of such set theories is presented.

(b) Selected set theories

The following list contains (by no means exhaustive) 33 of the most common set theory axioms used to form various theories of sets. Only the first three axioms will also be presented in some detail.

For symbolizations of the remainder and further details, see, e.g., Maydole [172], Cohen [39], Vopenka and Hajek [258], MacLane [165], Fraenkel and Bar-Hillel [62], Devlin [46''], Cohen and Hersh [40], Suppes [249], Pareigis [202] (Appendix), and the discussions of Cohen, Hajek and MacLane in [4']. All of the above, except Maydole, refer to classical 0 - 1 logic.

Before presenting the axioms, four distinguished binary function symbols in Foun(L) are reintroduced from section 2.2.2:

$$\text{(set)abstraction} \quad \{\cdot|\cdot\cdot\} : \text{Ob}(\mathcal{L}) \times \text{Ob}(\mathcal{L}) \times \text{Rel}(\mathcal{L}) \to \text{Ar}(\mathcal{L})$$

$$\text{(set)membership} \quad \in : \text{Ob}(\mathcal{L}) \to \text{Rel}(\mathcal{L})$$

$$\text{(set)exponentiation} \quad \Omega : \text{Ob}(\mathcal{L}) \to \text{Ob}(\mathcal{L})$$

$$\text{(set)equivalence} \quad \asymp : \text{Ob}(\mathcal{L}) \to \text{Rel}(\mathcal{L}) .$$

Note that all of the axioms presented below are in the form $(\vdash\Psi)$, for some $\Psi \in \text{Wff}(\mathcal{L})$. (See also section 2.3.3 (a) (viii) for a discussion of the different ways axioms may be presented.) In addition, only $\in$ and $\asymp$ appear explicitly in the axioms, while the class abstract operator $\{\cdot|\cdot\cdot\}$ is avoided by use of the contextual definition approach via

$$\{\alpha|\Psi(\alpha)\} \quad \text{for} \quad (\exists\beta)(\forall\alpha)((\alpha\in\beta) \Leftrightarrow \Psi(\alpha))$$

where $\alpha \in \mathrm{Wfv}_i(\ell)$, $B \in \mathrm{Wfv}_{\Omega^i}(\ell)$, and $\Psi \in \mathrm{Wff}_i(\ell)$, for the various concepts - such as unions, intersections, ordered pairs, etc. - produced by the set theory axioms. (See the discussion in [172], p. 70-76.) Furthermore, (compatible with the comments in [172], p. 248) we can evaluate

$$\|\{\alpha|\Psi(\alpha)\}\| \overset{d}{=} (\|i\|, \|\Psi\|) ,$$

where $\|\Psi\| : \|i\| \to H$, for example.

The basic table of axioms is as follows:

Axiom Un Universal

$$\vdash (\exists\alpha)(\forall\beta)((\beta\epsilon\alpha) \Leftrightarrow \beta \asymp \beta)) ,$$

where ϵ and $\asymp$ are abbreviated symbols and $\beta \in \mathrm{Wfv}_i(\ell)$, for some $i \in \mathrm{Var}(\mathrm{Ob}(\ell))$. Individual variables here, α , β , γ , ..., are considered sets in a general sense.

Axiom Z1(E1) Extension

$$\vdash (\forall\alpha)(\forall\beta)(\forall\gamma)((\gamma \in \alpha \Leftrightarrow \gamma \in \beta) \Rightarrow \alpha \asymp \beta) .$$

Many modifications of this axiom exist. (See Maydole [171], p. 66, 60, 63, 214, 222, 223.)

Axiom GC Generalized Comprehension

$$(\forall\alpha_1)\cdot\cdot(\forall\alpha_n)(\exists\alpha)(\forall\beta)(\beta \in \alpha \Leftrightarrow \Psi(\beta,\alpha,\alpha_1,\ldots,\alpha_n)) ,$$

for all $\Psi \in \mathrm{Wff}(\ell)$.

Thus formally, any *attribute* Ψ yields a corresponding *generalized set* α . Many variations or weakenings of GC exist, including Abstraction (see Maydole [172], pp. 65, et passim). (See also subsection (d) for further discussion.)

Also, note the following axioms:

Abbreviation	Axiom Common Name
Z2	Null set
Z3	Unordered pairs (union of pairs)
Z4	Arbitrary union
Z5	Infinity
Z6	Replacement
Z7	Power set
Z8	Regularity (Russell Paradox exclusion)
Z9	Choice
Z10	Continuum Hypothesis
Z11	Ordered pairs
Z12	(Relative) Complement
Z13	Cartesian product
Z14	Membership relation
Z15	Domain
Z16	Permutation (conversion)
Z17	Foundations
Z18	Restricted Comprehension
Z19	Transitivity
Z20	Mostowski

Z21	Singletons
Z22	Intersection
Z23	Existence
Z24	Restriction
Z25	Range
Z26	Relations
Z27	Nontriviality
Z28	Functionality
Z29	Double replacement
Z30	Separation
Z31	$\in$ - Induction
Z32	Collection
Z33	Double complement .

(A) A selected list of logical axioms used in developing various set theories

For all θ, Ψ, $\eta \in \mathrm{Wff}(\mathcal{L})$; all $\alpha \in \mathrm{Var}(\mathcal{L})$, $\rightarrow$ an implication operator, etc.:

Abbreviation — Axiom Name

A1 Deduction

$\vdash \quad \theta \Rightarrow (\Psi \Rightarrow \theta)$.

A2 Distribution of implication over implication

$\vdash \quad (\theta \Rightarrow (\Psi \Rightarrow \eta)) \Rightarrow ((\theta \Rightarrow \Psi) \Rightarrow (\theta \Rightarrow \eta))$.

A3 Modus Tollens

$\vdash \quad (\mathrm{nt}\ \Psi \Rightarrow \mathrm{nt}\ \theta) \Rightarrow (\theta \Rightarrow \Psi)$.

A4 Distribution of Universal Quantification over Implication

$\vdash \quad (\forall\alpha)(((\theta \Rightarrow \Psi(x)) \Rightarrow (\theta \Rightarrow ((\forall x)\Psi(x))))$,

α bound in θ .

A5 Universal instantiation

$\vdash \quad ((\forall\alpha)\Psi) \Rightarrow \theta$,

where θ is like Ψ with α replaced by β , etc.

A6 Equivalence

$\vdash \quad (\forall\alpha)(\alpha \asymp \alpha)$.

A7 Substitution

$\vdash \quad (\forall\alpha)(\forall\beta)((\alpha \asymp \beta) \Rightarrow (\theta(\alpha) \Leftrightarrow \theta(\beta)))$, where $\theta(\alpha)$ is like $\theta(\beta)$ with β substituted for α whenever α is free.

See Maydole [172], p. 50, et passim. Hay's Logic Axioms (H1) - (H9)((H1) = (A1) , (H2) = (A2)(modified) , (H4) = (A3)) are discussed in Maydole [172], p. 225, et passim, including various properties for Logic(ℓ) = $Ł_{\aleph_1}$ that hold when (H1) - (H9) are assumed.

Next, two inference rules are listed below which are used in conjunction with various collections of set theory and logical axioms to form set theories.

(B) <u>Basic inference rules use in set theories</u>

Abbreviation	Inference Rule
R1	Modus Ponens
	If $\vdash(\theta \Rightarrow \Psi)$ and $\vdash \theta$ then $\vdash \Psi$.
R2	Universal Instantiation
	If $\vdash \theta$, then $\vdash(\forall\alpha)\theta$.

(C) <u>Some basic set theories</u>

To each of the following eight axiom collections, Ax(ℓ) , may be added Rul(ℓ) = {(R1),(R2)} (with some redundancy possible) to form eight corresponding set theories $Th_x(\ell)$, where x = NST, MH, NGB, ZF, IZF, Ch, Wei, Nov.

1. NST - <u>Naïve Set Theories</u> ([104], [172])

   a. (A1) - (A5) , (Z1) , (Z9) , (GC) ,
   b. (A1) - (A7) , (Z1) , (Z9) , (GC) with an identity assignment (valuation) constraint.

2. MH - <u>Maydole-Hay Set Theories</u> ([172], Chapter 6).

   a. (A6) , (H1) - (H9) , (Z1)(modified)(GC) ,
   b. (H1) - (H9) , (Z1)(modified)(GC) with an identity assignment constraint.

3. NGB <u>Von Neumann-Gödel-Bernays Set Theory</u> [4'].

   (Z1) - (Z8) , (Z12) , (Z14) , (Z16) , (Z22) - (Z25) ; with some modifications.

4. ZF <u>Zermelo-Fraenkel Set Theory</u> [249], [4'], [62].

   (Z1) - (Z8)
   Optionally, add (Z9) and/or (Z10) .

5. IZF <u>Intuitionistic Zermelo-Fraenkel Set Theory</u> [97'].

   a. Grayson (Z1) , (Z3) - (Z7) , (Z30) - (Z31) ,
   b. Grayson (Z1) , (Z3) - (Z7) , (Z30) - (Z32) ,
   c. Powell (Z1) , (Z3) - (Z7) , (Z30) , (Z31) , (Z33) .

6. CH <u>Chapin's Set Theory</u> ([32], [33])

   Here, $\in$ is a trinary predicate symbol, between an element, a set, and degree of membership. The following axioms are thus appropriately modified: (Z1) - (Z3) , (Z5) - (Z9) , (Z11) , (Z13) , (Z26) , (Z27) ; presented within 14 axioms.

7. Wei <u>Weidner's Set Theory</u> [270].

   Similar restrictions hold for $\in$ as in Chapin's Theory:
   (Z1) , (Z3) , (Z5) - (Z8) , (Z11) , (Z28) , (Z29) , appropriately modified.

8. Nov <u>Novak's Set Theory</u> [195].

   Again, $\in$ is as in Chapin's Theory:
   (Z1) , (Z3) , (Z7) , (Z11) , (Z12) , (Z14) , (Z15) , (Z16) , (Z18) , (Z23) , (Z25) , Un .

(c) Basic relations among set theories

(1) For Naïve Set theory relative to Logic($\mathcal{L}$) = $Ł_2$:

$$(Z2) - (Z5) , (Z7) , (Z9) , (Z12) , (Z21) , (Z22) ,$$

are all theorem in $Ł_2$ (Maydole, [172], p. 77).

(2) For Maydole-Hay's theory relative to Logic($\mathcal{L}$) = $Ł_{\aleph_1}$: all ZF axioms, except possibly for (Z5) are theorems in $Ł_{\aleph_1}$. ([172], p. 241).

(3) (i) Zermelo-Fraenkel Theory (Z1) - (Z8) is consistent <u>iff</u> NGB is consistent.

(ii) It is not known whether ZF is consistent or not.

(iii) Essentially all (set-theoretic) theorems of ZF and NGB coincide.

(iv) If ZF is consistent, then it is not complete.

(v) (Z9) and (Z10) are consistent with, and independent of, (ZF), i.e., there are various models for (ZF) which make (Z9) , (Z10) have any combination of truth or falsity values (P. Cohen, 1963: [4'], [39], [40]).

(vi) {(Z1) - (Z3) , (Z7) , (Z11) , (Z12) - (Z16)} is equivalent deductively to {(Z1) - (Z4) , (Z7) , (Z11) , (Z18)} . (See Johnstone [127], p. 312-319.)

(4) If ZF is consistent then Weidner's Theory is consistent (Weidner [270], Theorem 11). Weidner's Theory extends ZF where the predicate membership symbol is trinary, accounting for membership levels.

(5) Maydole shows ([172], Chapter I, II):

(i) For any NST for $Ł_2$ GC yields Cantor's paradox and hence NST is model-inconsistent (for $Ł_2$) .

(ii) For any formal language $\mathcal{L}$ and corresponding Logic($\mathcal{L}$) , if the following inference rules involving evaluations can be shown to hold:

Existential instantiation	(EI)
Universal instantiation	(UI)
Material equivalence	(ME)
Simplification	(S)
Absorption of some order	(A)
Modus Ponens	(MP) ,

then any theory Th($\mathcal{L}$) containing also (GC) has a Curry-like paradox ([172], p. 121 et passim), and hence (GC) is model-inconsistent for Logic($\mathcal{L}$) . More explicitly, universal and existential instantiation may be written as:

Suppose $\| \ \| : \mathcal{L} \to (\text{SET}, H^{\cdot})$ with $\{0,1\} \subseteq H \subseteq [0,1]$.

<u>Universal Instantiation</u> (UI):

For any $i \in \text{Var}(\text{Ob}(\mathcal{L}))$, any $x \in \text{Wfv}_i(\mathcal{L})$ and any $\Psi \in \text{Wff}(\mathcal{L})$:
If

$$\|(\forall x)\Psi(x)\| = 1$$

then for all $t \in X_i \overset{d}{=} \|i\| \in \text{Ob}(\text{SET})$

$$\|\Psi\|(t) = 1 \ .$$

<u>Existential Instantiation</u> (EI):

For any $i \in \text{Var}(\text{Ob}(\mathcal{L}))$, any $x \in \text{Wfv}_i(\mathcal{L})$ and any $\Psi \in \text{Wff}(\mathcal{L})$;
If

$$\|(\exists x)\Psi(x)\| = 1$$

then there is a $t \in X_i$; such that

$$\|\Psi\|(t) = 1 \ .$$

(iii) If Logic($\mathcal{L}$) has a finite semantic truth value range, universal and existential instantiation always are valid (provided (R1), (R2) are inference rules, as usual) in any theory Th($\mathcal{L}$).

(iv) If for any formal language $\mathcal{L}$ and corresponding Logic($\mathcal{L}$), the six inference rules hold in (ii) in a weakened "quasi-" form (by modifying for various truth levels - see [172], pp. 123, 124), then a Curry-like paradox still holds for any Th($\mathcal{L}$) when (GC) is included; and hence, (GC) is model inconsistent for Logic($\mathcal{L}$).

More specifically, to illustrate the "quasi" form, (QUI) and (QEI) may be written as:

<u>Quasi-universal Instantiation</u> (QUI):

For any $\lambda \in [0,1]$ and any $i \in \mathrm{Var}(\mathrm{Ob}(\mathcal{L}))$ and any $x \in \mathrm{Wfv}_i(\mathcal{L})$, and any $\Psi \in \mathrm{Wff}(\mathcal{L})$:
If

$$\|(\forall x)\Psi(x)\| \geq \lambda ,$$

then for all $t \in X_i \overset{d}{=} \|i\| \in \mathrm{Ob}(\mathrm{SET})$:

$$\|\Psi\|(t) \geq \lambda .$$

<u>Quasi-existential Instantiation</u> (QEI):

For any $i \in \mathrm{Var}(\mathrm{Ob}(\mathcal{L}))$ and any $x \in \mathrm{Wfv}_i(\mathcal{L})$ and any $\Psi \in \mathrm{Wff}(\mathcal{L})$:
If

$$\|(\exists x)\Psi(x)\| = 1$$

then for each integer $m \geq 1$, there is a corresponding $t_m \in X_i$ such that

$$\|\Psi\|(t_m) \geq 1 - 1/m .$$

(v) As a consequence of (ii) or (iii) or (iv), Maydole shows that, except for $Ł_{\aleph_1}$, for all other logics considered ($Ł_k$, $2 \leq k < \aleph_0$, Bochvar, Prob. Logic, Gödel-Logic, etc.) when GC is added to any Th($\mathcal{L}$), a Curry-like paradox results and hence *except for* $Ł_{\aleph_1}$, Th($\mathcal{L}$), when GC is included in its axioms, is *model-inconsistent*. (See [172], [172'].)

(a) We do not know whether Th($\mathcal{L}$) with GC is model consistent for $Ł_{\aleph_1}$.

(b) Since $Ł_{\aleph_1}$ is not axiomitizable, no Th(ℓ) (including any set theory) can be both logically sound and logically complete.

(c) Any Th(ℓ) including both GC and (E1) is model-inconsistent for $Ł_{\aleph_1}$ with an identity assignment construct ([172], p. 203).

(d) By *suitably restricting* GC ([172], pp. 151-171), MH Set Theories (which all contain GC) *are* model-consistent for $Ł_{\aleph_1}$.

However, none of these theories can be both logically sound and complete. Indeed they all are deductively incomplete, logically incomplete, but logically sound. (See Maydole's discussions, pp. 236-245.) On the other hand, MH retains some form of (GC) and is a plausible candidate for set theory. (See [172], Chapter V.)

(6) Chapin's [32], [33] theory extends ZF ; some rudementary arithmetic and set theory relations are developed. The membership predicate symbol is considered trinary, hence, involving set membership level.

(7) Novak's theory extends NGB. Novak's membership predicate symbol is trinary analogous to Weidner and Chapin.

Novak, in a different direction [195"] from the above approach, uses the concept of semisets as originally expounded by Vopenka and Hajek [258], as the basis for a generalized, and in effect, multiple-valued logical set theory. (Roughly speaking, a semiset $X_\Psi = \{x \mid \Psi(x) \subseteq a\}$ where Ψ is a generalized (non-set one) property or predicate and a is an ordinary set.) Essentially, Novak first shows that all semisets are monotone approximable by nested sequences of ordinary sets, i.e., by flou classes and hence in turn by fuzzy sets. (See section 5.2 (B) for basic properties and background.) A number of points of difficulty arise in both the structure of the approximating collections of sets and set-like operations on them - in this approach. (Compare with the situation for elementary flou class representation of fuzzy sets by ordinary sets as, e.g., in Theorem 4, section 5.2 (B).) However, the approach does appear promising since the entire formulation is carried out completely within an axiom-like framework, as opposed to the usual situation, where fuzzy set membership functions are ideally exact numerical functions, estimated through empirical and psychological considerations. On the other hand, it seems that Novak can still not completely avoid, somewhere along the line, empirical subsets in the modeling of the original wffs or properties generating the semisets of interest.

(8) For Gödel-Intuitionistic logic, it can be shown (see Grayson [97']):

(ZF) is consistent relative to (IZF)(b)

(ZF) is consistent relative to (IZF)(c) .

(9) In a related vein, it can be shown that ([179]) (Z1) - (Z7) ((Z6) (weakened)) are valid for Gödel Logic relative to Higg(H) .

Other approaches to set theory through multi-valued logic include: Allen [2'], using the concept of "property systems"; Chang's infinite-valued logical set theory [31]; Smith's "textured sets", a concept using weighted sums for modeling membership-like functions [244']. See also Klaua's series of papers in the *Monat. Deutsche Akad. Wiss.*, Berlin, on a set theory based on multi-valued logic, analagous to - and, originally, independent of - Zadeh's work, beginning with [139] and [138']. Approaches to set theories and properties of generalized sets may be carried out through membership functions only (unlike Ch, Wei, Nov).

In another direction, Willmott [274] has investigated various ways of defining norms and distances between fuzzy sets which Warren [266] considered the equivalence relation of shape (up to scalar multiples) of fuzzy set membership functions. Kloeden [143] investigated the topological structure (through a Hausdorff metric distance) of the space of membership functions $[0,1]^X$.

See also section 2.4.2 (G) for a discussion of the connections between various set theories and topoi.

(d) The axiom of comprehension/abstraction revisited

Finally, let us tie-in the basic approach to set comprehension or abstraction through formal language $\mathcal{L}$ where some or all of appended theory $Th_K(\mathcal{L})$ (and the appropriate part of $Th_{syn_K}(\mathcal{L})$) is present, with the set theory axioms (and consequently, set theories) discussed earlier. (Again, the basic reference is [172], pp. 65-86, 246-254.)

Let $\mathcal{L}$ be a formal language as presented in 2.2.2, but with $Th_K(\mathcal{L})$ to be specified.

First note that for any $i,m \in Var(Ob(\mathcal{L}))$, with $m \geq i \times \Omega^i$, i.e., $m = i \times \Omega^i \times k$, etc., for some $k \in Var(Ob(\mathcal{L}))$ (possibly vacuous so that $m = i \times \Omega^i$) ,

$$\Psi \overset{d}{=} (x_m^{(i)} \in_i y_m^{(\Omega^i)})$$

$$= \in_i[\langle x_m^{(i)}, y_m^{(\Omega^i)}\rangle]$$

$$\in Wff(\mathcal{L}) ,$$

with

$$\sigma(\Psi) = m .$$

Now consider the converse problem: Given any $\Psi \in Wff(\mathcal{L})$ with $FV(\Psi) = x^{(i)} \times z^{(j)}$, without loss of generality, for some $i,j \in Var(Ob(\mathcal{L}))$, $x^{(i)},z^{(j)} \in Wfv(\mathcal{L})$, and writing, w.l.o.g. in substitution form

$$\Psi = \Psi[x^{(i)}, z^{(j)}] \ ,$$

does it follow that the following holds, connecting dummy variable and individual variable notation:

$$\text{(GC)} \quad (\forall z^{(j)})(\exists y^{(\Omega^i)})(\forall x^{(i)})((x^{(i)} \in_i y^{(\Omega^i)}) \Leftrightarrow \Psi[x^{(i)}, z^{(j)}]) \ ,$$

Generalized Comprehension or Abstraction?

Note first axioms $R_{I,Th,22}$ and $R_{I,Th,23}$ put in individual variable form imply the desirable property

$$\text{(GC')} \quad (x^{(i)} \in_i \{x^{(i)} \mid \Psi[x^{(i)}, z^{(j)}]\}) \ \vdash_{\ell}\dashv \Psi[x^{(i)}, z^{(j)}] \ ,$$

which in turn, because of the obvious fact that

$$a \ \vdash_{\ell}\dashv \ b$$

implies always

$$(a \Leftrightarrow b) \ ,$$

we then have the weaker form

$$\text{(GC")} \quad \vdash_{\ell}((\forall x^{(i)})(x^{(i)} \in_i \{x^{(i)} \mid \Psi[x^{(i)}, z^{(j)}]\}) \Leftrightarrow \Psi[x^{(i)}, z^{(j)}])) \ ,$$

the theorem of set compatibility.

But clearly by straightforward use of $\exists$, and in effect letting

$$y^{(\Omega^i)} \asymp \{x^{(i)} \mid \Psi[x^{(i)}, z^{(j)}]\} \ ,$$

(GC") implies (GC) .

Also, $R_{I,syn,35}$ implies the basic substitution form for $(f : \ell \to j) \in \mathrm{Var}(\mathrm{Ar}(\ell))$,

$$\vdash_{\ell} (\{x^{(i)} \mid \Psi[x^{(i)}, z^{(j)}]\} \circ f \asymp \{x^{(i)} \mid \Psi[x^{(i)}, z^{(j)} \circ f]\}) \ ,$$

etc. Furthermore, if $\| \ \| : \ell \to (\mathfrak{C}, \mathfrak{X})$ is a model, then for $\sigma(\Psi) = i \times j$, w.l.o.g. ,

$$\{x_m^{(i)} \mid \Psi[x_m^{(i)}, z_m^{(j)}]\} \in \mathrm{Ar}_{j,\Omega^i}(\mathrm{Var}(\ell)) \subseteq \mathrm{Var}(\mathrm{Ar}(\ell))$$

and

$$\|\{x_m^{(i)} \mid \Psi[x_m^{(i)}, z_m^{(j)}]\}\| : \|j\| \to \|\Omega^i\| \ .$$

(See 2.3.5 for further details.)

In addition, note that, e.g., axioms (Z12) , complements, (Z22) , intersections, and (Z4) , unions , all yield set compatible forms. For example,

$$(Z12)\ \vdash(\forall y^{(\Omega^i)})(\exists z^{(\Omega^i)})(\forall x^{(i)})((x^{(i)} \in_i z^{(\Omega^i)}) \Leftrightarrow nt(x^{(i)} \in_i y^{(\Omega^i)}))$$

yields

$$(Z12'')\quad \vdash_{\ell}((\forall y^{(\Omega^i)})(\exists z^{(\Omega^i)})(\forall x^{(i)})((x^{(i)} \in_i z^{(\Omega^i)}) \Leftrightarrow x^{(i)} \in_i \{x^{(i)} \mid nt(x^{(i)} \in_i y^{(\Omega^i)})\}))$$

and (Z22) specialized to binary intersections

$$(Z22')\quad \vdash_{\ell}((\forall y^{(\Omega^i)})(\forall w^{(\Omega^i)})(\exists z^{(\Omega^i)})(\forall x^{(i)}) (x^{(i)} \in z^{(\Omega^i)}) \Leftrightarrow ((x^{(i)} \in_i y^{(\Omega^i)}) \& (x^{(i)} \in_i w^{(\Omega^i)})))$$

implies

$$(Z22'')\quad \vdash_{\ell}((\forall y^{(\Omega^i)})(\forall w^{(\Omega^i)})(\exists z^{(\Omega^i)})(\forall x^{(i)})((x^{(i)} \in z^{(\Omega^i)}) \Leftrightarrow (x^{(i)} \in \{x^{(i)} \mid (x^{(i)} \in_i y^{(\Omega^i)}) \ \&\ (x^{(i)} \in_i w^{(\Omega^i)})\}))) .$$

Thus we make the new compound definitions for the arrows

$$Cy^{(\Omega^i)} \stackrel{d}{=} \{x^{(i)} \mid nt(x^{(i)} \in_i y^{(\Omega^i)})\} ,$$

$$y^{(\Omega^i)} \cap w^{(\Omega^i)} \stackrel{d}{=} \{x^{(i)} \mid (x^{(i)} \in_i y^{(\Omega^i)} \ \&\ (x^{(i)} \in_i w^{(\Omega^i)})\},$$

$$y^{(\Omega^i)} \cup w^{(\Omega^i)} \stackrel{d}{=} \{x^{(i)} \mid (x^{(i)} \in_i y^{(\Omega^i)}) \ \text{ or } \ (x^{(i)} \in_i w^{(\Omega^i)})\} ,$$

and more generally, for any combination of C , $\cap$, $\cup$,

$$\mathrm{comb}(C,\cap,\cup)(y_{(1)}^{(\Omega^i)},\ldots,y_{(n)}^{(\Omega^i)})$$
$$\stackrel{d}{=} \{x^{(i)} \mid \mathrm{comb}(C,\cap,\cup)((x^{(i)} \in_i y_{(i)}^{(\Omega^i)}),\ldots,(x^{(i)} \in_i y_{(m)}^{(\Omega^i)})\} ,$$

with similar definitions holding for multiple arguments (replacing single $x^{(i)}$) and cartesian products and sums.

For related results, see section 2.3.5 (b) .

(e) **Summary**

Many difficulties inherent in developing the basis for a multi-valued set theory are discussed in Chapter VI, [172] (especially, pp. 236-254). Many competing set theories abound. The positive results for Maydole's advanced set theory relative to $Ł_{\aleph_1}$ are encouraging. However, set theories for other logics such as the general truth functional one generated by triples of negations, t-norms, t-conorms (see section 2.3.5), may also be worthy, although for such logics, it may be difficult to show any soundness or completeness properties, or similarly, it may be difficult to show inconsistencies are not plausible.

2.3.5 General logical systems and dispersions.

(a) **Discussion**.

In addressing the problem of determining the state or states present (or partially present) of a given system of interest, i.e., the *uncertainty* of the system, an *uncertainty model* must be established, which in some sense captures both the system and its uncertainties. One way this can be accomplished is through a complete intuition/heuristic approach, where a single individual or panel of experts considers the problem at hand and in a coordinated manner, using his/her (or their) pooled knowledge, attempts a solution. This is based on the general principle that human beings can successfully attack very complicated problems by use of common sense and learned knowledge. Another approach is to establish a rigorous systematic model of the problem, consisting of a choice of measures or (possibly generalized) distributions or dispersions, together with some collection of logical and other types of operators acting upon them according to some prescribed calculus. We call such a model, a *general logical system*. Another approach is to attempt to integrate the first two approaches by some kind of feedback-loop procedure, so that the model of the problem reflects the experts' knowledge and, at the same time, these experts may be used to override all decision making outputs or to adjust or correct the model in an adaptive manner. The last approach serves as the basis for the concept of *knowledge-based systems*, which play a central role in the AI approach to complex problem solving.

In Chapters 8 and 9, some aspects of knowledge-based systems will be considered in addressing, especially, problems concerning the combining of evidence or clues describing the states of a system that are present, represented in terms of parameter vectors.

General logical systems may be considered from the following general viewpoint:

A general logical system is essentially a semantic evaluation of a formal language in a collection of (deduction) categories which in some sense generalize SET, the category of all ordinary sets. In general, these categories do not have a topos structure and consequently, may not be sound and complete (deductively). However, it is hoped that at least "locally" - in the same sense, that local theories are developed for disciplines such as for quantum mechanics, topology, mathematical-biological systems, and number theory - the system will be consistent. See related comments on adaptive or "local" logics by Bellman [13'] and Bellman and Zadeh [15]. The first reference also contains interesting comments on uncertainty decision making and artificial intelligence by one of the eminent scientists of our time. See also Haack's texts on nonstandard or deviant logics - [100] as well as [101]. In addition, see section 10.2 concerning the various controversies involving fuzzy logic.

The following discussion is based in part upon the properties of several categories and topoi which in a natural sense generalize or fuzzify SET: (See section 2.4 for a detailed presentation of these entities.)

Candidates for the range of the semantic evaluation representing a general logical system include, naturally, Higg(H) , Fuz(H) , $Fuz_{\asymp}(H)$, and Gog(H) . First, consider Higg(H) . As a topos, it has "nice" properties, as mentioned above. However, it is often too strict a structure, since $\wedge = \min$, $\vee = \max$, and the rest of the intuitionistic logic structure are not compatible with general negation, t-norm or t-conorm structure (see 2.3.6), the latter being more suitable for natural language/real-world use. (See, e.g., the comments of Thöle et al., [250], e.g.) In addition, Higg(H) has a more restricted and complex structure than Fuz(H) , as the investigations in 2.4 attest. On the other hand, Fuz(H) is not a topos, as seen in 2.4, and is also restrictive in that intuitionistic logic - except for equality ($\asymp$) - is required. Although some $Fuz_{\asymp}(H)$'s are topoi for appropriate choice of $\asymp$ (see 2.4) , they have relatively sparse structures. Hence, one is led to consider their union FUZ(H) . But FUZ(H) has still some typpe of intuitionistic logic on it; in particular, Fuz(H) still depends highly on $\wedge$ and $\vee$ in the definition of its arrows. (See also Pitts' recommendation for Higg(H) in place of FUZ(H) [203].)

The remaining candidate Gog(H) , which in one sense is close to Fuz(H) in structure - no intuitionistic logic structure - indeed, no logical structure - is required for its arrows. In particular, using the fact that t-conorms or copulas are bounded below by $\vee$, we can consider the subclass of arrows in Gog(H) exactly connecting objects in Gog . This subclass of arrows will yield a subcategory of Gog(H) , due to the associativity of t-conorms. However, even this may not capture all operations of importance, such as copulas and co-copulas - which may be non-associative - as used in Sklar's Theorem for joint distribution functions (see 2.3.9).

In any case, we will first define a general logical system as a semantic evaluation

$$\| \ \| : \mathcal{L} \to (\mathrm{GOG}, \mathrm{Sub})$$

where

$$\mathrm{GOG} \overset{d}{=} \bigcup_{\alpha \in I} (\mathrm{Gog}(H), \mathrm{Logic}_{\alpha})$$

for some index set I , and where each $(\mathrm{Gog}(H), \mathrm{Logic}_{\alpha})$ represents Gog(H) and a collection of logic, quantifier, and possibly, foundations operators (see 2.2.2) acting upon Gog(H) , which for simplicity is denoted Logic_{α} .

Often a general logical system contains only a small list of basic operators such as "nt","&", "or" as simply (nt, &, or) .

Next, for any choice of $i \in \mathrm{Var}(\mathrm{Ob}(\mathcal{L}))$, define

$$\|i\| \overset{d}{=} (\|i\|^{(1)}, \|i\|^{(2)}) \overset{d}{=} (X_i, \theta_i) \in \mathrm{Ob}(\mathrm{Gog}(H)) ,$$

where

$$X_i \in \mathrm{Ob}(\mathrm{SET}) , \ \theta_i : X_i \to H ,$$

and we define *generalized* or *fuzzy* set A_i as

$$A_i \overset{d}{=} i$$

with membership function

$$\phi_{A_i} \overset{d}{=} \|i\|^{(2)} = \theta_i .$$

For any $j \in \mathrm{Var}(\mathrm{Ob}(\ell))$ such that

$$\|j\|^{(2)} = \perp_H \,,\ \perp_H : X_j \to \perp_H \quad \text{(constant)} ,$$

identify $\|j\| = (X_j, \perp_H)$ with $\emptyset$.

For any $j \in \mathrm{Var}(\mathrm{Ob}(\ell))$ such that

$$\|j\|^{(2)} = T_H \,,\ T_H : X_j \to T_H \quad \text{(constant)} ,$$

identify $\|j\| = (X_j, T_H)$ with $X_j \in \mathrm{Ob(SET)}$.

Next, for any $X \in \mathrm{Ob(SET)}$, consider:

$$\mathcal{F}(X) \overset{d}{=} \{A_i \mid i \in \mathrm{Var}(\mathrm{Ob}(\ell)) \text{ and } \|i\|^{(1)} = X\}$$

and assume there exists $i_X \in \mathcal{F}(X)$ such that

$$\|i_X\| = X .$$

We call $\mathcal{F}(X)$ a class of *generalized* or *fuzzy subsets* A_i (=i) of X .

$$\mathcal{F}(X) \overset{d}{=} \{\|i\|^{(2)} \mid i \in \mathrm{Var}(\mathrm{Ob}(\ell) \text{ and } \|i\|^{(1)} = X\} \subseteq H^X .$$

We call $\mathcal{F}(X)$ a class of *dispersions* or *generalized* (or fuzzy) *set membership functions* $\phi_{A_i} (= \theta_i)$ over X .

Depending on $\|\ \|$, of course, often we may have $\mathcal{F}(X) = H^X$, for all $X \in \mathrm{Ob(SET)}$.

We assume that $\|\ \|^{(2)} : \mathrm{Var}(\mathrm{Ob}(\ell)) \to \mathrm{Ar(SET)}$ is injective. Related to this map is the membership function - map ϕ , where

$$\phi : \mathrm{Ob(SET)} \to \mathrm{Ar(SET)} ,$$

where for all $X \in \mathrm{Ob(SET)}$, $\phi(X) \in \mathcal{F}(X)$ where for all $A_i \in \mathcal{F}(X)$,

$$\phi(X)(A_i) \overset{d}{=} \phi_{A_i} \overset{d}{=} \|i\|^{(2)} = \theta_i .$$

Note that $\phi(X) : \mathcal{F}(X) \to \mathcal{F}(X)$ is also injective, for each $X \in \mathrm{Ob(SET)}$.

Suppose for convenience now $H = [0,1]$.

Let ϕ_{or} be a given t-conorm (see 2.3.6).

Let $f : X_i \to X_j$, $g : X_j \to X_k$ be ordinary functions with ordinary composition $g \circ f : X_i \to X_k$. Consider now any $\theta_i : X_i \to H$, but $\theta_j : X_j \to H$ and $\theta_k : X_k \to H$ defined by

$$\theta_j(y) \stackrel{d}{=} \phi_{or_{k \in f^{-1}(y)}} (\theta_i(x)) = \phi_{or}(\theta_i[f^{-1}](x)) \geq \bigvee_{x \in f^{-1}(y)} (\theta_i(x)) \ ;$$

all $y \in X_j$,

so that in particular, for any $x \in X_k$,

$$\theta_j(f(x)) = \phi_{or_{x' \in f^{-1}(f(x))}} (\theta_i(x')) \geq \theta_i(x) \ ,$$

and hence $f \in Ar_{(X_i,\theta_i),(X_j,\theta_j)}(Gog(H))$ in the above "exact" sense. Note the similarity of the approach here with that of a large class of functional extensions considered in 2.3.7.

Analagously, we may define for all $z \in X_k$,

$$\theta_k(z) = \phi_{or_{y' \in g^{-1}(z)}} (\theta_j(y')) \ ,$$

yielding similarly $g \in Ar_{(X_j,\theta_j),(X_k,\theta_k)}(Gog(H))$.

In turn because of the associativity of ϕ_{or} , it follows that for all $x \in X_i$,

$$\begin{aligned}\theta_k(g(f(x))) &= \phi_{or_{y' \in g^{-1}(g(f(x)))}} (\theta_j(y')) \\ &= \phi_{or_{\substack{x' \in f^{-1}(y') \\ y' \in g^{-1}(g(f(x)))}}} (\theta_i(x')) \\ &= \phi_{or_{x' \in (g \circ f)^{-1}(g \circ f)(x))}} (\theta_i(x')) \\ &= \theta_k((g \circ f)(x)) \ ,\end{aligned}$$

and hence $g \circ f \in Ar_{(X_i,\theta_i),(X_k,\theta_k)}(Gog(H))$, also in the exact sense as above.

Conversely, given any (X_i,θ_i) , and any $(X_j,\theta_j) \in Ob(Gog(H))$, does there exist some $f : X_i \to X_j$ such that

$$\theta_j(f(x)) = \phi_{or \atop x' \in f^{-1}(f(x))} (\theta_i(x')) \text{ , for all } x \in X_i \text{ ?}$$

At least one such f always exists, provided θ_i and θ_j are normable, i.e., there are points $x_o \in X_i$, $y_o \in X_j$ such that $\theta_i(x_o) = T_H$ and $\theta_j(x_o) = T_H$ and that θ_j is continuous.

In any case, we have a well-defined subcategory $(Gog(H),\phi_{or})$ of $Gog(H)$ with possibly some empty classes of arrows, i.e.,

$$Ar_{(X_i,\theta_i),(X_j,\theta_j)}(Gog(H),\phi_{or}) = \emptyset ,$$

for some pairs (X_i,θ_i) , $(X_j,\theta_j) \in Ob(Gog(H)) = Ob(Gog(H),\phi_{or})$.

Furthermore, we may afix other logical operators such as a negation $\phi_{nt} : H \to H$ and t-norm $\phi_{\&} : H \times H \to H$. Of course, these operations do not affect the category structure of $Gog(H)$ (and hence $(Gog(H),\phi_{or})$) except to be used in computing semantic evaluations for various elements of $Wfex(\ell)$, i.e., well-formed expressions, as shown, e.g., in sections 2.2.2, 2.3.2, and 2.3.6. (See also section 2.6 for extensive examples of the evaluation of natural language forms via formal language.)

Thus, in summary, an important class of general logical systems may be indicated as $(\mathcal{C},\otimes,\oplus;\ \mathcal{F})$ or $(\phi_{nt},\phi_{\&},\phi_{or};\ \mathcal{F})$ where

$\mathcal{F} : Ob(SET) \to Ob(SET)$ or more specifically $\mathcal{F}(X) \subseteq H^X$, for each set X .

General logical systems are related to L-valued logics, which are generalized by Czogala [44'''] to probabilistic L-valued logics, using Hirota's "probabilistic sets" [111].

Again, it should be emphasized that dispersions as discussed here generalize the concept of membership functions of ordinary sets, i.e., functions of the form

$$\phi_A(x) = \begin{cases} 1 & \text{iff } x \in A \\ 0 & \text{iff } x \notin A , \end{cases}$$

where A is an ordinary subset of X , $x \in X$; X also an ordinary set. Even before Zadeh [276'], Klaua [139] and others (such as Watanabe [268]) extended membership functions to, in effect, generalized or fuzzy subsets of an ordinary space. See also 2.3.6 for the development of families of operators upon such membership functions, extending ordinary set operations, including complement, intersection and union. Indeed, the manipulation of classical sets and functions, independent of any generalized set considerations, has often been facilitated by the employment of (classical) membership or "indicator" functions of sets, such as will be found in any standard textbook on Lebesgue integration. In conjunction with this idea, see the recent paper of Morrill [179'], where the use of membership functions for teaching set theory is emphasized - but completely ignoring the fact that the same or similar formal manipulations may be used to discuss generalized sets! Furthermore, after a moment's thought, the category theory concept of subobject (or functor Sub - see Appendix 1, end of section 2.4.2) is also compatible with the idea of a membership function.

Two obvious examples of generalized sets in our everyday lives are given below:

In the clothing business, size of women's clothing is in general determined by height and weight through a few simple natural language labels such as "petite", "average", "tall", "full figure short", full figure tall". Despite the common use of these terms to describe ordinary sets in height vs weight space, for purposes of convenience, the boundaries of these "sets" should actually be fuzzy and could be so indicated by lightening the colors near the boundaries, etc.

The above remarks also apply to visual examples such as a cloud in the sky. Thus, we could conceivably divide up a region of the sky into cells and determine the percentage of black vs white (vs grey, etc.) pixels or primitive picture dots within a given cell, and in turn convert the percentage of black ones directly into a membership function. Thus, for cells well within the "boundaries" of the cloud, membership levels are approximately unity, for cells near or on the boundary area, membership levels drop and for cells well outside the boundary area, membership levels are approximately zero.

These ideas appear also to be related to the classical notion of the density of a set (see, e.g., [181'], pp. 261-263) and, as well, to extended-dimension concepts as presented in Mandelbrot's exposition on fractals, i.e., highly irregularly-shaped geometric objects, typically appearing in nature [167']. In addition, independent of fuzzy set theory directly, Mandelbrot also considered, in effect, generalized set membership functions over "gaps" of fractals arising from random set coverages (167'], p. 366). See also Chapters 3 - 5 of our text, for various relations between random set coverages and generalized set membership functions.

Three general examples of general logical systems are given next.

In the previous paragraphs, we have seen how the membership symbol and its natural evaluation determine membership mappings. A membership mapping ϕ depends on $\|\cdot\|$. However, for simplicity, when no confusion is possible, we will drop this dependency in our writing, but not from our mind! The membership mappings turn out to play a crucial role in developing the concept of general logical systems as we now proceed. The motivation for out general definition below will be clarified through examples.

Examples.

1. **Boolean system.** Let $\mathcal{L}$ be the formal language of ordinary predicate calculus. For each set X , $\mathcal{F}(X)$ is the class of subsets of X , and $\mathcal{T}(X)$ is the class of all ordinary set membership functions over X .

2. **Zadeh's system.** Let $\mathcal{L}$ be the formal language with Lukasiewicz logic $\aleph_1$. For each set X , $\mathcal{F}(X)$ is the class of all generalized sets on X , and $\mathcal{T}(X) = [0,1]^X$, the class of all dispersions over X .

3. **Probabilistic system.** Let $\mathcal{L}$ be the formal language of Probability Logic (see section 2.3.3). Let $Y \in \mathrm{Ob(SET)}$ and choose $\mathcal{X} \subseteq \mathcal{P}(Y)$, where $\mathcal{X}$ is a σ-algebra of subsets of Y . Then $\mathcal{F}(\mathcal{X})$ corresponds bijectively to $\mathcal{T}(\mathcal{X})$, the class of all probability measures over Y . (See also section 2.3.9.)

b) Set operations for general logical systems.

Note again (see section 2.3.4 (b)) the relationship between Wff(ℓ) and all generalized sets through the Axiom of General Comprehension (GC) and/or the contextual or operator approach to class abstraction.

On the other hand, we have stated (2.3.4) that (see originally Maydole [172]) if set axiom (GC) is accepted in conjunction with any logic of interest (see again section 2.3.4 for the list), except for $Ł_{\aleph_1}$, a Curry-like paradox, and hence inconsistency, occurs. More generally, Maydole [172] showed that (GC) in such cases implies the validity of several inference rules for all logics of interest, including quasi-universal and quasi-existential instantiation, as well as other quasi-forms (quasi-modus ponens, simplification, absorption, etc.). (He also showed that whenever the above inference rules hold, a Curry-like paradox indeed results.)

Now, many set theory axioms (see 2.3.4 for various listings) will be of the form

$$Q(\phi \Leftrightarrow \Psi) \ ,$$

where Q consists of a string of universal and/or existential quantifiers and ϕ and Ψ are (in general, open) wff's for formal language ℓ. For example, complementation (Z12), cartesian products (Z13), unions (Z4), etc., all fall under this classification.

It follows readily that for a given general logical system with the usual logical constants nt, &, or, $\Rightarrow$, $\Leftrightarrow \in$ Loc(ℓ), if the quasi-form inference rules (section 2.3.4) such as (QUI), (QEI), (QME), (QS), etc., hold, than any such set theory axiom as mentioned above will imply at least in an asymptotic sense the existence of corresponding class abstract "sets". The term "asymptotic" may be omitted, if the stronger non-quasi inference rules, (UI), (EI), (ME), etc., hold.

As an illustration, consider the following development for (Z12), where $i \in$ Var(Ob(ℓ)) is arbitrary, $\epsilon_i(x,A)$ is replaced by simply $(x \in A)$, for any $x,y,z,\ldots \in \text{Wfv}_i(\ell)$ and general sets $A,B,C,\ldots \in \text{Wfv}_{\Omega^i}(\ell)$:

From, e.g., Maydole [172], p. 77,

$$(Z12) = Q(\phi \Leftrightarrow \Psi) \ ,$$

where

$$Q \overset{d}{=} (\forall\gamma)(\exists\alpha)(\forall\beta)$$

$$\phi = \phi(\beta,\alpha) \overset{d}{=} (\beta\in\alpha)$$

$$\Psi \overset{d}{=} \Psi(\beta,\gamma) \overset{d}{=} \text{nt}(\beta\in\gamma) \ .$$

Then, applying (QUI)

$$\|(Z12)\| = 1$$

implies that for all t

$$\|(\exists\alpha)(\forall\beta)(\phi(\beta,\alpha) \Leftrightarrow \Psi(\beta,t))\| = 1 .$$

In turn, applying (QEI), it follows that for all t and each integer $m \geq 1$, there is an α_m such that

$$\|\forall\beta(\phi(\beta,\alpha_m) \Leftrightarrow \Psi(\beta,t))\| \geq 1 - 1/m .$$

Next, again using (QUI) we obtain, for all t, each integer $m \geq 1$, a corresponding α_m, such that for all v,

$$\|\phi(v,\alpha_m) \Leftrightarrow \Psi(v,t)\| \geq 1 - 1/m .$$

Finally, if quasi-material equivalence and quasi-simplification hold for $\mathcal{L}$ (see Maydole [172], p. 124), then if $\| \ \|$ is truth function with respect to $\Rightarrow$ and $\|\Rightarrow\|$ is continuous, then for all t, each integer $m \geq 1$, a corresponding α_m exists such that for all v

$$|\|\phi(v,\alpha_m)\| \Leftrightarrow \|\Psi(v,t)\|| < 1/m .$$

We could call each such α_m as above the mth approximating complement $C_m(\gamma)$ of γ.

Hence in an asymptotic sense, for any given $\gamma \in \mathrm{Wfv}_{\Omega^i}(\mathcal{L})$ we can postulate $C\gamma \in \mathrm{Wfv}_{\Omega^i}(\mathcal{L})$ such that

$$\|\beta \in C\gamma\| = \|\mathrm{nt}(\beta \in \gamma)\| .$$

Of course, if the stronger inference rules (UI), (EI), (ME), etc., hold - as is true for $Ł_m$ or G_m - then the above proof may be appropriately modified so that the asymptotic interpretation may be omitted.

Furthermore, for $Ł_{\aleph_1}$ (as was stated in section 2.3.4), Maydole's modification of (GC) together with Hayes' logical axioms will imply the validity of the quasi-form inference rules and yet consistency will also hold (Maydole [172]), although the logic is deductively and logically incomplete. Hence, at least in an asymptotic sense, complementation, cartesian products, intersections, unions, etc., all may be safely defined - with no paradox derivable.

In any case, motivated by the above, we can define, for example, the following basic general set operations, for truth functional systems; through a class abstract-like approach. (See also the previous discussion in 2.3.4 (d).)

(i) **Complementation**

$$C : \mathrm{Wfv}_{\Omega^i}(\mathcal{L}) \to \mathrm{Wfv}_{\Omega^i}(\mathcal{L}) .$$

For any $A \in Wfv_{\Omega^i}(\ell)$, there is a $\complement A \in Wfv_{\Omega^i}(\ell)$ such that, for all $x \in Wfv_i(\ell)$,

$$nt(x \in A) = (x \in \complement A) ,$$

whence

$$\begin{aligned} \|nt(x \in A)\| &= \|nt\|(\|x \in A\|) = \|nt\|(\|A\|(\|x\|)) \\ &= \|nt\|(\phi_A(x)) = \phi_{nt}(\phi_A(x)) \\ &= \|x \in \complement A\| \\ &= \phi_{\complement A}(x) . \end{aligned}$$

(ii) **Cartesian product**

$$\times : Wfv_{\Omega^i}(\ell) \times Wfv_{\Omega^j}(\ell) \to Wfv_{\Omega^{i \times j}}(\ell) ,$$

For any $A \in Wfv_{\Omega^i}(\ell)$, $B \in Wfv_{\Omega^j}(\ell)$ and any $x \in Wfv_i(\ell)$, and $y \in Wfv_j(\ell)$,

$$(x \in A)\&(y \in B) = ((x,y) \in A \times B)) ,$$

whence

$$\begin{aligned} \|(x \in A)\&(y \in B)\| &= \|\&\|(\|A\|(\|x\|) , \|B\|(\|y\|)) \\ &= \phi_\&(\phi_A(x) , \phi_B(y)) \\ &= \|(x,y) \in A \times B\| \\ &= \phi_{A \times B}(x,y) . \end{aligned}$$

(iii) **Intersection**:

$$\cap : Wfv_{\Omega^i}(\ell) \times Wfv_{\Omega^i}(\ell) \to Wfv_{\Omega^i}(\ell) .$$

Specialize cartesian product in (ii) for $i = j$, $x = y$:

$$(x \in A)\&(x \in B) = ((x,x) \in A \times B) = (x \in A \cap B) ,$$

whence

$$\begin{aligned} \|(x \in A)\&(x \in B)\| &= \phi_\&(\phi_A(x), \phi_B(x)) \\ &= \phi_{A \times B}(x,x) \\ &= \|x \in A \cap B\| \\ &= \phi_{A \cap B}(x) . \end{aligned}$$

(iv) **Cartesian sum**

$$\dagger : Wfv_{\Omega^i}(\ell) \times Wfv_{\Omega^j}(\ell) \to Wfv_{\Omega^{i \times j}}(\ell) .$$

For any $A \in Wfv_{\Omega^i}(\ell)$, $B \in Wfv_{\Omega^j}(\ell)$ and any $x \in Wfv_i(\ell)$, $y \in Wfv_j(\ell)$,

$$(x \in A) \text{ or } (y \in B) = ((x,y) \in A \dagger B)$$

whence, analogous to (ii),

$$\|(x \in A) \quad \text{or} \quad (y \in B)\| = \phi_{or}(\phi_A(x),\ \phi_B(y))$$
$$= \phi_{A \dagger B}(x,y) \ .$$

(v) **Union**

$$\cup : \mathrm{Wfv}_{\Omega^i}(\mathcal{L}) \times \mathrm{Wfv}_{\Omega^i}(\mathcal{L}) \to \mathrm{Wfv}_{\Omega^i}(\mathcal{L}) \ .$$

Analogous to (iii), specialize cartesian sum in heading (iv) for $i = j$, $x = y$:

$$(x \in A) \quad \text{or} \quad (x \in B) = ((x,x) \in A \dagger B) = (x \in A \cup B) \ ,$$

whence

$$\|(x \in A) \quad \text{or} \quad (x \in B)\| = \phi_{or} \quad (\phi_A(x),\ \phi_B(x))$$
$$= \phi_{A \dagger B}(x,x)$$
$$= \|x \in A \cup B\|$$
$$= \phi_{A \cup B}(x) \ .$$

Symbolically, we may write more generally,

$$(x_1, \ldots, x_n) \in \mathrm{comb}(nt,\ \&,\ or)(A_1, \ldots, A_n)$$
$$= \mathrm{comb}(nt,\ \&,\ or)(\langle x_1 \in A_1\rangle, \ldots, \langle x_n \in A_n\rangle) \ ,$$

where some of the A_j's and/or x_j's , independently, may be the same, and "comb" refers to some combination of operators. In the above, we could also use nt, $\times$, $\dagger$, $\Rightarrow$, etc.

Of course, all of the above operations in (ii) - (v) may be extended in the obvious way to an arbitrary finite number of arguments, and further by standard limiting procedures, to an arbitrary number of arguments. Note the use of ϕ_{nt} for $\|nt\|$, $\phi_\&$ for $\|\&\|$, ϕ_{or} for $\|or\|$, reminiscent of negation, t-norm and t-conorm operators discussed in section 2.3.6. In fact, often the general logical system will be such that ϕ_{nt} , $\phi_\&$, ϕ_{or} are such operators.

For non-truth-functional logics such as Probability Logic, the above relations must be modified.

(vi) **Subset relations** may be defined in two different ways:

For any $i \in \mathrm{Typ}(\mathcal{L})$, $A,B \in \mathrm{Var}_{\Omega^i}(\mathcal{L})$,

(a) $A \subseteq B$ iff , by definition,

$\phi_A \le \phi_B$ pointwise over X_i

or

(b) $\|A \subseteq B\| \overset{d}{=} \| \underset{x \in X_i}{\&} ((x \in A) \Rightarrow (x \in B))\|$, etc.

Subset relations for generalized sets may be defined more systematically as follows:
Let $B \in Var(Ob(\ell))$. Then for any $A \in Var(Ob(\ell))$,

$$A \subseteq B \text{ iff } \|A\| \subseteq \|B\| \text{ iff } \|A\| \in Sub(\|B\|).$$

Now, the generalized power class of $\|B\| = (X_B, \theta_B)$ is

$$Sub(X_B, \theta_B) = \{\Psi \mid \Psi : X_B \to H , \Psi \leq \theta_B\}$$

and hence

$$\|A\| \subseteq \|B\|$$

iff

$$\|A\| = \Psi \text{ or } (X_B, \Psi) , \text{ such that } \Psi \leq \theta_B .$$

Also

$$\|\Omega^B\| = \|\Omega\|^{\|B\|} = (Sub(X_B, \theta_B), T)$$

(See 2.4.2 (D) for basic properties of Gog(H).)

(vii) **Membership relations** for generalized sets are obtained from:
Let $x \in Wfv_i(\ell)$, $A \in Wfv_{\Omega^i}(\ell)$, $i \in Var(Ob(\ell))$. Then

$$\|x \in A\| = \|x\| \, \|\in_i\| \, \|A\| .$$

Consider first $\|\in_i\|$:

$$\begin{aligned}\|\in_i\| &\in Sub(\|i\| \times \|\Omega^i\|)\\ &= Sub((X_i, \theta_i) \times (\{\Psi \mid \Psi : X_i \to H \text{ and } \Psi \leq \theta_i\}, T)\\ &= Sub(\{(x,\Psi) \mid x \in X_i, \Psi : X_i \to H \text{ and } \Psi \leq \theta_i\}, \theta_i) ,\end{aligned}$$

where for all $y \in X_i$, $\Psi : X_i \to H$, $\Psi \leq \theta_i$,

$$\begin{aligned}\|\in_i\|(x,\Psi) &\overset{d}{=} x \, \|\in_i\| \, \Psi\\ &\overset{d}{=} \Psi(x) \leq \theta_i(x) .\end{aligned}$$

Hence,

$$\begin{aligned}\|x \in A\| &= \|A\|(\|x\|)\\ &= \phi_A(\|x\|) .\end{aligned}$$

A linguistic example is "John is happy".

$\|x\| = \text{John}$,

$\|A\| = \text{happy} : X_i \to H \in \|\Omega^i\|$,

$\|i\| = X_i$ = set of humans ,

$\|\Omega^i\| = \|\Omega\|^{\|i\|} = H^{X_i}$,

$\|\in\| \ : X_i \times H^{X_i} \to H$ (with restriction) ,

"John is happy" = John $\in$ happy .

See also sections 2.3.2, 2.6 and Appendix 3 (iv) of section 2.4.

Let us consider in some detail the semantic evaluation in 2.3.4 (d):

$$q \overset{d}{=} \|\{x^{(i)} \mid \Psi[x_m^{(i)}, y_m^{(j)}]\}\| : \|j\| \to \|\Omega^i\| \in Ar_{\|j\|,\|\Omega^i\|}(Gog(H)) .$$

Thus,

$$q : X_j \to Sub(\|i\|) = \{f \mid f \in H^{X_i} \text{ with } f \le \theta_i \text{ pointwise}\}$$

with the restriction

$\theta_j \le T(q(\cdot))$, pointwise,

i.e., no restriction. Before defining θ_j , consider the semantic evaluation of Ψ and $\Psi[\cdot, y^{(j)}]$: Since the evaluation is essentially in $(Gog(H), Sub)$, it follows that

$$\begin{aligned} \|\Psi\| &\in Sub(\|\sigma(\Psi)\|) \\ &= Sub(\|i\| \times \|j\|) \\ &= \{f \mid f \in H^{X_i \times X_j}, f \le \theta_i(\cdot) \wedge \theta_j(\cdot\cdot), \text{ pointwise}\} . \end{aligned}$$

Next consider, for any $\ell \in Var(Ob(\mathcal{L}))$ and any $(g : \|l\| \to \|i\| \times \|j\| \overset{d}{=} \|k\|) \in Ar(Gog(H))$. It then follows from the definition of pullbacks (see 2.4.2, Appendix 1) that

$$Sub(g) : Sub\|\ell\| \to Sub\|k\|$$

where for any $h \in Sub(\|\ell\|)$, letting mono $(h : \|n\| \to \|\ell\|) \in Ar(Gog(H))$, for some $n \in Var(Ob(\mathcal{L}))$,

$$Sub(g)(h) = (proj_{\|k\|}^{(\|n\| \times_{h,g} \|k\|)} : \|n\| \times_{h,g} \|k\| \to \|k\|)$$

where

$$\|n\| \times_{h,g} \|k\| = (X_n \times X_k, h(\cdot) \wedge g(\cdot\cdot)) ,$$

so that for any $(s,t) \in X_n \times X_k$,

$$Sub(g)(h)(s,t) \overset{d}{=} h(s) \wedge g(t) .$$

In particular, note that

$$\|x_m^{(i)}\| : \|m\| \to \|i\| ,$$

$$\|y_m^{(j)}\| : \|m\| \to \|j\| ,$$

where $\|m\| = (X_m, \theta_m)$, $\|j\| = (X_j, \theta_j)$, etc.

Let $g \overset{d}{=} \|\langle x_m^{(i)}, y_m^{(j)}\rangle\|$, with $\ell = i \times j$ and $h \overset{d}{=} \Psi$. Then

$$\|\Psi[x_m^{(i)}, y_m^{(j)}]\| = \|\Psi\|[\|\langle x_m^{(i)}, y_m^{(j)}\rangle\|]$$

$$= (\mathrm{Sub}\ \|\langle x_m^{(i)}, y_m^{(j)}\rangle\|)(\|\Psi\|)$$

$$= \|\Psi\|(\cdot,\cdot\cdot) \wedge \langle \|x_m^{(i)}\|, \|y_m^{(j)}\|\rangle(\cdot\cdot\cdot)$$

$$= \|\Psi\|(\cdot,\cdot\cdot) \wedge \langle \|x_m^{(i)}\|(\cdot\cdot\cdot), \|y_m^{(j)}\|(\cdot\cdot\cdot)\rangle .$$

In any case, we simply define q as, for any $t \in X_j$, $s \in X_i$,

$$q(t)(s) \overset{d}{=} \|\Psi\|(s,t) .$$

If we use the generic term "comb" for an arbitrary combination, of operators $\complement$, $\times$, $\dagger$, etc., then for many systems, further compound set operators may be obtained through the relations

$$\mathrm{comb}(\mathrm{nt},\&,\mathrm{or})(\cdot\cdot(x \in A), (y \in B),\cdot\cdot)$$
$$= (\cdot\cdot x,y,\cdot\cdot) \in \mathrm{comb}(\complement,\cap,\cup)(\cdot\cdot A,B,\cdot\cdot) .$$

For example,

$$\mathrm{nt}((x \in A) \text{ or } (y \in B)) \ \& \ (z \in C)$$
$$= \mathrm{nt}((x,y) \in A \dagger B) \ \& \ (z \in C)$$
$$= ((x,y) \in \complement(A \dagger B)) \ \& \ (z \in C)$$
$$= ((x,y,z) \in (\complement(A \dagger B)\times C)) .$$

Algebraic properties of $\complement$, $\times$, $\dagger$, $\cup$, $\cap$, etc., all are derivable from the properties of nt , & , or , $\Rightarrow$ that are postulated for $\mathcal{L}$. For example, let us consider associativity: From the above definitions, it follows that for all x , y , z , A , B , C ,

$$(x \in A) \text{ or } (y \in B \text{ or } z \in C) = (x,y,z) \in (A \dagger (B \dagger C))$$

$$((x \in A) \text{ or } (y \in B)) \text{ or } (z \in C) = (x,y,z) \in (A \dagger B) \dagger C) .$$

Thus, *if* "or" is an associative logical operator for $\mathcal{L}$, then clearly, the two left hand sides of the above equations are equal and hence so are the two right hand sides. Thus, associativity holds for $\dagger$:

$$A \dagger (B \dagger C) = (A \dagger B) \dagger C .$$

Similar results hold for symmetry, idempotent, etc., for $\dagger$ as well as analogous properties for $\times$, replacing "or" everywhere by

"&" . Also, similar comments are valid for properties involving both $+$ and $\times$ such as various types of distributivity and modularity. Conversely, properties postulated for $\times$, $+$, C , become properties for & , or , nt , etc., in $\mathcal{L}$. Also, similar comments hold following semantic evaluations for the corresponding logics, truth functional or non-truth-functional. Again, see 2.3.4 for various types of operators with prescribed algebraic properties. For example, t-norms in addition to being required to have certain boundary conditions also must be symmetric and associative - and a subclass - the non Archimedean ones - will also be idempotent. Indeed, a re-examination of the various logics of interest, illustrates the various algebraic properties of the semantic evaluations of the basic logical connectors and hence (by the bijective mapping discussed earlier) of the corresponding general set theory operators.

Compound predicates may be formed in $\mathfrak{a}$, the formal language class (the counterpart of the natural language class) - and then evaluated for truth content by putting them into fuzzy set form.

By this procedure, other more complicated predicates and their quantifications may be evaluated, including universal and existential quantifiers, cartesian sums, and products, logical implications, and logical equivalences. Also, subset relations and relational and functional transforms may be evaluated.

As an example, consider the semantic evaluation here, in (Gog(H),Sub), for quantifications and substitution:

Let $\mathcal{L}$ be the basic formal language and $\Psi \in \mathrm{Wff}(\mathcal{L})$ with $\sigma(\Psi) = 1 \times j$, $i,j \in \mathrm{Var}(\mathrm{Ob}(\mathcal{L}))$, $x_m^{(i)}, y_m^{(j)} \in \mathrm{Wfv}(\mathcal{L})$ and write

$$\Psi(x^{(i)},y^{(j)}) \quad \text{for} \quad \Psi[<x^{(i)},y^{(j)}>] \text{ , etc.}$$

Then, as usual, letting $m = i \times j \times k$,

$$\| j\| = (X_i,\theta_i) \text{ , } \| j\| = (X_j,\theta_j) \text{ ,}$$
$$\| i\times j\| = \| i\| \times \| j\| = (X_i \times X_j,\ \theta_i(\cdot) \wedge \theta_j(\cdot\cdot)) \text{ , etc.,}$$
$$\|\Psi\| \in \mathrm{Sub}(\sigma(\|\Psi\|)) = \mathrm{Sub}(\| i\times j\|) \text{ ,}$$

i.e.,

$$\|\Psi\| : X_i \times X_j \to H \quad \text{with} \quad \|\Psi\| \le \theta_i(\cdot) \wedge \theta_j(\cdot\cdot) = \theta_{i\times j}(\cdot,\cdot\cdot) \text{ ,}$$

and, more generally, replacing $<x_m^{(i)},y_m^{(j)}>$ by $(f : m \to i \times j) \in \mathrm{Var}(\mathrm{Ar}(\mathcal{L}))$, we have for the substitution $\Psi[f]$ (noting formally $\sigma(\Psi[f]) = m$)

$$\|\Psi[f]\| = \mathrm{Sub}(\| f\|)(\|\Psi\|) \text{ .}$$

Now, $\| f\| : \| m\| \to \| i\times j\|$ in Gog(H) and it follows from 2.4.2 (D) that

$$\mathrm{Sub}(\| f\|)(\|\Psi\|) = \theta_m \wedge (\|\Psi\| \circ \| f\|) \text{ .}$$

Also,

$$\begin{aligned} &\| (\forall x_m^{(i)})\ \Psi(x_m^{(i)},y_m^{(j)})\| \\ &= \|\forall(i,j,\Psi)\| \\ &= \|\forall\| (\| i\|,\| j\|,\|\Psi\|) \\ &= \bigwedge_{t\in X_i} (\theta_i(t) \Rightarrow_H \|\Psi\|(t,\cdot)) \text{ ,} \end{aligned}$$

$$\|(\exists \underset{m}{x}^{(i)})(\Psi(\underset{m}{x}^{(i)}, \underset{m}{y}^{(j)}))\|$$
$$= \|\exists(i,j,\Psi)\|$$
$$= \bigvee_{t \in X_i} (\|\Psi\|(t,\cdot)) ,$$

See Kwakernaak [148], Goodman [88], Hisdal [114] and Dubois and Prade [51], p. 18, for techniques for evaluating "fuzzified" concepts. Bellman and Zadeh [15] (see also [14]) were among the first to use a restricted form of the Principle of Abstraction to fuzzify concepts, relying on Lukasiewicz ($Ł_{\aleph_1}$)-logic (i.e., min for & , max for or , 1 - (·) for negation, etc.) for evaluation. Giles [74] also has emphasized the connection with Lukasiewicz logic in developing fuzzy logic as part of his risk-based subjective approach to modeling of fuzzy set concepts. Skala [237] developed a number of interesting properties of Lukasiewicz logic for use in fuzzy set theory.

Albert [2] has proposed an alternative (but similar in many respects) development of fuzzy set theory and fuzzy logic, within an axiomatic viewpoint, including qualifiers such as "usually" and a new approach to deduction.

Bellman and Giertz [14] in addition to establishing the previously mentioned mutual distributivity characterization of $\mathcal{F}_0$ also suggested in effect use of a form of the Principle of Abstraction. In practice, the required mutual distribution conditions may be too restrictive. For example, Thöle, et al. [250] and Zimmermann [291] have shown through empirical considerations that other forms of $\phi_{\&}$ and ϕ_{or} may be more appropriate. Interestingly enough, a basic survey (see, e.g., Rescher [214]) of multi-valued logic shows a paucity of choices for "and", "or", and "not" - most picking some variation of Zadeh's original choice (independent usually of Zadeh's work). Other restrictions may be placed upon fuzzy set systems such as the DeMorgan relation or requiring the satisfying of certain functional relations (again, see, [140]).

Thus, a calculus of fuzzy set operations may be established. (See, e.g., Dubois and Prade [51] for extensive listings of operators, relations and applications.)

The basic problem of choosing, for a given situation, which fuzzy set system $(\phi_{nt}, \phi_{\&}, \phi_{or})$ is most appropriate may be approached by both empirical considerations and theoretical guidelines (by appealing to random set connections - see the last comments of this introduction). (See [250], [291]; also Goodman and Nguyen [92].) Also, modeling of possibility functions and their modifications poses a problem - but essentially no different than that of choosing a suitably large parameterized family of probability density functions. (See Lakoff [150], Hersh and Carramazza [109], MacVicar-Whelan [167], Kuzmin [147], Kochen and Badre [144], and Dubois and Prade [51], pp. 255-264, for various modeling of possibility functions and their operators.)

In addition, the work of Nanlun [181] should be mentioned in regard to empirical verification of fuzzy set membership functions through statistical data (random "appearences") in histograms representing overlapping classes - hence not necessarily adding up to unity.

Finally, the comprehensive approach of Norwich and Turksen [194''] in modeling membership functions should be mentioned where a number of representation and uniqueness theorems are obtained.

2.3.6 Families of truth functions.

At this point, let us summarize briefly some of the highlights of fuzzy set theory as originally conceived by Zadeh [276'] and some natural extensions of it. (Leech ([153], pp. 38-41 and Chapter 6 presents "fuzziness" from a linguistic viewpoint.)

The basic building block in the development of fuzzy set theory is the membership function

$$\phi: X \to [0,1]$$

which uniquely corresponds to a fuzzy subset A of ordinary set X. If the range of ϕ_A is a subset of $\{0,1\}$, then ϕ_A reduces to the classical ordinary characteristic or set membership function found in most textbooks on real analysis and Lebesgue integration. In a related vein, G.S. Goodman [93] has pointed out that the collection of all fuzzy subsets of a closed interval may be considered in a sense the weak*- completion (i.e., pointwise convergence) of the collection of all ordinary set membership functions. Operations on fuzzy set membership functions - or , in short, possiblity functions - therefore extend those on ordinary sets. Zadeh originally considered (pointwise) $1 - (\cdot)$, min, and max as the basic fuzzy set operations for, complement, intersection, and union, respectively. However, after some thought, it is clear that many other extensions for these operations can be considered as alternative definitions for fuzzy set complements, intersections, and unions. For example, complement could be represented by

$$\phi_{not}(x) = (1 - x^{\alpha})^{1/\alpha} ,$$

for all $x \in [0,1]$; $\alpha > 0$ constant. Note the involutive property

$$\phi_{not}(\phi_{not}(x)) \equiv x \ ; \text{ all } \ x \in [0,1] ,$$

and that $\phi_{not}(x)$ is decreasing in x with the required boundary (i.e., classical $0 - 1$ logic) conditions

$$\phi_{not}(0) = 1 \ ; \ \phi_{not}(1) = 0 . \tag{*}$$

Another possible definition for complement could be the intuitionistic one (2.3.3 (C))

$$\phi_{not}(x) = \begin{cases} 1 , & \text{if } \ x = 0 , \\ 0 , & \text{if } \ 1 \geq x > 0 . \end{cases}$$

But this ϕ_{not} fails to satisfy the involutive property and is not continuous.

All of the above definitions for ϕ_{not} satisfy the boundary conditions in eq. (*) and are non-increasing functions. We will call such a unary operator $\phi_{not} : [0,1] \to [0,1]$ a *negation operator* .

Intersection could be represented by

$$\phi_{\&}(x,y) = prod(x,y) \overset{d}{=} x \cdot y ,$$

or by

$$\phi_{\&}(x,y) = maxsum(x,y) \overset{d}{=} max(x + y - 1, 0) ,$$

or as proposed by Zadeh [276']

$$\phi_{\&}(x,y) = min(x,y) ,$$

etc., for all $x,y \in [0,1]$. All of the above definitions are bounded above by min , are nondecreasing in each argument, are symmetric, continuous and associative, as well as satisfying the 0 - 1 classical logic boundary conditions

$$\phi_{\&}(x,1) = \phi_{\&}(1,x) = x , \phi_{\&}(0,x) = \phi_{\&}(x,0) = \phi_{\&}(0,0) = 0 ,$$

for all $x \in [0,1]$. This implies that $\phi_{\&}$ may be extended to any number of arguments. Such a function $\phi_{\&} : [0,1]^2 \to [0,1]$ is called a *t-norm*. In a related manner, union could be represented by a function $\phi_{or} : [0,1]^2 \to [0,1]$ which is, similarly, nondecreasing in arguments, symmetric, continuous and associative so that is is extendable unambiguously recursively to arbitrary multiple arguments. In addition, ϕ_{or} is bounded below by max and satisfies the boundary conditions

$$\phi_{or}(1,x) = \phi_{or}(x,1) = \phi_{or}(0,1) = \phi_{or}(1,0) = \phi_{or}(1,1) = 1 ,$$

$$\phi_{or}(0,x) = \phi_{or}(x,0) = x ; \text{ all } x \in [0,1]$$

Possible definitions for ϕ_{or} include:

$$\phi_{or}(x,y) = probsum(x,y) \overset{d}{=} x + y - xy = 1 - (1 - x)(1 - y) ,$$

or

$$\phi_{or}(x,y) = bndsum(x,y) = minsum (x,y) \overset{d}{=} min(x + y, 1)$$

or Zadeh's originally proprosed

$$\phi_{or}(x,y) = max(x,y) ; \text{ all } x,y \in [0,1] ,$$

among infinitely many possible extensions. Such a function ϕ_{or} is called a *t-conorm*. (For background, see Klement [140], Goodman [91], and the comprehensive text of Schweizer and Sklar [226]. See also Frank [61] and Ling [159] and Alsina, et al., [4].)

Originally, t-norms and t-conorms arosefrom the concept of a probabilistic metric space, developed independently of fuzzy set theory [226]. The recent paper of Czogala and Drewniak [44'] extends the definitions of t-norms and t-conorms, including changes in min-bounds, max-bounds and other properties and applies these to random variables and fuzzy probabilistic sets. (See also the empirically-oriented paper of Czogala and Zimmermann [44"].) In addition, intermediate operators or generalized means are considered in some detail by Dyckhoff and Pedrycz [52'].

Let ϕ_{nt} , $\phi_{\&}$, ϕ_{or} be any negation operator, t-norm and t-conorm, respectively. Then since we may extend unambiguously, $\phi_{\&}$ and ϕ_{or} recursively (using symmetry and associativity) by, e.g.

$$\begin{aligned}\phi_{\&}(x_1,x_2,x_3) &= \phi_{\&}(\phi_{\&}(x_1,x_2),x_3) \\ &= \phi_{\&}(x_1,\phi_{\&}(x_2,x_3)) ,\end{aligned}$$

etc.,

then $\phi_{\&}$, ϕ_{or} : $[0,1]^n \rightarrow [0,1]$ are well-defined for all $n > 1$. For $n = 1$, define $\phi_{\&}(x) = \phi_{or}(x) = x$.

Call the triple of operators

$$\mathcal{F} = (\phi_{not}, \phi_{\&}, \phi_{or})$$

a *general (fuzzy) set system*, operating on some given class of fuzzy sets. Such a system extends the classical Aristotelian two-valued $\{0,1\}$ logical system.

A general fuzzy set system is said to be *DeMorgan* iff for any given ϕ_{nt} ,

$$\phi_{nt}(\phi_{\&}(x,y)) = \phi_{or}(\phi_{nt}(x), \phi_{nt}(y))$$

$$\phi_{nt}(\phi_{or}(x,y) = \phi_{\&}(\phi_{nt}(x), \phi_{nt}(y)) ,$$

for all $x,y \in [0,1]$, etc. For simplicity, for all of the following definitions, assume

$$\phi_{nt} = 1 - (\cdot), \text{ i.e., } \phi_{nt}(x) \equiv 1 - x .$$

Denote $\mathfrak{D}$ as the class of all DeMorgan systems. Thus,

$$\mathcal{F}_0 \stackrel{d}{=} (1 - (\cdot), \min, \max)$$

$$\mathcal{F}_1 \stackrel{d}{=} (1 - (\cdot), \text{prod}, \text{probsum})$$

and

$$\mathcal{F}_\infty \stackrel{d}{=} (1 - (\cdot), \text{maxsum}, \text{bndsum})$$

are all in $\mathfrak{D}$, but, e.g.,

$$\mathcal{F}' \overset{d}{=} (1-(\cdot),\ \text{prod},\ \text{bndsum}) \quad \text{is not in } \mathfrak{D} .$$

Note that if $\phi_{\&}$ is any t-norm,

$\phi_{or}(x,y) \overset{d}{=} 1 - \phi_{\&}(1-x,\ 1-y)$, all $x,y \in [0,1]$, always determines a well defined t-conorm and hence a DeMorgan system.

A *copula* is a cumulative probability distribution function (c.d.f.) over $\mathbb{R}^2$ such that its two one-dimensional marginal c.d.f.'s, each over $\mathbb{R}$, are identical in form to the c.d.f. of the uniform random variable U over $[0,1]$, i.e., the c.d.f. F_0 of U is at any $x \in [0,1]$

$$F_0(x) = x .$$

It can be shown that not only any *associative* copula is also a t-norm, but more generally, defining for any fixed integer $n \geq 1$ an *n-copula* as a c.d.f. over $\mathbb{R}^n$, all of whose one-dimensional marginal c.d.f.'s are the same as F_0 above (Sklar [238]):

(a) All associative n-copulas are t-norms.
All t-norms which are probability distribution functions in n-arguments are n-copulas. For any n-copula, $\phi_{\&}$ and

$$x = (x_1,\ldots,x_n)\ ,\ y = (y_1,\ldots,y_n) \in [0,1]^n ,$$

$$|\phi_{\&}(x) - \phi_{\&}(y)| \leq \sum_{j=1}^{n} |\phi_{\&}(x_j) - \phi_{\&}(y_j)| \leq \sum_{j=1}^{n} |x_j - y_j|$$

and hence $\phi_{\&}$ is uniformly continuous over $[0,1]^n$.

(b) For any arbitrary c.d.f. F over $\mathbb{R}^n$, there exists a unique corresponding n-copula $\phi_{\&}$ such that

$$F(x_1,\ldots,x_n) = \phi_{\&}(F_1(x_1),\ldots,F_n(x_n)) ;\quad \text{all } x_1,\ldots,x_n \in \mathbb{R} , \tag{**}$$

where $F_1,\ldots,F_n$ are the n one-dimensional marginal c.d.f.'s over $\mathbb{R}$ for F .

Indeed, $\phi_{\&} \equiv F(F_1^{\ddagger}(\cdot),\ldots,F_n^{\ddagger}(\cdot))$. (See subsection on pseudoinverses of distribution functions.)

(c) For any collection of n one-dimensional c.d.f.'s $F_1,\ldots,F_n$ over $\mathbb{R}$ and any choice of n-copula $\phi_{\&}$, defining F by eq. (**) yields F as a legitimate c.d.f. over $\mathbb{R}^n$. If $\phi_\&$ is a given copula such that the nth iterate of $\phi_\&$ is an n-copula, we say $\phi_\&$ is an n-copula by abuse of notation.

We call the above two results, Sklar's Theorem.

(1) First, note that if V and W are any 0 - 1 valued random variables with $Pr(V = 1) \overset{d}{=} x$ and $Pr(W = 1) \overset{d}{=} y$, say, $0 \le x,y \le 1$, then the following bounds occur: for the possible evaluation of the joint probability $Pr(V = 1 \;\&\; W = 1)$ and $Pr(V = 1 \text{ or } W = 1)$.

$$\text{maxsum}(x,y) \le Pr(V = 1 \;\&\; W = 1) \le \min(x,y)$$

$$\max(x,y) \le Pr(V = 1 \text{ or } W = 1) \le \text{bndsum}(x,y) \ , \qquad (***)$$

for all $0 \le x,y \le 1$, the upper bound occurring for maximally correlated V and W , while the lower bound occurs for V and W most negatively correlated. Note that the case of V and W being statistically independent yields $Pr(V = 1, W = 1) = x \cdot y$, somewhere in the middle of the two bounds.

(2) Let $\phi_\&$ be any (2-) copula. Then

$$\text{maxsum}(x,y) \le \phi_\&(x,y) \le \min(x,y) \ ; \text{ all } \ 0 \le x,y \le 1 \ ,$$

with the boundaries also being copulas, since we can write, for all $0 \le x,y \le 1$,

$$\phi_\&(x,y) = Pr(V' \le x, W' \le x) \ ,$$

for some uniform [0-1] r.v.'s V',W' over $\mathbb{R}$. Then define 0 - 1 r.v.'s V_x, W_x by:

$$V_x \overset{d}{=} \begin{cases} 1 & \text{iff } V' \le x \\ 0 & \text{iff } V' > x \end{cases}$$

$$W_x \overset{d}{=} \begin{cases} 1 & \text{iff } W' \le x \\ 0 & \text{iff } W' > x \end{cases} \ .$$

Hence,

$$\phi_\&(x,y) = Pr(V_x = 1, W_x = 1) \ ,$$

and we may apply eq. (***) .

(d) For any integer $n \ge 1$, define c_n as the class of all DeMorgan n-copula systems for $\phi_{not} = 1 - (\cdot)$. Thus, ϕ_{or} for any such system for $n = 2$ is easily shown to satisfy the relation

$$\max(x,y) \le \phi_{or}(x,y) \le \text{bndsum}(x,y) \ ; \text{ all } \ 0 \le x,y \le 1 \ ,$$

with the boundaries also achieved by ϕ_{or} being the DeMorgan transform of copulas min and maxsum.

(e) For any $n \ge 1$, min and prod are n-copulas, but maxsum although a t-norm is not an n-copula for $n \ge 3$, noting for all $x_1,\ldots,x_n \in [0,1]$, the evaluations

$$\begin{aligned} &\min(x_1,\ldots,x_n) \\ &\text{prod}(x_1,\ldots,x_n) = x_1\cdots x_n \ , \\ &\text{maxsum}(x_1,\ldots,x_n) = \max(x_1+\cdots+x_n - (n-1),\ 0) \ . \end{aligned}$$

Furthermore, for any n-copula $\phi_{\&}$, and all $x_1,\ldots,x_n \in [0,1]$,

$$\text{maxsum}(x_1,\ldots,x_n) \le \phi_{\&}(x_1,\ldots,x_n) \le \min(x_1,\ldots,x_n) \ ,$$

noting that for

$x = (x_1,\ldots,x_n) \le y = (y_1,\ldots,y_n) \in [0,1]^n$, the variations over the n-interval $J(x,y)$ are

$$\text{Var}_{J(x,y)}(\min) = \max(0,\min(y_1,\ldots,y_n)) - \max(x_1,\ldots,x_n) \ ,$$

$$\text{Var}_{J(x,y)}(\text{prod}) = (y_1 - x_1)\cdots(y_n - x_n) \ ,$$

and

$$\text{Var}_{J(\frac{1}{2}\underset{\sim}{1}_n,\underset{\sim}{1}_n)}(\text{maxsum}) = 1 - \frac{n}{2} \ ,$$

and hence maxsum is not an n-copula for $n \ge 3$ (but it can be verified to be a copula, i.e., 2-copula). Denote the class of all n-copulas by $\mathcal{C}_n$.

(f) Consider now Yager's family of t-norms [275'], $\phi_{\&,p}$. For all real p, $1 < p < +\infty$, each $\phi_{\&,(p)}$ is also an n-copula for any $n \ge 1$, since generator $h_p(t) = (1-t)^p$ as a function of $t \in [0,1]$ yields $h_p^{-1}(y) = 1 - y^{1/p}$, a complete monotone function over $\mathbb{R}^+$. (See later in this section for definitions and properties of generators.)

It also follows easily that for any $n \ge 1$

$$\begin{aligned} \lim_{p\to 1^+} \phi_{\&,(p)}(x_1,\ldots,x_n) &= \phi_{\&,(1)}(x_1,\ldots,x_n) \\ &= \text{maxsum}(x_1,\ldots,x_n) \end{aligned}$$

uniformly in all $x = (x_1,\ldots,x_n) \in [0,1]^n$.

In particular, let $x \in [0,1]^n$ be arbitrary and consider maxsum(x) :

$$x_1+\cdots+x_n < n - 1 .$$

This implies

$$(1 - x_1)+\cdots+(1 - x_n) > 1 .$$

Hence, there is a $p > 1$ such that

$$(1 - x_1)^p+\cdots+(1 - x_n)^p > 1 ,$$

whence

$$\begin{aligned}\phi_{\&,p}(x_1,\ldots,x_n) &= 1 - (\min(\sum_{J=1}^{n} (1 - x_j)^p, 1))^{1/p} \\ &= 0 = \text{maxsum}(x) .\end{aligned}$$

In any case, the above approximating property shows that the lower bound for n-copulas by maxsum cannot be improved upon. Similarly, for any n-copula

$$\max(x_1,\ldots,x_n) \le \phi_{or}(x_1,\ldots,x_n) \le \text{bndsum}(x_1,\ldots,x_n) ,$$

with Yager's, $\phi_{or,p}$ as $p \to 1^+$ uniformly approximating the upper bound bndsum (the latter, not an n-copula for $n \ge 3$) .

A general fuzzy set system $\mathcal{F}$ is said to be *mutually distributive* iff

$$\phi_\&(x, \phi_{or}(y,z)) = \phi_{or}(\phi_\&(x,y) \phi_\& (x,z))$$

$$\phi_{or}(x, \phi_\&(y,z)) = \phi_\&(\phi_{or}(x,y), \phi_{or}(x,z)) ,$$

for all $x,y,z \in [0,1]$.

A general fuzzy set system $\mathcal{F}$ is *idempotent* iff

$$\phi_\&(x,x) = \phi_{or}(x,x) = x ; \text{ all } x \in [0,1] .$$

A DeMorgan general fuzzy set system is said to be *semi-distributive* iff, for all $x,y,z \in [0,1]$,

$$\phi_\&(x, \phi_{or}(y,z)) = \phi_\&(x,y) + \phi_\&(x,z) - \phi_\&(x,y,z)) .$$

Let $\mathcal{S}$ denote the class of all semi-distributive families.

A general fuzzy set system $\mathcal{F}$ is said to be *Archimedean* iff

$$\phi_\&(x,x) < x ; \text{ for all } 0 < x < 1$$

and

$$\phi_{or}(x,x) > x ; \text{ for all } 0 < x < 1 .$$

Denote the class of all Archimedean systems by $\mathcal{A}r$.

Note that $F_0 = (1 - (\cdot), \min, \max)$ is not Archimedean. The following important result will be useful:

For any $x, y \in [0,1]$ and any t-norm $\phi_\&$, if $\phi_\&(x,x) = x$ or $\phi_\&(y,y) = y$, then $\phi_\&(x,y) = \min(x,y)$.

(<u>Proof:</u> Suppose $x < y$.

(1) If $\phi_\&(x,x) = x$, then since

$$x = \phi_\&(x,x) \le \phi_\&(x,y) \le \phi_\&(x,1) = x ,$$

the result follows.

(2) If $\phi_\&(y,y) = y$ and $\phi_\&(x,x) < x$ (by case (1)), assume $\phi_\&(x,y) < x$. The function $f_y \stackrel{d}{=} \phi_\&(\cdot, y)$ is continuous with $f_y(x) < x < y = f_y(y)$. Hence there is a z , $x < z < y$ with $f_y(z) = x$,

$$x > \phi_\&(x,x) = \phi_\&(\phi_\&(z,y),\ y) = \phi_\&(z,\ \phi_\&(y,y))$$
$$= \phi_\&(z,y) = x$$

yields a contradiction to the assumption.)

An Archimedean system $\mathcal{F}$ is *strict* iff $\phi_\&$ and ϕ_{or} are strictly increasing over $(0,1)^2$.

A DeMorgan system $\mathcal{F}$ such that

$$\phi_\&(x,y) + \phi_\&(x,\ 1-y) = y \ ; \text{ all } x,y \in [0,1]$$

is called *exchangable*.

A general fuzzy set system $\mathcal{F}$ such that

$$\phi_{or}(x,y) = x + y - \phi_\&(x,y) \ ; \text{ all } x,y \in [0,1]$$

is called *Frankian*. (See Frank [61] for properties.) Let $\mathcal{F}r$ be the class of all Frankian families. Note that the Frankian property has essentially the same form as a modular form or valuation for operators $\phi_\&$ and ϕ_{or} over $[0,1]$. (See, e.g., Birkhoff [17].)

Yager's family of DeMorgan fuzzy set systems $\mathcal{F}$ has the forms $\{\mathcal{F}_{(p)} \mid 1 \le p \le +\infty\}$, where

$$\mathcal{F}_{(p)} \stackrel{d}{=} (1 - (\cdot),\ \phi_{\&,(p)},\ \phi_{or,(p)}) ,$$

with

$$\phi_{\&,(p)}(x,y) = 1 - (\min((1-x)^p + (1-y)^p,\ 1))^{1/p}$$

all $x,y \in [0,1]$, etc. Denote this class by $\mathcal{Y}$.

Note that

$$\mathcal{F}_{(1)} = (1 - (\cdot),\ \text{maxsum},\ \text{bndsum})$$
$$\mathcal{F}_{(+\infty)} = (1 - (\cdot),\ \min,\ \max)\ .$$

Let J be any at most countable (or finite) non-vacuous index set. Let $\underset{\sim}{\mathcal{F}} \overset{d}{=} \{\mathcal{F}_j \mid j \in J\}$ be any collection of Archimedean fuzzy set systems $\mathcal{F}_j = (\phi_{not}, \phi_{\&}^{(j)}, \phi_{or}^{(j)})$, with ϕ_{not} fixed (usually to $1 - (\cdot)$) . Let mapping $\rho : J \to J$ be given and also let $K \overset{d}{=} \{[a_j,b_j] \mid 0 \le a_j < b_j \le 1$, with all closed intervals $[a_j,b_j]$ for distinct j's be disjoint, $j \in \rho(J)$, such that $\bigcup_{j\in\rho(J)} [a_j,b_j] \subset$ (proper) $[0,1]\}$.

Also, for any $\gamma \overset{d}{=} [a,b]$, $0 \le a < b \le 1$, define the affine operator $L_\gamma : [0,1] \to [0,1]$ and its inverse L_γ^{-1} , by, for all $u \in [0,1]$,

$$L_\gamma(u) \overset{d}{=} a + (b-a)\cdot u$$
$$L_\gamma^{-1}(u) = (u-a)/(b-a)\ ,$$
$$L\gamma(L_\gamma^{-1}(u)) = L_\gamma^{-1}(L_\gamma(u)) \equiv u\ .$$

Then the *ordinal sums* $\phi_{\&}(\underset{\sim}{\phi}_{\&}, \rho, K)$ and $\phi_{or}(\underset{\sim}{\phi}_{or}, \rho, K)$ are defined by, for any $x,y \in [0,1]$,

$$\phi_{\&}(\phi_{\&}, \rho, K)(x,u) \overset{d}{=} \begin{cases} L_{\gamma_j}(\phi_{\&}^{(j)}(L_{\gamma_j}^{-1}(x), L_{\gamma_j}^{-1}(y))), \\ \quad \text{iff } x,y \in \gamma_j \ , \\ \quad \text{for some } j \in \rho(J)\ ; \\ \min(x,y)\ , \\ \quad \text{iff } x,y \in [0,1] \text{ are otherwise}\ , \end{cases}$$

$$\phi_{or}(\underset{\sim}{\phi}_{or}, \rho, K)(x,y) \overset{d}{=} \begin{cases} L_{\gamma_j}(\phi_{or}^{(j)}(L_{\gamma_j}^{-1}(x), L_{\gamma_j}^{-1}(y)))\ , \\ \quad \text{iff } x,y \in \gamma_j\ , \\ \quad \text{for some } j \in \rho(J)\ ; \\ \max(x,y) \text{ iff } x,y \in [0,1] \text{ are} \\ \quad \text{otherwise}\ , \end{cases}$$

where

$$\gamma_j \overset{d}{=} [a_j,b_j]\ ,\ j \in \rho(J)\ ,$$

and

$$\mathcal{F}(\underset{\sim}{\mathcal{F}}, \rho, K) \overset{d}{=} (\phi_{not}, \phi_{\&}(\underset{\sim}{\phi}_{\&}, \rho, K)\ ,\ \phi_{or}(\underset{\sim}{\phi}_{or}, \rho, K))\ ,$$

is called an ordinal sum of systems $\underset{\sim}{\mathcal{F}}$, with $\sigma(\underset{\sim}{\mathcal{F}})$ defined as the collection of all possible ordinal sums over $\underset{\sim}{\mathcal{F}}$ fixed. Similar notation may be used for only the t-norm or t-conorm part.

Note that $\phi_{\&}(\underset{\sim}{\phi}_{\&}, \rho, K)$ is *locally Archimedean* over each $[a_j,b_j]^2$, since $\phi_{\&}(\underset{\sim}{\phi}_{\&}, \rho, K)(x,x) < x$ for all $x \in [a_j,b_j]$, and otherwise $\phi_{\&}(\underset{\sim}{\phi}_{\&}, \rho, K)$ is locally a min. Similar remarks hold for $\phi_{or}(\underset{\sim}{\phi}_{or}, \rho, K)$

Theorem

(i) Given any $\underset{\sim}{\mathcal{F}}$, ρ and K as above, $\mathcal{F}(\underset{\sim}{\mathcal{F}}, \rho, K)$ is a well defined non-Archimedean fuzzy set system - since for any $x \in [0,1] - \bigcup_{j\in\rho(J)} [a_j,b_j]$,

$$\phi_{\&}(\phi_{\&}, \rho, K)(x,x) = \min(x,x) = x ,$$

$$\phi_{or}(\phi_{or}, \rho, K)(x,x) = \max(x,x) = x .$$

(ii) Any t-norm $\phi_{\&}$ is either min, an Archimedean t-norm or an ordinal sum (of t-norms). Similar results hold for any t-conorm being either max, Archimedean or an ordinal sum.

Proof: Suppose $\phi_{\&}$ is neither Archimedean nor min. Then let

$$M \overset{d}{=} \{x \mid x \in [0,1] \& \ \phi_{\&}(x,x) < x\} .$$

It follows from the continuity and nondecreasing argument properties of $\phi_{\&}$, that we can write w.l.o.g.

$$M = \dot{\bigcup_{j\in J}} [a_j,b_j] ,$$

for some non vacuous, at most countable index set J with $[a_j,b_j]$'s all disjoint, $a_j < b_j$, and with $M \subset$ (proper)$[0,1]$, such that

$$\phi_{\&}(x,x) \cdot \begin{cases} = x & \text{for } x = a_j \text{ or } b_j \\ < x & \text{for all } a_j < x < b_j , \end{cases}$$

$j \in J$.

Now for each $j \in J$, and all $x,y \in [a_j,b_j]$, $j \in J$, we have the identity

$$\begin{aligned}\phi_{\&}(x,y) &= L_{\gamma_j}(L_{\gamma_j}^{-1}\phi_{\&}(L_{\gamma_j}(L_{\gamma_j}^{-1}(x)), L_{\gamma_j}(L_{\gamma_j}^{-1}(y)))) \\ &= L_{\gamma_j}(\phi_{\&}^{(j)}(L_{\gamma_j}^{-1}(x), L_{\gamma_j}^{-1}(y))) ,\end{aligned}$$

$$\phi_{\&}^{(j)}(u,v) \overset{d}{=} L_{\gamma_j}^{-1}(\phi_{\&}(L_{\gamma_j}(u), L_{\gamma_j}(v))) ;$$

for all $u,v \in [0,1]$, where it can be shown that $\phi_{\&}^{(j)}$ is a legitimate Archimedean t-norm (over $[0,1]^2$).

Also, for any $(x,y) \in [0,1]^2 \vdash \bigcup_{j\in J} [a_j,b_j]^2$, if $x = y$, then $\phi_{\&}(x,x) = x$, by construction. If $x < y$, say, then there exists z, $x < z < y$ such that $\phi_{\&}(z,z) = z$, from which it follows (see eq. (I)) that $\phi_{\&}(x,z) = \min(x,z)$ which implies, $\phi_{\&}(x,y) = \min(x,y)$.

Thus, for all $x,y \in [0,1]$,

$$\phi_{\&}(x,y) = \phi_{\&}(\underset{\sim}{\phi}_{\&}, \text{id}, K) ,$$

$\underset{\sim}{\phi}_{\&} = (\phi_{\&}^{(j)})_{j\in J}$, $\text{id} \equiv \rho : J \to J$, as given above.

Similar results hold for any t-conorm with respect to max, Archimedeaness, or being an ordinal sum.

Extend the definition of L_γ and L_γ^{-1} to be defined over $[0,1]^2$, where for any $V \in [0,1]^2$, letting $\underset{\sim}{1}_2 \overset{d}{=} \begin{bmatrix}1\\1\end{bmatrix}$, and $\gamma \overset{d}{=} (a,b)$,

$$L_\gamma(V) \overset{d}{=} a\underset{\sim}{1}_2 + (b-a)\cdot V$$

$$L_\gamma^{-1}(V) \overset{d}{=} (1/(b-a))(V-a\underset{\sim}{1}_2) ,$$

yielding $L_\gamma(L_\gamma^{-1}(V)) = L_\gamma^{-1}(L_\gamma(V)) = V$.

Thus, if F is any cumulative probability distribution function (c.d.f.) over $[0,1]^2$, $F\circ L_\gamma^{-1}$ is also a legitimate c.d.f. over $[0,1]^2$.

Hence if $\underset{\sim}{\phi}_{\&}$ is a family of associative Archimedean copulas so that for any $j \in \rho(J)$, $\phi_{\&}^{(j)}$ a copula and hence cumulative probability distribution function (with uniform marginals),

$$F_j \overset{d}{=} \phi_{\&}^{(j)}\circ L_{\gamma_j}^{-1}$$

is a legitimate c.d.f. over $[0,1]^2$, noting that for any $V = \begin{bmatrix}x\\y\end{bmatrix} \in [0,1]^2$, the special cases

$$F_j(V) = \begin{cases} 0\,, & \text{if } V \in J_{1,j} \overset{d}{=} \{V \mid x \le a_j \text{ or } y \le a_j\} \\ \dfrac{v_2 - a_j}{b_j - a_j}\,, & \text{if } V \in J_{2,j} \overset{d}{=} \{V \mid x \ge b_j \text{ and } a_j \le y \le b_j\} \\ \dfrac{v_1 - a_j}{b_j - a_j}\,, & \text{iff } V \in J_{3,j} \overset{d}{=} \{V \mid y \ge b_j \text{ and } a_j \le x \le b_j\} \\ 1\,, & \text{if } V \in J_{4,j} \overset{d}{=} \{V \mid x \ge b_j \text{ and } y \ge b_j\}\,. \end{cases}$$

Suppose w.l.o.g.

$$0 \le a_1 < b_1 < a_2 < b_2 < \cdots \le 1\,.$$

Define intervals

$$\tau_j \overset{d}{=} [b_{j-1}, a_j]\,, \quad j = 1,2,\ldots$$

where $b_0 \overset{d}{=} 0$, if $a_1 > 0$, etc.

Also, denote, as before, min to be the t-norm representing mini-mum, noting that min is a legitimate c.d.f. over $[0,1]$ representing the distribution of a point uniformly distributed over the main diagonal of $[0,1]^2$. Indeed, min is a non-Archimedean copula. Then, for $j = 1,2,3,\ldots$,

$$G_j \overset{d}{=} \min \circ L_{\tau_j}^{-1}$$

is also a legitimate c.d.f. over $[0,1]^2$, where

$$G_j(V) = \max(0, \min(\frac{x - b_{j-1}}{a_j - b_{j-1}}, \frac{y - b_{j-1}}{a_j - b_{j-1}}, 1))$$

with the special cases

$$G_j(V) = \begin{cases} 0\,, & \text{if } V \in K_{1,j} \overset{d}{=} \{V \mid x_1 \le b_{j-1} \text{ or } y \le b_{j-1}\} \\ \dfrac{v_2 - b_{j-1}}{a_j - b_{j-1}}\,, & \text{if } V \in K_{2,j} \overset{d}{=} \{V \mid x \ge a_j \text{ and } b_{j-1} \le y \le a_j\} \\ \dfrac{v_1 - b_{j-1}}{a_j - b_{j-1}}\,, & \text{if } V \in K_{3,j} \overset{d}{=} \{V \mid y \ge a_j \text{ and } b_{j-1} \le x \le a_j\} \\ 1\,, & \text{if } V \in K_{4,j} \overset{d}{=} \{V \mid x \ge a_j \text{ and } y \ge a_j\}\,. \end{cases}$$

It readily follows that all γ_j^2, τ_j^2, $J_{2,j}$, $J_{3,j}$, $K_{2,j}$, $K_{3,j}$, $j = 1,2,3,\ldots$ are essentially disjoint (except at boundaries - see diagram below).

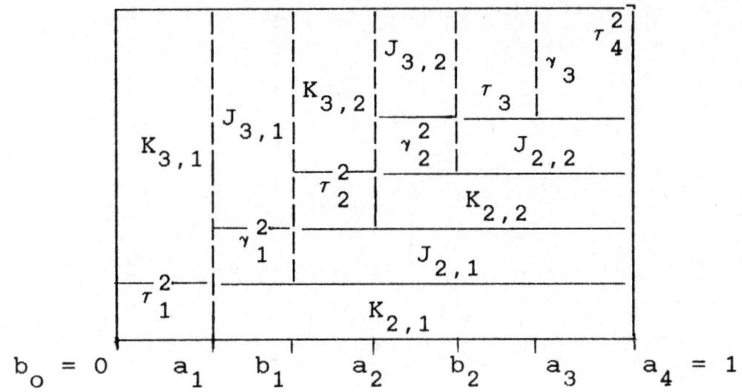

By using these properties, it can be verified directly that any ordinal sum of associative copulas is also an at most countable probability mixture of c.d.f.'s over $[0,1]^2$:

$$\phi_\&(\underset{\sim}{\phi}_\&,\ \rho,\ K) = \sum_{j\geq 1} (b_j - a_j)\cdot F_j + \sum_{j\geq 1} (a_j - b_{j-1})\cdot G_j ,$$

where

$$F_j = \phi_\&^{(j)} \circ L_{\gamma_j}^{-1} ,$$

$$\phi_\&^{(j)}(x,y) = h_j^{-1}(\min(h_j(x) + h_j(y),\ h_j(0))) ,$$

where $h_j : [0,1] \to [0,+\infty]$ is monotone (strict) decreasing convex with $h_j(1) = 0$, $0 < h_j(0) \leq +\infty$, and G_j is as before.

Now

(i) For all $V = \begin{bmatrix} x \\ y \end{bmatrix}$ with

$$V \in M_j \overset{d}{=} \{V \mid V \in [0,1]^2 \ \&\ h_j(x) + h_j(y) \geq h(0)\} ,$$

$$\frac{\partial^2 \phi_\&^{(j)}(x,y)}{\partial x \partial y} = \frac{\partial^2 0}{\partial x \partial y} = 0 .$$

(ii) For all $V = \begin{bmatrix} x \\ y \end{bmatrix}$ with

$$V \in N_j \overset{d}{=} \{V \mid V \in [0,1]^2 \ \&\ h_j(x) + h_j(y) \leq h(0)\} ,$$

$$0 \leq \frac{\partial^2 \phi_\&^{(j)}(x,y)}{\partial x \partial y} = \frac{\partial^2 h_j^{-1}(h_j(x) + h_j(y))}{\partial x \partial y}$$

$$= \frac{-Dh_j(x)\cdot Dh_j(y)\cdot (D^2 h_j)(\phi_\&^{(j)}(x,y))}{((Dh_j)(\phi_\&^{(j)}(x,y)))^3}$$

$$= (D^2 h_j^{-1})(h_j(x) + h_j(y)) \cdot Dh_j(x) \cdot Dh_j(y)$$

$$\stackrel{d}{=} \eta(h_j)(x,y)$$

$$\leq D^2 hj(\phi_{\&}^{(j)}(x,y)) / |Dh_j(\phi_{\&}^{(j)}(x,y))|$$

$$\stackrel{d}{=} \kappa(h_j)(x,y) \ ,$$

by using the fact that always

$$\phi_{\&}^{(j)}(x,y) \leq \min(x,y)$$

and the convexity of h_j .

Hence, for all $V = \begin{bmatrix} x \\ y \end{bmatrix} \in [0,1]^2$,

$$\frac{\partial^2 F_j(x,y)}{\partial x \partial y} \leq \frac{\eta(h_j)(L_{\gamma_j}^{-1}(V))}{(b_j - a_j)^2} \leq \frac{\kappa(h_j)(L_{\gamma_j}^{-1}(V))}{(b_j - a_j)^2} \ .$$

Consider now Frank's family (the modular t-norms) of Archimedean t-norms $\phi_{\&,s}$, $0 < s < +\infty$, where it can be shown each $\phi_{\&,s}$ is a copula, since the canonial form is

$$\phi_{\&,s}(x,y) = h_s^{-1}(h_s(x) + h_s(y))$$

$$= \log(1 + (s^x - 1)(s^y - 1)/(s-1))/\log s$$

with generator h_s given by

$$h_s(x) = -\log((s^x - 1)/(s-1)) \ ,$$

with limiting cases $s = 1$ and $s = +\infty$:

$$h_1(x) \equiv -\log x$$

and

$$h_{+\infty}(x) \equiv 1 - x$$

yielding

$$\phi_{\&,1}(x,y) \equiv x \cdot y \equiv \mathrm{prod}(x,y)$$

and

$$\phi_{\&,+\infty}(x,y) = \max(0,\ x + y - 1) = \text{maxsum}(x,y)\ ;$$

all $x,y \in [0,1]$,

and clearly $h_s : [0,1] \to [0,+\infty]$ is nonincreasing convex with $h_s(1) = 0$, $h_s(0) = +\infty$,

$$Dh_s(x) = -\log s\cdot\frac{s^x}{s^x - 1} = -\log s\cdot(1 + \frac{1}{s^x - 1})$$

$$D^2h_s(x) = (\log s)^2\cdot\frac{s^x}{(s^x - 1)^2} = (\log s)^2\cdot(\frac{1}{s^x - 1} + \frac{1}{(s^x - 1)^2})$$

$$\geq 0 .$$

Note also that since

$$-\log\left[\frac{(s^x - 1)(s^y - 1)}{(s - 1)^2}\right] = h_s(x) + h_s(y)$$

$$= h_s(\phi_{\&,s}(x,y))$$

$$= -\log\left[\frac{s^{\phi_{\&,s}(x,y)} - 1}{s - 1}\right] ,$$

$$s^{\phi_{\&,s}(x,y)} - 1 = (s^x - 1)(s^y - 1)/(s - 1) \ :\ \text{all}\ \ x,y \in [0,1] .$$

Thus, for all $x,y \in [0,1]$,

$$(D^2h_s)(\phi_{\&,s}(x,y)) = (\log s)^2\cdot\left[\frac{s - 1}{(s^x - 1)(s^y - 1)} + \frac{(s - 1)^2}{(s^x - 1)^2(s^y - 1)^2}\right] ,$$

$$Dh_s(\phi_{\&,s}(x,y)) = (-\log s)\cdot\left[1 + \frac{s - 1}{(s^x - 1)(s^y - 1)}\right]$$

and thus

$\eta(h_s)(x,y)$

$$= \frac{-(\log s)^4\cdot\left[1+\frac{1}{s^x-1}\right]\left[1+\frac{1}{s^y-1}\right]\cdot\left[\frac{s - 1}{(s^x- 1)(s^y - 1)} + \frac{(s - 1)^2}{(s^x-1)^2(s^y-1)^2}\right]}{(-\log s)^3\cdot\left[1+\frac{s - 1}{(s^x-1)(s^y - 1)}\right]^3}$$

$$= \frac{(\log s)\cdot(s - 1)\cdot(s^x - 1 + 1)(s^y - 1 + 1)}{((s^x - 1)(s^y - 1) + (s - 1)^2}$$

$$= \frac{(\log s)(s-1)\cdot s^{x+y}}{(s^{x+y} - s^x - s^y + s)^2}$$

$$\leq \log s\cdot(s-1)\cdot \sup_{(0\leq u,v\leq s-1)} \frac{(u+1)(v+1)}{(u\cdot v + (s-1))^2} ,$$

$$= \log s\cdot(s-1)\cdot \begin{cases} \dfrac{1}{(s-1)^2} , & \text{if } s < 1 , \text{ occurring for } u = v = 0 \text{ or } u = v = s-1 \\ \dfrac{s}{(s-1)^2} , & \text{if } s \geq 1 , \text{ occurring for } u = 0,\ v = s-1;\ u = s-1,\ v = 0 \end{cases}$$

$$= \frac{\log s}{s-1} \max(s,1) ,$$

by simple inspection.

Note also, for example,

$$\frac{\partial \phi_{\&,s}(x,y)}{\partial y} = \frac{Dh_s(y)}{Dh_s(\phi_{\&,s}(x,y))} = \frac{s^y}{s^y + \dfrac{s-1}{s^x - 1}} ,$$

noting for all $s \geq 0$, $\dfrac{s-1}{s^x - 1} \geq 0$; $x,y \in [0,1]$.

Thus, in turn, for all $s \geq 0$

$$\frac{\partial^2 \phi_{\&,s}(x,y)}{\partial^2 y} = \frac{(s-s^x)s^y \log s}{\left[s^y + \dfrac{s-s}{s^x - 1} - 1\right]^2} ,$$

for all $x,y \in [0,1]$.

Hence, for all $x,y \in [0,1]$

$$\left|\frac{\partial^2 \phi_{\&,s}(x,y)}{\partial y}\right| \leq \begin{cases} \dfrac{s\cdot(s^x - 1)}{s^x(s-1)} , & \text{if } 1 < s \\ \dfrac{s^x - 1}{s - 1} , & \text{if } 0 < s < 1 , \\ x , & \text{if } s = 1 , \end{cases}$$

Similarly,

$$\left|\frac{\partial^2 \phi_{\&,s}(x,y)}{\partial^2 y}\right| \leq \frac{\log s}{4} \cdot (s^x - 1) .$$

Note, finally, the evaluation

$$\left[\frac{\partial^2\phi_{\&,s}(x_1,\ldots,x_k)}{\partial x_1,\ldots,\partial x_k}\right]_{x_1=\cdots=x_k=0} = \begin{cases} \left[\dfrac{\log s}{s-1}\right]^{k-1} & , \ 0 < s < +\infty \ , \ s \neq 1 \\ 1 & , \ s = 1 \\ 0 & , \ \text{if} \ s = +\infty \ \text{for} \ k \geq 2 \end{cases}$$

For Yager's Family $\phi_{\&,(p)}$:

$$0 \leq \frac{\partial\phi_{\&,p}(x,y)}{\partial y} = \frac{1}{\left[1 + \left[\frac{1-x}{1-y}\right]^p\right]^{(p-1)/p}} \ , \ \text{all} \ \ x,y \in [0,1] \ ,$$

$$0 \leq \frac{\partial^2\phi_{\&,(p)}(x,y)}{\partial^2 y} = \frac{p-1}{1-x} \cdot \frac{((1-x)/(1-y))^{p+1}}{\left[1 + ((1-x)/(1-y))^p\right]^{2-(1/p)}} \ ,$$

all $x,y \in [0,1]$.

For $1 < p < 2$, $\dfrac{\partial^2\phi_{\&,p}(x,y)}{\partial^2 y}$ is the product of $\dfrac{p-1}{1-x}$ and a nondecreasing function in $\dfrac{1-x}{1-y}$ with limit as $y \to 1$ being $+\infty$.

$$\frac{\partial^2\phi_{\&,(p)}(x,y)}{\partial^2 y} \equiv 0 \ ; \ \text{for} \ \ p - 1 \ ,$$

$$\frac{\partial^2\phi_{\&,(p)}(x,y)}{\partial^2 y} \leq \frac{p-1}{1-x} \cdot \frac{(p+1)^{1+(1/p)} \cdot (p-2)^{1-(2/p)}}{(2p-1)^{2-(1/p)}} \ ;$$

for $2 \leq p \leq +\infty$.

Also, for all $n \geq 1$, $p \geq 1$, all $x_1,\ldots,x_n \in [0,1]$, the probability density function, when non-zero is

$$0 \leq \frac{\partial^2\phi_{\&,(p)}(x_1,\cdots,x_n)}{\partial x_1\cdots\partial x_n}$$

$$= \frac{1\cdot(p-1)\cdot(2p-1)\cdots((n-1)\cdot p-1)\cdot(1-x_1)^{p-1}\cdots(1-x_n)^{p-1}}{((1-x_1)^p+\cdots+(1-x_n)^p)^{n-(1/p)}}$$

$$\leq 1 \cdot (p-1)\cdot(2p-1)\cdots(n-1)\cdot p - 1) \cdot n^{-(n-(1/p))} \ .$$

Bellman-Giertz [14] and related theorems

(i) Bellman-Giertz theorem extended:
Given any general fuzzy set system $\mathcal{F}$, $\mathcal{F}$ is mutually distributive iff $\mathcal{F}$ is idempotent iff $\mathcal{F} = \mathcal{F}_0$. (See [14].)

(ii) From Goodman [91], we have:
Given any general fuzzy set system $\mathcal{F}$, $\mathcal{F}$ is exchangable with, for all $x,y \in [0,1]$

$$\left[\frac{\partial\phi_{\&}(x,y)}{\partial y}\right]_{y=0} \quad \text{existing,}$$

iff

$$\mathcal{F} = \mathcal{F}_1 .$$

(iii) Given any general fuzzy set system $\mathcal{F}$, $\mathcal{F}$ is semidistributive iff, for all finite index sets J_0 , and all $x_j \in [0,1]$ $j \in J_0$,

$$\underset{j\in J_0}{\phi_{or}}(x_j) = \sum_{\emptyset\neq K\subseteq J_0} (-1)^{\text{card } k+1} \cdot \underset{j\in K}{\phi_{\&}}(x_j) ,$$

and

$$\underset{j\in J_0}{\phi_{\&}}(x) = \sum_{\emptyset\neq K\subseteq J_0} (-1)^{\text{card } k+1} \cdot \underset{j\in K}{\phi_{\&}}(x_j) ,$$

noting the similarity of the above relations with the alternating (Poincare) sum expansions of probabilities of unions of events in terms of intersections and vice-versa.

Basic canonical expansion theorems

Ling [159] and others (see [226], [140]) have obtained the following:
Given any general fuzzy set system $\mathcal{F}$,

(a) $\mathcal{F}$ is Archimedean iff there are monotone decreasing continuous functions

$$h,h' : [0,1] \rightarrow [0,+\infty]$$

with $h(1) = h'(1) = 0$; $h(1)$, $h'(1) \leq +\infty$, called *generators*, such that for all $x_1,x_2,\ldots,x_n \in [0,1]$, $n \geq 1$,

$$\phi_{\&}(x_1,\ldots,x_n) = h^{-1}(\min(\sum_{j=1}^{n} h(x_j), h(0))) .$$

$$\phi_{or}(x_1,\ldots,x_n) = 1 - h'^{-1}(\min(\sum_{j=1}^{n} h'(1-x_j), h'(0))) .$$

h,h' are unique up to positive multiplicative constants.
Conversely, any choice of such h,h' as above generate an Archimedean system $\mathcal{F}$.
$\mathcal{F}$ is strict iff $h(0) = h'(0) = +\infty$, and this the min operator above may be omitted. Also, iff $\mathcal{F}$ is DeMorgan (for $\phi_{not} = 1-(\cdot)$) , $h = h'$.

(b) ϕ_{not} is involutive, continuous, and

$$\phi_{not}(x) - \phi_{not}(y) \equiv y - x \;;\; 1 \geq y \geq x \geq 0 \;,$$

iff $\phi_{not} = 1 - (\cdot)$.

(c) For any involutive ϕ_{not} , there is a monotone increasing continuous function $V : [0,1] \to \mathbb{R}^+$, with $V(0) = 0$ such that for all $x \in [0,1]$,

$$\phi_{not}(x) = V^{-1}(V(1) - V(x)) \;.$$

(d) Moynihan's theorem [226].

Given any DeMorgan fuzzy set system for $\phi_{not} = 1 - (\cdot)$,

$$\mathcal{F} \in \mathcal{C}_2 \quad \text{iff} \quad 0 \leq \begin{Bmatrix} \phi_{\&}(x,y) - \phi_{\&}(x,z) \\ \phi_{or}(x,y) - \phi_{or}(x,z) \end{Bmatrix} \leq z - y \;;\; \text{for all}$$

$x,y,z \in [0,1]$ with $y \leq z$.

(e) Given any general fuzzy set system $\mathcal{F}$; $\mathcal{F} \in \mathcal{C}_2 \cap \mathcal{A}r$ iff the monotone generator h is convex. The nth iteration $\mathcal{F}^n$ is an n-copula system iff h is convex and h^{-1} is a completely monotone function up to degree n , i.e.,
$(-1)^j \cdot d^j h^{-1}(x)/d^j x \geq 0$, for $j = 0,1,2,\ldots,n$; all x .

(f) Frank's theorem (Frank, [61])

$$\mathcal{F}r = (\mathcal{F}r \cap \mathcal{A}r) \,\dot{\cup}\, \mathcal{F}_0 \,\dot{\cup}\, \sigma(\mathcal{F}r \cap \mathcal{A}r) \;,$$

$$\mathcal{F}r \cap \mathcal{A}r = \{\mathcal{F}_s \mid 0 < s \leq +\infty\} \subseteq \mathfrak{D} \; (\text{for } \phi_{not} = 1-(\cdot))$$

$$\mathcal{F}_s \underline{\underline{d}} \, (1 - (\cdot) \;,\; \phi_{\&,s},\; \phi_{or,s}) \;,$$

and for all $x_1,\ldots,x_n \in [0,1]$; $0 < s \leq +\infty$,

$$\phi_{\&,s}(x_1,\ldots,x_n) = \log(1 + \prod_{j=1}^{n} (s^{x_j} - 1)/(s - 1)^{n-1})/\log s$$

$$= h_s^{-1} \Big(\sum_{j=1}^{n} h_s(x_j) \Big) \;,$$

$$\phi_{or,s}(x_1,\ldots,x_n) = 1 - \phi_{\&,s}(1 - x_1,\ldots,1 - x_n)$$

$$= 1 - h_s^{-1} \Big(\sum_{j=1}^{n} h_s(1 - x_j) \Big) \;, \text{ etc.},$$

where generator h_s is given by

$$h_s(x) = -\log((x^x - 1)/(s - 1)) \;,$$

and where the cases $s = 0$, 1, $+\infty$ are derived by limit considerations ($\mathcal{F}_0$, $\mathcal{F}_1$, $\mathcal{F}_{+\infty}$ already having been introduced). In particular, although h_0 does not exist as an ordinary function, for all $x \in [0,1]$

$$h_1(x) = -\log(x) \;,$$
$$h_{+\infty}(x) = 1 - x \;.$$

(See Frank [61], Goodman [91].) Also,

$$\mathcal{S} \subseteq \mathcal{C}_n \;; \quad \text{for all} \quad n \geq 2 \;,$$
$$\mathcal{F} = \{\mathcal{F}_0, \mathcal{F}_1\} \,\dot{\cup}\, \sigma(\mathcal{F}_0, \mathcal{F}_1\}$$
$$\subseteq \mathcal{F}r \subseteq \mathcal{C}_2 \;,$$
$$\{\mathcal{F}_0, \mathcal{F}_1\} \subseteq \{\mathcal{F}_s \mid 0 \leq s \leq 1\} \subseteq \mathcal{C}_n \subseteq \mathcal{C}_2$$

for all $n \geq 2$,

$$\mathcal{F}_{+\infty} \in \mathcal{C}_2 \rightarrow \mathcal{C}_n \quad \text{for} \quad n \geq 3 \;,$$
$$\mathcal{Y} \rightarrow \{\mathcal{F}_{+\infty}\} \subseteq \mathcal{C}_n \cap \mathcal{A}r \;,$$
$$\mathcal{F}_{+\infty} \in \mathcal{C}_2 \;.$$

For all $n \geq 2$,

$$\mathcal{C}_n = \{\mathcal{F}_0\} \,\dot{\cup}\, (\mathcal{C}_n \cap \mathcal{A}r) \,\dot{\cup}\, \sigma(\mathcal{C}_n \cap \mathcal{A}r) \;.$$

Let $\mathcal{F} = (\phi_{not}, \phi_{\&}, \phi_{or})$ be any fuzzy set system. Then

$$f_1(x,y) \leq \phi_{\&}(x,y) \leq \min(x,y) \;,$$
$$\max(x,y) \leq \phi_{or}(x,y) \leq f_2(x,y) \;,$$

for all $0 \leq x,y \leq 1$ where f_1 and f_2 is a *non-continuous* t-norm and t-conorm, respectively, which are in a DeMorgan relationship for $\phi_{not} = 1 - (\cdot)$, with

$$f_1(x,y) \overset{d}{=} \begin{cases} x & \text{iff} \quad y = 1 \\ y & \text{iff} \quad x = 1 \\ 0 & \text{iff} \quad 0 \leq x,y < 1 \end{cases}$$

$$f_2(x,y) \overset{d}{=} \begin{cases} x & \text{iff} \quad y = 0 \\ y & \text{iff} \quad x = 0 \\ 0 & \text{iff} \quad 0 \leq x,y < 1 \;. \end{cases}$$

Note that for any $\mathcal{F}_{(p)} \in \mathcal{Y}$, $1 \le p \le +\infty$, the generator $h_{(p)}$ for $\phi_{\&,(p)}$ and $\phi_{or,(p)}$ may be written

$$h_{(p)}(x) = (1 - x)^p \ ; \ \text{all} \quad x \ \phi \ [0,1] \ .$$

Extend now Yager's family $\mathcal{Y}$ to include all $\mathcal{F}_{(p)}$ for $0 < p < 1$, with generator $h_{(p)}$ given above. Then for any such $\mathcal{F}_{(p)}$, we can compare $\phi_{\&,(p)}$ and $\phi_{or,(p)}$ with the previous bounds for copulas (2): Since for any

$$1 \ge x,y > 0 \ ; \ 0 < p < 1 \ ,$$

$$(x^p + y^p)^{1/p} > x + y \ ,$$

it follows that

$$\phi_{\&,(p)}(x,y) \le \text{maxsum}(x,y) \ ; \ \text{all} \quad x,y \in [0,1]$$

with strict inequality holding for all $x,y \in [0,1]$ such that

$$(1 - x)^p + 1 - y)^p < 1 \ . \qquad \text{(A)}$$

Similarly, by taking the DeMorgan transform,

$$\phi_{or,(p)}(x,y) \ge \text{bndsum}(x,y) \ ; \ \text{all} \quad x,y \in [0,1] \ ,$$

for $0 < p < 1$, with strict inequality holding for all x,y as above in eq. (A).

Moreover, it easily follows that

$$\lim_{p \to 0} \phi_{\&,(p)}(x,y) = f_1(x,y)$$

and

$$\lim_{p \to 0} \phi_{or,(p)}(x,y) = f_2(x,y) \ ,$$

for all $x,y \in [0,1]$, so that these bound relations cannot in general be improved, noting $\{\mathcal{F}_{(p)} \mid 0 < p < 1\} \subseteq \mathcal{A}r$, but certainly $\{\mathcal{F}_{(p)} \mid 0 < p < 1\} \cap \mathcal{C}_2 = \emptyset$.

Min and max can be considered as limiting cases of Archimedean t-norms and t-conorms:

Consider Yager's DeMorgan Archimedean families of t-norms and t-conorms

$$\phi_{\&,p}(x_1,\ldots,x_n) = h_p^{-1}(\min(\sum_{j=1}^{n} h_p(x)_j), 1))$$

$$\phi_{or,p}(x_1,\dots,x_n) = 1 - \phi_{\&,p}(1 - x_1,\dots,1 - x_n)$$
$$= 1 - h_p^{-1}(\min(\sum_{j=1}^{n} h_p(x_j), 1)) ,$$

$x_1,\dots,x_n \in [0,1]$;

$$h_{(p)}(x) = (1 - x)^p , \text{ for } 0 \le x \le 1 ; p > 0 .$$

Then it can be shown although min, max are non-Archimedean and not in the family,

$$\begin{bmatrix} \min(x_1,\dots,x_n) \ge \phi_{\&,(p)}(x_1,\dots,x_n) \ge \min(x_1,\dots,x_n) - (n^{1/p} - 1) \\ \max(x_1,\dots x_n) + (n^{1/p} - 1) \ge \phi_{or,(p)}(x_1,\dots,x_n) \ge \max(x_1,\dots,x_n) , \end{bmatrix}$$

uniformly, for all $x_1,\dots,x_n \in [0,1]$.

On the other hand, Frank's family $\phi_{\&,s}$, $\phi_{or,s}$ as $s \to 0$, approaches min, max, respectively, non-uniformly.

For example,

$$\phi_{\&,s}(x,y) = \min(x,y) + \log(1 + s^{|x-y|} - s^{\max(x,y)} - s^{(1-\min(x,y))}) \frac{-\log(1-s)}{\log s} ,$$

noting the critical $s^{|x-y|}$ term, e.g.

Similarly, recalling that maxsum is not a copula (but is a t-norm) for $n \ge 3$ and bndsum is not a co-copula (but is a t-conorm) for $n \ge 3$, and for all $+\infty \ge p > 1$, $\phi_{\&,(p)}$ is a copula $\phi_{\&,1}$ = maxsum , and $\phi_{or,(p)}$ is a co-copula , $\phi_{or,1}$ = bndsum:

$$\begin{cases} (1 - \max(x_1,\dots,x_n))^{\frac{p-1}{p}} \cdot \text{maxsum}(x_1,\dots,x_n) \\ + 1 - (1 - \max(x_1,\dots,x_n))^{\frac{p-1}{p}} \\ \ge \phi_{\&,p}(x_1,\dots x_n) \ge \text{maxsum}(x_1,\dots,x_n) , \\ \text{bndsum}(x_1,\dots,x_n) \ge \phi_{or,(p)}(x_1,\dots,x_n) \\ \qquad \ge (1 - \max(x_1,\dots,x_n))^{\frac{p-1}{p}} \cdot \text{bndsum}(x_1,\dots,x_n) , \end{cases}$$

uniformly for all $x_1,\dots,x_n \in [0,1]$.

Thus maxsum and bndsum are uniform limiting cases of $\phi_{\&,p}$ and $\phi_{or,p}$, respectively, as $p \to 1^+$.

For further investigations into the definitions and relations for various fuzzy set operations see Dubois and Prade [51]. See also: [55], [160], [199], [200] for further discussions on negation; [65], [10], [112], [115] for implication operator modeling; and [275] and [50] for interesting general discussions of how fuzzy set operators should be defined. In addition, again see [4], [91], [140], [226] for background and other references. See also the recent comprehensive paper [44'].

Appendix. Pseudo-Inverses of Distribution Functions and Bounds on Probabilities of Events.

Let F be continuous from the right and non-decreasing over $\mathbb{R}$. For any $x \in \mathbb{R}$, define

$$x^* = \inf\{t \mid t \in \mathbb{R} \text{ and } F(t) = F(x)\}$$

$$= \inf F^{-1}(F(x)) \leq x .$$

Similarly define for all $y \in [0,1]$,

$$y \leq \rho_F(y) = \inf\{z \mid y \leq z \in \text{rng}(F)\} .$$

By the right continuity of F it follows that for all $x \in \mathbb{R}$ and $y \in [0,1]$,

$$x^{**} = x^* ,$$

$$F(x) = F(x^*) ,$$

$$\rho_F(\rho_F(y)) = \rho_F(y) .$$

Define for all $y \in [0,1]$

$$F^{\ddagger}(y) \overset{d}{=} \inf F^{-1}(\rho_F(y))$$

$$= \inf F^{-1}([\rho_F(y), 1])$$

$$= \inf(F^{-1}[y,1]) ,$$

$$= F^{\ddagger}(\rho_F(y)) .$$

In particular, when $y \in \text{rng}(F)$,

$$y = \rho_F(y) = F(x) = F(x^*) , \text{ for some } x \in \mathbb{R}$$

and

$$F^{\ddagger}(y) = F^{\ddagger}(\rho_F(y)) = F^{\ddagger}(F(x)) = x^* .$$

Thus, for all $x \in \mathbb{R}$,

$$F^{\ddagger}(F(x)) \equiv F^{\ddagger}(F(x^{*})) = x^{*} .$$

Hence for all $y \in [0,1]$, since $\rho_F(y) \in \text{rng}(F)$, there is a unique $x^{*} \in \mathbb{R}$ such that

$$F(x^{*}) = \rho_F(y)$$

and hence

$$F(F^{\ddagger}(y) = FF^{\ddagger}(\rho_F(y)) = F(F^{\ddagger}F(x^{*})) = F(x^{*}) = \rho_F(y) .$$

Furthermore, for all $x \in \mathbb{R}$, $y \in [0,1]$,

$$F(F^{\ddagger}(F(x))) = FF^{\ddagger}F(x^{*}) = F(x^{*}) = F(x)$$
$$F^{\ddagger}(F(F^{\ddagger}(y))) = F^{\ddagger}(FF^{\ddagger}\rho_F(y)) = F^{\ddagger}(\rho_F(y)) = F^{\ddagger}(y) .$$

Thus, $F^{\ddagger}$ is an actual pseudo-inverse operator.
Also, the above implies, for all $x \in \mathbb{R}$, $y \in [0,1]$,

$$\rho_F(F(x)) = \rho_F(F(x^{*})) = FF^{\ddagger}F(x^{*}) = F(x^{*}) = F(x)$$

Lemma 1

For any $x \in \mathbb{R}$, $y \in [0,1]$,

$$F^{\ddagger}(y) \le x \quad \text{iff} \quad y \le F(x) \quad \text{iff} \quad x \in F^{-1}[y,1]$$

i.e.,

$$[F^{\ddagger}(y), +\infty) = F^{-1}[y,1] .$$

Proof: (i) If $F^{\ddagger}(y) \le x$, then

$$y \le \rho_F(y) = F(F^{\ddagger}(y)) \le F(x)$$

(ii) If $y \le F(x)$, then

$$F^{\ddagger}(y) \le F^{\ddagger}F(x) = x^{*} \le x .$$

Application 1:

Let U be distributed uniformly on $[0,1]$ and r.v. X have c.d.f. F over $\mathbb{R}$. Then $F^{\ddagger}\circ(U)$ and X are identically distributed.

Lemma 2

For any $x \in \mathbb{R}$, $y \in [0,1]$,

$$x^* \le F^{\ddagger}(y) = F^{\ddagger}(\rho_F(y))$$

iff

$$F(x) = F(x^*) \le \rho_F(y) .$$

Proof: Use $FF^{\ddagger}(\rho_F(y)) = \rho_F(y)$ and $F^{\ddagger}F(x^*) = x^*$.

Application 2

Let X be any r.v. having c.d.f. F over $\mathbb{R}$. Then for all $x \in \mathbb{R}$, $y \in [0,1]$:

(i) Up to zero probability,

$$\begin{aligned} X \le x \quad &\text{iff} \quad X^* \le x^* \\ &\text{iff} \quad X^* \le F^{\ddagger}(F(x)) \\ &\text{iff} \quad F(X) \le \rho_F(F(x)) \\ &\text{iff} \quad F(X) \le F(x) . \end{aligned}$$

(ii)
$$\begin{aligned} F(X) \le y \quad &\text{iff} \quad F(X) \le \rho_F(y) \\ &\text{iff} \quad X^* \le F^{\ddagger}(y) \\ &\text{iff} \quad X \le F^{\ddagger}(y) . \end{aligned}$$

(iii)
$$\begin{aligned} \Pr(F(X) \le y) &= \Pr(X \le F^{\ddagger}(y)) \\ &= F(F^{\ddagger}(y)) \\ &= \rho_F(y) . \end{aligned}$$

Hence, the c.d.f. of $F(X)$ is ρ_F .

Application 3

Let F be any c.d.f. over $\mathbb{R}^n$ with marginal c.d.f's F_j corresponding to r.v. X_j, $j = 1,\ldots,n$. Then for all $x_1,\ldots,x_n \in \mathbb{R}$,

$$\begin{aligned} F(x_1,\ldots,x_n) &= \Pr\Big(\mathop{\&}_{j=1}^{n} (X_j \le x_j)\Big) \\ &= \Pr\Big(\mathop{\&}_{j=1}^{n} (X_j \le F^{\ddagger}(F(x_j)))\Big) \end{aligned}$$

$$= F(F_1^{\ddagger}(F_1(x_1)),\ldots,F_n^{\ddagger}(F_n(x_n)))$$
$$= G(F_1(x_1),\ldots,F_n(x_n)) \; ,$$

$$G(y_1,\ldots,y_n) = F(F_1^{\ddagger}(y_1),\ldots,F_n^{\ddagger}(y_n)) \; ; \quad \text{all} \quad y_j \in [0,1] \; .$$

Clearly G is the joint distribution of n unif $[0,1]$ r.v.'s $U_1,\ldots,U_n$. Also marginally, the above results imply each

$X_j = F_j^{\ddagger}(U_j)$ has c.d.f. F_j , $j = 1,\ldots,n$.

Suppose dually that F is a continuous from the left nondecreasing function over $\mathbb{R}$. For any $x \in \mathbb{R}$, define

$$\tilde{F}(x) \overset{d}{=} \sup\{t \mid t \in \mathbb{R} \;\&\; F(t) \le x\} \; .$$

Lemma 3

For any $x \in \mathbb{R}$, $y \in [0,1]$

$$\tilde{F}(y) \ge x \quad \text{iff} \quad y \ge F(x) \; .$$

Proof: (i) If $\tilde{F}(y) \ge x$, then immediately

$$y \ge F(\tilde{F}(y)) \ge F(x)$$

(ii) If $y \ge F(x)$, then using the definition of,
$$\tilde{F}(y) \ge \tilde{F}(F(x)) \ge x \; .$$

Lemma 4 (Bounds on the Joint Probability of Events)

Let $(X,\mathfrak{B},Pr)$ be a probability space. Then, for any $n \ge 1$ and $A_1,\ldots,A_n \in \mathfrak{B}$,

(i) $\text{maxsum}(Pr(A_1),\ldots,Pr(A_n)) \le Pr(A_1 \cap \cdot\cdot \cap A_n)$
$\le \min(Pr(A_1),\ldots,Pr(A_n))$,
$\max(Pr(A_1),\ldots,Pr(A_n)) \le Pr(A_1 \cup \cdot\cdot \cup A_n)$
$\le \text{bndsum}(Pr(A_1),\ldots,Pr(A_n))$,

where
$$\text{maxsum}(a_1,\ldots,a_n) \overset{d}{=} \max(a_1+\cdot\cdot+a_n - (n-1), 0)$$
$$\text{bndsum}(a_1,\ldots,a_n) \overset{d}{=} \min(a_1+\cdot\cdot+a_n, 1) \; .$$

(ii) $Pr(A_1 \cap \cdot\cdot \cap A_n) = \min(Pr(A_1),\ldots,Pr(A_n))$,

iff for any i, $1 \le 1 \le n$ such that

$$Pr(A_i) = \min(Pr(A_1),\ldots,Pr(A_n) \; ,$$
$$Pr(A_i \subseteq \bigcap_{\substack{1\le j\le n \\ j\ne i}} A_j) = 1 \; ,$$

i.e., there is a minimal set by set-inclusion.

In particular, if $A_1 = \cdot\cdot = A_n$, (ii) is clearly satisfied.

(iii) $Pr(A_1 \cup \cdot\cdot \cup A_n) = \max(Pr(A_1),...,Pr(A_n))$
iff for any i , $1 \le i \le n$ such that

$$Pr(A_i) = \max(Pr(A_1),...,Pr(A_n))$$

$$Pr(A_i \supseteq \bigcup_{\substack{1 \le j \le n \\ j \ne i}} A_j) = 1 ,$$

i.e., there is a maximal set by set-inclusion.

In particular, if $A_1 = \cdot\cdot = A_n$, (iii) is clearly satisfied.

(iv) $Pr(A_1 \cap \cdot\cdot \cap A_n) = \mathrm{maxsum}(Pr(A_1),...,Pr(A_n))$
iff either

$$Pr(A_1 \cap \cdot\cdot \cap A_n) = 0 \quad \text{or} \quad Pr(A_i \cup A_j = X) = 1 ,$$

for all i,j ; $1 \le i,j \le n$; $i \ne j$,
i.e., all A_1, ..., A_n are pairwise exhaustive.

In particular, if A_1, A_2, ..., A_n are all pairwise disjoint, (iv) is clearly satisfied.

(v) $Pr(A_1 \cup \cdot\cdot \cup A_n) = \mathrm{bndsum}(Pr(A_1),...,Pr(A_n))$
iff either

$$Pr(A_1 \cup \cdot\cdot \cup A_n) = 1 , \quad \text{i.e.,}$$

$$Pr(A_1 \cup \cdot\cdot \cup A_n = X) = 1 \quad \text{or} \quad Pr(A_i \cap A_j = \emptyset) = 1 ,$$

for all i,j ; $1 \le i,j \le n$, $i \ne j$, i.e., all $A_1,...,A_n$ are pairwise disjoint.

In particular, if $A_1,A_2,...,A_n$ are all pairwise disjoint (v) is satisfied.

Proof of Lemma:

Results (iii) and (v) follow by use of DeMorgan transforms upon arbitrary $A_1,...,A_n$.

For $n = 2$, simply use the modular expansion

$$Pr(A \cup B) = Pr(A) + Pr(B) - Pr(A \cap B).$$

For $n \ge 3$, use induction. For example, for (iv) for $n = 3$, if $Pr(A_1 \cap A_2 \cap A_3) > 0$, consider

$$Pr(A_1 \cap A_2 \cap A_3) = \max(Pr(A_1) + Pr(A_2) + Pr(A_3) -2, 0)$$

iff, by using the case for $n = 2$,

$$\begin{cases} Pr(A_1 \cap (A_2 \cap A_3)) = Pr(A_1) + Pr(A_2 \cap A_3) - 1 \\ Pr(A_2 \cap A_3) = Pr(A_2) + Pr(A_3) - 1 \end{cases}$$

iff

$$\begin{cases} Pr(A_1 \cup (A_2 \cap A_3) = X) = 1 \\ Pr(A_2 \cup A_3 = X) = 1 \end{cases}$$

iff

$$\begin{cases} Pr((A_1 \cup A_2) \cap (A_1 \cup A_3) = X) = 1 \\ Pr(A_2 \cup A_3 = X) = 1 \end{cases}$$

iff $Pr(A_i \cup A_j = X) = 1$, $i \neq j$, $i,j = 1, 2, 3$.

See also the very general bounds for the probability measure of any wff in PL developed by Hailperin ([102'], pp. 206-208), extending his and Frechet's earlier work on probability bounds. See also section 2.3.9 (A).

2.3.7 Functional extensions and embeddings

Extension or lifting procedures are done to enlargen the domain of point functions to set functions, and further, to generalize set-functions. Embedding here is restricted to the identification of points with certain dispersions or equivalently generalized sets: namely dirac-like forms. Generalizations of extension procedures and embeddings have been particularly developed by Manes [169]. The connections between the fuzzy theories of Manes and general logical systems will be established in Chapter 7.

Here we present essentially two natural approaches to function extensions and discuss briefly some connections between the two.

Let X and Y be arbitrary non-vacuous sets and $f : X \to Y$ a fixed function. Consider then the following extension and inverse operations:

$$f^{-1} : \mathcal{P}(Y) \to \mathcal{P}(X) ,$$

where for any $C \in \mathcal{P}(Y)$,

$$f^{-1}(C) \overset{d}{=} \{x \mid x \in X \ \&\ f(x) \in C\} = \bigcup_{y \in C} f^{-1}(y)$$

and where similar notation

$$f^{-1} : Y \to \mathcal{P}(X)$$

is used for $(f^{-1} \mid \{\{y\} \mid y \in Y\})$. Also,

$$\bar{f} : \mathcal{P}(X) \to \mathcal{P}(Y) ,$$

where for any $B \in \mathcal{P}(X)$

$$\bar{f}(B) \overset{d}{=} \{f(x) \mid x \in B\} .$$

Similarly, definitions hold for

$$\bar{f}^{-1} : \mathcal{P}\mathcal{P}(Y) \to \mathcal{P}\mathcal{P}(X) ,$$
$$\bar{f}^{-1} : \mathcal{P}(Y) \to \mathcal{P}\mathcal{P}(X),$$

and

$$\bar{\bar{f}} : \mathcal{P}\mathcal{P}(X) \to \mathcal{P}\mathcal{P}(Y) .$$

Standard relations which will be useful include:

For any $\mathfrak{B} \in \mathcal{P}\mathcal{P}(X)$ and $C \in \mathcal{P}(Y)$, if $\emptyset \neq f^{-1}(C) \in \mathfrak{B}$, then $C \cap \operatorname{rng} f \in \bar{\bar{f}}(\mathfrak{B})$,

$$f^{-1}(C) \in \mathfrak{B} \quad \text{iff} \quad (\exists B)(B \in \mathfrak{B} \ \& \ B = f^{-1}(C)) ,$$

$$\begin{aligned} C \in \bar{\bar{f}}(\mathfrak{B}) \quad & \text{iff} \quad (\exists B)(B \in \mathfrak{B} \ \& \ C = \bar{f}(B)) \\ & \text{iff} \quad (\exists B)(B \in \mathfrak{B} \ \& \ B \in \bar{f}^{-1}(C)) \\ & \text{iff} \quad \underset{(B\in\bar{f}^{-1}(C))}{\text{or}} \quad (B \in \mathfrak{B} \cap \bar{f}^{-1}(C)) \\ & \text{iff} \quad (B)_{B\in\bar{f}^{-1}(C)} \in \underset{(B\in\bar{f}^{-1}(C))}{\dagger} (\mathfrak{B} \cap \bar{f}^{-1}(C)) . \end{aligned}$$

Similar results hold at the point level for C replaced by $y \in Y$, $\mathfrak{B}$ by $B \in \mathcal{P}(X)$, etc.

Let H_0 be a fixed Heyting algebra and recall the category theory notation SET . (See section 2.4.2.)

Let $\mathcal{T} : \mathrm{Ob(SET)} \to \mathrm{Ar(SET)}$ be such that

$$\mathcal{T}(X) \subseteq H_0^{\,X} .$$

$\mathcal{T}(X) = \emptyset$ is also permissible.

Let $U : \mathrm{Ob(SET)} \to \mathrm{Ob(SET)}$ such that $\mathcal{F}(X) \subseteq U(X) \subseteq \mathcal{P}(X)$, where $\mathcal{F}(X)$ = class of all finite subsets of X .

Consider then the following extension relative to $\mathcal{T}$ and U : for $f : X \to Y$;

$$\bar{f} : U(X) \to U(Y) .$$

Suppose $\mathcal{K} : \mathcal{T}(X) \to \mathcal{T}(U(X))$ is given such that for any $x \in X$, defining $\delta_x \in \mathcal{T}(X)$, a dirac-like form, where

$$\delta_x(y) = \begin{cases} 1 & \text{iff } y = x \\ 0 & \text{iff } y \neq x , \end{cases}$$

$$\mathcal{K}(\delta_x)(B) = \begin{cases} 1 & \text{iff } x \in B \\ 0 & \text{iff } x \notin B , \end{cases}$$

all $B \in U(X)$.

Suppose also first $f^{-1} : Y \to U(X)$ with extension $f^{-1} : U(Y) \to U(X)$. Then $\hat{f} : \mathcal{F}(X) \to \mathcal{F}(Y)$ extends $f : X \to Y$: For any $g \in \mathcal{F}(x)$,

$$\hat{f}(g) = \mathcal{K}(g) \circ f^{-1} \in \mathcal{F}(Y) .$$

In particular,

$$\hat{f}(\delta_x) = \phi_{\{f(x)\}} \ : \ \text{all } x \in X .$$

In general, although $\hat{f}$ extends f , it need not extend $\bar{f}$. (This will be clarified a bit later.)

In turn, by considering $f^{-1} : U(Y) \to U(X)$, then $\hat{f} : \mathcal{F}(X) \to \mathcal{F}(U(Y))$ is also defined which extends $\hat{f} : \mathcal{F}(X) \to \mathcal{F}(Y)$.

Finally, consider $\underline{f} : \mathcal{F}(U(X)) \to \mathcal{F}(U(Y))$ as an extension of $\hat{f}$ or f , where for any $g \in \mathcal{F}(U(X))$, $\underline{f}(g)$ may be defined in two different natural ways:

(I) Now let $\mathcal{K} : \mathcal{F}(U(X)) \to \mathcal{F}(U(X))$ with similar restrictions as before. Then

$$\underline{f}(g) \overset{d}{=} \mathcal{K}(g) \circ f^{-1} .$$

(II) Simply let $\mathcal{K}(g) \equiv g$ and thus

$$\underline{f}(g) \overset{d}{=} g \circ f^{-1} ,$$

noting now that for $g = \delta_x$, assuming $\delta_x \in \mathcal{F}(U(X))$,

$$\delta_x(B) = \begin{cases} 1, & \text{iff } x \in B \\ 0 , & \text{iff } x \notin B , \end{cases}$$

for all $x \in X$,

$$\underline{f}(\delta_x) = \delta_x \circ f^{-1} = \phi_{\mathcal{C}_{\{f(x)\}}} ,$$

$$\mathcal{C}_{\{f(x)\}} \overset{d}{=} \{C \mid C \in U(Y) \ \& \ f(x) \in C\} ,$$

the filter class in $U(Y)$ on $f(x)$.

As was shown above, the function $\mathcal{K}$ plays a key role in determining expansions $\hat{f}$ or $\underline{f}$ of f . One basic procedure for determining the choice of $\mathcal{K}$ is as follows:

(i) First consider $\hat{f}$ as an extension of $f : X \to Y$.

Let $A \in \mathcal{F}(X)$ with $\phi_A \in \mathcal{F}(X)$ and let $y \in Y$.

First, formally treat A as an ordinary subset of X , $y \in Y$. We have

$$\begin{aligned}\hat{f}(\phi_A)(y) &= \phi_{\hat{f}(A)}(y) = \|\langle y \in \hat{f}(A)\rangle\| = \|\langle y \in \overline{f}(A)\rangle\| \\ &= \|(\langle \underset{x\in X}{\text{or}} (\langle x\in A\rangle \ \&\ \langle x\in f^{-1}(y)\rangle\| \\ &= \|((x,x)_{x\in X} \in \underset{x\in X}{\dagger} A\times f^{-1}(y))\| \\ &= \phi_{\underset{x\in X}{\dagger}(A\times f^{-1}(y))}((x,x)_{x\in X}) \\ &= \underset{x\in X}{\dagger}(\phi_A \times \phi_{f^{-1}(y)})((x,x)_{x\in X}) \\ &= \underset{(x\in f^{-1}(y))}{\dagger}(\phi_A)((x)_{x\in f^{-1}(y)}) ,\end{aligned}$$

since $\mathrm{rng}(\phi_{f^{-1}(y)}) \subseteq \{0,1\}$.

If the logical system $(\mathcal{C},\times,\dagger)$ is also truth functional derived from $\mathcal{F} = (\phi_{not}, \phi_{\&}, \phi_{or})$ (we write also, e.g., ϕ_{not} or ϕ_{nt} for $\|nt\|$) , then the above evaluation becomes simply

$$\|\langle y \in \hat{f}(A)\rangle\| = \underset{x\in f^{-1}(y)}{\phi_{or}} (\phi_A(x)) ,$$

noting again the relations,

$$\underset{(j=1,\ldots,n)}{\dagger} \phi_{A_j}(x_1,\ldots,x_n) = \phi_{or}(\phi_{A_1}(x_1),\ldots,\phi_{A_n}(x_n))$$

$$\underset{(j=1,\ldots,n)}{\times} \phi_{A_j}(x_1,\ldots,x_n) = \phi_{\&}(\phi_{A_1}(x_1),\ldots,\phi_{A_n}(x_n)) ,$$

for all $A_j \in \mathcal{F}(X_j)$, $x_j \in X_j$, $j = 1, \ldots, n$.

Thus, in the case, for all $\phi_A \in \mathcal{F}(X)$ and $B \in U(X)$,

$$\mathcal{K}(\phi_A)(B) = \underset{x\in B}{\phi_{or}}(\phi_A(x)) ,$$

noting, as a check, the boundary conditions

$$\mathcal{K}(\phi_{\{x\}})(B) = \begin{cases} 1 & \text{iff} \quad x \in B \in U(X) \\ 0 & \text{iff} \quad x \notin B \in U(X) \ . \end{cases}$$

Thus, because ϕ bijectively relates $\mathcal{F}(X)$ and $\mathcal{F}(X)$, $\hat{f}$ may be considered dually as an extension of f :

$$\hat{f} : \mathcal{F}(X) \to \mathcal{F}(Y)$$

as developed above, and

$$\hat{f} : \mathcal{F}(X) \to \mathcal{F}(Y) \ .$$

(ii) Next, consider $\underline{f}$ as an extension of $f : X \to Y$. Again, treat $\mathcal{A} \in \mathcal{F}(U(X))$ formally as an ordinary subset of $U(X)$ with $C \in U(X)$ arbitrary.

Approach (I):

$$\begin{aligned} \underline{f}(\hat{\phi}_{\mathcal{A}})(C) &= \phi_{\underline{f}(\mathcal{A})}(C) \\ &= \| \langle C \in \underline{f}\ (\mathcal{A}) \rangle \| \\ &= \| \langle C \in \bar{\bar{f}}(\mathcal{A}) \rangle \| \\ &= \underset{(B \in \bar{f}^{-1}(C))}{\dagger} (\phi_{\mathcal{A}})((B)_{B \in \bar{f}^{-1}(C)}) \ . \end{aligned}$$

Subcase 1: Logical system $(\mathbb{C}, \times, \dagger)$ is truth functional. Then it follows immediately that

$$\underline{f}(\phi_{\mathcal{A}})(C) = \underset{(B \in \bar{f}^{-1}(C))}{\phi_{or}} (\phi_{\mathcal{A}}(B)) \ ,$$

analogous to the truth functional case for evaluating $\hat{f}$.

The following refers to section 2.3.9 (B):

Subcase 2: Logical system $(\mathbb{C}, \times, \dagger)$ is Probability Logic (PL), which although extended from a truth functional system $\mathcal{F} = (\phi_{not}, \phi_{\&}, \phi_{or})$ (at the left-ray level) is itself <u>not</u> truth functional. For PL, denote $\mu = \phi_{\mathcal{A}}$; $\mathcal{A} = \phi^{-1}(\mu)$ (inverse of ϕ) and where for any $q \geq 1$,

$$\mathcal{F}(X) = U(X) = \varnothing \ , \ \text{if} \quad X \neq U(\cdots(U(\mathbb{R}^q))\cdots)$$
$$U(\mathbb{R}^q) = \mathbb{B}_q \ , \ \mathcal{F}(\mathbb{R}^q) = DPL_{\mathcal{F},q} \ , \ \mathcal{F}(\mathbb{D}_q) = PL_{\mathcal{F},q} \ ; \ q \geq 1 \ .$$

Assume $\mu \in \mathcal{P}r_q$ and $C \in \mathbb{B}_r$, with $f : \mathbb{R}^q \to \mathbb{R}^r$.
It then follows that

$$\underline{f}(\mu)(C) = \dagger_{B\in\overline{f}^{-1}(C)}(\mu)((B)_{B\in\overline{f}^{-1}(C)})$$

$$= (1 - \times_{B\in\overline{f}^{-1}(C)}(1-\mu))(\times_{B\in\overline{f}^{-1}(C)})$$

$$= \sum_{\emptyset\neq\mathfrak{B}\subseteq\overline{f}^{-1}(C)} (-1)^{\mathrm{card}\,\mathfrak{B}+1}(\times_{B\in\mathfrak{B}}\mu)(\times_{B\in\mathfrak{B}} B))$$

$$= \times_{B\in\overline{f}^{-1}(C)}(\mu)(\dagger_{B\in\overline{f}^{-1}(C)} B) ,$$

noting the complicated form of $\mathcal{X}(\mu)$ here.

Approach (II):

$$\underline{f}(\mu)(C) = \|\langle f^{-1}(C) \in \phi^{-1}(\mu)\rangle\| = \mu(f^{-1}(C)) ,$$

(same as the induced probability measure $\mu\circ f^{-1}$).

Returning now to $\hat{f}$, relative to PL, where $A \in \mathcal{F}(\mathbb{R}^q)$ is such that $\phi_A \in \mathbb{D}_q$, and $C = \mathrm{ray}_r(Y)$, for any $Y \in \mathbb{R}^r$,

$$\hat{f}(\phi_A)(C) = \dagger_{x\in f^{-1}(C)}(\phi_A)((x)_{x\in f^{-1}(C)})$$

$$= \sum_{\emptyset\neq G\subseteq f^{-1}(C)} (-1)^{\mathrm{card}\,G+1}(\times_{x\in G}\phi_A)((x)_{x\in G})$$

$$= \sum_{\emptyset\neq G\subseteq f^{-1}(C)} (-1)^{\mathrm{card}\,G+1}\phi_{\&\,x\in G}(\phi_A(x)) .$$

Furthermore, if $\phi_{\&}$ and ϕ_{or} are semi-distributive, it follows that the last expression (formally the same as the Poincaré alternating sign expansion of the probability of a union of sets) becomes simply

$$\hat{f}(\phi_A)(C) = \phi_{or\,x\in f^{-1}(C)}(\phi_A(x)) ,$$

the same formally as for a purely truth functional system! However, in general, even if $\phi_{\&}$ and ϕ_{or} are modular or Frankian, this does not at all imply semi-distributivity. (The latter class is much smaller than the modular class of copulas.)

Consider now the "extension principle", that is, the general fuzzy set extension of ordinary functional transforms. Thus, if $f : X \to Y$ is an ordinary function and C is an ordinary subset of X,

$$\overline{f}(C) = \{f(x) \mid x \in C\} \subseteq Y .$$

More generally, let A be any fuzzy subset of X and $y \in Y$ arbitrary, then using the previous mechanism in evaluating predicates

$$\begin{aligned}\phi_{\overline{f}(A)}(y) &= \| \langle y \in \overline{f}(A) \rangle \| \\ &= \| (\exists x)(x \in A \;\&\; y = f(x)) \| \\ &= \| (\underset{x \in X}{\text{or}})(x \in A \cap f^{-1}(y) \| \\ &= \underset{x \in X}{\phi_{or}} \phi_{\&}(\phi_A(x), \phi_{f^{-1}(y)}(x)) \\ &= \underset{x \in f^{-1}(y)}{\phi_{or}} (\phi_A(x)) .\end{aligned}$$

Note that $\phi_{\overline{f}(A)}$ has the same form as the transformed probability function for random variable $f(V)$, when V has probability function ϕ_A, for fuzzy set system $\mathcal{F}' = (1 - (\cdot)$, prod, bndsum) (where bndsum = sum, because of the probability functions present).

The above derivation should also serve as a partial response to Manes' criticism [170] concerning the "arbitrariness of the fuzzy set (function) extension principle". (In addition, using random set representations of fuzzy set theory, another justification for this definition may also be made. See section 5.2.)

Other fuzzy set operations, including various linguistic quantifiers, are also definable, as illustrated later in section 2.6 through examples of fuzzy set symbolization of natural language expressions.

We establish now some results needed for considering lifting operators.

Theorem I (See [181'], pp. 248, 249 for analogous results.)

Let $f : \mathbb{R}^q \to \mathbb{R}^r$ be Borel measurable such that if $C \subseteq \mathbb{R}^q$ is any closed set, then $f(C) \in \mathbb{B}_r$. Then:

(1) For all $B \in \mathbb{B}_q$, $f(B) \in \mathbb{B}_r$, up to Lebesgue r-measure 0

iff

(2) f possesses property (N), i.e., for all $A \subseteq \mathbb{R}^q$ with $vol_q(A) = 0$, $vol_r(f(A)) = 0$.

Proof:

If (2) holds: Let $B \in \mathbb{B}_q$ be arbitrary. Then for all $n \geq 1$, $\exists B_n \subseteq \mathbb{R}^q$ closed such that

$$B_n \subseteq B \quad \text{and} \quad vol_q(B) - \frac{1}{n} < vol_q(B_n) \leq vol_q(B) .$$

Define $B_\infty \overset{d}{=} \bigcup_{n=1}^{+\infty} B_n$. Then $B = B_\infty \dot{\cup} (B \dashv B_\infty)$ with $vol_q(B) = vol_q(B_\infty)$ and $vol_q(B) = vol_q(B \dashv B_\infty) = 0$. It readily follows that

$$f(B) = f(B_\infty) \dot{\cup} f(B \dashv B_\infty)$$

with $f(B_\infty) = \bigcup_{n=1}^{+\infty} f(B_n) \in \mathbb{B}_r$ and $vol_q(B \dashv B_\infty) = 0$, noting indeed

$$vol_r(f(B)) = vol_r(\bigcup_{n=1}^{+\infty} f(B_n)) .$$

If (1) holds: By the proof in Natanson [181'] (originally shown for f continuous, but not dependent on that property), if f did not have the (N) property, there exists, $A \subseteq \mathbb{R}^q$ with $vol_q(A) = 0$, but $vol_r(f(N)) > 0$. Hence, there is a non-measurable set $B \subseteq f(A)$. Hence, $A \cap f^{-1}(B) \subseteq A$ and thus $vol_q(A \cap f^{-1}(B)) = 0$ with $f(A \cap f^{-1}(B)) = B$. Thus (1) is violated.

Example: If f as above is absolutely continuous, then (1) and (2) both hold.

Recall for any set X ,

$$\mathfrak{I}(X) \subseteq U(X) \subseteq \mathcal{P}(X) .$$

Theorem II

Let $f : X \to Y$ be such that for $\mathcal{A} \in U(X)$ and $\mathcal{B} \in U(Y)$,

$$\overline{\overline{f^{-1}}}(\mathcal{B}) \overset{d}{=} \{f^{-1}(B) \mid B \in \mathcal{B}\} \subseteq \mathcal{A}$$

and

$$\overline{\overline{f}}(\mathcal{A}) \overset{d}{=} \{\overline{f}(A) \mid A \in \mathcal{A}\} \subseteq \mathcal{B} .$$

Then

$$\overline{\overline{f^{-1}}}(\overline{\overline{f}}(\mathcal{A})) \subseteq \overline{\overline{f^{-1}}}(\mathcal{B}) \subseteq \mathcal{A} .$$

Theorem III

Let $f : X \to Y$, inducing $\overline{f} : \mathcal{P}(X) \to \mathcal{P}(Y)$, and let

$\mathcal{A} \in U(X)$. Then

(1) $\overline{f^{-1}}(\overline{\overline{f}}(\mathcal{A})) \subseteq \mathcal{A}$, i.e., $f^{-1}(f(A)) \in \mathcal{A}$, for all $A \in \mathcal{A}$,
iff for all $C \in \mathcal{P}(Y)$,

(2) $C \cap \mathrm{rng}(f) \in \overline{\overline{f}}(A)$ iff $f^{-1}(C) \in \mathcal{A}$.

(**Proof**:

If (1) holds:

If $C \cap \mathrm{rng}(f) \in \overline{\overline{f}}(\mathcal{A})$, then $C \cap \mathrm{rng}(f)) = f(\mathcal{A})$, for some $A \in \mathcal{A}$. Thus, $f^{-1}(C) = f^{-1}(C \cap \mathrm{rng}(f)) \in \mathcal{A}$ by (1) .

If $f^{-1}(C) \in \mathcal{A}$, then $f(f^{-1}(C)) = f(f^{-1}(C) \cap \mathrm{rng}(f)) = C \cap \mathrm{ring}(f)$. Hence $C \cap \mathrm{rng}(f) \in \overline{\overline{f}}(\mathcal{A})$.

If (2) holds:
Let $A \in \mathcal{A}$ be arbitrary and $C = f(A)$. Since clearly $C \cap \mathrm{rng}(f) = f(A) \in \overline{\overline{f}}(A)$, it follows by (2) that $f^{-1}(f(A)) \in \mathcal{A}$.

Remark.

For any $A \in \mathcal{A}$, $f^{-1}(f(A)) = \bigcup_{B \in \overline{f}^{-1}(f(A))} B = \bigcup_{\left[\begin{smallmatrix} B \in \mathcal{P}(X) \\ \overline{f}(B) = A \end{smallmatrix}\right]} B$ = largest set B in $\mathcal{P}(X)$ with $\overline{f}(B) = A$.

Corollary 1

Let $f : \mathbb{R}^q \to \mathbb{R}^r$ be Borel-measurable (i.e., $f^{-1}(\mathbb{B}_r) \subseteq \mathbb{B}_q$) such that for all $B \in B_q$, if B is closed, then $f(B) \in \mathbb{B}_r$, or, if $\mathrm{vol}_q(B) = 0$, then $\mathrm{vol}_r(f(B)) = 0$. Then

(i) $\overline{f^{-1}}(\overline{\overline{f}}(\mathbb{B}_q)) \subseteq \mathbb{B}_q$,

and

(ii) For all $C \in \mathcal{P}(Y)$, with $\mathcal{A}$ as before

$$C \cap \mathrm{rng}(f) \in \overline{\overline{f}}(\mathcal{A}) \text{ iff } f^{-1}(C) \in \mathcal{A} .$$

In particular, if f is absolutely continuous, then (i) and (ii) hold.

Remark 1.

For any $C \in \mathcal{P}(Y)$,

$$\begin{aligned} & C \cap \text{rng}(f) \in \overline{\overline{f}}(\mathcal{A}) \\ \text{iff} \quad & (\exists A)(A \in \mathcal{A} \ \& \ \overline{f}(A) = C \cap \text{rng}(f)) \\ \text{iff} \quad & (\exists A)(A \in \mathcal{A} \cap \overline{f}^{-1}(C)) . \end{aligned}$$

Remark 2.

Note that, always, for any $C \in \mathcal{P}(Y)$, if $f^{-1}(C) \in \mathcal{A}$, then

$$C \cap \text{rng}(f) \in \overline{\overline{f}}(\mathcal{A}) .$$

Thus, when considering functional extensions, in general, two choices can arise: the lifting operator $\Uparrow$ can be defined as follows: for $f : X \to Y$, $\Uparrow(f) : \mathcal{F}(X) \to \mathcal{F}(Y)$, where for $A \in \mathcal{F}(X)$, and equivalently $\phi_A \in \mathcal{F}(X)$, and $y \in Y$, by treating formally A as an ordinary subset of X ,

$$\begin{aligned} & (\Uparrow(f)(\phi_A))(y) \\ & = \phi_{\hat{f}(A)}(y) \\ & = \begin{cases} \| \langle f^{-1}(y) \in A \rangle \| \\ \qquad \text{or} \\ \| \langle y \in \hat{f}(A) \rangle \| . \end{cases} \end{aligned}$$

The first interpretation - see Corollary 1 - is relatively simple: it is the same as $\phi_A(f^{-1}(y))$, a desirable form. However, this interpretation is only natural when $X \subseteq \mathcal{P}(X')$ and $Y \subseteq \mathcal{P}(Y')$ for some spaces X' and Y' , and where we interpret for any $y \in Y$, by abuse of notation

$$f^{-1}(y) = \bigcup_{z \in y} f^{-1}(z) = \cup f^{-1}(y) .$$

In particular, this holds for $X = \mathbb{B}_q$, $Y = \mathbb{B}_r$

$X' = \mathbb{R}^q$, $Y' = \mathbb{R}^r$, with $(\mathbb{R}^q, \mathbb{B}_q, \mu)$ any probability space,

$A \in \mathcal{F}(\mathbb{B}_q)$, $\phi_A = \mu \in \mathcal{F}(\mathbb{B}_q) = \mathcal{P}r_q$, $g : \mathbb{R}^q \to \mathbb{R}^r$, $f \overset{d}{=} \overline{g} : \mathbb{B}_q \to \mathbb{B}_r$,

and thus,

$$\| \langle f^{-1}(y) \in A \rangle \| = \phi_A(f^{-1}(y)) = \mu \circ f^{-1}(y) ,$$

noting $(\mathbb{R}^r, \mathbb{B}^r, \mu \circ f^{-1})$ is the induced probability space under f

and hence

$$\dagger\!\dagger(f) : \mathcal{P}r_q \to \mathcal{P}r_r .$$

On the other hand, the second interpretation though relatively complicated - see Remark 1, following Corollary 1 - can always be used, where here simply

$$f^{-1}(y) = \{x \mid x \in X \;\&\; f(x) = y\} .$$

Thus,

$$\| \langle y \in \hat{f}(A) \rangle \| = \| \langle (\exists x)(x \in A \cap \overline{f^{-1}}(y)) \rangle \|$$

$$= \| (\underset{x \in X}{\text{or}} \langle x \in A \cap \overline{f^{-1}}(y) \rangle) \|$$

$$= \| ((x)_{x \in X} \in \underset{x \in X}{\dagger} (A \cap \overline{f^{-1}}(y)) \|$$

$$= \phi_{\underset{x \in X}{\dagger} A(A \cap \overline{f^{-1}}(y)}((x)_{x \in X})$$

$$= \underset{x \in X}{\dagger} (\phi_{A \cap \overline{f^{-1}}(y)})((x)_{x \in X})$$

$$= \underset{x \in \overline{f^{-1}}(y)}{\dagger} (\phi_A)((x)_{x \in \overline{f^{-1}}(y)})$$

$$= \phi_{\underset{x \in \overline{f^{-1}}(y)}{\dagger A}} ((x)_{x \in \overline{f^{-1}}(y)}) ,$$

using the fact that $\overline{f^{-1}}(y)$ is an ordinary set and using the properties of $\dagger$.

Thus, e.g., for any truth functional system $\mathcal{F} = (\phi_{not}, \phi_{\&}, \phi_{or})$, $f : X \to Y$, and any $A \in \mathcal{F}(X)$, $y \in Y$,

$$\phi_{(\dagger\!\dagger(\hat{f})(A)}(y) = \phi_{\hat{f}(A)}(y) = \phi_{\underset{x \in \overline{f^{-1}}(y)}{or}}(\phi_A(x)) .$$

Also, note that Corollary 1 gives sufficient conditions when the two interpretations for $\dagger\!\dagger$ coincide.

Again, note that the two approaches are based upon, in general, two different appearing relations

$$\phi_{Rel_1}(y,A,f) = \| \langle (\exists x)(x \in A \cap \overline{f^{-1}}(y) \rangle \|$$

and

$$\phi_{Rel_2}(y,A,f) = \| \langle f^{-1}(y) \in A \rangle \| ,$$

for all $f : X \to Y$, $A \in \mathcal{P}(X)$, $y \in Y$.

When the sufficient conditions (Corollary 1) hold for f , say, all $f \in C(X,Y)$, then for all $y \in Y$, $A \in \mathcal{P}(X)$,

$$\phi_{Rel_1}(y,A,F) = \phi_{Rel_2}(y,A,f) .$$

Equivalently,

$(\forall y)(\forall A)$(If $y \in Y$ and $A \in \mathcal{P}(X)$ and $f \in C(X,Y)$, then

$(Rel_1(y,A)$ iff $Rel_2(y,A)))$.

Note that for $j = 1, 2$,

$$Rel_j \subseteq Y \times \mathcal{P}(X) \times Y^X$$

and may be considered equivalently

$$\phi_{Rel_j} : Y \times \mathcal{P}(X) \times Y^X \to \{0,1\}$$

or as the function

$$f_j : Y \to \mathcal{P}(\mathcal{P}(X) \times Y^X) ,$$

etc.

Thus, if a standardized extension procedure is adapted for all functions, e.g., then clearly since $Rel_1 = Rel_2$ over $Y \times \mathcal{P}(X) \times C(X,Y)$,

$$\dagger\dagger(Rel_1) = \dagger\dagger(Rel_2) : \mathcal{F}(Y \times \mathcal{P}(X) \times C(X,Y)) \to \mathcal{F}\{0,1\} .$$

However, in general, even if such a consistent procedure were adapted, a given relation could be reinterpreted distinctly.

For example, Rel_1 could be interpreted as

$$\phi_{Rel_1} : X \times \mathcal{P}(X) \to \{0,1\}$$

where

$$\phi_{Rel_1}(x,A) \overset{d}{=} \phi_{\overline{A \cap f^{-1}(y)}}(x) ,$$

or Rel_2 as

$$\phi_{Rel_2} : X \to \{0,1\} ,$$

where

$$\phi_{Rel_2}(A) = \phi_A(f^{-1}(y)) \ ,$$

etc.

Thus, much care must be exercised in the choice of definitions and in particular the application to the extension of functions. (See Manes' related approach to extensions and lifting, section 7.2.)

Extensions of classical logical connectors and semantic evaluations from classical logic to H_0-valued logic.

1. All statements in natural language must be put into formal language in terms of memberships w.r.t. attributes and use of the operations not, &, or, in perhaps some compound form.

2. Consequently, all propositions of interest in the formal language may be reduced to strings of the generic form

$$s = (\mathrm{comb}(\mathrm{not}, \&, \mathrm{or}))(<x_1 \in A_1), \ldots, <x_n \in A_n>) \ .$$

3. Each such string s may be further interpreted as

$$s = \underbrace{<(x_1, \ldots, x_n)}_{= x} \in \underbrace{(\mathrm{comb}(\mathrm{C}, \times, \dagger))(A_1, \ldots, A_n))}_{= B} \ .$$

4. The truth extension of any such s is:

$$\begin{aligned} \|s\| &= \phi_B(x) \\ &= ((\mathrm{comb}(\mathrm{C}, \times, \dagger))(\phi_{A_1}, \ldots, \phi_{A_n}))(x) \end{aligned}$$

(However, this does not necessarily imply truth functionality.)

5. If the system is truth functional, then step 4 may be carried further:

$$\|s\| = \mathrm{comb}(\hat{\phi}_{not}, \hat{\phi}_{\&}, \hat{\phi}_{or})(\phi_{A_1}(x_1), \ldots, \phi_{A_n}(x_n))$$

where the operators $\hat{\phi}_{not} \in \mathcal{FP}_1$, $\hat{\phi}_{\&}$, $\hat{\phi}_{or} \in \mathcal{FP}_2$ extend their classical counterparts $\phi_{not} \in \mathcal{BP}_1$, $\phi_{\&}$, $\phi_{or} \in \mathcal{BP}_2$, in some sense, where

$$\mathcal{BP}_n \stackrel{d}{=} \{f \mid f : \{-,1\}^n \to \{0,1\}\}$$

is the class of all n-argument Boolean polynomials (or truth table functions) for classical $0 - 1$ logic and where we could choose, e.g., $H_0 = [0,1]$, and

$$\mathcal{TP}_n \overset{d}{=} \{f \mid f : H_0^n \to H_0\} , \quad n = 1,2,...,$$

is the class of all generalized n-argument Boolean polynomials (or truth table functions) and where

$$\phi_{A_j}(x_j) = \|<x_j \in A_j>\| , \quad j = 1,...,n .$$

6. In place of step 5, for the non-truth functional system LSL (Lebesgue-Stieltjes Logic), $\|s\|$ must in general remain as in step 4 and be evaluated by relations established between C, $\times$, $\dagger$.

However, for the subsystem PL (Probability Logic), we do have the relation, where each $x_j \in \mathbb{B}_{q_j}$,

$\phi_{A_j} \in \mathcal{P}r_{q_j}$, $j = 1,...,n$,

$$\|s\| = (\phi_{A_1} \times \cdots \times \phi_{A_n})(\text{comb}(C,\times,\dagger))(x_1,...,x_n) .$$

(Note that each x_j here is a set, not a "point".)

Consider next step 2. It is well known (see, e.g., Enderton [54]) that in classical 0 - 1 logic, $(\phi_{not}, \phi_{\&}, \phi_{or})$ form a complete Boolean operator system, i.e.,

$$\mathcal{BP} \overset{d}{=} \bigcup_{n=1}^{\infty} \mathcal{BP}_n = \{\text{comb}(\phi_{not}, \phi_{\&}, \phi_{or}) \mid \text{comb is an arbitrary combination forming strings}\}.$$

The question of operator completeness for any [0,1]-valued logic becomes essentially a moot one. (See [54], pp. 62-66, 313-315.) In any case, the above property justifies step 2 for formal logical abstractions of two-valued logic to more general ([0,1]-valued, for example) logics.

However, consider the following alternative evaluations for $\|s\|$ in steps 4 and 5:

We can extend all at once $\mathcal{BP}$ to

$$\hat{\mathcal{BP}} = \{\hat{f} \mid f \in \mathcal{BP}\}$$

by use of either definition for $(\hat{\ })$ or $\dagger\dagger$, as discussed earlier. In particular, this means that for a truth functional system, the 0 - 1 logical connectors $\phi_{not} \in \mathcal{BP}_1$, $\phi_{\&}$, ϕ_{or}, $\phi_{\Rightarrow}$, $\phi_{\Leftrightarrow} \in \mathcal{BP}_2$ all extend (non-uniquely) to some $\hat{\phi}_{not}$, $\hat{\phi}_{\&}$, $\hat{\phi}_{or}$, $\hat{\phi}_{\Rightarrow}$, $\hat{\phi}_{\Leftrightarrow} \in \hat{\mathcal{BP}}$. In turn, these extensions may be used in steps 3, 4, 5 for modeling and evaluating sentences or strings s . (The triple of primitive operators (not, &, or) could be replaced by (not, &, or, $\Rightarrow$) , etc., in generating sentences through all choices of comb.) Hence, any s in step 5 is evaluated by this approach as

(i)

$$\|s\| = \text{comb}(\hat{\phi}_{not}, \hat{\phi}_{\&}, \hat{\phi}_{or})(\phi_{A_1}(x_1),\ldots,\phi_{A_n}(x_n))$$

or distinctly by

(ii)

$$\|s\| = \widehat{\text{comb}}(\phi_{not}, \phi_{\&}, \phi_{or})(\phi_{A_1}(x_1),\ldots,\phi_{A_n}(x_n)) ,$$

which are obviously not the same evaluation as the earlier approach, the latter being two-valued while the former is single-valued, etc.

For either variation of this approach each $f \in \mathcal{BP}_n$ of interest, such as $f = \phi_{not}, \phi_{\&}, \phi_{or}$, or $f = \text{comb}(\phi_{not}, \phi_{\&}, \phi_{or})$, etc., extends to some

$$\hat{f} \overset{d}{=} (\hat{f}_0, \hat{f}_1) : H_0^{2n} \to H_0^{2} ,$$

since we can identify, e.g., for $H_0 = [0,1]$,

$$[0,1]^{2n} = \mathcal{F}(\{0,1\}^n)$$

and

$$[0,1] = \mathcal{F}(\{0,1\}) ,$$

where for any $x \in [0,1]^{2n}$, $\hat{f}_0(x) \in [0,1]$ can be considered the degree of truth of $\hat{f}$ operating on x, while $\hat{f}_1(x) \in [0,1]$ can be considered the degree of falsehood of $\hat{f}(x)$. Manes ([169] and see also section 7.2) considers this approach to the extension of operators as well as to the extension of membership and equality relations. In general, we take the first approach for simplicity, with the other in mind. The resolution of choice of the most appropriate extension of classical logic operators to H_0-valued logic remains a difficult problem. Some progress at the practical level may be seen in the work of Zimmermann [291] and others [250], [275]. See also section 8.4 and Chapter 9 for related issues where asymptotic behavior may be utilized. Frank's or Yager's families can serve as natural parametrized classes of connectives - see section 2.3.6 again.

2.3.8 Further semantic evaluations

In sections 2.3.5 and 2.3.6, we have considered some basic formal language operations, and their direct general set operation interpretations, as well as, several possible corresponding semantic evaluations, depending of course on the particular logic chosen. These included:

nt (negation) - complement - $1 - (\cdot)$, etc.

& (conjunction) - intersection or more generally,- t-norms, etc.
cartesian product.

or (disjunction) - union, or more generally -t-conorms, etc.
cartesian sum

$\Rightarrow$ (implication) - if (·) then (··) - nt(·) or (··) , etc.

$\Leftrightarrow$ (double implication) - iff - (if(·) then (··)) and (if(··) then (·))) .

In addition, in section 2.3.7, we treated the important concepts of the formlization of ordinary functions (within a formal language) and the consequent semantic evaluations as extensions of these functions.

In this section, we look at some additional formal language concepts together with their corresponding semantic evaluations. All of these are related to functional extensions and, more generally, fuzzifications of classical concepts.

It should be noted that the term "projection" as used in subsection (D) should not be confused with the function symbol $proj : Ob(\mathcal{L}) \times Ob(\mathcal{L}) \to Ar(\mathcal{L})$ and its semantic evaluations. In addition, only two quantifier function symbols - together with the axioms and rules in which they appeared in $Th_{syn_K,K}$ and their semantic evaluations - were considered in some depth in sections 2.2.2 and 2.3.2, namely: $\forall$ and $\exists$. Even so, the axioms and rules governing these are compatible with essentially only intuitionistic logic and in particular not with general negations, t-norms, t-conorms, i.e., general fuzzy set systems. Furthermore, other quantifications - such as Mo and Abt(3/4) were listed as function symbols in 2.2.2, representing, "most", "about 3/4", respectively, but no axioms and rules were introduced in $Th_{syn_K,K}$ governing their behavior. Consequently, because of the nature of general quantification, an alternative approach - basically, only through semantic evaluations and not through any particular theory - is developed, as given briefly in subsection (F) here, although, of course, the function symbols for such quantifications do appear in the formal language. Note also that the extreme quantifiers, $\exists$ and $\forall$, can be considered as eliminative definitions in a natural sense in terms of interated or and & operators, respectively. However, as before, this approach and the axiomatic one developed in $Th_{syn_K,K}$ in general do not coincide. Nor do these coincide with the single "percentage" approach (II) used here in subsection (F).

A. Compound operators

"if (·) then (··) " can be defined compoundly:

(·) $\Rightarrow$ (··) as (not(·) or (··)) , or can be defined directly.

"iff" $\Leftrightarrow$ usually defined as

(if(·) then (··)) & if (··) then (·)) , i.e.,
(· ⇒ ··) & (·· ⇒ ·) .

The concepts of incidence and subset have already been approached through majorizing membership functions. Another (different) approach is through the compound formalizations:

$$(A \triangleleft B) = \underset{x \in X}{\text{or}} (x \in A \cap B) ,$$
$$(A \subseteq B) = \underset{x \in X}{\&} ((x \in A) \Rightarrow (x \in B)) .$$

This naturally leads to

$$(A = B) = (A \subseteq B \; \& \; B \subseteq A) .$$

But note that this does not in general imply the following semantic evaluations as $\phi_A = \phi_B$, i.e.,

$$\| x \in A \| = \| x \in B \| \; ; \text{ for all } x \in X .$$

Indeed, under a truth functional system,

$$\| A = B \| = \phi_{\&}(\underset{x \in X}{\phi_{\&}} (\phi_{\Rightarrow}(\phi_A(x), \phi_B(x)) ,$$
$$\underset{x \in X}{\phi_{\&}} (\phi_{\Rightarrow}(\phi_B(x), \phi_A(x)))) .$$

Other equivalence relations similar to equality of sets have been discussed in section 2.3.3 on Gödelian Logic and in section 2.2.2 (see "≍") , as well as in Appendix 3 (iv), section 2.4.2..

B. Intensifiers

For any $A \in \mathcal{F}(X)$ and non-negative integer n , define $A^{ⓝ}$, the nth *intensification* of A as, for all $x \in X$,

$$(x \in A^{ⓝ}) = \underset{j=1,...,n}{\&} (x \in A_j) ,$$

where

$$A_1 = A_2 = \cdot\cdot = A_n = A$$

and define the nth *extensification* or stretching of A as , for all $x \in X$,

$$(x \in A^{\boxed{n}}) = \underset{j=1,...,n}{\text{or}} (x \in A_j)$$

where again

$$A_1 = A_1 = \cdot\cdot = A_n = A .$$

Thus, if a truth functional system is present, typical evaluations are

$$\|x \in A^{\textcircled{n}}\| = \underset{j=1,\ldots n}{\phi_{\&}}(\phi_{A_j}(x))$$
$$= \phi_{A\times\cdots\times A}(x,\ldots,x)\ ,$$
$$\|x \in A^{\boxed{n}}\| = \underset{j=1,\ldots n}{\phi_{or}}(\phi_{A_j}(x_j))$$
$$= \phi_{A\dagger\cdots\dagger A}(x,\ldots,x_n)\ .$$

If further, $\phi_{\&}$ is a strict Archimedean t-norm with a canonical representation as given in section 2.3.6;

$$\phi_{\&}(u,v) = h^{-1}(h(u) + h(v))$$

then it readily follows that

$$\|x \in A^{\textcircled{n}}\| = h^{-1}(n\cdot h(\phi_A(x)))$$

with a dual representive for $\|x \in A^{\boxed{n}}\|$, when ϕ_{or} is a strict Archimedean t-conorm. In turn, these relations may be used to define immediately, arbitrary real-intensifications:

For any non-negative real r ,

$$\|x \in A^{\textcircled{r}}\| = h^{-1}(r\cdot h(\phi_A(x)))\ .$$

Note the basic exponential relation, for any $r,s \geq 0$, $x \in X$, $A \in \mathcal{F}(X)$,

$$\|x \in (A^{\textcircled{r}})^{\textcircled{s}}\| = \|x \in (A^{\textcircled{s}})^{\textcircled{r}}\|$$
$$= \|x \in A^{\textcircled{rs}}\|$$
$$= h^{-1}(rs\cdot h(\phi_A(x)))\ .$$

Thus, linguistic hedges such as "more or less", "very", "extremely", "little", etc., could all be defined through proper choice of exponent above. (But see also [51] and [167] for other approaches.)

C. <u>Conditioning</u> (See also section 2.3.9)

Let $A \in \mathcal{F}(X\times Y)$ and $B \in \mathcal{F}(X)$, noting that trivially $B \in \mathcal{F}(X\times Y)$ where for all $x \in X$, $y \in Y$,

$$\phi_B(x,y) = \phi_B(x)\ .$$

Suppose also that (in the membership function ordering sense)

$$A \subseteq B ,$$

i.e.,

$$\sup_{y \in Y} \phi_A(x,y) \leq \phi_B(x) \;;\; \text{all} \quad x \in X .$$

Suppose finally that $\phi_{\&}$ is continuous. Then by the basic (Darboux) property of continuous functions, if follows that there exists at least one

$$(A|x\in B) \in \mathcal{F}(Y) \;;\; \text{all} \quad x \in X$$

such that

$$\|(y\in(A|x\in B)) \;\&\; (x \in B)\| = \|(x,y) \in A\| ,$$

i.e., assuming truth functionality,

$$\phi_{\&}(\phi_{(A|x\in B)}(y) \, , \, \phi_B(x)) = \phi_A(x,y) \;;\; \text{all} \quad x \in X .$$

We call $(A|x\in B)$ the *conditional* generalized set A given $x \in B$.

The above relation is equivalent to

$$(A|x\in B) \times B = A .$$

If $\phi_{\&}$ is strictly increasing in its arguments, then the above conditional generalized set is uniquely determined.

D. <u>Projections and interactions of generalized sets</u>

Let $A \in \mathcal{F}(X\times Y)$. Then for any given ϕ_{or} , the X-projection of A is given by, for all $x \in X$

$$\begin{aligned} \phi_{proj_X(A)}(x) &\overset{d}{=} \phi_{\underset{y\in Y}{or}}(\phi_A(x,y)) \\ &= \| \underset{y\in Y}{or}((x,y) \in A)\| \\ &= \|(\exists y\in Y)((x,y) \in A)\| \quad , \end{aligned}$$

assuming a truth functional system.

Thus, using the basic property of t-conorms

$$\phi_{proj_X(A)}(x) \geq \sup_{y\in Y} \phi_A(x,y) \geq \phi_A(x,y) \; ,$$

for all $x \in X$, $y \in Y$, implying

$$\phi_A(x,y) = \phi_{\&}(\phi_{(A|x\in proj_X(A))}(y) \, , \, \phi_{proj_X(A)}(x)) .$$

Then,

$$(A|x \in proj_X(A)) = proj_Y(A)$$

iff

$$A = proj_Y(A) \times proj_X(A) \ ,$$

in which case, the two projections of A are said to be *non-interactive*, or, in particular, *independent*, for $\phi_\& = \text{prod}$.

For other approaches to projections and conditioning see Nguyen [188] and section 3.3. See also section 2.3.9 for related results for Probability Logic.

E. Bayes' theorem

Let X and Y be any two spaces and assume for each $x \in X$, a set $B_x \in \mathcal{F}(Y)$ exists. Also, let $C \in \mathcal{F}(X)$ be given. Then for any chosen ϕ_{or}, $(A|y \in proj_Y(A)) \in \mathcal{F}(X)$ exists for each $y \in Y$ such that for all $x \in X$,

$$\phi_A(x,y) \stackrel{d}{=} \phi_\&(\phi_{B_x}(y), \phi_C(x)) = \phi_\&(\phi_{(A|y \in proj_Y(A))}(x), \phi_{proj_Y(A)}) \ .$$

(The proof is immediate from the definition of conditional sets.)

We can identify without loss of generality (with abuse of notation)

$$\begin{cases} B_x = (A|x \in proj_X(A)) & \text{conditional set} \\ C = proj_X(A) & \text{prior-X set} \\ proj_Y(A) & \text{averaged-Y set} \\ (A|y \in proj_Y(A)) & \text{posterior-X set} \ . \end{cases}$$

However, in general, equality does not really hold for the first two relations. Indeed, if for each $x \in X$, there is a $y_x \in Y$ such that

$$\phi_{B_x}(y_x) = 1 \ ,$$

then

$$\phi_B(x) \le \phi_{proj_X(A)}(x) \le \underset{y \in Y}{\phi_{or}}(\phi_B(x))$$

and hence for a non-Archimedean t-norm such as sup, equality indeed does hold.

The use of Bayes' Theorem procedes analogously as in the classical probability situation, which incidently, is clearly a special case of the above development when discrete spaces are considered and $\phi_\& = \text{prod}$, $\phi_{or} = \text{bndsum}$ and ϕ_{B_x}, ϕ_C are ordinary probability functions. (See Chapter 9 for applications to combination of evidence problems.)

F. Quantification

Generally, quantification may be approached as follows: (See also Zadeh's extensive work, e.g., [283], [286].)

First assume as usual that a fixed logic and a logical system are present. Let "quant" be the linguistic form for any percentage quantifier such as: many, some, all, almost none, few, sometimes, about 3/4, two-thirds, most, etc. It is assumed that $\phi_{quant} : [0,1] \to [0,1]$. Note, however, some dichotomy for the extreme quantifications "for all," and "there exists": These, of course, may also be treated from an interactive conjunction and disjunction approach, respectively.

Let "pop" be the linguistic label for some fixed ordinary set representing the base population to be considered. Let $A,B \in \mathcal{F}(pop)$, representing two attributes. We wish to evaluate semantically the sentence

$$s \overset{d}{=} quant(A \text{ is (are) } B) .$$

For example:

"most men are short here", "several tall people have jaundice", "sometimes fat people have breathing problems", etc.

Approach I - Use of implication operator.

$$s = quant(\forall x \in pop)((x \in A) \Rightarrow (x \in B)) .$$

Assuming the logical system is sufficiently truth functional, the above evaluation becomes

$$\|s\| = \phi_{quant}(\underset{x \in pop}{\&} (\phi_{\Rightarrow}(\phi_A(x) , \phi_B(x)))) .$$

Approach II - Use of conditioning.

Suppose formally that "univ" stands for the ordinary set representing all possible populations or "worlds" of interest. Also, let "wt" be a weighting attribute. Then we may also formally consider $A,B \in \mathcal{F}(univ)$ and the wff's

$$a \overset{d}{=} (pop \in A) \overset{d}{=} (\exists x \in pop)(x \in A \;\&\; x \in wt) ,$$

$$b \overset{d}{=} (pop \in A \cap B) \overset{d}{=} (\exists x \in pop)(x \in A \cap B \;\&\; x \in wt) .$$

Note that from the above definitions, it does not follow in general that truth functionality holds for $A \cap B$ relative to A and B , i.e.,

$$\phi_{A\cap B}(\text{pop}) \neq \phi_{\&}(\phi_A(\text{pop}), \phi_B(\text{pop})) .$$

However, truth functionality may be applied to $x \in A \cap B$, i.e.,

$$\phi_{A\cap B}(x) = \phi_{\&}(\phi_A(x), \phi_B(x))$$

may hold.

Thus, typically,

$$\|a\| = \phi_{\substack{or \\ x\in pop}} (\phi_{\&}(\phi_A(x), \phi_{wt}(x)))$$

$$\|b\| = \phi_{\substack{or \\ x\in pop}} (\phi_{\&}(\phi_A(x), \phi_B(x), \phi_{wt}(x))) ,$$

and hence, $\|(b|a)\|$ is evaluated from

$$\|b\| = \phi_{\&}(\|(b|a)\|, \|a\|) .$$

In turn,

$$\|(\text{quant}(b|a))\| = \phi_{\text{quant}}(\|(b|a)\|) .$$

In particular, if $\phi_{wt}(x) \equiv 1/\text{card}(\text{pop})$, $\phi_{\&}$ = prod (or min), and ϕ_{or} = bndsum , then

$$\|(b|a)\| = \sum_{x\in pop} \phi_A(x)\cdot\phi_B(x) \Big/ \sum_{x\in pop} \phi_A(x) \equiv \text{card}(A\cap B)/\text{card } A ,$$

with $\|(\text{quant}(b|a))\|$ then obtainable - the same result as obtained by Zadeh, e.g., [283], [286] in his "fuzzy cardinality" approach to quantifications.

Again, as in the general case, modeling of quantifiers may be carried out in several different ways.

See section 2.3.9 (B) for more detailed development of conditioning, projections, Bayes' Theorem, and quantification as applied to probability and Lebesgue-Stieltjes logical systems.

G. Transformations of dispersions, induced measures and linguistic variables.

Recall that a dispersion space $(X,\mathcal{A},\mu)$ consists of a set X, $\mathfrak{f}(X) \subseteq \mathcal{A} \subseteq \mathcal{P}(X)$, with $\mathcal{A}$ possibly having additional structure such as being a σ-algebra, and $\mu : \mathcal{A} \to [0,1]$, also possibly having additional structure such as being a probability measure.

Let $(X,\mathcal{A},\mu)$ be an initial dispersion space $(Y,\mathcal{B})$ a space such that $\mathfrak{f}(Y) \subseteq \mathcal{B} \subseteq \mathcal{P}(Y)$, for some set Y, with $f : X \to Y$ being $\mathcal{A}-\mathcal{B}$ measurable, i.e.,

$$f^{-1}(\mathcal{B}) \stackrel{d}{=} \{f^{-1}(B) \mid B \in \mathcal{B}\} \subseteq \{f^{-1}(A) \mid A \in \mathcal{A}\} ,$$

where as usual $f^{-1} : \mathcal{P}(Y) \to \mathcal{P}(X)$, where

$$f^{-1}(A) = \{x \mid x \in X \ \& \ f(x) \in A\} .$$

Then f induces a (final) dispersion space $(Y,\mathcal{B},\nu)$, where

$$\nu \overset{d}{=} \mu \circ f^{-1} .$$

Example 1. Probability spaces

Here, $(X,\mathcal{A},\mu)$ is a probability space and hence $(Y,\mathcal{B},\nu)$ is also a probability space, the one induced by f , also considered a random variable.

Example 2. Linguistic variables (See also Zadeh [279].)

Let X be a measurement space. Typically, $X \subseteq \mathbb{R}^m$, or $X = \{\cdots \text{red, yellow, } \cdots\}$, etc. Let Y be a space representing a population, such as all living female humans between 30 and 40 years of age and holding a Ph.D. degree in Economics. Let $g : Y \to X$ representing a measurement mapping such as age, height, race, weight, etc. Indeed, X^Y may be considered the class of all measurement mappings. Next, $\text{ling} : X^Y \to \mathcal{P}\mathcal{F}(X)$ is the linguistic variable mapping where, for example

ling(age) = {·· old, young, very old, about 20 years old, middle age, ...}

ling(ht) = {·· tall, very tall, short, between 60 and 68 inches tall, ...} , etc.

A natural constraint is that

$$\text{ling}(X^Y) = \bigcup_{g \in X^Y} \text{ling}(g) ,$$

and a basic condition is that for any $g \in X^Y$ and any $C \in \text{ling}(g) \subseteq \mathcal{F}(X)$, there is a $\tau_C \in \mathcal{F}(Y)$ such that

$$\langle y \in \tau_C \rangle = \langle g(y) \in C \rangle , \text{ all } y \in Y$$

and hence taking semantic evaluations

$$\phi_{\tau_C}(y) = \|(y \in \tau_C)\| = \|(g(y) \in C)\| = \phi_C(g(y)) ,$$

for all $y \in Y$.
Thus, for example, for $y = \text{John} \in Y$, $g = \text{age}$ and $C = \text{young}$, τ_C = "young" and

$$\phi_{\text{young}}(\text{John}) = \phi_{\text{young}}(\text{age}(\text{John})) .$$

Now consider again any $g \in X^Y$. Then

$g^{-1} : rng(g) \to rng(g^{-1})$, where $rng(g) \subseteq X$, $rng(g^{-1}) \subseteq \mathcal{P}(Y)$,

is disjointly bijective (due to the partitioning of Y induced by g^{-1}), noting $(g^{-1})^{-1} = \bar{g} : \mathcal{P}(rng(g^{-1})) \to \mathcal{P}(rng(g))$. ($\bar{g}$ being the set extension of g as previously developed in 2.3.7.)

In this case, we let the initial dispersion space be $(rng(g), \mathcal{A}, \mu)$ where

$$\mathcal{A} \overset{d}{=} \mathcal{J}(rng(g))$$

$$\mu \overset{d}{=} \phi_C ,$$

with $C \in lng(g)$ arbitrary fixed, and where for any $Q \in \mathcal{A}$,

$$\phi_C(Q) \overset{d}{=} \underset{x \in Q}{\phi_\&} (\phi_C(x)) ,$$

for t-norm $\phi_\&$ fixed.

Then we may take for the transformation here

$$f \overset{d}{=} g^{-1} ,$$

resulting in induced dispersion space $(rng(g^{-1}), \mathcal{B}, \nu)$, where

$$\mathcal{B} = \mathcal{J}(rng(g^{-1})) ,$$

$$\nu \overset{d}{=} \phi_{\tau_C} ,$$

where for any $\mathcal{Q} \in \mathcal{J}(rng(g^{-1}))$,

$$\begin{aligned} \phi_{\tau_C}(\mathcal{Q}) &= \phi_C(\bar{g}(\mathcal{Q})) \\ &= \underset{Q \in \mathcal{Q}}{\phi_\&} (\phi_C(g(Q))) \\ &= \underset{y \in Q \in \mathcal{Q}}{\phi_\&} (\phi_C(g(y))) . \end{aligned}$$

2.3.9 Examples of semi-truth functional logical systems

In this section, the formal language $\mathcal{L}$ is for Probability Logic. (See Maydole [172], p. 145; Hailperin [102']; Rescher [214], pp. 184-188; also section 2.3.3.) We will first proceed to specify the concept of dispersion and show that the probability logical system is semi-truth functional (i.e., up to the rays-level) but not truth-functional. Next, we will extend the probability logical system to the Lebesgue-Stieltjes logical system.

A. Probability logical system.

I. As in 2.3.5, let $Y = \mathbb{R}$, and $X = \mathbb{B}_1$, the Borel σ-algebra of $\mathbb{R}$, so that $\mathcal{P}(X) = \mathcal{P}(\mathbb{R})$ = the class of all probability measures over $(\mathbb{R},\mathbb{B}_1)$. If $Pr \in \mathcal{P}(\mathbb{R})$, we write $A_{Pr} = \phi^{-1}(Pr) \in \mathcal{P}(\mathbb{R})$ for the generalized set on $\mathbb{B}_1$ with $\phi_{A_{Pr}} = Pr$. Pick $\phi_\&$ any ∞-copula, e.g., min, prod. Let ϕ_{or} be the DeMorgan transform of $\phi_\&$.

First, construct by Sklar's theorem (see 2.3.6 or [238]) all joint probability distribution functions $F_{1,\ldots,n}$ for any given $Pr_1,\ldots,Pr_n \in \mathcal{P}(\mathbb{R})$ using $\phi_\&$.

$$F_{1,\ldots,n}(a_1,\ldots,a_n) \overset{d}{=} \phi_\&(F_1(a_1),\ldots,F_n(a_n))$$

for all $a_j \in \mathbb{R}$ where F_j is the distribution function corresponding to Pr_j, $j = 1,\ldots,n$. Thus, for
$I_{a_j} \equiv (-\infty, a_n) \in \mathbb{B}_1$,

$$Pr_{1,\ldots n}(I_{a_1}\times\cdots\times I_{a_n}) = \phi_\&(Pr_1(I_{a_1}),\ldots,Pr_n(I_{a_n}))$$

(truth functionally over rays).

In turn this uniquely determines

$$(\mathbb{R}^n, \mathbb{B}_n, Pr_{1,\ldots n}) .$$

Note here $\times$ is defined (through $\phi_\&$) by

$$Pr_1\times\cdots\times Pr_n \overset{d}{=} Pr_{1,\ldots,n} .$$

We extend $\times$ to include forms such as $(1 - Pr_1) \times Pr_2$, $(1 - Pr_1) \times (1 - Pr_2)$, $Pr_1 \times (1 - Pr_2)$, for two arguments and similarly for three or more agruments, by formal expansion, where $\underset{\sim X}{1}(A) \equiv 1$ for all $A \in \mathbb{B}_1$, etc.

For example,

$$(1 - Pr_1) \times Pr_2 \overset{d}{=} \underset{\sim X}{1} \times Pr_2 - Pr_1 \times Pr_2$$

where it should be noted for any $A,B \in \mathbb{B}_1$,

$$\begin{aligned}((1-Pr_1) \times Pr_2)(A\times B) &= (\underset{\sim}{1}\times Pr_2)(A\times B) - (Pr_1\times Pr_2)(A\times B)\\ &= Pr_2(B) - Pr_{12}(A\times B)\end{aligned}$$

$$= Pr_{12}(\complement A \times B) ,$$

and for all $A, B \in \mathbb{B}_1$:

$$((1-Pr_1) \times (1-Pr_2))(A \times B) \stackrel{d}{=} (\underset{\sim}{1} \times \underset{\sim}{1} - Pr_1 \times \underset{\sim}{1} - \underset{\sim}{1} \times Pr_2 + Pr_1 \times Pr_2)(A \times B)$$
$$= 1 - Pr_1(A) - Pr_2(B) + Pr_{12}(A \times B)$$
$$= Pr_{12}(\complement A \times \complement B) .$$

It can be verified that here $\times$ is a legitimate cartesian product.

Note

$$\complement <G \in A_{Pr_1}> = <G \in \complement A_{Pr_1}>$$
$$= <G \in A_{1-Pr_1}>$$
$$= <\complement G \in A_{Pr_1}>$$

Note for any $A, B \in \mathbb{B}_1$,

$$A \dagger B = \complement(\complement A \times \complement B)$$
$$= (A \times \mathbb{R}) \cup (\mathbb{R} \times B) ,$$
$$A \times B = (A \times \mathbb{R}) \cap (\mathbb{R} \times B) ,$$
$$Pr_{12}(A \dagger B) \equiv Pr_1(A) + Pr_2(B) - Pr_{12}(A \times B)$$

$$\text{(modular form)} \equiv (Pr_1 \times \underset{\sim}{1})(A \times B) + (\underset{\sim}{1} \times Pr_2)(A \times B) - Pr_{12}(A \times B) .$$

$$\text{(DeMorgan form)} \equiv (1 - (1 - Pr_1) \times (1 - Pr_2))(A \times B)$$

Define for any

$$\alpha = Pr_1 \text{ or } 1 - Pr_1 ,$$
$$\beta = Pr_2 \text{ or } 1 - Pr_2 ,$$
$$\alpha \dagger \beta = (\alpha \times \underset{\sim}{1}) + (\underset{\sim}{1} \times \beta) - \alpha \times \beta .$$

Thus,

$$(Pr_1 \dagger Pr_2)(A \times B)$$
$$= Pr_{12}(A \dagger B) , \text{ etc.}$$

So $\dagger$ is a legitimate cartesian sum.

Thus, $\times$ and $\dagger$ form a DeMorgan and modular system here.

$$Pr_1 \dagger Pr_2 = (Pr_1 \times \underset{\sim}{1}) + (\underset{\sim}{1} \times Pr_2) - Pr_1 \times Pr_2 ,$$

noting $Pr_1 \times Pr_2 = Pr_{12}$.

In particular, if $\phi_{\&} \equiv \min$ and $Pr_1 = Pr_2$,

$$(Pr_1 \dagger Pr_1)(A \times B) = Pr_{12}(A \dagger B)$$
$$= Pr_1(A) \dagger Pr_2(B) - Pr_{12}(A \times B)$$

$$Pr_{12}(A \times B) = Pr_1(A \cap B) ,$$
$$(Pr_1 \dagger Pr_1)(A \times B) = Pr_{12}(A \dagger B) = Pr_1(A \cup B)$$

Use the notation

$$\text{comb}(C, \times, \dagger)(Pr_1, Pr_2, \ldots, Pr_n)$$

to indicate some combination of prob. measures, as for example:

$$(1 - Pr_1) \times (Pr_2 + (1 - Pr_3)) \times Pr_4 .$$

Theorem

For any probability spaces $(X_j, \mathcal{A}_j, Pr_j)$, $j = 1,\ldots,n$, and any $A_j \in \mathcal{A}_j$, $j = 1,\ldots,n$

$$\text{comb}(C, \times, \dagger)(Pr_1,\ldots,Pr_n)(A_1,\ldots,A_n)$$
$$= Pr_1 \times \cdots \times Pr_n(\text{comb}(C, \times, \dagger)(A_1,\ldots,A_n)) .$$

(Note that $Pr_1 \times \ldots \times Pr_n = Pr_{1,\ldots,n}$.)
Thus, e.g.,

$$((1 - Pr_1) \times (Pr_2 \dagger (1 - Pr_3)) \times Pr_4)(A, B, C, D)$$
$$\equiv Pr_{1,2,3,4}(CA \times (B \dagger CC) \times D) .$$

Examples:

$$(Pr_1 \times Pr_2)(A \times B) = Pr_{12}(A \times B) ;$$

$$\begin{aligned}(CPr_1 \times Pr_2)(A \times B) &= (1 - Pr_1 \times Pr_2)(A \times B)\\ &= (1 \times Pr_2)(A \times B) - Pr_1 \times Pr_2(A \times B)\\ &= Pr_2(B) - Pr_{12}(A \times B)\\ &= Pr_{12}(CA \times B) ;\end{aligned}$$

$$\begin{aligned}(CPr_1 \times CPr_2)(A \times B) &= ((1 - Pr_1) \times (1 - Pr_2))(A \times B)\\ &= 1 - Pr_2(B) - Pr_1(A) + Pr_{12}(A \times B)\\ &= Pr_{12}(CA \times CB) ;\end{aligned}$$

$$\begin{aligned}(Pr_1 \dagger Pr_2)(A \times B) &= Pr_1(A) + Pr_2(B) - Pr_{12}(A \times B)\\ &= 1 - ((1 - Pr_1) \times (1 - Pr_2))(A \times B)\\ &= Pr_{12}(A \dagger B) ;\end{aligned}$$

$$(CPr_1 \dagger Pr_2)(A \times B) = Pr_{12}(CA + B) ;$$

$$((\complement Pr_1 \dagger Pr_2) \times (Pr_3 \dagger Pr_4))(A \times B \times C \times D)$$
$$= ((\complement Pr_1 + Pr_2 - \complement Pr_1 \times Pr_2)\times(Pr_3 + Pr_4 - Pr_3 \times Pr_4))(A \times B \times C \times D)$$
$$= (\complement Pr_1 \times Pr_3 + \complement Pr_1 \times Pr_4 - \complement Pr_1 \times Pr_3 \times Pr_4$$
$$+ Pr_2 \times Pr_3 + Pr_2 \times Pr_4 - Pr_2 \times Pr_3 \times Pr_4 - \complement Pr_1 \times Pr_2 \times Pr_3$$
$$- \complement Pr_1 \times Pr_2 \times Pr_4 + \complement Pr_1 \times Pr_2 \times Pr_3 \times Pr_4)(A \times B \times C \times D)$$
$$= Pr_{13}(\complement A \times C) + Pr_{14}(\complement A \times D) - Pr_{134}(\complement A \times C \times D)$$
$$+ Pr_{23}(B \times C) + Pr_{24}(B \times D) - Pr_{234}(B \times C \times D)$$
$$- Pr_{123}(\complement A \times B \times C) - Pr_{124}(\complement A \times B \times D)$$
$$+ Pr_{1234}(\complement A \times B \times C \times D)$$
$$= Pr_{1234}((\complement A \dagger B) \times (C \dagger D)) .$$

II. By the bijection between probability measures and c.d.f.s over $\mathbb{R}^q$, $q \geq 1$, we consider

$$T(\mathbb{R}^q) \stackrel{d}{=} \{A \mid A \in \mathcal{F}(X) \ \& \ \phi_A = F \text{ where } F \text{ is a c.d.f. over } \mathbb{R}^q\}$$

Pick not, &, or to have their ordinary meanings, so that not is involutive, & , or are symmetric, associative distributive, etc.

Let $\phi_\&$ be an r-copula (not necessarily associative nor symmetric). Then by Sklar's Theorem (2.3.6), for any $A_j \in \mathcal{F}(\mathbb{R})$ (here $\phi_{A_j} = F_j$ c.d.f.) , $x_j \in \mathbb{R}$, $j = 1,\ldots,r$,

$$\begin{aligned}\phi_{A_1\times\cdots\times A_r}(x_1,\ldots,x_r) &= F_1\times\cdots\times F_n(x_1,\ldots,x_r)\\ &= \phi_\&(\phi_{A_1}(x_1),\ldots,\phi_{A_r}(x_r))\\ &= \phi_\&(F_1(x_1),\ldots,F_r(x_r))\\ &= \| <(x_1,\ldots,x_n) \in A_1\times\cdots\times A_r> \| ,\end{aligned}$$

is a legitimate c.d.f. - as a function of $\underset{\sim}{x} = (x_1,\ldots,x_r) \in \mathbb{R}^r$. Conversely, (by Sklar's Theorem), any c.d.f. F over $\mathbb{R}^r$ may be written as, for any $\underset{\sim}{x} = (x_1,\ldots,x_n) \in \mathbb{R}^n$,

$$F(x_1,\ldots x_r) = \phi_\&(F_1(x_1),\ldots,F_r(x_r)) ,$$

where $\phi_\& = F(F_1^{\ddagger},\ldots,F_r^{\ddagger})$ is an r-copula and $F_j = F(+\infty,\ldots,+\infty,\cdot,+\infty,\ldots,+\infty)$ is the jth marginal c.d.f. of F , $j = 1,\ldots,r$.

Define ϕ_{or} to be the modular complement of $\phi_\&$, i.e., for any $u_1,\ldots,u_r \in [0,1]$,

$$\phi_{or}(u_1,\dots,u_r) \overset{d}{=} \sum_{\emptyset \neq S \subseteq \{1,\dots,r\}} (-1)^{\text{card } S+1} \phi_{\underset{j\in S}{\&}} (u_j)$$

Thus, for all $u_1, u_2, u_3 \in [0,1]$

$$\phi_{or}(u_1) = u_1$$

$$\phi_{or}(u_1, u_2) = u_1 + u_2 - \phi_{\&}(u_1, u_2)$$

$$\phi_{or}(u_1, u_2, u_3) = u_1 + u_2 + u_3 - \phi_{\&}(u_1, u_2) - \phi_{\&}(u_1, u_3)$$

$$- \phi_{\&}(u_2, u_3) + \phi_{\&}(u_1, u_2, u_3) \text{ , etc.}$$

Define negation operator as simply

$$\phi_{not}(u) = 1 - u \text{ ; all } u \in [0,1] .$$

We can interpret, for any $x_j \in \mathbb{R}$, $A_j \in \mathcal{F}(\mathbb{R})$, $\phi_{A_j} = F_j$ c.d.f., corresponding to r.v. $V_j : \Omega \to \mathbb{R}$ where $(\Omega, \mathfrak{B}, Pr)$ is a fixed probability space and left ray $R_{x_j} = (-\infty, x_j]$, $j = 1,\dots,r$.

$<x_j \in A_j> = <V_j \in R_{x_j}>$, $j = 1,\dots,r$ and jointly,

$$<(x_1,x_2) \in A_1 \times A_2> = <(V_1,V_2) \in R_{x_1} \times R_{x_2}>$$

$$= <x_1 \in A_1> \& <x_2 \in A_2> = <V_1 \in R_{x_1}> \& <V_2 \in R_{x_2}> ,$$

$$<(x_1,x_2,x_3) \in A_1 \dagger A_2 \dagger A_3>$$

$$= <x_1 \in A_1> \text{ or } <x_2 \in A_2> \text{ or } <x_3 \in A_3>$$

$$= <V_1 \in R_{x_1}> \text{ or } <V_2 \in R_{x_2}> \text{ or } <V_3 \in R_{x_3}> ,$$ etc., where some of the x_j's or A_j's may be the same.

Thus, a typical string may be written as

$$s = \text{comb}(\text{not}, \&, \text{or})(<x_1 \in A_{j_1}>,\dots,<x_m \in A_{j_m}>) ,$$

where $A_{j_1},\dots,A_{j_m} \in \{A_1,\dots,A_r\}$, and hence

$$s = \text{comb}(\text{not}, \&, \text{or})(<V_{j_1} \in R_{x_1}>,\dots,<V_{j_m} \in R_{x_m}>)$$

$$= <(V_{j_1},\dots,V_{j_m}) \in \text{comb}(\complement, \times, \dagger)(R_{x_1},\dots,R_{x_m})> ,$$

by the usual relations between ordinary complement $\complement$, cartesian product $\times$, cartesian sum $\dagger$, and ordinary not, &, or, so that

$$s = <(x_1,\dots,x_m) \in \text{comb}(\complement, \times, \dagger)(A_{j_1},\dots,A_{j_m})> ,$$

so that

$$\|s\| = \phi_{\mathrm{comb}(C,\times,\dagger)(A_{j_1},\ldots,A_{j_m})}(x_1,\ldots,x_m)$$
$$\neq \mathrm{comb}(\phi_{not}, \phi_{\&}, \phi_{or})(\phi_{A_{j_1}}(x_1),\ldots,\phi_{A_{j_m}}(x_m)) ,$$

in general, and hence *non-truth functional*, although $\|s\|$ does depend on $\mathrm{comb}(\phi_{not}, \phi_{\&}, \phi_{or})$.

Example 1.

Let $r = 2$, and consider B as the shaded region:

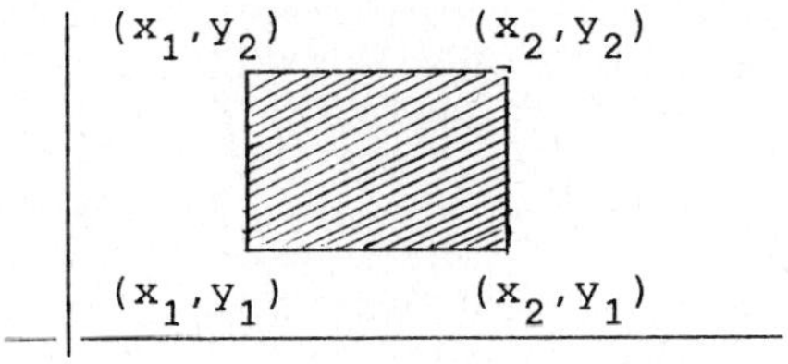

Let here $m = 4$, with

$$A_{j_1} = A_{j_2} = A_1 , \ \phi_{A_1} = F_1 ,$$
$$A_{j_3} = A_{j_4} = A_2 , \ \phi_{A_2} = F_2 , \text{ etc.}$$

$$\begin{aligned} s &= \langle x_1 \in A_1\rangle \ \& \ (\text{not } \langle x_2 \in A_1\rangle) \\ &\quad \& \ \langle y_1 \in A_2\rangle \ \& \ (\text{not } \langle y_2 \in A_2\rangle) \\ &= \langle (x_1,x_2,y_1,y_2) \in ((A_1 \times CA_2) \times (A_2 \times CA_2)) \\ &= \langle (V_1,V_1,V_2,V_2) \in (R_{x_1} \times CR_{x_1}) \times (R_{y_1} \times CR_{y_2}) \\ &= \langle (V_1,V_2) \in (R_{x_1} \dashv R_{x_2}) \times (R_{y_1} \dashv R_{y_2})\rangle \\ &= \langle (V_1,V_2) \in R_{x_1} \times R_{y_1} \dashv (R_{x_2} \times R_{y_1}) \dashv (R_{x_1} \times R_{y_2}) \cup (R_{x_2} \times R_{y_2}) \\ &= \langle V_1 \in R_{x_1} \dashv R_{x_2}\rangle \ \& \ \langle V_2 \in R_{y_1} \dashv R_{y_2}\rangle , \end{aligned}$$

with truth evaluation

$$\begin{aligned} \|s\| &= F_1 \times F_2((R_{x_1} \dashv R_{x_2}) \times (R_{y_1} \dashv R_{y_2})) \\ &= (F_1 \times F_2)(x_1,y_1) - (F_1 \times F_2)(x_2,y_1)) \\ &\quad - (F_1 \times F_2)(x_1,y_2) + (F_1 \times F_2)(x_2,y_2) \end{aligned}$$

Example 2.

$$s = (\langle x_1 \in A_1\rangle \ \& \text{ not } \langle x_2 \in A_1\rangle)$$

$$\text{or } (\langle y_1 \in A_2\rangle \ \& \text{ not } \langle y_2 \in A_2\rangle)$$
$$= \langle (x_1,x_2,y_1,y_2) \in ((A_1 \times CA_2) \dagger (A_2 \times CA_2))\rangle$$
$$= \langle (V_1,V_2) \in (R_{x_1} \dashv R_{x_2}) \dagger (R_{y_1} \dashv R_{y_2})\rangle$$

so that

$$\|s\| = (F_1 \times F_2)((R_{x_1} \dashv R_{x_2}) \dagger (R_{y_1} \dashv R_{y_2}))$$
$$= (F_1 \dagger F_2)((R_{x_1} \dashv R_{x_2}) \times (R_{y_1} \dashv R_{y_2})) .$$

In turn, by using standard extension procedures of measure, the above results may be extended from propositions $\langle x \in A\rangle$ to $\langle B \in \mathcal{A}\rangle$, where $\langle x \in A\rangle = \langle R_x \in \mathcal{A}\rangle$ and $\mu_F = \phi_{\mathcal{A}}$ is the probability measure corresponding to c.d.f. F and $B \in \mathbb{B}_q$, the Borel field or σ-algebra over $\mathbb{R}^q$. Marginals, conditionals, independence all hold as usual. Thus we identify

$$\text{comb}(C,\times,\dagger)(\mu_{F_1},\ldots,\mu_{F_m})(R_{x_1},\ldots,R_{x_m})$$
$$= \text{comb}(C,\times,\dagger)(F_1,\ldots,F_m)(x_1,\ldots,x_m).$$

Hailperin [102'] has recently contributed a most important paper concerning Probability Logic (PL).

First, a brief history is given for the problem of determining if probability theory can be viewed as a multiple-valued logic. Included is the Reichenbach-Tarski controversy, where Reichenbach considered, formally, probability analyzable as a truth functional multiple-valued logic, when conditional probabilities are also treated as (hidden) variables along with marginal probabilities; Tarski taking a critical view of this.

Hailperin's approach, avoiding the problems of quantification, etc,. is restricted to developing a semi-truth functional PL .

More specifically, Hailperin utilizes the normal disjunctive form available for any propositional wff Ψ in a formal language $\mathcal{L}$ where, say, $FV(\Psi) = \{x_1,\ldots x_n\}$, for some (free) variables $x_1,\ldots,x_n$, and some $n = n(\Psi) \geq 1$,

$$\Psi = \text{comb}(\text{not}, \&, \text{or})\ (x_1,\ldots,x_n)$$
$$= \text{comb}(\text{not}, \text{or})\ (\&\ B \mid B \subseteq \{x_1,\ldots,x_n\}) .$$

where for any $B = \{x_{j_i},\ldots,x_{j_m}\}$, say,

$$\&\ B \overset{d}{=} x_{j_1} \ \&\ldots\&\ x_{j_m} .$$

Then, generalizing the ordinary concept of a model (see section 2.3.3), in effect, a probability model P_M for a collection of propositions $\{\Psi_1,\ldots,\Psi_r\}$ with

$$A_o \overset{d}{=} \bigcup_{j=1}^{r} FV(\Psi_j)$$

is any probability function P_M over $\{\& B \mid B \subseteq A_o\}$.

In turn, if Ψ is any wff with $FV(\Psi) \subseteq A_o$, then

$$P_M(\Psi) \overset{d}{=} \sum_{\{B|B\subseteq A_o \text{ is such that } \&B \models \Psi\}} P_M(\&B)$$

where $B \models \Psi$ is the usual material implication in 0 - 1 logic (see section 2.3.3 (a)) .

A word of caution in the use of Hailperin's scheme: One must distinguish carefully between the primitive (author's term) conjunctions and similar appearing but different compound ones. For example, suppose that $A_o = \{x_1,x_2\}$. Then the four possible primitive conjunctions are,

$$\&\emptyset \ , \ \&x_1 \ , \ \&x_2 \ , \ \&\{x_1,x_2\} = x_1 \ \& \ x_2 \ ,$$

keeping (on purpose) the & notation on unary forms, where the corresponding probabilities satisfy

$$P_M(\emptyset) + P_M(x_1) + P_M(x_2) + P_M(x_1 \ \& \ x_2) = 1 \ .$$

But note that for x_j considered as a compound expression,

$$x_j = \&x_j \ \text{ or } \ (x_1 \ \& \ x_2)$$
$$\neq \&x_j \ , \ j = 1,2 \ ,$$

and since for ordinary 0 - 1 logic

$$x_j \models x_j \ \text{ and } \ (x_1 \ \& \ x_2) \models x_j \ , \ j = 1,2 \ ,$$

but it is not true that

$$\emptyset \models x_j \ \text{ nor } \ x_i \models x_j \ ; \ i \neq j \ ,$$

it follows that

$$P_M(x_j) = P_M(\&x_j) + P_M(x_1 \ \& \ x_2) \ , \ j = 1,2 \ ,$$

and hence

$$P_M(x_1 \ \& \ x_2) \leq \min P_M(x_1,x_2) \ ,$$

as should be, etc.

(Note the analogue of this situation with that in Chapter 9 (B).)

It follows that P_M obeys all the usual laws for a probability logic operator including, for all $\theta, \Psi \in Wff(\mathcal{L})$, x any variable

(a) $P_M(\Psi) = 0$, if $\Psi \models (x \& (\text{not } x))$

(b) $P_M(\theta) \leq P_M(\Psi)$, if $\theta \models \Psi$

(c) $P_M(\text{not}\theta) = 1 - P_M(\theta)$

(d) $P_M(\theta \vee \Psi) = P_M(\theta) + P_M(\Psi)$, if $(\theta \& \Psi) \models (x \& \text{not } x)$

where $\models$ is relative to ordinary 0 - 1 logic.

In turn, since (b) yields P_M having the same evaluation over 0 - 1 logically equivalent ($\models\!\dashv$) wff's, Hailperin uses the Lindenbaum-Tarski probability algebra which identifies all wff's $\in \mathcal{L}$ which are logically equivalent.

In addition, an extended material implication is defined: For any

$$(1) \qquad \Sigma \overset{d}{=} \{\theta_0, \theta_1, \ldots, \theta_m\} \subseteq Wff(\mathcal{L})$$

with, say,

$$(2) \qquad FV(\Sigma) = \bigcup_{j=0}^{m} FV(\theta_j) = \{x_1, \ldots, x_n\} ,$$

say, where $n = n(\Sigma)$, and hence we may write, w.l.o.g.

$$(3) \qquad \theta_i = \theta_i(x_1, \ldots, x_n) , \; i = 0,1,\ldots,n ,$$

and for any

$$(4) \qquad \alpha_0 \text{ and } \alpha \overset{d}{=} (\alpha_i)_{i=1,\ldots,m} ,$$

$$(5) \qquad \alpha_i \overset{d}{=} [a_i, b_i] \subseteq [0,1] \; ; \; i = 0,1,\ldots,m ,$$

define the (α, α_0)-level probabilistic implication.

$$(6) \qquad (\theta_1 \in \alpha_1, \ldots, \theta_m \in \alpha_m) \models_{\text{prob}} (\theta_0 \in \alpha_0) ,$$

iff, for all possible probability models P_M:
if $(P_M(\theta_1) \in \alpha_1, \ldots, P_M(\theta_m) \in \alpha_m)$, then $P_M(\theta_0) \in \alpha_0$.

The first basic result is the reaffirmation that the tautologies of standard PL and ordinary 0 - 1 logic coincide. (See also Rescher [214], pp. 184-188, for more details.)

Theorem (Hailperin [102'], Theorem 2.1)

For any $\theta \in Wff(\mathcal{L})$,

$\models_{prob} (\theta = 1)$ iff $\models \theta$, for

two-valued logic.

The next result is a further extension of Hailperin's generalization of Fréchet's theorem on the bounding of probabilities.

Theorem (Hailperin [102'], Theorem 3.2, 4.2)

Let $\Sigma \subseteq \text{Wff}(\mathcal{L})$ be arbitrary with all notation holding as in (1) - (3) .

Then there exists L_B , U_B : $[0,1]^{2m} \to [0,1]$, such that for any α_0 and α as in (4), (5) and

(i) for any probability operator P (including P_M) over $\mathcal{L}$, if

$$P(\theta_i) \in \alpha_i \ , \ i = 1,\ldots,m \ ,$$

then

$$L_B(\alpha) \leq P(\theta_0) \leq L_U(\alpha) \ ,$$

where $[L_B(\alpha), U_B(\alpha)]$ is the tightest possible bounding interval for $P(\theta_0)$. L_B, U_B are obtainable by solving a linear programming problem.

(ii) $$(\theta_1 \in \alpha_1,\ldots,\theta_m \in \alpha_m) \models_{prob} (\theta_0 \in \alpha_0)$$

iff

$$[L_B(\alpha), U_B(\alpha)] \subseteq \alpha_0 \ .$$

(iii) In particular, note that if $m = n$ and

$$\theta_j = \theta_j(x_1,\ldots,x_n) = x_j \ , \ j = 1,\ldots,n \ ,$$

then (ii) implies

$$(x_1 \in \alpha_1,\ldots,x_n \in \alpha_n) \models_{prob} (\theta_0 \in [L_B(\alpha), U_B(\alpha)]) \ .$$

Note that part (i) of the theorem may be interpreted as a sensitivity analysis for $P(\theta_0)$, when the initial θ_i (or x_i as in (iii)) have probability values known up to interval-values. In addition, note that the upper and lower bounding functions L_U and L_B *are* truth functional in form. Indeed, for θ_0 in pure disjunctive or conjunctive form and initial $\theta_i = x_i$, Lemma 4 of the Appendix, section 2.3.6, shows equivalently that L_U and L_B are in t-conorm or t-norm form, respectively.

See also Chapter 6, following Cor. 1 and section 5.3 B for

further discussion of probability bounds.

B. Lebesgue-Stieltjes logical system.

Use the basic theorem (McShane [174]: see also following Appendix) that if $f : \mathbb{R}^q \to [0,1]$ is of strong bounded variation (SBV), there is an $\tilde{f}$ such that the interval functions $Vr(f,\cdot) = Vr(\tilde{f},\cdot)$ and the extended measures $\mu_f = \mu_{\tilde{f}}$ where μ_f is a finite countably addi- tive complete regular signed measure, where w.l.o.g.

$$\mu_f = \mu_{f^+} - \mu_{f^-}$$

$$f = f^+ - f^- ,$$

f^+, f^- are nondecreasing positive increment monotone grounded continuous from the right - and hence are generalized c.d.f.'s yielding μ_{f^+}, μ_{f^-} non-negative complete regular finite countably additive measures. We say $\tilde{f}$ is *equivalent* to f.

Then replace in probability logic any c.d.f. by an SBV function and in the extension to the Borel set level, probability measures by these finite signed measures.

The interpretation and truth evaluation of strings proceeds analogously, except that Sklar's Theorem no longer holds, in the more general setting. It is assumed that $\phi_{\&}$, is sufficiently well-behaved that $\mathrm{comb}(\phi_{\mathrm{not}}, \phi_{\&}, \phi_{\mathrm{or}})$ preserves SBV, etc.

In summary, given any $A_j \in \mathcal{B}(\mathbb{R}^{q_j})$, $\phi_{A_j} = f_j$, assumed w.l.o.g. as in the basic theorem,

$$\phi_{CA_j}(x_j) = 1 - \phi_{A_j}(x_j) ,$$

and defining $C_j = \begin{cases} C \\ \quad \text{or} \\ id \end{cases}$

we can show that the following relations must hold

$$\phi_{\underset{j=1,\dots,r}{\times} C_jA_j}(x_1,\dots,x_r)$$

$$= \| < \underset{j=1,\dots,r}{\&} <x_j \in C_jA_j> \|$$

$$= \sum_{S\subseteq\{1,\dots,r\}\dashv C_r} (-1)^{\mathrm{card}\, S} \cdot \phi_{\underset{j\in C_r \cup S}{\times} A_j}((x_j)_{j\in S}) ,$$

where

$$C_r \overset{d}{=} \{j \mid 1 \le j \le r \;\&\; C_j = \mathrm{id}\} \,,$$

$$\phi_{\dagger A_j,\ j=1,\dots,r}(x_1,\dots,x_r) = \| \underset{j=1,\dots,r}{\mathrm{or}} \langle x_j \in C_j A_j \rangle \|$$

$$= \sum_{\emptyset \ne S \subseteq \{1,\dots,r\}} (-1)^{\mathrm{card}\,S+1} \phi_{\times A_j,\ j\in S}((x_j)_{j\in S}) = \phi_{\underset{j=1,\dots,r}{\mathrm{or}}}(\langle x_j \in A_j \rangle) \,.$$

Let us consider Lebesgue-Stieltjes Logic in further detail. Note that all the theorems referred to, unless otherwise notated, will be found in the Appendix at the end of this subsection.

Define the following important spaces:

$$\mathbb{S}_q \overset{d}{=} \{f \mid f \text{ is a (simple) step function over } \mathbb{R}^q\}$$

$$\mathbb{F}_q \overset{d}{=} \{f \mid f : \mathbb{R}^q \to \mathbb{R} \text{ (Borel) measurable}\}$$

$$\mathbb{BV}_q \overset{d}{=} \{f \mid f : \mathbb{R}^q \to \mathbb{R} \;\&\; f \text{ is BV (bounded variation)}\}$$

$$\mathbb{SBV}_q \overset{d}{=} \{f \mid f : \mathbb{R}^q \to \mathbb{R} \;\&\; f \text{ is SBV (strong bounded variation)}\}$$

$$\mathbb{D}_q = \{ f \mid f : \mathbb{R}^q \to [0,1] \text{ is a c.d.f.}\}$$

$$\mathbb{PM}_q \overset{d}{=} \{f \mid f : \mathbb{R}^q \to \mathbb{R} \text{ is PM (positive increment monotone)}\}$$

$$\mathbb{SPM}_q \overset{d}{=} \{f \mid f : \mathbb{R}^q \to \mathbb{R} \text{ is PM \& SBV}\}$$

Recall the spaces of all dispersions over $\mathbb{R}^q$, $[0,1]^{\mathbb{R}^q}$, and $\{0,1\}^{\mathbb{R}^q}$, the space of all ordinary set membership functions over $\mathbb{R}^q$.

Thus, e.g.,

$$\{0,1\}^{\mathbb{R}^q} \subseteq [0,1]^{\mathbb{R}^q} \cap \mathbb{F}_q \,,$$

$$\mathbb{S}_q \cap [0,1]^{\mathbb{R}^q},\ \mathbb{D}_q \subseteq \mathbb{SBV}_q \cap [0,1]^{\mathbb{R}^q} \subseteq \mathbb{BV}_q \cap [0,1]^{\mathbb{R}^q} \subseteq [0,1]^{\mathbb{R}^q} \cap \mathbb{F}_q \,.$$

By Theorem 2, e.g., $\mathbb{S}_q \cap [0,1]^{\mathbb{R}^q}$ and hence $\mathbb{SBV}_q \cap [0,1]^{\mathbb{R}^q}$ and $\mathbb{BV}_q \cap [0,1]^{\mathbb{R}^q}$ are all dense w.r.t. $[0,1]^{\mathbb{R}^q} \cap \mathbb{F}_q$ over arbitrary q-intervals $[-t,t]^q$, $t > 0$ in L^1-norm. By Theorems 6 - 8, we may always identify (or need only consider)

$$\mathbb{BV}_q = \{f \mid f : \mathbb{R}^q \to \mathbb{R} \text{ is a g.d.f. (generalized distribution function)}\} \,,$$

$$\mathbb{SBV}_q = \{f \mid f : \mathbb{R}^q \to \mathbb{R} \text{ is a SBV g.d.f.}\} \,,$$

$$\mathbb{P}\mathrm{M}_q = \{f \mid f : \mathbb{R}^q \to \mathbb{R}^+ \text{ is a PM g.d.f.}\} ,$$

$$\mathbb{S}\mathrm{PM}_q = \{f \mid f : R^q \to \mathbb{R}^+ \text{ is a SBV, PM g.d.f.}\} \subseteq \mathbb{D}_q .$$

Recall $\mathbb{C}_q$ is the class of all q-copulas $\phi_\&$, a subclss of all conjunction operators. Then Sklar's Theorem may be reformulated, involving in a key way generalized cartesian products,

$$\mathbb{D}_q = \bigcup_{\phi_\& \in \mathbb{C}_q} \underbrace{\mathbb{D}_1 \times_{\phi_\&} \cdots \times_{\phi_\&} \mathbb{D}_1}_{\text{q-factors}} , \quad \text{all } q \geq 1 ,$$

where for any q-copula $\phi_\&$.

$$\mathbb{D}_1 \times_{\phi_\&} \cdots \times_{\phi_\&} \mathbb{D}_q \overset{d}{=} \{f_1 \times_{\phi_\&} \cdots \times_{\phi_\&} f_q \mid f_j \in \mathbb{D}_j , \ j = 1,\ldots,q\} .$$

Define the q-right closed ray class as

$$\mathrm{Ray}_q \overset{d}{=} (J(-\infty \underset{\sim}{1}_q , y) \mid y \in \mathbb{R}^q)$$

and note the bijective mapping $\mathrm{ray}_q : \mathbb{R}^q \longleftrightarrow \mathrm{Ray}_q$, where for all $y \in \mathbb{R}^q$, $\mathrm{ray}_q(y) \overset{d}{=} J(-\infty \cdot 1_q, y)$. (We will interchange often ray_q and Ray_q .)

Define the class of all complete regular probability measures over $\mathbb{B}_q$ by

$$\mathcal{P}r_q \overset{d}{=} \{\mu_f \mid \mu_f , \mathbb{B}_q \to [0,1] \text{ is the unique complete regular probability measure induced by } f \text{ , for any } f \in \mathbb{D}_q\} , \text{ all } q \geq 1 .$$

It follows from bijection ray_q and the standard construction of complete regular probability measures μ_f associated with given c.d.f. f (a special case of the Lebesgue-Stieltjes measure construction) that a bijective relation exists between $\mathbb{D}_q$ and $\mathcal{P}r_q$; $\mu : \mathbb{D}_q \longleftrightarrow \mathcal{P}r_q$, where for all $f \in \mathbb{D}_q$,

$$\mu(f) = \mu_f ,$$

and where

$$\mu_f(\mathrm{ray}_q(y)) = f(y) \ ; \text{ all } y \in \mathbb{R}^q .$$

In turn, it follows that Sklar's Theorem yields

$$\mathcal{P}r_q = \bigcup_{\phi_\& \in \mathcal{C}_q} (\mathcal{P}r_q \times_{\phi_\&} \cdots \times_{\phi_\&} \mathcal{P}r_1) \text{ , all } q \geq 1 \text{ ,}$$

where for any q-copula $\phi_\&$,

$$\mathcal{P}r_1 \times_{\phi_\&} \cdots \times_{\phi_\&} \mathcal{P}r_q \stackrel{d}{=} \{\mu_{f_1} \times_{\phi_\&} \cdots \times_{\phi_\&} \mu_{f_q} \mid f_j \in \mathbb{D}_1 \text{ , } j = 1,\ldots,q\} \text{ ,}$$

and

$$\mu_{f_1} \times_{\phi_\&} \cdots \times_{\phi_\&} \mu_{f_q} \stackrel{d}{=} \mu_{f_1 \times_{\phi_\&} \cdots \times_{\phi_\&} f_q} \in \mathcal{P}r_q$$

is consistently defined by the unique extension property of probability measure μ_f given any c.d.f. f .

By considering co-$\mathcal{C}_q$, the class of all DeMorgan q-cocopulas, all possible generalized cartesian sums $\dagger_{\phi_{or}}$ may be obtained, generated by $\phi_{or} \in$ co-$\mathcal{C}_q$. Dual to the above development for $\times_{\phi_\&}$, strings of the form $f_1 \dagger_{\phi_{or}} \cdots \dagger_{\phi_{or}} f_q$ may be found as well as these involving C , noting for all $f \in \mathbb{D}_q$,

$$\mathrm{C}\mu_f = 1 - \mu_f = \mu_f(\mathrm{C}\cdot) \text{ ,}$$

and finally, strings involving arbitrary mixed finite combinations comb($\mathrm{C}, \times_{\phi_\&}, \dagger_{\phi_{or}}$) (or equivalently, comb($\phi_{not}, \phi_\&, \phi_{or}$)) . Special cases of these, as in the development of general logical systems, include the definitions for $\cap$, $\cup$, Δ , $\subseteq$, $\hat{f}$, etc., all depending on particular choices of truth functional system $\mathcal{F} = (\phi_{not}, \phi_\&, \phi_{or})$. Thus a probability logic in the extended sense may be considered as the class of all finite strings involving a fixed $\mathcal{F}$ and $\mathbb{D}_q$'s .

It is required that $\times_{\phi_\&}$ and $\dagger_{\phi_{or}}$ be symmetric and associative operations, and hence unambiguously extendable to any finite number of arguments.

In general, a probability logic is *not* truth functional - although clearly restricted to the left-ray level, since it reduces to all finite strings of c.d.f.'s involving $\mathcal{F}$, it is truth functional. Let us consider this in some more detail:

Let $f \in \mathbb{D}_q$, $g \in \mathbb{D}_r$, and define

$$\mathrm{C}\mu_f \times_{\phi_\&} \mu_g = (1 - \mu_f) \times_{\phi_\&} \mu_g \stackrel{d}{=} 1(q) \times_{\phi_\&} \mu_g - \mu_f \times_{\phi_\&} \mu_g \text{ ,}$$

where $1(q) : \mathbb{R}^q \to \{1\}$, and $1(q) \times \mu_g$ is the embedding of $\mu_g : \mathbb{B}_r \to [0,1]$ into $\mathbb{B}_{q+r}$, where for all $B \in \mathbb{B}_q$, $C \in \mathbb{B}_r$,

$$(1(q) \times_{\phi_\&} \mu_g)(B \times C) = \mu_{1(q)\times_{\phi_\&} g}(B \times C) = \mu_g(C) \quad .$$

Define, similarly $\mu_f \times_\phi 1(r)$. Also, define

$$1(q) \times_{\phi_\&} 1(r)(B \times C) \stackrel{d}{=} 1.$$

Note that $C\mu_f$ is not to be confused with μ_{Cf} , since for all $B \in \mathbb{B}_q$

$$\mu_{Cf}(B) = M_{1-f}(B) = \mu_{-f}(B) = -\mu_f(B)$$

from the Lebesgue-Stieltjes construction, noting $1 - f$ is *not* grounded but is equivalent to $-f$ which is grounded (see the Appendix). On the other hand, note $C\mu_f$ is *not* any type of measure (let alone, a probability measure) and thus

$$C\mu_f(B) = 1 - \mu_f(B) \neq \mu_{Cf}(B) \quad .$$

Also, define, for $B \in \mathbb{B}_q$, $C \in \mathbb{B}_r$ arbitrary

$$\begin{aligned}
&(C\mu_f \times_{\phi_\&} C\mu_g)(B \times C) \\
&= ((1 - \mu_f) \times_{\phi_\&} (1 - \mu_g))(B \times C) \\
&= (1(q + r) - \mu_f \times_{\phi_\&} 1(r) - 1(q) \times_{\phi_\&} \mu_g + \mu_f \times_{\phi_\&} \mu_g)(B \times C) \quad . \\
&= (1 - \mu_f(B) - \mu_g(C) + \mu_{f\times_{\phi_\&} g})(B \times C), \\
&= \mu_{f\times_{\phi_\&} g}(CB \times CC) \quad .
\end{aligned}$$

Similarly,

$$\begin{aligned}
&(\mu_f \dagger \mu_g)(B \times C) \\
&\stackrel{d}{=} C(C\mu_f \times_{\phi_\&} C\mu_g)(B \times C) \\
&= (\mu_f \times_{\phi_\&} 1(r) + (1(q) \times_{\phi_\&} \mu_g) - \mu_{f\times_{\phi_\&} g})(B \times C) \\
&= \mu_f(B) + \mu_g(C) - \mu_{f\times_{\phi_\&} g}(B \times C) \\
&= \mu_{f\times_{\phi_\&} g}(B \dagger C) \quad ,
\end{aligned}$$

where

$$B \dagger C \stackrel{d}{=} (B \times \mathbb{R}^r) \cup (\mathbb{R}^q \times C) \; , \; B \times C \stackrel{d}{=} (B \times \mathbb{R}^r) \cap (\mathbb{R}^q \times C) \quad .$$

Compatability between $\dagger$ and ϕ_{or} and C will be achieved by choosing $\mathcal{F}$ to be any Frankian or modular logical system (see section 2.3.6). Then let $\dagger = \dagger_{\phi_{or}}$.

More generally, if $\mathrm{comb}(\complement, \times_{\phi_\&}, \dagger_{\phi_{or}})$ denotes any given combination of probability operators which can be applied (in a well defined manner) to any collection of probability measures $\mu_{f_j} : \mathbb{B}_{q_j} \to [0,1]$, $j = 1,\ldots,n$, say, then it can be shown that the evaluation of the resulting (finite) string at any cartesian product (or cylinder) set is obtained by replacing all probability operators by the corresponding ordinary set operators in the comb function and in its arguments, each probability measure by a corresponding cartesian product factor relative to the joint probability measure. That is

$$(\mathrm{comb}(\complement,\times_{\phi_\&},\dagger_{\phi_{or}})(\mu_{f_1},\ldots,\mu_{f_n}))(B_1\times\cdots\times B_n) \qquad \text{(i)}$$
$$= (\mu_{f_1}\times_{\phi_\&}\cdots\times_{\phi_\&}\mu_{f_n})((\mathrm{comb}(\complement,\times,\dagger))(B_1,\cdots,B_n)),$$

for all $B_j \in \mathbb{B}_{q_j}$, $f_j \in \mathbb{D}_{q_j}$, $j = 1,\ldots,n$; $n \geq 1$.

Furthermore, if this result is specialized to $\mathbb{B}_j = \mathrm{ray}_{q_j}(Y_j)$, $y_j \in \mathbb{R}^{q_j}$, $j = 1,\ldots,n$, arbitrary, one readily obtains

$$(\mathrm{comb}(\complement, \times_{\phi_\&}, \dagger_{\phi_{or}})(\mu_{f_1},\ldots,\mu_{f_n}))(B_1\times\cdots\times B_n) \qquad \text{(ii)}$$
$$= \mathrm{comb}'(\phi_{not},\phi_\&,\phi_{or})(f_1(y_1),\ldots, f_n(y_n))$$
$$= \mathrm{comb}'(\phi_{not},\phi_\&,\phi_{or})(\mu_{f_1}(B_1),\ldots,\mu_{f_n}(B_n)),$$

a truth functional system, when B_j's are restricted to rays. But, for more general B_j's, even for $n = 2$, probability logic is *not* a truth functional system since there is no function τ such that, e.g.,

$$(\mu_{f_1} \times \mu_{f_2})(B_1 \times B_2) = \tau(\mu_{f_1}(B_1), \mu_{f_2}(B_2)),$$

for all $B_j \in \mathbb{B}_{q_j}$, $j = 1, 2$. (See the Preface for a specific example. See also Rescher [214] for further properties of probabibity logics.) The development of the concepts of marginal probability measures, statistical independence and conditional probability measures are all well known and will be omitted here. (See, e.g., Neveu [184'].)

Motivated by the above development for Probability Logic, let us reconsider Lebesgue-Stieltjes measures and Lebesgue-Stieltjes Logic:

First note that with respect to pointwise addition and scalar multiplication, $\mathbb{S}BV_q$ is a vector subspace of vector space $\mathbb{B}V_q$, in the sense that for any $n \geq 1$ and scalars $\lambda_1,\ldots,\lambda_n \in \mathbb{R}$, and $f_1,\ldots,f_n \in \mathbb{S}BV_q$ (or $\in \mathbb{B}V_q$), $\sum_{j=1}^{n} \lambda_j f_j \in \mathbb{S}BV_q$ (or $\in \mathbb{B}V_q$).

Denoting

$$\mathcal{BV}_q \overset{d}{=} \{\mu_f \mid f \text{ (g.c.d.)} \in \mathbb{BV}_q\} ,$$

where μ_f now represents a possibly signed measure corresponding to f:

$$\mathcal{SBV}_q \overset{d}{=} \{\mu_f \mid f \in \mathbb{SBV}_q\} ,$$

$$\hat{\mathcal{BV}}_q = \{\mu_f \mid f \in \mathbb{BV}_q \cap [0,1]^{\mathbb{R}^q}\} ,$$

$$\hat{\mathcal{SBV}}_q \overset{d}{=} \{\mu_f \mid f \in \mathbb{SB}\mathcal{V}_q \cap [0,1]^{\mathbb{R}^q}\} ,$$

it follows that for $\lambda_1,\ldots,\lambda_n \in \mathbb{R}$, $\mu_{f_1},\ldots,\mu_{f_n} \in \mathcal{SBV}_q$ (or $\mathcal{BV}_q$) ,

$$\sum_{j=1}^{n} \lambda_j \mu_{f_j} = \mu_{\sum_{j=1}^{n} \lambda_j f_j} \in \mathcal{SBV}_q (\text{or} \in \mathcal{BV}_q)$$

and hence $\mathcal{SBV}_q$ is a vector subspace of vector space $\mathcal{BV}_q$ w.r.t. scalar multiplication and addition as defined. Similarly, since for $0 \le \lambda_1,\ldots,\lambda_n \le 1$, $\sum_{j=1}^{n} \lambda_j = 1$ and any $\mu_{f_1},\ldots,\mu_{f_n} \in \hat{\mathcal{SBV}}_q$ (or $\in \hat{\mathcal{BV}}_q$) ,

$$\sum_{j=1} \lambda_j \mu_j = \mu_{\sum_{j=1}^{n} \lambda_j f_j} \in \hat{\mathcal{SBV}}_q \text{ (or } \in \hat{\mathcal{BV}}_q) .$$

Hence $\hat{\mathcal{SBV}}_q$ is a positive convex cone of $\mathcal{SBV}_q$ and $\hat{\mathcal{BV}}_q$ is a positive convex cone of $\mathcal{BV}_q$, noting that

$$\mathcal{P}r_q \subseteq \hat{\mathcal{SBV}}_q \text{ ; all } q \ge 1 \text{ , etc.}$$

Metrics and norms can be introduced on any of the above spaces, using the relation for any μ_f, μ_g ,

$$\text{dist}(\mu_f,\mu_g) = \text{dist}(f,g) ,$$

where dist may be determined by any appropriate function space norm such as L^1- , L^2- , or sup-norms.

Analogous to the Probability Logic development, let us next enlarge $\mathcal{BV}_q$ by the introduction of constants $c : \mathbb{B}_q \to \{c\}$ which, unless $c \equiv 0$, are non-measures;

$$\mathbb{C}\mathcal{BV}_q \overset{d}{=} \{c + \mu_f \mid \mu_f \in \mathcal{BV}_q \text{ , } c \in \mathbb{R} \}$$

$$\supseteq \mathbb{C}\mathcal{SBV}_q \overset{d}{=} \{c + \mu_f \mid \mu_f \in \mathcal{SBV}_q \text{ , } c \in \mathbb{R}\} ,$$

where $c \in \mathbb{R}$ is identified with $c : \mathbb{B}_q \to \{c\}$ and $c + \mu_f : \mathbb{B}_q \to \mathbb{R}$, $(c + \mu_f)(B) \overset{d}{=} c + \mu_f(B)$, for all $B \in \mathbb{B}_q$.

Again, $\mathcal{CBV}_q$ is a vector subspace of $\mathcal{CSBV}_q$ under scalar multiplication and addition. In particular, consider any $\hat{\mu}_f \in \mathcal{BV}_q(\hat{\mathcal{SBV}}_q)$. Then $-\mu_f = \mu_{-f} \in \mathcal{BV}_q$ $(\mathcal{SBV}_q)$ and $1 - \mu_f \in \mathcal{CBV}_q(\mathcal{CSBV}_q)$.

We can denote $1 - \mu_f$ as $\complement\mu_f$, the generalized complement of μ_f since for any $y \in \mathbb{R}^q$,

$$(1 - \mu_f)(\mathrm{ray}_q(y)) = 1 - f(y) = \complement f(y) .$$

However, if $\mu_f \in \mathcal{CSBV}_q$ then for all $B \in \mathbb{B}_q$,

$$(1 - \mu_f)(B) = \mu_f(\complement B) + 1 - \mu_f(\mathbb{R}^q)$$

which will coincide with a measure complement only when, e.g., f is a c.d.f. and hence μ_f is a probability measure (and thus $1 - \mu_f(\mathbb{R}^q) = 0$).

Note as in the probability logic case, for any $f \in \mathbb{BV}_q \cap [0,1]^{\mathbb{R}^q}$,

$$\complement f = 1 - f \in \mathbb{BV}_q \cap [0,1]^{\mathbb{R}^q} \text{ and}$$
$$\mu_{\complement f} = \mu_{-f} = -\mu_f ,$$

and for any $g : \mathbb{R}^q \to \mathbb{R}$ Borel measurable,

$$\int_{x\in\mathbb{R}^q} g(x)d\mu_{\complement f}(x) = -\int_{x\in\mathbb{R}^q} g(x)d\mu_f(x) ,$$

and that $\complement f$ is *not* grounded in general, especially when f is a g.d.f. Hence, again

$$\mu_{\complement f} = -\mu_f \neq 1 - \mu_f = \complement\mu_f .$$

Now, analogous to Sklar's Theroem mentioned previously, define for any $n \geq 1$

$$\mathbb{C}_n \overset{d}{=} \bigcup_{\substack{q\geq 1,\\ j=1,\ldots,n\\ \phi_\&\in\mathcal{C}_q}} (\mathbb{SBV}_q \cap ((\mathbb{SBV}_{q_1} \cap [0,1]^{\mathbb{R}^{q_1}}) \times_{\phi_\&} \cdots \times_{\phi_\&} (\mathbb{SBV}_{\phi_n} \cap [0,1]^{\mathbb{R}^{q_1}}))) .$$

Sufficient conditions (for the cases $q_1 = \cdots = q_n = 1$) for membership in $\mathbb{C}_n$ is given in Theorem 12. (It would be of some interest to develop practical necessary and sufficient conditions for membership in $\mathbb{C}_n$.)

As in the Probability Logic case, the more general Lebesgue-Stieltjes development established that $\mu : \mathbb{S}BV_q \cap [0,1]^{\mathbb{R}^q} \leftrightarrow \hat{\mathcal{SBV}}_q$, $\mu(f) \overset{d}{=} \mu_f$, all $f \in \mathbb{S}BV_q \cap [0,1]^{\mathbb{R}^q}$ is bijective where again

$$\mu_f(\mathrm{ray}_q(Y)) = f(Y) \ ; \text{ all } Y \in \mathbb{R}^q ,$$

and in turn

$$c_{(n)} \overset{d}{=} \{\mu_f \mid f \in \mathbb{C}_n\}$$

$$= \bigcup_{\left[\begin{array}{l} q_j \geq 2, j=1,\ldots,n, \\ \phi_\& \in C_q \end{array}\right]} (\mathcal{SBV}_q \cap (\hat{\mathcal{SBV}}_{q_1} \times_{\phi_\&} \cdots \times_{\phi_\&} \hat{\mathcal{SBV}}_{q_n})) .$$

Thus, the $\mathbb{C}_n$'s are the classes of relevant Lebesgue-Stieltjes measures which arise as generalized cartesian products.

Note that for all $y_j \in \mathbb{R}^{q_j}$, $j = 1,\ldots,n$,

$$(\mu_{f_1} \times_{\phi_\&} \cdots \times \mu_{f_n})\underbrace{(\mathrm{ray}_{q_1}(y_1) \times \cdots \times \mathrm{ray}_{q_n}(y_n))}_{= \mathrm{ray}_q(y_1 \times \cdots \times y_n)}$$

$$= (f_1 \times_{\phi_\&} \cdots \times f_n)(y_1,\ldots,y_n)$$

$$= \phi_\&(f_1(y_1),\ldots,f_n(y_n))$$

$$= \phi_\&(\mu_{f_1}(\mathrm{ray}_{q_1}(y_1)),\ldots,\mu_{f_n}(\mathrm{ray}_{q_n}(y_n))) ,$$

analogous to the Probability Logic case.

On the other hand, eq. (i) does not in general carry over here. Also, since probability logic is not truth functional, Lebesgue-Stieltjes logic is not also, at the Borel set level - even over cartesian products of Borel sets.

Of course, all evaluations for any $\mu_f \in \hat{\mathcal{SBV}}_q$, e.g., may be carried out by use of the minimal decomposition

$$f = (f)^+ - (f)^-$$

$(f)^+$, $(f)^-$ being strong BV PM g.c.d.'s. Thus, for any $B \in \mathbb{B}_q$,

$$\mu_f(B) = \mu_{(f)^+}(B) - \mu_{(f)^-}(B) ,$$

etc.

Analogous to the Probability Logic case, define also $+_{\phi_{or}}$.

Again, as in the Probability Logic case, it follows immediately that $\mathbb{C}$, $\times_{\phi_\&}$, $+_{\phi_\&}$ (at both the left ray and, more generally, Borel σ-algebra level) are unambiguously well-defined eneralized complements, cartesian products and sums, i.e., symmetric, associative, min bounded above for $\times_{\phi_\&}$, max bounded below for $+_{\phi_\&}$ and having marginal properties w.r.t. unity and zero, respectively.

Define also for $\mathcal{C}\mathcal{F}\mathcal{B}\mathcal{V}_q$, e.g., generalized cartesian products distributive-wise, analogous to the Probability Logic case, except that $1(q)$ is replacable by a more general constant $c(q)$. Thus (noting again, $c = 0$ reduces to the pure measure situation) for any

$\mu_{f_1} \pm c_1 \in \mathcal{C}\mathcal{F}\mathcal{B}\mathcal{V}_q$ and $\mu_{f_2} \pm c_2 \in \mathcal{C}\mathcal{F}\mathcal{B}\mathcal{V}_r$,

$$(\mu_{f_1} \pm c_1) \times_{\phi_\&} (\mu_{f_2} \pm c_2)$$
$$= \mu_{f_1} \times_{\phi_\&} \mu_{f_2} \pm c_1(q) \times_{\phi_\&} \mu_{f_2} \pm \mu_{f_1} \times_{\phi_\&} c_2(r) + c_1(q) \cdot c_2(r)$$
$$= \mu_{f_1 \times_{\phi_\&} f_2} \pm \mu_{c_1(q) \times_{\phi_\&} f_2} \pm \mu_{f_1 \times_{\phi_\&} c_2(r)} + c_1(q) \cdot c_2(r) ,$$

Similar expansion definitions hold for $\mathbb{C}$ and $+_{\phi_{or}}$, so that again arbitrary finite strings of $\text{comb}(\mathbb{C}, \times_{\phi_\&}, +_{\phi_{or}})$ may be defined unambiguously upon those μ_f's $\in \mathcal{F}\mathcal{B}\mathcal{V}_q$'s yielding cartesian products in some $\mathcal{C}_n$.

For example for any g.c.d., f and g , the following DeMorgan and modular property of $+$ and $\times$ hold:

$$\begin{aligned} \mu_f + \mu_g &\overset{d}{=} 1 - (1 - \mu_f) \times_{\phi_\&} (1 - \mu_g) \\ &= 1 - (1 - \mu_f \times 1 - 1 \times \mu_g + \mu_f \times \mu_g) \\ &= \mu_f \times 1 + 1 \times \mu_g - \mu_f \times \mu_g \\ &= \mu_{f+g} , \end{aligned}$$

where ϕ_{or} may be chosen modular and DeMorgan w.r.t. $\phi_\&$: For all $x,y \in [0,1]$,

$$\begin{aligned} (f + g)(x,y) &= \phi_{or}(f(x),g(y)) \\ &= f(x) + g(y) - \phi_\&(f(x),g(y)) , \end{aligned}$$

i.e., $\mathcal{F} = (\phi_{not}, \phi_\&, \phi_{or})$ is Frankian (see 2.3.6), as in the probability logic development.

As a check on the associativity and symmetry of $\dagger_{or}$, note that, e.g.,

$$\begin{aligned}\mu_f \dagger (\mu_g \dagger \mu_h) &= 1 - ((1 - \mu_f) \times (1 -(\mu_g \dagger \mu_h)))\\ &= 1 - (1 - \mu_f) \times (1 - \mu_g) \times (1 - \mu_h)\\ &= (\mu_f \dagger \mu_g) \dagger \mu_h .\end{aligned}$$

Returning to marginal measures, let $f_j \in \mathrm{SBV}_{q_j} \cap [0,1]^{\mathbb{R}^{q_j}}$, $j = 1,\ldots,n$. Suppose also that each f_j is *normable*, i.e., there exists $x_j^{(0)} \in \mathbb{R}^{q_j} \cup \{+\infty 1_{\sim a_j}\}$ such that

$1 = f_j(x_j^{(0)}) = \sup_{x_j \in \mathbb{R}^{q_j}} f_j(x_j)$; $j = 1,\ldots,n$.

Then for any $\emptyset \neq C \subseteq \{1,\ldots,n\}$, the C-marginals $(f_1 \times \cdot\cdot \times f_n)_C : \mathbb{R}^{q_j} \to [0,1]$ are all well-defined strong BV g.d.f. functions, where $q_C = \sum_{j \in C} q_j$ and where

$$(f_1 \times \cdot\cdot \times f_n)_C = \times_{j \in C} f_j .$$

In turn, these induce (via Theorems 6, 7, and Corollary 1) complete regular countably additive signed measures extending the corresponding interval functions generated by the increments, $\mu_{f_j} : \mathbb{B}_{q_j} \to [0,1]$, $j = 1,\ldots,q_j$, $\mu_{f_1 \times \cdot\cdot \times f_n} : \mathbb{B}_q \to \mathbb{R}$, $\mu_{(f_1 \times \cdot\cdot \times f_n)_C} : \mathbb{B}_{q_C} \to \mathbb{R}$, for all $\emptyset \neq C \subseteq \{1,\ldots,n\}$. In addition, define the C-marginal measure $(\mu_{f_1 \times \cdot\cdot \times f_n})_C : \mathbb{B}_{q_C} \to \mathbb{R}$, by uniquely extending the definition over right closed $q - C$ rays $\mathrm{ray}_q(y)$, $y = (y_j)_{j \in C} \in \mathbb{R}^{q_C}$,

$$\begin{aligned}&(\mu_{f_1 \times \cdot\cdot \times f_n})_C(\mathrm{ray}_q(y))\\ &\overset{d}{=} \mu_{f_1 \times \cdot\cdot \times f_n}\left(\times_{j=1}^{n} (-\infty, z_j]\right) ,\end{aligned}$$

where

$$z_j = \begin{cases} x_i^{(0)} , & \text{if } j \in \{1,\ldots,n\} \dashv C \\ y_j , & \text{if } j \in C \end{cases} ,$$

$$= (f_1 \times \cdot\cdot \times f_n)(z_1,\ldots,z_n)$$

$$= \underset{j\in C}{\times} f_j(y_j)$$
$$= (f_1\times\cdot\cdot\times f_n)_C(y) \ .$$

Hence, for all $\emptyset \neq C \subseteq \{1,\ldots,n\}$

$$(\mu_{f_1\times\cdot\cdot\times f_n})_C = \mu_{(f_1\times\cdot\cdot\times f_n)_C} = \underset{j\in C}{\times} f_j \ .$$

Let us call this condition, *marginal consistency*.

For given $\phi_\&$, marginals $\mu_{f_1},\ldots,\mu_{f_n}$ are thus $\phi_\&$-*independent* or *non-interactive* w.r.t. *joint measure* $\mu_{f_1\times_{\phi_\&}\cdot\cdot\times_{\phi_\&} f_n}$.

More generally, if $f \in \mathrm{SBV}_q \cap [0,1]^{\mathbb{R}^q}$ is normable with $\emptyset \neq C \subseteq \{1,\ldots,q\}$ such that

$$\sup_{\begin{bmatrix} x_j\in\mathbb{R} , \\ j\in\{1,\ldots,q\}\dashv C\end{bmatrix}} f(x_1,\ldots,x_q) \text{ occurs for } x_j = x_j^{(0)}, \text{ all } j \in 1,\ldots q\} \dashv C ,$$

not depending on any x_j, $j \in C$, then the C-marginal function $f_C : \mathbb{R}^{\text{card } C} \to [0,1]$ exists and w.l.o.g. is a g.d.f. strong BV. This induces marginal measure $\mu_{f_C} : \mathbb{B}_{\text{card } C} \to [0,1]$ w.r.t. $\mu_f : \mathbb{B}_q \to [0,1]$. (In the case of f being a c.d.f., one can choose $x_j^{(0)} = +\infty$, $j \in C$.) Again, it follows that

$$(\mu_f)_C = \mu_{f_C} \ .$$

If $\emptyset \neq C,D \subseteq \{1,\ldots,q\}$ with $C \cap D = \emptyset$ and marginal g.d.f.'s f_C and exist, then f_C and f_D – and equivalently μ_{f_C} and μ_{f_D} w.r.t. μ_f – are said to be $\phi_\&$-independent or non-interactive w.r.t. f iff

$$f_{C\cup D} = f_C \times_{\phi_\&} f_D$$

(up to appropriate ordering of components), i.e.,

$$\mu_{f_{C\cup D}} = \mu_{f_C} \times_{\phi_\&} \mu_{f_D} ,$$

noting f_C, f_D, $f_{C\cup D}$ are all normable, since f is. Conversely, if only $f = f_C \times_{\phi_\&} f_D$ is required, f_C, f_D normable, then as in the previous development f_C and f_D are appropriate marginals,

etc.

Consider now any t-conorm (or t-co-copula) ϕ_{or} . Since sup is a special case of ϕ_{or} , the following extends the previous concepts for marginals: Let $G^q \subset \mathbb{R}^q$ be at most countable. Let $f : G^q \to [0,1]$ be a strong BV g.d.f.

Again, let $\emptyset \neq C \subseteq \{1,...q\}$ be given. Define the C-ϕ_{or}-projection, $proj(\phi_{or})_C(f) : G^{card\ C} \to [0,1]$ for a given truth functional system $(\phi_{not}, \phi_\&, \phi_{or})$

$$proj(\phi_{or})_C(f)((x_j)_{j\in C}) = \underset{\begin{bmatrix} x_j \in G \\ j\in\{1,...,q\}\dashv C \end{bmatrix}}{\phi_{or}} (f(x_1,...,x_q)) ,$$

(without requiring the ϕ_{or} process to achieve its limit, independent of the remaining x_j's) . Then define for any $\emptyset \neq C,D \subseteq \{1,...,q\}$, $C \cap D = \emptyset$, $proj(\phi_{or})_C(f)$ and $proj(\phi_{or})_D(f)$ to be $\phi_{or} - \phi_\&$ independent or noninteractive w.r.t. $f_{C\cup D}$ (and similarly projection measures $\mu_{proj(\phi_{or})_C(f)}$ and $\mu_{proj(\phi_{or})_D(f)}$ w.r.t. $\mu_{f_{C\cup D}}$) , iff

$$f_{C\cup D} = proj(\phi_{or})_C(f) \times_{\phi_\&} proj(\phi_{or})_D(f) ,$$

and hence

$$\mu_{f_{C\cup D}} = \mu_{proj(\phi_{or})_C(f)} \times_{\phi_\&} \mu_{proj(\phi_{or})_D}(f) .$$

A natural question to ask here is what is the analogue of the marginal consistency relation? Suppose f is normable. Then since $\phi_{or} \geq max$ pointwise, it follows that $proj(\phi_{or})_C(f)$ and $proj(\phi_{or})_D(f)$ are normable. Suppose also that $\phi_\&$ is right distributive over ϕ_{or} . (Examples of this include (min,max) and (prod,max).) Then it follows that,

$$\begin{aligned} &proj(\phi_{or})_C(f_{C\cup D})(x) \\ &= \phi_\&(proj(\phi_{or})_C(f), \underset{y\in G_D}{\phi_{or}} (proj(\phi_{or})_D(f)(y))) \\ &= \phi_\&(proj(\phi_{or})_C(f) , 1) \\ &= proj(\phi_{or})_C(f) . \end{aligned}$$

A similar projection consistency relation holds for $proj(\phi_{or})_D(f)$.

Note the relationship between truth functionality and $\phi_\&$-independence: Even when f_C and f_D are $\phi_\&$-independent w.r.t.

$f_{C\cup D}$, e.g., truth functionality still does not hold for $\mu_{f_{C\cup D}}$ relative to μ_{f_C} and μ_{f_D} in general, unless $\phi_\&$ = prod, in which case (for Probability Logic) statistical independence and $\phi_\&$-independence coincide.

More generally, for a given logical system $(\mathbb{C},\times,\dagger)$, define projection by, for f and C as above,

$$\mathrm{proj}(\dagger)_C(f)((x_j)_{j\in C}) = \underset{\begin{bmatrix} x_j\in G \\ j\in\{1,\ldots,q\}\dashv C\end{bmatrix}}{\dagger} f(x_1,\ldots,x_q) \ ,$$

completely analogous to the truth functional case.

Conditioning

Recall that if X and Y are any sets and $f : X\times Y \to [0,1]$, $g : Y \to [0,1]$ with f dominated by g pointwise, i.e.,

$$f(x,y) \le g(y) \ ; \ \text{all} \ x\in X \ , \ y\in Y \ ,$$

and $\phi_\&$ is a given continuous t-norm, by the Darboux Theorem there is a class of functions $\{f_Y(\cdot|y)_{\phi_\&} \mid f_Y(\cdot|y)_{\phi_\&} : X \to [0,1] \ , \ y\in Y\}$ such that

$$f(x,y) = \phi_\&(f_Y(x|y) \ , \ g(y)) \ ; \ \text{all} \ x\in X \ , \ y\in Y \ .$$

If $\phi_\&$ is strict Archimedean , then for each $y\in Y$, $f_Y(\cdot|y)_{\phi_\&}$ will be uniquely determined. Each $f_Y(\cdot|y)_{\phi_\&}$ is called the *conditional dispersion* of f given y w.r.t. $\phi_\&$. This result is related to the Radon-Nikodym Theorem. Indeed, if now $X = \mathbb{R}^q$, $Y = \mathbb{R}^r$ with $f \in \mathbb{S}BV_q \cup [0,1]^{\mathbb{R}^q}$, $g \in \mathbb{S}BV_r \cup [0,1]^{\mathbb{R}^r}$, consider $\mu_f : \mathbb{B}_q \to [0,1]$ and $\mu_g : \mathbb{B}_r \to [0,1]$, the associated Lebesgue-Stieltjes measures. In particular, one could have here $g = \mathrm{proj}_Y(\phi_{or})(f)$ (changing notation) since

$$\begin{aligned} g(y) = \mathrm{proj}_Y(\phi_{or})(f)(y) &= \underset{\text{all } x\in X}{\phi_{or}} (f(x,y)) \\ &\ge \max_{\text{all } x\in X} f(x,y) \\ &\ge f(x,y) \ , \ \text{all} \ x\in X \ , \ y\in Y \ . \end{aligned}$$

Assuming all $f(\cdot|y) \in \mathbb{S}BV_q \cap [0,1]^{\mathbb{R}^q}$, $y \in \mathbb{R}^r$ and $g \in \mathbb{S}BV_r \cap [0,1]^{\mathbb{R}^r}$, then $\mu_f : \mathbb{B}_q \to [0,1]$ and $\mu_{f(\cdot|y)} : \mathbb{B}_r \to [0,1]$ exist. Thus, for all $x \in \mathbb{R}^q$, $y \in \mathbb{R}^r$

$$\begin{aligned}
&(\mu_{f(\cdot|y)_{\phi_\&}} \times_{\phi_\&} \mu_g)(ray_q(x) \times ray_r(y)) \\
&= (f_Y(\cdot|y)_{\phi_\&} \times_{\phi_\&} g)(x,y) \\
&= \phi_\&(f_Y(x|y)_{\phi_\&}, g(Y)) \\
&= f(x,y) \\
&= \mu_f(ray_q(x) \times ray_r(Y)) ,
\end{aligned}$$

and hence for all $g : \mathbb{R}^{q+r} \to \mathbb{R}$ measurable,

$$\int_{x,y\in\mathbb{R}^{q+r}} h(x,y)\, d\mu_f(x,y) = \int_{x,y\in\mathbb{R}^{q+r}} h(x,y) d(\mu_{f_Y(\cdot|y)_{\phi_\&}} \times_{\phi_\&} \mu_g)(x,y) .$$

If in particular $\mu_f(B,\cdot)$ is absolutely continuous w.r.t $\mu_g(\cdot)$, i.e.,
$\mu_f(B \times C) \le \mu_g(C)$; all $B \in \mathbb{B}_q$, $C \in \mathbb{B}_r$, then by the Radon-Nikodym Theorem, up to μ_g-measure zero,

$$d\mu_f(x,y) \equiv \frac{d\mu_f(x,y)}{d\mu_g(y)} \cdot d\mu_g(y) ,$$

noting that the conditional - Radon-Nikodym derivative $\frac{d\mu_f(x,y)}{d\mu_d(y)}$ can be identified with $\mu_{f_Y(\cdot|y)_{\phi_\&}}$ when $\phi_\& = \text{prod}$.

For example, if f is a c.d.f. with $g = proj_Y(\phi_{or})(f)$, then g and f will satisfy the above conditions.

Bayes' theorem

Fix a truth functional system $\mathcal{F} = (\phi_{not}, \phi_\&, \phi_{or})$.

Let, for all $x \in X$, $f(\cdot|x) : \mathbb{R}^r \to [0,1]$ in $\mathbb{S}BV_r$ be given, using conditioning notation, interpreted as the *conditional data* (y) *g.d.f.* and $g : \mathbb{R}^q \to [0,1]$ in $\mathbb{S}BV_q$ given, interpreted as the *prior parameter* (x) *g.d.f.* Then as a converse to the previous development form *joint parameter and data* (x,y) *g.d.f.*,

$f : \mathbb{R}^{q+r} \to [0,1]$, where for all $x \in \mathbb{R}^q$, $y \in \mathbb{R}^r$

$$f(x,y) \overset{d}{=} \phi_\&(g(x), f(y|x)) .$$

Under reasonable conditions (see, e.g., Theorem 12),

$$f : \mathbb{R}^{q+r} \to [0,1] \in \mathrm{SBV}_r .$$

Analogous to the previous result, if $f(\cdot|x)$ is normable for all $x \in X$ and $\phi_\&$ is right distributive over ϕ_{or} then projection consistency holds for g w.r.t. f . Call this *condition star* (*).

In any case, determine $\mathrm{proj}_Y(\phi_{or})(f) : \mathbb{R}^r \to [0,1]$, the *averaged data* g.d.f. and finally $f(\cdot|y) : \mathbb{R}^q \to [0,1]$, the *posterior* g.d.f. implicitly via the relation

$\phi_\&(g(x), f(y|x)) = f(x,y) = \phi_\&(f(x|y), \mathrm{proj}_Y(\phi_{or})(f))$, for all $x \in \mathbb{R}^q$, $y \in \mathbb{R}^r$.

As usual, these relations may be lifted to the corresponding Lebesgue-Stieltjes measure level over the appropriate Borel σ-algebras.

Under the condition (*) , assumptions for $\phi_\&$, ϕ_{or} and g.d.f.'s involved, essentially all (implicit form) analogues of conditional Probability Logic calculus extend to the situation here. For example, using abridged notation, the following hold:

For all variables x , y , z , and $f : \mathbb{R}^{p+q+r} \to [0,1]$, SBV g.c.d.:

(1) $f(x,z,y) = \phi_\&(f(x,z|y),f(y))$.

Fixing y ,

(2) $f(x,z|y) = \phi_\&(f((x|z)|y), f(z|y))$.

Substituting (2) into (1)) ,

(3) $f(x,z,y) = \phi_\&(f((x|z)|y), f(z|y),f(y))$

Projecting out z (using condition (*) yields

$$f(x,y) = \phi_\&(f(z|y),f(y)) ,$$

so that $f(z|y)$ is consistently defined, and hence (3) becomes

$$f(x,z,y) = \phi_\&(f((x|z)|y) , f(z,y)) ,$$

whence we may identify

$$f((x|z)|y) = f(x|z,y) .$$

Also, we may always identify

$$f(x,z|y) = f((x|y),(z|y)) .$$

Thus, eq.(2) becomes

$$(4) \quad f((x|y),(z|y)) = \phi_{\&}(f(x|z,y) , f(z|y))$$
$$= \phi_{\&}(f((x|y)|(z|y)) , f(z|y)) .$$

Hence, we may identify,

$$f(x|z,y) = f((x|y)|(z|y)) ,$$

the analogue of the well-known classical Bayesian sequential "learning" equation.

Again, the Lebesgue-Stieltjes measure extensions of these results should be mentioned.

Quantifications carry over to this example as in the general situation with little change in forms. (See below.)

It follows from the previous results, given any truth functional copula system $\mathcal{F} = (\phi_{not}, \phi_{\&}, \phi_{or})$, the resulting Probability Logic (PL) may be identified with the class $DPL_{\mathcal{F}}$ of all well-formed strings over all c.d.f's $f_1,\ldots,f_n$, i.e., all

$$comb(C,\times_{\phi_{\&}},\dagger_{\phi_{or}})(f_1,\ldots,f_n)$$

extending uniquely to the class $PL_{\mathcal{F}}$ of all well formed strings over probability measures $\mu_{f_1},\ldots,\mu_{f_n}$, i.e., all

$comb(C,\times_{\phi_{\&}},\dagger_{\phi_{or}})(\mu_{f_1},\ldots,\mu_{f_n})$, which can be further evaluated using previous results.

Quantifiers.

Let Z be a given space called the *base population*. Let X and Y be two other spaces called the *X-attribute* and *Y-attribute* spaces, and form X × Y the *joint attribute* space.

Let $h_X : Z \to X$ and $h_Y : Z \to Y$ be measurement functions. Thus, e.g., Z = set of all Australians living in June, 1933, h_X = ht (in feet), h_Y = wt (in lbs.), X = [0,10] (in feet), Y = [0,2000] (in lbs).

We wish to symbolize for two particular attributes $B \in \mathcal{F}(X)$, $C \in \mathcal{F}(Y)$

‖<quantification (for Z having B given C)>‖ .

Let $\mathbb{Q}(Z)$ represent the class of all *discrete* probability functions over Z (including deficient ones).

Let $A \in \mathcal{F}(X \times Y)$ represent a binary compound attribute of X × Y and consider $proj_Y(A) \in \mathcal{F}(Y)$.

Define also, for some fixed weighting-function $p \in \mathbf{Q}(Z)$, corresponding to $\phi^{-1}(p) \in \mathcal{F}(Z)$,

$$C_1(A) = \underset{z \in Z}{\dagger} ((h_X, h_Y)^{-1}(A) \cap \phi^{-1}(p))$$

$$C_2(A) \overset{d}{=} \underset{z \in Z}{\dagger} (h_Y^{-1}(\mathrm{proj}_Y(A)) \cap \phi^{-1}(p)) .$$

Since $C_2(A)$ can be written

$$C_2(A) = \underset{z \in Z}{\dagger} ((h_X, h_Y)^{-1}(X \times \mathrm{proj}_Y(A)) \cap \phi^{-1}(p))$$

and

$$\begin{aligned} \phi_{X \times \mathrm{proj}_Y(A)}(s,y) &= (\phi_X \times \underset{x \in X}{\dagger} \phi_A)(s,(x)_{x \in X}) \\ &\geq (\underset{x \in X}{\dagger} \phi_A)((s,x)_{x \in X}) \\ &\geq \max_{x \in X}(\phi_A(s,x)) \\ &\geq \phi_A(s,y) \ ; \text{ all } \ s \in X \ , \ y \in Y \end{aligned}$$

then

$$\begin{aligned} &\phi_{(h_{X_1}, h_Y)^{-1}(X \times \mathrm{proj}_Y(A))}(z_1, z_2) \\ &\quad = \phi_{X \times \mathrm{proj}_Y(A))}(h_X(z_1), h_Y(z_2)) \\ &\quad \geq \phi_A(h_X(z_1), h_Y(z_2)) \\ &\quad = \phi_{(h_X, h_Y)^{-1}(A)}(z_1, z_2) . \end{aligned}$$

Assuming $\cap \phi^{-1}(p)$ and $\underset{z \in Z}{\dagger}(\cdot)$ preserve the above inequality, it follows that $\phi_{C_1(A)} \leq \phi_{C_2(A)}$ pointwise.

Hence, $(C_1(A) \mid C_2(A))$ exists, where

$$\phi_{C_1(A)}(u,v) = \phi_\&(\phi_{(C_1(A) \mid C_2(A))}(u) \ , \ \phi_{C_2(A)}(v)) \ ; \text{ all } \ u,v \in [0,1] .$$

Now the class of all quantifiers such as "most", "some", "all", "at least one", "none", "about 3/4", "sometimes", "6/7", etc. may be identified with $\mathcal{F}(H)$, and for any quant $\in \mathcal{F}(H)$ with $\phi_{quant} \in \mathcal{F}(H)$, and any $B \in \mathcal{F}(W)$, it is assumed $\mathrm{quant}(B) \in \mathcal{F}(W)$ also with

$$\phi_{quant(B)} = \phi_{quant} \circ \phi_B .$$

Thus, letting $\hat{z} = (z,z)_{z\in Z}$, form

$$\|(\hat{z} \in \text{quant}(C_1(A)|C_2(A)))\|$$

$$= \phi_{\text{quant}(\phi(C_1(A))|C_2(A))}(\hat{z})) \ .$$

$$= \|(\text{quant of } \hat{z} \text{ (population) w.r.t } C_2(A) \text{ have } c_1(A))\| \ .$$

To indicate the restriction of all c.d.f.'s to a fixed $\mathbb{R}^q$, e.g., we use the notation $DPL_{\mathcal{F},q}$.

Lebesgue-Stieltjes Logic (LSL) includes Probability Logic as a special case and centers about the development of the class $DLSL_{\mathcal{F}}$ of all well-formed strings over all g.d.f.'s $f_1,...,f_n$, i.e., all

$$\text{comb}(C,\times_{\phi_\&},\dagger_{\phi_{or}})(f_1,..,f_n) \ ,$$

which induces a corresponding class $LSL_{\mathcal{F}}$ of Lebesgue-Stieltjes measures

$$\mu_{\text{comb}(C,\times_{\phi_\&},\dagger_{\phi_{or}})(f_1,...,f_n)}$$

$$\stackrel{d}{=} \text{comb}(C,\times_{\phi_\&},\dagger_{\phi_{or}})(\mu_{f_1},...\mu_{f_n}) \ ,$$

for a large class of such g.d.f.'s. Furthermore, the restriction of $f_1,...,f_n$ to be also SBV and/or to have ranges in $[0,1]$, carries over to the corresponding measures. (For example, Corollary 2 (Appendix) states that $f_1,...,f_n$ g.d.f. SBV implies $\mu_{f_1},...,\mu_{f_n}$ are finite.).

Note that when $f_1,...,f_n$ are restricted to have ranges in $[0,1]$, then any string will also have range in $[0,1]$, for either Probability Logic or Lebesgue-Stieltjes Logic. In either case, using the fundamental membership function ϕ , we can bijectively assign attribute A_j to f_j :

$$A_j \stackrel{d}{=} \phi^{-1}(f_j) \in \mathcal{F}(\mathbb{R}^{q_j}) \leftrightarrow (f_j : \mathbb{R}^{q_j} \to [0,1]) \ ,$$

so that

$f_j = \phi_{A_j}$, $j = 1, ..., n$, say, and define attribute

$$\text{comb}(C,\times_{\phi_\&},\dagger_{\phi_{or}})(A_1,...,A_n) \in \mathcal{F}(\mathbb{R}^{q_1+\cdots+q_n}) \ ,$$

by

$$\phi_{\text{comb}(C,\times_{\phi_\&},\dagger_{\phi_{or}})(A_1,...,A_n)}$$

$$= \text{comb}(C,\times_{\phi_\&},\dagger_{\phi_{or}})(f_1,...,f_n) \ ,$$

with truth evaluation, for any $y_j \in \mathbb{R}^{q_j}$, $j = 1,\ldots,n$,

$$\| \langle (y_j)_{j=1,\ldots,n} \in \mathrm{comb}(C,\times_{\phi_\&},\dagger_{\phi_{or}})(A_1,\ldots,A_n) \rangle \|$$

$$= \phi_{\mathrm{comb}(C,\times_{\phi_\&},\dagger_{\phi_{or}})(A_1,\ldots,A_n)}(y_1,\ldots,y_n) \in [0,1] .$$

A similar procedure may be carried out at the Borel σ-algebra level. Thus, for any $B_j \in \mathbb{B}_{q_j}$, $j = 1,\ldots,n$, with $f_1,\ldots,f_n$ c.d.f.'s, now letting attribute $\mathcal{A}_j$ correspond uniquely to μ_{f_j}:

$$\mathcal{A}_j = \phi^{-1}(\mu_{f_j}) \in \mathcal{G}(\mathbb{B}_{q_j}) \longleftrightarrow (\mu_{f_j} : \mathbb{B}_{q_j} \to [0,1]) , \quad j = 1,\ldots,n ,$$

$$\| \langle (B_j)_{j=1,\ldots,n} \in \mathrm{comb}(C,\times_{\phi_\&},\dagger_{\phi_{or}})(\mathcal{A}_1,\ldots,\mathcal{A}_n) \rangle \|$$

$$= \phi_{\mathrm{comb}(C,\times_{\phi_\&},\dagger_{\phi_{or}})(\mathcal{A}_1,\ldots,\mathcal{A}_n)}(B_1,\ldots,B_n)$$

$$= \mathrm{comb}(C,\times_{\phi_\&},\dagger_{\phi_{or}})(\mu_{f_1},\ldots,\mu_{f_n})(B_1,\ldots,B_n) \in [0,1] .$$

This symbolization allows a natural setting in extending classical set relations and definitions to attribute forms. Definitions for generalized unions $\cup$, intersections $\cap$, subset relations $\subseteq$, incidence relations $\mathcal{A}$ and functional transforms $\hat{\hat{f}}$ may all be motivated by this structure, even though the logics involved are strictly not truth functional. The latter condition only limits the full evaluatoin of $\times$ and $\dagger$ in terms of marginal components. Instead, evaluation of all relevant joint c.d.f.'s or measures must be determined.

Discrete spaces

If in all of the previous development, either $\mathbb{R}^q$'s are replaced everywhere by discrete subspaces or all relevant functions are restricted to be purely step functions, then the results specialize appropriately. PL is thus not only generated by strings over $\mathbb{D}'_q$ (the prime from here on will indicate appropriate restriction to a discrete subspace $X^{(q)}$ of $\mathbb{R}^q$, etc.) but also, equivalently by strings over $\mathbb{Q}'_q$, where

$$\mathbb{Q}'_q = \{h \mid h \text{ is an ordinary or deficient probability function over } X^{(q)}, \text{ i.e., } h \in [0,1]^{X^{(q)}} \text{ with } \sum_{x \in X^{(q)}} h(x) \le 1\} .$$

Thus,

$$\mathbb{Q}'_q = \{\mu_f(\{\cdot\}) \mid f \in \mathbb{D}'_q \text{ (including deficient c.d.f.'s)}\}, \text{etc.}$$

Attribute-events (This extends Zadeh's concept of fuzzy events [285].)

For any $f \in \mathbb{BV}_q \cap [0,1]^{\mathbb{R}^q}$, and $B \in \mathbb{B}_q$, as we have seen

$\mu_f(B) = \int_{x \in \mathbb{R}^q} \phi_B(x) df(X)$ is the μ_f-measure of B.

In turn, for any attribute $A \in \mathcal{F}(\mathbb{R}^q)$ with $\phi_A \in \mathbb{F}_q$, we may define

$$\mu_f(A) \overset{d}{=} \int_{x \in \mathbb{R}^q} \phi_A(x) df(x) .$$

Thus, the first extension of $\mathbb{BV}_q \cap [0,1]^{\mathbb{R}^q}$ and its class of strings $DLSL_{\mathcal{F}}$ over points in $\mathbb{R}^q$, to $LSL_{\mathcal{F}}$ over Borel sets in $\mathbb{B}_q$ may be once more extended in its domain to "Borel" attributes as above.

Also note that if $B \in \mathbb{R}^q$ is a finite set, then ϕ_B induces μ_{ϕ_B} which is equivalent to 0.

Appendix to 2.3.9.B Functions of Bounded Variation in $\mathbb{R}^q$

The partial order $\leq$ over $\mathbb{R}^q$ is defined by, for all $y = \begin{bmatrix} y_1 \\ \vdots \\ y_q \end{bmatrix}$

$x = \begin{bmatrix} x_1 \\ \vdots \\ x_q \end{bmatrix} \in \mathbb{R}^q$, $x \leq y$ iff $x_j \leq y_j$, for $j = 1,\ldots,q$.

For any $x,y \in \mathbb{R}^q$ such that $x \leq y$, define the corresponding closed q-interval $J(x,y)$ by

$$J(x,y) = \{v \mid v \in \mathbb{R}^q \ \& \ x \leq v \leq y\} = \mathop{\times}_{j=1}^{q} [x_j,y_j] ,$$

noting

$$J(x,y) = [x,y] , \text{ for } x,y \in \mathbb{R}$$

and for $x \leq y$,

$$J(x\cdot \underset{\sim}{1}_q , y\cdot \underset{\sim}{1}_q) = [x,y]\times\cdots\times[x,y] = [x,y]^q .$$

Also, define for any $x = \begin{bmatrix} x_1 \\ \vdots \\ x_q \end{bmatrix}$, $y = \begin{bmatrix} y_1 \\ \vdots \\ y_q \end{bmatrix} \in \mathbb{R}^q$,

$$x \wedge y \stackrel{d}{=} \begin{bmatrix} x_1 \wedge y_1 \\ \vdots \\ x_q \wedge y_q \end{bmatrix} , \quad x \vee y = \begin{bmatrix} x_1 \vee y_1 \\ \vdots \\ x_q \vee y_q \end{bmatrix} ,$$

$$x_j \wedge y_j = \min(x_j,y_j) , \quad x_j \vee y_j \stackrel{d}{=} \max(x_j,y_j) \ ; \ j = 1,2,\ldots,q .$$

Then

$$\mathfrak{J}(x,y) \stackrel{d}{=} J(x\wedge y, x\vee y) .$$

Hence

$$\mathfrak{J}(\underset{\sim}{0}_q,x) = J(\underset{\sim}{0}_q,x) , \text{ if } x \geq \underset{\sim}{0}_q ,$$

$$\mathfrak{J}(\underset{\sim}{0}_q,x) = J(x,\underset{\sim}{0}_q) , \text{ if } x \leq \underset{\sim}{0}_q .$$

For $f : \mathbb{R} \to \mathbb{R}$, define for any $x \leq y \in \mathbb{R}$, the *first difference*

$$\Delta_1(f,J(x,y)) \stackrel{d}{=} f(y) - f(x) .$$

For $f : \mathbb{R}^2 \to \mathbb{R}$ define for any

$$x = \begin{bmatrix} x_1 \\ x_2 \end{bmatrix} \leq y = \begin{bmatrix} y_1 \\ y_2 \end{bmatrix} \in \mathbb{R}^2 ,$$

the *second difference*

$$\begin{aligned}\Delta_2(f,J(x,y)) &= \Delta_1(\Delta_1(f(\cdot,x_2) , J(x_1,y_1)) , J(x_2,y_2)) \\ &= f(x_1 ,x_2) - f(y_1,x_2) - f(x_1,y_2) + f(y_1,y_2)\end{aligned}$$

In general, for $f : \mathbb{R}^q \to \mathbb{R}$, and

$$x = \begin{bmatrix} x_1 \\ \vdots \\ x_q \end{bmatrix} \leq y = \begin{bmatrix} y_1 \\ \vdots \\ y_q \end{bmatrix} \in \mathbb{R}^q ,$$ the qth *difference*

$$\Delta_q(f,J(x,y)) \overset{d}{=} \Delta_1(\Delta_{q-1}(f(\cdot,x_q), J(\begin{bmatrix} x_1 \\ \vdots \\ x_{q-1} \end{bmatrix} , \begin{bmatrix} y_1 \\ \vdots \\ y_{q-1} \end{bmatrix})) , J(x_q,y_q))$$

$$= \sum_{j=0}^{q} (-1)^{q-j} \cdot \sum_{\begin{bmatrix}\theta_1,\ldots,\theta_q \in \{0,1\}, \\ \theta_1+\ldots+\theta_q = j\end{bmatrix}} f(x_1 + \theta_1\cdot(y_1-x_1),\ldots,x_q + \theta_q\cdot(y_q-x_q)) .$$

Let $J(x_j,y_j)$, $j = 1,\ldots,m$, be m disjoint or contiguous closed q-intervals and region $K \overset{d}{=} \bigcup_{i=1}^{m} J(x_j,y_j)$. Let $\mathcal{Q}$ be any partitioning of K , where each $J(x_j,y_j)$ is partitioned into disjoint or contiguous q-sub-intervals. Define the *variation of f over K w.r.t.* $\mathcal{Q}$ as

$$Vr(f,K,\mathcal{Q}) \overset{d}{=} \sum_{J(u,v)\in\mathcal{Q}} | \Delta_q(f,J(u,v))|$$

and the *total variation of f over K* as

$$Vr(f,K) \overset{d}{=} \sup_{(\text{all } \mathcal{Q} \text{ over } K)} Vr(f,K,\mathcal{Q}) .$$

The total variation of f over $\mathbb{R}^{q_+}$ and $\mathbb{R}^q$ are defined, respectively, by

$$Vr(f,\mathbb{R}^{q_+}) = \lim_{t\to+\infty} Vr(f,J(\underset{\sim}{0}_q,t\cdot\underset{\sim}{1}_q))$$

$$Vr(f,\mathbb{R}^q) = \lim_{t\to+\infty} Vr(f,J(-t\cdot 1_q,t\cdot 1_q)) ,$$

etc.

$f : \mathbb{R}^q \to \mathbb{R}$ is of *bounded variation over region* $K \subseteq \mathbb{R}^q$ iff, by definition,

$$0 \le V_r(f,K) < +\infty .$$

$f : \mathbb{R}^q \to \mathbb{R}$ is of *bounded variation* (BV) iff for all bounded $K \subseteq \mathbb{R}^q$,

$$V_r(f,K) < +\infty .$$

$f : \mathbb{R}^q \to \mathbb{R}$ is of *strong bounded variation* (SBV) iff f is of bounded variation over $\mathbb{R}^q$, i.e.,

$$Vr(f,\mathbb{R}^q) < +\infty .$$

$f : \mathbb{R}^q \to \mathbb{R}$ is *nondecreasing* (ND) iff for all $x \le y \in \mathbb{R}^q$, $f(x) \le f(y)$. It follows that f is nondecreasing iff f is nondecreasing in each argument separately.

$f : \mathbb{R}^q \to \mathbb{R}$ is *positive increment monotone* (PM) iff, for $x \le y \in \mathbb{R}^q$, $\Delta_q(f,J(x,y)) \ge 0$.

Clearly, if $q = 1$, $f : \mathbb{R} \to \mathbb{R}$ is ND iff f is PM . However, for $q \ge 2$, neither property in general implies the other. For example:

If $f,g : \mathbb{R} \to \mathbb{R}$ are arbitrary, then $h : \mathbb{R}^2 \to \mathbb{R}$ defined by, for all $x,y \in \mathbb{R}$,

$$h(x,y) \stackrel{d}{=} f(x) + g(y) ,$$

is such that for all $x = \begin{bmatrix} x_1 \\ x_2 \end{bmatrix} \le y = \begin{bmatrix} y_1 \\ y_2 \end{bmatrix} \in \mathbb{R}^2$,

$$\Delta_2(h,J(x,y)) \equiv 0 ,$$

yet f and g may be chosen each, e.g., decreasing in x and y separately and hence h is not ND but rather decreasing.

On the other hand, $f : \mathbb{R}^2 \to \mathbb{R}$ given by, for all $x,y \in \mathbb{R}$,

$$f(x,y) \stackrel{d}{=} \max(0,\min(1,1-(1-x)(1-y))) ,$$

is ND , but for any $x = \begin{bmatrix} x_1 \\ x_2 \end{bmatrix} \leq y = \begin{bmatrix} y_1 \\ y_2 \end{bmatrix} \in \mathbb{R}^2$,

$$\Delta_2(f, J(x,y)) = -(y_1 - x_1)\cdot(y_2 - x_2) \ .$$

Let $f : \mathbb{R}^q \to \mathbb{R}$, $C \dot{\cup} D = \{1,2,\ldots,q\}$, with $C = \{j_1,\ldots,j_m\}$, $1 \leq j_1 < \cdots < j_m \leq q$, $1 \leq m \leq q$,

$D = \{k_1,\ldots,k_{q-m}\}$, $1 \leq k_1 < \cdots < k_{q-m} \leq q$ and $y = \begin{bmatrix} y_{k_1} \\ \vdots \\ y_{k_{q-m}} \end{bmatrix} \in \mathbb{R}^{q-m}$.

Then the (C,y)-*marginal* function $f_{C,y} : \mathbb{R}^m \to \mathbb{R}$ is defined by, for all $x = \begin{bmatrix} x_{j_1} \\ \vdots \\ x_{j_m} \end{bmatrix} \in \mathbb{R}^m$,

$$f_{C,y}(x) \stackrel{d}{=} f(\gamma(x,y)) \ ,$$

where

$$\gamma(x,y) \stackrel{d}{=} \begin{bmatrix} z_1 \\ z_2 \\ \vdots \\ z_q \end{bmatrix} \ ; \ z_i = \begin{cases} x_{j_\ell} \ , & \text{if } i = j_\ell \ , \ 1 \leq \ell \leq m \\ y_{k_t} \ , & \text{if } i = k_t \ , \ 1 \leq t \leq q-m \ . \end{cases}$$

If also, $\sup\limits_{y \in \mathbb{R}^{q-m}} (f_{C,y}) < +\infty$, occurring at some $y_o \in \mathbb{R}^{q-m} \cup \{+\infty \cdot \underset{\sim}{1}_{q-m}\}$, then $f_C = f_{(C,y_o)} : \mathbb{R}^m \to \mathbb{R}^q$ is called the Cth *marginal function* of f .

Let $f : \mathbb{R}^q \to \mathbb{R}$. Define f to be *hereditary PM iff* for all $\emptyset \neq C \subseteq \{1,\ldots,q\}$, and all $x \in \mathbb{R}^m$, $f_{C,x} : \mathbb{R}^{\mathrm{card}(C)} \to \mathbb{R}$ is PM . On the other hand, define f to be *grounded* iff for any $x = \begin{bmatrix} x_1 \\ \vdots \\ x_q \end{bmatrix} \in \mathbb{R}^q$, $f(x) = 0$, if there is at least one value x_i ; $1 \leq i \leq q$ such that $x_i = -\infty$.

Lemma 1.

Let $f : \mathbb{R}^q \to \mathbb{R}$.

(i) If f is PM and grounded, then f is hereditary PM.

(ii) Suppose f is PM. Then if either f is hereditary PM or grounded, f is also ND. In the case of f being grounded, ND, in turn, implies that $f \geq 0$.

Proof:

(i) For example, for $q = 2$, for $\Delta_2(f,J(x,y))$,

$$x = \begin{bmatrix} x_1 \\ x_2 \end{bmatrix} < y = \begin{bmatrix} y_1 \\ y_2 \end{bmatrix}, \text{ letting } x_2 \to -\infty ,$$

yields $0 \leq f_{\{1\},y_2}(y_1) - f_{\{1\},y_2}(y_2) = f(y_1,y_2) - f(x_1,y_2) - 0 + 0$.

(ii) From the definition of Δ_q , for $x \leq y \in \mathbb{R}^q$,

$$f(y) - f(x) = \sum_{\begin{bmatrix} \emptyset \subseteq C \subseteq \{1,\ldots,q\}, \\ D \overset{d}{=} \{1,\ldots,q\} \dashv C \end{bmatrix}} \Delta_{\mathrm{card}(C)} \left(f_{C,(x|C)}, J\left((x|D), (y|D)\right)\right) ,$$

$(x|C)$ indicating the restriction of x to C , etc.
Thus, hereditary PM implies ND .
If f is grounded, let

$$x = \begin{bmatrix} -\infty \\ \vdots \\ -\infty \\ x_j \\ -\infty \\ \vdots \\ -\infty \end{bmatrix} \leq y = \begin{bmatrix} x_1 \\ \vdots \\ x_{j-1} \\ y_j \\ x_{j+1} \\ \vdots \\ x_q \end{bmatrix}, \quad j = 1,2,\ldots,q .$$

Then, taking limits

$$0 \leq \Delta_q(f,J(x,y)) = f\left(\begin{bmatrix} x_1 \\ \vdots \\ x_{j-1} \\ y_j \\ x_{j+1} \\ \vdots \\ x_q \end{bmatrix}\right) - f\left(\begin{bmatrix} x_1 \\ \vdots \\ x_{j-1} \\ x_j \\ x_{j+1} \\ \vdots \\ x_q \end{bmatrix}\right) ,$$

$j = 1,2,\ldots,q$, implying f is ND .

For any $f : \mathbb{R}^q \to \mathbb{R}$ define the *total variation function*

$$\tau(f) : \mathbb{R}^q \to \mathbb{R}^+ \text{ by, for all } x = \begin{bmatrix} x_1 \\ \vdots \\ x_q \end{bmatrix} \in \mathbb{R}^q ,$$

$$\tau(f)(x) \overset{d}{=} (-1)^{\nu_q(x)} \cdot Vr(f, \tilde{J}(\underset{\sim}{0}_q, x)) ,$$

where

$$\nu_q(x) \overset{d}{=} \text{card}\,\{j \mid 1 \le j \le q \;\&\; x_j < 0\} .$$

Lemma 2

Let $f : \mathbb{R}^q \to \mathbb{R}$.

(i) If f is PM then f is BV with for all $x \le y \in \mathbb{R}^q$,

$$\begin{aligned} Vr(f,J(x,y)) &= Vr(\tau(f),J(x,y)) \\ &= \Delta_q(f,J(x,y)) \\ &= \Delta_q(\tau(f),J(x,y)) . \end{aligned}$$

(ii) If f is BV , then for all $x \le y \in \mathbb{R}^q$,

$$\begin{aligned} Vr(f,J(x,y)) &= Vr(\tau(f),J(x,y)) \\ &= \Delta_q(\tau(f),J(x,y)) , \\ &\ge |\Delta_q(f,J(x,y))| , \end{aligned}$$

and hence $\tau(f)$ is PM . In addition, $Vr(f,J(x,y))$ as a function of intervals $J(x,y) \subseteq \mathbb{R}^q$ is finitely additive.

(iii) If f is PM and grounded, then for all $x \in \mathbb{R}^q$,

$$Vr(f,J(-\infty \underset{\sim}{1}_q ,x)) = \Delta_q(f,J(-\infty \underset{\sim}{1}_q,x)) = f(x) .$$

Theorem 1 (McShane, [174], p. 250)

(i) Let $f : \mathbb{R}^q \to \mathbb{R}$ be BV . Then there exist $(f)^+,(f)^- : \mathbb{R}^q \to \mathbb{R}$, PM such that

$$f = (f)^+ - (f)^-$$

is a minimal decomposition, i.e., for all such possible representations, $(f)^+$ and $(f)^-$ have minimal total variation. $(f)^+$ and $(f)^-$ may be defined by

$$(f)^+ = \frac{1}{2}(\tau(f)+f) \ ; \ (f)^- = \frac{1}{2}(\tau(f)-f) \ ,$$

Thus,

$$\tau(f) = (f)^+ + (f)^- \ .$$

Also, for all $x \leq y \in \mathbb{R}^q$,

$$\begin{aligned} +\infty > Vr(f,J(x,y)) &= Vr(\tau(f),J(x,y)) \\ &= Vr((f)^+,J(x,y)) + Vr((f)^-, - J(x,y)) \\ &= \Delta_q((f)^+,J(x,y)) + \Delta_q((f)^-,J(x,y)) = \Delta_q(\tau(f),J(x,y)) \ . \end{aligned}$$

If also $(f)^+,(f)^-$ are grounded - and hence f is grounded then for all $y \in \mathbb{R}^q$,

$$\begin{aligned} \Delta_q(f,J(-\infty\underset{\sim}{1}_q,y)) &= \Delta_q((f)^+,J(-\infty\underset{\sim}{1}_q,y)) - \Delta_q((f)^-,J(-\infty\underset{\sim}{1}_q,y)) \\ &= (f)^+(y) - (f)^-(y) = f(y) \ . \end{aligned}$$

(ii) Conversely, if $f_1,f_2 : \mathbb{R}^q \to \mathbb{R}$ are arbitrary and PM then $f = f_1 - f_2 : \mathbb{R}^q \to \mathbb{R}$ is BV .

Remarks.

1. The identity function $id : \mathbb{R} \to \mathbb{R}$ is PM with $Vr(f,J(-t,t)) = 2t$, for all $t > 0$.

2. Let $\mathbb{Q} = \{J(x_j,y_j) \mid j = 1,\ldots,m\}$ be any collection of disjoint or contiguous closed q-intervals and $\lambda_1,\ldots,\lambda_m$ any constants. Then the step function $f = \sum_{j=1}^{m} \lambda_j \phi_{J(x_j,y_j)}$ is of BV with

$$Vr(f,[-t,t]^q) = \sum_{j=1}^{m} |\lambda_j| \cdot 2^q \ .$$

3. For any $f : \mathbb{R} \to \mathbb{R}$, if f is PM or NM (non-increasing), or a finite sum of bounded unimodal or multimodal (finite number of modes) functions, then f is BV .

Lemma 3

Let $f : \mathbb{R}^q \to \mathbb{R}$ be PM (and hence BV) and grounded (and hence by Lemma 1, ND). Then

f is bounded iff $f(+\infty\underset{\sim}{1}_q) < +\infty$ iff f is of SBV .

Proof:

If f is ND and bounded, it follows that $f(+\infty \underset{\sim}{1}_q) < +\infty$.
If $f(+\infty \underset{\sim}{1}_q) < +\infty$, then for all $t > 0$

$$\begin{aligned} Vr(f,[-t,+\infty]^q) &= \Delta_1(f, J(-t\cdot \underset{\sim}{1}_q, +\infty \underset{\sim}{1}_q)) \\ &\leq \sum_{j=o}^{q} \sum_{\begin{bmatrix}\theta_1,\ldots,\theta_q \in \{0,1\} \\ \theta_1+\cdots+\theta_q = j\end{bmatrix}} f(+\infty \underset{\sim}{1}_q) \\ &\leq \sum_{j=o}^{q} \cdot \begin{bmatrix} q \\ j \end{bmatrix} \cdot f(+\infty \underset{\sim}{1}_q) = 2^q \cdot f(+\infty \underset{\sim}{1}_q) < +\infty . \end{aligned}$$

Taking limits as $t \to +\infty$, yields f is SBV.
Finally, if f is SBV, by evaluating for $t > 0$

$$+\infty > Vr(f,[-t,+\infty]^q) = f(+\infty \underset{\sim}{1}_q) + \sum_{j=o}^{q-1} (-1)^{q-j} \cdot g_j(t) ,$$

each $g_j(t)$ is a sum of $\begin{bmatrix} a \\ j \end{bmatrix}$ terms, each of which contains at least one term of the form $f(\cdots,-t,\cdots)$, which by the grounding property of f, for t sufficiently large, is arbitrarily small. Hence, $f(+\infty \underset{\sim}{1}_q) < +\infty$.

Theorem 2 (McShane [174], pp. 125, 230) - Basic approximation I.

(i) Let $f : \mathbb{R}^q \to \mathbb{R}$ be bounded and (Borel) measurable. Then, for each $t > 0$, f is thus (Lebesgue) integrable over $[-t,t]^q$ and hence there exists a sequence of step functions and hence strong BV functions such that

$$f_{t,n} \overset{d}{=} \sum_{j=1}^{m_{t,n}} \lambda_{t,n,j} \cdot \phi_{J(x_{t,n,j}, y_{t,n,j})}$$

in $\mathbb{R}^q$, $n = 1,2,3,\ldots$.

such that the L^1-norm convergence

$$\lim_{n\to\infty} \left[\int_{x\in[-t,t]^q} |f(x) - f_{t,n}(x)|dx \right] = 0$$

holds.

(ii) Let $f : \mathbb{R}^q \to \mathbb{R}$ be integrable over $\mathbb{R}^q$. Then there is a sequence of step functions - and hence strong BV functions,

$$f_n \overset{d}{=} \sum_{j=1}^{m_n} \lambda_{nj} \cdot \phi_{J(x_{nj}, y_{nj})}$$

in $\mathbb{R}^q$, $n = 1,2,3...$, such that

$$\lim_{n\to\infty} \int_{x\in\mathbb{R}^q} | f(x) - f_n(x) | \, dx = 0 .$$

(iii) Let $f : \mathbb{R}^q \to \mathbb{R}$ be such that there is an $t_o > 0$ such that (locally) over $\mathbb{R}^q \dashv [-t_o, t_o]^q$, f is of BV . For example, f may be PM or NM over $\mathbb{R}^q \dashv [-t_o, t_o]^q$. Suppose over $[-t_o, t_o]^q$ f is bounded and measurable or integrable. Then there exists a sequence $(f_n)_{n=1,2,...}$ of BV functions $f_n : \mathbb{R}^q \to \mathbb{R}$ such that

$$\lim_{n\to\infty} \int_{x\in\mathbb{R}} | f(x) - f_n(x) | \, dx = 0 .$$

Proof: For example, if f is bounded and measurable over $[-t_o, t_o]^q$, and f is BV over $\mathbb{R}^q \dashv [-t_o, t_o]^q$, define

$$f_n = \phi_{[-t_o,t_o]^q} \cdot f_{t_o,n} + \phi_{\mathbb{R}^q \dashv [-t_o,t_o]^q} \cdot f \; ; \; n = 1,2,\ldots .$$

Remark: Result (iii) above can be modified for f assumed to be SBV, whence $(f_n)_{n=1,2...}$ becomes a sequence of SBV functions.

Let $f : \mathbb{R}^q \to \mathbb{R}$ be PM . Recall that $Vr(f,J(x,y)) = \Delta(f,J(x,y))$, as a function of closed intervals $J(x,y) \subseteq \mathbb{R}^q$ is a finitely additive non-negative interval function. Then from standard measure theory constructions (analogous, e.g., to Lebesgue measure theory), a countably additive non-negative measure μ_f extending $\Delta(f,\cdot)$ is induced over $\mathcal{S}(\mu_f, \mathbb{R}^q)$, the *class of all* μ_f*-measurable subsets* of $\mathbb{R}^q$, a σ-algebra. In addition, let $\mathcal{F}(\mu_f, \mathbb{R}^q)$ be the *class of all* μ_f*-measurable functions* g , i.e., $g^{-1}(B) \in \mathcal{S}(\mu_f, \mathbb{R}^q)$ for all $B \in \mathbb{B}_1$ and $L^1(\mu_f, B) \subseteq \mathcal{F}(\mu_f, B))$ to be the class of all μ_1*-integrable functions* over B .

Theorem 3 (McShane [174], pp. 262-263, extended)

Let $f : \mathbb{R}^q \to \mathbb{R}$ be PM (and hence BV) . Then

(i) $\mathbb{B}_q \subseteq \mathcal{I}(\mu_f, \mathbb{R}^q)$

and

(ii) $\mathbb{F}_q \subseteq \mathcal{I}(\mu_f, \mathbb{R}^q)$

(since for any $B \in \mathbb{B}_1$, and $g \in \mathbb{F}_q$, $g^{-1}(B) \in \mathbb{B}_q$ and hence $g^{-1}(B) \in \mathcal{I}(\mu_g, \mathbb{R}^q))$.

(iii) If $g = \sum_{j=1}^{n} \lambda_j \phi_{A_j}$, $A_1, \ldots, A \in \mathbb{F}_q$ with $\lambda_1, \ldots, \lambda_n$ real constants, then

$$\int_{x \in \mathbb{R}^q} g(x)df(x) = \int_{x \in \mathbb{R}^q} g(x)d\mu_f(x) = \sum_{j=1}^{n} \lambda_j \cdot \int_{x \in \mathbb{R}^q} \phi_{A_j}(x)d\mu_f(x) ,$$

$$\int_q \phi_{A_j}(x)d\mu_f(x) = \int_{x \in A_j} d\mu(x) = \mu_f(A_j) ,$$

etc.

Theorem 4 (Dominated convergence, McShane [174], p. 276)

Let $f : \mathbb{R}^q \to \mathbb{R}$ be PM. Let $g : \mathbb{R}^q \to \mathbb{R}$ be such that $g \in \mathcal{I}(\mu_f, \mathbb{R}^q)$ and g is bounded by, say, $M_o < +\infty$. (This is guaranted if $g \in \mathbb{F}_q$ and g is bounded by M_o.) Then, for any $J(u,v) \in \mathbb{R}^q$ and

$$\begin{aligned} \left| \int_{x \in J(u,v)} g(x)df(x) \right| &\le \int_{x \in J(u,v)} |g(x)|df(x) \\ &\le M_o \cdot \int_{x \in J(u,v)} df(x) \\ &= M_o \cdot \mu_f(J(u,v)) \\ &= M_o \cdot Vr(f, J(u,v)) \\ &< +\infty , \end{aligned}$$

and hence

$$g \in L^1(\mu_f, J(u,v)) .$$

Theorem 5 (McShane [174], p. 287)

Given $f : \mathbb{R}^q \to \mathbb{R}$ BV, let for any $t > 0$,

$$f = (f)^+ - (f)^-$$

be any minimal decomposition of f into $(f)^+$ and $(f)^-$ (PM).

Then f induces a complete regular countably additive, signed, measure μ_f which extends interval function

$$\Delta_q(f,\cdot) = \Delta_q((f)^+,\cdot) - \Delta_q((f)^-,\cdot) = Vr((f)^+,\cdot) - Vr((f)^-,\cdot)\ , \text{ such}$$

that

$$\mathbb{B}_q \subseteq \mathcal{S}(\mu_f,\mathbb{R}^q) = \mathcal{S}(\mu_{(f)^+},\mathbb{R}^q) \cap \mathcal{S}(\mu_{(f)^-},\mathbb{R}^q)\ ,$$

and

$$\mathbb{F}_q \subseteq \mathcal{S}(\mu_f,\mathbb{R}^q) = \mathcal{S}(\mu_{(f)^+},\mathbb{R}^q) \cap \mathcal{S}(\mu_{(f)^-},\mathbb{R}^q)\ ,$$

and for any $B \in \mathcal{S}(\mu_f,\mathbb{R}^q)$

$$L^1(\mu_f,B) = L^1(\mu_{(f)^+},B) \cap L^1(\mu_{(f)^-},B)\ ,$$

Also, for any $g \in L^1(\mu_f,B)$,

$$\int_{x\in B} g(x)d\mu_f(x) = \int_{x\in B} g(x)df(x) = \int_{x\in B} g(x)d(f)^+(x) - \int_{x\in B} g(x)d(f)^-(x)$$

is consistently defined, independent of the particular (minimal) decomposition.

Remark:

If in Theorem 5, c is any constant, $(f)^+$ may be replaced by $(f)^+ + c$ and $(f)^-$ by $(f)^- + c$, with no other changes.

Theorem 6. (McShane [174], pp. 291-292)

Let $f : \mathbb{R}^q \to \mathbb{R}$ be PM. Then there exists $\tilde{f} : \mathbb{R}^q \to \mathbb{R}$ which is PM, right continuous and grounded and hence ND and non-negative, such that

(i) $\mathcal{S}(\mu_f, \mathbb{R}^q) \subseteq \mathcal{S}(\mu_{\tilde{f}}, \mathbb{R}^q)$,

and if $B \in \mathcal{S}(\mu_f, \mathbb{R}^q)$ with $\mu_{f(B)} < +\infty$ then $\mu_f(B) = \mu_{\tilde{f}}(B)$.

(ii) For any $J(x,y) \in \mathbb{B}_o \subseteq \mathcal{S}(\mu_f, \mathbb{R}^q)$,

$$\mu_f(J(x,y)) = \mu_{\tilde{f}}(J(x,y)) = \Delta_q(f, J(x,y)) \text{ , etc.}$$

Also, as in Theorem 1,

$$\mu_{\tilde{f}}(J(-\infty \underset{\sim}{1}_q, y)) = \Delta_q(\tilde{f}, J(-\infty \underset{\sim}{1}_q, y)) = \tilde{f}(y) \text{ ,}$$

(iii) $\mathcal{S}(\mu_f, \mathbb{R}^q) \subseteq \mathcal{S}(\mu_{\tilde{f}}, \mathbb{R}^q)$,

(iv) $L^1(\mu_f, B) \subseteq L^1(\mu_{\tilde{f}}, B)$; all $B \in \mathcal{S}(\mu_f, \mathbb{R}^q)$ and if $g \in L^1(\mu_f, B)$, then

$$\int_{x \in b} g(x)df(x) = \int_{x \in B} g(x)d\tilde{f}(x) \text{ .}$$

Call any such $\tilde{f}$ as in Theorem 6, the equivalent PM *generalized distribution function* (g.d.f.) w.r.t. f .

Corollary 1

Let $f : \mathbb{R}^q \to \mathbb{R}$ be BV with minimal decomposition $f = (f)^+ - (f)^-$. It follows immediately from Theorem 6 that extending the above definition, there is an equivalent generalized distribution function $\tilde{f}$ w.r.t. f , i.e., $\tilde{f} = (\tilde{f})^+ - (\tilde{f})^-$ is BV, right continuous and grounded such that all of the results in Theorem 6 now hold for this f , since $(\tilde{f})^+$ is a PM g.d.f. equivalent to $(\tilde{f})^-$ and $(\tilde{f})^-$ is a PM g.d.f. equivalent to $(f)^-$. Hence

$$\mu_f(J(-\infty \underset{\sim}{1}_q, y)) = \mu_{\tilde{f}}(J(-\infty \underset{\sim}{1}_q, y)) = \Delta_q(\tilde{f}, J(-\infty \underset{\sim}{1}_q, y)) = \tilde{f}(y) \text{ ,}$$

all $y \in \mathbb{R}^q$, etc.

Theorem 7

Let $f : \mathbb{R}^q \to \mathbb{R}$ be of SBV.
Then

(i) There is an equivalent generalized distribution function $\tilde{f} : \mathbb{R}^q \to \mathbb{R}$ w.r.t. f with

$$\tilde{f} = (\tilde{f})^+ - (\tilde{f})^-$$

a minimal decomposition, $(\tilde{f})^+$ equivalent to f^+ and $(\tilde{f})^-$ equivalent to f^- (generalized PM distributions) such that $(\tilde{f})^+$, $(\tilde{f})^-$, and $\tilde{f}$ are all SBV .

(ii) If also, f is *c-grounded* for some constant c, i.e., for any $x = \begin{bmatrix} x_1 \\ \vdots \\ x_q \end{bmatrix} \in \mathbb{R}^q$, $f(x) = c$, if $x_i = -\infty$ for some i, $1 \le i \le q$, then we can define,

$$\tilde{f} = \alpha_f \cdot (\check{f})^+ - \beta_f \cdot (\check{f})^- + c ,$$

where α_f, $\beta_f \ge 0$ constants and $(\check{f})^+$ and $(\check{f})^-$ are legitimate cumulative probability distribution functions over $\mathbb{R}^q$ (c.d.f.'s), i.e., $(\check{f})^+$ and $(\check{f})^-$ are: PM, grounded and hence nondecreasing nonnegative right continuous, and SBV with

$$(\check{f})^+ (+\infty \underset{\sim}{1}_q) = (\check{f})^-(+\infty \underset{\sim}{1}_q) = 1.$$

(iii) Conversely, if $f = f_1 - f_2$, where f_1 and f_2 are PM generalized distribution functions, then f is a g.d.f.

(iv) Conversely, if $f = a \cdot f_1 - bf_2 + c$, where $a,b \ge 0$ constants and c is a constant and f_1 and f_2 are c.d.f.'s, then f is a c-grounded generalized distribution function. Note that for any q-interval K,

$$Vr(f,K) = aVr(f_1,K) + bVr(f_2,K) .$$

Proof:

(i) f SBV implies for the minimal decomposition $f = (f)^+ - (f)^-$, $(f)^+$ and $(f)^-$ are PM and SBV . Theorem 6 implies $\tilde{f}^+$ and $\tilde{f}^-$ are equivalent PM generalized distribution functions which are strong BV and by Lemma 3.

$$0 \le \alpha_f \overset{d}{=} (\tilde{f})^+(+\infty \underset{\sim}{1}_q) \ , \ \beta_f = (\tilde{f})^-(+\infty \cdot \underset{\sim}{1}_q) < +\infty \ , \text{ etc.}$$

Theorem 8 (McShane [174], pp. 258, 291,301)

Let $\mathcal{A} \subseteq \mathcal{P}(\mathbb{R}^q)$ be a (non-empty) σ-algebra and $\mu : \mathcal{A} \to \mathbb{R}$ a complete regular countably additive signed measure over $\mathcal{A}$. Then there exists $f : \mathbb{R}^q \to \mathbb{R}$ g.d.f. such that μ extends interval function $\Delta(f,\cdot)$ and such that

(i) $\mathcal{A} \subseteq \mathcal{S}(\mu_f, \mathbb{R}^q)$,

(ii) $\mathcal{S}(\mu, \mathbb{R}^q) \subseteq \mathcal{S}(\mu_f, \mathbb{R}^q)$ with $\mu(B) = \mu_f(B)$, for all $B \in \mathcal{S}(\mu, \mathbb{R}^q)$ with $\mu(B)$ finite,

(iii) $L^1(\mu, B) \subseteq L^1(\mu_f, B)$; all $B \in \mathcal{A}$ and for all $f \in L^1(\mu, \mathbb{R}^q)$,

$$\int_{x \in B} f(x) d\mu(x) = \int_{x \in B} f(x) d\mu_f(x) \ .$$

Corollary 2

(i) Let $\mu : A \to \mathbb{R}$ be a complete regular countably additive finite signed measure over $\mathcal{A}$. Then there is an $f : \mathbb{R}^q \to \mathbb{R}$ generalized distribution function which is SBV such that (i), (ii), (iii) all hold in Theorem 8 (μ extending interval function $Vr(f,\cdot)$) .

(ii) If $f : \mathbb{R}^q \to \mathbb{R}$ is SBV , then there exists a complete regular countably additive finite signed measure μ_f over $\mathcal{A}$, extending interval function $Vr(f,\cdot)$.

Proof:

(i) Use Theorem 8 to obtain f inducing μ . Then since

$$+\infty > \mu(\mathbb{R}^q) = \mu_f(\mathbb{R}^q) = Vr(f, \mathbb{R}^q) \ ,$$

f must be SBV.

(ii) Use Theorem 7, yielding $\tilde{f}$ SBV general distribution function equivalent to f and hence

$$\mu_f(\mathbb{R}^q) = \mu_{\tilde{f}}(\mathbb{R}^q) = Vr(\tilde{f}, \mathbb{R}^q) = Vr(f, \mathbb{R}^q) < +\infty \ .$$

Call, for any BV $f : \mathbb{R}^q \to \mathbb{R}$, $\mu_f : \mathbb{B}_q \to [0,1]$, the associated Lebesgue-Stieltjes signed measure.

Theorem 9 (Hahn-Jordan decomposition)

Let f be any c.d.f. over $\mathbb{R}^q$. Then there exist constants $1 \geq \lambda_1(f), \lambda_2(f), \lambda_3(f) \geq 0$, $\lambda_1(f) + \lambda_2(f) = 1$, $\lambda_2(f) = \lambda_3(f) + \lambda_4(f)$ and hence $\lambda_1(f) + \lambda_2(f) + \lambda_3(f) = 1$ and c.d.f.'s f_1, f_2, f_3, f_4 , according as $\lambda_1(f), \lambda_2(f), \lambda_3(f), \lambda_4(f)$ are positive such that f_1 is discrete (finite or countable), f_2 is continuous, f_3 is absolutely continuous and hence probability density function (p.d.f.) $\frac{\partial^q f_3}{\partial \cdots \partial}$ exists in $\mathbb{R}^q$ almost everywhere (Lebesgue) and f_4 is continuous and singular, where there is a set $\emptyset \neq A \subseteq \mathbb{R}^q$ with $\mathrm{vol}_q(A) = 0$ and $\int_{t \in A} df_4(t) = \mu_{f_4}(A) = 1$, and

$$\begin{aligned} f &= \lambda_1(f)\cdot f_1 + \lambda_2(f)\cdot f_2 \\ &= \lambda_1(f)\cdot f_1 + \lambda_3(f)\cdot f_3 + \lambda_4(f)\cdot f_4 , \\ f_2 &= (\lambda_3(f)/\lambda_2(f))\cdot f_3 + (\lambda_4(f)/\lambda_2(f)).f_4 , \text{ etc.} \end{aligned}$$

Conversely, any probability mixture $f = \lambda_1 \cdot f_1 + \lambda_2 \cdot f_2 + \lambda_3 \cdot f_3$ as above determines a legitimate c.d.f.

Remarks:

Thus, if $f : \mathbb{R}^q \to \mathbb{R}$ is of strong BV , then f may not only be decomposed into its minimal forms, written w.l.o.g. through Theorem 7 as

$$f \equiv (f)^+ - (f)^- \equiv \alpha_f \cdot \overset{\vee}{(f)}{}^+ - \beta_f \cdot \overset{\vee}{(f)}{}^- + c ,$$

but by Theorem 9, the c.d.f.'s $\overset{\vee}{(f)}{}^+$, $\overset{\vee}{(f)}{}^-$ may be further decomposed so that

$$f \equiv \eta_f^{(1)} \cdot f_{(1)} + \eta_f^{(3)} \cdot f_{(3)} + \eta_f^{(4)} \cdot f_{(4)} ,$$

where

$$\eta_f^{(j)} = \alpha_f \cdot \lambda_j(\overset{\vee}{(f)}{}^+) - \beta_f \cdot \lambda_j(\overset{\vee}{(f)}{}^-) ,$$

$$f_{(j)} \stackrel{d}{=} \alpha_f \cdot (\check{f})_j^+ - \beta_f \cdot (\check{f})_j^- \quad ; \; j = 1,3,4 \; ,$$

$f_{(1)}$ is a discrete generalized distribution function,

$f_{(3)}$ is an absolutely continuous generalized distribution function,

$f_{(4)}$ is a continuous and singular generalized distribution function,

etc.

Hence,

$$\mu_f = \mu_{(f)^+} - \mu_{(f)^-} = \alpha_f \cdot \mu_{(\check{f})^+} - \beta_f \cdot \mu_{(\check{f})^-} \; ,$$

etc.

Lemma 4

Let $a < b$ be constants and define for all $u,v \in \mathbb{R}$,

$$G(u,v) = \max\left[0, \min\left[\frac{u-a}{b-a}, \frac{v-a}{b-a}, 1\right]\right] .$$

Then for any $h,k \geq 0$,

$$\Delta(G, J(\begin{bmatrix} u \\ v \end{bmatrix}, \begin{bmatrix} u+h \\ v+k \end{bmatrix})) = \begin{cases} \frac{1}{b-a} \min(h,k) \; , & \text{if } \begin{cases} u < v < u+h & \text{or} \\ v < u < v+k \end{cases} \\ 0 \; , & \text{if } u+h \leq v \text{ or } v+k \leq u \; . \end{cases}$$

Lemma 5

Let $a < b$ be constants and define for all $u,v \in \mathbb{R}$,

$$H(u,v) \stackrel{d}{=} \begin{cases} F(\frac{u-a}{b-a}, \frac{v-a}{b-a}) \; , & \text{if } a \leq u,v \leq b \\ \max\left[0, \min\left[\frac{u-a}{b-a}, 1\right]\right], & \text{if } v > b \\ \max\left[0, \min\left[1, \frac{v-a}{b-a}\right]\right] \; , & \text{if } u > b \\ 0 \; , & \text{if } u \leq a \text{ or } v \leq a \; , \end{cases}$$

where F is an absolutely continuous c.d.f. over $[0,1]^2$ with p.d.f. f bounded by c_o .

Then for any $h,k \geq 0$,

$$\Delta(H, J(\begin{bmatrix} u \\ v \end{bmatrix}, \begin{bmatrix} u+h \\ v+k \end{bmatrix})) = \iint\limits_{\substack{\max(a,u) \leq x \leq \min(b,u+h) \\ \max(a,v) \leq y \leq \min(b,v+k)}} \frac{1}{(b-a)^2} f\left[\frac{x-a}{b-a}, \frac{y-a}{b-a}\right] dxdy$$

$$\leq \frac{c_o}{(b-a)^2} \, h \cdot k \; .$$

Theorem 10

Let $f,g : \mathbb{R} \to \mathbb{R}$ both be of BV.

Let $H : \mathbb{R}^2 \to \mathbb{R}$ be defined as in Lemma 5 and define $H : \mathbb{R}^2 \to \mathbb{R}$ by, for all $x,y \in \mathbb{R}$,

$$\tilde{H}(x,y) \overset{d}{=} H(f(x),g(y)) \; .$$

Then $\tilde{H}$ is of BV .
Specifically, for all $t > 0$

$$Vr(\tilde{H},K_t) \leq \frac{c_o}{(b-a)^2} \cdot Vr(f,[-t,t]) \cdot Vr(g,[-t,t]) \; .$$

Proof: Use Lemma 5 directly.

Remark:

Theorem 10 may be extended in the obvious way to n variables. It also can be modified - by replacing BV by SBV for f and g - to yield $\tilde{H}$ being SBV .

Theorem 11

Let $f,g : \mathbb{R} \to \mathbb{R}$ both be of BV.
Also suppose, for any $t > 0$, f is continuous over $[-t,t]$, except possibly on a finite subset of $[-t,t]$ of cardinality $m_{f,t}$ and similarly for g over $[-t,t]$, continuity holds except possibly over a finite subset of cardinality $m_{g,t}$.
Suppose finally that for all $t > 0$, over $[-t,t]$, f and g are such that there exist finite integers $n_{f,t}$ and $n_{g,t}$, such that for any $u \in rng(f)$, $v \in rng(g)$,

$$f^{-1}(u) = \bigcup_{k=1}^{n_{f,t,u}} I_{f,t,u,k} ; \quad g^{-1}(v) = \bigcup_{k=1}^{n_{g,t,v}} I_{g,t,v,k}$$

where each $I_{f,t,u\,k}$, $I_{g,t,v,k}$ denotes a general interval in $\mathbb{R}$ (i.e., either a single point, an open or closed or half-open, half-closed interval or a ray, etc.), and where

$$n_{f,t,u} \leq n_{f,t} \; , \quad n_{g,t,v} \leq n_{g,t} \; .$$

(This concept is related to the Banach indicatrix. See, e.g.,

[181'], pp. 225-229.)

Let $G : \mathbb{R}^2 \to \mathbb{R}$ be defined as in Lemma 1. Let $\tilde{G} : \mathbb{R}^2 \to \mathbb{R}$ be defined by, for all $x,y \in \mathbb{R}$,

$$\tilde{G}(x,y) \stackrel{d}{=} G(f(x),g(y)) .$$

Then $\tilde{G}$ is of BV.

Specifically, there is a finite constant $\gamma_t > 0$, not dependent on a or b, such that

$$Vr(\tilde{G},K_t) \leq \gamma_t/(b - a) \; ; \text{ all } \; t > 0 .$$

Proof:

Let $t > 0$ be arbitrary fixed.

Let the discontinuities of f over $[-t,t]$ be denoted

$$-t \leq x^{(1,t)} < x^{(2,t)} < \cdots < x^{(m_{f,t},t)} \leq t$$

while the discontinuities of g over $[-t,t]$ be denoted

$$-t \leq y^{(1,t)} < y^{(2,t)} < \cdots < y^{(m_{g,t},t)} \leq t .$$

Let

$$\mathcal{Q}_1 = \{x_0,x_1,\ldots,x_m\} ,$$

where

$$-t = x_0 < x_1 < \cdots < x_m = t$$

represent any partitioning of $[-t,t]$ as x-axis and

$$\mathcal{Q}_2 \stackrel{d}{=} \{y_0,y_1,\ldots,y_n\} .$$

where

$$-t = y_0 < y_1 < \cdots < y_n = t$$

is any partitioning of $[-t,t]$ as y-axis,

Thus $\mathcal{Q}_1 \times \mathcal{Q}_2$ is the corresponding rectangular (product) partitioning of $K_t = [-t,t]^2$.

Refine $\mathcal{Q}_1$ and $\mathcal{Q}_2$ to $\mathcal{Q}_1'$ and $\mathcal{Q}_2'$, respectively, so that for any r, $1 \leq r \leq m_{f,t}$ and any s, $1 \leq s \leq m_{g,t}$, there are unique integers $i(r)$, $0 \leq i(r) \leq m-1$, $j(s)$, $1 \leq j(s) \leq n-1$, using w.l.o.g. , the same notation for $\mathcal{Q}_j$ as for $\mathcal{Q}_j'$, $j = 1,2$, such that

$$x_{i(r)} \le x^{(r)} < x_{i(r)+1} < x_{i(r)+2} < \cdots < x_{i(r+1)} \le x^{(r+1)} ,$$

suitably modified if needed for $r = m_{f,t}$, and similarly

$$y_{j(s)} \le y^{(s)} < y_{j(s)+1} < \cdots < y_{j(s+1)} \le y^{(s+1)} < y_{j(s+1)} + 1 .$$

In turn, define for all $1 \le r \le m_{f,t}$, $1 \le s \le m_{g,t}$.

$$C_r \overset{d}{\equiv} [x_{i(r)-1} , x_{i(r)+1}] \times [-t,t] ,$$

$$D_r \overset{d}{\equiv} [-t,t] \times [y_{j(s)-1}, y_{j(s)+1}] ,$$

and partitionings of C_r and D_s ,

$$\mathfrak{C}_r \overset{d}{\equiv} \{x_{i(r)-1}, x_{i(r)}, x_{i(r)+1}\} \times [-t,t] ,$$

$$\mathfrak{D}_r \overset{d}{\equiv} [-t,t] \times \{y_{j(s)-1}, y_{j(s)}, y_{j(s)+1}\} .$$

Also, define w.l.o.g.

$$E_{r,s} = [x_{i(r)+1}, x_{i(r+1)-1}] \times [y_{j(s)+1}, y_{j(s+1)-1}] ,$$

noting that f is continuous, and hence uniformly continuous over the first factor and similarly, g is uniformly continuous over the second factor.

Let

$$\mathcal{E}_{r,s} \overset{d}{\equiv} \{x_{i(r)+1}, x_{i(r)+2}, \ldots, x_{i(r+1)-1}\} \times \{y_{j(s)+1}, y_{j(s)+2}, \ldots, y_{j(s+1)-1}\}$$

be the corresponding rectangular partitioning of $\mathcal{E}_{r,s}$.

It follows from the additivity property of $V_r(\tilde{G},[-t,t],\mathcal{P})$ w.r.t. $\mathfrak{a}$-intervals in $\mathcal{P}$ for any partitioning $\mathcal{P}$ of $[-t,t]$ that

$$V_r(\tilde{G},K_t,\mathfrak{a}_1\times\mathfrak{a}_2) \le \sum_{r=1}^{m_{f,t}} V_r(\tilde{G},C_r,\mathfrak{C}_r) + \sum_{s=1}^{m_{g,t}} V_r(\tilde{G},D_s,\mathfrak{D}_s) + \sum_{\substack{1\le r\le m_{f,t}\\ 1\le s\le m_{g,t}}} V_r(\tilde{G},E_{r,s},\mathcal{E}_{r,s}) .$$

Consider now Lemma 5. Define the range values (not necessarily distinct)

$$u_i \overset{d}{\equiv} f(x_i) , \ i = 0,1,\ldots,m ,$$

$$v_j \overset{d}{=} g(y_j) \quad , \quad j = 0,1,\ldots,n \; .$$

Define the relations

$$\mathcal{A} \overset{d}{=} \{(u_i,v_j) \mid u_i \le v_j < u_{i+1} \quad \text{or} \quad u_i < v_j \le u_{i+1} \quad \text{or} \quad u_{i+1} < v_j \le u_i \quad \text{or} \quad u_{i+1} \le v_j < u_i\}$$

and the dual

$$\mathcal{B} \overset{d}{=} \{(u_i,v_j) \mid v_j \le u_i < v_{j+1} \quad \text{or} \quad v_j < u_i \le v_{j+1} \quad \text{or} \quad v_{j+1} < u_i \le v_j \quad \text{or} \quad v_{j+1} \le u_i < v_j\} \; .$$

For any x_i , y_j,

$$\Delta\left(G,J\left(\begin{bmatrix}x_i\\y_j\end{bmatrix} , \begin{bmatrix}x_{i+1}\\y_{j+1}\end{bmatrix}\right)\right) \begin{cases} = 0 \; , \; \text{if} \begin{cases} u_{i+1} = u_i \quad \text{or} \quad v_{j+1} = v_j \\ \text{or} \quad u_i,u_{i+1} \le v_i,v_{j+1} \\ \text{or} \quad v_j,v_{j+1} \le u_i,u_{i+1} \end{cases} \\ \ne 0 \; , \; \text{if} \quad (u_i,v_j) \in \mathcal{A}_t \cup \mathcal{B}_t \end{cases} .$$

For any $1 \le r \le m_{f,t}$, $1 \le s \le m_{g,t}$, define

$$\mathcal{F}_r \overset{d}{=} \{u_i \mid i(r) + 1 \le i \le i(r+1) - 1\} \; ,$$

$$\mathcal{G}_s \overset{d}{=} \{v_j \mid j(s) + 1 \le j \le j(s+1) - 1\} \; ,$$

$$\mathcal{K}_{r,s} \overset{d}{=} \{u_i \mid u_i \in \mathcal{F}_r \;\&\; \exists\; v_j \in \mathcal{G}_s \quad \text{with} \quad (u_i,v_j) \in \mathcal{A}\} \; .$$

For any $v_j \in \mathcal{G}_s$, define

$$\mathcal{I}_{r,s}(v_j) = \{u_i \mid u_i \in \mathcal{F}_r \quad \text{with} \quad (u_i,v_j) \in \mathcal{A}\} \; .$$

Also,

$$V_r(\tilde{G},C_r,c_r) = \sum_{s=0}^{m-1} \left| \Delta\left(\tilde{G},J\left[\begin{bmatrix}x_{i(r)-1}\\y_s\end{bmatrix} , \begin{bmatrix}x_{i(r)}\\y_{s+1}\end{bmatrix}\right]\right)\right|$$

$$+ \sum_{s=0}^{m-1} \left| \Delta\left(\tilde{G},J\left[\begin{bmatrix}x_{i(r)}\\y_s\end{bmatrix} , \begin{bmatrix}x_{i(r)+1}\\y_{s+1}\end{bmatrix}\right]\right)\right|$$

$$\le \frac{2n_{g,t}}{b-a} \cdot \left(\sum_{j=0}^{m-1} \min(|u_{i(r)}-u_{i(r)-1}|,|v_{j+1} - v_j|) \right.$$

$$+\sum_{j=0}^{m-1} \min(|u_{i(r)+1}-u_{i(r)}|,|v_{j+1}-v_j|)$$

$$\leq \frac{4n_{g,t}}{b-a} \cdot \sum_{j=0}^{n-1} |v_{j+1}-v_j| .$$

Similarly,

$$V_r(\tilde{G},D_s,\mathfrak{D}_s) \leq \frac{4n_{f,t}}{b-a} \cdot \sum_{i=0}^{m-1} |u_{i+1}-u_i| .$$

Now, fix any $1 \leq r \leq m_{f,t}$, $1 \leq s \leq m_{g,t}$, and consider

$$V_r(G,E_{r,s},\mathcal{E}_{r,s}) :$$

Given $\mathcal{Q}_1$ refined to $\mathcal{Q}_1'$, $\mathcal{Q}_2$ refined to $\mathcal{Q}_2'$, fix $\mathcal{Q}_2'$ and refine $\mathcal{Q}_1'$ further to $\mathcal{Q}_1''$ over $[x_{i(r)+1},x_{i(r+1)-1}]$ such that again w.l.o.g. using the same notation,

$$\max_{(i(r)+1 \leq i \leq i(r+1)-1)} |u_{i+1} - u_i| < \min_{\begin{bmatrix} j(s)+1\leq j\leq j(s+1)-1 \\ \text{over distinct } v_j \end{bmatrix}} |v_{j+1} - v_j| .$$

This implies

$$\mathcal{F}_r = \bigcup_{v_j \in \mathcal{G}_s} \mathcal{J}_{r,s}(v_j) .$$

Let

$$\mathcal{K}_{r,s} \stackrel{d}{=} \{(x_i,y_j) \mid i(r)+1 \leq i \leq i(r+1)-1,\ j(s)+1\leq j\leq j(s+1)-1 ,\ (u_i,v_j) \in \mathcal{A}\} .$$

Hence, using Lemma 2,

$$\sum_{(x_\alpha,y_\beta) \in \mathcal{K}_{r,s}} \left| \Delta(\tilde{G},J(\begin{bmatrix} x_\alpha \\ y_\beta \end{bmatrix} , \begin{bmatrix} x_{\alpha+1} \\ y_{\beta+1} \end{bmatrix})) \right|$$

$$= \sum_{v_j\in\mathcal{G}_s} \ \sum_{u_i\in\mathcal{J}_{r,s}(v_j)} \ \sum_{\begin{Bmatrix} x_\alpha\in f^{-1}(u_i) \\ y_\beta\in g^{-1}(v_j) \end{Bmatrix}} \left|\Delta(\tilde{G},J(\begin{bmatrix} x_\alpha \\ y_\beta \end{bmatrix} , \begin{bmatrix} x_{\alpha+1} \\ y_{\beta+1} \end{bmatrix}))\right|$$

$$\leq \sum_{v_j\in\mathcal{G}_s} \ \sum_{u_i\in\mathcal{J}_{r,s}(v_j)} \ \sum_{\begin{Bmatrix} x_\alpha\in f^{-1}(u_i) \\ y_\beta\in g^{-1}(v_j) \end{Bmatrix}} (|u_{i+1}-u_i|/(b-a))$$

$$\leq \sum_{v_j \in \mathcal{G}_s} \sum_{u_i \in \mathcal{F}_{rs}(v_j)} (4n_{f,t} \cdot n_{g,t} \cdot |u_{i+1} - i_i| / (b-a))$$

$$\leq \frac{4n_{f,t} \cdot n_{g,t}}{b - a} \cdot \sum_{i=i(r)+1}^{i(r+1)-1} |u_{i+1} - u_i| \quad .$$

Next, define

$$\ell_{r,s} \overset{d}{=} \{(x_i, y_j) \mid i(r)+1 \leq i \leq i(r+1)-1,\ j(s) + 1 \leq j \leq j(s+1)-1,\ (u_i, v_j) \in \mathcal{B} \dashv \mathcal{A}\}$$

and

$$\mathcal{M}_{r,s} \overset{d}{=} \{v_j \mid v_j \in \mathcal{G}_s \ \&\ \exists\ u_i \in \mathcal{F}_r \text{ with } (u_i, v_j) \in \mathcal{B} \dashv \mathcal{A}\} .$$

Now, defining w.l.o.g.

$$\alpha_{r,s}(\mathcal{Q}_1'') \overset{d}{=} \min_{(1(r)+1 \leq i \leq i(r+1)-1)} u_i < \beta_{r,s}(\mathcal{Q}_1'') \overset{d}{=} \max_{(i(r)+1 \leq i \leq i(r+1)-1)} (u_i) ,$$

it follows that if $v_j \in \mathcal{M}_{r,s}$ then

$$v_j \leq \alpha_{rs} < v_{j+1} \quad \text{or} \quad v_{j+1} \leq \alpha_{r,s} < v_j \quad \text{or}$$
$$v_j < \beta_{r,s} \leq v_{j+1} \quad \text{or} \quad v_{j+1} < \beta_{r,s} \leq v_j .$$

Consider, e.g., $v_j \leq \alpha_{r,s} < v_{j+1}$. By continuity of g, $\exists\ y_o \in g^{-1}(\alpha_{r,s})$ with $y_j \leq y_o < y_{j+1}$ with $y_o \in I_{s,t,\alpha_{r,s},k}$, for some k, $1 \leq k \leq n_{g,t,\alpha_{r,s}} \leq n_{g,t}$. Thus by Lemma 5, we must have

$$y_j \leq I_{g,t,\alpha_{r,s,k}} < y_{j+1} .$$

Hence, for a given $\mathcal{Q}_1''$, there can be at most $2 \cdot n_{g,t}$ $v_j \in \mathcal{M}_{r,s}$. Thus,

$$\sum_{(x_\alpha, y_\beta) \in \ell_{r,s}} \left| \Delta(\tilde{G}, J(\begin{bmatrix} x_\alpha \\ y_\beta \end{bmatrix}, \begin{bmatrix} x_{\alpha+1} \\ y_{\beta+1} \end{bmatrix})) \right|$$

$$\leq \sum_{v_j \in \mathcal{M}_{r,s}} 4n_{f,t} \cdot n_{g,t} \quad \cdot \quad \sum_{i=i(r)+1}^{i(r+1)-1} (|u_{i+1}-u_i|/(b - a))$$

$$\leq \frac{8n_{f,t} \cdot n_{g,t}^2}{b - a} \sum_{i=i(r)+1}^{i(r+1)-1} |u_{i+1} - u_i|$$

Hence,

$$Vr(\tilde{G},E_{r,s},\mathcal{E}_{r,s}) = \sum_{(x_\alpha,y_\beta) \in \mathcal{K}_{r,s} \cup \mathcal{L}_{r,s}} |\Delta(\tilde{G},J(\begin{bmatrix} x_\alpha \\ y_\beta \end{bmatrix}, \begin{bmatrix} x_{\alpha+1} \\ y_{\beta+1} \end{bmatrix}))|$$

$$\leq \frac{4n_{f,t} \cdot n_{g,t} \cdot (1+2n_{g,t})}{b - a} \cdot \sum_{i=i(r)+1}^{i(r+1)-1} |u_{i+1}-u_i| \ .$$

Thus, combining the above results,

$$V_r(\tilde{G},K_t,\mathcal{Q}_1 \times \mathcal{Q}_2) \leq V_r(\tilde{G},K_t,\mathcal{Q}_1'' \times \mathcal{Q}_2')$$

$$\leq \frac{1}{b - a} \cdot (4m_{f,t} \cdot n_{g,t} \cdot \sum_{j=0}^{n-1} |v_{j+1}-v_j| + 4m_{g,t} \cdot n_{f,t} \sum_{i=0}^{m-1} |u_{i+1}-u_i|$$

$$+ 4n_{f,t} \cdot n_{g,t}(1 + 2n_{g,t}) \cdot \sum_{i=0}^{m-1} |u_{i+1}-u_i|)$$

$$\leq \frac{1}{b - a} \cdot \gamma_t \ .$$

where

$$\gamma_t \stackrel{d}{=} 4n_{f,t}(m_{g,t} + n_{g,t} \cdot (1 + 2n_{g,t})) \cdot d_{1,t} + 4m_{f,t} \cdot n_{g,t} \cdot d_{2,t} \ ,$$

where by BV, $\exists \ d_{1,t}, d_{2,t} > 0$ constants with

$$\sum_{i=0}^{m-1} |u_{i+1}-u_i| < d_{1,t} \quad \text{and} \quad \sum_{j=0}^{n-1} |v_{j+1}-v_j| < d_{2,t} \ .$$

Remarks

1. If f = const. and g is arbitrary, then $V_r(\tilde{G},K_t) \equiv 0$ for all $t > 0$. In particular g may not be of BV although clearly here $\tilde{G}$ is BV for Theorem 11.

2. However, if f even has one discontinuity at, say, x_o with

jump $f(x_o+) > f(x_o)$, say, and g is such that there exist constants $a < b$ such that for all $a \le x \le b$,

$$f(x_o+) \ge g(y) \ge f(x_o)$$

and g is not of BV , over $[a,b]$, then $\tilde{G}$ is not of BV .

3. Theorem 11 may be extended from two one-dimensional arguments for G to any number, where

$$G(x_1,\ldots,x_n) \overset{d}{=} \max\left(0,\min\left(1,\frac{f_1(x_1)-a}{b-a},\ldots,\frac{f_n(x_n)-a}{b-a}\right)\right)$$

for all $x_1,\ldots,x_n \in \mathbb{R}$. Thus here

$$Vr(\tilde{G},[-t,t]^n) \le \gamma_{n,t}/(b-a) \text{ , for } \gamma_{n,t} < +\infty \text{ .}$$

4. Theorem 11 and its extension mentioned above may be modified to yield $\tilde{G}$ being of strong BV , when in the assumptions of the theorem, all dependency on t is omitted.

Theorem 12 (Sufficiency for BV of cartesian product).

Let $\phi_\&$ be any n-copula with probability mixture representation for c.d.f.'s H_j , G_j ,

$$\phi_\&(u_1,\ldots,u_n) = \sum_{j=1}^{\infty}(b_j-a_j)\cdot H_j(u_1,\ldots,u_n)+\sum_{j=1}^{\infty}(a_j-b_{j-1})\cdot G_j(u_1,\ldots,u_n)$$

for all $u_1,\ldots,u_n \in [0,1]$, where constants

$$0 = b_o \le a_1 \le b_1 \le a_2 \le b_2 \le \cdots \le 1 \text{ ,}$$

$$\sum_{j=1}^{\infty}(b_j-a_j) + \sum_{j=1}^{\infty}(a_j-b_{j-1}) = 1 \text{ ,}$$

$$H_j(u_1,\ldots,u_n) = \phi_\&^{(j)}\left(\frac{u_1-a_j}{b_j-a_j},\ldots,\frac{u_n-a_j}{b_j-a_j}\right) \text{ ,}$$

where $\phi_\&^{(j)}$ is an Archimedean n-copula with p.d.f. g_j bounded over $[0,1]^n$ by $C_j < +\infty$,

$$G_j(u_1,\ldots,u_n) \overset{d}{=} \max\left(0,\min\left(1,\frac{u_1-b_{j-1}}{a_j-b_{j-1}},\ldots,\frac{u_n-b_{j-1}}{a_j-b_{j-1}}\right)\right) \text{ ,}$$

for all $u_1,\dots,u_n \in [0,1]$; $j = 1,2,\dots$

Suppose $f_1,\dots,f_n$ satisfy Theorem 11. Define

$$C_{j,t} \overset{d}{=} C_j \cdot Vr(f_1,[-t,t]) \cdots Vr(f_n,[-t,t])$$

and $f_1 \times \cdots \times f_n : \mathbb{R}^n \to [0,1]$ by,

$$(f_1 \times \cdots \times f_n)(x_1,\dots,x_n) \overset{d}{=} \phi_\&(f_1(x_1),\dots,f_n(x_n)) \, ,$$

for all $x_1,\dots,x_n \in \mathbb{R}$. Then Theorems 10 and 11 yield:

(i) $Vr(f_1 \times \cdots \times f_n, [-t,t]^n)$

$$\le \sum_{j=1}^{\infty} \frac{C_{j,t}}{(b_j - a_j)^{n-1}} + \sum_{j=1}^{+\infty} \gamma_{j,t} \, .$$

(ii) Thus, if also, e.g.,

$0 = b_0 < a_1 < b_1 < a_2 < b_2 < \cdots < a_n < b_n = 1$, then $f_1 \times \cdots \times f_n$ is BV .

(iii) With obvious modifications, SBV holds for $f_1 \times \cdots \times f_n$.

We will say that a copula $\phi_\&$ has a bounded-finite probability mixture representation iff the conditions of Theorem 12 (ii) hold for $\phi_\&$.

Theorem 13 (Basic approximation II)

Let $\phi_\&$ be a copula with a bounded-finite probability mixture representation.

Let $f,g : \mathbb{R} \to \mathbb{R}$ be arbitrary, bounded and Borel measurable. Then there exist sequences $(f_m)_{m=1,2,\dots}$, $(g_m)_{m=1,2,\dots}$ of BV functions

$f_m, g_m : \mathbb{R} \to \mathbb{R}$ for which for all $t > 0$

$$0 = \lim_{m\to\infty} \int_{x=-t}^{t} | f(x) - f_m(x) | \, dx = \lim_{m\to\infty} \int_{y=-t}^{t} | g(y) - g_m(y) | \, dy$$

and which are BV and satisfy the conditions of Theorem 12 so that $f_m \times g_m$ is BV for $m = 1,2,\dots$, and for all $t > 0$, $(f_m \times g_m)$, $m = 1,2,\dots$, converges in L^1-norm to $f \times g$ over $[-t,t]^2$:

$$0 = \lim_{n\to\infty} \iint_{x,y \in [-t,t]} | (f\times g)(x,y) - (f_m\times g_m)(x,y) | \, dxdy .$$

In particular f_m and g_m may be chosen as step functions; $m = 1,2,\ldots$.

Proof:

First choose f_m and g_m as step functions as in Theorem 3 (i), $m = 1,2,\ldots$. Clearly each f_m and g_m satisfy the hypotheses of Theorem 11, and by Theorem 12 (ii) , $f_m \times g_m$ is BV ; $m = 1,2,\ldots$.

It also follows readily for all $x,y \in [-t,t]$, by use of the triangle inequality and Moynihan's Theorem (see section 2.3.6).

$$|(f\times g)(x,y) - (f_m\times g_m)(x,y)|$$

$$\le |\phi_{\&}(f(x),g(y)) - \phi_{\&}(f_m(x),f(y))|$$

$$+ |\phi_{\&}(f_m(x),g(y)) - \phi_{\&}(f_m(x),g_m(y))|$$

$$\le |f(x) - f_m(x)| + |g(y) - g_m(y)| ,$$

whence

$$\int_{x,y \in [-t,t]} |(f\times g)(x,y) - (f_m\times g_m)(x,y)| \, dxdy$$

$$\le 2t\cdot(\int_{x=-t}^{t} |f(x) - f_m(x)| \, dx + \int_{y=-t}^{t} |g(y) - g_m(y)| \, dy .$$

Theorem 14 (Helly-Bray-like theorem)

Let $g : \mathbb{R}^q \to \mathbb{R}$ be continuous over closed q-interval K .

(i) Let $f_n : \mathbb{R}^q \to \mathbb{R}$ be uniformly bounded over K and uniformly BV over K : $Vr(f_n,K) \le \gamma_o < +\infty$, for all $n \ge 1$. Then independent of g , $\exists$ subsequence $(f_{n_j})_{j=1,2,\ldots}$ of $(f_n)_{n=1,2,\ldots}$ and there exists $f_o : \mathbb{R}^q \to \mathbb{R}$ BV such that

(a) $\lim_{j\to+\infty} f_{n_j}(x) = f_o(x)$ for all $x \in K$

(b) $Vr(f_o,K) \le \gamma_o$

(c) $\lim_{j\to+\infty} \int_{x\in K} g(x)df_{n_j}(x) = \int_{x \in K} g(x)df_o(x)$.

(ii) If (i)(a) holds for $f_{n_j} \equiv f_j$, $j = 1,2,\ldots$ then (i)(b),(c) also hold.

Proof: See, e.g., [181'], pp. 233-234.

Theorem 15 (Basic convergence theorem)

Let K be a closed q-interval. Let $f : \mathbb{R}^q \to \mathbb{R}$ be BV . Let $g_n : \mathbb{R}^q \to \mathbb{R}$ and $g_o : \mathbb{R}^q \to \mathbb{R}$, $n = 1,2,\ldots$ all be continuous with

$$\lim_{n\to\infty} g_n(x) = g_o(x) \text{ , uniformly in } x \in K \text{ .}$$

Then

$$\lim_{n\to\infty} \int_{x\in K} g_m(x)df(x) = \int_{x\in K} g_o(x)df(x) \text{ .}$$

Proof: Standard; see, e.g., [181'], p. 232.

Remarks:

1. Theorems 14 and 15 may be extended to where g_n , $n = 1,2,\ldots$ and g are finitely piecewise continuous but such that over all regions of their discontinuities, all f_n are simultaneously continuous.

2. For the space

$\mathcal{F}^{(q)} \overset{d}{=} \{f \mid f : \mathbb{R}^q \to \mathbb{R}$ is measurable, bounded and of BV$\}$, for each $t > 0$, the L^1-norm over $[-t,t]^q$ may be used, but clearly Theorem 3 (i) shows that it is not complete since any bounded measurable non-BV function may be $L^1([-t,t]^q)$ - approximated by a sequence of $f_n \in \mathcal{F}^{(q)}$, $n = 1,2,\ldots$.

The supremum norm furnishes an alternative norm for $\mathcal{F}^{(q)}$ (over all $\mathbb{R}^q$) , but approximations analogous to Theorem 3 must be modified (Lusin's and Egorov's Theorems) up to sets of arbitrary small positive measure. Theorems 14 and 15 imply that in general convergence under the sup norm can only occur for uniformly bounded and uniformly BV functions, in which case a form of completeness then holds.

3. For the subspace $\mathcal{D}^{(q)}$ (of $\mathcal{F}^{(q)}$) of all c.d.f.'s over $\mathbb{R}^q$, the Lévy metric over $\mathbb{R}^q$ furnishes a genuine complete metric (and norm) where convergence in the Lévy metric is equivalent to weak convergence (i.e., pointwise over all points of continuity of the limit

function). (See, e.g., Schweizer and Sklar [26], Chapter 4.)

Consider now the following discrete case which will be useful in the next theorem:

Let $D_j \subseteq \mathbb{R}$ be discrete, $j = 1,\ldots,q$, such that for

$D_j = \{x_{j,\ell} \mid \ell = \ldots -2,-1,0,1,2,\ldots\}$ with

$$\ldots < x_{j,-2} < x_{j,-1} < x_{j,0} < x_{j,1} < \ldots$$

and

$$\inf(x_{j,\ell+1} - x_{j,\ell}) > 0$$
all j,ℓ.

Let $f : \overset{q}{\underset{j=1}{\times}} D_j \to \mathbb{R}$ be arbitrary. Let

$$\mathbb{Q} \overset{d}{=} \{J(x) \mid x \in \overset{q}{\underset{j=1}{\times}} D_j\}$$

be a semi-closed-open partitioning of $\mathbb{R}^q$ such that for all

$$x = \begin{bmatrix} x_{1,\ell_1} \\ \vdots \\ x_{q,\ell_q} \end{bmatrix} \in \overset{q}{\underset{j=1}{\times}} D_j \ , \quad x^+ \overset{d}{=} \begin{bmatrix} x_{1,\ell_1+1} \\ \vdots \\ x_{q,\ell_q+1} \end{bmatrix} \in \overset{q}{\underset{j=1}{\times}} D_j \ ,$$

$$J(x) = \overset{q}{\underset{j=1}{\times}} [x_{j,\ell}\ , x_{j,\ell+1}),\ \bar{J}(x) = \overset{q}{\underset{j=1}{\times}} [x_{j,\ell}\ , x_{j,\ell+1}] = J(x,x^+) \ .$$

In turn, define $f_{\mathbb{Q}_q}$, the *step function imbedding* of f into $\mathbb{R}^{\mathbb{R}^q}$, where for any $y \in \mathbb{R}^q$, let $J(x) \in \mathbb{Q}$ be unique such that

$$y \in J(x) \ .$$

Then

$$f_{\mathbb{Q}}(y) = f(x) \ .$$

It follows that for any $g : \mathbb{R}^q \to \mathbb{R}$ such that f is continuous at all $x \in D \overset{d}{=} \overset{q}{\underset{j=1}{\times}} D_j$,

$$\int_{(y \in \mathbb{R}^q)} g(y)df_{\mathbb{Q}}(y) = \sum_{x \in D} g(x) \cdot \Delta_q(f_{\mathbb{Q}},\bar{J}(x))$$

$$= \sum_{x \in D} g(x)\ \Delta_q(f,\bar{J}(x)) \ ,$$

$f_{\mathbb{Q}}$ being BV . Also, $f_{\mathbb{Q}}$ is SBV with

$$Vr(f_{\mathbb{Q}}) = \sum_{x \in D} |\Delta_q(f, \bar{J}(x))|$$ iff that series converges.

Theorem 15' (Fundamental approximation of Lebesgue-Stieltjes measure and integration)

(i) Let $g : \mathbb{R}^q \to \mathbb{R}$ be continuous.

Let $f : \mathbb{R}^q \to \mathbb{R}$ be bounded, measurable and BV . Thus, w.l.o.g. $f = f_1 - f_2$ with f_1, f_2 both g.d.f.'s and hence both are continuous over $\mathbb{R}^q$ except on at most a countable subset, say, G_o of $\mathbb{R}^q$.

For each integer $n \geq 1$, define

$$D_n \overset{d}{=} \{-n + k/2^n \mid k = 0,1,2,\ldots,n \cdot 2^{n+1}\} \subseteq [-n,n]$$

with mesh $1/2^n$. Thus, for any $n \geq 1$, D_{n+1} refines D_n . Also, define $B_n \overset{d}{=} (D_n)^q = D_n \times \cdots \times D_n \subseteq [-n,n]^q$ and note that B_{n+1} refines B_n , for all $n \geq 1$. For each $n \geq 1$, let $\mathbb{Q}_n$ be the associated semi-closed-open partitioning of $[-n,n]^q$. Hence $\mathbb{Q}_{n+1}$ refines $\mathbb{Q}_n$ over both $[-(n+1),n+1]^q$ and hence $[-n,n]^q$.

Then define for each $n \geq 1$,

$$f_n \overset{d}{=} \begin{cases} (f|B_n)_{\mathbb{Q}_n} & \text{over } [-n,n]^q , \\ 0 & \text{over } [-n,n]^q . \end{cases}$$

It then follows that for any $t > 0$, (see also Theorem 2)

(a) $(f_n)_{n=1,2,\ldots} \to f$ pointwise over $[-t,t]^q$ except possibly over G_o ,

(b) $(f_n)_{n=1,2,\ldots} \xrightarrow{L^1} f$ over $[-t,t]^q$,

(c) $$Vr(f_n,[-t,t]^q) = \sum_{x \in B_n} |\Delta_q((f \mid B_n),\bar{J}(x))|$$
$$\leq Vr(f,[-t,t]^q)$$
$$< +\infty ,$$

for all $n \geq t$.

Hence by Theorem 14, for any $t > 0$,

(d) $$\int_{x \in [-t,t]^q} g(x)df(x) = \lim_{n \to \infty} \int_{x \in [-t,t]^q} g(x)df_n(x) .$$

$$= \lim_{n \to \infty} \sum_{x \in D_n} g(x) \cdot \Delta_q(f, \overline{J}(x)) .$$

(ii) Result (i) can be extended w.l.o.g. by slight changes in the constrution of the f_n's so that g may be considered continuous except on a finite number of points or piecewise continuous, etc.

Theorem 16 (BV measure reduced to copula measure)

Let $f : \mathbb{R}^q \to \mathbb{R}$ be a c.d.f. with one dimensional marginal c.d.f.'s $f_1, \ldots, f_q : \mathbb{R} \to \mathbb{R}$ which by Sklar's Theorem (section 2.3.6) yields

$$f(x_1, \ldots, x_q) = \phi_\&(f_1(x_1), \ldots, f_q(x_q)) ,$$

for all $x_1, \ldots, x_q \in \mathbb{R}$ and some n-copula $\phi_\&$.

Let $g : \mathbb{R}^q \to \mathbb{R}$ be measurable.

Recall the quasi-inverse $f_j^{\ddagger}$ (see also Appendix, 2.3.6) defined by

$$f_j^{\ddagger}(x) \stackrel{d}{=} \inf f_j^{-1}(x,1] \; ; \; x \in [0,1] ,$$

for $j = 1,2,\ldots$. Then

$$\int_{x_1, \ldots, x_n \in \mathbb{R}} g(x_1, \ldots, x_n) df(x_1, \ldots, x_n)$$

$$= \int_{x_1, \ldots, x_n \in \mathbb{R}} g(x_1, \ldots, x_n) d\phi_\&(f_1(x_1), \ldots, f_n(x_n))$$

$$= \int_{u_1, \ldots, u_n \in [0,1]} g(f_1^{\ddagger}(u_1), \ldots, f_n^{\ddagger}(u_n)) d\phi_\&(u_1, \ldots, u_n) .$$

Proof: See Schweizer and Sklar [266], section 6.5.

Marginal functions

Recalling the previous definition of C-marginal

$f_C : \mathbb{R}^{card(C)} \to \mathbb{R}$ for any given $f : \mathbb{R}^q \to \mathbb{R}$ and $\emptyset \neq C \subseteq \{1,\ldots,q\}$, suppose first that f is PM. This condition is not sufficient for all marginals to be also PM. For example, $h(x,y) \equiv f(x) + g(y)$ is PM since $\Delta_2(h,k) \equiv 0$, for all 2-intervals K, for *any* choice of $f,g : \mathbb{R} \to \mathbb{R}$.

However, the following holds

Theorem 17

Let $f : \mathbb{R}^q \to \mathbb{R}$ be given.

(i) If f is a PM g.d.f. which is bounded - equivalently f is also SBV and thus $f(+\infty 1_q) < +\infty$ is the supremum of f, then for all $\emptyset \neq C \subseteq \{1,\ldots,q\}$, C-marginal $f_C : \mathbb{R}^{card(C)} \to \mathbb{R}^+$ exists and is a g.d.f.

(ii) If f is g.d.f. with minimal decomposition

$$f = (f)^+ - (f)^-$$

such that $(f)^+$, $(f)^-$ and hence f are all SBV and hence all bounded, then for all $\emptyset \neq C \subseteq \{1,\ldots,q\}$, C-marginal f_C exists, although in general

$$f_C \neq (f)_C^+ - (f)_C^- ,$$

and f_C is a g.d.f. which is also SBV. The result may be modified, if f being SBV is replaced by BV and bounded.

Proof: Use hereditary properties of groundedness, right continuity and, by Lemma 1, PM.

Remark:

Theorems 7 and 17 (ii) imply that if $f : \mathbb{R}^q \to \mathbb{R}$ is SBV, for all $\emptyset \neq C \subseteq \{1,\ldots,q\}$, $\tilde{f}_C$ is a generalized distribution function which is SBV, for f equivalent to f.

It is of some interest to relate measures $\mu_{\tilde{f}_C}$ induced by the marginals of f and marginal measures (to be defined) of $\mu_{\tilde{f}}$.

2.4 Category and topos theory viewpoint of generalized set theory.

2.4.1 Introduction.

A logical basis for fuzzy set theory may be established using [0,1] - valued logic and its semantic evaluations as presented in previous sections 2.3.2 and 2.3.3.

An alternative approach, entails the imbedding of Zadeh's min-max fuzzy set theory ($\mathcal{F}_o$) into a special category theory structure called a topos, so that formal language and set theory investigations may be carried out. (See Johnstone [127], MacLane [166], and Lawvere [152].) In the following discussion [0,1] is replaced by the more general structure of a complete Heyting algebra H. (See, e.g., Ponasse [204]). Nothing is gained by restricting H = [0,1] and analysis is eased by use of the more general structure. Goguen [96] using six axioms abstracting properties from Fuz(H) - Zadeh's fuzzy set theory with [0,1] replaced by H, the objects of category Fuz(H) being fuzzy set membership functions and the arrows fuzzified functional transforms between objects - showed that any category satisfying them necessarily must be the category Gog(H), where the object collection Ob(Gog(H)) consists of all possible pairs (X,ϕ_A), where A is any fuzzy subset of X and the morphism or arrow collection Ar(Gog(H)) consists of

$$\mathrm{Ar}(\mathrm{Gog}(H)) = \bigcup_{\substack{\text{over all} \\ (X,\phi_A),(Y,\phi_B) \\ \in \mathrm{Ob}(\mathrm{Gog}(H))}} \mathrm{Ar}_{((X,\phi_A),(Y,\phi_B))}(\mathrm{Gog}\ (H)),$$

$$\mathrm{Ar}_{((X,\phi_A),(Y,\phi_B))}(\mathrm{Gog})(H))$$

$$\overset{d}{=} \{f \mid f : X \to Y \text{ and } \phi_B(f(x)) \geq \phi_A(x), \text{ all } x \in X\} .$$

The motivation for the last definition comes from the extension principle applied to Zadeh's fuzzy set system (1 - (·), min, max), i.e., for any

$$f : X \to Y$$

and fuzzy subset A of X, for all $x \in X$, it follows that for all $x \in X$

$$\phi_{f(A)}(f(x)) \geq \phi_A(x) .$$

See subsection 2.4.2 (D) for further details for Gog(H).

Chapin [32], [33], Weidner [270] and Novak [195] considered the membership operator $\in$ and fuzzy set-like extensions connected with it. All of these and Albert [2], as well, have approached fuzzy set theory through an axiom system with deductive rules. For example, Chapin uses 14 axioms, but one difficulty with his system - unlike Goguen's [96], mentioned above - is the possible lack of uniqueness of the resulting model of fuzzy set theory. (See again, 2.3.4.)

Eytan [56] produced a variation Fuz(H) of Gog(H). (Subsection 2.4.2 discusses Eytan's formulated of Fuz(H).) Indeed, Carrega [29] demonstrated easily that Fuz(H) and $\mathrm{Gog}^*(H)$ - Gog(H) having all of its objects (fuzzy sets) restricted to their supports - when

H is a complete chain (the case of course for [0,1]), are isomorphic.

Fuz(H) is a category where for any $(X,\phi_A) \in Ob(Fuz(H))$, the identity arrow (under $\circ$) in $Ar_{((X,\phi_A),(X,\phi_A))}(Fuz(H))$ is $id_{(X,\phi_A)}$, where

$$id_{(X,\phi_A)} \stackrel{d}{=} \phi_A(\cdot) \wedge \phi_A(\cdot\cdot) \wedge \delta_{X}\cdot,\cdot\cdot : X \times X \to [0,1] .$$

(For Gog(H) , composition of arrows is the same as ordinary composition of functions and the identity arrows are the same as the ordinary identity functions over sets.)

Eytan [56] also claimed that Fuz(H) was a topos. However, Carrega [29], Ponasse [204] and Pitts [203] all pointed out the incorrectness of Eytan's results. (H necessarily must be a Boolean algebra which is not the case for [0,1].) Indeed, Carrega specifically showed that Fuz(H) was a pseudotopos, i.e., possessed all of the required basic properties to be a topos, except that it has no subobject classifier ([127], pp. 23,24). Also, Pitts [203] claims that Higg(H) is a better candidate than Fuz(H) for developing a "fuzzy" set theory, since Higg(H) is not only a category, but a topos and the quotient object completion of Fuz(H) , Higg(H) (which as shown below contains Fuz(H) as a diagonal imbedding) treats simultaneous membership - as opposed to Fuz(H) treating single memberships, although Fuz(H) is extendable to non-interactive multiple membership functions by repeating the $\phi_{\&}$ (here,min) operation:

$$\phi_A(x_1,\ldots,x_n) \stackrel{d}{=} \phi_{\&}(\phi_A(x_1),\ldots,\phi_A(x_n)) \ ; \text{ all } x_1,\ldots,x_n \in X .$$

More tie-ins with multiple point coverage functions of random sets will be treated later. (See subsection 2.4.2 for further details concerning Higg(H).)

Since min is the maximal t-norm, a more general class of Higg's objects is obtained by replacing min by $\phi_{\&}$ in the above definitions. In a sense, each Higg object f is a kind of equality over $X \times X$.

If $(X,\phi_A) \in Ob(Fuz(H))$ is arbitrary, then clearly

$$(X, id_{(X,\phi_A)}) \in Ob(Higg(H)) .$$

Conversely, if $(X,f) \in Ob(Higg(H))$,

$$(X,D(f)) \in Ob(Fuz(H)) ,$$

where D(f) is the diagonal part of f :

$$D(f)(x) \stackrel{d}{=} f(x,x) ,$$

for all $x \in X$.

See Fourmann and Scott [59] for basic properties of Higg(H) , which is shown to be the Grothendieck topos of all sheaves over H . Furthermore (see [59] and [56]) Higg(H) can be used to realize general formal higher order many-sorted languages through a form of intuitionistic logic yielding sound and complete semantics. (See also subsection 2.3.3.)

In a second (unpublished) paper, Eytan [57], whose earlier work was to a large degree based on Coste's construction [41] being a topos, extended Fuz(H) by weakening the single-valued condition for the arrows of Fuz(H).

2.4.2 Basic concepts

A. Basic fuzzy set category Fuz(H) (Eytan [56].)

SET = (Ob(SET), Ar(SET)) is the category of all well-formed ordinary sets with Ob(SET), the object part, being the collection of all well-formed sets and Ar(SET) the collection of all arrows for SET - in this case

$$Ar(SET) = \bigcup_{X,Y \in Ob(SET)} Ar_{X,Y}(SET) ,$$

$$Ar_{X,Y}(SET) \stackrel{d}{=} Y^X \stackrel{d}{=} \{f \mid f : X \to Y\} ,$$

for all $X, Y \in Ob(SET)$.

We use similar notation for any category $\mathbb{C} = (Ob(\mathbb{C}), Ar(\mathbb{C}))$,

$$Ar(\mathbb{C}) = \bigcup_{X,Y \in Ob(\mathbb{C})} Ar_{X,Y}(\mathbb{C}) .$$

For any fixed complete Heyting algebra H and $X \in Ob(SET)$, define

$$Ob_X(Fuz(H) \stackrel{d}{=} \{(X,\eta) \mid \eta : X \to H\}$$
$$= \{(X,\eta) \mid \eta \in H^X\}$$

the class of all H-valued membership functions on X, and in turn

$$Ob(Fuz(H)) \stackrel{d}{=} \bigcup_{X \in Ob(SET)} Ob_X(Fuz(H))$$

is the class of all H-valued membership functions.

Note that for any $X \in Ob(SET)$:

(1) $Ob_X(Fuz(H)) \supseteq \phi_X \stackrel{d}{=} \{(X,\eta) \mid \eta \in \{0,1\}^X\}$, the class of all ordinary set membership functions on X, i.e., membership functions of X.

(2) The operations $\wedge$, $\vee$, $\Rightarrow$, $\complement$ over H may all be used to define operations on $Ob_X(Fuz(H))$, where, for any $\eta_1, \eta_2, \ldots \in H^X$,

$$(X,\eta_1) \wedge (X,\eta_2) \overset{d}{=} (X,(\eta_1 \wedge \eta_2)) \ ,$$
$$(X,\eta_1) \vee (X,\eta_2) \overset{d}{=} (X,(\eta_1 \vee \eta_2)) \ ,$$
$$(X,\eta_1) \Rightarrow (X,\eta_2) = (X,(\eta_1 \Rightarrow \eta_2))$$
$$C(X,\eta_1) \overset{d}{=} (X,(C\eta_1)) \ ,$$

where for all $x \in X$,

$$(\eta_1 \wedge \eta_2)(x) \overset{d}{=} \eta_1(x) \wedge \eta_2(x)$$
$$(\eta_1 \vee \eta_2)(x) \overset{d}{=} \eta_1(x) \vee \eta_2(x)$$
$$(\eta_1 \Rightarrow \eta_2)(x) \overset{d}{=} \eta_1(x) \Rightarrow \eta_2(x)$$
$$(C\eta_1)(x) \overset{d}{=} C(\eta_1(x)) \qquad , \text{etc.}$$

Furthermore, because of commutativity and associativity of $\wedge$ and $\vee$, we can define similarly unambiguously recursively

$$(X,\eta_1)\wedge(X,\eta_2) \wedge \cdots \overset{d}{=} (X,\eta_1\wedge\eta_2\wedge\cdots)$$
$$(X,\eta_1)\vee(X,\eta_2) \vee \cdots \overset{d}{=} (X,\eta_1\vee\eta_2\vee\cdots) \ , \text{etc.}$$

(3) Also, we can define the cartesian products and cartesian sums for any $X_j \in Ob(SET)$, $\eta_j \in H^{X_j}$, $j = 1,2,\ldots$.

$$(X_1,\eta)\times_\wedge(X_2,\eta_2)\times_\wedge\cdots = (X_1\times X_2\times\cdots, \ \eta_1\times_\wedge\eta_2\times_\wedge\cdots)$$
$$(X_1,\eta_1) \dagger_\vee(X_2,\eta_2) +_\vee\cdots = (X_1\times X_2\times\cdots,\eta_1\dagger_\vee\eta_2\dagger_\vee\cdots)$$

where, for any $x_j \in X_j$, $j = 1,2,\ldots$

$$(\eta_1\times_\wedge\eta_2\times_\wedge\cdots)(x_1,x_2,\cdots) \overset{d}{=} \eta_1(x_1)\wedge\eta_2(x_2)\wedge\cdots \ ,$$
$$(\eta_1\dagger_\vee\eta_2\dagger_\vee\cdots)(x_1,x_2,\cdots) \overset{d}{=} \eta_1(x)\vee\eta_2(x_2)\vee\cdots \ .$$

(4) For any $X \in Ob(SET)$ and $n \geq 1$ and $\eta \in H^{X^n} = H^{X\times X\times\cdots\times X}$, define $D(\eta) \in H^X$ by, for all $x \in X$, the diagonal part of η at x ,

$$D(\eta)(x) \overset{d}{=} \eta(x,x,\cdots,x) \ ,$$

and in turn, define for any $(X^n,\eta) \in Ob_{X^n}(Fuz(H))$,

$$D(X^n,\eta) \overset{d}{=} (X,D(\eta)) \in Ob_X(Fuz(H)) \ .$$

Thus, for any $n > 1$ and $\eta_1, \eta_2, \ldots, \eta_n \in H^X$,

$$D((X,\eta_1)\times_\wedge \cdots \times_\wedge (X,\eta_n))$$

$$= (X, \eta_1 \wedge \cdots \wedge \eta_n) ;$$

$$D((X,\eta_1)\dagger_\vee \cdots \dagger_\vee (X,\eta_n))$$

$$= (X, \eta_1 \vee \cdots \vee \eta_n) .$$

(5) It follows readily that

(i) For any $X \in Ob(SET)$ and any $A_1, \ldots, A_n \in \mathcal{P}(X)$, with

$$\phi_X(A_j) \overset{d}{=} (X, \phi_{A_j}) ,$$

where ϕ_B denotes the membership function for $B \in \mathcal{P}(X)$, i.e.

$$\phi_B(x) = \begin{cases} 1 & \text{iff } x \in B \\ 0 & \text{iff } x \notin B , \end{cases}$$

for all $x \in X$, and any B ; $j = 1, \ldots, n$, then

$$(X,\phi_{A_1}) \wedge \cdots \wedge (X,\phi_{A_n}) = (X, \phi_{A_1} \wedge \cdots \wedge \phi_{A_n})$$

$$= (X, \phi_{A_1 \cap \cdots \cap A_n}) ,$$

$$(X,\phi_{A_1}) \vee \cdots \vee (X,\phi_{A_n}) = (X, \phi_{A_1 \cup \cdots \cup A_n}) ,$$

$$C(X,\phi_{A_1}) = (X, C\phi_{A_1}) = (X, 1-\phi_{A_1}) = (X, \phi_{CA_1}) .$$

(ii) Similarly for any $X_j \in Ob(SET)$ and $A_j \in \mathcal{P}(X_j)$, $j = 1, \ldots, n$,

$$(X_1,\phi_{A_1})\times_\wedge \cdots \times_\wedge (X_n,\phi_{A_n}) = (X_1\times\cdots\times X_n, \phi_{A_1\times\cdots\times A_n}) ,$$

$$(X_1,\phi_{A_1})\dagger_\vee \cdots \dagger_\vee (X_n,\phi_{A_n}) = (X_1\times\cdots\times X_n, \phi_{A_1\dagger\cdots\dagger A_n}) .$$

(6) If H has additional structure, other operations in addition to the ones above may be defined over $Fuz(H)$ which in a natural way extend ordinary set operations. In particular, if $H = [0,1]$, we can let $\phi_\& : H \times H \to H$ be any t-norm, with $\phi_{or} : H \times H \to H$ any t-conorm, and $\phi_{nt} : H \to H$ be any negation - or even more generally, $\phi_\&$ could be any conjunction operator and ϕ_{or} any disjunction operator.

(7) One approach to a relation on $Ob(Fuz(H))$ which extends ordinary subset inclusion is to define for any $X \in Ob(SET)$ any

$\eta_1, \eta_2 \in H^X$

$$((X,\eta_1) \subseteq_H (X,\eta_2))$$

iff

$$\eta_1 \in \mathrm{Sub}(X,\eta_2)$$

iff

$\eta_1 \leq \eta_2$ pointwise over X, i.e.,

$$\eta_1(x) \leq_H \eta_2(x) \;;\; \text{for all} \;\; x \in H .$$

Thus, for any $A_1, A_2 \in \mathcal{P}(X)$

$$(X,\phi_{A_1}) \subseteq_H (X,\phi_{A_2}) \;\; \text{iff} \;\; A_1 \subseteq A_2 .$$

Define $\mathrm{Ar}(\mathrm{Fuz}(H))$ as follows.
For any (X_1,η_1) , $(X_2,\eta_2) \in \mathrm{Ob}(\mathrm{Fuz}(H))$, let

$$\mathrm{Ar}_{(X_1,\eta_1),(X_2,\eta_2)}(\mathrm{Fuz}(H))$$

$$\stackrel{d}{=} \{g \mid g : X_1 \times X_2 \to J \;\&$$

(F1) $$(g(\cdot,\cdot\cdot) \leq \eta_1(\cdot) \wedge \eta_2(\cdot\cdot)) \;\&$$

(F2) $$\bigvee_{x_2 \in X_2} g(\cdot,x_2) = \eta_1(\cdot) \qquad \&$$

(F3) $$g(\cdot,\cdot\cdot) \wedge g(\cdot,\cdot\cdot\cdot) \leq \delta_{\cdot\cdot,\cdot\cdot\cdot}\} ,$$

where we use the Krönecker delta notation

$$\delta_{x,y} = \begin{cases} 1 , & \text{if} \;\; x = y \\ 0 , & \text{if} \;\; x \neq y \end{cases}$$

and alternatively, $\delta_{x,y}(X)$ is used to indicate that x and y are restricted to be in space X .

It follows from (F2) and (F3) for any $g \in \mathrm{Ar}_{(X_1\eta_1),(X_2,\eta_2)}(\mathrm{Fuz}(H))$, there exists a unique $h_g : (X_1 \dashv \eta_1^{-1}(0)) \to X_2$, such that for all $x_1 \in X_1 \dashv \eta_1^{-1}(0)$, i.e., $\eta_1(x_1) > 0$,

$$\bigvee_{x_2 \in X_2} g(x_1,x_2) = g(x_1,h_g(x_1)) = \eta_1(x_1)$$

and for all $x_2 \in X_2$

$$g(x_1,x_2) = \delta_{h_g(x_1),x_2} \wedge \eta_1(x_1) .$$

But (F1) implies that at $x_2 = h_g(x_1)$,

$$g(x_1,h_g(x_1)) = \eta_1(x_1) \le \eta_1(x_1) \wedge \eta_2(h_g(x_1))$$

whence

$$\eta_1(x_1) \le \eta_2(h_g(x_1)) ,$$

for all $x_1 \in X_1 \dashv \eta_1^{-1}(0)$.

This thus implies trivially that for all $x_1 \in X_1 \dashv \eta_1^{-1}(0)$ and all $x_2 \in X$

$$g(x_1,x_2) = \delta_{h_g(x_1),x_2} \wedge \eta_1(x_1) \wedge \eta_2(x_2) .$$

On the other hand, if $\eta_1(x_1) = 0$, then (F2) and (F3) imply that for all $x_2 \in X_2$,

$$0 = g(x_1,x_2) .$$

Hence, if we (arbitrarily) extend

$$h_g : X_1 \to X_2 ,$$

it follows that, for all $x_1 \in X_1$, $x_2 \in X_2$,

$$g(x_1,x_2) = \delta_{h_g(x_1),x_2} \wedge \eta_1(x_1) \wedge \eta_2(x_2) .$$

Note also that it follows that for all $x_1 \in X_1$,

$$\eta_1(x_1) \le \eta_2(h_g(x_1)) .$$

Conversely, if $h : X_1 \to X_2$ is arbitrary, define

$$g_{(h)}(\cdot,\cdot\cdot) \overset{d}{=} \delta_{h(\cdot),\cdot\cdot} \wedge \eta_1(\cdot) \wedge \eta_2(\cdot\cdot) .$$

Then it follows (see Eytan [56], p. 59, Proposition 3.3.1) that

$$g_{(h)} \in Ar_{(X_1,\eta_1),(X_2,\eta_2)}(\text{Fuz}(H))$$

iff

$$\eta_1(x_1) \le \eta_2(h(x_1)) ,$$

for all $x_1 \in X_1$.

Hence, in summary:

$$Ar_{(X_1,\eta_1),(X_2,\eta_2)}(\text{Fuz}(H))$$

$$= \{\delta_{h(\cdot),\cdot\cdot} \wedge \eta_1(\cdot) \wedge \eta_2(\cdot\cdot) \mid h : X_1 \to X_2 \ \& \ \eta_1(\cdot) \le \eta_2(h(\cdot))\}$$

$$= \{\delta_{h(\cdot),\cdot\cdot} \wedge \eta_1(\cdot) \mid h : X_1 \to X_2 \ \& \ \eta_1(\cdot) \le \eta_2(h(\cdot))\} ,$$

$$Ar(Fuz(H)) \overset{d}{=} \bigcup_{\substack{X_1, X_2 \\ \in Ob(SET)}} Ar_{(X_1,\eta_1),(X_2,\eta_2)}(Fuz(H)) .$$

B. A connection between Ar(Fuz(H)) and extension maps.

Let $\phi_{\&}$ be any fixed t-norm, such as $\phi_{\&} = \wedge$ and ϕ_{or} be any t-conorm such as $\phi_{or} = \vee$. Then define the extension or lifting operator

$$\# : Ar(SET) \to Ar(Ob(Fuz(H))) ,$$

where for any X_1 , $X_2 \in Ob(SET)$, and any $h : X_1 \to X_2$,

$$\#(h) : Ob_{X_1}(Fuz(H)) \to Ob_{X_2}(Fuz(H)) ,$$

by, for any $\eta_1 \in H^{X_{-1}}$,

$$(\#(h))(X_1,\eta_1) \overset{d}{=} (X_2,\#(h)(\eta_1))$$

where, $\#(h)(\eta_1) \in H^{X_2}$ is given by, for any $x_2 \in X_2$:

$$((\#(h))(\eta_1))(x_2) \overset{d}{=} \phi_{\substack{or \\ x_1 \in h^{-1}(x_2)}} (\eta_1(x)) \in H .$$

This implies

(i) If $x_2 \notin rng(h)$, $h^{-1}(x_2) = \emptyset$ and

$$((\#(h))(\eta_1))(x_2) = 0 ,$$

(ii) For all $x_1 \in X_1$,

$$\eta_1(x_1) \le ((\#(h))(\eta_1))(h(x_1)) ,$$

(iii) For any $c \in H$, $x_1 \in X_1$,

$$(\#(h))(\delta_{x_1,\cdot} \wedge c) = \delta_{h(x_1),\cdot\cdot} \wedge c ,$$

(iv) Thus, using (iii) in the definition, for any $x_2 \in X_2$,

$$((\#(h))(\eta_1))(x_2) = \phi_{\substack{or \\ x_1 \in X_1}} (\delta_{h(x_1),x_2} \wedge \eta_1(x_1))$$

$$= \phi_{\substack{or \\ x_1 \in X_1}} ((\#(h))(\delta_{x_1,\cdot} \wedge \eta_1(x_1)))(x_2) ,$$

i.e.

$$(\#(h))(\eta_1) = \phi_{\substack{or \\ x_1 \in X_1 \\ \text{(pointwise)}}} ((\#(h))(\delta_{x_1,\cdot} \wedge \eta_1(x_1)))$$

$$\geq \delta_{h(\cdot),\cdot\cdot} \wedge \eta_1(\cdot) .$$

Hence, if

$$(X_2,\eta_2) = \#(h)((X_1,\eta_1)) ,$$

then

$$\eta_1(x_1) \leq \eta_2(h(x_1)) \; ; \text{ all } \; x_1 \in X_1$$

and

$$\eta_2(\cdot\cdot) \geq \delta_{h(\cdot),\cdot\cdot} \wedge \eta_1(\cdot) \in Ar_{(X_1,\eta_1,(X_2,\eta_2)}(Fuz(H)) , \text{ etc.}$$

C. General compositions of binary mappings.

Let $\phi_{\&}$ and ϕ_{or} be any fixed t-norm and t-conorm.

Let X_1 , X_2 , $X_3 \in Ob(SET)$ be arbitrary with $f : X_1 \times X_2 \to H$ and $g : X_2 \times X_3 \to H$ also arbitrary. Then define composition or relational product mapping $g \circ f : X_1 \times X_3 \to H$ by, for all $x_1 \in X_1$, $x_3 \in X_3$,

$$(g \circ f)(x_1,x_3) = \phi_{\substack{or \\ x_2 \in X_2}} (\phi_{\&}(f(x_1,x_2), g(x_2,x_3)) .$$

In particular, note that if $h : X_2 \to X_3$. $f(\cdot,\cdot\cdot) = \eta(\cdot\cdot)$ and $g(\cdot\cdot,\cdot\cdot\cdot) = \delta_{h(\cdot\cdot),\cdot\cdot\cdot}$, then

$$(g \circ f)(\cdot,\cdot\cdot\cdot) = \#(h)(\eta)(\cdot\cdot\cdot) ,$$

etc.

It follows that, if $\phi_{\&}$ is distributive over ϕ_{or} , then $\circ$ is associative, as is the case for $(\wedge,\vee)$ or $(\wedge,\text{bndsum})$. In any case, for any X_1 , X_2 and any $f : X_1 \times X_2 \to H$, letting $\eta_1 \in H^{X_1}$, $\eta_2 \in H^{X_2}$ be arbitrary such that $f(\cdot,\cdot\cdot) \leq \eta_1(\cdot) \wedge \eta_2(\cdot\cdot)$ (we can always choose $\eta_1(\cdot) = \eta_2(\cdot\cdot) = 1$) , then $\eta_1(\cdot) \wedge \delta_{\cdot,\cdot\cdot}(X_1) : X_1 \times X_1 \to H$ and $\eta_2(\cdot\cdot) \wedge \delta_{\cdot\cdot,\cdot\cdot\cdot}(X_2) : X_2 \times X_2 \to H$ act as (nonunique) local identity maps relative to $\circ$, i.e.,

$$\begin{cases} f\circ\left[\eta_1(\cdot) \wedge \delta_{\cdot,\cdot\cdot}(X_1)\right] = f \\ \left[\eta_2(\cdot\cdot) \wedge \delta_{\cdot\cdot,\cdot\cdot\cdot}(X_2\right] \circ f = f \,. \end{cases}$$

In particular, define composition $\circ$ for Ar(Fuz(H)) as above using $\wedge$ and $\vee$. It follows that $\circ$ is indeed associative and for all $f \in Ar_{(X_1,\eta_1),(X_2,\eta_2)}(Fuz(H))$, $\eta_1(\cdot) \wedge \delta_{\cdot,\cdot\cdot}(X_1)$ and $\eta_2(\cdot\cdot) \wedge \delta_{\cdot,\cdot\cdot\cdot}(X_2)$ act as simultaneous local identity arrows.

It follows that $Fuz(H) = (Ob(Fuz(H)),Ar(Fuz(H))$ is a category. Note that explicitly, if $f \in Ar_{(X_1,\eta_1),(X_2,\eta_2)}(Fuz(H))$ and $g \in Ar_{(X_2,\eta_2),(X_3,\eta_3)}(Fuz(H))$, then since

$$f = \delta_{h_f(\cdot),\cdot\cdot} \wedge \eta_1(\cdot)$$

for some $h_f : X_1 \to X_2$; $\eta_1(\cdot) \le \eta_2(h_f(\cdot))$, and

$$g = \delta_{h_g(\cdot\cdot),\cdot\cdot\cdot} \wedge \eta_2(\cdot\cdot)$$

for some $h_g : X_2 \to X_3$; $\eta_2(\cdot\cdot) \le \eta_3(h_g(\cdot\cdot))$, then for all $x_1 \in X_1$, $x_3 \in X_3$,

$$\begin{aligned}(g\circ f)(x_1,x_3) &= \bigvee_{x_2 \in X_2} (\delta_{h_f(x_1),x_2} \wedge \eta_1(x_1) \wedge \delta_{h_g(x_2),x_3} \wedge \eta_2(x_2)) \\ &= \delta_{h_g(h_f(x_1)),x_3} \wedge \eta_1(x_1) \wedge \eta_2(h_f(x_1)) \\ &= \delta_{h_g(h_f(x_1)),x_3} \wedge \eta_1(x_1) \,,\end{aligned}$$

since

$$\eta_1(\cdot) \le \eta_2(h_f(\cdot)) \,,$$

and hence as a check,

$$g\circ f \in Ar_{(X_1,\eta_1),(X_3,\eta_3)}(Fuz(H)) \,.$$

We summarize some of the basic properties of Fuz(H) :
For any $(X_i,\eta_1) \in Ob(Fuz(H))$, $i = 1,2,\ldots$.

Cartesian products: $\underset{i=1,2,\ldots}{\times}(X_i,\eta_i) = (\underset{i=1,2,\ldots}{\times} X_i, \eta_1(\cdot)\wedge\eta_2(\cdot\cdot)\wedge\cdots)$

Power class and subobject class (up to isomorphisms):

$$\tilde{\mathcal{P}}(X_1,\eta_1) = \{(X_1,\Psi) \mid \Psi\in \mathrm{Sub}(X_1,\eta_1)\}$$

where

$$\mathrm{Sub}(X_1,\eta_1) = \{\Psi \mid (X_1,\Psi) \in \mathrm{Ob}(\mathrm{Fuz}(H)) \text{ and } \Psi \le \eta_1 (\text{pt-wise}\} .$$

For any $f,g \in \mathrm{Ar}_{(X_1,\eta_1),(X_2,\eta_2)}(\mathrm{Fuz}(H))$:

Equalizer: $\gamma_{(X_1,\eta_1),(X_2,\eta_2),f,g} \overset{d}{=} (X_1, \bigvee_{y\in X_2}(f(\cdot,y)\wedge g(\cdot,y)))$.

Monic: f is a monic iff

$$f(x',y) \wedge f(x'',y) = \delta(x',x'') \wedge f(x',y)$$

for all $x',x'' \in X_1$, $y \in X_2$.

Epi: f is an epi iff

$$\eta_2(y) = \bigvee_{x\in X_1} f(x,y) \;;\; \text{all } y \in X_2 .$$

Initial object: $\emptyset_{\mathrm{Fuz}(H)} = (\emptyset,0)$

Terminal object(s): $T_{\mathrm{Fuz}(H)} = (\{x\},T_H)$,
where $\{x\}$ is any singleton set and as usual T_H is the maximal element under $\le_H$ of H . (See, e.g., Eytan [57].)

Pullbacks: Let $f \in \mathrm{Ar}_{(X,\Psi),(Z,\theta)}(\mathrm{Fuz}(H))$,

$g \in \mathrm{Ar}_{(Y,\eta),(Z,\theta)}(\mathrm{Fuz}(H))$. Then the following commutative diagram holds

$$\begin{array}{ccc}
\xi \overset{d}{=} (W,\kappa) & \xrightarrow{\ \mathrm{proj}^{(\xi)}_{(Y,\eta)}\ } & (Y,\eta) \\
\mathrm{proj}^{(\xi)}_{(X,\Psi)} \big\downarrow & & \big\downarrow g \\
(X,\Psi) & \xrightarrow[\ f\ ]{} & (Z,\theta)
\end{array}$$

where pullback $\xi = (X,\Psi) \underset{f,g}{\times} (Y,\eta)$, and $W = X \times Y$,

$$\kappa(.,..) \overset{d}{=} \bigvee_{z \in Z} (f(.,z) \wedge g(..,z)) ,$$

with e.g., first projection determined by

$$\mathrm{proj}^{(\xi)}_{(X,\Psi)}(\cdot,\cdot\cdot,x) \overset{d}{=} \xi(\cdot,\cdot\cdot) \wedge \Psi(\cdot) \wedge \Psi(x) \wedge \eta(\cdot\cdot) \wedge \delta_{\cdot,x}$$

for all $x \in X$, where δ is the Krönecker delta function.

D. Goguen's category Gog(H)

Independently, Goguen developed category theory connections with Fuzzy sets [96].

Specifically,

$$\mathrm{Gog}(H) = (\mathrm{Ob}(\mathrm{Gog}(H)),\ \mathrm{Ar}(\mathrm{Gog}(H)),$$

where

$$\mathrm{Ob}(\mathrm{Gog}(H)) = \mathrm{Ob}(\mathrm{Fuz}(H)) ,$$

and it follows immediately from the above results that, for any (X_1,η_1) , $(X_2,\eta_2) \in \mathrm{Ob}(\mathrm{Gog}(H))$,

$$\mathrm{Ar}_{(X_1,\eta_1),(X_2,\eta_2)}(\mathrm{Gog}(H))$$
$$= \{h \mid h : X_1 \to X_2 \ \&\ \eta_1(\cdot) \le \eta_2(h(\cdot))\}$$

may be identified with $\mathrm{Ar}_{(X_1,\eta_1),(X_2\eta_2)}(\mathrm{Fuz}(H))$, where composition here is ordinary functional composition and identity maps $id_{(X,\eta)} \equiv id_X$, i.e., ordinary identity maps. In addition, for any $(X,\eta) \in \mathrm{Ob}(\mathrm{Gog}(H))$, the class of all category subobjects denoted $\tilde{\mathcal{P}}(X,\eta)$, analogous to ordinary power class and fuzzy class notations, is isomorphic to

$$\{(X',\eta') \mid X' \subseteq X \ \&\ \eta' \le \eta \ \text{ pointwise over } X'\} .$$

Thus, order $\le_H$ for H induces an order over $\tilde{\mathcal{P}}(X,\eta)$.

Consider next the following 6 properties which any given category $\mathcal{C} = (\mathrm{Ob}(\mathcal{C}),\mathrm{Ar}(\mathcal{C}))$ may or may not satisfy:

(G1) $\mathcal{C}$ has *initial* and *terminal* objects called $\emptyset_{\mathcal{C}}$ and $T_{\mathcal{C}}$, respectively

(G2) $\mathcal{C}$ has *associative images*, i.e., for $A_1,A_2,A_3 \in \mathrm{Ob}(\mathcal{C})$, and $f \in \mathrm{Ar}_{A_1,A_2}(\mathcal{C})$, $g \in \mathrm{Ar}_{A_2,A_3}(C)$,

$$g(f(A_1)) = (g \circ f)(A_1) ,$$

where image $f(A_1)$ is defined to be the smallest - through functional composition - subobject relative to f and A_1, etc.

(G3) $\mathcal{C}$ is *disjointly a complete distributive lattice*. That is: for each $A \in Ob(\mathcal{C})$, $\mathcal{P}(A)$, the class of all subobjects of A, is a complete distributive lattice ordered according to subobject orderings, i.e., composition with $\vee$ defined here as a least upper bound operator and $\wedge$ as a greatest lower bound one. In addition, noting $\emptyset_C, T_C \in \tilde{\mathcal{P}}(A)$, for any $B,C \in \tilde{\mathcal{P}}(A)$, if $B \neq C$ and B,C are atoms, i.e., for any $D \in \tilde{\mathcal{P}}(A)$, if $\emptyset_C \leq D \leq B$, either $D = \emptyset_{\mathcal{C}}$ or $D = B$, and similarly for C, and noting also that $\complement B \overset{d}{=} \vee \{x \mid x \in \tilde{\mathcal{P}}(A) \ \& \ x \wedge B = \emptyset_{\mathcal{C}}\} \in \tilde{\mathcal{P}}(A)$ and similarly $\complement C \in \tilde{\mathcal{P}}(A)$, then $\complement B \vee \complement C = T_{\mathcal{C}}$.

(G4) For any $\Psi_j \in \tilde{\mathcal{P}}(A)$, $\Psi_j \in Ar_{A_j,A}(\mathcal{C})$, $j \in J$, J any index set, where if $i,j \in J$, $i \neq j$, then $A_i \underset{\tilde{\mathcal{P}}(A)}{\wedge} A_j = \emptyset_C$, the *disjoint union* $\underset{j \in J}{\vee} \Psi_j \in \tilde{\mathcal{P}}(A)$ and the latter may be considered also as the coproduct of all injections Ψ_j from A_j into A, $j \in J$. Conversely, any coproduct (or cartesian sum) of injections in $\mathcal{C}$ may be considered a disjoint union of the injections.

(G5) $\mathcal{C}$ has an *atomic-monic, generator* P which is *projective*, i.e., $P \in Ob(\mathcal{C})$ is such that

(i) For any $A \in Ob(\mathcal{C})$, $Ar_{P,A}(\mathcal{C})$ is a (nonempty for $A \neq \emptyset$) *collection of monomorphisms, such that for any* $\Psi \in \mathcal{P}(A)$, with $\Psi \in Ar_{P,A}(\mathcal{C})$, Ψ is atomic.

(ii) For any $A,B \in Ob(\mathcal{C})$ and $f \neq g$, $f,g \in Ar_{A,B}(\mathcal{C})$, there is $m \in Ar_{P,A}(\mathcal{C})$ such that $f \circ m \neq g \circ m$.

(iii) For each $A,B \in Ob(\mathcal{C})$ and any $f \in Ar_{A,B}(\mathcal{C})$, and $m \in Ar_{P,B}(\mathcal{C})$, there is an $m' \in Ar_{P,A}(\mathcal{C})$ such that

$$f \circ m' = m .$$

(G6) For any $P \in Ob(\mathcal{C})$, $P + P$, the co-product of P with itself is not isomorphic to P.

Theorem (Goguen [96], Carrega [29].)

For any completely distributive lattice H and hence for any Heyting algebra H, $Gog(H)$ satisfies properties (G1) - (G6). In conjunction with this, $Gog(H)$ is a pseudotopos, i.e., it satisfies properties (i) - (iv) (but not in general necessarily (v)) for the definition of a topos in Appendix 1 (9)(xiii).

(a) The initial object $\emptyset_{Gog(H)}$ for $Gog(H)$ is given by,

$$\emptyset_{Gog(H)} = (\phi, 0)$$

which has the basic property that for any $(Y,\eta) \in Ob(Gog(H))$,

$$Ar_{\emptyset_{Gog(H)},(Y,\eta)}(Gog(H)) = \{f_{(Y,\eta)}\}$$

where $f_{Y,\eta} : \emptyset \to Y$ is symbolicly defined.

(b) The terminal object $T_{Gog(H)}$ for $Gog(H)$ is given by

$$T_{Gog(H)} = (\{x\}, T_H)$$

where $x \in X \in Ob(SET)$ is arbitrary fixed; all $T_{Gog(H)}$ are isomorphic; and for any $(Y,N) \in Ob(Gog(H))$,

$$Ar_{(Y,\eta),T_{Gog(H)}}(Gog(H)) = \{f_{(Y,\eta)}\},$$

where here for all $y \in Y$

$$f_{Y,\eta}(y) = x$$

(c) $Gog(H)$ has all products existing, where for any $(X_j,\eta_j) \in Ob(Gog(H))$, $j \in J$, J any index set,

$$\underset{j\in J}{\times} (X_j,\eta_j) \text{ is isomorphic to } (\underset{j\in J}{\times} X_j, \underset{j\in J}{\wedge} \eta_j(\cdot_j)) .$$

(d) Let $(X_j,\eta_j) \in Ob(Gog(H))$, $j \in J$. Thus, w.l.o.g. $(X_j,\eta_j) \in \tilde{\mathcal{P}}(X,\eta)$ for $X = \underset{j\in J}{\times} X_j$, $\eta = \underset{j\in J}{\vee} \eta_j$ pointwise. Then the category definitions for unions and intersections of (X_j,η_j), $j \in J$ in terms of least upper bounds and greatest lower bounds for the order induced on $\tilde{\mathcal{P}}(X,\eta)$ coincides with the Zadehian definitions

$$\underset{j\in J}{\cup} (X_j,\eta_j) = (\underset{j\in J}{\cup} X_j, \underset{j\in J}{\vee_H} \eta_j)$$

$$\underset{j\in J}{\cap} (X_j,\eta_j) = (\underset{j\in J}{\cap} X_j, \underset{j\in J}{\wedge_H} \eta_j) .$$

Similarly for $C(X,\eta) = (X, C_H\eta)$ complementation. $\cup, \eta, C$ all have the usual properties.

(e) An atomic projective generator P for $Gog(H)$ is given by (up to isomorphic uniqueness) for any $x \in X \in Ob(SET)$, $P \overset{d}{=} (\{x\},0)$.

(f) For any (x_1,η_1) , $(X_2,\eta_2) \in Gog(h)$ and any

$$f,g \in Ar_{(X_1,\eta_1),(X_2,\eta_2)}(Gog(H)) ,$$

an equalizer of (f,g) is:

$$id_{X_3} \in Ar_{(X_3,\eta_3),(X_1,\eta_1)}(Gog(H)) .$$

where

$$X_3 = \{x \mid x \in X_1 \ \& \ f(x) = g(x)\} ,$$

$$\eta_3 \overset{d}{=} (\eta_1 \mid X_3) .$$

(g) For any (X_1,η_1) , $(X_2,\eta_2) \in Ob(Gog(H))$, the exponential object

$$(X_2,\eta_2)^{(X_1,\eta_1)} \overset{d}{=} (X_2^{X_1},\eta_{12}) \in Ob(Gog(H))$$

where for any $f : X_1 \to X_2$,

$$\eta_{12}(f) \overset{d}{=} \vee_H\{t \mid t \in H \ \& \ \eta_1(x) \wedge_H t \le \eta_2(f(x)) , \text{ for all } x \in X_1\} ,$$

and associated evaluation

$$ev \in Ar_{(X_1,\eta_1)\times(X_2,\eta_2)^{(X_1,\eta_1)},(X_2,\eta_2)}(Gog(H))$$

$$= Ar_{(X_2^{X_1},\eta_{12}),(X_2,\eta_2)}(Gog(H)) ,$$

given by, for any $f : X_1 \to X_2$ and $x \in X_2$,

$$ev(f,x) \overset{d}{=} f(x) .$$

__**Theorem**__ (Goguen [96])

Let $\mathbb{C}$ be any category satisfying properties (G1) - (G6). Then, up to isomorphism, there exist a unique completely distributive lattice H such that $Gog(H)$ and $\mathbb{C}$ are equivalent in the sense that there is a functor $F : \mathbb{C} \to Gog(H)$ such that for all $A,B \in Ob(\mathbb{C})$, $(F|Ar_{A,B}(\mathbb{C}))$ is isomorphic to $Ar_{F(A),F(B)}(Gog)(H)$ and for any $(X,\eta) \in Ob(Gog(H))$, there exists $C \in Ob(\mathbb{C})$ such that $F(\mathbb{C})$ is isomorphic to (X,η) .

Stout [249'] has pointed out that (G1) (G2) (G4) (and (G6) in a trivial-like sense) hold for all topoi, whereas (G3) and (G5), in general, do not.

Another property of Gog(H) that is desirable is the determination of pullbacks. It follows by using the property of pullbacks for Fuz(H) in 2.4.2 (C) and the representation of Gog(H) in Fuz(H) (via its arrows) in 2.4.2 (F)(2), that we have the following:

For any $f \in Ar_{(X,\Psi),(Z,\theta)}(Gog(H))$,

$g \in Ar_{(Y,\eta),(Z,\theta)}(Gog(H))$, the following commutative diagram holds

$$\begin{array}{ccc} \xi = (W,\kappa) & \xrightarrow{\ proj^{(\xi)}_{(Y,\eta)}\ } & (Y,\eta) \\ {\scriptstyle proj^{(\xi)}_{(X,\Psi)}}\downarrow & & \downarrow{\scriptstyle g} \\ (X,\Psi) & \xrightarrow[\ f\ ]{} & (Z,\theta) \end{array}$$

where pullback $\xi = (X,\Psi) \underset{f,g}{\times} (Y,\eta)$,

where

$$W \overset{d}{=} X \times Y$$

$$\kappa(x,y) \overset{d}{=} \Psi(x) \wedge \eta(y) \wedge \theta(f(x)) \wedge \delta(f(x),g(y)) \ ,$$

for all $x \in X$, $y \in Y$, and

$$proj^{(\xi)}_{(X,\Psi)} = proj_X(W)$$

In particular, if $g \in Sub(Z,\theta)$, we may write (from 2.4.2 (D)) w.l.o.g.

$$Y = Z \ , \quad g = id_Z \ , \quad \eta \le \theta \ .$$

and define

$$Sub(f) : Sub(Z,\theta) \to Sub(X,\Psi)$$

by, for all $x \in X$,

$$\begin{aligned} Sub(f)(g)(x) &\overset{d}{=} \kappa(x,f(x)) \\ &= \Psi(x) \wedge \eta\,(f(x)) \wedge \theta\,(f(x)) \\ &= \Psi(x) \wedge \eta\,(f(x)) \ . \end{aligned}$$

E. <u>Higg's topos Higg(H) .</u>

Higgs developed a category connected with sheaf theory [59]. First define

$$Higg(H) = (Ob(Higg(H)) \ , \ Ar(Higg(H))) \ ,$$

where: for any $X \in Ob(SET)$,

$$Ob_X(Higg(H)) = \{(X,\theta) \mid \theta : X \times X \to H \ \&$$

(H1) θ is symmetric,

(H2) $\theta \circ \theta \le \theta$.

i.e.,

$$\theta(x,y)) \wedge \theta(y,z) \le \theta(x,z), \quad \text{all} \quad x,y,z \in X\}$$

Thus, by setting $x = z$ and using symmetry, it follows that for all $(X,\theta) \in Ob_X(Higg(H))$,

(1) $\theta(\cdot,\cdot\cdot) \le (D(\theta)(\cdot) \wedge D(\theta)(\cdot\cdot))$,

(ii) $(X,D(\theta)) \in Ob_X(Fuz(H))$,

where we recall the diagonalization $D(\theta)$ of θ is

$$D(\theta)(x) \overset{d}{=} \theta(x,x) , \quad \text{for all} \quad x \in X .$$

Also, for any $(X_1,\theta_1),(X_2,\theta_2) \in Ob(Higg)$,

$$Ar_{(X_1,\theta_1),(X_2,\theta_2)}(Higg) = \{f \mid f : X_1 \times X_2 \to H \ \&$$

(H3) $f \circ \theta_1 \le f$, $\theta_2 \circ f \le f$,

i.e.,

$$\begin{cases} \theta_1(x_1',x_1) \wedge f(x_1,x_2) \le f(x_1',x_2) \\ f(x_1,x_2) \wedge \theta_2(x_2,x_2') \le f(x_1,x_2') \end{cases} ,$$

for all $x_1,x_1' \in X_1$, $x_2,x_2' \in X_2$, &

(H4) $f^T \circ f \le \theta_2$,

i.e.,

$$f(x_1,x_2) \wedge f(x_1,x_2') \le \theta_2(x_2,x_2')$$

for all $x_1 \in X_1$, $x_2,x_2' \in X_2$ &

(H5) $\bigvee_{x_2 \in X_2} f(\cdot,x_2) = D(\theta_1)(\cdot)$,

(H6) $f(\cdot,\cdot\cdot) \le D(\theta_1)(\cdot) \wedge D(\theta_2)(\cdot\cdot)\}$.

Composition of arrows for Higg(H) is the same as introduced earlier for $f : X_1 \times X_2 \to H$, $g : X_2 \times X_3 \to H$, etc. The identity arrow under composition is, for any $(X,\theta) \in Higg(H)$

$$id_{(X,\theta)} \overset{d}{\equiv} \theta : X \times X \to H .$$

Theorem (Fourmann and Scott [59], [226']).

$Higg(H)$ is a Grothendieck topos equivalent to the category of sheaves over H, with subobject classifier Ω being

$$\Omega \overset{d}{\equiv} (H, 1_H),\ 1_H : H\times H \to H\ ,\ 1_H(x,y) \equiv 1_H\ .$$

We can write symbolically (see Johnstone [127], pp. 8 - 12)

$$Higg(H) = Sh\circ(SET^{H^{op}})\ ,$$

where $Sh \equiv \Gamma L$ is the associated sheaf functor and $SET^{H^{op}}$ is the category of all presheaves:

First, Identify Heyting algebra H as a category where $Ob(H) = H$ and for any $h_1, h_2 \in H$,

$$Ar_{h_1,h_2}(H) \overset{d}{\equiv} \begin{cases} \emptyset\ , & \text{if } h_1 >_H h_2 \\ (h_1 \Rightarrow h_2)\ , & \text{if } h_1 \le_H h_2\ , \end{cases}$$

where $\Rightarrow\ = \ \Rightarrow_H$ is the implication operator for H (see section 2.3.3 (C)(3)).

Then

$$SET^{H^{op}} = (Ob(SET^{H^{op}})\ ,\ Ar(SET^{H^{op}}))$$

where

$$Ob(SET^{H^{op}}) = \{F \mid F : H \to SET \text{ is a contravariant functor}\}$$

and for all $F,G \in Ob(SET^{H^{op}})$,

$$Ar_{F,G}(SET^{H^{op}}) = \{g \mid g : F \overset{\cdot}{\longrightarrow} G \text{ is a natural transform}\}$$

Theorem (Pitts [203])

For any $(X_j,\theta_j) \in Ob(Higg)$, $j = 1,2, \ldots$ and

$$f \in Ar_{(X_1,\theta_1),(X_2,\theta_2)}(Higg(H))\ ,$$

(a) f is a monomorphism iff $f o f^T \le \theta_1$

(b) f is an epimorphism iff $\bigvee_{x \in X_1} f(x_1, \cdot) = D(\theta_2)(\cdot)$

(c) f is an isomorphism iff f is a mono and epi.

The subobjects, terminal objects, initial objects, etc., for Higg(H) are completely analagous to those for Fuz(H). (See also Eytan [57] for a listing of various properties of $Fuz_{\times}(H)$ (see the next subsection F) which in turn can be directly translated in terms of Higg(H).)

Now consider Higg's category and two point coverage functions (see Chapter 5). This is a special case of the problem, given any $f : \mathcal{P}_n(X) \to [0,1]$, where

$$\mathcal{P}_n(X) \stackrel{d}{=} \{A \mid A \subseteq X \ \& \ \text{card}(A) \le n\} ,$$

for some fixed integer n, to determine which, if any, random subsets S of X are such that their n point coverage functions match f, that is, for all $A \in \mathcal{P}_n(X)$,

$$f(A) = Pr(A \subseteq S)$$

Clearly, when $n = 1$, we have the well investigated one point coverage problem for fuzzy sets. When $n = 2$ and $f \in Ob(Higg([0,1]))$ (letting once more $H = [0,1]$ from now on), this reduces to the two point coverage problem for Higg objects.

Clearly, for any random subset S of X and any $x,y \in X$

(1)

$$\max(Pr(x\in S)+Pr(y\in S)-1,0) \le Pr(\{x,y\} \subseteq S) \le \min(Pr(x\in S),Pr(y\in S)) ,$$

noting that upper and lower bounds also coincide with the maximal and minimal copulas possible with respect to the possibility function $Pr(\cdot\in S)$ evaluated at x and y. (See also section 2.3.6 on t-norms, t-conorms for similar bounds and Chapter 6.)

First, let us remark that in general it is <u>not</u> true there exists

$$f : [0,1] \times [0,1] \to [0,1]$$

such that for given random subset S of X, for all $x,y \in X$,

(2) $$Pr(\{x,y\} \subseteq S) = f(Pr(x \in S) , Pr(y \in S)) ,$$

unlike the analogue in Sklar's theorem for probability distribution functions [226]: Reconsider the above relations in terms of zero-one random variables representing whether a point is, or is not, covered by S and show for two distinct sets $\{x,y\}$, $\{x',y'\} \subseteq X$,

$$Pr(x \in S) = Pr(x' \in S) , Pr(y \in S) = Pr(y' \in S) ,$$

but

$$Pr(\{x,y\} \subseteq S) \neq Pr(\{x',y'\} \subseteq S).)$$

However, for certain random subsets, this is not only true, but f is also a t-norm. For random sets of the form $S(\underset{\sim}{A};\phi_{\&})$ where here $\underset{\sim}{A} \equiv A$, a single fuzzy subset of X, for any $n \geq 1$ and $x_1,\ldots,x_n \in X$,

$$Pr(\{x_1,\ldots,x_n\} \subseteq S(A;\phi_{\&}))$$

$$= \phi_{\&}(Pr(x_1 \in S(A;\phi_{\&}),\cdots,Pr(x_n \in S(A;\phi_{\&})))$$

$$= \phi_{\&}(\phi_A(x_1),\cdots,\phi_A(x_n)) .$$

(Special cases of this random set, include $S_U(A) = \phi_A^{-1}[U,1]$, for $\phi_{\&} = \min$ and $T(A)$, for $\phi_{\&} = \text{prod}$. See Chapter 6.)

Because of eq. (1), eq. (2) may have no solution in S, depending on choice of f. For example, if we choose the Higg's object (X,f), where $D(f)$ is arbitrary over $\text{diag}(X{\times}X)$, but such that there are at least two distinct points $x_o,y_o \in Y$ such that

$$f(x_o,y_o) + f(y_o,y_o) - 1 > f(x_o,y_o) \geq 0 ,$$

then eq. (2) has no solution. Or, if X is discrete, let

$$f(x,y) = \begin{cases} > 0 & \text{if} \quad x = y \\ = 0 & \text{iff} \quad x \neq y , \end{cases}$$

such that

(3) $$\sum_{x \in X} f(x,x) > 1 .$$

Thus, if an S satisfies eq.(2), then for any $x \neq y$,

$$0 = Pr(\{x,y\} \subseteq S) ,$$

which implies $S = \{V\}$, V a random variable over X, but letting $x = y$ arbitrary in eq. (2), eq. (3) yields a contradiction.

The following positive result does obtain:

1. Given any space X and a random subset S of X, there is a copula $\phi_{\&}$ such that

(4) $$\phi_{\&}(f(x,y),f(y,z)) \leq f(x,z) ,$$

for all $x,y,z \in X$, where for all $x,y \in X$

$$f(x,y) = Pr(\{x,y\} \subseteq S) .$$

2. Given any space X and $\phi_{\&} = \min$, a solution class of f's satisfying (4) is given by

$$f = \phi_A(\cdot) \wedge \phi_A(\cdot\cdot) ,$$

for all fuzzy subsets A of X . Note that since min is the maximal t-norm, any solution of (3) for $\phi_{\&} = \min$, i.e., any Higg's object (X,f) (assuming f symmetric) must also satisfy eq. (3) , for $\phi_{\&}$ but not conversely.

3. Given any space X and $\phi_{\&}$, any strict Archimedean t-norm [140] (such as prod) then the solution class of all f's satisfying eq.(3) is

$$\{f \mid f = h^{-1} \circ d \text{ , } d \text{ is any pseudometric over } X\} ,$$

where $\circ$ is ordinary function composition and

$$\phi_{\&}(x,y) = h^{-1}(h(x) + h(y)) ,$$

$h : [0,1] \to \mathbb{R}^+$, $h(0) = +\infty$, $h(1) = 0$, h decreasing, is the canonical representation of $\phi_{\&}$. (See 2.3.6.)

Finally, it should be noted that Cerruti [30] has investigated the category of fuzzy set relations.

For some set theory connections involving Higg(H) , see subsection G of this section.

Next, we will consider several important relations between Fuz(H) , a class of modifications of Fuz(H) , $Fuz_{\asymp}(H)$, and Higg(H) as well as some connections with Gog(H) .

For more general constructions of which Gog(H) , Fuz(H) , $Fuz_{\asymp}(H)$ and Higg(H) are special cases, see Apendix 3, at the end of 2.4.

F. Relations between the basic categories.

We present a list of relevant results connecting Gog(H) , Fuz(H) , modifications of Fuz(H) and Higg(H) . Some of these results are motivated by the desire to determine which of the above categories are topoi - topoi being in a sense kinds of generalized sets. (See also the discussion in (G) following this subsection.) In the following, H is some fixed Heyting algebra.

(1) Fuz(H) is the type II Bénabou extension $\mathcal{F}_{II}(SET,H^{\cdot})$ of the deduction category $(SET,H^{\cdot})$ *with the proviso*: $\asymp$ as developed in the formal language in section 2.2.2 is to be replaced formally by ordinary equality (via the Krönecker delta function. This shows up in the construction in constraint (F3) , Appendix 3, section 2.4.2.

(See also Remark 3 of the Appendix.)

(2) Carrega [29] showed that for any complete chain H (and H is thus a Heyting algebra), $Fuz(H)$ and $Gog(H)$ are isomorphic under the isomorphism functor $F : Gog(H) \to Fuz(H)$, where for any (X,θ), $(Y,\Psi) \in Ob(Gog(H))$ and for any $f \in Ar_{(X,\theta),(Y,\Psi)}(Gog(H))$,

$$F((X,\theta)) \overset{d}{=} (X,\theta) ,$$

$F(f) : X \times Y \to H$ is such that, for all $x \in X$, $y \in Y$,

$$F(f)(x,y) \overset{d}{=} \delta_{f(x),y}(Y) \wedge \theta(x) \wedge \Psi(y) .$$

It follows from Appendix 3 (at the end of 2.4.2), (iii) and Remark 3, Case (4), that for H, a general Heyting algebra, and F as above

$$F : Gog(H) \to Fuz(H)$$

is a (non-faithful, in general) functor.

In addition, Stout [249'] has indicated differences in structure between $Ar(Gog(H))$ and $Ar(Fuz(H))$ through the fact that for any $(X,\eta) \in Ob(Fuz(H)) = Ob(Gog(H))$ and any singleton $\{x\}$,

$$Ar_{(\{x\},0),(X,\eta)}(Gog(H))$$

$$= \{f \mid f : \{x\} \to X \text{ and } \eta \circ f \geq 0\}$$

$$= X^{\{x\}} ,$$

but by (F1),

$$Ar_{(\{x\},0),(X,\eta)}(Fuz(H)) = \{f_o\} ,$$

where

$$f_o : \{x\} \times X \to H ; \ f_o \equiv 0 .$$

(3) It should be noted (see Appendix 3 (iv), Remark 3) that $Gog(H)$ is a type-I Benabou extension of the deduction category $(SET,H^{\cdot})$, again as in (1), with $\asymp$ interpreted as ordinary equality. Thus $Gog(H) = \mathcal{F}_I(SET,H^{\cdot})$.

(4) Next, let us modify Eytan's original $Fuz(H)$ [56] to $Fuz_{\asymp}(H)$, where in the type II Benabou construction in (1) - and in particular in (F3) - , $\asymp$ is retained. See, e.g., Appendix 3 (iv) and section 2.3.3 (C), Gödel-intuitionistic logic, for the procedure for generating the intuitionistic Krönecker delta e_θ from any object (X,θ) in $Higg(H)$; in turn e_θ defines a corresponding $\asymp$ over (X,θ). Similarly, we can modify $Gog(H)$ to be $Gog_{\asymp}(H)$.

(5) Thus, it follows from Appendix 3 (Theorem 2) that

$F_{\asymp}$: Gog $_{\asymp}$(H) → Fuz $_{\asymp}$(H) where $F_{\asymp}$ is the same as F in (2) but with δ replaced by a suitable e_θ's , is a faithful factor.

(6) Eytan claimed in [56] that Fuz(H) was indeed a topos, because (mistakenly) of Theorem 2, Appendix 3. But since $(SET, H^{\cdot})$, in effect, due to ≍ being forced to be ordinary equality and hence not in general compatible with the $Th_{syn_K, K}(\ell)$ (see 2.2.2), is *not* a formal topos, $\mathcal{F}_{II}(SET, H^{\cdot})$ need not be a topos. In conjunction with this problem, the following results are pertinant:

(i) Carrega [29] showed that Gog(H) is a pseudo topos (again, see subsection D). In addition, if H is a complete chain (with at least three elements), then Gog(H), and hence by (2) above, Fuz(H) have no subobject classifier. (See Appendix 1, end of section 2.4.3, for pertinent definitions.) Thus, in this case, Gog(H) and Fuz(H) are not topoi.

(ii) Ponasse [204] and Pitts [203], in effect, showed that: Fuz(H) is a topos iff H is a Boolean algebra, in which case Fuz(H) is equivalent to Higg(H) .

Note that H = {0,1} is a (trivial) Boolean algebra and as a check, indeed Fuz({0,1}) may be identified with the topos SET . There is a great potential for applying the last mentioned theorem to set-valued (or interval-valued) logics, i.e., logics in which truth values are actually sets of numbers. (See the interesting work of Shoesmith and Smiley [234'].)

Pitts [203] concluded from this analysis that Higg(H) , not Fuz(H) , is the appropriate vehicle to "fuzzify" SET , noting that Higg objects simultaneously fuzzify membership and a kind of equality.

(iii) More directly, and apropos to the previous comments, if $(\mathcal{C}, \mathfrak{R})$ is a formal topos then (Appendix 3, Theorem 2) $\mathcal{F}_{II}(\mathcal{C}, \mathfrak{R})$ must be a topos. In particular, for $(SET, H^{\cdot})$ (see comment (4) above) it must follow that $(SET, H^{\cdot})$ when ≍ is interpreted as ordinary equality (=) , in general, is not a formal topos. Indeed we can show, through a simple counterexample to deduction rule $R_{I,Th,24}$ (2.2.2) that this is so:

Choose any X,Y ∈ Ob(SET) , $\phi \in H^Y$, y ∈ Y , x ∈ X , $s,t \in \mathcal{P}(X)^Y$, $0 < \|\phi(y)\| < \|x \in s(y)\| < \|x \in t(y)\| \le 1$. Then the hypothesis of $R_{I,Th,24}$ will hold:

$$\begin{cases} \|\phi(y)\| \wedge \|x \in s(y)\| \le \|x \in t(y)\| \\ \|\phi(y)\| \wedge \|x \in t(y)\| \le \|x \in s(y)\| \end{cases} .$$

But the conclusion

$$\|\phi(y)\| \le \|s(y) \asymp t(y)\|$$

is contradicted since

$$0 = \|s(y) \asymp t(y)\| < \|\phi(y)\| \ .$$

On the other hand, not any choice of $\asymp$ will work, since for $\asymp$ being interpreted as being derived from e_θ , $\theta \in Ob(Higg)$, by choosing $\theta = \delta$, we know $e_\delta = \delta$, which in turn yields $\asymp$ interpreted as ordinary equality. However, if we choose $\theta : H \times H \to H$ to be of the form $\theta(x,y) = \eta(x) \wedge \eta(y)$, for all $x,y \in H$, then, e_θ will indeed generate $\asymp$ so that all axioms and rules of $Th_{syn_K,K}$ are valid and $(SET,H^\cdot)$ is indeed a formal topos, as is seen by inspection. In turn, this choice for $(SET,H^\cdot)$ yields $\mathcal{S}_{II}(SET,H^\cdot) = Fuz_{\asymp}(H)$ as a topos by Theorem 2, Appendix 3.

(iv) Pitts [203] also related Fuz(H) with Higg(H) in the following way:

Define the categories

$$Higg_{const}(H) \subseteq Higg_{subconst}(H) \subseteq Higg(H) \ ,$$

where

$$Higg_{const}(H) \overset{d}{=} Ob(Higg_{const}(H)) \ , Ar(Higg_{const}(H))) \ ,$$

$$Ob(Higg_{const}(H)) \overset{d}{=} \{(X,\delta(X{\times}X) \mid X \in Ob(SET)\} \ ,$$

noting $\delta(X)$ is the ordinary Krönecker delta function over X .

$$Ar(Higg_{const}(H)) = \bigcup_{\substack{X,Y \\ \in Ob(SET)}} Ar(Higg_{(X,\delta(X\times X)),(Y,\delta(Y\times Y))}(H)) \ ,$$

$$Higg_{subconst}(H) = (Ob(Higg_{subconst}(H)),Ar(Higg_{subconst}(H))) \ ,$$

$$Ob(Higg_{subconst}(H)) = \{(X,\theta) \mid X \in Ob(SET) \ , \theta \in Sub(X,\delta(X{\times}X), \text{ i.e., } \theta : X \times X \to H \text{ with } \theta(x,y) \le \delta_{x,y}(X{\times}X)\} \ ,$$

$$Ar(Higg_{subconst}(H)) = \bigcup_{\left[\substack{(X,\theta),(Y,\gamma) \\ \in Ob(Higg_{subconst}(H))}\right]} Ar_{(X,\theta)(Y,\gamma)}(Higg(H)) \ .$$

Define also the mapping

$$G : Fuz(H) \to Higg(H) \ ,$$

where, for all $X \in Ob(SET)$, $\eta \in H^X$

$$G((X,\eta)) \overset{d}{=} (X,G(\eta)) \ ,$$

$$G(\eta) \overset{d}{=} \delta_{(\cdot,\cdot\cdot)}(X \times X) \wedge \eta(\cdot) ,$$

and for any (X,η) , $(Y,\xi) \in Ob(Fuz(H))$, and any $f \in Ar_{(X,\eta),(Y,\xi)}(Fuz(H))$,

$$G(f) \overset{d}{=} f \in Ar_{G((X,\eta)),G((y,\xi))}(Higg(H)) .$$

Note $G(\eta) \in Sub(X,\delta(X{\times}X))$. Conversely, if $f \in Ar_{(Y,\theta),(X,\delta(X\times X))}(Higg(H))$ is a monic, i.e., $f \in Sub(X,\delta(X{\times}X))$, for some $(Y,\theta) \in Ob(Higg(H))$, then also f is an isomorphism from (Y,θ) to $G(X,\Psi)$, where $(X,\Psi) \in Ob(Fuz(H))$, and where

$$\Psi(\cdot) \overset{d}{=} \bigvee_{y \in Y} f(y,\cdot) .$$

G is a full and faithful functor imbedding $Fuz(H)$ into the subcategory $Higg_{subconst}(H)$ of $Higg(H)$.

Furthermore, consider the mapping $D : Higg(H) \to Fuz(H)$, where for any $f \in Ar(Higg(H))$, $D(f) = f$ and for any $(X,\theta) \in Ob(Higg(H))$,

$$D((X,\theta)) = (X,D(\theta)) \in Ob(Fuz(H)) ,$$
$$D(\theta) \overset{d}{=} \theta(\cdot,\cdot) : X \to H .$$

Then the following diagram holds:

For any $(X,\theta) \in Ob(Higg(H))$:

$$\begin{array}{ccc} G(D(X,\theta)) \in Ob(Higg_{subconst}(H)) & \xrightarrow[\text{an epi}]{\theta} & (X,\theta) \\ \Big\downarrow \; G(D(X,\theta)) \text{, a mono} & & \\ (X,\delta(X \times X)) \in Ob(Higg_{const}(H)) . & & \end{array}$$

Thus, (X,θ) is a quotient object of $G(D(X,\theta))$, which in turn is the domain of a subobject of $(X,\delta(X{\times}X))$. Hence, $Higg(H)$ is the quotient object completion of the subcategory $Higg_{subconst}(H)$, which may be identified with $Fuz(H)$.

(v) We can establish two additional interesting connections between $Fuz(H)$, and more generally $Fuz_{\ast}(H)$, and $Higg(H)$.

First choose any function

$$g : Ob(SET) \to Rel(SET,H^{\cdot}) ,$$

where for any $X \in Ob(SET)$,

$$g(X) \in H^{X\times X} \overset{d}{=} Rel_{X\times X}(SET,H^{\cdot}) .$$

Let $(X,g(X))$, $(Y,g(Y)) \in Ob(Higg(H))$ and consider any $f \in Ar_{(X,g(X)),(Y,g(Y))}(Higg(H))$. Then noting $g \le e_g$ (see Appendix 3 (iv) at the end of 2.4.2), (H4) implies (F3) with right upper bound e_g. Also (H4), (H5) imply (F1) holds with right upper bound the same as in $Higg(H) : D(g(X)) \wedge D(g(Y))$. (F2) and (H5) are the same. Thus $f \in Ar_{(X,D(g(X))),(Y,D(g(Y)))}(Fuz_{\check{g}}(H))$, and hence

(a) $$Ar_{(X,g(X)),(Y,g(Y))}(Higg(H)) \subseteq Ar_{(X,D(g(X))),(Y,D(g(Y)))}(Fuz_{\check{g}}(H)) ,$$

for all $X \in Ob(SET)$.

Secondly, choose any

$$f : Ob(SET) \to Rel(SET,H^{\cdot})$$

where for any $X \in Ob(SET)$,

$$f(X) \in H^{X} = Rel_{X}(SET,H^{\cdot})$$

and in turn define

$$g_f : Ob(SET) \to Rel(SET,H^{\cdot})$$

where for all $X \in Ob(SET)$, $x,y \in X$

$$g_f(x,y) \overset{d}{=} \varepsilon_f(x,y) \overset{d}{=} f(X)(x) \wedge f(X)(y) .$$

Then for all $X \in Ob(SET)$

(b) $$Ar_{(X,f(X)),(Y,f(Y))}(Fuz_{\check{g}_f}(H)) \cap Ar_{(X,g_f(X)),(Y,g_f(Y))}(Higg(H)) = \{\varepsilon_{f(X),f(Y)}\}$$

where

$$\varepsilon_{f(X),f(Y)}(x,y) \overset{d}{=} f(X)(x) \wedge f(Y)(y) ,$$

for all $x \in X$, $y \in Y$.

Proof: Clearly for all $X \in Ob(SET)$, $(X, g_f(X)) \in Ob(\mathcal{F}_{III}(SET, H^{\cdot}))$.
In turn, replace $\asymp$ by $\asymp_{g_f} = e_{g_f}$ and consider $Fuz_{\asymp_{g_f}}(H)$:

For any $f \in Ar_{(X,f(X)),(Y,f(Y))}(Fuz_{\asymp_{g_f}}(H))$, (F1), (F2), (F3) all hold for f with right hand side upper bounds being $f(X) \wedge f(Y)$, for (F1) and e_{g_f} for (F3), etc.

Now form:

$$f(x,y) \wedge f(x,y') \le f(X)(x) \wedge f(Y)(y) \wedge f(X)(x) \wedge f(Y)(y') \wedge e_{g_f}(y,y') ,$$

for all $x \in X$, $y,y' \in Y$.
But

$$\begin{aligned} & f(X)(x) \wedge f(Y)(y) \wedge f(X)(x) \wedge f(Y)(y') \wedge e_{g_f}(y,y') \\ &= f(X)(x) \wedge f(Y)(y) \wedge f(Y)(y') \\ &\le f(Y)(y) \wedge f(Y)(y') \\ &= g_f(Y)(y,y') . \end{aligned}$$

Hence (H4) holds:

$$f(x,y) \wedge f(x,y') \le g_f(Y)(y,y')$$

for all $x \in X$, $y,y' \in Y$.
In addition, since $D(g_f) = f$, (F2) and (H5) are the same with this use.
All that remains is (H3), which becomes here, for all $x,x' \in X$, $y,y' \in Y$,

$$\begin{aligned} g_f(X)(x,x') \wedge f(x,y) &= f(X)(x) \wedge f(X)(x) \wedge f(x,y) \\ &\le f(x',y) \ ? \end{aligned}$$

$$f(x,y) \wedge g_f(Y)(y,y') = f(x,y) \wedge f(Y)(y) \wedge f(Y)(y') \le f(x,y') \ ?$$

Equivalently,

$$\begin{cases} f(X)(x') \wedge f(x,y) \le f(x',y) & ? \\ f(x,y) \wedge f(Y)(y') \le f(x,y') & ? \end{cases}$$

Taking supremums over x in the bottom inequality and using (F2) implies

$$f(X)(x) \wedge f(Y)(y') \le f(x,y') .$$

But by (F1)

$$f(x,y') \le f(X)(x) \wedge f(Y)(y') .$$

Hence, we must have for all $x \in X$, $y' \in Y$,

$$f(X)(x) \quad \wedge \quad f(Y)(y') = f(x,y') ,$$

i.e.,

$$f(x,y) = \varepsilon_{f(X),f(Y)}(x,y) .$$

Combining (a) and (b), noting g_f is a particular g, we obtain for all $X \in Ob(SET)$

$$\text{(c)} \quad \{\varepsilon_{f(X),f(Y)}\} = Ar_{(X,g_f(X)),(Y,g_f(Y))}(Higg(H))$$
$$\subseteq Ar_{(X,f(X)),(Y,f(Y))}(Fuz_{\overset{\asymp}{g}_f}(H)) .$$

Thus, we can consider the basic mapping

$$\mathfrak{Q} : Higg(H) \to Fuz(H) ,$$

where

$$Fuz(H) \overset{d}{\equiv} \bigcup_{\begin{bmatrix}\text{over all}\\ \text{such } g\end{bmatrix}} Fuz_{\overset{\asymp}{g}}(H) ,$$

so that for all (X,Ψ), $(Y,\theta) \in Ob(Higg(H))$ and $f \in Ar_{(X,\Psi),(Y,\theta)}(Higg(H))$,

$$\mathfrak{Q}(X,\Psi) \overset{d}{\equiv} (X,D(\Psi)) ,$$
$$\mathfrak{Q}(f) \overset{d}{\equiv} f \in Ar_{\mathfrak{Q}(X,Y),\mathfrak{Q}(Y,\theta)}(Fuz_{\overset{\asymp}{g}}(H)) ,$$

and hence in a sense $\mathfrak{Q}$ may be considered a functor.

We can also define

$$Higg(H) \overset{d}{\equiv} \bigcup_{\text{all } g} Higg_g(H) ,$$

where $Higg_g(H)$ is like $Higg(H)$ except that $Higg_g(H)$ is restricted to objects generated by g and arrows are likewise developed. It follows, that for any choice of g there is a mapping

$$\mathfrak{Q}' : Higg(H) \to Fuz(H)$$

where for any g as before

$$\mathfrak{Q}' : Higg_g(H) \to Fuz_g , \text{ etc.}$$

Eytan's [57] claimed that $Fuz_{\asymp}(H)$ and $Higg(H)$ are equivalent under the mapping D , but this does not appear so.

(vi) Stout [249'] has shown a natural relation directly between $Gog(H)$ and $Higg(H)$ via the level sets functor $\mathcal{L}$. (See also

Chapters 5 and 6 for related results, where level set mappings are used to connect fuzzy sets, random sets and/or flou sets.):

$$\mathcal{S} : \text{Gog}(H) \to \text{SET}^{H^{op}} ,$$

where for all $(X,\eta) \in \text{Ob}(\text{Gog}(H))$,

$$\mathcal{S}(X,\eta) \overset{d}{=} \eta^{-1}[h,T_H]$$

$$\overset{d}{=} \{x \mid x \in X \ \text{ and } \ \eta(x) \geq h\} ,$$

and for any h_1 , $h_2 \in H$, $h_1 \leq h_2$, and hence arrow $((h_1 \Rightarrow h_2) : h_1 \to h_2)$ of H ,

$$\mathcal{S}(X,\eta(h_1 \Rightarrow h_2) \overset{d}{=} \text{id}_{\mathcal{S}(X,\eta)(h_2)} : \mathcal{S}(X,\eta)(h_2) \to \mathcal{S}(X,\eta)(h_1) ,$$

and hence $\mathcal{S}(X,\eta) \in \text{SET}^{H^{op}}$. Also, for any $f \in \text{Ar}_{(X_1,\eta_1),(X,\eta_2)}(\text{Gog}(H))$, define the natural transform

$$\mathcal{S}(f) : \mathcal{S}(X_1,\eta_1) \overset{\cdot}{\longrightarrow} \mathcal{S}(X_2,\eta_2) ,$$

by, for all $h \in H$,

$$\mathcal{S}(f)(h) : \mathcal{S}(X_1,\eta_1)(h) \to \mathcal{S}(X_2,\eta_2)(h) ,$$

an ordinary function $(\in \text{Ar}(\text{SET}))$, where for all $k \in \mathcal{S}(X_1,\eta_1)(h)$,

$$\mathcal{S}(f)(h)(k) \overset{d}{=} f(k) \in \mathcal{S}(X_2,\eta_2)(h) ,$$

since

$$\eta_2(f(k)) \geq \eta_1(k) \geq h ,$$

etc.

$\mathcal{S}$ preserves limits and monics and the composition and extension (see also 2.4.2 (E)) functor

$$F_o \overset{d}{=} \text{Sh} \circ \mathcal{S} : \text{Gog}(H) \to \text{Higg}(H)$$

preserves all finite limits and colimits (and hence is "exact") as well as all monics, but not in general epis and is hence not a faithful functor. In addition, it has a right adjoint (see [249'], Prop. 3).

Next, let us reconsider the functor in subsection 2.4.2 (F)(2)

$$F_1 : \text{Gog}(H) \to \text{Fuz}(H)$$

where we add the subscript 1 for notational purposes and we do not assume necessarily that H is a complete chain. Also, reconsider from subsection 2.4.2 (F) (6) (iv), the faithful functor

$$G_o : \mathrm{Fuz}(H) \to \mathrm{Higg}(H) ,$$

with added notational subscript o .

In summary, F_o , F_1 and G_o all preserve finite limits and colimits and all monos, but in general, F_o and F_1 are not faithful, while G_o is. As Stout concludes, in any case, this implies that all three functors do preserve all power class and hence subobjects, G_o being of course injective.

Extending Goguen's observations [96] (see also 2.4.2 (D), (G4)) , Stout points out the basic idea that for any category $\mathbb{C}$ with all limits and colimits (finite) existing, for any $A,B,C \in \mathrm{Ob}(\mathbb{C})$ and $(f : B \to A)$, $(g : C \to A) \in \tilde{\mathcal{P}}(A)$, the intersection and union of f and g can be defined as equalizer $(\gamma_{B,C,f,g})$ and similarly for coequalizer of f and g .

Let $(X,\eta) \in \mathrm{Ob}(\mathrm{Fuz}(H)) = \mathrm{Ob}(\mathrm{Gog}(H))$.

Thus, for $\mathrm{Gog}(H)$, and any (X_1,η_1) , $(X_2, \eta_2) \in \tilde{\mathcal{P}}(X,\eta)$, i.e., $X_1, X_2 \subseteq X$, $\eta_1, \eta_2 \le \eta$,

$$(X_1,\eta_1) \cup (X_2,\eta_2) = (X_1 \cup X_2, \eta_1 \vee \eta_2)$$

where $\eta_1 \vee \eta_2 = \eta_1$ or η_2 , for appropriate values not in $X_1 \cup X_2$,

$$(X_1,\eta_1) \cap (X_2,\eta_2) = (X_1 \cap X_2, \eta_1 \wedge \eta_2) .$$

For $\mathrm{Fuz}(H)$, and any (X_1,η_1) , $(X_2,\eta_2) \in \tilde{\mathcal{P}}(X,\eta)$, i.e.,

$$X_1 = X_2 = X , \quad \eta_1,\eta_2 \le \eta ,$$

the same formal definitions hold.

Similar properties hold for $\mathrm{Higg}(H)$. But in addition, as a topos, noting that for any $(X,\Psi) \in \mathrm{Ob}(\mathrm{Higg}(H))$,

$$\phi : \tilde{\mathcal{P}}(X,\Psi) \to \Omega^{(X,\Psi)}$$

is bijective, where $\Omega = (H,T_H)$ is the subobject classifier for $\mathrm{Higg}(H)$, all set-like operations on subobjects of $\mathrm{Higg}(H)$ can be naturally defined in terms of membership functions in $\Omega^{(X,\Psi)} = \{f \mid f \in \mathrm{Ar}_{(X,\Psi),\Omega}(\mathrm{Higg}(H))\}$ where analagous to the situation for general logical systems (see 2.3.5), we can define for any $(X,\lambda) \in \tilde{\mathcal{P}}(X,\Psi), \lambda \in \mathrm{Sub}\,(X,\Psi)$,

$$\phi(X,\lambda) = \phi_{X,\lambda} : X \times H \to H$$

where for all $x \in X$, $h \in H$,

$$\phi_{(X,\lambda)}(x,h) \overset{d}{=} \begin{cases} 1 & \text{iff } \exists\ y \in X \text{ with } h = \lambda(x,y) \\ 0 & \text{iff otherwise} \end{cases} .$$

In turn, we can then consider basic arrows acting like & , or , if( ) , nt (abusing notation)

$$\phi_{\&} = \wedge\ ,\ \phi_{or} = \vee\ ,\ \phi_{if(\cdot)} = \Rightarrow\ \in Ar_{\Omega\times\Omega,\Omega}(Higg(H))$$

and

$$\phi_{nt} = \ulcorner \in Ar_{\Omega,\Omega}(Higg(H))\ ,$$

and then compose these appropriately. For example, for any (X,Ψ_1), $(X,\Psi_2) \in \tilde{\mathcal{P}}(X,\Psi)$,

$$(X,\Psi_1) \cup (X,\Psi_2) \overset{d}{=} \phi^{-1}(\phi_{(X,\Psi_1)} \wedge \phi_{(X,\Psi_2)})\ ,$$

etc.

It follows that F_o , F_1 and G_o all preserve unions and intersections as well as all natural orders relative to H .

Stout further defines implication and negation intuitionistically (see again 2.3.3 (C) (3)) for Gog(H) and Fuz(H) and remarks that the usual Zadeh fuzzy negation $\phi_{nt} = 1 - (\cdot)$ can be obtained in the compatible (adjoint) intuitionistic form

$$\phi_{nt}(h) = \phi_{\Rightarrow}(h,0)\ ,$$

with $\phi_{\Rightarrow}(a,b) \overset{d}{=} \phi_{or}(1-a,b)$, ϕ_{or} = (min)bndsum and $\phi_{\&}$ = maxbndsum.

In addition, Stout establishes a formal language and a basic semantic evaluation for each of Gog(H) , Fuz(H) , and Higg(H) , analogous to the development in 2.3.2 and Appendix 2 for deduction categories $(\mathcal{C},\mathfrak{X})$ where $\mathfrak{X}$ = Sub . It follows that F_o , F_1 and G_o all preserve semantic evaluations. Finally, Stout establishes sufficient conditions on Heyting algebra maps $f : H \to H'$ so that the naturally induced functors $F_{f,1} : Gog(H) \to Gog(H')$, $F_{f,2} : Fuz(H) \to Fuz(H)$, and $F_{f,3} : Higg(H) \to Higg(H')$ preserve certain logical properties. For example (Theorem 9 [249']), if f preserves $\wedge$, $\vee$, T_H , then $F_{f,\alpha}$, $\alpha = 1,2,3$, all preserve universal quantification of implications of wff's composed of compounds of atomic formula, $\wedge$, $\vee$, $\exists$, T_H , $\perp_H$, i.e., geometric statements. $F_{f,1}$ can be defined as

$$F_{f,1}(X,\eta) \overset{d}{=} (X,\ f\circ\eta)\ ,$$

for all $(X,\eta) \in Ob(Gog(H))$, and for any $g \in Ar(Gog(H))$,

$$F_{f,1}(g) \overset{d}{=} f o g \ .$$

G. Some connections between set theory and topos theory

As mentioned previously, one of the motivations for considering topoi is the set-like structure they have. That is, as shown in 2.2 and 2.3, the set foundations part Foun(ℓ) of a class of formal languages ℓ can be semantically modeled - as indeed all of ℓ - within an appropriate topos. Moreover, there is always a canonical model and canonical formal topos, and by the Bénabou constructions, a topos, in which Foun(ℓ) can be evaluated compatibly.

We present here a summary of the development in Johnstone [127], Chapter 9 which directly connects various set theory models and topos theory models - or equivalently topoi, themselves.

First, recall the notation and results of section 2.3.4. Define a weakened form of Zermelo-Fraenkel set theory (ZF) as

$$Ax_{zer_o}(\ell) \overset{d}{=} \{(Z1), (Z2), (Z7), (Z11), (Z12), (Z13), (Z14), (Z15), (Z16), (Z17)\} ,$$

which can be shown to be essentially equivalent to $\{(Z1), (Z2), (Z4), (Z77), (Z18)\}$.

Define the somewhat stronger

$$Ax_{zer}(\ell) \overset{d}{=} Ax_{zer_o}(\ell) \cup \{Z19, Z20\} \ .$$

Also, define $wpt = Th_{Wpt}(\ell)$, the theory of well-pointed topoi by

$$Ax_{wpt}(\ell) \overset{d}{=} Ax_{topos} \cup \{wellpt\}$$

where it should be noted via the identification of $(\mathcal{C},Sub)$ with $\mathcal{C}$, when $\mathcal{C}$ is a topos, that Ax_{topos} can then be chosen as Ax_K (together with Ax_{syn_K} for required syntax) in 2.2. The axiom of well-pointedness "wellpt" is given in [127], p. 314, in concrete form, which may be abstracted in a straightforward manner.

In addition, consider the topos-like axioms PT , "partial transitivity" and TR, an axiom connected with transitivity. (See [127], pp. 303-315.)

Define then the axiom systems

$$Ax_{wtt}(\ell) = Ax_{wpt}(\ell) \cup \{PT\} ,$$

$$Ax_{wtr}(\ell) = Ax_{wpt}(\ell) \cup \{TR\} ,$$

$$Ax_{wttr}(\ell) = Ax_{wpt}(\ell) \cup \{PT, TR\} .$$

In turn, we consider the set theories $Th_{zer_o}(\ell)$, $Th_{zer}(\ell)$,

$Th_{ZF}(\mathcal{L})$ and the topos theories $Th_{topos}(\mathcal{L})$, $Th_{wpt}(\mathcal{L})$, $Th_{wtt}(\mathcal{L})$, $Th_{wtr}(\mathcal{L})$, $Th_{wttr}(\mathcal{L})$.

Note that if $\mathcal{C}$ is a category and $\| \ \| : \mathcal{L} \to \mathcal{C}$ (i.e., $(\mathcal{C},Sub)$) is a model for $Th(\mathcal{L}) \subseteq Th_{zer_o}(\mathcal{L})$, then necessarily $\mathcal{C}$ must be at least a topos.

For a model $\| \ \| : \mathcal{L} \to (\mathcal{C},Sub)$ of $Th(\mathcal{L})$ with $\mathcal{C}$ a topos, we will write

$$\| \ \| : Th(\mathcal{L}) \to \mathcal{C} .$$

Two topoi constructed from $\| \ \|$ are of importance here:

$$S(\| \ \|) \subseteq \mathcal{C} ,$$

where construction S is given in Johnstone [127], p. 315, and where

$$\mathcal{S}(\| \ \|) \overset{d}{=} \| \ \|(Var(\mathcal{L})) = Var(\|\mathcal{C}\|) \subseteq \mathcal{C} .$$

Then abusing notation somewhat

(i) If $\| \ \| : Th_{zer_o}(\mathcal{L}) \to \mathcal{C}$, then

$$\mathcal{S}(\| \ \|) : Th_{wpt}(\mathcal{L}) \to \mathcal{S}(\| \ \|)$$

(ii) If $\| \ \| : Th_{zer}(\mathcal{L}) \to \mathcal{C}$, then indeed

$\mathcal{S}(\| \ \|) : Th_{zer_o}(\mathcal{L}) \to \mathcal{C}$ and hence

$$\mathcal{S}(\| \ \|) : Th_{wpt}(\mathcal{L}) \to \mathcal{S}(\| \ \|) ,$$

but in addition,

$$\mathcal{S}(\| \ \|) : Th_{wttr}(\mathcal{L}) \to \mathcal{S}(\| \ \|) .$$

(iii) Conversely to (i) and (ii):
If $\| \ \| : Th_{wpt}(\mathcal{L}) \to \mathcal{C}$, then

$$S(\| \ \|) : Th_{zer}(\mathcal{L}) \to S(\| \ \|)$$

and in turn from (ii)

$$\mathcal{S}(S(\| \ \|)) : Th_{wttr}(\mathcal{L}) \to \mathcal{S}(S(\| \ \|))$$

and if also $\| \ \| : Th_{wtr}(\mathcal{L}) \to \mathcal{C}$, then it can be shown that $\mathcal{S}(S(\| \ \|))$ is equivalent to the subcategory of all partially transitive objects of $\mathcal{C}$ (see [127], p. 311).

(iv) An improvement to (ii), using (iii):
If $\| \ \| : Th_{zer}(\mathcal{L}) \to \mathcal{C}$, then from (ii)

$$\mathcal{S}(\| \ \|) : Th_{wttr}(\mathcal{L}) \to \mathcal{S}(\| \ \|) ,$$

and hence

$$\mathcal{S}(\| \ \|) : Th_{wpt}(\mathcal{L}) \to \mathcal{S}(\| \ \|) ,$$

which in turn from (III) implies

$$S\mathcal{S}(\| \|)) : Th_{zer}(\ell) \to S(\mathcal{S}(\| \|)) ,$$

but in addition, it can be shown that $S(\mathcal{S}(\| \|))$ is isomorphic to $\| \|$

(v) Note that if

$$\| \| : Th_{wttr}(\ell) \to \mathcal{C} ,$$

then

$$\| \| : Th_{wpt}(\ell) \to \mathcal{C} , \text{ and (iii) applies,}$$

(vi) Thus, in the above cyclical construction sense: $Th_{zer}(\ell)$ and $Th_{wttr}(\ell)$ are "logically" equivalent.

(vii) In a similar vein, strengthening $Th_{zer}(\ell)$ further to $Th_{ZF}(\ell)$ and $Th_{wttr}(\ell)$ sufficiently to, say, $Th_{wq}(\ell)$, then $Th_{ZF}(\ell)$ and $Th_{wq}(\ell)$ are "logically" equivalent. (See [127], p. 318.)

(viii) On the other hand (as Johnstone also remarks), replacing $Th_{zer}(\ell)$ and, in effect, weakening) by $Th_K(\ell)$, as given in section 2.2.2, yields the result that (omitting the necessary syntax theory and choosing for the range of semantic evaluations $(\mathcal{C},Sub)$, $\mathcal{C}$ a topos - see 2.3.2) $Th_K(\ell)$ and $Th_{Topos}(\ell)$ are "logically" equivalent.

(ix) Note that Higg(H) is a well-pointed topos. (Apply Freyd's theorem to: any terminal object in Higg(H)) , $(\{a\},T_H)$, $\{a\}$ any singleton set, is a generator - see Johnstone [127], p. 314 and Appendix 1, 9 (xii); see also a similar property for the non-topos Gog(H) in subsection (D).) Hence, by result (iii), a model (using the S construction) can be constructed from Higg(H) for $Th_{zer}(\ell)$.

(x) For applications of topos theory to the investigation of consistency, independence, and other set foundations problems, again see [127]. See also Mitchell's interesting exposition [179].

Appendix 1

Basic category and topos definitions

1. For any category $\mathcal{C} = (Ob(\mathcal{C}), Ar(\mathcal{C}))$:

$$Ar(\mathcal{C}) = \bigcup_{\alpha,\beta\in Ob(\mathcal{C})} Ar_{\alpha,\beta}(\mathcal{C}) = \text{class of all arrows for } \mathcal{C},$$

$Ar_{\alpha,\beta}(\mathcal{C})$ = class of all arrows from α to β for $\mathcal{C}$, $\alpha,\beta \in Ob(\mathcal{C})$,

$Ob(\mathcal{C})$ = class of all objects,

$S,B : Ar \to Ob$,

where for any $f \in Ar_{\alpha,\beta}(\mathcal{C})$, $\alpha,\beta \in Ob(\mathcal{C})$,

$$S(f) \overset{d}{=} \alpha \text{ (source or domain of } f),$$
$$B(f) \overset{d}{=} \beta \text{ (end or codomain of } f),$$

$$D(\mathcal{C}) \overset{d}{=} \{(f,g) \mid f,g \in Ar(\mathcal{C}) \ \& \ S(f) = B(g)\} \subseteq Ar(\mathcal{C}) \times Ar(\mathcal{C}),$$

$$E(\mathcal{C}) \overset{d}{=} \{(f,g) \mid f,g \in Ar(\mathcal{C}) \ \& \ S(f) = S(g)\} \subseteq Ar(\mathcal{C}) \times Ar(\mathcal{C}),$$

$Id : Ob(\mathcal{C}) \to Ar(\mathcal{C})$, identity map,

$\circ : D(\mathcal{C}) \to Ar(\mathcal{C})$, composition,

where for all $(f,g), (g,h) \in D(\mathcal{C})$, $\alpha \in Ob(\mathcal{C})$,

$$Id(\alpha) \in Ar_{\alpha,\alpha}(\mathcal{C}),$$
$$S\circ Id = Id\circ B = id,$$
$$S(f\circ g) = S(g), \ B(f\circ g) = B(f),$$
$$(f\circ g)\circ h = f\circ (g\circ h).$$

2. In addition, category $\mathcal{C}$ may have

$$\times : Ob(\mathcal{C}) \times Ob(\mathcal{C}) \to Ob(\mathcal{C})$$

a finite cartesian product operator

$$\langle , \rangle : E(\mathcal{C}) \to Ar(\mathcal{C}),$$

ordered pair operator,

$$proj_1 : Ob(\mathcal{C}) \times Ob(\mathcal{C}) \to Ar(\mathcal{C})$$

$proj_2 : Ob(\mathcal{C}) \times Ob(\mathcal{C}) \to Ar(\mathcal{C})$, projections,

satisfying, for all $f,g \in Ar(\mathcal{C})$, $\alpha,\beta \in Ob(\mathcal{C})$,

$$S(\langle f,g\rangle) = S(f) = S(g),$$
$$B(\langle f,g\rangle) = B(f) \times B(g),$$

$$S(proj_1(\alpha,\beta)) = S(proj_2(\alpha,\beta)) = \alpha \times \beta ,$$
$$B(proj_1(\alpha,\beta)) = \alpha ,$$
$$B(proj)_2(\alpha,\beta) = \beta ,$$
$$proj_1(B(f),B(g)) \circ <f,g> = f$$
$$proj_2(B(f),B(g)) \circ <f,g> = g .$$

If $Bf = \alpha \times \beta$, then

$$<proj_1(\alpha,\beta)\circ f \ , \ proj_2(\alpha,\beta)\circ f> = f .$$

3. **Category SET** .

$$SET = (Ob(SET), Ar(SET)) ,$$

Ob(SET) = class of all ordinary sets

$$Ar(SET) = \bigcup_{\substack{X,Y \\ \in Ob(SET)}} Ar(SET)_{X,Y} ,$$

$$Ar_{X,Y}(SET) \overset{d}{=} Y^X \overset{d}{=} \{f \mid f : X \to Y \text{ in ordinary sense}\}$$

for all $X,Y \in SET$

$$Id = id ,$$

i.e., for all $X \in Ob(SET)$,

$$Id(X) = id(X) : X \to X$$

where for all $x \in X$,

$$id(X)(x) \overset{d}{=} x .$$

$$\circ : D(SET) \to Ar(SET)$$

is such that for all $(f,g) \in D(SET)$,

$f\circ g \overset{d}{=} f$ composed with g in ordinary sense.

Clearly SET has $\times$, ordinary cartesian product, and $proj_1$, $proj_2$, ordinary projections.

4. **Categories $Preord_{\le}$** .

Let $\le : Ob(SET) \to Ob(SET)$ be a fixed mapping such that for any $X \in Ob(SET)$, $\le_X \subseteq X \times X$ is a fixed preorder on X . Then

$$Preord_{\le} = (Ob(Preord_{\le}), Ar(Preord_{\le}))$$

is such that

$$\mathrm{Ob}(\mathrm{Preord}_{\le} = \{(X,\le_X) \mid X \in \mathrm{Ob}(\mathrm{SET})\}$$

$$\mathrm{Ar}(\mathrm{Preord}_{\le}) = \bigcup_{\substack{X,Y \\ \in \mathrm{Ob}(\mathrm{SET})}} \mathrm{Ar}_{(X,\le_X),(Y,\le_Y)}(\mathrm{Preord}_{\le}) ,$$

$$\begin{aligned} \mathrm{Ar}_{(X,\le_X),(Y,\le_Y)Y}(\mathrm{Preord}_{\le}) &= \{f \mid f : X \to Y \text{ and for all } x_1,x_2 \in X , \\ &\qquad \text{if } x_1 \le_X x_2 , \text{ then } f(x_1) \le_Y f(x_2)\} \\ &= \text{class of all preorder-preserving} \\ &\quad\ \text{functions} \subseteq Y^X . \end{aligned}$$

$\circ$ is usual functional composition,

Id = id .

5. Deduction categories.

$(\mathcal{C},\mathfrak{R})$ is a deduction category iff $\mathcal{C}$ is a category with a finite product $(\times)$ operator and $\mathfrak{R} : \mathcal{C} \to \mathrm{Preord}_{\le}$, for some fixed choice of $\le$, is a contravariant functor, i.e., for any $\alpha,\beta,\gamma \in \mathrm{Ob}(\mathcal{C})$, and any $f \in \mathrm{Ar}_{\beta,\gamma}(\mathcal{C})$, $g \in \mathrm{Ar}_{\alpha,\beta}(\mathcal{C})$,

$$\mathfrak{R}(\alpha),\ \mathfrak{R}(\beta),\ \mathfrak{R}(\gamma) \in \mathrm{Ob}(\mathrm{Preord}_{\le}) ,$$

$$\mathfrak{R}(f) \in \mathrm{Ar}_{\mathfrak{R}(\gamma),\mathfrak{R}(\beta)}(\mathrm{Preord}_{\le}) ,$$

$$\mathfrak{R}(g) \in \mathrm{Ar}_{\mathfrak{R}(\beta),\mathfrak{R}(\alpha)}(\mathrm{Preord}_{\le}) ,$$

and noting $f \circ g \in \mathrm{Ar}_{\alpha,\gamma}(\mathcal{C})$,

$$\mathfrak{R}(f \circ g) = \mathfrak{R}(g) \circ \mathfrak{R}(f) \in \mathrm{Ar}_{\mathfrak{R}(\gamma),\mathfrak{R}(\alpha)}(\mathrm{Preord}_{\le}) .$$

It follows from part (4) that for all $x_1,x_2 \in \mathfrak{R}(\gamma)$ such that $x_1 \le_{\mathfrak{R}(\gamma)} x_2$, then

$$\mathfrak{R}(f)(x_1) \le_{\mathfrak{R}(\beta)} \mathfrak{R}(f)(x_2) .$$

6. Let $\mathcal{C}$ be any category with not only a finite product operator, but with all finite limits existing. Then $(\mathcal{C},\mathrm{Sub})$ is a deduction category, where

$$\mathrm{Sub} : \mathcal{C} \to \mathrm{Preord}_{\le_{\mathrm{Sub}}}$$

is the subobject functor and $\le_{\mathrm{Sub}}$ is chosen as follows :

Let $\alpha \in \mathrm{Ob}(\mathcal{C})$ be arbitrary. Let $f,g \in \mathrm{Ar}(\mathcal{C})$ also be any two monics, i.e., for any $f_1,f_2,g_1,g_2 \in \mathrm{Ar}(\mathcal{C})$ with

$$B(f_1) = B(f_2) = S(f) , S(f_1) = S(f_2)$$
$$B(g_1) = B(g_2) = S(g) , S(g_1) = S(g_2) , \text{ if}$$

$$f \circ f_1 = f \circ f_2 , \text{ then } f_1 = f_2$$

and if

$$g \circ g_1 = g \circ g_2 \text{ , then } g_1 = g_2 \text{ .}$$

Suppose also $B(f) = B(g) = \alpha$. Define $f \leq_{Sub(\alpha)} g$, iff $f = g \circ h$, for some (monic) $h \in Ar(\mathbb{C})$ $(B(h) = S(g), S(h) = S(f))$, and define

$$f =_{Sub(\alpha)} g$$

iff

$$f \leq_{Sub(\alpha)} g \text{ and } g \leq_{Sub(\alpha)} f \text{ .}$$

Then it follows that for each $\alpha \in Ob(\mathbb{C})$, $=_{Sub;\alpha}$ generates an equivalence relation among the class of all monics with codomain α , partially ordered by $\leq_{Sub(\alpha)}$. Call this class the class of sub-objects of α , denoted $(Sub(\alpha) , \leq_{Sub(\alpha)})$, and the resulting order is $\leq_{Sub}$.

For any $\alpha,\beta \in Ob(\mathbb{C})$, let $f \in Ar_{\alpha,\beta}(\mathbb{C})$ be arbitrary and $(g : \gamma \rightarrow \beta) \in Sub(\beta)$ arbitrary $(\gamma \in Ob(\mathbb{C}))$. Then obtain *pullback* $\xi \stackrel{d}{=} \gamma \underset{g,f}{\times} \alpha$, where, in the following diagram all maps commute under compositions (well-defined) $\in Ob(\mathbb{C})$, projections $proj_{\gamma}^{(\xi)} \in Ar_{\xi,\alpha}(\mathbb{C})$ are all unique such that for any $\eta \in Ob(\mathbb{C})$ with $s \in Ar_{\eta,\gamma}(\mathbb{C})$, $t \in Ar_{\eta,\alpha}(\mathbb{C})$ such that $g \circ s = f \circ t$, there is a unique $r \in Ar_{\eta,\xi}(\mathbb{C})$ making all maps commute:

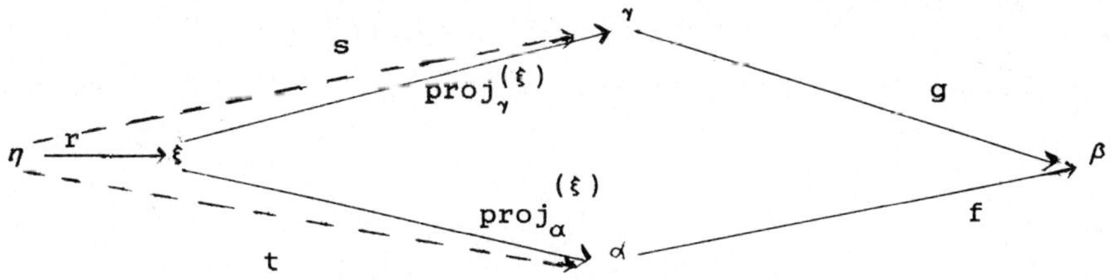

Then define the monic

$$Sub(f)(g) \stackrel{d}{=} proj_{\alpha}^{(\gamma \underset{\beta}{\times} \alpha)} ,$$

identifying the equivalence class under $=_{Sub(\alpha)}$ with $proj_{\alpha}^{(\gamma \underset{\beta}{\times} \alpha)} \in Sub(\alpha)$.

Also note that if $(h : \delta \rightarrow \beta) \in Sub(\beta)$ is also arbitrary such that $g \leq_{Sub(\beta)} h$, then $g = h \circ k$, for some $(k : \gamma \rightarrow \delta)$ and similarly,

$$Sub(f)(h) = proj_{\alpha}^{(\delta \underset{\beta}{\times} \alpha)} \text{ , relative to } =_{Sub(\alpha)} \text{ .}$$

Since

$$\mathrm{proj}_{\alpha}^{(\gamma \underset{\beta}{\times} \alpha)} = \mathrm{proj}_{\alpha}^{(\delta \underset{\beta}{\times} \gamma)} \circ (k \underset{\beta}{\times} \mathrm{id}_{\alpha})^{(\delta \times \gamma)}$$

it follows that

$$\mathrm{Sub}(f)(g) \le_{\mathrm{Sub}(\alpha)} \mathrm{Sub}(f)(h) \ ,$$

and hence

$$\mathrm{Sub}(f) \in \mathrm{Ar}_{\mathrm{Sub}(\beta),\mathrm{Sub}(\alpha)}(\mathrm{Preord}_{\le_{\mathrm{Sub}}}) \ ,$$

and hence $\mathrm{Sub} : C \to \mathrm{Preord}_{\le_{\mathrm{Sub}}}$ is a contravariant functor and thus (C,Sub) is a deduction category.

7. **The deduction category (SET,Sub)** .

First note the following construction and commutative diagram for any (non-vacuous) $X,Y \in \mathrm{Ob(SET)}$ and any $f \in \mathrm{Ar}_{X,Y}(\mathrm{SET})$, i.e., $f \in Y^X$ in the ordinary sense:

Define

$$\mathrm{rng}(f) \overset{d}{=} \{f(x) \mid x \in X\} \subseteq Y$$

with

$$f_{\mathrm{rng}} : X \to \mathrm{rng}(f) \ , \quad \text{(surjective)}$$

$$\mathrm{Sub}(Y)(\mathrm{rng}(f)) : \mathrm{rng}(f) \to Y \ , \quad \text{(identity)}$$

given by, for all $x \in X$ and all $y \in \mathrm{rng}(f)$,

$$f_{\mathrm{rng}}(x) \overset{d}{=} f(x)$$

$$\mathrm{Sub}(Y)(\mathrm{rng}(f))(y) = \mathrm{id}_Y(y) = y \ .$$

Noting that $F_f \overset{d}{=} \{f^{-1}(x) \mid x \in \mathrm{rng}(f)\}$ forms a disjoint exhaustive partitioning of X , let $g_f : F_f \to X$ be an arbitrary choice function such that for each $x \in \mathrm{rng}(f)$,

$$g_f(f^{-1}(x)) \in f^{-1}(x) \ .$$

Then define

$$X_f = \mathrm{rng}(g_f)$$

and define

$$f_{sur} : X \to X_f \quad , \quad \text{(surjective)}$$
$$Sub(X)(X_f) : X_f \to X \quad , \quad \text{(identity)}$$
$$f_{inj} : X_f \to Y \quad , \quad \text{(injective)}$$
$$f_{bij} : X_f \to rng(f) \quad , \quad \text{(bijective)}$$

where, for all $x \in X$ and all $z \in X_f$,

$$f_{sur}(x) \stackrel{d}{=} g_f(f^{-1}(x))$$
$$Sub(X)(X_f)(z) \stackrel{d}{=} id_X(z) = z$$
$$f_{inj}(z) \stackrel{d}{=} f_{bij}(z) = id_Y(z) = z \quad .$$

Thus,

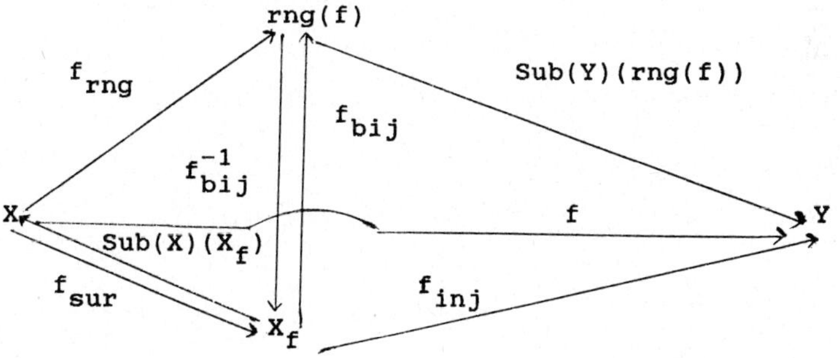

Hence, in particular,

$$(*) \quad \begin{cases} f = Sub(Y)(rng(f)) \circ f_{rng} \quad , \\ Sub(Y)(rng(f)) = f \circ Sub(X)(X_f) \circ f_{bij}^{-1} \quad . \end{cases}$$

Thus (without even assuming f is a monic) indeed, f is $=_{Sub(Y)}$ - equivalent to the monic $Sub(Y)(rng(f))$.

Furthermore, if $Z \in Ob(SET)$ and $h : X \to Z$, $g : Z \to Y$ are arbitrary such that

$$(**) \quad f = g \circ h \quad ,$$

Since analogous to the above development

$$g = Sub(Y)(rng(g)) \circ g_{rng} \quad ,$$

eqs. (*), (**) imply

$$Sub(Y)(rng(f)) = Sub(Y)(rng(g)) \circ k$$
$$\leq_{Sub(Y)} Sub(Y)(rng(g)) \quad ,$$

where

$$k \stackrel{d}{=} g_{rng} \circ h \circ Sub(X)(X_f) \circ f_{bij}^{-1} \quad .$$

Hence, for (SET,Sub) , the preorder reation for Preord must be $\leq \, = \, \subseteq$, i.e., ordinary subset inclusion, and for all $X \in Ob(SET)$, we may take equivalently

$$Sub(X) = (\mathcal{P}(X), \subseteq_{\mathcal{P}(X)}) .$$

In addition, in SET for any $X,Y,Z \in Ob(SET)$ with $f : X \to Y$, $g : Z \to Y$, the pullback

$$\xi = Z \underset{g,f}{\times} X = \{(z,x) \mid z \in Z , x \in X , \text{ and } f(x) = g(z)\}$$
$$= g^{-1}(rng(f) \cap rng(g)) \times f^{-1}(rng(f) \cap rng(g)) \subseteq Z \times X ,$$

and $proj_X^{(\xi)}$, $proj_Z^{(\xi)}$ become ordinary X- , Z - projection, respectively over ξ .

Hence, for any $X,Y \in Ob(SET)$ and any $W \in Sub(Y)$, i.e., we can let $W \in \mathcal{P}(Y)$, and identify further W with the identity imbedding

$$g_o \overset{d}{=} Sub(Y)(W) : W \to Y ,$$

$$Sub(f)(W) = Sub(f)(Sub(Y)(W))$$
$$= proj_X^{(\xi)} , \text{ relative to } \subseteq_{\mathcal{P}(X)} ,$$

where now

$$\xi = W \underset{g_o,f}{\times} X$$
$$= \{(w,x) \mid w \in W , x \in X \text{ and } f(x) = w\}$$

which may be identified with the inverse mapping $f^{-1} : W \to \mathcal{P}(X)$.

Hence, we can let

$$Sub(f)(W) = f^{-1}(W) ,$$

and check the contravariance:

For any $V \subseteq_{\mathcal{P}(X)} W$, i.e.,

$$V \subseteq W \subseteq X , \quad V , W , X \in Ob(SET) ,$$

$$Sub(f)(V) = f^{-1}(V) \subseteq Sub(f)(W) = f^{-1}(W) ,$$

etc.

In summary, (SET,Sub) is equivalent to $Sub: SET \to Preord_{\subseteq}$ where

$$Ob(Preord_{\subseteq} = \{(\mathcal{P}(X), \subseteq_X) \mid X \in Ob(SET)\} ,$$

$$Ar(Preord_{\subseteq}) = \bigcup_{\begin{bmatrix} X,Y \\ \in Ob(SET) \end{bmatrix}} Ar_{(\mathcal{P}(X), \subseteq_{\mathcal{P}(X)}),(\mathcal{P}(Y), \subseteq_{\mathcal{P}(Y)})}(Preord_{\subseteq}) ,$$

$$Ar_{(\mathcal{P}(X),\subseteq_{\mathcal{P}(X)}),(\mathcal{P}(Y),\subseteq_{\mathcal{P}(Y)})}(Preord_{\subseteq})$$
$$= \{f^{-1} \mid f^{-1} : \mathcal{P}(Y) \to \mathcal{P}(X) \text{ , where } f : X \to Y \text{ is arbitrary}\} ,$$

under the usual relation composition

$(f \circ g)^{-1} = g^{-1} \circ f^{-1}$, etc.,

and for all $X, Y \in Ob(SET)$, $f : X \to Y$,

$$Sub(X) = (\mathcal{P}(X), \subseteq_{\mathcal{P}(X)}) ,$$
$$Sub(f) = f^{-1} : \mathcal{P}(Y) \to \mathcal{P}(X) .$$

8. The deduction category $(SET, H^{\bullet})$.

Let $H \in Ob(Preord)$ to be specified later, with partial order $\le_H$. Define contravariant functor $H^{\bullet} : SET \to$ **Preord** by:
For all $X \in Ob(SET)$ (i.e., for any ordinary set X) ,

$$H^{\bullet}(X) \overset{d}{=} H^X = \{f \mid f : X \to H \text{ in the usual sense}\} .$$

Define the partial order $\le_{H^X}$ on H^X by if $f, g \in H^X$,

$$f \le_{H^X} g \text{ iff } f(x) \le_H g(x) \text{ , for all } x \in X .$$

For all $X, Y \in Ob(SET)$ and any $h \in Ar_{X,Y}(SET)$ (i.e., for any $h \in Y^X$ or $h : X \to Y$, in the usual sense) , define

$$H^{\bullet}(h) : H^Y \to H^X ,$$

by, for any $f \in H^Y$,

$H^{\bullet}(h)(f) \overset{d}{=} f \circ h$ (ordinary composition) and note that if $f, g \in H^Y$ with $f \le_{H^Y} g$, then $H^{\bullet}(f), H^{\bullet}(g) \in H^X$ with $H^{\bullet}(f) \le_{H^X} H^{\bullet}(g)$, since $f(h(x)) \le_H g(h(x))$ for all $x \in X$.

Now depending on the choice of H , $(SET, H^{\bullet})$ may have additional properties.

Note first that here

$$Rel(SET, H^{\bullet}) = \bigcup_{X \in Ob(C)} Rel_X(SET, H^{\bullet}) ,$$

where

$$Rel_X(SET, H^{\bullet}) = H^X ,$$

and hence substitution here becomes, for any $r \in H^X$ - noting

$\sigma(r_X) = X$, and $r : X \to H$ is an ordinary function, and for any $h : Y \to X$, $Y \in Ob(SET)$,

$$r[h] = H^{\cdot}(h)(r) = r \circ h ,$$

i.e., for all axioms and rules involving the substitution operation $\cdot[\cdot\cdot]$, the latter becomes simply ordinary composition (in the same order).

Thus, e.g., if H has structure so that H has a largest element, say $T_H \in H$ and a smallest element $\perp_H \in H$, with respect to $\leq_H$, then conditions (T) ($R_{I,syn,18}$, $R_{I,Th,3}$, $R_{I,syn,19}$) and ($\perp$) ($R_{I,syn,22}$, $R_{I,Th,7}$, $R_{I,syn,23}$) are immediately satisfied, by using the mappings

$$T, \perp : Ob(SET) \to Rel(SET, H^{\cdot}) \text{ as}$$

$$T(X)(x) \overset{d}{=} T_H ,$$

$$\perp(X)(x) \overset{d}{=} \perp_H , \text{ for all } x \in X , \text{ for all } X \in Ob(SET) .$$

Next, we consider some structure on H , $\wedge_H$, to correspond to $\wedge$, although not necessarily the "and" axioms and rules given in $Loc(\mathcal{C}, \mathfrak{R})$ before ($R_{I,syn,20}$, $R_{I,syn,21}$, $R_{I,Th,4}$, $R_{I,Th,5}$, $R_{I,Th,6}$) .

For example, if we choose H to have an operation corresponding to $\wedge = \min$, then we require $\wedge_H$ over H to satisfy formally $R_{I,Th,4,5,6,}$, i.e., for all elements $r,s,t \in H$,

$$\text{if } r \leq_H s , \text{ then } t \wedge_H r , r \wedge_H t \leq_H s ;$$

$$\text{if } r \leq_H s,t , \text{ then } r \leq_H s \wedge_H t .$$

On the other hand, if we choose H to have the more general structure of a t-norm $\&_H$, replacing $\wedge_H$ (see the remarks in 2.2.2 VI and section 2.3.6) , then this structure will be reflected in the mapping $\& : Rel(SET,H^{\cdot})^n \to Rel(SET,H^{\cdot})$, where for example for $n = 2$, and any $X \in Ob(SET)$, $r,s : X \to H$ relations in $Rel_X(SET,H^{\cdot})$, $\&(r,s) = r \& s : X \to H$ so that for all $x \in X$,

$$(r \& s)(x) \overset{d}{=} r(x) \&_H s(x)$$

with the t-norm properties of symmetry, associativity (so that unambiguously $\&_H$ can be recursively extended to any number of arguments - see 2.3.6), nondecreasing, bounded above by min, and having the marginal properties, with possibly additional properties such as idempotence, etc.

Similar remarks hold for or_H and a t-conorm structure, as well as for other operators such as negation, and universal and existential quantification, as well as for equivalence and set membership. In particular, see section 2.3.3 (C) , Gödel-Intuitionistic Logic, for a brief summary of Heyting algebras (choosing in effect H to be a Heyting algebra) and intuitionistic logic operators over them. See also Remark 3 at the end of Appendix 3.

9. Some miscellaneous basic category concepts.

We will exploit *commutative diagrams* for all definitions: Let $\mathbb{C} = (\mathrm{Ob}(\mathbb{C}),\mathrm{Ar}(\mathbb{C}))$ be any category.

(i) If

$$\mathrm{Id}_\alpha \circlearrowright \alpha \underset{g}{\overset{f}{\rightleftarrows}} \beta \circlearrowright \mathrm{Id}_\beta ,$$

i.e., $\alpha,\beta \in \mathrm{Ob}(\mathbb{C})$, $f \in \mathrm{Ar}_{\alpha,\beta}(\mathbb{C})$, $g \in \mathrm{Ar}_{\beta,\alpha}(\mathbb{C})$,

with

$$g\cdot f = \mathrm{Id}_\alpha \;;\; f\circ g = \mathrm{Id}_\beta ,$$

then we say f and g are *inverses* of each other (with either one uniquely determined by the other) and α and β are *isomorphic* objects.

(ii) If, for some $\alpha,\beta \in \mathrm{Ob}(\mathbb{C})$, $f \in \mathrm{Ar}_{\alpha,\beta}(\mathbb{C})$: For all $\gamma \in \mathrm{Ob}(\mathbb{C})$, all $f_1,f_2 \in \mathrm{Ar}_{\gamma,\alpha}(\mathbb{C})$,

$$\left[\; \gamma \;\underset{f_2}{\overset{f_1}{\rightrightarrows}}\; \alpha \xrightarrow{\;f\;} \beta \;\right] \quad \text{implies} \quad f_1 = f_2 ,$$

then we say $f \in \mathrm{Ar}_{\alpha,\beta}(\mathbb{C})$ is a *monic* (or monomorphism).

(iii) If, for some $\alpha,\beta \in \mathrm{Ob}(\mathbb{C})$, $f \in \mathrm{Ar}_{\alpha,\beta}(\mathbb{C})$: For all $\gamma \in \mathrm{Ob}(\mathbb{C})$, all $f_1,f_2 \in \mathrm{Ar}_{\beta,\gamma}(\mathbb{C})$

$$\left[\; \alpha \xrightarrow{\;f\;} \beta \;\underset{f_2}{\overset{f_1}{\rightrightarrows}}\; \gamma \;\right] \quad \text{implies} \quad f_1 = f_2 ,$$

then we say $f \in \mathrm{Ar}_{\alpha,\beta}(\mathbb{C})$ is an *epi* (morphism) .

(iv) Let $\alpha \in \mathrm{Ob}(\mathbb{C})$. If for all $\beta \in \mathrm{Ob}(\mathbb{C})$, there is a unique $f_{\beta,\alpha} \in \mathrm{Ar}_{\beta,\alpha}(\mathbb{C})$, called a *terminal arrow* then α is called a *terminal object*, in which case, necessarily, $f_{\alpha,\alpha} = \mathrm{Id}_\alpha$, and any two terminal objects are isomorphic. Often we write 1 for the terminal arrow.

(v) Let $\alpha \in Ob(\mathbb{C})$. If for all $\beta \in Ob(\mathbb{C})$, there is a unique $g_{\alpha,\beta} \in Ar_{\alpha,\beta}(\mathbb{C})$, called an *initial arrow*, then α is called an *initial object*, in which case, necessarily, $g_{\alpha,\alpha} = Id_{\alpha}$, and any two initial objects are isomorphic. We denote $\alpha = \emptyset$.

Note that for SET , monos are the same as ordinary injective functions, epis are the same as ordinary surjective functions, isomorphisms are the same as bijective functions - and hence, in this sense all sets having the same cardinality are isomorphic; any singleton set is a terminal object, the null set is an initial object (by definition).

(vi) Subobjects have been discussed, the definition being motivated by monos. Dually, *quotient objects* may be defined, relative to all epis (for a fixed category) where ordering $\leq_{Quo}$ epis f,g with $S(f) = S(g)$, is

$$f \leq_{Quo} g \quad \text{iff} \quad f = h \circ g ,$$

and where $=_{Quo}$ g is defined by the usual relation

$$f =_{Quo} g \quad \text{iff} \quad (f \leq_{Quo} g) \quad \text{and} \quad (g \leq_{Quo} f) ,$$

etc.

For SET , it follows that for any $X \in Ob(SET)$, Quo(X) , the class of all quotient objects over X , can be identified with $\{Y \mid Y \in Ob(SET) \text{ and } X \subseteq Y\}$.

(vii)(a) *Finite products* are defined analogous to pullbacks with the right half of the commutative diagram removed - as in (6), so that $\overset{g}{\underset{f}{\rightrightarrows}}\beta$ is removed, etc.

Thus, for example, for two objects: Let $\alpha, \beta \in Ob(\mathbb{C})$. Then the *product* $\alpha \times \beta \in Ob(\mathbb{C})$, if it exists, where α and β are called its *factors* and arrows $proj_{\alpha}$, $proj_{\beta}$ (see below) called the *projections*, are such that for each $\gamma \in Ob(\mathbb{C})$ and each $f \in Ar_{\gamma,\alpha}$, $g \in Ar_{\gamma,\beta}(\mathbb{C})$, there is a unique $k_{f,g} \in Ar_{\gamma,\alpha\times\beta}(\mathbb{C})$ such that the following diagram commutes:

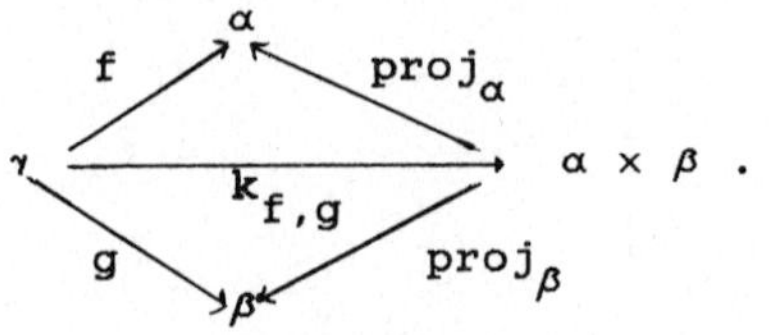

(b) *Finite coproducts:* For example, for two objects: Let $\alpha, \beta \in Ob(\mathbb{C})$. Then the co-product $\alpha \coprod \beta$ (or $\alpha + \beta$) $\in \mathbb{C}$, if it exists, where α and β are called its *summands* and arrows inj_{α} , inj_{β} (see below) called *injections*, are such that, for each $\gamma \in Ob(\mathbb{C})$, and each $f \in Ar_{\alpha,\gamma}(\mathbb{C})$, there is a unique $h_{f,g} \in Ar_{\alpha\coprod\gamma}(\mathbb{C})$, $g \in Ar_{\beta,\gamma}(\mathbb{C})$ such that the following diagram commutes:

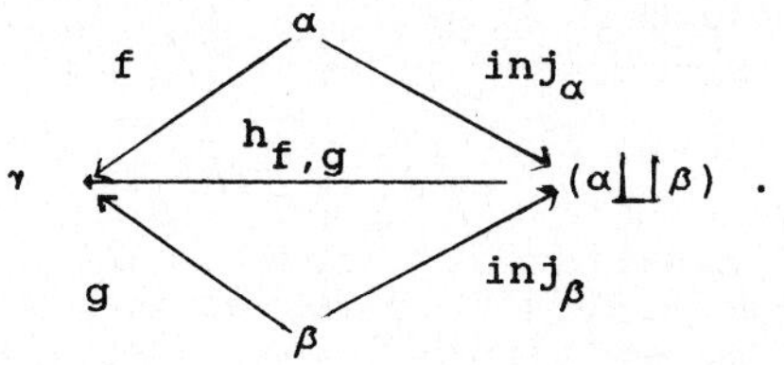

Note, for SET , all products coincide with the usual cartesian products of sets and all co-products with the usual cartesian sums of sets.

(viii) If, for some $\alpha, \beta \in Ob(\mathcal{C})$, $f, g \in Ar_{\alpha,\beta}(\mathcal{C})$: For all $\eta \in Ob(\mathcal{C})$, all $k \in Ar_{\eta,\gamma}(\mathcal{C})$, all $\ell \in Ar_{\eta,\alpha}(\mathcal{C})$

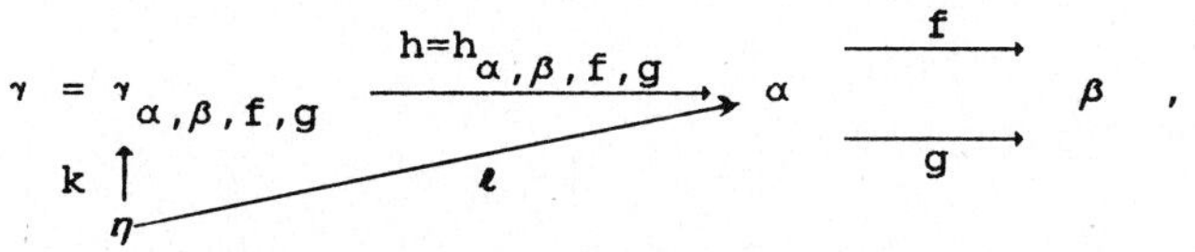

then we say $\gamma_{\alpha,\beta,f,g}$ is an *equalizer* for α , β , f , g with unique arrow $h_{\alpha,\beta,f,g} \in Ar_{\gamma_{\alpha,\beta,f,g},\alpha}(\mathcal{C})$.

For SET , and any X , $Y \in Ob(SET)$ with $f, g : X \to Y$,

$\gamma_{X,Y,f,g} = \{x \mid x \in X \text{ and } f(x) = g(x)\}$.

(ix) Suppose category $\mathcal{C}$ has all finite products existing.
For some $\alpha, \beta \in Ob(\mathcal{C})$: If for each $\gamma \in Ob(\mathcal{C})$ and each $f \in Ar_{\gamma\times\alpha,\beta}(\mathcal{C})$, there is a unique $h = h_{\alpha,\beta,\gamma} \in Ar_{\gamma,\beta^\alpha}(\mathcal{C})$ such that

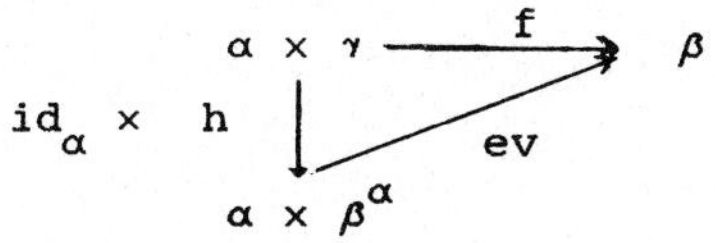

then we say, for that $\alpha, \beta \in Ob(\mathcal{C})$, *exponential* $\beta^\alpha \in Ob(\mathcal{C})$ exists with *evaluation* $ev \in Ar_{\alpha\times\beta^\alpha,\beta}(\mathcal{C})$.

For SET , for all $X, Y \in Ob(SEt)$,

$Y^X = \{f \mid f : X \to Y\}$ and $ev : X \times Y^X \to Y$ is such that for all $x \in X$, $f \in Y^X$, $ev(x,f) = f(x)$.

(x) If there is some terminal object $U \in Ob(\mathcal{C})$ and an object $\Omega \in Ob(\mathcal{C})$ and $g_o \in Ar_{U,\Omega}(\mathcal{C})$ such that for any $\beta \in Ob(\mathcal{C})$ and any representative subobject $(f : \alpha \to \beta)$ of β , there is a unique $h_f \in Ar_{\beta,\Omega}$ such that subobject $(proj_\beta(\xi) \to \alpha)$ and $(f : \alpha \to \beta)$ are $\le_{Sub(\beta)}$ equivalent, where $\xi \overset{d}{=} U {}_{g_o}\!\times_{h_f} \beta$:

$$\begin{array}{ccc} \xi & \xrightarrow{\ \mathrm{proj}_U\ } & U \\ {\scriptstyle \mathrm{proj}_\beta}\downarrow & & \downarrow{\scriptstyle g_o} \\ \beta & \xrightarrow[\ h_f\ ]{} & \Omega \end{array} \quad .$$

Then g_o is called the *true-mapping*, h_f the *classifying* or *characteristic map*, Ω the *subobject classifier*, and the power object is Ω^β (from part (ix)).

For SET, we may choose for any $X \in Ob(SET)$, $W \in Sub(X)$, i.e., $W \subseteq X$,

$$\begin{array}{ccc} \{1\}\times W & \xrightarrow{\ \ 1\ \ } & \{1\} \\ {\scriptstyle Sub(Y)(W)}\downarrow & & \downarrow{\scriptstyle id} \\ Y & \xrightarrow[\ \phi_W\ ]{} & \{0,1\} \end{array} \quad .$$

That is, the subobject classifier is $\Omega = \{0,1\}$, the true-mapping $g_o = id : \{1\} \to \{0,1\}$, $id(1) = 1$, and the classifying map here is $h_f = \phi_W : Y \to \{0,1\}$, where ϕ_W is the ordinary membership (or characteristic function) map.

(xi) More on subobjects of a category $\mathcal{C}$.

(a) $\mathcal{C}$ has *associative images* iff, by definition, for all $\alpha,\beta,\gamma \in Ob(\mathcal{C})$, and all $f \in Ar_{\alpha,\beta}(\mathcal{C})$, $g \in Ar_{\beta,\gamma}(\mathcal{C})$, there are (unique) smallest (in sense of $\le_{Sub(\beta)}$, $\le_{Sub(\gamma)}$) subobjects, written $f(\alpha)$ of β and $g(\beta)$ of γ such that

$$f \le_{Sub(\beta)} f(\alpha) \ , \quad g \le_{Sub(\gamma)} g(\beta)$$

and such that

$$g(f(\alpha)) = (g \circ f)(\alpha) \ .$$

(b) $\mathcal{C}$ is said to be *complete distributive lattice* (c.d.l.) - ordered, iff, by definition, for all $\alpha \in \mathcal{C}$, $Sub(\alpha)$ under $\le_{Sub}$ is a complete distributive lattice (c.d.l.)

(c) If $\mathcal{C}$ is a c.d.l., then for $\mathcal{C}$ all classical unions and intersections of subobjects exist, where we define for any $\alpha \in Ob(\mathcal{C})$ and any $\beta,\gamma \in Sub(\alpha)$, $\beta \cup \gamma$, $\beta \cap \gamma \in Sub(\alpha)$, as the least upper bound, greatest lower bound for β and γ relative to $\le_{Sub(\alpha)}$, respectively. In turn, the *pseudo-complement* β' of $\beta \in Sub(\alpha)$ is the least upper bound for the class of all $\eta \in Sub(\alpha)$ with $\eta \cap \beta = m_\alpha$, where m_α is the minimal element in $Sub(\alpha)$ relative to $\le_{Sub(\alpha)}$. We say $\beta,\gamma \in Sub(\alpha)$ are *disjoint* iff $\beta \cap \gamma = m_\alpha$, etc.

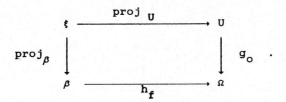

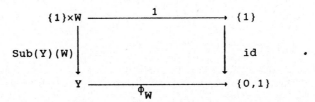

(xii) An object $\alpha \in Ob(\mathbb{C})$ is called *monic* iff for all $f \in Ar(\mathbb{C})$ with $S(f) = \alpha$, f is monic.

An object $\alpha \in Ob(\mathbb{C})$ is called *atomic-monic*, iff: (i) α is monic; (ii) for each $\gamma \in Sub(\alpha)$, γ is *atomic*, i.e., (assuming $Sub(\alpha)$ is a c.d.l.) if $\gamma \neq m_\alpha$ (the minimal element in $Sub(\alpha)$ w.r.t. $\leq_{Sub(\alpha)}$ and if $\eta \in Sub(\alpha)$ is such that $m_\alpha \leq_{Sub(\alpha)} \eta \leq_{Sub(\alpha)} \gamma$, then $\eta = m_\alpha$ or $\eta = \gamma$; (iii) for any $\beta \in Ob(\mathbb{C})$, $Ar_{\alpha,\beta} \neq \emptyset$.

An object $\alpha \in Ob(\mathbb{C})$ is called a *generator* (or separator) of $\mathbb{C}$, iff, for any $\beta,\gamma \in Ob(\mathbb{C})$ and any $f,g \in Ar_{\beta,\gamma}(\mathbb{C})$ with $f \neq g$, there is some $h_{f,g} \in Ar_{\alpha,\beta}(\mathbb{C})$ such that $f \circ h_{f,g} \neq g \circ h_{f,g}$. More generally, a set $\{\alpha_1,\ldots,\alpha_n\} \subseteq Ob(\mathbb{C})$ is called a *generating* (or separating) set of objects for $\mathbb{C}$, iff, for all $\beta,\gamma \in Ob(\mathbb{C})$ and $f,g \in Ar_{\beta,\gamma}(\mathbb{C})$ with $f \neq g$, there is some j, $1 \leq j \leq h$, and $h_j \in Ar_{\alpha_j,\beta}(\mathbb{C})$ such that $f \circ h_j \neq g \circ h_j$.

An object $\alpha \in Ob(\mathbb{C})$ is called *projective* iff, for each $f \in Ar(\mathbb{C})$ and each epi $g \in Ar(\mathbb{C})$ with $\alpha = S(f)$ and $B(f) = B(g)$ there is some $h_{f,g} \in Ar(\mathbb{C})$ such that $f = g \circ h_{f,g}$ (and hence $S(h_{f,g}) = S(f)$, $B(h_{f,g}) = S(g)$) :

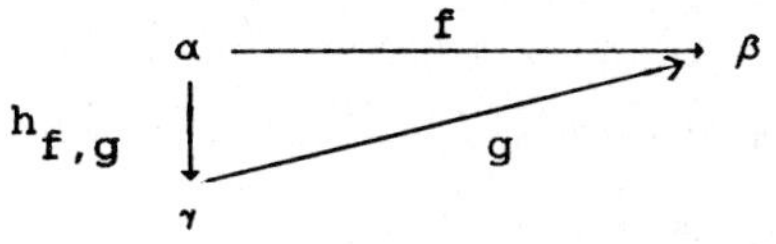

, all $\beta,\gamma \in Ob(\mathbb{C})$.

For SET :

For any $X,Y \in Ob(SET)$, $f \in Ar_{X,Y}(SET) = Y^X$, the image $f(X) = Sub(Y)(rng(f))$ with $f \leq_{Sub(Y)} f(X)$ and clearly SET has associative images and is a c.d.l. under $\leq_{Sub} = \subseteq$ with unions and intersections of any subobjects $W \in Sub(X) = \mathcal{P}(X)$ being ordinary unions and intersections of W's ; $m_X = \emptyset$; pseudo-complement W' of $W \in Sub(X)$ is the ordinary complement $\complement W = X \dashv W$.

The monic objects of SET consist of all singleton sets $\{x\}$, $x \in X$, $X \in Ob(SET)$, i.e., the monic objects and terminal object(s) coincide. The atomic objects of SET are also the singleton sets, while any nonvacuous $X \in Ob(SET)$ is a projective generator, since, for any $Y,Z \in Ob(SET)$ and any $f : X \to Y$ and $g : Z \to Y$ surjective, we can define $h_{f,g} : X \to Z$ by choosing for each $x \in X$, $h_{f,g}(x)$ arbitrary fixed $\in g^{-1}(f(x))$. For SET, the atomic-monic projective generators are the same as the singleton sets.

(xiii) A *topos* is a category for which
- (a) All finite products $\times$ exist,
- (b) Has a terminal object,
- (c) Has equalizers for all pairs of objects in it,
- (d) Has exponents and evaluation maps existing for all pairs of objects in it,
- (e) Has a subobject classifier.

In a topos, an arrow is an isomorphism iff it is both an epi and a mono.

(xiv) Some basic properties of functors and related concepts.

(A) Let $\mathcal{C}$, $\mathfrak{D}$ be two categories. A functor $\mathfrak{F} : \mathcal{C} \to \mathfrak{D}$ consists of two maps

(i) $\mathfrak{F} : \mathrm{Ob}(\mathcal{C}) \to \mathrm{Ob}(\mathfrak{D})$
(ii) $\mathfrak{F} : \mathrm{Ar}(\mathcal{C}) \to \mathrm{Ar}(\mathcal{C})$

such that either

(a) For all $f,g \in \mathrm{Ar}(\mathcal{C})$, $\alpha \in \mathrm{Ob}(\mathcal{C})$

$S(\mathfrak{F}(f)) = \mathfrak{F}(S(f))$, $B(\mathfrak{F}(f)) = \mathfrak{F}(B(f))$,
If $S(f) = B(g)$,
$\mathfrak{F}(f \circ g) = \mathfrak{F}(f) \circ \mathfrak{F}(g)$,
$\mathfrak{F}(\mathrm{Id}_\alpha) = \mathrm{Id}_{\mathfrak{F}(\alpha)}$,

in which case $\mathfrak{F}$ is said to be a *covariant functor*;
or

(b) For all $f,g \in \mathrm{Ar}(\mathcal{C})$, $\alpha \in \mathrm{Ob}(\mathcal{C})$,
$S(\mathfrak{F}(f)) = \mathfrak{F}(B(f))$, $B(\mathfrak{F}(f)) = \mathfrak{F}(S(f))$
If $S(f) = B(g)$,
$\mathfrak{F}(f \circ g) = \mathfrak{F}(g) \circ F(f)$
$\mathfrak{F}(\mathrm{Id}_\alpha) = \mathrm{Id}_{\mathfrak{F}(\alpha)}$,

in which case $\mathfrak{F}$ is said to be a *contravariant functor*.

(B) Let $f : \mathcal{C} \to \mathfrak{D}$ be a functor. Then:

(1) $\mathfrak{F}$ is *full* iff, by definition, for all $\alpha,\beta \in \mathrm{Ob}(\mathcal{C})$,

$$\mathfrak{F}(\mathrm{Ar}_{\alpha,\beta}(\mathcal{C})) \overset{d}{=} \{\mathfrak{F}(f) \mid f \in \mathrm{Ar}_{\alpha,\beta}(\mathcal{C})\} = \mathrm{Ar}_{\mathfrak{F}(\alpha),\mathfrak{F}(\beta)}(\mathfrak{D}) .$$

(2) F is *faithful* iff, by definition, for all $f,g \in \mathrm{Ar}(\mathcal{C})$, if $f \neq g$, then $\mathfrak{F}(f) \neq \mathfrak{F}(g)$, i.e., $\mathfrak{F} : \mathrm{Ar}(\mathcal{C}) \to \mathrm{Ar}(\mathfrak{D})$ is injective.

(C) $\mathfrak{F}$ is *representative* iff, by definition, for all $\alpha \in \mathrm{Ob}(\mathfrak{D})$, there is some $\beta \in \mathrm{Ob}(\mathcal{C})$ such that α is isomorphic to $\mathfrak{F}(\beta)$.

(D) $\mathfrak{F}$ is an *equivalence* between $\mathcal{C}$ and $\mathfrak{D}$ (or $\mathcal{C}$ and $\mathfrak{D}$ are equivalent w.r.t. $\mathfrak{F}$) iff, by definition, $\mathfrak{F}$ is full, faithful and representative. iff (a theorem - see, e.g., MacLane [165] , p. 91) there is a functor $\mathfrak{G} : \mathfrak{D} \to \mathcal{C}$ and natural isomorphisms between $\mathfrak{G}\circ\mathfrak{F} : \mathcal{C} \to \mathcal{C}$ and $\mathrm{Id}_{\mathcal{C}} : \mathcal{C} \to \mathcal{C}$ and natural isomorphisms between $\mathfrak{F}\circ\mathfrak{G} : \mathfrak{D} \to \mathfrak{D}$ and $\mathrm{Id}_{\mathfrak{D}} : \mathfrak{D} \to \mathfrak{D}$. In particular, if, more strongly, $\mathfrak{G}\circ\mathfrak{F} = \mathrm{Id}_{\mathcal{C}}$ and $\mathfrak{F}\circ\mathfrak{G} = \mathrm{Id}_{\mathfrak{D}}$ then we say $\mathfrak{F}$ is an isomorphism between $\mathcal{C}$ and $\mathfrak{D}$, where natural transforms and natural isomorphisms are defined below:

Let $\mathcal{C}$, $\mathfrak{D}$ be two categories.

Let $\mathcal{F},\mathcal{G} : \mathcal{C} \to \mathcal{D}$ be two functors. Then the mapping $\tau : \mathrm{Ob}(\mathcal{C}) \to \mathrm{Ar}(\mathcal{D})$ such that for all $\alpha \in \mathrm{Ob}(\mathcal{C})$, $\tau(\alpha) \in \mathrm{Ar}_{\mathcal{F}(\alpha),\mathcal{G}(\alpha)}(\mathcal{D})$ such that for all $\beta \in \mathrm{Ob}(\mathcal{C})$ and all $f \in \mathrm{Ar}_{\alpha,\beta}(\mathcal{C})$, the following diagram is commutative

$$\begin{array}{ccc} \mathcal{F}(\alpha) & \xrightarrow{\tau(\alpha)} & \mathcal{G}(\alpha) \\ \downarrow \mathcal{F}(f) & & \downarrow \mathcal{G}(f) \\ \mathcal{F}(\beta) & \xrightarrow[\tau(\beta)]{} & \mathcal{G}(\beta) \end{array},$$

and we denote symbolically: $\tau : \mathcal{F} \stackrel{\cdot}{\longrightarrow} \mathcal{G}$ and call τ a natural transform from $\mathcal{F}$ to $\mathcal{G}$. If $\tau : \mathcal{F} \stackrel{\cdot}{\longrightarrow} \mathcal{G}$ is a *natural transform* from functors $\mathcal{F}$ to $\mathcal{G}$, where $\mathcal{F}, \mathcal{G} : \mathcal{C} \to \mathcal{D}$, for categories $\mathcal{C}$, $\mathcal{D}$, and if also, for each $\alpha \in \mathrm{Ob}(\mathcal{C})$, $\tau(\alpha)$ is an isomorphism (as previously defined), we say τ is a *natural isomorphism* from $\mathcal{F}$ to $\mathcal{G}$.

Summary of isomorphism concepts

Let $\mathcal{C}$, $\mathcal{D}$ be any categories:

(1) A given $\alpha,\beta \in \mathrm{Ob}(\mathcal{C})$ are isomorphic iff an isomorphism $f \in \mathrm{Ar}_{\alpha,\beta}(\mathcal{C})$ exists iff there is $f \in \mathrm{Ar}_{\alpha,\beta}(\mathcal{C})$, $g \in \mathrm{Ar}_{\beta,\alpha}(\mathcal{C})$ such that

$$f \circ g = \mathrm{Id}_\beta \quad \text{and} \quad g \circ f = \mathrm{Id}_\alpha .$$

(2) A given $f,g \in \mathrm{Ar}(\mathcal{C})$ are isomorphic iff there are isomorphisms $h,k \in \mathrm{Ar}(\mathcal{C})$ such that

$$h \circ f = g \circ k ,$$

in which case where well-defined $f \circ g$ is an isomorphism; Id_α is always an isomorphism, for all $\alpha \in \mathrm{Ob}(\mathcal{C})$; if $f \in \mathrm{Ar}_{\alpha,\beta}(\mathcal{C})$ is an isomorphism between α and $\beta \in \mathrm{Ob}(\mathcal{C})$ then so is $\mathcal{F}(f) \in \mathrm{Ar}_{\mathcal{F}(\alpha),\mathcal{F}(\beta)}(\mathcal{D})$, for any functor $\mathcal{F} : \mathcal{C} \to \mathcal{D}$.

(3) Let $\mathcal{F},\mathcal{G} : \mathcal{C} \to \mathcal{D}$ be two functors. The $\tau : \mathcal{F} \stackrel{\cdot}{\longrightarrow} \mathcal{G}$ is a natural isomorphism iff there is a $\sigma : \mathcal{G} \stackrel{\cdot}{\longrightarrow} \mathcal{F}$, natural transformation such that $\sigma \circ \tau = \mathrm{Id}_{\mathcal{F}}$ and $\tau \circ \sigma = \mathrm{Id}_{\mathcal{G}}$, iff, by definition, $\mathcal{F}$ and $\mathcal{G}$ are isomorphic (relative to τ or to σ - both σ and τ being natural isomorphisms).

(4) Let $\mathcal{C}$ and $\mathcal{D}$ be two given categories. Then

(i) $\mathcal{C}$ and $\mathcal{D}$ are isomorphic iff there are functors $\mathcal{F} : \mathcal{C} \to \mathcal{D}$, $\mathcal{G} : \mathcal{D} \to \mathcal{C}$ such that $\mathcal{F} \circ \mathcal{G} = \mathrm{Id}_{\mathcal{D}}$, $\mathcal{G} \circ \mathcal{F} = \mathrm{Id}_{\mathcal{C}}$.

(ii) $\mathcal{C}$ and $\mathcal{D}$ are equivalent iff there are functors $\mathcal{F} : \mathcal{C} \to \mathcal{D}$, $\mathcal{G} : \mathcal{D} \to \mathcal{C}$ such that $\mathcal{F} \circ \mathcal{G}$ is isomorphic (via a natural isomorphisms) to $\mathrm{Id}_{\mathcal{D}}$ and $\mathcal{G} \circ \mathcal{F}$ is isomorphic to $\mathrm{Id}_{\mathcal{C}}$.

(xv) <u>Adjoints</u>

Let $\mathfrak{F} : \mathfrak{C} \to \mathfrak{D}$ and $\mathfrak{G} : \mathfrak{D} \to \mathfrak{C}$ be two functors for categories $\mathfrak{C}$ and $\mathfrak{D}$.

Then we say $\mathfrak{F}$ is *left adjoint* to $\mathfrak{G}$ and $\mathfrak{G}$ is *right adjoint* to $\mathfrak{F}$ iff, by definition; $(\ )^*$, $^*(\ )$ are bijections, where

(i) For all $\alpha, \beta \in \mathrm{Ob}(\mathfrak{C})$, $\gamma, \eta \in \mathrm{Ob}(\mathfrak{D})$ and all $f \in \mathrm{Ar}_{\mathfrak{F}(\alpha),\gamma}(\mathfrak{D})$, $h \in \mathrm{Ar}_{\beta,\alpha}(\mathfrak{C})$, $k \in \mathrm{Ar}_{\gamma,\eta}(\mathfrak{D})$,

$$\begin{array}{ccccccc}
\mathfrak{F}(\beta) & \xrightarrow{\mathfrak{F}(h)} & \mathfrak{F}(\alpha) & \xrightarrow{f} & \gamma & \xrightarrow{k} & \eta \\
\uparrow \mathfrak{F} & & \uparrow \mathfrak{F} & & \downarrow \mathfrak{G} & & \downarrow \mathfrak{G} \\
\beta & \xrightarrow{h} & \alpha & \xrightarrow{f^*} & \mathfrak{G}(\gamma) & \xrightarrow{\mathfrak{G}(k)} & \mathfrak{G}(\eta)
\end{array}$$

$$(f \circ \mathfrak{F}(h))^* = f^* \circ h$$
$$(k \circ f)^* = \mathfrak{G}(k) \circ f^* ,$$

f^* being the right adjoint of f,

(ii) Equivalently, for all $\alpha, \beta \in \mathrm{Ob}(\mathfrak{C})$, $\gamma, \eta \in \mathrm{Ob}(\mathfrak{D})$, and all $g \in \mathrm{Ar}_{\alpha,\mathfrak{G}(\gamma)}(\mathfrak{C})$, $h \in \mathrm{Ar}_{\beta,\alpha}(\mathfrak{C})$, $k \in \mathrm{Ar}_{\gamma,\eta}(\mathfrak{D})$,

$$\begin{array}{ccccccc}
\mathfrak{F}(\beta) & \xrightarrow{\mathfrak{F}(h)} & \mathfrak{F}(\alpha) & \xrightarrow{^*g} & \gamma & \xrightarrow{k} & \eta \\
\uparrow \mathfrak{F} & & \uparrow \mathfrak{F} & & \downarrow \mathfrak{G} & & \downarrow \mathfrak{G} \\
\beta & \xrightarrow{h} & \alpha & \xrightarrow{g} & \mathfrak{G}(\gamma) & \xrightarrow{\mathfrak{G}(k)} & \mathfrak{G}(\eta)
\end{array}$$

$$^*(\mathfrak{G}(k) \circ g) = k \circ {}^*g$$
$$^*(g \circ h) = {}^*g \circ \mathfrak{F}(h)$$

Note that for any $f \in \mathrm{Ar}_{\mathfrak{F}(\alpha),\gamma}(\mathfrak{D})$ and any $g \in \mathrm{Ar}_{\alpha,\mathfrak{G}(\gamma)}(\mathfrak{C})$, as above,

$$^*(f^*) = f \ ; \ (^*g)^* = g .$$

Appendix 2

Deduction Categories and Formal Topos Properties

Let $(\mathcal{C},\mathfrak{R})$ be a deduction category, with the usual notation

$\mathcal{C} = (Ob(\mathcal{C}),Ar(\mathcal{C}))$, $Ar(\mathcal{C}) = \bigcup_{i,j\in Ob(\mathcal{C})} Ar_{i,j}(\mathcal{C})$, the arrow class, and $Ob(\mathcal{C})$, the object class. We assume the initial object $\emptyset \in Ob(\mathcal{C})$.

In addition, define the $\mathfrak{R}$*-relation* (object) class

$$Rel(\mathcal{C},\mathfrak{R}) \overset{d}{=} \bigcup_{i\in Ob(\mathcal{C})} \mathfrak{R}(i) \subseteq Ob(Preord_{\leq})$$

the $\mathfrak{R}$*-relation arrow* class,

$$ArRel(\mathcal{C},\mathfrak{R}) = \bigcup_{f\in Ar(\mathcal{C})} \mathfrak{R}(f) \subseteq Ar(Preord_{\leq})$$

and the *signature* (object) mapping

$$\sigma : Rel(\mathcal{C},\mathfrak{R}) \to Ob(\mathcal{C}) ,$$

where for any $r \in Rel(\mathcal{C},\mathfrak{R})$, $\sigma(r) \in Ob(\mathcal{C})$ is that unique object such that

$$r \in \mathfrak{R}(\sigma(r)) .$$

In particular, note the special case (assuming $\mathcal{C}$ has all finite limits and products) for $(\mathcal{C},Sub)$, and further (SET,Sub) , where indeed any relation r is such that

$$r \in Sub(\sigma(r)) = \mathcal{P}(\sigma(r)) ,$$

i.e.,

$$r \subseteq \sigma(r) .$$

That is, a relation is simply a subset of a given set. For example, let $X,Y \in Ob(SET)$. Thus, $X \times Y \in Ob(SET)$. Let $r \subseteq X \times Y$ be arbitrary fixed (binary) relation relative to X and Y . Thus, $\sigma(r) = X \times Y$ here.

Note also as usual, for any $i,j \in Ob(\mathcal{C})$ and, say, $f \in Ar_{i,j}(\mathcal{C})$, $\mathfrak{R}(f) \in Ar_{\mathfrak{R}(j),\mathfrak{R}(i)}(Preord_{\leq})$ and $\mathfrak{R}$-relations $r,s \in \mathfrak{R}(j)$ such that $r \leq_{\mathfrak{R}(j)} s$, $\mathfrak{R}(f)(r) \leq_{\mathfrak{R}(i)} \mathfrak{R}(f)(s)$; $\mathfrak{R}(f)(r)$, $\mathfrak{R}(f)(s) \in \mathfrak{R}(i)$.

Also consider the following basic results:

$Cat(\mathcal{C},\mathfrak{R})$ $\quad S,B : Ar(\mathcal{C}) \to Ob(\mathcal{C})$,

$\quad Id : Ob(\mathcal{C}) \to Ar(\mathcal{C})$,

$\quad \circ : Ar(\mathcal{C})\,{}_{S}{\times}_{B}\,Ar(\mathcal{C}) \overset{d}{=} \{(f,g) \mid f,g \in Ar(\mathcal{C})$ and $S(f) = B(g)\} \to Ar(\mathcal{C})$,

where S is the *source* of domain map
B is the *codomain* ($\subseteq$ range) map ,
Id is the *identity* association map,
$\circ$ is the (binary) *composition* map,

where for all $i,j \in Ob(\mathcal{C})$, $f \in Ar_{i,j}(\mathcal{C})$

$$S(f) \stackrel{d}{=} i \ , \ B(f) \stackrel{d}{=} j \ , \ Id(i) \in Ar_{i,j}(\mathcal{C}) \ ,$$

the identity arrow, and for any $(f,g) \in Ar(\mathcal{C})_{S}\times_{B} Ar(\mathcal{C})$,

$$\circ\ (f,g) = f \circ g \ , \text{ arrow composition.}$$

Basic first level syntax rules

For all $i \in Ob(\mathcal{C})$, all $k \in Ar(\mathcal{C})$, all $(f,g) \in Ar(\mathcal{C})_{S}\times_{B} Ar(\mathcal{C})$, $(g,h) \in Ar(\mathcal{C})_{S}\times_{B} Ar(\mathcal{C})$,

$R_{I,syn,1}$: $S(Id(i)) = B(Id(i)) = i$,

$R_{I,syn,2}$: $k \circ (Id(S(k))) = Id(B(k)) \circ k = k$,

$R_{I,syn,3}$: $S(f \circ g) = S(g)$, $B(f \circ g) = B(f)$,

$R_{I,syn,4}$: $(f \circ g) \circ h = f \circ (g \circ h)$.

$$\times : Ob(\mathcal{C}) \times Ob(\mathcal{C}) \to Ob(\mathcal{C}) \text{ (object) product map ,}$$

$$\langle , \rangle : Ar(\mathcal{C}) \underset{S,S}{\times} Ar(\mathcal{C}) = \{(f,g) \mid f,g \in Ar(\mathcal{C}) \text{ and } S(f) = S(g)\} \to Ar(\mathcal{C}) \text{ , arrow product map ,}$$

$proj_1$, $proj_2$: $Ob(\mathcal{C}) \times Ob(\mathcal{C}) \to Ar(\mathcal{C})$, *projection* map , where for all $f,g \in Ar(\mathcal{C}) \underset{S,S}{\times} Ar(\mathcal{C})$, all $i,j \in Ob(\mathcal{C})$,

$R_{I,syn,5}$: $S(\langle f,g \rangle) = S(f) = S(g)$

$R_{I,syn,6}$: $B(\langle f,g \rangle) = \times(B(f),B(g)) \stackrel{d}{=} B(f) \times B(g)$

$R_{I,syn,7}$: $S(proj_1(i \times j)) = S(proj_2(i \times j)) = i \times j$

$R_{I,syn,8}$: $B(proj_1(i \times j)) = i$, $B(proj_2(i \times j)) = j$

$R_{I,syn,9}$: $proj_1(B(f),B(g)) \circ \langle f,g \rangle = f$

$R_{I,syn,10}$: $proj_2(B(f),B(g)) \circ \langle f,g \rangle = g$

$R_{I,syn,11}$: If

$$B(f) = i \times j$$

then

$$\langle proj_1(i,j) \circ f, \ proj_2(i,j) \circ f \rangle = f \ .$$

Define also

$$\times : Ar(\mathcal{C}) \times Ar(\mathcal{C}) \to Ar(\mathcal{C}) \ ,$$

unrestricted arrow product map, where, for all $f,g \in Ar(\mathcal{C})$,

$$f \times g \stackrel{d}{=} \langle f \circ proj_1(S(f),S(g)), \ g \circ proj_2(S(f),S(g)) \rangle \ .$$

Next, define:

$$\cdot[\cdot\cdot] \equiv \text{Subst} : \text{Rel}(\mathbb{C},\mathfrak{R}) \underset{\sigma,B}{\times} \text{Ar}(\mathbb{C}) \to \text{Rel}(\mathbb{C},\mathfrak{R}) ,$$

the *substitution* mapping, where for any $(r,f) \in \text{Rel}(\mathbb{C},\mathfrak{R}) \underset{\sigma,B}{\times} \text{Ar}(\mathbb{C})$, recalling $r \in \mathfrak{R}(\sigma(r))$, $\sigma(r) \in \text{Ob}(\mathbb{C})$,

$$\begin{aligned} T(r,f) &\overset{d}{\equiv} r[f] \\ &\overset{d}{\equiv} (\mathfrak{R}(f))(r) \in \mathfrak{R}(S(f)) \subseteq \text{Rel}(\mathbb{C},\mathfrak{R}) \\ &\overset{d}{\equiv} \text{substitution of } f \text{ into } r . \end{aligned}$$

The following properties hold:
For $(r,f) \in \text{Rel}(\mathbb{C},\mathfrak{R}) \underset{\sigma,B}{\times} \text{Ar}(\mathbb{C})$ and all $(f,g) \in \text{Ar}(\mathbb{C}) \underset{B,S}{\times} \text{Ar}(\mathbb{C})$,

$R_{I,syn,12}$: $\sigma(r[f]) = S(f)$,

$R_{I,syn,13}$: $(r[f])[g] = r[f \circ g]$,

$R_{I,syn,14}$: $r[Id(\sigma(r))] = r$

Also, for any $r,s \in \text{Rel}(\mathbb{C},\mathfrak{R})$,

$R_{I,syn,15}$: If

$$r \leq_{\mathfrak{R}(\sigma(r))} s ,$$

then

$$\sigma(r) =_{Ob} \sigma(s) .$$

$R_{I,Th,0}$: If

$$(r,f),(s,f) \in \text{Rel}(\mathbb{C},\mathfrak{R}) \underset{\sigma,B}{\times} \text{Ar}(\mathbb{C}) ,$$

and if

$$r \leq_{\mathfrak{R}(\sigma(r))} s ,$$

then, by the order preserving property,

$$\mathfrak{R}(f)(r) \leq_{\mathfrak{R}(\sigma(r))} \mathfrak{R}(f)(s) ,$$

i.e.,

$$r[f] \leq_{\mathfrak{R}(\sigma(r))} s[f] .$$

In particular, note the special case $\mathfrak{R} = \text{Sub}$ (and $\mathbb{C}$ having all finite limits and products). Furthermore, for the case of (SET,Sub) , we note now that for all $(r,f) \in \text{Rel(SET,Sub)} \underset{\sigma,B}{\times} \text{Ar(SET)}$:

$$r \in \text{Sub}(\sigma(r)) = \mathcal{P}(\sigma(r)) ,$$

i.e.,

$$r \subseteq \sigma(r) \in \text{Ob(SET)} ,$$

$$r[f] = f^{-1}(r) \subseteq B(f) \in \text{Ob(SET)} .$$

Also, note the terminal arrow maps

$$p_a : Ob(\mathbb{C}) \to Ar(\mathbb{C})$$

where for each $i \in Ob(\mathbb{C})$, $\{p_a(i)\} = Ar_{i,1_a}(\mathbb{C})$, where 1_a is any terminal object in $Ob(\mathbb{C})$, and hence

$R_{I,syn,16}$: $\quad S(p_a(i)) =_{Ob} i\ ,\quad B(p_a(i)) =_{Ob} 1_a$

and for all $f \in Ar(\mathbb{C})$ with $B(f) = 1_a$

$R_{I,syn,17}$: $\quad f =_{Ar} p_a(S(f))$.

Note also that for all $r,s\ t \in Rel(\mathbb{C},\mathfrak{R})$,

$R_{I,Th,1}$: $\quad r \le_{\mathfrak{R}(\sigma(r))} r \quad$ (indeed, $r =_{\mathfrak{R}(\sigma(r))} r$) .

$R_{I,Th,2}$: $\quad$ If

$$r \le_{\mathfrak{R}(\sigma(r))} s \quad \text{and} \quad s \le_{\mathfrak{R}(\sigma(s))} t$$

then

$$\sigma(r) = \sigma(s) = \sigma(t)$$

and

$$r \le_{\mathfrak{R}(\sigma(r))} t_\circ$$

(Modus Ponens) .

In addition, we may have:

$Loc(\mathbb{C},\mathfrak{R})$ $\quad T : Ob(\mathbb{C}) \to Rel(\mathbb{C},\mathfrak{R})$, truth mapping

where for all $i \in Ob(\mathbb{C})$, all $f \in Ar(\mathbb{C})$ and all $r \in Rel(\mathbb{C},\mathfrak{R})$

$R_{I,syn,18}$: $\quad \sigma(T(i)) =_{Ob} i$,

$R_{I,Th,3}$: $\quad r \le_{\mathfrak{R}(\sigma(r))} T(\sigma(r))$,

$R_{I,syn,19}$: $\quad T(B(f))[f] =_{Ob} T(S(f))$.

$$\& = \wedge : Rel(\mathbb{C},\mathfrak{R}) \underset{\sigma,\sigma}{\times} Rel(\mathbb{C},\mathfrak{R}) \to Rel(\mathbb{C},\mathfrak{R})$$

conjunction mapping, where, for all $r,s,t \in Rel(\mathbb{C},\mathfrak{R})$, $f \in Ar(\mathbb{C})$ with $\sigma(r) = \sigma(s) = \sigma(t) = B(f)$,

$$\wedge(r,s) \overset{d}{=} r \wedge s\ ,$$

where

$R_{I,syn,20}$: $\quad \sigma(r \wedge s) = \sigma(r) = \sigma(d)$,

$R_{I,syn,21}$: $\quad (r \wedge s)[f] = r[f] \wedge s[f]$.

$R_{I,Th,4,5}$: If

$$r \leq_{\mathfrak{R}(\sigma(r))} s \; ,$$

then

$$t \wedge r,\; r \wedge t \leq_{\mathfrak{R}(\sigma(r)} s \; .$$

$R_{I,Th,6}$: If

$$r \leq_{\mathfrak{R}(\sigma(r))} s, t$$

then

$$r \leq_{\mathfrak{R}(\sigma(r))} s \wedge t \; .$$

$\perp : Ob(\mathfrak{C}) \to Rel(\mathfrak{C},\mathfrak{R})$, *false* mapping where for all $i \in Ob(\mathfrak{C})$, all $f \in Ar(\mathfrak{C})$, and all $r \in Rel(\mathfrak{C},\mathfrak{R})$,

$R_{I,syn,22}$: $\sigma(\perp(i)) = i$

$R_{I,Th,7}$: $\perp(\sigma(r)) \leq_{\mathfrak{R}(\sigma(r))} r$

$R_{I,syn,23}$: $\perp(B(f))[f] = \perp(s(f))$.

or $= \vee : Rel(\mathfrak{C},\mathfrak{R}) \underset{\sigma,\sigma}{\times} Rel(\mathfrak{C},\mathfrak{R}) \to Rel(\mathfrak{C},\mathfrak{R})$, *disjunction* mapping, where, for all $r,s,t \in Rel(\mathfrak{C},\mathfrak{R})$, $f \in Ar(\mathfrak{C})$ with $\sigma(r) = \sigma(s) = \sigma(t) = B(f)$,

$$\vee\,(r,s) \overset{d}{=} r \vee s \; ,$$

where

$R_{I,syn,24}$: $\sigma(r \vee s) = \sigma(r) = \sigma(s)$.

$R_{I,syn,25}$: $(r \vee s)[f] = r[f] \vee s[f]$.

$R_{I,Th,9,10}$: If

$$r \leq_{\mathfrak{R}(\sigma(r))} s \; ,$$

then

$$r \leq_{\mathfrak{R}(\sigma(r))} s \vee t \; , \; t \vee s \; .$$

$R_{I,Th,8}$: If

$$r \wedge s \; , \; r \wedge t \leq_{\mathfrak{R}(\sigma(r))} u$$

then

$$r \wedge (s \vee t) \leq_{\mathfrak{R}(\sigma(r))} u$$

(distributivity) .

$\Rightarrow \; : \; \mathrm{Rel}(\mathcal{C},\mathfrak{R}) \underset{\sigma,\sigma}{\times} \mathrm{Rel}(\mathcal{C},\mathfrak{R}) \to \mathrm{Rel}(\mathcal{C},\mathfrak{R})$, *implication* mapping is defined to be such that for all $r \in \mathrm{Rel}(\mathcal{C},\mathfrak{R})$ and the mapping

$$id_{\mathfrak{R}(\sigma(r))} \wedge r : \mathfrak{R}(\sigma(r)) \to \mathfrak{R}(\sigma(r)) ,$$

where for all $s \in \mathfrak{R}(\sigma(r))$,

$$(id_{\mathfrak{R}(\sigma(r))} \wedge r)(s) \overset{d}{=} s \wedge r ,$$

$$(\Rightarrow)(r,s) \overset{d}{=} r \Rightarrow s$$

$$\overset{d}{=} (id_{\mathfrak{R}(\sigma(r))} \wedge r)^{*}(s) ,$$

where the following diagram commutes:

$$\left[\mathfrak{R}(\sigma(r)) \xrightarrow{id_{\mathfrak{R}(\sigma(r))} \wedge r} \mathfrak{R}(\sigma(r)) \right]^{*}$$

$$||$$

$$\begin{array}{ccccc} \mathfrak{R}(\sigma(r)) & \xrightarrow{(r \Rightarrow \cdot)} & \mathfrak{R}(\sigma(r)) & \qquad & S(f) \\ \mathfrak{R}(f) \downarrow & & \downarrow \mathfrak{R}(f) & & \downarrow f \\ \mathfrak{R}(S(f)) & \xrightarrow{\mathfrak{R}(f)(r) \Rightarrow \mathfrak{R}(f)(\cdot)} & \mathfrak{R}(S(f)) & & \sigma(r) \end{array} .$$

We can show, for all $r,s,t,u \in \mathrm{Rel}(\mathcal{C},\mathfrak{R})$ and $f \in \mathrm{Ar}(\mathcal{C})$ with $\sigma(r) = \sigma(s) = \sigma(t) = \sigma(u) = B(f)$, corresponding to the diagram

$R_{I,syn,26}$: $\sigma(r \Rightarrow s) = \sigma(r) = \sigma(s)$,

$R_{I,syn,27}$: $(r \Rightarrow s)[f] = r[f] \Rightarrow s[f]$.

In addition, we require:

$R_{I,Th,11}$: If

$$r \leq_{\mathfrak{R}(\sigma(r))} s \quad \text{and} \quad t \leq_{\mathfrak{R}(\sigma(r))} u ,$$

then

$$(r \wedge (s \Rightarrow t)) \leq_{\mathfrak{R}(\sigma(r))} u .$$

$R_{I,Th,12}$: If

$$(r \wedge S) \leq_{\mathfrak{R}(\sigma(r))} t$$

then

$$r \leq_{\mathfrak{R}(\sigma(r))} (s \Rightarrow t) .$$

$\mathrm{Quan}(\mathbb{C},\mathfrak{R})$ $\forall : (\mathrm{Ob}(\mathfrak{R}) \times \mathrm{Ob}(\mathfrak{R})) \underset{(id,\sigma)}{\times} \mathrm{Rel}(\mathbb{C},\mathfrak{R}) \to \mathrm{Rel}(\mathbb{C},\mathfrak{R})$ *universal quantifier* mapping, where for all $i,j \in \mathrm{Ob}(\mathbb{C})$, for the mapping

$$\mathfrak{R}(\mathrm{proj}_2(i,j)) : \mathfrak{R}(j) \to \mathfrak{R}(i\times j) ,$$

and all $r \in \mathrm{Rel}(\mathbb{C},\mathfrak{R})$ with $\sigma(r) = i \times j$ (i.e., $r \in \mathfrak{R}(i \times j)$),

$$\forall(i,j,r) \overset{d}{=} (\mathfrak{R}(\mathrm{proj}_2(i,j)))^*(r) ,$$

where the following diagram commutes:

$$\left[\ \mathfrak{R}(j) \xrightarrow{\ \mathfrak{R}(\mathrm{proj}_2(i\times j))\ } \mathfrak{R}(i\times j)\ \right]^*$$

$$||$$

$$\begin{array}{ccccc} \mathfrak{R}(i\times j) & \xrightarrow{\ \forall(i,j)\ } & \mathfrak{R}(j) & & k \\ {\scriptstyle \mathfrak{R}(Id(i)\times f)}\downarrow & & \downarrow{\scriptstyle \mathfrak{R}(f)} & & \downarrow{\scriptstyle f} \\ \mathfrak{R}(i\times k) & \xrightarrow{\ \forall(i,k)\ } & \mathfrak{R}(k) & & j \end{array} .$$

We can show, for all $i,j,k \in \mathrm{Ob}(\mathbb{C})$, all $r,s,t \in \mathrm{Rel}(\mathbb{C},\mathfrak{R})$, all $f \in \mathrm{Ar}_{k,j}(\mathbb{C})$, all $g \in \mathrm{Ar}_{i\times j,k}(\mathbb{C})$, $\sigma(r) = i \times j$, $\sigma(s) = k \times j$, $\sigma(t) = j$, corresponding to the diagram

$$\begin{array}{ll} R_{I,syn,28}: & \left\{ \begin{array}{l} \sigma(\forall(i,j,r)) = j \\ \forall(i,j,r)[f] = \forall(i,k,r[Id(i)\times f]) . \end{array} \right. \\ R_{I,syn,29}: & \end{array}$$

In addition, we require

If

$R_{I,Th,13}$: $\quad s[\langle g,\mathrm{proj}_2(i,j)\rangle] \le_{\mathfrak{R}(\sigma(r))} r ,$

then

$$\forall(k,j,r)[\mathrm{proj}_2(i,j)] \le_{\mathfrak{R}(\sigma(r))} r .$$

If

$R_{I,Th,14}$: $\quad t[\mathrm{proj}_2(i\times j)] \le_{\mathfrak{R}(\sigma(r))} r ,$

then

$$t \le_{\mathfrak{R}(\sigma(w))} \forall(i,j,r) .$$

$$\exists : (\mathrm{Ob}(\mathbb{C}) \times \mathrm{Ob}(\mathbb{C})) \underset{id,\sigma}{\times} \mathrm{Rel}(\mathbb{C},\mathfrak{R}) \to \mathrm{Rel}(\mathbb{C},\mathfrak{R})$$

existential quantifier mapping, is defined analogous to $\forall$, as, for all $i,j \in \mathrm{Ob}(\mathbb{C})$, $r \in \mathrm{Rel}(\mathbb{C},\mathfrak{R})$ with $\sigma(r) = i \times j$,

$$\exists(i,j,r) \overset{d}{=} {}^{*}(\mathfrak{R}(proj_2(i\times j)))(r) ,$$

with associated commutivity of diagram, implying

$$R_{I,syn,30}: \quad \sigma(\exists(i,j,r)) = j$$

$$R_{I,syn,31}: \quad \exists(i,j,r)[f] = \exists(i,k,r[Id(i)\times f]) ,$$

for all $i,j,k \in Ob(\mathcal{C})$, all $r,s,t,u,v \in Rel(\mathcal{C},\mathfrak{R})$, all $f \in Ar_{k,j}(\mathcal{C})$, all $g \in Ar_{i\times j,k}(\mathcal{C})$, $\sigma(r) = i \times j$, $\sigma(s) = k \times j$, $\sigma(t) = \sigma(u) = j$.

$R_{I,Th,15}$: If

$$r \le_{\mathfrak{R}(\sigma(r))} t[proj_2(i\times j)] \le_{\mathfrak{R}(\sigma(r))} u[proj_2(i\times j)]$$

then

$$(\exists(i,j,r) \wedge t) \le_{\mathfrak{R}(\sigma(r))} u[proj_2(i\times j)] .$$

$R_{I,Th,16}$: If

$$r \le_{\mathfrak{R}(\sigma(r))} t[\langle g,proj_2(i\times j)\rangle]$$

then

$$r \le_{\mathfrak{R}(\sigma(r))} (\exists(i,j,t))[proj_2(i\times j)] .$$

Foun($\mathcal{C},\mathfrak{R}$) $\asymp : Ob(\mathcal{C}) \to Rel(\mathcal{C},\mathfrak{R})$, the *equivalence* mapping is defined to satisfy the usual;
For all $i,\in Ob(\mathcal{C})$,

$$R_{I,syn,32}: \quad \sigma(\asymp(i)) = i \times i .$$

Also define the associated mapping

$$\asymp_{\cdot} : Ob(\mathcal{C}) \underset{id,B\circ proj_1}{\times} (Ar(\mathcal{C}) \underset{(S,B),(S,B)}{\times} Ar(\mathcal{C}) \to Rel(\mathcal{C},\mathfrak{R}) ,$$

where for any $i,j \in Ob(\mathcal{C})$ and any $f,g \in Ar_{j,i}(\mathcal{C})$,

$$f \asymp_i g \overset{d}{=} \asymp_i(f,g)$$
$$= \asymp(i)[\langle f,g\rangle] ,$$

noting here

$$\sigma(f \asymp_i g) = j .$$

In addition, we require, for all $i \in Ob(\mathcal{C})$,

$$R_{I,Th,17}: \quad T(i) \le_{\mathfrak{R}(i)} (Id(i) \asymp_i Id(i)) \qquad \text{(reflexivity)}$$

$R_{I,Th,18}$: $(proj_1(i\times i) \asymp_i proj_2(i\times i) \leq_{\mathfrak{R}(i\times i)} (proj_2(i\times i) \asymp_i proj_1(i\times i))$. (symmetry)

$R_{I,Th,19}$:

$$\left[\left[\underbrace{(proj_1(i\times i)\circ proj_1((i\times i)\times i))}_{\overset{d}{=}\ proj_1(i\times i\times i)} \asymp_i \underbrace{(proj_2(i\times i)\circ proj_1((i\times i)\times i))}_{\overset{d}{=}\ proj_2(i\times i\times i)}\right]\right]$$

$$\wedge \left[\left[\underbrace{(proj_2(i\times i)\circ proj_1((i\times i)\times 1))}_{=\ proj_2(i\times i\times i)} \asymp_i \underbrace{(proj_2((i\times i)\times i)}_{\overset{d}{=}\ proj_3(i\times i\times i)}\right]\right]$$

$$\leq_{R(i\times i\times i)} \left[\left[\underbrace{(proj_1(i\times i)\circ proj_1((i\times i)\times i))}_{=\ proj_1(i\times i\times i)} \asymp_i \underbrace{(proj_2((i\times i)\times i)}_{=\ proj_3(i\times i\times i)}\right]\right] .$$

(transitivity)

Clearly $\leq_{\mathfrak{R}(\cdot)}$ can be replaced by $\asymp_{\mathfrak{R}(\cdot)}$, using (T) , etc.
In addition, we require for all $r \in Rel(\mathcal{C},\mathfrak{R})$ with $\sigma(r) = i$, all $f \in Ar(i,j)$, all $i,j \in Ob(\mathcal{C})$

$R_{I,Th,20}$: $((proj_1(i\times i) \asymp_i (proj_2(i\times i)) \wedge r[proj_1(i\times i)])$
$\leq_{\mathfrak{R}(i\times i)} r[proj_2(i\times i)]$, (substitution for relations)

$R_{I,Th,21}$: $((proj_1(i\times i)) \asymp_i proj_2(i\times i))$

$\leq_{\mathfrak{R}(i\times i)}((f\circ proj_1(i\times i)) \asymp_j (f\circ proj_2(i\times i))$
(substitution for arrow composition; also the natural generalization of functional extensions by fuzzification),

$(((proj_1(i\times j\times i\times j) \asymp_i proj_3(i\times j\times i\times j))\wedge$
$((proj_2(i\times j\times i\times j) \asymp_j proj_4(i\times j\times i\times j)))$

$\leq_{\mathfrak{R}(i\times j\times i\times j)}(proj_{12}(i\times j\times i\times j) \asymp_{i\times j} proj_{34}(i\times j\times i\times j))$.

Note also the definition, for all $i,j \in Ob(\mathcal{C})$,

$$proj_1(i) \overset{d}{=} Id(i) \ , \ proj_{1,2}(i\times j) = Id(i\times j) \ , \ etc.$$

Need also to consider:

$\Omega : Ob(\mathbb{C}) \rightarrow Ob(\mathbb{C})$, *exponential mapping*

$\{\cdot|\cdot\cdot\} : (Ob(\mathbb{C}) \times Ob(\mathbb{C}) \underset{id,\sigma}{\times} Rel(\mathbb{C},\mathfrak{R}) \rightarrow Ar(\mathbb{C})$,

class (or set) *abstraction mapping*,

$\in : Ob(\mathbb{C}) \rightarrow Rel(\mathbb{C},\mathfrak{R})$, *membership mapping* with basic properties.

For all $i,j,k,\ell \in Ob(\mathbb{C})$ and all $r \in Rel(\mathbb{C},\mathfrak{R})$ with $\sigma(r) = i \times j$, all $f \in Ar_{\ell,j}(\mathbb{C})$

$R_{I,syn,33}$: $S(\{i \mid j,r\}) = j$, $B(\{i \mid j,r\}) = \Omega(i) \overset{d}{=} \Omega^i$

$R_{I,syn,34}$: $\sigma(\in(i)) = i \times \Omega^i$,

$R_{I,syn,35}$: $\{i \mid j,r\}\circ f = \{i \mid \ell,r[Id(i) \times f]\}$.

In addition, is associated the mapping

$\in : Ob(C) \times (Ar(C) \times Ar(\mathbb{C})) \rightarrow Rel(\mathbb{C},\mathfrak{R})$,
$(id,B\circ proj_1)(S,\Omega\circ B),(S,B))$

where for any $i,j \in Ob(\mathbb{C})$ and any $f \in Ar_{i,j}(\mathbb{C})$, $g \in Ar_{i,\Omega^j}(\mathbb{C})$,

$$\in_j(f,g) \overset{d}{=} f \in_j g \overset{d}{=} \in(j)[<f,g>] \in \mathfrak{R}(i) ,$$

i.e.,

$$\sigma(f \in_j g) = i .$$

Also, for all $i,j,k \in Ob(\mathbb{C})$, $f,h \in Ar(\mathbb{C})$, $r,s,t,u \in Rel(\mathbb{C},\mathfrak{R})$, $h \in Ar_{k\times j,i}$, $\sigma(r) = i \times j$, $\sigma(s) = k \times j$, $\sigma(t) = k \times j$, $f,m \in Ar_{j,\Omega^i}(\mathbb{C})$, $g \in Ar_{j,i}(\mathbb{C})$ $\sigma(u) = j$.

$R_{I,Th,22}$: If

$$(r[<h,proj_2(k\times j)>] \le_{\mathfrak{R}(i\times j)} h)$$

then

$$((h \in_i (\{i \mid j,r\} \circ proj_2(k\times j)) \le_{\mathfrak{R}(i\times j)} h) .$$

$R_{I,Th,23}$: If

$$(t \le_{\mathfrak{R}(k\times j)} s[<h,proj_2(k\times j)>])$$

then

$$t \leq_{\mathfrak{R}(k\times j)} s \in_i (\{i \mid j,r\} \circ \mathbf{proj}_2(k\times j)) .$$

$R_{I,Th,24}$: If

$$(u[\mathbf{proj}_2(i\times j)] \wedge (\mathrm{proj}_1(i\times j) \in_i (f\circ\mathbf{proj}_2(i\times j)))$$
$$\leq_{\mathfrak{R}(i\times j)} (\mathrm{proj}_1(i\times j) \in_i (m\circ \mathrm{proj}_2(i\times j)))$$

and

$$(u[\mathbf{proj}_2(i\times j)] \wedge (\mathrm{proj}_1(i\times j) \in_i (m\circ\mathbf{proj}_2(i\times j)))$$
$$\leq (\mathbf{proj}_1(i\times j) \in_i (f\circ \mathrm{proj}_2(i\times j)))$$

then

$$u \leq_{\mathfrak{R}(j)} (f \asymp_{\Omega} {}_i m) .$$

A deduction category $(\mathbb{C},\mathfrak{R})$ satisfying properties $\mathrm{Loc}(\mathbb{C},\mathfrak{R})(T, \wedge = \&, \perp = F, \vee = or, \Rightarrow)$, $\mathrm{Quan}(\mathbb{C},\mathfrak{R})(\forall, \exists)$, $\mathrm{Foun}(\mathbb{C},\mathfrak{R})$ $(\asymp, \Omega, \{\cdot|\cdot\cdot\}, \in)$ is called a *formal topos*.

It follows readily (see Coste [41], pp. 9, 10) that letting $\mathfrak{R} = \mathrm{Sub}$, $(\mathbb{C},\mathrm{Sub})$ is a formal topos *iff* $\mathbb{C}$ is a topos.

Note the following specialization as an example of a formal topos

$$(\mathbb{C},\mathfrak{R}) = (\mathrm{Higg}(H),\mathrm{Sub})$$

Note also, e.g., for (Fuz(H),Sub) noting Fuz(H) is not topos, as mentioned before, that, e.g., $R_{I,Th,4,5}$ is satisfied for $\wedge$ interpreted as ordinary minimum: $(\Psi_r \leq \Psi_s)$ implies $(\Psi_t \wedge \Psi_r = \Psi_r \wedge \Psi_t \leq \Psi_s)$ pointwise over X, where $\Psi_r, \Psi_s, \Psi_t : X \to [0,1]$ for some $X \in \mathrm{Ob(SET)}$. (Abusing notation, $X = \sigma(r) = \sigma(s) = \sigma(t)$.)

Similarly, $\wedge$ interpreted as ordinary minimum satisfies $R_{I,Th,6}$

$(\Psi_r \leq \Psi_s, \Psi_t)$ implies $(\Psi_r \leq \Psi_s \wedge \Psi_t)$ point-wise over X.

But, $\wedge$ interpreted more generally, such as in t-norm form $\phi_\&$ will not satisfy $R_{I,Th,6}$ since $\phi_\& \leq \min = \wedge$ pointwise over $[0,1]^2$ and indeed if

$$\Psi_s = \Psi_r \leq \Psi_t \text{ , pointwise over } X$$

then choose any t-norm $\phi_\& < \wedge$ (such as prod, e.g.), whence, in general,

$$\phi_\&(\Psi_s, \Psi_t) < \Psi_s .$$

Similar remarks hold for some of the rules for $\vee$, $\forall$, $\exists$, $\Rightarrow$.

Thus, the concept of a formal topos must be modified to allow natural evaluations for more general negations, t-norms, t-conorms, in the class of generalized set systems. This remains at present as an open problem. One could state there are enough difficulties even with Fuz(H) and $\phi_{\&} = \wedge = \min$, $\phi_{or} = \vee = \max$, $\phi_{nt} = 1 - (\cdot)$, since Fuz(H) is not a topos and hence (Fuz(H),Sub) is not a formal topos, since Fuz(H) - although a category and hence (Fuz(H),Sub) is a deduction category - lacks a subobject classifier Ω . (See, e.g., Carrega [29].)

Nevertheless, semantic evaluation can be carried out into generalized set systems, but the soundness and completeness property may not in general hold.

Appendix. 3

Extensions of deductive categories ([41], Chapter III)

This appendix establishes a category structure, extending Zadeh's and others' "fuzzification" or generalization of ordinary sets and functions and relations on them.

The Bénabou constructions imbed deduction categories within categories, and formal topoi within topoi, in a way so that any results involving deduction categories (or formal topoi) may be - in a natural way - re-interpreted in terms of (ordinary) categories and topoi. The latter two structures have received more attention in the literature involving formal language and set theory (for example, Johnstone [127]) than the former. Furthermore, by specializing these constructions over $(SET, H^{\cdot})$, the categories Fuz(H) and Gog(H) are obtained representing generalizations of Zadeh's fuzzy set theory. (See section 2.4.) In addition, Higgs' and other extensions are considered.

In the following results, we refer to deduction categories all having syntax structure furnished by Th_{syn_0} plus possible additional syntactic structure, depending on the additional pure theoretical structure required, as presented in 2.2.2 (and a basic concrete example in Appendix 2), through the corresponding axioms and rules. If a deduction category satisfies "all" additional structure, it is a *formal topos* (i.e., T, $\wedge$, $\perp$, $\vee$, $\asymp$, $\Rightarrow$, $\exists$, Ω, making up $Foun(\mathfrak{C},\mathfrak{R})$, $Loc(\mathfrak{C},\mathfrak{R})$, $Quan(\mathfrak{C},\mathfrak{R})$); if it satisfies additionally all but Ω (i.e., T, $\wedge$, $\perp$, $\vee$, $\asymp$, $\Rightarrow$, $\exists$), it is called a *formal logos*; if it only satisfies additionally (T, $\wedge$, $\asymp$, $\exists$), it is called a *formal regular category*; and if it satisfies additionally merely (T, $\wedge$, $\asymp$), it is called a formal finite limit category.

It follows that (extending the previous result at the end of Appendix 2), assuming $\mathfrak{C}$ is a category with finite limits existing:

$(\mathfrak{C}, Sub)$ is a formal regular category iff $\mathfrak{C}$ is a regular category;

$(\mathfrak{C}, Sub)$ is a formal logos iff $\mathfrak{C}$ is a logos;

$(\mathfrak{C}, Sub)$ is a formal topos iff $\mathfrak{C}$ is a topos.

(i) Bénabou type I construction

Let $(\mathfrak{C},\mathfrak{R})$ be a deduction category with additional property $\asymp$. Then define category $\mathcal{F}_I(\mathfrak{C},\mathfrak{R})$ as follows:

$$Ob(\mathcal{F}_I(\mathfrak{C},\mathfrak{R})) \overset{d}{=} \{(i,\Psi) \mid i \in Ob(\mathfrak{C}),\ \Psi \in \mathfrak{R}(i)\},$$

$$Ar(\mathcal{F}_I(\mathfrak{C},\mathfrak{R})) = \bigcup_{((i,\Psi),(j,\theta)\in Ob(\mathcal{F}_I(\mathfrak{C},\mathfrak{R}))} Ar_{(i,\Psi),(j,\theta)}(\mathcal{F}_I(\mathfrak{C},\mathfrak{R})) ,$$

where for any (i,Ψ), $(j,\theta) \in Ob(\mathcal{F}_I(\mathfrak{C},\mathfrak{R}))$,

$$\mathrm{Ar}_{(i,\Psi),(j,\theta)}(\mathcal{F}_I(\mathbb{C},\mathfrak{R})) \stackrel{d}{=} \{((f))_{\Psi,\theta} \mid f \in \mathrm{Ar}_{i,j}(\mathbb{C}) \text{ and } f \text{ satisfies condition (G1)}\},$$

where

(B1) $\Psi \leq_{\mathfrak{R}(i)} \theta[f]$,

and where $((\ ))_{\Psi,\theta}$ is an equivalence relation (depending also on i,j) upon $\mathrm{Ar}_{i,j}(\mathbb{C})$, so that for any $f,g \in \mathrm{Ar}_{i,j}(\mathbb{C})$,

$$((f))_{\Psi,\theta} = ((g))_{\Psi,\theta}$$

iff

(B2) $\Psi \leq_{\mathfrak{R}(i)} (f \approx_j g)$.

Composition $\circ$ is defined by, for any (i,Ψ) , (j,θ) , $(k,\lambda) \in \mathrm{Ob}(\mathcal{F}_I(\mathbb{C},\mathfrak{R}))$, $f \in \mathrm{Ar}_{i,j}(\mathbb{C})$, $h \in \mathrm{Ar}_{j,k}(\mathbb{C})$, $h \circ f \in \mathrm{Ar}_{i,k}(\mathbb{C})$, and

$$((h))_{\theta,\lambda} \circ ((f))_{\Psi,\theta} \stackrel{d}{=} ((h \circ f))_{\Psi,\lambda}$$

is well-defined, since

$$\theta \leq_{\mathfrak{R}(i)} \lambda[h]$$

implies , by $R_{I,Th,0}$ (substitution) and $R_{I,syn,13}$

$$\theta[f] \leq_{\mathfrak{R}(i)} \lambda[h][f] =_{\mathfrak{R}(i)} \lambda[h \circ f]$$

and since

$$\Psi \leq_{\mathfrak{R}(i)} \theta[f] ,$$

by $R_{I,Th,2}$ (modus ponens) ,

$$\Psi \leq_{\mathfrak{R}(i)} \lambda[h \circ f] .$$

Similarly, we can show the above holds for any h replacing h' , f' replacing f satisfying analogous of (B2) , etc., as well as associativity.

For each $(i,\Psi) \in \mathrm{Ob}(\mathcal{F}_I(\mathbb{C},\mathfrak{R}))$, the identity arrow $\mathrm{Id}_{(i,\Psi)}$ is merely $((\mathrm{Id}_i))_{\Psi,\Psi}$, where Id_i is the identity arrow for i in $\mathbb{C}$. $\Psi =_{\mathfrak{R}(i)} \Psi[\mathrm{Id}_i]$, by $R_{I,Syn,14}$.

Theorem 1

Let $(\mathbb{C},\mathfrak{R})$ be a formal finite limit category. Then $\mathcal{F}_I(\mathbb{C},\mathfrak{R})$ is a category with finite limits, $(\mathcal{F}_I(\mathbb{C},\mathfrak{R}),\mathrm{Sub})$ is a formal finite limit category, and there is a universal arrow which is order preserving, etc.,

$$(F_{(\mathcal{C},\mathfrak{R})}, \alpha_{(\mathcal{C},\mathfrak{R})}) \in Ar_{(\mathcal{C},\mathfrak{R}),(\mathcal{S}_I(\mathcal{C},\mathfrak{R}),Sub)}(DeCat) ,$$

where $F_{(\mathcal{C},\mathfrak{R})} : \mathcal{C} \to \mathcal{S}_I(\mathcal{C},\mathfrak{R})$ is the faithful functor determined by

(a) For all $i \in Ob(\mathcal{C})$,

$$F_{(\mathcal{C},\mathfrak{R})}(i) \stackrel{d}{=} (i,T(i)) \in Ob(\mathcal{S}_I(\mathcal{C},\mathfrak{R})) .$$

(b) For all $i,j \in Ob(\mathcal{C})$, $f \in Ar_{i,j}(\mathcal{C})$,

$$F_{(\mathcal{C},\mathfrak{R})}(f) \stackrel{d}{=} ((f))_{T(i),T(j)} \in Ar_{F_{(\mathcal{C},\mathfrak{R})}(i),F_{(\mathcal{C},\mathfrak{R})}(j)}(\mathcal{S}_I(\mathcal{C},\mathfrak{R})) ,$$

and where the natural transform $\alpha_{(\mathcal{C},\mathfrak{R})} : \mathfrak{R} \stackrel{\cdot}{\longrightarrow} Sub \circ F_{(\mathcal{C},\mathfrak{R})}$ is given as:

For all $i \in Ob(\mathcal{C})$,

$$\alpha_{(\mathcal{C},\mathfrak{R})}(i) \in Ar_{\mathfrak{R}(i),Sub\circ F_{(\mathcal{C},\mathfrak{R})}(i)}(Preord) ,$$

i.e.,

$$\alpha_{(\mathcal{C},\mathfrak{R})}(i) : \mathfrak{R}(i) \to Sub(F_{(\mathcal{C},\mathfrak{R})}(i)) ,$$

where, for all $\varphi \in \mathfrak{R}(i)$, noting that $\varphi \leq_{\mathfrak{R}(i)} T(i)$, and hence, for $(Id_i : i \to i)$ the identity arrow on i in $Ar(\mathcal{C})$, we have

$$\alpha_{(\mathcal{C},\mathfrak{R})}(i)(\varphi) \stackrel{d}{=} ((Id_i))_{\varphi,T(i)} \in Ar_{(i,\varphi),(i,T(i))}(\mathcal{S}_I(\mathcal{C},\mathfrak{R})) .$$

and hence $\alpha_{(\mathcal{C},\mathfrak{R})}(i)(\varphi) \in Sub\circ F_{(\mathcal{C},\mathfrak{R})}(i)$.

(See Theorem 2 for the definition of the term "universal".)

(ii) <u>Bénabou type II construction</u>

Now consider a similar - but differently appearing construction - for $(\mathcal{C},\mathfrak{R})$ being a formal topos. The connection between type I and type II constructions will be given in part (iii):

Let $(\mathcal{C},\mathfrak{R})$ be a formal topos. Define category $\mathcal{S}_{II}(\mathcal{C},\mathfrak{R})$ as follows:

$$Ob(\mathcal{S}_{II}(\mathcal{C},\mathfrak{R})) \stackrel{d}{=} Ob(\mathcal{S}_I(\mathcal{C},\mathfrak{R}))$$

$$Ar(\mathcal{S}_{II}(\mathcal{C},\mathfrak{R}) = \bigcup_{(i,\varphi),(j,\theta)\in Ob(\mathcal{S}_{II}(\mathcal{C},\mathfrak{R}))} Ar_{(i,\varphi),(j,\theta)}(\mathcal{S}_{II}(\mathcal{C},\mathfrak{R})) ,$$

where for any (i,Ψ) , $(j,\theta) \in Ob(\mathcal{F}_{II}(\mathcal{C},\mathfrak{X}))$,

$$Ar_{(i,\Psi),(j,\theta)}(\mathcal{F}_{II}(\mathcal{C},\mathfrak{X})) \overset{d}{=} \{(((\lambda)))_{\Psi,\theta} \mid \lambda \in \mathfrak{X}(i\times j) \text{ and } \lambda \text{ satisfies conditions (F1), (F2), (F3)}\} .$$

(F1) $\lambda \le_{\mathfrak{X}(i\times j)} \Psi[proj_i(i\times j)],\ \theta[proj_j(i\times j)]$

(F2) $\Psi[proj_i(i\times j)] =_{\mathfrak{X}(i\times j)} (\exists k)(i\times j, \lambda[proj_{i\times j}(k\times i\times j)])$

(F3) $\lambda[proj_{i\times j}(i\times j\times k)] \wedge \lambda[proj_{i\times j}(i\times k\times j)] \le_{\mathfrak{X}(i\times j\times k)} (proj_j(i\times j\times k) \asymp_j proj_j(i\times k\times j))$

(abusing notation) .

In individual variable form, equivalently, we have, for all $x^{(i)}$, $y^{(j)}$, $w^{(j)}$, $z^{(k)}$

(F1) $\lambda[<x^{(i)},y^{(j)}>] \le \Psi[x^{(i)}],\ \theta[y^{(j)}]$,

(F2) $\Psi[<x^{(i)},y^{(j)}>] = (\exists z^{(k)})(\lambda(z^{(k)},x^{(i)},y^{(j)}))$,

(F3) $\lambda[<x^{(i)},y^{(j)}>] \wedge \lambda[<x^{(i)},w^{(j)}>] \le (y^{(j)} \asymp w^{(j)})$,

where $\le$ is $\le_{\mathfrak{X}(\cdot)}$.

$(((\lambda)))_{\Psi,\theta}$ is to be interpreted as the equivalence class of all $\lambda' \in \mathfrak{X}(i\times j)$ such that $\lambda' =_{\mathfrak{X}(i\times j)} \lambda$, i.e.,

$$\lambda' \le_{\mathfrak{X}(i)} \lambda \quad \text{and} \quad \lambda \le_{\mathfrak{X}(i)} \lambda' .$$

Composition $\circ$ for $Ar(\mathcal{F}_{II}(\mathcal{C},\mathfrak{X}))$ is defined by, for any two arrows $(((\lambda))) \in Ar_{(i,\Psi)(j,\theta)}(\mathcal{F}_{II}(\mathcal{C},\mathfrak{X}))$ and $(((\mu))) \in Ar_{(j,\theta),(k,\nu)}(\mathcal{F}_{II}(\mathcal{C},\mathfrak{X}))$,
$(((\mu)))\circ(((\lambda))) \overset{d}{=} (((\mu\circ\lambda)))$, where noting $\mu \in \mathfrak{X}(i\times j)$, $\lambda \in \mathfrak{X}(j\times k)$

$$\begin{aligned}\mu\circ\lambda &\overset{d}{=} (\exists\ j)(i \times k,\ \mu[proj_{j\times k}(i\times j\times k)] \wedge \lambda[proj_{i\times j}(i\times j\times k)]) \\ &= (\exists\ y^{(j)})(\lambda(x^{(i)},y^{(j)}) \wedge \mu(y^{(j)},z^{(k)})) \in \mathfrak{X}(i \times k) ,\end{aligned}$$

and where for any $(i,\Psi) \in Ob(\mathcal{F}_{II}(\mathcal{C},\mathfrak{X}))$, the identity arrow is

$$\begin{aligned}&Id_{(i,\Psi)} \\ &\overset{d}{=} (((\Psi[proj_{(1)i}(i\times i) \wedge \Psi[proj_{(2)i}(i\times i)] \wedge (proj_{(1)i}(i\times i) \asymp_i proj_{(2)i}(i\times i))\ ))) \\ &= (((\Psi(x^{(i)}) \wedge \Psi(y^{(i)}) \wedge (x^{(i)} \asymp_i y^{(i)})\ ))) .\end{aligned}$$

Theorem 2

Let $(\mathcal{C},\mathfrak{X})$ be a formal topos. Then $\mathcal{S}_{II}(\mathcal{C},\mathfrak{X})$ is a topos, $(\mathcal{S}_{II}(\mathcal{C},\mathfrak{X}),\mathrm{Sub})$ is a formal topos, and there exists a faithful (order preserving, etc.) universal arrow

$$(G_{(\mathcal{C},\mathfrak{X})},\beta_{(\mathcal{C},\mathfrak{X})}) \in \mathrm{Ar}_{(\mathcal{C},\mathfrak{X}),(\mathcal{S}_{II}(\mathcal{C},\mathfrak{X}),\mathrm{Sub})}(\mathrm{DeCat}) ,$$

where $G_{(\mathcal{C},\mathfrak{X})} : \mathcal{C} \to \mathcal{S}_{II}(\mathcal{C},\mathfrak{X})$ is the faithful functor determined by:

(a) For all $i \in \mathrm{Ob}(\mathcal{C})$,

$$G_{(\mathcal{C},\mathfrak{X})}(i) \stackrel{d}{=} (i,T(i)) \in \mathrm{Ob}(\mathcal{S}_{II}(\mathcal{C},\mathfrak{X})) ,$$

(b) For all $i,j \in \mathrm{Ob}(\mathcal{C})$, $f \in \mathrm{Ar}_{i,j}(\mathcal{C})$,

$$\begin{aligned} G_{(\mathcal{C},\mathfrak{X})}(f) &\stackrel{d}{=} (((\mathrm{proj}_j(i\times j) \asymp_j (f\circ \mathrm{proj}_i(i\times j))))) \\ &= (((y^{(j)} \asymp_j f(x^{(i)})))) \\ &\in \mathrm{Ar}_{G_{(\mathcal{C},\mathfrak{X})}(i),G_{(\mathcal{C},\mathfrak{X})}(j)}(\mathcal{S}_{II}(\mathcal{C},\mathfrak{X})) , \end{aligned}$$

and where the natural transform

$$\beta_{(\mathcal{C},\mathfrak{X})} : \mathfrak{X} \xrightarrow{\cdot} \mathrm{Sub}\circ G_{(\mathcal{C},\mathfrak{X})} \quad \text{is given as :}$$

For all $i \in \mathrm{Ob}(\mathcal{C})$,

$$\beta_{(\mathcal{C},\mathfrak{X})}(i) \in \mathrm{Ar}_{\mathfrak{X}(i),\mathrm{Sub}\circ G_{(\mathcal{C},\mathfrak{X})}(i)}(\mathrm{Preord}) ,$$

i.e.,

$$\beta_{(\mathcal{C},\mathfrak{X})}(i) : \mathfrak{X}(i) \to \mathrm{Sub}(G_{(\mathcal{C},\mathfrak{X})}(i)) ,$$

where for all $\Psi \in \mathfrak{X}(i)$,

$$\begin{aligned} &\beta_{(\mathcal{C},\mathfrak{X})}(i)(\Psi) \\ &\stackrel{d}{=} (((\Psi[\mathrm{proj}_{(1)i}(i\times i)] \wedge (\mathrm{proj}_{(1)i}(i\times i) \asymp_i \mathrm{proj}_{(2)i}(i\times i))))) \\ &\in \mathrm{Ar}_{(i,\Psi),(i,T(i))}(\mathcal{S}_{II}(\mathcal{C},\mathfrak{X})) , \end{aligned}$$

and hence,

$$\beta_{(\mathcal{C},\mathfrak{X})}(i)(\Psi) \in \mathrm{Sub}(G_{(\mathcal{C},\mathfrak{X})}(i)) .$$

By $(G_{(\mathcal{C},\mathfrak{X})},\beta_{(\mathcal{C},\mathfrak{X})})$ being universal we mean that for all $(\mathcal{C}',\mathfrak{X}') \in \mathrm{DeCat}$ and each $(G',\beta') \in \mathrm{Ar}_{(\mathcal{C},\mathfrak{X}),(\mathcal{C}',\mathfrak{X}')}(\mathrm{DeCat})$, there is a unique $(G'',\beta'') \in \mathrm{Ar}_{(\mathcal{S}_{II}(\mathbb{C},\mathfrak{X}),\mathrm{Sub}),(\mathbb{C}',\mathfrak{X}')}(\mathrm{DeCat})$ such that the followng diagram commutes:

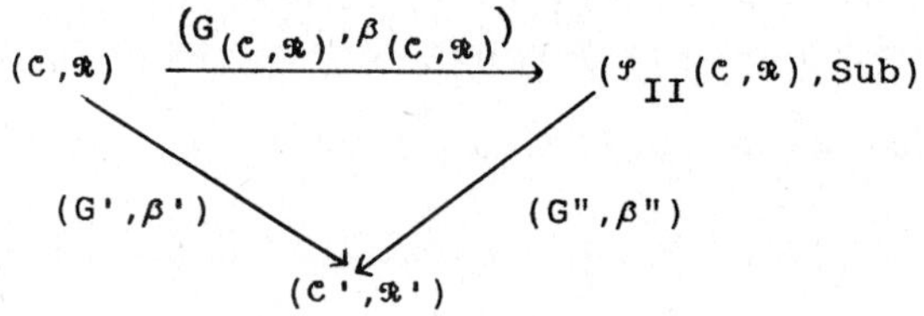

Remark 1.

Note that if $(\mathbb{C},\mathfrak{X})$ is a formal regular deduction category or, further, a formal logos, then the construction $\mathcal{S}_{II}(\mathbb{C},\mathfrak{X})$ remains valid. In turn, Theorem 2 holds with the appropriate modifications ("formal regular deduction category" and "regular category", used in place of "formal topos" and "topos", respectively, for example).

(iii) Connection between type I and type II constructions

The following result shows that for $(\mathbb{C},\mathfrak{X})$ a formal topos, type I constructions may be considered a subclass of type II .

Theorem 3.

Let $(\mathbb{C},\mathfrak{X})$ be a formal topos. Then there is a faithful functor (i.e., a one-to-one injection which is a functor) $\mathcal{G} : \mathcal{S}_I(\mathbb{C},\mathfrak{X}) \to \mathcal{S}_{II}(\mathbb{C},\mathfrak{X})$. More specifically, we may choose $\mathcal{G}$ as follows:

For any (i,Ψ), $(j,\theta) \in \mathrm{Ob}(\mathcal{S}_I(\mathbb{C},\mathfrak{X}))$, and $((f))_{\Psi,\theta} \in \mathrm{Ar}_{(i,\Psi),(j,\theta)}(\mathcal{S}_I(\mathbb{C},\mathfrak{X})$ where $f \in \mathrm{Ar}_{i,j}(\mathbb{C})$,

$$\mathcal{G}((i,\Psi)) = (i,\Psi) \;;\; \mathcal{G}((j,\theta)) = (j,\theta) \;,$$

$$\mathcal{G}(((f))_{\Psi,\theta}) \overset{d}{=} (((\mathcal{G}(f))))_{\Psi,\theta} \;,$$

where

$$\mathcal{G}(f) \overset{d}{=} (f\circ x^{(i)}_{i\times j} \asymp_j y^{(j)}_{i\times j}) \wedge \Psi[x^{(i)}_{i\times j}] \wedge \theta[y^{(j)}_{i\times j}]$$

recalling the notation $x^{(i)}_{i\times j} \overset{d}{=} \mathrm{proj}_i(i\times j)$, $y^{(j)}_{i\times j} \overset{d}{=} \mathrm{proj}_j(i\times j)$.

Proof:

First, it follows easily that for any fixed (i,Ψ), $(j,\theta) \in \mathrm{Ob}(\mathcal{S}_I(\mathbb{C},\mathfrak{X}))$ and any $f \in \mathrm{Ar}_{i,j}(\mathbb{C})$, that $\mathcal{G}(f)$ satisfies properties **(F1)**, **(F2)**, **(F3)** iff f satisfies property (B1).

Next, we can show $\mathcal{G}$ is one-to-one w.r.t. (( )) and ((( ))) :

Noting that since $(\mathfrak{C},\mathfrak{R})$ is a formal topos, the following axioms and rules invoked are valid:

Let $f,g \in Ar_{i,j}(\mathfrak{C})$ with $((f)),((g)) \in Ar_{(i,\Psi),(j,\theta)}(\mathcal{F}_I(\mathfrak{C},\mathfrak{R}))$, and suppose $\mathcal{G}(f) =_{\mathfrak{R}} \mathcal{G}(g)$. Thus, trivially, $\mathcal{G}(f) \leq_{\mathfrak{R}} \mathcal{G}(g)$ and by use of the substitution rule $(R_{I,Th,0})$, replacing $y^{(j)}_{i\times j}$ by $g\circ x^{(j)}_{i\times j}$ everywhere yields (using now simplified notation)

$$((f(x) \asymp f(x))\wedge\Psi[x]\wedge\theta[f(x)]) \leq_{\mathfrak{R}} ((f(x) \asymp g(x))\wedge\Psi[x]\wedge\theta[f(x)]) .$$

But since (by $R_{I,Th,17}$ and the definition of T)

$$T = (f(x) \asymp f(x))$$

and hence by $R_{I,Th,1}$ and $R_{I,Th,4}$ for any $\kappa \in \mathfrak{R}(i\times j)$,

$$\kappa \wedge T \leq_{\mathfrak{R}} \kappa$$

and by (6), since $\kappa \leq_{\mathfrak{R}} \kappa$ and $\kappa \leq_{\mathfrak{R}} T$,

$$\kappa \leq_{\mathfrak{R}} \kappa \wedge T ,$$

and hence

$$\kappa =_{\mathfrak{R}} \kappa \wedge T ..$$

Thus,

$$(f(x) \asymp f(x))\wedge\Psi[x]\wedge\theta[f(x)] =_{\mathfrak{R}} \Psi[x]\wedge\theta[f(x)]$$

and hence by $R_{I,Th,2}$ (modus ponens) ,

$$\Psi[x]\wedge\theta[f(x)] \leq_{\mathfrak{R}} (f(x) \asymp g(x))\wedge\Psi[x]\wedge\theta[f(x)] .$$

Then by use of $R_{I,Th,5}$ and $R_{I,Th,2}$ (modus ponens) we obtain

$$\text{(a)} \qquad \Psi[x] \wedge \theta[f(x)] \leq_{\mathfrak{R}} (f(x) \asymp g(x)) .$$

Now note the following theorem.

For any $\kappa\ \lambda \in \mathfrak{R}(i\times j)$,

$$\kappa \leq_{\mathfrak{R}} \lambda \quad \text{iff} \quad \kappa =_{\mathfrak{R}} \kappa \wedge \lambda$$

(See Theorem 1 (ii), section 2.2.2 (VI).)

Now since $((f)) \in Ar_{(i,\Psi),(j,\theta)}(\mathcal{F}_I(\mathfrak{C},\mathfrak{R}))$, then condition (B1) holds:

$$\Psi[x] \leq \theta[f(x)] .$$

Hence applying the above theorem, where

$\kappa = \Psi[x]$ and $\lambda = \theta[f(x)]$, we have

(b) $\Psi[x] =_{\mathfrak{R}} \Psi[x] \wedge \theta[f(x)]$.

Hence combining (a) and (b) by $R_{I,Th,2}$, we have

$\Psi[x] \leq_{\mathfrak{R}} (f(x) \asymp g(x))$,

i.e., (B2) is satisfied by f and g and hence by definition

$((f))_{\Psi,\theta} = ((g))_{\Psi,\theta}$.

(vi) <u>Higg's construction extended</u>

Let $(\mathcal{C},\mathfrak{R})$ be a deduction category with additional properties where required, beginning with $\wedge$, $\vee$, $\perp$, T .

Define $\mathcal{F}_{III}(\mathcal{C},\mathfrak{R})$ as follows:

$$Ob(\mathcal{F}_{III}(\mathcal{C},\mathfrak{R}) \stackrel{d}{=} \{(i,\Psi) \mid i \in Ob(\mathcal{C}),\ \Psi \in \mathfrak{R}(i\times i) \text{ with } \Psi \text{ satisfying (H1), (H2)}\} ,$$

(H1) $\Psi[<x^{(i)},y^{(i)}>] =_{\mathfrak{R}(i\times i\times i)} \Psi[<y^{(i)},x^{(i)}>]$

(i.e., $R_{I,Th,18}$, symmetry, holds for $\asymp$ replaced by Ψ) ,

(H2) $\Psi[<x^{(i)},y^{(i)}>] \wedge \Psi[<y^{(i)},z^{(i)}>] \leq \Psi\ [<x^{(i)},z^{(i)}>]$

(i.e., $R_{I,Th,19}$, transitivity, holds for $\asymp$ replaced by Ψ) ,
$x^{(i)} = x^{(i)}_{i\times i\times i}$, $y^{(i)} = y^{(i)}_{i\times i\times i}$, $z^{(i)} = z^{(i)}_{i\times i\times i}$.

$$Ar(\mathcal{F}_{III}(\mathcal{C},\mathfrak{R})) \stackrel{d}{=} \bigcup_{\begin{bmatrix}\text{all } (i,\Psi),(j,\theta) \\ \in Ob(\mathcal{F}_{III}(\mathcal{C},\mathfrak{R}))\end{bmatrix}} Ar_{(i,\Psi),(j,\theta)}(\mathcal{F}_{III}(\mathcal{C},\mathfrak{R})) ,$$

where for any (i,Ψ) , $(j,\theta) \in Ob(\mathcal{F}_{III}(\mathcal{C},\mathfrak{R}))$,

$$Ar_{(i,\Psi),(j,\theta)}(\mathcal{F}_{III}(\mathcal{C},\mathfrak{R})) \stackrel{d}{=} \{f \mid f \in \mathfrak{R}(i\times j) \text{ and } f \text{ satisfies (H3), (H4), (H5)}\}$$

(We assume $\mathfrak{R}(\cdot)$ - equivalence here as in type II constructions.)
Simplifying notation somewhat

(H3) $\Psi[<x^{(i)},y^{(i)}>] \wedge f[<y^{(i)},z^{(j)}>] \leq f[<x^{(i)},z^{(j)}>]$,
$f[<y^{(i)},z^{(j)}>] \wedge \theta[<z^{(j)},w^{(j)}>] \leq f[<y^{(i)},w^{(j)}>]$,

(i.e., $R_{I,Th,20}$, substitution for relations, holds for f and $\asymp$ replaced by Ψ)

(H4) $f[<y^{(i)},z^{(j)}>] \wedge f[<y^{(i)},w^{(j)}>] \leq \theta[<z^{(j)},w^{(j)}>]$,

(H5)
$$\bigvee_{\substack{\text{all } g \in Ar(\mathcal{C}),\\ B(g) = j}} (f[\langle y^{(i)},g\rangle]) = D(\Psi)[y^{(i)}] \stackrel{d}{=} \Psi[\langle y^{(i)},y^{(i)}\rangle] \ ,$$

where $D(\Psi) \in \mathfrak{X}(i)$ is the *diagonal* part of Ψ .

Composition $\circ$ for $\mathcal{S}_{III}(\mathcal{C},\mathfrak{X})$ is defined by, for any (i,Ψ), (j,θ), $(k,\lambda) \in Ob(\mathcal{S}_{III}(\mathcal{C},\mathfrak{X}))$ and $f \in Ar_{(i,\Psi),(j,\theta)}(\mathcal{S}_{III}(\mathcal{C},\mathfrak{X}))$, $g \in Ar_{(j,\theta),(k,\lambda)}(\mathcal{S}_{III}(\mathcal{C},\mathfrak{X}))$,

$$g\circ f = (g\circ f)[\langle x^{(i)},z^{(k)}\rangle] \stackrel{d}{=} \bigvee_{\substack{h \in Ar(\mathcal{C}),\\ B(h) = j}} (f[\langle x^{(i)},h\rangle] \wedge g[\langle h,z^{(k)}\rangle]) \ .$$

For each $(i,\Psi) \in Ob(\mathcal{S}_{III}(\mathcal{C},\mathfrak{X}))$, $Id_{(i,\Psi)} \stackrel{d}{=} \Psi$ is the identity arrow on (i,Ψ) .

It easily follows that for any $(i,\Psi) \in Ob(\mathcal{S}_{III}(\mathcal{C},\mathfrak{X}))$, (from (H2)) ,

$$\Psi = \Psi[\langle x^{(i)},y^{(i)}\rangle] \leq D(\Psi)[x^{(i)}] \wedge D(\Psi)[y^{(i)}]$$ and (from (H4), (H5)) for any $f \in Ar_{(i,\Psi),(j,\theta)}(\mathcal{S}_{III}(\mathcal{C},\mathfrak{X}))$,

$$f = f[\langle x^{(i)},y^{(j)}\rangle] \leq D(\Psi)[x^{(i)}] \wedge D(\theta)[y^{(j)}] \ .$$

Note that (H2) - (H5) are equivalent to the following composition equations:

$\mathcal{S}_{III}(\mathcal{C},\mathfrak{X})$ is a category under $\cdot$, and in particular, for any $f \in Ar_{(i,\Psi),(j,\theta)}(\mathcal{S}_{III}(\mathcal{C},\mathfrak{X}))$,

$$f\circ Id_{(i,\Psi)} = Id_{(j,\theta)}\circ f = f \qquad ((H3)),$$

$$\Psi = Id_{(i,\Psi)}\circ Id_{(I,\Psi)} = Id_{(i,\Psi)} \qquad ((H1),\ (H2)),$$

together with (due to the associativity of $\vee$ - see 2.2.2, VI),

$f\circ(g\circ h) = (f\circ g)\circ h)$, all $f,\ g,\ h \in Ar(\mathcal{S}_{III}(\mathcal{C},\mathfrak{X}))$, where well-defined, the usual properties for arrows in a category.

In addition,

$$f^{op}\circ f \leq \Psi \qquad (H4)$$
$$f\circ D(\theta) = D(\Psi) \qquad (H5)$$

where $(f^{op} : (j,\theta) \rightarrow (i,\Psi))$ is the "opposite" of f .

For any (i,Ψ), $(j,\theta) \in Ob(\mathcal{S}_{III}(\mathcal{C},\mathfrak{X}))$, define:

$$\kappa_{\Psi,\theta} \overset{d}{=} \{f \mid f \in Ar_{i,j}(\mathcal{C}) \text{ and } D(\Psi) \leq_{\mathfrak{X}(i)} D(\theta)[f]\} ,$$

i.e., $f \in \mathcal{G}_{\Psi,\theta}$ satisfies (G1), and hence essentially, $\mathcal{G}_{\Psi,\theta}$ is the same as $Ar_{(i,D(\Psi)),(j,D(\theta))}(\mathcal{S}_I(\mathcal{C},\mathfrak{X}))$.

Next, define

$$\mathcal{H}_{\Psi,\theta} = \{f \mid f \in Ar_{i,j}(\mathcal{C}) \text{ and } \Psi[<x^{(i)},y^{(i)}>] \leq \theta[<f\circ x^{(i)},f\circ y^{(i)}>]\}$$

and in turn, define

$$\mathcal{G}_{\Psi,\theta} = \{G(f) \mid f \in \mathcal{H}_{\Psi,\theta}\} ,$$

where here

$$\mathcal{G}(f) \overset{d}{=} \Psi(f\circ x^{(i)},y^{(j)}) \wedge D(\Psi)[x^{(i)}] \wedge D(\theta)[y^{(j)}] .$$

It follows immediately that

$$\mathcal{H}_{\Psi,\theta} \subseteq \kappa_{\Psi,\theta} \subseteq Ar_{i,j}(\mathcal{C})$$

and by using (H1) - (H5) ,

$$\mathcal{G}_{\Psi,\theta} \subseteq Ar_{(i,\Psi),(j,\theta)}(\mathcal{S}_{III}(\mathcal{C},\mathfrak{X})) \subseteq \mathfrak{X}(i\times j) .$$

Now define

$$\mathcal{N} \overset{d}{=} \{(i,\Psi) \mid (i,\Psi) \in Ob(\mathcal{S}_{III}(\mathcal{C},\mathfrak{X})) \text{ and there is some } f \in Ar(\mathcal{C}) \text{ with } B(f) = i \text{ such that } D(\Psi)[f] =_{\mathfrak{X}(i)} T(i)\}$$

the class of all normalized (or normable) objects of $\mathcal{S}_{III}(\mathcal{C},\mathfrak{X})$.

It then follows that for any (i,Ψ) and $(j,\theta) \in \mathcal{N}$,

$$\emptyset \neq \mathcal{H}_{\Psi,\theta}$$

and hence

$$\emptyset \neq \mathcal{H}_{\Psi,\theta} \subseteq \kappa_{\Psi,\theta} \subseteq Ar_{i,j}(\mathcal{C}) ,$$

$$\emptyset \neq \mathcal{G}_{\Psi,\theta} \subseteq Ar_{(\Psi,i),(\theta,j)}(\mathcal{S}_{III}(\mathcal{C},\mathfrak{X})) \subseteq \mathfrak{X}(i\times j) ,$$

and

$\mathcal{S}_{III,\mathcal{N}}(\mathcal{C},\mathfrak{X}) \overset{d}{=} (Ob(\mathcal{S}_{III,\mathcal{N}}(\mathcal{C},\mathfrak{X})), Ar(\mathcal{S}_{III,\mathcal{N}}(\mathcal{C},\mathfrak{X})))$ is a well-defined subcategory of $\mathcal{S}_{III}(\mathcal{C},\mathfrak{X}))$ where

$$Ob(\mathcal{S}_{III,\mathcal{N}}(\mathcal{C},\mathfrak{X})) \overset{d}{=} \mathcal{N} ,$$

$$Ar(\mathcal{S}_{III,\mathcal{N}}(\mathcal{C},\mathfrak{R})) = \bigcup_{\substack{\text{over all} \\ (i,\Psi),(j,\theta) \\ \in \mathcal{N}}} Ar_{(i,\Psi),(j,\theta)}(\mathcal{S}_{III}(\mathcal{C},\mathfrak{R})) .$$

Note that for the ordinary Krönecker delta $\delta(i) \in \mathfrak{R}(i\times i)$, where for all $f,g \in Ar(\mathcal{C})$, $S(f) = S(g) = j$ $G(f) = B(g) = i$,

$$\delta(i)[<f,g>] = \begin{cases} T(i) & \text{iff } f =_{\mathfrak{R}(i)} g , \\ \bot(i) & \text{iff } f \neq_{\mathfrak{R}(i)} g , \end{cases}$$

$(i,\delta(i)) \in Ob(\mathcal{S}_{III,\mathcal{N}}(\mathcal{C},\mathfrak{R}))$. In addition the constant relation $T(i\times i)$ identified as

$$T(i\times i)[<f,g>] = T(i) \text{ , all } f,g ,$$

is such that $(i,T(i)) \in Ob(\mathcal{S}_{III,\mathcal{N}}(\mathcal{C},\mathfrak{R}))$.

Suppose now $(\Rightarrow)$ (i.e., $R_{I,Th,11,12}$ hold) is valid for $(\mathcal{C},\mathfrak{R})$. Then for each $(i,\Psi) \in Ob(\mathcal{S}_{III}(\mathcal{C},\mathfrak{R}))$, the *intuitionistic Krőnecker* delta is defined as

$$e_\Psi = e_\Psi[<x^{(i)},y^{(i)}>] \stackrel{d}{=} (D(\Psi)[x^{(i)}] \vee D(\Psi)[y^{(i)}]) \Rightarrow \Psi$$

noting

$$\Psi = \Psi[<x^{(i)},y^{(i)}>] .$$

Some basic properties (see also Fourmann and Scott [59] and Scott [226']) are:

For all (i,Ψ), $(j,\theta) \in Ob(\mathcal{S}_{III}(\mathcal{C},\mathfrak{R}))$:

(1) $$\Psi[<x^{(i)},y^{(i)}>] \leq e_\Psi[<x^{(i)},y^{(i)}>] .$$

Indeed,

(2) $$\begin{aligned}\Psi[<x^{(i)},y^{(i)}>] &= D[x^{(i)}] \wedge D[y^{(i)}] \wedge e_\Psi[<x^{(i)},y^{(i)}>] \\ &= (D[x^{(i)}] \vee D[y^{(i)}]) \wedge e_\Psi[<x^{(i)},y^{(i)}>] .\end{aligned}$$

(**<u>Proof</u>**: Theorem 9, 2.2.2, VI, with $a = D[x^{(i)}] \wedge D[y^{(i)}]$ and $b = \Psi[<x^{(i)},y^{(i)}>]$, yields $\leq$ for (2). Also, $R_{I,Th,12}$, where $r = b$ and $s = a$, as above, yields $\geq$ for (2).)

(3) $$e_\Psi[<x^{(i)},y^{(i)}>] = T ,$$

if

$$D[x^{(i)}] \vee D[y^{(i)}] = \Psi[<x^{(i)},y^{(i)}>]$$

i.e.,

$$D[x^{(i)}] = D[y^{(i)}] = \Psi[<x^{(i)},y^{(i)}>] .$$

(Proof is immediate from Theorem 9, 2.2.2, VI.)

(4) $(i,e_\Psi) \in Ob(\mathcal{F}_{III}(\mathbb{C},\mathfrak{R}))$.

Proof that transitivity holds for $\asymp$ replaced by e_Ψ is complicated. Note however:

(5) Define for any $i \in Ob(\mathbb{C})$ and any $r,s \in \mathfrak{R}(i)$,

$$r <_{\mathfrak{R}(i)} s \qquad (\text{or } s >_{\mathfrak{R}(i)} r)$$

iff $r \leq_{\mathfrak{R}(i)} s$, but $r \neq_{\mathfrak{R}(i)} s$.

Then we can choose (compatible with $R_{I,Th,11}$ and $R_{I,Th,12}$)

$$(r \Rightarrow s) = \begin{cases} T(i) , & \text{if } r \geq_{R(i)} s \\ s , & \text{if } r <_{R(i)} s , \end{cases}$$

in which case e_Ψ simplifies to

$$e_\Psi[<x^{(i)},y^{(i)}>] = \begin{cases} T \text{ iff } D(\Psi)[x^{(i)}] \vee D(\Psi)[y^{(i)}] \\ \qquad = \Psi[<x^{(i)},y^{(i)}>] \\ \quad \text{iff } D(\Psi)[x^{(i)}] = D(\Psi)[y^{(i)}] \\ \qquad = \Psi[<x^{(i)},y^{(i)}>] , \\ \Psi[<x^{(i)},y^{(i)}>] , \text{ otherwise} . \end{cases}$$

(In this case, the proof of (4) becomes easy, by considering $e_\Psi[<x^{(i)},y^{(i)}>] \wedge e_\Psi[<y^{(i)},z^{(i)}>]$ and $e_\Psi[<x^{(i)},z^{(i)}>]$, and considering all possible cases when $e_\Psi = T$ or $< T$.)

Note the following special cases for $(i,\Psi) \in Ob(\mathcal{F}_{III}(\mathbb{C},\mathfrak{R}))$ and the resulting e_Ψ :

(i) $\varepsilon_\Psi[<x^{(i)},y^{(i)}>] \overset{d}{=} D(\Psi)[x^{(i)}] \wedge D(\Psi)[y^{(i)}]$

$$e_{\varepsilon_\Psi}[<x^{(i)},y^{(i)}>] = \begin{cases} T , \text{ if } D(\Psi)[x^{(i)}] = D(\Psi)[y^{(i)}] \\ \Psi[<x^{(i)},y^{(i)}>] , \text{ if } D(\Psi)[x^{(i)}] \\ \qquad \neq D(\Psi)[y^{(i)}] . \end{cases}$$

Equivalently, we can begin with any $\eta \in \mathfrak{R}(i)$ and define $\varepsilon_\eta [<x^{(i)},y^{(i)}>] \overset{d}{=} \eta[x^{(i)}] \wedge \eta[y^{(i)}]$, yielding

$(i,\varepsilon_\eta) \in Ob(\mathcal{P}_{III}(\mathcal{C},\mathfrak{R}))$ and

$$e_{\varepsilon_\eta}[<x^{(i)},y^{(i)}>] = \begin{cases} T \text{ iff } \eta[x^{(i)}] = \eta[y^{(i)}] , \\ \varepsilon_\eta[<x^{(i)},y^{(i)}>] \text{ iff } \\ \qquad \eta[x^{(i)}] \neq \eta[y^{(i)}] . \end{cases}$$

(ii) $\quad \Psi[<x^{(i)},y^{(i)}>] = T$,
$e_\Psi[<x^{(i)},y^{(i)}>] = T$.

(iii) $$\Psi[<x^{(i)},y^{(i)}>] \stackrel{d}{=} \delta(i)[<x^{(i)},y^{(i)}>]$$
$$\stackrel{d}{=} \begin{cases} T \text{ iff } x^{(i)} = y^{(i)} \\ \perp \text{ iff } x^{(i)} \neq y^{(i)} , \end{cases}$$

the ordinary Krönecker delta function over i ,

$$e_\Psi[<x^{(i)},y^{(i)}>] = \delta(i)[<x^{(i)},y^{(i)}>] .$$

(6) For any $f \in Ar_{(i,\Psi),(j,\theta)}(\mathcal{P}_{III}(\mathcal{C},\mathfrak{R}))$, e_Ψ and e_θ satisfy (H3) formally, where Ψ is replaced by e_Ψ and θ by e_θ .

(**Proof**: Consider, e.g., e_Ψ : By (H3) and property (2) above,

$$D(\Psi)[x^{(i)}] \wedge D(\Psi)[y^{(i)}] \wedge e_\Psi[<x^{(i)},y^{(i)}>] \wedge f[<y^{(i)},z^{(j)}>]$$
$$\leq f[<x^{(i)},z^{(j)}>] .$$

But since $f[<y^{(i)},z^{(j)}>] \leq D(\Psi)[y^{(i)}]$, the right hand factor is absorbed, and since

$$D(\Psi)[x^{(i)}] \wedge e_\Psi[<x^{(i)},y^{(i)}>] \wedge f[<y^{(i)},z^{(j)}>]$$
$$= e_\Psi[<x^{(i)},y^{(i)}>] \wedge f[<y^{(i)},z^{(j)}>] ,$$

the desired result obtains.)

(7) Noting that $\mathcal{K}_{e_\Psi,e_\theta} \subseteq \mathcal{K}_{\Psi,\theta}$, we let $g : Ob(\mathcal{C}) \to Rel(\mathcal{C},\mathfrak{R}))$ be arbitrary fixed so that for all $i \in Ob(\mathcal{C})$, $g(i) \in \mathfrak{R}(i\times i)$ so that $(i,g(i)) \in Ob(\mathcal{P}_{III}(\mathcal{C},\mathfrak{R}))$. Define then the contravariant functor $\mathfrak{R}_g : \mathcal{C} \to$ Preord, by, for all $i \in Ob(\mathcal{C})$,

$$\mathfrak{R}_g(i) \stackrel{d}{=} Ar_{(i,g(i)),(i,g(i))}(\mathcal{P}_{III}(\mathcal{C},\mathfrak{R})) \cup \{e_{g(i)}\} ,$$

with $\mathfrak{R}_g(h) = \mathfrak{R}(h)$, for all $h \in Ar(\mathcal{C})$. Define $\mathcal{K}_e = \bigcup_{\text{all } i,j\in Ob(\mathcal{C})} \mathcal{K}_{e_{g(i)},e_{g(j)}}$. Then $(Ob(\mathcal{C}),\mathcal{K}_e)$ is a category and

$((\mathrm{Ob}(\mathcal{C}),\mathcal{K}_e),\mathcal{R}_g))$ is a deduction category with equivalence $\asymp_g$ represented by e_g, i.e., e_g satisfies $R_{I,Th,17} - R_{I,Th,21}$ with $\asymp$ replaced by $\asymp_g \overset{d}{=} e_g$ (slightly abusing notation). We call e_g an intuitionistic equivalence, due to the structure of Th_K.

At the formal language level, we may consider distinguished function symbol $(g : \mathrm{Ob}(\mathcal{L}) \to \mathrm{Rel}(\mathcal{L}))$ representing "partial equivalence" with syntax rule added: $\sigma(g(i)) = i \times i$ and with $\asymp$ temporarily omitted, with only $R_{I,Th,18}$ and $R_{I,Th,19}$ satisfied by g, replacing $\asymp$, and where distinguished function symbol $(Ex_g : \mathrm{Ob}(\mathcal{L}) \to \mathrm{Rel}(\mathcal{L}))$ representing "existence" or "extent"

$$Ex_g(i) \overset{d}{=} D(g(i)) \overset{d}{=} g(i)[<x^{(i)},x^{(i)}>]$$

(where $Id_i = <x^{(i)},y^{(i)}>$). In turn, define equivalence $\asymp_g : \mathrm{Ob}(\mathcal{L}) \to \mathrm{Rel}(\mathcal{L})$ by

$$\begin{aligned}\asymp_g(i) &\overset{d}{=} \asymp_g(i)[<x^{(i)},y^{(i)}>] \\ &\overset{d}{=} (Ex_g(i)[x^{(i)}] \vee Ex_g(i)[y^{(i)}]) \\ &\Rightarrow g(i)[<x^{(i)},y^{(i)}>] .\end{aligned}$$

The obvious compatable model $\| \ \|$ for $\mathcal{L}_{syn_K,K}$ preserving these relations yields the following:

$$\begin{aligned}\|\asymp_g(i)[<x^{(i)},y^{(i)}>]\| &= \|Ex_g(i)[x^{(i)}]\| \ \|\vee\| \ \|Ex_g(i)[y^{(i)}]\| \\ &= \|\Rightarrow\| \ \|g(i)[<x^{(i)},y^{(i)}>]\| \\ &= e_{g(i)}([<\|x^{(i)}\|,\ \|y^{(i)}\|>]) ,\end{aligned}$$

$$\begin{aligned}\|Ex_g(i)[x^{(i)}]\| &= \|Ex_{g(i)}[x^{(i)}]\| \\ &= \|D(g(i))\|[<\|x^{(i)}\|,\ \|y^{(i)}\|>] , \\ &= \|g(i)\|[<\|x^{(i)}\|,\ \|x^{(i)}\|>] ,\end{aligned}$$

etc.

Remarks 2

Analagous to Theorem 3, $(\mathcal{C},\mathcal{R})$ can be imbedded within $(\mathcal{F}_{III}(\mathcal{C},\mathcal{R}),\mathrm{Sub}))$ by use of the map $(H_{(\mathcal{C},\mathcal{R})}, \gamma_{(\mathcal{C},\mathcal{R})}) : (\mathcal{C},\mathcal{R}) \to \mathcal{F}_{III}(\mathcal{C},\mathcal{R})$ where for all $i \in \mathrm{Ob}(\mathcal{C})$,

$$H_{(\mathcal{C},\mathcal{R})}(i) \overset{d}{=} (i,\delta_i)$$

and, for all $f \in Ar_{i,j}(\mathcal{C})$,

$$H_{(\mathcal{C},\mathfrak{R})}(f)[<x^{(i)},y^{(j)}>] \stackrel{d}{=} \delta_i[<f\circ x^{(i)},y^{(j)}>]$$

and $\gamma_{(\mathcal{C},\mathfrak{R})} : \mathfrak{R} \xrightarrow{\cdot} \mathrm{Sub}\circ\mathcal{H}_{(\mathcal{C},\mathfrak{R})}$ is defined as, for any $i \in \mathrm{Ob}(\mathcal{C})$, $\gamma_{(\mathcal{C},\mathfrak{R})}(i) \in \mathrm{Ar}_{\mathfrak{R}(i),\mathrm{Sub}(i,\delta_i)}(\mathrm{Preord})$, given by, for any $r \in \mathfrak{R}(i)$,

$$\gamma_{(\mathcal{C},\mathfrak{R})}(i)(r) = r[x^{(i)}] \wedge \delta_i[<x^{(i)},y^{(i)}>] ,$$

etc.

More generally, we can replace for $H_{(\mathcal{C},\mathfrak{R})}$ the relation $i \to \delta_i$, $i \in \mathrm{Ob}(\mathcal{C})$, by , e.g., g , as defined earlier in this section. To what extent any such mapping (whether for g arbitrary or for $g = \delta_.$) is a functor and whether $\mathcal{F}_{III}(\mathcal{C},\mathfrak{R})$ is a topos remains open for the general case. For the particular case $\mathfrak{R} = H^{\cdot}$, see the related results in section 2.4 and the following remarks here.

Remark 3

All of the previous development specializes to well-known structures when the base deduction category $(\mathcal{C},\mathfrak{R})$ is chosen to be $(\mathrm{SET},H^{\cdot})$:

Case (1) : $\mathcal{F}_I(\mathrm{SET},H^{\cdot})$,for H a complete lattice such that $\asymp$ is formally treated as ordinary equality (see Case (2) for a similar situation) is essentially Gog(H) , Goguen's category of fuzzy sets [96], obtained originally as the characterizing category satisfying six basic conditions. (See section 2.4.2 D.)

Case (2): $\mathcal{F}_{II}(\mathrm{SET},H^{\cdot})$, for H a complete Heyting algebra, except for having $\asymp$ formally used as ordinary equality in the definitions of $\mathrm{Ar}(\mathcal{F}_{II}(\mathrm{SET},H^{\cdot}))$ (see property (F3)), is the same as Eytan's category Fuz(H) , another extension of fuzzy set theory [56], [57]. When H is not, in effect so constrained, but rather allowed to have its "natural" full Heyting algebra structure, including $\asymp$ properly interpreted by, say, $e_{\asymp}$, then the resulting category, $\mathrm{Fuz}_e(H)$ is indeed a topos. (See 2.4.2, A, B, F.)

Case (3): $\mathcal{F}_{III}(\mathrm{SET},H^{\cdot})$, for H a complete Heyting algebra, with all of its intuitionistic structure, is always a topos - Higg's topos Higg(H) - and indeed is the Grothendieck topos of sheaves Sheave(H) [59], [226']. (See 2.4.2, E, F.)

Case (4): The relationship ("representativeness") mentioned in Eytan [56], between Gog(H) and Fuz(H) is a special case of Theorem 3, for $(\mathcal{C},\mathfrak{R}) = (\mathrm{SET},H^{\cdot})$.

For further comments on the above categories and relations between them, see section 2.4.2, (F).

2.5 Probabilistic and approximate reasoning

2.5.1 General comments

It appears that relatively few individuals recognize that set theory based on probability logic (a multi-valued logic) is the basis of standard statistical approaches to problems involving uncertainty. (See section 2.3.9.) With this in mind, it should be pointed out that many semantic evaluations exist for set theories relative to logic, including classical two-valued logic (the deterministic approach), intuitionistic logic, and Lukasiewicz $\aleph_1$-logic (section 2.3.4). In addition, why choose the particular logic of probability when there are infinitely many alternatives, some of which were outlined in section 2.3.3? Why cannot we switch logics for various problems involving uncertainty? On the other hand, it has been shown that quite different appearing set theories/logics may be directly related, such as probability logic with Lukasiewicz logic or with a variation of Lukasiewicz logic. This has been accomplished, e.g., through the coverage functions of random sets. See section 2.3.8, Chapters 5, 6, and section 8.3. Thus these relations embrace the choice of probability logic; however, the latter must be suitably modified. The difficulty in choosing a particular logic lies essentially in the choice of logical operators comprising the logic. Since any problem can be described by an appropriate formal language, one can use the data to guide the choice of the most appropriate logics. (See Chapter 9 or section 2.3.5.)

In this section, we outline an approach to the manipulation and explanation of uncertainty in knowledge-based systems, employing "fuzzy" logic as a basis for approximate reasoning. For further background motivations and various applications of fuzzy logic, we refer the reader to Zadeh's work, e.g., Zadeh [280].

We can view fuzzy logic as a *semantic* deduction procedure as opposed to just deduction.

Specifically, let $\mathcal{L}$ be a formal language, $\|\cdot\|$ be a fixed semantic evaluation, and $\mathrm{Loc}(\mathcal{L})$ a fixed logic. We assume at least for the present, no additional theory $\mathrm{Th}_K(\mathcal{L})$. In particular, consider $\Rightarrow$ (implication) in $\mathrm{Loc}(\mathcal{L})$.

Define, for any wff's $\phi, \Psi \in \mathrm{wff}(\mathcal{L})$, the deduction sequent $(\phi \dashv \Psi)$ or $\frac{\phi}{\Psi}$ iff $\|\phi \Rightarrow \Psi\| = 1$. Note that, for the logics $\L_k$ and G_k , $k = 2,3,\ldots,\aleph_1$, $\phi \vdash \Psi$ iff $\|\phi\| \le \|\Psi\|$ (semantics entailment). (See section 2.3.3.) Similarly, deduction holds for

$$\phi_1, \phi_2, \ldots, \phi_m \vdash \Psi \quad \text{iff} \quad \|\phi_j \Rightarrow \Psi\| = 1 \ , \ j = 1,2,\ldots,m \ .$$

Note that Zadeh's fuzzy logic is not typically formalized in terms of a formal language and semantic evaluation framework. In fuzzy logic, the truth values - as typically occur in multi-valued logic - in the unit interval are replaced by linguistic truth quantifiers such as "very true", "slightly false", etc., and the numerical descriptions are in general replaced by linguistic ones - i.e., linguistic variables such as age, with typical values: young, very young, old, middle age, ... These linguistic values in turn have numerical representations in the form of fuzzy set membership or possibility functions. (See Haack [102] and section 10.2 A(I) for criticisms of fuzzy logic.)

At this present stage of designing knowledge-based systems, statistical reasoning and techniques of artificial intelligence (AI-based techniques) are the two main approaches to the analysis of uncertainty. Much research remains to be done in order to see whether or not a combined approach of statistical/probabilistic and other techniques (e.g., AI techniques) will lead to a better way of modeling of expert knowledge systems. (See the recent paper of Spiegelhalter and Knill-Jones [246].) As far as meaning representation in natural language is concerned, an attempt will be made in the following chapters to establish some connections between possibility theory and random sets.

2.5.2 Approximate reasoning

Approximate reasoning (e.g., inexact reasoning in clinical decision-support systems) is commonly used in knowledge-based systems, in particular in expert systems. In general, the data base in a knowledge-based system comprises:

(i) facts expressed by sentences

(ii) rules expressed by conditional sentences (where conditioning is expressed as a binary logical connective).

All sentences in a knowledge-based system have an associated *certainty factor*, i.e., numerical value lying in the unit interval expressing the degree of confirmation associated with the sentence in question (See, e.g., Shortliffe and Buchanan [236].).

The basic problem in the analysis of uncertainty consists of assigning an associated degree of uncertainty to conclusions from various combinations of hypotheses from (i) using (ii).

Zadeh argued that if (i) and (ii) are imprecise, due, e.g., to natural language, then the computation of certainty factors is not obtainable in classical form. But, if we accept a weaker replacement - linguistic certainty for numerical certainty - then fuzzy logic may be used as a basis to carry out approximate reasoning. In the latter, classical deduction reasoning is carried out, modified by the use of imprecise sentences, and thus hypotheses and conclusions modified likewise.

To illustrate the use of fuzzy logic in deriving inference rules for quantified propositions, we examine below an example from Zadeh [289] and show that these deductions are semantically consistent.

Let X be a finite set, and A , B , C be attributes with domains in X . Let Q_1 , Q_2 be linguistic quantifiers, e.g., "most", with domains in $[0,1]$. We write, e.g., ϕ_A for the membership or possibility function of A ; and $Q_1 \otimes Q_2$ as the product of fuzzy numbers , an extension of the product operation on ordinary numbers - considered as singleton sets (see, e.g., Dubois and Prade [51]).

Consider the following deduction

$$\begin{array}{l} P_1 \stackrel{d}{=} Q_1 \text{ A's are B's} \\ P_2 \stackrel{d}{=} Q_2 \text{ (A and B)'s are C's} \\ \hline P_3 \stackrel{d}{=} (Q_1 \otimes Q_2) \text{ A's are (B and C)'s .} \end{array}$$

To evaluate $P_1, P_2, P_3,$ we use the approach to quantification (section 2.3.8) using conditioning with

$$\phi_{wt} \equiv 1/\mathrm{card}(X)\ ,\ \phi_{\&} = \wedge\ ,\ \phi_{or} = \Sigma\ (\mathrm{bndsum})\ .$$

Let $u = \sum_x (\phi_A(x) \wedge \phi_B(x)) / \sum_x \phi_A(x)$,

$$v = \sum_x (\phi_A(x) \wedge \phi_B(x) \wedge \phi_C(x)) \ / \sum_x (\phi_A(x) \wedge \phi_B(x))\ ,$$

$$w = \sum_x (\phi_A(x) \wedge \phi_B(x) \wedge \phi_C(x)) \ / \sum_x \phi_A(x)\ .$$

Now

$$\text{(i)}\quad \|P_3\| = \phi_{Q_1 \otimes Q_2}(w) \overset{d}{=} \sup_{\begin{cases} s,t \\ st=w \end{cases}} (\phi_{Q_1}(s) \wedge \phi_{Q_2}(t))$$

$$= \sup_s (\phi_{Q_1}(s) \wedge \phi_{Q_2}(w/s))$$

$$\geq \phi_{Q_1}(u) \wedge \phi_{Q_2}(v) \qquad \text{(i)}$$

$$= \|P_1 \text{ and } P_2\|\ .$$

Next, if $z \overset{d}{=} \sum_x (\phi_A(x) \wedge \phi_C(x)) \ / \sum_x \phi_A(x)$

then $$\phi_{(\geq \circ Q_1 \otimes Q_2)}(z) \overset{d}{=} \sup_{\begin{cases} s,t \\ s\cdot t \leq z \end{cases}} (\phi_{Q_1}(s) \wedge \phi_{Q_2}(t))$$

$$\geq \sup_{\begin{cases} s,t \\ s\cdot t = z \end{cases}} (\phi_{Q_1}(s) \wedge \phi_{Q_2}(t))$$

$$\geq \phi_{Q_1 \otimes Q_2}(w)\ , \qquad \text{(ii)}$$

since $v \leq \sum_x (\phi_A(x) \wedge \phi_C(x)) \ / \sum_x (\phi_A(x) \wedge \phi_B(x)) = \frac{z}{u}$ and $w = uv$.

The inequality (i) means that $(P_1$ and $P_2) \vdash P_3$, and (ii) means $(P_3 \vdash \text{wff})$ for any wff whose truth value is $\phi_{\geq \circ Q_1 \otimes Q_2}(z)$.

See Zadeh [288] - [290] and the development of the calculus of deduction sequents, similar to the case illustrated above.

2.6 Examples of meaning representation of natural language

This section through a large number of examples, extends Zadeh's approach to modeling natural language [15], [277], [279], [280], [283], [286] - [290].

The basic goal of modeling natural language may be formulated as the determination of the "most appropriate" mapping $\rho : \mathcal{S} \to \mathcal{P}$, where $\mathcal{S}$ is the class of all sentences (or open wff's, etc.) of interest and $\mathcal{P}$ is the class of all formal strings or wff's. This is based on the results of the rest of section 2. (For convenience, we have slightly changed some notation.) See also the Appendix, Chapter 10.

(i) All predicates of the form $<x \in A>$ are in $\mathcal{P}$ where $x \in X$ and A is any fuzzy subset of X , x , A , X otherwise arbitrary

(ii) If $p_1,...,p_n \in \mathcal{P}$, then arbitrary (well-defined) combinations of not , & , or operating on $p_1,...,p_n$ are also $\in \mathcal{P}$.

(iii) If $p_1,p_2 \in \mathcal{P}$, then $(p_1|p_2) \in \mathcal{P}$ where the conditional operator $(\cdot|\cdot\cdot)$ is defined implicitly by

$$p_1 \otimes p_2 = (p_1|p_2) \ \& \ p_2 ,$$

$\otimes$ "joint product",
and

$$\text{quant}(p_1|p_2) \in \mathcal{P} ,$$

for any allowable quantifier "quant", such as: many, few, several, all, sometimes, etc.

(iv) If $p \in \mathcal{P}$, then $\text{int}(p) \in \mathcal{P}$, where "int" is any intensifier (or extensifier) such as "very", "little", etc.

By considering a large number of sentences empirically, the above four conditions appear sufficient to characterize sentences. These cover:

I . Modal/mood operators - include:

(a) alethic - necessity, possibility (= necessary not), probably likely, etc.

(b) deontic - permission, exclusion - may, allow, imperitives/jussives;

(c) obligative - must, ought to, should, etc.;

(d) volitive - want, hope, expect, wish;

(e) epistemic - belief, doubt, knows;

(f) threat;

(g) potentiality , etc.

All of the above forms may be treated by suitable indexing in conjunction with the compatibility of the (mood) index with the particular type of mood considered. For example,

$$\rho(\text{"John wants very much to run"}) = \text{"}(\text{Or}(\text{John} \in \text{runners}_{\alpha}) \ \& \ (\alpha \in \text{very(volition)}))\text{"}$$

where the degree of volation is measured on a scale from 0 to 1 . (See also, e.g., Snyder [245] for development of modal logic.)

II. <u>Temporal operators</u> - past, remote past, future, completion of action vs. incompletion of action - "used to", etc. - may be similarly modeled:

$$\rho(\text{"John was a good man"}) = \text{" } \underset{t\leq 0}{\text{Or}}(\text{John} \in (\text{good men})_t \ \& \ t \in \text{was})\text{"},$$

t being the time index (domain $\mathbb{R}$, present nominally 0) "was", a fuzzy subset of $\mathbb{R}^-$, with membership function being decreasing. (See also Rescher and Urquhart [215] or McDermott [173'] for development of temporal logics.)

III. n-ary relations are the same as n-ary verbal forms. For example,

$$\rho(\text{"John runs quickly to the store for her"}) = \text{"}(\text{John, store, her}) \in \text{run quickly - for}\text{"}$$

In addition, as mentioned previously, for each choice of arbitrary fuzzy set system

$$\mathcal{F} \overset{d}{=} (\phi_{not}, \phi_{\&}, \phi_{or})$$

there is a truth mapping

$$\|\cdot\| : \mathcal{P} \to [0,1] ,$$

where the following isomorphic-like (or commutative) forms hold for any $p \in \mathcal{P}$, assuming truth functionality ,

$$\|(\text{not}(p))\| = \phi_{not}(\|p\|)$$

$$\|(\underset{j\in J}{\&} p_j)\| = \underset{j\in J}{\phi_{\&}}(\|p\|)$$

$$\|(\underset{j\in J}{\text{Or}} p_j)\| = \underset{j\in J}{\phi_{or}}(\|p\|) ,$$

$$\|(\langle x\in A\rangle)\| = \phi_A(x) \ ; \text{ all } x , A , X , \text{etc.}$$

Hence, the composite mapping

$$\|\cdot\|\circ\rho : \mathcal{F} \to [0,1]$$

is a truth evaluation mapping from sentences into their corresponding truth values.

Some additional comments concerning the modeling of natural language:

1. Many sentences have ambiguous interpretations which can often be resolved through disambiguating context. For example:

"He uses her well." (two meanings)
"John found a book on Third Avenue." (three meanings)

As Leech points out ([153], pp. 78, 79) probabilistic (or for that matter, possibilistic - the authors) weights could be assigned to the various interpretations, based on usual understanding of the sentence. See Oden [196] for an extensive fuzzy set analysis of this problem and an excellent survey of the field.

2. The cardinality of a fuzzy subset A of an ordinary space X,

$$\text{card}(A) = \sum_{x \in X} \phi_A(x)$$

has played a large role in symbolizing quantifications. (See, e.g., almost any of the Zadeh references.) However, as natural as the concept appears, in general, it is not representable as a compound definition based on a given fuzzy set system $(\phi_{not}, \phi_{\&}, \phi_{or})$ as is the well-used ratio

$$\text{card}(A \cap B) \,/\, \text{card}(B) = \sum_{x \in X} \phi_{\&}(\phi_A(x), \phi_B(x)) \,/\, \sum_{x \in X} \phi_B(x) ,$$

where usually $\phi_{\&}$ is chosen as min. (There is also an obvious tie-in with the averaging operator and fuzzy set partitioning. See [91], Theorem 6.5 and Cor. 6.2.)

An alternative to the above approach, using only the basic fuzzy set operators $\phi_{\&}$ and ϕ_{or} is given:

Let X be a fixed ordinary set and let

$$u : X \to Y \quad \text{and} \quad v : X \to Z$$

be two mappings, each representing a linguistic or numerical measurable such as $u = ht(\cdot)$, $v = age(\cdot)$, $w = color(\cdot)$, $x =$ distance between $(\cdot,\cdot)$, etc.

Also let

$$q : X \to [0,1]$$

be a possibility function (or in particular, a probability function) representing the weight of importance attached to each $x \in X$, corresponding to fuzzy subset wt of X. Let C and D be two fuzzy subsets of X.

Then defining

$$S_C \stackrel{d}{=} ((\exists x)(x\in X \ \&\ u(x) \in C \ \&\ x \in wt)$$

$$\|S_C\| = \phi_{\underset{x\in X}{or}}(\phi_\&(\phi_C(u(x)),q(x))) ,$$

and

$$S_{C\otimes D} \stackrel{d}{=} (\exists x)(x \in X \ \&\ u(x) \in C \ \&\ v(x) \in D \ \&\ x \in wt) ,$$

$$\|(S_{C\otimes D})\| = \phi_{\underset{x\in X}{or}}(\phi_\&(\phi_C(u(x)), \phi_D(v(x)), q(x))) .$$

See the previous analysis of conditioning and quantification in sections 2.3.9 (B) and 2.3.8.

Then analogous to the development of conditional possibility functions, note that it always follows (from basic properties of t-norms) that

$$\|(S_C)\| \geq \|(S_{C\otimes D})\|$$

and it is natural to define $S_{D|C}$ implicitly by

$$S_{C\otimes D} = (S_C \ \&\ S_{D|C}) ,$$

whence (using the continuity property of $\phi_\&$ as in the definition of conditional possibilities)

$$\|(S_{C\otimes D})\| = \|(S_C \ \&\ S_{D|C})\|$$
$$= \phi_\&(\|S_C\|, \|S_{D|C}\|) .$$

Note (as in the conditional possibility definition), if $\phi_\&$ = prod, then

$$\|S_{D|C}\| = \|S_{C\otimes D}\| \ / \ \|S_C\| ,$$

and, if further, ϕ_{or} = bndsum and q is chosen as probability function, then

$$\|S_C\| = \sum_{x\in X} \phi_C(u(x))\cdot q(x) ,$$

$$\|S_{C\otimes D}\| = \sum_{x\in X} \phi_C(u(x))\cdot\phi_D(v(x))\cdot q(x) ,$$

yielding a result quite similar in form to Zadeh's procedure for forming fuzzy cardinalities and fuzzy precentages - except for min being replaced by prod - in order to model quantifications. However, note for Zadeh's fuzzy set system $(1-(\cdot),\min,\max)$,

$$\|S_{D|C}\| = \|S_{C\otimes D}\| = \|S_{C|D}\|$$

$$= \max_{x\in X}(\min(\phi_C(u(x)),\phi_D(c(x)),q(x))) ,$$

which is less close to Zadeh's fuzzy cardinality and fuzzy quantification modeling!

3. The modeling of interrogatives has been omitted. (See Zadeh [290'] for one approach to the symbolization of questions.)

4. It has been proposed (L.A. Zadeh, 1983, personal communications) that quantifiers are essentially generalizations of probability measures and hence may be further characterized through this approach.

The following examples illustrate the mappings ρ , $\|\cdot\|$ and $\|\cdot\|\circ\rho$ in evaluating a number of different sentences. Note that in most uses of quantifications, we employ Zadeh's approach using fuzzy cardinality [277], [283], [286] - [290] - for simplicity - rather than by use of the above more complicated (but closer to first principles), alternative approach. However, one example illustrating both approaches will first be given.

For further discussion of the formal language interpretation of natural language, see the Appendix at the end of Chapter 10.

Note: In the beginning examples, we use both p and ϕ to indicate possibility/membership functions.

Example 1.

$S_1 \overset{d}{=}$ "Perhaps there are a hundred happy people in the world".

Using Zadeh's approach:

$$\|S_1\| = \phi_{perhaps}(\phi_{\approx 100}(\sum_{x\in X}\phi_{happy}(x))) ,$$

where

$$\phi_{perhaps} : [0,1] \to [0,1] ,$$
$$\phi_{\approx 100} : [70,130] \to [0,1] ,$$

and

$$X \overset{d}{=} \text{set of all people in world.}$$

Using the alternative approach presented above,

$$\|S_1\| = \phi_{or_{B\subseteq X}}(\phi_{\&}(\phi_{\approx 100}(\mathrm{card}(B)),\phi_{\&_{x\in B}}(\phi_{happy}(x))))$$

where now

$$\phi_{\approx 100} : \text{Set of integers} \to [0,1]$$

and

$$\mathrm{card}(B) \overset{d}{=} \text{no. of elements (i.e., cardiality) of } B .$$

Example 2.

$S_2 \overset{d}{=}$ "If visibility is very good then most likely a type A submarine will not be found in area III over the standard search period."

Suppose (maximum) visibility is defined in terms of miles over a possible continuum $[0,m_o]$, where m_o is some sufficiently large upper bound. Then "at least good" relative to this scale is represented by a monotone increasing possibility function p_G and "at least very good" is represented by p_{VG} monotone increasing with

$$p_{VG} \geq p_G \ .$$

This can be accomplished simply by either use of the transforms

$$p_{VG}(\cdot) \overset{d}{=} p_G(\cdot + \alpha) \quad \text{or} \quad p_{VG}(\cdot) \overset{d}{=} p_G(\cdot)^{\beta+1} \ ,$$

for constants $\alpha,\beta > 0$, after first modeling p_G . In this case, p_{VG} is considered as an intensification of p_G . On the other hand, p_{VG} could be modeled directly.

"Most likely" is a truth quantification and is represented by

$$p_{ML} : [0,1] \to [0,1] \ ; \ p_{ML}(x) \leq x \ , \ \text{all} \ \ x \in [0,1] \ ,$$

due to loss of truth values.

Let X be the set of ships of interest.

For each time t , let

$$p_{F_{III,t}} : X \to [0,1]$$

represent the fuzzy set of submarines found in (fuzzy) area III at time t . Also, let

$$p_T : \mathbb{R}^+ \to [0,1]$$

represent the standard search time period - symmetric and unimodal, etc.

"Will" is represented by

$$p_W : \mathbb{R}^+ \to [0,1] \ ,$$

a monotone increasing function, with $\mathbb{R}^+$ identified with time; present time being 0 .

Some fuzzy set system $(\phi_{not},\phi_{\&},\phi_{or})$ is chosen. If $(\cdot)$ then $(\cdot\cdot)$ - implication - is evaluated through binary operator

$$\phi_{\Rightarrow} : [0,1]^2 \to [0,1] \ ; \ \phi_{\Rightarrow}(u,v) \overset{d}{=} \phi_{or}(\phi_{not}(u),v) \ ,$$

for all $u,v \in [0,1]$.

$$p_A : X \to [0,1]$$

represents type A submarines.

Evaluating the truth of sentence S_2,

$$\|S_2\| = \|([If(mi(vis) \in VG)] \text{ then } [(ML)(not\{(\exists t)(\exists x)[(t \in T\cap W)\&(x \in A\cap F_{III,t})]\})])\|$$

$$= \phi_{\Rightarrow}(\|(mi(vis) \in VG)\|, (ML)(not) \underset{t\in\mathbb{R}^+}{Or} \underset{x\in X}{Or} \|(t \in T\cap W)\&(x \in A\cap F_{III,t})\|)$$

$$= \phi_{\Rightarrow}(p_{VG}(mi(vis)), p_{ML}(\phi_{not}\, \underset{t\in\mathbb{R}^+}{\phi_{or}}((\underset{x\in X}{\phi_{or}}(\phi_{\&}(p_T(t), p_W(t), p_A(x), p_{III,t}(x)))))) .$$

__**Example 3**__.

S_3 = "Based on very reliable sources, Ship B will soon arrive in area II along with most of their heavily equipped carriers that are within about 100 miles of B at present".

"Based on very reliable sources" is a modification of truth increasing curve p_R, $p_R : [0,1] \to [0,1]$, where compared to p_{ML} in Example 2, we have for all $x \in [0,1]$

$$x \geq p_R(x) \geq p_{ML}(x) .$$

This could be modeled directly or, analogous to the situation for p_{VG} vs p_G, by some (perhaps exponential or translational) relation with p_{ML} or some common base such as the identity function $id : [0,1] \to [0,1]$, $id(x) \equiv x$, all $x \in [0,1]$, identified as the truth level function.

Similarly "will soon" is a modification of "will" and thus we may have

$$p_{WS} = p_W^{1+\gamma}$$

or

$$p_{WS} = p_W(\cdot + \delta) ,$$

for some suitably chosen $\gamma, \delta > 0$.

"at present, within about 100 miles of" is a symmetric fuzzy relation

$$p_Q : D \times D \to [0,1] ,$$

where D is some suitably large region of the earth's surface measured in latitude , and perhaps the shape of $p_{W,100}$ could be

$$p_Q(x,y) = \begin{cases} 1 , & \text{if } \|x-y\| \leq 100 \\ 1 - e^{-a\cdot\|x-y\|^2} , & \text{if } \|x-y\| > 100 \end{cases} ,$$

for some suitably chosen constant $a > 0$.

Thus, if

$C(B) \overset{d}{=}$ set of all heavily equipped carriers within about 100 miles of B at present that will arrive soon,

then letting

$X \overset{d}{=}$ set of enemy ships of interest ,

and for each time t ,

$Ar_{II,t} \overset{d}{=}$ fuzzy set of all enemy ships arriving in area II at time t ,

and

$H \overset{d}{=}$ fuzzy subset of X representing heavily equipped carriers,

then for all $x \in X$,

$$\begin{aligned}\phi_{C(B)}(x) &= \|(x \in C(B)\| \\ &= \|(\exists t)((t \in WS) \ \& \ (x \in Ar_{II,t}) \ \& \ (x \in H) \ \& \ ((x,B) \in Q))\| \\ &= \phi_{\underset{t \in \mathbb{R}^+}{or}}(\phi_\&(p_{WS}(t), p_{Ar_{II,t}}(x), p_H(x), p_Q(x,B)))\ .\end{aligned}$$

Then the (fuzzy) cardinality of $C(B)$ is

$$\text{card}(C(B)) = \sum_{x \in X} \phi_{C(B)}(x)\ .$$

Also, if

$E(B) \overset{d}{=}$ set of all heavily equipped carriers within 100 miles of B at present,

then similarly for any $x \in X$

$$p_{E(B)}(x) = \phi_\&(p_H(x), p_Q(x,B))$$

and we can show, using the properties of $\phi_\&$ and ϕ_{or} that - as a check, as should be -

$$p_{E(B)}(x) \geq p_{C(B)}(x)\ ;\ \text{all}\ \ x \in X\ ,$$

i.e.,

$$E(B) \supseteq C(B)\ ,$$

(one version of fuzzy subset relations). As before,

$$\text{card}(E(B)) = \sum_{x \in X} p_{E(B)}(x)\ .$$

Now, "most" may be considered to be represented by

$$p_M : [0,1] \to [0,1]\ ;\ p_M(x) = 0\ ,\ \text{for}\ \ 0 \leq x < \tfrac{1}{2}\ ,$$

and over $[\frac{1}{2},1]$, p_M is monotone increasing to 1 .

Then "most of their heavily equipped carriers that are within about 100 mile of B at present will soon arrive in area II" becomes $\phi_M(\mathrm{card}(C(B)/\mathrm{card}(E(B)))$.

Thus, sentence 3 has truth evaluation

$$\| S_3 \| = p_R(\phi_\&(\phi_{C(B)}(B), \phi_M(\mathrm{card}(C(B))/\mathrm{card}(E(B))))) .$$

Example 4.

S_4 = "Intelligence reports that during the past month, between eight and ten of the largest ships spotted in region I were observed to be carrying a total of perhaps a dozen missiles, some of which may be of class G; this could indeed lead to a world crisis."

First let sentence S_4 be broken up to the left and right of the semi-colon as $(K;L)$. Clearly,
$\| S_4 \| = \phi_\&(\|K\|, \|L\|)$.

Let
$X \overset{d}{=}$ the ordinary set of all ships of interest and for each $t \in \mathbb{R}^-$,

$S_{I,t} \overset{d}{=}$ the fuzzy set of all ships of interest spotted in region I at time t . For any $X \in X$, suppose

$p_L(x) \overset{d}{=}$ degree to which x is large ,

$f(x) \overset{d}{=}$ no. of missiles x is observed to carry ,

and

$g(x) \le f(x)$; $g(x) \overset{d}{=}$ no. of G-type missiles x may carry,
f is known, while g is unknown.

Then for any integer m and $x_1, \ldots, x_m \in X$,

$$p_{PM} : \mathbb{R}^- \to [0,1]$$

represents the fuzzy time period "past month",

$p_{S_I}(x_1, \ldots, x_m)$

$$\overset{d}{=} \|(x_1, \ldots, x_m \text{ were spotted in } I \text{ during the past month})\|$$
$$= \underset{t \in \mathbb{R}^-}{\phi_{or}}(\phi_\&(p_{PM}(t) , p_{S_{I,t}}(x_1), \ldots, p_{S_{I,t}}(x_m))) ,$$

with corresponding ordering by size indicated by

$$p_L(x_{(1)}) \ge p_L(x_{(2)}) \ge \cdots \ge p_L(x_{(m)}) .$$

Let

$$p_F : \{6,7,8,9,10,11,12\} \to [0,1]$$

be the possibility function (peaking to one at 8,9,10) representing "between eight and ten".

Similarly,

$$p_{\approx 12} : \{7,8,9,10,11,12,13\} \to [0,1]$$

represents "perhaps a dozen" , "Some" is represented by

$$p_{Som} : [0,1] \to [0,1] ,$$

generally unimodal and peaking to one prior to 1/2 . Note that "intelligence reports that" acts only as a truth modification on the rest of K , and may be represented by some suitably chosen

$$p_{int} : [0,1] \to [0,1] ,$$

which may be compared to the truth modifications (or intransifications) in sentences S_2 and S_3.

Thus,

$$\|K\| = \|(int((\exists x_1)\cdots(\exists x_m)\ (\{x_1,\ldots,x_m\} \subseteq X$$
$$\&(x_1,\ldots,x_m \text{ spotted in I during past month})$$
$$\&\ (\exists n)(1 \le n \le m\ \&\ (n \in F)\ \&\ (\sum_{i=1}^{n} f(x_{(i)}) \in 12))\ \&$$
$$((\sum_{i=1}^{n} g(x_{(i)})/\sum_{i=1}^{n} f(x_{(i)})) \in Som)\}))\|$$

$$= p_{int}(\phi_{or\ \text{over all}\ \{x_1,\ldots,x_m\}\subseteq X,\ m \ge 1}(\phi_\&[p_{S_I}(x_1,\ldots,x_m) ,$$

$$\phi_{or\ 1\le n\le m}(\phi_\&(p_F(n),\ p_{\approx 12}(\sum_{i=1}^{n} f(x_{(i)}),\ p_{Som}(\sum_{i=1}^{n} g(x_{(i)}))/\sum_{i-1}^{n} f(x_{(i)})))))])) .$$

Next, note that "could indeed" is a modification of truth which if compared with "will" and "will soon" looks like:

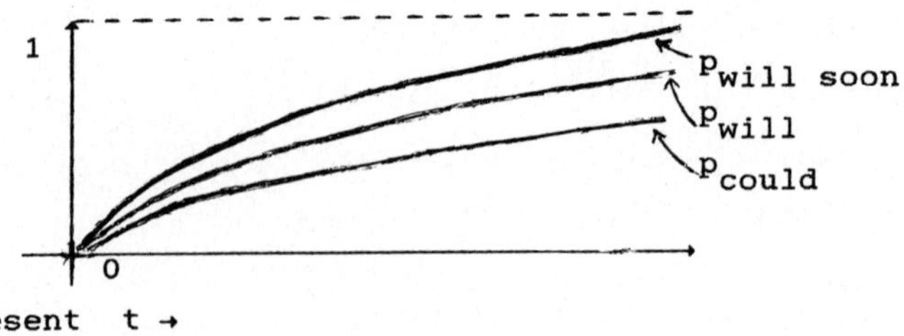

Let "world crisis" be represented by

$$p_{WC} : Y \to [0,1]$$

where Y represents the states of the world which for simplicity could be n by 1 vectors, each entry being some measure of potentitial crisis such as "troop buildup in area IV", "defense expenditures over time t_1", "trade-level", etc. Then for any

$y \in Y$,

$$\|L(y)\| = p_{cou}(\phi_G(\|K\|,\ p_{WC}(y)))$$

__Example 5.__

$S_5 \overset{d}{\equiv}$ "For any $0 < \alpha < 1$, let C_α be defined by $F_2(C_\alpha) = 1 - \alpha$, where F_2 is the cumulative probability distribution function of χ_2^2 (a chi-square random variable with two degrees of freedom). Then decide H_o with probability γ and H_1 with probability $1 - \gamma$ iff $\lambda(Z) < C_\alpha$ for test statistic $\lambda(Z)$, assuming $\lambda(Z)$ given H_o is distributed as χ_2^2; otherwise decide H_1 with probability one."

The above sentence, a combination of mathematical and logical terms may be evaluated a few different ways: Let

$$p_<,\ p_= : \mathbb{R} \times \mathbb{R} \to [0,1]$$

be the possibility functions representing the binary relations of (either fuzzy or crisp) inequality and equality of real numbers.

For any $\lambda(z) \geq 0$, let

$$p_{d|\lambda(z)} : \{H_o, H_1\} \to [0,1]$$

be the possibility (in actuality, probability) function corresponding to the fuzzy subset "decision given $\lambda(z)$ observed".

Then one interpretation is:

$$\|S_5\| = \underset{0<\alpha<1}{\phi_\&} (\phi_\&(p_= (C_\alpha, F_2^{-1}(1-\alpha)), Q_\alpha)) ,$$

$$Q_\alpha \overset{d}{\equiv} \underset{(\lambda(z)\geq 0)}{\phi_\&} (\phi_\&(Q_{1\alpha}(\lambda(z)), Q_{2\alpha}(\lambda(z))))$$

where

$$Q_{1\alpha}(\lambda(z)) = \phi_{\Leftrightarrow}(p_<(\lambda(z), C_\alpha), \phi_\&(p_=(p_{d|\lambda(z)}(H_o), \gamma) , p_=(p_{d|\lambda(z)}(H_1), 1-\gamma))) ,$$

$$Q_{2\alpha}(\lambda(z)) = \phi_{\Leftrightarrow}(1-p_<(\lambda(z), C_\alpha), \phi_\&(p_=(p_{d|\lambda(z)}(H_o), 0) , p_=(p_{d|\lambda(z)}(H_1), 1))) .$$

Alternatively, if $p_<$, $p_=$ strictly represent classical inequality and equality, respectively,

$$\|S_5\| = \|(S_5(\alpha, \lambda(z)))\| ,$$
$$0 \leq \alpha \leq 1 ,$$
$$\lambda(z) \geq 0 ,$$

where for any $0 \le \alpha \le 1$, $\lambda(z) \ge 0$,

$$\|(S_5(\alpha,\lambda(z)))\| = 1$$

iff α and $\lambda(z)$ are such that

$$\begin{cases} C_\alpha = F_2^{-1}(1-\alpha) \quad \text{and} \\ \text{if } \lambda(z) > C_\alpha \text{ , then } \begin{cases} p_{d|\lambda(z)}(H_0) = \gamma \\ p_{d|\lambda(z)}(H_1) = 1-\gamma \end{cases} \\ \text{if } \lambda(z) \le C_\alpha \text{ , then } \begin{cases} p_{d|\lambda(z)}(H_0) = 0 \text{ ,} \\ p_{d|\lambda(z)}(H_1) = 1 \text{ ;} \end{cases} \end{cases}$$

$$\|(\alpha,\lambda(z))\| = 0 \text{ ; otherwise.}$$

Example 6.

S_6 = "The probability that the target of interest contains on-board many more systems of the form A than that of B is not really very high."

Let the number of systems on-board the target of forms A and B be represented by the joint probability (and possibility) function

$$p_{A,B} : J_o \times J_o \to [0,1] \text{ ,}$$

where J_o is the set of all nonnegative integers.

Let "many more" correspond to

$$p_{M,M} : J_o \times J_o \to [0,1] \text{ ,}$$

where, e.g., $p_{M,M}(x,x) = 0$, but $p_{M,M}(x,y)$ is nondecreasing in y , etc.,

If "high" is first modeled as a truth modifier with possibility function

$$p_H : [0,1] \to [0,1] \text{ , } p_H \text{ nondecreasing,}$$

etc., then one way to model "not really very high" is by

$$p_N \overset{d}{=} 1 - p_M^{\;1+\alpha} \text{ ; constant } \alpha > 0 \text{ .}$$

Then,

$\|S_6\|$

$$= \|(N\!H((\exists x)(\exists y)((x,y) \in (A,B) \;\&\; (x,y) \in MM)))\|$$
$$= p_{N\!H}(\phi_{or\,x,y\in J_o}(\phi_\&(p_{A,B}(x,y),\, p_{MM}(x,y)))) \text{ .}$$

If $\phi_\&$ = prod and ϕ_{or} = bndsum is chosen, then it follows that

$$\|S_6\| = p_N(E_X(p_{M,M}(X))) ,$$

where X is a random variable over $J_o \times J_o$ corresponding to $p_{A,B}$ and $E_X(\cdot)$ is statistical expectation.

The following additional examples illustrate further the usefulness of general fuzzy set systems in modeling and interpreting unertainties in decision and estimation problems where evidence may consist of a mixture of probabilistic and natural language information, or only the latter. Abbreviations for fuzzy sets or attributes will be self explanatory as much as possible.

Example 7.

$$\|(\text{Men are better operators than women.})\| = \sum_{\substack{x\in \text{Men},\\ y\in \text{Women}}} \phi_{\leq}(\text{lev. op}(x), \text{lev. op}(y))/\text{card(Men)}\cdot\text{card(Women)}$$

or, alternatively,

$$= \phi_{\leq}\Big(\sum_{x\in\text{Men}} \text{lev. op}(x)/\text{card(Men)},\ \sum_{y\in\text{Women}} \text{lev. op}(y)/\text{card(women)}\Big)$$

where

$$\phi_{\leq} : \mathbb{R} \times \mathbb{R} \to [0,1]$$

is a fuzzification of ordinary inequality or equality.

Example 8.

$$\|(\text{Most men are better operators than most women.})\|$$
$$= \|\Big(\phi_{\text{Most}}\Big[\frac{\text{card}\{x|x \in \text{Men \& lev. op}(x) \text{ is better than most women.}}{\text{card(Men)}}\Big]\Big)\|$$

where

$\phi_{\text{Most}} : [0,1] \to [0,1]$; $\phi(x) \equiv 0$, for $x \leq 1/2$,
with ϕ_{Most} monotone increasing up to 1 after that;

$$\text{card}\{x \mid x \in \text{Men \& lev. op}(x) \text{ is better than most women}\}$$
$$= \sum_{x\in\text{Men}} \phi_{\left[\substack{\text{is better than}\\ \text{most women}}\right]}(x) ,$$

$$\phi_{\substack{\text{is better}\\ \text{than most}\\ \text{women}}}(x) = \phi_{\text{Most}}\Big[\frac{\text{card}\{y|y \in \text{Women} \ \& \ \phi_{\leq}(\text{lev. op}(y),\text{lev. op}(x))\}}{\text{card(Women)}}\Big] ,$$

$$\text{card}(\{y \mid y \in \text{Women} \ \& \ \phi_{\leq}(\text{lev. op}(x), \text{lev. op}(x))\})$$
$$= \sum_{y\in\text{Women}} \phi_{\leq}(\text{lev. op}(y), \text{lev, op}(x)) .$$

Example 9.

‖(The identities of A and B are believed to be incorrect; most likely they should be reversed.)‖

$$= \phi_{\&}(\phi_{believe}(\phi_{\&}(\phi_{not}(\phi_{=}(ident_{true}(A), ident_{past\ est.}(A))), \phi_{not}(\phi_{=}(ident_{true}(B), ident_{past\ est.}(B))))), \phi_{\substack{most\\likely}}(\phi_{\&}(\phi_{=}(ident_{true}(A), ident_{past\ est.}(B)), \phi_{=}(ident_{true}(B), ident_{past\ est.}(A))))$$

where

$$ident_{true}, ident_{past\ est} : Ships \xrightarrow{injective} Names .$$

Example 10.

‖(I intend to launch system C against D and E in order to help F)‖

=‖(My intended launching of C against D and E is to help F)‖

$$= \phi_{\substack{or\\(0\le t,t')}}(\phi_{\&}(\phi_{because}(\phi_{\substack{launch\\against,t}}(I,C;D,E), \phi_{help,t'}(I,F)), \phi_{intend}(t))) .$$

Example 11.

‖(Country A's ships are now widely distributed with no unusual activities.)‖

$$= \phi_{\substack{or\\t\in\mathbb{R}}}(\phi_{\&}(\phi_{high}(scatter(ships(A))), \phi_{now}(t), \phi_{usual}(activ.\ level(ships(A)))) ,$$

where

$$scatter(Ships(A)) = \sum_{x,y\in Ships(A)} dist(loc(x), loc(y))/(card\ Ships(A))^2 ,$$

etc.

Example 12.

‖(It always rains in Minnesota, according to Sam)‖

= ‖(Very often it rains in Minnesota according to Sam)‖

$$= \phi_{v.often}(\sum_{t\in D_{Sam}} \phi_{rain,t}(Minn.)/card\ D) ,$$

where D_{Sam} is some sufficiently large set of days of recording according to Sam.

Example 13.

‖(It sometimes rains here at night a couple of days later following an unusually hot day)‖

$$= \phi_{some}\left(\sum_{t\in D}\left(\phi_{\substack{or\\ t'\geq t\\ t'\in D}}\left(\phi_{\&}(\phi_{\substack{usually\\ high}}(\phi_{hot,day(t)}(here)),\right.\right.\right.$$

$$\left.\left.\left.\phi_{rain,night(t)}(here)\ ,\ \phi_{\substack{couple\ of\\ days\ between}}(t,t')))\right)/card(D)\right)\ ,$$

where D is some sufficiently large set of integers representing days of weather reporting.

Example 14.

"(Green flares were sighted shortly after the initial contact which used equipment A)"

$$= \phi_{\substack{or\\ x\in Flare\\ t,t'\leq 0}}\left(\phi_{\&}(\phi_{green}(color(x),\phi_{sight,t}(system,x),\ \phi_{was}(t),\right.$$

$$\left.\phi_{\substack{shortly\\ after}}(\phi_{\leq}(t',t)),\ \phi_{use,t'}(system,A),\phi_{\substack{initial\\ contact}}(t'))\right)\ .$$

Example 15.

"(Contact with A was held for a long time)"

$$= \phi_{\substack{or\\ t,t'\leq 0}}\left(\phi_{\&}(\phi_{contact,t}(system,A),\phi_{C_{t'}}(t)\ ,\ \phi_{was}(t))\right)\ ,$$

where $C_{t'}$ is the fuzzy interval representing "for a long time beginning at about t'". Thus

$$\phi_{C_{t'}}(t) = \phi_{\substack{or\\ t',t\leq 0,\\ t'+t''\leq 0}}\left(\phi_{\&}(\phi_{\leq}(t',t),\ \phi_{\leq}(t,t'+t'')\ ,\phi_{\substack{long\\ time}}(t''))\right)\ .$$

Example 16.

"(A is continuing his search of targets in B despite heavy losses to his vessel)"

$$= \phi_{\substack{or\\ x\in Targets\\ t\geq 0}}\left(\phi_{\&}(\phi_{search\ of,t}(A,x),\phi_{B}(loc(x)),\ \phi_{\substack{now\\ continue}}(t)\ ,\right.$$

$$\left.\phi_{heavy}(loss(A)))\right)\ .$$

Example 17.

"I tracked the ship for (about) 2 hours and (then) lost contact)"

$$= \phi_{\substack{or \\ t \le t'' \le 0 \\ t' \le 0}} (\phi_\&(\phi_{track,t}(I,ship), \phi_{A_{t'}}(t), \phi_{not}(\phi_{track,t''}(I,ship)), \phi_{B_{t',t'''}}(t'')))$$

where $A_{t'}$ is the fuzzy time interval from fuzzy time around t' to fuzzy time two hours later (around $t' + 2$), and thus for any t

$$\phi_{A_{t'}}(t) = \phi_\&(\phi_\le(t',t), \phi_\le(t,t' + 2)) ,$$

$\phi_\le : \mathbb{R} \times \mathbb{R} \to [0,1]$ is a fuzzification of ordinary equality.

$B_{t',t''}$ is the fuzzy time interval from around time $t' + 2 + t''$ until 0 (present). Thus, for any t

$$\phi_{B_{t',t''}}(t) = \phi_\&(\phi_\le(t' + 2 + t'',t) , \phi_\le(t,0)) .$$

Example 18.

‖(It is possible to stop action C)‖

$$= \phi_{\substack{or \\ 0 \le \alpha \le 1, \\ t \ge 0}} (\phi_\&(\phi_{poss}(\alpha), \phi_{stop;\alpha,t}(system,C), \phi_{will}(t)))$$

where

$$\phi_{poss}(\alpha) = \phi_{not}(\phi_{necess}(1 - \alpha)) .$$

Example 19.

‖(Most likely, action C can be stopped)‖

$$= \phi_{\substack{or \\ 0 \le \alpha \le 1, \\ t \ge 0}} (\phi_\&(\phi_{\substack{most \\ likely}} (\phi_{poss}(\alpha)), \phi_{stop;\alpha,t}(system,C), \phi_{will}(t))).$$

Example 20.

‖(It is impossible to stop action C)‖

$$= \phi_{\substack{or \\ 0 \le \alpha \le 1, \\ t \ge 0}} (\phi_\&(\phi_{not}(\phi_{poss}(\alpha)), \phi_{stop,\alpha,t}(system\ C), \phi_{will}(t)))$$

Example 21.

‖(A employed system B but was unable to follow the target)‖

$$= \phi_{\substack{or \\ t \le 0}} \phi_\&(\phi_{use,t}(A,,B), \phi_{was}(t), \phi_{not}(\phi_{follow,t}(A,target))))$$

Example 22.

$\|$(It was stated yesterday that "because of several factors, A will not be able to refuel at B")$\|$

$$= \phi_{\substack{or \\ t\le t'\le 0}} (\phi_{\&}(\phi_{yest}(t), \phi_{because}(\phi_{var\ fact,t}(A), \phi_{not}(\phi_{refuel\ at,t}(A,B))), \phi_{will}(t' - t))),$$

where

$$\phi_{var\ fact,t}(A) = \phi_{several}(\sum_{j\in J} \phi_{fact\ j,t}(A)/card(J))$$

and

J = set of all relevant factors.

Example 23.

$\|$(It may be necessary to stop action C)$\|$

$$= \phi_{\substack{or \\ 0\in\alpha\le 1 \\ t\ge 0}} (\phi_{\&}(\phi_{may}(\phi_{necess}(\alpha)), \phi_{stop;\alpha,t}(system,C), \phi_{will}(t))) ;$$

$\|$(It will be necessary to stop action C)$\|$

$$= \phi_{\substack{or \\ 0\le\alpha\le 1 \\ t\le 0}} (\phi_{\&}(\phi_{necess}(\alpha), \phi_{stop;\alpha,t}(system,C), \phi_{will}(t))) .$$

Example 24.

$\|$(We were going to do this but instead because of condition A we did that)$\|$

$$= \phi_{\substack{or \\ t\le 0, \\ t'\le t''\le 0}} (\phi_{\&}(\phi_{do,t}(we,this), \phi_{\substack{were \\ going,to}}(t), \phi_{because}(\phi_{A,t'}(we), \phi_{do,t''}(we,that)), \phi_{was}(t'), \phi_{was}(t''))),$$

where for all $u,v \in [0,1]$,

$$\phi_{because}(u,v) \equiv \phi_{\&}(\phi_G(u,v),u)$$

Diagramatically, we have:

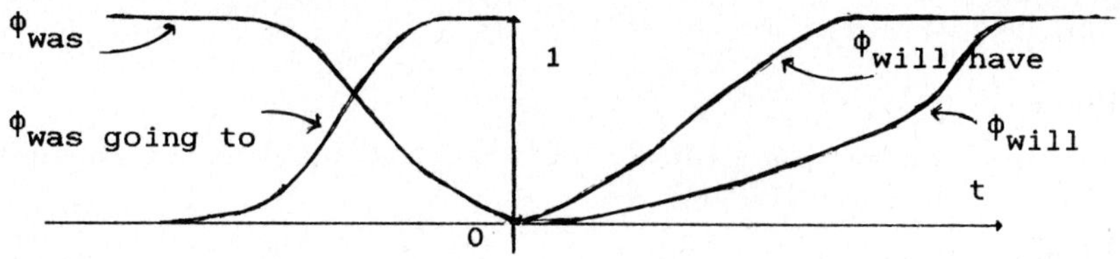

Example 25.

Law of excluded middle need not hold here:

‖(On the whole, some small countries are both friendly and not so friendly to strangers)‖

$$= \phi_{on\ wh}\left(\phi_{some}\left[\frac{\text{card(small coun.} \cap \text{fr.} \cap \text{not so fr.)}}{\text{card(small coun.)}}\right]\right),$$

where

card(small coun. ∩ fr. ∩ not so fr.)

$$\sum_{x \in \text{countries}} \phi_{\&}(\phi_{small}(\text{popul}(x)), \phi_{fr.\cap not\ so\ fr.}(x)),$$

$$\phi_{fr.\cap not\ so\ fr.}(x) = \frac{\sum_{(y \in \text{Vist.to } x)} \phi_{\&}(\phi_{fr}(x,y), \phi_{not\ so}(\phi_{fr}(x,y)))}{\text{card(Vist.to } x)},$$

$$\text{card(small coun.)} = \sum_{x \in \text{countries}} \phi_{small}(\text{popul}(x)).$$

Example 26.

‖(John is tall, yet not that tall)‖

$$= \phi_{\&}(\phi_{tall}(\text{ht(John)}), \phi_{not\ so}(\phi_{tall}(\text{ht(John)}))).$$

Example 27.

Redundancies are employed here:

‖(He is a large man; indeed he is!)‖

$$= \phi_{\&}(\phi_{\substack{large\\man}}(\text{ht(he)}, \text{wt(he)}), \phi_{\substack{large\\man}}(\text{ht(he)}, \text{wt(he)})).$$

Example 28.

‖(A little more than one third of the ships observed were from country B)‖

$$= \phi_{or}\phi_{\&}(\phi_{little\ more \geq\ 1/3}$$

$$\left(\sum_{x \in \text{Ships}} \phi_{\&}(\phi_{observ,t}(x), \phi_B(x)) / \sum_{x \in \text{Ships}} \phi_{observ,t}(x)\right), \phi_{was}(t))),$$

where for all $0 \le u \le 1$,

$$\phi_{\text{little more} \ge 1/3}(u) = \phi_{\substack{\text{little}\\\text{more}}}(\phi_{\ge}(u,1/3)) \ .$$

Example 29.

$$\|(\text{Ships are gray})\|$$
$$= \|(\text{Usually ships are gray color})\|$$
$$= \phi_{\text{usual}}\Big(\sum_{x\in \text{Ships}} \phi_{\text{Gray}}(\text{color}(x))/\text{card}(\text{Ships})\Big)$$

where

$$\phi_{\text{usual}} = \phi_{\text{most}} \ , \text{ etc.}$$

Example 30.

$$\|(\text{I really want to run someday!})\|$$
$$= \phi_{\substack{\text{or}\\ 0\le\alpha\le 1,\\ t\ge 0}}(\phi_{\&}(\phi_{\text{run},\alpha,t}(\text{I}),\phi_{\substack{\text{really}\\\text{want}}}(\alpha),\phi_{\text{someday}}(t))) \ .$$

Example 31.

$$\|(\text{He cannot start the engine.})\|$$
$$= \phi_{\text{not}}\big(\phi_{\substack{\text{or}\\ 0\le\alpha\le 1}}(\phi_{\&}(\phi_{\text{start},\alpha}(\text{He},\text{engine}) \ , \ \phi_{\text{able}}(\alpha)))\big) \ .$$

Example 32.

$$\|(\text{John, keep all day old eggs under refrigeration!})\|$$
$$= \phi_{\substack{\&\\ x\in \text{Eggs}}}(\phi_{\Rightarrow}(\phi_{\text{day old}}(\text{age}(x)) \ , \ \phi_{\&}(\phi_{\text{refrig};\alpha}(\text{John},x),\phi_{\text{imper}}(\alpha)))) \ ,$$

or, alternatively,

$$= \phi_{\text{all}}\left[\sum_{x\in \text{Eggs}} \phi_{\&}(\phi_{\text{day old}}(\text{age}(x)),\phi_{\text{refrig};\alpha}(\text{John},x),\phi_{\text{imper}}(\alpha))/\sum_{x\in \text{Eggs}} \phi_{\text{day old}}(\text{age}(x))\right].$$

Example 33.

$$\|(\text{Some balls were chosen two days ago, others, yesterday.})\|$$
$$= \phi_{\&}\Big(\phi_{\text{some}}\Big(\sum_{x\in \text{Balls}} \phi_{\substack{\text{or}\\ t\le 0}} \phi_{\&}(\phi_{\text{choose},t}(x),\phi_{\text{2 days ago}}(t))/\text{card}(\text{Balls})\Big) \ ,$$
$$\phi_{\text{some}}\Big(\sum_{x\in \text{Balls}} \phi_{\substack{\text{or}\\ t\le 0}} \phi_{\&}(\phi_{\text{choose},t}(x),\phi_{\text{yesterday}}(t))/\text{card}(\text{Balls})\Big)\Big) \ .$$

Example 34.

$$\|(\text{All of my goats eat about three times a day})\| = \phi_{\underset{x\in \text{Goat}}{\&}}(\phi_{\Rightarrow}(\phi_{\text{Goat(Me)}}(x), \phi_{\substack{\text{eat about three}\\ \text{times a day}}}(x))),$$

where

$$\phi_{\substack{\text{eat about three}\\ \text{times a day}}}(x) = \phi_{\underset{(n=1,2..)}{or}}(\phi_{\underset{(0\le t_1<t_2<\cdots<t_n\le t_0)}{\&}}(\phi_{\underset{(i=1,..,n)}{or}}(\phi_{\&}(\phi(x)_{\substack{\text{eats around}\\ \text{time } t_i}}), \phi_{\substack{\text{about}\\ \text{three}}}(n))))),$$

and for each i,

$$\phi_{\substack{\text{eat around}\\ \text{time } t_i}}(x) = \phi_{\underset{0\le t\le t_0}{or}}(\phi_{\&}(\phi_{\text{eat},t}(x), \phi_{\text{around } t_i}(t)));$$

$$t_0 \overset{d}{=} \text{end of day in hours, e.g.}$$

Example 35.

$\|(\text{All of my goats eat very frequently each day})\|$
is the same as the above example, except for the replacement of $\phi_{\substack{\text{about}\\ \text{three}}}(n)$ by $\phi_{\substack{\text{very}\\ \text{frequently}}}(n)$, for all $n = 1,2...$.

Example 36.

$$\|(\text{A fat man who hates himself was talking to a thin one.})\| = \phi_{\underset{t\le 0}{or}}(\phi_{\underset{x,y\in \text{Men}_t}{or}}(\phi_{\&}(\phi_{\text{fat}}(wt(x),ht(x)), \phi_{\text{hate},t}(x,x), \phi_{\text{was}}(t), \phi_{\text{talk},t}(x,y), \phi_{\text{thin}}(wt(y),ht(y))))).$$

Example 37.

$$\|(\text{John hasn't been here for a month, but Bill has.})\| = \phi_{\&}(\phi_{\underset{t\in\mathbb{R}}{or}}(\phi_{\&}(\phi_{\text{is},t}(\text{John,here}), \phi_{\substack{<\text{ past}\\ \text{month}}}(t), \phi_{\text{now}}(t))),$$
$$\phi_{\underset{t\le 0}{or}}\phi_{\&}(\phi_{\text{is},t}(\text{Bill,here}), \phi_{\substack{\ge\text{past}\\ \text{month}}}(t), \phi_{\text{now}}(t)))).$$

Example 38.

$$\|(\text{Larry and Luke punch each other, but Pat and Mike don't})\| = \phi_{\&}(\phi_{\text{punch}}(\text{Larry,Luke}), \phi_{\text{punch}}(\text{Luke,Larry}),$$
$$\phi_{\text{not}}(\phi_{\text{punch}}(\text{Pat,Mike}), \phi_{\text{not}}(\phi_{\text{punch}}(\text{Mike,Pat}))).$$

Example 39.

$$\|(\text{Bill asks John about himself (John)})\| = \phi_{\text{ask about}}(\text{Bill},\text{John},\text{John}) .$$

Example 40.

$$\|(\text{Bill asks John about himself (Bill)})\| = \phi_{\text{ask about}}(\text{Bill},\text{John},\text{Bill}) .$$

Example 41.

$$\|(\text{John is being easy to please})\| = \phi_{\underset{t\in\mathbb{R}}{\text{or}}}(\phi_{\&}(\phi_{\text{easy to please},t}(\text{John}),\phi_{\text{now}}(t))) .$$

Example 42.

$$\|(\text{John's intelligence, which is his most remarkable quality, exceeds his foresight.})\|$$
$$= \phi_{\&}(\phi_{\geq}(\text{meas}(\text{intell}(\text{John})),\ \text{meas}(\text{forsight}(\text{John}))),$$
$$\phi_{=}(\max_{x\in \text{Qual}(\text{John})} \text{meas}(x),\ \text{meas}(\text{intell}(\text{John}))))$$

Example 43.

$$\|(\text{What Thompson said, which Smith criticized him for, is that we should visit Bolivia})\|$$
$$= \phi_{\&}(\phi_{\underset{t\leq 0}{\text{or}}}(\phi_{\&}(\phi_{\text{say},t}(\text{Thompson},x_o),\phi_{\text{was}}(t))) ,$$
$$\phi_{\underset{t\leq 0}{\text{or}}}(\phi_{\&}(\phi_{\text{criticize for},\ t}(\text{Smith},\text{Thompson},x_o),\phi_{\text{was}}(t)))) ,$$
$$x_o \overset{d}{=} \text{"we should visit Bolivia"} ,$$

and

$$\phi_{\text{say},t} : (\text{People})\times(\text{statements made at } t) \to [0,1] ,$$
$$\|x_o\| = \phi_{\underset{0\leq\alpha\leq 1}{\text{or}}}(\phi_{\&}(\phi_{\text{visit},\alpha}(\text{we},\text{Bolivia}),\phi_{\text{should}}(\alpha))) .$$

Remark.

As a final note to this section, complete truth functionality has been assumed for $\|\cdot\|$ of the logics involved. Alternatively, semi-truth functional logics could have been utilized, such as probability logic. (See section 2.3.9).

CHAPTER 3

UNCERTAINTY MEASURES

This chapter is devoted to the study of different measures of uncertainty. The major application of this - as will be seen later - is to knowledge-based systems. (See Chapters 8 and 9.)

By an uncertainty measure for a given system, we mean a numerical valued function, usually in the form of a membership function or dispersion, which reflects the degrees of certainty or uncertainty of various objects of interest or events from the system.

In the spirit of Chapter 2, uncertainty measures, alternatively, may be thought of as special cases of dispersions and may be directly connected with formal language and semantic evaluations: They are semantic evaluations of certain relations, whose signatures, when evaluated, become the universes of discourse or semantical domains of the uncertainty measures at hand. For example, probability measures and related measures and their generalizations including Dempster-Shafer or Choquet capacity-type measures all may be considered in this light. See sections 2.3.3 (C)(4) and 2.3.9.

Typically, for a probability space, uncertainty is measured by $\mu : \mathcal{A} \to [0,1]$ where $\mathcal{A} \subseteq \mathcal{P}(X)$ for some base space X , with $\mathcal{A}$ being also a σ-algebra and μ satisfying the standard normalized measure axioms (as formulated by Kolmogorov, e.g.). The higher the value $\mu(A)$ for $A \in \mathcal{A}$ the more certain or "probable" A is. By weakening (or omitting altogether) the structures on $\mathcal{A}$ and/or μ above, more generalized concepts of uncertainty measures are obtained such as the Choquet-type measures or possibility measures, among others. (See Dubois and Prade [51] for a summary of axiom inclusion relations between various proposed measures of uncertainty.) On the other hand, many kinds of uncertainty measures may be derived from probability measures by use of suitable transformations such as the logarithmic one yielding statistical information measures and in turn (through the expectation) statistical entropy.

In summary, uncertainty measures may be considered essentially as structured dispersions, often unnormalized, as in the case of information measures, but usually normalized or bounded as in probability measures, possibility measures, or Choquet-type measures.

3.1 Probability theories and information theory.

The most common approach to uncertainty modeling is based upon some form of probability theory. For an excellent treatise on various theories of probability, including Kolmogorov-axiomatic, Von Mises' frequentist and Savage's subjective interpretations, we refer the reader to Fine [58]. For logical and philosophical issues entailed in the application of probability theory and its derivative field, mathematical statistics, to uncertainty modeling, see, e.g., the excellent papers of Good [76], Savage [221], De Finetti [46'], Lindley [158'].

From probability theory, the logical path to statistical information theory was established by Shannon [232]. Obviously, general information theory plays an important role in the theory of knowledge. In statistical information theory, the measure of information supplied by probabilistic experiments is connected to the amount of uncertainty. Specifically, the information measure is defined as follows:

Let $(\Omega, \mathcal{A}, P)$ be a probability space. Define $J : \mathcal{A} \to \mathbb{R}^+$ by;

$$J(A) \overset{d}{=} -\log P(A) \; ; \text{ all } A \in \mathcal{A} .$$

General information theory (Kampé de Fériet and Forte [132]; see also Guiasu [99]) is based essentially on the idea that it is possible to define information measures by a set of axioms. More precisely, if $\mathcal{B}$ is a class of subsets of Ω, then a mapping $J : \mathcal{B} \to \mathbb{R}^+$ is called an information measure if:

(i) $A, B \in \mathcal{B}$ and $A \subseteq B \Rightarrow J(A) \geq J(B)$.

(ii) If $\emptyset, \Omega \in \mathcal{B}$, then $J(\emptyset) = +\infty$, $J(\Omega) = 0$.

Several information measures are defined with additional structures. E.g., when $\mathcal{B}$ is an algebra of sets, J is said to possess a regular composition operation F if

$$J(A \uplus B) = F(J(A), J(B)) \; ; \text{ all } A, B \in \mathcal{B} ,$$

where $\uplus$ denotes disjoint union and

(a) $F : \mathbb{R}^+ \times \mathbb{R}^+ \to \mathbb{R}^+$, continuous ,

(b) $F(x,y) = F(y,x), \forall x,y \in \mathbb{R}^+$,

(c) $F[x, F(y,z)] = F[F(x,y), z]$, (associativity)

(d) $F(x, +\infty) = +\infty$

(e) $x_1 < x_2 \Rightarrow F(x_1, y) \leq F(x_2, y)$, for all $y \in \mathbb{R}^+$.

Note that such an F induces a topological semi-group on $\mathbb{R}^+$ (see, e.g., Paalman de Miranda [201]). For example, for the Wiener-Shannon information measure, we have

$$F(x,y) = \max\left(0, -c \log\left(e^{-\frac{x}{c}} + e^{-\frac{y}{c}}\right)\right) , \quad c > 0 .$$

If $J(A) = 1/\mu(A)$ where μ is a measure on a measurable space $(\Omega, \mathcal{A})$, then $F(x,y) = (\frac{1}{x} + \frac{1}{y})^{-1}$ (hyperbolic semi-group). (See also [136].)

An important class of information measures related to possibility theory (Zadeh [218]) and Choquet's capacity (Choquet [36]) is the class of information measures of type Inf (see, e.g., Nguyen [185], Langrand and Nguyen [151]) defined as follows:

Let $\varphi : \Omega \to \mathbb{R}^+$ such that

$$\inf\{\varphi(\omega) \mid \omega \in \Omega\} = 0$$

Define $J : \mathcal{P}(\Omega) \to \mathbb{R}^+$ by:

$$J(A) \overset{d}{=} \inf\{\varphi(\omega) \mid \omega \in A\} .$$

The regular composition operation of the above J is

$$F(x,y) = x \wedge y \ ; \text{ all } x , y .$$

For example, (see Kampé de Fériet and Nguyen [133]) let $f : \overline{\mathbb{R}}^+ \to U$, and for $A \subseteq U$,

$$J(A) = \inf\{t \geq 0 \mid f(t) \in A\} .$$

It is clear that $J(A)$ (the hitting time of A) is an information measure of type Inf. If we extend this notion of hitting time to multi-valued mappings, then all information measures of type Inf can be constructed this way. Indeed, if $f : \overline{\mathbb{R}}^+ \to \mathcal{P}(U)$, then

$$J(A) = \sup\{t \geq 0 \mid [\bigcup_{0 \leq s \leq t} f(s)] \cap A = \emptyset\} .$$

Conversely, if $J(A) = \inf\{\varphi(u) \mid u \in A\}$, then J is the hitting time of the set $f(t) = \{u \in U \mid \varphi(u) < t\}$.

In a narrow sense of information theory, the concept of probabilistic entropy is the cornerstone of theoretical investigation of the transmission of information over communication channels. More generally, the uncertainty about a stochastic system can be measured by the entropy of the random vector or random set describing the system. When the probabilities cannot be directly evaluated but some evidence about the system is available, say, in the form of expectation, or higher moments, the principle of maximum entropy (or minimum cross entropy) (Jaynes [123]), extending Laplace's principle of insufficient reason, can be used as a selection criterion for constructing probability distributions. We will discuss this principle in the context of random sets in 5.4. For an axiomatic foundation of the principle of maximum entropy and of minimum cross-entropy, see Shore and Johnson [235]. For the applications of the maximum entropy principle to statistics and statistical mechanics, see, e.g., Kampé de Fériet [130]; see also Kullback [145'].

Remark.

We present an example connecting basic set operations as formal language descriptions, semantic evaluations, logical validity, and probabilistic and informational change relative to Probability Logic. (See again Chapter 2 for background especially sections 2.3.3 (C), 2.3.4, 2.3.5 and 2.3.9 (A).)

For any $i,j \in Var(Ob(\mathcal{L}))$, letting

$$m \overset{d}{=} i \times \Omega^i \times j$$

and choosing any individual variables (projections) $x_m^{(i)}$, $y_m^{(\Omega^i)}$, $z_m^{(\Omega^i)}$, recalling the specially designated function symbol for set membership (in the general sense) $(\in : Ob(\mathcal{L}) \rightarrow Rel(\mathcal{L}))$, consider wff's

$$\Psi_1 \overset{d}{=} \in_i[<x_m^{(i)}, y_m^{(\Omega^i)}>] = (x_m^{(i)} \in_i y_m^{(\Omega^i)})$$

and

$$\Psi_2 \overset{d}{=} \in_i[<x_m^{(i)}, z_m^{(\Omega^i)}) = (x_m^{(i)} \in_i z_m^{(\Omega^i)}) .$$

Suppose that (Z4) unions hold as either an axiom or theorem (see 2.3.4 or [172], pp. 70 - 86).

$$\vdash ((\forall \gamma_m^{(\Omega^i)}, \xi_m^{(\Omega^i)})(\exists \alpha_m^{(\Omega^i)})(\forall \beta_m^{(i)})((\beta_m^{(i)} \in_i \alpha_m^{(\Omega^i)}) \Leftrightarrow \eta)) ,$$

$$\eta \overset{d}{=} (\beta_m^{(i)} \in_i \gamma_m^{(\Omega^i)}) \text{ or } (\beta_m^{(i)} \in_i \xi_m^{(\Omega^i)})$$

is in $Wff_m(\mathcal{L})$, for all i in $Var(Ob(\mathcal{L}))$, where $\gamma^{(\Omega^i)}$, $\xi^{(\Omega^i)}$, $\alpha^{(\Omega^i)}$, $\beta^{(i)}$ are all arbitrary individual variables of the appropriate types, where we define via class abstraction

$$\gamma^{(\Omega^i)} \cup \xi^{(\Omega^i)} \overset{d}{=} \alpha^{(\Omega^i)} .$$

Alternatively, we can use the class abstraction function symbol $\{\cdot|\cdot\cdot\}$ and a natural associated tautology

$$\vdash ((\beta_m^{(i)} \in_i (\gamma^{(\Omega^i)} \cup \xi^{(\Omega^i)})) \Leftrightarrow \eta) ,$$

where we recall from 2.2.2,

$$(\{\cdot|\cdot\cdot\} : Ob(\mathcal{L}) \times Ob(\mathcal{L}) \times Rel(\mathcal{L}) \rightarrow Ar(\mathcal{L}))$$

and

$$\gamma^{(\Omega^i)} \cup \xi^{(\Omega^i)} \overset{d}{=} \{i \mid \Omega^i \times j , \eta\} \overset{d}{=} \{\beta_m^{(i)} \mid \eta\} ,$$

using individual variable notation.

In turn, this implies in a natural way

$$\gamma^{(\Omega^i)} \subseteq_{\Omega^i} \left(\gamma^{(\Omega^i)} \cup \xi^{(\Omega^i)}\right),$$

implicitly defining generalized subset relation $\subseteq_{\Omega^i}$.

Specializing these results,

$$w_m^{(\Omega^i)} \stackrel{d}{=} y_m^{(\Omega^i)} \cup z_m^{(\Omega^i)} \supseteq_{\Omega^i} y_m^{(\Omega^i)}, \; z_m^{(\Omega^i)},$$

define

$$\begin{aligned}\Psi_3 &\stackrel{d}{=} \in_i[<x_m^{(i)}, w_m^{(\Omega^i)}>] \\ &= (x_m^{(i)} \in_i w_m^{(\Omega^i)}) \\ &= \Psi_1 \text{ or } \Psi_2 .\end{aligned}$$

Let $\| \; \| : \mathcal{L} \to (\mathrm{SET}, H^{\cdot})$, $H = [0,1]$ be a semantic evaluation for PL. Thus $\|i\|$ is some σ-algebra over X_i , some ordinary set, with similar remarks for $\|j\|$, $\|\Omega\| = \{0,1\}$ and $\|\Omega^i\| = \sigma(\{0,1\}^{\|i\|})$, by identification $\|x_m^{(i)}\| : \|m\| \to \|i\|$, $\|y_m^{(\Omega^i)}\| : \|m\| \to \|\Omega^i\|$, $\|z_m^{(\Omega^i)}\| : \|m\| \to \|\Omega^i\|$, are projections, where $\|m\| = \sigma(\|i\| \times \|\Omega^i\| \times \|j\|)$.

Also, recall that $\|\in_i\| : \|i{\times}\Omega^i\| \to H$ is a probability measure, where $\|i{\times}\Omega^i\| = \sigma(\|i\| \times \|\Omega^i\|)$. Then

$$\begin{aligned}\Pr(\Psi_1) &\stackrel{d}{=} (\|x_m^{(i)}\| \; \|\in_i\| \; \|y_m^{(\Omega^i)}\|) \\ &\stackrel{d}{=} \|\Psi_1\| \\ &= \|\in_i\| \; (\|x_m^{(i)}\| \times \|y_m^{(\Omega^i)}\|) \\ &= \|\in_i\| \; (\|x_m^{(i)}\| \, (\cdot) \times (\|y_m^{(\Omega^i)}\| \, (\cdot\cdot)) \circ \|x_m^{(i)}\|(\cdot))\end{aligned}$$

and similarly,

$$\begin{aligned}\Pr(\Psi_2) &\stackrel{d}{=} \|\Psi_1\| \\ &= \|\in_i\| \circ (\|x_m^{(i)}\|(\cdot) \times (\|z_m^{(\Omega^i)}\|(\cdot\cdot)) \circ \|x_m^{(i)}\|(\cdot)) .\end{aligned}$$

But compatible with the definition for unions and $\|\text{or}\|$,

$$\|w_m^{(\Omega^i)}\| = \|y_m^{(\Omega^i)}\| \cup \|z_m^{(\Omega^i)}\| : \|m\| \to \|\Omega^i\| .$$

Then

$$\begin{aligned}
\Pr(\Psi_3) &= (\|x_m^{(i)}\| \ \|\epsilon_i\| \ \|w_m^{(\Omega^i)}\|) \\
&= \|\Psi_3\| \\
&= \|\epsilon_i\|\circ(\|x_m^{(i)}\|(\cdot)\times(\|w_m^{(\Omega^i)}\|(\cdot\cdot))\circ\|x_m^{(i)}\|(\cdot))) \\
&= \|\epsilon_i\|\circ(\|x_m^{(i)}\|(\cdot)\times((\|y_m^{(\Omega^i)}\|(\cdot\cdot)\circ\|x_m^{(i)}\|(\cdot)) \\
&\qquad\qquad \cup \|z_m^{(\Omega^i)}\|(\cdot\cdot)\circ\|x_m^{(i)}\|(\cdot)))) \\
&= \Pr(\Psi_1) + \Pr(\Psi_2) - \Pr(\Psi_4) ,
\end{aligned}$$

using the ordinary modular property of probability, noting

$$\begin{aligned}
\Pr(\Psi_4) &= \|\epsilon_i\|\circ(\|x_m^{(i)}\|(\cdot)\times((\|y_m^{(\Omega^i)}\|(\cdot\cdot)\circ\|x_m^{(i)}\|(\cdot)) \\
&\qquad\qquad \cap (\|z_m^{(\Omega^i)}\|(\cdot\cdot)\circ\|x_m^{(i)}\|(\cdot)))) ,
\end{aligned}$$

is compatibly defined, if (Z22) intersections holds if the class abstraction function symbol is appropriately applied, where

$$\begin{aligned}
\Psi_4 \overset{d}{=} \Psi_1 \,\&\, \Psi_2 &= \epsilon_i[\langle x_m^{(i)}, v_m^{(\Omega^i)}\rangle] , \\
&= (x_m^{(i)} \ \epsilon_i \ v_m^{(\Omega^i)}) , \\
v_m^{(\Omega^i)} \overset{d}{=} y_m^{(\Omega^i)} &\cap z_m^{(\Omega^i)} .
\end{aligned}$$

(See also the discussion in 2.3.4 (D) concerning the definition of set operations.)

Thus,

$$\Pr(\Psi_1), \Pr(\Psi_2) \le \Pr(\Psi_3) ,$$

and equivalently, in terms of *negative information*, defining

$$I(\Psi) \overset{d}{=} \log \Pr(\Psi) = -J(\Psi) ,$$

for any $\Psi \in \mathrm{Wff}(\mathcal{L})$,

$$I(\Psi_1), I(\Psi_2) \le I(\Psi_3) .$$

Note that this is equivalent to the sequents $(\Psi_1 \vdash \Psi_3)$, $(\Psi_2 \vdash \Psi_3)$ being valid relative to $\| \ \|$ as used here, i.e., *negative* information increase or, equivalently probability increase on wff's is the same as validity for PL.

Analagous results are obtainable for other set operations such as complementations, cartesian products and sums, and more general compound set operations.

3.2 Choquet-type measures: Basic Properties

In this subsection, the Choquet-type family of uncertainty measures is presented. The following development is based on the works of Choquet [36], Shafer [228], Dempster [46], as well as Nguyen [187], Goodman [90] and Höhle [116].

Let X be a fixed base space with $\mathfrak{B} \subseteq \mathcal{P}(X)$ with either $\mathfrak{B}$ closed under all finite intersections - indicated by $\mathfrak{B}_{\cap}$ - or closed under all finite unions - indicated by $\mathfrak{B}_{\cup}$. Let $\mathfrak{B}$ denote generally either situation. Let $\mu : \mathfrak{B} \to [0,1]$ be an uncertainty measure over $\mathfrak{B}$ for X. We say μ is *monotone increasing* iff $\forall\ C \subseteq D \in \mathfrak{B}$, $\mu(C) \le \mu(D)$ and μ is *monotone decreasing* iff $\forall\ C \subseteq D \in \mathfrak{B}$, $\mu(C) \ge \mu(D)$. In addition, let $(*',*'') = (\cap,\cup)$ or $= (\cup,\cap)$. Define for any integer $n \ge 1$, the *Choquet operators* $\Delta_n, \nabla_n : \times_{j=1}^{n} \mathfrak{B} \to [0,1]$: for any

$\underset{\sim}{B}_n = (B_1,\ldots,B_n)$, $B_j \in \mathfrak{B}$, $j = 1,\ldots,n$,

$$\Delta_n(\mu,*'',\underset{\sim}{B}_n) \overset{d}{=} \sum_{K \subseteq \{1,\ldots,n-1\}} (-1)^{\text{card } K} \mu\Big(\underset{j\in K}{*''} B_j *'' B_n \Big)$$

$$\nabla_n(\mu,*',*'',\underset{\sim}{B}_n) \overset{d}{=} \mu\Big(\underset{j\in\{1,\ldots,n\}}{*'} B_j \Big) - \sum_{\emptyset \ne K \subseteq \{1,\ldots,n\}} (-1)^{\text{card}(K)+1} \mu\Big(\underset{j\in K}{*''} B_j \Big)$$

Definitions:

Let $\mu : \mathfrak{B} \to [0,1]$ be an uncertainty measure.

μ is a *plausibility* or *upper probability* ***measure*** iff $\forall n$ and $\underset{\sim}{B}_n$, $\Delta_n(\mu,\cup,\underset{\sim}{B}_n) \le 0$ & $\mu(\emptyset) = 0$.

μ is a *belief* or *credibility* or *lower probability* ***measure*** iff $\forall n$ and $\underset{\sim}{B}_n$, $\Delta_n(\mu,\cap,\underset{\sim}{B}_n) \ge 0$ & $\mu(X) = 1$.

μ is a *doubt* or ***commonality measure*** iff $\forall n$ and $\underset{\sim}{B}_n$, $\Delta_n(\mu,\cup,\underset{\sim}{B}_n) \ge 0$ & $\mu(\emptyset) = 1$.

μ is a *disbelief* or *incredibility* ***measure*** iff $\mu(X) = 0$ & $\forall n$ and $\underset{\sim}{B}_n$, $\Delta_n(\mu,\cap,\underset{\sim}{B}_n) \le 0$.

Remark:

Following Choquet's original nomenclature [36], a plausibility measure is a "$\cup$-alternating (Choquet) capacity of ∞-order", a belief measure is a "$\cap$-monotone Choquet capacity of ∞-order"; a doubt measure is a "$\cup$-monotone Choquet capacity of ∞-order", a disbelief measure is a "$\cap$-alternating capacity of ∞-order".

Lemma 1 Fix $n = 2$.

If $\forall \underset{\sim}{B}_2$, $\nabla_2(\mu,\cap,\cup,\underset{\sim}{B}_2) \left.\begin{matrix}\ge\\ \le\end{matrix}\right\} 0$ & $\mu(X) = \left\{\begin{matrix}0\\ 1\end{matrix}\right.$ or

if $\forall \underset{\sim}{B}_2$, $\Delta_2(\mu,\cup,\underset{\sim}{B}_2) \left.\begin{matrix}\ge\\ \le\end{matrix}\right\} 0$, then

μ is monotone $\left\{\begin{matrix}\text{decreasing}\\ \text{increasing}\end{matrix}\right.$.

If $\forall \underset{\sim}{B}_2, \nabla_2(\mu,\cup,\cap,\underset{\sim}{B}_2) \left.\begin{matrix}\ge\\ \le\end{matrix}\right\} 0$ & $\mu(\emptyset) = \left\{\begin{matrix}0\\ 1\end{matrix}\right.$

or if $\forall \underset{\sim}{B}_2$, $\Delta_2(\mu,\cap,\underset{\sim}{B}_2) \left.\begin{matrix}\ge\\ \le\end{matrix}\right\} 0$, then

μ is monotone $\left\{\begin{matrix}\text{increasing}\\ \text{decreasing}\end{matrix}\right.$.

Lemma 2 Fix n .

If $\mu(X) = 0$, then $\forall \underset{\sim}{B}_n$, $\nabla_n(\mu,\cap,\cup,\underset{\sim}{B}_n) \ge 0$ iff $\forall \underset{\sim}{B}_{n+1}$, $\Delta_{n+1}(\mu,\cup,\underset{\sim}{B}_{n+1}) \ge 0$.

If $\mu(X) = 1$, then $\forall \underset{\sim}{B}_n$, $\nabla_n(\mu,\cap,\cup,\underset{\sim}{B}_n) \le 0$ iff $\forall \underset{\sim}{B}_{n+1}$, $\Delta_{n+1}(\mu,\cup,\underset{\sim}{B}_{n+1}) \le 0$.

If $\mu(\emptyset) = 0$, then $\forall \underset{\sim}{B}_n$, $\nabla_n(\mu,\cup,\cap,\underset{\sim}{B}_n) \ge 0$ iff $\forall \underset{\sim}{B}_{n+1}$, $\Delta_{n+1}(\mu,\cap,\underset{\sim}{B}_{n+1}) \ge 0$.

If $\mu(\emptyset) = 1$, then $\forall \underset{\sim}{B}_n$, $\nabla_n(\mu,\cup,\cap,\underset{\sim}{B}_n) \le 0$ iff $\forall \underset{\sim}{B}_{n+1}$, $\Delta_{n+1}(\mu,\cap,\underset{\sim}{B}_{n+1}) \le 0$.

Proof: $\Rightarrow$: Given the form $\Delta_{n+1}(\mu,*'',\underset{\sim}{B}_{n+1}) \left.\begin{matrix}\ge\\ \le\end{matrix}\right\} 0$ choose $B_{n+1} \overset{d}{=} *' \underset{\sim}{B}_n$. $\Leftarrow$: Given the form $\nabla_n(\mu,*',*'',\underset{\sim}{B}_n) \begin{matrix}\ge\\ \le\end{matrix} 0$, $\forall \underset{\sim}{B}_n$, replace B_j by $B_j *'' \underset{\sim}{B}_{n+1}$, $j = 1,\ldots,n$, and then use Lemma 1.

Lemma 3

If μ is a plausibility measure or a belief measure, it is monotone increasing.

If μ is a doubt measure or a disbelief measure, it is monotone decreasing.

Lemma 4

μ is a plausibility measure over $\mathfrak{B}_{\dot{\cup}}$ iff $1 - \mu$ is a doubt measure over $\mathfrak{B}_{\dot{\cup}}$.

μ is a belief measure over $\mathfrak{B}_{\cap}$ iff $\mu(\underline{\mathfrak{C}}\cdot)$ is a doubt measure over $X \underline{\dashv} \mathfrak{B}_{\cap}$.

μ is a disbelief measure over $\mathfrak{B}_{\cap}$ iff $1 - \mu(\underline{\mathfrak{C}}\cdot)$ is a doubt measure over $X \underline{\dashv} \mathfrak{B}_{\cap}$, where

$$X \underline{\dashv} \mathfrak{B}_{\cap} \overset{d}{=} \{X \dashv B \mid B \in \mathfrak{B}_{\cap}\} = \{\mathfrak{C}B \mid B \in \mathfrak{B}_{\cap}\} \text{ , etc.}$$

The following theorems have straightforward proofs which involve some messy computations.

Theorem 1

Let μ be an uncertainty measure over $\mathfrak{F}(X)$ (class of all finite subsets of X) or over $X \dashv \mathfrak{F}(X)$, whichever is appropriate. Then:

(i) μ is a doubt measure over $\mathfrak{F}(X)$ *iff* $\mu(\emptyset) = 1$ & $\forall G \in \mathfrak{F}(X)$, $\mu_G^{(1)} \geq 0$, where for any $C \subseteq G$,

$$\mu_G^{(1)}(\{C\}) \overset{d}{=} \Delta_{m+1}(\mu, \cup, \{x_1\}, \ldots, \{x_n\}, C)$$

$$= \sum_{K \subseteq G \dashv C} (-1)^{\mathrm{card}(K)} \mu(C \,\dot{\cup}\, K) \text{ ,}$$

where $G \dashv C = \{x_1, \ldots, x_m\}$, $x_j \in X$, $j = 1, \ldots, m$.

(ii) μ is a belief measure over $X \underline{\dashv} \mathfrak{F}(X)$ *iff* $\mu(X) = 1$ & $\forall\, G \in \mathfrak{F}(X)$, $\mu_{X \dashv G}^{(2)}(\{X \dashv C\}) \geq 0$, where for any $C \subseteq G$,

$$\mu_{X \dashv G}^{(2)}(\{X \dashv C\}) \overset{d}{=} \Delta_{m+1}(\mu, \cap, X \dashv \{x_1\}, \ldots, X \dashv \{x_m\}, X \dashv C)$$

$$= \sum_{K \subseteq G \dashv C} (-1)^{\mathrm{card}(K)} \mu(X \dashv (C \,\dot{\cup}\, K)) \text{ .}$$

(iii) μ is a plausibility measure over $\mathfrak{F}(X)$ iff $\mu(\emptyset) = 0$ & $\mu_G^{(1)} \leq 0$, $\forall\, G \in \mathfrak{F}(X)$.

(iv) μ is a disbelief measure over $X \underline{\dashv} \mathfrak{F}(X)$ iff

$$\forall\, C \subseteq G \in \mathfrak{F}(X) \text{ , } \mu_{X \dashv G}^{(2)}(\{X \dashv C\}) \leq 0 \text{ .}$$

Theorem 2

If μ is a doubt measure over $\mathfrak{F}(X)$, then $\forall\, G \in \mathfrak{F}(X)$,

(i) $0 \leq \mu_G^{(1)} \leq 1$; indeed $\mu_G^{(1)}$ is a probability measure over $\mathfrak{P}\mathfrak{P}(G)$ corresponding to random subset $S_G^{(1)}$ of G .

(ii) $\forall\ C \subseteq G$,

$$\sum_{C \subseteq B \subseteq G} \mu_G^{(1)}(\{B\}) = \mu(C) = \Pr(C \subseteq S_G^{(1)}) \overset{d}{=} \mu_G^{(1)}(\mathcal{C}_C(\mathcal{P}(G))) ,$$

where $\mathcal{C}_C(\mathcal{P}(G)) \overset{d}{=} \{B \mid C \subseteq B \subseteq G\}$ is the superset or filter class on C in $\mathcal{P}(G)$.

In particular,

$$\mu_G^{(1)}(\{\emptyset\}) = \sum_{B \subseteq G} (-1)^{\text{card } B} \cdot \mu(B) , \quad \mu_G^{(1)}(\{G\}) = \mu(G) ,$$

and as a check

$$\mu_G^{(1)}(\mathcal{P}(G)) = \mu(\emptyset) = 1 ; \quad \mu_G^{(1)}(\emptyset) = 0 .$$

(iii) If $C \subseteq G_1 \subseteq G_2$

$$\mu_{G_1}^{(1)}(\{C\}) \overset{d}{=} \mu_{G_2}^{(1)}(\mathcal{C}_C(\mathcal{P}(G_2))) ,$$

and more generally, for any $\mathcal{A} \subseteq \mathcal{P}(G_1)$,

$$\mu_{G_1}^{(1)}(\mathcal{A}) = \sum_{C \in \mathcal{A}} \mu_{G_1}^{(1)}(\{C\}) = \mu_{G_2}^{(1)}(p_{G_1}^{-1}(\mathcal{A}) \underline{\cap} \{G_2\}) ;$$

$$p_{G_1}^{-1}(\mathcal{A}) \underline{\cap} \{G_2\}) \overset{d}{=} \{C \mid C \subseteq G_2 \ \&\ C \cap G_1 \in \mathcal{A}\} ,$$

where p_{G_1} is the standard projection: $p_{G_1}(A) \overset{d}{=} G_1 \cap A$. (See section 4.2.)

Remark.

For Theorem 2 above and for the following two theorems, all results involving probability measures over classes of sets may be reinterpreted directly in terms of random sets. (See Chapter 4.)

Theorem 3

If μ is a belief measure over $X \underline{\dashv} \mathcal{J}(X)$, then $\forall\ G \in \mathcal{J}(X)$,

(i) $\mu_{X \dashv G}^{(2)}$ is a probability measure over $\mathcal{P}\mathcal{P}(X \dashv G)$, corresponding to a random subset $S_{X \dashv G}^{(2)}$ of $X \dashv G$.

(ii) $\forall\ C \subseteq G$,

$$\sum_{(X \dashv G \subseteq B \subseteq X \dashv C)} \mu_{X \dashv G}^{(2)}(\{B\}) = \mu(X \dashv C) = \Pr(S_{X \dashv G}^{(2)} \subseteq X \dashv C)$$

$$= \mu_{X \dashv G}^{(2)}(\mathcal{D}_{X \dashv C}(\underline{\mathcal{P}}(X \dashv G))) , \text{ where}$$

$\mathcal{P}(X \dashv G) \overset{d}{=} \{X \dashv B \mid B \subseteq G\}$ and $\mu^{(2)}_{X \dashv G}(\mathfrak{B})$, for any $\mathfrak{B} = X \underline{\dashv} \mathcal{A}$, $\mathcal{A} \subseteq \mathcal{P}(G)$, is defined analagous to $\mu^{(1)}_{G}(\mathcal{A})$.

Proof: Use Theorem 2 and Lemma 4.

Remark

Analogues of Theorems 2 and 3 for plausibility and disbelief measures may also be established, utilizing Lemma 4. An alternative approach to the uncertainty measures discussed above is presented in section 4.3, where Choquet's capacity theorem is used.

Theorem 4

(i) Let $\mathfrak{B}$ be a fixed Boolean ring. Then μ is a finitely additive probability measure over $\mathfrak{B}$ iff μ is both a plausibility and a belief measure over $\mathfrak{B}$.

(ii) If μ is a semi-distributive t-norm possibility measure, i.e., μ is a monotone and $\forall\ C,D \in \mathfrak{B}_o$, $\mu(C \cup D) = \mu(C) + \mu(D) - \phi_{\&}(\mu(C),\mu(D))$, for t-norm $\phi_{\&}$, then μ is a plausibility measure.

(iii) If $\phi_{\&}$ is a semi-distributive t-norm, then for any $A \in \mathcal{F}(X)$, $\mu_{A,\&}(\cdot) \overset{d}{=} \underset{x \in (\cdot)}{\phi_{\&}} (\phi_A(x)) : \mathfrak{F}(X) \to [0,1]$ is a doubt measure.

(iv) If ϕ_{or} is a semi-distributive t-conorm, then for any $A \in \mathcal{F}(X)$, $\mu_{A,or}(\cdot) \overset{d}{=} \underset{x \in (\cdot)}{\phi_{or}} (\phi_A(x)) : \mathfrak{F}(X) \to [0,1]$ is a plausibility measure.

(v) If $\phi_{\&}$, ϕ_{or} are a DeMorgan pair with respect to $\phi_{nt} \equiv 1 - (\cdot)$, then $\mu_{A,or} = 1 - \mu_{CA,\&}$.

(vi) In general, no μ is both a finitely additive probability measure and a t-norm possibility measure.

Remark.

Recall (see section 2.3.5) that a dispersion space (X,A,μ) consists of $\mathfrak{F}(X) \subseteq \mathcal{A} \subseteq \mathcal{P}(X)$ and $\mu : A \to [0,1]$, an uncertainty measure. μ can arise as simply a given function or μ may be derivable from an initial function such as from $\phi_A : X \to [0,1]$ and a fixed function such as a t-norm (inf, e.g.) or t-conorm (sup, e.g.) as given above in Theorem 4 (iii), (iv). In the latter case, μ may be thought of as an extension of ϕ_A , with the identification

$$\mu(\{x\}) = \phi_A(x) \ ; \text{ all } \ x \in X .$$

3.3 Possibility and related measures.

The notion of possibility distributions was introduced by Zadeh [281] for the analysis of situations in which the uncertainty is not statistical in nature, especially in "humanistic" systems.

With the notation of 3.2:

Definition.

Let $\mathfrak{B} \subseteq \mathcal{P}(X)$ and $\mu : \mathfrak{B} \to [0,1]$ be an uncertainty measure. Then μ is a t-possibility measure iff μ is a monotone measure and $\mu(B_1 \cup B_2) = \mu(B_1) + \mu(B_2) - t(\mu(B_1),\mu(B_2))$ for all $B_1,B_2 \in \mathfrak{B}$, where t is a (mutually) distributive t-norm $(t = \phi_{\&})$. In particular, Zadeh's possibility measure $\mu_o(B) \overset{d}{=} \sup_{x\in B} \pi(x)$ for any $B \subseteq X$ and given π, where $\pi : X \to [0,1]$ is any dispersion (or fuzzy set membership function or possibility distribution function) is a t-possibility measure, where $t \overset{d}{=} \wedge$ (min). (See Klement [140] or others for extensions of Zadeh's theory.) Note that the possibility measure μ_o satisfies the following property:

For any index set I, and $A_i \subseteq X$, $i \in I$,

$$\mu_o(\bigcup_{i\in I} A_i) = \sup\{\mu(A_i) \mid i \in I\} .$$

Conversely, given any t-possibility measure μ the associated possibility distribution function π_μ is defined to be:

$$\pi_\mu : X \to [0,1] ,$$

where

$$\pi_\mu(x) \overset{d}{=} \mu(\{x\}) \ ; \text{all } x \in X .$$

When X is a topological space, a possibility measure μ can be a precapacity or even a special Choquet capacity, for example $\mu(A) \overset{d}{=} 1/J(A)$ where $J(A) \overset{d}{=} \inf\{\phi(x) \mid x \in A\}$; $A \subseteq X$, with $\phi : X \to \overline{\mathbb{R}}^+$ being lower-semi-continuous.

In an approach to the problem of meaning representation in natural language (Zadeh [283]), the law which governs the variable V in a proposition of the form <V is A> , $A \in \mathcal{F}(X)$, is defined as a possibility distribution $\pi = \phi_A$, expressing the degree to which each element $x \in X$ "belongs" to the generalized set A . It should also be noted that, in the formulation of the concept of values for non-atomic games, Aumann and Shapley [9] are led to consider "ideal sets" which are formally fuzzy sets in the sense of Zadeh.

We specialize now the general formulation of conditioning, projections and interactions (see section 2.3.8) to the case where $\phi_{\&} = \wedge$ and $\phi_{or} = \vee$. (See also Nguyen [188].)

Recall that (section 2.3.8) if $A \in \mathcal{F}(X\times Y)$ and $B \in \mathcal{F}(X)$, then the conditional generalized set $(A \mid x \in B) \in \mathcal{F}(Y)$ exists for all $x \in X$ provided $\sup_{y \in Y} \phi_A(x,y) \le \phi_B(x)$, $\forall x \in X$, and t-norm $\phi_\&$ is continuous. Furthermore, denoting truth content by $\| \ \|$,

$$\|(y \in (A \mid x \in B)) \ \& \ (x \in B)\| = \|(x,y) \in A\| ,$$

i.e., assuming truth functionality,

(1) $$\phi_\&(\phi_{(A|x \in B)}(y) \ , \ \phi_B(x)) = \phi_A(x,y) \ , \ \forall \ x \in X .$$

Also, the X-projection of A is defined as

(2) $$\phi_{proj_X(A)}(x) = \phi_{or_{y \in Y}}(\phi_A(x,y)) \ , \ \forall \ x \in X ,$$

and the two projections $proj_X(A)$ and $proj_Y(A)$, are said to be non-interactive iff

(3) $$A = proj_X(A) \times proj_Y(A) .$$

When $\phi_\& = \wedge$ and $\phi_{or} = \vee$, (1), (2) and (3) become, respectively:

(4) $$\phi_{(A|x \in B)}(y) \wedge \phi_B(x) = \phi_A(x,y) \ , \ \forall \ x,y \in X \times Y ,$$

(5) $$\phi_{proj_X(A)}(x) = \sup_{y \in Y} \phi_A(x,y) \ , \ \forall \ x \in X ,$$

(6) $$\phi_A(x,y) = \phi_{proj_X(A)}(x) \wedge \phi_{proj_Y(A)}(y) \ , \ \forall \ x,y \in X \times Y .$$

An explicit form for $\phi_{(A|x \in B)}(y)$ is given as follows:

$$\phi_{(A|x \in B)}(y) = \begin{cases} \phi_A(x,y) \ , \ \text{iff} \ \ \phi_{proj_X(A)}(x) \ge \phi_{proj_Y(A)}(y) \\ \phi_A(x,y) \cdot \phi_{proj_Y(A)}(y) \ / \ \phi_{proj_X(A)}(x) \qquad , \\ \qquad \text{iff} \ \ \phi_{proj_X(A)}(x) < \phi_{proj_Y(A)}(y) . \end{cases}$$

Now let μ be a possibility measure with associated possibility distribution function $\pi = \pi_\mu$. In constrast to probability theory, the non-interaction of variables has to be defined (as above) directly from possibility distributions and not from possibility measures. This is due to the fact that $\mu(A \cap B) = \mu(A) \wedge \mu(B)$ does not imply necessarily one of the following relations:

(i) $\mu(A \cap CB) = \mu(A) \wedge \mu(CB)$,

(ii) $\mu(CA \cap B) = \mu(CA) \wedge \mu(B)$.

(iii) $\mu(CA \cap CB) = \mu(CA) \wedge \mu(CB)$.

The extension of the domain of possibility measures to include generalized sets is as follows:

For $A \in \mathcal{F}(X)$,

$$\mu(A) \overset{d}{=} \sup \{\Pi(x) \wedge \phi_A(x) \mid x \in X\} .$$

Another extension is based upon integration with respect to capacities:

For $A \in \mathcal{F}(X)$, we have

$$\mu(A) \overset{d}{=} \sup \{\Pi(x) \mid x \in A\} = \int_0^1 \mu(A_t)\, dt$$

where we note $\mu(A_t)$ is well-defined for

$$A_t \overset{d}{=} \{x \in X \mid \phi_A(x) > t\} .$$

For the connections between dispersions or possibility distributions and probability theory, via random sets, see Chapter 4.

We mention now a problem of inference using possibility theory. Let U be a variable taking values in X with possibility distribution $\Pi_U = \phi_A$ induced by the proposition <U is A> . From this proposition, one can infer that:

$$\text{Poss}(U \text{ is } B) \overset{d}{=} \mu_U(B) = \sup \{\phi_A(x) \wedge \phi_B(x) \mid x \in X\} .$$

This inference rule can be interpreted intuitively as follows: For each $x \in X$, the dirac measure δ_x is a possibility measure with the following interpretation of conditioning: Knowing that x is the only possible value, the conditional possibility measure of a crisp set B is

$$\delta_x(B) = \begin{cases} 1 & \text{iff } x \in B \\ 0 & \text{iff } x \notin B \end{cases} .$$

More generally,

$$\delta_A(B) = \begin{cases} 1 & \text{if } A \cap B \neq \emptyset \\ 0 & \text{if } A \cap B = \emptyset \end{cases} , \quad \text{for any } A \subseteq X .$$

Note that

$$\delta_A(B) \overset{d}{=} \sup \{\phi_A(x) \wedge \phi_B(x) \mid x \in X\} .$$

Again, it is natural to extend conditional possibility measures to generalized sets by the same formula, replacing A and B .

Now if U is a random variable, defined on the probability space $(\Omega, \mathcal{A}, \Pr)$, with probability distribution P_U on X , and V is a (fuzzy) variable taking values in Y depending on U in the following way: given that $U = x$, the strict range of V is some subset T_x of Y . Thus,

$$\text{Poss}(V = y \mid U = x) = \begin{cases} 1 & \text{if } y \in T_x \\ 0 & \text{otherwise} \end{cases},$$

and $\text{Poss}(V \mid U = x) = \phi_{T_x}$ or more generally $\text{Poss}(V|U) = \phi_{T \circ U}$, where $\circ$ is functional composition.

If we identify P_U with (U, P_U) and T with $\text{Poss}(V|U)$, we can consider an *evidence* $\mathcal{E} \overset{d}{=} (P_U, \text{Poss}(V|U))$. Note that $\text{Poss}(V|U = x)$ is a random set in Y. It is easy to see that

$$\text{Poss}(V|U = x) = \emptyset \Leftrightarrow T_x = \emptyset$$

$$A \subseteq Y \,,\; A \cap T_x \neq \emptyset \Leftrightarrow A \cap \text{Poss}(V|U = x) \neq \emptyset$$

$$T_x \subseteq A \Leftrightarrow \text{Poss}(V|U = x) \subseteq A \,.$$

Therefore

$$Pr_*(A) = Pr(\text{Poss}(V|U) \subseteq A)$$

$$Pr^*(A) = Pr(\text{Poss}(V|U) \cap A \neq \emptyset)$$

where Pr_*, Pr^* are lower and upper probabilities (Dempster [46]) associated with $(\Omega, \mathcal{A}, Pr)$ and the multi-valued mapping $\text{Poss}(V|U)$. (See also Chapter 4, especially Theorems 2 and 3.)

The random set $\text{Poss}(V|U = x)$ induces a possibility measure defined by

$$\text{Poss}(V \in A \mid U = x) = \sup \{\text{Poss}(V = y \mid U = x) \mid y \in A\}$$

or a random possibility measure:

$$\text{Poss}(V \in A \mid U) = \begin{cases} 1 & \text{if } A \cap T_X \neq \emptyset \\ 0 & \text{otherwise} \end{cases}.$$

Note that $E_U(\text{Poss}(V \in A|U)) = Pr^*(A)$ where E_U denotes probabilistic expectation with respect to the random variable U.

The concept of conditional possibility measure can be used in the analysis of evidence (see, e.g., Zadeh [282]). For example, consider the problem of making inference about probability laws of random variables. As before, let U be a random variable with values in a measurable space $(X, \mathcal{C})$. Denote by D the set of all probability densities on X. By an evidence $\mathcal{E}$, we mean propositions which specify that the true density f_o of U lies in some subset $D(\mathcal{E})$ of D. The subset $D(\mathcal{E})$ is referred to as the constraint. The inference procedure consists of finding an estimate of f_o based upon the information contained in the evidence $\mathcal{E}$. As a classical example, let X be the state space of some stochastic system, and $\mathcal{E}$ is expressed in the form of a constraint on the expectation of U, say, $E(U) = a$. The evidence $\mathcal{E}$ specifies the subset:

$$D(\mathcal{E}) = \{f \in D \mid \int x f(x)\, dx = a\} \,.$$

An estimate, say $\hat{f}$, of f_o can be obtained by using the principle of maximum entropy (Jaynes [123], see also section 5.4). If $B \in \mathcal{C}$, we infer that:

$$\Pr(U \in B \mid \mathcal{E}) = \int_B \hat{f}(x)\,dx$$

Now if the evidence $\mathcal{E}$ is of the form <U is A> such that ϕ_A is measurable, then $\mathcal{E}$ does not specify the true density f_o but does specify a weaker law, namely, a possibility distribution expressed as $\pi_U = \phi_A$, and in this spirit, if B is another fuzzy event, i.e., $B \in \mathcal{F}(X)$, with ϕ_B measurable, we have:

$$\begin{aligned}\text{Poss}(U \text{ is } B \mid \mathcal{E}) &= \mu(B \mid A) \overset{d}{=} \mu(B \mid \pi_U = \phi_A) \\ &= \sup\{\phi_A(x) \wedge \phi_B(x) \mid x \in X\} .\end{aligned}$$

Relations between possibility theory and other uncertainty measures.

First, the concept of fuzzy measures is given by Sugeno [248'] as follows:

Let $(X,\mathcal{A})$ be a measurable space. A mapping $g : \mathcal{A} \to [0,1]$ is called a fuzzy measure iff

(i) $g(\emptyset) = 0$, $g(X) = 1$,

(ii) $A,B \in \mathcal{A}$, $A \subseteq B \Rightarrow g(A) \le g(B)$,

i.e., g is monotone increasing, and g satisfies the following monotone continuity condition:

(iii) $A_n \in \mathcal{A}$ and $(A_n)\uparrow_{n=1,2,...}$ (resp., $(A_n)\downarrow_{n=1,2,...}$) implies

$$g\left(\bigcup_{n=1}^{\infty} A_n\right) = \lim_{n\to+\infty} g(A_n) .$$

$$\left(\text{resp., } g\left(\bigcap_{n=1,2,...}^{\infty} A_n\right) = \lim_{n\to+\infty} g(A_n).\right)$$

Secondly, Sugeno defined a λ-fuzzy (or λ-additive) measure as the mapping

$$g_\lambda : \mathcal{A} \to [0,1] \ ; \ -1 < \lambda < +\infty$$

such that

(a) $g_\lambda(X) = 1$.

(b) $g_\lambda(A \cup B) = g_\lambda(A) + g_\lambda(B) + \lambda \cdot g_\lambda(A) g_\lambda(B)$.

(c) g_λ satisfies condition (iii) above.

It is easy to verify that (see, e.g., Dubois and Prade [51]).

(α) All probability measures are fuzzy measures.

(β) Any λ-fuzzy measure is a fuzzy measure.

(γ) Banon [11] has shown, the following:

Let g_λ be any λ-fuzzy measure. Then

(i) If $\lambda \geq 0$, g_λ is a belief measure.

(ii) If $-1 < \lambda \leq 0$, g_λ is a plausibility measure.

(iii) If $\lambda = 0$, g_λ is an ordinary probability measure.

(δ) Kruse [146] developed an extension theorem for λ-fuzzy measures, and showed that the unique translation invariant λ-fuzzy measure over $\mathcal{C}$ (= $\mathbb{B}[0,1]$) , the σ-algebra of all Borel subsets of [0,1] , is given by

$$g_\lambda(A) \overset{d}{=} \frac{1}{\lambda}\cdot((1+\lambda)^{\mathrm{vol}_1(A)} - 1) \ ; \ A \in \mathcal{C} \ ,$$

where vol_1 is Legesgue measure over [0,1] .

(ε) Banon [11] also showed that a (Zadeh) possibility measure is a belief measure (or a λ-fuzzy measure) iff it is a dirac (i.e., one mass point) measure.
(See Banon [11] for a summary of various relations for uncertainty measures.)

However, as shown in Puri and Ralescu [206], in general a (Zadeh) possibility measure is not a fuzzy measure.

Finally, note that the concept of probabilities of fuzzy events (Zadeh [285]) is formulated in Klement [139'] as follows:

Again, let $(X,\mathcal{A})$ be a measurable space, and let $\mathcal{C}$ be the Borel σ-algebra of [0,1] . Denote $\sigma(\mathcal{A})$ the fuzzy σ-algebra generated by $\mathcal{A}$, i.e.,

$$\sigma(\mathcal{A}) = \{f \mid f : X \rightarrow [0,1] \mid f \text{ is } \mathcal{A}-\mathcal{C} \text{ measurable}\} \ .$$

A *fuzzy probability* measure is a mapping $m : \sigma(\mathcal{A}) \rightarrow [0,1]$ such that

(i) $m(0) = 0$, $m(1) = 1$ (for the 0- and 1- constant functions)

(ii) modularity holds, i.e.,

$$\forall f,g \in \sigma(\mathcal{A}) \ ,$$
$$m(f \vee g) + m(f \wedge g) = m(f) + m(g) \ ,$$

(iii) increasing continuity holds, i.e.,

if $f_n \in \sigma(\mathcal{A})$ and $f_n \uparrow f$ then
$m(f_n) \uparrow m(f)$.

If $m : \sigma(\mathcal{A}) \to \mathbb{R}$ satisfies (ii), (iii) and $m(\emptyset) = 0$, then m is called a fuzzy measure in Klement's sense. It should be noted that this concept of fuzzy measure is different from Sugeno's fuzzy measure in general. The characterization of this type of fuzzy measures is given in Klement [139']: if m is a finite fuzzy measure, then there exists a unique finite measure P on $(X,\mathcal{A})$ and a P - almost everywhere unique Markoff-kernel K such that:

$$\forall\ f \in \sigma(\mathcal{A}),\ m(f) = \int_{x \in X} K(x,[0,f(x))) \, dP(x) \ .$$

(See also Klement, Schwyhla and Lowen [141].)

Remark.

From a semantic evaluation viewpoint, the above investigation can be enlarged by replacing $\wedge$, $\vee$ by other t-norms and t-conorms.

CHAPTER 4

RANDOM SET THEORY: INTRODUCTION

This chapter contains necessary background on the theory of random sets which will be used in Chapters 5 and 6 to establish formal connections between possibility and probability theories.

4.1 Background.

By random sets we mean random elements whose possible outcomes are subsets of some given space. Random sets often arise in statistical problems in the form of families of confidence sets. In sampling from a finite population, a sampling design is precisely a random set. The theory of random sets has been mainly developed by Kendall [137] and Matheron [171].

Let $(\Omega, \mathcal{A}, Pr)$ be a probability space, and X be an arbitrary set. Let $\mathcal{C} \subseteq \mathcal{P}(X)$, and $\hat{\mathcal{C}}$ be a σ-algebra on $\mathcal{C}$. A random set S is an $\mathcal{A}-\hat{\mathcal{C}}$ measurable mapping from $(\Omega, \mathcal{A}, Pr)$ to $(\mathcal{C}, \hat{\mathcal{C}})$. The induced probability measure on $(\mathcal{C}, \hat{\mathcal{C}})$ is $P_S = Pr \circ S^{-1}$. As in the case of random vectors, given a probability space of the form $(\mathcal{C}, \hat{\mathcal{C}}, P_S)$, $id : \mathcal{C} \to \hat{\mathcal{C}}$ is referred to also as a random set. When X is arbitrary, $\mathcal{C}$ can be $\mathcal{P}(X)$, and $\hat{\mathcal{C}} = \sigma(\mathcal{D})$, the σ-algebra generated by $\mathcal{D}$, where

$$\mathcal{D} \stackrel{d}{=} \{M(I,I') \mid I,I' \in \mathcal{F}(X)\}$$

where $\mathcal{F}(X)$, or simply $\mathcal{F}$, is the class of all finite subsets of X, and

$$M(I,I') \stackrel{d}{=} \{A \in \mathcal{P}(X) \mid A \supseteq I,\ A \cap I' = \emptyset\}$$

When $(X, \mathcal{B})$ is a measurable space, one might take $\mathcal{C} = \mathcal{B}$, and hence $\hat{\mathcal{C}}$ is a σ-algebra on $\mathcal{B}$. In practice, X will be a locally compact Hausdorff and separable space, e.g., $\mathbb{R}^d$ and $\mathcal{B}$ is its Borel σ-algebra. In this topological setting, compact-convex-valued random sets generalize random vectors (when restricting to singleton sets). Some natural extensions of results for random vectors have been obtained for random sets - for mostly compact-valued random sets; other analogues remain to be established. When the base space X is a metric space, the class of non-empty compact sets $\mathcal{K}' = \mathcal{K} - \{\emptyset\}$ is a metric space with the Hausdorff distance, so that compact-valued random sets are measurable mappings taking values in $(\mathcal{K}', \mathcal{B}(\mathcal{K}'))$, where $\mathcal{B}(\mathcal{K}')$ is the Borel σ-algebra of $\mathcal{K}'$. The fact that $\mathcal{K}'$ is a metric space allows us to consider weak convergence of probability measures on $\mathcal{K}'$ and study asymptotic problems, e.g., central limit theorems. Also, the integration of multi-valued mappings (see, e.g., Debreu [45], and section 4.4) can be formulated so that the problems of the law of large numbers for random sets can be addressed.

When X is locally compact, the class $\mathcal{F}$ of closed sets of X can be topologized in a suitable way (Matheron, [171]) to yield a compact space, and closed random sets can be defined. For these random sets, incidence functions play the role of distribution functions of random vectors. Specifically, the incidence function T_o of the random set S , a special type of Choquet's capacity, is defined as follows:

$$T_o : \mathcal{K} \to [0,1],$$

$$T_o(K) = \Pr(S \cap K \neq \emptyset) ,$$

(Kendall [137] uses the terminology "trapping functions".) Note that T characterizes an equivalence class of closed random sets (Matheron, [171]).

In the case of $(X,\sigma(\mathfrak{D}))$, the space law

$$T_o : \mathcal{I}(X) \to [0,1] \quad \text{defined by}$$

$$T_o(I) \overset{d}{=} \Pr(S \cap I \neq \emptyset) \; ; \; I \in \mathcal{I}(X) ,$$

characterizes also an equivalent class of general random sets.

In this book, we will mainly consider random sets on $(\mathcal{P}(x), \sigma(\mathfrak{D}))$. A characterization of these random sets will be given in terms of probability coverage functions which are relevant to our analysis of uncertainty (see Chapter 5). However, to compute expected measure of random sets and higher moments, since elementary proofs are not available, we will call upon topological structures and abstract measure theory.

The reader interested in the development of random set theory towards statistical applications can find main references on these issues in the bibliography at the end of the book. We will not discuss random sets arising from stochastic point processes or geometric covering problems. However, we will say a few words, in 5.5, about randomized set estimators (and tests) because of the analogy in spirit with the investigation we are going to carry out.

The fact that random set theory can be viewed as a tool toward providing a unified treatment of uncertainty measures is the main reason why it will occupy a large portion of this book.

4.2 Structure.

In this section, we study structures of random sets and their connections with uncertainty measures. As stated before, random sets are essentially set-valued random variables or vectors. Ordinary random variables are singleton-valued random sets. More rigorously, consider the following: The natural topology on $\{0,1\}^X$ is $\mathcal{T}(X)$, the product topology induced by the discrete topology over each factor space $\{0,1\}$. $\mathcal{T}(X)$ is a compact Hausdorff, totally disconnected (and separable, if X is at most countable) topology. It follows that the same properties hold for

$$\mathscr{T}(\mathfrak{B}_o) \overset{d}{=} \phi^{-1}(\mathscr{T}(X)) \underline{\cap} \mathfrak{B}_o ,$$

the natural topology for power class $\mathfrak{B}_o$, where it is always assumed that

$$\emptyset, X \in \mathfrak{B}_o \subseteq \mathscr{P}(X) .$$

A typical open set for $\mathscr{T}(X)$ is an arbitrary union of sets of the form

$$\sigma_{\tilde{x},\tilde{a}} \overset{d}{=} \{f \mid f \in \{0,1\}^X \ \& \ f(x_j) = a_j , \ j \in I_m\} ;$$

$$x_j \in X_j, \ a_j \in \{0,1\}, \ m \geq 1 .$$

A typical open set for $\mathscr{T}(\mathfrak{B}_o)$ is a union of sets of the form

$$\phi^{-1}(\sigma_{\tilde{x},a}) \underline{\cap} \mathfrak{B}_o = \mathfrak{C}_{C'} \cap \mathfrak{D}_{X \dashv (G' \dashv C')} = M(C', G' \dashv C')(\text{extended}) ;$$

$$C' \overset{d}{=} \{x_j \mid a_j = 1 , \ j \in I_m\} \subseteq G' = \{x_j \mid j \in I_m\} ,$$

where the following is defined: Let $B \in \mathscr{P}(X)$ be arbitrary fixed. The *superset coverage class* on B , which becomes the *one-point coverage class* on x when $B = \{x\}$, $x \in X$; the *subset coverage class* under B ; and the *incidence* (or trapping) *class* relative to $B \in \mathscr{P}(X)$, respectively;

$$\mathfrak{C}_B \overset{d}{=} \{C \mid B \subseteq C \in \mathfrak{B}_o\} ; \ \mathfrak{D}_B \overset{d}{=} \{C \mid \emptyset \neq C \subseteq B , \ C \in \mathfrak{B}_o\} ;$$

$$\mathfrak{E}_B \overset{d}{=} \{C \mid C \mathbin{\Delta} B, \ C \in \mathfrak{B}_o\} .$$

The above concepts are closely related to that of filter classes. Indeed, relative to $\mathfrak{B}_o$, subset coverage classes are all ultrafilters. (See the remark at the end of the appendix of this section).

$\mathfrak{C}_B$, $\mathfrak{D}_B$, and $\mathfrak{E}_B$ are all closed-compact for $\mathscr{T}(\mathfrak{B}_o)$. If $B \in \mathfrak{F}(X)$, then additionally they are all open. Define also the *special projection* map

$$p_G : \mathscr{P}(X) \to \mathscr{P}(G) ; \ p_G(C) \overset{d}{=} C \cap G ; \text{ all } G \in \mathfrak{F}(X) , \ C \in \mathscr{P}(X) .$$

Then letting

$$\mathscr{W}(\mathfrak{B}_o) \overset{d}{=} \bigcup_{G \in \mathfrak{F}(X)} \mathscr{W}_G(\mathfrak{B}_o) ; \ \mathscr{W}_G(\mathfrak{B}_o) \overset{d}{=} p_G^{-1}(\mathscr{P}\mathscr{P}(G)) \underline{\cap} \mathfrak{B}_o ,$$

the first being a Boolean ring over $\mathfrak{B}_o$, the second a σ-algebra for each G ;

$$\mathcal{T}(\mathcal{B}_o) = \text{top}(\mathcal{W}(\mathcal{B}_o)) = \sigma(\mathcal{W}(\mathcal{B}_o)) = \sigma(\mathcal{C}_{\{x\}} \mid x \in X) \subseteq \sigma(\mathcal{T}(\mathcal{B}_o))$$
$$= \sigma(\mathcal{C}_1(\mathcal{B}_o)) ,$$

where $\mathcal{C}_1(\mathcal{B}_o)$ is the class of all compact sets relative to $\mathcal{T}(\mathcal{B}_o)$. In addition, it easily follows that $\mathcal{C}_B$, $\mathcal{D}_B$, $\mathcal{E}_B \in \sigma(\mathcal{W}(\mathcal{B}_o))$; all $B \in \mathcal{P}(X)$. All the above equations and all related results carry over to $\{0,1\}^X$ and $\mathcal{F}(X)$ via the membership function ϕ .

A *primitive random set* (see also Wang and Sanchez [262]) is a mapping S_o , where for given probability space $(\Omega,\mathcal{A},Pr)$ and any $\mathcal{C}_{\{x\}}$, assumed $\in \mathcal{B}_o$, all $x \in X$,

$$S_o : \Omega \to \mathcal{B}_o \ ; \ S_o^{-1}(\mathcal{C}_{\{x\}}) \in \mathcal{A} \ ; \text{ all } x \in X .$$

Any primitive random subset S_o of X can be extended uniquely, using the above equations and standard measure extension procedures to correspond to the complete regular Borel probability space (with regularity involving finite coverages)

$$(\mathcal{B}_o, \sigma(\mathcal{C}_1(\mathcal{B}_o)), \nu_{S_o}) \ ; \ \nu_{S_o} \overset{d}{=} Pr \circ S_o^{-1} .$$

This extension, also denoted as S_o , is called a *random subset* of X with range $\mathcal{B}_o$ generated by the primitive random set. Corresponding to the above coverage classes, S_o generates *coverage functions* (by computing probabilities of coverages).

Note the distinction between specifying a one-point coverage function $Pr(x \in S_o) = \nu_{S_o}(\mathcal{C}_{\{x\}})$ as a function of x , and S_o itself as a primitive random set. The former in general is highly nonunique. Thus, for any $C \in \mathcal{P}(X)$,

$$Pr(S \in \mathcal{C}_C) = Pr \circ S^{-1}(\mathcal{C}_C) = Pr(C \subseteq S)$$

as a function of C, $\mu_{(S)}(C)$, is the *subset coverage function* $\mu_{(S)}$ for S . In particular, for $C = \{x\}$, $x \in X$;

$$Pr(S \in \mathcal{C}_{\{x\}}) = Pr(x \in S)$$

as a function of all $x \in C$ is the <u>one point coverage function</u> $\mu_{(S)}(\{\cdot\})$ for S ;

$$Pr(S \in \mathcal{D}_C) = Pr \circ S^{-1}(\mathcal{D}_C) = Pr(\emptyset \neq S \subseteq C)$$

as a function of C, $\mu_{(S)^{(1)}}(C)$, is the *superset coverage function* $\mu_{(S)^{(1)}}$ for S ;

$$Pr(S \in \mathcal{E}_C) = Pr\circ S^{-1}(\mathcal{E}_C) = Pr(S \mathrel{\Lambda} C)$$

as a function of C, $\mu_{(S)^{(2)}}(C)$, is the *incidence function* $\mu_{(S)^{(2)}}$ of S ; $Pr(S \in \mathcal{E}_{CC}) = Pr\circ S^{-1}(\mathcal{E}_{CC}) = Pr(S \not\subseteq C)$, as a function of C , $\mu_3(C)$, is the *complement-incidence function* $\mu_{(S)}(3)$ of S .

The basic construction of random sets will now be given in detain in Theorem 1.

Theorem 1 (Construction of Random Sets from Primitive Random Sets).

If S_o is a primitive random subset of X with range $\mathfrak{B}_o$, then S_o induces the unique probability space $(\mathfrak{B}_o, \sigma(\mathcal{C}_o(\mathfrak{B}_o)), \nu_{S_o})$, where ν_{S_o} can be uniquely extended in stages over the nested σ-algebras $\sigma(\mathcal{C}_o(\mathfrak{B}_o)) \subseteq \sigma(\mathcal{C}_1(\mathfrak{B}_o)) \subseteq \bar{\sigma}(\mathcal{C}_1(\mathfrak{B}_o))$, the Baire, Borel, and complete σ-algebras, respectively.

Proof:

The construction of ν_{S_o} proceeds as follows:

(I) Define for each $x \in X$, $\nu_{S_o}(\mathcal{C}_{\{x\}}) \overset{d}{=} Pr(S_o^{-1}(\mathcal{C}_{\{x\}}(\mathfrak{B}_o))$ and more generally, for any $C \in \mathfrak{F}(X)$ by

$$\mu_{(S_o)}(C) \overset{d}{=} \nu_{S_o}(\mathcal{C}_C(\mathfrak{B}_o) \overset{d}{=} Pr(S_o^{-1}(\bigcap_{x\in C} \mathcal{C}_{\{x\}}(\mathfrak{B}_o))) = Pr(\bigcap_{x\in C} S_o^{-1}(\mathcal{C}_{\{x\}}(\mathfrak{B}_o))).$$

Similarly, define the collection of 0 - 1 random variables $\underset{\sim}{V}(S_o) \overset{d}{=} (V_x(S_o))_{x\in X}$ through the joint probability relations,

$$Pr(\underset{x\in C}{\&}(V_x(S_o) = 1)) = \mu_{(S_o)}(C) \ , \ C \in \mathfrak{F}(X) \ .$$

Note that $\mu_{(S_o)}(C)$ as a function of C is a doubt measure over $\mathfrak{F}(X)$, since, for $B_1, \ldots, B_n \in \mathfrak{F}(X)$ arbitrary,

$$0 \le \mu_{(S_o)}(\mathcal{C}_{B_n} \dashv \bigcup_{j=1}^{n-1} \mathcal{C}_{B_j \cup B_n}) = Pr(S_o^{-1}(\mathcal{C}_{B_n} \dashv \bigcup_{j=1}^{n-1} \mathcal{C}_{B_j \cup B_n}))$$

$$= Pr(S_o^{-1}(\mathcal{C}_{B_n}) \dashv \bigcup_{j=1}^{n-1} S_o^{-1}(\mathcal{C}_{B_j \cup B_n}))$$

$$= 1 - \Pr((\Omega \dashv S_o^{-1}(\mathcal{C}_{B_n})) \cup \bigcup_{j=1}^{n-1} S_o^{-1}(\mathcal{C}_{B_j \cup B_n}))$$

$$= \Pr(S_o^{-1}(\mathcal{C}_{B_n})) - \sum_{\emptyset \neq K \subseteq \{1,\ldots n-1\}} (-1)^{\text{card } K+1} \Pr(\bigcap_{j \in K} S_o^{-1}(\mathcal{C}_{B_j \cup B_n}))$$

$$= \Pr(S_o^{-1}(\mathcal{C}_{B_n})) + \sum_{\emptyset \neq K \subseteq \{1,\ldots,n-1\}} (-1)^{\text{card } K} \cdot \Pr(S_o^{-1}(\mathcal{C}_{\bigcup_{(j \in K)} B_j \cup B_n}))$$

$$= \Delta_n(\mu_{(S_o)}, \cup, \underset{\sim}{B}_n) .$$

(II) Thus, by part (I), $\underset{\sim}{V}(S_o)$ is a well-defined (consistent) 0 - 1 stochastic process uniquely determined by $\mu_{(S_o)}$. Then there is a unique probability measure $\nu_{(S_o)}$ which extends $\underset{\sim}{V}(S_o)$ to the Baire and Borel σ-algebra levels, the latter yielding a regularity property, and may be further extended to the complete σ-algebra. (This is due to standard results as may be found in, e.g., Halmos [104'])

(III) By employing the fundamental one-to-one onto mapping $\phi : \mathcal{P}(X) \to \{0,1\}^X$, cut down to $\mathcal{B}_o$, all of these results carry over to $\mathcal{B}_o$ and $\sigma(\mathcal{C}_o(\mathcal{B}_o))$, etc.

More specifically:

(i) Over the Boolean ring $\mathcal{W}(\mathcal{B}_o)$,

$$\nu_{(S_o)}(p_G^{-1}(A)) = \mu^{(1)}_{(S_o)_G}(\mathcal{A}) = \sum_{C \in \mathcal{A}} \mu_{(S_o)_G}(C) , \quad \mathcal{A} \subseteq \mathcal{P}(G) ,$$

$G \in \mathcal{J}(X)$, is well-defined from properties of $\mu_{(S_o)_G}$ (see Theorem 1). Then, using the finite additivity of $\nu_{(S_o)}$ over $\mathcal{W}(\mathcal{B}_o)$ and its downward continuity at $\emptyset$ (using properties of topology $\mathcal{T}(\mathcal{B}_o)$, $\nu_{(S_o)}$ is indeed a probability measure over $\mathcal{W}(\mathcal{B}_o)$. (Note $p_{G_j}^{-1}(\mathcal{A}_j)$, $j = 1,\ldots,n$, will be disjoint iff all the A_j's are disjoint collections of sets and $\mathcal{A}_1,\ldots,\mathcal{A}_m \subseteq \mathcal{P}(\bigcap_{j=1}^{m} G_j)$.)

(ii) Extend $\nu_{(S_o)}$ up to $\sigma(\mathcal{C}_o(\mathcal{B}_o))$ by the usual outer measure procedure. (See, e.g., Halmos [104']) Then, in turn, extend up to $\sigma(\mathcal{C}_1(\mathcal{B}_o))$, noting the regularity property associated with $\sigma(\mathcal{C}_1(\mathcal{B}_o))$. (Again, see Halmos [104'].) However, the last property may be improved upon by using the structure of $\mathcal{T}(\mathcal{B}_o)$:

Let $\mathcal{A} \in \sigma(\mathcal{C}_1(\mathcal{B}_o))$ be arbitrary. Then by regularity of $\nu_{(S_o)}$ over $\sigma(\mathcal{C}_1(\mathcal{B}_o))$, $\exists$ sequences of classes of sets from $\mathcal{B}_o$, $\mathcal{C}_{(1)} \subseteq \mathcal{C}_{(2)} \subseteq \cdots \subseteq \mathcal{A} \subseteq \cdots \subseteq \mathcal{A}_{(2)} \subseteq \mathcal{A}_{(1)}$, where $\mathcal{C}_{(j)} \in \mathcal{C}_1(\mathcal{B}_o)$ and $\mathcal{A}_{(j)} \in \mathcal{Y}(\mathcal{B}_o)$, $j = 1,2,\ldots,$ with $\lim_{j\to\infty} \uparrow \nu_{(S_o)}(\mathcal{C}_{(j)}) = \nu_{(S_o)}(\mathcal{A}) = \lim_{j\to\infty} \downarrow \nu_{(S_o)}(\mathcal{A}_{(j)})$. But $\mathcal{A}_{(j)}$ as an open set for $\mathcal{Y}(\mathcal{B}_o)$ is in the form $\mathcal{A}_{(j)} = \bigcup_{\alpha\in J_1} p_{G_\alpha}^{-1}(\{C_\alpha\})$, for some $C_\alpha \subseteq G_\alpha \in \mathcal{J}(X)$, J_1 an arbitrary index set. Then by the compactness of say $\mathcal{C}_{(j)}$, $\exists$ finite integer m_j , say, such that $\mathcal{C}_{(j)} \subseteq \mathcal{E}_{(j)} \overset{d}{=} \bigcup_{k=1}^{m_j} p_{G_{j_k}}^{-1}(\{C_{j_k}\})$. By choosing j such that $\mathcal{C}_{(j)} \subseteq A$, $\nu_{(S_o)}(\mathcal{C}_{(j)}) \le \nu_{(S_o)}(\mathcal{A}) \le \nu_{(S_o)}(\mathcal{C}_{(j)}) + 1/j$ we finally obtain

$$\nu_{(S_o)}(\mathcal{E}_j) - 1/j \le \sum_{k=1}^{m_j}\left(\nu_{(S_o)}(p_{G_{j_k}}^{-1}(\{C_{j_k}\}))\right) - 1/j \le \nu_{(S_o)}(\mathcal{A}) \le$$

$$\nu_{(S_o)}(\mathcal{E}_{(j)}) + 1/j \le \sum_{k=1}^{m_j}\left(\nu_{(S_o)}(p_{G_{j_k}}^{-1}(\{C_{j_k}\}))\right) + 1/j ,$$

yielding, without loss of generality,

$$\nu_{(S_o)}(\mathcal{A}) = \lim_{j\to\infty} \downarrow \nu_{(S_o)}(\mathcal{E}_{(j)}) = \lim_{j\to\infty} \downarrow \sum_{k=1}^{m_j}\left(\nu_{(S_o)}(p_{G_{j_k}}^{-1}(\{C_{j_k}\}))\right)$$

with $\nu(\mathcal{A} \dashv \mathcal{E}_{(j)}) < 1/j$ and $\mathcal{A} \cap \mathcal{C}_{(j)} = \mathcal{C}_{(j)} \subseteq \mathcal{E}_{(j)}$, for $j = 1,2,\ldots$

In particular, for $\mathcal{A} = \mathcal{C}_C(\mathcal{B}_o)$, $C \in \mathcal{P}(X)$, we can show

$$\mathcal{E}_{(j)} = \bigcup_{k=1}^{m_j} p_{G_{j_k}}(\{G_{j_k}\}) = \bigcup_{k=1}^{m_j} \mathcal{C}_{G_{j_k}}$$ may be chosen, etc.

(iii) Finally, letting (see Halmos, Theorem D, p. 239)

$\mathcal{N}_{\nu_{(S_o)}}(\mathcal{B}_o) \overset{d}{=} \{\mathcal{A} \mid \mathcal{A} \in \mathcal{B}_o \ \&\ \exists\ \mathcal{A}' \in \mathcal{B}_o$ with $\mathcal{A} \subseteq \mathcal{A}'$, $\nu_{(S_o)}(\mathcal{A}') = 0\}$, we can let $\bar{\sigma}(\mathcal{C}_1(\mathcal{B}_o)) = \sigma(\mathcal{C}_1(\mathcal{B}_o)) \,\underline{\cup}\, \mathcal{N}_{\nu_{(S_o)}}(\mathcal{B}_o) = \sigma(\mathcal{C}_1(\mathcal{B}_o) \,\underline{\cup}\, \mathcal{N}_{\nu_{(S_o)}}(\mathcal{B}_o))$, where for any

$$\mathcal{A} \in \sigma(\mathcal{C}_1(\mathcal{B}_o)) \text{ and } \mathcal{B} \in \mathcal{N}_{\nu_{(S_o)}}(\mathcal{B}_o) \text{ , } \nu_{S_o}(\mathcal{A} \underline{\cup} \mathcal{B}) = \nu_{S_o}(\mathcal{A}) \text{ .}$$

Remark

The following natural relations hold for any $\mathcal{A} \in \bar{\sigma}(\mathcal{C}_1(\mathcal{B}_o))$, $C \in \mathcal{P}(X)$.

$$\nu_{(S_o)}(\mathcal{A}) = \Pr(S_o \in \mathcal{A}) = \Pr(S_o^{-1}(\mathcal{A})) \text{ .}$$

$$\nu_{(S_o)}(\mathcal{C}_C(\mathcal{B}_o)) = \Pr(S_o \in \mathcal{C}_C(\mathcal{B}_o)) = \Pr(C \subseteq S_o) = \mu_{(S_o)}(C) \text{ .}$$

In particular, for $C = \{x\}$, $x \in X$,

$$\nu_{(S_o)}(\mathcal{C}_{\{x\}}(\mathcal{B}_o)) = \Pr(S_o \in \mathcal{C}_{\{x\}}(\mathcal{B}_o)) = \Pr(x \in S_o)$$
$$= \nu_{(S_o)}(\mathcal{E}_{\{x\}}(\mathcal{B}_o)) = \mu_{(S_o)}(\{x\}) \text{ .}$$

$$\nu_{(S_o)}(\mathcal{D}_C(\mathcal{B}_o)) = \Pr(S_o \in \mathcal{D}_C(\mathcal{B}_o)) = \Pr(S \subseteq C) \text{ ,}$$

$$\nu_{(S_o)}(\mathcal{E}_C(\mathcal{B}_o)) = \Pr(S_o \in \mathcal{E}_C(\mathcal{B}_o)) = \Pr(S \cap C \neq \emptyset) \text{ ,}$$

$$\nu_{(S_o)}(\mathcal{E}_{X \dashv C}(\mathcal{B}_o)) = \Pr(S_o \in \mathcal{E}_{X \dashv C}(\mathcal{B}_o)) = \Pr(S \not\subseteq C) \text{ ,}$$

$$S_o = \phi^{-1}(\underset{\sim}{V}(S_o)) \cap \mathcal{B}_o \text{ ,}$$

$$(\phi(S_o))(\{x\}) = \phi_{S_o}(\{x\}) = V_x(S_o) \text{ , etc.}$$

Dempster [46] first obtained the following important relations.

Theorem 2 (Dempster's Theorem [46] - Justification for the Use of Terms Upper and Lower Probability Measures as Alternates for Plausibility and Belief Measures.)

Let $(\Omega, \mathcal{G}, \Pr)$ be a given probability space with $S_o : \Omega \to \mathcal{B}_o$, $\{\emptyset, X\} \subseteq \mathcal{B}_o \subseteq \mathcal{P}(X)$, S_o being a random subset of X , thus inducing probability space $(\mathcal{B}_o, \bar{\sigma}(\mathcal{C}_1(\mathcal{B}_o)), \nu_{S_o})$.

Then, for any $f : \Omega \to X$ such that f is $(\mathcal{G}, \mathcal{D})$-measurable, where $\mathcal{D} \subseteq \mathcal{B}_o$ is a σ-algebra, and $f(\omega) \in S_o(\omega)$, $\forall\, \omega \in \Omega$, the induced probability measure under f , $\Pr \circ f^{-1}$ over $\mathcal{D}$ satisfies the inequalities

$$\mu_{(S_o)(1)}(C) \overset{d}{=} \Pr(\emptyset \neq S_o \subseteq C) \leq \Pr \circ f^{-1}(C) \leq \Pr(S_o \cap C \neq \emptyset)$$
$$\overset{d}{=} \mu_{(S_o)(2)}(C)$$

for all $C \in \mathcal{D}$.

Proof:

Straightforward, see Dempster [46] for further details and related results.

Note that for $C = \{x\}$, $x \in X$, Dempster's inequality becomes

$$\Pr(S_o = \{x\}) \le \Pr\circ f^{-1}(x) \le \Pr(x \in S_o) .$$

Theorem 3 (Uncertainty Measures as Random Set Coverage Functions)

Let X be a given base space with $\{\emptyset, X\} \subseteq \mathfrak{B}_o \subseteq \mathcal{P}(X)$. Then

(i) If μ is a doubt measure over $\mathfrak{F}(X)$, then μ can be extended uniquely to $\mathcal{P}(X)$ such that there exists a (unique) complete - (finitely) regular probability space, i.e.,

$(\mathfrak{B}_o, \bar{\sigma}_\mu(\mathcal{C}_1(\mathfrak{B}_o)), \nu_{S_\mu})$ corresponding to random subset S_μ of X with range $\mathfrak{B}_o$ such that for all $C \in \mathcal{P}(X)$

$$\mu(C) = \Pr(S_\mu \in \mathcal{C}_C(\mathfrak{B}_o)) = \nu_{S_\mu}(\mathcal{C}_C(\mathfrak{B}_o))$$
$$(= \Pr(C \subseteq S_\mu)) .$$

(ii) If μ is a plausibility measure over $\mathfrak{F}(X)$, then μ can be uniquely extended to $\mathcal{P}(X)$ such that there exists a (unique) complete - (finitely) regular probability space, i.e.,

$(\mathfrak{B}_o, \bar{\sigma}_{1-\mu}(\mathcal{C}_1(\mathfrak{B}_o)), \nu_{S_{1-\mu}}(\underline{\complement}\cdot))$ corresponding to random subset $\underline{\complement}\cdot S_{1-\mu}$ of X with range $\mathfrak{B}_o$ such that for all $C \in \mathcal{P}(X)$

$$\mu(C) = \Pr(\underline{\complement}\cdot S_{1-\mu} \in \mathcal{E}_C(\mathfrak{B}_o))$$
$$= 1 - \nu_{S_{1-\mu}}(\mathcal{C}_C(\mathfrak{B}_o))$$
$$(= \Pr(C \cap \underline{\complement}S_{1-\mu} \ne \emptyset)) .$$

(iii) If μ is a belief measure over $\mathcal{P}(X) \dashv \mathfrak{F}(X)$ then μ can be uniquely extended to $\mathcal{P}(X)$ such that there exists a (unique) complete (finitely) regular probability space

$(\mathfrak{B}_o, \bar{\sigma}_{\mu(\underline{\complement}\cdot)}(\mathcal{C}_1(\mathfrak{B}_o)), \nu_{S_{\mu(\underline{\complement}\cdot)}}(\underline{\complement}\cdot))$ corresponding to random subset $\underline{\complement}\cdot S_{\mu(\underline{\complement}\cdot)}$ of X with range $\mathfrak{B}_o$ such that for all $C \in \mathcal{P}(X)$,

$$\mu(C) = \Pr(\underline{\complement}\cdot S_{\mu(\underline{\complement}\cdot)} \in \mathfrak{D}_C(\mathfrak{B}_o))$$
$$= \nu_{S_{\mu(\underline{\complement}\cdot)}}(\underline{\complement}\cdot\mathfrak{D}_C(\mathfrak{B}_o)) \ (= \Pr(\emptyset \ne \underline{\complement}\cdot S_{\mu(\underline{\complement}\cdot)} \subseteq C)) .$$

(iv) If μ is a disbelief measure over $\mathcal{P}(X) \dashv \mathfrak{F}(X)$ then μ can be extended uniquely to $\mathcal{P}(X)$ such that there exists a (unique) complete (finitely) regular probability space

$(\mathfrak{B}_o, \bar{\sigma}_{1-\mu(\underline{\complement}\cdot)}(\mathcal{C}_1(\mathfrak{B}_o)), \nu_{1-\mu(\underline{\complement}\cdot)}(\underline{\complement}\cdot))$ corresponding to random subset $\underline{C}S_{1-\mu(\underline{C}\cdot)}$ of X with range $\mathfrak{B}_o$ such that for all $C \in \mathcal{P}(X)$,

$$\mu(C) = \Pr(\underline{C}\cdot S_{1-\mu(\underline{C}\cdot)} \in \mathcal{E}_{CC}(\mathfrak{B}_o))$$
$$= 1 - \nu_{1-\mu(\underline{C}\cdot)}(\underline{C}\cdot\mathfrak{D}_C(\mathfrak{B}_o))$$
$$(= \Pr(CC \cap \underline{C}\, S_{1-\mu(\underline{C}\cdot)} \neq \emptyset)) .$$

Proof:

First consider $\mathcal{I}(X)$ and $\mathcal{P}(X) \dashv \mathcal{I}(X)$, where appropriate. For (i), since μ is a doubt measure, we can replace in part (I) of the construction in Theorem 1, $\mu_{(S_o)}$ by μ. Parts (II) and (III) follow, (ii) - (iv) follow by using Lemma 4, Chapter 3 in conjunction with part (i) above.

Finally, consider again (i) for the unique extension from $\mathcal{I}(X)$ to $\mathcal{P}(X)$. Cases (ii) - (iv) will follow similarly. The finite regularity property for S_o, shown in III (ii) of Theorem 1 and the result shown first - $\mu(C) = \nu_{S_o}(\mathcal{C}_C), \forall\ C \in \mathcal{I}(X)$, demonstrate that for $C \in \mathcal{P}(X)$ arbitrary, we should define

$$\mu(C) \overset{d}{=} \lim_{j\to\infty} \downarrow \sum_{k=1}^{m_j} \mu(G_{j_k}) ,$$

the definition not depending on the particular convergence sequence, etc. (See also related results of Höhle [116] and Goodman [90].)

Theorem 4 (Natural Imbedding of a Random Variable as a Random Set.)

Let μ be a finitely additive probability measure over the Boolean ring $\mathcal{I}(X) \cup (X \dashv \mathcal{I}(X))$. Then μ can be uniquely extended to $\mathcal{P}(X)$ such that there exists a unique (complete finitely regular) probability space $(\mathcal{P}(X), \mathcal{P}\mathcal{P}(X), \nu_{(\mu)})$ corresponding to random subset $S_{\nu_{(\mu)}}$ of X such that for all $C \in \mathcal{P}(X)$,

$$\mu(C) = \Pr(\emptyset \neq S_{\nu_{(\mu)}} \subseteq C) = \Pr(S_{\nu_{(\mu)}} \cap C \neq \emptyset) .$$

More specifically $S_{\nu_{(\mu)}}$ can be shown to correspond to probability subspace $(\hat{X}, \mathcal{P}(\hat{X}), \nu_{(\mu)})$, where for any $C \in \mathcal{P}(X)$, $\hat{C} \overset{d}{=} \{\{x\} \mid x \in C\} \subseteq \mathcal{P}(X)$, and where, for any $\mathcal{A} \in \mathcal{P}\mathcal{P}(X)$,

$$\nu_{(\mu)}(\mathcal{A}) = \nu_{(\mu)}(\mathcal{A} \cap \hat{X}) = \mu(\cup(\mathcal{A} \cap \hat{X})) .$$

In particular, for any C

$$\nu_{(\mu)}(\mathcal{C}_C(\mathcal{P}(X))) = \begin{cases} 0 & \text{iff} \quad \text{card}\, C \geq 2\ , \quad C \in \mathcal{P}(X) \\ \mu(\{x\}) & \text{iff} \quad C = \{x\}\ , \quad x \in X\ . \end{cases}$$

(<u>**Proof**</u>:

From Theorem 4, Chapter 3, μ is both a plausibility and belief measure. Then $S_{\nu_{(\mu)}}$ satisfies these conditions; then use uniqueness of constructions as in previous theorems.)

<u>**Theorem 5**</u> (Converse to Theorem 3:) (Random Set Coverage Functions as Uncertainty Measures)

Let X be a given base space, with $\{\emptyset, X\} \subseteq \mathcal{B}_o \subseteq \mathcal{P}(X)$ and S_o some random subset of X with range $\mathcal{B}_o$ corresponding to probability space $(\mathcal{B}_o, \overline{\sigma}(\mathcal{C}_1(\mathcal{B}_o)), \nu_{S_o})$. Then as functions of $C \in \mathcal{P}(X)$,

$$\mu_{(S_o)}(C) \overset{d}{=} \nu_{S_o}(\mathcal{C}_C(\mathcal{B}_o)) = \Pr(C \subseteq S_o)\ ,$$

$$\nu_{S_o}(\mathcal{D}_C(\mathcal{B}_o)) = \Pr(S_o \subseteq C)\ ,$$

$$\nu_{S_o}(\mathcal{E}_C(\mathcal{B}_o)) = \Pr(S_o \cap C \neq \emptyset)\ ,$$

$$\nu_{S_o}(\mathcal{E}_{X \dashv C}(\mathcal{B}_o)) = \Pr(S_o \not\subseteq C)\ ,$$

the first is a doubt measure, the second is a belief measure, the third a plausibility measure, and the fourth is a disbelief measure.

<u>**Proof**</u>:

Let $\underset{\sim}{B}_n = (B_1, \ldots, B_n)$, $B_j \in \mathcal{P}(X)$, $j = 1, \ldots, n$. For the first, use

$$0 \leq \nu_{S_o}(\mathcal{C}_{B_n}(\mathcal{B}_o) \dashv \bigcup_{j=1}^{n-1} \mathcal{C}_{B_j \cup B_n}(\mathcal{B}_o))$$

$$= 1 - \nu_{S_o}(\mathcal{B}_o \dashv \mathcal{C}_{B_n}(\mathcal{B}_o)) - \nu_{S_o}(\bigcup_{j=1}^{n-1} \mathcal{C}_{B_j \cup B_n}(\mathcal{B}_o))\ .$$

Expand the last union in terms of intersections. Then use Lemma 4, Chapter 3. For example, $\nu_{S_o}(\mathcal{E}_C(\mathcal{B}_o))$ is a plausibility measure w.r.t. C iff $1 - \nu_{S_o}(\mathcal{E}_C(\mathcal{B}_o)) = \nu_{\underline{\mathcal{C}}S_o}(\mathcal{C}_C(\mathcal{B}_o))$ is a doubt measure, which follows from the first part of the proof, replacing S_o by $\underline{\mathcal{C}}\, S_o$.

Remark.

Many additional results relating uncertainty measures with random sets may be obtained. For example, Dempster's combination of evidence operator $\oplus$ (see [282], [228]) can be reinterpreted in terms of statistically independent random sets, each representing a doubt measure. Specifically, we can let

$$Bel_i(C) = Pr(\emptyset \neq S_j \subseteq C) \ , \ j = 1,2 \ , \ C \subseteq X \ , \ S_1, \ S_2$$

being statistically independent random subsets of X . Then

$$(Bel_1 \oplus Bel_2)(C) = Pr(\emptyset \neq S_1 \cap S_2 \subseteq C \mid S_1 \cap S_2 \neq \emptyset) \ .$$

Theorem 6 (Approximations)

Let S_o be a random subset of X with range $\mathfrak{B}_o$ corresponding to probability space $(\mathfrak{B}_o, \bar{\sigma}(\mathcal{C}_1(\mathfrak{B}_o)), \nu_{(S_o)})$. Let $f : \mathcal{P}(X) \to \mathbb{R}$ be any $(\bar{\sigma}(\mathcal{C}_1(\mathfrak{B}_o)), \mathbb{B})$-measurable function ($\mathbb{B}$ being the real Borel field) such that f is uniformly bounded by, say M_f . Then defining $E(f(S_o)) \overset{d}{=} \int_{C\in\mathfrak{B}_o} f(C)\, d\nu_{S_o}(C)$, expectation of $f(S_o)$, in the usual way.

For any $j > 0$, $\exists\ G_j \in \mathcal{F}(X)$ such that

(i) $$|E(f(S_o)) - E((f\circ p_{G_j})(S_o))| < 2(M_f + 1)\cdot 1/j \ ,$$

noting

(ii) $$E((f\circ p_{G_j})(S_o)) = \int_{C\in\mathfrak{B}_o} f(p_{G_j}(C))\, d\nu_{(S_o)}(C)$$

$$= \int_{D\in\mathcal{P}(G_j)} f(D)\, d\nu_{(S_o)}(p_{G_j}^{-1}(D)) = \int_{D\in\mathcal{P}(G_j)} f(D)\, d\mu^{(1)}_{(S_o)_{G_j}}(D)$$

$$= E(f(S^{(1)}_{G_j})) \ .$$

(iii) In particular, if $f = \phi_{\mathcal{A}}$, where $\mathcal{A} \in \bar{\sigma}(\mathcal{C}_1(\mathfrak{B}_o))$, then

$$E(f(S_o)) = \nu_{(S_o)}(\mathcal{A}) = Pr(S_o) \in \mathcal{A}) \ ,$$

$$E((f\circ p_{G_j})(S_o)) = \nu_{(S_o)}(p_{G_j}^{-1}(\mathcal{A})) = \mu^{(1)}_{(S_o)_{G_j}}(\mathcal{A} \underline{\cap} G_j)$$

$$= \Pr(S^{(1)}_{G_j} \in \mathcal{A} \sqcap G_j) \ .$$

Note also the regularity approximations from Theorem 1 .

Proof:

First use a form of Lusin's Theorem (Halmos [104'], pp. 242, 243) to obtain $\mathcal{A}_j \in \mathcal{C}_1(\mathfrak{B}_o)$ with $\nu_{(S_o)}(\mathfrak{B}_o \dashv \mathcal{A}_j) \leq 1/j$ and $(f|A_j)$ continuous. Then consider $\mathcal{K}_j \stackrel{d}{=} \{g\circ(p_G|\mathcal{A}_j) \mid G \in \mathfrak{f}(X),\ g : \mathcal{P}(G) \to \mathbb{R}\}$. Each g, $(p_G|A_j)$ and hence $g\circ(p_G|\mathcal{A}_j) \in \mathcal{K}_j$ is continuous. For $* = +$ or $\cdot$, $(g_1\circ p_{G_1})*(g_2\circ p_{G_2}) = ((g_1\circ p_{G_1})*(g_2\circ p_{G_2}))\circ p_{G_1\cup G_2} \in \mathcal{K}_j$, implying that $\mathcal{K}_j$ is an algebra of functions including all constant functions $\lambda\circ p_G \equiv \lambda$, $\lambda \in \mathbb{R}$. Let $G_1, G_2 \in \mathfrak{f}(X)$ be such that $G_1 \neq G_2$, $\emptyset$, say. Then $p_{G_1 \dashv G_2}(\{G_2\}) = \emptyset$ and $p_{G_1\dashv G_2}(G_1) = G_1 \dashv G_2 \neq \emptyset$. Since $\mathcal{T}(\mathfrak{B}_o)$ is compact Hausdorff, it is normal and T_1 , the latter implying $\{\emptyset\}$, $\{G_1 \dashv G_2\}$ are closed sets. Urysohn's Lemma then implies $\exists$ g continuous $g : \mathfrak{B}_o \to [0,1]$ such that $g(\emptyset) = 0$, $g(G_1 \dashv G_2) = 1$. Hence $(g\circ p_{G_1\dashv G_2})(\{G_2\}) = 0$, $(g\circ p_{G_1\dashv G_2})(\{G_1\}) = 1$, and thus $\mathcal{K}_j$ is a separating algebra. Hence by the Stone-Weierstrass Theorem, $\exists$ $G_j \in \mathfrak{f}(X)$, $g_j : \mathcal{P}(G_j) \to \mathbb{R}$ such that $\sup_{C\in\mathcal{A}_j} |f(C) - (g_j\circ p_{G_j})(C)| < 1/j$. Then for $C \in \mathcal{A}_j$,

$$|E(f(S_o)) - E((f\circ p_{G_j})(S_o))|$$

$$\leq \int_{C\in\mathfrak{B}_o \dashv \mathcal{A}_j} (|f(C)| + |f(C \cap C_j)|)d\nu_{(S_o)}(C)$$

$$+ \int_{C\in\mathcal{A}_j} |f(C) - (g_j\circ p_{G_j})(C)|d\nu_{(S_o)}(C)$$

$$+ \int_{C\in\mathcal{A}_j} |(f\circ p_{G_j})(C) - (g_j\circ p_{G_j})(C)|d\nu_{(S_o)}(C)$$

$$\leq (1/j)\cdot(M_f + M_f) + (1/j)\cdot 1 + (1/j)\cdot 1$$

Remark.

The degree of information lost by S_o approximating f may be measured by the *cross entropy*, assuming X is finite, letting $V = \mathrm{id}$ correspond to $(\Omega,\mathcal{A},\Pr)$, where

$$\mathrm{Ent}(f(V),S_o) \overset{d}{=} \sum_{\begin{bmatrix}\text{all } x\in X\\ B\in\mathcal{B}_o\end{bmatrix}} - \Pr(f^{-1}(x) \mid S_o^{-1}(B))\cdot\log(\Pr(f^{-1}(x)\mid S_o^{-1}(B))) ,$$

subject to the constraint

$$S_o \in \mathcal{R}_f(X) = \{S_o \mid S_o \in \mathcal{R}(X) \ \&\ f(\omega) \in S_o(\omega) , \text{ all } \omega \in \Omega\} ,$$

where $\mathcal{R}(X)$ is the class of all random subsets of X.

Then clearly for any given $f : \Omega \to X$ as above

$$\sup_{S_o \in \mathcal{R}_f(X)} \mathrm{Ent}(f(V),S_o) = \mathrm{Ent}(f(V)) = \sum_{x\in X} - \Pr(f^{-1}(x))\cdot\log \Pr(f^{-1}(x)) ,$$

occurring for $S_o \equiv X$, and

$$\inf_{S_o \in \mathcal{R}_f(X)} \mathrm{Ent}(f(V),S_o) = 0 ,$$

occurring for $S_o = \{f(V)\}$, i.e., $S_o(\omega) \equiv \{f(\omega)\}$.

Remarks. Marginal and Joint Random Sets and Functions.

Let $(\Omega,\mathcal{G},\Pr)$ be a given probability space with $S_o : \Omega \to \mathcal{B}_o$ a random subset of X with range $\mathcal{B}_o \subseteq \mathcal{P}(X)$.

Often, in practice, there is some index set J_o such that $\Omega = \times_{j\in J} \mathcal{B}_j$, $\emptyset \neq \mathcal{B}_j \subset \mathcal{P}(X_j)$, $j \in J_o$, with

$$\mathcal{G} \supseteq \bigotimes_{j\in J_o} \mathcal{G}_j \overset{d}{=} \sigma(\{ \times_{j\in J_1} \mathcal{A}_j \times \times_{j\in J_o - J_1} \mathcal{B}_j \mid \mathcal{A}_j \in \mathcal{G}_j,\ j \in J_1 \subseteq J_o \text{ arb. finite}\}) ,$$

where for each $j \in J_1$, $\mathcal{G}_j \supseteq \mathcal{C}_1(\mathcal{B}_j)$ or $\supseteq \mathcal{V}(\mathcal{B}_j)$. It can be shown that for $\bigotimes_{j\in J_o} \mathcal{G}$, we can replace $\mathcal{A}_j$ by $\mathcal{C}_{\{x_j\}}$ or $\mathcal{C}_{C_j}$ or $\{\mathcal{C}_{C_j},\mathcal{D}_{X_j - B_j}\}$, for $x_j \in X_j$, C_j, $B_j \in \mathcal{I}(X_j)$ arb., $j \in J_1$. In addition, we may take $S_k = \mathrm{proj}_k$, where for any $\underset{\sim}{B} \overset{d}{=} (B_j)_{j\in J_o} \in \Omega$, $B_j \in \mathcal{B}_j$, $j \in J_o$, $\mathrm{proj}_k(\underset{\sim}{B}) \overset{d}{=} B_k$, for some fixed $k \in J_o$. (In particular, if J_o is a singleton, say $\{0\}$, then $\Omega = \mathcal{B}_o$ and $S_o = \mathrm{id}$ over $(\Omega,\mathcal{A},\Pr)$.) We say that S_k, $k \in J_o$, is a *marginal random subset* of X_j corresponding to probability space $(\mathcal{B}_k,\mathcal{G}_k,\Pr_{S_k})$, $\Pr_{S_k} = \Pr\circ\mathrm{proj}_k^{-1}$, and $(S_k)_{k\in J_o}$ is a J_o*-joint collection of random subsets* of each X_j, $j \in J_o$.

Other relations between random subsets are required. For example, if $J_o = \{1,2\}$, $X_1 = X_2 = X$ and $\forall\ C \in \mathcal{P}(X)$, $\mathcal{C}_C \in \mathcal{B}_o$,

$(\mathfrak{B}_1 = \mathfrak{B}_2 = \mathfrak{B}_o)$ and the conditional probability measure here is well defined, then

$$Pr(S_1 \subseteq S_2) = E_{S_1}(Pr_{(S_2|S_1)}(S_1 \subseteq S_2 \mid S_1)\ , \text{ etc.}$$

Let $\underset{\sim}{S} \overset{d}{=} (S_j)_{j\in J_o}$ be a J_o-joint family of random subsets corresponding to probability space $(\underset{j\in J_o}{\times} \mathfrak{B}_j, \mathcal{G}, Pr)$ as above. Let $* : \underset{j\in J_o}{\times} \mathcal{P}(X_j) \to \mathcal{P}(X_o)$ be a given ordinary set operation such that $*$ is $(\underset{j\in J_o}{\otimes} \mathcal{G}_j, \mathcal{C}_{\{x\}}(rng(*)))$-measurable for all $x \in X_o$. Then $*\circ\underset{\sim}{S}$ is a random subset of X_o, since functional inverses preserve all ordinary set operations, noting $X \dashv \mathcal{C}_{\{x\}} = \mathfrak{D}_{X\dashv\{x\}}$, etc.

$$(*\circ\underset{\sim}{S})^{-1}(\mathcal{V}(rng(*))) = \underset{\sim}{S}^{-1}(*^{-1}\mathcal{V}(rng(*))) \subseteq \underset{\sim}{S}^{-1}(\underset{j\in J_o}{\otimes} \mathcal{G}_j) = \underset{j\in J_o}{\otimes} \mathcal{G}_j\ .$$

Hence $(*\circ\underset{\sim}{S})^{-1}(\sigma(\mathcal{V}(rng(*)))) \subseteq \underset{j\in J_o}{\otimes} \mathcal{G}_j$. $*\circ\underset{\sim}{S}$ corresponds to probability space $(rng(*), \sigma(\mathcal{V}(rng(*))), Pr\circ *^{-1})$.

Example 1. Let $f : X_1 \to X_o$ be arbitrary. Let S_1 be a random subset of X_1, corresponding to probability space $(\mathfrak{B}_1, \mathcal{G}_1, Pr_{S_1})$, where $\mathfrak{B}_1 \subseteq \mathcal{P}(X)$, $\mathcal{G}_1 \supseteq \nu(\mathfrak{B}_1)$ is a σ-algebra over $\mathfrak{B}_1$. Consider then the induced set function $\hat{f} : \mathcal{P}(X_1) \to \mathcal{P}(X_o)$. Then for any $x \in X_o$, $\hat{f}^{-1}(\mathcal{C}_{\{x\}}(rng(f))) \cap \mathfrak{B}_1 = \mathcal{C}_{f^{-1}(x)}(\mathfrak{B}_1)$. Thus, if either f is such that f^{-1} is at most countably infinitely valued or $\mathcal{C}_C(\mathfrak{B}_1) \in \mathcal{G} \supseteq \underset{j\in J_o}{\otimes} \mathcal{G}_j$, $\mathcal{G}$ a σ-algebra, then $\hat{f}(S_1)$ will be a random subset of X_o .

Example 2. Consider spaces $\underset{j\in J_o}{\times} \mathcal{P}(X_j)$ and $\mathcal{P}(X_o)$, with joint random sets $\underset{\sim}{S}$ corresponding to probability space $(\underset{j\in J_o}{\times} \mathfrak{B}_j, \mathcal{G}, Pr)$ as above. Let $* : \underset{j\in J_o}{\times} \mathcal{P}(X_j) \to \mathcal{P}(X_o)$ as before. Form the (compact Hausdorff, etc.) topologies $\mathcal{T}(B_j)$, $j \in J_o$ and $\mathcal{T}(rng(*))$. Form the natural product topology

$$\underset{j\in J_o}{\otimes} \mathcal{T}(\mathcal{B}_j) = \left\{ \underset{j\in J_1}{\times} A_j \times \underset{j\in J_o \dashv J_1}{\times} \mathcal{T}_j \mid A_j \in \mathcal{T}_j,\ j \in J_1 \subseteq J_o,\ J_1 \text{ arb.} \right\}^{\cup}$$

which is also compact Hausdorff, etc. Then if $*$ is $(\underset{j\in J_o}{\otimes} \mathcal{T}(\mathcal{B}_j),$ $\mathcal{T}(\mathrm{rng}(*)))$-continuous, then it follows immediately that $*$ is $(\mathcal{G}, \sigma(\mathcal{T}(\mathrm{rng}(*))))$-measurable and hence $*\underset{\sim}{S}$ is a random subset of X_o .

In particular, if $*$ is a composition operation, i.e., $\exists\ \phi_* : \{0,1\}^{J_o} \to \{0,1\}$ such that for any $C_j \in \mathcal{P}(X_j)$, $j \in J_o$, letting $\underset{\sim}{C} \overset{d}{=} (C_j)_{j\in J_o}$, $\phi_{\underset{\sim}{C}} \overset{d}{=} (\phi_{C_j})_{j\in J_o}$,

$$\phi(*(\underset{\sim}{C})) = \phi_* \circ \phi_{\underset{\sim}{C}} ,$$

then $*$ is also continuous in the above sense. Thus, $\cap$, $\cup$, $\dashv$, Δ , etc., are all continuous and hence measurable operations yielding in turn, $\cap \underset{\sim}{S}$, $\cup \underset{\sim}{S}$, $X \dashv \underset{\sim}{S}$ (when $J_o = \{0\}$) , all legitimate random sets.

Specifically, note for $\mathcal{B}_j \subseteq \mathcal{P}(X_j)$ $(X_j \equiv X_1)$

$\cap^{-1}\mathcal{C}_{\{x\}}(\mathrm{rng}(\cap)) = \underset{j\in J_o}{\times} \mathcal{C}_{\{x\}}(\mathcal{B}_j) \in \underset{j\in J_o}{\otimes} \mathcal{G}_j$, and for J_o countably infinite or finite

$$\cup^{-1}\mathcal{C}_{\{x\}}(\mathrm{rng}(\cup)) = \underset{j\in J_o}{\cup} (\mathcal{C}_{\{x\}}(\mathcal{B}_j) \times \underset{k\in J\dashv\{j\}}{\times} \mathcal{B}_k) \in \underset{j\in J_o}{\otimes} \mathcal{G}_j ,$$

$$C^{-1}(\mathcal{C}_{\{x\}}(\mathrm{rng}(\underline{\dashv}))) = C(\mathcal{C}_{\{x\}}(\mathrm{rng}\underline{\dashv})) = \mathcal{D}_{X\dashv\{x\}}(\mathrm{rng}\underline{\dashv}) \in \mathcal{G}_o .$$

All operations on random sets here can be shown to be at least measurable, if not continuous.

Appendix

The Natural Topologies and Sigma Algebras for the Power Class and Membership Function Space of a Given Base Space.

Let X be a given base space, $\{\emptyset, \mathcal{P}(X)\} \subseteq \mathcal{B}_o \subseteq \mathcal{P}(X)$ fixed and recall the definitions for $\mathcal{C}_C(\mathcal{B}_o)$, $\mathcal{D}_C(\mathcal{B}_o)$ and $\mathcal{E}_C(\mathcal{B}_o)$, for any $C \in \mathcal{P}(X)$, and for $\sigma_{\underset{\sim}{x},\underset{\sim}{a}}$, for any $\underset{\sim}{x} = (x_j)_{j\in J_o}$, $\underset{\sim}{a} = (a_j)_{j\in J_o}$, $x_j \in X$, $a_j \in \{0,1\}$, $j \in J_o$, as well as for ϕ the fundamental membership mapping. For each $x \in X$, the set $\{0,1\}^x$ can be identified with $\{0,1\}$ and is assigned the natural discrete topology $\mathcal{T}_x = \mathcal{T} = \mathcal{P}\{0,1\} = \{\emptyset, \{0\}, \{1\}, \{0,1\}\}$, i.e., all subsets of

$\{0,1\}$ are considered open relative to $\mathcal{T}_x$. It is trivially verified that indeed $\mathcal{T}_x$ is a totally disconnected compact Hausdorff space. Hence the cartesian product topology (or topology of pointwise convergence), the smallest topology making all $proj_x : \{0,1\}^X \to \{0,1\}^X$, $x \in X$, continuous, is

$$\mathcal{T}'(X) \overset{d}{=} top(\{proj_x^{-1}(\mathcal{T}) \mid x \in X\}) = \{proj_x^{-1}(\mathcal{T}) \mid x \in X\}^{\cap\cup}$$

$$= (\{\sigma_{\underset{\sim}{x}_{J_o},\underset{\sim}{a}_{J_o}}(X) \mid \text{for all } \underset{\sim}{x}, \underset{\sim}{a}, J_o \text{ finite}\} \cup \{\{0,1\}^X\} \cup \{\emptyset\})^{\cup}$$

$$= (\{\sigma_{x_j,1}(X) \mid x_j \in X,\ j = 1,\dots,m\ ;\ m \geq 1\} \cup \{\sigma_{y_j,0} \mid y_j \in X,$$

$$j = 1,\dots,n\ ;\ n \geq 1\} \cup \{\{0,1\}^X\} \cup \{\emptyset\})^{\cap\cup}.$$

$\mathcal{T}'(X)$ is the natural topology for $\{0,1\}^X$. As a product topology, it follows that $\mathcal{T}'(X)$ is also a totally disconnected compact Hausdorff topology over $\{0,1\}^X$.

Now recalling that ϕ is a one-to-one onto mapping, $\mathcal{T}(\mathcal{B}_o) \overset{d}{=} \phi^{-1}(\mathcal{T}'(X)) \underline{\cap}\ \mathcal{B}_o$ is a disconnected compact Hausdorff topology over $\mathcal{B}_o$ and is called the *natural topology* (or the power class on X relative to $\mathcal{B}_o$). Note the correspondences for any $x, x_1, x_2, \dots, x_m, y_1, \dots, y_n \in X$

$$\mathcal{C}_{\{x\}}(\mathcal{B}_o) = \phi^{-1}(\sigma_{x,1}(X)) \cap \mathcal{B}_o\ ,$$

$$\mathcal{D}_{X\dashv\{x\}}(\mathcal{B}_o) = \phi^{-1}(\sigma_{x,o}(X)) \cap \mathcal{B}_o\ ,$$

$$\mathcal{C}_{\{x_1,\dots,x_m\}}(\mathcal{B}_o) = \bigcap_{j=1}^{m} \mathcal{C}_{\{x_j\}}(\mathcal{B}_o) = \phi^{-1}(\sigma_{\underset{\sim}{x},\underset{\sim}{1}}) \cap \mathcal{B}_o\ ,$$

$$\mathcal{D}_{X\dashv\{y_1,\dots,y_n\}}(\mathcal{B}_o) = \bigcap_{j=1}^{m} \mathcal{D}_{X\dashv\{x_j\}}(\mathcal{B}_o) = \phi^{-1}(\sigma_{\underset{\sim}{y},\underset{\sim}{o}}) \cap \mathcal{B}_o\ ,$$

$$\mathcal{E}_{\{y_1,\dots,y_n\}}(\mathcal{B}_o) = \mathcal{B}_o \dashv \mathcal{D}_{X\dashv\{y_1,\dots,y_n\}}$$

$$= \cup\ \{\phi^{-1}(\sigma_{\underset{\sim}{y},\underset{\sim}{a}}) \mid \underset{\sim}{a} \not\equiv \underset{\sim}{o}\}\ ,$$

since $\mathcal{C}\,\sigma_{x,1} = \sigma_{x,0}$. This also implies that all $\sigma_{\underset{\sim}{x}_{J_o},\underset{\sim}{a}_{J_o}}$, J_o finite, are clopen (closed and open) and hence also compact relative to $\mathcal{T}'(X)$; hence all $\phi^{-1}(\sigma_{\underset{\sim}{x}_{J_o},\underset{\sim}{a}_{J_o}}) \cap \mathcal{B}_o$, for J_o finite, are clopen compact,

Note also,

$$\phi^{-1}(\sigma_{\underset{\sim}{x}_{J_o},\underset{\sim}{a}_{J_o}}(X)) \cap \mathfrak{B}_o = \mathfrak{C}_{\{x_1,\ldots,x_m\}}(\mathfrak{B}_o) \cap \mathfrak{D}_{X\dashv\{y_1,\ldots,y_n\}}(\mathfrak{B}_o)$$

where

$$((\underset{\sim}{x}_{J_o}),\underset{\sim}{a}_{J_o}) =$$

$$((x_j)_{j=1,\ldots,m},(1)_{j=1,\ldots,m}) \,\dot{\cup}\, ((y_j)_{j=1,\ldots,n},(0)_{j=1,\ldots,m})\ ;$$

$$\mathfrak{B}_o \dashv (\phi^{-1}(\sigma_{\underset{\sim}{x}_{J_o},\underset{\sim}{a}_{J_o}}(X)) \cap \mathfrak{B}_o) = \cup\, \phi^{-1}(\sigma_{\underset{\sim}{x}_{J_o},\underset{\sim}{a}'_{J_o}} \mid \underset{\sim}{a}'_{J_o} \not\equiv \underset{\sim}{a}_{J_o})$$

$$= \bigcup_{j=1}^{m} \mathfrak{D}_{X\dashv\{x_j\}}(\mathfrak{B}_o) \cup \bigcap_{j=1}^{m} \mathfrak{C}_{y_j}(\mathfrak{B}_o)\ .$$

Thus, in summary, for any $C \in \mathfrak{F}(X)$, $\mathfrak{C}_C(\mathfrak{B}_o)$, $\mathfrak{D}_{X\dashv C}(\mathfrak{B}_o)$, $\mathcal{E}_C(\mathfrak{B}_o)$ and all finite unions intersections and complements (relative to $\mathfrak{B}_o$) are clopen-compact for $\mathcal{T}(\mathfrak{B}_o)$.

As also a T_1-space (and compact), it follows that any finite subclass of $\mathfrak{B}_o$ is closed (and compact) relative to $\mathcal{T}(\mathfrak{B}_o)$.

Furthermore, for *any* $C \in \mathcal{P}(X)$, since $\mathfrak{C}_C(\mathfrak{B}_o) = \bigcap_{x\in\mathfrak{B}_o} \mathfrak{C}_{\{x\}}(\mathfrak{B}_o)$, $\mathfrak{C}_C(\mathfrak{B}_o)$ is closed and thus compact relative to $\mathcal{T}(\mathfrak{B}_o)$. Similarly, $\mathfrak{D}_C(\mathfrak{B}_o)$ is closed-compact relative to $\mathcal{T}(\mathfrak{B}_o)$, while $\mathcal{E}_C(\mathfrak{B}_o)$ is open relative to $\mathcal{T}(\mathfrak{B}_o)$, for any $C \in \mathcal{P}(X)$.

An alternative equivalent approach is through projections: For any $C \in \mathfrak{F}(X)$, define the general projection mapping $p_C : \mathcal{P}(X) \to \mathcal{P}(C)$, where for any $D \in \mathcal{P}(X)$, $p_C(D) \overset{d}{=} D \cap C$. Thus, for any $C \subseteq G \in \mathfrak{F}(X)$,

$$p_G^{-1}(\{C\}) \cap \mathfrak{B}_o = (\{C\} \,\underline{\cap}\, \mathcal{P}(X\dashv G)) \cap \mathfrak{B}_o\ ,$$

$$= \mathfrak{C}_C(\mathfrak{B}_o) \cap \mathfrak{D}_{X\dashv(G\dashv C)}(\mathfrak{B}_o)\ ,$$

$$p_G^{-1}(\{\emptyset\}) \cap \mathfrak{B}_o = \mathfrak{D}_{X\dashv G}(\mathfrak{B}_o)\ ;\ p_\emptyset^{-1}(\{\emptyset\}) \cap \mathfrak{B}_o = \mathfrak{D}_X(\mathfrak{B}_o) = \mathfrak{B}_o$$

$$p_G^{-1}(\{G\}) \cap \mathfrak{B}_o = \mathfrak{C}_G(\mathfrak{B}_o)\ .\ p_\emptyset^{-1}(\{G\} \cap \mathfrak{B}_o) = \mathfrak{C}_\phi(\mathfrak{B}_o) = \mathfrak{B}_o$$

$$p_G^{-1}(\emptyset) \cap \mathfrak{B}_o = \emptyset\ .$$

Now for any $G \in \mathfrak{F}(X)$,
$p_G^{-1}(\mathcal{P}\mathcal{P}(G)) \,\underline{\cap}\, \mathfrak{B}_o = \{p_G^{-1}(\mathcal{A}) \cap \mathfrak{B}_o \mid \mathcal{A} \subseteq \mathcal{P}(G)\}$ is a σ-algebra (of

clopen compact sets relative to $\mathcal{T}(\mathfrak{B}_o)$) over $\mathfrak{B}_o$, where $p_G^{-1}(\mathcal{A}) = \bigcup_{C \in \mathcal{A}} p_G^{-1}(C)$: For any $\mathcal{A}_j \subseteq \mathcal{P}(G)$, $j = 1,2,\ldots,$

$$\bigcup_{j=1}^{+\infty} (p_G^{-1}(\mathcal{A}_j) \cap \mathfrak{B}_o) = p_G^{-1}(\bigcup_{j=1}^{+\infty} \mathcal{A}_j) \cap \mathfrak{B}_o ,$$

$$\bigcap_{j=1}^{+\infty} (p_G^{-1}(\mathcal{A}_j) \cap \mathfrak{B}_o) = p_G^{-1}(\bigcap_{j=1}^{+\infty} \mathcal{A}_j) \cap \mathfrak{B}_o ,$$

$$\mathfrak{B}_o \dashv (p_G^{-1}(\mathcal{A}_1) \cap \mathfrak{B}_o) = p_G^{-1}(\mathcal{P}(G) \underline{\dashv} \mathcal{A}_1) \cap \mathfrak{B}_o . \qquad (*)$$

Furthermore, $\mathcal{W}(\mathfrak{B}_o) \stackrel{d}{=} \bigcup_{G \in \mathcal{T}(X)} (p_G^{-1}(\mathcal{P}\mathcal{P}(G)) \underline{\cap} \mathfrak{B}_o)$ is a Boolean ring over $\mathfrak{B}_o$, since for any $\mathcal{A}_j \subseteq \mathcal{P}(G_j)$, $G_j \in \mathcal{T}(X)$, $j = 1,\ldots,m$,

$$\bigcup_{j=1}^{m} (p_G^{-1}(\mathcal{A}_j) \cap \mathfrak{B}_o) = p^{-1}_{\left[\bigcup_{j=1}^{m} G_j\right]}(\bigcup_{j=1}^{m} (\mathcal{A}_j \underline{\cup} \mathcal{P}(\bigcup_{\ell=1}^{m} G_\ell \dashv G_j)) \cap \mathfrak{B}_o),$$

$$\bigcap_{j=1}^{m} (p_{G_j}^{-1}(\mathcal{A}_j) \cap \mathfrak{B}_o) = p^{-1}_{\left[\bigcap_{j=1}^{m} G_j\right]}(\bigcap_{j=1}^{m} (\mathcal{A}_j \underline{\cap} \mathcal{P}(\bigcup_{\ell=1}^{m} G_\ell \dashv G_j)) \cap \mathfrak{B}_o),$$

(and equation (*) still remaining valid).

It is not difficult to see that

$$\mathcal{T}(\mathfrak{B}_o) = \text{top}\,(\mathcal{W}(\mathfrak{B}_o)) = (\mathcal{W}(\mathfrak{B}_o))^{\cap\cup} = \mathcal{W}(\mathfrak{B}_o))^{\cup}$$

$$= \text{top}\,(\{\mathcal{C}_{\{x\}}(\mathfrak{B}_o) \mid x \in X\} \cup \{\mathfrak{D}_{X \dashv \{x\}}(\mathfrak{B}_o) \mid x \in X\} \cup \{\mathfrak{B}_o\} \cup \{\varnothing\})$$

$$= \text{top}\,(\{\mathcal{C}_C(\mathfrak{B}_o) \mid C \in \mathcal{J}(X)\} \cup \{\mathfrak{D}_{X \dashv C}(\mathfrak{B}_o) \mid C \in \mathcal{J}(X)\} \cup \{\varnothing\})$$

$$= \{\mathcal{C}_C(\mathfrak{B}_o) \cap \mathfrak{D}_{X \dashv (G \dashv C)}(\mathfrak{B}_o) \mid C \subseteq G \in \mathcal{J}(X)\}^{\cup} ,$$

noting that for any $C_j \in \mathcal{P}(X)$, $j \in J_o$, arbitrary index set,

$$\bigcap_{j \in J_o} \mathcal{C}_{C_j}(\mathfrak{B}_o) = \mathcal{C}_{\left[\bigcup_{j \in J_o} C_j\right]}(\mathfrak{B}_o) , \quad \bigcap_{j \in J_o} \mathfrak{D}_{C_j}(\mathfrak{B}_o) = \mathfrak{D}_{\bigcap_{j \in J_o} C_j}(\mathfrak{B}_o) .$$

For any $\mathcal{A}_j \subseteq \mathcal{P}(G_j)$, $G_j \in \mathcal{J}(X)$, $j = 1,2$, $p_{G_1}^{-1}(\mathcal{A}_1) = p_{G_2}^{-1}(\mathcal{A}_2)$ iff $G_1 \subseteq G_2$ and $\mathcal{A}_2 = p_{G_1}^{-1}(\mathcal{A}_1) \underline{\cap} \{G_2\}$, or vice versa with $G_2 \subseteq G_1$, etc. In particular, note

$$p_{G_1}^{-1}(\{G_1\}) = p_{G_2}^{-1}(\{C \mid G_1 \subseteq C \subseteq G_2\}) .$$

First consider the Baire σ-algebra (Halmos, Theorem C, p. 221)

$$\sigma(\{\mathcal{C}_{\{x\}}(\mathcal{B}_o) \mid x \in X\} \cup \{\mathcal{B}_o\}) = \sigma(\mathcal{W}(\mathcal{B}_o)) = \sigma(\mathcal{C}_o(\mathcal{B}_o)) = \sigma(\mathcal{U}_o(\mathcal{B}_o)) ,$$

where

$$\mathcal{C}_o(\mathcal{B}_o) \overset{d}{=} \{\mathcal{A} \mid \mathcal{A} \subseteq \mathcal{B}_o \ \& \ \mathcal{A} \text{ is compact } G_\delta \text{ (at most countable intersection of open sets for } \mathcal{T}(\mathcal{B}_o))\} ,$$

$$\mathcal{U}_o(\mathcal{B}_o) \overset{d}{=} \sigma(\mathcal{C}_o(\mathcal{B}_o)) \cap \mathcal{T}(\mathcal{B}_o) .$$

In turn, the Baire σ-algebra is contained within the Borel σ-algebra:

$$\sigma(\mathcal{W}(\mathcal{B}_o)) \subseteq \sigma(\mathcal{C}_1(\mathcal{B}_o)) = \sigma(\mathcal{T}(\mathcal{B}_o)) ,$$

where

$$\mathcal{C}_1(\mathcal{B}_o) \overset{d}{=} \{\mathcal{A} \mid \mathcal{A} \subseteq \mathcal{B}_o \ \& \ \mathcal{A} \text{ is compact (equivalently closed) relative to } \mathcal{T}(\mathcal{B}_o)\} .$$

Clearly, for any $C \in \mathcal{P}(X)$, $\mathcal{C}_C(\mathcal{B}_o)$, $\mathcal{D}_C(\mathcal{B}_o)$, $\mathcal{E}_C(\mathcal{B}_o) \in \sigma(\mathcal{W}(\mathcal{B}_o))$ (since already, the first two classes are closed compact for $\mathcal{T}(\mathcal{B}_o)$; while the last class is the complement of a closed-compact set for $\mathcal{T}(\mathcal{B}_o)$) .

Finally, using ϕ , note the analagous Baire and Borel σ-algebras with respect to $\underset{x\in X}{\times} \{0,1\}^x = \{0,1\}^X$ are

$$\sigma(\{\sigma_{x_{j},1}(X) \mid x_j \in X , j = 1,\ldots,m , m \geq 1\} \cup \{\{0,1\}^X\})$$

$$= \sigma(\{\sigma_{\underset{\sim}{x}_{J_o},\underset{\sim}{a}_{J_o}}(X) \mid \text{for all } \underset{\sim}{x}, \underset{\sim}{a}, J_o \text{ finite}\} \cup \{\{0,1\}^X\})$$

$$= \sigma(\mathcal{C}_o'(X)) = \phi(\sigma(\mathcal{C}_o(\mathcal{P}(X)))) ,$$

where $\mathcal{C}_o'(X)$ is the set of all compact (equivalently closed) G_δ subsets of $\{0,1\}^X$ relative to $\mathcal{T}'(X)$,
$\sigma(\mathcal{C}_1'(X)) = \sigma(\mathcal{T}'(X)) = \phi(\sigma(\mathcal{C}_1(\mathcal{P}(X))))$ (Borel σ-algebra), where $\mathcal{C}_1'(X)$ = class of all compact (equivalently closed) subsets of $\{0,1\}^X$ relative to $\mathcal{T}'(X)$.

See also Michael [176] for basic background. For further development of the topologies of collections of subsets, see also Badard [9'], where also applications to uniform structures for flou classes are given, which in turn are used in fuzzy analysis and extensions of fixed point theorems.

4.3 Coverage/Incidence functions and Choquet's theorem on capacities.

In Chapter 3, an alternative approach to uncertainty measures was developed with enphasis on the finite case, although extended to more general situations. In this section, Choquet's Capacity Theorem is used.

As in 4.1, let X be an arbitrary set, and T_o be the space law of a random set S taking values in $(\mathcal{P}(X),\sigma(\mathfrak{D}))$. Note that $T_o : \mathfrak{I}(X) \to [0,1]$, $T_o(I) = Pr(S \cap I \neq \emptyset)$ and T_o is characterized as follows:

Theorem 7 (Matheron [171])

If $T' : \mathfrak{I}(X) \to [0,1]$ is a given functional, define $P' : \mathfrak{I}(X) \times \mathfrak{I}(X) \to [0,1]$ by $P'(\emptyset,I') = 1 - T'(I')$, and recursively

$$P'(I \cup \{x\},I') = P'(I,I') - P'(I,I' \cup \{x\}) ,$$

then T' is a space law, i.e., T' determines a unique probability measure on $(\mathcal{P}(X),\sigma(\mathfrak{D}))$ iff

(i) $T'(\emptyset) = 0$

(ii) $P' \geq 0$.

Note that Matheron's theorem is a strengthening of Theorems 3 (ii) and 5 of section 4.2.

Now, such a space law T_o defines a sequence $\Psi = (\Psi_n, n \geq 1)$ of functions as follows:

For $I = \{x_1, x_2, \ldots, x_n\} \in \mathfrak{I}(X)$,

$$\Psi_n(x_1,x_2,\ldots,x_n) = T_o(I) = Pr(S \cap \{x_1,\ldots,x_n\} \neq \emptyset) .$$

In a dual way, we define *n-point probability coverage function* of a random set S as follows:

For $n \geq 1$, $\Phi_n(x_1,x_2,\ldots,x_n) = Pr(S \supseteq \{x_1,x_2,\ldots,x_n\})$, we have

(i) For each $n \geq 1$, $\Phi_n : X^n \to [0,1]$.

(ii) For each $n \geq 1$, Φ_n is symmetric.

(iii) $(\Phi_n, n \geq 1)$ is decreasing in the following sense:

$$\forall_n \geq 1, \forall_j \leq n, \Phi_n(x_1,\ldots,x_n) \leq \Phi_j(x_1,\ldots,x_j) .$$

(iv) If $x_1=\ldots=x_m$, $m \leq n$, then

$$\Phi_n(x_1,\ldots,x_m,x_{m+1},\ldots,x_n) = \Phi_{n-m+1}(x_1,x_{m+1},\ldots,x_n) .$$

(v) For each $n \ge 1$,

$$\Sigma\ (-1)^{K+1}\Phi_K(x_{i_1},x_{i_2},\ldots,x_{i_k}) \in [0,1] ,$$

where the summation is taken over all integers $i_1,i_2,\ldots,i_K$ $(1 \le k \le n)$ such that $1 \le i_1 < i_2 < \ldots < i_k \le n$. This can be seen by observing that $(\Psi_n,\ n \ge 1)$ and $(\Phi_n,\ n \ge 1)$ are dually related as follows:

(a) $\Psi_n(x_1,\ldots,x_n) = \sum (-1)^{k+1}\Phi_k(x_{i_1},x_{i_2},\ldots,x_{i_k})$,

(b) $\Phi_n(x_1,\ldots,x_n) = \sum (-1)^{k+1}\Psi_k(x_{i_1},x_{i_2},\ldots,x_{i_k})$.

Indeed, since

$$(S \cap \{x_1,\ldots,x_n\} \ne \emptyset) = \bigcup_{i=1}^{n} (x_i \in S) ,$$

$$(S \supseteq \{x_1,\ldots,x_n\}) = \bigcap_{i=1}^{n} (x_i \in S) ,$$

therefore, by Poincaré's expansion

$$\Psi_n(x_1,\ldots,x_n) = \Pr[\bigcup_{i=1}^{n} (x_i \in S)] =$$

$$\sum (-1)^{k+1}\Pr[x_{i_1} \in S) \cap\ldots\cap(x_{i_k} \in S)]$$

$$= \sum (-1)^{k+1}\Phi_k(x_{i_1},\ldots,x_{i_k}) .$$

__Examples.__

1. Let $f : X \to [0,1]$ be given.
   Define $\Phi_1(x_1) = f(x_1)$, and

$$\Phi_n(x_1,\ldots,x_n) = \bigwedge_{i=1}^{n} f(x_i) .$$

2. Let F be a distribution function of a real-valued random variable Y . Then the random set $S = [Y,+\infty)$ has

$$\Phi_n(x_1,\ldots,x_n) = F(\bigwedge_{i=1}^{n} x_i) .$$

Remark.

For $f : X \to [0,1]$, the sequence of functions

$f_n(x_1,\ldots,x_n) = \overset{n}{\underset{i=1}{\times}} f(x_i)$ is similar to the one used in symmetric statistics of infinite order (Dynkin and Mandelbaum, [53]). By considering symmetric functions as functions defined on sets, we define $\Phi_n(\{x_1,\ldots,x_n\}) = \prod(f(x))$ where the product $\prod$ is taken over $x \in \{x_1,\ldots,x_n\}$.

The following form of Choquet's theorem on capacities (see Matheron, [171]) is useful for establishing connections between random sets and uncertainty measures. (See, e.g., Goodman [90], Shafer [228], Höhle [116]).

Let X be a locally compact and separable space. Denote by $\mathcal{F}$, $\mathcal{K}$ the class of closed, compact sets of X, respectively. Denote by $\mathcal{B}(\mathcal{F})$ the Borel σ-algebra of the topological space $\mathcal{F}$.

Theorem 8 (Choquet [36])

Let T' be a function defined on $\mathcal{K}$. Then there exists a unique probability measure Pr on $(\mathcal{F},\mathcal{B}(\mathcal{F}))$ satisfying

$$\Pr\{F \in \mathcal{F} \mid F \cap K \neq \emptyset\} = T'(K),\ \forall\ K \in \mathcal{K},$$

iff T' is a $\cup$-alternating Choquet capacity of infinite order such that $0 \le T' \le 1$ and $T'(\emptyset) = 0$.

Remark.

For the use of Choquet's theorem, and Matheron's theorem (Matheron [171], p. 41) in establishing a connection between random sets and possibility distributions, see, e.g., Nguyen [187]. Note also that the above theory essentially may be thought of as the plausibility measure analogue of Theorem 2 or Theorem 3 of section 3.2, or as a form of Theorem 3 of section 4.2.

4.4 Multi-valued mappings and integration.

The concept of expectation of a random set S can be formally defined if the base space X possesses an appropriate topological structure. For example, when $X = \mathbb{R}^d$, one defines:

$$A + B = \{x + y \mid x \in A,\ y \in B\},\ A,B \subseteq \mathbb{R}^d.$$
$$\alpha A = \{\alpha x \mid x \in A\},\ \alpha > 0, A \subseteq \mathbb{R}^d.$$

More generally, if S takes values in a separable Banach space X with norm $\|\cdot\|$, and Borel σ-algebra $\mathcal{B}$, then first the random set S will be called simple if the set of possible values of S is at most countable. Let random set $S \overset{d}{=} \sum_{j=1}^{\infty} B_j \phi_{A_j}$ with $\|S\|$ Pr-integrable, so that $\sum_{j=1}^{\infty} \Pr(A_j)B_j$ converges absolutely, where $B_j \in \mathcal{B}$ and $A_j \in \mathcal{A}$, for probability space $(\Omega,\mathcal{A},\Pr)$, $\sum_{j=1}^{\infty} \Pr(A_j)B_j$

is called the *Bochner integral* of S, noting ϕ_{A_j} is the indicator function of A_j. For a general random set S, it can be shown that $\|S\|$ is Pr-integrable iff S is Bochner integrable, i.e., there exists a sequence of simple random sets S_n such that $(S_n)_{n=1,2,...} \to S$, Pr-almost surely, and for each n, $\|S_n\|$ is Pr-integrable and $\int_{\omega\in\Omega} \|S_n - S\| dP(\omega) \to 0$, as $n \to +\infty$. (For a treatise on integration of multivalued mappings, see Debreu [45].)

We proceed now to point out Robbins' formula (Robbins, [219], p. 72) relating the computation of the expected volumn of a random set to its probability coverage functions.

Let S be a random set taking values in $\mathbb{C} \subseteq \mathbb{B}_m$ (the Borel σ-algebra of $\mathbb{R}^m$), $\hat{\mathbb{C}}$ a σ-algebra on $\mathbb{C}$, and μ_m or vol_m the Lebesgue measure on $\mathbb{R}^m$. If the measure $\mu_m(S)$ is a random variable, then under suitable conditions, its expectation $E(\mu_m(S))$ can be obtained as follows (by use of Fubini's iteration theorem).

Theorem 9 (Robbins [219]).

Define

$$g : \mathbb{R}^m \times \mathbb{C} \to [0,1] \quad \text{by}$$

$$g(x,A) = \begin{cases} 1 & \text{if} \quad x \in A \\ 0 & \text{if} \quad x \notin A \end{cases} = \phi_A(x) .$$

If g is $\mathbb{B}_m \otimes \hat{\mathbb{C}}$-measurable, then

$$E(\mu_m(S)) = \int_{x\in\mathbb{R}^m} \pi(x) d\mu_m(x)$$

where $\pi(x) \overset{d}{=} Pr(x \in S)$, $x \in \mathbb{R}^m$.

By considering many-point coverage functions, and under suitable measurability conditions, higher moments of $\mu_m(S)$ are obtained as follows:

For $k \geq 1$, $E(\mu_m(S)^k) =$

$$\int_{\mathbb{R}^{mk}} \pi(x_1,...,x_k) \bigotimes_{i=1}^{k} \mu_m^{(i)} (dx_1,...,dx_k)$$

where $\mu_m^{(i)} = \mu_m$ for $i = 1,2,...,k$, and $\bigotimes_{i=1}^{k} \mu_m^{(i)}$ denotes the product measure on $\mathbb{R}^{mk}$.

Remark.

In the case $k = 1$, the measurability of $g(x,A)$ implies that $\pi(x)$ is measurable and that $\mu_m(S)$ is a random variable. One can view $(g(x,\cdot) \mid x \in \mathbb{R}^m)$ as a $0 - 1$ stochastic process on the measurable space $(\mathcal{C},\hat{\mathcal{C}})$, so that the measurability condition of g is equivalent to the fact that this stochastic process is a measurable process. The following is a concrete situation where Robbins' formula is valid: $\mathcal{C} = \mathcal{K}$, $\hat{\mathcal{C}} = \mathcal{B}(\mathcal{K})$, i.e., S is a compact-valued random set on $\mathbb{R}^m$. Indeed, the stochastic process $(g(x,\cdot) \mid x \in \mathbb{R}^m)$ on $(\mathcal{K},\mathcal{B}(\mathcal{K}))$ is measurable. That can be shown as follows: It is enough to show that

$$g^{-1}(\{1\}) \in \mathbb{B}_m \otimes \mathcal{B}(\mathcal{K}).$$

Now, viewing $\mathcal{K}$ as a set whose "points" are compact sets, and defining a multi-valued mapping

$$\Gamma : (\mathcal{K},\mathcal{B}(\mathcal{K})) \to \mathcal{P}(\mathbb{R}^m)$$

by

$$\Gamma(K) = K \quad ,$$

i.e., $\Gamma : (\mathcal{K},\mathcal{B}(\mathcal{K})) \to (\mathcal{K},\mathcal{B}(\mathcal{K}))$, but the second space is considered as the collection of all possible values of the multi-valued mapping in $\mathbb{R}^m$. It is obvious that Γ is $\mathcal{B}(\mathcal{K}) - \mathcal{B}(\mathcal{K})$-measurable. Next, observe that $g^{-1}(\{1\}) = G(\Gamma)$, the graph of Γ, defined as:

$$G(\Gamma) = \{(x,K) \mid x \in \Gamma(K)\} \subseteq \mathbb{R}^m \times \mathcal{K} .$$

Since $\mathbb{R}^m$ is metric and separable, and Γ is $\mathcal{B}(\mathcal{K}) - \mathcal{B}(\mathcal{K})$-measurable, it follows that $G(\Gamma) \in \mathbb{B}_m \otimes \mathcal{B}(\mathcal{K})$, Q.E.D.

This last statement is a special case of the following theorem.

Theorem 10 (Debreu [45], p. 360)

Let X be a metric space, $\mathcal{T}$ its Borel σ-algebra and Γ a multi-valued mapping from an arbitrary measurable space $(H,\mathcal{H})$ to $\mathcal{P}(X)$, with values in $\mathcal{K}$ (of X). If X is separable and Γ is $\mathcal{H} - \mathcal{B}(\mathcal{K})$ measurable, then the graph of Γ is in the product σ-algebra $\mathcal{H} \otimes \mathcal{T}$.

Remark.

If f is a single-valued mapping from V to W (Hausdorff topological spaces), then the graph of f, defined as $\{(v,w) \mid w = f(v)\} \subseteq V \times W$, is closed in $V \times W$ (with product topology) if f is continuous. But the Borel σ-algebra of $V \times W$ contains the product σ-algebra $\sigma(V) \otimes \sigma(W)$, with equality if, in addition, both V and W have countable bases for their topology (see, e.g., Courrège [42]).

More generally, for random closed sets, we have:

Theorem 11 (Matheron [171], p. 47)

Let X be a locally compact, Hausdorff and separable space (with topology $\mathcal{F}$, and Borel σ-algebra denoted by $\sigma(\mathcal{T})$). Then any random closed set S is measurable in the following sense: The mapping $g : X \times \mathcal{F} \to \{0,1\}$ is $\sigma(\mathcal{T}) \otimes \mathcal{B}(\mathcal{F})$-measurable.

Indeed, let $\mathcal{D}$ be a countable base for the topology $\mathcal{T}$. Then $x \notin F$ (for $F \in \mathcal{F}$) is equivalent to: there exists $D \in \mathcal{D}$ such that $x \in D$ and $F \cap D = \emptyset$. Thus,

$$g^{-1}(\{0\}) = \bigcup_{D \in \mathcal{D}} \{D \times \mathcal{F}^D\} \in \sigma(\mathcal{T}) \otimes \mathcal{B}(\mathcal{F}) ,$$

where $\mathcal{F}^D = \{F \in \mathcal{F} \mid F \cap D = \emptyset\}$.

Corollary.

(Matheron) With the conditions of the above theorem, let μ be a positive measure on $(X,\sigma(\mathcal{T}))$. Then the mapping $(F \in \mathcal{F}) \to \mu(F) = \int_{x \in X} g(x,F)\, d\mu(x)$, from $(\mathcal{F},\mathcal{B}(\mathcal{F}))$ into $\mathbb{R}^+$, is a positive random variable (i.e., $\mu(S)$ is a positive random variable), the expectation of which is

$$E(\mu(S)) = \int_{x \in X} Pr(x \in S)\, d\mu(x) .$$

Indeed, by the previous theorem, g is $\sigma(\mathcal{T}) \otimes \mathcal{B}(\mathcal{F})$-measurable, hence $F \to \mu(F)$ is $\mathcal{B}(\mathcal{F})$-measurable. Next, by Fubini's theorem, we have:

$$E(\mu(S)) = \int_{F \in \mathcal{F}} \mu(F) dP_S(F) = \int_X \int_{\mathcal{F}} g(x,F) dP_S(F) d\mu(x)$$

$$= \int_{x \in X} P_S\{F \in \mathcal{F} \mid x \in F\} d\mu(x)$$

$$= \int_{x \in X} Pr\{\omega \mid x \in S(\omega)\} d\mu(x) .$$

Some applications of Robbins' Theorem to the problem of determining the class of random sets having given coverage functions up to some order will be treated in section 5.4. This is also intimately included with the problem of relating dispersions to random sets.

CHAPTER 5

RANDOM SETS AND DISPERSIONS

In this chapter, we establish connections between random sets and dispersions, discuss the principle of maximum entropy for random sets, and relate our analysis to some familiar situations in statistics.

5.1 Zero-one stochastic processes.

An alternative approach to the development of random subsets from primitive ones and relations between random sets and uncertainty measures may be expressed through zero-one processes.

A zero-one stochastic process $V \overset{d}{=} (V_j)_{j\in J_o}$ is a collection of random variables $V_j : \Omega \to \{0,1\}$, $j \in J_o$ which are consistently determined, i.e., if $K' \subseteq K'' \subseteq J_o$, then the joint marginal distribution of $(V_j)_{j\in K'}$ remains the same relative to K' or K'' . We can identify each V_j with the probability space $(\{0,1\},\mathcal{P}\{0,1\}, \nu_j)$, $Pr(V_j = 1) = \nu_j(\{1\}) \overset{d}{=} a_j$, $Pr(V_j = 0) = 1 - a_j$, $j \in J_o$. Since each such space is trivially a Polish space (a complete separable metric space - see, e.g., Neveu [184'], pp. 64 et passim; p. 83) then there exists a unique probability measure ν which *extends* all of the ν_j's to two levels as follows in terms of probability spaces:

$$\text{Baire-level} : (\{0,1\}^{J_o}, \sigma(\mathfrak{C}_o^{\prime}(J_o)), \nu) ,$$

$$\text{Borel-level} : (\{0,1\}^{J_o}, \sigma(\mathfrak{C}_1^{\prime}(J_o)), \nu) ,$$

noting $\sigma(\mathfrak{C}_o^{\prime}(J)) \subseteq \sigma(\mathfrak{C}_1^{\prime}(J_o))$. For any $C \subseteq G \in \mathfrak{z}(J_o)$,

$$Pr(\underset{j\in C}{\&} (V_j = 1) \& \underset{j\in G\dashv C}{\&} (V_j = 0))$$

$$= \mu_G^{(1)}(C) = \sum_{K\subseteq G\dashv C} (-1)^{\text{card } K} \cdot \mu(C\dot{\cup}K)$$

$$= \nu(\sigma_{\underset{\sim}{Y},\underset{\sim}{a}}) ,$$

where $\mu : \mathfrak{F}(G) \rightarrow [0,1]$ is the doubt measure determined by

$$\mu(B) \overset{d}{=} \Pr(\underset{j \in B}{\&} (V_j = 1)) \; ; \; B \subseteq G \; ,$$

where here $\underset{\sim}{y} = (j)_{j \in G}$, $\underset{\sim}{a} = (a_j)_{j \in G}$; for $j \in C$, $a_j = 1$; for $j \in G \dashv C$, $a_j = 0$. Further properties such as finite-regularity and completeness of measure (at the Borel level extension) also hold, completely analogous to the situation for $\mathcal{P}(J_o)$ through the ϕ-mapping.

In particular, letting $J_o = X$:

Theorem 1

Given any base space X , $\{\varnothing, X\} \subseteq \mathcal{B}_o \subseteq \mathcal{P}(X)$, and any zero-one stochastic process $\underset{\sim}{V} = (V_x)_{x \in X}$ indexed by X , there is a unique corresponding random subset S_o of X with range $\mathcal{B}_o$ corresponding to probability space $(\mathcal{B}_o \, , \, \sigma(\mathcal{C}_1(\mathcal{B}_o)), \, \nu_{S_o})$ induced by the always measurable mapping ϕ^{-1} , i.e., $\nu_{S_o} = \nu \circ \phi$, and $\sigma(\mathcal{C}_1(\mathcal{B}_o)) = \phi^{-1}(\sigma(\mathcal{C}_1^{!}(X))) \cap \mathcal{B}_o$, etc.

Remark.

The mapping $(\phi \mid \mathcal{B}_o)$ may be thought of as a *random ordinary membership function* corresponding to probability space $(\{0,1\}^{J_o}, \sigma(\mathcal{C}_1^{!}(X)), \nu)$. The above result also shows that a zero-one process is uniquely specified by all of its joint one-values.

Theorem 2

(i) If μ is a doubt measure over $\mathfrak{F}(J_o)$, then μ determines a unique $0 - 1$ stochastic process $\underset{\sim}{V} = (V_j)_{j \in J_o}$ such that

$$\Pr(\underset{j \in C}{\&} (V_j = 1)) = \mu(C) \; , \; \forall \; C \in \mathfrak{F}(J_o) \; .$$

Indeed, it follows that for any $C \subseteq G \in \mathfrak{F}(J_o)$,

$$\Pr(\underset{j \in C}{\&} (V_j = 1) \; \& \underset{j \in G \dashv C}{\&} (V_j = 0)) = \mu_G^{(1)}(\{C\}) \; ,$$

where $\mu_G^{(1)}$ is defined as before in Chapter 4.

(ii) Conversely, if $\underset{\sim}{V} = (V_j)_{j \in J_o}$ is any $0 - 1$ stochastic process, then $\underset{\sim}{V}$ is uniquely determined by the specifications

$$\mu(C) \overset{d}{=} \Pr(\underset{j \in C}{\&} (V_j = 1)) \; ; \; C \in \mathfrak{F}(J_o) \; ,$$

where it can be shown μ is a legitimate doubt measure over $\mathfrak{F}(J_o)$ and all results in (i) are valid for μ .

Remark.

Thus, the class of all zero-one processes can be placed in a one-to-one correspondence with the class of all doubt measures.

Corollary 1

Let $\phi_{\&}$, ϕ_{or} be any semi-distributive DeMorgan t-norm and t-conorm pair.

Then for any $A \in \mathfrak{F}(X)$, the doubt measure $\mu_{A,\&}$ and plausibility measure $\mu_{A,or} = 1 - \mu_{CA,\&}$ we have the following properties:

(i) $\mu_{A,\&}$ determines a unique $0 - 1$ stochastic process $\underset{\sim}{V}_{A,\&} = (V_{A,\&,j})_{j \in J_o}$ such that for all $C \in \mathfrak{F}(J_o)$,

$$\Pr(\underset{j \in C}{\&} (V_{A,\&,j} = 1)) = \mu_{A,\&}(C) = \underset{x \in C}{\phi_{\&}} (\phi_A(x))$$

with eq. (*) of the Appendix, section 4.2, also valid for μ *replaced by* $\mu_{A,\&}$, V_j by $V_{A,\&,j}$.

(ii) $\mu_{A,or}$ determines the $0 - 1$ stochastic process

$$\underset{\sim}{V}_{A,or} \overset{d}{=} (V_{A,or,j})_{j \in J_o} \overset{d}{=} (1 - V_{CA,\&,j})_{j \in J_o}$$ such that for all

$C \in \mathfrak{F}(J_o)$,

$$\Pr(\underset{j \in C}{Or}(V_{A,or,j} = 1)) = \mu_{A,or}(C) = \underset{x \in C}{\phi_{or}}(\phi_A(x)) \; .$$

5.2 One-point coverage problem.

A. Background.

Now, given any space X and any fuzzy subset A of X , there always exist (in general, many, unless A is an ordinary set) random subsets S of X such that S , under its one-point-coverage function is the same as the corresponding possibility function of A :

$$\phi_A(x) = Pr(x \in S) \text{ , for all } x \in X .$$

We write:

$$A \approx S .$$

In particular, we may choose

$$S = S_{U(A)} \stackrel{d}{=} \phi_A^{-1}[U,1] ,$$

a nested random subset of X one point coverage equivalent to A, where U is a random variable uniformly distributed over $[0,1]$.

If it is subsumed (and it is throughout where required) that $(\Omega,\mathfrak{B},Pr)$ is some non-atomic probability space, then such a $U : \Omega \to [0,1]$, may always be chosen. (See Theorem 3.)

Or choose $S = T(A)$, where $T(A)$ has a (random) membership function

$$\phi_{T(A)} \equiv (\phi_{T(A)}(x))_{x \in X}$$

which may be considered as a mutually statistically independent zero-one stochastic process, where

$$Pr(\phi_{T(A)}(x) = 1) = \phi_A(x),$$

$$Pr(\phi_{T(A)}(x) = 0) = 1 - \phi_A(x) ,$$

for all $x \in X$. (See, e.g., Goodman [90], [77], [78] and Nguyen [190].)

Conversely, it is clear that *any* random subset S of X generates a uniquely determined one point coverage equivalent fuzzy set $A = A(S)$ by defining

$$\phi_{A(S)}(x) = Pr(x \in S) \text{ ; all } x \in X .$$

Thus each fuzzy subset of a space may be represented by an entire class of random subsets of the same space through the common one point coverage function. This also implies that $\mathfrak{R}(X)$, the class of all random subsets of X, is partitioned into subclasses of random subsets of X, which each such class represents the equivalence class of all random subsets of X, all one point coverage equivalent to a given (and arbitrary) fuzzy subset of X.

Thus, we are led to the definition:

A (random set) *choice function* S is an injective mapping,

$$S : \mathfrak{F}(X) \to \mathfrak{R}(X) \text{ ; } S(A) \approx A \text{ ; all } A \in \mathfrak{F}(X) ,$$

i.e.,

$$\phi_A(x) = Pr(x \in S(A)) \text{ ; all } x \in X .$$

Hence, S_U and T are examples of choice functions.

More specifically, $S_U(A)$ has a nested range $\mathfrak{B}_o \overset{d}{=} r_A([0,1])$, where

$$r_A(x) \overset{d}{=} \phi_A^{-1}([x,1]) \; ; \; x \in [0,1] .$$

S_U corresponds to induced probability space

$$(r_A([0,1]) \, , \, r_A(\mathbb{B}_1), \, \nu_A') \; ; \; \nu_A' \overset{d}{=} vol_1 \circ r_A^{-1} \, ,$$

where $\mathbb{B}_1$ is the real Borel field over $[0,1]$. In addition, for all $C \in \mathcal{P}(X)$,

$$\mathfrak{C}_C = r_A[0, \inf_{x \in C} \phi_A(x)] \; ; \; \mathfrak{D}_C = r_A[\sup_{x \in C} \phi_A(x), \, 1] \; ;$$

$$\mathcal{E}_C = r_A[0, \, \sup_{x \in C} \phi_A(x)] \, ,$$

with evaluations

$$Pr(C \subseteq S_U(A)) = \inf_{x \in C} \phi_A(x) \; ; \; Pr(\emptyset \neq S_U(A) \subseteq C) = 1 - \sup_{x \in C} \phi_A(x) \; ;$$

$Pr(S_U(A) \; \Lambda \; C) = \sup_{x \in C} \phi_A(x)$, where Λ is the incidence relation (Chapter 3).

S_U also has the maximal coverage function among all choice functions S :

$$Pr(C \subseteq S_U(A)) \geq Pr(C \subseteq S(A)) \; ; \text{ for all } A \in \mathcal{F}(X) \, , \, C \in \mathcal{P}(X) .$$

In addition, S_U as a mapping from the class of all fuzzy subsets of any given space onto the class of all nested random subsets of the same space is an isomorphism - up to the one point coverage equivalence $\approx$ - between the following Zadeh's fuzzy set operations: $\mathcal{F}_o = (1 - (\cdot) \, , \min, \max)$ is the choice of the fuzzy set system - and corresponding ordinary set operations: complements, cartesian products, intersections, cartesian sums, unions, projections, subset relations, (defined here by ordering the membership functions pointwise), functional and inverse functional transforms. (See, e.g., Goodman [88].) For example, for any $f : X \to Y$, and any fuzzy subset A of X ,

$$f(A) \approx S_U(f(A)) \approx f(S_U(A)) \, ,$$

i.e., for any $x \in X$,

$$\phi_{f(A)}(x) = Pr(x \in S_U(f(A))) = Pr(x \in f(S_U(A))) .$$

Indeed, for S_U , there are even stronger relationships:

$$S_U(A \cup B) = S_U(A) \cup S_U(B)$$

$$S_U(A \cap B) = S_U(A) \cap S_U(B)$$

$$S_U(\mathrm{proj}(A)) = \mathrm{proj}(S_U(A))$$

$$S_U(f(A)) = f(S_U(A)) ,$$

but note that although

$$S_U(X \dashv A) \approx X \dashv S_U(A) ,$$

$$S_U(X \dashv A) = X \dashv S_{1-U}(A) \qquad (+)$$

for all $A,B \in \mathcal{F}(X)$.

Eq. (+) serves as a check on the prevention of the violation of the Law of Excluded Middle for ordinary sets: For any $x \in X$,

$$\begin{aligned} 0 &= \Pr(x \in \emptyset) = \Pr(x \in S_U(A) \cap (X \dashv S_U(A))) \\ &\le \Pr(x \in S_U(A) \cap S_U(X \dashv A)) \\ &= \Pr(x \in S_U(A) \cap (X \dashv S_{1-U}(A))) \\ &= \phi_{A\cap(X\dashv A)}(x) \\ &= \min(\phi_A(x), \phi_{X\dashv A}(x)) \\ &= \min(\phi_A(x), 1 - \phi_A(x)) . \end{aligned}$$

The range for $T(A)$ is $\mathcal{B}_o = \mathcal{P}\{x \mid \phi_A(x) > 0\}$ and

$$\Pr(C \subseteq T(A)) = \prod_{x\in C} \phi_A(x) \ ; \ \Pr(\emptyset \ne T(A) \subseteq C) = \prod_{x\in C} (1 - \phi_A(x)) \ ;$$

$$\Pr(T(A) \mathbin{\triangle} C) = 1 - \prod_{x\in C} (1 - \phi_A(x)) .$$

For fuzzy set system $\mathcal{F}_1 = (1 - (\cdot), \mathrm{prod}, \mathrm{probsum})$, T induces isomorphic-like relations for complements, cartesian products, intersections, cartesian sums, unions, projections, etc. (See [90] and [88].)

See also the following papers for related results in establishing one point coverage representations of fuzzy sets by random sets: Orlov [197], Wang [261], Wang and Sanchez [262], Nguyen [187], [190], and Höhle [116], [117]. Also, Wang and Sanchez (e.g., [264], [265]), extend earlier work in relating fuzzy sets to random sets by introducing the general notion of "hyperfields" to motivate random set definitions and properties, and as well, the concept of random fuzzy sets.

B. Flou classes, level sets and nested random sets.

With a random variable interpretation for indices, Zadeh's early result [278], as well as, Negoita and Ralescu's extensions

[184] of Gentilhomme's flou sets [69] (essentially a collection of nonrandomized nested sets) may be tied in with one point random set coverage representations of fuzzy sets via choice function S_U

The choice function S_U is definable through the mappings Γ_A, $A \in \mathcal{F}(X)$. The ordinary set $\Gamma_A(\alpha)$ is often called in the fuzzy set literature the α-level or α-cut set formed from A, $\alpha \in [0,1]$. As early as 1971 ([278]), Γ_A was employed in representations of fuzzy sets in terms of ordinary ones, via the equation

$$\phi_A(x) = \sup_{0<\alpha\leq 1} (\alpha \cdot \phi_{\Gamma_A(\alpha)}(x)) \; ; \text{ all } x \in X, \; A \in \mathcal{F}(X), \qquad (\ddagger)$$

later extended by Sugeno [248'] for defining fuzzy integrals. (Note that integrating both sides of $(\ddagger)$ with respect to x leads to the standard simple function representation for a Lebesgue integral.) α-cuts may also be used to motivate techniques for the combination of evidence.

But notice that for any outcome U

$$\begin{aligned} x \in S_U(A) \quad &\text{iff} \quad \phi_A(x) \geq U \\ &\text{iff} \quad x \in \Gamma_A(U) \\ &\text{iff} \quad \phi_{\Gamma_A(U)}(x) = 1 \; ; \\ x \notin S_U(A) \quad &\text{iff} \quad \phi_{\Gamma_A(U)}(x) = 0 \; , \end{aligned}$$

whence

$$\begin{aligned} Pr(x \in S_U(A)) &= E(\phi_{\Gamma_A(U)}(x)) \\ &= \int_{\alpha=0}^{1} \alpha \cdot \phi_{\Gamma_A(\alpha)}(x) \, d\alpha = \sup_{0\leq\alpha\leq 1} (\alpha \cdot \phi_{\Gamma_A(\alpha)}(x)) \; , \end{aligned}$$

the same as $(\ddagger)$.

Originally, in 1968, Gentilhomme [69] independent of Zadeh, envisioned the extension of an ordinary set by the addition of a zone where set membership would not be certain. Negoita and Ralescu [184] extended this concept, called *flou set*, to that of an arbitrary collection $(A_\alpha)_{0\leq\alpha\leq 1}$ of nested sets, sufficiently continuous with respect to the index α. A typical flou set as defined here will be $\underset{\sim}{C} = (C_\alpha)_{\alpha\in[0,1]}$, where $\underset{\sim}{C} \in \mathcal{P}(X)$,

$$X = C_0 \supseteq \cdots \supseteq C_\alpha \supseteq C_\beta \supseteq \cdots \supseteq C_1 \; ; \; 1 \geq \beta \geq \alpha \geq 0 \; ,$$

with continuity condition

$$C_{\vee(K)} = \bigcap_{\alpha\in K} C_\alpha \; ; \text{ all } K \subseteq [0,1] \; ,$$

$\vee$ being the sup operation.

Operations $\complement$, $\cup$, $\cap$ and subset ordering $\subseteq$ may be defined over $\mathcal{FL}(X)$, the class of all flou subsets of X , by requiring these operators and relations to hold component-wise for the flou sets involved (in the proper order). Ralescu and Negoita [184] first showed (replacing the unit interval range of fuzzy set membership functions by a lattice L with sufficient ordering properties) that

$$\Gamma : \mathcal{F}(X) \to \mathcal{FL}(X) \;;\; \Gamma(A) \overset{d}{=} \Gamma_A \overset{d}{=} (\Gamma_A(\alpha))_{\alpha\in[0,1]} \;;\; A \in \mathcal{F}(X) , \qquad (\#)$$

is a bijective mapping, which is in fact an isomorphism preserving $\complement$, $\cup$, $\cap$, and $\subseteq$, where the fuzzy set counterparts correspond to fuzzy set system $\mathcal{F}_0$, with $\subseteq$ defined here by, for any $A,B \in \mathcal{F}(X)$,

$$A \subseteq B \quad \text{iff} \quad \phi_A(x) \le \phi_B(x) \;;\; \text{all} \quad x \in X .$$

In addition, Γ_A (analogous to the isomorphism-like properties of S_U) also preserves functional and inverse functional transforms. Extensions of these relations for other fuzzy concepts, including fuzzy groups and fuzzy dynamic systems, have also been accomplished [184]. In a related area, Radecki [209] independently obtained similar isomorphic relations for level set mappings. Earlier, Goodman (1976), referenced in Nguyen [190]), in effect, replaced the non-random parameter α in eq. (#) by the random variable U , uniformly distributed over $[0,1]$. This has the effect of replacing each flou set in eq. (#) by a corresponding *nested random set*, namely $\Gamma_A(U) = S_U(A)$. In addition, there is an obvious bijective correspondence between $\mathcal{FL}(X)$ and $\mathcal{NR}(X)$, the class of all nested random subsets of X . Before detailing these results, it is of some importance to establish the following necessary and sufficient conditions when a uniformly distributed random variable may be used in terms of non-atomic probability spaces and other criteria. (See [89].)

Theorem 3

Let $P = (\Omega,\mathcal{B},Pr)$ be a probability space. Define a flou class $A = (A_\alpha)_{\alpha\in[0,1]} \subseteq \mathcal{B}$ to be a nested class of sets which are non-increasing inclusion-wise with respect to index α and which are continuous with respect to union and intersection relative to index α . Then the following statements are equivalent:

1. There is a random variable $U : \Omega \to [0,1]$ uniformly distributed.

2. For any probability distribution function F over $\mathbb{R}$, there is a random variable $V : \Omega \to \mathbb{R}$ such that V has probability distribution function F .

3. There is a flou subclass $A = (A_\alpha)_{\alpha\in[0,1]}$ of $\mathcal{B}$ such that for all $\alpha \in [0,1]$,

$$Pr(A_\alpha) = 1 - \alpha .$$

4. $\mathcal{P}$ is a non-atomic probability space.

Proof.

1 implies 2: Let

$$V = F^\dagger(U) ,$$

where pseudoinverse $F^\dagger$ is defined by

$$F^\dagger(t) = \inf F^{-1}(\inf\{x \mid t \le x \in \mathrm{range}(F)\}) ,$$

whence for all $t \in [0,1]$, $x \in \mathbb{R}$,

$$F^\dagger(t) \le x \quad \text{iff} \quad t \le F(x) .$$

1 implies 3: Let

$$A_\alpha = U^{-1}([\alpha,1]) , \text{ for all } \alpha \in [0,1] .$$

3 implies 1: For all $\omega \in \Omega$, define

$$U(\omega) = \sup \{\alpha \mid \alpha \in [0,1] \ \& \ \omega \in A_\alpha\} ,$$

which implies for all $\alpha \in [0,1]$

$$Pr(U^{-1}([0,\alpha])) = Pr(\Omega \dashv A_\alpha) = \alpha .$$

4 implies 3: Use, e.g., the standard result [104'], pp. 168, 174.
3 implies 4: Suppose there is an atom $B \in \mathfrak{D}$. Then use continuity of probability to obtain the desired contradiction.

Thus, from now on, $\mathcal{P}$ is assumed to be some fixed non-atomic probability space, which thus may also be used to generate $\mathfrak{R}(X) = \{S \mid S : \Omega \to \mathcal{P}(X)$ is measurable$\}$ which will include all random sets of interest such as $S_U(A)$, $T(A)$, etc.

Let $A \in \mathcal{F}(X)$ be arbitrary. Consider now the mapping S without regard to the random variable U . That is, define the family of all level sets associated with A as in eq. (#):

$$\Gamma(A) = (\phi_A^{-1}([\alpha,1]))_{\alpha\in[0,1]} ,$$

and $Lev(X)$ as the collection of all level families $\Gamma(A)$ for all $A \in \mathcal{F}(X)$. Operations between level families are defined componentwise in terms of ordinary set operations at each level α , including complements, intersections, union, subset relations, functional transforms, projections, etc.

Theorem 4

Let X be any fixed space and defined $\mathcal{FL}(X)$ as the collection of all flou classes of X : $\underset{\sim}{A} = (A_\alpha)_{\alpha\in[0,1]} \subseteq \mathcal{P}(X)$ with $A_0 = X$. Then

1. $\mathcal{FL}(X) = \mathrm{Lev}(X)$, where for any $\underset{\sim}{A} \in \mathcal{FL}(X)$

$$\underset{\sim}{A} = \Gamma(B_{\underset{\sim}{A}}) , \quad B_{\underset{\sim}{A}} \in \mathcal{F}(X) ,$$

where, letting U be a random variable distributed uniform [0,1] ,

$$\phi_{B_{\underset{\sim}{A}}}(x) = \sup \{\alpha \mid \alpha \in [0,1] \ \&\ x \in A_\alpha\}$$

$$= \Pr(x \in A_U) \ ; \ \text{all} \quad x \in X .$$

Conversely, if $A \in \mathcal{F}(X)$, then $\Gamma(A) \in \mathcal{FL}(X)$.

2. Let the collection of all nested random subsets of X be denoted by $\mathcal{NR}(X)$, where it is assumed that for any $S \in \mathcal{NR}(X)$, $\mathrm{range}(S) \in \mathcal{FL}(X)$. Then $\mathcal{F}(X)$, $\mathcal{FL}(X)$, and $\mathcal{NR}(X)$ are all bijectively related as in the following diagram:

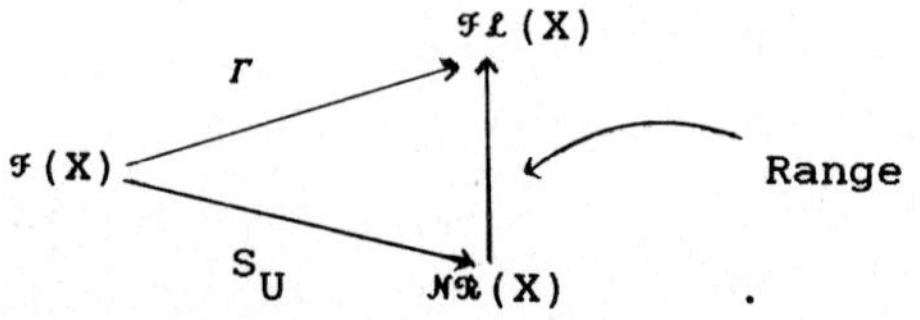

Isomorphisms or isomorphic-like relations hold for all of the abovementioned operations defined over each of the three spaces.

Proof.

The only thing new to show is that S_U is surjective. Let S be any nested random subset of X with the property of $\mathrm{range}(S) = (A_\alpha)_{\alpha\in[0,1]} \in \mathcal{FL}(X)$. Thus, there is a random variable $V : \Omega \to [0,1]$ such that for all $\omega \in \Omega$, $S(\omega) = A_{V(\omega)}$. By part 1 of this theorem,

$$S(\omega) = \phi^{-1}_{B_{\mathrm{range}(S)}}([V(\omega),1]) \ : \ \text{all} \quad \omega \in \Omega .$$

Then letting F be the probability distribution function for V and using the proof of Theorem 3, for any $x \in X$,

$$x \in S \ \text{ iff } \ V \le \phi_{B_{\mathrm{range}(S)}}(x) \ \text{ iff } \ F^{\dagger}(U) \le \phi_{B_{\mathrm{range}(S)}}(x)$$

$$\text{iff } \ U \le F(\phi_{B_{\mathrm{range}(S)}}(x)) \ \text{ iff } \ x \in S_U(C) ,$$

where

$$\phi_C(x) = F(\phi_{B_{\text{range}(S)}}(x)) \;;\; \text{all} \quad x \in X \; .$$

Hence, $S = S_U$ (in distribution).

An immediate consequence of Theorem 4 is that for any $A \in \mathcal{F}(X)$, there is a unique nested random subset of X, $S(A) \approx A$, namely, $S(A) = S_U(A)$. (See again [89] for further details.)

C. <u>Additional results for the one point coverage problem</u>.

<u>Case I</u>.

Let X be a finite space and $A \in \mathcal{F}(X)$ with $\phi_A : X \to [0,1]$ given.

Let $S \in \mathcal{R}(X)$ be arbitrary, i.e., $S : \Omega \to \mathcal{P}(X)$ with $S^{-1}(C_{\{x\}}) \in \mathcal{B}$ for all $x \in X$, where $(\Omega, \mathcal{B}, Pr)$ is a given probability space. Note that S is bijectively related to $\phi_S = (\phi_S(x))_{x \in X}$, a zero-one stochistic process, where for any $C \in \mathcal{P}(X)$,

$$\begin{aligned} Pr(S = C) &= Pr(\phi_S = \phi_C) \\ &= Pr(\underset{x\in X}{\&}(\phi_S(x) = \phi_C(x))) \\ &= Pr(\underset{x\in C}{\&}(\phi_S(x) = 1) \;\&\; (\underset{x\in X \dashv C}{\&}(\phi_S(x) = 0))) \\ &= \sum_{K \subseteq X \dashv C} (-1)^{\text{card } K} \cdot \mu_S(C \cup K) \; , \end{aligned}$$

for any $B \in \mathcal{P}(X)$,

$$\mu_S(B) \overset{d}{=} Pr(\underset{x\in B}{\&}(\phi_S(x) = 1)) = Pr(B \subseteq S) \; .$$

Now by Theorem 4 of Chapter 3, since $Pr(S = \cdot)$ is a probability function over $\mathcal{P}(X)$, it follows that μ_S is a doubt measure over $\mathcal{P}(X)$ which uniquely determines S. Note the convention

$$\mu_S(\emptyset) = 1 \; .$$

In particular, if S is constrained so that $S \approx A$, i.e., they are one point converage equivalent, this is equivalent to requiring for each $x \in X$

$$Pr(\phi_S(x) = 1) = \phi_A(x)$$

yielding

$$\Pr(\phi_S(x) = 0) = 1 - \phi_A(x) ,$$

which means, for all $x \in X$

$$\mu_S(\{x\}) = \Pr(x \in S) = \Pr(\phi_S(x) = 1) = \phi_A(x) .$$

Now let, for each $x \in X$, U_x be such that w.l.o.g. $U_x : \Omega \to [0,1]$ is a uniformly distributed random variable, and $\underset{\sim}{U} = (U_x)_{x\in X}$ is a stochastic process (with all well-defined and consistent joint c.d.f.'s). Identify the events

$$\phi_S(x) = 1 \quad \text{iff} \quad U_x \le \phi_A(x)$$

$$\phi_S(x) = 0 \quad \text{iff} \quad U_x > \phi_A(x)$$

for all $x \in X$. Thus, here

$$S \approx A .$$

Thus, for any $B \in \mathcal{P}(X)$,

$$\mu_S(B) = \Pr(\underset{x\in B}{\&} (U_x \le \phi_A(x)))$$

and thus μ_S and hence S are specified by $\underset{\sim}{U}$.

In particular, choose $\phi_\&$, any n-copula. This uniquely determines $U_{\phi_\&}$ a corresponding well-defined process, where for any $B \in \mathcal{P}(X)$ and constants $\{c_x \mid x \in B\}$, $c_x \in [0,1]$, $x \in B$,

$$\Pr(\underset{x\in B}{\&} (U_x \le c_x)) \stackrel{d}{=} \underset{x\in B}{\phi_\&} (c_x) .$$

In turn, $\phi_\&$ yields $S_\&$, where for any $B \in \mathcal{P}(X)$,

$$\mu_{S_\&}(B) = \Pr(\underset{x\in B}{\&} (\phi_{S_\&}(x) = 1)) = \Pr(B \subseteq S_\&)$$

$$= \Pr(\underset{x\in B}{\&} (U_x \le \phi_A(x))) = \underset{x\in B}{\phi_\&} (\phi_A(x)) ,$$

and hence, for any $C \in \mathcal{P}(X)$

$$\Pr(S_\& = C) = \sum_{K\subseteq X\dashv C} (-1)^{\text{card } K} \cdot \mu_{S_\&}(C \cup K) .$$

For $\phi_\& = \min$, $U_x \equiv U$, all $x \in X$ and

$$S_\& = S_U(A) .$$

For $\phi_{\&}$ = prod, all U_x's are statistically independent, for $x \in X$ and

$$S_{\&} = T(A) .$$

For $\phi_{\&}$ = maxsum and $n = 2$, letting $X = \{x_1,x_2\}$ with $\phi_A(x_1) + \phi_A(x_2) \le 1$, i.e., ϕ_A is a deficient or ordinary probability function, depending on whether $\phi_A(x_1) + \phi_A(x_2) < 1$ or $\phi_A(x_1) + \phi_A(x_2) = 1$, respectively, it follows that

$$Pr(S_{\&} = \{x_1,x_2\}) = \mu_{S_{\&}}(\{x_1,x_2\}) = 0 ,$$

$$Pr(S_{\&} = \{x_1\}) = \mu_S(\{x_1\}) - \mu_S(\{x_1,x_2\}) = \phi_A(x_1) ,$$

$$Pr(S_{\&} = \{x_2\}) = \mu_S(\{x_2\}) - \mu_S(\{x_1,x_2\}) = \phi_A(x_2) ,$$

$$\begin{aligned} Pr(S_{\&} = \emptyset) &= \mu_S(\{x_1\}) - \mu_S(\{x_2\}) + \mu_S(\{x_1,x_2\}) + \mu_S(\emptyset) \\ &= 1 - \phi_A(x_1) - \phi_A(x_2) . \end{aligned}$$

Thus, here $S_{\&}$ coincides essentially with the random variable determined by ϕ_A. This case corresponds to $U_{x_2} = 1 - U_{x_1}$.

More generally, if $\sum_{x \in X} \phi_A(x) \le 1$, again, ϕ_A corresponding to a deficient or ordinary probability function, S may be identified with the random variable V, say, determined by ϕ_A, i.e.,

$$S = \{V\} .$$

Equivalently, for any $C \in \mathcal{P}(X)$,

$$Pr(S = C) = \begin{cases} 0 , & \text{if } \text{card } C \ge 2 \\ \phi_A(x) , & \text{if } C = \{x\} \\ 1 - \sum_{x \in X} \phi_A(x) , & \text{if } C = \emptyset , \end{cases}$$

and thus $(\phi_S(x))_{x \in X}$ is a disjoint $0 - 1$ process, i.e., at most only one $\phi_S(x)$ may take one in value. Of course, this implies $S \approx A$.

Case II

Let $Y \subseteq \mathbb{R}^n$ be arbitrary with $\phi_A : Y \to [0,1]$ given. Then for any finite subset X of Y, construct random set $S_X : \Omega \to \mathcal{P}(X)$ or equivalently, zero-one process $(\phi_{S_X}(x))_{x \in X}$ as in

Case I. Clearly, the entire collection $(\phi_{S_X}(x))_{x \in X,\ X \in \mathfrak{F}(Y)}$ yields all joint c.d.f.'s being consistent. Thus Kolmogorov's Extension Theorem may be applied to yield a probability space $(\{0,1\}^Y, \mathbb{B}_Y, \nu)$ such that all finite joint c.d.f.'s of $(\phi_{S_X}(x))_{x \in X}$ are marginal c.d.f.'s relative to ν, and thus relabelling, $\Upsilon \overset{d}{=} (\phi_S(x))_{x \in Y}$ is a well-defined stochastic process with joint probability measure ν and hence we may take

$$S = \phi^{-1}(\Upsilon) ,$$

i.e.,

$$\phi_S = \Upsilon ,$$

as the desired random set.

In particular, any choice of infinite-copula $\phi_\&$ results in a well-defined uniform process $(U_x)_{x \in Y}$, each U_x distributed uniform $[0,1]$, in turn determining a unique zero-one process $(\phi_S(x))_{x \in Y}$ over Y and equivalently $S \in \mathfrak{R}(Y)$.

D. <u>The one point random set coverage problem: a general solution for the finite case</u>.

A basic question may be posed: Given $A \in \mathcal{F}(X)$, what other random subsets S of X exist besides $S_U(A)$ and $T(A)$ such that $S \approx A$? Some results are given in [88], [89] where a family of random subsets of X is obtained, which includes $S_U(A)$ and $T(A)$ as members, all one point coverage equivalent to a given A. However, this does not exhaust all possible such random sets. The problem of determining all possible random sets one point equivalent to a given fuzzy set is called the one point coverage problem. (The problem of determining all random sets m point coverage equivalent to a given fuzzy set is treated in the following section.) Let

$$\mathcal{F}_1(A) = \{S \mid S \in \mathfrak{R}(X) \ \& \ A \approx S\} .$$

Suppose form now on, X is any space with $n = \text{card}(X) \geq 3$ and order all 2^n sets $C \in \mathcal{P}(X)$ by order $\leq$ where if $\text{card}(C') < \text{card}(C'')$ then $C' \leq C''$ and if $\text{card}(C') = \text{card}(C'')$, determine an arbitrary but fixed and consistent order also. The notation

$$\binom{m}{j} = m!/((m-j)!j!) , \ j = 0,1,\ldots,m \ ; \ \underset{\sim}{1}_m = \begin{bmatrix}1\\ \vdots \\ 1\end{bmatrix} ; \ \underset{\sim}{0}_m = \begin{bmatrix}0\\ \vdots \\ 0\end{bmatrix} ;$$

$$a_n = 2^n - n - 1$$

will be used, and denoting vector and matrix transposes by superscript Tr, define:

$$\kappa_{(n)}^{Tr} = (1\cdot \underset{\sim}{1}_{\binom{n}{2}}^{Tr},\ 2\cdot \underset{\sim}{1}_{\binom{n}{3}}^{Tr}, \ldots, (n-1)\cdot \underset{\sim}{1}_{\binom{n}{n}}^{Tr}) \quad (1 \text{ by } a_n) \ ;$$

$$\xi_x = (\phi_C(x))_{\substack{C\in\mathcal{P}(X)\\ \mathrm{card}(C)\geq 2}} \quad (a_n \text{ by } 1) \ , \text{ all } x \in X \ ;$$

$$\xi_{(n)} = (\xi_x)_{x\in X} \quad (a_n \text{ by } n) \ ;$$

$$\gamma^{(2)}(S) = (\Pr(S = C))_{\substack{C\in\mathcal{P}(X)\\ \mathrm{card}(C)\geq 2}} \quad (a_n \text{ by } 1) \ ; \text{ all } S \in \mathfrak{R}(X) \ ;$$

$$\nu(A) = (\phi_A(x))_{x\in X} \quad (n \text{ by } 1) \ ; \ \tau(A) = \max\left(\sum_{x\in X} (\phi_A(x)) - 1,\ 0\right) \ ;$$

all $A \in \mathcal{F}(X)$.

Theorem 5

For any finite space X (with notation as above) and any $A \in \mathcal{F}(X)$,

1. $\mathcal{S}_1(A) = \{S \mid S \in \mathfrak{R}(X) \ \& \ \gamma^{(2)}(S) \in \mathfrak{R}_1(A)\}$

where

$\mathfrak{R}_1(A) = \{W \mid W \in \mathbb{R}^{a_n}$ is arbitrary satisfying eqs. (1) - (3)} ,

$$\begin{cases} \tau(A) \leq \kappa_{(n)}^{Tr}\cdot W & (1) \\ \nu(A) \geq \xi_{(n)}^{Tr}\cdot W & (2) \\ \underset{\sim}{0}_{a_n} \leq W \quad . & (3) \end{cases}$$

2. $\mathfrak{R}_1(A)$ is a closed convex region in $\mathbb{R}^{a_n}$ having in general $1 + n + a_n = 2^n$ hyperplane bounds with an uncountable infinity of possible elements $\gamma^{(2)}(S)$ in it, or equivalently, $S \in \mathcal{S}_1(A)$.

3. There is a bijective correspondence between $\mathcal{S}_1(A)$ and $\mathfrak{R}_1(A)$, where for any given $W \in \mathfrak{R}_1(A)$, $S \in \mathcal{S}_1(A)$ is uniquely determined (in distribution) by

$$\begin{cases} \gamma^{(2)}(S) = W \\ \Pr(S = \emptyset) = 1 - \sum_{x\in X} (\phi_A(x)) + \kappa_{(n)}^{Tr} \cdot W \\ \Pr(S = \{x\}) = \phi_A(x) - \underset{\sim}{1}_{a_n}^{Tr} \cdot W \ ; \text{ all } x \in X \ . \end{cases}$$

Define now the vertex set $\mathcal{V}_1(A)$ of $\mathfrak{X}(A)$ as the set of $W \in \mathfrak{X}_1(A)$ such that equality holds in eqs. (1) - (3) for a_n linearly independent columns of $(\kappa_{(n)}, \xi_{(n)}, I_{a_n})$. There can be at most $\binom{2^n}{a_n} = \binom{2^n}{n+1}$ vertex elements. It also follows that for all $A \in \mathcal{F}(X)$:

(a) $\text{Range}(S_U(A)) = \{\phi_A^{-1}([y_j(A),1]) \mid j = 1,..,r\}$,

where

$$\text{range}(\phi_A) = \{y_1(A),..,y_r(A)\} \; ; \; 0 \le y_1(A) < \cdots < y_r(A) \le 1 .$$

Hence,

$$\Pr(S_U(A) = C) = \begin{cases} y_j(A) - y_{j-1}(A) \quad \text{if} \quad C = \phi_A^{-1}([y_j(A),1]) \\ \quad \text{for } j = 1,..,r \; ; \; y_0(A) = 0 , \\ 0 , \quad \text{for } C \text{ otherwise} . \end{cases}$$

$\gamma^{(2)}(S_U(A)) \in \mathcal{V}_1(A)$, where

$$\kappa_{(n)}^{Tr} \cdot \gamma^{(2)}(S_U(A)) = \sum_{x \in X} (\phi_A(x)) \ge \tau(A) ,$$

$$\xi_{(n)}^{Tr} \cdot \gamma^{(2)}(S_U(A)) = \nu(A) .$$

(b) $\Pr(T(A) = C) = \prod_{x \in C} (\phi_A(x)) \cdot \prod_{x \in X \dashv C} (1 - \phi_A(x))$;
all $C \in \mathcal{P}(X)$.

$\gamma^{(2)}(T(A)) \in \text{interior}(\mathfrak{X}_1(A))$ in general, where

$$\kappa_{(n)}^{Tr} \cdot \gamma^{(2)}(T(A)) = \sum_{x \in X} (\phi_A(x)) - 1 + \prod_{x \in X} (1 - \phi_A(x)) \ge \tau(A)$$

and

$$\xi_x^{Tr} \cdot \gamma^{(2)}(T(A)) = \phi_A(x) \cdot (1 - \prod_{y \in X \dashv \{x\}} (1 - \phi_A(y))) \le \phi_A(x) \; ; \text{ all } x \in X .$$

(c) It should be noted that the condition given in eq. (1) is superfluous iff

$$\sum_{x \in X} (\phi_A(x)) \le 1 , \qquad (4)$$

i.e., ϕ_A is either an ordinary probability function (equality holding in (4) or a deficient probability function (inequality holding in (4) over X, in which case random set $S'(A) \in \mathcal{S}_1(A)$, where $S'(A)$ may be identified with a random variable over X having ϕ_A as its probability function (possibly deficient). Thus

$$\gamma^{(2)}(S'(A)) = \underset{\sim}{0}_{a_n} ,$$

and hence $\gamma^{(2)}(S'(A)) \in \mathcal{V}_1(A)$. Also,

$$\Pr(S'(A) = \emptyset) = 1 - \sum_{x \in X} \phi_A(x) ,$$

$$\Pr(S'(A) = \{x\}) = \phi_A(x) \text{ ; all } x \in X .$$

E. <u>One point coverage functions and random intervals</u>. [89]

An important class of random sets is the random intervals. In this section, the one point coverage problem is specialized to the case where base space $X = \mathbb{R}, A \in \mathcal{F}(\mathbb{R})$, and $\mathcal{S}_1(A)$ is replaced by a more restrictive class $\mathcal{S}_1(A,Q)$, the class of all $S \in Q$ such that $S \approx A$, for various classes $\mathcal{Q} \subseteq \mathcal{R}(\mathbb{R})$ of random closed intervals of $\mathbb{R}$.

Define first $\mathcal{Q}_1$ as the class of all random closed intervals and $\mathcal{Q}_2$ as the class of all random closed intervals S with $\Pr(S = \emptyset) = 0$. Then:

(1) There is a natural identification between $\mathcal{Q}_1$ and the class of all bivariate random variables $Z = \begin{bmatrix} V \\ W \end{bmatrix}$ over the upper half diagonal plane in $\mathbb{R}^2$, and between $\mathcal{Q}_2$ and the class of all random variables over $\mathbb{R}^2$. From now on, let $S = [V,W]$ denote a random interval with V and W r.v.'s over $\mathbb{R}$ with marginal c.d.f. for V denoted by F_1, for W denoted by F_2, and joint c.d.f. by F, etc. The convention $[a,b] = \emptyset$ for $a > b$ will be used.

(2) For any $A \in \mathcal{F}(\mathbb{R})$, $S = [V,W] \in \mathcal{S}_1(A,\mathcal{Q}_1)$ iff

$$\phi_A(x) = F_1(x) - F(x,x) \text{ ; all } x \in \mathbb{R} ,$$

the solution which for F_1 and F in terms of ϕ_A may be complicated unless ϕ_A is further specified.

(3) Letting $\mathcal{Q}_3$ be the class of all random intervals $S = [V,W]$ with V and W statistically independent,

$$\Pr(S \neq \emptyset) = \int_{x \in \mathbb{R}} F_1(x) \cdot dF_2(x) ,$$

and for any $A \in \mathcal{F}(\mathbb{R})$, $S = [V,W] \in \mathcal{F}_1(A,\mathcal{Q}_3)$ iff

$$\phi_A(x) = F_1(x) \cdot (1 - F_2(x)) \ ; \ \text{all} \ \ x \in \mathbb{R} , \qquad (1)$$

which implies that $\log(\phi_A)$ is of bounded variation with $\lim_{x \to \pm\infty} \phi_A(x) = 0$.

(4) If $A \in \mathcal{F}(\mathbb{R})$ is such that ϕ_A is unimodal (which will be in the sense that possibly a neighborhood of modal points exists and continuity from the right holds) at some x_o say at which $\phi_A(x_o) = 1$, then $S = [V,W] \in \mathcal{F}_1(A,\mathcal{Q}_3)$ where

$$F_1(x) = \begin{cases} \phi_A(x) , & \text{if} \ \ x \leq x_o \\ 1 , & \text{if} \ \ x \geq x_o \end{cases} \ ; \quad F_2(x) = \begin{cases} 0 , & \text{if} \ \ x \leq x_o \\ 1 - \phi_A(x) , & \text{if} \ \ x \geq x_o \end{cases}$$

(5) Let $\mathcal{Q}_4$ be the class of all random intervals $S = [V,W]$ with V and W statistically independent and identically distributed. If $A \in \mathcal{F}(\mathbb{R})$, then $\mathcal{F}_1(A,\mathcal{Q}_4) \neq \emptyset$ iff $\lim_{x \to \pm\infty} (\phi_A(x)) = 0$ and ϕ_A is unimodal at some x_o with $\phi_A(x_o) \leq 1/4$, in which case $\mathcal{F}_1(A,\mathcal{Q}_4) = \{S(A)\}$ where $S(A) = [V,W]$ is determined by solving eq.(1) for $F_1 = F_2$ in terms of ϕ_A :

$$F_1(x) = F_2(x) = \begin{cases} (1 - (1 - 4 \cdot \phi_A(x))^{1/2})/2 , & \text{if} \ \ x < x_o \\ (1 + (1 - 4 \cdot \phi_A(x))^{1/2})/2 , & \text{if} \ \ x \geq x_o . \end{cases}$$

(6) Let $\mathcal{Q}_5$ be the class of all nested random closed intervals. Then using Theorem 2,

$$\mathcal{Q}_5 = \{S_U(A) \mid A \in \mathcal{F}(\mathbb{R}) \ \& \ \phi_A \ \text{is continuous and either: unimodal, non-increasing, or non-decreasing over} \ \mathbb{R}\} ,$$

where as usual, U is a fixed random variable uniformly distributed over $[0,1]$.

Also, for any $A \in \mathcal{F}(\mathbb{R})$ with ϕ_A continuous and either: unimodal, non-increasing, or non-decreasing, $\mathcal{F}_1(A,\mathcal{Q}_5) = \{S_U(A)\}$, where it should be noted that

$$S_U(A) = \begin{cases} (-\infty, \sup(\phi_A^{-1}(U))] & , \text{ if } \phi_A \text{ is non-increasing} \\ [\inf(\phi_A^{-1}(U)), +\infty] & , \text{ if } \phi_A \text{ is non-decreasing} . \end{cases}$$

(Examples of monotone fuzzy sets include: "tall", "short", "old", etc.)

In a related vein, note that if ϕ_A is any prob. dist. func. over $\mathbb{R}$ coresponding to random variable Z, say, then Z can be identified with $\phi_A^{\dagger}(U)$ (see Theorem 3), $S_U(A) = [Z,+\infty)$ and

$$\phi_A(x) = Pr(Z \leq x) = Pr(x \in [Z,+\infty)) \text{ ; all } x \in \mathbb{R} .$$

Two more interesting classes of random intervals remain to be discussed.

Theorem 6

Let $\mathcal{Q}_6$ denote the class of all fixed length random closed intervals. Let $A \in \mathcal{F}(\mathbb{R})$. Then $\mathcal{F}_1(A,\mathcal{Q}_6) \neq \emptyset$ iff there exists prob. dist. func. F_A and positive real constant b_A such that for all $x \in X$,

$$\phi_A(x) = F_A(x + b_A) - F_A(x - b_A)$$

iff ϕ_A is integrable over $\mathbb{R}$ and defining

$$2 \cdot b_A = \int_{x \in \mathbb{R}} \phi_A(x) \cdot dx$$

and

$$F_A(x + (2k+1) \cdot b_A) = \sum_{j=-\infty}^{k} (\phi_A(x + 2j \cdot b_A)) \text{ ; all } x \in [0, 2b_A] ,$$

$$k = 0, \pm 1, \pm 2, \ldots ,$$

F_A is a legitimate prob. dist. func., in which case
$\mathcal{F}_1(A,\mathcal{Q}_6) = \{S(A)\}$, where

$$S(A) = [V - b_A , V + b_A] ,$$

where V is a random variable having prob. dist. func. F_A.

Theorem 7

Let $\mathcal{Q}_7$ denote the class of random closed intervals of the form $S = [V - W_1, V + W_2]$, where V is a random variable over $\mathbb{R}$ statistically independent of random variables W_1 and W_2 jointly defined over $\mathbb{R}^+ \times \mathbb{R}^+$. Then for any $A \in \mathcal{F}(\mathbb{R})$, $\mathcal{F}_1(A,\mathcal{Q}_7) \neq \emptyset$ iff

$$\phi_A = f_A * G_A$$

where $f_A : \mathbb{R} \to [0,1]$ is unimodal at 0 with $f_A(0) = 1$, $\lim_{x\to\pm\infty} (f_A(x)) = 0$, G_A is some prob. dist. funct. over $\mathbb{R}$, and $*$ denotes the convolution operator; in which case, $S(A) = [V - W_1, V + W_2] \in \mathcal{F}_1(A,\mathcal{Q}_7)$ where V has prob. dist. func. G_A, W_1 has prob. dist. func. $1 - f_A(-\cdot)$ over $\mathbb{R}^+$, W_2 has prob. dist. func. $1 - f_A(\cdot)$ over $\mathbb{R}^+$, with W_1, W_2 jointly arbitrary and statistically independent of V.

It follows that any $A \in \mathcal{F}(\mathbb{R})$ for which ϕ_A is uniformly continuous and integrable over $\mathbb{R}$ may be arbitrarily uniformly closely approximated, in the one point coverage sense, up to some scalar multiple, by some S in $\mathcal{Q}_7$. (Approximate ϕ_A by $c \cdot f * G$, where $c = c_o/((2\pi)^{1/2} \cdot \sigma)$, $c_o = \int_{x\in\mathbb{R}} \phi_A(x)dx$, $f = (2\pi)^{1/2} \cdot \sigma \cdot f_\sigma$, f_σ being the probability density function for Gaussian distribution $N(0,\sigma^2)$.)

The construction of such an approximation (given in [85]), $f * G$ to ϕ_B, thus yields the approximation desired one-point-coverage equivalent closed random interval $S \in \mathcal{Q}_7$.

On the other hand, the exact solution (if it exists) of the convolution equation

$$\phi_B = f * G$$

for some f and G as above for $\mathcal{Q}_7$, can entail difficulties, which may be alleviated to some degree by use of the characteristic function transform $ch(g)(S) = \int_{x\in\mathbb{R}} e^{isx} g(x)dx$, etc., which converts the above equation to

$$ch(\phi_B) = ch(f) \cdot ch(G) .$$

Also, solutions of these equations may be related to unimodal infinitely divisible distributions, but we leave this for future work. (See also, Lukacs [161].)

Lastly, we wish to indicate connections between random intervals and interval mathematics in general (see, e.g., Nickel [194]) could be explored further in relation to dispersions.

F. A connection between fuzzy sets, random sets and random variables

So far in this paper, connections have been established between the membership functions of generalized sets and the one point coverage functions of random sets. Recently [86], [89] it has been shown that random variable evaluation functions may also be directly related to membership functions and one point coverage functions. This result is restated.

If Y is any space of elementary events and $\mathfrak{B} \subseteq \mathcal{P}(Y)$ is any collection of compound or elementary events for random variable V over Y (i.e., $\mathfrak{B} \subseteq \mathcal{A}$, the σ-algebra over Y for V), the function $g_V : \mathfrak{B} \to [0,1]$ where for any $B \in \mathfrak{B}$, $g_V(B) = Pr(V \in B)$, is called the evaluation function for V over event collection $\mathfrak{B}$. Recall the notation f_S as the one point coverage function for any $S \in \mathfrak{R}(X)$ for any space X.

Theorem 8

1. Let X be any space and $S \in \mathfrak{R}(X)$. Then X may be identified as a collection of events $\mathfrak{B}$ for some random variable V over say Y such that

$$S = \mathfrak{C}_{\{V\}} \tag{1}$$

and whose evaluation function over $\mathfrak{B}$ is the same as f_S.

2. Let V be any random variable over, say, Y with $\mathfrak{B}$ any collection of events for V. Then letting $X = \mathfrak{B}$ and defining S by eq. (1), evaluation function g_V for V over $\mathfrak{B}$ and f_S both coincide.

3. Let X be any space and let $A \in \mathcal{F}(X)$ be arbitrary. Let $S \in \mathfrak{R}(X)$ be arbitrary with $S \in \mathcal{F}_1(A)$ such as $S_U(A)$, $T(A)$, for example. Then applying part 1 above, X may be identified as a collection of events $\mathfrak{B}$ for some random variables V over say, Y such that eq. (1) holds and ϕ_A, f_S, and g_V all coincide. That is, any fuzzy set is one point equivalent to the evaluation function of suitably chosen random variables over event collections.

Proof and constructions for Parts 1 and 2:

1: First, suppose that $S : \Omega \to \mathcal{P}(X)$ is a random set relative to initial probability space $(\Omega,\mathfrak{D},Pr)$ and induced probability space

$$(\mathrm{range}(S),\mathfrak{B},Pr\circ S^{-1}) , \quad \mathrm{range}(S) \subseteq \mathcal{P}(X) .$$

Now,

$$\mathcal{G}(S) \overset{d}{=} \{\mathcal{C}_{\{x\}}(\mathrm{rng}(S)) \mid x \in X\}$$
$$= \{\mathcal{C}_{\{x\}}(\mathrm{rng}(S)) \mid x \in X'\} \subseteq \mathcal{B} ,$$

where $X' \subseteq X$ is chosen so that the mapping $\varphi : X' \to \mathcal{G}(S)$ is bijective, where for any $x \in X'$,

$$\varphi(x) \overset{d}{=} \mathcal{C}_{\{x\}}(\mathrm{rng}(S)) .$$

Clearly,

$$\mathcal{K}(S) \overset{d}{=} \{\{B\} \mid B \in \mathrm{rng}(S)\}$$

is a disjoint exhaustive partitioning of rng(S) with unique representation

$$\mathcal{C}_{\{x\}}(\mathrm{rng}(S)) = \bigcup_{B \in \mathcal{C}_{\{x\}}(\mathrm{rng} S)} \{B\} ,$$

for each $x \in X'$. Thus $\{S^{-1}(\{B\}) \mid B \in \mathrm{rng}(S)\}$ is a disjoint exhaustive partitioning of Ω .

For each $B \in \mathrm{rng}(S)$, let

$$V_B : S^{-1}(B) \to Y_B$$

be any surjective random variable for non-empty arbitrary measure space $(Y_B, \mathcal{A}_B)$ such that all Y_B's are disjoint. Then define

$$Y \overset{d}{=} \dot{\bigcup_{B \in \mathrm{rng}(S)}} Y_B$$

and define random variable

$$V : \Omega \to Y$$

where for any $\omega \in \Omega$, there is a unique $B(\omega) \in \mathrm{rng}(S)$ such that

$$\omega \in S^{-1}(B(\omega))$$

and hence

$$V(\omega) \overset{d}{=} V_{B(\omega)}(\omega)$$

is unambiguously defined, and without loss of generality V may be assummed measurable.

Define the mapping $\wedge : X' \to \mathcal{P}(Y)$ by, for any $x \in X'$,

$$\hat{x} \overset{d}{=} V(S^{-1}(\mathcal{C}_{\{X\}}(\mathrm{rng}(S))))$$
$$= \dot{\bigcup_{B \in \mathcal{C}_{\{x\}}(\mathrm{rng}(S))}} Y_B .$$

Then it follows that $\wedge$ is injective and for any $x \in X'$,

$$V^{-1}(\hat{x}) = S^{-1}(\mathcal{C}_{\{x\}}(\mathrm{rng}(S)))$$

which is equivalent, for all $\omega \in \Omega$,

$$\hat{S}(\omega) = \mathcal{C}_{\{V(\omega)\}}(\hat{X}) ,$$

and which implies, for all $x \in X'$,

$$\Pr(V^{-1}(\hat{x})) = \Pr(S^{-1}(C_{\{x\}}(\mathrm{rng}(S)))) ,$$

i.e.,

$$g_V(\hat{x}) \overset{d}{=} \Pr(V \in \hat{x}) = \Pr(x \in S) \overset{d}{=} f_S(x) \ ; \text{ all } \ x \in X' .$$

Hence (1) holds with S identified with $\hat{S}$ and $\hat{X} = \mathfrak{B}$.

2: Let $V : \Omega \to Y$ be a random variable for measure space $(Y,\mathfrak{B})$. Then eq. (1), which is the same as

$$S(\omega) = \mathcal{C}_{\{V(\omega)\}} \ ; \text{ all } \ \omega \in \Omega ,$$

is equivalent to

$$V^{-1}(x) = S^{-1}(\mathcal{C}_{\{x\}}(\mathrm{rng}(S)))$$

and hence

$$g_V(x) = f_S(x) \ ; \text{ all } \ x \in X' .$$

One consequence of Theorem 8 is a new interpretation for possibities or equivalently, values $\phi_A(x)$, for $x \in X$, where $A \in \mathcal{F}(X)$ is given through membership function $\phi_A : X \to [0,1]$:

For any $x \in X$,

$$\begin{aligned} \text{Possibility of } \ x \in A &= \mathrm{Poss}(x \in A) \\ &= \Pr(x \in S(A)) = \Pr(V(A) \in x) , \end{aligned}$$

and since the events $x \in X$ can also be considered compound or elementary events for $V(A)$ over Y which may well be overlapping and perhaps exhaustive, possibilities need not sum to unity when X is discrete. However, when - and only when - ϕ_A is an ordinary or deficient probability function, possibilities will sum to unity or to less that unity, possibilities and probabilities coincide, and the events for $V(A)$ are all necessarily elementary and disjoint, with $V(A)$ and $S(A)$ also being identifiable.

5.3 Multiple point coverage problem [89].

A. The multiple point random set coverage problem.

For any integer $m \geq 1$, define $\mathscr{P}_{(m)}(X)$ as the collection of all non-vacuous subsets of X with cardinality $\leq m$. Then define

$$\begin{aligned}\mathscr{F}_{(m)}(X) = \{f \mid f : \mathscr{P}_{(m)}(X) \to [0,1] \ \& \\ &\text{there is an } S \in \mathscr{R}(X) \text{ such that} \\ &f(C) = Pr(C \subseteq S) \ ; \text{ all } C \in \mathscr{P}_{(m)}(X)\} \\ \subseteq \{f \mid f : \mathscr{P}_{(m)}(X) \to [0,1]\} ,\end{aligned}$$

with, in general, strict subset inclusion holding above. That is, there are functions $f : \mathscr{P}_{(m)} \to [0,1]$ which are not the m point coverage function of some random subset of X. A simple example of this is generated for the case $m = 2$ by first noting the basic constraints for any random subset S of X and any $x,y \in X$:

$$\max(Pr(x \in S) + Pr(y \in S) - 1,0) \leq Pr(\{x,y\} \subseteq S) \leq \min(Pr(x \in S), Pr(y \in S)) \qquad (\cdot)$$

and then choosing, e.g., any such f with at least some $x,y \in X$ such that

$$\min(f(\{x\}),f(\{y\})) < f(\{x,y\}) .$$

This situation contrasts sharply with the case $m = 1$ where indeed

$$\mathscr{F}(X) = \mathscr{F}_{(1)}(X) = \{f \mid f : \mathscr{P}_{(1)}(X) \to [0,1]\} ,$$

abusing notation somewhat in identifying A with ϕ_A, for any $A \in \mathscr{F}(X)$.

In the following discussion, X need not be finite nor even discrete. Clearly,

$$\mathscr{F}_{(1)}(X) \supseteq \mathscr{F}_{(2)}(X) \supseteq \mathscr{F}_{(3)}(X) \supseteq \cdots \supseteq \mathscr{F}_{(\infty)}(X) \overset{d}{=} \bigcap_{j=1}^{\infty} \mathscr{F}_{(j)}(X)$$

and if for any $f \in \mathscr{F}_{(m)}(X)$,

$$\mathscr{S}_{(m)}(f) = \{S \mid S \in \mathscr{R}(X) \ \& \ f(C) = Pr(C \subseteq S) \ ; \text{ all } C \in \mathscr{P}_{(m)}(X)\} ,$$

then

$$\mathscr{S}_1(f) = \mathscr{S}_{(1)}(f) \supseteq \mathscr{S}_{(2)}(f) \supseteq \cdots \supseteq \mathscr{S}_{(m)}(f) .$$

Letting $\mathfrak{I}(X)$ be the class of all finite subsets of X ,

$$\mathcal{F}_{(\infty)}(X) = \{f \mid f : \mathfrak{I}(X) \to [0,1] \ \& \ \text{there is an } S \in \mathfrak{R}(X) \text{ such that } f(C) = \Pr(C \subseteq S) \ ; \text{ all } C \in \mathfrak{I}(X)\} \ .$$

Define also for any $f \in \mathcal{F}_{(\infty)}(X)$,

$$\mathcal{S}_{(\infty)}(f) = \{S \mid S \in \mathfrak{R}(X) \ \& \ f(C) = \Pr(C \subseteq S) \ ; \text{ all } C \in \mathfrak{I}(X)\} \ .$$

Then gathering all of these definitions together yields the following theorem:

Theorem 8.

For any space X :

1. $\mathcal{F}_{(\infty)}(X)$ is the class of all doubt measures over $\mathfrak{I}(X)$.

2. For any integer $m \geq 1$, $\mathfrak{R}(X)$ is disjointly partitioned as

$$\mathfrak{R}(X) = \dot{\bigcup_{f \in \mathcal{F}_{(m)}(X)}} (\mathcal{S}_{(m)}(f)) \ .$$

3. For $f \in \mathcal{F}_{(\infty)}(X)$, there is a unique $S_f \in \mathfrak{R}(X)$ such that

$$\mathcal{S}_{(\infty)}(f) = \{S_f\} \ ,$$

with the converse, for each $S \in \mathfrak{R}(X)$ determining the coverage function f_S by

$$f_S(C) = \Pr(C \subseteq S) \ ; \text{ all } C \in \mathfrak{I}(X) \ .$$

4. $\mathcal{F}_{(\infty)}(X)$, $\mathfrak{R}(X)$, and $\mathfrak{Y}(X)$, the class of all zero-one stochastic processes over X , are all in a bijective relationship as in the diagram:

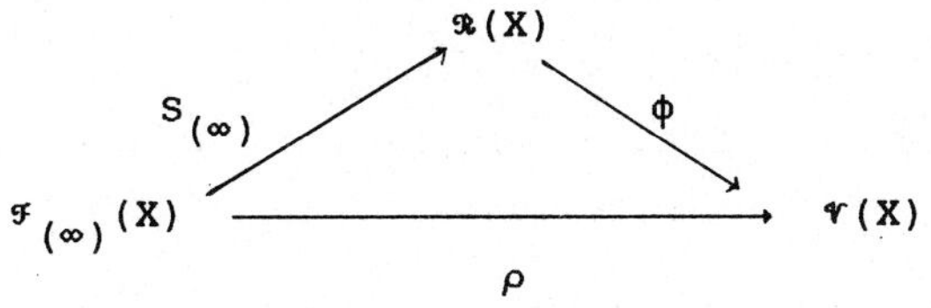

where for any $S \in \mathfrak{X}(X)$, $\phi(S) = (\phi_S(x))_{x\in X}$ and ρ is determined by the Kolmogorov Extension Theorem applied to the relations in 5.

5. For any $V = (V(x))_{x\in X} \in \mathcal{V}(X)$ and any $C,D \in \mathcal{J}(X)$ disjoint,

$$Pr((\underset{x\in C}{\&}(V(x) = 1)) \& (\underset{x\in D}{\&}(V(x) = 0))) = \sum_{K\subseteq D}((-1)^{card(K)} \cdot f_V(C\cup K))$$

where $f_V \in \mathcal{F}_{(\infty)}(X)$ is given by, for any $B \in \mathcal{J}(X)$ as

$$f_V(B) = Pr(\underset{x\in B}{\&}(V(x) = 1)) .$$

Thus in terms of degree of coverages, $\mathcal{F}(X)$ and $\mathfrak{X}(X)$ represent opposite extremes.

Returning to the case for X finite, let $m \geq 1$ be arbitrary fixed with $card(X) = n \geq 3$. Define for any $S \in \mathfrak{X}(X)$, recalling the total order defined over $\mathcal{P}(X)$,

$$\gamma^{(m+1)}(S) = (Pr(S = C))_{\substack{C\in\mathcal{P}(X)\\ card(C)\geq m+1}} \qquad (a_{n,m} \text{ by } 1) .$$

$$a_{n,m} = \sum_{k=m+1}^{n} \left(\binom{n}{k}\right) ;$$

$$C_{B,j}(X) = \{C \mid B \subseteq C \in \mathcal{P}(X) \;\&\; card(C) = j\} ;$$

all $C \in \mathcal{P}(X)$; $0 \leq j \leq n$.

Also, define for any $n \geq m \geq r,s \geq 0$ and all $f \in \mathcal{F}_{(m)}(X)$ and $C \in \mathcal{P}(X)$, $card(C) = r$,

$$\nu_{r,0}(f,C) = f(C) ; \quad \text{for } s = 0$$

$$\nu_{r,s}(f,C) = f(C) + \sum_{t=1}^{s}((-1)^t \cdot \sum_{B\in C_{C,t+r}} (f(B))) ; \; s \geq 1 ;$$

$$\begin{bmatrix}\geq\\<\end{bmatrix}_j = \begin{cases}\geq & \text{iff } j \text{ is even}\\ \leq & \text{iff } j \text{ is odd} .\end{cases}$$

Theorem 9

For any finite space X , with notation as above, for any $f \in \mathcal{F}_{(m)}(X)$:

1.

$$\mathcal{F}_{(m)}(f) = \{S \mid S \in \mathfrak{X}(X) \;\&\; \gamma^{(m+1)}(S) \in \mathfrak{X}_{(m)}(f)\} .$$

where

$\mathfrak{R}_{(m)}(f) = \{W \mid W \in \mathbb{R}^{a_{n,m}}$ is arbitrary satisfying eqs. (*), (**) below\} ,

$$\begin{cases} (-1)^j \cdot \nu_{m-j,j}(f,C) \begin{bmatrix} \geq \\ < \end{bmatrix}_j \sum_{t=m+1}^{n} \left[\begin{bmatrix} t-m+j-1 \\ j \end{bmatrix} \cdot \sum_{B \in \mathcal{C}_{C,t}(X)} (W_B)\right] \quad (*); \\ \text{all } C \in \mathcal{P}(X) \text{ with } \mathrm{card}(C) = m - j, \text{ for } j = 0,1,2,\ldots,m ; \\ W_B \geq 0 ; \text{ all } B \in \mathcal{P}(X) \text{ with } \mathrm{card}(B) \geq m+1 ; \quad (**) \\ \text{all } f \in \mathcal{F}_{(m)}(X) , \\ W = (W_B)_{\substack{B \in \mathcal{P}(X) \\ \mathrm{card}(B) \geq m+1}} \in \mathbb{R}^{a_{n,m}} . \end{cases}$$

2. $\mathfrak{R}_{(m)}(f)$ is a closed convex region in $\mathbb{R}^{a_{n,m}}$ having, in general, $a_{n,m} + \sum_{t=0}^{m} (\begin{bmatrix} n \\ t \end{bmatrix}) = 2^n$ hyperplane bounds, and thus, in general, there is an uncountable infinity of possible $\gamma^{(m+1)}(S)$ in it or equivalently $S \in \mathcal{S}_{(m)}(f)$.

3. There is a bijective correspondence between $\mathcal{S}_{(m)}(f)$ and $\mathfrak{R}_{(m)}(f)$, where for any given $W \in \mathfrak{R}_{(m)}(f)$, $S \in \mathcal{S}_{(m)}(f)$ is uniquely determined by

$$\begin{cases} \gamma^{(m+1)}(S) = W , \\ \Pr(S = C) = \nu_{m-j,j}(f,C) + (-1)^{j+1} \cdot \sum_{t=m+1}^{n} \left[\begin{bmatrix} t-m+j-1 \\ j \end{bmatrix} \cdot \sum_{B \in \mathcal{C}_{C,t}(X)} (W_B)\right] \end{cases}$$

for all $C \in \mathcal{P}(X)$ with $\mathrm{card}(C) = m - j$, $j = 0,1,\ldots,m$.

Outline of proofs for Theorems 4 and 9.

First obtain Theorem 4 by simply extending the basic identity $\phi_A(x) = \Pr(x \in S(A))$ in terms of $\Pr(S = C)$'s together with the standard probability constraints and solve in terms of $\gamma^{(2)}(S)$. Theorem 9 is obtained by tedious induction. The key computational identity useful in the proofs is

$$\sum_{B\in \mathcal{C}_{C,k}(X)} \left(\sum_{D\in \mathcal{C}_{B,j}(X)} (f(D)) \right) = \begin{bmatrix} j-\ell \\ k-\ell \end{bmatrix} \cdot \sum_{D\in \mathcal{C}_{C,j}(X)} \left(f(D) \right) ,$$

for any $f : \mathcal{P}(X) \to \mathbb{R}$; $j \geq k \geq \ell$, and any $C \in \mathcal{P}(X)$ with $\mathrm{card}(C) = \ell$.

Remark.

In Chapters 3 and 4, explicit relations were developed between random sets and uncertainty measures in terms of subset coverage functions for doubt measures, superset coverage functions for belief measures, and incidence functions for plausibility measures. Thus, a restricted form of the multiple point coverage problem (obviously including the one point coverage problem) where multiple point coverages are given in terms of a doubt measure of sets of multiple points is solved by construction of a random set as given in Chapters 3 and 4. In the multiple point coverage problem) discussed here, *no* restriction in general (except to allow some random set representation) is required on the coverage function.

Recall (see Chapter 3.3) that Zadeh's possibility measure is a special case of a semi-distributive t-norm possibility measure, where the t-norm is min. (See Theorem 4, Chapter 3, where these possibility measures are related to random set coverage and incidence functions.) In the same spirit of Theorems 2 and 3 (see also the following remark) of Chapter 3, a relation may be established between Zadeh's possibility measure and random sets, by direct use of random set theory (à la Matheron):

Proposition 1

Let Π be a possibility measure on X , with possibility distribution function f . Then there exists a random set S on X such that:

$$\forall\ A \subseteq X\ ,\ \Pi(A) = \sup\ \{\Pi(I)\ |\ I \subseteq A,\ I \in \mathcal{I}(X)\}$$

with $\Pi(I) = \Pr(S \cap I \neq \emptyset)$.

Proof:

It is clear that the restriction of Π to $\mathcal{I}(X)$ is a space law, and hence by Matheron's theorem [171], there exists a unique probability measure Q on $(\mathcal{P}(X),M)$ such that:

$$\forall\ I \in \mathcal{I}(X),\ \Pi(I) = Q\{A\ |\ A \cap I \neq \emptyset\}$$

Let S be a random set with Q as probability law, i.e.,

$$\Pi(I) = \Pr\{S \cap I \neq \emptyset\}\ ,\ \forall\ I \in \mathcal{I}(X)\ .$$

The result follows from the fact that •

$$\forall A \subseteq X\ ,\ \Pi(A) = \sup\ \{\Pi(I),\ I \subseteq A,\ I \in \mathcal{I}(X)\}\ .$$

A similar result for the topological setting is:

Proposition 2

Let X be a locally compact and separable space, and $f : X \to [0,1]$ upper-semicontinuous (u.s.c.). Then there exists a random set S on $(\mathcal{F},\sigma(\mathcal{F}))$ such that:

$$\forall\ A \subseteq X\ ,\ \Pi(A) = \inf\ \{\Pi(G)\ |\ A \subseteq G,\ G \in \mathcal{G}\}$$

where $\Pi(A) = \sup\ \{f(x)\ |\ x \in A\ \}$, and

$$\Pi(G) = \sup\ \{\Pr(S \cap K \neq \emptyset)\ |\ K \in \mathcal{K},\ K \subseteq G\}\ .$$

Proof:

First, let us show that there exists a unique probability measure Q on $(\mathcal{F},\sigma(\mathcal{F}))$ such that

$$\forall\ K \in \mathcal{K},\ \Pi(K) = Q\{F\ |\ F \cap K \neq \emptyset\}\ .$$

By Choquet's theorem, it suffices to verify that Π is a Choquet capacity, alternating of infinite order. The fact that Π is alternating of infinite order is obvious. Now let $K_n \in \mathcal{K}$, $n \geq 1$, and $K \in \mathcal{K}$ such that $K_n \downarrow K$. Let $\alpha = \inf \Pi(K_n)$ and $\beta = \Pi(K)$. It is obvious that $\beta \leq \alpha$. Now let $\epsilon > 0$, and set $\delta = \alpha - \epsilon < \alpha$. It follows that $\forall n \geq 1$, $\Pi(K_n) > \delta$, i.e., $\sup\ \{f(x)\ |\ x \in K_n\} > \delta$, $\forall n \geq 1$.

Hence: $A_n \overset{d}{=} \{x \in X\ |\ f(x) \geq \delta\} \cap K_n \neq \emptyset$ and since by construction, $\forall_n \geq 1$, $A_n \subseteq K_n \subset K_1$ (compact), and the A_n's are closed (since f is u.s.c. by hypothesis), we have

$$A \overset{d}{=} \bigcap_{n=1}^{+\infty} A_n \neq \emptyset\ .$$

Now $A \subseteq K$; we have $\Pi(A) \leq \Pi(K) = \beta$. But, by construction, of the A_n's , $\Pi(A) \geq \delta$; thus, $\delta \leq \beta$, therefore $\alpha = \beta$.

Finally, since X is locally compact and separable, any Borel set A is capacitable, i.e.,

$$\Pi(A) = \sup\ \{\Pi(K)\ |\ K \in \mathcal{K},\ K \subseteq A\}\ ,$$

in particular, for $A \in G$. Let S be a random set on $(\mathcal{F},\sigma(\mathcal{F}))$ having Q as probability law,

$$\Pi(K) = Pr(S \cap K \neq \emptyset) \ , \ K \in \mathcal{K} \ .$$

The approximation of $\Pi(A)$, for $A \subseteq X$, from $\Pi(G)$, $G \in \mathcal{G}$ and $G \supseteq A$, is the usual extension of capacity.

B. Multiple point coverage functions and Higg's topos.

Lemma

Let $X = \{0,1\} \times \{0,1\}$ and P be a given bivariate probability function over X . Denote the x - and y - marginal probabilities of P , respectively, by

$$P_1 \stackrel{d}{=} P(1,1) + P(1,0)$$

$$P_2 = P(1,1) + P(0,1) \ .$$

Then

$\{q \mid q$ is a probability function over X such that the x- and y- marginal probabilities of q are the same as that for $P\}$

$= \{q_\epsilon \mid -\min(P(1,1), P(0,0)) \leq \epsilon \leq \min(P(1,0), P(0,1), P(1,1)\}$

where for any such ϵ ,

$$q_\epsilon(i,j) \stackrel{d}{=} P(i,j) + (-1)^{i+j}.\epsilon$$

for any $(i,j) \in X$.

For any such q_ϵ , in particular,

$$q_\epsilon(1,1) = P(1,1) + \epsilon \ .$$

Application:

Consider a random subset S of a space Y and its local behavior at two fixed subsets of Y : $\{x,y\}$ and $\{x',y'\}$. Now the local behavior of S at any point $z \in Y$ may be identified with a marginal zero-one random variable $V_Z = \phi_S(Z)$, where ϕ_S is the random characteristic function induced by S . Thus,

$$V_Z = 1 \quad \text{iff} \quad Z \in S$$

$$V_Z = 0 \quad \text{iff} \quad Z \notin S \ .$$

Hence, we may define

$$Pr(x,y \in S) = Pr(V_x = 1, V_y = 1)$$

$$Pr(x \in S) = Pr(V_x = 1)$$

$$Pr(y \notin S) = Pr(V_y = 0) \text{ , etc.}$$

Thus by choosing S such that

$$Pr(V_{x'} = i, V_{y'} = j) = q_\epsilon(i,j) \text{ ,}$$

for any fixed ϵ as above, in general,

$$Pr(x \in S) = Pr(x' \in S)$$
$$Pr(y \in S) = Pr(y' \in S) \text{ ,}$$

but

$$Pr(x \in S,\ y \in S) = Pr(x' \in S,\ y' \in S) + \epsilon$$
$$\neq Pr(x' \in S,\ y' \in S) \text{ ,}$$

in general.

Hence, in general, it is not true
$\exists\ f : [0,1] \times [0,1] \rightarrow [0,1]$ such that for all $x,y \in Y$,

(I) $\quad Pr(\{x,y\} \subseteq S) = f(Pr(x \in S) , Pr(y \in S))$.

On the other hand, for certain random sets this is not only true but f is also a t-norm:

Let $\phi_\& : [0,1] \times [0,1] \rightarrow [0,1]$ be any semi-distributive t-norm. Then for any Y (see Goodman [91] or Höhle [116] for further details) and any given mapping $\phi_A : Y \rightarrow [0,1]$, there exists a random subset $S_{A;\&}$ of Y such that for all $y_1,\ldots,y_m \in Y$, $m \geq 1$,

(i) $\quad Pr(\{y_1,\ldots,y_m\} \subseteq S_{A;\&})$
$= \phi_\&(Pr(y_1 \in S_{A;\&}),\ldots, Pr(y \in S_{A;\alpha}))$,

(ii) $\quad Pr(y_j \in S_{A;\alpha}) = \phi_A(y_j)$; $j = 1,\ldots,m$.

In particular;

(iii) For $\phi_\& = \min$,

$$S_{A,\&} = S_U(A) \stackrel{d}{=} \phi_A^{-1}[U,1] \text{ ,}$$

where U is a r.v. uniformly distributed over $[0,1]$.

(iv) For $\phi_{\&} = \text{prod}$,

$S_{A,\&} = T$,

where T is such that the corresponding random membership function ϕ_T is equivalent to a statistically independent $0 - 1$ process, i.e.,

$$\Pr(\{y_1,\ldots,y_m\} \subseteq T) \equiv \Pr(y_1 \in T)\cdot\cdot\Pr(y_m \in T)$$
$$= \phi_A(y_1)\cdot\cdot\phi_A(y_m) .$$

Note also, for any random subset S of Y , the inequalities in eq. $(\cdot)$, section 5.3 (A), are

$$(*) \quad \max(0,\Pr(x\in S)+(\Pr(y\in S)-1) \le \Pr(\{x,y\}\subseteq S) \le \min(\Pr(x \in S), \Pr(y\in S))$$

the same bounds formally for any continuous t-norm $\phi_{\&}$ as a function of $\Pr(x \in S)$, $\Pr(y \in S)$.

Note some formal similarities in eq. (I) with Sklar's Theorem.

Now consider the converse problem:

Let Y be an arbitrary space and let $J^{(2)}(Y)$ denote $\{C \mid C \in \mathcal{P}(Y) \,\&\, \text{card } C \le 2\}$.

Let $g : J^{(2)}(Y) \to [0,1]$ be a given function. Then we wish to find all random subsets S , if any, such that for all $C \in J^{(2)}(Y)$,

$$g(C) = \Pr(C \subseteq S) .$$

Equivalently, let $g : Y \times Y \to [0,1]$ be symmetric and S a random subset of Y such that for all $x,y \in Y$,

$$\text{(II)} \qquad g(x,y) = \Pr(\{x,y\} \subseteq S) .$$

Letting $x = y$, this includes the condition

$$\text{(III)} \qquad g(x,x) = \Pr(x \in S) \ ; \text{ all } \ x \in Y .$$

But because of the negation of relation (I), we know (II) (and III) in general, may have no solution for an S given a g :

In particular, pick any $g : Y \times Y \to [0,1]$ symmetric such that g is arbitrary over diag $(Y \times Y)$, and such that there is at least two distinct points $x_o,y_o \in Y$ such that

$$1 \ge g(y_o,y_o) > 1 - g(x_o,x_o) \ge 0 .$$

Then define g otherwise off the main diagonal to be arbitrary symmetric such that at (x_o, y_o)

$$0 \le g(x_o, y_o) = g(y_o, x_o) < g(x_o, x_o) + g(y_o, y_o) - 1 .$$

Then equation $(\cdot)$ will be violated, no matter what choice of S .

Recall that any random variable V over Y may be considered a random set $S = \{V\}$. Another example of the impossibility in general, of II, III admitting a solution S for a given g is obtained by choosing, for example, Y to be discrete

$$g_o(x,y) \overset{d}{=} g_o(x,x) \cdot \delta_Y^{(0)}(x,y) \ ; \text{ all } \ x,y \in Y ,$$

$\delta_Y^{(0)}$ the classical Krönecker delta function, and such that

$$\sum_{x \in Y} g(x,x) > 1 \ ; \ 0 \le g_o(x,x) \le 1 \ , \text{ all } \ x \in Y .$$

It then follows that if $\exists S$ satisfying (II,III), then $S = \{V\}$ for some r.v. V over Y . But

$$1 = \Pr(V \in Y) = \sum_{x \in Y} \Pr(V = x) = \sum_{x \in Y} g(x,x) > 1$$

a contradiction!

Let $H = [0,1]$. Let $X \in$ SET . Recall (see section 2.4.2 (E)) $g \in Ob_X(Higg(H))$ iff

$$\begin{cases} (1) & g : X \times X \to H \ \text{ is symmetric} \\ (2) & g(x,y) \wedge g(y,z) \le g(x,z) \\ & \text{for all } \ x,y,z \in X . \end{cases} \qquad (\cdot\cdot)$$

In general, given any g satisfying $(\cdot\cdot)$, no random subset S of X exists such that g and S satisfy (II, III): In particular, choose $g = g_o$. It is clear that g_o satisfies $(\cdot\cdot)$, but as the previous example has shown, no S satisfies (II,III) for given g_o . On the other hand, there are g's satisfying $(\cdot\cdot)$ which admit random subsets S of X such that (II,III) are satisfied. For example, let $(X,\varphi) \in Ob_X(Fuz(H))$ be arbitrary. Then let, for all $x,y \in X$,

$$g(x,y) \overset{d}{=} \varphi(x) \wedge \varphi(y) .$$

Then the previous example shows $S_U(\varphi) \overset{d}{=} \varphi^{-1}[U,1]$, U uniform on $[0,1]$ will satisfy (II,III) for g here.

More generally, we have the following positive result

Lemma

Given any space X and any random subset S of X, $\exists$ a t-norm (continuous) $\phi_{\&}$ such that

$$\phi_{\&}(g(x,y),\ g(y,z)) \leq g(x,z)\ , \qquad (\cdots)$$

where

$$g(x,y) \overset{d}{=} \Pr(\{x,y\} \subseteq S)\ ,$$

for all $x,y,z \in X$.

Proof:

Since the minimal (continuous) t-norm is minbndsum, $\phi_{\&}^{(0)}$ where

$$\phi_{\&}^{(0)}(u,v) \overset{d}{=} \max(u + v - 1, 0)\ ,$$

for all $u,v \in [0,1]$, all we have to do is verify $(\cdots)$ for $\phi_{\&} = \phi_{\&}^{(0)}$:

Pick any three points $x,y,z \in X$.

Consider $g(x,y) + g(y,z)$

$$\begin{aligned}
&= \Pr(x \in S,\ y \in S) + \Pr(y \in S,\ z \in S) \\
&= (\Pr(x \in S \mid y \in S) + \Pr(z \in S \mid y \in S)) \cdot \Pr(y \in S) \\
&\leq \max_{\substack{a_{01}, a_{10} \\ \text{such that } a_{11} \text{ is} \\ \text{fixed, with} \\ a_{11}+a_{10}+a_{01}+a_{00}=1}} (a_{11} + a_{10} + a_{11} + a_{01}) \cdot \Pr(y \in S)\ ,
\end{aligned}$$

where

$$\begin{aligned}
a_{11} &\overset{d}{=} \Pr(x \in S,\ z \in S \mid y \in S) \\
a_{10} &\overset{d}{=} \Pr(x \in S,\ z \notin S \mid y \in S) \\
a_{01} &\overset{d}{=} \Pr(x \notin S,\ z \in S \mid y \in S) \\
a_{00} &\overset{d}{=} \Pr(x \notin S,\ z \notin S \mid y \in S\ ) \\
&= (2a_{11} + 1 - a_{11}) \cdot \Pr(y \in S) \\
&= (a_{11} + 1) \cdot \Pr(y \in S)\ .
\end{aligned}$$

Hence

$$g(x,y) + g(y,z) \le (Pr(x \in S,\ z \in S \mid y \in S) + 1)\cdot Pr(y \in S)$$
$$= Pr(x \in S,\ z \in S,\ y \in S) + Pr(y \in S)$$
$$\le Pr(x \in S,\ z \in S) + 1\ .$$

Thus,

$$\phi_{\&}^{(0)}(g(x,y),\ g(y,z)) \le Pr(x \in S,\ z \in S) = g(x,z)\ .$$

If $\phi_{\&} = \wedge$ (i.e., min), a solution set of g's satisfying $(\cdots)$ is given by

$$g(x,y) \overset{d}{=} \Psi(x) \wedge \Psi(y)\ ,$$

for any $(X,\Psi) \in Ob_X(Fuz(H))$.

If $\phi_{\&}$ is any Archimedean t-norm, then since $\exists$ unique $h : [0,1] \to [0,+\infty]$ monotone decreasing with $h(1) = 0$, with

$$\phi_{\&}(u,v) = h^{-1}(\min(h(u) + h(v),h(0)))$$

for all, $u,v \in [0,1]$ (see section 2.3.6), whence $(\cdots)$ becomes

$$h^{-1}(\min(h\circ g(x,y) + h\circ g(y,z),\ h(0))) \le g(x,z)$$

and hence

$$\min(h\circ g(x,y) + h\circ g(y,z),\ h(0)) \le h\circ g(x,z)\ .$$

In particular, if $\phi_{\&}$ is strict Archimedean, $h(0) = +\infty$: Then the above relation is equivalent to $h\circ g$ being a pseudometric d over X ; conversely, given any pseudometric d over X , $g \overset{d}{=} h^{-1}\circ d$ will satisfy $(\cdots)$.

Finally, note that it easily follows from the property of t-norms that if g,g' are any solutions for $(\cdots)$, then so is $\phi_{\&}(g,g')$.

Thus again, Higg(H) - or more generally - the extension Higg(H; $\phi_{\&}$, ϕ_{or}) defined through $(\cdots)$ plays a natural role in extending fuzzy sets to a joint membership definition ($\vee$, "or", is similarly replaced by ϕ_{or}).

The natural questions we thus pose are:

(1) What are the properties of Fuz(H; $\phi_{\&}$, ϕ_{or}) when $\wedge$ = min is everywhere replaced in Fuz(H) by $\phi_{\&}$, an arbitrary but fixed t-norm?

(2) What are the properties of Higg(H, $\phi_{\&}$, ϕ_{or}) ?

5.4 Entropy of Random Set Systems and Coverages.

Another basic problem associated with generalized sets or possibility theory, or more generally, multiple-point coverage functions and random sets is the determination of meaningful criteria for ordering, in some sense, random sets in terms of "best" representing coverage functions. Among natural criteria, should be mentioned: expected volume (or expected cardinality in the finite case) and entropy.

Denote by f_S the coverage function of a random set S on an arbitrary space X. Recall Robbins' formula (section 4.4):

(i) If $X \subseteq \mathbb{R}^n$, then under suitable measurability conditions, we have, for any $m \geq 1$,

$$E(\mu_n(S)^m) = \int_{\mathbb{R}^{mn}} f_S(x_1,\ldots,x_m) \bigotimes_{i=1}^{m} \mu_n^{(i)}(dx_i) .$$

(ii) If X is a finite space,

$$E((\mathrm{card}(S))^m) = \sum_{(x_1,\ldots,x_m \in X)} \cdots \sum f_S(x_1,\ldots,x_m) .$$

Thus, for any $f \in \mathcal{F}_{(m)}(X)$,
$E((\mu_n(S)^k) = \text{constant}, k = 1,2,\ldots,m$, regardless of the S chosen from $\mathcal{F}_{(m)}(X)$. Thus, another criterion must be sought which is sensitive to variable $S \in \mathcal{F}_{(m)}(X)$.

Remark.

Robbins' formula was later independently rediscovered by Pratt [205], and in turn used by Hooper [119] in demonstrating that most common figures - of merit - for randomized test procedures and randomized confidence sets involve the random sets determining these procedures only through their one point coverage functions. (See section 5.5.)

We proceed now to discuss maximal and minimal entropy problems for discrete spaces.

A. Fundamental maximal entropy theorem for discrete spaces.
(See, e.g., Jaynes [123].)

Let X be any fixed discrete space. For any probability function $P \in \mathcal{P}r(X)$, the class of all probability functions over X, define the entropy of P by

$$\mathrm{Ent}(P) \overset{d}{=} \sum_{x \in X} -\log P(x)\cdot P(x) .$$

Let J_o be any finite index set.

Let

$$g \overset{d}{=} (g_j)_{j\in J_o} \quad \text{(column vector of functions)},$$

$$\gamma \overset{d}{=} (\gamma_j)_{j\in J_o} \quad \text{(column vector)},$$

$$\lambda \overset{d}{=} (\lambda_j)_{j\in J_o} \quad \text{(column vector)},$$

where for each $j \in J_o$, $g_j : X \to \mathbb{R}$ is an arbitrary fixed function, $\gamma_j \in \mathbb{R}$ arbitrary fixed constant.

Next, (assuming convergence) define

$$\mathcal{P}_{(g,\gamma)}(X) \overset{d}{=} \{P \mid P \in \mathcal{P}r(X) \ \&\ \sum_{x\in X} p(X)\cdot g_j(x) = \gamma_j\ ,\ j \in J_o\} .$$

Then

$$\sup_{P\in\mathcal{P}_{(g,\gamma)}(X)} \mathrm{Ent}(P) = \log\,(G(\lambda)) - \lambda^T\cdot\gamma\ ,$$

occurring for $P = P_{(g,\gamma)}$, where $P_{(g,\gamma)}$ is determined by:

$$P_{(g,\lambda)}(x) = (1/G(\lambda))\cdot e^{\lambda^T\cdot g(x)}$$

$$G(\lambda) = \sum_{x\in X} e^{\lambda^T\cdot g(x)}\ ,\ x\in X,$$

and λ is a constant vector determined by

$$\sum_{x\in X} g(x)\cdot e^{\lambda^T\cdot g(x)} = \gamma\ .$$

or equivalently,

$$\gamma\cdot\log G(\lambda)/\partial\lambda_j = \gamma_j\ ,\ \text{all}\ \ j \in J_o\ . \tag{1}$$

Let $X \subseteq \mathbb{R}^n$, X discrete.

In particular, let m be such that $m \geq 1$ fixed and choose

$$J_o \overset{d}{=} \bigcup_{k=1}^{m} J_{(k)}\ .$$

where

$$J_{(k)} \overset{d}{=} \{1,2,\ldots,n\}^k = \{(j_1,\ldots,j_k) \mid j_1,\ldots,j_k \in \{1,\ldots,n\}\}\ ,$$

$k = 1,2,\ldots,m$.

For each $j \overset{d}{=} (j_1,\ldots,j_k) \in J_{(k)}$, $k = 1,2,\ldots,m$, define g_j by,

$$g_j(x) \stackrel{d}{=} x_{j_1} \cdots x_{j_k} ,$$

for any $x = \begin{bmatrix} x_1 \\ \vdots \\ x_n \end{bmatrix} \in X , \; x_i \in \mathbb{R}$.

This is the first m-moment constraint problem with solution for maximal entropy being

$$P_{(g,\gamma)}(x) \equiv \mathrm{const}(\lambda) \cdot e^{\left[\sum_{1 \le j_1 \le n} \lambda_{j_1} x_{j_1} + \cdots + \sum_{1 \le j_1, \ldots, j_m \le n} \lambda_{j_1 \cdots j_m} \cdot x_{j_1} \cdots x_{j_m} \right]}$$

with λ determined from eq. (1).

In particular, let $X = \{a + j \cdot \Delta \mid j = 0,1,\ldots,n-1\}^n$, a lattice structure.

For $m = 1$, we obtain

$$J_o = J_{(1)} = \{1,\ldots,n\} ,$$

$$G(\lambda) = \prod_{k=1}^{n} \left[e^{a\lambda_k} \circ \frac{e^{\lambda_k \Delta \cdot r} - 1}{e^{\lambda_k \Delta} - 1} \right]$$

and hence eq. (1) reduces to

$$\lambda_j = (1/\Delta) \log (\tau_j) , \; j = 1,\ldots,n ,$$

where each τ_j is determined from

$$\frac{\Delta \cdot r \tau_j^{\,r}}{\tau_j^{\,r} - 1} - \frac{\Delta \cdot \tau_j}{\tau_j - 1} = \gamma_j - a ; \; j = 1,\ldots,n .$$

Specializing further, suppose $a = 0$, $\Delta = 1$, and $r = 2$, i.e., $X = \{0,1\}^n$, $m = 1$ and $n \ge 1$ as before. Then here

$$G(\lambda) = \prod_{k=1}^{n} (e^{\lambda_k} + 1) ,$$

$$\tau_j = \gamma_j/(1 - \gamma_j) , \; j = 1,\ldots,n ,$$

implying

$$G(\lambda) = 1/\prod_{j=1}^{n} (1 - \gamma_j)$$

and finally

$$P_{(g,\gamma)}(x) = \prod_{j=1}^{n} \left[\gamma_j^{x_j} \cdot (1 - \gamma_j)^{1-x_j} \right] ,$$

all $x \in X$.

(For $a = 0$, $\Delta = 1$, $r = 2$, but $m \geq 2$, the solution form remains as in eq. (1) with λ no longer in simple form for the λ's as the case $m = 1$, because of the relatively complicated form of $G(\lambda)$.)

The above special case thus yields the same result $S = T$ for the problem

$$\sup_{S \in \mathcal{F}_{(1)}(g)} (\mathrm{Ent}(S))$$

where $g = \phi_A$ and $P_{(g,\gamma)}$ is the probability function of random variable ϕ_T .

Other maximal entropy problems involving m point coverages may be similarly approached.

B. **Case for finite base space**. (See also [89].)

Consider now the case where the base space X is finite. Recall that the entropy of a random set S on X is

$$\mathrm{Ent}(S) = - \sum_{C \in \mathcal{P}(X)} \Pr(S = C) \log \Pr(S = C).$$

Theorem 10

For any $A \in \mathcal{F}(X)$,

$$\sup_{S \in \mathcal{F}_1(A)} (\mathrm{Ent}(S)) = \sum_{x \in X} (-\phi_A(x) \log \phi_A(x) - (1 - \phi_A(x)) \log(1 - \phi_A(x))),$$

occurring uniquely for $S = T(A)$.

Proof:

Either use the fundamental information theory inequality applied to ϕ_S - which is equivalent to a specialization of the well-known result that given any marginal probability distributions, the joint probability distribution function maximizing the entropy corresponds to the marginal random variables being statistically independent, or specialize the exponential family characterization of maximal entropy (see part A) to this case.

Remark.

The above Theorem 10 is also well-known in the theory of sample surveys; see Hajek [103]. Specifically, in sampling from a finite population X, a sampling design is a probability distribution Q on the collection of all 2^n subsets of X (assuming $\text{card}(X) = n$). In other words, Q is the induced probability measure of a random set S on X. The inclusion probabilities (first and second-order) are precisely the values of the coverage functions of S, i.e.,

$$\Pr(x \in S) = \sum_{\substack{x \in A, \\ A \in \mathcal{P}(X)}} Q(A)$$

$$\Pr(\{x,y\} \subseteq S) = \sum_{\substack{A \supseteq \{x,y\}, \\ A \in \mathcal{P}(X)}} Q(A)$$

The entropy of S is a measure of spread-out for sampling probabilities. For the choice of a random set representation (a sampling design) of a given one-point coverage function (first-order inclusion probabilities), one is in favor of the maximum entropy principle as an appropriate criterion. More precisely, given $\Pr(x \in S)$, for all $x \in X$, the random set S which has maximum entropy is the one with probability measure Q on $\mathcal{P}(X)$ given by:

$$A \in \mathcal{P}(X),\ Q(A) = \prod_{x \in A} \Pr(x \in S) \times \prod_{y \notin A} (1 - \Pr(y \in S))$$

(Poisson sampling design).

Now, motivated by Robbins' formula, consider the weaker constraint

$$E(\text{card}(S)) = \sum_{x \in X} \Pr(x \in S) = \gamma ,$$

$(1 < \gamma < n = \text{card}(S))$, γ given.

Using the Lagrange multiplier technique as in the case of random variables, we obtain:

Theorem 11

The solution of the optimization problem

$$\begin{cases} \text{maximize} & -\sum_{A \in \mathcal{P}(X)} \Pr(S = A) \log \Pr(S = A) \\ \text{subject to} & \sum_{x \in X} \Pr(x \in S) = \gamma \end{cases}$$

is given by:

$$Pr(S = A) = \frac{1}{g(\beta)} e^{-\beta \cdot card(A)} , \quad A \in \mathscr{P}(X) ,$$

where β is the unique solution of the equation

$$g'(\beta) + \gamma g(\beta) = 0$$

with $g(\beta) = \sum_{A \in \mathscr{P}(X)} e^{-\beta \cdot card(A)}$.

C. Minimal entropy problem.

On the other hand, the minimal entropy problem here poses more difficulties. It can be shown that [89]:

Theorem 12

Let $card(X) = n$. Then for any $A \in \mathscr{F}(X)$,

$$\inf_{S \in \mathscr{F}_1(A)} (Ent(S)) = \min_{(\gamma^{(2)}(S) \in \mathscr{V}_1(A))} (Ent(S)) .$$

Proof:

By Theorem 4(3), the minimization problem reduces to the routine minimizing of the sum of a strictly convex function $(-x \cdot \log x)$ of linear combinations of components of $\gamma^{(2)}(S)$ over the region $\mathfrak{R}_1(A)$.

Even though (see remarks (a) and (c) following Theorem 4 , $\gamma^{(2)}(S_U(A)) \in \mathscr{V}_1(A)$, and if $\sum_{x \in X} (\phi_A(x)) \le 1$, $S'(A)$ is well- defined with $\gamma^{(2)}(S'(A)) \in \mathscr{V}_1(A)$, it is not always true that the global minimal entropy occurs for either one. A simple example illustrates this. Let $n = 2$ with $X = \{x_1, x_2\}$, $A \in \mathscr{F}(X)$ with $\phi_A(x_1) \le \phi_A(x_2)$. Let $h(x) = -x \cdot \log x$, all x , and define $y_1 = \phi_A(x_1)$ and $y_2 = \phi_A(x_2)$. Finally, let $G(A) = \inf_{S \in \mathscr{F}_{(1)}(A)} (Ent(S))$. Then:

(i) If $\tau(A) = 0$ and $y_2 > 1/2$, then

$$G(A) = h(y_1) + h(y_2) + h(1 - y_1 - y_2) ,$$

occurring uniquely for $S = S'(A)$.

(ii) If either $\tau(A) = 0$ and $y_2 < 1/2$ or $\tau(A) > 0$ and $y_1 \ge 1/2$, then

$$G(A) = h(y_1) + h(y_2 - y_1) + h(1 - y_2) \ ,$$

occurring uniquely for $S = S_U(A)$.

(iii) If $\tau(A) > 0$ and $y_1 < 1/2$, then

$$G(A) = h(1 - y_1) + h(1 - y_2) + h(y_1 + y_2 - 1) \ ,$$

occurring uniquely for $S = S''(A)$, where $S''(A)$ is determined by

$$Pr(S''(A) = \{x_1\}) = 1 - y_2 \ , \ Pr(S''(A) = \{x_2\}) = 1 - y_1 \ ,$$

$$Pr(S''(A) = X) = \tau(A) \ , \ Pr(S''(A) = \emptyset) = 0 \ .$$

Extensions of the entropy problem to multiple coverage functions and general spaces X have yet to be addressed.

5.5 Randomized tests and confidence region procedures.

Consider the following extensions of Lehmann [154]:

Let $Y \subseteq \mathbb{R}^m$ be a data or sample space, $X \subseteq \mathbb{R}^n$ a parameter space, $(V|\theta)_{\theta\in X}$ a family of data random variables over Y with corresponding well-defined probability distribution functions $(P_\theta)_{\theta\in X}$.

Let $(\Omega,\mathfrak{D},Pr)$ be a fixed non-atomic probability space and denote

$$\mathfrak{R}(Y) \overset{d}{=} \{S \mid S : \Omega \to \mathcal{P}(Y) \ , \ S \text{ a random subset of } Y\}$$

and similarly denote $\mathfrak{R}(X)$ and $\mathfrak{R}(X \times Y)$ as the classes of all random subsets of X and $X \times Y$, respectively.

The class of all *randomized confidence set procedures* is denoted by

$$\mathfrak{R} \overset{d}{=} \{R \mid R : Y \to \mathfrak{R}(X) \ \ (\text{measurable, etc.})\}$$

and the class of all *randomized acceptance region procedures* is given by

$$\mathcal{A} \overset{d}{=} \{A \mid A : X \to \mathfrak{R}(Y) \ \ (\text{measurable, etc.})\} \ .$$

Let

$$\mathcal{H} \overset{d}{=} ((H_0(\theta), H_1(\theta)) \mid \theta \in X)$$

be the fixed family of *hypotheses*, where for any $\theta \in X$,

$$H_0(\theta) \overset{d}{=} \{\theta\} \ , \ H_1(\theta) \overset{d}{=} X \dashv \{\theta\} \subseteq X \ .$$

Let $(V|\theta)_{\theta\in X}$ be a family of observation random variables over Y (i.e., $(V|\theta) : \Omega \to Y$ (measurable, etc.) with corresponding probability distribution functions $(P_\theta)_{\theta\in X}$.

There is a bijective correspondence between $\mathcal{T}$, the class of all *randomized decision or test procedures* $(\text{test}(\theta))_{\theta\in X}$ concerning $\mathcal{H}$, and $\mathcal{A}$, given by

$$\text{test}(\theta) : \begin{cases} \text{Decide } H_0(\theta) & \text{iff observe } y \in A(\theta) \\ \text{Decide } H_1(\theta) & \text{iff observe } y \in Y \dashv A(\theta), \end{cases}$$

for all $\theta \in X$.

There is a bijective correspondence between $\mathfrak{R}$ and $\mathcal{A}$ and hence $\mathcal{T}$, given by:

(i) Given any $R \in \mathfrak{R}$, define $A_R \in \mathcal{A}$ by, for any $\theta \in X$,

$$A_R(\theta) \overset{d}{=} \{y \mid y \in Y \;\&\; \theta \in R(y)\}.$$

Then, if one defines $S_R \in \mathfrak{R}(X \times Y)$ by

$$S_R \overset{d}{=} \{(\theta,y) \mid \theta \in X,\ y \in Y \;\&\; \theta \in R(y)\},$$

it follows that for all $\theta \in X$, $y \in Y$,

$$\begin{aligned} S_R(\theta,\cdot) &\overset{d}{=} \text{section of } S_R \text{ at } \theta \\ &= \{y \mid y \in Y \;\&\; (\theta,y) \in S_R\} = A_R(\theta) \end{aligned}$$

$$\begin{aligned} S_R(\cdot,y) &\overset{d}{=} \text{section of } S_R \text{ at } y \\ &= \{\theta \mid \theta \in X \;\&\; (\theta,y) \in S_R\} = R(y). \end{aligned}$$

(ii) Given any $A \in \mathcal{A}$, define $R_A \in \mathfrak{R}$ by, for any $y \in Y$,

$$R_A(y) \overset{d}{=} \{\theta \mid \theta \in X \;\&\; y \in A(\theta)\}.$$

Then, if one defines $S_A \in \mathfrak{R}(X \times Y)$ by

$$S_A \overset{d}{=} \{(\theta,y) \mid \theta \in X,\ y \in Y \;\&\; y \in A(\theta)\},$$

it follows that, for all $\theta \in X$, $y \in Y$,

$$\begin{aligned} S_A(\theta,\cdot) &\overset{d}{=} \text{section of } S_A \text{ at } \theta \\ &= \{y \mid y \in Y \;\&\; (\theta,y) \in S_A\} = A(\theta) \end{aligned}$$

$$\begin{aligned} S_A(\cdot,y) &\overset{d}{=} \text{section of } S_A \text{ at } y \\ &= \{\theta \mid \theta \in X \;\&\; (\theta,y) \in S_A\} = R_A(y). \end{aligned}$$

Call any pair (A,R_A) or (A_R,R) *compatible*.

Conversely, it follows that $\mathfrak{R}(X \times Y)$ generates all possible compatable pairs of randomized confidences set procedures:

Let $S \in \mathfrak{R}(X \times Y)$ be arbitrary.

Define $A_S \in \mathcal{A}$ and $R_S \in \mathfrak{R}$ by, for all $\theta \in X$, $y \in Y$,

$$A_S(\theta) \overset{d}{=} \text{section of } S \text{ at } \theta$$
$$= \{y \mid y \in Y \ \& \ (\theta,y) \in S\},$$
$$R_S(y) \overset{d}{=} \text{section of } S \text{ at } y$$
$$= \{\theta \mid \theta \in X \ \& \ (\theta,y) \in S\},$$

and

$$A_{R_S} \equiv A_S, \quad R_{A_S} \equiv R_S .$$

Thus, for any $S \in \mathfrak{R}(X \times Y)$, there is $\text{test}_S = (\text{test}_S(\theta))_{\theta \in X}$ determined by randomized acceptance region procedure A_S corresponding to confidence set procedure R_S such that, for all $\theta \in X$,
$\Pr(\text{Decide(for test}_S(\theta))H_0(\theta) \mid \theta) = 1 - \Pr(\text{Decide } H_1(\theta) \mid \theta)$

$$= \Pr(V \in A_S(\theta) \mid \theta) = \int_{y \in A_S(\theta)} dP_\theta(y)$$

$$= \Pr(\theta \in R_S(V) \mid \theta) \quad \text{(two-stage randomness due to } V \text{ and } S\text{).}$$

In particular, these relations show:

(i) For any $0 < \alpha < 1$: $\text{test}_S \in \mathcal{T}$ is an α - level test procedure, i.e.,

$$\Pr(\text{Decide(for test}_S(\theta)) \ H_1(\theta) \mid \theta) \geq \alpha \ ; \text{ for all } \theta \in X$$

iff R_S is an $(1 - \alpha)$-level confidence set procedure, i.e.,

$$\Pr(\theta \in R_S(V) \mid \theta) \geq 1 - \alpha \ ; \text{ for all } \theta \in X .$$

(ii) Let $0 < \alpha < 1$ and $\theta_0 \in X$. Then $\text{test}_S(\theta_0)$ is a uniformly most powerful α-level test for $H_0(\theta_0)$ vs. $H_1(\theta_0)$ iff R_S, among all $(1 - \alpha)$-level confidence set procedures R, minimizes $\Pr(\theta_0 \in R(y) \mid \theta)$, simultaneously, for all $\theta \in H_1(\theta_0)$.

(See Lehmann [154] for other properties.)

In addition, Robbins' result [219] (also independently rediscovered by Pratt [205]) applied here yields (see also section 4.4):

$$E_V(vol_n(R_S(V))) = \int_{B\in\mathbb{B}_n} \int_{\theta\in B} d\theta \; dPr\circ(R_S(V))^{-1}(B)$$

$$= \int_{\theta\in X} \int_{B\in C_{\{\theta\}}(\mathbb{B}_n)} d\; Pr\circ(R_S(V))^{-1}(B)\; d\theta$$

$$= \int_{\theta\in X} Pr(\theta \in R_S(V) \mid \theta)\; d\theta$$

$$= \int_{\theta\in X} Pr(V \in A_S(\theta) \mid \theta)\; d\theta$$

$$= \int_{\theta\in X} Pr(\text{Decide } H_0(\theta) \mid \theta)\; d\theta \; .$$

Also, note the evaluation of the one-point coverage function $\phi_{(S)} : X \times Y \to [0,1]$ of S at any $\theta \in X$ and $y \in Y$

$$\phi(S)(\theta,y) = Pr((\theta,y) \in S)$$

$$= Pr(V \in A_S(\theta) \mid V = y) = Pr(y \in A_S(\theta))$$

$$= Pr(\theta \in R_S(V) \mid V = y) = Pr(\theta \in R_S(y))$$

$$= Pr(\text{Decide (for } test_S(\theta))\; H_0(\theta) \mid V = y\; ;\; \theta)\; .$$

Note also the reductions of all of the above results when $S \equiv C \subseteq X \times Y$, i.e., for the non-random case.
Thus, in this notation, for all $\theta \in X$, $y \in Y$,

$$E(vol_n(R_S(V) \mid V = y) = \int_{\theta\in X} \phi_{(S)}(\theta,y)\; d\theta \; ,$$

$$E(vol_n(R_S(V))) = \int_{\theta\in X} \int_{y\in Y} \phi_{(S)}(\theta,y)\; dP_\theta(y)\; d\theta \; ,$$

$$Pr(\text{Decide(for } test_S(\theta))\; H_0(\theta) \mid \theta) = Pr(V \in A_S(\theta) \mid \theta)$$

$$= Pr(\theta \in R_S(V) \mid \theta)$$

$$= \int_{y\in Y} \phi_S(\theta,y)\; dP_\theta(y)\; .$$

Then define the joint admissibility measure map $\rho : \mathcal{T} \to ([0,1]^2)^{X\times Y}$ for $\mathcal{H}$ by, for any $S \in \mathfrak{R}(X \times Y)$ and hence any $test_S \in \mathcal{T}$, as the map $\rho(S) : X \times Y \to [0,1]^2$ where for any $\theta \in X$ and any $y \in Y$,

$\rho(S)(\theta,y)$

$$\stackrel{d}{=} \Big(\Pr(\text{Decide}(\text{for } \text{test}_S(\theta))H_1(\theta) \mid \theta) \text{ , } E(\text{vol}_n(R_S(V)) \mid V = y)\Big) \text{ .}$$

Partially order $\mathcal{T}$ by, for any $S_1, S_2 \in \mathfrak{R}(X \times Y)$,

$$\text{test}_{S_1} = \text{test}_{S_2} \quad \text{iff} \quad \rho(S_1) = \rho(S_2)\text{, a.e.,}$$

$$\text{test}_{S_1} \le \text{test}_{S_2} \quad \text{iff} \quad \rho(S_1) \le \rho(S_2) \text{ , a.e.,}$$

$$\text{test}_{S_1} < \text{test}_{S_2} \quad \text{iff} \quad \rho(S_1) \le \rho(S_2) \text{ ,}$$

for all $\theta \in X$ and for a.e. $y \in Y$ with strict inequality holding for either the first component at some $\theta \in X$ or for the second component at some set of $y \in Y$ of positive Lebesgue measure.

Then the admissible tests in $\mathcal{T}$ are those which are not less than some other test in $\mathcal{T}$. Other criteria may be designated for comparing the worthiness of tests. In any case, these comparisons may be carried out essentially through use of the functions $\phi_{(S)}$ and not necessarily directly using the actual corresponding tests $\in \mathcal{T}$. Joshi [125] was apparently one of the first to recognize this principle, where he showed the admissibility of the usual confidence set procedure for the means of one-and-two-dimensional Gaussian distributions. (For three or more dimensions, the procedure is inadmissible as Joshi showed in an earlier paper.) Joshi also claimed ([125]) that given any $\phi_C : X \times Y \to [0,1]$ in the form of a simple or elementary (a countable weighted sum of membership functions of ordinary sets) function corresponds to a randomized confidence set procedure, i.e., an $S \in \mathfrak{R}(X \times Y)$ and that any (suitably measurable) ϕ_C represents the limit of a sequence of such procedures. (See G. S. Goodman [93] for some related results from a fuzzy set viewpoint.) Carrying this idea further, Hooper ([118], [119]) showed that given any suitably measurable $\phi_C : X \times Y \to [0,1]$, there was at least one random set $S \in \mathfrak{R}(X \times Y)$ whose one point coverage function was ϕ : namely $S = S_U(C)$! Hooper, clearly, was unaware of the extensive literature devoted to the basic one point coverage problem, but indeed did use the fundamental transform S_U in reconstructing random set S whose one point coverage function was specified. (See the earlier part of this section for various results in this problem.) Furthermore, Hooper ([119], p. 550) also developed independent of any fuzzy set literature connections (as extensively described in this text) in effect, that the class $\mathfrak{R}(X \times Y)$ partitions into one point coverage equivalence classes indexed by all possible distinct $\phi_C \in \mathcal{T}(X \times Y)$! (Hooper [239], [240] also developed important natural generalizations of sufficiency and invariance techniques for confidence set procedures in terms of the one point coverage function representations.)

Thus we have a basic tie-in between some basic fuzzy set-random set relations and results in classical hypotheses testing and confidence interval theory!

In summary:

(a) There is essentially (up to measurability considerations) a bijective relationship between all random subsets of a parameter space, cross a data space, $X \times Y$, all randomized test procedures for all simple null hypotheses vs. complement alternatives of the parameter space and all compatible pairs of randomized acceptance regions and confidence set procedures. A similar relation holds for all ordinary subsets of $X \times Y$ and all non-randomized tests and confidence set procedures.

(b) Most criteria of interest involving such tests or equivalently confidence set procedures may be formulated in terms of the one point coverage function of random subsets of $X \times Y$ and (hence by the use of the canonical transform S_U, etc.), in effect (up to suitable measurability conditions), in terms of all fuzzy subsets of $X \times Y$ only. For example Robbins' result [207] shows expected volumes of a randomized confidence set procedure are the integrals of fuzzy set membership functions - the one point coverage functions of the random subsets of $X \times Y$.

CHAPTER 6

ISOMORPHIC-LIKE RELATIONS BETWEEN RANDOM SETS AND GENERAL LOGICAL SYSTEMS.

Mappings S_U and T (Chapter 5) are special one-argument cases of multiple argument mappings $\underset{\sim}{S}$ from cartesian products of all, generalized subsets of given spaces to cartesian products (as well-defined random objects) of all random subsets of the same spaces which marginally produce one point coverage-equivalences between the generalized and random sets involved. Again (see [90], [88]), these are called *choice function families*. Next, let $X_1,\ldots,X_n$ and X be any $n+1$ given spaces and

$$* : \mathcal{P}(X_1)\times\cdots\times\mathcal{P}(X_n) \to \mathcal{P}(X)$$

any given n-ary ordinary set operation. Often (but not necessarily so, in general), $*$ is the power extension of the mapping

$$*' : X_1 \times\cdots\times X_n \to X ,$$

where for any $C_j \in \mathcal{P}(X_j)$, $j = 1,\ldots,n$,

$$*(C_1,\ldots,C_n) \overset{d}{=} \{*'(x_1,\ldots,x_n) \mid x_j \in C_j , \ j = 1,\ldots,n\} .$$

Also, let

$$\bar{*} : \mathcal{F}(X_1)\times\cdots\times\mathcal{F}(X_n) \to \mathcal{F}(X)$$

be any given n-ary generalized set operation (defined through the membership functions, of course).

Finally, let $\underset{\sim}{S} = (S_j)_{j=1,\ldots,n}$ be a choice function family of random set maps, i.e., for any space X ,

$$S_j \equiv S : \mathcal{F}(X) \to \mathcal{R}(X) ,$$

such that for any spaces X_j , and any $A_j \in \mathcal{F}(X_j)$, $j = 1,\ldots,n$, the random sets

$$S_j(A_j) : \Omega \to \mathcal{P}(X_j) , \ j = 1,\ldots,n ,$$

with respect to some initial probability space Ω , yield

$$(S_j(A_j))_{j=1,\ldots,n} : \Omega \to \times_{j=1}^{n} \mathcal{P}(X_j)$$ as a well defined random set, where marginally

$$S_j(A_j) \approx A_j \ , \ j = 1,\ldots,n \ .$$

Then we say that the triple $(\bar{*} \ ; \ *,\underset{\sim}{S})$ is in an isomorphic-like relation, also called a w-hom (weak-homomorphism), iff

$$\bar{*}\underset{\sim}{A}_n \approx S(\bar{*}\underset{\sim}{A}_n) \approx *\underset{\sim}{S}(\underset{\sim}{A}_n) \ ,$$

i.e., for all $A_j \in \mathcal{F}(X_j)$, $j = 1,\ldots,n$, $x \in X$,

$$\phi_{\bar{*}\underset{\sim}{A}_n}(x) \overset{d}{=} \phi_{\bar{*}(A_j)_{j=1,\ldots,n}}(x) = \Pr(x \in S(\bar{*}\underset{\sim}{A}_n))$$

$$= \Pr(x \in * \ \underset{\sim}{S}(\underset{\sim}{A}_n)) = \Pr(x \in \underset{(j=1,\ldots,n)}{*} (S_j(A_j))) \ .$$

Note that in the above equation, it is assumed that $* \ \underset{\sim}{S}(\underset{\sim}{A}_n)$ is a well defined random set. More on this:

Using standard procedures, it is easily shown that if I is *any* index set,

$$\underset{\sim}{S}(\underset{\sim}{A}_I) \overset{d}{=} (S(A_j))_{j\in I} : \Omega \to \times_{j\in I} \mathcal{P}(X_j)$$

where $(\Omega,\mathfrak{D},\Pr)$ is some fixed probability space and for all $\omega \in \Omega$, $\underset{\sim}{S}(\underset{\sim}{A}_I)(\omega) \overset{d}{=} (S(\underset{\sim}{A}_j)(\omega))_{j\in I}$, $\underset{\sim}{S}(\underset{\sim}{A}_I)$ will be $(\mathfrak{D},\mathcal{E})$-measurable, where $\mathcal{E} \overset{d}{=} \sigma(\times_{j\in I} \bar{\sigma}(\mathcal{C}_2(\mathcal{B}_o(X_j))))$, inducing probability space $(\times_{j\in I} \mathcal{P}(X_j), \ \mathcal{E}, \ \nu)$, $\nu \overset{d}{=} \Pr\circ\underset{\sim}{S}(\underset{\sim}{A}_I)^{-1}$. Furthermore, if $* : \times_{j\in I} \mathcal{P}(X_j) \to \mathcal{P}(Y)$ is any $(\mathcal{E},\mathcal{F})$-measurable mapping for some σ-algebra $\mathcal{F}$ over $\mathcal{P}(Y)$, then $*\circ\underset{\sim}{S}(\underset{\sim}{A}_I) : \Omega \to \mathcal{P}(Y)$ will also be measurable. In particular, since ordinary set operations $*$ including $\cup$, $\cap$ and $\complement$ are measurable, (and continuous relative to the natural topologies involved), it follows that $*\circ\underset{\sim}{S}(\underset{\sim}{A}_I)$ for $* = \cup \ , \cap \ , \complement$, etc., are all measurable and hence random subsets of appropriate Y's.

Define for any $A \in \mathcal{F}(X)$ here the complement of A , $\bar{\complement}A$ (or $X \dashv A$, etc.) by

$$\phi_{\overline{CA}}(x) = 1 - \phi_A(x) \ ; \ \text{all} \ \ x \in X \ ,$$

and similarly, if $f : X \to Y$ is any ordinary function, for any $B \in \mathcal{F}(Y)$, $x \in X$,

$$\phi_{\overline{f^{-1}}(B)}(x) = \phi_B(f(x)) \ .$$

Then, it can be shown that if S is any choice function, then $(\bar{C} ; C, S)$ is a w-hom and if $f : X \to Y$ is sufficiently measurable, then $(\overline{f^{-1}} ; f^{-1}, S)$ is a w-hom. If fuzzy set system $\mathcal{F}$ is non-Archimedean, and S is any choice function, then f and projection, proj, induce modified w-hom's, where $\approx$ is replaced by $\lesssim$. Furthermore, if $(\bar{\times}, \times, \underset{\sim}{S})$ is a w-hom for fuzzy set system $\mathcal{F}$, then for any $A \in \mathcal{F}(X)$, $x_j \in X_j$, $x_k \in X_k$, the pair-wise correlation of random set coverage $\text{correl}(\phi_{S_j(A_j)}(x_j), \phi_{S_k(A_k)}(k_j))$ – is:

(i) maximized for the evaluation $\mathcal{F} = \mathcal{F}_0$,

(ii) made zero, i.e., uncorrelated, for $\mathcal{F} = \mathcal{F}_1$.

(iii) minimized, i.e., made most negative, for $n = 2$, for $\mathcal{F} = \mathcal{F}_\infty$.

It can be shown ([91], Theorem 5.1) that if $(\bar{\times}, \times, \underset{\sim}{S})$ is a w-hom, then $(\bar{\dagger}, \dagger, \underset{\sim}{S})$ is also a w-hom (for the same $\underset{\sim}{S}$) iff the corresponding fuzzy set system is semi-distributive. (See section 2.3.6 for notation.)

Let us consider now some particular classes of choice function families and associated w-hom's.

First, let $\phi_\&$ be any J_o-copula (see [91]) and let stochastic process $\underset{\sim}{U} \stackrel{d}{=} (U_j)_{j \in J_o}$ be such that each U_j is a random variable uniformly distributed over $[0,1]$ with joint probability distribution function furnished by $\phi_\&$:

$$\Pr(U_1 \le x_1, \dots, U_n \le x_n) = \phi_\&(x_1, \dots, x_n) \ ,$$

for any $x_1, \dots, x_n \in [0,1]$. Then it follows that $\underset{\sim}{U}$ induces choice function family $S_{\underset{\sim}{U}} \stackrel{d}{=} (S_{U_j})_{j \in J_o}$ where for DeMorgan fuzzy set system $\mathcal{F} = (1-(\cdot), \phi_\&, \phi_{or})$, it readily follows that $(\bar{*} ; * ; S_{\underset{\sim}{U}})$ is a w-hom for $* = \times, \cap, \dagger, \cup$. Also, for any $C_j \in \mathcal{P}(X_j)$,

$A_j \in \mathcal{F}(X_j)$; $j \in K \subseteq J_o$,

$$\Pr(\underset{j\in K}{\&} (C_j \subseteq S_{U_j}(A_j))) = \Pr(\underset{j\in K}{\&} (C_j \subseteq \phi_{A_j}^{-1}[U_j,1]))$$
$$= \Pr(\underset{j\in K}{\&} (U_j \le \inf_{x\in C_j} \phi_{A_j}(x)))$$
$$= \phi_{\underset{j\in K}{\&}} (\inf_{x\in C_j} \phi_{A_j}(x)) .$$

Note that when $\phi_{\&} = \min$, we obtain $S_{\underset{\sim}{U}} = S_U$ and all of the w-hom results remain valid. Also, for $\phi_{\&} = \text{prod}$, $\underset{\sim}{U}$ becomes a statistically independent uniform [0,1] process and $S_{\underset{\sim}{U}}$ likewise induce statistically independent $S_{U_j}(A_j)$'s and w-hom's for unions, intersections, and projections, etc.

Next, let $\mathcal{F} \in \mathcal{F}_{e}$ (semi-distributive class) and for any $\underset{\sim}{A} = (A_j)_{j\in J_o}$, $A_j \in \mathcal{F}(X)$, for all $j \in J_o$, let

$$\phi_{\underset{\sim}{T}(\underset{\sim}{A})} \overset{d}{=} (\phi_{\underset{\sim}{T}(\underset{\sim}{A})}(x))_{x\in X} \overset{d}{=} (V_{\underset{\sim}{A},\&,x})_{x\in X} \overset{d}{=} V_{\underset{\sim}{A},\&}$$

be a zero-one process such that each $V_{\underset{\sim}{A},\&,x}$ is statistically independent with respect to different $x \in X$ and where each

$$V_{\underset{\sim}{A},\&,x} \overset{d}{=} (V_{A_j,\&,x,j})_{j\in J_o}$$

is a zero-one process finitely consistently generated by the relations

$$\Pr(\underset{j\in K}{\&} (V_{A_j,\&,x,j} = 1)) = \phi_{\underset{j\in K}{\&}} (\phi_{A_j}(x)) \ ; \ K \subseteq \mathfrak{F}(J_o) .$$

Each $T_j(A_j)$, uniquely corresponds to

$$\phi_{T_j(A_j)} = V_{A_j,\&,j} = (V_{A_j,\&,x,j})_{x\in X} ,$$

a T-type random subset of X .

For any $C_j \in \mathcal{P}(X)$ and $A_j \in \mathcal{F}(X)$; $j \in K \subseteq J_o$,

$$\Pr(\underset{j\in K}{\&} (C_j \subseteq T_j(A_j))) = \prod_{x \in \bigcup_{j\in K} C_j} \Big(\phi_{\underset{\{k|x\in C_k, k\in K\}}{\&}} (\phi_{A_k}(x))\Big) ,$$

implying that $(\bar{\cap} \ ; \cap \ , \underset{\sim}{T})$ is a w-hom.

Another family (see Höhle [116] and [117] - the latter presenting very general results) of choice functions may be generated by choosing any fuzzy set system $\mathcal{F} = (1-(\cdot), \phi_{\&}, \phi_{or}) \in \mathcal{F}_e$ (the semi-distributive class - see earlier remarks, recalling that examples of these fuzzy set systems include $(1-(\cdot)$, prod, probsum$)$, $(1-(\cdot)$, min, max$)$ and all ordinal sums of these (section 2.3.6).

Then for any fixed collection of spaces $\underset{\sim}{X} = (X_j)_{j=1,\dots,n}$, and a collection of fuzzy subsets $\underset{\sim}{A} = (A_j)_{j=1,\dots,n}$ from $\underset{\sim}{X}$, first a doubt measure $\mu_{\underset{\sim}{A},\phi_{\&}}$ is determined over the class of all subsets $\underset{\sim}{C}$ of $\underset{\sim}{X}$ by (first evaluating for finite sets and extending)

$$\mu_{\underset{\sim}{A},\phi_{\&}}(\underset{\sim}{C}) \overset{d}{=} \underset{\begin{bmatrix} x_j \in C_j, \\ j=1,\dots,n \end{bmatrix}}{\phi_{\&}} (\phi_{A_j}(x_j)) .$$

Similarly, define plausibility measure $\mu_{\underset{\sim}{A},\phi_{or}}$ by

$$\mu_{\underset{\sim}{A},\phi_{or}}(\underset{\sim}{C}) \overset{d}{=} \underset{\begin{bmatrix} x_j \in C_j, \\ j=1,\dots,n \end{bmatrix}}{\phi_{or}} (\phi_{A_j}(x_j)) .$$

Then, by previous results, there are uniquely determined joint random set families

$$\underset{\sim}{S}_{\&}(\underset{\sim}{A}) = (S_j(A_j,\phi_{\&}))_{j=1,\dots,n}$$

and

$$\underset{\sim}{S}_{or}(\underset{\sim}{A}) = (S_j(A_j,\phi_{or}))_{j=1,\dots,n}$$

such that not only for all $\underset{\sim}{A}$ fuzzy sets

$$\underset{\sim}{S}_{\&}(\underset{\sim}{A}) \approx \underset{\sim}{A} \; ; \; \underset{\sim}{S}_{or}(\underset{\sim}{A}) \approx \underset{\sim}{A} ,$$

yielding $\underset{\sim}{S}_{\&}$ and $\underset{\sim}{S}_{or}$ as choice function families, but also such that for all combinations of $\phi_{\&}$ and ϕ_{or} (and cartesian product and sum - and, in particular, intersection and union)

$$\Pr(\underset{\text{all } j,k}{\text{comb}} (\&,or)(C_{j,k} \subseteq S_j(A_j,\phi_{\&})))$$

$$\equiv \underset{\text{all } j,k}{\text{comb}} (\phi_{\&},\phi_{or})(\underset{x_j \in C_{j,k}}{\phi_{\&}} (\phi_{A_j}(x_j))) \; ; \; \text{all } C_{j,k} , A_j ,$$

with a similar relation holding for $\underset{\sim}{S}_{or}(\underset{\sim}{A})$, with respect to incidences in place of inclusions. This implies isomorphic-like relations between multiple argument fuzzy $\bar{f}$ and ordinary set operation $f : \underset{\sim}{X} \to Y$ extended to the respective power classes,

where $\bar{f}$ as obtained by the extension principle discussed earlier, i.e., for all $y \in Y$ and all (fuzzy) $\underset{\sim}{A}$,

$$\phi_{\bar{f}(\underset{\sim}{A})}(y) = \underset{\left((x_j)_{j=1,\dots,n} \in f^{-1}(y)\right)}{\phi_{or}} (\underset{j=1,\dots,n}{\phi_\&} (\phi_{A_j}(x_j))) .$$

Thus, for all $\underset{\sim}{A}$

$$\bar{f}\,(\underset{\sim}{A}) \approx S_\&(\,\bar{f}\,(\underset{\sim}{A})\,;\,\phi_\&) \approx f(\underset{\sim}{S}_\&(\times\underset{\sim}{A};\phi_\&)) .$$

This should serve as a second response to Manes' complaints [170] (see also 10.2 A), since the cartesian products and sums (for $\mathcal{F} \in \mathcal{F}_e$) form simultaneous w-hom's with respect to members of the families. Arithmetic operations (such as fuzzy sums, functional-cartesian product transforms, fuzzy products, etc.) also form w-hom's for $\underset{\sim}{S}_\&$ and $\underset{\sim}{S}_{or}$.

For subset inclusions, the following holds for any A_1 , $A_2 \in \mathcal{F}(X)$:

$$\| \langle A_1 \mathrel{\bar{\subseteq}} A_2 \rangle \| = \underset{x \in X}{\phi_\&} (\phi_{A_1 \bar{\Rightarrow} A_2}(x)) = Pr(S_{\&,1}(A_1) \subseteq S_{or,2}(A_2)) .$$

The above results generalize the single argument choice functions $S_\&$ and S_{or} where, for any $A \in \mathcal{F}(X)$, $\mu_{A,\&}$ is a doubt measure and $\mu_{A,or}$ is a plausibility measure obtained by, for all $C \in \mathfrak{F}(X)$,

$$\mu_{A,\&}(C) = \underset{x \in C}{\phi_\&} (\phi_A(x)) ,$$

$$\mu_{A,or}(C) = \underset{x \in C}{\phi_{or}} (\phi_A(x)) ,$$

$$S_\&(A) \stackrel{d}{=} S_{\mu_{A,\&}} \; ; \; S_{or}(A) \stackrel{d}{=} S_{\mu_{A,or}} = \complement\, S_{1-\mu_{A,\&}} .$$

A basic characterizing property of this class of choice functions is given by

$$Pr(C \subseteq S_{\mu_{A,\&}}) = \mu_{A,\&}(C) \; ; \; Pr(S_{\mu_{A,or}} \mathbin{\Lambda} C) = \mu_{A,or}(C) \; ; \; C \in \mathcal{P}(X) ,$$

by extending the domains from $\mathfrak{F}(X)$ to $\mathcal{P}(X)$ via Theorem 3, Chapter 4. Note also that

$$S_U(A) = S_{\mu_{A,\min}} \;;\; T(A) = S_{\mu_{A,\mathrm{prod}}} \;;\; \text{all } A \in \mathcal{F}(X) \;.$$

$S_{\underset{\sim}{U}}$ is not a part of the $\underset{\sim}{S}_{\&}$ nor $\underset{\sim}{S}_{or}$ family, in general, except when $\underset{\sim}{U}$ is chosen to be identical to U , i.e., $U_j = U$, for all $j \in J$, whence $\phi_{\&} = \min$.

T is not a part of the $\underset{\sim}{S}_{\&}$ nor $\underset{\sim}{S}_{or}$ family, in general, unless $\phi_{\&}$ is chosen to be prod, in which case, $V_{\underset{\sim}{A},\&}$ becomes a completely statistically independent (with respect to all indices) zero-one process.

A basic question is to determine what fuzzy set systems exist which lead to simultaneous w-hom's, for either the $S_{\underset{\sim}{U}}$ family or the $\underset{\sim}{T}$ family, for cartesian sums and products and possibly complements, and for arbitrary combinations of these operations. In the last case, it may be interpreted that a generalized set system involved in such a relationship is identifiable with a corresponding random set system.

Theorem 1 (Identification of Generalized Set Systems with Random Set Systems.)

(a) $\mathcal{F}$ is semi-distributive iff $(\bar{\times} \;;\; \times \;,\; \underset{\sim}{S})$ and $(\bar{\dagger} \;;\; \dagger,\; \underset{\sim}{S})$ are simultaneously w-hom's for $\underset{\sim}{S}$

$$\text{iff } (\mathrm{combo}(\bar{\times} \;,\; \bar{\dagger}) \;,\; \mathrm{combo}(\times,\dagger),\; \underset{\sim}{S}) \text{ is a w-hom,}$$

where $\underset{\sim}{S} = \underset{\sim}{S}_{\underset{\sim}{U}}$ or $\underset{\sim}{S} = \underset{\sim}{T}$; in the latter case, replace $\times$ by $\cap$ and $\dagger$ by $\cup$ everywhere.

(b) $\mathcal{F}$ is semi-distributive and DeMorgan iff (a) holds with the inclusion of C in the combo operators and a modification of certain random set representations (those corresponding to an odd number of DeMorgan transposes to be clear of all complements) where in places $S_j(A_j)$ is replaced by $CS_j(\bar{C}\, A_j)$.

(c) Assuming for $\mathcal{F}$ that $(\partial\phi_{\&}(x,y)/\partial y)_{y=0}$ exists for all $x \in [0,1]$, then $\mathcal{F} = \mathcal{F}_1$ iff (b) holds with no modifications of random set representations.

(d) Consider the case $\underset{\sim}{S} = S_{\underset{\sim}{U}}$ and $\mathcal{F}$ a DeMorgan fuzzy set system:

(i) $\underset{\sim}{U}$ is a statistically independent process iff $\mathcal{F} = \mathcal{F}_1$, whence (c) applies;

(ii) $\underset{\sim}{U}$ is an identical process, i.e., $U_j \equiv U$, iff $\mathcal{F} = \mathcal{F}_0$, whence (b) is applicable with

$$C\, S_U(\bar{C}\, A_j) = S_{1-U}(A_j) \quad \text{(with probability one)};$$

(iii) For $\underset{\sim}{U} = (U_1, U_2)$ only : $U_2 = 1 - U_1$ iff $\mathcal{F} = \mathcal{F}_\infty$. However, although $(\bar{x}\ ;\ x,\ S_{\underset{\sim}{U}})$ is a w-hom,

$(\tilde{t}\ ; t, S_{\underset{\sim}{U}})$ is not simultaneously a w-hom.

(e) Yager's DeMorgan family $\mathcal{Y}$ yields for each p, and corresponding $\phi_{\&,(p)}$, generating uniform [0,1] process $\underset{\sim}{U}_p$: $(\bar{x}_p ; x, S_{\underset{\sim}{U}_p})$ is a w-hom, but $(\bar{t}_p\ ;\ t,\ S_{\underset{\sim}{U}_p})$ is not simultaneously a w-hom. Parameter p can be shown to be directly proportional to the pairwise correlation of random set coverage here [91].

Three basic problems arise concerning relations between fuzzy and ordinary set operations with respect to weak homomorphism.

Basic Problem 1.

Given any ordinary n-ary set operation $*$, what choice function families $\underset{\sim}{S}$ exist and what fuzzy set operations $\bar{*}$ exist such that $(\bar{*}\ ;\ *, \underset{\sim}{S})$ is a w-hom?

Theorem 2 (Solution to Basic Problem 1 - See [81].)

Given any $*$ and any $\underset{\sim}{S}$, there exists a unique $\bar{*}$ such that $(\bar{*},\ *,\ \underset{\sim}{S})$ is a w-hom. The relationship is given explicitly by, for all $x \in X$, $\underset{\sim}{A} \in \mathcal{F}(\underset{\sim}{X})$,

$$\phi_{\bar{*}\,\underset{\sim}{A}}(x) = \Pr(\phi_{\underset{\sim}{S}(\underset{\sim}{A})} \in \phi_*^{-1}(\sigma_{x,1})) = \int_{z \in Z_n} \phi_{\phi_*^{-1}(\sigma_{x,1})}(z)\, d\,\nu_{\underset{\sim}{S}(\underset{\sim}{A})}(z) ;$$

$$\phi_*(\phi_{\underset{\sim}{C}}) = \phi_{*(\underset{\sim}{C})} \ ;\ Z_n \overset{d}{=} \underset{j \in I_n}{\times} \{0,1\}^{X_j} \ ;\ \underset{\sim}{C} \in \mathcal{P}(\underset{\sim}{X}) .$$

In addition, $\bar{*}$ extends $*$, i.e., for all $\underset{\sim}{C} \in \mathcal{P}(\underset{\sim}{X})$,

$$\bar{*}\, \underset{\sim}{C} = *\underset{\sim}{C} .$$

Corollary 1 (Basic Problem 1 for Compositional Operations.)

If $*$ is a composition, i.e., there is a fixed function $g_* : \{0,1\}^n \to \{0,1\}$, with

$$\phi_*(\phi_{\underset{\sim}{C}}) = g_* \circ (\phi_{\underset{\sim}{C}}) \ ; \text{ all } \underset{\sim}{C} \in \mathcal{P}(\underset{\sim}{X}) ,$$

then

$$\phi_{\bar{*}\underset{\sim}{A}}(x) = \sum_{\underset{\sim}{a} \in [0,1]^n} (g_*(\underset{\sim}{a}) \cdot Pr(x \in (\bigcap_{a_j=1} S_j(A_j) \dashv (\bigcup_{a_j=0} S_j(A_j)))) \ ; x \in X .$$

Ordinary binary composition set operations.

Let $g_* : \{0,1\}^2 \to \{0,1\}$ be arbitrary. There are 16 possible g_*'s , analogous to the 16 possible classical logical binary truth operators. Let $X_1 = X_2 = X$ be arbitrary spaces. Then, each g_* corresponds uniquely to a $\phi_* : Z_2 \overset{d}{=} \{0,1\}^X \times \{0,1\}^X \to \{0,1\}^X$ and $* : X \times X \to X$ such that for any $C_j \in \mathcal{P}(X)$, $j = 1,2$,

$$\phi(*(C_1,C_2)) = \phi(C_1 * C_2) = \phi_*(\phi_{C_1},\phi_{C_2}) = g_* \circ (\phi_{C_1},\phi_{C_2}) .$$

Now let $S_j : \mathcal{F}(X) \to \mathcal{R}(X)$ be arbitrary such that for any $A_j \in \mathcal{F}(X)$

$$S_j(A_j) \approx A_j \ ; \ j = 1,2 . \qquad (\cdot)$$

It follows readily that the joint random sets $(S_1(A_1),\ S_2(A_2))$ may be arbitrary such that for all $x \in X$,

$$f(A_1,A_2;x) \overset{d}{=} Pr(x \in S_1(A_1) \cap S_2(A_2)) = Pr(x \in S_1(A_1),\ x \in S_2(A_2))$$
$$= Pr(\phi_{A_1}(x) = 1, \phi_{A_2}(x) = 1) \ ;$$

$$L(A_1,A_2;x) \le f(A_1,A_2;x) \le U(A_1,A_2;x) ,$$

$$U(A_1,A_2;x) \overset{d}{=} \min Pr(x \in S_1(A_1),\ Pr(x \in S_2(A_2)))$$
$$= \min (\phi_{A_1}(x),\ \phi_{A_2}(x)) ,$$ the maximal t-norm evaluation,

$$L(A_1,A_2;x) \overset{d}{=} \max\ (Pr(x \in S_1(A_1)) + Pr(x \in S_2(A_2)) - 1,0)$$
$$= \text{minsum}\ (\phi_{A_1}(x),\ \phi_{A_2}(x))\ ,\ \text{the minimal t-conorm evaluation,}$$

where, in general, there does not necessarily exist $g : \{0,1\}^2 \to \{0,1\}$, such that

$$Pr(\phi_{S_1(A_1)}(x) = 1\ ,\ \phi_{S_2(A_2)}(x) = 1) = g(\phi_{A_1}(x),\ \phi_{A_2}(x))$$

for all $x \in X$, $j = 1,2$. (Sklar's Theorem [226] is too weak for use here. See also the more general bounds L,U discussed in section 2.3.9 (A).)

Next, for each given choice function family $\underset{\sim}{S}_2 = (S_1,S_2)$, (with S_1,S_2 arbitrary satisfying eq. $(\cdot)$ and for any $A_j \in \mathcal{F}(X)$, $j = 1,2$, $(S_1(A_1),\ S_2(A_2))$ being a well-defined joint random set), by either direct expansions of each of the 16 operators $*$ or by specializing Corollary 1 to $n = 2$, it follows that 16 unique binary generalized set operations $\bar{*}$ may be defined such that $(\bar{*}\ ,\ *,\ \underset{\sim}{S}_2)$ is a w-hom, i.e., for all $A_j \in \mathcal{F}_j(X_j)$, all $x \in X$, $j = 1,2$,

$$Pr(x \in (S_1(A_1) * S_2(A_2))) = \phi_{A_1 \bar{*} A_2}(x)\ :$$

Operator No.	g_* defined by its evaluation over: (1,1)	(1,0)	(0,1)	(0,0)	$C_1 * C_2$ for any $C_1, C_2 \in \mathcal{P}(X)$	$\phi_{A_1 \bar{*} A_2}(x)$ for any $A_1, A_2 \in \mathcal{F}(X)$; $x \in X$
1	1	1	1	1	X	1
2	1	1	1	0	$C_1 \cup C_2$	$\phi_{A_1}(x) + \phi_{A_2}(x) - f$
3	1	1	0	1	$C_1 \cup (X \dashv C_2)$	$1 - \phi_{A_2}(x) + f$
4	1	1	0	0	C_1	$\phi_{A_1}(x)$
5	1	0	1	1	$C_2 \cup (X \dashv C_1)$	$1 - \phi_{A_1}(x) + f$
6	1	0	1	0	C_2	$\phi_{A_2}(x)$
7	1	0	0	1	$X \dashv (C_1 \triangle C_2)$	$1 - \phi_{A}(x) - \phi_{A_2}(x) + 2f$
8	1	0	0	0	$C_1 \cap C_2$	f
9	0	1	1	1	$X \dashv (C_1 \cap C_2)$	$1 - f$
10	0	1	1	0	$C_1 \triangle C_2$	$\phi_{A_1}(x) + \phi_{A_2}(x) - 2f$
11	0	1	0	1	$X \dashv C_2$	$1 - \phi_{A_2}(x)$
12	0	1	0	0	$C_1 \dashv C_2$	$\phi_{A_1}(x) - f$
13	0	0	1	1	$X \dashv C_1$	$1 - \phi_{A_1}(x)$
14	0	0	1	0	$C_2 \dashv C_1$	$\phi_{A_2}(x) - f$
15	0	0	0	1	$X \dashv (C_1 \cup C_2)$	$1 - \phi_{A_1}(x) - \phi_{A_2}(x) + f$
16	0	0	0	0	$\emptyset$	0

Table I.

Generalized Set Operator Extensions Isomorphic-Like (w-hom) to Ordinary Binary Composition Set Operators.

Thus, for example, consider operator 2, union. By first choosing

$$f = \min\,(\phi_{A_1}(\ ),\ \phi_{A_2}(\ ))\ ,$$

occurring, for example, for $S_j(A_j) \equiv S_U(A_j) = \phi_{A_j}^{-1}[U,1]$, U a uniform [0,1] random variable, then for all $x \in X$, $A_j \in \mathcal{F}(X)$, $j = 1,2$.

$$\phi_{A_1 \bar{\cup} A_2}(x) = \max(\phi_{A_1}(x), \phi_{A_2}(x))$$
$$= \Pr(x \in S_U(A_1) \cup S_U(A_2)) .$$

Or by choosing

$$f = \phi_{A_1}(\cdot)\cdot\phi_{A_2}(\cdot) ,$$

occurring, for example, for $S_j(A_j) = S_{U_j}(A_j) = \phi_{A_j}^{-1}[U,1]$, $j = 1,2$, where U_1 and U_2 are statistically independent uniform [0,1] random variables,

$$\phi_{A_1 \bar{\cup} A_2}(x) = \phi_{A_1}(x) + \phi_{A_2}(x) - \phi_{A_1}(x)\cdot\phi_{A_2}(x) ,$$
$$= \text{probsum}(\phi_{A_1}(x), \phi_{A_2}(x)) .$$

Or by choosing

$$f = \max(\phi_{A_1}(\cdot) + \phi_{A_2}(\cdot) - 1,0) ,$$

occurring, for example, for $S_j(A_j) = S_{U_j}(A_j) = \phi_{A_j}^{-1}[U,1]$, $j = 1,2$, where $U_1 = 1 - U_2$ are uniform [0,1] random variables,

$$\phi_{A_1 \cup A_2}(x) = \min(\phi_{A_1}(x) + \phi_{A_2}(x), 1)$$
$$= \text{minsum}(\phi_{A_1}(x), \phi_{A_2}(x)) .$$

Note also the table includes the four unary composition extension forms:

Operation No.	g_* defined by its evaluation over: 1	0	$*(C)$ for any $C \in \mathcal{P}(X)$	$\phi_{\bar{*}(A)}(x)$, for any $A \in \mathcal{F}(X)$; $x \in X$
1	1	1	X	1
2	1	0	C	$\phi_A(x)$
3	0	1	$X \dashv C$	$1 - \phi_A(x)$
4	0	0	$\emptyset$	0

<u>Table II.</u>

Generalized Set Operator Extensions
Isomorphic-Like to Unary Compositions.

Basic Problem 2.

Given an n-ary generalized set operation $\bar{*}$, does there exist a choice function family $\underset{\sim}{S}$ and an ordinary n-ary set operation $*$ such that $(\bar{*}\ ;\ *,\ \underset{\sim}{S})$ is a w-hom?

First, it can be shown that *there is at most one* $*$ such that $(\bar{*};\ *,\ \underset{\sim}{S})$ is a w-hom (for any possible $\underset{\sim}{S}$): namely, $\bar{*}$ restricted to ordinary subsets. (Proof: Restrict the definition of a w-hom to ordinary subsets and use the fact that the one-element equivalence classes under $\approx$ are generated by the class of all ordinary subsets.)

Secondly, the aforementioned examples of choice function families $S_{\underset{\sim}{U}}$, $\underset{\sim}{T}$, $\underset{\sim}{S}_{\&}$, $\underset{\sim}{S}_{or}$ show that many such w-hom's exist. In addition, it can also be shown (Goodman [91], Cor. 6.2) that fuzzy partitionings, and in particular, all fuzzy weighted sum operators (not t-norms nor t-conorms, in general), have natural corresponding weak homomorphic random set representations. These are in the form of disjoint unions of intersections of corresponding pairs of statistically independent weak homomorphic T – type random sets. Nevertheless, there do exist classes of fuzzy set operations which have no random set counterparts which preserve the number of arguments of the operator. (See also, Theorem 4 here.)

Some binary fuzzy set operations with no binary random set operation representations.

Let D_1 be the open unit interval, D_2 be the open unit square, and g_2 be such that for all $x,y \in D_2$,

$$g_2 : D_2 \to D_1 \ ;\ g_2(x,y) \overset{d}{=} x \ .$$

Then let g be arbitrary such that $g : [0,1] \times [0,1] \to [0,1]$, $g \not\equiv g_2$ (over D_2) , $g(0,0) = g(0,1) = 0$; $g(1,0) = g(1,1) = 1$.

In turn, define the binary fuzzy set operator $(\bar{*})_g$ over $\mathcal{F}(X)$ by

$$\phi_{A_1(\bar{*})_g A_2}(x) \overset{d}{=} g(\phi_{A_1}(x),\ \phi_{A_2}(x)) \ ;\ A_1,A_2 \in \mathcal{F}(X) \ ,\ x \in X \ .$$

Then $((\bar{*})_g\ ;\ *',\ \underset{\sim}{S})$ is <u>never</u> a w-hom, no matter what ordinary binary operator $*'$ and choice function family $\underset{\sim}{S} = (S_1,S_2)$ are selected.

A related construction yields an analagous lack of possible unary set operator representations for a class of unary fuzzy set operators: Choose $g : [0,1] \to [0,1]$ to be arbitrary such that $g \not\equiv$ identity, 1-identity, 0, 1 . In particular, this implies if $\mathcal{F}$ is Archimedean, the qth intensification operator, which linguistically can correspond to "very(·)", "very, very(·)", etc., depending on the integer q chosen, where for all $x \in X$ and all $A \in \mathcal{F}(X)$,

$$\phi_{A^{\textcircled{q}}}(x) \equiv \phi_{A^{q}}(x) \stackrel{d}{=} \phi_{\&}(\phi_A(x), \phi_A(x)), \ldots, \phi_A(x)) \quad (q \text{ factors}) ,$$

has no random set unary operator counterpart, although by Theorem 2, for many such fuzzy set systems, $(\cdot)^{(\bar{q})}$ does have a q-ary random set representation with $A_1 = A_2 = \cdots = A_q = A$ for the w-hom $((\ )^{\bar{q}} ; \cap, \underset{\sim}{S})$, i.e., for all $A \in \mathcal{F}(X)$,

$$A^{\bar{q}} \approx S(A^{\bar{q}}) \approx S(A \mathbin{\bar{\cap}} A \mathbin{\bar{\cap}} \cdots \mathbin{\bar{\cap}} A) \approx S_1(A) \cap S_2(A) \cap \cdots \cap S_q(A) .$$

Basic Problem 3.

Are there weak homomorphic relations between given generalized set operators which do not depend on specific choice function subfamilies for some large class of choice function families? Equivalently, how closely do weak homomorphic generalized and ordinary set operations resemble true algebraic equivalence class operations, where the operations do not depend on the particular choice of equivalence class representative?

A partial affirmation to Problem 3 is given in

Theorem 3 (Some Equivalence Class Operations Involved in Weak Homomorphisms)

Let $f : \{0,1\}^{I_n} \to \{0,1\}$ be fixed but arbitrary and for each $\underset{\sim}{k} \stackrel{d}{=} (k_1, \ldots, k_n) \in f^{-1}(1)$, define

$$\tau_{\underset{\sim}{k},j} : [0,1] \to [0,1] ;$$

$$\tau_{\underset{\sim}{k},j}(x) \stackrel{d}{=} \begin{cases} x & , \text{ if } k_j = 1 \\ 1 - x & , \text{ if } k_j = 0 \end{cases} ; \quad x \in [0,1] ,\ j \in I_n .$$

Then define n-ary generalized set operator $(\bar{*})_f$ over $\mathcal{F}(\underset{\sim}{X})$, by, for all $\underset{\sim}{A} \in \mathcal{F}(\underset{\sim}{X})$, $x \in X$,

$$\phi_{(\bar{*})_f \underset{\sim}{A}}(x) \overset{d}{=} \sum_{k\in f^{-1}(1)} \left[\prod_{j\in I_n} \tau_{k,j}(\phi_{A_j}(x)) \right] .$$

If n-ary composition operator $(*)_f$ over $\mathcal{P}(\underset{\sim}{X})$ is defined by, for all $\underset{\sim}{C} \in \mathcal{P}(\underset{\sim}{X})$, $x \in X$,

$$\phi_{(\bar{*})_f(\underset{\sim}{C})}(x) \overset{d}{=} f(\phi_{C_1}(x)) ,\ldots,\phi_{C_n}(x)) ,$$

then it follows that for any statistically independent choice function family $\underset{\sim}{S} = (S_j)_{j\in I_n}$ (i.e., for any $\underset{\sim}{A} \in \mathcal{P}(\underset{\sim}{X})$, the $S_j(A_j)$'s are all statistically independent), $((\bar{*})_f \, ; \, *_f \, , \underset{\sim}{S})$ is a w-hom.

In [91] (Theorem 6.5 and Corollary 6.2), isomorphic-like relations were established between fuzzy partitionings - and in particular, between weighted sums of membership functions and random set partitionings:

Theorem 4. (Weak-Homomorphic Representations for Fuzzy Partitionings.)

Let $K \overset{d}{=} \{1,\ldots,m\}$ and let $\underset{\sim}{B} \overset{d}{=} (B_j)_{j\in K}$ be a *fuzzy partitioning* of X , i.e.,

$$\sum_{j\in K} \phi_{B_j}(x) = 1 \text{ , for all } x \in X .$$

Then $\underset{\sim}{T}^{(1)}(\underset{\sim}{B}) \overset{d}{=} (T_j^{(1)}(\underset{\sim}{B}))_{j\in K}$ is a *random partitioning* of X , i.e.,

$$1 = \Pr(X = \bigcup_{j\in K} T_j^{(1)}(B_j)) ,$$

with each $T_j^{(1)}$ being a T-type choice function;

$$\underset{\sim}{T}^{(1)}(\underset{\sim}{B}) \approx \underset{\sim}{B} \; ; \; T_j^{(1)}(\underset{\sim}{B}) \approx \underset{\sim}{B}; g \in K .$$

$\underset{\sim}{T}^{(1)}$ may be constructed as follows: Let

$\underset{\sim}{V}(\underset{\sim}{B}) \overset{d}{=} (V_{j,x}(\underset{\sim}{B}))_{\substack{j\in K\\ x\in X}}$ be a zero-one process where,

$$V_{1,x}(\underset{\sim}{B}) \overset{d}{=} W_{1,x}(B_1) ,$$

$$V_{j,x}(\underset{\sim}{B}) \overset{d}{=} (1 - W_{1,x}(B_1))\cdots(1 - W_{j-1,x}(B_{j-1}))\cdot W_{j,x}(B_j) ,$$

for $j = 2,\ldots,m-1$,

$$V_{m,x}(\underset{\sim}{B}) \overset{d}{=} (1 - W_{1,x}(B_1))\cdots(1 - W_{m,x}(B_m)) \text{ , where}$$

$(W_{j,x}(B_j))_{\substack{j\in K\\ x\in X}}$ is a statistically independent zero-one process

with $\Pr(W_{m,x}(B_j) = 1) = \phi_{B_j}(x)/\sum_{i=j}^{m} \phi_{B_i}(x)$; $j \in K$, $x \in X$. Then define $\phi_{T_j^{(1)}(\underset{\sim}{B})}(x) \overset{d}{=} V_{j,x}(\underset{\sim}{B})$, $j \in K$, $x \in X$: thus

$\phi_{\underset{\sim}{T}^{(1)}(\underset{\sim}{B})} = \underset{\sim}{V}(\underset{\sim}{B})$, and $\underset{\sim}{T}^{(1)}(\underset{\sim}{B}) = \phi^{-1}(\underset{\sim}{V}(\underset{\sim}{B}))$, ϕ being the 1 - 1 onto membership function mapping $\phi : \mathcal{P}(X) \to \{0,1\}^X$.

Corollary (Weak-Homomorphic Representation for Weighted Sum Operator.)

For any constant $\tau, 0 \le \tau \le 1$, define $\theta_\tau \in \mathcal{F}(X)$ by $\phi_{\theta_\tau}(x) \equiv \tau$, for all $x \in X$. Let $K \overset{d}{=} \{1,...,m\}$ and let $0 < \lambda_j < 1$ be arbitrary constant, $j \in K$, with $\sum_{j\in K} \lambda_j = 1$. Let $\theta_{\underset{\sim}{\lambda}} \overset{d}{=} (\theta_{\lambda_j})_{j\in K}$. Define the *extended weighted sum operator* $\text{wtdsum}_{\underset{\sim}{\lambda}} : \mathcal{F}(X)^K \to \mathcal{F}(X)$, by, for any

$\underset{\sim}{A} \overset{d}{=} (A_j)_{j\in K}$, $A_j \in \mathcal{F}(X)$, $j \in K$, $x \in X$,

$$\phi_{\text{wtdsum}_{\underset{\sim}{\lambda}}(\underset{\sim}{A})}(x) \overset{d}{=} \sum_{j\in K} \lambda_j \cdot \phi_{A_j}(x) = \sum_{j\in K} \phi_{(\theta_{\lambda_j} \bar{\cap} A_j)}(x),$$

where $\bar{\cap}$ is determined by $\phi_{\&} \equiv$ prod. Then

$\underset{\sim}{T}^{(1)} \overset{d}{=} (T_j^{(1)})_{j\in K}$ and $\underset{\sim}{T}^{(2)} \overset{d}{=} (T_j^{(2)})_{j\in K}$ are two statistically independent T-type choice function families such that $\underset{\sim}{T}^{(1)}(\theta_{\underset{\sim}{\lambda}})$ is a random partitioning of X and

$$\text{wtdsum}_{\underset{\sim}{\lambda}}(\underset{\sim}{A}) \approx \bigcup_{j\in K} (T_j^{(1)}(\theta_{\lambda_j}) \cap T_j^{(2)}(A_j)) .$$

$\underset{\sim}{T}^{(1)}(\underset{\sim}{B})$ is the same as in Theorem 4 with $\underset{\sim}{B}$ replaced by $\theta_{\underset{\sim}{\lambda}}$.

$\underset{\sim}{T}^{(2)}(\underset{\sim}{A}) = (T_j^{(2)}(A_j))_{j\in K}$ is such that $(\phi_{T_j^{(2)}(A_j)}(x))_{\substack{j\in K\\ x\in X}}$ is a statistically independent zero-one process which is also independent of $\underset{\sim}{T}^{(1)}(\theta_{\underset{\sim}{\lambda}})$ such that

$$Pr(\phi_{T_j^{(2)}(A_j)}(x) = 1) = \phi_{A_j}(x) \ , \text{ for } \ j \in K \ , \ x \in X \ .$$

The proofs of Theorem 3, Theorem 4 and its corollary can be found in Goodman [91].

When there is no confusion, unless otherwise indicated, we will use the same notation for ordinary set operations and their generalized set extensions.

Summary

Thus, in summary, any generalized subset A of X may be considered as a weakened form of a random set S ; A corresponds to the collection of all random sets one-point coverage equivalent to it. At the same time, the corresponding possibility function of A may be considered as the evaluation function of a random variable, over an elementary event space, for corresponding compound events which may be identified with the elements of X . By choosing particular random set representations for generalized sets, isomorphic-like (or "weak-homomorphic") relations may be established between generalized set and ordinary set operations, etc.

One application of the above can be made to the use of a panel of experts in obtaining distributional information concerning a collection of objects (such as possible classifications of a ship) when the values of the "distribution" do not add up to unity - often the sum will exceed one). It does not mean the laws of probability are being violated nor should normalization be carried out to make the "distribution" formally a legitimate one. Indeed, the distribution represents probability values of properly chosen compound overlapping events which the panel as human integrators of information in effect tacitly employ - or equivalently the distribution represents coverage probabilities of a suitably implicitly chosen random set of interactions. (See Chapter 9 for more details.)

Finally, note that the field of random set theory is not as well known as other branches of probability theory. For background, see the general works of Kendall [137], Matheron [171] and Ripley [217]. See also Cressie [43], Ripley [217] and Artstein and Vitale [7] for results concerning random set versions of the Laws of Large Numbers and the Central Limit Theorem.

CHAPTER 7

SOME THEORIES OF UNCERTAINTY

In this chapter, we discuss different approaches to the problem of uncertainty modeling. These include Manes' distributional theory, Watanabe's system, Gaines' uncertainty logic and Schefe's agreement probabilities.

7.1 Introduction

Generalized set theory in its general formulation, as mentioned previously, already is an extension of probability theory over discrete spaces. (Thus there may be no need to construct systems which formally generalize both fuzzy set theory and probability theory). This is true by simply recognizing that:

(1) All probability functions p (over a discrete space) are also possibility functions (but of course, not conversely). (Indeed, all cumulative and anti-cumulative distribution functions are also possibility functions.)

(2) The usual probability operations may be interpreted through the particular fuzzy set system

$$\mathfrak{F}' \overset{d}{=} (1-(\cdot), \text{prod}, \text{sum}) ,$$

noting the operation sum is the same as bndsum (or maxsum) over the cone of all probability functions.

(3) Complete analogues (as mentioned previously) may be established between the concepts of joint conditional, marginal and (via Bayes' theorem) posterior possibility and probability functions. Hence, all possibilistic forms will reduce to ordinary probabilistic counterparts when $\mathfrak{F}'$ is employed with respect to probability functions only. This may be summarized by the many-to-one correspondences (over spaces):

$$\left.\begin{array}{ccc} \text{p-possibility function} & \leftrightarrow & \text{p-probability function} \\ \phi_{not} & \leftrightarrow & 1-(\cdot) \\ \phi_{\&} & \leftrightarrow & \text{prod} \\ \phi_{or} & \leftrightarrow & \text{sum} \quad . \end{array}\right\}$$

(4) It should also be mentioned that an obvious interpretation of any probability measure Pr over a σ-algebra $\mathfrak{B}$ of subsets of

its base space X : Pr : $\mathfrak{B} \to [0,1]$ is a fuzzy set membership function representing a fuzzy subset of $\mathfrak{B}$.

(5) On the other hand, note that probability theory is *not* a truth functional system as Zadeh's fuzzy set theory is. (See the remarks in 7.4 for Gaines' system. See also section 2.3.9 (A).)

Figure A presents some relations between various logical systems.

In the wake of the criticisms of Zadeh's fuzzy sets, several systems have been developed which simultaneously extend both Zadeh's original formulation of fuzzy set theory and classical probabilistic concepts. Among these are Hirota's "probabilistic sets" [111] - essentially, randomized fuzzy sets (perhaps more accurately, randomized fuzzy set membership functions), and the large literature devoted to fuzzifying probability spaces and random variables. (See the survey in [51], as well as Kwakernaak [148] and Klement and Schwyhla [142].) Manes [169], based upon his previous work with Arbib [5] in developing category theory models for fuzzy machines, used a form of the Kleisli category theorem [165] in deriving a very general theory of distributions which extend not only Zadeh's (min-max, etc.) fuzzy set concepts and classical probability relations, but also generalizes the basic structure of topological neighborhood theory, credibility theory and other approaches to the modeling of uncertainties. (However - see Goodman and Nguyen [92] for a characterization of Manes' system which shows that although it generalizes Zadeh's original concept of fuzzy set theory, it is not compatible with more general fuzzy set systems $(\phi_{not}, \phi_{\&}, \phi_{or})$. See also the following section.)

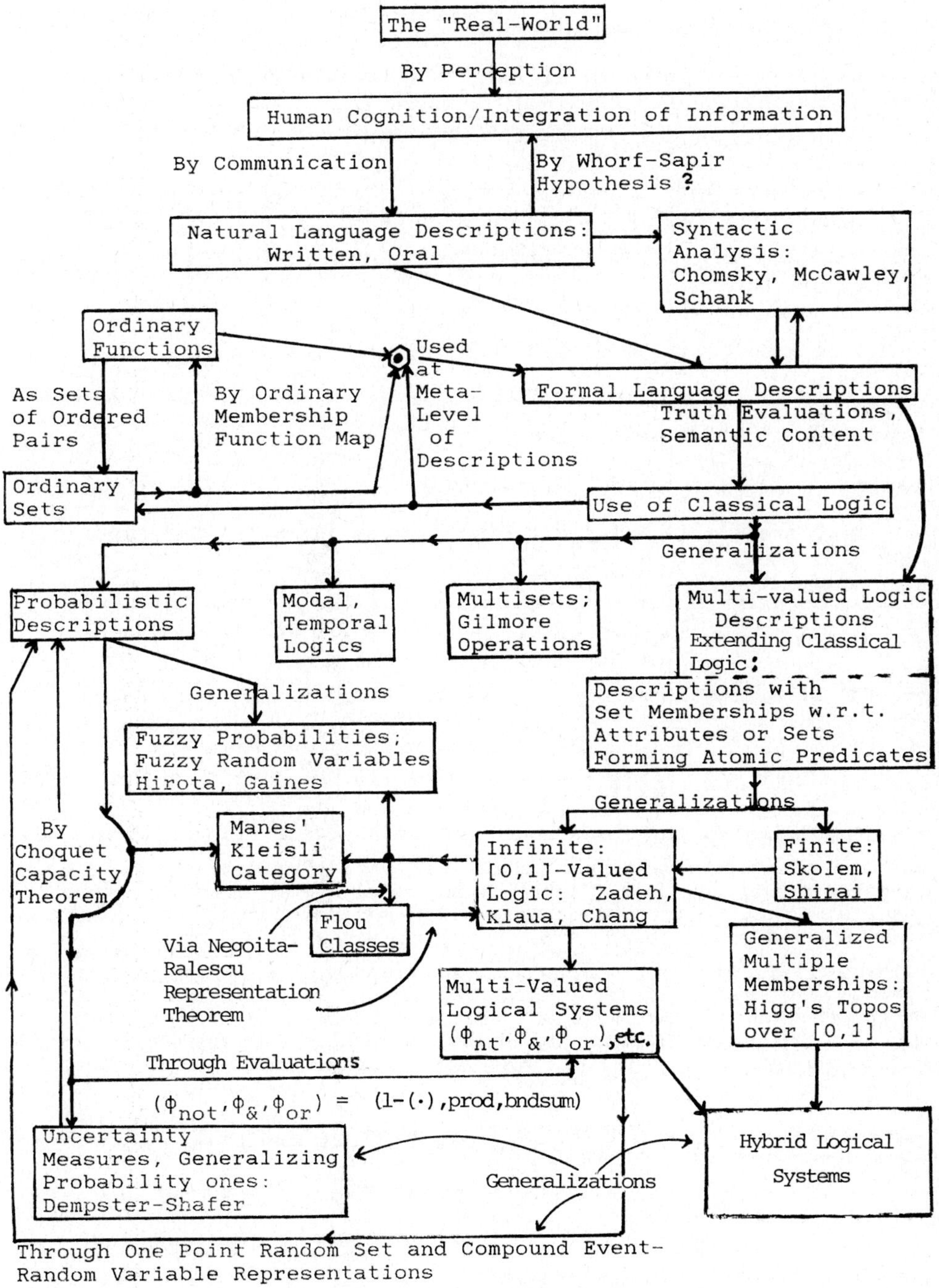

Figure A. Processing flow of information and relationships between some selected logical systems.

7.2 Manes' distributional theory

A. Summary of Manes' basic work.

Manes [169] developed a theory of "fuzzy" theories as an outgrowth of his earlier work [5].

1. **Consider the category SET.**

(a) Given a monad $(\mathcal{T}, e, \mu)$ over SET, i.e., $\mathcal{T} : \text{SET} \to \text{SET}$ is a functor and $e : \text{Id} \xrightarrow{\cdot} \mathcal{T}$ and $\mu : \mathcal{T} \circ \mathcal{T} \xrightarrow{\cdot} \mathcal{T}$ are natural transforms satisfying certain commutative relations (see, e.g., S. MacLane [165]), then by defining $\#$, where for any sets X, Y and $\alpha \in \text{Ar}(X, \mathcal{T}(Y))$,

$$\#(\alpha) \overset{d}{=} \mu(y) \circ \mathcal{T}(\alpha) \in \text{Ar}(\mathcal{T}(X), \mathcal{T}(Y)) ,$$

then $K_{\mathcal{T}}$ is a category - the Kleisli category associated with $\mathcal{T}$ (again, see [169]) where

$$\text{Ob}(K_{\mathcal{T}}) = \{\mathcal{T}(X) \mid X \text{ any set}\}$$

$$\text{Ar}(K_{\mathcal{T}}) = \{\#(\alpha) \mid \alpha \in \text{Ar}(X, \mathcal{T}(Y)) , X, Y \text{ any sets}\}$$

with composition $\circ$ defined by

$$\#(\beta) \circ \#(\alpha) \overset{d}{=} \#(\#\beta \circ \alpha) ; \qquad \text{(M3)}$$

and with identity maps

$$\#(e(X)) = \text{id}_{\mathcal{T}(X)} ; \qquad \text{(M2)}$$

and finally, with the relation

$$\#(\alpha) \circ e(X) = \alpha ; \qquad \text{(M1)}$$

holding for all $\alpha \in \text{Ar}(X, \mathcal{T}(Y))$, all $\beta \in \text{Ar}(Y, \mathcal{T}(Z))$, and all sets X, Y, Z. (M1) and (M2) imply $e(X)$ is uniquely determined.

(b) Conversely, given a mapping $\mathcal{T} : \text{Ob(SET)} \to \text{Ob(SET)}$ a mapping $e : \text{Ob(SET)} \to \text{Ar(SET)}$, where for any set X, $e(X) \in \text{Ar}(X, \mathcal{T}(X))$, and mapping

$$\# : \bigcup_{\substack{\text{all sets} \\ X,Y}} \text{Ar}(X, \mathcal{T}(Y)) \to \bigcup_{\substack{\text{all sets} \\ X,Y}} \text{Ar}(\mathcal{T}(X), \mathcal{T}(Y)) \text{ satisfying (M1) ,}$$

(M2), (M3). Then by defining $\mu : \text{Ob(SET)} \to \text{Ar(SET)}$ by, for any set X,

$$\mu(X) \overset{d}{=} \#(\text{id}_{\mathcal{T}(X)}) ,$$

and defining for any $f \in \text{Ar}(X, Y)$,

$$\mathcal{T}(f) \overset{d}{=} \#(e(Y)\circ f) \in Ar(\mathcal{T}(X),\mathcal{T}(Y)) ,$$

and composition via (M3) , it follows that $\mathcal{T}$ is a functor, $e : id \xrightarrow{\cdot} \mathcal{T}$ and $\mu : \mathcal{T}\circ\mathcal{T} \xrightarrow{\cdot} \mathcal{T}$ are natural transforms and $(\mathcal{T},e,\mu)$ is a monad, etc.

Manes calls $(\mathcal{T},e,\#)$ a *theory*, when case (b) holds (which is thus equivalent to specifying monad $(\mathcal{T},e,\mu)$ and case (a)). $\mathcal{T}$ is the *distribution map*, e is the *imbedding map* and # is the *domain extension* or *lifting operator*. This is motivated by the special cases presented next.

2. Some specializations of the general case.

(i) For any set X :

$\mathcal{T}(X) \overset{d}{=} [0,1]^X$ is identified with $\mathcal{F}(X)$, the class of all fuzzy subsets of X .

$$e(X)(x) \overset{d}{=} \phi_{\{x\}} \text{ (relative to } X \text{) ; all } x \in X ,$$

$$(\#(\alpha))(\phi_A)(y) \overset{d}{=} \sup_{x\in X} \min (\phi_A(x), \phi_{\alpha(x)}(y))$$

for any $\alpha : X \to \mathcal{F}(Y)$, any $A \in \mathcal{F}(X)$ and any $y \in Y$.

Thus, if $f : X \to Y$ for any sets X , Y , it follows that $\mathcal{T}(f)$ may be identified as the operator $\mathcal{T}(f) : \mathcal{F}(X) \to \mathcal{F}(Y)$, where for any $A \in \mathcal{F}(X)$,

$$\mathcal{T}(f)(A) = \hat{f}(A) ,$$

where (see also 2.3.7)

$$\phi_{\hat{f}(A)}(y) = \sup_{x\in f^{-1}(A)} \phi_A(x) ,$$

i.e., $\hat{f}$ is the Zadeh fuzzy set extension of f . More generally, if $A \in \mathcal{F}(X \times Y)$, $B \in \mathcal{F}(Y \times Z)$ since the identifications

$$A \longleftrightarrow (\alpha_A : X \to \mathcal{F}(Y)) ,$$

where for any $x \in X$, $y \in Y$,

$$(\alpha_A(x))(y) = \phi_A(x,y) ,$$

and similarly

$$B \longleftrightarrow (\alpha_B : Y \to \mathcal{F}(Z))$$

may be made, then (M3) implies that composition $\circ$ is the same as fuzzy relational product

$$\phi_{\hat{B}(A)}(x,z) = \sup_{y \in Y} \min (\phi_A(x,y), \phi_B(y,z))$$

for all $x \in X$, $z \in Z$, which is an associative operation.

(ii) For any set X :

$\mathcal{T}(X) \overset{d}{=} \{p \mid p : X \to [0,1]$ & p is a finite (supported) probability function over $X\}$,

$e(X)(x) \overset{d}{=} \phi_{\{x\}}$ (relative to X) ; all $x \in X$

$(\#(\alpha)(p)(y) \overset{d}{=} \sum_{x \in X} (p(y) \cdot \alpha(x)(y))$, for any $\alpha : X \to \mathcal{T}(Y)$, all $y \in Y$.

In this case, for any $f : X \to Y$, for any sets X and Y , $\mathcal{T}(f) : \mathcal{T}(X) \to \mathcal{T}(Y)$, where for any $p \in \mathcal{T}(X)$ and any $y \in Y$,

$$\mathcal{T}(f)(p)(y) = \sum_{x \in f^{-1}(Y)} p(x) ,$$

i.e., $\mathcal{T}(f)(p)$ is the probability function of r.v. $f(V)$ where r.v. V has prob. function p .

(iii) For any Set X :

$\mathcal{T}(X) \overset{d}{=} \mathcal{P}(X)$, the class of all ordinary subsets of X ,

$e(X)(x) \overset{d}{=} \{x\}$; all $x \in X$,

$$(\#(\alpha))(C) = \bigcup_{x \in C} \alpha(x) = \alpha(C) ,$$

for any $\alpha : X \to \mathcal{P}(Y)$, and any $C \in \mathcal{P}(X)$.

Manes calls this case "possibilistic" set theory.

Manes also specializes theory $(\mathcal{T},e,\#)$ to a number of other systems including "crisp" set theory with $\mathcal{T}(X) = X$, priority theory, credibility theory and topological neighborhood theory.

3. Additional comments.

Thus Manes cleverly shows that the concept of a Kleisli category associated with a monad over SET is sufficient to describe not only Zadeh's fuzzy set theory and classical discrete probability theory but a number of other theories of uncertainties. He obtains a number of basic properties common to all of these theories. In summary, this includes:

(a) Development of maps between theories as essentially "natural" (i.e., commutative-form) mappings between the three corresponding components of theories, which, following category theory concepts, is specialized to quotient or surjective types, subobject or injective types, and, further, to isomorphisms (which are characterized as both surjective and injective types). Also, cartesian products of theories are defined in the obvious way. Examples include: for any fixed $\lambda \in [0,1]$, consider the level set mapping T_λ, where for any set X and any $A \in \mathcal{T}(X)$, $T_\lambda(A) = \phi_A^{-1}[\lambda,1]$ yields $(T_\lambda, e^*, \#_\lambda)$ as a quotient theory of Zadeh's fuzzy set theory, where $e^*(X)(x) = \{x\}$, all $x \in X$, and for any $\alpha : X \to T(Y)$, $T_\lambda(\alpha) : X \to \mathcal{P}(X)$, where for all $x \in X$, $T_\lambda(\alpha)(x) \overset{d}{=} T_\lambda(\alpha(x))$, and for any $A \in \mathcal{T}(X)$, and thus $\phi_A^{-1}[\lambda,1] \in \mathcal{P}(X)$,

$$\#_\lambda(\phi_A^{-1}[\lambda,1]) = (\#(\alpha))(\phi_A))^{-1}[\lambda,1] .$$

On the other hand, $(\mathcal{T},e,\#)$ where $\mathcal{T}(X) = \{A \mid A \in \mathcal{T}(X) \ \&\ \sup_{x\in X} \phi_A(X) = 1\}$, for any set X is a subtheory of Zadeh's fuzzy set theory. ($\mathcal{T}(X)$ is the class of normable membership functions.)

(b) Development of equality and membership relations:

Define for any theory $\underset{\sim}{\mathcal{T}} = (\mathcal{T},e,\#)$, $\mathcal{T}(\{0,1\})$ as the theory truth values. Define the general membership function ϕ, for any set X, $\phi(X) : \mathcal{P}(X) \times \mathcal{T}(X) \to \mathcal{T}(\{0,1\})$, by, for any $C \in \mathcal{P}(X)$, $A \in \mathcal{T}(X)$,

$$\phi(X)(C,A) = \phi(X)_A(C) \overset{d}{=} \mathcal{T}(\phi_C)(A) ,$$

$\phi_C : X \to \{0,1\}$ ordinary membership function of C.

Define the equality map eq, where for any set X, $eq(X) : \mathcal{T}(X) \times \mathcal{T}(X) \to \mathcal{T}(\{0,1\})$ where first for any $x \in X$ and $A \in \mathcal{T}(X)$,

$$eq(X)(e(X)(x),A) = \mathcal{T}(\phi_{\{x\}}(A)) ,$$

and for any $A,B \in \mathcal{T}(X)$

$$eq(X)(B,A) = (\#(\mathcal{T}(\phi_{\{\cdot\}}(A))))(B) .$$

Alternatively, Manes could have developed a one-branch truth theory based on $\mathcal{T}(\{1\})$ instead of $\mathcal{T}(\{0,1\})$; evaluations are similar for only this one component. (The idea of using $\mathcal{T}\{0,1\}$ is based on Gaines' earlier approach.) Or, one could choose any number of values $0 = a_0 < \cdots < a_n = 1$ and use $\mathcal{T}(\{a_0,\ldots,a_n\})$.

For Zadeh's fuzzy set theory

$$\mathcal{T}(\phi_C)(A) = \phi_C(A) \ ; \text{ all } A \in \mathcal{T}(X) ,\ C \in \mathcal{P}(X)$$

where $\phi_C(A) \in \mathcal{T}\{0,1\}$,

$$\begin{cases} \phi_{\phi_C(A)}(0) = \sup_{x \in \phi_C^{-1}(0)} (\phi_A(x)) = \sup_{x \notin C} \phi_A(x) \\ \phi_{\phi_C(A)}(1) = \sup_{x \in \phi_C^{-1}(1)} (\phi_A(x)) = \sup_{x \in C} \phi_A(x) \end{cases} ,$$

and for any $A,B \in \mathcal{F}(X)$, $eq(X)(B,A) \in \mathcal{F}\{0,1\}$,

$$\begin{cases} \phi_{eq(X)(B,A)}(0) = \sup_{\substack{x,y \in X \\ x \neq y}} \min (\phi_A(x), \phi_B(y)) \\ \phi_{eq(X)(B,A)}(1) = \sup_{x \in X} \min (\phi_A(x), \phi_B(x)) \end{cases} .$$

For discrete probability theory, $\mathcal{F}(\phi_C)(p)$ is the probability function of r.v. $\phi_C(V)$ where V is a r.v. corresponding to probability function $p \in \mathcal{F}(X)$, i.e.,

$$\phi_C(V) = 1 \quad \text{iff} \quad V \in C$$

$$\phi_C(V) = 0 \quad \text{iff} \quad V \notin C$$

and hence

$$\mathcal{F}(\phi_C)(p)(0) = Pr(V \notin C) = \sum_{x \notin C} p(x) = 1 - \sum_{x \in C} p(x)$$

and

$$\mathcal{F}(\phi_C)(p)(1) = Pr(V \in C) = \sum_{x \in C} p(x) .$$

For any $p,q \in \mathcal{F}(X)$,

$$eq(X)(p,q)(0) = \sum_{\substack{x,y \in X \\ x \neq y}} p(x)q(y) = 1 - \sum_{x \in X} p(x)q(x)$$

$$eq(x)(p,q)(1) = \sum_{x \in X} p(x)q(x) .$$

(c) Manes defines

I. $eq(X)(p,p)$ as *degree of vagueness* of $p \in \mathcal{F}(X)$,

II. A theory $\underset{\sim}{\mathcal{F}} = (\mathcal{F},e,\#)$ is *anti-reflexive* iff for all sets X and $A \in \mathcal{F}(X)$, if $eq(X)(A,A) \equiv 1$, then $A = e(X)(\{x\})$ for some $x \in X$, i.e., A is "crisp".

III. A theory $\underset{\sim}{\mathcal{T}}$ has *symmetric equality* iff for all sets X, and all $A, B \in \mathcal{T}(X)$,

$$eq(X)(A,B) = eq(X)(B,A) ,$$

IV. A theory $\underset{\sim}{\mathcal{T}}$ *satisfies* the *eigenstate condition* iff for all sets X and all $x \in X$ and $A \in \mathcal{T}(X)$, if $\phi(X)(\{x\},A) \equiv 1$, then A is crisp where $A = e(X)(x)$.

V. For any set X,

$$\mathrm{Prop}(X) \overset{d}{=} (\mathcal{T}\{0,1\})^X ,$$

is defined as the class of all *propositions over* X. A theory $\underset{\sim}{\mathcal{T}}$ is *faithful* iff for all sets X, the mapping

$$\rho(X) : \mathcal{T}(X) \to \mathrm{Prop}(X) ,$$

where for any $A \in \mathcal{T}(X)$, and $x \in X$

$$(\rho(X)(A))(x) \overset{d}{=} \phi(X)(\{x\},A) ,$$

is injective.

VI. A theory $\underset{\sim}{\mathcal{T}}$ is *propositionally complete* (or separating) iff for all sets X and any $A, B \in \mathcal{T}(X)$, $A \neq B$, there is $\alpha \in \mathrm{Prop}(X)$ such that

$$(\#(\alpha))(A) \neq (\#(\alpha))(B) .$$

VII. A theory $\underset{\sim}{\mathcal{T}}$ is *consistent* iff $\mathcal{T}$ is injective relative to $\mathrm{Ar}(\mathrm{SET})$ or equivalently, iff for each set X, $e(X) : X \to \mathcal{T}(X)$ is injective.

VIII. A theory $\underset{\sim}{\mathcal{T}}$ is *noise-free* iff $\mathcal{T}(\emptyset) = \emptyset$.

IX. A theory $\underset{\sim}{\mathcal{T}}$ has *crisp points* iff for any set X, $x \in X$, $\mathcal{T}(\{x\}) = \{x\}$.

A number of the above definitions have direct category theory counterparts (for example, "faithful" in V).

It follows that: any faithful theory is propositionally complete and if $f \in \mathrm{Ar}(X,Y)$ is injective (bijective) so is $\mathcal{T}(f)$ (bijective). Any consistent theory with crisp points is noise-free and a theory has crisp points iff for all sets X, and $A \in \mathcal{T}(X)$, $\phi(X)(X,A) \equiv 1$. Any theory has a largest subtheory with crisp points. Zadeh's fuzzy set theory, finite probability theory and possibilistic set theory satisfy conditions II - VIII. Probabilistic set theory has crisp points but Zadeh's fuzzy set theory doesn't, nor does possibilistic set theory.

(d) X_0-ary operations and homomorphisms in Manes' sense:

Fix theory $\underset{\sim}{\mathcal{T}} = (\mathcal{T}, e, \#)$.

Fix set X_o . Then there is a bijection ρ_{X_o} between $\mathcal{T}(X_o)$ and $Q(X_o)$, where for any $A \in \mathcal{T}(X_o)$, $\rho_{X_o}(A) \in Q(X_o)$, where for any set Y , $\rho_{X_o}(A)(Y) : \mathcal{T}(Y)^{X_o} \to \mathcal{T}(Y)$ where for any $\alpha : X_o \to \mathcal{T}(Y)$,

$$(\rho_{X_o}(A)(Y))(\alpha) \overset{d}{=} (\#(\alpha))(A) .$$

$Q(X_o)$ is called the class of all (abstract) X_o*-ary* $\mathcal{T}$*-operations*.

For any sets X , Y and $f : \mathcal{T}(X) \to \mathcal{T}(Y)$, f is a *homomorphism* w.r.t. X and Y and $\mathcal{T}$, *iff* for any set X_o , any $A \in \mathcal{T}(X_o)$, and hence any $\rho_{X_o}(A) \in Q(X_o)$,

$$f \circ \rho_{X_o}(A)(X) = \rho_{X_o}(A)(Y)(f \circ (\ ))$$

iff $f = \#(\alpha)$, for some $\alpha : X \to \mathcal{T}(Y)$ in which case α may be arbitrary in general and

$$\alpha = f \circ e(X) .$$

For any sets $X_1, \ldots, X_n$, Y and $f : \mathcal{T}(X_1) \times \ldots \times \mathcal{T}(X_n) \to \mathcal{T}(Y)$, f is an *n-homomorphism iff* all marginals $f_j : \mathcal{T}(X_j) \to \mathcal{T}(Y)$, $j = 1, \ldots, n$ of f are (1-) homomorphisms.

(e) Joint distributions and independence.
Suppose $\underset{\sim}{\mathcal{T}} = (\mathcal{T}, e, \#)$ is a theory.

Let $\alpha : X_1 \times X_2 \to \mathcal{T}(Y)$ be arbitrary for any sets X_1, X_2, Y . Then define $\alpha_{(1)}, \alpha_{(2)} : \mathcal{T}(X_1) \times \mathcal{T}(X_2) \to \mathcal{T}(Y)$ by

$$\alpha_{(1)} = (\#(((\#(\alpha(x_1,\cdot)))_{x_1 \in X_1})(A_2)))_{A_2 \in \mathcal{T}(X_2)}$$

$$\alpha_{(2)} = (\#(((\#(\alpha(\cdot,x_2)))(A_1))_{x_2 \in X_2}))_{A_1 \in \mathcal{T}(X_1)} .$$

α_1 and α_2 are the natural component-wise ways to extend α via # . Similar constructions hold for any $\alpha : X_1 \times \cdots \times X_n \to \mathcal{T}(Y)$. If $\alpha_{(1)} = \cdots = \alpha_{(n)}$, denote the common value by $\bar{\alpha}$; $\bar{\alpha}$ is the basic *commutative domain lifting or extension operator* for α .

It can be verified by use of (M3) that for any α as above,

$$\alpha_{(1)} \circ (e(X_1) \times e(X_2)) = \alpha_{(2)} \circ (e(X_1) \times e(X_2)) = \alpha .$$

In particular, consider $\alpha = e(X_1 \times X_2)$ for any sets X_1 , X_2 .

Then, if $e_{(1)}(X_1 \times X_2) = e_{(2)}(X_1 \times X_2)$,

$$\bar{e}(X_1 \times X_2) : \mathcal{F}(X_1) \times \mathcal{F}(X_2) \rightarrow \mathcal{F}(X_1 \times X_2)$$

is called the *independence* map and

$$\mathrm{Ind}(X_1 \times X_2) \overset{d}{=} \{\bar{e}(X_1 \times X_2)(A \times B) \mid A \in \mathcal{F}(X_1) , B \in \mathcal{F}(X_2)\}$$

is called the class of all independent distributions of $X_1 \times X_2$.

Manes showed for any theory $\underset{\sim}{\mathcal{F}}$:

(i) For all sets X_1 , X_2 , $\bar{e}(X_1 \times X_2)$ exists and is thus a 2-homomorphism iff

(ii) For all integers $n \geq 1$, and sets $X_1,\ldots,X_n$, Y and any $\alpha : X_1 \times X_2 \times\ldots X_n \rightarrow \mathcal{F}(Y)$, $\bar{\alpha} : \mathcal{F}(X_1)\times\cdot\cdot\times\mathcal{F}(X_n) \rightarrow \mathcal{F}(Y)$ exists and is an n-homomorphism, iff

(iii) For any sets X_o , Y_o and all $A \in \mathcal{F}(X_o)$, $B \in \mathcal{F}(Y_o)$ and any set Z ,

$$\rho_{X_o}(A)\circ\rho_{Y_o}(B)(Z)\circ = \rho_{Y_o}(B)(Z)\circ\rho_{X_o}(A)\circ$$

for suitable composition arguments, in which case $\underset{\sim}{\mathcal{F}}$ is called a *commutative* theory.

If $\underset{\sim}{\mathcal{F}}$ is a commutative theory:

(I) For any $\alpha : X_1\times\cdot\cdot\cdot\times X_n \rightarrow Y$;

$$\bar{\alpha}\circ e(X_1)\times\cdot\cdot\times e(X_n) = \alpha$$

(II) For $n = 2$,

$$\#(\alpha)\circ\bar{e}(X_1 \times X_2) = \bar{\alpha}$$

(III) For $n = 1$,

$$\#(\alpha) = \bar{\alpha}$$

which justifies $\bar{\alpha}$ being also called the *n-homomorphic extension* of α , although $\#(\alpha)$ is also an extension of α (but not n-homomorphic in general).

(IV) The equality mapping for $\underset{\sim}{\mathcal{F}}$ is symmetric.

(V) $\underset{\sim}{\mathcal{F}}$ has crisp points iff for all sets X and Y ,

$\bar{e}(X \times Y) : \mathcal{F}(X)\times\mathcal{F}(Y) \to \mathcal{F}(X \times Y)$ is injective.

(VI) Let $X_1,\ldots,X_n,Y$ be any sets and let $f : X_1\times\cdots\times X_n \to Y$, $n \geq 1$, all be arbitrary. Then, define the n-homomorphic extension or basic commutative multiple domain and range lifting or extension: $\hat{f} : \mathcal{F}(X_1)\times\cdots\times\mathcal{F}(X_n) \to \mathcal{F}(Y)$ by

$$\hat{f} = (e(Y)\circ f)^{-} ,$$

analogous to

$\mathcal{F}(f) : \mathcal{F}(X_1\times\cdots\times X_n) \to \mathcal{F}(Y)$, defined by

$$\mathcal{F}(f) = \#(e(Y)\circ f) .$$

Thus the operator $\wedge$ extends Zadeh's fuzzy set extension principle.

(VII) It follows that Zadeh's fuzzy set theory, finite probability theory, and possibilistic set theory as well as other theories are all commutative theories.

In the following, let $n \geq 1$ be any integer and $X_1,\ldots,X_n,Y$ arbitrary sets;

(i) Zadeh's fuzzy set theory:
For all $A \in \mathcal{F}(X)$, $B \in \mathcal{F}(Y)$

$$\bar{e}(X \times Y)(A,B) = A \times B ,$$

i.e., for all $x \in X$, $y \in Y$

$$\phi_{\bar{e}(X\times Y)(A,B)}(x,y) = \min\,(\phi_A(x),\ \phi_B(y)) .$$

For any $\alpha : X_1\times\cdots\times X_n \to \mathcal{F}(Y)$,
and any $A_j \in \mathcal{F}(X_j)$, $j = 1,\ldots,n,$ and any $y \in Y$,

$$\phi_{\bar{\alpha}(A_1,\ldots,A_n)}(y) = \sup_{\begin{bmatrix}x_j\in X_j,\\ j=1,\ldots,n\end{bmatrix}} \min\,(\phi_{A_1}(x_1),\ldots,\phi_{A_2}(x_n),\phi_{\alpha(x_1,\ldots,x_n)}(y))$$

and hence for any $f : X_1\times\cdots\times X_n \to Y$, any $A_j \in \mathcal{F}(X_j)$, $j = 1,\ldots,n$, and any $y \in Y$, letting $\alpha = e(Y)\circ f$,

$$\phi_{\hat{f}(A_1,\dots,A_n)}(y) = \sup_{\left[\begin{array}{c} x_j \in X_j, \\ j=1,\dots,n, \\ f(x_1,\dots,x_n)=y \end{array}\right]} \min(\phi_{A_1}(x_1),\dots,\phi_{A_n}(x_n)) .$$

(ii) Finite probability theory:

For any (probability functions) $p \in \mathcal{F}(X)$ and $q \in \mathcal{F}(Y)$, and all $x \in X$, $y \in Y$,

$$\bar{e}(X \times Y)(p,q)(x,y) = p(x)\cdot q(y) ,$$

i.e., $\bar{e}(X \times Y)(p,q)$ corresponds to the ordinary statistically independent joint probability funcions.

For any $\alpha : X_1 \times\cdots\times X_n \to \mathcal{F}(Y)$, and any $p_j \in \mathcal{F}(X_j)$, $j = 1,\dots,n$, and any $y \in Y$,

$$\begin{aligned}\bar{\alpha}(p_1,\dots,p_n)(y) &= \sum_{\substack{x_j \in X_j, \\ j=1,\dots,n}} p_1(x_1)\cdots p_n(x_n)\cdot\alpha(x_1,\dots,x_n)(y) \\ &= E(\alpha(V_1,\dots,V_n)(y))\end{aligned}$$

with V_j, r.v., corresponding to probability function p_j, $j = 1,\dots,n$; all V_j's being statistically independent.

Hence for any $f : X_1\times\cdots\times X_n \to Y$, and $p_j \in \mathcal{F}(X_j)$, $j = 1,\dots,n$ and any $y \in Y$,

$$\hat{f}(p_1,\dots,p_n)(y) = \sum_{\left[\begin{array}{c} x_j \in X_j, \\ j=1,\dots,n, \\ f(x_1,\dots,x_n)=y \end{array}\right]} p_1(x_1)\cdots p_n(x_n)$$

(iii) Possibilistic set theory:

For any $C \in \mathcal{P}(X)$, $D \in \mathcal{P}(Y)$,

$$\bar{e}(X \times Y)(C,D) = C \times D .$$

For any $\alpha : X_1\times\cdots\times X_n \to \mathcal{P}(Y)$, and any $C_j \in \mathcal{P}(X_j)$, $j = 1,\dots,n$,

$$\bar{\alpha}(C_1,\dots,C_n) = \bigcup_{\left[\begin{array}{c} x_j \in C_j, \\ j=1,\dots,n \end{array}\right]} \alpha(x_1,\dots,x_n) .$$

Thus, for any $f : X_1\times\cdots\times X_n \to Y$, and any $C_j \in \mathcal{P}(X_j)$, $j = 1,\dots,n$,

$$\hat{f}(C_1,\ldots,C_n) = \bigcup_{\substack{x_j \in C_j, \\ j=1,\ldots,n}} \{f(x_1,\ldots,x_n)\} = f(C_1\times\cdots\times C_n) .$$

(VIII) In particular, consider for any integer $n \geq 1$,

$$\text{Bool}_n \overset{d}{=} \{f \mid f : \{0,1\}^n \to \{0,1\}\} ,$$

the set of all classical n-ary truth functions or Boolean polynomials and define

$$\hat{\text{Bool}}_n \overset{d}{=} \{\hat{f} \mid f \in \text{Bool}_n\} .$$

Hence, any $\hat{f} \in \hat{\text{Bool}}_n$ is such that

$f : (\mathcal{F}(\{0,1\}))^n \to \mathcal{F}(\{0,1\})$ is the n-homomorphic extension of truth function $f : \{0,1\}^n \to \{0,1\}$.

In particular, consider the classical Boolean polynomials:

$n = 2 : f = \& : \&(0,0) = \&(1,0) = \&(0,1) = 0 ; \&(1,1) = 1$

$n = 2 : f = \text{or} : \text{or}(0,0) = 0 ; \text{or}(1,0) = \text{or}(0,1) = \text{or}(1,1) = 1$

$n = 1 : f = \text{not} : \text{not}(0) = 1 , \text{not}(1) = 0$

$n = 1 : f = \text{id} : \text{id}(0) = 0 , \text{id}(1) = 1$.

Then for

(a) Zadeh's fuzzy set theory, it follows for any $n \geq 1$ and any $\hat{f} \in \hat{\text{Bool}}_n$, any $A_j \in \mathcal{F}(\{0,1\})$, $j = 1,\ldots,n$,

$$\phi_{\hat{f}(A_1,\ldots,A_n)}(y) = \sup_{\begin{bmatrix} x_1,\ldots,x_n \in \{0,1\} \text{ with} \\ f(x_1,\ldots,x_n) = y \end{bmatrix}} \min (\phi_{A_1}(x_1),\ldots,\phi_{A_n}(x_n))$$

for $y \in \{0,1\}$.

Thus, for $n = 1$ and any $A \in \mathcal{F}\{0,1\}$,

$$\phi_{\hat{\text{id}}(A)}(0) = \phi_A(0) , \phi_{\hat{\text{id}}(A)}(1) = \phi_A(1) ,$$

i.e.,

$$\hat{\text{id}}(A) \equiv A ,$$

but note

$$\phi_{\hat{\text{not}}(A)}(0) = \phi_A(1) , \phi_{\hat{\text{not}}(A)}(1) = \phi_A(0)$$

For $n = 2$, and any A_1 , $A_2 \in \mathcal{F}\{0,1\}$

$$\phi_{\hat{\&}(A_1,A_2)}(0) = \max(\min(\phi_{A_1}(0),\ \phi_{A_2}(0)),\ \min(\phi_{A_1}(0),\ \phi_{A_2}(1))\ ,$$

$$\min(\phi_{A_1}(1),\ \phi_{A_2}(0)))\ ,$$

$$\phi_{\hat{\&}(A_1,A_2)}(1) = \min\ (\phi_{A_1}(1),\ \phi_{A_2}(1))$$

$$\phi_{\hat{or}(A_1,A_2)}(0) = \min\ (\phi_{A_1}(0),\ \phi_{A_2}(0))$$

$$\phi_{\hat{or}(A_1,A_2)}(1) = \max\ (\min(\phi_{A_1}(1),\ \phi_{A_2}(1)),\ \min(\phi_{A_1}(1),\ \phi_{A_2}(0))\ ,$$

$$\min\ (\phi_{A_1}(0),\ \phi_{A_2}(1)))\ .$$

(b) For finite probability theory:
For $n = 1$ and any $p \in \mathcal{T}(\{0,1\})$,

$$\hat{id}(p) = p$$

and

$$\hat{not}(p)(0) = p(1)\ ;\ \hat{not}(p)(1) = p(0) = 1 - p(1)\ .$$

For $n = 2$, and any $p,q \in \mathcal{T}\{0,1\}$,

$$\hat{\&}(p,q)(1) = p(1)\cdot q(1)$$

$$\hat{\&}(p,q)(0) = 1 - p(1)\cdot q(1)$$

$$\hat{or}(p,q)(1) = 1 - p(0)\cdot q(0) = 1 - (1 - p(1))(1 - q(1))$$
$$= p(1) + q(1) - p(1)q(1)$$

$$\hat{or}(p,q)(0) = p(0)\cdot q(0)$$
$$= (1-p(1))(1-q(1)) = 1-p(1) - q(1)) + p(1)\cdot q(1)\ .$$

(c) For possibilistic set theory:
Note that $\mathcal{P}\{0,1\} = \{\emptyset\ ,\ \{0\},\ \{1\},\ \{0,1\}\}$.

For $n = 1$, and any $C \in \mathcal{P}\{0,1\}$,

$$\hat{id}(C) = C\ ,$$

$$\hat{not}(\emptyset) = \emptyset\ ,\ not(\{0,1\}) = \{0,1\}$$
$$not(\{0\}) = \{1\},\ not(\{1\}) = \{0\}\ .$$

For $n = 2$:

$\hat{\&}$ is symmetric and

$$\hat{\&}(\emptyset,\emptyset) = \hat{\&}(\emptyset,\{1\}) = \emptyset\ ,$$

$$\hat{\&}(\emptyset,\{0\}) = \hat{\&}(\emptyset,\{0,1\}) = \hat{\&}(\{0\},\{0\})\ ,$$

$$= \hat{\&}(\{0\},\{1\}) = \hat{\&}(\{0\},\{0,1\}) = \{0\},$$

$$\hat{\&}(\{1\},\{1\}) = \{1\}$$

$$\hat{\&}(\{1\},\{0,1\}) = \hat{\&}(\{0,1\},\{0,1\}) = \{0,1\} .$$

$\hat{or}$ is symmetric and

$$\hat{or}(\emptyset,\emptyset) = \hat{or}(\emptyset,\{0\}) = \hat{or}(\emptyset,\{0,1\}) = \emptyset$$

$$\hat{or}(\emptyset,\{1\}) = \hat{or}(\{0\},\{1\}) = \hat{or}([1\},\{1\})$$

$$= \hat{or}(\{1\},\{0,1\}) = \{1\} ,$$

$$\hat{or}(\{0\},\{0,1\}) = \hat{or}(\{0,1\},\{0,1\}) = \{0,1\} .$$

Manes interprets:

$\emptyset$ = "undefined"	$\{1\}$ = "yes"
$\{0\}$ = "no"	$\{0,1\}$ = "maybe".

B. Major issues concerning Manes' theory.

Manes' extremely attractive theory of "fuzzy" theories essentially postulates that all of these theories (Zadeh's system, finite probability theory, etc.) have the form of a monad and the associated Kleisli category relative to SET. However, these results - as typical of a category theory setting - depend to a degree upon commutativity of operations. This can result in rather restrictive applications relative to general fuzzy set theory as developed here. More specifically, the following result holds:

Theorem (Goodman-Nguyen) [92].

Let $\mathcal{F} = (\phi_{not}, \phi_{\&}, \phi_{or})$ be an arbitrary generalized (fuzzy) set system.

Define $\mathcal{F}$ by, for all sets X ,

$$\mathcal{F}(X) \overset{d}{=} \mathcal{F}(X) .$$

Define e by, for all sets X

$$e(X) : X \to \mathcal{F}(X)$$

where for all $x \in X$,

$$e(X)(x) = \{x\} .$$

Finally, define # by, for any sets X , Y , and $R \in \mathcal{F}(X \times Y)$,

$$\#(R) : \mathcal{F}(X) \to \mathcal{F}(Y) ,$$

where for any $A \in \mathcal{F}(X)$ and any $y \in Y$,

$$\phi_{(\#(R)(A)}(y) = \phi_{R\circ A}(y)$$
$$= \phi_{\underset{x\in X}{or}}(\phi_\&(\theta_A(X), \phi_R(X,Y))) \ . \qquad (1)$$

This definition is also motivated by [0,1]-logic considerations as the evaluation

$$\| (y \in R\circ A) \|$$
$$= \| ((\exists X)((x \in A) \ \& \ ((x,y) \in R))) \| \ ,$$

through $\mathcal{F}$. (See Chapter 2.)

Then for these definitions for $\mathcal{F}$, e and # :

(a) Axioms (M1) and (M2) hold.

(b) Axiom (M3) holds
iff $\phi_\&$ is right distributive over ϕ_{or} , i.e.

$$\phi_\&(a, \phi_{or}(b,c)) = \phi_{or}(\phi_\&(a,b), \phi_\&(a,c)) \ ;$$

all $a,b,c \in [0,1]$ (2)

iff composition $\circ$ is associative

$$S\circ(R\circ P) = (S\circ R)\circ P \ ; \text{ all } R, S, P,$$

where

$$P \in \mathcal{F}(W \times X), \ R \in \mathcal{F}(X \times Y), \ S \in \mathcal{F}(Y \times Z) \ ;$$

all sets W, X, Y, Z , where composition is typically given in eq. (1) , in which case $\underset{\sim}{\mathcal{F}} = (\mathcal{F},e,\#)$ is a theory in Manes' sense.

Proof (2): For any sets X, Y, Z , for any $R \in \mathcal{F}(X \times Y)$, $S \in \mathcal{F}(Y \times Z)$, $A \in \mathcal{F}(X)$, $x \in X$, $y \in Y$, $z \in Z$:

$$\text{LHS(M3)} = \phi_{\underset{y\in Y}{or}}(\phi_\&(\phi_{R\circ A}(y), \phi_S(y,z))) \ , \qquad (3)$$

(left hand side of M3)

$$\text{RHS(M3)} = \phi_{\underset{x\in X}{or}}(\phi_\&(\phi_{S\circ R}(x,z), \phi_A(x))) \ , \qquad (4)$$

(right hand side of M3)

where $\phi_{R\circ A}(y)$ is given in eq(1) and

$$\phi_{S\circ R}(x,z) = \phi_{\underset{y\in Y}{or}}(\phi_\&(\phi_R(x,y), \phi_S(y,z))) \ . \qquad (5)$$

If $\phi_\&$ is right distributive over ϕ_{or} , then

$$\phi_{\&}(\phi_{R\circ A}(y),\ \phi_S(y,z)) = \phi_{\underset{x\in X}{or}}(\phi_M(x,y,z)) \tag{6}$$

where

$$\phi_M(x,y,z)) \overset{d}{=} \phi_{\&}(\phi_A(x),\ \phi_R(x,y),\ \phi_S(y,z))\ , \tag{7}$$

and

$$\phi_{\&}(\phi_{S\circ R}(x,z),\ \phi_A(x)) = \phi_{\underset{y\in Y}{or}}(\phi_M(x,y,z))\ . \tag{8}$$

Hence, substituting (7) into (3) and (8) into (4) yields

$$\mathrm{LHS(M3)} = \phi_{\underset{\substack{x\in X,\\ y\in Y}}{or}}(\phi_M(x,y,z)) = \mathrm{RHS(M3)}\ .$$

Conversely, if Axiom (M3) holds, choose $A = X = \{x_1,x_2\}$, $Y = \{y\}$, $\phi_R(x_1,y) = b$, $\phi_R(x_2,y) = c$, $\phi_S(y,z) = a$, otherwise arbitrary. Hence eq.(2) holds.

As a consequence of the above theorem, since as a check, Zadeh's system $\mathcal{F}_o = (1-(\cdot),\min,\max)$ and $\mathcal{F}' = (1-(\cdot),\mathrm{prod},\max)$ are always right distributive, both satisfy (M1), (M2) and (M3) and yield Manes' theories. On the other hand, $\mathcal{F}_1 = (1-(\cdot),\mathrm{prod},\mathrm{probsum})$, $\mathcal{F}'' = (1-(\cdot),\mathrm{prod},\mathrm{minsum})$ and many other systems such as non-Archimedean semi-distributive ones are in general not right distributive and hence are not compatible with Manes' theories. The latter class of systems plays a key role in the weak-homomorphic approach to fuzzy set systems (see Chapter 6).

Although the above theorem shows composition with respect to binary fuzzy relations for general fuzzy set systems is associative iff right distributivity holds, it is always true that functional transforms for general fuzzy set systems are always associative since the $\phi_{\&}$ operator is not used here:

For any $f : X \to Y$, $g : Y \to Z$, $h : Z \to W$, X, Y, Z, W any sets, associativity holds

$$h\circ(g\circ f) = (h\circ g)\circ f\ ,$$

where, e.g., for any $A \in \mathcal{F}(X)$, $y \in Y$,

$$\phi_{f(A)}(Y) = \phi_{\underset{x\in f^{-1}(y)}{or}}(\phi_A(x))\ ,$$

and any $z \in Z$,

$$\begin{aligned}\phi_{(g\circ f)(A)}(z) &= \phi_{\underset{x\in (g\circ f)^{-1}(z)}{or}}\ \phi_A(x)\\ &= \phi_{\underset{x\in f^{-1}(y)}{or}}(\phi_{\underset{y\in g^{-1}(z)}{or}}\ \phi_A(x))\\ &= \phi_{g(f(A))}(z)\ ,\end{aligned}$$

etc.

A basic question then is to determine which of Manes' developments are compatible with general fuzzy set systems: in particular, when can axiom (M3) be eliminated?

Eytan [57] (despite his mistaken idea that Fuz(H) is a topos - see [29] or [204]) compares Manes' approach with his own which utilizes Coste's construction. (See also section 2.4.) Both approaches rely on commutativity of basic system operators, which as stated before, may be somewhat restrictive. Further effort must be expanded in comparing Manes' approach, Fuz(H) and Higg(H) (see section 2.4) and in determining what extensions to general fuzzy set systems are possible.

Next, suppose that Manes' theory is replaced by the following generalized logical system type theory:

$\mathcal{T}$: SET → Ar(SET)	attribute or dispersion operator,
e : SET → Ar(SET)	imbedding operator,
$\dagger\dagger$: Ar(SET) → Ar(SET)	lifting operator (modified)

are such that for any X, Y, Z ∈ SET , $\mathcal{T}(X), \mathcal{T}(Y), \mathcal{T}(Z) \neq \emptyset$:

(a) $e(X) : X \to \mathcal{T}(X)$

where for any $x \in X$,

$$\delta_X = (e(X))(x) \in \mathcal{T}(X) \subseteq \{0,1\}^X .$$

(b) $\dagger\dagger(Y^X) : Y^X \to \mathcal{T}(Y)^{\mathcal{T}(X)}$

where for any $f \in Y^X$, slightly abusing notation,

$$\dagger\dagger(f) \overset{d}{=} (\dagger\dagger(Y^X))(f) .$$

(c) For any $\phi_A \in \mathcal{T}(X)$ and $x \in X$

$$(\dagger\dagger(e(X))(\phi_A))(\delta_x)) = \phi_A(x) .$$

(d) For any $f \in Y^X$, $x \in X$

$$\dagger\dagger(f)(\delta_x) = \delta_{f(x)}$$

(e) Recall that id : SET → Ar(SET) where for any X ∈ SET ,

$$id\ (X) : x \to X$$

where, for any $x \in X$,

$$id(X)(x) \overset{d}{=} x .$$

Then

$$\pi(id)(X) = id(\mathcal{T}(X)) .$$

(f) For any $x \in X$ and any $\phi_A \in \mathcal{T}(X)$,

$$(\pi(\delta_x)(\phi_A))(1) = \phi_A(x) .$$

(g) For any $f \in Y^X$, $g \in Z^Y$ noting the composition $g \circ f \in Z^X$,

$$\pi(g \circ f) = \pi(g) \circ \pi(f) ,$$

implying π is a functor.

Examples.

Ex. 1. $\mathcal{T} = \mathcal{F}$ (i.e., no restriction).
Pick $\mathcal{F} = (\phi_{not}, \phi_{\&}, \phi_{or})$.
Define, for any $x,y \in X$

(a') $$\delta_x(y) = \delta_{x,y} \quad \text{(Krönecker delta)}$$

and for any $f \in Y^X$, $\phi_A \in \mathcal{F}(X)$, $y \in Y$,

(b') $$(\pi(f)(\phi_A))(y) \overset{d}{=} \underset{x \in f^{-1}(y)}{\phi_{or}} (\phi_A(x)) ,$$

i.e.,

$$\pi(f) = \hat{f} \quad (\text{relative to } \phi_{or}) .$$

Then for any $\phi_A \in \mathcal{T}(X)$, $x \in X$

(c') $$(\pi(e(X))(\phi_A))(\delta_A)$$
$$= \underset{(\delta \in e(X)^{-1}(\delta_x))}{\phi_{or}} (\phi_A(\delta))$$
$$= \phi_A(x) ,$$

since $e(X)(x) = \delta_x$, uniquely.

(d') For any $f \in Y^X$, $x \in X$, $y \in Y$
$$(\pi(f)(\delta_x))(y)$$
$$= \underset{\delta \in f^{-1}(y)}{\phi_{or}} (\delta_x(s))$$

$$= \begin{cases} \phi_{or}(\cdots 0 \cdots, 1, \cdots 0) = 1, & \text{if } x \in f^{-1}(y) \\ \phi_{or}(\cdots 0 \cdots, 0, \cdots, 0) = 0, & \text{if } x \notin f^{-1}(y) \end{cases}$$

$$= \delta_{f(x)}(y) ,$$

(e') For any $\phi_A \in \mathcal{F}(X)$, $x \in X$,

$$(\dagger(id)(X))(\phi_A))(x) = \phi_{\substack{or \\ (s \in id(X)^{-1}(x))}}(\phi_A(s)) = \phi_A(x) ,$$

since $x = id(X)^{-1}(x)$, uniquely.

(f') For any $\phi_A \in \mathcal{F}(X)$, $x \in X$,

$$(\dagger(\delta_x)(\phi_A))(1) = \phi_{\substack{or \\ (s \in \delta^{-1}(1))}}(\phi_A(s)) = \phi_A(x) ,$$

since $\delta_x(x) = 1$ uniquely.

Note also that

$$(\dagger(\delta_x)(\phi_A))(0) = \phi_{\substack{or \\ s \in \delta_x^{-1}(0)}}(\phi_A(s)) = \phi_{\substack{or \\ (s \in X \dashv \{x\})}}(\phi_A(s))$$

(g') For any $f \in Y^X$, $g \in Z^Y$, $\phi_A \in \mathcal{F}(X)$, $z \in Z$,

$$(\dagger(g \circ f))(\phi_A)(z) = \phi_{\substack{or \\ s \in (g \circ f)^{-1}(z)}}(\phi_A(s)) = \phi_{\substack{or \\ s \in f^{-1}(g^{-1}(z))}}(\phi_A(s))$$

$$= \phi_{\substack{or \\ t \in g^{-1}(z)}}(\phi_{\substack{or \\ s \in f^{-1}(t)}} \phi_A(s)) = (\dagger(g)(\dagger(f)(A))(t) ,$$

provided ϕ_{or} is associative.

Ex. 2. $\mathcal{F}(X) = \varnothing$ if $X \not\subseteq \mathbb{R}$, etc.

For $\mathcal{F}(X) \neq \varnothing$, let

$$\mathcal{F}(\mathbb{R}) = \{F \mid F \text{ is a c.d.f. over } \mathbb{R}\} .$$

Let $\phi_{not} = 1 - (\cdot)$

$\phi_{\&}$ = r-copula, etc., by Sklar's theorem (2.3.6).

Define, for any $x, y \in X$

$$\delta_x(Y) = H_x(Y) \quad \text{(heavyside function)}$$

$$= \begin{cases} 0 & \text{iff } y < x \\ 1 & \text{iff } y \geq x \end{cases}$$

and for any $f \in Y^X$, $F \in \mathcal{F}(X)$, $y \in Y$,

$$(\pi(f)(F))(y) = \mu_F \circ f^{-1}(R_{y-})$$

where μ_F is probability measure over $\mathbb{B}$ determined by c.d.f. F and $R_a \overset{d}{=} [a,+\infty)$ (right ray), etc.

Then

(c'') For any $F \in \mathcal{F}(X)$, $x \in X$,

$$(\pi(e(X))(F))(H_x) = \mu_F \circ e(X)^{-1}(R_{H_x})$$

where the natural ordering of c.d.f.'s by R_{H_x} is given as

$$R_{H_x} \overset{d}{=} \{G \mid G \text{ is a c.d.f. over } \mathbb{R} \text{, with } G > H_x\} ,$$

since the rth moment $m_r(G) < M_r(H_x)$; all $r > 0$,
and hence

$$e(X)^{-1}(R_{H_x}) = \{y \mid y \in \mathbb{R} \ \& \ H_y \geq H_x\} = (-\infty, x) ,$$

and thus,

$$\mu_F \circ e(X)^{-1}(R_{H_{x-}}) = \mu_F(-\infty, x) = F(x) .$$

(d'') For any $f \in Y^X$, $x \in X$, $y \in Y$

$$(\pi(f)(H_x))(y) = (\mu_{H_x} \circ f^{-1})(R_{y-}) = H_{f(x)}(y) \quad \text{(essentially)}.$$

(e'') For any $F \in \mathcal{F}(X)$, $x \in X$

$$(\pi(id)(X)(F)(x) = (\mu_F \circ id(X)^{-1})(R_x-) = \mu_F \circ (R_x) = F(x) .$$

(f'') For any $F \in \mathcal{T}(X)$, $x \in X$,

$$(\text{tt}(H_x)(F))(1) = \mu_F \circ H_x^{-1}(R_{1-}(in\{0,1\}))$$

$$= \mu_F \circ H_x^{-1}(0)$$

$$= \mu_F(-\infty, x)$$

$$= F(x) \; .$$

Note that

$$(\text{tt}(H_x)(F))(0)$$

$$= \mu_F \circ H_x^{-1}(R_{0-}(in\{0,1\}))$$

$$= \mu_F(H_x^{-1}(\emptyset))$$

$$= \mu_F(\emptyset))$$

$$= 0 \; .$$

(g'') For any $f \in Y^X$, $g \in Z^Y$, $F \in \mathcal{T}(X)$, $z \in Z$,

$$\text{tt}(g \circ f)(F)(z) = \mu_F \circ (g \circ f)^{-1}(R_z) = (\mu_F(f^{-1}(g^{-1}(R_z)))$$

$$= (\mu_{\text{tt}(f)}(g^{-1}(R_z)) = \text{tt}(g)(\text{tt}(f)(F))(z) = \text{tt}(g) \circ \text{tt}(f)(F)(z) \; .$$

Ex. 3. Manes' system revisited.

Suppose once again $(\mathcal{T}, e, \#)$ is a given Manes theory. Then define tt by, for any $X, Y \in$ SET and $f \in Y^X$, $\phi_A \in \mathcal{T}(X)$,

$$\text{tt}(f) \overset{d}{=} \mathcal{T}(f) \overset{d}{=} (\text{tt}(Y^X))(f) \overset{d}{=} \#(e(Y) \circ f) \; .$$

Consider:

(d''') $\text{tt}(f)(\delta_x) = (\#(e(Y) \circ f))(\delta_x) = (e(Y) \circ f)(x)$,

by (M1)

$$= \delta_{f(x)} \; .$$

(e''') $\text{tt}(id)(X) = \#(e(X) \circ id(X)) = \#(e(X))$

$$= id(\mathcal{T}(X)) ,$$

by (M2) .

(g''') $\text{tt}(g \circ f) = \#(e(Z) \circ g \circ f)$.

Now

$\text{tt}(g) \circ \text{tt}(f) = \#(e(Z) \circ g) \circ \#(e(Y) \circ f) = \#(\#(e(Z) \circ g) \circ e(Y) \circ f)$,
by (M3)

$$= \#((e(Z)\circ g)\circ f) = \#(g\circ f),$$

using (M3) and (M1).

In general, c) and f) from part (2) will not be satisfied for Manes' theory.

However, if we define # by,

For any $\phi_R : X \to \mathcal{T}(Y)$, $\#(\phi_R) : \mathcal{T}(X) \to \mathcal{T}(Y)$

where, for any $\phi_A \in \mathcal{T}(X)$ and $y \in Y$,

$$((\#(\phi_R))(\phi_A))(y) = \phi_{\underset{s\in X}{or}}(\phi_\&(\phi_A(s), (\phi_R(s))(y))$$

and hence for any $f : X \to Y$, $\phi_A \in \mathcal{T}(X)$, $y \in Y$

$$(\#(f))(\phi_A))(y) \stackrel{d}{=} (\#(e(Y)\circ f))(\phi_A)(y)$$

$$= \phi_{\underset{s\in X}{or}}(\phi_\&(\phi_A(s), e(Y)(f(s)))(y)))$$

$$= \phi_{\underset{s\in f^{-1}(y)}{or}}(\phi_A(S)) .$$

(Note: $e(Y)(f(s))(y) = \delta_{f(s)}(y)$.)

(f''') For any $\phi_A \in \mathcal{T}(X)$, $x \in X$,

$$(\#(\delta_x)(\phi_A))(1)$$

$$= ((\#(e(\{0,1\})\circ\delta_x))(\phi_A))(1)$$

$$= \phi_{\underset{s\in X}{or}}(\phi_\&(\phi_A(S), (e(\{0,1\})\circ\delta_x)(s)(1)))$$

$$= \phi_{\underset{s\in X}{or}}(\phi_\&(\phi_A(s)) , \begin{bmatrix} \delta_1 & \text{for} & s = x \\ \delta_0 & \text{for} & s \neq x \end{bmatrix} (1)))$$

$$= \phi_{\underset{s\in X}{or}}(\phi_\&(\phi_A(s) , \begin{bmatrix} 1 & \text{for} & s = x \\ 0 & \text{for} & s \neq x \end{bmatrix}))$$

$$= \phi_A(x) .$$

Also:

(c''') For any $\phi_A \in \mathcal{T}(X)$, $x \in X$,

$$(\#(e(x))(\phi_A))(\delta_x)$$

$$= ((\#\underbrace{(e(\mathcal{T}(X))\circ e(X))}_{X \to \mathcal{T}(\mathcal{T}(X))})(\phi_A))(\delta_x)$$

$$= \phi_{\underset{s\in X}{or}}(\phi_\&(\phi_A(s) , ((e(\mathcal{T}(X))\circ e(X))(s))(\delta_x))$$

$= \phi_A(x)$

(Note: $(e(\mathcal{F}(X)\circ e(X))(s) = \delta_{\delta_s}$ and $(e(\mathcal{F}(X))\circ e(X))(s))(\delta_x) = \delta_{s,x}$.)

In addition, # as defined above also is such that:

For (M1) : For any $\alpha : X \to \mathcal{F}(Y)$ and any $x \in X$,

$((\#(\alpha))\circ e(X))(x) = (\#(\alpha))(\delta_x)$

$= \phi_{\substack{or \\ s\in X}}(\phi_\&(\delta_x(s), \alpha(s)(\cdot)))$

$= \alpha(x)(\cdot)$

Thus (M1) holds.

For (M2) : For any $\phi_A \in \mathcal{F}(X)$, $x \in X$,

$(\#(e(X)))(\phi_A)(x)) = \phi_{\substack{or \\ s\in X}}(\phi_\&(\phi_A(s) , e(X)(s)(x))) = \phi_A(x)$,

Thus (M2) holds.

In addition, note again

(i) If $\phi_R : X \to \mathcal{F}(Y)$ is such that $\exists\ f : X \to Y$ where for all $x \in X$, $y \in Y$,

$$(\phi_R(x))(y) = \delta_{y,f(x)} ,$$

then for all $\phi_A \in \mathcal{F}(X)$, $y \in Y$,

$$(\#(\phi_R))(\phi_A)(y)$$

$$= \phi_{\substack{or \\ x\in f^{-1}(y)}}(\phi_A(x))$$

$$= (\dagger\dagger(f)(\phi_A))(y) .$$

(ii) # as defined above, satisfies (M3) iff, assuming for $\phi_\&$, ϕ_{or} , $\phi_\&$ is right distributive over ϕ_{or} (such as (min,max) or (prod, bndsum) , in which case fuzzy composition * is defined by

$$\phi_R : X \to \mathcal{F}(Y)$$

$$\phi_S : Y \to \mathcal{F}(Z)$$

$$\phi_{S*R} : X \to \mathcal{F}(Z) ,$$

where for any $x \in X$, $z \in Z$,

$$(\phi_{S*R}(x))(z) = \phi_{\substack{or \\ y\in Y}}(\phi_\&((\phi_R(x))(y), (\phi_S(y))(z))$$

$$= (((\#(\phi_S))\circ\phi_R)(x))(z) ,$$

i.e.,

$$\phi_{S*R} = \#(\phi_S)\circ\phi_R \ .$$

and $*$ is associative.

C. <u>A modification of Manes' theory</u>.

Many of Manes' Fuzzy Theory concepts simplify when the lifting operator relation

$$(1) \quad f : X \to \mathcal{T}(Y) \quad \text{to} \quad (\#)f : \mathcal{T}(X) \to \mathcal{T}(Y)$$

is replaced by the relation

$$(2) \quad f : X \to Y \quad \text{to} \quad \pi(f) : \mathcal{T}(X) \to \mathcal{T}(Y) \ .$$

For example, for Manes' axiom (M3) , an associativity form of # is actually quite stringent. It was shown previously that indeed a general truth functional fuzzy set system satisfies (M3) iff $\phi_{\&}$ is right distributive over ϕ_{or} (and hence includes Zadeh's original min-max system). On the other hand, it is shown in this section that with the relation (2) , (M3) can be replaced by a simple associative form which holds for <u>all</u> truth functional fuzzy set systems as well as probability measure systems.

Some additional modifications, in addition to those already presented in this section include:

1. <u>Theory maps</u>:

$$\lambda : (\mathcal{T},e,\pi) \to (\mathcal{T}',e',\pi')$$

is a theory map iff for all $X \in$ SET .

(i) $\lambda(X) : \mathcal{T}(X) \to \mathcal{T}'(X)$

and for all $X,Y \in$ SET and $f : X \to Y$.

(ii) $\lambda(X)(\delta_x) = \delta'_x$, for all $x \in X$,

(iii) $\pi'(f)\circ\lambda(X) = \lambda(Y)\circ\pi(f)$.

In a quotient theory, each $\lambda(X)$ is required to be surjective.

If $(\mathcal{T},e,\pi)$ is a theory and for all $X \in$ SET , $\lambda(X) : \mathcal{T}(X) \to H^X$ is *arbitrary*, first define $\mathcal{T}'(X)$ by (i), for all $x \in X$, δ'_x by (ii), and define π' by (iii). Thus, $(\mathcal{T},e,\pi)$ and λ always induces a unique quotient theory, where λ is a surjective theory map to the quotient theory.

In particular, if $(\mathcal{T},e,\pi)$ is a theory, and for all $X \in$ SET , $\mathcal{E}(X)$ is an equivalence relation on $\mathcal{T}(X)$, then define $\lambda(X) : \mathcal{T}(X) \to \mathcal{T}(X)/\mathcal{E}(X)$ a surjective map which yields a quotient theory symbolized as $(\mathcal{T}/\varepsilon,\ e/\varepsilon,\ \pi/\varepsilon)$, with λ the theory map.

In a *subtheory*, each $\lambda(X)$ is required to be injective. Then the converse of the above holds:

If $(\mathcal{T}',e',\pi')$ is a theory and for all $X \in SET$, $\lambda(X) : \mathcal{T}(X) \to \mathcal{T}'(X)$ is injective, then there is a unique way to define theory $(\mathcal{T},e,\pi)$ such that λ is an injective theory map from $(\mathcal{T},e,\pi)$ into $(\mathcal{T}',e',\pi')$. In particular, given any theory $(\mathcal{T}',e',\pi')$ and for each $X \in SET$, define $\mathcal{T}(X) \subseteq \mathcal{T}'(X)$, then the mapping

$$\lambda(X) : T(X) \xrightarrow{id} \mathcal{T}(X) \subseteq \mathcal{T}'(X)$$

with e and π cut down to $\mathcal{T}$, yields an imbedding of $(\mathcal{T},e,\pi)$ into $(\mathcal{T}',e',\pi')$ uniquely.

2. Membership functions and extensions.

(a) Consider first any $f : X \to \{0,1\}$, $f \in \mathcal{T}(X)$. Then $\pi(f) : \mathcal{T}(X) \to \mathcal{T}(\{0,1\})$.

In particular, for any set $C \in \mathcal{P}(X)$, if $\phi_C \in \mathcal{T}(X)$, then $\pi(\phi_C)$ may be considered the natural extension of ϕ_C and hence of C . Note the range of $\pi(f)$ is $\mathcal{T}(\{0,1\})$ not just, e.g., $\mathcal{T}(\{1\})$.

(b) Similarly for any $f : X \to H$, $f \in \mathcal{T}(X)$, $\pi(f) : \mathcal{T}(X) \to \mathcal{T}(H)$ may be considered the natural extension of f and hence letting $f = \phi_A$, $A \in \mathcal{T}(H)$, $\pi(\phi_A)$ is the natural extension of A . Again, note the range of $\pi(f)$ being $\mathcal{T}(H)$ not just $\mathcal{T}(1)$, e.g.

3. Equality maps.

Note that classical equality between points in a space X is given by as the diagonal relation

$$"=" \subseteq X \times X ,$$

and

$$\phi_= : X \times X \to \{0,1\} ,$$

where

$$\phi_=(x,y) = \begin{cases} 1 , & \text{if } x = y \\ 0 , & \text{if } x \neq y . \end{cases}$$

and equivalently the associated function is

$$id : X \to X .$$

Then using approach 2 to extensions, as presented in section 2.3.7, it follows easily that

$$\hat{\phi}_{=} : \mathcal{F}(X \times X) \to \mathcal{F}\{0,1\}$$

where for any $\phi_A \in \mathcal{F}(X \times X)$, $\ell \in \{0,1\}$

$$\phi_{\hat{\phi}_{=}(\phi_A)}(\ell) = \Big(\underset{\substack{z \in X \times X \\ =(z)=\ell}}{\dagger} (\phi_A))((z)_{\left[\substack{z \in X \times X \\ =(z)=\ell}\right]})$$

$$= \begin{cases} \underset{x \in X}{\dagger} \phi_A((x,x)_{x \in X}) & , \text{ if } \ell = 1 \\ \underset{\substack{x,y \in X \\ x \neq y}}{\dagger} \phi_A((x,y)_{\substack{x,y \in X \\ x \neq y}}) & , \text{ if } \ell = 0 \end{cases} .$$

Note the special case $\phi_A = \phi_{\{y\}} \times \phi_B$ for some fixed $y \in X$, $B \in \mathcal{F}(X)$, yields

$$\phi_A(x,x) = \begin{cases} \phi_B(y) & , \text{ if } x = y \\ 0 & , \text{ if } x \neq y \end{cases} .$$

whence

$$\phi_{\hat{\phi}_{=}(\phi_{\{y\}} \times \phi_B)}(\ell) = \begin{cases} \phi_B(y) & \text{for } \ell = 1 \\ 0 & \text{for } \ell = 0 \end{cases} ,$$

an interesting check that membership should be a special case of equality.

More generally, note the case $\phi_A = \phi_C \times \phi_B$, for $C,B \in \mathcal{F}(X)$ does not really simplify, except that it extends Manes' equality map specialized to Zadeh's min - max system.

Alternatively, if approach 1 to extensions (section 2.3.7) is formally applied to $\phi_{=}$, then for any $A \in \mathcal{F}(X \times X)$,

$$\phi_{\hat{\phi}_{=}(\phi_A)}(\ell) = \phi_A \circ (\hat{\phi}_{=})^{-1}(\ell) ,$$

yielding a similar result.

On the other hand, if we consider $id(X) : X \to X$, it follows immediately that $\dagger\dagger(id(X)) = id(\mathcal{F}(X))$, i.e.,

$$\phi_{\hat{id}(X)} = \phi_{id(\mathcal{F}(X))} .$$

Note that Manes considers as basic, the asymmetric extension procedure $f : X \to \mathcal{F}(Y)$ extended to $\#(f) : \mathcal{F}(X) \to \mathcal{F}(Y)$. Instead, we have considered the full extension $\dagger\dagger(f) : \mathcal{F}(X) \to \mathcal{F}(Y)$ from $f : X \to Y$. However, note: if $f : X \to \mathcal{F}(Y)$ then

$$\dagger\dagger(f) : \mathcal{F}(X) \to \mathcal{F}(\mathcal{F}(Y)) ,$$

by the usual extension. Let $g \in \mathcal{F}(X)$. Thus,

$(\dagger(f))(g) \in \mathcal{F}(\mathcal{F}(Y))$ and hence $(\dagger(f))(g) : \mathcal{F}(Y) \to H$.

In particular, for any $y \in Y$, $\delta_y \in e(Y) \subseteq \mathcal{F}(Y)$. Thus,

$$((\dagger(f))(g))(\delta_\cdot) : Y \to H$$

where for each $y \in Y$,

$$((\dagger(f))(g))(\delta_\cdot)(y) \overset{d}{=} ((\dagger(f))(g))(\delta_y) .$$

Hence, in general, $(\dagger(f))(g))(\delta_\cdot) \in \mathcal{F}(Y)$. Thus, for $f : X \to \mathcal{F}(Y)$, we define:

$$\#(f) : \mathcal{F}(X) \to \mathcal{F}(Y) ,$$

where, for any $g \in \mathcal{F}(X)$ and $y \in Y$,

$$(\#(f))(g)(y) \overset{d}{=} ((\dagger(f))(g))(\delta_y) .$$

Thus, $\#$ as used here corresponds to Manes' $\#$.

Furthermore, note that $\#$ is an extension, since, for any $x \in X$ and hence $\delta_x \in e(X) \subseteq \mathcal{F}(X)$, $y \in Y$

$$(\#(f))(\delta_x)(y) = (\dagger(f)(\delta_x))(\delta_y) = \delta_{f(x)}(\delta_y) .$$

Define

$\bar{\bar{e}}(X) : X \to \mathcal{F}(X)$, where for any $X \in X$, $\bar{\bar{e}}(X)(x) \overset{d}{=} \delta_x$.

Then consider Manes' axiom (M1) :

For any $\alpha : X \to \mathcal{F}(Y)$, $y \in Y$,

$$(\#(\alpha)\circ\bar{\bar{e}}(X))(y)$$

$$= ((\dagger(\alpha))\circ\bar{\bar{e}}(X)(x))(\delta_y)_{x\in X}$$

$$= ((\dagger(\alpha))\circ\delta_x)(\delta_y))_{x\in X}$$

$$= ((\delta_{\alpha(x)})(\delta_y))_{x\in X} = \begin{cases} 1 & \text{iff} \quad \alpha(x) = \delta_y \\ 0 & \text{iff} \quad \alpha(x) \neq \delta_y \end{cases}$$

$$\neq \alpha .$$

Next consider Manes' axiom (M2):

For any $g \in \mathcal{F}(X)$, $x \in X$,

$$((\#)(\bar{\bar{e}}(X)))(g))(x)$$

$$= ((\dagger(\bar{\bar{e}}(X)))(g)(\delta_x)$$

$$\equiv ((\dagger(\delta_y))_{y\in X}(g))(\delta_x)$$

$$\equiv g(x) .$$

Hence, $(\#)(\bar{\bar{e}}(X))(g) = g$, i.e.,

$$\#(\bar{\bar{e}}(X)) = id_{\mathcal{F}(X)} .$$

Finally, it should be remarked that, in general, we cannot derive Manes' axiom M3 for # . Indeed, for the truth functional system $(\phi_{nt}, \phi_{\&}, \phi_{or})$:

For any $\alpha : X \to \mathcal{F}(Y)$, $\beta : Y \to \mathcal{F}(Z)$, for all $f \in \mathcal{F}(X)$, $z \in Z$,

$$((\#(\beta)\circ\#(\alpha))(f))(z)$$

$$= \underset{\begin{bmatrix} x\in\alpha^{-1}(\delta_y) \\ x\in\beta^{-1}(\delta_z) \end{bmatrix}}{\phi_{or}} (f(x))$$

On the other hand, it can be shown

$$((\#(\#(\beta)\circ\alpha))(f))(z)$$

$$= \underset{x \in \alpha^{-1}((\#(\beta))^{-1}(\delta_z))}{\phi_{or}} (f(x)) ,$$

where

$$(\#(\beta))^{-1}(\delta_z) = \{g \mid g \in \mathcal{F}(Y) \ \& \ \text{for all } z' \in Z ,\ z' \neq z ,\ (g \mid \beta^{-1}(\delta_{z'},\cdot)) = 0 \ \& \ \underset{(y\in\beta^{-1}(\delta_z))}{\phi_{or}} (g(y)) = 1\}$$

$$\geq e_{\beta,\delta_z} \overset{d}{=} \{\delta_y \mid y \in \beta^{-1}(\delta_z)\} .$$

Hence using the monotonic property of t-conorms: If $C \subseteq D$, then $\underset{x\in C}{\phi_{or}}(h(x)) \geq \underset{x\in D}{\phi_{or}}(h(x))$, it follows that for all $f \in \mathcal{F}(X)$, $z \in Z$,

$$((\#(\beta)\circ\#(\alpha))(f))(z) \geq ((\#(\#(\beta)\circ\alpha))(f))(z) ,$$

with strict inequality holding in general unless

$$(\#(\beta))^{-1}(\delta_z) = e_{\beta,\delta_z} .$$

Furthermore, as mentioned previously, a necessary and sufficient condition for Manes axiom (M3) to hold for the interpretation of # , given in section B and below, is that the truth functional system $(\phi_{not}, \phi_{\&}, \phi_{or})$ be such that $\phi_{\&}$ is right distributive over ϕ_{or} .

Again, conversely, let $(\mathcal{F},e,\#)$ be a given Manes theory. Then define operator Π by, for any sets X,Y and $f : X \to Y$, first noting

$$e(Y)\circ f : X \to e(Y) \subseteq \mathcal{F}(Y) ,$$

and hence

$$\Pi(f) : \mathcal{F}(X) \to \mathcal{F}(Y) ,$$

where

$$\Pi(f) \overset{d}{=} \#(e(Y)\circ f) .$$

It follows readily that all of the axioms we require for Π (and $\mathcal{F}$ and e) to satisfy for a general logical system indeed hold!

Thus, Manes' theory may be considered, in so far as the lifting operator $\#$ is concerned (in conjunction with $\mathcal{F}$ and e), a somewhat more restricted logical system. Hence, we cannot expect, in general, certain of his results to be applicable to general logical systems. In particular, it can be shown that Manes' concept of independence of distributions and homomorphisms do not apply here, in general. However, consider the following example:

As an illustration of the previous point, consider Manes' system as applied to Zadeh's min-max system and its natural generalizations:

For any $f : X \to \mathcal{F}(Y)$ define $\#(f) : \mathcal{F}(X) \to \mathcal{F}(Y)$ by, for all $g \in \mathcal{F}(X)$ and all $y \in Y$,

$$((\#(f))(g))(y) = \sup_{x\in X} (\min (g(x), f(x)(y))) .$$

More generally, for any truth functional system $(\phi_{not}, \phi_{\&}, \phi_{or})$ consider

$$((\#(f))(g))(y) \overset{d}{=} \underset{x\in X}{\phi_{or}}(\phi_{\&}(g(x), f(x)(y))) .$$

Now, $\#$ is a legitimate lifting operator in Manes' sense, except that axioms M1, M3 are violated, unless, as stated before $\phi_{\&}$ is right distribution over ϕ_{or} - which is the case for Zadeh's min-max system. (Again, see subsection B.)

Then define Π by, for any $f : X \to Y$,

$$\Pi(f) = \#(e(Y)\circ f) \ ; \ \Pi(f) : \mathcal{F}(X) \to \mathcal{F}(Y) .$$

Thus, for any $g \in \mathcal{F}(X)$ and $y \in Y$,

$$(\Pi(f))(g))(y) = ((\#(e(Y)\circ f))(g))(y)$$

$$= \underset{x\in X}{\phi_{or}}(\phi_{\&}(g(x), (e(Y)\circ f)(x)(y)))$$

$$= \underset{x\in X}{\phi_{or}}(\phi_{\&}(g(x), \delta_{f(x)}(y)))$$

$$= \phi_{\substack{or \\ x \in f^{-1}(y)}} (g(x)) \; .$$

Thus indeed, ⫪ as defined above coincides with ⫪ as previously defined for truth functional systems! Hence the above
alternative definition for ⫪ for truth functional systems is
justifiable.

Analogous to Manes' development of the concept of independence,
first define the following natural extensions of any
$f : X \times Y \to \mathcal{S}(Z)$ by use of # or some equivalent.

Define variables by

$$\cdot \in X, \;\; \cdot\cdot \in Y, \;\; \cdots \in Z, \;\; :: \in \mathcal{S}(X), \;\; ::. \in \mathcal{S}(Y) \; .$$

Then with obvious notation, for any $x \in X$,
$f(x,\cdot\cdot) : Y \to \mathcal{S}(Z)$, and hence $\#\cdot\cdot f(x,\cdot\cdot) : \mathcal{S}(Y) \to \mathcal{S}(Z)$, and hence

$$\#\cdot\cdot f(\cdot,\cdot\cdot) : X \to \mathcal{S}(Z)^{\mathcal{S}(Y)} \; ,$$

equivalently

$$\Gamma_1(f) \stackrel{\mathrm{d}}{=} (((\#\cdot\cdot f(\cdot,\cdot\cdot)(\cdot))(::.) : X \to \mathcal{S}(Z)^{\mathcal{S}(Y)} \; ,$$

where for any $g \in \mathcal{S}(Y)$,

$$((\#\cdot\cdot f(\cdot,\cdot\cdot))(\cdot))(g) : X \to \mathcal{S}(Z) \; .$$

Thus,

$$\#(\Gamma_1(f)) = (\#(((\#\cdot\cdot f(\cdot,\cdot\cdot))(\cdot))(::.))) : \mathcal{S}(X) \to \mathcal{S}(Z)^{\mathcal{S}(Y)}$$

yielding equivalently

$$\#(\Gamma_1(f)) : \mathcal{S}(X) \times \mathcal{S}(Y) \to \mathcal{S}(Z) \; .$$

Similarly by reversing first y for x ,

$$\#(\Gamma_2(f)) : \mathcal{S}(X) \times \mathcal{S}(Y) \to \mathcal{S}(Z) \; .$$

In particular, letting $f = \bar{\bar{e}}(X \times Y) : X \times Y \to \mathcal{S}(X \times Y)$, if, as
before

$$\#(\Gamma(X \times Y)) \stackrel{\mathrm{d}}{=} \#(\Gamma_1(\bar{\bar{e}}(X \times Y))) = \#(\Gamma_2(\bar{\bar{e}}(X \times Y))) \; ,$$

for all sets X and

$$\#(\Gamma(X \times Y)) : \mathcal{S}(X) \times \mathcal{S}(Y) \to \mathcal{S}(X \times Y)$$

is the independence mapping.

It can be verified that for $\#$ as defined previously for truth functional system $(\phi_{not}, \phi_{\&}, \phi_{or})$, the independence mapping exists and is given by, for all $f \in \mathcal{F}(X)$, $g \in \mathcal{F}(Y)$ and all $x \in X$, $y \in Y$

$$((\#(\Gamma(X \times Y)))(f,g))(x,y) = \phi_{\&}(f(x),g(y))$$
$$= (f \times g)(x,y) .$$

Also, one can define for any

$$\alpha : X_1 \times X_2 \rightarrow \mathcal{F}(Z) ,$$
$$\#(\alpha) : \mathcal{F}(X_1 \times X_2) \rightarrow \mathcal{F}(Z) ,$$

as usual, and assuming

$$\Gamma(X_1 \times X_2) : \mathcal{F}(X_1) \times \mathcal{F}(X_2) \rightarrow \mathcal{F}(X_1 \times X_2)$$

exist,

$$\overline{\alpha} \overset{d}{=} (\#(\alpha))\circ\Gamma(X_1 \times X_2) : \mathcal{F}(X_1) \times \mathcal{F}(X_2) \rightarrow \mathcal{F}(Z) ,$$

and it follows that $\#(\alpha)$ and $\overline{\alpha}$ extend α :

$$\overline{\alpha}\circ\overline{\overline{e}}(X_1 \times X_2) = \alpha = \#(\alpha)\circ\overline{\overline{e}}(X_1 \times X_2) .$$

A natural question: What is the relation between $\overline{\alpha}$, $\#(\alpha)$ and $\#(\Gamma(\alpha)) = \#(\Gamma_1(\alpha)) = \#(\Gamma_2(\alpha))$, when the latter exists? In Manes' theory, it follows by uniqueness of 2-homomorphic extensions and the construction of $\Gamma(\alpha)$ (see his theorem 5.7 [169]), that $\overline{\alpha} = \Gamma(\alpha)$. However, due to the failure of axiom (M3) to hold in general, each $\overline{\alpha}$ need not be a 2-homomorphism in Manes' sense, the multiple factor generalization of a function arising as an extension through $\#$; although when $\Gamma(\alpha)$ is well defined, the latter clearly is such an extension. Thus also, Manes' characterization (again see Theorem 5.7 [169]) of universally commutative Y-ary operations being equivalent to unique multi-homomorphism extensions fail here.

Again, two important special cases should be mentioned where all three Manes axioms hold and hence where all of Manes' results on n-homomorphism extensions and commutative systems, among others, hold are:

(1) Zadeh's fuzzy set system $(1 - (\cdot),\min,\max)$ where for any X,

$$\mathcal{F}(X) = [0,1]^X , \quad U(X) = X$$

$\overline{\overline{e}}(X) : X \rightarrow \mathcal{F}(X)$, where for all $x,y \in X$, $\overline{\overline{e}}(X)(x)(y) = \delta_{x,y}$, and for $f : X \rightarrow \mathcal{F}(Y)$, for all $g \in \mathcal{F}(X)$, $y \in Y$,

$$((\#(f))(g))(y) = \sup_{x \in X} \min ((f(x))(y), g(x)) .$$

(2) Discrete probability theory: the same as the fuzzy set system (1-(·), prod, bndsum) where

$$\mathcal{F}(X) \overset{d}{=} \begin{cases} \emptyset, \text{ if } X \text{ is not discrete ,} \\ \text{class of all prob. fucntions over } X , \\ \text{if } X \text{ is discrete} \end{cases}$$

$\bar{\bar{e}}(X) : X \to \mathcal{F}(X)$, where for all $x,y \in X$,

$$(\bar{\bar{e}}(X)(x))(y) = \delta_{x,y}$$

and for $f : X \to \mathcal{F}(Y)$, for all $g \in \mathcal{F}(X)$, $y \in Y$,

$$((\#(f))(g))(y) = \sum_{x \in X} (f(x))(y) \cdot g(x) = E_g(f(\cdot)(\cdot\cdot)) .$$

Note that both examples above are special cases of the system $(\phi_{not}, \phi_{\&}, \phi_{or})$, with # defined as before, where in (1) $\phi_{\&}$ = min, ϕ_{or} = max and in (2) $\phi_{\&}$ = prod, ϕ_{or} = bndsum . Note also that for both systems - as a check with the characterization of such Manes' truth functional systems - have $\phi_{\&}$ right distributive over ϕ_{or} .

So far, we have considered the extension operations ⇈ , lifting functions $f : X \to Y$ to $⇈(f) : \mathcal{F}(X) \to \mathcal{F}(Y)$ and # lifting functions $\alpha : X \to \mathcal{F}(Y)$ to $\#(\alpha) : \mathcal{F}(X) \to \mathcal{F}(Y)$ and the imbedding operation $e : X \to \bar{\bar{e}}(X) \subseteq \mathcal{F}(X)$.

The question then arises as to the converses of these operations.

For example, consider the converse of the imbedding operation e . Can we obtain a natural "subjection" (in order to avoid confusion with "projection") S, where for all X , and given $U(X) \subseteq \mathcal{P}(X)$, $S(X) : \mathcal{F}(X) \to U(X)$ is surjective. Watanabe's example [267] furnishes such as mapping, when $U(X) = \mathcal{P}(X)$, $\mathcal{F}(X) = [0,1]^X$ and under $S(X)$, any $f \in \mathcal{F}(X)$ is pushed to an image representing the membership function of an ordinary set.

In turn, any mapping such as $h : \mathcal{F}(X) \to \mathcal{F}(Y)$ may be reduced in two easy stages, using again the notation $e(X)(x) = \delta_x$, for all $x \in X$,

(i) $s(h) : X \to \mathcal{F}(Y)$,
where for any $x \in X$, $s(h)(x) \overset{d}{=} h(\delta_x)$.

(ii) $t(h) : X \to U(Y)$
where

$$t(h) \overset{d}{=} s(Y) \circ s(h) .$$

Note, of course, the compatibility of step (i) when $h = \#(f)$, $f : X \to \mathcal{T}(Y)$, i.e.,

$$s(\#(f)) = f .$$

In summary, a certain arbitrariness marks any logical system. Even Manes' very structured system with many useful properties - such as the uniqueness of homomorphic extensions (see his Theorem 5.7 [169]) - still depends on the choice of lifting operator (in his case #) and $\mathcal{T}$ operation. (The imbedding operation is usually naturally determined.)

As Klement mentions in his paper on triangular norms [140], empirical investigations (such as those by Zimmermann, et al. [250], [291]) are also needed for better semantic modeling.

Summary of extensions

All the results below may be extended in the obvious way to an arbitrary number of finite factors, by replacing $\Gamma(X_1 \times X_2)$ by $\Gamma(X_1 \times \ldots \times X_n)$.

I. $f : X_1 \times X_2 \to Y$, given

We always have

$$e(X_1 \times X_2) : X_1 \times X_2 \to \bar{\bar{e}}(X_1 \times X_2) \subseteq \mathcal{T}(X_1 \times X_2) .$$

Assuming Γ exists,

$$\Gamma(X_1 \times X_2) : \mathcal{T}(X_1) \times \mathcal{T}(X_2) \to \mathcal{T}(X_1 \times X_2) .$$

Thus,

$$e(Y) \circ f : X_1 \times X_2 \to \mathcal{T}(Y) .$$

(i) If # is first available, define †† by

$$\dagger\dagger(f) \overset{d}{=} \#(e(Y) \circ f) = \mathcal{T}(f) : \mathcal{T}(X_1 \times X_2) \to \mathcal{T}(Y) .$$

In addition,

$$\bar{f} \overset{d}{=} \#(f) \circ \Gamma(X_1 \times X_2) : \mathcal{T}(X_1) \times \mathcal{T}(X_2) \to \mathcal{T}(Y) .$$

(ii) If †† is first available, then directly

$$\dagger\dagger(f) : \mathcal{T}(X_1 \times X_2) \to \mathcal{T}(Y) ,$$

and again in turn

$$\bar{f} \overset{d}{=} \dagger\dagger(f) \circ \Gamma(X_1 \times X_2) : \mathcal{T}(X_1) \times \mathcal{T}(X_2) \to \mathcal{T}(Y) .$$

II. $f : X_1 \times X_2 \to \mathcal{F}(Y)$, given

(i) If $\#$ is first available, then directly

$$\#(f) : \mathcal{F}(X_1 \times X_2) \to \mathcal{F}(Y)$$

and hence assuming Γ exists

$$\overline{f} \overset{d}{=} \#(f) \circ \Gamma(X_1 \times X_2) : \mathcal{F}(X_1) \times \mathcal{F}(X_2) \to \mathcal{F}(Y) .$$

(ii) If $\dagger\dagger$ is first available, then

$$\dagger\dagger(f) : \mathcal{F}(X_1 \times X_2) \to \mathcal{F}(\mathcal{F}(Y))$$

and in turn, letting $\cdot \in \mathcal{F}(X_1 \times X_2)$, $\cdot\cdot \in Y$,

$$\#(f) \overset{d}{=} ((\dagger\dagger(f))(\cdot))(e(Y)(\cdot\cdot)))$$
$$: \mathcal{F}(X_1 \times X_2) \to \mathcal{F}(Y) ,$$

and hence

$$\overline{f} \overset{d}{=} \#(f) \circ \Gamma(X_1 \times X_2) : \mathcal{F}(X_1) \times \mathcal{F}(X_2) \to \mathcal{F}(Y) .$$

In particular, all of these results could be applied to the classical Boolean polynomials - or truth table function operators, given by the classes

$$\mathrm{Bool}_n \overset{d}{=} \{f \mid f : \{0,1\}^n \to \{0,1\}\} \ ; \ n = 1,2,...$$

Lastly, consider Manes' concept of "distributions as operations" (see [169], Theorem 3.3).

(1) If $\#$ is first available, Manes shows for any $Y \in \mathrm{SET}$, the class of all *commutative Y-ary $\mathcal{F}$-operations* satisfies:

$c_Y \overset{d}{=} \{\mathcal{F}_Y \mid \mathcal{F}_Y : \mathrm{SET} \to \mathcal{P}(\mathrm{Ar}(\mathrm{SET}))$, where for all $X \in \mathrm{SET}$,

$\mathcal{F}_Y(X) : \mathcal{F}(X)^Y \to \mathcal{F}(X)$ and for all $Z \in \mathrm{SET}$ and all $\beta : X \to \mathcal{F}(Z)$,

$$\#(\beta) \circ \mathcal{F}_Y(X) = \mathcal{F}_Y(Z) \circ (\#(\beta))^Y$$

where $(\#(\beta))^Y : \mathcal{F}(X)^Y \to \mathcal{F}(Z)^Y$, where for all $\alpha : Y \to \mathcal{F}(X)$, and $y \in Y$,

$$(\#(\beta))^Y(\alpha)(y) \overset{d}{=} (\#(\beta) \circ \alpha)(y)\} ,$$

$= \{\tilde{f} \mid \tilde{f} : \mathrm{SET} \to \mathcal{P}(\mathrm{Ar}(\mathrm{SET}))$, where $f \in \mathcal{F}(Y)$ and for all

$X \in SET$, $\tilde{f}(X) : \mathcal{F}(X)^Y \to \mathcal{F}(X)$ where for all $\alpha : Y \to \mathcal{F}(X)$,

$$(\tilde{f}(X))(\alpha) \stackrel{d}{=} (\#(\alpha))(f) ,$$

with the bijective relation,

$$f \longleftrightarrow \tilde{f} , \text{ all } f \in \mathcal{F}(Y) ,$$

and where for any $\mathcal{F}_Y$,

$$\mathcal{F}_Y = ((\mathcal{F}_Y(Y))(e(Y)))^{\sim}\} .$$

(2) If the less restrictive $\dagger\dagger$ is first available, analogous to Manes' proof, we can show

$$\mathcal{C}_Y \stackrel{d}{=} \{\mathcal{F}_Y \mid \mathcal{F}_Y : SET \to \mathcal{P}(Ar(SET)) \text{ , where for all } X \in SET ,$$
$$\mathcal{F}_Y(X) : X^Y \to \mathcal{T}(X) \text{ and for all } Z \in SET \text{ and all}$$
$$\beta : X \to Z , \dagger\dagger(\beta)\circ\mathcal{F}_Y(X) = \mathcal{F}_Y(Z)\circ\beta^Y , \text{ where}$$
$$\beta^Y : X^Y \to Z^Y , \text{ where for all } \alpha : Y \to X , \text{ and all}$$
$$y \in Y , (\beta^Y(\alpha))(y) \stackrel{d}{=} (\beta\circ\alpha)(y) \in Z\} .$$

$$= \{\tilde{f} \mid \tilde{f} : SET \to \mathcal{P}(Ar(SET))\} \text{ , where for all } X \in SET ,$$
$$\tilde{f}(X) : X^Y \to \mathcal{F}(X) \text{ where for all } \alpha : Y \to X ,$$
$$(\tilde{f}(X))(\alpha) \stackrel{d}{=} (\dagger\dagger(\alpha))(f) \text{ , with the bijective relation}$$
$$f \longleftrightarrow \tilde{f} \text{ , all } f \in \mathfrak{I}(Y) \text{ , and where for any } \mathfrak{I}_Y ,$$

$$\mathcal{F}_Y = ((\mathcal{F}_Y(Y))(id_Y))^{\sim}\} .$$

Note also,

$$(\tilde{f}(Y))(id_X) = f .$$

Thus the interesting characterization by Manes for all commutative Y-ary operations does not in general extend to the less restrictive $\dagger\dagger$ system. However, by specializing Y to $\{1,\dots,n\}$, say, the second result shows for cartesian n-products there is a bijective relation between commutative n-ary functions $\mathcal{F}_Y(X) : X^n \to \mathcal{F}(X)$, X arbitrary, and $\tilde{f}$ for all $f \in \mathcal{T}\{1,\dots,n\}$, where for any $x \in X^n$ considered as a function $x : \{1,\dots,n\} \to X$, where $x(j) = x_j$, $j = 1,\dots,n$; $x = (x_1,\dots,x_n)$,

$$\tilde{f}(X)(x) = (\dagger\dagger(x))(f) .$$

Thus, because of the excessive restriction of axiom (M3), many (but not all) of Manes'elegant results do not hold for the $\dagger\dagger$ system but of course will hold when $\#$ is replaced by $\dagger\dagger$ (which is always compatible, as shown previously).

7.3 <u>Watanabe's system.</u>

Consider now in some detail Watanabe's fuzzy set theory which also has a strong probabilistic connection [268]:

Let X be an fixed nonvacuous space of points or objects and $\mathcal{F}_1(X)$ (corresponding to $\mathcal{F}(X)$) a space of attributes or predicates or fuzzy sets, etc. Let $\phi : X \times \mathcal{F}_1(X) \to [0,1]$ be fixed such that for any $x \in X$ and $A \in \mathcal{F}_1(X)$, $\phi(x,A) = \phi_A(x) \in [0,1]$. Identify $x = y$, iff $\phi_A(x) = \phi_A(y)$ for all $A \in \mathcal{F}_1$ and dually $A = B$ iff $\phi_A(x) = \phi_B(x)$ for all $x \in X$. Suppose also $\varnothing$, $\square \in \mathcal{F}_1(X)$ with the evaluations: $\phi_\varnothing \equiv 0$, $\phi_\square = 1$. (For convenience, let $X = \square$.)

Let $\rho : X \times \mathcal{F}_1(X) \to \mathcal{F}_1(X)$ be fixed and define composition $\circ$: $\mathcal{F}_1(X) \times \mathcal{F}_1(X) \to \mathcal{F}_1(X)$ by, for any $A,B \in \mathcal{F}(X)$, and $x \in X$,

$$\phi_{A\circ B}(x) \overset{d}{=} \phi_A(\rho(x,B))\cdot\phi_B(x) .$$

$\circ$ is not associative nor symmetric in general.

Let the *simple* predicate class $\mathcal{S}(X)$ be defined by

$$\begin{aligned}\mathcal{S}(X) &\overset{d}{=} \{A \mid A \in \mathcal{F}_1(X) \ \&\ A\circ A = A\} \\ &= \{A \mid \text{For all } x \in \operatorname{supp}(A) \overset{d}{=} \{x \mid \phi_A(x) > 0\} , \\ &\qquad \phi_A(\rho(x,B)) = 1 , \text{ i.e., } \rho(x,B) \in A\}.\end{aligned}$$

Thus, $\varnothing, X \in \mathcal{S}(X)$.

(i) If $A,B \in \mathcal{S}(X)$ and $A\circ B = B\circ A$, then

$$A\circ B = B\circ A \in \mathcal{S}(X) .$$

(ii) If $A,B \in \mathcal{S}(X)$ with $A\circ B = B\circ A = A$, we write $A \mapsto B$, an implication or deduction sequent between A and B, noting $\phi_B \geq \phi_A$ pointwise over X, if $A \mapsto B$. Also,

$$\begin{aligned}&A \mapsto A \ ; \ A \mapsto B ,\ B \mapsto C \text{ implies } A \mapsto C ; \\ &A = B \text{ iff } (A \mapsto B \ \&\ B \mapsto A) ; \\ &\varnothing \mapsto A \mapsto X , \text{ for all } A,B,C \in \mathcal{S}(X) .\end{aligned}$$

(iii) Thus $\mapsto$ induces a partial order over $\mathcal{S}(X)$, which in turn yields least upper bound and greatest lower bound operators

$$\cup,\cap : \mathcal{S}(X) \times \mathcal{S}(X) \to \mathcal{S}(X)$$

E.g., $A,B \mapsto A \cup B$ and if $A,B \mapsto C$ then $A \cup B \mapsto C$, which explicitly is the same as, for any $A,B \in \mathscr{F}_1(X)$,

$$A \cup B = C(\cdots \circ C(A) \circ C(B) \circ C(A) \circ C(B)) \in \mathscr{F}(X)$$

(unambiguously well-defined)

$$A \cap B = (\cdots \circ A \circ B \circ A \circ B) \in \mathscr{F}(X) \quad \text{(unambiguous well-defined)}$$

where complemental operator $C : \mathscr{F} \to \mathscr{F}$ is also assumed well-defined, where $\phi_{CA}(x) \overset{d}{=} 1 - \phi_A(x)$; $x \in X$.

If $A \circ B = B \circ A$ then it can be shown

$$A \cap B = B \cap A = A \circ B = B \circ A .$$

(iv) It also follows that $(\mathscr{F}(X), \cap, \cup, C)$ is a complete complemented lattice which is also symmetric, associative, idempotent and DeMorgan, but in general, *not distributive*. Also, C is involutive with the Law of Excluded Middle holding:

$$A \cap CB = \emptyset \ , \ A \cup CA = X \ , \text{ and } \ A \circ C(A) = C(A) \circ A = \emptyset \ ;$$

the Law of Self-Contradiction:

$$A \mapsto CA \quad \text{iff} \quad A = \emptyset .$$

If $A \circ B = B \circ A$, then $A \circ C(B) = C(B) \circ A$ and $C(A) \circ C(B) = C(B) \circ C(A)$, and

$$\phi_{B \circ A} + \phi_{B \circ C(A)} = \phi_B \qquad \text{(pointwise)} ;$$

$$A \cap C(B) = \emptyset \ \& \ A \circ B = B \circ A \ \text{ implies } \ A \mapsto B$$

$$A \mapsto B \ \text{ implies } \ A \cap C(B) = \emptyset ,$$

$$A \mapsto B \ \text{ iff } \ C(B) \mapsto C(A) \ \text{(Modus Tollens)} .$$

(v) Iff for all $A,B \in \mathscr{F}(X)$, $A \circ B = B \circ A$, $\mathscr{F}(X)$ is also distributive; in which case, for any $x \in X$, $\phi_{(\cdot)}(x) : \mathscr{F}(X) \to [0,1]$ is a finitely additive probability measure over $\mathscr{F}$. Hence in the latter case, $(\phi_{(\cdot)}(x))_{x \in X}$ is a family of probability measures.

(vi) If for all $A,B \in \mathscr{F}(X)$, $A \circ B = B \circ A$ and $\mathscr{F}(X)$ is finite in cardinality, then in addition to the results of (v) , there exist $A_1,\ldots,A_n \in \mathscr{F}(X)$ for some $n \geq 1$, called atoms, such that w.r.t. $\cap$ and $\cup$, they form a disjoint partitioning of X and such that for any $A \in \mathscr{F}(X)$, if $A \mapsto A_j$, then either $A = \emptyset$ or $A = A_j$; $j = 1,\ldots,n$. This implies that any $A \in \mathscr{F}(X)$ can be written uniquely

$$A = \bigcup_{\substack{1 \leq j \leq n ,\\ A_j \mapsto A}} A_j ,$$

which in turn implies for any $x \in X$, we have a probability function

$$\phi_{(\cdot)}(x) : \{A_1, \ldots, A_n\} \to [0,1]$$

with

$$\sum_{0=1}^{n} \phi_{A_j}(x) = \phi_X(x) = 1$$

and for any $A \in \mathscr{S}(X)$,

$$\phi(x) = \sum_{\substack{1 \le j \le n, \\ A_j \mapsto A}} \phi_{A_j}(x) \; ; \text{ for all } x \in X .$$

Suppose now $X \supseteq \{a_1, \ldots, a_n\}$, such that

$$\phi_{A_i}(a_j) = \delta_{ij} \; ; \text{ all } i,j \; ; \; 1 \le i,j \le n \text{ (Krönecker delta)} .$$

Then for any such $a_j \in X$ and $A \in \mathscr{S}$,

$$\phi_A(a_j) = \sum_{\substack{1 \le k \le n \\ A_k \mapsto A}} \phi_{A_k}(a_j) = \begin{cases} 1 & \text{iff } A_j \mapsto A \\ 0 & \text{iff otherwise} , \end{cases}$$

and hence

$$\phi_A(x) = \sum_{j=1}^{n} \phi_A(a_j) \cdot \phi_{A_j}(x) \; ; \text{ all } x \in X .$$

Watanabe realized the above scheme in a geometric setting. However, his important example appears somewhat ambiguous in regard to the interpretation of the composition operation and whether $\mathscr{S}(X)$ in the example should be distributive or not. We present a simple unified approach here, interpreting composition as ordinary matrix multiplication:

Let X correspond to a subclass of all products G of positive semidefinite matrices G_j , where G is normalized with respect to the trace operation, i.e., $G = (1/tr(G_1 \cdot\cdot G_n)) \cdot G_1 \cdot G_2 \cdot\cdot G_n$, $n \ge 1$, whence $tr(G) = 1$. (Thus any $(1/trG_j)G_j$ is a quantum mechanics object.)

Let $\mathscr{S}_1(X)$ correspond to some subclass of all A or $I_n - A$, where $A = A_1 \cdot\cdot A_m$ and matrices A_j are positive semidefinite with maxeig $(A_j) \le 1$. Let composition $\circ$ be ordinary matrix multiplication so that $\mathscr{S}(X)$ is the class of all idempotent (or projection) matrices intersected with $\mathscr{S}_1(X)$ with typical element

$C = \sum_{j=1}^{m} P_j P_j^T$, for some $P_1, \ldots, P_m \in \mathbb{R}^n$ orthonormal, $m \le n$. It then follows by the fundamental commutativity theorem, for any

$$A = \sum_{j=1}^{m} P_j' P_j'^T \ , \ B = \sum_{j=1}^{m} P_j'' P_j''^T \in \mathcal{G}(X) \ , \text{ letting}$$

$$P' \overset{d}{=} \{P_1', \ldots, P_{m'}'\} \ ; \ P'' \overset{d}{=} \{P_1'', \ldots, P_{m''}''\} \ ,$$

AB is symmetric

iff $AB \in \mathcal{G}(X)$
iff $AB = BA$
iff $P' \cup P'' \subseteq \{P_1, \ldots, P_n\}$ orthonormal in $\mathbb{R}^n$,

in which case,

$$AB = BA = \sum_{\begin{bmatrix} 1 \le j \le n \\ P_j \in P' \cap P'' \end{bmatrix}} P_j P_j^T \in \mathcal{G}(X) \ .$$

Define ϕ for any $G \in X$, $A \in \mathcal{G}_1(X)$, by

$$\phi_A(G) \overset{d}{=} tr(A \cdot G) \le 1 \ .$$

Note also that ρ here becomes

$$\rho(G,B) = (1/tr(BG) \cdot B \cdot G \ ,$$

for all $G \in X$, $B \in \mathcal{G}_1(X)$.

Then for any $A,B \in \mathcal{G}(X)$, $A \mapsto B$ becomes the relation $B \subseteq A$, i.e., w.l.o.g.

$$A = \sum_{j \in \Lambda_1} P_j P_j^T \ , \ B = \sum_{j \in \Lambda_2} P_j P_j^T \ ; \ \Lambda_2 \subseteq \Lambda_1 \ .$$

Also, $A \cap B$ and $A \cup B$ have interpretations in terms of matrix products. In particular, if $AB = BA$, then letting

$$A = \sum_{j \in \Lambda_1} P_j P_j^T \ , \ B = \sum_{j \in \Lambda_2} P_j P_j^T \quad \text{for some } \Lambda_1 \ , \Lambda_2 \subseteq \{1, \ldots, n\} \ ,$$

$$A \cap B = AB = BA = \sum_{j \in \Lambda_1 \cap \Lambda_2} P_j P_j^T \ ,$$

and

$$A \cup B = \sum_{j \in \Lambda_1 \cup \Lambda_2} P_j P_j^T$$

in which case for all $G \in X$,

$$\phi_A(G) = \sum_{j \in \Lambda_1} P_j^T \cdot GP_j \quad ; \quad \phi_B(G) = \sum_{j \in \Lambda_2} P_j^T GP_j \ ,$$

$$\phi_{A\cap B}(G) = \sum_{j\in\Lambda_1\cap\Lambda_2} P_j^T G P_j \quad ; \quad \phi_{A\cup B}(G) = \sum_{j\in\Lambda_1\cup\Lambda_2} P_j^T G P_j ,$$

where it can be shown that the same bounds, as obtained for all copulas and their Demorgan t-conorm transforms, hold here.

In addition, define

$$CA \overset{d}{=} I_n - A .$$

Note that if $A = \sum_{j\in\Lambda} P_j P_j^T \in \mathcal{P}(X)$, $\Lambda \subseteq \{1,...,n\}$,

then

$$CA = I_n - A = \sum_{j\in\{1,...,n\}-\Lambda} P_j P_j^T \in \mathcal{P}(X) .$$

Also, for any $A \in \mathcal{P}_1(X)$, $G \in X$,

$$\phi_{CA}(G) + \phi_A(G) = tr(AG + (I_n - A)G) = tr(G) = 1 ,$$

etc.

Thus all desired results in the general case may be realized in this example, which, in general, yields $(\mathcal{P}(X), \cap, \cup, C)$ as a non-distributive system (with all other properties for the general case being valid). Thus the system will become distributive (by (v)) iff for all $A,B \in \mathcal{P}(X)$, $AB = BA$, i.e., there exists a fixed orthonormal matrix $P = (P_1,...,P_n)$ such that all $A \in \mathcal{P}(X)$ may be written as $A = \sum_{j\in\Lambda_A} P_j P_j^T$ for some $\Lambda_A \subseteq \{1,...,n\}$, etc.

In addition, Watanabe defines an extended information theory, where for any $G = G(P,W) \in X$,

$$Ent(G) = -tr(G\cdot(\log G)) = Ent(W) = \sum_{j=1}^{n} - w_j \log w_j .$$

Watanabe then extends the following basic theroem in a natural way to the above example: The entropy of a joint probability function which has independent marginals is the sum of the entropies of both and exceeds the entropy of any other joint probability function with the same specified marginals.

Finally, Watanabe proposes that in the pattern recognition or classification problem, one may re-interpret the membership function within the same basic geometric setting as

$$\phi_A(x) \overset{d}{=} \|A\cdot x\|^2/\|x\|^2$$

where $A = \sum_{j\in\Lambda_1} P_j P_j^T \in \mathcal{P}(X)$ as before; A is interpreted as the class or pattern against which observation $x = \begin{bmatrix} x_1 \\ \vdots \\ x_n \end{bmatrix} \in X \subseteq \mathbb{R}^n$ is to be tested for membership. In practice, Watanabe concludes, rnk(A) will be of a relatively low dimension compared to both n and sample sizes used to empirically establish a typical candidate A .

7.4 Gaines' uncertainty logic.

We discuss here a simplified but more general variation of Gaines' uncertainty logic [66], [68] which simultaneously extends ordinary probability logic and Zadeh's fuzzy sets.

Let X be any nonvacuous set of predicates and "&" , "or" be two arbitrary binary operations defined on X which are symmetric and associative and "not" a unary operator on X . Let $\mathcal{P}(X)$ be the class of all finite well-formed strings from X under these operations with distinguished elements T and $F \in \mathcal{P}(X)$ such that for all $p \in \mathcal{P}(X)$,

$$\begin{cases} (T \mathbin{\&} p) = p = (F \text{ or } p) \\ (T \text{ or } p) = T \; ; \; (F \mathbin{\&} p) = F \; . \end{cases}$$

(Note the similarity to the usual meaning of $\mathcal{P}(X)$: the power class on X .)

For any sequence $p_1, p_2, \cdots \in \mathcal{P}(X)$,

$$p_1 \& p_2 \& \cdots \in \mathcal{P}(X) \; ; \; p_1 \text{ or } p_2 \text{ or } \cdots \in \mathcal{P}(X) \; .$$

Let $\|\cdot\| : \mathcal{P}(X) \to [0,1]$ be a *truth mapping* such that

(1) $\|(T)\| = 1 \; , \; \|(F)\| = 0 \; ;$

For any $p,q \in \mathcal{P}(X)$,

(2) $\|(p \mathbin{\&} q)\| \le \min(\|p\|,\|q\|)) \; ;$

(3) $\|(p \text{ or } q)\| \ge \max(\|p\|,\|q\|) \; ;$

(4) $\|\cdot\|$ is continuous from above and below, i.e., for any sequence $p_1, p_2, \cdots \in \mathcal{P}(x)$,

$$\|(p_1 \mathbin{\&} p_2 \mathbin{\&} \cdots)\| = \lim_{n\to\infty} \|(p_1 \mathbin{\&} p_2 \mathbin{\&} \cdots \mathbin{\&} p_n)\|$$

$$\|(p_1 \text{ or } p_2 \text{ or} \cdots)\| = \lim_{n\to\infty} \|(p_1 \text{ or } p_2 \text{ or} \cdots \text{or } p_n)\| \; .$$

Call the system $(\mathcal{P}(X), \&, \text{or})$ an *uncertainty logic*.

Now suppose in addition to $(\mathcal{P}(X), \&, \text{or})$ being an uncertainty logic,

(PI) "&" and "or" satisfy in addition the basic relations of mutual distributivity and

(PII) $\|\cdot\|$ is a valuation mapping:
For all $p,q \in \mathcal{P}((X)$,

$$\|(p \text{ or } q)\| = \|p\| + \|q\| - \|(p \mathbin{\&} q)\|$$

and the negation law holds.

(PIII) $1 = \|(p \text{ or } \text{not}(p)\| = \|p\| + \|(\text{not } p)\|$.

From this, we can show for any $p,q \in \mathcal{P}(X)$: the Law of Excluded Middle holds:

$\|(p \& \text{ not } p)\| = 0$, since $1 = \|(p \text{ or not } p)\| = \|p\| + \|(\text{not } p)\|$

$- \|(p \& \text{ not } p)\| = 1 - \|(p \& \text{ not } p)\|$,

$\|q\| = \|((p \& \text{ not } p)\text{or } q)\| = \|(p \text{ or } q)\&(\text{not } p \text{ or } q)\|$

$= \|((p \text{ or not } p)\& q)\| = \|(p \& q)\text{or}(\text{not } p \& q))\|$

$= \|(p \& q)\| + \|(\text{not } p \& q)\|$.

Also,

$\|(p \text{ or } q)\| = \|p\| + (\|q\|-\|(p \& q)\|) = \|p\| + \|(\text{not } p \& q)\|$

noting $\|(p \&(\text{not } p \& q)\| \equiv 0$.

If $\|(p \& q)\| = \|(p \text{ or } q)\|$, then

$$\|(p)\| = \|(p \& q)\| = \|(p \text{ or } q)\| = \|q\| .$$

Also, idempotency holds

$\|p\| = \|(p \&(p \text{ or not } p))\|$

$= \|((p \& p) \text{ or } (p \& \text{ not } p))\| = \|(p \& p)\|$.

Also, DeMorgan's Laws hold

$$\begin{aligned}
\|(\text{not } p \text{ or not } q)\| &= \|(\text{not } p)\| + \|(\text{not } q)\| - \|(\text{not } p \& \text{ not } q)\| \\
&= \|(\text{not } p)\| = \|(\text{not } p \& \text{ not } q)\| + \|\text{not } q\| \\
&= \|(\text{not } p \& q)\| + \|\text{not } q\| \\
&= (\|q\| - \|(p \& q)\|) + \|\text{not } q\| \\
&= 1 - \|(p \& q)\| \\
&= \|(\text{not}(p \& q))\| ,
\end{aligned}$$

$$\begin{aligned}
\|(\text{not } p \& \text{ not } q)\| &= \|\text{not } p\| + \|\text{not } q\| - \|(\text{not } p \text{ or not } q)\| \\
&= 1 - \|p\| + 1 - \|q\| - \|(\text{not}(p \& q))\| \\
&= 1 - (\|p\| + \|q\| - \|(p \& q))\|) \\
&= 1 - \|(p \text{ or } q)\| \\
&= \|(\text{not}(p \text{ or } q))\|
\end{aligned}$$

Also, we have countable additivity:
For any $p_1,p_2,\ldots \in \mathcal{P}(X)$ with $\|(p_i \& p_j))\| = 0$ for all $i \neq j$,

$$\|(p_1 \text{or } p_2 \text{or} \cdots \text{or} \cdots)\| = \lim_{n\to\infty} \|(p_1 \text{or} \cdots \text{or } p_n)\|$$

$$= \lim_{n\to\infty} \sum_{j=1}^{n} \|p_j\| = \sum_{j=1}^{\infty} \|p_j\| .$$

This yields a probability logic (see section 2.3.9 (A) and Rescher [214]), where it should be noted that here the mapping $\|\cdot\| : \mathcal{P}(X) \to [0,1]$ is not, in general, a truth functional in the sense that there is no function such as $\phi_\&$ for "&" nor ϕ_{or} for "or" nor ϕ_{not} for "not", such that for all $p,q \in \mathcal{P}(X)$,

$$\|(p \& q)\| = \phi_\&(\|p\|,\|q\|) ,$$

as is true for many general logical systems - including general fuzzy set systems, where $\phi_{\&}$ is a t-norm, ϕ_{or}, a t-conorm, ϕ_{not}, a negation, etc. However, do not confuse this with the probability algebra system $\mathcal{F}' = (\phi_{not}, \phi_{\&}, \phi_{or}) = (1 - (\cdot), \text{prod}, \text{bndsum})$ relative to discrete spaces, where, in effect, the predicates $p \in \mathcal{P}(X)$ are replaced by probability functions over X.

Thus, e.g., suppose we let $\mathcal{P}(X)$ be $\mathbb{B}_2$ (the real Borel field on $\mathbb{R}^2$) with $\& = \cap$, or $= \cup$, not $= C$, $T = \mathbb{R}^2$, $F = \emptyset$ and $\|\cdot\|$ be any probability measure over $\mathbb{B}_2$, then we do have a truth functional system over all pairs of events of the form

$$p_x \overset{d}{=} (-\infty, x] \times \mathbb{R}, \quad q_y \overset{d}{=} \mathbb{R} \times (-\infty, y]$$

for any $x, y \in \mathbb{R}$, since by Sklar's theorem, corresponding to $\|\cdot\|$ there is a unique *copula* $\phi_{\&}$ such that for all $x, y \in \mathbb{R}$

$$\|(p_x \;\&\; q_y)\| = \phi_{\&}(\|p_x\|, \|q_y\|),$$

and hence

$$\|(p_x \text{ or } q_y)\| = \|p_x\| + \|q_y\| - \phi_{\&}(\|p_x\|, \|q_y\|)$$

(although in general, unless $\phi_{\&}$ is Frankian in form - see 2.3.6 - $\|(p_x \text{or } q_y)\|$ is not a legitimate t-conorm) and

$$\|\text{not } p_x\| = 1 - \|p_x\|.$$

Particular examples of choices for $\|\cdot\|$ include $\phi_{\&} = \min$, corresponding to the two marginal random variables being maximally (positively) correlated, $\phi_{\&} = \text{prod}$, which Gaines calls the "stochastic logic" case, corresponding to statistical independence of the marginal random variables, and $\phi_{\&} = \text{maxsum}$, corresponding to the marginal random variables being most negatively correlated.

However, in general, for the same probability space as above, we do not have a truth functional system over all $\mathcal{P}(X)$, since, e.g., take p to be any fixed subset of $\mathbb{B}_2$ such that (assuming one exists) $\|p\| = 1/2$. But then take not $p = Cp$. In this case, $\|Cp\| = 1/2$ also, but note

$$\|(p \;\&\; p)\| = 1/2 > 0 = \|(p \;\&\; Cp)\|.$$

On the other hand, it follows that any general fuzzy set system $\mathcal{F} = (\phi_{not}, \phi_{\&}, \phi_{or})$ - ϕ_{not} a negation, $\phi_{\&}$ a t-norm and ϕ_{or} a t-conorm - over $\mathcal{P}(X)$ is also an uncertainty logic where $\|\cdot\|$ may be extended unambiguously to satisfy the continuity conditions, by using the continuity and nondecreasing properties of $\phi_{\&}$ and ϕ_{or}.

Gaines presents a scheme for empirically modeling any truth mapping over an uncertainty logic. (Again, we modify it to fit our more general approach.):

Evaluate empirically first X by the usual sample percentage response of a population answering affirmatively to the question "Is p true or not?" , for each $p \in X$. This corresponds formally to the estimation of unknown parameter $\|p\|$ for a zero-one random variable V_p . For a probability logic approach, interpret "&", "or", "not" in the usual senses and estimate compound predicate truth evaluations such as $\|(p \& q)\|$ by those who replied "yes" to both "p true?" and "q true?" , while for $\|(p \text{ or } q)\|$, obtain the percentage who reply affirmatively to one or both questions, etc. In this case, it follows that the estimator $\widehat{\|\cdot\|}$ of $\|\cdot\|$ can easily be made to fit the required probability logic structure. Since a general fuzzy set system is truth functional we need only obtain, in addition to $\widehat{\|p\|}$, $p \in X$, as above, empirically $\hat{\phi}_{\&}$, $\hat{\phi}_{or}$, $\hat{\phi}_{not}$ by discretizing $[0,1]$ into disjoint cells $C_j = [\frac{j}{m}, \frac{j+1}{m}]$, $j = 0,1,\ldots,m-1$, picking any two cells C_i and C_j , obtaining all $p,q \in X$ for which $\widehat{\|p\|} \in C_i$ and $\widehat{\|q\|} \in C_j$, then computing for each such pair p,q , $\hat{\phi}_{\&}(p,q) \overset{d}{=} \|(p,\hat{q})\|$ as obtained in the probability logic approach, and finally compute the pooled sum $\sum\limits_{\substack{\text{over all } p,q \\ \widehat{\|p\|} \in C_i, \widehat{\|q\|} \in C_j}} (\|(p,\hat{q})\|/\text{card}(C_i)\cdot\text{card}(C_j))$ where $\text{card}(C_k)$ is the number of $p \in X$ which have $\widehat{\|p\|} \in C_k$, $k = i,j$. Analagous computations should be carried out for $\hat{\phi}_{or}$ and $\hat{\phi}_{not}$.

Gaines' original version is directed to specifically generalizing Lukasiewicz $\aleph_1$-logic and Rescher's probability logic, so that he also considers, e.g., the Lukasiewicz implication operator. Although Lukasiewicz $\aleph_1$-logic corresponds to $\mathcal{F}_o = (1 - (\cdot),\ \min,\ \max)$, its implication operator in effect, in the form $\phi_{\Rightarrow}(u,v) = \phi_{or}(1 - u,v)$, actually corresponds to ϕ_{or} = bndsum, yielding

$$\phi_{\Rightarrow}(u,v) = \min\ (1 - u + v,1) ,$$

whence equivalence $\phi_{\Leftrightarrow}$ is given by $\phi_{\Leftrightarrow}(u,v) = 1 - |u-v|$, for all $u,v \in [0,1]$.

Figure A presents a simplified view of the general processing flow of acquired information and the relative degrees of generality of some of the more important logical systems discussed previously which can treat this information.

7.5 Schefe's agreement probabilities.

Schefe [224] presents both criticism of Zadeh's fuzzy logic and an attempt at replacing fuzzy set theory by a system closely aligned to probability theory.

Schefe desires to connect Zadeh's basic (first order) fuzzy set theory with probabilities, but rejects the fuzzy set membership concept. In place of membership-grade mapping, equivalently, he replaces the values of a membership function in the unit interval [0,1] by subsets of the unit interval. We simplify and extend his concepts:

Let X be a fixed space and define set-valued map $f_o : \mathcal{P}(X) \to \mathbb{B}[0,1]$, the real Borel field over $[0,1]$, generated, e.g., by the class $\mathcal{B}_o \overset{d}{=} \{[0,x] \mid 0 \le x \le 1\}$, where f_o is bijective (thus limiting the possible elements of $\mathcal{P}(X)$), $\mathcal{P}(X)$ is the class of all (compound) predicates of interest and $\mathcal{P}_o(X) \subseteq \mathcal{P}(X)$ is such that f_o is bijective over $\mathcal{P}_o(X)$ relative to $\mathcal{B}_o$, where for any $a \in \mathcal{P}_o(X)$, a is typically of the form $(y \in A)$ (A to be defined), $y \in X$ with $f_o(a) = f_o((y \in A)) = [0,x_a] \in \mathcal{B}_o$. Thus $[0,1]$-Lebesgue probability space $([0,1], \mathbb{B}[0,1], vol_1)$ induces probability space $(\mathcal{P}(X), f_o^{-1}(\mathcal{B}_o[0,1]), P)$, with

$$P \overset{d}{=} vol_1 \circ f_o$$

called the *agreement probability*.

In addition, using f_o, in a natural way, we can define operations $\vee, \wedge, C, \Rightarrow$ over $\mathcal{P}(X)$: For any $a_1,\ldots,a_n \in \mathcal{P}(X)$,

$$\bigvee_{j=1}^{n} a_j \overset{d}{=} f_o^{-1}\Big(\bigcup_{j=1}^{n} f_o(a_j)\Big)$$

$$\bigwedge_{j=1}^{n} a_j \overset{d}{=} f_o^{-1}\Big(\bigcap_{j=1}^{n} f_o(a_j)\Big) ,$$

$$C a_1 \overset{d}{=} f_o^{-1}(C\, f_o(a_1))$$

$$(a_1 \Rightarrow a_2) \overset{d}{=} f_o^{-1}(C\, f_o(a_1) \cup f_o(a_2)) , \text{ etc.}$$

Hence f_o is a lattice isomorphism for $\vee$, $\wedge$, etc. Also

$$P\Big(\bigvee_{j=1}^{n} a_j\Big) = vol_1\Big(\bigcup_{j=1}^{n} f_o(a_j)\Big)$$

$$P(C\, a_1) = vol_1(C\, f_o(a_1)) , \text{ etc.}$$

In particular, for all $a_1,\ldots,a_n \in \mathcal{P}_o(X)$, it follows that

$$P(\bigvee_{j=1}^{n} a_j) = \max_{1 \le j \le n} x_{a_j}$$

$$P(\bigwedge_{j=1}^{n} a_j) = \min_{1 \le j \le n} x_{a_j}$$

$$P(C\, a_1) = 1 - x_{a_1}$$

$$P(a_1 \Rightarrow a_2) = \min(1, 1 - x_{a_1} + x_{a_2}) \text{ , etc.}$$

On the other hand, for $a_1, a_2 \in \mathcal{P}(X)$ with $f_o(a_1)$ and $f_o(a_2)$ independent events w.r.t. vol_1,

$$P(a_1 \wedge a_2) = P(a_1)\cdot P(a_2)$$

$$P(a_1 \vee a_2) = P(a_1) + P(a_2) - P(a_1)\cdot P(a_2) \text{ .}$$

In turn, define

$$\mathcal{A}_o(X) \overset{d}{=} \{A \mid A \overset{d}{=} (a_y)_{y\in X} \text{ , } a_y \in \mathcal{P}_o(X) \text{ , } y \in X\} \text{ ,}$$

$$\subseteq \mathcal{A}(X) \overset{d}{=} \{A \mid A \overset{d}{=} (a_y)_{y\in X} \text{ , } a_y \in \mathcal{P}(X) \text{ , } y \in X\} \text{ .}$$

Any $A \in \mathcal{A}_o(X)$ is called an *elementary agreement probabilistic set*, while $A \in \mathcal{A}(X)$ in general is a compound agreement probabilistic set with membership-grade mapping $\tau_A : X \to (P(a_y))_{y\in X}$ with the following operations defined over $\mathcal{A}_o(X)$: For any

$$A = (a_y)_{y\in X} \text{ , } B = (b_y)_{y\in X} \text{ , define}$$

$$A \cup B \overset{d}{=} (a_y \vee b_y)_{y\in X}$$

whence for any $y \in X$,

$$\tau_{A\cup B}(y) = (P(a_y \vee b_y))_{y\in X} \text{ ,}$$

and similarly for $A \cap B$, CA , $A \Rightarrow B$, etc.

Hence it follows immediately that $\mathcal{A}_o(X)$ and $\mathcal{F}(X)$ are bijective under, mapping $\tau(\cdot)$ which is also an isomorphism w.r.t. $\cap$ and $\cup$. But note that C and $\cap$, e.g., preserve the Law of Excluded Middle unlike fuzzy set theory or more generally, for generalized logical systems.

For any $A \in A_o(X)$,

$$\tau_{A\cap CA} = 0 = (0)_{y\in X} \text{ .}$$

Similarly, other classical relations no longer true in fuzzy set theory remain true for agreement probabilistic sets and their operations. In addition, Schefe investigates, to some degree, possible definitions for conditional agreement probabilities.

Schefe is unaware of any of the more direct natural relations between fuzzy sets and random sets as set membership functions as well as with the evaluation of random variables over compound events ([90], [116], [86] and Chapters 3 - 6).

Schefe's criticism of Zadeh's fuzzy logic is illuminating:

(i) He points out that the subjective interpretation of a fuzzy set membership function (e.g., [105] or [71] or Chapter 8), $\phi_A(x)$ at some point $x \in X$, is the degree of certainty or precision that x has property A interpreted as non-fuzzy by Schefe - indeed in terms of his agreement probabilities and membership-grade mappings, rather than the interpretation that x has A or x is in A to degree $\phi_A(x)$. Furthermore, he claims that taking $1 - (\cdot)$ as a standard negation operation, $1 - \phi_A(x)$ is to be interpreted as "$x \in A$ is $(1-\phi_A(x))$-uncertain" but not as "$(x \notin A)$ is $(1 - \phi_A(x))$-certain". Hence, according to Schefe, we must obtain additional evidence concerning x not having property A, even when we have the certainty level for x having A. In this regard, Schefe examines Shortliffe's certainty factors approach to combining evidence [236] (or [120]) and exhibits similarities and differences (such as inducing the ability to handle conjunctions of independent events) with his agreement probability model. (See also section 8.3.)

(ii) Difficulties occur in modeling fuzzy set membership functions, including these due to statistical and cognition uncertainties. But again, Schefe fails to see that the same problems arise in the modeling of probability distributions. Suitable parameterization of the family of membership functions being considered can be a reasonable approach to this problem analogous to classical statistical modeling.

(iii) However, Schefe's criticism that the intersection of fuzzy sets (under min) produces subnormal (i.e., maximal value of the membership functions being less than unity) fuzzy sets, which may not reflect the linguistic situation, is not on firm ground. (See a similar type argument in 10.2 A (I).) Consider Schefe's example of "large" $\wedge$ "not large" = "moderate size". This should really be replaced by "not small" $\wedge$ not large" = "moderate size" where "large" $\neq$ "not small". Indeed, Schefe himself points out Hersh and Carramazza's empirical results [109], indicating that "not large" is less precise than "small". In the second definition of "moderate," the following more compatible result may well abtain:

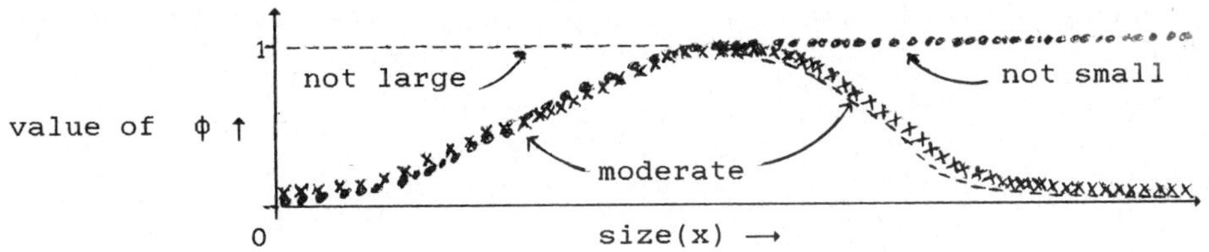

(iv) Problems in modeling hedges (as well as negations) are indicated by Schefe. Zadeh's square transform ([15], e.g.) or, more generally, exponential transform on fuzzy set membership functions to indicate an intensification such as "very ( )" as indicated in [109] by emperical studies, probably would be better modeled by a translation operation. (See also section 9 (C).) In a related vein, as pointed out above, the antonym "not small" ≠ "large" and a new operation are required to captive the lack of precision in "not small" as compared to the simple negation of "large". (See [199] for some related topics. See also the comments in, 2.3.8 (B).)

(v) Finally, Schefe points out some inadequacies in fuzzy set models involving vague inference, including one treating the premises " x knows y", "y knows z" with fuzzy conclusion "x may know Z , too". However, if more information in the conclusion were desired, a more specific binary relation should be used such as $(x,y,z) \in X \stackrel{d}{=}$ set of all people who work at A and "know" replaced by "know well". As premises become more descriptive so do conclusions. Schefe's appeal to simple statistical correlation as a measure of friendship itself is inadequate, since a multiple attribute approach would probably be more appropriate: " x knows y" can be measured in terms of frequency of lunches together, visitations to common work areas, number of items borrowed from each other over a time period, reference to each other's names, lengths of natural conversations, etc.

Additional remarks.

Lake [149] has suggested use of the function (in place of set) - axiom approach of Von Neumann, which would encompass ordinary set theory, fuzzy set theory and multiset concepts.

Birkhoff in Chapter 10 of his basic book [17] presents a most succinct account of attributes, propositional calculus, quantum mechanics, modal and multivalued logic, and probability theory.

CHAPTER 8

INFERENCE USING GENERAL LOGICAL SYSTEMS

This chapter is devoted to the development of inference procedures useful in knowledge-based systems.

8.1 Knowledge representation

The problem of analyzing and representing states of knowledge has been basically treated in AI systems as in classical probabilistic approaches by establishing models using:

(1) Conditional (possibilistic or probabilistic) distributions (or dispersions) representing e.g., in medical diagnoses problems, relationships between patients' symptoms and disease states, and

(2) Conditional distributions representing observed data errors.

Tribus [252] considers probability assignments to information available as a numerical encoding of states of knowledge. For the linguistic information analogue, possibility assignments, such as proposed by Zadeh [290], may suffice as the numerical evaluation of states of knowledge. See also Felsen [57'].

Due to the concept of a general logical system, as developed in Chapter 2, both Zadeh's possibilistic and the more classical probabilistic, approach to knowledge representation may be treated in a general unified manner.

As mentioned at the end of the Preface, this treatise is concerned with developing appropriate models for handling different types of uncertainty involved in knowledge-based systems, and is not about the "theory" of knowledge-based systems per se. However, we will summarize here some of the relevant issues involved in knowledge-based systems.

In addition to the reference cited in the preface ([12']), the interested reader should consult Bellman [13'], Davis and Lenat [44^{iv}], and Rich [216'], where knowledge-based systems are viewed as part of AI. In addition, the work of Spiegelhalter and Knill-Jones [246], where comparisons between AI and statistical techniques are presented, may be applied to the analysis of knowledge-based systems.

Knowledge-based systems are basically systems which can use human knowledge (sometimes, expert knowledge) to perform tasks through some reasoning process. At an "intelligent" level, these systems should be able to do things which require some form of human intelligence, e.g., decision-making under uncertainty.

As stated earlier (see section 2.1), natural language is a priviledged channel of communications of humans, so it is therefore reasonable, for example, to consider understanding natural language as an appropriate (albeit, ideal) goal for machine intelligence.

This requires the modeling of knowledge acquisition, knowledge representation, and knowledge utilization. (In this text, emphasis is mostly upon the latter two areas.) Often, part of the modeling is based upon knowledge gleaned from experts - leading to the design of "expert" systems. On the other hand, mathematical logic can also be used in the modeling, especially in the representational aspect. However, as Rich [216'] points out, it may be more appropriate to use more flexible logics than simply the classical one, such as Probability Logic, Fuzzy Logic or some "non-monotone" logic. For example, in the case of incomplete information, a type of "default" reasoning is suggested.

At this state-of-the-art, basic objectives in the field of knowledge-based systems can be handled by declarative methods (consisting of facts and procedures/rules for manipulating facts) or by procedural methods (where knowledge is represented as procedures/rules for using it). Examples of declarative representations of knowledge are conceptual dependency, frames, semantic networks, and scripts. Default reasoning and probabilistic reasoning can be considered as procedural methods. Often, a combination of the two above methods is used. Knowledge representation structures can be syntactically oriented - where, e.g., classical predicate calculus and logic are utilized - or can be more semantically oriented - where conceptual dependency, frames and semantic networks are employed, etc. In a related vein, Zadeh's PRUF [283] approach should be again mentioned.

Analysis of knowledge-based systems also requires the modeling of perception, judgment, integration of knowledge, and cognitive processes in general [98'], [25], [38], [157], [274']. Another related area involved in knowledge modeling is that of the mental representation of concepts and concept prototypes. See, e.g., Cohen and Murphy [40'] also Osherson and Smith [198'], where the theory of fuzzy sets has been considered. Specifically, a concept is regarded as a definition of a term (in some natural language) or a statement of the defining conditions for membership in the class designated by the term . A theory of prototype was suggested as follows: a concept C (in a given natural language), e.g., "bird", "red", "table", "red table", is not sharply defined, and hence should be considered as a fuzzy set of some universe of discourse, say, a base space X , elements of which are objects related to C . The notion of membership in C is specified by a membership function $\phi_C : X \to [0,1]$. A special member $x_o \in X$ is chosen based upon some criterion determined by a given metric d on X . This special x_o is called the concept's prototype. Thus a mental representation of C is a quadruple of the form $\langle X, D, x_o, \phi_C\rangle \overset{d}{\equiv} MR(C)$. In order to represent more complex concepts, in natural language, (e.g., as expressed by adjective-noun, noun-noun, such as "ocean drive", "night flight", etc.), the problem of conceptual combination, based on generalized set theory, has been discussed. As was pointed out in [198'], there is a need for considering different logical systems other than ("nt", "&", "or") = (1-(·), min, max) . Nevertheless, the negative conclusions of [198'] concerning the use of fuzzy set theory due to apparent "fallacies" is basically unfounded. (See section 10.2(A) for further discussions.)

8.2 A decision theory based on dispersions.

A generalized decision theory based on semantic evaluations of possible losses may be developed, extending the classical notions of probabilistic decision theory and statistical inference.

Let X be a fixed parameter space and D a fixed decision space and suppose L and A represent, respectively, loss and true values, jointly relative to $X \times D$. Indeed, assume L and A are both generalized subsets of $X \times D$, where

$$\phi_L \, , \, \phi_A \, : X \times D \to [0,1] \, .$$

In turn, expected loss in ordinary decision theory is replaced by the semantic evaluation for any $\tau \in D$,

$$\begin{aligned} E(\phi_{(D|\cdot)}) &\overset{d}{=} \|(\exists x)((x,\tau) \in L \cap A)\| \\ &= \phi_{\underset{x\in X}{or}}(\phi_{\&}(\phi_L(x,\tau), \phi_A(x,\tau))) \\ &= \phi_{\underset{y\in Y}{or}}(\phi_{\&}(\phi_{(L|y)}(\tau) \, , \, \phi_{(D|Y)}(\tau), \phi_B(y))) \, , \end{aligned}$$

assuming the Y-projection may be consistently carried out (see section 2.3.8 E), where

$$\phi_{(L|Y)}(\tau) \overset{d}{=} \phi_{\underset{x\in X}{or}}(\phi_{\&}(\phi_L(x,\tau), \phi_{(C|y)}(x))) \, ,$$

where it is assumed for all $\tau \in D$, $y \in Y$, $x \in X$,

$$\phi_{((A|y)|\tau)}(x) \equiv \phi_{(C|y)}(x)$$

and $\phi_B : Y \to [0,1]$ is given.

Thus, the Bayes decision function $\phi^*_{(D|\cdot)}$ will satisfy

$$\inf_{\substack{\text{all} \\ \phi(D|\cdot)}} E(\phi_{(D|\cdot)}) = E(\phi^*_{(D|\cdot)}) \, ,$$

where for all $y \in Y$,

$$\phi^*_{(D|y)}(\tau) = \delta_{\tau,\tau_y} \qquad \text{(Krönecker delta)},$$

where τ_Y is determined from

$$\phi_{(L|y)}(\tau_y) = \inf_{\tau\in D} \phi_{(L|y)}(\tau) \, .$$

For example, analagous to ordinary decision theory, if

$$L_\alpha(x,\tau) = \begin{cases} 1 & \text{if } \|x-\tau\| \le \alpha \\ 0 & \text{if } \|x-\tau\| > \alpha \end{cases} ,$$

then in a limiting sense, as α approaches zero, the Bayes decision function which yields $\inf_{\phi_{(D|\cdot)}} E(\phi_{(D|\cdot)})$ is

$$\phi_{(D|y)}(\tau) = \delta_{\tau,\phi_{(C|y)}} , \text{ for all } \tau \in D .$$

For simple hypotheses testing

$$\left.\begin{array}{ll} L(x,\tau) = a > 0 , & \text{iff } x \in H_1 \; \tau = H_o \\ L(x,\tau) = b > 0 , & \text{iff } x \in H_o , \tau = H_1 \\ L(x,\tau) = \;\; 0 \quad , & \text{iff } x \text{ and } \tau \text{ are} \\ & \text{otherwise.} \end{array}\right\} ,$$

where

$$X = H_o \cup H_1 , \; D = \{H_o,H_1\} ,$$

the Bayes decision function is equivalent to deciding H_1 *iff*

$$\phi_\&(a,\phi_{\underset{(x\in H_1)}{or}}(\phi_{(C|y)}(x))) \ge \phi_\&(b,\phi_{\underset{(x\in H_o)}{or}}(\phi_{(C|y)}(x))) ,$$

noting the further simplication of omitting $\phi_\&$, a , and b , when a = b = 1 .

Analogues to several concepts in ordinary statistical theory may be developed here, including maximum likelihood estimators, likelihood comparisons, invariant estimators, Neyman-Pearson-like hypotheses tests and confidence sets. However, these will differ in form - in some cases considerably - due to the lack of the constraint of summing to one for the possibility functions involved and due to the general forms for ϕ_{not} , $\phi_\&$, ϕ_{or} . It should be noted, if $\phi_{not} = 1 - (\cdot)$, $\phi_\& =$ prod, and $\phi_{or} =$ bndsum , and the possibility functions representing parameters and data are probability functions, then *all* of the above decision theory concepts reduce to the classical probabilistic counterparts.

The above development in general, is in contrast to other attempts to "fuzzify" ordinary decision theory, by replacing ordinary sets or operations involved by fuzzy ones. (See Dubois and Prade [51], pp. 277-296.)

To illustrate the above remarks, consider the following example of the construction of a possibilistic confidence set.

Let unknown parameter $\theta \in X = D = \mathbb{R}^P$, and suppose observed data vector $y \in Y = \mathbb{R}^m$, where

$$y = f(\theta) + \nu \; ; \quad \text{all } \theta \in X , \text{ all } \nu \in Y$$

with

$$f : X \to Y \quad \text{known.}$$
$$\hat{\theta} : Y \to X \quad \text{estimating function being h-invariant,}$$

where

$$h : Y \to X \quad \text{known,}$$

i.e.,

$$\hat{\theta}(y) = \theta + h(\nu) \; ; \text{ all } \theta \in X \, , \, \nu \in Y \, .$$

Let ν have possibility function ϕ_A not dependent on θ. Define, for any possible $\mathring{\theta} \in X$, $c > 0$, region $R_{\mathring{\theta},c} \subseteq X$ by

$$R_{\mathring{\theta},c} = \{\theta \mid \theta \in X \; \& \; |||\theta - \mathring{\theta}||| \le c\} \, .$$

$|||\cdot|||$ denoting vector norm (while $\|\cdot\|$ denotes truth value).

Then, for all $\theta \in X$,

$$\|(\theta \in R_{\hat{\theta}(\cdot),c} \mid \theta)\| = \| \underset{\text{all } \mathring{y}}{\text{Or}} (\theta \in R_{\hat{\theta}(y),c} \; \& \; y = \mathring{y})\|$$

$$= \| \underset{\{\mathring{y} \mid \; |||\hat{\theta}(\mathring{y}) - \theta||| \le c\}}{\text{Or}} (y = \mathring{y})\| \qquad = \| \underset{\{\mathring{\nu} \mid \; |||\mathring{\nu}||| \le c\}}{\text{Or}} (\nu = \mathring{\nu}) \|$$

$$= \underset{\{\mathring{\nu} \mid \; |||\mathring{\nu}||| \le c\}}{\phi_{or}} (\phi_A(\mathring{\nu})) \quad \overset{d}{=} \phi_{B(A)}(c) \, ,$$

a result not dependent on θ, assuming the truth functionality of evaluations relative to ϕ_{or}. Thus, $\phi_{B(A)} : \mathbb{R}^+ \to [0,1]$ is monotone increasing, in general.

Hence for any $0 < \alpha < 1$, defining C_α by

$$C_\alpha \overset{d}{=} g_A^{-1} \, (1 - \alpha) \, ,$$

$R_{\hat{\theta}(\cdot),C_\alpha}$ is a $(1 - \alpha)$-level possibility confidence region for θ, analagous to the classical statistical concept. Especially note, the linear regression reduction when B is m by p of rank p, $h(\nu) = \mathcal{A}\cdot\nu$, where $\mathcal{A} = (B^{T}\text{Cov}^{-1}(\nu)B)^{-1}B^{T}\text{Cov}^{-1}(\nu)$, $\phi_{or} = \text{bndsum}$, etc. (See, e.g., C.R. Rao [212].)

8.3 Combination of evidence problem.

Knowledge representation techniques play an important role in the design of expert systems; see, e.g., Nau [183] and Davis and Lenat [44']. At the control level, the problem of combining of evidences becomes essential in the technique known as problem reduction, e.g., in MYCIN (see Shortliffe and Buchanan [236]) where each problem can be decomposed into several simpler sub-problems.

Formally, Bayes' theorem for manipulation of conditional probabilities (in statistical systems) provides a rigorous probabilistic analysis.

Recall that the probabilistic combining function is derived as follows (see also Ishizuka, et al., [121]):

Let (Ω, A, Pr) be a probability space and $A, B, D \in \mathcal{A}$ such that $Pr(A)$, $Pr(B)$, $Pr(D)$ and $P(\bar{D})$ (where $\bar{D}$ is the set-complement of D) are all positive. Then we have:

$$Pr(D \mid A \cap B) = \left[1 + \frac{Pr(\bar{D}|A)Pr(\bar{D}|B)}{Pr(D|A)Pr(D|B)} \cdot \frac{Pr(D)}{Pr(\bar{D})} \right]^{-1}$$

provided $Pr(A \cap B|D) = Pr(A|D)Pr(B|D)$ and

$$Pr(A \cap B|\bar{D}) = Pr(A|\bar{D})Pr(B|\bar{D}) .$$

Indeed,

$$Pr(D|A \cap B) = \frac{Pr(A \cap B|D)Pr(D)}{Pr(A \cap B)}$$

$$= \frac{Pr(A|D)Pr(B|D)Pr(D)}{Pr(A \cap B)} = \frac{Pr(D|A)Pr(D|B)}{Pr(D)} \cdot \frac{Pr(A)Pr(B)}{Pr(A \cap B)} .$$

But $Pr(A \cap B) = Pr(A \cap B|D)Pr(D) + Pr(A \cap B|\bar{D})Pr(\bar{D})$

$$= \left[\frac{Pr(D|A)Pr(D|B)}{Pr(D)} + \frac{Pr(\bar{D}|A)Pr(\bar{D}|B)}{Pr(\bar{D})} \right] \cdot Pr(A)Pr(B) .$$

Thus:

$$\frac{Pr(A)Pr(B)}{Pr(A \cap B)} = \left[\frac{Pr(D|A)Pr(D|B)}{Pr(D)} + \frac{Pr(\bar{D}|A)Pr(\bar{D}|B)}{Pr(\bar{D})} \right]^{-1} .$$

In medicine for example, due to the lack of sufficient data and the imperfectness of judgmental knowledge, one is led to consider a more realistic measure of uncertainty known as the *certainty factor* (Shortliffe and Buchanan, [236]) which is an approximation of conditional probability. The problem of combining of certainty factors, or of other uncertainty measures, is important for decision processes. Dempster [46], followed by Shafer [228], generalized classical Bayesian analysis. Dempster in essence worked with multi-valued mappings (or random sets), while Shafer presented an axiomized version of the approach in the form of his "belief functions". Both addressed the problem of combination of evidence based upon Dempster's earlier work, Dempster [46]. The Dempster-Shafer theory of belief functions, which claims to provide a mechanism for handling doubt, ignorance and conflicting evidence, is receiving increasing attention in the AI literature. (See Spielgelhater and Knill-Jones [246].)

However, it should be emphasized that Dempster-Shafer theory is completely analyzable through the use of random sets and the Choquet capacity theorem (see section 3.2 or Nguyen [187], etc.). For example, the Dempster-Shafer rule of combination of evidence is in actuality the superset coverage function of the intersection of statistically independent random sets (see Goodman's comments [90] or the remark following Theorem 5, section 4.2).

Let us return to the concept of certainty factors.

Let $(\Omega, \mathcal{A}, Pr)$ be a probability space. For an event $H \in \mathcal{A}$, considered as a hypothesis, and an event $E \in \mathcal{A}$, considered as an evidence, the 'certainty factor for H in the light of E' is defined, assuming $0 < Pr(H) < 1$,

$$CF(H,E) \overset{d}{=} \begin{cases} \dfrac{Pr(H|E) - Pr(H)}{1 - Pr(H)}, & \text{if } Pr(H|E) \geq Pr(H), \\[2ex] \dfrac{Pr(H|E) - Pr(H)}{Pr(H)}, & \text{if } Pr(H|E) < Pr(H). \end{cases}$$

Remark:

The set function $\alpha : \mathcal{A} \to \overline{\mathbb{R}}^+$, where

$$\alpha(A) \overset{d}{=} \frac{Pr(A)}{1 - Pr(A)} \; ; \; A \in \mathcal{A}, \; Pr(A) \neq 1,$$

is the (prior) odds ratio of the event A. The conditional odds ratio of A given B is

$$\alpha_B(A) = \frac{Pr(A|B)}{1 - Pr(A)} .$$

Note also that, when $Pr(H|E) \geq Pr(H)$,

$$CF(H,E) = \alpha_E(H) - \alpha(H) .$$

Heuristically, the same interpretation of CF applies to the case $Pr(H|E) < Pr(H)$ with appropriate odds ratios.

The set-function α satisfies the following properties:

(i) $\alpha(A) \cdot \alpha(\complement A) = 1, \; \forall A \in \mathcal{A}$,

(ii) $A, B \in \mathcal{A}, \; A \subseteq B \Rightarrow \alpha(A) \leq \alpha(B)$

(iii) $A, B \in \mathcal{A}, \; A \cap B = \emptyset \Rightarrow \alpha(A \cup B) \geq \alpha(A) + \alpha(B)$ (superadditive),

(iv) If $A_n, B_n \in \mathcal{A}$, and $A_n \uparrow$ (Resp. $B_n \downarrow$), then $\alpha(A_n) \uparrow \alpha(\bigcup_n A_n)$ (resp. $\alpha(B_n) \downarrow \alpha(\bigcap_n A_n)$) (sequential ascending and descending continuity).

We can extend α from $\mathcal{A}$ to $\mathcal{P}(\Omega)$ by replacing Pr in the definition of α by its induced outer measure. If Ω is a topological space and $\mathcal{A}$ is its Borel σ-algebra, then it can be verified that α(or α_E) is a Choquet capacity.

Now, from the definition of CF(H,E), the problem of combination of evidence - namely, given $C(H,E_i)$, $i = 1,2$, say, find $CF(H,E_1$ and $E_2)$ - is centered around the following problem of calculus of probabilities: given $Pr(H|E_i)$, $i = 1,2$, find $Pr(H|E_1 \cap E_2)$.

Assuming independency between evidences, i.e., $Pr(E_1 \cap E_2|H) = Pr(E_1|H)Pr(E_2|H)$, an ad hoc combining function was proposed in MYCIN [236] in the following "truth functional" form:

$$CF(H,E_1 \cap E_2) = g[CF(H,E_1), CF(H,E_2)]$$

where

$$g(x,y) \overset{d}{=} \begin{cases} 1 & \text{if } x = 1 \text{ or } y = 1 \\ x + y - xy & \text{if } x > 0 \text{ and } y > 0 \\ x + y & \text{if } x \neq \pm 1,\ y \neq \pm 1 \text{ and } xy \leq 0 \\ x + y + xy & \text{if } x < 0 \text{ and } y < 0 \\ -1 & \text{if } x = -1 \text{ or } y = -1 \end{cases}$$

As it was pointed out in Ishizuka, et al. [120], $CF(H,E_1 \cap E_2)$, which is obtained by using the above combining function, is only an approximation since

$$g[CF(H,E_1), CF(H,E_2)] \neq \frac{Pr(H|E_1 \cap E_2) - Pr(H)}{1 - Pr(H)} .$$

A consistent combining function, always holding in the case of independent evidences, was proposed in Ishizuka, et al., [120]. The combining function turns out to be a function of $CF(H,E_i)$, $i = 1,2$, and of the prior odds ratio $\alpha(H)$. See also Ishizuka, et al., [121] for the problem of combination of evidence using Dempster and Shafer's theory.

In summary it has been proposed to combine evidence in the forms of:

(1) conditional probabilities using the classical Bayes' theorem,

(2) belief (and related) measures using Dempster-Shafer's rule of combination evidence,

(3) certainty factors (as approximating to conditional probabilities) using ad hoc procedures.

Typically, in applying Dempster-Shafer theory to problems of combining evidence or in estimating unknown parameters, the relevant belief measures, doubt measures, plausibility measures, etc., must be known exactly or up to some class. (See, e.g., Shafer [228].) However, the results of section 3.2 show that there is, up to distributional considerations, bijective relations between such uncertainty measures and corresponding random sets, and as well, between belief and doubt measures, doubt and plausibility measures, etc. In practice, it may be too difficult to obtain the necessary probability measures corresponding to the random sets of interest. This is often due to combinatorial considerations: for a space X, $2^{\mathrm{card}(X)} = \mathrm{Card}\,\mathcal{P}(X)$ probability values are involved for S, any random subset of X. A reasonable weakening of the above requirements is a specification of only the k-coverage functions of the random sets involved for some suitable finite k. In particular, $k = 1$ yields the weakest level of specifying information, $k = 2$, less weak, etc. See sections 5.2, 5.3 for further details concerning the spectrum of specification of random sets through their multiple point coverage functions. Also, it has been shown (section 5.2) that the k-point coverage determination of random sets is essentially equivalent to the specification of a corresponding multiple membership function, i.e., the semantic evaluation of the distinguished k-place signature membership predicate symbol $\in_{i_1 \times \cdots \times i_k}$ between k variables and k-place attributes of generalized sets. In particular, the case $k = 1$ corresponds to the simple membership symbol $\in_i$ (or just $\in$). (See section 2.3.5.)

With the above in mind, we can consider for purposes of simplicity only the case $k = 1$ and develop an approach to the combination of evidence through simple dispersions representing the semantic evaluation of the relevant membership relations between the unknown parameters of interest and their attributes.

Finally, it should be noted that this approach is a generalization of the case involving conditional probabilities, when Probability Logic is used for the semantic evaluations.

The following approach to the combination of evidence within a general multi-valued logical set theory context may be modified in a straightforward way for changes in the assumptions. Here it is assumed that:

(a) A collection of joint posterior membership functins ϕ_{C_k} is available:

$$\phi_{C_k}(\theta_k, z_k \mid y_k) \; ; \; k \in J ,$$

where $C_k \in \mathcal{F}(X \times D_k)$; $\theta_k \in X$ represents the common values of unknown parameter vector $\theta \in X$, $z_k \in D_k$ represents a nuisance parameter; and $y_k \in Y_k$ represents data, all for source $k \in J$, the collection index set of sources. J may be finite or infinite.

(b) A fuzzy set system $(\phi_{nt}, \phi_{\&}, \phi_{or})$ is chosen for the logical operators. More generally, a single logical system or a collection of logical systems could be chosen, but for simplicity, only the former will be treated. For justification for choosing a particular fuzzy set system (or systems), see Chapter 9.

Then, assuming no interactions from the overall joint posterior function,

$$\phi_{C_o}(\underset{\sim}{\theta},\underset{\sim}{z}|\underset{\sim}{y}) = \text{"}(\underset{\sim}{\theta},\underset{\sim}{z}) \in \underset{k\in J}{\times} C_k \mid \underset{\sim}{y}\text{"}$$

$$= \underset{k\in J}{\phi_\&} (\phi_{C_k}(\theta_k, z_k|y_k)) ,$$

$$(= \phi_{\underset{k\in J}{\times} C_k}(\underset{\sim}{\theta},\underset{\sim}{z}|\underset{\sim}{y})) ,$$

where

$$\underset{\sim}{\theta} \overset{d}{=} (\theta_k)_{k\in J} , \underset{\sim}{z} \overset{d}{=} (z_k)_{k\in J} ; \underset{\sim}{y} \overset{d}{=} (y_k)_{k\in J} .$$

In turn, the nuisance parameters may be eliminated by the projection

$$\phi_{\text{proj}_X(C_o)}(\underset{\sim}{\theta}|\underset{\sim}{y}) = \text{"} \underset{\underset{\sim}{z}\in D_o}{\text{Or}} (\phi_{C_o}(\underset{\sim}{\theta},\underset{\sim}{z}|\underset{\sim}{y}))\text{"}$$

$$= \underset{\underset{\sim}{z}\in D_o}{\phi_{or}} (\phi_{C_o}(\underset{\sim}{\theta},\underset{\sim}{z}|\underset{\sim}{y})) ,$$

where

$$D_o \overset{d}{=} \underset{k\in J}{\times} D_k .$$

The unnormalized diagonal set diag $\in \mathcal{F}(X)$ is determined by the constraint

$$\phi_{diag}(\theta|\underset{\sim}{y}) = (\phi_{\text{proj}_X(C_o)}(\underset{\sim}{\theta}|\underset{\sim}{y})) , \theta_k = \theta , k \in J ; \text{ all } \theta \in X .$$

Let univ $\in \mathcal{F}(\mathcal{F}(X))$ be a universal set representing all possible (fuzzy) sets describing θ . Then at diag ,

$$\phi_{univ}(\text{diag}) = \underset{\theta\in X}{\phi_{or}}(\phi_{diag}(\theta|\underset{\sim}{y})) .$$

Noting the identification

$$\phi_{diag\text{-}univ}(\theta,\text{diag}|\underset{\sim}{y}) = \phi_{diag}(\theta|\underset{\sim}{y}) ,$$

the desired conditional possibility function $\phi(\theta|\text{diag}, \underset{\sim}{y})$ is obtained from the relation

$$\phi_{diag}(\theta|\underset{\sim}{y}) = \phi_\&(\phi(\theta|\text{diag},\underset{\sim}{y}), \phi_{univ}(\text{diag})) .$$

In particular, suppose : $X = \mathbb{R}^j$, J finite, $\phi_\& = \text{prod}$, $\phi_{or} = \text{probsum}$, $D_o = \emptyset$,

$$\phi(\theta_k \mid y_k ; k) = \Psi_j(\theta_k - \mu_k(y_k), C_k)\cdot \Delta_k(\theta_k)$$

where Ψ_j is the j-dimensional multivariate Gaussian p.d.f., $\mu_k(y_k)$ is an estimator of the true value for θ_k, C_k is a corresponding covariance matrix of error, and $\Delta_k(\theta_k)$ is the X-volume of a sufficiently small X-cube (cell) $C_k(\theta_k)$ surrounding $\theta_k \in X$, $k \in J$.

It then follows that (approximately, becoming more accurate as $\Delta_k(\theta_k) \to 0$, $k \in J$)

$$\phi(\theta \mid \text{diag}, \underset{\sim}{y})$$
$$= \Psi(\theta - \overline{\mu}(\underset{\sim}{y}), \overline{C})\cdot \Delta_k(\theta_k),$$

where

$$\overline{\mu}(\underset{\sim}{y}) \stackrel{d}{=} \overline{C}\cdot \sum_{k\in J} (C_k^{-1}\cdot \mu_k(y_k)),$$

$$\overline{C} = \left[\sum_{k\in J} C_k^{-1}\right]^{-1}.$$

Note that $(\overline{\mu}(\underset{\sim}{y}), \overline{C}_j)$ represents the standard BLUE (best linear unbiased estimator) statistical estimator of θ.

Consider again the ϕ_{C_k}'s in general where

$\phi_{C_k}(\theta_k, z_k \mid y_k)$; all $\theta_k \in X$, $z_k \in Z_k$, $k \in J$, with all of the above definitions holding.

The following theorems are direct consequences of these definitions (see Goodman [86]):

Theorem 1

If $J = \{1,2,3,\ldots\}$,

$$\varnothing = \{\theta \mid \theta \in X \ \& \ \lim_{k\to+\infty} \phi_{C_k}(\theta, z_k \mid y_k) = 1\},$$

for all $z \in D_o$, and if $\phi_\&$ is an Archimedean t-norm (see section 2.3.6), then

$$\phi_{\text{diag}}(\theta \mid \underset{\sim}{y}) = 0 \ ; \ \text{all} \ \theta \in X.$$

Remark 1.

If $\phi_\& = \min$, then in general

$$\phi_{diag}(\theta|\underset{\sim}{y}) > 0 \ ; \text{ all } \ \theta \in X \ .$$

Recall from section (5.2) the bijective relation between flou classes (or collections of nested level sets) and membership functions. Thus

$$r(C_o|\underset{\sim}{y}) \stackrel{d}{=} (\phi_{C_o}^{-1}[\alpha,1])_{\alpha\in[0,1]}$$

corresponds uniquely to ϕ_{C_o} .

Define also for any t-norm $\phi_\&$ the flou class of conjunctive information as

$$M(\underset{\sim}{C}, \phi_\&|\underset{\sim}{y}) = \left[\bigcap_{k\in J} \phi_{C_k}^{-1}[\alpha,1]\right]_{\alpha\in[0,1]} .$$

Then

Theorem 2

$$r(C_o|\underset{\sim}{y}) \subseteq M(C,\phi_\&|\underset{\sim}{y}) ,$$

for all $\underset{\sim}{y}$, with equality holding iff $\phi_\& = \min$.

Remark 2

In a sense, Theorem 2 indicates no information loss when $\phi_\& = \min$ is chosen. (See Goodman [86], [82], [91'''] for related results.)

8.4 Some asymptotic results

Most results involving general logical systems and fuzzy systems are concerned with fixed finite structures.

In response to the criticism of Arbib [6] and Manes [170], [168] concerning the lack of asymptotic results, Dishkant [48] has made progress in addressing this issue. He shows for general fuzzy set system $\mathcal{F}'' \stackrel{d}{=} (1-(\cdot)$, minsum, max) , for any sequence $(A_j)_{j=1,2,\ldots}$ of fuzzy subsets of $\mathbb{R}$ with sufficiently well-behaved derivatives for ϕ_{A_j} , which have only one modal point yielding value one and having finite interval support,

$$\left(\phi_{\underset{(1\le j\le n)}{\Sigma A_j}}(x) - \rho(x)\right)_{n=1,2,\ldots} \to 0 ,$$

uniformly in x , for all $x \in \mathbb{R}$, where

$$\rho(x) \stackrel{d}{=} \max\,(1 - (c/2)(x - a)^2, 0)$$

$$\sim \exp\left(-(c/2)(x-a)^2\right) ;$$

for constants $c > 0$ and $a \in \mathbb{R}$ which functionally depend on the "well-behaved" conditions of the derivatives. In addition, Dishkant discusses estimation of a and c from empirical evidence.

Concerning Manes' last criticism, see section 2.3.7 where two justifications for the extension principle - in its general form - are given.

It also can be shown there are general fuzzy set system analogues of the Law of Large Numbers and related results. Specifically, the following properties may be easily obtained:

(1) Following the extension principle, justified by multivalued logical considerations, let $A_1, A_2, \ldots$ be arbitrary fuzzy subsets of $X \subseteq \mathbb{R}$, where X is a discrete (finite or countable) space. Then, defining the function $h_n : \mathbb{R}^n \to \mathbb{R}$;

$$h_n(x_1,\ldots,x_n) \stackrel{d}{=} \frac{1}{n}\sum_{i=1}^{n} x_i \;, \text{ all } x_1,\ldots,x_n \in \mathbb{R} \;,$$

the mean or least squares estimator, etc., without any appeal to statistical theory. Then for any $y \in \mathbb{R}$,

$$\phi_{h_n(A_1,\ldots,A_n)}(y) = \|(y \in h_n(A_1,\ldots,A_n))\|$$

$$= \phi_{or}\, \phi_{\&}(\phi_{A_1}(x_1),\ldots, \phi_{A_n}(x_n))$$

$$\left[(x_1,\ldots x_n) \in h_n^{-1}(y) \cap X\right] .$$

For any $\epsilon > 0$, consider:

$$\underset{(|y-\mu_n|\geq\delta)}{\phi_{or}} \quad \phi_{h_n(A_1,\ldots,A_n)}(y)$$

$$= |\underset{x\in X}{\mathrm{Or}}\, (|y-\mu_n| \geq \delta \;\&\; y \in h_n(A_1,\ldots,A_n))| \;, \quad \text{for all } y \in X \;, \qquad (1)$$

where

$$\mu_n \stackrel{d}{=} \frac{1}{n}\sum_{j=1}^{n} \mu_j \;,$$

$\mu_1, \mu_2, \ldots$, a sequence of constants in $\mathbb{R}$. Note that the number of arguments of ϕ_{or} is at most countable here (while that of $\phi_{\&}$ is finite).

Thus, if, e.g., $\mu_1,\ldots,\mu_n$ are some measures of central tendency such as, e.g., means

$$\mu_j \overset{d}{=} \sum_{x \in X} x \cdot \phi_{A'_j}(x) \ ,$$

where for all $x \in \mathbb{R}$,

$$\phi_{A'_j}(x) = (1/\gamma_j)\phi_{A_j}(x) \ ,$$

and

$$\gamma_j \overset{d}{=} \sum_{x \in X} \phi_{A_j}(x)$$

is assumed finite; $j = 1,2,\ldots,n$,

then eq.(1) represents the general fuzzy set extension of the probability form

$$\Pr(|\overline{X}_n - \mu_n| \geq \epsilon) \ ,$$

where

$$\overline{X}_n \overset{d}{=} h_n(X_1,\ldots,X_n) \ ;$$

random variable X_j having $\phi_{A'_j}$ as its probability function, $j = 1,\ldots,n$, with $X_1,\ldots,X_n$ being statistically independent. As before, merely specialize $(\phi_{nt}, \phi_{\&}, \phi_{or}) = (1-(\cdot), \text{prod}, \text{bndsum})$ (bndsum = sum over probability functions) to obtain the probability analogues.

Assume now

(i) $\gamma_1, \gamma_2, \ldots, \leq \gamma_o < +\infty$,

(ii) $\mu_1, \mu_2, \ldots, < +\infty$,

(iii) $\sigma_j^2 \overset{d}{=} \sum_{x \in X} (x-\mu_j)^2 \ \phi_{A'_j}(x) \leq \sigma_o^2 < +\infty \ , \ j = 1,2,\ldots$,

(iv) $\phi_{\&}$ is any t-norm bounded above by prod ,

(v) ϕ_{or} is any copula.

Then for any $\delta > 0$,

$$J_{n,\delta} \overset{d}{=} \underset{\substack{|y-\mu_n| \geq \delta \\ y \in X}}{\phi_{or}} (\phi_{h_n(A_1,\ldots,A_n)}(y))$$

$$\leq \sum_{\substack{(x_1,\ldots,x_n)\in h_n^{-1}(y)\cap X \\ |y-\mu_n|\geq\delta,\, y\in X}} \left(\phi_{A_1}(x_1)\cdots\phi_{A_n}(x_n)\right),$$

since

$$\phi_{or} \leq \text{bndsum} \leq \text{sum} \qquad (2)$$

$$\leq \gamma_o^{\,n} \cdot \sum_{\substack{(x_1,\ldots,x_n)\in h_n^{-1}(y)\cap X \\ |y-\mu_n|\geq\delta,\, y\in X}} \phi_{A'_1}(x_1)\cdots\phi_{A'_n}(x_n)$$

$$= \gamma_o^{\,n} \cdot \Pr(|\overline{X}_n - \overline{\mu}_n| \geq \delta)$$

$$\leq \gamma_o^{\,n} \cdot \frac{\sigma_o^{\,2}}{n\cdot\delta^2},$$

noting that now $\overline{X}_n$ is the sample mean of statistically independent random variables, which by use of Chebyshev's inequality yields the standard upper bound for Weak Law of Large Number convergence. (See, e.g., Revesz [216].)

Note that

(a) If all $\gamma_1, \gamma_2, \ldots < 1$,

i.e., $\phi_{A_1}, \phi_{A_2}, \ldots$ all represent deficient probability functions, then

$$0 = \lim_{n\to\infty} J_{n,\delta} \leq \sigma(\gamma_o^{\,n}/n),$$

better than exponential rate convergence to zero.

(b) If all $\gamma_1 = \gamma_2 = \cdots = 1$,

i.e., $\phi_{A_1}, \phi_{A_2}, \ldots,$ all represent ordinary probability functions, then

$$0 = \lim_{n\to\infty} J_{n,\delta} \leq \sigma(\tfrac{1}{n}).$$

(c) However, if

$$\gamma_1, \gamma_2, \ldots \geq 1,$$

then the upper bound on $J_{n,\delta}$ diverges, although for any fixed n, by choosing $\delta > 0$ suitably large $J_{n,\delta}$ may be made small.

(2) The last situation can be improved upon by considering first the continuous analogue of (1) and within it the class of Gaussian-like fuzzy set membership functions:

Suppose t-norm $\phi_{\&}$ is arbitrary differentiable in all of its arguments at 0 and

$$\phi_{A_1}, \phi_{A_2}, \ldots : \mathbb{R} \to [0,1],$$

with $B_n \subseteq \mathbb{R}^n$, an open connected domain.

Also, for each $m \geq 1$, define for any $\Delta_k^{(m)} > 0$, $k = 1,..,n$; $n \geq 1$,

$$M_{m,n} \overset{d}{=} \mathop{\times}_{k=1}^{m} \{j \cdot \Delta_k^{(n)} \mid j = 0, \pm 1, \pm 2, \ldots\}$$

and

$$K_{m,n} \overset{d}{=} B_n \cap M_{m,n} .$$

Suppose the grid

$$\lim_{m\to\infty} \max (\Delta_1^{(m)}, \ldots, \Delta_n^{(m)}) = 0$$

for any $m \geq 1$. Finally, suppose ϕ_{or} is any Archimedean copula (see 2.3.6) which implies there is a decreasing convex h

$$h : [0,1] \to \mathbb{R}^+ ; \; h(1) = 0 ,$$

such that for all $y_1, \ldots, y_n \in [0,1]$,

$$\phi_{or}(y_1, \ldots, y_n) = 1 - h^{-1}(\min(h(0), \sum_{j=1}^{n} h(1 - y_j))) ,$$

assuming also $h(1 - u)$ is differentable in u at 0.

Then for any $n \geq 1$, defining

$$x^{(n)} \overset{d}{=} (x_1, \ldots, x_n) \in \mathbb{R}^n ,$$

$$\mathop{\phi_{or}}_{x^{(n)}\in B_n} (\phi_{\&}(\phi_{A_1}(x_1)dx_1, \ldots, \phi_{A_n}(x_n)dx_n))$$

$$\overset{d}{=} \lim_{m\to\infty} \mathop{\phi_{or}}_{x^{(n)}\in K_{m,n}} (\phi_{\&}(\phi_{A_1}(x_1)\cdot\Delta_1^{(m)}, \ldots, \phi_{A_n}(x_n)\cdot\Delta_n^{(m)}))$$

$$= 1 - h^{-1}(\min(h(0), \left[\frac{\partial h(1-y)}{\partial y}\right]_{y=0} \cdot N_n)) \leq N_n ,$$

by suitable multiplying and dividing by arguments, use of the definition of integration, and eq.(2) , where

$$N_n \overset{d}{=} \left[\frac{\partial^n \phi_\&(y_1,\ldots,y_n)}{\partial y_1,\ldots,\partial y_n}\right]_{y_1=\cdots=y_n=0} \cdot \int_{x^{(n)}\in B} \phi_{A_1}(x_1)\cdots\phi_{A_n}(x_n)dx_1\cdots dx_n .$$

If now for $j = 1,2,\ldots$

(i) $\gamma_j \overset{d}{=} \int_{x\in\mathbb{R}} \phi_{A_j}(x)dx \le \gamma_o < +\infty$,

defining probability density function $\phi_{A'_j}$ by

$$\phi_{A'_j}(x) \overset{d}{=} \frac{1}{\gamma_j}\phi_{A_j}(x) \; ; \quad \text{all} \quad x \in \mathbb{R} ,$$

(ii) $\mu_j \overset{d}{=} \int_{x\in\mathbb{R}} x\phi_{A'_j}(x)dx < +\infty$,

(iii) $\sigma_j^2 \overset{d}{=} \int_{x\in\mathbb{R}} (x-\mu_j)^2\phi_{A'_j}(x)dx < \sigma_o^2 < +\infty$,

(iv) $\phi_\&$ is any t-norm bounded above by prod ,

(v) ϕ_{or} is any Archimedean copula ,

(vi) $B_n = \{(x_1,\ldots,x_n) \mid |\overline{x}_n - \overline{\mu}_n| \ge \delta\}$, for all $n \ge 1$,

then for any $n \ge 1$ and any $\delta > 0$, by a slight modification of the last result,

$$J_{n,\delta} \overset{d}{=} \underset{x^{(n)}\in B_n}{\phi_{or}} (\phi_\&(\phi_{A_1}(x_1)dx_1,\ldots,\phi_{A_n}(x_n)dx_n))$$

$$\le \gamma_o^{\,n} \cdot \Pr(|\overline{X}_n - \overline{\mu}_n| \ge \delta) ,$$

where now random variables $X_1,\ldots,X_n$ correspond to p.d.f.'s $\phi_{A'_1},\ldots,\phi_{A'_n}$, respectively,

$$\le \gamma_o^{\,n} \cdot \frac{\sigma_o^2}{n\delta^2} .$$

Again, the same convergence conditions hold analogous to the discrete case. However, in this case, if these conditions can be improved upon by suitably restricting the shapes of ϕ_{A_1} , ϕ_{A_2}, ... , then convergence can take place. That is, geometric convergence in n can be assured for $\Pr(|\overline{X}_n - \overline{\mu}_n| \ge \delta)$, by the Baum-Katz-Read Theorem [13], which gives necessary and sufficient conditions for such convergence: essentially, the moment generating function of $\bar{X}_n$, $E(e^{\bar{X}_n t})$ as a function of t for any $\delta > 0$, and t sufficiently small satisfies

$$E(e^{\bar{X}_n \cdot t}) \le \text{const}_\delta \cdot e^{|t|\delta} .$$

This condition is satisfied by the Gaussian-like forms (or by suitably bounded mixtures of them)

$$\phi_{A_j}(x) \overset{d}{=} c_j e^{-a_j \cdot (x-\mu_j)^2} ; \text{ all } x \in \mathbb{R} ,$$

where $a_j > 0$ is arbitrary fixed and where $1 \ge c_j > 0$ is arbitrary fixed, whence

$$\phi_{A_j'}(x) = (1/\gamma_j) \cdot \phi_{A_j}(x) ; \text{ all } x \in \mathbb{R} ,$$

is a p.d.f. for $\text{Gauss}(\mu_j, \frac{1}{\sqrt{2a_j}})$, where

$$\gamma_j \overset{d}{=} c_j \cdot \sqrt{\frac{\pi}{a_j}} , \; j = 1,\ldots,n .$$

(These forms are closely related to those often chosen for "fuzzy numbers". See [51].)

Hence, for these substitutions, by direct computations, for any integer $n \ge 1$, and any $\delta > 0$, since $\bar{X}_n$ is distributed $\text{Gauss}(\bar{\mu}_n, \bar{\sigma}_n^2 \overset{d}{=} \frac{1}{n^2} \sum_{j=1}^{n} \sigma_j^2)$,

$$J_{n,\delta} \le \left[\max_{1\le j\le n} \left[c_j \cdot \sqrt{\frac{\pi}{a_j}} \right]\right]^n \cdot \int_{|x-\bar{\mu}_n|\ge\delta} \frac{1}{\sqrt{2\pi}\,\bar{\sigma}_n} e^{-\frac{1}{2}\left[\frac{x-\bar{\mu}_n}{\sigma_n}\right]^2} dx$$

$$\le \left[\sqrt{\pi} \cdot \max_{1\le j\le n} \left[\frac{c_j}{\sqrt{a_j}}\right]\right]^n \cdot 2 \int_{v=\delta/\bar{\sigma}_n}^{\infty} \frac{1}{\sqrt{2\pi}} e^{-\frac{1}{2}v^2} dv \qquad (\delta \ge \bar{\sigma}_n)$$

$$\le \left[\sqrt{\pi} \cdot \max_{1\le j\le n}\left[\frac{c_j}{\sqrt{a_j}}\right]\right]^n \cdot \frac{2}{\sqrt{\pi}} \cdot \frac{e^{-\delta^2/2\bar{\sigma}_n^2}}{\frac{\delta}{\sqrt{2}\,\bar{\sigma}_n} + \sqrt{\left[\frac{\delta}{\sqrt{2}\,\bar{\sigma}_n}\right]^2 + 4/\pi}} ,$$

by standard inequalities (see, e.g., [1], p. 296, # 7.1.13).

Thus,

$$c_j/\sqrt{a_j} \le \eta_o < +\infty \qquad \text{implies} \qquad J_{\eta,\delta} \le a_\delta \cdot (b_\delta)^n/\sqrt{n} ,$$

where

$$a_\delta \overset{d}{=} \sqrt{\frac{2}{\pi}} \cdot (\sigma_o/\delta) \ ,$$

$$b_\delta \overset{d}{=} \sqrt{\pi} \cdot \eta_o \cdot e^{-\delta^2/\sigma_o^2} \ .$$

Hence, if δ is chosen such that

$$\delta > \sigma_o^2 \cdot \log (\sqrt{\pi} \cdot \eta_o) \ ,$$

then

$$0 = \lim_{n\to\infty} J_{n,\delta} = \sigma(b_\delta^{\ n}/\sqrt{n}) \ .$$

(See also [52] for some related results involving asymptotic properties of sums of fuzzy numbers.)

For other asymptotic results involving ϕ_{or} and $\phi_{\&}$ operations, see Chapter 9 (E).

For a recent paper on the Strong Law of Large Numbers for fuzzy random variables, following up on Kwakernaak's concept of fuzzy random variables [148], see Miyakoshi and Shimbo [179"].

(3) Walley and Fine [259] establish parallels to the classical laws of large numbers linking sampling frequencies of events through use of limsup and liminf operations with upper and lower probability measures, as well as generalizing probabilistic concepts of independence and estimability.

Noting that both upper and lower probability measures correspond uniquely to random sets (see Chapters 3 and 4), an empirical link as described above is not surprising. Indeed, if a random set $S \in \mathfrak{R}(X)$ has a known distribution, the incidence function $\mu_{(S)^{(2)}}$ given in section 4.2 where for all sets $C \in \mathcal{P}(X)$ of interest,

$$\mu_{(S)^{(2)}}(C) \overset{d}{=} P_1(S \cap C \neq \emptyset),$$

is an upper probability (or plausibility) measure. Similarly, if S is actually unknown but is estimated by any standard procedure by, say, $\hat{S}$, then again $\mu_{(\hat{S})^{(2)}}$ will be an upper probability measure, which if $\hat{S}$ is close to S in any reasonable sense, so will $\mu_{(\hat{S})^{(2)}}$ be close to $\mu_{(\hat{S})^{(2)}}$.

A similar situation holds for the other extreme: fuzzy or generalized sets, but in this case, the random set S involved in generating a given membership function is not uniquely determined - only up to one point coverages. Or alternatively, using the random variable representation of a fuzzy set membership function, one can choose a space X and a fixed collection $\mathcal{A}$ of, in general, overlapping compound events from a σ-algebra on X and a given sequence of independent identically distributed random variables $V_1, V_2, \ldots$ and compute by any standard zero-one averaging procedure the asymptotic probabilities $1/n \sum_{j=1}^{n} \Pr(V_j \in C) \overset{d}{=} \hat{g}_n(C)$, for each $C \in \mathcal{A}$ to obtain $\hat{g}_n$ as an estimator of true membership function g over $\mathcal{A}$ where each C is formally now a "point" in $\mathcal{A}$.

Of course, another alternative to the modeling of membership functions is to use formally a zero-one random process which may be repeatedly sampled, to represent a subjective determination. (See also section 5.1.)

(4) Goodman [79] has obtained asymptotic forms for generalized weighted sums representing averaged fuzzy data and corresponding posterior fuzzy parameter sets. First recall the following concepts (see also section 8.2):

Definitions

Let X_1 and X_2 be two given base spaces and $\phi_\&$ any t-norm. For any $A \in \mathcal{F}(X_1 \times X_2)$, define a projection $p_1(A) \in \mathcal{F}(X_1)$ by $\phi_{p_1(A)}(x_1) \overset{d}{=} \phi_{\substack{or \\ x_2 \in X_2}}(\phi_A(x_1, x_2))$; $x_1 \in X_1$ and similarly define $p_2(A) \in \mathcal{F}(X_2)$. Then it follows from basic properties of t-norms that all $x_j \in X_j$, $j = 1, 2$, there are $(p_1(A) \mid x_2) \in \mathcal{F}(X_1)$ and $(p_2(A) \mid x_1) \in \mathcal{F}(X_2)$, called conditional fuzzy sets, such that for all x_1, x_2

$$\begin{aligned} \phi_A(x_1, x_2) &= \phi_\&(\phi_{(p_1(A)|x_2)}(x_1), \phi_{p_2(A)}(x_2)) \\ &= \phi_\&(\phi_{(p_2(A)|x_1)}(x_2), \phi_{p_1(A)}(x_1)) \end{aligned} \tag{1}$$

which are uniquely determined over $\operatorname{supp}(\phi_A) \overset{d}{=} \{(x_1, x_2) | \phi_A(x_1, x_2) > 0\}$, provided $\phi_\&$ is strictly increasing in each argument. Note that if $A \in \mathcal{P}(X_1 \times X_2)$ then $p_j(A)$ is the ordinary projection of d $(p(A)|x)$, A into x_j and $(p_2(A)|x_1)$, say, is the section of A in x_2, given x_1. (See also section 2.3.8 for background.)

It then follows immediately that a fuzzy set form of Bayes' theorem is obtainable.

Theorem 0 (Fuzzy Bayes')

Let $A \in \mathcal{F}(X_1 \times X_2)$ with $\phi_\&$ a strictly increasing t-norm.

Then over supp(A) , $(p_1(A)|x_2)$ is a function of $(p_2(A)|\cdot)$ and $p_1(A)$, determined implicity from the following equations:

$$\phi_{\&}(\phi_{(p_1(A)|x_2)}(x_1),\ \phi_{p_2(A)}(x_2)) = \phi_{\&}(\phi_{(p_2(A)|x_1)}(x_2),\ \phi_{p_1(A)}(x_1)) \ , \tag{2}$$

where

$$\phi_{p_2(A)}(x_2) = \phi_{\substack{or \\ x_1 \in X_1}} (\phi_{\&}(\phi_{(p_2(A)|x_1)}(x_2),\ \phi_{p_1(A)}(x_1))) \tag{3}$$

Remark 1.

An obvious analogy holds here with respect to standard Bayesian modeling. We can interpret $(p_2(A)|\cdot)$ to be the conditional fuzzy data set, $p_1(A)$ to be the prior fuzzy parameter set , $(p_1(A)|x_2)$ to be the posterior fuzzy parameter set, and $p_2(A)$ to be the averaged fuzzy data set, where x_2 may be considered a fuzzy outcome. (In the classical Bayesian formulation, $\phi_{\&}$ = prod and ϕ_{or} is replaced by an intergral or sum which is possibly weighted.)

In conjunction with the above remarks, we will assume that the following general fuzzy sampling experiment holds:

(a) $p_1(A)$ is known, but A itself is not known beforehand.

(b) $(p_2(A)|\cdot)$ is obtained empirically, sometimes through human sources, via a panel of "experts" (rather than from the unknown A via Bayes' theorem).

Bayes' theorem can then be applied, with the above interpretation, to obtain the desired posterior fuzzy parameter set. The key computation lies in the evaluation of $\phi_{p_2(A)}$ in equation (3). In addition to (a) and (b), assume that the following modification holds:

First define the weighted averages

$$w_{n,j} \overset{d}{=} w'_{n,j} / \sum_{j=1}^{n} w'_{n,j} \ ; \ j = 1,...,n \tag{4}$$

where $w'_{n,j} \geq 0$ are constants, and the normalized n^{th} fuzzy prior set ω_n is given by

$$\phi_{\omega_n}(y_j) = w_{n,j} \ ; \ j = 1,...,n \ ; \tag{5}$$

otherwise, ϕ_{ω_n} is zero.

If a panel of experts is used, each y_j represents expert j, where $y_j \in X_1$, $j = 1,2,\ldots$.

(c) Formally replace for each $n \geq 1$ in eqs. (1),(2), $p_1(A)$ everywhere by ω_n and denote the subsequent value of $\phi_{p_2(A)}$ by ϕ_{A_n} and $\phi_{(p_1(A)|x_2)}$ by $\phi_{(B_n|x_2)}$.

The next theorem concern the asymptotic behavior of ϕ_{A_n} and hence of $\phi_{(B_n|x_2)}(y_j)$ as $n \to \infty$. First define

$$a_{n,j}(x_2) \stackrel{d}{=} \phi_{(p_2(A)|y_j)}(x_2)\cdot w_{n,j} \ , \tag{6}$$

$$a_j(x_2) \stackrel{d}{=} \phi_{(p_2(A)|y_j)}(x_2) \ , \tag{7}$$

$$\phi_{\overline{A}_n}(x_2) \stackrel{d}{=} \sum_{j=1}^{n} a_{n,j}(x_2) \ . \tag{8}$$

Asymptotic behavior of average buzzy data and posterior fuzzy parameter sets.

Theorem 1

Suppose the conditions for Theorem 0 hold with modifications (a), (b), (c), for each $n \geq 1$, and suppose the constant sample means converge:

$$\lim_{n\to\infty} \phi_{\overline{A}_n}(x_2) \stackrel{d}{=} \phi_{\overline{A}_\infty}(x_2) \quad \text{exists; } x_2 \in X_2 \ . \tag{9}$$

Suppose also for all $n \geq 1$,

$$a\cdot n^{-\epsilon_1} \leq w'_{n,j} \leq b\cdot n^{\epsilon_2} \ , \tag{10}$$

where $0 < a \leq b$ and $\epsilon_1, \epsilon_2 > 0$ are all constants, with $\epsilon_1 + \epsilon_2 < 1$.

Thus,

$$0 < C_n \leq w_{n,j} \leq D_n \ ; \ j = 1, \ldots, n \ , \tag{11}$$

$$0 < C_n \stackrel{d}{=} (a/b)\cdot n^{-(1+\epsilon_1+\epsilon_2)} < 1 \ , \tag{12}$$

$$0 < D_n \stackrel{d}{=} (b/a)\cdot n^{-(1-\epsilon_1-\epsilon_2)} < 1 \ , \tag{13}$$

where it is assumed that $n > n_o \overset{d}{=} (b/a)^{1/(1-\epsilon_1-\epsilon_2)}$. Note that for $w'_{n,j} = 1$, $w_{n,j} \equiv 1/n$ satisfies (11) .

Then for the fuzzy set system determined by $(\phi_{not}, \phi_\&, \phi_{or}) = (1-(\cdot),$ prod, probsum$)$, for all n , and all $x_2 \in X_2$,

$$\phi_{A_n}(x_2) = 1 - \prod_{j=1}^{n} (1-a_{n,j}(x_2)) , \quad (14)$$

$$\phi_{\bar{A}_n}(x_2) \le -\log(1 - \phi_{A_n}(x_2)) \le \phi_{\bar{A}_n}(x_2)\cdot(1 + J_n) , \quad (15)$$

equivalently,

$$1 - \exp(-\phi_{\bar{A}_n}(x_2)) \le \phi_{\bar{A}_n}(x_2) \le 1 - \exp(-(\phi_{\bar{A}_n}(x_2)\cdot(1 + J_n)) \quad (15')$$

where,

$$J_n \overset{d}{=} -(\log(1 - D_n) + D_n)/D_n . \quad (16)$$

$$\lim_{n\to\infty} J_n = \lim_{n\to\infty} (D_n/(1 - D_n)) = 0 . \quad (17)$$

Thus,

$$\lim_{n\to\infty} \phi_{A_n}(x_2) \overset{d}{=} \phi_{A_\infty}(x_2) = 1 - \exp(-\phi_{\bar{A}_\infty}(x_2)) , \quad (18)$$

uniformly in $x_2 \in X_2$, with convergence rate determined by eqs. (15'), (16) . Thus, for large n , all $y_j \in X_1$,

$$\phi_{(B_n|x_2)}(y_j) \sim a_{n,j}(x_2)/(1 - \exp -\phi_{\bar{A}_\infty}(x_2)) . \quad (19)$$

Theorem 2 (Central limit type theorem for a class of analytic operator pairs.)

Suppose assumptions (a), (b), (c) and eq. (10) all hold. Suppose also that $(1 - (\cdot), \phi_\&, \phi_{or})$ is a DeMorgan system where $\phi_\&$ has a generator $h : [0,1] \to [0,+\infty]$ which is strictly decreasing with $h(0) = +\infty$, $h(1) = 0$. Then

(i) $$\phi_{A_n}(x_2) = 1 - h^{-1}\left(\sum_{j=1}^{n} h(1 - \phi_\&(w_{nj}, a_j(x_2)))\right)$$

$$\le 1 - h^{-1}\left(\sum_{j=1}^{m} h(1 - w_{nj})\right)$$

$$\leq 1 - h^{-1}(n \cdot h(1 - D_n)) \ . \qquad (20)$$

Thus, if

$$\lim_{n \to +\infty} (n \cdot h(1 - D_n)) = 0 \ ,$$

then

$$\lim_{n \to +\infty} \phi_{A_n}(x_2) = 0 \ .$$

(ii) Suppose also that for any fixed $c \in [0,1]$, $\phi_{\&}(z,c)$ is analytic in z about some neighborhood of 0 and that h is analytic within some fixed neighborhood of, and below, 1. Suppose, further, that in eq. (10),

$$0 < \epsilon_1 + \epsilon_2 < \frac{1}{2}$$

and that

$$\lim_{n \to +\infty} \left(\sum_{j=1}^{n} \beta_j(x_2) \cdot w_{nj} \right) \overset{d}{=} \alpha(x_2) \quad \text{exists,}$$

where for $j = 1,2,\ldots,$

$$\beta_j(x_2) \overset{d}{=} (\partial \phi_{\&}(z, a_j(x_2))/\partial z)_{z=0} \ .$$

Finally, define

$$\lambda_o = -(dh(z)/dz)_{z=1} \geq 0 \ .$$

Then, uniformly in all $x_2 \in X_2$,

$$\phi_{A_\infty}(x_2) \overset{d}{=} \lim_{n \to \infty} \phi_{A_n}(x_2) = 1 - h^{-1}(\lambda_o \cdot \alpha(x_2))$$

exists, and for large n

$$\phi_{(B_n | x_2)}(y_j) = h^{-1}(h(w_{nj}) + h(a_j(x_2))) - h(\phi_{A_\infty}(x_2)) \ .$$

Proof:

(i) follows from the monotone property of h. For (ii): expand out in a power series the function $h(1 - \phi_{\&}(z,c))$ in z, yielding for all sufficiently small z, for $c = a_j(x_2)$ at $z = w_{nj}$:

$$h(1 - \phi_{\&}(z,c)) = \lambda_o \cdot \beta_j(x_2) \cdot z + o(z^2) \ , \qquad (21)$$

$\sigma(z^2)$ indicating the remaining series has powers of z to at least 2. Substitute (21) into the first part of eq. (20), noting that

$$\sum_{j=1}^{n} \sigma(w_{nj}^2) \leq n\cdot\sigma(D_n^2) = \sigma(n^{-(1-2(\epsilon_1+\epsilon_2))}) .$$

The next results are concerned with asymptotic properties of combination of evidence, when discretization of possibility functions is involved, as occurs typically when attributes concerning an unknown papameter vector are statistical in nature and are represented by probability density functions.

First, let $B \in \mathcal{F}(\mathbb{R}^n)$, where for any positive integer p, the pth discretization $\phi_{B_p} : D_p \to [0,1]$ of ϕ_B is constructed typically as

$$\phi_{B_{(p)}}(x) \overset{d}{=} \phi_B(x) \ ; \text{ all } \ x \in D_p ,$$

where $D_p \subseteq \mathbb{R}^n$ is a discrete equally spaced lattice, where each $\mathbb{R}^n$-cube $C_p(x)$ of D_p is such that $\lim_{p\to+\infty} \Delta_p(x) = 0$ and such that for all integers $p \geq q \geq 1$, D_p refines D_q. (D_p may be modified for truncations.) Then for any t-conorm ϕ_{or}:

Theorem 3 (Simple limit theorem for discretizations)

If ϕ_{or} is an Archimedean t-conorm, then

$$\lim_{p\to+\infty} (\phi_{or}{}_{x\in D_p} (\phi_{B_{(p)}}(x)) = 1 .$$

Remark 2.

If $\phi_{or} = \max$, then in general

$$\lim_{p\to+\infty} \phi_{or}{}_{x\in D_p} (\phi_{B_{(p)}}(x)) < 1 .$$

The following theorem extends Theorem 2.

Theorem 4 (Limit theorem as information granularity approaches zero)

(a) For each positive integer p, let D_p be a discretization of $\mathbb{R}^n$ as before and let $\phi_{C_p} : D_p \to [0,1]$. Also, let $\phi_G : X \times \mathbb{R}^n \to [0,1]$ be continuous, where X is any fixed space.

(b) Suppose $\phi_\&$ is a fixed t-norm such that there is a fixed δ , $0 < \delta < 1$, such that for each $u \in [0,1]$, $\partial\phi_\&(u,v)/\partial v$ and $\partial^2\phi_\&(u,v)/\partial^2 v$ are finitely bounded as functions of $v \in [0,\delta)$.

(c) Suppose ϕ_{or} is an Archimedean t-conorm with canonical generator h , i.e. (see section 2.3.6)

$$\phi_{or}(u,v) = 1 - h^{-1}(\min\ (h(1-u) + h(1 - v),\ h(0)))$$

for all $u,v \in [0,1]$, where $h : [0,1] \to [0,+\infty)$ is monotone decreasing continuous with $h(1) = 0$.

Also, assume there is a fixed K , $0 < K < 1$, such that $dh(v)/dv$ and $d^2h(v)/d^2v$ are finitely bounded functions of $v \in [K,1]$.

Then for all $\theta \in X$,

$$\lim_{p\to+\infty} (g_p(\theta)) = 1 - h^{-1}(\min\ (\tau(\theta),\ h(0))) \ ,$$

where

$$g_p(\theta) \overset{d}{=} \underset{x\in D_p}{\phi_{or}} (\phi_\&(\phi_G(\theta,x),\ \phi_{C_p}(x))) \ ,$$

$$\tau(\theta) \overset{d}{=} \lim_{p\to\infty} \sum_{x\in D_p} (\phi_{C_p}(x)\cdot\nu(\phi_G(\theta,x))) \ ,$$

$$\nu(u) \overset{d}{=} -(dh(v)/dv)_{v=1}\cdot(\partial\phi_\&(u,v)/\partial v)_{v=0} \ ,$$

for all $u \in [0,1]$.

Proof: First note that

$$g_p(\theta) = 1 = h^{-1}(\min\ (\sum_{x\in D_p} h(1 - \phi_\&(\phi_G(\theta,x),\ \phi_{C_p}(x))),\ h(0))) \ .$$

Then for each u , expand $h(1 - \phi_\&(u,v))$ as a function of v about $v = 0$, up to second order.

Corollary 1.

(a) Let $f_k : \mathbb{R}^{m_k} \to \mathbb{R}^+$ be a bounded continuous probability density function, $k = 1,2,\ldots$.

(b) Let q be any fixed positive integer.

(c) Suppose $\phi_{\&,1}$ is any fixed t-norm such that

$$+\infty > r_q \overset{d}{=} \partial^q\phi_{\&,1}(u_1,\ldots,u_q)/\partial u_1\cdots\partial u_q)_{u_1=\cdots=u_q=0} \;.$$

(d) As before, denote $D_{k,p}$ as the pth discretization (with all previous properties holding) for $\mathbb{R}^{m_k}$, so that letting

$$f_{k,p}(x_k) \overset{d}{=} f_k(x_k)\cdot\Delta_{k,p}(x_k) \;,$$

for all $x_k \in D_{k,p}$; $k = 1,2,\ldots$; $p = 1,2,\ldots$, with

$$\sum_{x_k\in D_{k,p}} f_{k,p}(x_k) = 1 \;,$$

i.e., $f_{k,p}$ is a probability function.

In turn, define

$$\underset{\sim}{x}_q \overset{d}{=} (x_1,x_2,\ldots,x_q) \in D_p^{(q)} \overset{d}{=} D_{1,p}\times\cdots\times D_{q,p} \;,$$

$$f_p^{(q)}(\underset{\sim}{x}_q) \overset{d}{=} \phi_{\&,1}(f_{1,p}(x_1),\ldots,f_{q,p}(x_p)) \;.$$

(e) Next, suppose $\phi_{\&,2}$ is a fixed t-norm such that there is a fixed δ, $0 < \delta < 1$ such that for each $u \in [0,1]$, $\partial\phi_{\&,2}(u,v)/\partial v$ and $\partial^2\phi_{\&,2}(u,v)/\partial^2 v$ are finitely bounded as functions of $v \in [0,\delta)$.

(f) Let X be any space and let

$$\phi_{G_q} : X \times \mathbb{R}^{m^{(q)}} \to [0,1]$$

be any continuous function, where

$$m^{(q)} \overset{d}{=} m_1+\cdots+m_q \;.$$

(g) Let ϕ_{or} be any Archimedean t-conorm with canonical generator h,

$$\phi_{or}(u,v) = 1 - h^{-1}(\min\,(h(1-u) + h(1-v),\, h(0))) \;,$$

for all $u,v \in [0,1]$, where $h : [0,1] \to [0,+\infty)$ is monotone decreasing continuous, with $h(1) = 0$.

Also, assume there is a fixed K, $0 < K < 1$, such that

$dh(v)/dv$ and $d^2h(v)/d^2v$ are finitely bounded functions of $v \in [K,1]$.

Then, for all $\theta \in X$

$$\lim_{p\to+\infty} (g_p^{(q)}(\theta)) = 1 - h^{-1}(\min(\tau_q(\theta), h(0))) ,$$

where for all $\theta \in X$,

$$g_p^{(q)}(\theta) \overset{d}{=} \phi_{\substack{or \\ (\underset{\sim}{x}_q \in D_p^{(q)})}} (\phi_{\&,2}(\phi_{G_q}(\theta, \underset{\sim}{x}_q), f_p^{(q)}(\underset{\sim}{x}_q))) ,$$

$$\tau_q(\theta) \overset{d}{=} r_q \cdot \int_{\left(\underset{\sim}{x}_q \in \mathbb{R}^{m(q)}\right)} \nu(\phi_{G_q}(\theta, \underset{\sim}{x}_q)) \cdot \prod_{k=1}^{q} f_k(\underset{\sim}{x}_k) d\underset{\sim}{x}_k ,$$

$$\nu(u) \overset{d}{=} -(dh(v)/dv)_{v=1} \cdot (\partial\phi_{\&,2}(u,v)/\partial v)_{v=0} ,$$

for all $u \in [0,1]$.

Remark.

Frank's Archimedean family (see section 2.3.6) can be used to supply $\phi_{\&,1}$, $\phi_{\&,2}$, ϕ_{or} for Theorem 4 or Corollary 1.

8.5 Subjective probability and general logical systems.

There have also been a number of papers attempting to interpret fuzzy set concepts within the purview of subjective probability theory. (See, e.g., Nalimov [180], Hanrahan [105], [106]. Nativig [182], Hisdal [113]).

In particular, consider the important independent work of Watanabe [268] and Giles [70 - 73]. Both have developed a basic mathematical theory for fuzzy sets, in a somewhat different context from Zadeh, in which they are concerned also with an empirical basis for the numerical evaluation of the membership functions, the various logical connections, and other relations involved in fuzzy set models. Consider the following:

Let X be a fixed space of *points* or *objects* and $\mathcal{F}_1(X)$ a fixed space of *properties*, *attributes*, *predicates* or *fuzzy sets*. Define for any $C \subseteq X$ and $A \in \mathcal{F}_1(X)$, $(C \subseteq A)$ or $A(C)$ as that *atomic* or *primitive proposition* representing compatability or truth that C has property or attribute A or C is a subset of fuzzy set A . Introduce also the operators "not," "&," "or" which formally have the usual classical logical interpretations, and then form the class of all compound propositions as the well-formed strings, under not , & , or , of the primitive propositions, so that at least a Boolean algebra $\mathfrak{B}$ results. (See also 2.2.) A similar result holds for all well-formed strings of predicates. Watanabe restricts himself to the special case of $C = \{x\}$, $x \in X$, resulting in fuzzy set membership forms $(x \in A)$, $A \in \mathcal{F}_1(X)$ and fuzzy set membership functions $\phi_A(x)$.

In addition, he uses first a fundamental composition operator on $\mathcal{F}_1(X)$ to develop his logical operators over a subspace $\mathcal{F}(X)$ of $\mathcal{F}_1(X)$, where the composition operator is idempotent. Both Watanabe and Giles approach the evaluation of a proposition throuth the concept of a "test" in an extended sense. Watanabe stresses more the nonsubjective probability ideas that in effect - again restricting himself to $(x \in A) - \phi_A(x)$, the fuzzy set membership level of x in A, is to be interpreted not as the truth $(x \in A) - (x \in A)$ being either true or not - but rather as the probability of observing (at least theoretically) that $x \in A$ or equivalently, the probability that zero-one r.v. $V_{x,A} = 1$, with $1 - \phi_A(x) = \text{probability } (V_{x,A} = 0)$, where $\phi_A(x)$, can be estimated by a test procedure which counts the percentage of successes. If the test for a proposition can not be repeated - due, for example, to a time factor t occurring for $A_t \in \mathcal{F}_1(X)$, where for $t' \neq t''$, in general, $A_{t'} \neq A_{t''}$ - the test is called *dispersive* (as, e.g., in a micro-level or single sample situation), otherwise the test is called *non-dispersive*. Giles differs from Watanabe in that he stresses the subjective and, in general, non-probabilistic, i.e., possibilistic interpretation: Using a pragmatic approach through a "rational" betting scheme, he first considers prob(A(C)), which, when it exists is the classical Savage Baysian subjective probability that A(C) occurs, relative to a test individual. In general, however, prob(A(C)) cannot be obtained but rather a probability interval, [low prob A(C), upp prob (A(C))], is identified with upp prob A(C). For compound propositions, Giles establishes a dialogue procedure for evaluation. The result is that in addition to the numerical evaluations being obtainable by this procedure, a particular specialization of Giles' system is seen to be the same as Lukasiewicz $\aleph_1$-logic (both semantically and syntactically) [214]. On the other hand, Watanabe's system differs considerably in form (q.v.). Giles obtains a number of interesting relations between probabilities, possibilities, and Zadeh's original concept of possibilities, which may be proved with a set-theoretic context not dependent upon the original betting scheme. Some of these results are similar to other relations developed between various definitions of uncertainty measures. (See Dubois and Prade [51], Chapter II.5 for a more comprehensive listing. See also Banon [11], Kruse [146] and Puri and Ralescu [206] as well as the extensive work of Klement and Schwyhla [142] and Klement et al. [141] in developing fuzzy probability measures and their relations to classical probability. See also section 3.3.)

(i) A (Giles) possibility function p may be defined by $p : \mathfrak{B} \to [0,1]$, where $\mathfrak{B}$ may be identified with some Boolean algebra of subsets of X, say, (by Stone's Representation Theorem) with p being nondecreasing w.r.t. subset inclusion, $p(\emptyset) = 0$, $p(X) = 1$ and for all $A,B \in \mathfrak{B}$,

$$\max(p(A),p(B)) \leq p(A \cup B) \leq p(A) + p(B) .$$

(ii) Every finite additive probability function is a (Giles) possibility one.

(iii) The argument-wise (w.r.t. sets $A \in \mathfrak{B}$) supremum of any collection of (Giles) possibility functions is also a (Giles possibility.

(iv) Any (Giles) possibility function is the argument-wise supremum of a class of (finitely additive) probability functions.

(v) A Zadeh possibility function $p : \mathfrak{B} \to [0,1]$ where for all $A,B \in \mathfrak{B}$,

$$p(A \cup B) = \max(p(A), p(B)) ,$$

is of course a (Giles) possibility function and for any fuzzy set membership function, $\phi_A : X \to [0,1]$, $\sup_{x \in B} \phi_A(x)$ is a Zadeh possibility function of $B \in \mathfrak{B}$.

See also Smets (e.g. [243]) for a subjectivist - betting approach to fuzzy set modeling.

Remark.

Subjective probability and possibility are a necessity in general decision analysis.

In expert systems, estimates of uncertainty quantities of interest, e.g., certainty factors in MYCIN, weights of evidences in clinical decision-support systems (see, e.g., Spiegelhalter and Knill-Jones, [246]), are obtained subjectively. The subjectivity is also dominant in applications of possibility theory. However, possibility measures, as proposed by Zadeh to model expert knowledge, differ from other uncertainty measures in particular, from subjective probability (e.g., Fine, [58], Good, [76]) by their interpretation and their associated calculus. Different modeling processes lead to different mechanisms for combining of evidence. Thus, for example, when probabilities are used to express prior knowledge, then Bayes' formula is used to update information or to combine evidence. On the other hand, in statistical systems, the concept of weight of evidence (Good, [76]), can be used to represent concepts such as "doubt," "ignorance" and "conflict of evidence". (See Spiegelhalter and Knill-Jones [246].) More precisely, following Good [76], the information concerning a proposition A provided by a proposition B, given a proposition G, is defined to be:

$$\log \frac{\Pr(A \mid B,G)}{\Pr(A \mid G)} .$$

The weight of evidence in favor of an hypothesis H_1 as compared with hypothesis H_2 provided by the evidence E, given G, is defined by:

$$W(H_1/H_2 : E \mid G) = \log \frac{\Pr(E \mid H_1, G)}{\Pr(E \mid H_2, G)} .$$

Note that, both information measure and weight of evidence have the additivity property.

The situation where expert knowledge should be taken into account is very common in systems engineering. For example, in

Structural Engineering (e.g., Au, et al., [8]), due mainly to insufficient statistical data, the ignorance of structures and the doubt in the actual hypothesis considered by a design engineer, field observations of experts should be used in any final decision analysis. More precisely, the reliability of engineering structures, the factor of safety and the margin of safety, which are defined in terms of the imposed load effects S and the structure resistance R (considered as random variables), are appropriate measures of reliability. The probability of structure failure P_f can be computed if the joint probability distribution of (S,R) is known. However, in practice, often this is not the case! On the other hand, the degree of "doubt" for the hypotheses considered in computing P_f should be assigned somehow to reflect this type of system uncertainty. The value of P_f is then used in the optimization, say, of the utility function relating the risk of failure to economical and social consequences. This decision making problem is clearly more general than traditional statistical decision problems due mainly to the kind of data available and the type of uncertainty measures involved. A procedure for computing P_f is suggested in Au, et al., [8] where subjective expert knowledge is expressed in the form of "judgmental factors" reflecting the uncertainty in assigning a joint probability distribution to (S,R). The question is then: how to effectively assign these judgmental factors in a given situation, or, to put it in another way, how to model or encode expert knowledge? Once these factors have been subjectively assigned by an "objective" procedure or by ad hoc quantification, we are facing two different types of uncertainty measures in a single decision problem.

Some of the above concepts will also be found in Chapter 9, where an application to data association is considered.

CHAPTER 9

AN APPLICATION OF GENERAL LOGICAL DECISION THEORY TO A PROBLEM OF DATA ASSOCIATION

This chapter contains a detailed application of our theory developed in previous chapters to a problem of data association.

A. Description of the problem.

Too often in the past, linguistic based information has been neglected in favor of "hard" numerical or statistical data. However, with the advent of rule-based systems and new approaches to the modeling of uncertainties, both literal and statistical information may be treated from a common basis and effectively combined.

The following example illustrates how general logical systems may be used to model linguistic and numerical information in order to estimate a parameter of interest.

Although the problem considered here will be the target data association one, obvious changes in notation and forms yield a similar model for medical or fault diagnoses. The results are based on the work developed in [80], [77], [82], [83], [86], [91"], [91'''].

By a target history, we mean a collection of data concerning a single target of interest which is sorted in two different ways: by time and by attribute. Time indices correspond to report samplings and could vary from a single report to a large collection of reports. Examples of attributes include: geolocation (2 - or 3 - dimensional positions with possible additional parameters: velocity or even acceleration information), classification-type, on-board sensor characteristics, hull lengths, or even visual descriptions, the latter resulting from an actual sighting of a vessel. This may also be interpreted in linguistic form such as "irregular hull appearance", "oblong shape like a type Q", "is approximately x yards long", "appears to be flying a dark triangular-shaped flag - maybe Antartica", or "has two or perhaps three missile launchers on-board". Other attributes that may be present at various times include: emitter fundamental frequencies of equipment (numerical), tentative classification by intelligence sources (numerical or literal), mode of operation (literal), as well as various measurements of system parameters obtained by various sensor systems. Each of these attributes, of course, could vary as a function of time. The domain of possibile values for each such attribute is assumed known and may vary considerably.

For example, the domain for geolocation could be

$$\mathrm{dom(geo)} = \{(x,\Sigma) \mid x \in \mathfrak{R},\ \Sigma \in \mathfrak{P}\} ,$$

where $\mathfrak{R} \subseteq \mathbb{R}^2$ is some region of interest and $\mathfrak{P}$ is the set of all positive definite 2 by 2 matrices or equivalently ellipses of some fixed confidence level. In general, $\mathfrak{R}$ and $\mathfrak{P}$ are time dependent.

The domain for classification could typically consist of the labels $C_1, C_2, \ldots, C_m$, which can well represent overlapping sets. The domain for frequency could be a range of numerical values in hertz, while a typical visual description attribute could be observed ship flag color with domain consisting of {red, dark red, orange, yellow, pink, white, ...} , or the attribute representing ship length could be in pure linguistic terms: very short, short, long, about 300 feet, very long, etc. Although the possible domain values for each attribute could also vary, let us assume that relative to some common fixed reference time - say, to the present - all information has been suitably updated for both target histories and all attribute domain values, with no missing attribute for either target history.

A track history may contain as little as a single report or it may consist of a large and growing (in time) number of reports assembled from one or more mechanical or human sensor sources over an extended period of time. Often, due to independent information sources, two or more track histories may be established which are suspected (or actually equated) of representing in reality the same target or platform. Most commonly, this is based on either simple unimpeachable identifications or upon reasonable matching of geolocation information, which may be further enhanced by a comparison of other attributes. All comparisons are carried out, of course, with respect to suitable common updatings (or smoothings or predictions) of the reports in the track history files. In the past, both the preliminary screening phase and the more refined final decision phase in determining whether two or more track histories "correlate", i.e., associate to the same platform, or not, were based typically upon a combination of heuristic and statistical hypotheses testing procedures with emphasis placed upon geolocation attribute information. In turn, if two or more histories were decided to represent the same object, the geolocation information was combined and most often some variation of the well-known Kalman filter procedure was used for the ensuing tracking aspect. If the track histories were decided as being associated with distinct targets, similar tracking procedures were carried out for the separate tracks. (For further background, see the extensive surveys of the field made in [87] and [273]. In addition, [84] presents a general mathematical model of the correlation problem, again with emphasis on the geolocation aspect. See also Bowman [23].)

For simplicity, consider two target histories, each arising from separate data/sensor sources. The more general situation of n target histories could be handled either by a direct generalization of the procedure developed here or, pairwise, by the establishement of a confusion - or likelihood matrix of possible associations (see Table 0) in which a number of standard algorithms, e.g., [146'] are available for converting to an assignment, i.e., permutation matrix. This is also related to the Birkhoff decomposition theorem which exhibits the (nonunique) probability distributions of a random assignment matrix, whose expectation is the given "confusion" matrix, [178].

TRACK HISTORY \ TRACK HISTORY	1	2	3	4	5
1	1.0	0.8	0.2	0.1	0.3
2	0.8	1.0	0.5	0.2	0.1
3	0.2	0.5	1.0	0.7	0.6
4	0.1	0.2	0.7	1.0	0.4
5	0.3	0.1	0.6	0.4	1.0

Entries represent likelihoods or possibilities of correlation between arbitrary pairs of track histories. Clustering techniques may be used to group these histories. Tentatively, two groups here may be formed by inspection: {1,2} and {3,4,5} .

Table 0

An Example of a Correlation or Confusion Matrix

Table 1 illustrates symbolically a tableau comparing data by attribute for two given track histories.

Attribute	Track history 1 updated to time t_o	Track history 2 updated to time t_o
A_1	$\overset{\circ}{Z}_1^{(1)}$	$\overset{\circ}{Z}_1^{(2)}$
A_2	$\overset{\circ}{Z}_2^{(1)}$	$\overset{\circ}{Z}_2^{(2)}$
A_3	$\overset{\circ}{Z}_3^{(1)}$	$\overset{\circ}{Z}_3^{(2)}$
.	.	.
.	.	.
.	.	.
A_m	$\overset{\circ}{Z}_m^{(1)}$	$\overset{\circ}{Z}_m^{(2)}$

Table 1

Tableau of Observed Attribute Data.

In Table 1, the values $\overset{\circ}{Z}_j^{(1)}$, $\overset{\circ}{Z}_j^{(2)} \in D_j \overset{d}{=} \text{dom}(A_j)$, represent observed, measured, or reported values, $j = 1,...,m$.

Symbolically, we may write

$$\overset{\circ}{Z} = (\overset{\circ}{Z}^{(1)}, \overset{\circ}{Z}^{(2)}) = \left[\begin{array}{c|c} \overset{\circ}{Z}_1^{(1)} & \overset{\circ}{Z}_1^{(2)} \\ \vdots & \vdots \\ \overset{\circ}{Z}_m^{(2)} & \overset{\circ}{Z}_m^{(2)} \end{array} \right] . \quad (1)$$

It should be noted that any or all of the attributes $A_1,...,A_m$ could themselves represent compound forms of simpler attributes. For example, A_1 could represent jointly geolocation and frequency or geolocation, frequency and ship length, etc. Table 2 illustrates these ideas further by displaying a simulated typical data comparison by attributes. (Due to paging error, Table 2 is located on page 542.)

B. Error tables.

In addition, it is assumed that associated with each attribute A_k is a known error table P_k of size n_k by n_k where $n_k \overset{d}{=} \text{card}(\text{dom}(A_k))$, where for any two values Z_k' , $Z_k'' \in \text{dom}(A_k)$, the entry

$$P_k(Z_k' \mid Z_k'') = \text{probability or possibility that } Z_k' \text{ is the true value given } Z_k'' \text{ is observed value.} \quad (2)$$

Thus, for any $Z_k'' \in \text{domain}(A_k)$, $P_k(\cdot | Z_k'')$ is either a probability function or, more generally, due to possible overlapping of events, representing values in $\text{dom}(A_k)$ (to be made clearer below), $P_k(\cdot | Z_k'')$ is a possibility function, $k = 1,2,...,m$. If P_k represents a probability function and perfect errorless measurements were always made, then

$$P_k = I_{n_k} \qquad (n_k \text{ by } n_k) , \quad (3)$$

identity matrix, for some k, $k = 1,...,m$.

In general, any P_k can be obtained in one of two ways; either analytically or subjectively. The former typically occurs for geolocation, frequency, and other attributes where the number of contributing factors may be determined so that all relevant physical and statistical relations may be modeled reasonably faithfully. Thus, geolocation has typically associated with it multivariate Gaussian error distributions; on the other hand, frequency can have a more complicated analytic form for its error table derived from e.g., dopplar shift considerations, using transformation of probabibility techniques. Of course, all such distributions must be suitably discretized and localized over the regions of interest. In these analytic cases, the entire error tables P_k could be tabulated or more conveniently written in formula form with evaluations held back until needed.

On the other hand, if attribute A_k represents relatively complex concepts which cannot be easily treated by an encompassing statistical model - such as involving many contributing factors which either cannot be fully quantified and/or where there is only incomplete knowledge of the actual conditional and joint probabilities involved, then in such a case, P_k may be more appropriately and simply obtained by querying directly a panel of experts. In this situation, P_k appears in numerical form - although the domain of A_k may be linguistic or numerical in nature. The panel of experts act as human integrators of knowledge in producing P_k. See Table 3 for a simple numerical example of an error table.

Z_2'' \ Z_2'	A	B	C	D	E	F
A	0.9	0.4	0.7	0.3	0.0	0.5
B	0.3	0.8	0.4	0.5	0.1	0.5
C	0.6	0.4	0.9	0.7	0.8	0.6
D	0.2	0.5	0.7	1.0	0.9	0.2
E	0.0	0.0	0.7	0.9	0.9	0.4
F	0.4	0.3	0.5	0.1	0.3	0.1

Entries represent the possibilities that a value Z_2' is true given value Z_2'' reported or observed, for the attribute Class. Note the absence of summing to unity for rows or columns due to overlapping sets of elementary events each class represents.

Table 3

A Typical Example of Error Table P_k Obtained from Directly Pooling a Panel of Experts for A_4 = Class.

Let us illustrate both the analytic and subjective modeling of P_k's by the example of classification:

Consider first the situation where classification can be obtained analytically:

For simplicity, consider the situation described, more

generally, in section 5.2 (F): Let $G_1 \stackrel{d}{=} \{a,b,c\}$, $G_2 \stackrel{d}{=} \{I,II\}$, $G_3 \stackrel{d}{=} \{1,2\}$, be the domain sets of the only factors considered for possible classes. For example, G_1 could represent lengths, G_2 , weights (heavy, light), and G_3 , shapes (of type 1 or type 2). Define then the classes $C_1,\ldots,C_6$ by the following table:

Class C_j	$G_{1j}=G_1$ values for C_j	$G_{2j}=G_2$ values for C_j	$G_{3j}=G_3$ values for C_j
C_1	a,b	I	1,2
C_2	b,c	I	1
C_3	a,c	II	1,2
C_4	a,b	II	1,2
C_5	a,b,c	II	1
C_6	c	I	2

Table 4

Definitions of Classes.

Define the following elementary events - possible triples of values from G_1 , G_2 , G_3 that determine the classes:

x_1 = (a,I,1)	x_4 = (a,II,2)	x_7 = (b,II,1)	x_{10} = (c,I,2)
x_2 = (a,I,2)	x_5 = (b,I,1)	x_8 = (b,II,2)	x_{11} = (c,II,1)
x_3 = (a,II,1)	x_6 = (b,I,2)	x_9 = (c,I,1)	x_{12} = (c,II,2)

Table 5

Multiplicative Definitions of Elementary Events.

Thus we can tabulate for each class which elements are in it, and, conversely, for each element, which classes contain it:

Class C_j	Elements in C_j	Class C_j	Elements in C_j
C_1	x_1, x_2, x_5, x_6	C_4	x_3, x_4, x_7, x_8
C_2	x_5, x_9	C_5	x_3, x_7, x_{11}
C_3	x_3, x_4, x_{11}, x_{12}	C_6	x_{10}

Table 6

Elementary Events in Each Class.

Here, $X = \{x_1, x_2, \ldots, x_{12}\}$, $\mathcal{A} = \{C_1, \ldots, C_6\} \subseteq \mathcal{P}(X)$, and the collection of all classes containing x_j is $\mathcal{C}_{\{x_j\}}(\mathcal{A})$.

x_j	$\mathcal{C}_{\{x_j\}}(\mathcal{A})$	x_j	$\mathcal{C}_{\{x_j\}}(\mathcal{A})$	x_j	$\mathcal{C}_{\{x_j\}}(\mathcal{A})$	x_j	$\mathcal{C}_{\{x_j\}}(\mathcal{A})$
x_1	$\{C_1\}$	x_4	$\{C_3, C_4\}$	x_7	$\{C_4, C_5\}$	x_{10}	$\{C_6\}$
x_2	$\{C_1\}$	x_5	$\{C_1, C_2\}$	x_8	$\{C_4\}$	x_{11}	$\{C_3, C_5\}$
x_3	$\{C_3, C_4, C_5\}$	x_6	$\{C_1\}$	x_9	$\{C_2\}$	x_{12}	$\{C_3\}$

Table 7

Classes Containing Elementary Events.

Next, let V_j be a random variable over G_j corresponding to the true value of factor j and $\mathring{V}_j$ a random variable also over G_j corresponding to the observed value of factor j , for $j = 1,2,3$. Suppose also that (V_1, V_2, V_3) are a mutually statistically independent triple, as are: $(\mathring{V}_1, \mathring{V}_2, \mathring{V}_3)$, $(V_1, \mathring{V}_2, \mathring{V}_3)$, $(\mathring{V}_1, V_2, V_3)$, and $(\mathring{V}_1, \mathring{V}_2, V_3)$. Suppose further that the probability functions $p(V_j | \mathring{V}_j)$ and $p(\mathring{V}_j)$, $j = 1,2,3$, are all known, where we use the convention of identifying, where necessary, random variable and their probability functions through their typical outcomes. Define random variable $V \stackrel{d}{=} (V_1, V_2, V_3)$ corresponding to the true joint factor values determining the true class, and similarly, $\mathring{V} \overset{d}{=} (\mathring{V}_1, \mathring{V}_2, \mathring{V}_3)$ for the observed (or reported) class. Then it follows that:

$$p(V \mid \mathring{V} \in C_k) =$$

$$\left[\prod_{j=1}^{3} \sum_{t \in G_{jk}} p(V_j \mid \mathring{V}_j = t) \cdot p(\mathring{V}_j = t) \right] \Big/ \prod_{j=1}^{3} \sum_{t \in G_{jk}} p(\mathring{V}_j = t) \tag{4}$$

and

$$p(C_m \text{ is true} \mid C_k \text{ is observed}) = p(V \in C_m \mid \mathring{V} \in C_k) \overset{d}{=} \phi_B(C_m \mid \mathring{V} \in C_k) =$$

$$\left[\prod_{j=1}^{3} \sum_{\begin{bmatrix} t \in G_{jk} \\ t' \in G_{jm} \end{bmatrix}} p(V_j = t' \mid \mathring{V}_j = t) \cdot p(\mathring{V}_j = t) \right] \Big/ \prod_{j=1}^{3} \sum_{t \in G_{jk}} p(\mathring{V}_j = t) \ . \tag{5}$$

Thus, $p(C_m \text{ true} \mid C_k \text{ observed})$ is a computable function of C_m for each C_m in $\mathcal{A}$ and may be interpreted as the fuzzy set membership function or possibility function ϕ_B for possible choices of which class gave rise to the observation C_k , for any fixed k , $k = 1,2,\ldots,6$. These functions are generated by the conditional random variables $(V \mid \mathring{V} \in C_k)$ evaluated over the collection of compound events $\mathcal{A}$. In turn, the possibility functions ϕ_B are also represented as the one point coverage functions of the random subsets $(S \mid \mathring{V} \in C_k)$ of $\mathcal{A}$ which represent the possible interactions of the classes $k = 1,2,\ldots,6$. (See Chapter 5.) Here, for any k , a typical outcome of $(S \mid \mathring{V} \in C_k)$ is some $c_{\{x_j\}}(\mathcal{A})$, the collection of all classes $C_1, C_2, \ldots$ such that they interact with respect to x_j , i.e., contain x_j . Table 6 presents the ten distinct such collections of classes making up the range of $(S \mid \mathring{V} \in C_k)$. The probability function for this random subset is obtained from

$$(S \mid \mathring{V} \in C_k) = c_{\{V\}}(\mathcal{A}) \ , \tag{6}$$

with

$$p(S = S' \mid \mathring{V} \in C_k) = p\,(V = V') \ , \tag{7}$$

for any outcome S' of S corresponding to V' of V , which, in summary, imply

$$\phi_B(C_m|\overset{o}{V} \in C_k) = p(C_m \in S \mid \overset{o}{V} \in C_k) = p(V \in C_m \mid \overset{o}{V} \in C_k) \ , \quad (8)$$

for all $C_m \in A = \{C_1,\ldots,C_6\}$, for $k = 1,\ldots,6$, where the probability function for random set $(S \mid \overset{o}{V} \in C_k)$ is given in (see also Table 7) eq. (9).

$$\left.\begin{array}{l} p(S = \{C_1\} \mid \overset{o}{V} \in C_k) = \sum\limits_{i=1,2,6} (p(V = x_1 \mid \overset{o}{V} \in C_k)) \ , \\ p(S = \{C_3,C_4,C_5\} \mid \overset{o}{V} \in C_k) = p(V = x_3 \mid \overset{o}{V} \in C_k) \ , \\ p(S = \{C_3,C_4\} \mid \overset{o}{V} \in C_k) = p(V = x_4 \mid \overset{o}{V} \in C_k) \ , \\ p(S = \{C_1,C_2\} \mid \overset{o}{V} \in C_k) = p(V = x_5 \mid \overset{o}{V} \in C_k) \ , \\ p(S = \{C_6\} \mid \overset{o}{V} \in C_k) = p(V = x_{10} \mid \overset{o}{V} \in C_k) \ , \text{ etc.,} \end{array}\right\} \quad (9)$$

which may be evaluated through eq. (4) .

Note that the function $\phi_B(\cdot|\overset{o}{V} \in C_k)$, in general, does not sum to 1 over A , since the outcomes $C_1,\ldots,C_6$ are compound events which are not all disjoint for random variable $(V \mid \overset{o}{V} \in C_k)$, $k = 1,\ldots,6$. Thus, we should *not* normalize ϕ_B to make it a probability function: it is a possibility function even though it was obtained analytically.

Consider now the converse of the first situation :

We know the classes of relevance $A = \{C_1,\ldots,C_6\}$, but we do not know all the contributing factors and/or we do not have a handle on all the required probability functions involved in the factors; but we do have before us a panel of experts who will give the possibilities of true class values given observed ones. To simplify notation, assume that a particular C_k is chosen and all results, as above, are conditioned upon the event $\overset{o}{V} \in C_k$. Suppose then the possibilities of a particular class being the true one, given C_k is observed, is determined by the panel to represent in effect the fuzzy subset B of A which is given through the membership (or possibility) function $\phi_B : A \to [0,1]$, where without loss of generality

$$0 < \phi_B(C_1) < \phi_B(C_2) <\cdots< \phi_B(C_6) = 1 \ .$$

First recall the fundamental results previously mentioned in section 5.2 (F):

There are random subsets S of A such that

$$\phi_B(C_m) = Pr(C_m \in S) \ ; \text{ all } C_m \in A \ . \quad (10)$$

Guided by (also previously mentioned) the results concerning minimal entropy or nested forms, we may choose, e.g.,

$$S = S_U(B) = \phi_B^{-1}[U,1] , \tag{11}$$

U uniformly distributed random variable over $[0,1]$. In this case, the probability function for S is, by defining for $m = 1,\ldots,6$,

$$C^{(m)} \overset{d}{=} \{C_m, C_{m+1},\ldots,C_6\} \ ; \ \phi_B(C_0) = 0 , \tag{12}$$

$$p(S = C^{(m)}) = \phi_B(C_m) - \phi_B(C_{m-1}),\ m = 1,\ldots,6 . \tag{13}$$

Thus,

$$\mathrm{rng}(S) = \{C^{(m)} \mid m-1,\ldots,6\} \subseteq \mathcal{P}(\mathcal{A}) , \tag{14}$$

$\mathcal{A} = \mathcal{A}'$, and

$$\begin{aligned} \mathcal{C}_{\{C_m\}}(\mathrm{rng}(S)) &= \{\mathcal{B} \mid C_m \in \mathcal{B} \subseteq \mathrm{rng}(S)\} \\ &= \{C^{(1)},\cdots,C^{(m)}\} \ ; \ m = 1,\ldots,6 . \end{aligned} \tag{15}$$

Let

$$\mathcal{G}(S) = \bigcup_{m=1}^{6} \mathcal{C}_{\{C_m\}}(\mathrm{rng}(S)) = \{C^{(2)},\ldots,C^{(6)}\} . \tag{16}$$

Noting here for $S : \Omega \to \mathcal{P}(\mathcal{A})$, we may choose $\Omega = [0,1]$, with $U(\omega) = \omega$, for all $\omega \in \Omega$. Then it follows that:

$$S^{-1}(C^{(m)}) = (\phi_B(C_{m-1}),\ \phi_B(C_m)] , \tag{17}$$

$m = 1,\ldots,6$.

In turn, define random variables $V_{(m)}$ and space $X_{(m)}$ arbitrary such that

$$(\text{surjective})\ V_{(m)} : (\phi_B(C_{m-1}),\ \phi_B(C_m)] \to X_{(m)} ,\ m = 1,\ldots,6 .$$

Then define space X by

$$X \overset{d}{=} \dot{\bigcup_{m=1}^{6}} X_{(m)} , \tag{18}$$

and random variable

$$V : \Omega \to X$$

by: for each $\omega \in \Omega$, there is a unique $m(\omega)$, $1 \le m(\omega) \le 6$

such that $\omega \in (\phi_B(C_{m(\omega)-1}), \phi_B(C_{m(\omega)})]$,
whence

$$V_{(\omega)} \overset{d}{=} V_{(m(\omega))}(\omega) . \tag{19}$$

Next, define mapping $\wedge$:

$$\wedge : \mathcal{A} \rightarrow \mathcal{P}(X)$$

($\mathcal{P}(X)$ being the collection of all ordinary subsets of X), by, for any $C_m \in \mathcal{A}$,

$$\hat{C}_m \overset{d}{=} V(S^{-1}(\mathscr{C}_{\{C_m\}}(rng(S))))$$

$$= V([0,\phi_B(C_m)]) = \bigcup_{j=1}^{m} X_{(j)} \; ; \; m = 1,\ldots,6 . \tag{20}$$

Then $\wedge$ is an injective mapping and it follows that for any outcome

$$\hat{S} = \mathscr{C}_{\{V\}}(\hat{\mathcal{A}}) , \tag{21}$$

$$p(V \in \hat{C}_m) = p(C_m \in S) = \phi_B(C_m) , \tag{22}$$

for all $C_m \in \mathcal{A}$.

In particular, we may let each $X_{(m)}$ be minimally any (disjoint) singleton:

$$X_{(m)} = \{y_{(m)}\} , \; m = 1,\ldots,6 . \tag{23}$$

Altermatively, let each

$$X_{(m)} = C^{(m)} , \tag{24}$$

implying

$$V = S \; ; \; X = rng(S) = \{C^{(1)},\ldots,C^{(6)}\} . \tag{25}$$

In any case, we have obtained *both* (nonuniquely) a random subset S of $\mathcal{A}$, representing interactions of the classes, and a random variable V , as above, such that the evaluation of V over certain compound events from its elementary event space and the one point coverage function of S all coincide with ϕ_B , analogous to the first situation. (See [86] for further details and the general set of constructions.) Thus, again, the function ϕ_B obtained from the panel of experts is a possibility function and not a probability function in general: it need not sum to one - as in the first situation - due to the presence of overlapping events (shown by the random variable V over X).

C. Inference rules and matching tables

Inference rules connect possible combinations of matchings of attributes (to various degrees) of any two given track histories to the correlation levels of the histories. We denote inference rules as R_t , $t = 1,2,\ldots,r$, where the tth inference rule R_t is of the form "if - or iff - (antecedent) attribute A_k $\alpha_{t,k}$ - matches for any two target histories, for all $k \in J_t$, then (consequent) the two target histories are considered to represent the same target (or not to represent the same target) to degree γ_t " , where

$$\emptyset \neq J_t \subseteq \{1,2,\ldots,m\} , \tag{26}$$

$$0 \leq \alpha_{t,k} , \gamma_t \leq 1 \quad ; \tag{27}$$

for all $k \in J_t$, $t = 1,\ldots,r$.

$\alpha_{t,k}$ represents the degree of matching relative to attribute A_k for any two target histories, and may be originally in linguistic form such as high, medium, low, etc., or in numerical form. Similarly $0 \leq \gamma_t \leq 1$ represents the degree of data association (or lack of it), $k \in J_t$, $t = 1,\ldots,r$.

In symbolic form, analagous to the results obtained earlier, the truth of rule R_t is evaluated for any possible set of values (or "dummy" data)

$$Z_{J_t} = (Z_{J_t}^{(1)}, Z_{J_t}^{(2)}) , \tag{28}$$

where

$$Z_{J_t}^{(j)} = (Z_k^{(j)})_{k \in J_t} , \quad Z_k^{(j)} \in \mathrm{dom}(A_k) , \tag{29}$$

for $j = 1,2,$ arbitrary fixed, and prior target association possibility or probability function

$$Q = f(\theta) , \tag{30}$$

evaluated at any possible association level $\theta \in [0,1]$ (suitably discretized, if required):

$$\begin{aligned} &\| (R_t(Q|A_{J_t})\| \\ &= \phi_*(M_{J_t}(Z_{J_t}^{(1)}, Z_{J_t}^{(2)}) , \begin{bmatrix} Q^{g_t} \\ (1 - Q)^{g_t} \end{bmatrix} \end{aligned} \tag{31}$$

where

$$* \stackrel{d}{=} \Rightarrow \quad \text{or} \quad * \stackrel{d}{=} \Leftrightarrow \,, \tag{32}$$

$$\phi_{\Rightarrow}(u,v) \equiv \| (\text{if} \quad u \quad \text{then} \quad v) \|$$

for example,

$$\equiv \phi_{or}(\phi_{not}(u),v) \; ; \tag{33}$$

$$\phi_{\Leftrightarrow}(u,v) = \| (\text{iff}(u, \text{ then } v)) \|$$

$$= \phi_{\&}(\phi_{\Rightarrow}(u,v), \phi_{\Rightarrow}(v,u)), \tag{34}$$

for all $u,v \in [0,1]$;

$$M_{J_t}(Z_{J_t}{}^{(1)}, Z_{J_t}{}^{(2)})$$

$$\stackrel{d}{=} \underset{k \in J_t}{\phi_{\&}} (\phi_{((\alpha_{t,k}))}(M_k(Z_k{}^{(1)}, Z_k{}^{(2)}))) \tag{35}$$

where

$$\phi_{((\alpha_{t,k}))} : [0,1] \to [0,1]$$

represents $\alpha_{t,k}$ - intensification (or extensification), such as by exponentiation as in

$$\phi_{((\alpha_{t,k}))}(y) = y^{\alpha_{t,k}/(1-\alpha_{t,k})} \; ; \; y \in [0,1] \,, \tag{36}$$

and

$$M_k : \text{dom}(A_k) \times \text{dom}(A_k) \to [0,1]$$

is a possibility function (actually a fuzzy set - binary relation) representing the matching table corresponding to attribute A_k, $k \in J_t$; $t = 1,\ldots,r$: (More on construction of the M_k's later.)

Analagous to the modeling of the error tables P_k, inference rules R_t may be obtained from analytic considerations or subjectively, by polling a panel of experts. (The latter procedure has been well developed in a number of related artificial intelligence - expert systems, but usually within the framework of classical logic and probability theory. (See e.g., [24] or [236].)

Consider the case of "analytic" inference rules. These are based - and essentially equivalent to, or extensions of - classical hypotheses tests:

Let $\tau \geq 0$ be an unknown paremeter and for each possible τ, $(Y^{(j)}|\tau)$, $j = 1,2$, be two random variables (possibly vector valued and often assumed statistically independent) representing observations of data for some attribute A_1, say, given τ, where it is assumed the relevant probability functions or probability density functions are all known. Let $\lambda = \lambda(Z)$, where $Z \overset{d}{=} (Z^{(1)}, Z^{(2)})$, be a test statistic, with scalar function $\lambda \geq 0$ having, for each fixed value τ, known prob. dist. function F_τ which is assumed increasing over $[0,b]$, b - a pos. const., possibly infinite, and such that, pointwise, F_τ is increasing in τ. Then λ may be chosen based on invariance, uniformly most powerful test properties or other considerations. (See, e.g., [154].)

Then a typical test for

$$\left.\begin{array}{l} H_o : 0 \leq \tau \leq \tau_o \\ \text{vs.} \\ H_1 : \tau_o \leq \tau \leq b \end{array}\right\} \tag{37}$$

is given by, at any fixed significance level α, $0 < \alpha < 1$:

For any observed Z :

$$\left.\begin{array}{l} \text{Decide } H_o \text{ iff } \lambda(Z) \leq D_\alpha \\ \quad \text{iff } 1 - F_{\tau_o}(\lambda(Z)) \geq 1 - F_{\tau_o}(D_\alpha) \equiv \alpha \text{ ;} \\ \text{Decide } H_1 \text{ iff } \lambda(Z) > D_\alpha \\ \quad \text{iff } 1 - F_{\tau_o}(\lambda(Z)) < 1 - F_{\tau_o}(D_\alpha) \equiv \alpha \text{ ,} \end{array}\right\} \tag{38}$$

where thus

$$\Pr(\text{Decide } H_1 \mid H_o \text{ true}) \leq \alpha \text{ .} \tag{39}$$

Thus if data association for the two target histories is to be based solely on this test of hypotheses, i.e.,

$$\left.\begin{array}{l} \text{Decide } Q = 1 \text{ iff } H_o \text{ is accepted ,} \\ \text{Decide } Q = 0 \text{ iff } H_1 \text{ is accepted ,} \end{array}\right\} \tag{40}$$

then the entire procedure is mathematically equivalent to the inference rule evaluation

$$\| (R_1^{(\alpha)}(Q|Z)) \| = \phi_{\Leftrightarrow}(M_1^{(\alpha)}(Z) \text{ , } Q^0 \equiv 1) \tag{41}$$

where the matching table here $M_1^{(\alpha)}$ is

$$M_1^{(\alpha)}(Z) = \begin{cases} 1 & \text{iff} \quad 1 - F_{\tau_o}(\lambda(Z)) \geq \alpha \ , \\ 0 & \text{iff} \quad 1 - F_{\tau_o}(\lambda(Z)) < \alpha \ , \end{cases} \tag{42}$$

for any $Z \in \text{dom}(A_1) \times \text{dom}(A_1)$.

Clearly, a "softer" more general form is obtained by replacing $M_1^{(\alpha)}$ by the natural full non-truncated matching table M_1 where for all such Z as above,

$$M_1(Z) = 1 - F_{\tau_o}(\lambda(Z)) \ , \tag{43}$$

the *randomized significance level*, and replacing exponent 0 by, say, $0 \leq \gamma_1 \leq 1$, so that $R_1^{(\alpha)}$ becomes

$$\|(R_1(Q|Z))\| = \phi_{\Leftrightarrow}(M_1(Z), Q^{\gamma_1}) \ . \tag{44}$$

An example of the above is A_1 = geolocation, with r.v. $(Z|\tau)$ distributed statistically independent $\text{Gauss}_2(\mu^{(j)}, \Sigma^{(j)})$, $j = 1,2$, such that

$$\lambda(Z) = (Z^{(1)} - Z^{(2)})^T(\Sigma^{(1)} + \Sigma^{(2)})^{-1}(Z^{(1)} - Z^{(2)}) \tag{45}$$

with

$$\tau \overset{d}{=} (\mu^{(1)} - \mu^{(2)})^T \cdot (\Sigma^{(1)} + \Sigma^{(2)})^{-1} \cdot (\mu^{(1)} - \mu^{(2)}) \ , \tag{46}$$

where τ_o is some upper bound chosen for maximal separation distance (or $\tau_o = 0$ could be chosen) , and hence $(\lambda(Z)|\tau)$ is distributed noncentral chi-square with two degrees of freedom and noncentrality parameter τ , etc.

If several attributes, say, $A_1,\ldots,A_n$ each has an associated statistical test with test statistics $\lambda_j = \lambda_j(Z_{(j)})$ and well-behaved cumulative prob. dist. functions F_j , $j = 1,\ldots,n$, with $Z_{(1)},\ldots,Z_{(n)}$ all statistically independent, then these may be combined into one compound test for compound attribute $(A_1 \cdot \cdots \cdot A_n)$ by, e.g., the construction of the minimum of individual randomized significance levels

$$K(Z) \overset{d}{=} \min\,(1 - F_j(\lambda_j(Z_{(j)}))) \ , \tag{47}$$

For any Z :

$$\begin{cases} \text{Accept } H_o & \text{iff } \textit{all } 1 - F_j(\lambda_j(Z_{(j)})) \ge \alpha \;, \\ & \qquad j = 1,\ldots,n \\ & \text{iff } K(Z) \ge \alpha \;; \\ \text{Accept } H_1 & \text{iff } K(Z) < \alpha \;, \end{cases} \tag{48}$$

where we note the level of the test is

$$\Pr(\text{Decide } H_1 | H_o \text{ true}) \le 1 - (1 - \alpha)^n \;. \tag{49}$$

(For background or more general constructions of compound hypothese tests, see, e.g., [154] and [18].)

Thus, if data association were based only on this compound test, one would have equivalently

$$\| R_C^{(\alpha)}(Q|Z) \| = \phi_{\Leftrightarrow}(M^{(\alpha)}(Z), Q^0 \equiv 1) \tag{50}$$

where compound matching table is

$$M_C^{(\alpha)}(Z) = \begin{cases} 1 & \text{iff } K(Z) \ge \alpha \\ 0 & \text{iff } K(Z) < \alpha \;. \end{cases} \tag{51}$$

However, as in the modeling of the error tables, in general, not all of the relationships between data association and attribute matching is obtainable as above; a panel of experts may be utilized to derive further relationships - especially those involving non-statistically oriented attributes such as flag color, classification, visual sightings, etc.

Again, as before, the inference rule corresponding to the compound test described above in fully general form is

$$\| (R_C(Q|Z)) \| = \phi_{\Leftrightarrow}(M_C(Z), Q^{\gamma}) \tag{52}$$

where

$$M_C(Z) \equiv K(Z) \tag{53}$$

and

$$0 \le \gamma \le 1 \;.$$

In general - especially for those attributes involved in statistical hypotheses tests - matching tables are distinct in form from error tables. However, in the case of many subjective oriented attributes, matching tables may be reasonably assumed the same.

See Table 8 below for an illustration of a typical inference rule.

1. Natural Language Form From Combination of Panel of Experts and Standard Statistical Hypotheses Testing:

   R_1 = "*If* two track histories are close to each other and have somewhat similar fundamental frequencies, but differ considerably with respect to motion type, *then* there is some - but not much - chance that they correlate."

2. Formal Language Form:
   For any Z and θ,

$$\text{Truth } (\textit{if } \text{modifier}_{\text{high}}((Z_1^{(1)} \text{ in } M_1) \,\&\, (Z_1^{(2)} \text{ in } M_1)) \,\&\, \text{modifier}_{\text{med}}((Z_5^{(1)} \text{ in } M_5) \,\&\, (Z_5^{(2)} \text{ in } M_5)) \,\&\, \text{modifier}_{\text{low}}((Z_6^{(1)} \text{ in } M_6) \,\&\, (Z_6^{(2)} \text{ in } M_6)) \; \textit{then } \text{modifier}_{\text{very low}}(\theta \text{ IN } Q))\,.$$

3. Full Truth Evaluation-Possibility Function Form;
   for any Z and θ,
   $\phi_{\rightarrow}(\text{anteced}(Z)\,,\ \text{conseq}(Q(\theta)))\,,$

$$\text{anteced}(Z) = \phi_{\&}(M_1(Z_1^{(1)},Z_1^{(2)})^{E_1}, M_5(Z_5^{(1)},Z_5^{(2)})^{E_2}, M_6(Z_6^{(1)},Z_6^{(2)})^{E_3})\,,$$

$$\text{conseq}(Q(\theta)) = Q(\theta)^{G}\,.$$

(i) The constants to be chosen such that

$$0 < G < E_3 < E_2 < E_1\,.$$

(ii) Logical System $\mathcal{F} = (\phi_{\text{not}}, \phi_{\&}, \phi_{\text{or}}) = (1 - (\cdot), \text{prod}, \text{sum})$ chosen.

(iii) $M_1(Z_1^{(1)},Z_1^{(2)}) = 1 -$ cumul. distrib. funct. of chi-square random variable with 2 degrees of freedom evaluated at $W = (Z_1^{(1)}-Z_1^{(2)})^T\cdot(\Sigma_1+\Sigma_2)^{-1}\cdot(Z_1^{(1)}-Z_1^{(2)})$, Σ_1,Σ_2 error covariance matrices.

(iv) M_5 is similarly evaluated from a closed-form formula while M_6 is obtained from a numerical table.

Table 8

An Example of Symbolization of an Inference Rule.

D. Additional comments on error tables, matching tables, and inference rules.

Error tables and matching tables

An elaborate example of an analytically obtained error table for an ideal classification attribute has already been presented (Tables 4 - 8, etc.). The actual error table for this attribute would then be a 6 by 6 table of numbers lying between 0 and 1, being evaluated correspondingly. (See eqs. (4), (5)).

Another example may be furnished by the attribute A_3 = length, with $dom(A_3) = \{B_1, B_2, B_3, B_4\}$,
where

$$\left.\begin{array}{lll} B_1 \overset{d}{\equiv} \text{very short} & : & \text{approx. less than 50 ft.} \\ B_2 \overset{d}{\equiv} \text{short} & : & \text{approx. between 50 and 100 ft.} \\ B_3 \overset{d}{\equiv} \text{moderate} & : & \text{approx. between 100 and 200 ft.} \\ B_4 \overset{d}{\equiv} \text{long} & : & \text{appprox. over 200 ft.} \end{array}\right\} \quad (54)$$

Thus, P_3 consists simply of a 4 by 4 table furnished by the consensus of a panel of experts in response to the question:

$$p(\text{true length} = B_m \mid \text{observed length} = B_k) \ ? \quad (55)$$

for $1 \le k,m \le 6$, p being probability or possibility.

Table 9 presents plausible values for the above equation (55):

True \ Observed	B_1	B_2	B_3	B_4
B_1	0.9	0.6	0.4	0.5
B_2	0.5	0.8	0.2	0.6
B_3	0.4	0.1	1.0	0.2
B_4	0.4	0.6	0.1	0.9

Table 9

Error Table for Eq. (55).

Thus, Table 9 shows

$$P_3(Z_3^{(j)} = B_2 \mid \tilde{Z}_3^{(j)} = B_3) = 0.8 , \quad (56)$$

regardless of $j = 1$ or 2.

It is not unreasonable here to allow the matching and error tables for A_3 to coincide, following suitable symmetrization, i.e., $M_3 = P_3$. Similar remarks hold for the classification example previously presented (for the second situation, not the first).

Consider now some examples of analytically obtained error and matching tables. These could typically involve attributes such as geolocation, frequency or class (as under the first situation in the previous example).

Thus, for A_1 = geolocation, we may have, regardless of $j, j = 1,2$,

$$P_1(Z_1^{(j)} \mid \mathring{Z}_1^{(j)}) = \text{dirac}(\Sigma - \mathring{\Sigma}) \cdot \text{Gauss}_2'(\mathring{X}, \mathring{\Sigma}) \tag{57}$$

where $Z_1^{(j)}$ and $\mathring{Z}_1^{(j)}$ are arbitrary with

$$Z_1^{(j)} \overset{d}{=} (X, \Sigma) \; ; \; Z_1^{(j)} \overset{d}{=} (\mathring{X}, \mathring{\Sigma}) \; , \tag{58}$$

$X, \mathring{X} \in \mathfrak{R} \subseteq \mathbb{R}^2$; $\mathfrak{R}$ suitably discretized, $\Sigma, \mathring{\Sigma} \in \mathfrak{P}$ = class of all 2 by 2 positive definite matrices, and hence

$$Z_1^{(j)}, \mathring{Z}_1^{(j)} \in \text{dom}(A_1) = \mathfrak{R} \times \mathfrak{P} \; ,$$

and Gauss_2' is a probability function over $\mathfrak{R}$ formed by suitably discretizing the bivariate distribution Gauss_2.

However, as noted previously, the associated matching table M_1 is quite different from P_1 here:

$$M_1(Z_1^{(1)}, Z_1^{(2)}) = 1 - F_{\tau_0}(\lambda(Z_1^{(1)}, Z_1^{(2)})) \; , \tag{59}$$

for all $Z \equiv (Z_1^{(1)}, Z_1^{(2)}) \in \text{dom}(A_1) \times \text{dom}(A_1)$, with λ given in eq. (45)).

Another example of an analytically derived error table is that for A_2 = signal frequency:

From simplified physical considerations, the relationship between true source frequency and received frequency is given by the doppler shift equation [255] given, regardless of $j, j = 1,2$, by

$$\mathring{Z}_2^{(j)} = (1 - (V_T/V_S) \cdot \cos\theta) \cdot Z_2^{(j)}$$

$$\overset{d}{=} \text{observed frequency at-rest receive} \tag{60}$$

$$V_T \overset{d}{=} \text{target speed,} \tag{61}$$

$$V_S \overset{d}{=} \text{speed of sound in water} \tag{62}$$

(assumed constant),

$Z_2^{(j)} \overset{d}{=}$ true frequency at source, (63)

$\theta \overset{d}{=}$ angle between receiver position, target location and target motion velocity measured counterclockwise. (See Figure 1) (64)

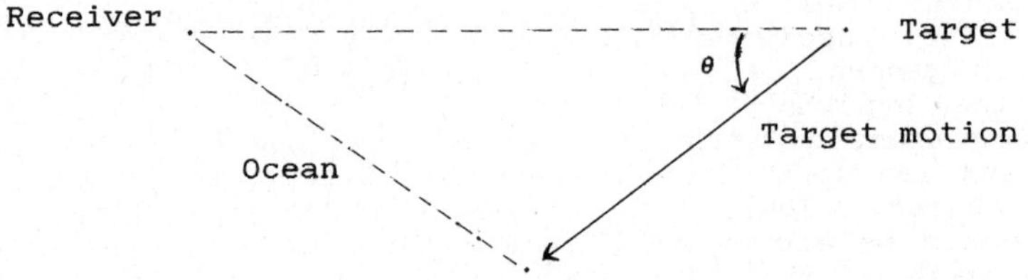

Figure 1. Basic geometry of droppler shift.

Suppose then θ is distributed uniformly over $[0,2\pi]$ and V_T is distributed uniformly over $[a,b]$ for some suitable chosen range $0 < a < b$, with θ, V_T, and $\tilde{Z}_2^{(j)}$ all statistically independent. Then it follows by use of standard transformation of probability techniques that we can derive the conditional probability density function

$$p_2(Z_2^{(j)} | \tilde{Z}_2^{(j)}) = (1/(\pi\cdot(b-a)))\cdot W'\cdot \begin{cases} g_o(W/a, W/b), & \text{if } W < 0 \\ g_o(W/b, W/a), & \text{if } W > 0, \end{cases} \tag{65}$$

where for all $u,v \in [0,1]$,

$$g_o(u,v) \overset{d}{=} (1/2)\log\left[\frac{1+\sqrt{1-u^2}}{1-\sqrt{1-u^2}}\cdot\frac{1-\sqrt{1-v^2}}{1+\sqrt{1-v^2}}\right], \tag{66}$$

$$W \overset{d}{=} V_S\cdot((\tilde{Z}_2^{(j)}/Z_2^{(j)}) - 1), \tag{67}$$

$$W' \overset{d}{=} V_S\cdot(\tilde{Z}_2^{(j)}/(Z_2^{(j)})^2). \tag{68}$$

Again, by suitable discretization over $\mathrm{dom}(A_2) \subseteq \mathbb{R}^+$, the corresponding error table P_2 can be constructed from p_2 in eq. (65).

On the other hand, the matching table M_2 here may be treated simply by first assuming $Z_2^{(1)}$, $Z_2^{(2)}$ are statistically independent Gaussian. (See also eqs. (37) - (46).)

Inference rules

Eqs. (37)-(53) adequately cover inference rules analytically obtained through statistical tests of hypotheses. However, it should be pointed out again, that the relationship between the rejecting or, accepting of the hypothesis concerning a single attribute or, more generally, a collection of attributes (in the case of a combined test of hypotheses), and the final decision to "correlate" - i.e., decide the target histories represent the same target, is, in general, a *subjective* choice of how much weight or reliability the hypotheses test has with respect to the final decision. For example, two different targets could truly possess the same or similar locations, frequencies and classes and yet not be the same object. Thus, *all* factors contributing to this identification should be accounted for, and since in practice this is not always feasible, this may be incorporated into the inference rules, by softening the consequents, i.e., replacing $Q^0 \equiv 1$ by Q^{γ_1} as in eq. (44) or eq. (52) .

On the other hand, inference rules may be formulated completely subjectively, by querying a panel of experts in the field. Two typical examples of this include:

(a) R_1 = "If A_3 0.6 - matches and A_8 0.8 - matches, then 0.7 - level intensification holds for Q." (69)

Here, $J_1 = \{3,8\}$, and we may symbolize , for any

$$Z_{J_1} = (z_3^{(1)}, z_3^{(3)}, z_8^{(1)}, z_8^{(2)}) , \quad (70)$$

$z_3^{(1)}, z_3^{(2)} \in \mathrm{dom}(A_3)$, $z_8^{(1)}, z_8^{(2)} \in \mathrm{dom}(A_8)$, and for any $Q \in [0,1]$:

$$R_1(Q \mid Z_{J_1}) = \phi_{\rightarrow}(\phi_{\&}((M_3(z_3^{(1)}, z_3^{(2)}))^{1.5}, (M_8(z_8^{(1)}, z_8^{(2)}))^4), Q^{2.3}) . \quad (71)$$

(b) R_2 = "Iff A_1 does not match that well but A_2 highly matches, then correlation probably does not occur". (72)

Here, $J_2 = \{1,2\}$, and we may symbolize, using the techniques illustrated previously as, e.g.:

$$R_2(Q \mid Z_{J_2}) = \phi_{\Leftrightarrow}(\phi_{\&}(\phi_{low}(M_1(z_1^{(1)}, z_1^{(2)})), \phi_{high}(M_2(z_2^{(1)}, z_2^{(2)}))), \phi_{prob}(1-Q)) , \quad (73)$$

where ϕ_{low}, ϕ_{high}, ϕ_{prob} : $[0,1] \to [0,1]]$ may be modeled as exponents as before or otherwise, as in the previous examples.

E. Combination of evidence for the correlation problem.

The basic structure of the technique for combining of evidence may be summarized as follows:

(a) Observed data: $\overset{\circ}{Z}$ categorized by attributes and target history.

(b) Error tables P_k, $k = 1,\dots,m$, which can be used to connect $\overset{\circ}{Z}$ with any Z.

(c) Matching tables M_k, (with $P_k = M_k$ or $P_k \neq M_k$) $k = 1,\dots,m$, leading to:

(d) Inference rules R_t, $t = 1,\dots,r$ which can be used to connect any Z and $Q \equiv P(\theta)$.

Now, let

$$\underset{\sim}{R} \overset{d}{=} \{R_t \mid t = 1,2,\dots,r\} ,$$

$$\underset{\sim}{P} \overset{d}{=} \{P_k \mid k = 1,\dots,m\} .$$

Then from the property of conditional possibility functions - see also the more general results of section 8.3 - the posterior possibility function for θ is given by, omitting the subscripts $proj_X(C_o)$, C_k, $k = 1,2,\dots$, C_o, etc. for simplicity, prior to diagonalization and normalization,

$$\phi(\underset{\sim}{\theta} \mid \underset{\sim}{\overset{\circ}{Z}} ; \underset{\sim}{R},\underset{\sim}{P}) = \underset{\underset{\sim}{Z} \in G_o}{\phi_{or}} \phi(\underset{\sim}{\theta},\underset{\sim}{Z} \mid \underset{\sim}{\overset{\circ}{Z}} ; \underset{\sim}{R},\underset{\sim}{P}) , \tag{74}$$

where

$$G_o \overset{d}{=} \mathop{\times}_{k=1}^{m} (\mathrm{dom}(A_k) \times \mathrm{dom}(A_k)) , \tag{75}$$

and general fuzzy set system $(\phi_{not},\phi_{\&},\phi_{or})$ is chosen, where

$$\begin{aligned}\phi(\underset{\sim}{\theta},\underset{\sim}{Z} \mid \underset{\sim}{\overset{\circ}{Z}} ; \underset{\sim}{R},\underset{\sim}{P}) &\equiv \phi_{\&}\left(\phi(\underset{\sim}{\theta} \mid \underset{\sim}{Z},\underset{\sim}{\overset{\circ}{Z}} ; \underset{\sim}{R},\underset{\sim}{P}) , \phi(\underset{\sim}{Z} \mid \underset{\sim}{\overset{\circ}{Z}} ; \underset{\sim}{R},\underset{\sim}{P})\right) \\ &\equiv \phi_{\&}\left(\phi(\underset{\sim}{\theta} \mid \underset{\sim}{Z} ; \underset{\sim}{R}) , \phi(\underset{\sim}{Z} \mid \underset{\sim}{\overset{\circ}{Z}} ; \underset{\sim}{P})\right)\end{aligned} \tag{76}$$

assuming that sufficiency relations for the inference rule and error table effects hold:

$$\phi(\underset{\sim}{\theta} \mid \underset{\sim}{Z},\underset{\sim}{\mathring{Z}} ; \underset{\sim}{R},\underset{\sim}{P}) \equiv \phi(\underset{\sim}{\theta} \mid \underset{\sim}{Z} ; \underset{\sim}{R}) , \tag{77}$$

$$\phi(\underset{\sim}{Z} \mid \underset{\sim}{\mathring{Z}} ; \underset{\sim}{R},\underset{\sim}{P}) \equiv \phi(\underset{\sim}{Z} \mid \underset{\sim}{\mathring{Z}} ; \underset{\sim}{P}) . \tag{78}$$

Consider now the error table effects. This expression does not really represent combination of evidence, but rather the joint error function. Hence, a natural evaluation is

$$\phi(\underset{\sim}{Z} \mid \underset{\sim}{\mathring{Z}} ; \underset{\sim}{P}) = \underset{k=1,\ldots,m}{\phi_{\&}} (P_k(Z_k \mid \mathring{Z}_k)) , \tag{79}$$

where

$$P_k(Z_k \mid \mathring{Z}_k)$$
$$= \phi_{\&}(P_k(Z_k^{(1)} \mid \mathring{Z}_k^{(1)}), P_k(Z_k^{(2)} \mid \mathring{Z}_k^{(2)})) , \tag{80}$$

for all $Z_k^{(j)}, \mathring{Z}_k \in \mathrm{dom}(A_k)$, $j = 1,2,$; $k = 1,\ldots,m$.

On the other hand, the inference rule effect *does* represent combination of evidence.

The first approach follows the idea of the extension principle, a specific case of which is related to the fuzzy set extension of the Weak Law of Large Numbers (see section 8.4):

Approach 1.

Let $g_r : [0,1]^r \to [0,1]$ be a given function such as

$$\text{(a)} \quad g_r(y_1,\ldots,y_r) \equiv \sum_{j=1}^{r} w_{rj} \cdot y_j \tag{81}$$

$$0 < w_{rj} < 1 , \quad \sum_{j=1}^{r} w_{rj} = 1 ,$$

or

$$\text{(b)} \quad g_r(y_1,\ldots,y_r) \equiv \delta_{y_1,\ldots,y_r} \cdot y_1$$

$$= \begin{cases} 0 & \text{iff } \exists\, y_i \neq y_j \\ & \quad 1 \le i,j \le r \\ y_1 & \text{iff } y_1 = \cdots = y_r , \end{cases} \tag{82}$$

where g_r represents some combination of descriptions of Q by each rule. Then by the "extension principle"

$$\phi(\underset{\sim}{\theta} \mid \underset{\sim}{Z} ; \underset{\sim}{R}) = \phi_{g_r(R_1,\ldots,R)}(Z,Q) \begin{bmatrix} \text{relative to} \\ Q(\theta_1) = q(\theta_1) \\ \vdots \\ Q(\theta_r) = q(\theta_r) \end{bmatrix}$$

$$= \underset{\begin{bmatrix} (\theta_1,\ldots,\theta_r) \\ \in g_r^{-1}(\theta) \\ \text{(discretized)} \end{bmatrix}}{\phi_{or}} \left[\underset{t=1,\ldots,r}{\phi_{\&}} (\| R_r(q(\theta_t) | Z_{J_t})) \|) \right] \tag{83}$$

In the case of (b) ,

$$\phi(\underset{\sim}{\theta} \mid \underset{\sim}{Z} ; \underset{\sim}{R}) = \underset{(t=1,\ldots,r)}{\phi_{\&}} (\| R_t(q(\theta_t) \mid Z_{J_t}) \|) \ . \tag{84}$$

For simplicity, from now on, we drop the notation $\|(R_t)\|$ for the simpler R_t .

Approach 2: (See [80], [82], [83].)

Let $g_r : [0,1]^r \to [0,1]$ be a nondecreasing combining function, such as $g_r = \phi_{\&}$ or $g_r = \text{wtdsum}$ as in (a) of Approach 1. Then there is a unique fuzzy subset A of $G_o \times [0,1]$ such that for all $\alpha_1,\ldots,\alpha_r \in [0,1]$,

$$\phi_A^{-1}[g_r(\alpha_1,\ldots,\alpha_r),1] \geq \bigcap_{j=1}^{r} (R_t^{-1}[\alpha_j,1]) \tag{85}$$

minimally with respect to set ordering. Indeed,

$$\phi_A = g_r \circ (R_1,\ldots,R_r) \ . \tag{86}$$

If $g_r = \phi_{\&}(,\ldots,)$ is a strict Archimedean t-norm, then there is an $h : [0,1] \to \mathbb{R}^+$ with h decreasing, $h(1) = 0$, such that

$$g_r(y_1,\ldots,y_r) \equiv h^{-1}\left(\sum_{t=1}^{r} h(y_t)\right) \tag{87}$$

(See [140].)

Then

$$w_r(\alpha_1,\ldots,\alpha_r) \overset{d}{=} (g_r \circ (R_1,\ldots,R_r))^{-1}[g_r(\alpha_1,\ldots,\alpha_r),1]$$

$$= \{V \mid h^{-1}\left(\sum_{t=1}^{r} h(R_t(V))\right) \geq h^{-1}\left(\sum_{t=1}^{r} h(\alpha_t)\right)\}$$

$$= \{V \mid \sum_{t=1}^{r} h(R_t(V)) \leq \sum_{t=1}^{r} h(\alpha_t)\} \; . \tag{88}$$

In particular, for $\alpha_1 = \cdots = \alpha_r = \alpha$,

$$w_r(\alpha,\ldots,\alpha) = \{V \mid \frac{1}{r} \cdot \sum_{t=1}^{r} h(R_t(V)) \leq h(\alpha)\} \; . \tag{89}$$

Note - as seen in previous examples - when fuzzy set systems $\mathcal{F}' = (1-(\cdot),\text{prod},\text{bndsum})$ is chosen and all possibility functions involved are also probability functions, then the above equations all reduce to the classical Bayesian forms.

See Figure 2 for a flow chart summary of the combination of evidence technique used here. This presents only a simplified scheme for combining evidence. Based on the results in section 8.3, (see Remarks 1,2) and in 8.4 (Theorems 3 and 4), in general, it may be better to use a hybrid logical system in evaluating the posterior function for θ . Thus, if $A_1,\ldots,A_{m'}$ denote statistically based attributes, while $A_{m'+1},\ldots,A_{m''}$ denote subjective based ones, it may be appropriate to choose a $\phi_{\&,1}$ to combine the first group for error table effect and some $\phi_{\&,2}$ for the second group, in place of a single $\phi_{\&}$. Moreover, $\phi_{\&,1}$, $\phi_{\&,2}$ may well be chosen as Archimedean t-norms. On the other hand, since inference rules typically operate on combinations of common or similar attributes - varying basically only on intensification modifications for possible attribute matches - $\phi_{\&} = \min$ may be most appropriate for obtaining the overall inference rule effect. Also, in obtaining the marginal posterior function for $\underset{\sim}{\theta}$, it follows from the above quoted results of sections 8.3 , 8.4 that the single projection operator ϕ_{or} may be replaced by max over $\underset{\sim}{Z}'' \overset{d}{=} (Z_k)_{k=m'+1,\ldots,m''}$ and by some Archimedean t-norm over $\underset{\sim}{Z}' \overset{d}{=} (Z_k)_{k=1,\ldots,m'}$, where as usual, $Z_k \overset{d}{=} (Z_k^{(i)}, Z_k^{(j)})$, for track histories i and j ; $k = 1,\ldots,m''$. In addition, $\phi_{or} = \max$ seems most appropriate, according to the above reasoning, for obtaining normalization as in section 8.3. See also the comments in Goodman [91'''], where several principles or guidelines are developed for choosing types of t-norms and t-conorms. Unfortunately, the choice of the most appropriate logical operators, except for the above general guidelines, still involves a mixture of art and intuition.

As an application of the above principles, the combination of evidence technique (based on eqs. (74)-(80), (84), etc.) becomes:

$$\phi_{diag}(\theta \mid \overset{\circ}{\underset{\sim}{Z}},\underset{\sim}{R},\underset{\sim}{P}) = \phi_{\&,4}(\phi(\theta \mid diag;\, \overset{\circ}{\underset{\sim}{Z}},\underset{\sim}{R},\underset{\sim}{P}),\, \phi_{univ}(diag)) , \tag{90}$$

solving for $\phi(\theta \mid diag;\, \overset{\circ}{\underset{\sim}{Z}},\underset{\sim}{R},\underset{\sim}{P})$, $0 \leq \theta \leq 1$,

$$\phi_{univ}(diag) = \max_{0 \leq \theta \leq 1} (\theta \mid \overset{\circ}{\underset{\sim}{Z}},\underset{\sim}{R},\underset{\sim}{P}) \; , \tag{91}$$

$$\phi_{diag}(\theta \mid \overset{\circ}{\underset{\sim}{Z}},R,P) = \phi(\underset{\sim}{\theta} \mid \overset{\circ}{\underset{\sim}{Z}},\underset{\sim}{R},\underset{\sim}{P})_{(\theta_k=\theta)_{k=1,\ldots,m''}} \tag{92}$$

$$\phi(\theta \mid \overset{\circ}{\underset{\sim}{Z}},\underset{\sim}{R},\underset{\sim}{P}) = \max_{\text{all } \underset{\sim}{Z}''} \left[\phi_{\substack{or \\ \text{all } \underset{\sim}{Z}'}} (\phi(\underset{\sim}{\theta},\underset{\sim}{Z} \mid \overset{\circ}{\underset{\sim}{Z}},\underset{\sim}{R},\underset{\sim}{P}) \right] \tag{93}$$

$$\phi(\underset{\sim}{\theta},\underset{\sim}{Z} \mid \overset{\circ}{\underset{\sim}{Z}},\underset{\sim}{R},\underset{\sim}{P}) = \phi_{\&,2}(\phi_G(\underset{\sim}{\theta},\underset{\sim}{Z}),\ \underset{\sim}{P}'(\underset{\sim}{Z}' \mid \overset{\circ}{\underset{\sim}{Z}}')) \tag{94}$$

$$\phi_G(\underset{\sim}{\theta},\underset{\sim}{Z}) \overset{d}{=} \phi_{\&,2}(P''(\underset{\sim}{Z}'' \mid \overset{\circ}{\underset{\sim}{Z}}''),\ R(\underset{\sim}{\theta} \mid \underset{\sim}{Z}))\ , \tag{95}$$

$$R(\underset{\sim}{\theta},\underset{\sim}{Z}) = \min_{t=1,2,\ldots,r} (R_t(\theta_t \mid \underset{\sim}{Z}))\ , \tag{96}$$

$$P'(\underset{\sim}{Z}' \mid \overset{\circ}{\underset{\sim}{Z}}') = \phi_{\substack{\&,1 \\ k=1,2,\ldots,m'}}(\phi_{\&,1}(P_k(Z_k^{(1)} | \overset{\circ}{Z}_k^{(1)}),\ P_k(Z_k^{(2)} | \overset{\circ}{Z}_k^{(2)}))) \tag{97}$$

$$P''(\underset{\sim}{Z}'' | \overset{\circ}{\underset{\sim}{Z}}'') = \phi_{\substack{\&,3 \\ k=m'+1,\ldots,m''}}(\phi_{\&,3}(P_k(Z_k^{(1)} | \overset{\circ}{Z}_k^{(1)}), P_k(Z_k^{(2)} | \overset{\circ}{Z}_k^{(2)})) \tag{98}$$

where $\underset{\sim}{Z} = (\underset{\sim}{Z}',\underset{\sim}{Z}'')$, $\overset{\circ}{\underset{\sim}{Z}} = (\overset{\circ}{\underset{\sim}{Z}}',\overset{\circ}{\underset{\sim}{Z}}'')$, etc., and $\phi_{\&,1}$, $\phi_{\&,2}$, $\phi_{\&,3}$, $\phi_{\&,4}$ are Archimedean t-norms and ϕ_{or} is an Archimedean t-conorm such as chosen, e.g., conveniently from Frank's family - see section 2.3.6.

For other approaches to the combination of uncertainties, see [23], [24], [236], the critique of [236] as presented in [120] as well as the discussions in Chapter 8.

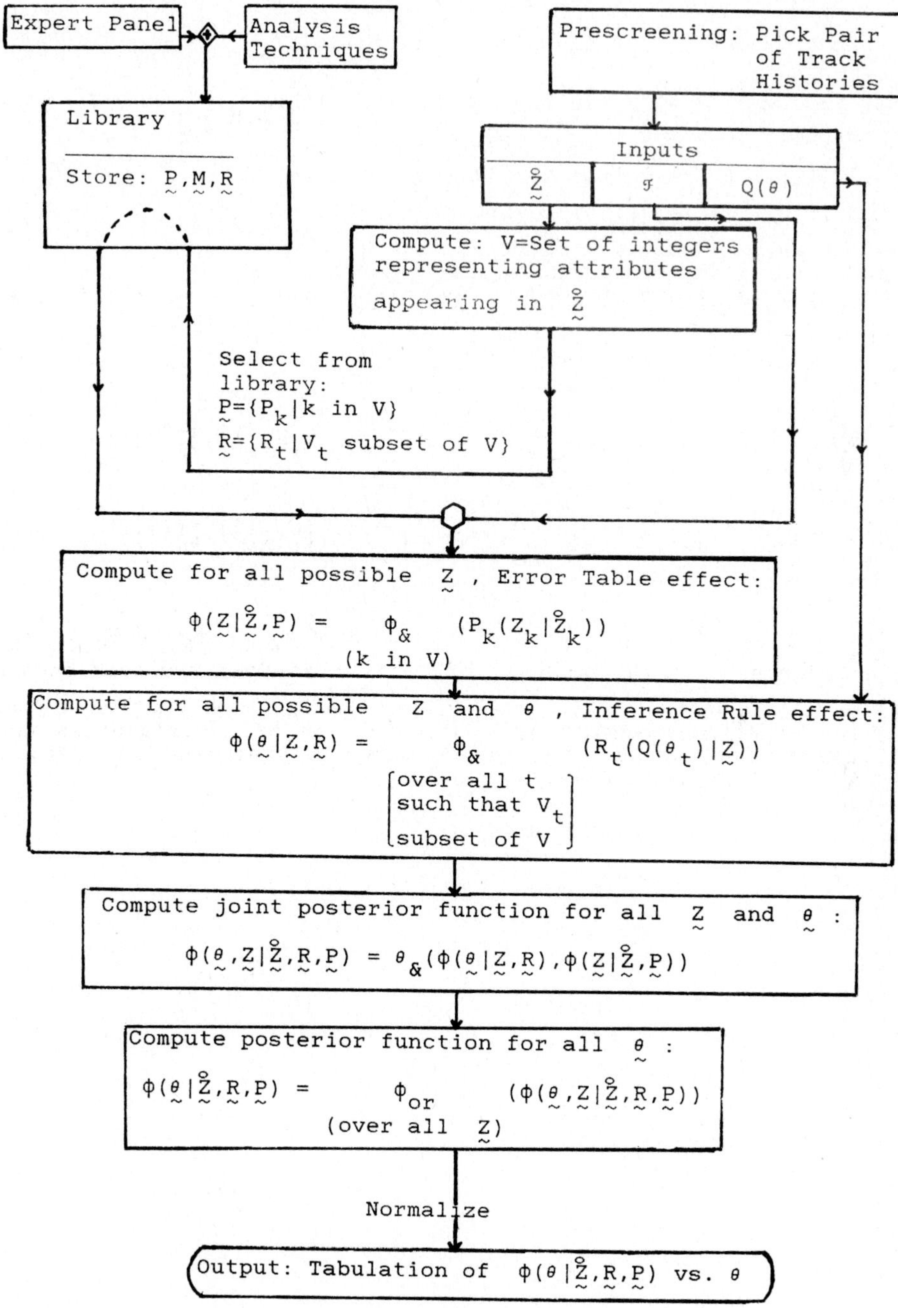

Figure 2. Flow chart structure for combination of evidence algorithm applied to correlation problem.

In Figure 2, the following legend holds:

$\overset{o}{\underset{\sim}{Z}}$ is observed data, $\underset{\sim}{Z}$ is variable dummy data,
$\underset{\sim}{P} = \{P_1, P_2, \ldots\}$ is set of all error tables,
$\underset{\sim}{R} = \{R_1, R_2, \ldots\}$ is set of all inference rules,
$\underset{\sim}{M} = \{M_1, M_2, \ldots\}$ is set of all matching tables,
$Q(\theta)$ is prior possibility function of θ ,
θ is correlation level between two track histories,
$\mathcal{F} = (\phi_{not}, \phi_{\&}, \phi_{or})$ is logical system chosen.

The computation of $\phi(\theta|\overset{\circ}{\underset{\sim}{Z}}\ ;\ \underset{\sim}{R},\underset{\sim}{P})$, etc. has been established as an algorithm in PACT - Possibilistic Approach to Correlation and Tracking [80], [82], [86]. This involves two looping processes: computations of $\underset{\sim}{Z}$ and $Q = q(\theta)$. As an approximation, whenever an attribute A_k is such that either a difficulty arises in the obtaining of P_k or $dom(A_k)$, although discrete, is too large, or simply to reduce computations of looping through Z , one has the option of assuming formally that P_k represents errorless measurements, i.e., $P_k = I$. In this case, this is equivalent in the computations for $\phi(\theta \mid \underset{\sim}{Z};\ \underset{\sim}{R},\underset{\sim}{P})$ for any $R_t(Q \mid \underset{\sim}{Z})$ with $k \in J_t$ (i.e., involving A_k) to, in effect, replace $M_k(Z_k)$ in the antecedent of R_t by $M_k(\overset{\circ}{Z}_k)$. See again Figure 2 for an outline of the PACT algorithm.

The PACT algorithm may be considered an example of a nonsequential inference rule expert system approach. More dynamic inference rule systems are described in [24], [236] - but with non-fuzzy set approaches, where inference rules are "fired" (or activated) or not, depending on whether the antecedents are satisfied or not. See also the surveys in [183] and [260]. Again, we ask: How to choose the particular fuzzy set system $(\phi_{not},\phi_{\&},\phi_{or})$. Recall that these operations may be considered infinite-valued (i.e., [0,1]-valued) extensions of classical logical operations. These extensions are highly nonunique. Two guidelines may be used in choosing a particular fuzzy set system: theoretical considerations via isomorphic-like relations between, e.g., semidistributive systems and random set operations (Chapter 6) and empirical considerations ([250], [291], and Chapters 8 and 2.3.5 . See, also [92] for further discussion.) In dealing with human informants, care must be exercised in extracting the maximal amount of unbiased information, especially in the modeling of inference rules. This requires improvement of psychometric techniques in modeling such as outlined in [195'] or [21] (especially, the first chapter). See also [220] and [63] for systematic approaches to modeling of membership functions from a subjective viewpoint.)

An alternative to obtaining inference rules completely empirically is to use an inductive procedure on selected samples of input attribute matching intensities and corresponding observed consequent (i.e., correlation level) matching intensities analogous to that found in [177] or [208].

It is often desirable to be able to interpret the output of the combination of evidence - the tabulation of the (normalized) posterior function $\phi(\theta \mid \text{diag}\ ;\ \overset{\circ}{\underset{\sim}{Z}},\underset{\sim}{R},\underset{\sim}{P})$ vs. θ , for all $\theta \in [0,1]$. If the function is monotone increasing, it follows that it may be formally interpreted as a probability distribution function over [0,1] . On the other hand, in general, this will not be so, and a Lebesgue-Stieltjes signed measure interpretation may be most appropriate. (See section 2.3.9.) Correspondingly, a natural single figure-of-merit appears to be the Lebesgue-Stieltjes total variation mean

$$\mu_1 \overset{d}{=} \int_{\theta=0}^{1} \theta \mid d\,\phi(\theta \mid \text{diag} \; ; \; \overset{\circ}{\underset{\sim}{Z}}, \underset{\sim}{R}, \underset{\sim}{P}) \mid . \tag{99}$$

Another figure-of-merit is based upon the conditional random variable $(W \mid S_U(B_o))$, where B_o is the fuzzy set represented by the above posterior function, and S_U is the one point equivalent nested random set (see Chapter 5) equivalent to B_o , i.e., letting

$\phi_{C_o} = \phi(\cdot \mid \text{diag} \; ; \; \overset{\circ}{\underset{\sim}{Z}}, \underset{\sim}{R}, \underset{\sim}{P})$,

$$S_U(B_o) = \phi_{B_o}^{-1}[U,1]$$

where U is a random variable uniformly distributed over $[0,1]$. For any outcome $S_U(B_o)$, $(W \mid S_U(B_o))$ is uniformly distributed over $S_U(B_o)$. Then the desired figure-of-merit here is

$$\mu_2 \overset{d}{=} E(W \mid S_U(B_o)) \quad \text{(two-stage mean)} = E(W) . \tag{100}$$

It easily follows that if the posterior function is unimodal at say $\theta = \theta_o$, then

$$\mu_2 = (1/2)\mu_1 , \tag{101}$$

$$\mu_1 = 2\theta_o - \phi_{B_o}(1) + \int_{\theta=\theta_o}^{1} \phi_{B_o}(\theta)d\theta - \int_{\theta=0}^{\theta_o} \phi_{B_o}(\theta)d\theta . \tag{102}$$

When ϕ_{B_o} is monotone increasing (and hence $\phi_{B_o}(1) = 1$) , then the above finally reduces to

$$\mu_2 = (1/2)\mu_1 = (1/2)(1 - \int_{\theta=0}^{1} \phi_{B_o}(\theta)d\theta) . \tag{103}$$

Other figures-of-merit may be constructed. An open question connected with this problem is the determination of such a value which is invariant with respect to any random set one-point-coverage-equivalent to ϕ_{B_o} .

F. Some asymptotic results.

Asymptotic results were previously obtained for the general combination of evidence problem in section 8.4. Here, more specific results are obtained for the correlation problem. Consider two fixed track histories $i = 1$, $j = 2$.

Without loss of generality, suppose $A_1,\ldots,A_{m'}$ are statistical attributes, where for each A_k, the discretization result

$$P_{k,p}(Z_k^{(\ell)} \mid \mathring{Z}_k^{(\ell)}) = f_k(Z_k^{(\ell)} \mid \mathring{Z}_k^{(\ell)})\cdot\Delta_{k,p}(Z_k^{(\ell)}) \qquad (104)$$

holds, for all $Z_k^{(\ell)}, \mathring{Z}_k^{(\ell)} \in \mathrm{dom}(A_k) \subseteq \mathbb{R}^{m_k}$, where $f_k(\cdot \mid \mathring{Z}_k^{(\ell)})$ is a bounded continuous p.d.f., $\ell = 1,2$ and $\Delta_{k,p}(Z_k^{(\ell)}) \subseteq \mathbb{R}^{m_k}$ is a sufficiently small m_k-cell, so that $P_{k,p}(\cdot \mid \mathring{Z}_k^{(\ell)})$ is a probability function ; $k = 1,\ldots,m'$. Here p indicates the pth discretization state and it is assumed that cells $\Delta_{k,p}(Z_k^{(\ell)})$ forming the discretization $D_{k,p}$ of $\mathbb{R}^{m_k}$ refine each other to- ward 0 as $p \to +\infty$. Since for these statistical attributes, although in general $M_k \neq P_k$, M_k has a form derived from P_k or at least the domain for P_k (based on statistical hypotheses testing using randomized significance levels - see eqs. (37)-(53)), M_k is also affected, through its domain $D_{k,p}$ replacing D_k, etc. Thus, if affected, $M_{k,p}$ replaces M_k, $k = 1,\ldots,m'$.

Next, suppose $A_{m'+1},\ldots,A_{m''}$ are subjective attributes so that error and matching tables coincide:

$$P_{k,p}(Z_k^{(\ell)} \mid \mathring{Z}_k^{(\ell)}) = M_{k,p}(Z_k^{(\ell)},\mathring{Z}_k^{(\ell)}) \;,\; \ell = 1,2 \;, \qquad (105)$$

for all $Z_k^{(\ell)},\mathring{Z}_k^{(\ell)} \in \mathrm{dom}(A_k)$, $k = m'+1,\ldots,m''$, where p here indexes the pth time of knowledge concerning P_k (and thus M_k). The contribution of the pth discretization $M_{k,p}$ for M_k, for all k, $k = 1,\ldots,m''$, in turn, when substituted into any inference rule R_t, yields the corresponding $R_{t,p}$, $t = 1,2,\ldots,r$.

Suppose that the posterior function, adding subscript p, is indicated by

$$\phi_{B_o,p}(\theta) = \phi_p(\theta \mid \mathrm{diag} \;;\; \underset{\sim}{\mathring{Z}},\underset{\sim}{R},\underset{\sim}{P}) \;;\; \theta \in [0,1] \;, \qquad (106)$$

where equations (90)-(98) hold (with subscript p properly added).

Suppose also $\phi_{\&,1}$, $\phi_{\&,2}$ and ϕ_{or}, with generator h, satisfy differentiability conditions (c), (e), (g), respectively, of Corollary 1, section 8.4.

Then the following result obtains:

Theorem (See also Goodman [91'''].)

Under the above assumptions,

$$\phi_{diag,+\infty}(\theta \mid \mathring{\underset{\sim}{Z}},\underset{\sim}{R},\underset{\sim}{P}) \overset{d}{=} \lim_{p\to+\infty} \phi_{diag,p}(\theta \mid \mathring{\underset{\sim}{Z}},\underset{\sim}{R},\underset{\sim}{P})$$

$$= 1 - h^{-1}(\min(\xi(\theta,\mathring{\underset{\sim}{Z}}),h(0))) , \tag{107}$$

$$\xi(\theta;\mathring{\underset{\sim}{Z}}) \overset{d}{=} \max_{(\text{all } \underset{\sim}{Z}")} (\tau(\theta,\underset{\sim}{Z}";\mathring{\underset{\sim}{Z}})) , \tag{108}$$

$$\tau(\theta,\underset{\sim}{Z}";\mathring{\underset{\sim}{Z}}) \overset{d}{=} r_{2m'} \cdot \underset{(\underset{\sim}{Z}'|\mathring{\underset{\sim}{Z}}')}{E} (\nu(\phi_{G_o}(\theta,\underset{\sim}{Z};\mathring{\underset{\sim}{Z}}")) \mid \mathring{\underset{\sim}{Z}}') , \tag{109}$$

where the statistical expectation $\underset{(\underset{\sim}{Z}'|\mathring{\underset{\sim}{Z}}')}{E}(\cdot)$ is with respect to $\underset{\sim}{Z}'$, considered now formally as a random variable with p.d.f. $f'(\cdot \mid \mathring{\underset{\sim}{Z}}')$, given by

$$f'(\underset{\sim}{Z}' \mid \mathring{\underset{\sim}{Z}}') \overset{d}{=} \prod_{\substack{1\le k\le m',\\ \ell=1,2}} (f_k(Z_k^{(\ell)} \mid \mathring{Z}_k^{(\ell)})) , \tag{110}$$

for all $\underset{\sim}{Z}' = (Z_k)_{1\le k\le m'}$, $Z_k^{(\ell)} \in \mathbb{R}^{m_k}$, $1 \le k \le m'$, $\ell = 1,2$, where constant r_q for $q = 2m'$ is given in (a), Corollary 1, section 8.4 and function ν is given in the conclusion of the Corollary;

$$\phi_{G_o}(\theta,\underset{\sim}{Z};\mathring{\underset{\sim}{Z}}") \overset{d}{=} \lim_{p\to+\infty} \phi_{G,p}(\theta,\underset{\sim}{Z};\mathring{\underset{\sim}{Z}}") \tag{111}$$

and as in eq. (95)

$$\phi_{G,p}(\theta,\underset{\sim}{Z};\overset{o}{\underset{\sim}{Z}}") \overset{d}{=} \phi_{\&,2}(P"_{(p)}(\underset{\sim}{Z}" \mid \overset{o}{\underset{\sim}{Z}}"), R_{(p)}(\theta \mid \underset{\sim}{Z})) , \tag{112}$$

for all $\underset{\sim}{Z} = (\underset{\sim}{Z}',\underset{\sim}{Z}")$ and all $\theta \in [0,1]$; $p \ge 1$.

Proof: Immediate from Corollary 1, section 8.4.

A simple example.

Suppose $m' = 1$, $\phi_{\&,1} = \phi_{\&,2} = \phi_{\&,3} = \phi_{\&,4} = \text{prod}$,

ϕ_{or} = probsum , $\lim_{p\to+\infty} P''_{(p)}(\underset{\sim}{Z}'' \mid \underset{\sim}{\overset{\circ}{Z}}'') = \delta_{\underset{\sim}{Z}'',\underset{\sim}{\overset{\circ}{Z}}''}$, and $r = 1$ with

$$R_{(p)}(\theta \mid \underset{\sim}{Z}) = R_1(\theta \mid \underset{\sim}{Z}')$$

$$= \phi_{or}(1 - M_1(Z_1^{(1)},Z_1^{(2)})^{\alpha_1} , \theta^{\gamma_1})$$

$$= 1 - M_1(Z_1^{(1)},Z_1^{(2)})^{\alpha_1} \cdot (1 - \theta^{\gamma_1}) , \tag{113}$$

for some fixed α_1 , $\gamma_1 > 0$; all $\theta \in [0,1]$. Then $r_{2m'} = 1$, $\nu(x) = x$, all $x \in [0,1]$. Suppose also, $f_1(Z_1^{(\ell)} \mid \overset{\circ}{Z}_1^{(\ell)})$ is the p.d.f. at $Z_1^{(\ell)}$ corresponding to the Gaussian-Dirac delta

$$\frac{1}{(2\pi)^{\frac{m'}{2}}\sqrt{\det \overset{\circ}{\Sigma}_1^{(\ell)}}} e^{-\frac{1}{2}\lambda_1(Z_1^{(\ell)},\overset{\circ}{Z}_1^{(\ell)})} \cdot \delta\left[\Sigma_1^{(\ell)} - \overset{\circ}{\Sigma}_1^{(\ell)}\right] , \tag{114}$$

$$\lambda_1(Z_1^{(\ell)},\overset{\circ}{Z}_1^{(\ell)}) \overset{d}{=} (Y_1^{(\ell)} - \overset{\circ}{Y}_1^{(\ell)})^T . \overset{\circ}{\Sigma}_1^{(\ell)^{-1}} \cdot (Y_1^{(\ell)} - \overset{\circ}{Y}_1^{(\ell)}) , \tag{115}$$

$$Z_1^{(\ell)} \overset{d}{=} (Y_1^{(\ell)},\Sigma_1^{(\ell)}) , \tag{116}$$

$$\overset{\circ}{Z}_1^{(\ell)} \overset{d}{=} (\overset{\circ}{Y}_1^{(\ell)},\overset{\circ}{\Sigma}_1^{(\ell)}) , \tag{117}$$

where $Y_1^{(\ell)},\overset{\circ}{Y}_1^{(\ell)} \in \mathbb{R}^{n_1}$, $\Sigma_1^{(\ell)}$, $\overset{\circ}{\Sigma}_1^{(\ell)} \in \mathbb{R}^{n_1,n_1}$ positive definite, so that without loss of generality $m_1 = n_1 + n_1^2$, $\ell = 1,2$. Suppose, finally, M_1 arises from the standard test statistic (see subsection (C) of this chapter.);

$$M_1(Z_1^{(1)},Z_1^{(2)}) = 1 - F_{n_1}(\lambda_2(Z_1^{(1)},Z_1^{(2)})) \tag{118}$$

where F_{n_1} is the probability distribution function of a $\chi^2_{n_1}$ random variable and

$$\lambda_2(\underset{\sim}{Z}') = \lambda_2(Z_1^{(1)},Z_1^{(2)})$$

$$\overset{d}{=} (Y_1^{(1)}-Y_1^{(2)})(\Sigma_1^{(1)}+\Sigma_1^{(2)})^{-1}(Y_1^{(1)}-Y_1^{(2)}) \tag{119}$$

for all $Z_1^{(1)},Z_1^{(2)}$.

Then it follows that

$$\phi_{diag,+\infty}(\theta \mid \overset{\circ}{\underset{\sim}{Z}},\underset{\sim}{R},\underset{\sim}{P}) = 1 - e^{-\xi(\theta;\overset{\circ}{\underset{\sim}{Z}}')} , \tag{120}$$

where

$$\xi(\theta;\overset{\circ}{\underset{\sim}{Z}}') \overset{d}{=} 1 - (1-\theta^{\gamma_1}) \cdot E_{\chi^2_{n_1,\lambda_2(\overset{\circ}{\underset{\sim}{Z}}')}}((1 - F_{n_1}(\chi^2_{n_1,\lambda_2(\overset{\circ}{\underset{\sim}{Z}}')}))^{\alpha_1}), \tag{121}$$

a monotone increasing function in θ , so that

$$\phi_{univ;+\infty}(\text{diag}) = 1 - e^{-1} \tag{122}$$

and hence for all $\theta \in [0,1]$

$$\phi_{+\infty}(\theta \mid \text{diag} ; \overset{\circ}{\underset{\sim}{Z}},\underset{\sim}{R},\underset{\sim}{P}) = (1 - e^{-\xi(\theta;\overset{\circ}{\underset{\sim}{Z}}')}) / (1 - e^{-1}). \tag{123}$$

If n_1 is even, a relatively simple form exists for F_{n_1} . In particular, for $n_1 = 2$, $F_2(x) = 1 - e^{-x/2}$, $x \geq 0$, and hence

$$\xi(\theta;\overset{o}{\underset{\sim}{Z}}') = 1 - (1 - \theta^{\gamma_1}) \cdot \omega(\alpha_1;\overset{o}{\underset{\sim}{Z}}') , \tag{124}$$

where

$$\omega(\alpha_1,\overset{\circ}{\underset{\sim}{Z}}') \overset{d}{=} E_{\chi^2_{2,\lambda_2(\overset{\circ}{\underset{\sim}{Z}}')}}\left[e^{-\frac{\alpha_1}{2}\cdot\chi^2_{2,\lambda_2(\overset{\circ}{\underset{\sim}{Z}}')}}\right] ,$$

$$= \frac{1}{\alpha_1 + 1} \cdot e^{-\frac{\alpha_1}{2(\alpha_1+1)}\lambda_2(\overset{\circ}{\underset{\sim}{Z}}')} , \tag{125}$$

by straightforward manipulation of a noncentral chi-square p.d.f. as a Poisson mixture of central ones. Note that $\phi_{+\infty}(\theta \mid \text{diag};\overset{\circ}{\underset{\sim}{Z}},\underset{\sim}{R},\underset{\sim}{P})$ is monotone increasing in θ , up to 1 at $\theta = 1$, and for any fixed θ , α_1 , γ_1 , is monotone increasing in the weighted squared "distance" $\lambda_2(\overset{\circ}{\underset{\sim}{Z}}')$ compatible with $\phi_{+\infty}$ viewed essentially as a formal probability distribution function (except for $\phi_{+\infty}(0) > 0$ in general). Finally, note that as $\alpha_1 \to 0$,

$$\phi_{+\infty}(\theta \mid \text{diag};\overset{\circ}{\underset{\sim}{Z}},\underset{\sim}{R},\underset{\sim}{P}) \to (1 - e^{-\theta^{\gamma_1}}) / (1 - e^{-1}) ,$$

which in turn approaches the Krönecker delta $\delta_{1,\theta}$, $0 \leq \theta \leq 1$, representing perfect or complete correlation!

Further asymptotic consistency results may be obtained for the general case by making additional assumptions concerning the intensification (increasing) in the consequences and extensification in the antecedents of inference rules. Or, consistencies in P_k tables may be assumed. (See Goodman [91'''], where some quantitative results are obtained.) Clearly, the asymptotic result in the theorem is the ideal form for the posterior function of θ, where instead of discretizing the statistical attributes, the corresponding limiting continuous error table and matching table forms are used instead. It is of some interest to determine what trade-offs exist in terms of computing times for the evaluation of the expectation in eq. (109) (which in general will not be in complete closed form, unlike the above special example) as opposed to the computations in eq. (93), for the full discretization approach.

Finally, analogous to the use of Kalman filters for geolocation data, other appropriate "filters" (recursive, if possible) must be developed for updating/smoothing all relevant attributes being carried for each track history. This is done in conjunction with all decisions to merge track histories or keep them separate, based on, e.g., a correlation matrix (Table O) built up from out-puts of figure-of-merit "averages" for the posterior correlation functions.

k	A_k ATTRIBUTE	INFORMATION TYPE	$dom(A_k)$ DOMAIN OF VALUES	$\overset{o}{Z}{}_k^{(1)}$ TYPICAL EXAMPLES OF REPORTED VALUES TRACK HIST.1	$\overset{o}{Z}{}_k^{(2)}$ TRACK HIST.2
1	GEOLOCATION	STATISTICAL (GAUSSIAN MODEL)	SET OF ALL PAIRS OF VALUES IN FIXED REGION OF INTEREST SUITABLY DISCRETIZED WITH ERROR ELLIPSES FIXED	x_1 MILES y_1 MILES	x_2 MILES y_2 MILES
2	CLASS	NON-STATISTICAL	$C_1, C_2, \ldots, C_N$ (OVERLAPPING)	TYPE C_{17}	TYPE C_8
3	VISUAL SHAPE	NON-STATISTICAL	$B_1, B_2, \ldots, B_L$	B_4 = DOME-SHAPED SUPER STRUCTURE AND SHORT DECK	B_{46} = LONG SUPER-STRUCTURE AND FAIRLY SHORT DECK
4	OBSERVED FLAG	NON-STATISTICAL	SET OF FINITE COMBINATIONS OF COLORS AND SHAPES	DARK-SQUARE	REDDISH OBLONG
5	FUNDAMENTAL FREQ. OF EQUIPMENT	STATISTICAL (MODEL CAN USE DOPPLER SHIFT, UNIFORM RANDOM SIGNAL DIR. AND INITIAL GAUSSIAN POS. DISTRIB.)	FINITE SET OF EQUALLY SPACED VALUES IN HZ.	D_1 HZ.	D_2 HZ.
6	PATH BEHAVIOR	ESSENTIALLY NON-STATISTICAL WITH SOME STATISTICAL EVALUATIONS	FINITE SET OF POSSIBLE TYPES OF MOTION	HIGH-MANEUVER	STRAIGHT-LINE WITH SOME ACCELERATION
7	HULL LENGTH	NON-STATISTICAL	FINITE SET OF LENGTHS IN EITHER LITERAL OR APPROXIMATE NUMERICAL FORM	VERY LONG: OVER 1000 FT	LONG: FROM ABOUT 800 - 1000 FT

Table 2

Examples of Attributes, Domains of Possible Values, and Observed Data.

For further background on the data association problem, see, e.g., [84], [12], and [213].

CHAPTER 10

SUMMARY OF THE MAIN RESULTS AND OPEN QUESTIONS

10.1 Summary

In this section, a brief description of the main results in previous chapters is presented together with concluding remarks.

In the Preface, several technical and mathematical definitions concerning uncertainty modeling were discussed, including: systems, states, processes, attributes, system uncertainties, experiments, dispersions, generalized sets, general logical systems, truth functionality, multi-valued logic, negations, t-norms or conjunction operators, t-conorms or disjunction operators and copulas.

Chapter 1 provides a basic introduction to the subject matter. Section 1.1 develops motivation and a basic framework of analysis for problems involving linguistic information. The use of observed data (numerical or linguistic), error distributions or dispersions, and inference rules (by experts, if possible) is emphasized. The general combination of evidence problem is also introduced as an important objective of knowledge-based systems. The problem of internal vs. external modeling and the development of general logical systems is also discussed, with some emphasis upon the major problem of resolving ambiguities that arise in modeling linguistic information.

In section 1.2, a presentation is made of the modeling and use of natural language information for multiple-valued logical set theories. In addition, some basic connections with random set theory are also mentioned. Finally, section 1.3 presents a brief outline of the contents of the text.

Chapter 2, symbolization and evaluation of language, constitutes a large section of the text - necessarily so because of the foundations it lays for investigating uncertainty modeling. Section 2.1 is succinctly summarized in Figure I, where the flow of knowledge from conception to evaluation is symbolized. The pertinant aspects of this transition include: the real world as a problem generator, systems of interest, cognition, which through communications gives rise to natural language expressions, which in turn through appropriate parsing techniques, lead to formal language definitions, which in turn through semantic evaluations, lead to general logical systems. Finally, combination of evidence problems - arising from real world generations - may be treated via knowledge-based systems, consisting of a general logical system and a feedback loop to both a panel of experts in terms of their ideas and thoughts and to the real-world effect of the tentative problem solution.

Section 2.2.2 presents the basic structure of a formal language. A summary of this highly detailed section is given in part V of the section. A formal language $\mathcal{L}$ contains a category Core($\mathcal{L}$) of types and sorts (kinds of things), basically consisting of formal objects, arrows and relations, together with function symbols (constituting Ar(Core ($\mathcal{L}$))) representing: Cat($\mathcal{L}$), category-function concepts; Foun($\mathcal{L}$), set theory concepts such as exponentiation, membership, equivalence, set abstraction; Loc($\mathcal{L}$), logical connectors, including negations, conjunctions, disjunctions and implications; and Quan($\mathcal{L}$), quantifiers, including universal, existential and possibly various partial quantifications. In addition, $\mathcal{L}$ contains $Th_{syn}(\mathcal{L})$, a theory of syntax establishing the relations between the functional symbols acting upon the deduction category $\widetilde{Var}(\mathcal{L})$ of all basic variables of $\mathcal{L}$. Thus, $\widetilde{Var}(\mathcal{L})$ consists of objects which will later be interpreted as generalized or fuzzy sets or universes of discourse under semantic evaluations, arrows, which play the role of functions among the objects, and relations. Next, $\mathcal{L}$ contains Wfex($\mathcal{L}$), the class of well-formed (according to $Th_{syn}(\mathcal{L})$) expressions of $\mathcal{L}$ - essentially compound relations or well-formed formulas Wff($\mathcal{L}$) and compound terms Wft($\mathcal{L}$). Also, $\mathcal{L}$ contains the total, free, and bound individual variable maps TV($\mathcal{L}$), FV($\mathcal{L}$), BnV($\mathcal{L}$), where (well-formed) individual variables are the same as projection arrows denoted as a class, Wfv($\mathcal{L}$), a subclass of Wft($\mathcal{L}$). Those maps count the free individual variables vs the bound ones in any given expression. Finally, $\mathcal{L}$ contains some theory $Th_K(\mathcal{L})$, in addition to the basic syntax. As presented in parts of the text - but not necessarily so everywhere - $Th_K(\mathcal{L})$ is chosen as an entire, or fragment of an, intuitionistic theory, encompassing logical, quantitative and set theoretic aspects. Basic theorems or deducts, elements of $De(Th_k(\mathcal{L}))$, are given in subsection (VI).

Section 2.3.2 concerns semantic evaluations $\| \ \|$ of a formal language $\mathcal{L}$ within a deduction category $(\mathcal{C},\mathfrak{R})$. Basically, we restrict ourselves to the case where $\| \ \| : \mathcal{L} \to (\mathcal{C},\mathfrak{R})$ is a model for $Th_{syn}(\mathcal{L})$ and if possible also for $Th(\mathcal{L})$, if $(\mathcal{C},\mathfrak{R})$ has additional structure, such as that of a topos. In these cases, the semantic evaluations, i.e., the ranges of $\| \ \|$ in $(\mathcal{C},\mathfrak{R})$ are compatible with the structure of $\mathcal{L}$, i.e., are isomorphic-alike.

In section 2.3.3, semantic evaluations are specialized further to $Loc(\mathcal{L}) \cup Quan(\mathcal{L})$, each class of evaluations, determining a particular logic L. A number of basic definitions is given here concerning the properties of semantic evaluations $\| \ \|$, theories Th($\mathcal{L}$), logics L, and related concepts may possess. These include: logical implication, validity, satisfiability, tautology, contradiction, tautologic equivalence, truth functionality, truth functional completeness, consistency, inconsistency, deductive soundness and completeness, logical soundness and completeness, model consistency, axiomatizability and compactness. Subsection 2.3.3(b) establishes the very important result — Theorem 1 (rephrased, due originally to Coste):

(a) $\widetilde{Var}(\mathcal{L})$ is a natural deduction category (indeed the canonical one) for evaluating $\mathcal{L}$ with model $\| \ \|_{\widetilde{Var}(\mathcal{L})} : \mathcal{L} \to Var(\mathcal{L})$.

(b) Any model $\| \ \| : \mathcal{L} \to (\mathcal{C},\mathfrak{R})$ (where $(\mathcal{C},\mathfrak{R})$ may have additional structure up to a topos) may be decomposed into a composition of a map from $\widetilde{\mathrm{Var}}(\mathcal{L})$ to $(\mathcal{C},\mathfrak{X})$ with $\| \ \|_{\widetilde{\mathrm{Var}}(\mathcal{L})}$.

(c) Consequently $\mathrm{Th}_K(\mathcal{L})$ (with $\mathrm{Th}_{syn}(\mathcal{L})$) is a sound and complete theory. By identifying any category $\mathcal{C}$, or more generally any category with additional properties up to a topos, with the deduction category $(\mathcal{C},\mathrm{Sub})$, Theorem 1 can be reformulated for ordinary categories or topoi, etc., (Theorem 2). 2.3.3(c) consists of a brief survey of various particular logics, including Lukasiewicz of all orders (including classical logic), Bochvarian, Gödel-Intuitionistic (compatible with $\mathrm{Th}_K(\mathcal{L})$ here), all truth-functional logics, and the non-truth functional Probability Logic.

Set theory concepts are discussed in section 2.3.4, beginning with a selected collection of set theories, including Naïve Set Theory, Zermelo-Fraenkel, Maydole-Hay, Intuitionistic, Novak's and Weidner's theories. Some emphasis at the end of 2.3.4 is placed upon the Comprehension/Abstraction Principle in forming generalized sets corresponding to wff's, and,in particular, in defining general set operations. Maydole's results concerning the consistency of Lukasiewicz $\aleph_1$-logic and Maydole-Hay set theory - with a modified form of the Comprehension Principle included as an axiom - are pointed out as a positive step in the establishment of a global generalized set theory. In any case, in 2.3.5, general logical systems, are introduced, in which it is hoped that in some "logical sense", at least consistency may hold. These logical systems are treated from a general deduction category approach. Connections with knowledge-based systems are discussed. A model $\| \ \| : \mathcal{L} \to (\mathrm{GOG},\mathrm{Sub})$, where GOG is a union of Goguen's category of fuzzy sets , Gog(H) , with appended logical operators, is chosen as the formal definition of a general logical system. In practice, GOG could be replaced simply by a single category Gog(H) and a single collection of logical operators. In conjunction with general logical systems, the class of generalized or fuzzy subsets of a space, and, correspondingly the class of dispersions on a space, are introduced. Essentially each object variable i in $\widetilde{\mathrm{Var}}(\mathcal{L})$, is evaluated as $\|i\| = (X_i,\theta_i) \in \mathrm{Ob}(\mathrm{Gog}(H))$, i.e., $\theta_i : X_i \to H$, H a fixed Heyting algebra (truth space), X_i an ordinary set, with $i = A_i$ identified as the generalized set and $\theta_i = \phi_{A_i}$ as its dispersion or membership function relative to X_i . The evaluations under $\| \ \|$ of logical connectors "nt" , "&" , "or" in $\mathrm{Loc}(\mathcal{L})$ are denoted $\|\mathrm{nt}\| = \phi_{nt}$, $\|\&\| = \phi_{\&}$, $\|\mathrm{or}\| = \phi_{or}$, if the logic is truth functional. Various set operations (for generalized sets here) are defined, including products, unions, intersections complements, relating to the results in 2.3.4. In addition set relations, set abstractions of wffs , and power class and subset relations among generalized sets are evaluated. Thus the wff $\varphi_1 = (x^{(i)} \in_i y^{(\Omega^i)})$, where $x^{(i)}$, $y^{(\Omega^i)}$ are in $\mathrm{Wfv}(\mathcal{L})$ and $(\in : \mathrm{Ob}(\mathcal{L}) \to \mathrm{Rel}(\mathcal{L}))$ is the distinguished function symbol representing generalized set membership relation, i an object in $\widetilde{\mathrm{Var}}(\mathcal{L})$, can be evaluated as

$\|\varphi_1\|$ where, letting

$$m = i \times \Omega^i \times j \ ,$$

$$\|j\| = (X_j, \theta_j) \ ,$$

$$\|i\| = (X_i, \theta_i) \ ,$$

$$\|\Omega^i\| = (\|\Omega^i\|^{(1)}, T_{\Omega}i) \ , \ \|\Omega\| = (H,T) \ ,$$

$$\|\Omega^i\|^{(1)} = (\|\Omega\|^{\|i\|})^{(1)} = ((H,T)^{(X_i,\theta_i)})^{(1)} = \{f \mid f \in H^{X_i}, \ f \le \theta_i\} \ ,$$

$$\|m\| = \|i\| \times \|\Omega^i\| \times \|j\| = (Y_m, \theta_m) \ ,$$

$$Y_m = X_i \times \| \ \Omega^i \ \|^{(1)} \times Y_j \ ,$$

$$\theta_m = \theta_i(\cdot) \wedge T_{\Omega}i(\cdot\cdot) \wedge \theta_j(\cdot\cdot\cdot)$$
$$= \theta_i(\cdot) \wedge \theta_j(\cdot\cdot\cdot) \ ,$$

$$\|x_m^{(i)}\| : Y_m \to X_i \ , \text{ projection,}$$

$$\|y_m^{(\Omega^i)}\| : Y_m \to \|\Omega^i\|^{(1)} \ , \text{ projection,}$$

$$\|\varphi_1\| = \|\epsilon_i\|[\langle\|x_m^{(i)}\| \ , \ \|y_m^{(\Omega^i)}\|\rangle]$$
$$= (\|x_m^{(i)}\| \ \|\epsilon_i\| \ \|y_m^{(\Omega^i)}\|)$$
$$= (\|y_m^{(\Omega^i)}\|(\cdot)) \circ \|x_m^{(i)}\|(\cdot\cdot)$$
$$= \phi_{y_m^{(\Omega^i)}}(\|x_m^{(i)}\|) \ ,$$

then we can find k , an object in $\widetilde{V}ar(\mathcal{L})$, such that

$$\|k\| = (X_i, \ \phi_{y_m^{(\Omega^i)}}) \ ; \ \ \phi_{y_m^{(\Omega^i)}} = \|y_m^{(\Omega^i)}\| \ (\cdot) \ .$$

Similarly, the wff representing a union is

$$\varphi \overset{d}{=} \varphi_1 \text{ or } \varphi_2$$
$$= \langle x_m^{(i)} \ \epsilon_i \ y_m^{(\Omega^i)}\rangle \text{ or } \langle x_m^{(i)} \ \epsilon_i \ z_m^{(\Omega^i)}\rangle$$

$$\stackrel{d}{=} \langle x_m^{(i)} \in_i (y_m^{(\Omega^i)} \cup z_m^{(\Omega^i)})\rangle \text{ (formal)}$$

where

$$\varphi_2 = \langle x_m^{(i)} \in z_m^{(\Omega^i)}\rangle \text{ , etc.}$$

Then

$$\begin{aligned} \|\varphi\| &= \|\varphi_1\| \ \|or\| \ \|\varphi_2\| \\ &= \phi_{or}(\|\varphi_1\|, \|\varphi_2\|) \\ &= \phi_{or}(\phi_{y_m^{(\Omega^i)}}(\|x_m^{(i)}\|) , \phi_{z_m^{(\Omega^i)}}(\|x_m^{(i)}\|)) \\ &= \phi_{y_m^{(\Omega^i)} \cup z_m^{(\Omega^i)}}(\|x_m^{(i)}\|) , \end{aligned}$$

with similar results holding for intersection, complementation and other generalized set operations. Hence a calculus of generalized set operations and relations can be established.

Furthermore, wff's need not be restricted to only membership relations (again see 2.2.2), but because of the Comprehension/Abstraction Principle, can w.l.o.g. be considered to be in that form.

Section 2.3.6 presents an extensive survey of various families of operators ϕ_{nt} , representing (through semantic evaluations) negation, $\phi_{\&}$, representing conjunction, and ϕ_{or} representing disjunction. $\phi_{\&}$ is usually called a t-norm and ϕ_{or} a t-conorm. A number of important properties are presented for various subclasses of such operators, including Archimedean, DeMorgan, distributive, semi-distributive, copulas and co-copulas, Frank's family, Yager's family and others. Sklar's Theorem, canonical forms and ordinal sums, as well, are discussed.

The problem of extending ordinary functions whose domains are ordinary sets to those whose domains are generalized sets is discussed in 2.3.7. Basically, two approaches are considered: If $f : X \to Y$ is an ordinary function, A is a generalized subset of X , $A \in \mathcal{F}(X)$, $\mathcal{J}(X) \subseteq U(X) \subseteq \mathcal{P}(X)$, then two approaches to extending f to $\underline{f} : \mathcal{F}(U(X)) \to \mathcal{F}(U(Y))$ are considered for any $C \in U(X)$, $A \in \mathcal{F}(U(X))$,

$$\text{Approach (I):} \quad \phi_{\underline{f}(A)}(C) = \|\langle C \in \bar{\bar{f}}(A)\rangle\|$$

$$\text{Approach (II):} \quad \phi_{\underline{f}(A)}(C) = \|\langle f^{-1}(C) \in A\rangle\|$$

(the second approach being compatible with uncertainty measures). Applications to the extension of classical logical (Boolean) connectors are also presented. Additionally, semantic evaluations, including compound operators, intensifications, conditioning, projections and interactions, Bayes' theorem, quantifications, and transformations of dispersions and linguistic variables are all considered in section 2.3.8. Especially new is the approach to conditioning (and hence quantification), which generalizes Zadeh's fuzzy cardinality approach in a natural way.

Section 2.3.9 (A) treats in some detail Probability Logic (PL) (briefly considered in 2.3.3(C)). Included is an analysis of Hailperin's approach to PL and a discussion of his extension of Fréchet's bounds on joint probabilities. Section 2.3.9 (B) extends PL to the more general Lebesgue-Stieltjes Logic (LSL), where essentially, probability measures are replaced by differences of such, corresponding to their distribution functions being replaced by the less restrictive class of functions of bounded variation with ranges in the unit interval. An extensive appendix on functions of bounded variation in $\mathbb{R}^q$ is added at the end of 2.3.9 (B) for convenience of reference.

Section 2.4 presents a category and topos theory viewpoint of generalized set theory. The basic categories Gog(H) (proposed by Goguen) and Fuz(H) (proposed by Eytan), forming pseudotopoi, and extending Zadeh's fuzzy set theory, are discussed and compared. In addition, the intuitionistic modification $\mathrm{Fuz}_\times(H)$ of Fuz(H) and Higg's topos Higg(H) are also analyzed. Relations between those categories are estabished and the controversy over which candidate category, or suitable modification, is most appropriate for presenting a theory of generalized sets is detailed. Tie-ins with models of Zermelo-Fraenkel set theory are also briefly considered in section 2.4.2 (G). Three appendices are given at the end of 2.4.2 covering basic category and topos definitions, deduction categories and formal topos properties, including a natural realization of $\mathrm{Th}_K(\mathcal{L})$ within a deduction category or topos, and the Bénabou and other constructions of standardized deduction categories and formal topoi. The latter extend in a natural sense arbitrary deduction categories and formal topoi and provide a general basis for establishing generalized or fuzzy sets, GOG being a particular case.

Section 2.5 briefly presents Zadeh's approximate reasoning and fuzzy logic as a legitimate logic, with an associated deduction system compatible with the semantic evaluations present.

Finally, Chapter 2 concludes with section 2.6, where a number of different natural language sentences are translated into formal language, and in turn, semantically evaluated.

In Chapter 3, a basis is established for investigating uncertainty measures - i.e., dispersions whose domains of definitions are collections of subsets of given spaces. A brief survey of basic information theory concepts is presented in 3.1. Choquet-type measures, including plausibility, belief and doubt measures - all generalizing ordinary probability measures are introduced in 3.2. Following the establishment of preliminary relations, characterizations are obtained for doubt, belief and plausibility measures in terms of alternating signed sums (Theorem 1). Further characterizations relating to coverage (subset and superset) and incidence functions of random subsets of finite (or complementary-finite) spaces are presented in Theorems 2 - 4.

Section 3.3 considers possibility and related uncertainty measures and, to some extent, conditional possibility measures. In addition, basic relations between various classes of possibility and other uncertainty measures are shown.

Chapter 4 provides an introduction to random set theory. The natural topologies, σ-algebras and coverage and incidence functions associated with (non-finite, in general) random sets are presented in section 4.2. (An appendix treating this from a projection viewpoint is given at the back of 4.2.) Theorem 1 establishes the construction of random sets from primitive ones. Theorem 2 rephrases Dempster's result justifying the alternative names "upper" and "lower" probability measures for plausibility and belief measures, respectively, in terms of non-precisely known (up to set values) transformations of probabilities. Theorem 3 establishes for general spaces, doubt measures as coverage functions of certain regular random sets (or subsets) and plausibility measures as incidence functions for certain regular random sets. Similar results are also established for belief and disbelief measures. Theorem 4 presents the natural imbedding of a random variable as a random set, compatible with the results of the previous theorems. The converse of Theorem 3 is presented in Theorem 5: Given any random subset of a space, its subset coverage function is a doubt measure, its superset coverage function is a belief measure, its incidence function is a plausibility measure, etc. Theorem 6 treats approximations to arbitrary functional transforms of random sets. Joint random sets and set operations on random sets are also considered. General results involving Choquet's theorem on capacities are presented in 4.3. Multi-valued mappings and Bochner integrals relative to random sets are considered briefly in section 4.4.

Chapter 5 treats random sets and dispersions. In 5.1, zero-one stochastic processes are analyzed and related to random sets (Theorem 1) and to doubt measures (Theorem 2) and, in particular, to semi-distributive t-norms and t-conorms (Corollary 1). The one-point coverage problem is treated in 5.2, where the basic nested canonical random set $S_U(A)$ and the maximal entropy random set $T(A)$ are considered, among others. Flou classes, level sets and nested random sets are connected in Theorems 3 and 4, extending previous work in [184]. Additional properties are obtained in subsection, 5.2 (C) involving isomorphic-like relations, based on one point random set coverages between operators on generalized sets and corresponding ones on random sets. Some emphasis is given to the S_U-type of random sets. (See also Chapter 6.) A general solution to the one point random set coverage problem for the finite case is presented (with some geometrical flavor) in Theorem 5. One point coverage functions generated by random intevals are considered in subsection 5.2 (E), culminating in Theorems 6 and 7. Theorem 8 connects random variables, generalized sets and random sets. This results in the relationship, for any generalized subset A of space X and $x \in X$,

$$\begin{aligned} \|(x \in A)\| &= \text{Poss}(x \in A) \\ &= \Pr(x \in S(A)) \\ &= \Pr(V(A) \in x) , \end{aligned}$$

where $S(A)$ is some appropriate random subset of X and $V(A)$ is some random variable, where x is considered a compound set.

Theorem 9 of section 5.3 treats the multiple point random set coverage problem for finite spaces. Also, in section 5.3 (Propositions 1 and 2) relations are established between Zadeh's possibility measure and random sets by a direct use of Matheron's techniques [171]. Higg's category (topos) and multiple point coverage functions are also considered to some extent. In 5.4, the problem of determining extremal - entropy random sets, one point coverage -

equivalent to given generalized sets is presented. Tie-ins with Robbins' earlier results concerning expected volumes or lengths of random sets are also pointed out. The fundamental maximal entropy theorem for discrete spaces is reviewed. Theorem 10 presents the (otherwise, unconstrained) maximal entropy solution to the one point coverage problem, while Theorem 11 considers the problem with an expected cardinality constraint. Theorem 12 treats the minimal entropy problem for one point coverages by random sets, followed by some simple examples and counterexamples. In section 5.5, inspired by the independent work of Hooper ([118]), randomized tests of classical statistical hypotheses, confidence region procedures and the one point coverage problems in section 5.4 are related.

Chapter 6 concerns general problems arising in the isomorphic-like (or "weak" homomorphic) relations between operators on random sets and those on generalized sets. Following an extensive development of mappings relating generalized sets to one point coverage-equivalent random sets, called choice function families, Theorem 1 presents conditions when arbitrary combinations of cartesian sum and product (or union and intersection, essentially, equivalently) operations have isomorphic-like counterparts in both general set systems and random set ones. Theorem 2 determines which general set operations are weak homomorphic to given set operations on random sets. Specialization to compositional ordinary set operations is also carried out in Corollary 1.

The converse problem is also discussed: Given any generalized set operations, which ordinary set operations on random sets are weak homomorphic? Some examples are shown where generalized set operations admit no natural corresponding (weak homomorphic) random set operations. Theorem 3 addresses the problem of constructing weak homomorphisms between generalized and random set operations which depend as little as possible on a particular choice function family. Theorem 4 represents weak homomorphic representations of fuzzy partitionings, with an application to weighted sum operators (Corollary).

Chapter 7 presents theories of uncertainty. Some connections between various logical (and other) systems involving information/knowledge flow is given in Figure 1 in section 7.1. Manes' very encompassing "fuzzy theories" is treated in some detail in 7.2 and related to general logical systems and functional extensions or lifting operators. Watanabe's fuzzy set theory is analyzed in 7.3. Gaines' uncertainty logic, an attempt at simultaneously generalizing both probability logic and Lukasiewicz logic, identified with fuzzy sets, is presented and critiqued in 7.4. Finally, in section 7.5, Schefe's "agreement probability" approach is reviewed. (This approach mimics to a certain degree ordinary probabilities.) In addition some of the controversies involving fuzzy set modeling are discussed.

In Chapter 8, inference procedures are developed for use in knowledge-based systems. Knowledge representation in general is discussed briefly in 8.1. Section 8.2 presents the outline of a general decision theory based on dispersions, replacing classical probabilistic notions. In section 8.3, a brief description is given of established approaches to the combination of evidence problem. This includes the following: classical Bayes' theorem, belief and related (Dempster-Shafer) uncertainty measures, and certainty factors. An alternative theory, applying the spirit of section 8.2, is presented in a general setting. Two short results (Theorems 1 and 2) are used as guidelines in the development of the approach, an application of which is given in Chapter 9. Section 8.4 presents some asymptotic results connected with generalized decision theory. The first result (8.4 (1)) is an analogue of the classical Law of Large Numbers, involving t-norm and t-conorm operators in place of the (classical) product and sum operations. The next result (8.4 (2)), in effect, is a continuous extension of the first to an uncountable number of arguments for the t-conorm operator. In 8.4(3), a few miscellaneous approaches are presented for estimating unknown dispersions. (See also 8.5 and Chapter 9.) In 8.4 (4) additional asymptotic properties of t-conorm, t-norm forms arising when "fuzzy" data is averaged are obtained (Theorems 1, 2). Asymptotic properties for combination of evidence forms, when information granularity approaches zero is given in Theorem 4 and Corollary 1, Theorem 3 being a "guideline" theorem in the sense of Theorems 1 and 2 of 8.3. More specifically, under relatively mild analytic conditions and appropriate segregation of data and inference rules into "analytic" and "subjective" groups, the limiting posterior dispersion of the unknown parameter vector is a computable transform of an integral - which can be interpreted as a classical probabilistic expectation.

Chapter 9 consists of an application of the approach developed in Chapter 8 for general knowledge-based systems to the specific problem of data association in multiple target tracking. The general problem and background information are given in part (A). The concept of error tables, as conditional dispersions, is presented in (B) with tie-ins to one point coverages of random sets and random variables (see also Chapter 5). In part (C), inference rules based on matching tables are analyzed and related, where appropriate, to classical statistical tests of hypotheses and decision procedures. In part (D) further problems involving modeling of error tables and inference rules are presented. In part (E), the actual combination of evidence is carried out, in the form of a posterior dispersion describing the unknown parameter θ - in this case the true level of association for any given pair of track histories. Interpretations and further uses of this output are also presented, including approaches to obtaining a final figure-of-merit description of θ, representing in a general sense the posterior expectation of θ. Finally, in part (F), Corollary 1 of section 8.4 (4) is applied to the situation considered here to obtain asymptotic forms for the posterior dispersions of θ.

Chapter 10 concludes the text with a subsection (10.1) devoted to summaring the basic results of the text (as presented above). In 10.2 (A), a survey of controversies and criticisms is presented, detailing particularly 10.2 (A)(II), Watanabe's criticism of Zadeh and his alternative theory. In 10.2 (A)(III), Lindley's approach to defining admissibility of uncertainty measures is given together with a number of responses to his claims that only probability measures, up to suitable transforms, are admissible. Finally, 10.2 (B) deals with the various research problems and open questions that have occurred throughout the text. At the back of section 10 is added an appendix on the modeling and semantic evaluation of natural language information.

10.2 Unresolved issues

A. Criticisms, controversies involved in generalized set theory and probability theory.

(I). General comments

Despite apparent success in applying fuzzy set theory to diverse disciplines - including medical and fault diagnoses, pattern recognition, clustering techniques, and various social/psychological areas (see again, Dubois and Prade [51] for a full survey) as well as several military applications (see, e.g., Dockery [49] and Watson et al., [269]), much controversy has raged between those advocating use of fuzzy set theory, probability theory and other approaches to the modeling of uncertainties. See Stallings [247], [248] vs. Jain [122]; Tribus [253], [254] vs. Kandel [129] and Zadeh [284]; Zadeh's criticism of the Dempster-Shafer theory [282], Johnson and Shore's claim [126] that maximal entropy and other standard statistical techniques supersede fuzzy set modeling. In addition, concerning the use of fuzzy logic and approximate reasoning, Haack [102], Tong and Efstathiou [251], Schefe [224], and Watanabe [267], [268] have all been quite critical; Fox [60], on the other hand supports its use. (See also chapter 7 for several proposed theories of uncertainties.)

Let us consider some of these criticisms and suggestions of alternative theories in some more detail.

Haack's criticism is basically directed to Zadeh's second order fuzzy logic [280], [289], where fuzzy set membership functions, in effect, have ranges of values (i.e., "truth" values) which themselves are fuzzy sets, as opposed to Zadeh's first order logic, where ordinary numerical values or more generally lattice-values are employed for the membership functions. (It is the latter approach we take throughout most of this text, not the second order approach.) Haack's main points of contention include: lack of closure, lack of use of formal inference rules and no soundness-completeness properties. But the latter are missing in most multiple-valued logics anyway - not just Zadeh's approach. (See section 2.3.3 or Rescher's comments on general multi-valued logic systems [214], pp. 161-166.) (By soundness of a logical system, we mean that any predicate (or relation or formula) which is deducible from the system's axiom set by use of its inference mechanisms, is also truth-table-wise, or tautologically, verifiable. By completeness of a logical system we mean that any predicate which is tautologically true or verifiable is also deducible from the axiom set of the system.) Other desirable properties of logical systems include compactness, decidability, and consistency. (See section 2.3.3 for discussions of these concepts for classical logic, where, e.g., for first order predicate calculus, soundness, completeness compactness, and consistency all hold. Again see Rescher for the problem in multi-valued logics [214], pp. 62-66 of the failure in general of such logics to have all possible operators reducible to a primitive set of operators - as is the case in classical logic.) Again, it should be reiterated that Zadeh's fuzzy set system $\mathcal{F}_0$ is relatable directly to Lukasiewicz $\aleph_1$- logic. See, e.g., Giles [70 - 73] where also a subjective probability approach (see also section 8.5) involving betting is established for fuzzy set membership and operator modeling, although it should be noted that Lukasiewicz Logic does not handle fuzzy quantifications such as "some", "many", etc. (See e.g. Zadeh [283].) Finally we note Gottwald's work on

Lukasiewicz Logic [94], [95].

However, if enough mathematical structure is present in the form of a topos (see also section 2.4), then by use of an appropriate formal language (see, e.g., Johnstone [127], pp. 152 - 64, or see sections 2.2 and 2.3 here) , a theory based on a variation of intuitionism, may be developed, with corresponding axioms and deduction rules, which is sound and complete. In particular, the important topos Higg (H) which includes Zadeh's system $\mathcal{F}_0$, i.e., Fuz(H) as a subcategory, has such a propety. (See again section 2.4.)

In addition, Haack complains of undue formalism in Zadeh's treatment of vagueness and artificial precision (in the form of the numerical valued membership functions) - but of course Haack tacitly accepts an analagous precision for probability functions or distributions in probability theory - which we have seen is a special case of general (fuzzy) set theory. She also indicates confusion by Zadeh in the interpretation of linguistic quantifiers. Fox offers reconciliation of classical logic and Zadeh's second order logic by suggesting use of "truth-prominance" priorities (borrowed from production rule techniques in artificial intelligence theory) in place of fuzzy truths.

Tong and Efstathiou argue that fuzzy truth values, such as "it is very truth that", do not need to be formalized relative to the truth of sentences. They also agree, in effect, with Haack's criticism of lack of closure properties for fuzzy truths with respect to fuzzy set operations. In addition, they claim Zadeh's linguistic approximation procedure results in cumbersome forms that are not very useful.

In Figure I, section 2.1, a summary of knowledge flow from conception to evaluation is presented. This text has emphasized natural language, formal language, general logical systems and knowledge-based systems (the latter mainly in Chapters 8 and 9) in treating combination of evidence problems arising from real-world situations (see especially Chapter 9). However, relatively little attention was paid to the upper left side box in Figure I: cognition. Some of the controversial work of Cohen [38] and Kahneman and Tversky [128] has been cited, as indeed was the linguistic-cognitive compendium of Winograd [274']. See also Anderson [4'] for a general psychological approach to cognition. Another area, that of "prototype theory", bears some comments. Originally, [40'] prototype theory, as based on Zadeh's fuzzy set theory (for other approaches see the listed references in [198']) was typified by the definition of a "concept" or perhaps better, "extension of a concept": A concept A is identified as the four-tuple $A = (X,d,x_0,\phi_A)$, where X is some ordinary set (universe of discourse), $d : X \times X \to \mathbb{R}^+$ is a metric, $x_0 \in X$ is the "prototype" and $\phi_A : X \to [0,1]$ is the membership function of A , so that for any $x, y \in X$, if $d(x,x_0) \leq d(y,x_0)$, then $\phi_A(x) \geq \phi_A(y)$.

Thus, in effect, this forces fuzzy (or generalized) subset A of X and $x_0 \in X$ to be such that ϕ_A is unimodal and normalized (i.e., $\phi_A(x_0) = 1$) at x_0 . Psychological research in this area looks promising in spite of the rather weak mathematical efforts. In fact, the gulf between psychological and mathematical analysis of cognition is no more apparent than in the above-referenced paper [198'], where Mssrs. Osherson and Smith purport to show Zadeh's fuzzy set theory as employed in prototype theory leads to contradictions, but classical set theory doesn't. As one example of this, consider their "incompatibility with concept combination" via conjunction: They believe that if X = all fruit, A_1 = all apples, A_2 = all striped fruit and $A_3 = A_1 \cap A_2$, x_0 or an x close to x_0 through d (as illustrated in their paper) is the prototypical striped apple, then in effect

$$\phi_{min}(\phi_{A_1}(x_0), \phi_{A_2}(x_0)) = \phi_{A_3}(x_0) > \phi_{A_1}(x_0) ,$$

violating the obvious condition $\phi_{A_3}(x) \le \phi_{A_1}(x)$, all $x \in X$, by supposed intuition!!

Similar gross misunderstandings of basic mathematical relations take place in their second "incompatibility with truth conditions of inclusion", given by the interpretation of the sentence "All grizzly bears are inhabitants of North America" as:

$$\text{For all } x \in X , (\phi_A(x) \le \phi_B(x)) ,$$

where X is the class of all animals, A is the fuzzy subset of all bears and B that of all inhabitants of North America. Obviously, this interpretation is too strong when they obtain the "fallacy" for x = Sam, a squirrel living on Mars,

$$\phi_A(\text{Sam}) > \phi_B(\text{Sam}) !$$

As a quantification, this could be treated as

$$\phi_{\underset{x \in X}{\&}}(\phi_{\Rightarrow}(\phi_A(x), \phi_B(x))) ,$$

or through Zadeh's fuzzy cardinality approach

$$\phi_{all}(\sum_{x \in X} \phi_{\&}(\phi_A(x), \phi_B(x)) / \sum_{x \in X} \phi_B(x)) ,$$

or even better through the general conditioning approach outlined in 2.3.8 (C) and (F).

On the other hand, the recent paper of Cohen and Murphy [40'] extends the idea of "concept" in natural language to a "knowledge representation model", in the sense of AI knowledge representation through a schematic display of the various subordinate roles a concept possesses. In turn, this leads to a reasonable approach to quantifications and combinations of concepts (in their sense). However, they accept the fallacies of [198'] and indeed attempt naïvely to avoid, as much as possible, both classical set theory and Zadeh's set theory in a formal sense. Oden and Lopes [196"], independently using fuzzy set theory (and fuzzy logic), developed a more detailed and rigorous approach to modeling concepts, but still retained psychological aspects of cognition. Their approach-in contradistinction to the "similarity-to-ideal" or "to-instances" approaches, compatible with [198'] - apply Zadeh's original ideas of fuzzy propositions, as espoused originaly in [290'] and continued, e.g., in [286]. See also Niedenthal and Cantor [194'] for further discussions. See Kempton [136'] for interview techniques for modeling category prototypes.

(II) Watanabe's criticism

Watanabes criticism and proposed modification of fuzzy set theory [267] also bear some additional analysis. (See also section 7.3.)

On the positive side, he establishes two interesting related mappings connecting fuzzy sets and their operations with ordinary sets and their operations in a nonprobabilistic setting:

For any (ordinary) set X, define

$$Q(X) \overset{d}{=} \{A \mid A \in \mathcal{F}(X) \ \&\ 0 \le \phi_A(x) < 1/2 \ , \quad \text{for all} \quad x \in X\} \ ,$$

where as usual $\mathcal{F}(X)$ is the class of all fuzzy subsets of X while $\mathcal{P}(X) \subseteq \mathcal{F}(X)$ is the class of all ordinary subsets of X. Then define the mapping $\rho : \mathcal{P}(X) \times Q(X) \to \mathcal{F}(X)$, where for any $C \in \mathcal{P}(X)$ and $B \in Q(X)$, $\rho(C,B) \in \mathcal{F}(X)$, where for all $x \in X$

$$\phi_{\rho(C,B)}(x) \overset{d}{=} \phi_C(x) + (-1)^{\phi_C(x)} \phi_B(x) \ .$$

Then,

(i) ρ is bijective (1-1, onto) with inverse ρ^{-1} given by, for any $A \in \mathcal{F}(X)$, $\rho^{-1}(A) \overset{d}{=} (\theta(A) \ , \omega(A))$, where $A = \rho(\theta(A) \ , \omega(A))$ as above and for the given A, the *core* $\theta(A) \in \mathcal{P}(X)$ and *frill* $\omega(A) \in Q(X)$ are given for all $x \in X$:

$$x \in \theta(A) \quad \text{iff} \quad 1 \ge \phi_A(x) \ge 1/2$$

$$x \notin \theta(A) \quad \text{iff} \quad 1/2 > \phi_A(x) \ge 0 \ ,$$

$$\phi_{\omega(A)}(x) \overset{d}{=} | \ \phi_A(x) - \phi_{\theta(A)}(x) \ | \ .$$

The core map $\theta : \mathcal{F}(X) \to \mathcal{P}(X)$ is of course surjective, but infinitely many-to-1.

(ii) Let $k_2, k_3 : \mathcal{F}(X) \times \mathcal{F}(X) \to Q(X)$
and $k_1 : \mathcal{F}(X) \to Q(X)$, all be arbitary but fixed.

Then define the fuzzy set operations for complement, intersection and union as follows

$$C_{k_1} : \mathcal{F}(X) \to \mathcal{F}(X) \ ,$$

where for any $A \in \mathcal{F}(X)$,

$$C_{k_1}(A) \overset{d}{=} \rho(C(\theta(A)) \ , k_1(A))$$

$$\cap_{k_2}, \cup_{k_3} \ : \mathcal{F}(X) \times \mathcal{F}(X) \to \mathcal{F}(X) \ ,$$

where for any $A,B \in \mathcal{F}(X)$,

$$A \cap_{k_2} B \overset{d}{=} \rho(\theta(A) \cap \theta(B) \ , \ k_2(A,B))$$

$$A \cup_{k_3} B \overset{d}{=} \rho(\theta(A) \cup \theta(B) \ , \ k_3(A,B)) \ .$$

Then it follows immediately that for all $A , B \in \mathcal{F}(X)$

$$\theta(A) = \emptyset \quad \text{iff} \quad \sup_{x \in X} \theta_A(X) < 1/2 \ ;$$

$$\theta(C_{k_1}(A)) = C(\theta(A)) \ ;$$

$$\theta(A \cap_{k_2} B) = \theta(A) \cap \theta(B)$$

$$\theta(A \cup_{k_3} B) = \theta(A) \cup \theta(B) \ ,$$

and hence θ is also a homomorphism w.r.t. $(C_{k_1}, \cap_{k_2}, \cup_{k_3})$ and $(C, \cap, \cup)$, etc.

(iii) We can extend Watanabe's results further. Consider first any binary fuzzy set operation $\circledast : \mathcal{F}(X) \times \mathcal{F}(X) \to \mathcal{F}(X)$ which extends some ordinary set operation $*$, i.e.,

$$(\circledast \ | \ \mathcal{P}(X) \times \mathcal{P}(X)) \equiv * \ ,$$

where

$$* : \mathcal{P}(X) \times \mathcal{P}(X) \to \mathcal{P}(X)$$

may be arbitrary (but fixed). Define function $\ddagger$ by

$$\ddagger(u) \overset{d}{=} \begin{cases} 0 & \text{iff} \quad 0 \le u < 1/2 \\ 1 & \text{iff} \quad 1/2 \le u \le 1 \ . \end{cases}$$

Suppose also $\circledast$ is in composition form i.e. there is a $g : [0,1]^2 \to [0,1]$ with $g\{0,1\}^2 \to \{0,1\}$ such that for all $A,B \in \mathcal{F}(X)$, and $x \in X$,

$$\phi_{A \circledast B}(x) = g(\phi_A(x), \ \phi_B(x)) \ .$$

Then it follows readily that θ is a homomorphism with respect to $\circledast$ defined through g iff for all $u,v \in [0,1]$,

$$g(\ddagger u, \ \ddagger v) = \ddagger g(u,v)$$

iff for all $u,v \in [0,1]$,

$$g(u,v) = g(\ddagger u, \ \ddagger v) + (-1)^{g(\ddagger u, \ \ddagger v)} \cdot h(u,v) \ ,$$

where $0 \le h\,(u,v) < 1/2$ is arbitrary .

In particular, for $* = \cap$, g must satisfy the boundary condition

$$g(0,0) = g(0,1) = g(1,0) = 0 \; ; \; g(1,1) = 1 \; .$$

Thus for θ to be a homomorphism for Ⓝ defined through g and for $\cap$, we must have:

$1 \geq g(u,v) \geq 1/2$ for all $1 \geq u,v \geq 1/2$, $0 \leq g(u,v) < 1/2$ for all $0 \leq u,v \leq 1$, otherwise.

Hence, $g = \min$ as shown in the paper will do, but $g = \text{prod}$ will not, since for example $\text{prod}(1/2,1/2) = 1/4 < 1/2$.

Similarly for $* = \cup$, g must satisfy $g(0,0) = 0$, $g(0,1) = g(1,0) = g(1,1) = 1$, implying for θ to be a homomorphism for Ⓤ and $\cup$, we must have for Ⓤ through g : $0 \leq g(u,v) < 1/2$ for all $0 \leq u,v < 1/2$; $1 \geq g(u,v) \geq 1/2$ for all $0 \leq u,v \leq 1$, otherwise. Hence $g = \max$ will work but $g = \text{probsum}$ will not since, for example, $\text{probsum}(3/8, 3/8) = 39/64 > 1/2$.

Next if ⊛ : $\mathcal{F}(X) \to \mathcal{F}(X)$ is a unary operator, extending $* : \mathcal{P}(X) \to \mathcal{P}(X)$ which corresponds to ⓖ : $[0,1] \to [0,1]$, with $g : \{0,1\} \to \{0,1\}$, then for all $A \in \mathcal{F}(X)$, $x \in X$

$$\phi_{\circledast A}(x) = g(\phi_A(x)) \; .$$

Then as above, θ is a homomorphism w.r.t. ⊛ and $*$, iff, for all $u \in [0,1]$,

$$g(\ddagger u) = \ddagger g(u)$$

iff

$$g(u) = g(\ddagger u) + (-1)^{g(\ddagger u)} \cdot h(u) \; , \; 0 < h(u) < 1/2 \text{ arbitrary.}$$

Hence for $* = C$, g must satisfy $g(0) = 1$, $g(1) = 0$, whence for θ to be a homomorphism for Ⓒ and C, we must have for Ⓒ, through g :

$$0 \leq g(u) < 1/2 \; , \text{ for } 1 \geq u \geq 1/2$$

$$1/2 \leq g(u) \leq 1 \; , \text{ for } 1/2 > u \geq 0 \; ,$$

yelding many choices for ⊛ including that for $g(u) = 1 - u$.

On the critical side, Wantanabe joins Schefe (see section 7.5) in the desire to preserve all of the basic laws of Classical Logic, especially the Law of the Excluded Middle, and criticizes the fuzzy set membership concept as involving over-precifications and adds (with Manes [170]) the lack of empirical ways of verifying fuzziness. (See also Chapter 7 for various theories of uncertainty.)

Arbib [6] has raised the issue of the lack of well-organized texts in fuzzy set theory, while Manes [168], [170], questions (1) the validity of fuzzy set theory as a legitimate branch of mathematics, by pointing up the lack of analogues with the Central Limit Theorem and Law of Large Numbers of probability theory as well as the apparent arbitrariness and (2) inconsistencies occurring in "fuzzifying" or extending ordinary set concepts such as the "extension principle" - the fuzzy set extensions of ordinary functional transforms operating on ordinary set or points. (See also section 7.2.)

(III) Admissibility of uncertainty measures [91'].

Recall that an uncertainty measure can be considered as a mapping $\tau : \mathcal{A} \to I_o$, where $(X,\mathcal{A})$ is a measurable space, i.e., $\mathcal{A} \subseteq \mathcal{P}(X)$ is a σ-algebra and $I_o \subseteq \mathbb{R}$ is a closed interval. A number of relations were developed between various classes of uncertainty measures in Chapters 3, 4 and 5, but no specific comparisons were established showing one class of uncertainty measures was "better" than another. Indeed the theme has been: each situation dictates a perhaps different appropriate uncertainty measure. However, Lindley [158] generalizing Savage's earlier work [221'], pointed out that by using additive scores, uncertainty measures can be considered as decision functions relative to event sequences. Consequently it is meaningful to consider the class of Bayes uncertainty measures, etc., among the many items one can investigate within a statistical decision theory framework.

Lindley concluded that only uncertainty measures that are certain transforms of probability measures are admissible and large classes of nonstandard ones, i.e., upper and lower probabilities, confidence statements, and possibilities, are all inadmissible. Because of these rather strong conclusions and the informality of Lindley's argument, a more detailed decision-theoretic presentation is given here together with some clarifications and modifications of the original conclusions.

(I) Uncertainty measures can be considered as decision functions relative to the following framework:

Let : $H_0 \overset{d}{=} \{0,1\}$, $H_1 \overset{d}{=} [0,1]$. Let $(X,\mathcal{A})$, $(Y,\mathcal{B})$, $(Z,\mathcal{C})$ be measurable spaces, i.e., $\mathcal{A} \subseteq \mathcal{P}(X)$, $\mathcal{B} \subseteq \mathcal{P}(Y)$, $\mathcal{C} \subseteq \mathcal{P}(Z)$ are σ-algebras, $\mathcal{I}_\infty(\mathcal{A}) \overset{d}{=} \{\mathcal{E} \mid \mathcal{E} \subseteq \mathcal{A}$ and $\mathcal{E}$ is at most countable$\}$,

$p : Y \to \mathcal{I}_\infty(\mathcal{A})$, $q : Z \to \mathcal{A}^{\mathcal{A}}$ arbitrary known, fixed maps, representing *choice* maps.

$\mathcal{A}$ is the collection of *basic events* on X ,

$\Omega \overset{d}{=} X \times \mathcal{I}_\infty(\mathcal{A})$ = *parameter space*,

$\mathcal{Y} \overset{d}{=} \{((g(B))_{B\in\mathcal{E}},g) \mid \mathcal{E} \in \mathcal{I}_\infty(\mathcal{A})$, $g \in \mathcal{A}^{\mathcal{A}}\}$ = *data space*,

$\mathcal{D} \overset{d}{=} \bigcup_{\mathcal{E}\in\mathcal{I}_\infty(\mathcal{A})} [a,b]^{\mathcal{E}}$ ($a < b$ fixed real constants) = *decision space*,

$\theta : X \times Y \to \Omega$ is the *parameter* map, where for all $\omega \in X$, $\eta \in Y$,

$\theta(\omega,\eta) \overset{d}{=} (\omega,p(\eta))$,

$V : \Omega \to \mathcal{Y}^Z$ is the *data map*, where for all $\theta \stackrel{d}{=} (\omega,\mathcal{E}) \in \Omega$, all $\gamma \in Z$,

$$V(\theta)(\gamma) \stackrel{d}{=} ((q(\gamma)(B)_{B,\ \omega\in B\in\mathcal{E}}, q(\gamma)) ,$$

$\mathcal{G} \subseteq \mathfrak{D}^{\mathcal{Y}}$ is the *decision function space*, so that any $\tau \in \mathcal{G}$, and any $y \stackrel{d}{=} ((g(B)_{B\in\mathcal{E}}, g) \in \mathcal{Y}$, $\mathcal{E} \in \mathcal{F}_\infty(\mathcal{A})$, $g \in \mathcal{A}^{\mathcal{A}}$,

$$\tau(y) \stackrel{d}{=} (\tau_B(g(B)))_{B\in\mathcal{E}} \text{ , where for all } B \in \mathcal{E} ,$$

$\tau_B(g(B)) \stackrel{d}{=}$ *uncertainty of event* B occurring, given $g(B)$ is observed to occur.

Each such $\tau : \mathcal{Y} \to \mathfrak{D}$ is a *conditional uncertainty measure map*, and we use the notation, for any $g \in \mathcal{A}^{\mathcal{A}}$, $(\tau|g) : \mathcal{F}_\infty(\mathcal{A}) \to \mathfrak{D}$, where for any $\mathcal{E} \in \mathcal{F}_\infty(\mathcal{A})$,

$$(\tau|g)(\mathcal{E}) \stackrel{d}{=} (\tau_B(g(B)))_{B\in\mathcal{E}} .$$

Also define the *score function class*

(0) $\mathcal{K} \stackrel{d}{=} \{f | f : [a,b] \times H_0 \to \mathbb{R}^+$ satisfies regularity condition (1)$\}$

(1) $\begin{cases} f \text{ is continuously differentiable in its first argument} \\ \text{with } f(x,t) \text{ nonincreasing in } x \text{ , for all } t \in H_0 , \\ x \le x_{t,f} \text{ , for some } x_{t,f} \text{ , for some } x_{t,f} , \\ \partial f(x_{t,f},t)/\partial x_{t,f} = 0 , \\ \text{and } f(x,t) \text{ nondecreasing in } x \text{ , for all } x \ge x_{t,f} , \\ \text{and } +\infty > M_f \stackrel{d}{=} \max_{t\in H_0} \sup_{x\in[a,b]} f(x,t) ; \\ a < x_{0,f} < x_{1,f} < b . \end{cases}$

Define for each $f \in \mathcal{K}$, *loss function*

$$L_f : \mathfrak{D} \times \Omega \to \mathbb{R}^+$$

where, for any $\mathcal{E}' \in \mathcal{F}_\infty(\mathcal{A})$ and $h \in [a,b]^{\mathcal{E}'}$, and any $\theta = (\omega,\mathcal{E}'') \in \Omega$, we have the additive form

$$L_f(h,\theta) \stackrel{d}{=} \begin{cases} +\infty \text{ , if } \mathcal{E}' \ne \mathcal{E}'' \\ \sum_{B\in\mathcal{E}'} f(h(B),\phi_B(\omega)) \text{ , iff } \mathcal{E}' = \mathcal{E}'' , \end{cases}$$

where $\phi : \mathcal{A} \to \{0,1\}$ is the ordinary membership function map, i.e., for any $B \in \mathcal{A}$

$$\phi_B(x) = \begin{cases} 1 & \text{iff} \quad x \in B \\ 0 & \text{iff} \quad x \notin B \,. \end{cases}$$

Assume all maps θ, V, τ, L_f are measurable in the usual sense for the appropriate measurable spaces.

In turn, the usual decision theory definitions apply here including conditional risks, posterior risks and Bayes decision functions with the above interpretations.

Define also for each $f \in \mathcal{K}$, the class of all *$\mathcal{Y}$-admissible uncertainty measures*

$$\mathcal{Y}\text{-admiss}_f \overset{d}{=} \{\tau \mid \tau \in \mathcal{G} \text{ and for each } y \overset{d}{=} (g(B))_{B\in\mathcal{E}} \in \mathcal{Y}\,, \text{ there is no } \tau' \in \mathcal{G} \text{ such that eq.(2) holds}\}$$

(2) $L_f(\tau'(y),\theta) \le L_f(\tau(y),\theta)$, all $\theta \in \Omega$ with strict inequality holding for at least some $\theta \in \Omega$.

Define also the class of all *locally admissible uncertainty measures* as

$$\text{loc-admis}_f \overset{d}{=} \{\tau \mid \tau \in \mathcal{G} \text{ and there is no}$$

$$y \overset{d}{=} ((g(B))_{B\in\mathcal{E}}, g) \in \mathcal{Y} \text{ such that eq.(3) holds}\}$$

(3) (total differential) $(d_u L_f(u,\theta))_{u=\tau(y)} \le 0$; all $\theta \in \Omega$, with strict inequality holding for at least some $\theta \in \Omega$.

Equivalently,

$$(3') \qquad \sum_{B\in\mathcal{E}} \left[\frac{\partial f(x,\phi_B(\omega))}{\partial x} \right]_{x=\tau_B(g(B))} \cdot \Delta_B \le 0 \,,$$

for all $\theta = (\omega,\mathcal{E}) \in \Omega$, with strict inequality holding for at least some θ.

Similarly, for each $y \in Y$, define

$$\text{loc-admiss}_{f,y} \overset{d}{=} \{\tau \mid \tau \in \mathcal{G} \text{ and eq.(3) does not hold}\}.$$

Next, define the *Lindley-transform*

$$P_{\cdot} : \mathcal{K} \to \mathcal{K} \qquad \text{(surjective)}$$

where

$$\mathcal{K} \overset{d}{=} \{Q \mid Q : [a',b'] \to [0,1] \text{ is continous, nondecreasing and such that } Q(a') = 0\,,\ Q(b') = 1\}\,;$$

$a \le a' < b' \le b$

and for any $f \in \mathcal{K}$, and all $x_{0,f} \leq x \leq x_{1,f}$, define

(4) $$P_f\ (x) \overset{d}{=} \frac{(\partial f(x,0)/\partial x)}{\partial f(x,0)/\partial x) - (\partial f(x,1)/\partial x)}\ .$$

In turn, define for each $f \in \mathcal{K}$, Lindley's class of uncertainty measures as

$$\mathrm{Lind}_f \overset{d}{=} \{\tau \mid \tau \in \mathcal{G} \text{ and there is a probability measure } \nu \text{ making } (X,\mathcal{A},\nu) \text{ a probability space such that eq.(5) holds}\}$$

(5) $$P_f(\tau_B(g(B))) = \nu\ (B \mid g(B)) \overset{d}{=} \nu\ (B \cap g(B))/\nu(g(B))\ ,$$

for $\nu(g(B)) > 0$, for all $B \in \mathcal{A}$, $g \in \mathcal{A}^{\mathcal{A}}$, i.e.,

$$P_f(\tau_B(F)) = \nu(B \mid F)\ ;\ \text{for all } B,F \in \mathcal{A}\ .$$

(II) It follows that for all $f \in \mathcal{K}$

(6) $$\mathcal{Y}\text{-admiss}_f \subseteq \text{loc-admiss}_f = \bigcap_{y \in \mathcal{Y}} \text{loc-admiss}_{f,y} \subseteq \mathcal{Z}_1 \cap \mathcal{Z}_2 \cap \mathcal{Z}_3 = \mathrm{Lind}_f\ ,$$

where

(7) $$\mathcal{Y}_1 \overset{d}{=} \{y \mid y = (g(B))_{B \in \mathcal{E}} \in \mathcal{Y}\ ;$$

$$g(B) \overset{d}{=} \begin{cases} C, & \text{if } B = F \\ \emptyset, & \text{if } B \neq F \end{cases},\ \text{all } C,\ F \in \mathcal{A}\},$$

(8) $$\mathcal{Y}_2 \overset{d}{=} \{y \mid y = (g(B))_{B \in \mathcal{E}} \in \mathcal{Y}\ ;$$

$$g(B) \overset{d}{=} \begin{cases} C, & \text{if } B = F,\ \complement F \\ \emptyset, & \text{if } B \neq F,\ \complement F \end{cases},\ \text{all } C,\ F \in \mathcal{A}\}$$

(9) $$\mathcal{Y}_3 \overset{d}{=} \{y \mid y = (g(B))_{B \in \mathcal{E}} \in \mathcal{Y}\ ;$$

$$g(B) \overset{d}{=} \begin{cases} G & \text{if } B = F,\ F \cap H \\ F \cap G, & \text{if } B = H \\ \emptyset, & \text{if } B \neq F,\ F \cap H, H \end{cases}\ \text{all } B,\ F,\ H,\ G \in \mathcal{A}\},$$

(10) $$\mathcal{Z}_1 \overset{d}{=} \bigcap_{y \in \mathcal{Y}_1} \text{loc-admiss}_{f,y}$$
$$= \{\tau \mid \tau \in \mathcal{F} \text{ and for all } F,\ C \in \mathcal{A}\ , \text{ if } C \neq \emptyset\ ,\ \tau_C(C) = x_{1,f}\ ,\ \tau_{\complement C}(C) = x_{0,f}\ ,$$

$$\tau_F(C) \in [x_{0,f}, x_{1,f}]\},$$

(11) $\mathcal{Z}_2 \overset{d}{=} \bigcap_{y\in\mathcal{Y}} \text{loc-admiss}_{f,y} = \{\tau \mid \tau \in \mathcal{G}$ and for all $F, C \in \mathcal{A}$,

$$P_f(\tau_F(C)) + P_f(\tau_{CF}(C)) = 1\},$$

(12) $\mathcal{Z}_3 \overset{d}{=} \bigcap_{y\in\mathcal{Y}} \text{loc-admiss}_{f,y} = \{\tau \mid \tau \in \mathcal{G}$ and for all $F, G, H \in \mathcal{A}$,

$$P_f(\tau_{F\cap H}(G)) = P_f(\tau_F(G)) \cdot P_f(\tau_H(F\cap G))\}.$$

(III) Now let

(13) $\mathcal{H}_0 \overset{d}{=} \{f \mid f \in \mathcal{H}$ is such that in eq. (1) "nonincreasing" and "nondecreasing" are replaced by "strictly decreasing" and "strictly increasing", respectively}.

Then it follows that for all $f \in \mathcal{H}_0$:

$P_f : [x_{0,f}, x_{1,f}] \to [0,1]$ is continuous and "strictly increasing", and for any $t \in H_1$,

$$\inf_{x\in[x_{0,f},x_{1,f}]} \big(f(x,1)\cdot t + f(x,0)\cdot(1-t)\big)$$

occurs uniquely at $x = x_{t,f}$, where by differentiating w.r.f. x.

(14) $p_f(x_{t,f}) = t$,

i.e.,

(14') $x_{t,f} = P_f^{-1}(t)$, for all $t \in H_1$.

(IV) Now for any $f \in H$, any probability measure μ such that $(X \times Y \times Z, \sigma(\mathcal{A} \times \mathcal{B} \times \mathcal{C}), \mu)$ is a probability space such that marginal probability measures μ_X and $\mu_{Y\times Z}$ are independent, for any $\tau \in \mathcal{G}$ and for any $y \overset{d}{=} (y_B)_{B\in\mathcal{E}} \overset{d}{=} (\tau_B(g(B)), g)_{B\in\mathcal{E}}$, the posterior risk is

(15) $r_f(\mu,\tau,y) \overset{d}{=}$

$$E(L_f(\tau(V(\theta(\cdot,\cdot\cdot))(\cdot\cdot\cdot)), \theta(\cdot,\cdot\cdot)) \mid V(\theta(\cdot,\cdot\cdot))(\cdot\cdot\cdot) = y)$$

$$= \sum_{B\in\mathcal{E}} K_f(y_B)\cdot \mu_{Y\times Z}(p^{-1}(\mathcal{E}) \times q^{-1}(g)),$$

where

(16) $K_f(y_B)$

$$\overset{d}{=} E(f(\tau_B(g(B)), \phi_B(\cdot)) \mid (q(\cdot\cdot)(B), q(\cdot\cdot)) = y_B)$$

$$= f(\tau_B(g(B)),1)\cdot\mu_X(g(B) \cap B) + f(\tau_B(g(B)),0) \cdot \mu_X(g(B) \dashv B)$$
$$= \nu_X(g(B))\cdot \big(f(\tau_B(g(B),1)\cdot\mu_X(B|g(B))+f(\tau_B(g(B)),0)\cdot$$
$$\cdot(1-\mu_X(B|g(B)))\big) .$$

Then applying the results in (III) to eqs. (15) and (16), $\inf_{\tau\in G} r_f(\mu,\tau,Y)$ occurs uniquely for the *Bayes uncertainty measures* $\tau = \tau^{(\mu,f)} \in \mathcal{G}$, where

$$(17) \qquad P_f(\tau_B^{(\mu,f)}(g(B))) = \mu_X(B|g(B)) ,$$

for all $B \in \mathcal{A}$, $g \in \mathcal{A}^{\mathcal{A}}$.

Conversely, if equation (17) holds for some $\tau^{(\mu,f)}$, then $\tau(\mu,f)$ is a (unique) Bayes uncertainty measure for the posterior risk. Since all uniquely determined Bayes decision functions are $\mathcal{Y}$-admissible, combining these results with eq.(6) yields

$$(18) \quad \text{Bayes}_f = \mathcal{Y}\text{-admis}_f = \text{loc-admiss}_f = \text{Lind}_f ,$$

for all $f \in \mathcal{K}_0$, with the form of the Bayes decision functions given above in eq. (17).

Remark 1.

Lindley shows that a number of well-known classes of uncertainty measures-including one-sided confidence intervals, significance statements, Zadeh's possibility measures and upper and lower probability measures - are not $\mathcal{Y}$-admissible. This is accomplished, noting eq. (6), for any such candidate uncertainty measure τ , that $\tau \notin \text{Lind}_f$, i.e.,

$$P_f(\tau_{\cdot}(\cdot\cdot)) \neq \nu_X(\cdot|\cdot\cdot) ;$$

for all probability measures ν_X over X relative to $\mathcal{A}$, and all $f \in \mathcal{K}$ (or $f \in \mathcal{K}_0$). This is equivalent to showing either (or both) eqs. (19) and (20) do not hold:

$$(19) \quad P_f(\tau_F(C)) + P_f(\tau_{CF}(C)) = 1 , \text{ all } C, F \in \mathcal{A}$$

and/or

$$(20) \quad P_f(\tau_{F\cap H}(G)) = P_f(\tau_F(G)) \cdot P_f(\tau_H(F\cap G)) , \text{ for all } F, G, H \in \mathcal{A} .$$

However, Lindley does not consider (except for his "proper" case of f constrained so that $P_f(x) \equiv x$) the validity of the class of all $\tau \in G$ such that $\tau_{\cdot}(\cdot\cdot)$ itself is a (conditional) probability measure family.

Indeed, the answer in general is negative:

Theorem 1

Under the same basic assumptions as in part (I), where now $x_0 = 0$, $x_1 = 1$:
If $\tau \in \mathcal{G}$ is such that $\tau_{\cdot}(\cdot\cdot)$ is a non-atomic conditional probability measure family, i.e. there is a non-atomic probability measure ν making $(x, \mathcal{A}, \nu)$ a probability space, such that

(21) $\tau_F(C) = \nu(F|C)$, all $C, F \in \mathcal{A}$,
with $\nu(C) \neq 0$, then:

(i) Unless f is constrained so that

(22) $P_f(x) = x$, for all $x \in H_1$,

such as for Savage's choice [221],

(23) $f(x,t) = (x-t)^2$, all $x \in [a,b]$, $\tau \in H_0$,

then τ is not $\mathcal{Y}$-admissible.

(ii) When f is chosen so that eq. (22) holds, then τ is $\mathcal{Y}$-admissible.

Proof: The proof involves a basic technique in functional equations. Since $\tau_{\cdot}(\cdot\cdot)$ is non-atomic, eqs. (19) and (20) become

(24) $P_f(x) + P_f(1-x) = 1$, all $x \in [0,1]$,

(25) $P_f(w \cdot z) = P_f(w) \cdot P_f(z)$, all $w,z \in [0,1]$.

Differentiating eq. (25) first w.r.t. w and then w.r.t. z yields, for all $w,z \in [0,1]$, the primes denoting derivatives,

$$z \cdot P_f'(w \cdot z) = P_f'(w) \cdot P_f(z) ,$$
$$w \cdot P_f'(w \cdot z) = P_f(w) \cdot P_f'(z) ,$$

whence

$$P_f'(w) \cdot P_f(z)/z \equiv P_f'(z) \cdot P_f(w)/w ,$$

i.e.

$$z \cdot d \log P_f(z)/dz \equiv w \cdot d \log P_f(w)/dw ,$$

implying

$$z \cdot d \log P_f(z)/dz = \text{const}, \; ; \text{ all } z \in [0,1] ,$$

which yields the solution

$$P_f(z) = z^k \; ; \text{ all } \; z \in [0,1] \; ,$$

for any fixed $k > 0$.

However, use of eq. (25) immediately implies that $k = 1$.

Corollary 1

Under the same basic assumptions: If τ is $\mathcal{Y}$-admissible and is such that it can continuously assume all values in $[0,1]$, then $P(\tau_{.}(\cdot\cdot))$ is an atomic probability nonsure family and hence not $\mathcal{Y}$-admissible, unless eq. (22) holds. Similarly, in general, all iterates $P^j(\tau_{.}(\cdot\cdot))$, for $j = 1,2,\ldots$, are not $\mathcal{Y}$-admissible.

Remark 2.

The above result may be weakened as follows; If τ is complementary, i.e. satisfies eq. (19) and continuously assumes all values in H_1 , then if τ is $\mathcal{Y}$-admissible , eq. (24) must hold, i.e.,

$$(26) \qquad f'(x,1) \cdot f'(1-x,1) = f'(x,0) \cdot f'(1-x,0)$$

for all $x \in [0,1]$.

Thus, e.g.,

$$(27) \qquad f(x,t) \overset{d}{=} t\cdot|x-t|^{k_1} + (1-t)x^{k_2} \; ,$$

for all $x \in [0,1]$, with $k_1,k_2 > 1$, $k_1 \neq k_2$ constants, will not satisfy (26), and consequently τ connot be $\mathcal{Y}$-admissible for that choice of f .

Remark 3.

All uncertainty measures can be extended-in the sense to be described below - to probability measures over higher order spaces, which in turn are all $\mathcal{Y}$-admissible relative to f chosen as in eq. (23):

Let$(\Omega,\mathcal{B},Pr)$ be a fixed non-atomic probability space and $U : \Omega \to H_1$, a uniformly distributed random variable. Let $(X,\mathcal{A})$ be a measurable space, i.e., $\mathcal{A} \subseteq \mathcal{P}(X)$, is a σ-algebra on X , and in turn, $(\mathcal{A},\underset{\sim}{B})$ be a measurable space.

For each $A \in \mathcal{A}$, define the filter class

$$(28) \qquad c_A \overset{d}{=} \{\mathcal{E} \mid A \in \mathcal{E} \in \underset{\sim}{\mathcal{B}}\} \; ,$$

and let

(29) $\underset{\sim}{C} \overset{d}{=} \sigma\{C_A \mid A \in \mathcal{A}\} \subseteq \mathcal{P}(\underset{\sim}{\mathfrak{B}})$,

forming the measurable space $(\underset{\sim}{\mathfrak{B}}, \underset{\approx}{C})$.

Define also the class of uncertainty measures on $\mathcal{A}$:

(30) $\mathcal{M}(\mathcal{A}) \overset{d}{=} \{\tau \mid \tau : \mathcal{A} \to H_1$ is a random variable, i.e., τ is $(\underset{\sim}{\mathfrak{B}}, \mathbb{B}_1)$ - measurable$\}$

and the class of all probability measures on $\underset{\approx}{C}$:

(31) $\mathcal{P}r(\underset{\approx}{C}) \overset{d}{=} \{\nu \mid (\underset{\sim}{\mathfrak{B}}, \underset{\approx}{C}, \nu)$ is a probability space$\}$.

Consider also the following mappings:

(32) $S : \mathcal{M}(\mathcal{A}) \to \underset{\sim}{\mathfrak{B}}^{\Omega}$

where for all $\tau \in \mathcal{M}(\mathcal{A})$, $S(\tau) : \Omega \to \underset{\sim}{\mathfrak{B}}$ where for all $\omega \in \Omega$,

(33)
$$\begin{aligned} S(\tau)\ (\omega) &\overset{d}{=} \tau^{-1}[U(\omega),1] \\ &= \{B \mid B \in \mathcal{A} \text{ and } \tau(B) \in [U(\omega), 1]\} \\ &= \{B \mid B \in \mathcal{A} \text{ and } U(\omega) \le \tau(B)\} \\ &= \{B \mid B \in \mathcal{A} \text{ and } \omega \in U^{-1}\ [0, \tau(B)]\} , \end{aligned}$$

(34) $h : \mathcal{M}(\mathcal{A}) \to \mathcal{P}r(\underset{\approx}{C})$ is injective,

where for all $\tau \in \mathcal{M}(\mathcal{A})$,

(35) $h(\tau) \overset{d}{=} \mathrm{Pr}\circ(S(\tau))^{-1}$,

noting that for all $A \in \mathcal{A}$,

(36)
$$\begin{aligned} (S(\tau)^{-1}(C_A) &= \{\omega \mid \omega \in \Omega \text{ and } A \in S(\tau)(\omega)\} \\ &= \{\omega \mid \omega \in \Omega \text{ and } U(\omega) \le \tau(A)\} \\ &= U^{-1}[0,\tau(A)] \in \mathfrak{B} , \end{aligned}$$

$(\underset{\sim}{\mathfrak{B}}, \underset{\approx}{C}, \mathcal{P}r\circ(S(\tau))^{-1})$ is the induced probability space under $S(\tau)$, and hence

$$\mathrm{Pr}\circ(S(\tau))^{-1} \in \mathcal{P}r(\underset{\approx}{C}) .$$

The above result directly implies

(37)
$$\begin{aligned} h(\tau)\ (C_A) &= \mathcal{P}r\circ U^{-1}[0,\tau(A)] \\ &= \tau(A)\ ;\ \text{all } A \in \mathcal{A} . \end{aligned}$$

Also define

(38) $k : \mathcal{P}r(\underset{\approx}{C}) \to \mathcal{M}(\mathcal{A})$,

surjective, where for all $\nu \in \mathcal{P}r(\underset{\approx}{C})$, $k(\nu) \overset{d}{=} \nu(C_{\cdot})$
Note the surjectivity of k holds since: For any

$\tau \in \mathcal{M}(\mathcal{A})$, $h(\tau) \in \mathcal{P}r(\underset{\approx}{C})$,

and

(40) $k(h(\tau)) = h(\tau)(C_{\cdot}) = \tau(\cdot)$

Note also that for any element $\mathcal{W} \in \underset{\approx}{C}$, writing it symbolically as

(41) $\mathcal{W} = \text{comb}(C,\cap,\cup)(\cdot\cdot C_A\cdot\cdot)$,
and any $\tau \in \mathcal{M}(\mathcal{A})$, extending eq. (36) ,

(42)
$$\begin{aligned}(S(\tau))^{-1}(\mathcal{W}) &= \text{comb}(C,\cap,\cup)(\cdot\cdot(S(\tau))^{-1}(C_A)\cdot\cdot)\\ &= \text{comb}(C,\cap,\cup)(\cdot\cdot U^{-1}[0,\tau(A)]\cdot\cdot)\\ &= U^{-1}(\text{comb}(C,\cap,\cup)(\cdot\cdot[0,\tau(A)]\cdot\cdot)) ,\end{aligned}$$

because inverse functions preserve all ordinary set operations, and which now can be conveniently computed. In turn $\text{Pr}\circ(S(\tau))^{-1}(\mathcal{W})$ can be obtained as $\text{Pr}\circ U^{-1}(\text{comb}(C,\cup,\cap)(\cdot\cdot[0,\tau(A)]\cdot\cdot))$ from eq. (42). Thus $h(\tau)$ can be obtained essentially in a natural constructive sense over $\underset{\approx}{C}$.

(i) In summary, noting the mapping

(41) $C_{\cdot} : \mathcal{A} \to \{C_A \mid A \in \mathcal{A}\} \subseteq \underset{\approx}{C}$, is bijective and hence injective in $\underset{\approx}{C}$; h in eq. (34) is injective; eqs. (37) and (42) all imply that in a natural way $\mathcal{M}(\mathcal{A})$ is imbedded within $\text{Pr}\circ(\underset{\approx}{C})$. (Indeed, this development is essentially equivalent to the representation of dispersions through one point coverage functions of nested random sets as developed in Chapters 4-6.)

(ii) Also, referring to the notation in part (I), replacing $\mathcal{A}$ there by $\underset{\approx}{C}$, etc., then for all f such as in eq. (23), so that eq. (22) holds, it follows from Theorem 1 that all probability measures $\nu \in \mathcal{P}r(\underset{\approx}{C})$ are $\mathcal{Y}$-admissible$_f$ (making the obvious identifications as need, e.g. in eq. (21)).

Hence, results (i) and (ii) imply in the above sense that all $\tau \in \mathcal{M}(\mathcal{A})$ are $\mathcal{Y}$-admissible$_f$!

B. Research issues

The development of generalized set theory - as opposed to Zadeh's fuzzy set theory and classical probability - is truly a brand new area. The applications to natural language modeling may enable feasible use in a systematic manner for information that was previously ignored to be fully integrated with statistical descriptions of unknown parameters, including data association, search parameters, and fault diagnosis levels. The basic combination of evidence algorithms presented in Chapters 8 and 9 in their present form have the capability of treating both literal and numerical information. This should be tested against simulated real-world situations. All of these developments rest on the theoretical bases established previously. The research issues to be presented consequently, must have an impact on the design of these algorithms. Choice of the most appropriate general logical system is another very important factor, as is resolution of random set representation ambiguity for modeling input information. Modeling of natural language forms is of course also critical. Thus, all of the research issues really drive the design of the algorithms in a true symbiotic relationship.

In this section, we pose a number of basic questions (with not enough answers at present!) for issues that arise concerning the role of natural language information, semantic evaluation of formal language, general logical systems, and other concepts in the modeling of uncertainty. Unfortunately, a number of basic problems remain concerning the foundation and implementation of the combination of evidence problem, discussed in Chapters 8 and 9. Even more basic than this are open problems involving the representation of natural language information, semantic evaluations, and a number of other important issues.

Issue #1 **Combination of evidence** (Chapters 8 and 9).

Primary on the list is that of the problem of combining evidence. Although some results have been obtained in the direction of generalizing the classical probability form of the Weak Law of Large Numbers to generalized set theory (section 8.4), more satisfactory upper bounds on convergence or firming-up rates must be obtained. The new idea of extending a t-conorm to an uncountable number of arguments, analagous to the role integration plays with averaged summations, should prove useful-as developed in section 8.4. In a related manner, suppose there are n probability or fuzzy set descriptions - noting that in the context of generalized set theory, unlike Zadeh's original development, all probability functions and their operators can be shown to be special cases of the general system:

$$\phi_{A_1}, \ldots, \phi_{A_n} : X \to [0,1]$$

for common unknown parameters $\theta \in X$, which also may contain some nuisance subparameters. In the basic combination of evidence algorithm, (see Chapters 8 and 9) θ may be identified with the pair (Z,Q), where Z, the dummy data parameter may be later projected out and where Q represents the prior data association level between two given track histories. Clearly, for any choice of confidence levels $\alpha_1, \ldots, \alpha_n$, the region

$$R_n(A_1,\ldots,A_n;\ \alpha_1,\ldots,\alpha_n) \overset{d}{=} \bigcap_{j=1}^{n} \phi_{A_j}^{-1}([\alpha_j,1]) \subseteq X$$

represents in a natural way the joint $(\alpha_1,\ldots,\alpha_n)^{th}$ level set in describing θ . Thus, any additional piece of evidence as given e.g., by

$$\phi_{A_{n+1}} : X \to [0,1] ,$$

results in clearly

$$R_{n+1}(A_1,\ldots,A_{n+1};\alpha_1,\ldots,\alpha_{n+1}) \subseteq R_n(A_1;\alpha_1,\ldots,\alpha_n) .$$

Thus in an inclusion set-sense , $R_n(A_1,\ldots,A_n;\alpha_1,\ldots,\alpha_n)$ is decreasing in n , for $n = 1, 2,$. However, this decrease is not necessarily to a single point $\{\theta\}$ as would be desirable and occur under reasonable asymptotic conditions within a pure probabilistic setting - i.e. classical consistency would hold. Indeed, the above sets are, in general, not compact, so the convergence is not necessarily to a simple set. What is sought is a single generalized set $A_{(n)}$ of X and some combining confidence level function g_n ,

$g_n : [0,1]^n \to [0,1]$ for each n , such that

$$R_n(A_1,\ldots,A_n;\alpha_1,\ldots,\alpha_n) \subseteq \phi_{A_{(n)}}^{-1}([g_n(\alpha_1,\ldots,a_n),1])$$

and the expression on the right-hand side of the above equation decreases in a set inclusion-sense for all n sufficiently large, although not necessarily to only θ . Also, numerical upper bounds on these expressions and rates of decrease are desirable. Previous results were obtained only when g_n was given in nondecreasing form[80].Here we wish to derive g_n under no restrictons, if possible. (See also section 8.4 and Chapter 9 (F) for related results concerning the asymptotic behavior of combination of evidence estimation as information granularity decreases.)

That the combination of evidence problem-even for classical statistical modeling - in expert rule-based systems is still an open issue, can be affirmed by the many discussions and ad hoc results. Finally, it should be remarked that the random set one point coverage representations mentioned earlier could play a useful role in approaching this problem by transferring known properties of combining random sets to the fuzzy set images.

Issue #2. One point coverage functions of random sets and equivalent dispersions (Chapters 5 and 6).

Another issue of importance is the resolution of the ambiguity of the one-point coverage representation of dispersions, or equivalently, generalized sets by random sets - and analogously, of the compound set evaluation representation of generalized sets by random variables. Some progress has been made on this problem in the case of finitely discrete spaces, by making use of entropy as a measure of ordering the representative random sets. (See section 5.4.) It is known that the minimal entropy set must lie in the vertex set of a space which is bijective to the class of all representing random subsets to the given fuzzy set. However, further characterizations are not known at present. On the other hand, it is easily shown that the maximal entropy solution is given by the choice of the random set T(A) , for given fuzzy set A , where the ordinary random membership function for T(A) corresponds to a mutually statistically independent zero-one process, with one-values corresponding to the values of the dispersion ϕ_A . (See section 5.4.)

The extension of the problem to a more general setting for the base space is of course desirable. This also must entail - as has been carried out for the previous special case - characterizations of the entire solution class of random set representations for each fuzzy set. Other measures of the ordering of uncertainty should also be considered, such as generalized variances, volume coverages, and variations of classical information measures.

Issue #3. Random variable representations of dispersions (Chapter 6).

It has been shown (as briefly mentioned above in #2) that not only do all generalized sets have random set representations, but also possess, in a canonically corresponding way to each such random set representation, random variable representations, where: given a base space X and fuzzy subset A with membership function $\phi_A : X \to [0,1]$, a random set representation S (in general; S is not unique, since for example $S_U(A) = \phi^{-1}([U,1])$ or T(A) as described briefly in item #2, may be chosen, among many others [77]), $S \subseteq X$, holds with

$$\phi_A(x) = Pr(x \in X).$$

In addition, a space of elementary events, say, Y , exists and a random variable V (in general not unique, but determined through S) exists over Y such that all points x in X may be considered also as compound events from Y , i.e., subsets of Y , such that

$$Pr(V \in x) = \phi_A(x) \; ; \text{ all } x \in X .$$

Analogous to the isomorphic-like or weak-homomorphis relationships developed in this book between fuzzy set operations and random set operations, similar relationships are sought for random variable representations.

Issue #4. Multiple point coverage representations

The problem of multiple point coverage function representation by random sets also remains an open problem. In the extreme cases where all possible subsets and incidences for random sets are specified, a number of results have been obtained by exploiting the Choquet capacity theorem and its variations. Also tie-ins with the Dempster-Shafer theory of uncertainty have been established as part of this work. (See especially, Chapters 4 and 5.) In addition, the other extreme case has also been investigated with many fruitful results: namely, the one point coverage case described in the above items. However, little progress, except for the work in discrete spaces characterizing all random set representations, has been carried out for the following n-point coverage problem:

Let $\mathcal{P}_n(X)$ denote the class of all ordinary subsets of space X which have at most n elements (distinct). Let

$$f : \mathcal{P}_n(X) \to [0,1]$$

be a given function. (When $n = 1$, this is the same as a fuzzy set membership function.) Then conditions are sought for f and a random subset S of X is sought, such that

$$f(C) = \Pr(C \subseteq S) \ ; \text{ all } \ C \in \mathcal{P}_n(X) \ .$$

This problem entails many more difficulties than the one point coverage problem, since in general it can be shown that unless f is suitably restricted, no solution exists for the above equation for S .

Issue #5. Extension of category and topos theory formulations of generalized set theory and relations with general logical systems (section 2.4).

Recall the extensive discussion in section 2.4.2 (F) concerning the relations between Goguen's category, Gog , Eytan's original category Fuz and modified category (and indeed in some cases, topos) $\text{Fuz}_\asymp$, and Higg's topos Higg .

(1) Is Higg the smallest topos containing Fuz , whose subobject classifier is H , the natural complete Heyting algebra generalization of the unit interval [0,1]?

(2) What functors can be established imbedding the extensions or variations of them into Higg? It should be mentioned that Eytan attempted a second time (unpublished personal communications [57]) to show that Fuz suitably enlargened was a topos. (However, see the construction of $\text{Fuz}_\asymp$ in section 2.4.2.)

(3) Can we extend Fuz and Higg to reflect the generalized (fuzzy) set theory established here? (This is in place of Zadeh's system.) Of course, since the mutual distributivity property will fail in general for the "and" and "or" operations, we may no longer have classical categories, but a good deal of structure remains. For example, Manes proposed a generalization of Fuz which is not compatible with generalized set systems. Yet, we can show the following extension of Manes' ideas: (See also section 7.2.)

Define function $T : SET \to SET$, where SET is the topos of all well-formed sets. The object class is indeed all sets, while the arrow class is all ordinary functions between all (ordinary) sets. Let $(\phi_{not}, \phi_{\&}, \phi_{or})$ be a fixed general logical system, where the first operator is realized as a negation, the second as a t-norm, and the third as a t-conorm. Then for any set X, define

$$\mathcal{T}(X) \overset{d}{=} \text{the class of all generalized subsets of } X .$$

For any fucntion $f : X \to Y$ (thus in $Ar(X,Y)$), define

$$\mathcal{T}(f) : \mathcal{T}(X) \to \mathcal{T}(Y) \text{, where for any } A \in \mathcal{T}(X) \text{, } (\mathcal{T}(f))(A) \overset{d}{=} f(A) ,$$

where for any $y \in Y$, the evaluation of $f(A) \in \mathcal{T}(Y)$ is given by

$$\begin{aligned}\phi_{f(A)}(y) &= \| y \in f(A)) \| \\ &= \| ((\exists x)((x \in A) \ \& \ (f(x) = y))) \| \\ &= \underset{\left[x \in f^{-1}(y))\right]}{\phi_{or}} (\phi_A(x)) .\end{aligned}$$

It then follows immediately from the above form that for any $f \in Y^X$ and any $g \in Z^Y$, that

$$\mathcal{T}(g \circ f) = \mathcal{T}(g) \circ T(f) \quad \text{and} \quad \mathcal{T}(ident_X) = ident_{\mathcal{T}(X)} ,$$

which in turn implies that $\mathcal{T}$ is a functor from SET back into itself (properly)!

Thus, we pose the following basic problem:

Extend the definition of $\mathcal{T}$ and investigate all possible relevant properties of $\mathcal{T}$ and relate this to Manes' "fuzzy theories".

Issue #6. <u>Extensions of classical estimation, hypotheses testing and other decision porcedures</u> (Chapter 8).

Dubois and Prade ([51], pp. 255-264) have devoted a section of their compendium on fuzzy set theory to the modeling of fuzzy set membership functions. A number of basic approaches are considered, with some emphasis on the empirical aspects of the modeling. In this vein, it should be added that the weak homomorphic theory developed for example in Chapters 4 - 6 shows that the idea of computing the degree to which a fixed value possesses a given attribute may be interpreted as the evaluation of the number of times (a fixed value possesses a given attribute), which in turn is interpreted as the evaluation of the corresponding fuzzy set membership function (see also section 8.5), as is typically done by survey sampling of individuals. This may be identified with the empirical one point coverage probability function generated by a random sample of random sets that are identically distributed and are one point coverage equivalent to the attribute or generalized set in question. However, the following issue has not been sufficiently emphasized: In classical statistical techniques, modeling of distribution functions is often carried out in two basic steps. First, a parametrized family of distributions is chosen. This may be done using invariance, shape, use of Central Limit Theory, or via trends of earlier empirical evidence. The family is chosen so that it reasonably contains the viable alternatives for the true distribution and its size is adjusted accordingly. Then empirical data or restrictions are imposed - such as unbiasedness, sufficiency, minimal risk with respect to some choice of loss function on errors and estimates of the unknown parameter value - yielding either a unique value or a reduced set of values where the unknown parameter lies. This argument leads to the conclusion that the same procedure should be applied to more general approaches to uncertainty modeling, where dispersions, replacing the classical probabilistic ones, play a key role in the theory. Examples of this are fuzzy set theory, with its fuzzy set membership functions, flou set theory with its index functions relative to the individual sets forming a given flou set, and topological neighborhood theory with its neighborhood filters. (See Manes' unified treatment of these theories as described in section 7.2.)

Other analogues can be established between generalized set theory as applied to parameter estimation and classical statistical estimation theory (see Chapter 8). For example, one can assume a linear regression model is valid connecting observations with an unknown parameter vector, with no specification of the relevant distributions involved - at least, at first. Then least squares, or more generally, a least weighted functional defined on the potential errors between observations and possible values of the parameter in question, is derived, yielding a reasonable value of the unknown parameter as a function of the observations, i.e., a statistic, if distributional assumptions were to be made. Then if a fuzzy set modeling approach is taken, the observations could be assumed to be generated from corresponding generalized set membership functions, yielding in turn through the standard extension of an ordinary function (see section 2.3.7) the generalized set membership function of the "statistic". In turn, this leads in a natural way to confidence sets for the unknown parameter vector, by, for example, considering the level sets associated with the aforementioned membership function. (See sections 8.2 and 8.3 for a related technique.) Asymptotic properties of these (general set) estimators may also be obtained as the sample sizes are increased. (See section 8.4.) Bayesian techniques may also be developed involving conditional distributions in the generalized set sense. (See sections 2.3.8 and 8.2 for development of these concepts for generalized sets.)

Can we develop a comprehensive decision theory directly extending classical probability and statistical theory, by utilizing both numerical and linguistic data sources through generalized set theory? The beginnings of such a theory, where independence, conditioning, Bayesian forms, loss functions, invariance techniques, etc., are given in Chapter 8. In addition, as mentioned previously, an extension of the Weak Law of Large Numbers, involving both discrete and a continuous infinity of operator arguments, has been carried out. This impinges directly upon the combination of evidence problem (item #1) and is illustrated by the algorithm development given in Chapter 9. As mentioned before, the entire approach to generalizing classical set theory and probability theory uses the Principle of Abstraction: evaluation of the concept through formal expression in classical logic relations, followed by choice of a particular logical system. The interpretation is often carried out through an isomorphism between truth evaluation and logical operators and the membership or dispersion interpretation of atomic predicates $(x \in A)$. (A simple example of this was given in issue #5 for the truth evaluation of $f(A)$.) This approach stands in contradistinction to the many brute force "fuzzifying" procedures available.

Finally, can figures-of-merit representing the central tendancy, variances, etc., be developed for generalized sets?

In conjunction with the issues raised above, we pose two related questions:

(a) What specific logical system should be chosen for a particular problem? As mentioned, a combination of theoretical and empirical guidelines seems the most appropriate approach. The theoretical part stems from the weak homomorphic relations between classes of fuzzy set systems - such as the semi-distributive or copula systems - and random set systems and their operators. The empirical may be based upon the many studies of Zimmermann [291], e.g., but then suitably combined with necessary parameterizations.

(b) Similar remarks hold for the modeling of generalized set membership functions.

Both problems, to a certain extent, imitate the situation in classical statistical modeling: How do we choose the appropriate dispersions and what independence/dependence assumptions should we make? Do we use invariance or loss function theory as a guideline? In the case of natural language modeling, in general, more emphasis must be placed upon subjectively obtained data and cognitive processes.

Issue #7. Formal language representation of natural language information and related problems (section 2.2).

Inference rules constitute the heart of any combination of evidence algorithm. Thus the faithful modeling of natural language descriptions is a key concern. This entails the ability to handle not only simple declarative sentences but other modal forms, complicated predicates, tenses, clausal forms, multiple argument predicate-relations, and quantifications which may be crisp or fuzzy.

Systematic symbolization of natural language is a much sought after goal. Some progress in this is shown in the appendix at the end of this section and the examples of section 2.6. (See also the numerous references mentioned throughout section 2.)

Consider first the following questions:

Can we express all human ideas or concepts in terms of natural language? Can these ideas be reduced to primitives and operators involving them? Can a mathematical/logical procedure be developed for describing and analyzing natural language in a unified way, including attributes and operators? What quantitative relationships can be established between prelinguistic ideas and natural language? How sensitive or robust - and how subjective - are concepts translated into natural language with respect to the particular language chosen (the Whorf-Sapir hypothesis is involved), the individual, and the medium used? Is there always inherent ambiguity in modeling a given concept in natural language? Can we make use of the enormous body of literature available which treats formal linguistics and semantics to develop a systematic unified framework directly relatable to multivalued logic theory? In a related manner, we may ask if a unified approach to uncertainty models (à la Manes - see Chapter 7 for further details on Manes' proposed answer to Zadeh's fuzzy set theory as well as theories (and criticisms) of Gaines, Schefe, Watanabe and others), and to natural language would be possible? Can the efficiency of the various approaches to modeling uncertainty be meaningfully compared?

In a more specific direction, it is clear that we must continue the development of a taxonomy of language forms relative to symbolizations as illustrated in the text. Thus, modal and temporal forms should be treated by a combination of ϕ_{not}, $\phi_{\&}$, ϕ_{or}, generalized set system operators. These act upon time and other variables in the form of both indices and elements of generalized sets. Compound relations may be best treated as formally n-ary generalized set relations. These new results replace Zadeh's well known fuzzy cardinality approach. They are based upon first principles - only, the generalized system chosen, and the resulting conditioning of predicates - rather than upon summation of membership functions with respect to their arguments.

Much interest has appeared (personal communications) for this new approach. In any case, a comprehensive procedure must be developed for systematic symbolization, extending Zadeh's previous work.

Finally, we ask:

Can we use formal linguistic/semantic metrics for determining accuracy of symbolizations? For example, see the well-established techniques of Osgood, et al., [198], Standard analysis of variance techniques properly applied or factor analysis as used in psychometrics, and specialized isolation of concept techniques such as Nowakowska's [195'] can be pooled. Or, tree-diagramming and parsing techniques and checks could be useful in comparing variations in symbolizations due to inherent ambiguity of forms in language or the necessary nonuniqueness in extending classical two-valued logic to infinitely-based logic via the Principle of Abstraction. (See [172].) As Chomsky has been often paraphrased: the efficacy of a linguistic theory is its test against actual ("randomly" chosen) linguistic situations.

Issue #8. Semantic evaluations, logics, soundness, completeness, consistency (sections 2.3, 2.4).

The problem of choosing the most appropriate logic as the vehicle for modeling natural language information has been mentioned already in #6. Do we choose a truth functional system or a probabilistic-like one, such as Lebesgue-Stieltjes logic (2.3.9)? Truth functional systems are easier to work with but may not reflect empirical conditions. In conjunction with this, we may pose the following: can any non-truth functional system be in some way approximated by a truth functional one? Can a logic be chosen together with a corresponding general set theory which is sound and complete, or at least consistent, in possibly some "local" sense? (See the various discussions throughout Chapter 2.)

Issue #9. Knowledge-based systems

There is a clear-cut need for a more comprehensive design of knowledge-based systems as developed here. As presented in this text, such systems are only informally organized as a feedback-loop between a panel of experts and the chosen general logical system(s).

In addition, there is always room for improvement in how information is extracted from experts. Improved questionnaire techniques and psychometric procedures (some of which were mentioned in #7) can be helpful. In short, what is needed is a specialization of the general theory of systems - many lucid articles of which can be found in the International Journal of General Systems (Great Britian) - to knowledge-based systems as interpreted here. The recent text of Hayes-Roth, et al. [107'] provides an excellent overview of knowledge acquisition and architecture, as well as evaluations and syntheses of knowledge-based (and expert) systems.

Issue #10. Miscellaneous comments on uncertainty modeling

In classical statistical decision theory, for finite sample sizes, non-zero lower bounds - of the Rao-Cramer-Fisher type [212] - exist for the second moment matrix of parameter estimator errors under sufficient regularity conditions. In conjunction with this, at the quantum level, the well-known Heisenberg uncertainty principle furnishes lower bounds on simultaneous variances of position and momentum measurements. General dispersion analogues to the above precision (or equivalently, entropy) bounds are sought. However, as pointed out in issue #6, development of measures of central tendency and higher order moment analogues for dispersions remain to be fully developed, and so all subsidiary investigations, including the above for precision bounds, must be held in abeyance.

In another direction, the role of idempotence and *fixed point theorems* in uncertainty modeling should be pointed out. (We have already considered idempotent t-norms and t-conorms in section 2.3.6.) Such mathematical tools have been well-developed in both existence forms (such as generalizations of Schauder's fixed point theorem for continuous functions over convex subsets of Banach spaces) and construction forms (being essentially an eigenvector-eigenvalue problem for unit eigenvalues).

In classical estimation, under reasonable conditions, it can be shown directly that if X and Y are random vectors representing an unknown (state) parameter vector and observed data, respectively, L is an estimation loss function and the Bayes estimators $\hat{X}(Y)$ is unique, etc., then the idempotence relation

$$\hat{X}(Y) = \hat{X}(\hat{X}(Y))$$

holds.

For any feedback-loop system - such as a knowledge-based system amenable to design changes via a panel of experts - we compare

$$y_t \quad \text{and} \quad \hat{y}_{t^-} = \Psi_t(\hat{x}_{t^-}(y_{t^-}, \hat{R}_{t^-}), \hat{S}_{t^-})$$

where subscript t indicates present time, t^-, indicates predicted to t, y indicates observed or potentially observable data, x unknown parameter vector and R and S design matrices, which include error covariance matrices, transition matrices, and measurement matrices as components, in the case of Kalman filtering.

If the system reaches a *steady state* level, i.e., y_t and $\hat{y}_{t^-}$ approach a common constant value with $\hat{X}_{t^-}$, $\hat{R}_{t^-}$, $\hat{S}_{t^-}$ all approaching constants as $t \to \infty$, then the relation becomes approximately the following fixed point one:

$$y_\infty = g(y_\infty; Q_\infty) ,$$

where

$$g(y_\infty; Q_\infty) \stackrel{d}{=} \Psi_\infty(\hat{X}_\infty(y_\infty, \hat{R}_\infty), \hat{S}_\infty) .$$

Note also the widespread use of fixed point theorems in obtaining various properties about logics such as in Rescher [214], Chapter III, where a modified form of the Axiom of Comprehension is shown to be model consistent with a variation of logic $L_{\aleph_1}$. On the other hand, more constructive aspects of fixed point theory can be utilized in the modeling and semantic evaluation of reflexive or self-referencing sentences. Interestingly enough, as Bellman points out in Chapter 9 of his book on AI [13'], such sentences are often the sources of humor, such as the statement telling us to plan ahead, which itself is not well-planned relative to page spacing or the one proclaiming that no one should use profane language, described through the use of such language.

Consider the following examples of reflexive statements:

$S_1 \stackrel{d}{=}$ "This sentence is true."

$S_2 \stackrel{d}{=}$ "This sentence is false."

$S_3 \stackrel{d}{=}$ "This sentence is q-true."

(q-true is some linguistic quantifier such as "mostly", "approximately 3/4", etc.)

$S_4 \stackrel{d}{=}$ "This sentence contains essentially gray colored characters."

$S_5 \stackrel{d}{=}$ "This sentence contains mostly roundish shaped letters."

$S_6 =$ "This sentence cannot be deduced within classical logic and the theory of arithmetic."

If we apply the general principles developed within the text, it follows that:

$$S_1 = \langle \| S_1 \| \in \{1\} \rangle ,$$
$$\| S_1 \| = \phi_{\{1\}}(\| S_1 \|) ; \qquad (1)$$

$$S_2 = \langle \| S_2 \| \in \{0\} \rangle ,$$
$$\| S_2 \| = \phi_{\{0\}}(\| S_2 \|) , \qquad (2)$$

and more generally,

$$S_3 = \langle \| S_3 \| \in q \rangle ,$$
$$\| S_3 \| = \phi_q(\| S_3 \|) . \quad (3)$$

Clearly, if {1} represents the crisp set singleton 1, then a natural solution for the semantic evaluation in eq. (1) is

$$\| S_1 \| = 1 .$$

However, if {0} represents the crisp set singleton 0, eq. (2) has no solution for $\| S_2 \|$ and leads to the famous "Liar's paradox". But, if {0} is replaced by a fuzzy number, i.e., $\phi_{\{0\}}$ is a monotone continuous decreasing function around 0 with $\phi_{\{0\}}(0) = 1$ and $\phi_{\{0\}}(c) = 0$ for some minimally chosen c, $0 < c \leq 1$, then eq. (1) does have (a fixed point) solution (as is easily seen graphically), which approaches 0 as c approaches 0.

In general, eq. (3) will have at least one (if ϕ_q is non-trivial symmetric unimodal, normalized at some $x_0 \in (0,1)$, then in general, two) solution(s) for $\| S_3 \|$.

On the other hand, S_4 is more difficult of evaluate, since

$$S_4 = \langle \mathrm{color}(S_4) \in \mathrm{Gray} \rangle ,$$
$$\| S_4 \| = \phi_{\mathrm{Gray}}(\mathrm{color}(S_4)) , \quad (4)$$

with $\| S_4 \|$ not appearing on the right hand side of eq. (4).

Similar remarks hold for S_5 and the Gödelian-like sentence S_6. Satisfactory analysis of these forms analogous to the first three examples is yet to be worked out.

APPENDIX

Modeling Natural Language and Semantic Evaluations

A good deal of this appendix is based upon the paper [91"].

INTRODUCTION

A procedure for combining evidence based upon linguistic and numerical/statistical sources is presented in Chapter 8. A more specific application to tracking and target data association problems is given in Chapter 9. The center of these approaches consists of inference rules and error tables (and matching tables used in the inference rules) modeled within a framework of multiple-valued logic. It is clear that the widest possible scope in modeling and evaluating natural language information must be sought in order to be able to carry out efficient programs of combining evidence. Natural language sentences are often complex in form. For example, the following sentences could occur within a military context:

S^* = In Ocean region V , and usually in Region W , if the weather is poor and the sea state corresponds to relatively high turbulance, then indications by sensor system A that a submarine was in the area are not that reliable and probably should be discounted in favor of geolocation matching information obtained from sensor system B , although exceptions to this can occur when visibility is up to about two miles, in which case, it has been shown that A-data matching should be assigned a much higher degree of importance in its effect upon correlation."

S^{**} = "Contact with the ship was held for about two hours, but was lost just before the Straights of Skagerrak were sighted, although purple side-insignias may have been spotted as well as an oval-shaped dome near the rear of the ship, but a foggy condition prevaded the area preventing any further identification."

Such examples as above illustrate the typical problems faced in modeling and symbolizing natural language. This includes the interpretation of modifiers such as "usually", "relatively high", "not that reliable", modal and temporal operators such as "probably should be", "was held for about two hours", and verb/predicative relations such as "Contact with the ship", "was lost", "foggy condition prevaded the area". (See [46'''], [46^{iv}] for related linguistic problems arising in expert systems.)

A systematic approach to the full symbolization of language is thus most desirable. In this text, some modest efforts in this direction are made. Conditional expressions, such as "most tall ships in region 5 are enemy ones of type F" are considered. The approach here is in contrast to Zadeh's rather arbitrary "fuzzy cardinality" approach which cannot be directly derived from multi-valued truth considerations [286], [289]. A comprehensive approach is taken to the modeling of temporal and modal relations, extending earlier ideas of Zadeh's PRUF technique [286]. Some examples are presented illustrating these ideas with an important application to the combination of evidence procedure. A number of other modeling procedures, in addition to those presented here, is given in section 2.6.

NATURAL LANGUAGE, FORMAL LANGUAGE, AND SEMANTIC EVALUATIONS

Too often in the past, natural language information was neglected in favor of "more precise" numerical data. Or, such information at times was arbitrarily made more precise to be in numerical form. Since the onset of Chomsky and others, more rigorous outlooks have been taken toward the understanding and modeling of information content in language [163], [47]. With the work of Zadeh on PRUF [286] began a new era in the development of a calculus for semantic evaluation of natural language. The following basic premises are assumed:

(a) All natural language information is translatable into sequences of English sentences. The problem of whether a given natural language molds the speaker's thoughts due to its structure and limitations - the Whorf-Sapir hypothesis, or whether this is not valid as Berlin and Kay claim (see [153] for comments) - will not be dealt with here.

(b) Ambiguity of meaning is expressed by (subjectively) weighting the possibility of interpretations. Thus, e.g., the expression "I like her well." could be

S_1 = "I really like her."

S_2 = "I wish she remains well (in good health)."

S_3 = "I want her to become well."

S_4 = "I like the well that she owns."

Weight w_i, could be assigned to S_i, $i = 1,\ldots,4$. Usually context allows for resolution of these possible branches of meaning. For simplicity, it will be assumed here no ambiguity is present. (See [153] for further discussion. See also the related idea of probabilistic grammars [249"] and Oden's fuzzy set approach [196], [196'].)

(c) Any given sentence in actuality represents an equivalence class of possibly differently appearing - i.e., syntactically different - sentences, all having the same semantic evaluation, a number lying in the unit interval [0,1] representing its truth value. This is related to Chomsky's concepts of transformational generative grammar, where changes in forms of sentences are due to word order rearranged, use of synonyms, change of voice from active to passive, or other superficialities [163], [47].

(d) Parsing Principle: Given any sentence (or any equivalence class of sentences) there exists an analytic form or parsing which is semantically the same but is structured within a formal language. This is related to Chomsky's deep structure analysis [163], [47]. (For further details on formal language and multivalued logic, see

[214], [172].) Attempts at establishing automatic procedures for parsing natural language into a corresponding formal language form, such as Schank's approach [223] are many and the area remains a lively one for research. (See the large compendium of approaches in [274'].)

A typical parsing analysis yields, for any given compound sentence S

$$S = \text{comb}(\ldots,\text{not},\&,\text{or},\ \text{if}(\ )\ ,\ \text{then},\ldots)(S_1,S_2,\ldots,S_r) \tag{1}$$

where the operators "not", "&", "or", etc., all indicate the usual unary or binary linguistic connectors and comb indicates some sequential combination of these connectors with sentences $S_1,S_2,\ldots,S_r$, the latter all having simpler forms than S_i does. In turn, each S_i also has a parsed form in terms of relatively simpler sentences, etc.

(e) Modified Principle of Abstraction: Any sufficiently simple sentence, such as the components S_i in (1), has a unique corresponding semantically equivalent form

$$(x \in A) \tag{2}$$

where A represents a generalized set, property, or attribute, x is a possible vector of elements in the ordinary sense, and $\in$ is the extended set membership relation for generalized sets. (See 2.2.) As in ordinary set relations, A is considered a subset of an ordinary set X called the universe of discourse or base space and in the ordinary sense, x is in X , i.e., $x \in X$. It should be noted that this apparently reasonable principle can lead to paradoxes in formal logical systems, such as in classical naïve set theory or even in set theory based on multiple-valued logic, for a wide variety of logics (except for Lukasiewicz-$\aleph_1$ Logic - see section 2.3.3.). In the work here, these difficulties will be ignored for the time being.

Thus, (1) and (2) yield for sentences S

$$\begin{aligned} S &= \text{comb}(\ldots,\text{not},\&,\text{or},\ldots)(x_1 \in A_1,\ x_2 \in A_2,\ldots,x_r \in A_r) \\ &= (x \in A)\ , \end{aligned} \tag{3}$$

where

$$x = (x_1,x_2,\ldots,x_r) \tag{4}$$

$$A = \text{comb}'(\ldots,\complement,\times,\dagger,\Rightarrow,\ldots)(A_1,A_2,\ldots,A_r)\ , \tag{5}$$

where comb' is some other combination function and $\complement$ is the complement operator on generalized sets, corresponding to "not", $\times$ is the cartesian product operator corresponding to "&" , $\dagger$ is the cartesian sum operator corresponding to "or" , etc. (See also 2.3.8.)

(f) Principle of Semantic Evaluation: Any sentence S has a truth value $\|S\|$, a number in [0,1] which can be evaluated through the values of the semantic function $\|\cdot\|$ over component parts of S , given the particular semantic function, or equivalently, logic chosen (section 2.3).

(i) If the semantic function is truth functional, then eq. (3) is evaluated as

$$\|S\| = \text{comb}(\ldots,\phi_{nt},\phi_{\&},\phi_{or},\phi_{\Rightarrow},\ldots)(\phi_{A_1}(x_1),\ldots,\phi_{A_r}(x_r))$$
$$= \phi_A(x) \ , \qquad (6)$$

where

$$\phi_{A_i}(x_i) = \|x_i \in A_i\| \ , \ i = 1,\ldots,r \qquad (7)$$

yielding in general the membership or possibility function $\phi_{A_i} : X_i \to [0,1]$, and where

$$\phi_{nt} = \|\text{not}\| : [0,1] \to [0,1] \qquad (8)$$

is a nonincreasing function with $\phi_{nt}(0) = 1$ and $\phi_{nt}(1) = 0$, the classical truth table relations, and similarly,

$$\phi_{\&} = \|\&\| : [0,1] \times [0,1] \to [0,1] \qquad (9)$$

is a nondecreasing function usually assumed to be bounded above pointwise by the function min, continuous, symm., associative - so that it is unambiguously extendable recursively to any finite number of arguments - and has the boundary truth table values $\phi_{\&}(0,y) = 0$, $\phi_{\&}(1,y) = y$, for all y in $[0,1]$. An analagous form holds for

$$\phi_{or} = \|\text{or}\| : [0,1] \times [0,1] \to [0,1] \ , \qquad (10)$$

nondecreasing, etc., bounded below pointwise by max, and having boundary truth table values $\phi_{or}(0,y) = y$, $\phi_{or}(1,y) = 1$, for all y in $[0,1]$.

The above functions are called negations (with often the added property of being an involution), t-norms, and t-conorms, respectively. (See section 2.3.6 for various properties of these operators.)

(ii) If $\|\cdot\|$ is not truth functional, then the evaluation in eq. (6) does not hold and a more complicated evaluation procedure is valid. One example of this is Probability Logic (section 2.3.9), where, e.g.,

$$\|S_1 \text{ or } S_2\| = \|S_1\| + \|S_2\| - \|S_1 \ \& \ S_2\| \ , \qquad (11)$$

$$\|\text{not } S\| = 1 - \|S\| \ , \qquad (12)$$

but in general there is *no* fixed $\phi_{\&}$, not dependent on any particular S_1 or S_2 such that

$$\|S_1 \ \& \ S_2\| = \phi_{\&}(\|S_1\|,\|S_2\|) \ ,$$

where S_1, S_2, S are any sentences. (See [214] and section 2.3.3 for further discussions concerning truth functional vs. non-truth functional evaluations.)

In addition, for a given set of natural language connectors, more than one semantic evaluation function may be used throughout a given sentence or in certian different sentences.

SOME LANGUAGE OPERATORS AND RELATIONS

In this section, some common (but by no means exhaustive) language operators and relations are considered.

(a) Linguistic/logical connectors.

The basic connectors representing negation (not), conjunction (&), disjunction (or), implication (if( ) then ( )) , have already been introduced. The last could also be defined, as in the classical logic case, in terms of "not" and "or". More compound operators such as "iff" may also be defined. Purely linguistic connectors such as "although " and "but" can be defined entirely in terms of the basic connectors also. For example, "although" may be identified with implication and "but" with conjunction, with some possible modifications.

(b) Hedges.

Hedges are intensifiers or modifiers operating on attributes. If one lets "hedge" represent generically any hedge, such as "extremely", "very", "little", "quite", then any choice of semantic evaluation function $\|\cdot\|$ leads to the function $\phi_{hedge} = \|hedge\| : [0,1] \to [0,1]$. Some controversy exists concerning how to generate spectra of hedges from a neutral hedge, where exponentiation and translation parameter families have been compared empirically as candidates [150], [147], [167]. An alternative, and perhaps more general, approach is to consider first the simple hedges corresponding to integral iterations of conjunction. Thus, for any positive integer j , and any sentence $S = \langle x \in A\rangle$; x and A are as before:

$$\begin{aligned} S^{(j)} &= \text{"x has property A to the } j^{th} \text{ intensity"} \\ &= \text{"x has property } A^{(j)}\text{"} \\ &= (x \in A^{(j)}) \ . \end{aligned} \qquad (13)$$

In turn, assuming truth functionality here,

$$\|S^{(j)}\| = \phi_{\&}(\phi_A(x),\ldots,\phi_A(x)) \ . \qquad (14)$$

However, for the choice $\phi_{\&} = \min$, no change in semantic value for the jth intensity is reflected here! On the other hand, if $\phi_{\&}$ is an Archimedean t-norm such as prod (i.e., ordinary product with respect to its arguments) then it follows from the canonical representation (see 2.3.6) that there exists a continuous monotone decreasing function $h : [0,1] \to \mathbb{R}^+$ with $h(0) \le +\infty$ and $h(1) = 0$ such that

$$\phi_{\&}(x_1,\ldots x_r) = h^{-1}(\min(h(x_1)+\ldots+h(x_r),\ h(0)))\ . \tag{15}$$

for all x_i in $[0,1]$, $i = 1,\ldots,n$, n arbitrary positive. (Conversely, any choice of such an h generates an Archimedean $\phi_{\&}$ as in (15), where one need only take $n = 2$.) It follows immediately that (15) implies that j in eq. (14) may be replaced by *any* positive real number so that (14) becomes

$$\| S^{(j)} \| = h^{-1}(\min(j\cdot h(\phi_A(x))\ ,\ h(0)))\ . \tag{16}$$

Analagous forms may be obtained relative to ϕ_{or} , and negation as well may be employed. In (16), when $j_o > 1$, $S^{(j_o)}$ can be called an intensification, where somewhat arbitrarily, one denotes "very(S)" as $S^{(j_o)}$, "very very(S)" as "very(very(S))" = $S^{(2j_o)}$, etc. When $j_1 < 1$, $S^{(j_1)}$ similarly can be identified with "little of (S)", etc. Some tie-ins between hedges and quantifiers will be discussed in subsection (e).

(c) <u>Modal operators.</u> (See [245] for background.)

Alethic modality concerns itself with the spectrum - together with negations - of indicativeness. Thus for example: "impossible," "improbable", "possible", "is", "likely", "probable", "certain" is one such collection. Indeed, correspondences have been established between a simple numerical scale of subjective confidences between 0 and 1 and such alethic forms for a number of applications (personal observations). Using negation, the operators of necessity and entailment, among others , may be defined [245]. Deontic modality concerns, analagously, the spectrum of permission or obligation. Other modal families of operators may concern hope, desire, hate, etc.

In any case, a reasonable way to generate such families or spectra of modal operators is to choose some base or anchor within a given family, denoted as modal_o , say, and simply define

$$\text{modal} = \text{hedge}(\text{modal}_o) \tag{17}$$

where hedge is some suitably chosen modifier, as in subsection (e), depending of course on modal. Hence,

$$\begin{aligned} S &= \text{modal}(x \in A) \\ &= (x \in \text{modal}(A)) \\ &= (x \in \text{hedge}(\text{modal}_o(A)))\ , \end{aligned} \tag{18}$$

with semantic evaluation, assuming truth functionality,

$$\begin{aligned} \| S \| &= \phi_{\text{modal}}(\phi_A(x)) \\ &= \phi_{\text{hedge}}(\phi_{\text{modal}_o}(\phi_A(x)))\ . \end{aligned} \tag{19}$$

(d) Temporal Operators. (See [215] for the related area of temporal logics.)

Consider first the case for past time operators and in particular the expression

$$S = \text{"y had property A"} . \tag{20}$$

Suppose that A is a generalized subset of domain $X = Y \times \mathbb{R}^-$, where Y is some fixed population (an ordinary set) and $\mathbb{R}^-$, the negative real with zero, represents the flow of time, with the present being identified with $t = 0$. It is also supposed that $\phi_A : X \to [0,1]$ is known. Thus for any $t \in \mathbb{R}^-$, the sentence

$$S_t = \text{"y had property A at time t"} \tag{21}$$

has the semantic evaluation

$$\|S_t\| = \phi_A(y,t) , \tag{22}$$

for any $y \in Y$. Next, identify "was" as a generalized subset of $\mathbb{R}$, so that

$$\|\text{was}\| = \phi_{was} : \mathbb{R}^- \to [0,1] \tag{23}$$

is some monotonically decreasing function with $\phi_{was}(-\infty) = 1$ and $\phi_{was}(0) = 0$. At this point it should be remarked that empirical investigations have to be made to determine what the actual membership functions involved in this modeling - and all previously mentioned models - are numerically. Putting together eqs. (21) - (23) yields the reasonable interpretation for eq. (20) :

$$S = \underset{\begin{bmatrix}\text{over all}\\ t \text{ in } \mathbb{R}^-\end{bmatrix}}{\text{Or}} (S_t \;\&\; \langle t \in \text{was}\rangle) , \tag{24}$$

which under the usual truth functionality assumptions yields

$$\|S\| = \underset{\begin{bmatrix}\text{over all}\\ t \text{ in } \mathbb{R}^-\end{bmatrix}}{\phi_{or}} (\phi_{\&}(\phi_A(y,t), \phi_{was}(t))) . \tag{25}$$

Note also, that in practice, $\mathbb{R}^-$ will be replaced by a suitable discretization, unless $\phi_{or} = \max$ is chosen. (The problem of extending t-norms and t-conorms to a continuum of arguments is discussed in section 8.4. A related result may also be found in [91'''], section 5.) Similar analysis can be carried out for remote past, future, future anterior, and many other temporal relations.

(e) Conditioning and quantification.

Zadeh's contributions to this area have already been mentioned [286]. See also the discussion of other approaches in [51], pp. 138-140. The approach presented here is quite general and reduces to Zadeh's and others for particular evaluations. Let A be a generalized subset of base space X and B a generalized subset of Y . Let quant stand for any quantification involving percentages such as "some", "all", "few", many", "sometimes", "often", "most", "about 3.4", "0.456", etc. Let pop be a fixed population of individuals (an ordinary finite set) and suppose that measurement functions $f : pop \to X$ and $g : pop \to Y$ are given so that for any z in pop ,

$(z \in A)$ = "z has attribute A" = "f(z) has attribute A"

and

$(z \in B)$ = z has attribute B" = "g(z) has attribute B". (26)

Furthermore, pop can be considered to be an element - in the ordinary sense - of a super-universal set Pop , the collection of all populations of possible interest. In turn, A and B may also be considered generalized subsets of Pop , so that for any member of Pop , such as pop , one can define in a reasonable way membership of pop in A and in B as

$$(pop \in A) = \underset{\begin{bmatrix}\text{over all}\\ z \in pop\end{bmatrix}}{\mathrm{Or}} ((z \in A) \mathbin{\&} (z \in wt))$$

and

$$(pop \in B) = \underset{\begin{bmatrix}\text{over all}\\ z \in pop\end{bmatrix}}{\mathrm{Or}} (z \in B) \mathbin{\&} (z \in wt)) , \qquad (27)$$

where wt is some generalized subset of pop representing weighting of importance of each individual for either attribute A or B (assuming here for simplicity that wt is the same for both attributes). If equally likely weighting is desired, $\phi_{wt} \equiv 1/\mathrm{card}(pop)$. Thus, under the usual truth functionality assumptions, it follows that

$$\phi_A(pop) = \| (pop \in A) \| = \underset{\begin{bmatrix}\text{over all}\\ z \in pop\end{bmatrix}}{\phi_{or}} (\phi_{\&}(\phi_A(f(z)), \phi_{wt}(z))) \qquad (28)$$

with a similar expression holding for $\phi_B(pop)$, where f is replaced by g . Similarly, the evaluation of $\phi_{A\cap B}(pop)$ is given, if no interaction is assumed between A and B (see [51] for further details) as:

$$\phi_{A\cap B}(pop) = \| (pop \in A\cap B) \|$$
$$= \underset{\begin{bmatrix}\text{over all}\\ x \in pop\end{bmatrix}}{\phi_{or}} (\phi_{\&}(\phi_A(f(z)), \phi_B(g(z)), \phi_{wt}(z))) . \qquad (29)$$

The sentences

S_1 = "individuals have A , given individuals have B"

$= (pop \in A \mid pop \in B)$ (30)

and

$$S_2 = \text{"If individuals have B they also have A"}$$
$$= \text{"If (pop} \in \text{B) then (pop} \in \text{A)"}$$
$$= ((\text{pop},\text{pop}) \in (B \Rightarrow A)) = ((\text{pop} \in B) \Rightarrow (\text{pop} \in A)) \qquad (31)$$

are slight variations of each other. The first is an example of conditioning, where here conditioning is defined as in section 2.3.8. Thus the semantic evaluation $\|S_1\|$ satisfies the relation

$$\phi_{A\cap B}(\text{pop}) = \|S_1 \ \& \ (\text{pop} \in B)\|$$
$$= \phi_{\&}(\|S_1\|, \ \phi_B(\text{pop})) \ . \qquad (32)$$

The second is evaluated, as before, as

$$\|S_2\| = \phi_{\Rightarrow}(\phi_B(\text{pop}),\phi_A(\text{pop})) \ , \qquad (33)$$

under the usual assumptions. Then, a sentence such as "Most ships that have long hulls also have maneuvering problems" may be expressed in the general form

$$S_3 = \text{quant}(S_1) \quad \text{or} \quad S_4 = \text{quant}(S_2) \ , \qquad (34)$$

leading directly to the evaluations (under truth functionality assumptions)

$$\|S_3\| = \phi_{\text{quant}}(\|S_1\|)$$

and

$$\|S_4\| = \phi_{\text{quant}}(\|S_2\|) \ , \qquad (35)$$

where

$$\phi_{\text{quant}} = \|\text{quant}\| : [0,1] \to [0,1] \qquad (36)$$

is obtained beforehand. For example, ϕ_{Q_1} is conveniently modeled as a unimodal normalized function about 3/4 , while ϕ_{Q_2} is a non-decreasing function, being zero over $[0,1/2]$ and then becoming monotone increasing over $[1/2,1]$, where Q_1 = "about 3/4" and Q_2 = "most".

Zadeh's fuzzy cardinality approach to quantification is obtained by choosing $\phi_{\&}$ = prod , $\phi_{wt}(z) = 1/\text{card(pop)}$, for all z in pop , and by choosing ϕ_o = bndsum (i.e., for any $v_1,\ldots,v_n$ in $[0,1]$, $\text{bndsum}(v_1,\ldots,v_n) = \min(1,v_1+\ldots+v_n)$) :

$$\|S_3\| = \phi_{\text{quant}}\Big(\sum_{\substack{\text{all } z \\ \text{in pop}}} (\phi_A(f(z))\cdot\phi_B(g(z)))/\sum_{\substack{\text{all } z \\ \text{in pop}}} (\phi_B(g(z)))\Big) \ . \qquad (37)$$

Finally, it should be noted that ambiguity arises in the modeling of exact quantifiers. For example, "all" can be approached as above through the function $\phi_{all} = \delta_{\cdot,1}$ (Krönecker delta function for 1) or it can be modeled by the hedge corresponding to the operation $S^{(j)}$ for any sentence S , where here $j = \text{card(pop)}$, i.e.,

$$\text{"all z's have A "} = \mathop{\&}_{\begin{Bmatrix}\text{over all}\\ \text{z in pop}\end{Bmatrix}} (\phi_A(f(z))) \ . \tag{38}$$

If "softening" is really intended as in "about 5/7" for "5/7", "almost all" for "all", "a few" or "there is", etc., then the approach given in this subsection is most appropriate. Conversely, if an exact cardinality is specified as in "at least 2" and is meant literally, then combinatoric considerations have to be made:

"At least two s's in the population which have B , have also A"

$$= \mathop{\text{Or}}_{\begin{bmatrix}\text{over all } z', z''\\ \text{in pop, } z' \neq z''\end{bmatrix}} ((z' \in A) \& (z'' \in A) | (z' \in B) \& (z'' \in B)) \ . \tag{39}$$

(f) Verb and predicative relations.

Three different approaches to the modeling of such relations are presented here.

(i) The relations may be defined operationally - i.e., only directly through a membership function. For example, the binary relation "runs to" as in "John runs to the store" can be defined over the domain $X = Y \times Z$, where Y is some relevant human population and Z is a collection of possible objects of the verb "run to" .

(ii) The relations may be defined indirectly through the use of measurement functions, as introduced earlier. Thus "gross", "fat", "small", depending of course on the context, can be directly defined on the domain $\mathbb{R}^+ \times \mathbb{R}^+$ after introducing the natural measurement functions $f : \text{pop} \to \mathbb{R}^+$, $g : \text{pop} \to \mathbb{R}^+$, representing height in inches and weight in pounds, respectively.

(iii) The relations may be analyzed further, analogous to a dictionary definition of a relatively compound concept in terms of more primitive ones. In turn, these relations could be used to form constraints between the components, which would be then modeled. The usefulness of this approach remains to be established.

EXAMPLES ILLUSTRATING SOME OF THE PRINCIPLES

The above stated principles serve as guidelines in the modeling of natural language information. In practice, much ingenuity must be exercised (in a sense, this is an art, based upon intuition) in properly capturing the essence of the meaning of a given sentence. Such will continue to be the case until a universal parsing procedure is discovered (see the comments earlier in the previous subsections)!

Example 1.

Consider the compound sentence S^* in the Introduction:

Let: pop_1 = set of all days of interest , (40)

pop_2 = set of all ocean regions of interest
$= \{V, W, \ldots\}$, (41)

pop_3 = set of all submarines of interest, (42)

X = (range of possible temperatures in degrees)
× (range of possible wind velocities in m.p.h.)
× (range of %'s possible representing cloudiness, etc.)
× (range of possible no. of representing precip. inten.)
× (range of average maximal visibility in miles)
$\subseteq \mathbb{R} \times \mathbb{R}^+ \times [0,1] \times \mathbb{R}^+ \times \mathbb{R}^+$, representing weather measurements, (43)

Y = (range of wave-chop heights)×(range of max.water vel.)
$\subseteq \mathbb{R}^+ \times \mathbb{R}^+$, representing sea state conditions, (44)

with also domains $V, W, \ldots \subseteq \mathbb{R}^2$ (in latitude and longitude).

Also define (errorless) measurement functions.

$wem : pop_1 \times pop_2 \to X$, weather measurement funct. (45)

$ssm : pop_1 \times pop_2 \to Y$, sea state meas. function, (46)

$loc : pop_3 \to V \cup W \cup \cdots$, geolocation meas. function. (47)

In particular, for any $z_j \in pop_j$, j = 1,2,

$$wem(z_1, z_2) = (wem_1(z_1, z_2), \ldots, wem_5(z_1, z_2)) \ , \qquad (48)$$

so that $wem_5(z_1, z_2)$ is the av. max. visibility during day z_1 in region z_2 (z_2 = V or W) .

Next, define generalized set C by, for all $z_j \in pop_j$, j = 1,2 ,

$$\phi_C(z_1, z_2) = \phi_\&(\phi_{poor}(wem(z_1, z_2)), \ \phi_{\substack{rel\ h. \\ turb.}}(ssm(z_1, z_2))) \qquad (49)$$

noting that ϕ_{poor} must be modeled and

$$\phi_{\substack{\text{rel h.}\\ \text{turb.}}}(x) = \phi_{\text{hedge}_1}(\phi_{\text{normal}}(x)) \ , \text{ all } \ x \in [0,1] \ , \tag{50}$$

for some properly chosen hedge_1 , etc.

Define generalized set D , where for any z_2 in pop_2 ,

$$\phi_D(z_2) = \phi_{\substack{\text{or}\\ \left[\substack{\text{over all}\\ z_3 \text{ in pop}_3}\right]}} (\text{"}z_3 \text{ was in } z_2\text{"}) \ , \tag{51}$$

where

$$\text{"}z_3 \text{ was in } z_2\text{"} = \phi_{\substack{\text{or}\\ (\text{all } t \text{ in } \mathbb{R}^-)}} (\phi_\&(\phi_{z_2(A)}(\text{loc}(z_3),t),\phi_{\text{was}}(t))) \ . \tag{52}$$

Define generalized set E , for any z_3' , $z_3'' \in \text{pop}_3$,

$$\phi_E(z_3',z_3'') = \phi_{\left[\substack{\text{geo}\\ \text{match-B}}\right]} (\text{wtd dist}(\text{loc}(z_3'),\text{loc}(z_3''))) \ , \tag{53}$$

where $\phi_{\left[\substack{\text{geo}\\ \text{match-B}}\right]}$ arises from, typically, hypotheses testing of equality of means from gaussian data, and is thus exponential in form (see Chapters 8 and 9 for further details relating statistical procedures with this modeling). $\phi_{z_2(A)}(\text{loc}(z_3),t)$, typically may be obtained as the probability function evaluation corresponding to the output of a Kalman filter, for sensor system A.

Next, define generalized set F , where for all $z \in \text{pop}_1$, $z_2 \in \text{pop}_2$, z_3' , $z_3'' \in \text{pop}_3$, $\theta \in [0,1]$ - representing possible correlation levels; and for all $\phi_{K_j} : [0,1] \to [0,1]$, for $j = 1,2,3$,

$$\begin{aligned} &\phi_F(z_1,z_2,z_3',z_3'',\theta,\phi_{K_1},\phi_{K_2},\phi_{K_3}) \\ &= \phi_\Rightarrow\big(\phi_\&(\phi_C(z_1,z_2),\phi_{K_3}(\phi_{\underset{\sim}{\geq}2}(\text{wem}_5(z_1,z_2))))) \ , \\ &\quad (\phi_\Rightarrow(\phi_\&(\phi_{K_1}(\phi_D(z_2)),\phi_{K_2}(\phi_E(z_3',z_3''))),\phi_{\text{hedge}_2}(\phi_{\text{corr}}(\theta))))\big) \ . \end{aligned} \tag{54}$$

Then define generalized set G , by for all $z_3',z_3'' \in \text{pop}_3$, with $z_2 = V$, and for all ϕ_{K_j} , $j = 1,2,3,$ and all θ ,

$$\phi_G(z_3', z_3'', \theta, \phi_{K_1}, \phi_{K_2}, \phi_{K_3}) = \phi_{\&\,\left[\substack{\text{all } z_1 \\ \text{in pop}_1}\right]} (\phi_F(z_1, V, z_3', z_3'', \theta, \phi_{K_1}, \phi_{K_2}, \phi_{K_3})) \,. \qquad (55)$$

Define generalized set H by the conditioning procedure where for all $z_3', z_3'', \theta, \phi_{K_j}$, $j = 1,2,3$, with $z_2 = W$,

$$\phi_H(z_3', z_3'', \theta, \phi_{K_1}, \phi_{K_2}, \phi_{K_3}) = \phi_{most}(\text{pop}_1 \in F(\cdot\,|z_3', z_3'', \theta, \phi_{K_1}, \phi_{K_2}, \phi_{K_3}))$$
$$= \phi_{most}(\phi_{or\,\left[\substack{\text{all } z_1 \\ \text{in pop}_1}\right]} (\phi_\&(\phi_F(z_1, W, z_3', z_3'', \theta, \phi_{K_1}, \phi_{K_2}, \phi_{K_3}), \phi_{wt}(z_1)))) \,. \qquad (56)$$

Finally, define generalized set L, corresponding to inference rule $S^*(\theta|z_3', z_3'')$, indicating the functional dependencies, as, for all $z_3', z_3'' \in \text{pop}_3$, $\theta \in [0,1]$,

$$\phi_L(\theta, z_3', z_3'') = \|S^*(\theta|z_3', z_3'')\| = \phi_\&\Big(\phi_G(z_3', z_3'', \theta, \phi_{\left[\substack{\text{low} \\ \text{effect}}\right]}, \phi_{\left[\substack{\text{high} \\ \text{effect}}\right]}, \phi_{iden}),$$
$$\phi_H(z_3', z_3'', \theta, \phi_{(improve)}(\phi_{\left[\substack{\text{low -} \\ \text{effect}}\right]}(\cdot)), \phi_{\left[\substack{\text{high -} \\ \text{effect}}\right]}, \phi_{nt})\Big) \,, \qquad (57)$$

with the required models assumed obtainable for the hedges "improve", "low effect", "high effect", etc.

Example 2.

Consider the compound sentence S^{**} in the Introduction: Let all notation be as in Example 1, where required: Without loss of generality, fix time interval $[a,b]$ compatible with a fixed single day $z_1^* \in \text{pop}_1$. Let

pop_4 = set of all surface ships of interest. (57')

Assume that z_4^* is our own ship and z_4 is the target one with $z_4, z_4^* \in \text{pop}_4$. Fix also region T^* = region around the Straights of Skagerrak, and let $T^* \in \text{pop}_2$. Suppose also that

Z = (range of possible hul lengths × ⋯
× (range of possible side-insignia colors) ×⋯
× (range of possible descriptions-locations of prominent objects on ship surfact) ×⋯

$$\subseteq \mathbb{R}^{+}\times\cdots\times\{\ldots,\text{red},\text{purple},\ldots\}\times\cdots\times(\ldots,\text{sq.box},\text{front},\ldots,(\text{oval-dome},\text{rear}),\ldots\}\times\cdots \quad , \tag{58}$$

and (errorless) measurement function is given

$$\text{des} : \text{pop}_4 \to Z \text{ , a description function,} \tag{59}$$

where for any z_4 in pop_4 ,

$$\text{des}(z_4) = (\text{des}_1(z_4),\ldots,\text{des}_3(z_4),\ldots,\text{des}_{17}(z_4),\ldots) \ . \tag{60}$$

Let "foggy" be a generalized subset of the range of the average maximal visibility in miles, for simplicity. Define genralized set A , where for any times t' , t", t''' , and z_4 ,

$$\phi_A(t',t'',t''',z_4) = \phi_{\&}\Big(\phi_{z_4^*\left[\begin{smallmatrix}\text{holds contract}\\ \text{over } [t',t'']\end{smallmatrix}\right]}(z_4),\ \phi_{\approx 2}(t''-t') ,$$

$$\phi_{\text{small}}(t'''-t''),\ \phi_{\left[\begin{smallmatrix}\text{posterior}\\ \text{geo}\end{smallmatrix}\middle|\, \text{wem}_5(z_1^*,T^*)\in\text{foggy}\right]}(\text{loc}(z_4^*),t''') ,$$

$$\phi_{\text{was}}(t',t'',t''')\Big) \ , \tag{61}$$

and in turn, define generalized set B , where for all z_4 ,

$$\phi_B(z_4) = \phi_{\text{or}\left[\begin{smallmatrix}\text{over all } t',t'',t''', \text{ with}\\ a\le t'\le t''\le t'''\le b\end{smallmatrix}\right]}(\phi_A(t',t'',t''',z_4)) \ . \tag{62}$$

Next, define the generalized set C , where for all z_4 ,

$$\phi_C(z_4) = \phi_{\&}\Big(\phi_{\left[\begin{smallmatrix}\text{posterior}\\ \text{descrip}_3\end{smallmatrix}\middle|\,\begin{smallmatrix}(\text{wem}_5(z_1^*,T^*)\in\text{foggy})\&\\ (\text{maybe}(\text{observ}(\text{des}_3(z_4))=\text{purple}))\end{smallmatrix}\right]}(\text{des}_3(z_4)) ,$$

$$\phi_{\left[\begin{smallmatrix}\text{posterior}\\ \text{descrip}_{17}\end{smallmatrix}\middle|\,\begin{smallmatrix}(\text{wem}_5(z_1^*,T^*)\in\text{foggy})\&\\ (\text{maybe}(\text{observ}(\text{des}_{17}(z_4))=(\text{oval-dome},\text{rear}))\end{smallmatrix}\right]}(\text{des}_{17}(z_4)) ,$$

$$\phi_{\left[\begin{smallmatrix}\text{conditional}\\ \text{set of ship}\\ \text{names}\end{smallmatrix}\middle|\,\text{des}_3(z_4)\ ,\ \text{des}_{17}(z_4)\right]}(\text{des}_2(z_4)) \quad , \tag{63}$$

where des_2 is the naming description such as "Jones", "S.S. Jackson", etc., and where all conditional or conditional posterior generalized sets as above must be appropriately modeled. Then, finally, define the generalized set M , corresponding to information $S^{**}(z_4)$, for all z_4 in pop_4 , as

$$\phi_M(z_4) = \|S^{**}(z_4)\| = \phi_\&(\phi_B(z_4), \phi_C(z_4)) . \quad (64)$$

Modeling of inference rules such as given in Example 1 and error distribution information as given in Example 2 can be used to extend the usefulness of combination of evidence procedures. It is essentially the semantic evaluation of the disjunction over all nuisance parameter values of the conjunction of all relevant information - in the case in Chapter 9, being the conjunction of all relevant inference rules connecting matching levels for attributes with correlation levels and error tables in the form of possibility or membership functions for the attributes in posterior forms, given observed data [80].

SUMMARY AND CONCLUSIONS

An outline has been presented for the modeling and semantic evaluation of linguistic information. The implementation of this depends heavily upon the appropriate modeling of the relevant component membership functions of the generalized sets involved. (See [51], pp. 255 - 264 for approaches to the latter problem.) Much work remains to be done in the general area.

REFERENCES

[1] Abramowitz, M. and Stegun, I. A. (Eds.) (1972). *HandBook of Mathematical Functions with Formulas, Graphs and Mathematical Tables*. National Bureau of Standards, U. S. Government Printing Office, Washington, D.C.

[2] Albert, P. (1978). The algebra of fuzzy logic. *Fuzzy Set and Systems*, **1**, 203-230.

[2'] Allen, A. D. (1974). Measuring the empirical properties of sets. *IEEE Trans. Syst. Man and Cybern.*, **SMC-4, No. 1**, 66-73.

[3] Allerton, D. J.(1979). *Essentials of Grammatical Theory* Routledge and Kegan Paul, London.

[4] Alsina, C., Trillas, E. and Valverde, L. (1980). On non-distributive logical connectives for fuzzy set theory. *BUSEFAL* , **3**, 18-29.

[4'] American Math. Soc., (Ed.) (1971). *Axiomatic Set Theory*. Providence, R. I.

[4"] Anderson, J. R. (Ed.) (1981). *Cognitive Skills and Their Acquisition*. L. Erlbaum Assoc., Hillsdale, N. J.

[5] Arbib, M. A. and Manes, E. G. (1975). A category-theoretic approach to systems in a fuzzy world. *Synthese*, **30**, 381-406.

[6] Arbib, M. A. (1977). Review of three fuzzy sets papers. *Bull. Am. Math. Soc*, **83, No. 5**, 946-951.

[7] Artstein, Z. and Vitale, R. A.(1975). A strong law of large numbers for random compact sets. *Ann. Prob.*, **3, No. 5**, 879-882.

[8] Au, T., Shane, R. M. and Hoel, L. A. (1972). *Fundamentals of Systems Engineering: Probabilistic Models*. Addison-Wesley, Reading, Mass.

[9] Aumann, R. J. and Shapley, L. S. (1974). *Values of Non-Atomic Games*. Princeton Univ. Press.

[9'] Badard, R. (1984). Fixed point theorems for fuzzy numbers. *Fuzzy Sets and Systems*, **13**, 291-302.

[10] Baldwin, J. F. and Pilsworth, B. W. (1980). Axiomatic approach to implication for approximate reasoning with fuzzy logic. *Fuzzy Sets and Systems*, **3**, 193-219.

[11] Banon, G. (1981). Distinction between several subsets of fuzzy measures. *Fuzzy Sets and Systems*, **5**, 291-305.

[12] Bar-Shalom, Y. (1978). Tracking methods in a multitarget environment. *IEEE Trans. Aut. Control*, **AC-23**, 618-626.

[12'] Barr, A. and Feigenbaum, E. A. (Eds.) (1981). *Handbook of Artificial Intelligence*. Heuris Tech Press, Stanford, Calif.

[13] Baum, L. E., Katz, M. and Read, R. R. (1962). Exponential convergence rates for the law of large numbers. *Trans. Am. Math. Soc.*, **102, No. 2**, 187-199.

[13'] Bellman, R. E. (1978). *Artificial Intelligence*. Boyd and Fraser, Boston.

[14] Bellman, R. E. and Giertz, M. (1973). On the analytic formalism of fuzzy sets. *Inf. Sci.*, **5**, 149-157.

[15] Bellman, R. E. and Zadeh, L. A. (1977). Local and fuzzy logics. In *Modern Uses of Multi-valued Logic* (J. M. Dunn and G. Epstein, Eds.), D. Reidel, Dordrecht, Holland, 103-165.

[16] Bertsekas, D. P. and Rhodes, I. B. (1971). Recursive state estimation for a set-membership description of uncertainty. *IEEE Trans. Aut. Control*, **AC-16, No. 2**, 117-128.

[17] Birkhoff, G. (1961). *Lattice Theory*. Am. Math. Soc., Newport, R.I.

[18] Birnbaum, A. (1954). Combining independent tests of significance. *J. Am. Statist. Assoc.*, **49**, 559-574.

[19] Black, M. (1937). Vagueness. *Phil. of Sci.*, **4**, 427-455.

[20] Bloomfield, L. (1935). *Language*. Allen and Unwin, London.

[21] Bock, R. D. (1975). *Multivariate Statistical Methods in Behavioral Research*. McGraw-Hill, N.Y.

[22] Borel, E. (1950). *Probabilite et Certitude*. Presse Univ. de France, Paris.

[23] Bowman, C. L. (1981). An architecture for fusion of multi-sensor ocean surveillance data. *Proc. 20th Conf. Decis. and Control*, 1419-1420.

[24] Buchanan, B. G. and Duda, R. O. (1983). Principles of rule-based expert systems. In *Advances in Computers*, **22**, (M. Yovits, Ed.). Academic Press, N.Y.

[25] Brown, R. V. and Lindley, D. V. (1982). Improving judgment by reconciling incoherence. *The behavioral and brain Sciences*, **4**, 317-370.

[26] Carnap, R. (1958). *Introduction to Symbolic Logic and its Applications*. Dover, N. Y.

[27] Carnap, R. (1959). *The Logical Syntax of Language*. Littlefield, Adam and Co., Paterson, New Jersey.

[28] Carnap, R. (1960). *Meaning and Necessity, a Study in Semantic and Modal Logic*. Phoenix Books, Univ. of Chicago.

[29] Carrega, J. C. (1983). The categories Set H and Fuz H . *Fuzzy Sets and Systems*, **9**, 327-332.

[30] Cerruti, U. (1981). Categories of L-fuzzy relations on L-fuzzy sets. In *Applied Syst. and Cybrn*, *VI*, (G. E. Lasker, Ed.), Pergamon Press, N. Y., 2912-2920.

[31] Chang, C. C. (1965). Infinite valued logic as a basis for set theory. In *Proc. 1964 Inter. Congress on Logic, Methodology and Philosophy of Science* (Y. Bar-Hillel, Ed.), North-Holland, N. Y., 93-100.

[32] Chapin, E. W. (1975). Set-valued set theory, part I. *Notre Dame J. Form. Logic*, **15**, **No. 4**, 619-634.

[33] Chapin, E. W. (1976). Set-valued set theory,part II. *Notre Dame J. Form. Logic*, **16**, **No. 2**, 255-267.

[34] Chomsky, N. (1957). *Syntactic Structures*. Mouton and Co., The Hague, Netherlands.

[35] Chomsky, N. (1965). *Aspects of the Theory of Syntax*. MIT Press, Cambridge, Mass.

[36] Choquet, G. (1954). Theory of capacities. *Ann. Inst. Fourier*, Univ. Grenoble, **V**, 131-296.

[37] Cohen, L. J. (1977). *The Probable and the Provable*. Clarendon Press, Oxford.

[38] Cohen, L. J. (1981). Can human irrationality be experimentally demonstrated? The *Behavioral and Brain Sciences*, **4**, 317-370.

[39] Cohen, P. J. (1966). *Set Theory and the Continuum Hypothesis*. W. H. Benjamin, Reading, Mass.

[40] Cohen, P. J. and Hersh, R. (1967). Non-Cantorian set theory. *Sci. Am.*, **217, No. 6**, Dec. 67, 104-116.

[40'] Cohen, B. and Murphy, G. L. (1984). Models of concepts. *Cognitive Science*, **8**, 27-58.

[41] Coste, M. (1974). Logique d'ordre superieur dans les topos elementaires. Seminaire de Théorie des Categories (under J. Bénabou), Univ. Paris.

[42] Courrège, P. (1966). *Théorie de la Mesure*. Centre de Documentation Univ., Paris.

[43] Cressie, N. (1979). A central limit theorem for random sets. *Z. Wahr*, **49**, 37-47.

[44] Curry, H. B. (1963). *Foundations of Mathematical Logic*. McGraw-Hill N.Y.

[44'] Czogala, E. and Drewniak, J. (1984). Associative monotone operations in fuzzy set theory. *Fuzzy sets and systems*, **12**, 249-269.

[44"] Czogala, E. and Zimmermann, H. J. (1984). The aggregation operations for decision making in probabilistic fuzzy environment. *Fuzzy sets and Systems*, **13**, 223-239.

[44'''] Czogala, E. (1984). An introduction to probabilistic L-valued logic. *Fuzzy Sets and Systems*, **13**, 179-185.

[44^{iv}] Davis, R. and Lenat, D. B. (1982). *Knowlege-Based Systems in Artificial Intelligence*. McGraw-Hill, N.Y.

[45] Debreu, G.(1967). Integration of correspondences. *Proc.5th Berkeley Symp. Math. Statist. and Prob.*, **2**, Univ. of Calif., 351-372.

[45'] DeGlas, M. (1984). Representation of Łukasiewicz many-valued algebras. The atomic case. *Fuzzy Sets and Systems*, **14**, 175-183.

[46] Demspter, A. P. (1967). Upper and lower probabilities induced by a multivalued mapping. *Ann. Math. Statist*, **38**, 325-339.

[46'] De Finetti, B. (1974). *Theory of Probability, Vol. I, II*, J. Wiley, N. Y.

[46"] Devlin, K. J. (1977). The axiom of constructability. *Lecture Notes in Math*, **No. 617**, Springer-Verlag, N. Y.

[46'''] Dillard, R. A. (1983). Representation of Tactical Knowledge Shared by Expert Systems. NOSC Tech. Doc. 632 (1 October 1983), Naval Ocean Systems Center, San Diego, Cal.

[46^{iv}] Dillard, R. A. (1981). Integration of Narrative Processing Data Fusion and Data Base Updating Techniques in an Automated System. NOSC Tech. Report 480 (29 Oct. 1981) Naval Ocean System Center, San Diego, Cal.

[47] Dingwall, W. O. (Ed., 1978). *A Survey of Linguistic Science*. Greylock Publishers, Stamford, Conn.

[48] Dishkant, H. (1981). About membership function estimation. *Fuzzy Sets and Systems*, **5**, 141-147.

[49] Dockery, J. T. (1982). Fuzzy design of military information systems. *Inter. J. Man-Machine Studies*, **16**, 1-38.

[50] Dombi, J. (1982). A general class of fuzzy operators, the Demorgan class of fuzzy operators and fuzziness measures induced by fuzzy operators. *Fuzzy Sets and Systems*, **8**, 149-163.

[51] Dubois, D. and Prade, H. (1980). *Fuzzy Sets and Systems.* Academic Press, N. Y.

[52] Dubois, D. and Prade, H. (1982). What does convergence mean for fuzzy numbers? *IFAC, New Delhi*, India.

[52'] Dyckhoff, H. and Pedrycz, W. (1984). Generalized means as model of compensative connectives. *Fuzzy Sets and Systems*, **14**, 143-154.

[53] Dynkin, E. B.and Mandelbaum, A. (1983). Symmetric statistics, Poisson point process and multiple Wiener integrals. *Ann. Statist*, **11**, 739-745.

[53'] Eco, U. (1976). *A Theory of Semiotics.* Indiana Univ. Press.

[54] Enderton, H. B. (1972). *A Mathematical Introduction to Logic.* Academic Press, N. Y.

[55] Esteva, F., Trillas, E. and Domingo, X. (1981). Weak and strong negation functions for fuzzy set theory. *Proc. 11 Inter. Symp. Multi. Logic*, 23-26.

[56] Eytan, M. (1981). Fuzzy sets: a topos-logical point of view. *Fuzzy sets and systems*, **5**, 47-67.

[57] Eytan, M. (1982). Fuzzy sets: a topos-logical point of view, II. Unpublished manuscript.

[57'] Felsen, J. (1976). *Decision Making Under Uncertainty: An Artificial Intelligence Approach.* CDS Publ. Co., N. Y.

[58] Fine, T. L. (1973). *Theories of Probability: An Examination of Foundations.* Academic Press, N. Y.

[59] Fourmann, M. P. and Scott, D. S. (1979). Sheaves and logic. *Lecture Notes in Math*, **No. 753**: Applications of Sheaves, Proc. Durham, Springer-Verlag, N. Y., 302-401.

[60] Fox, J. (1981). Towards a reconciliation of fuzzy logic and standard logic. *Inter. J. Man-Machine Studies*, **15**, 213-220.

[61] Frank, M. J. (1979). On the simultaneous associativity of F(x,y) and x + y-F(x,y) . *Aeq. Math.*, **19**, 194-226.

[62] Fraenkel, A. A. and Bar-Hillel, Y. (1958). *Foundations of Set Theory.* North-Holland, N. Y.

[63] Franksen, O. I. (1979). On fuzzy sets,subjective measurements and utility. *Inter. J. Man-Machine Studies*, **11**, 521-545.

[64] Freeling, A. N. (1981). Alternate theories of belief and the implications for incoherence,reconciliation and sensitivity analysis. Decision Science Consortium, Inc. Technical Report No. 81-4 (prepared for ONR).

[65] Fukami, S., Mizumoto, M. and Tanaka, K. (1980). Some considerations on fuzzy conditional inference. *Fuzzy Sets and Systems*, **4**, 243-273.

[66] Gaines, B. R. (1975), Stochastic and fuzzy logic. *Elect. Letters*, **11**, **No. 9**, 188-189.

[67] Gaines, B. R. (1976). Foundations of fuzzy reasoning. *Inter. J. Man-Machine Studies*, **8**, 623-668.

[68] Gaines, B. R. (1978). Fuzzy and probability uncertainty logics. *Inf. and Control*, **38**, 154-169.

[68'] Gardner, M. (1981). Two books on talking apes. In *Science: Good, Bad and Bogus*. Prometheus books, Buffalo, N. Y., 391-408.

[69] Gentilhomme, Y. (1968). Les ensembles flous en linguistique. *Cahiers de Ling. Théor. et Appl.*, **5**, 47-65.

[70] Giles, R. (1976). Łukasiewicz logic and fuzzy theory. *Inter. J. Man-Machine Studies*, **8**, 313-327.

[71] Giles, R. (1979). A formal system for fuzzy reasoning. *Fuzzy Sets and Systems*, **2**, 233-257.

[72] Giles, R. (1981). Foundations for a Theory of Possibility. Queen's Math. Reprint No. 1981-20, Queen's Univ., Kingston, Ontario, Canada..

[73] Giles, R. (1981). Semantics for Fuzzy Reasoning. Queen's Math. Reprint No. 1981-14, Queen's Univ.Kingston, Ontario, Canada.

[74] Gilmore, P. C. (1960). An alternative to set theory. *Am. Math. Monthly*, **67**, 621-632.

[75] Godal, R. C. and Goodman, T. J.(1980). Fuzzy sets and Borel. *IEEE Trans. Syst. Man and Cybern.*, **SMC-10**, 637.

[76] Good, I. J. (1983). *Good Thinking. The Foundations of Probability and its Applications*. Univ. of Minnesota Press, Minneapolis.

[77] Goodman, I. R. (1980). Identification of fuzzy sets with class of canonically induced random sets. *Proc. 19 IEEE Conf. Decis. and Control*, 352-357.

[78] Goodman, I. R. (1981). Fuzzy sets as random level sets: implications and extensions of basic results. In *Applied Syst. and Cybern., Vol. VI*, (G. Lasker, Ed.), Pergamon Press, N.Y., 2757-2766.

[79] Goodman, I. R. (1982) Some asymptotic properties of fuzzy set systems. *Proc.* 2nd *World Conf. Math. Ser. Man.* Univ. Pol. de Las Palmas, Can. Is., 312-317.

[80] Goodman, I. R. (1982). An approach to the data association problem through possibility theory. *Proc. 5th ONR/MIT C^3 Workshop*, 209-215

[81] Goodman, I. R. (1982). Characterizations of n-ary fuzzy set operations which induce homomorphic random set operations. *In Fuzzy Information and Decision Processes*, (M. M. Gupta and E. Sanchez, Eds.), North-Holland, N. Y., 203-212.

[82] Goodman, I. R. (1981). Application of a combined probabilistic and fuzzy set technique to the attribute problem in ocean surveillance. *Proc. 20th IEEE Conf. Decis. and Control*, 1409-1412.

[83] Goodman, I. R. (1982). PACT: Possibilistic approach to correlation and tracking. *Proc. 16th Asilomar Conf. Circuits, Syst., Comp. (IEEE)*, Nov. 82, 359-363.

[84] Goodman, I. R. (1980). A general model for the multiple target correlation and tracking problem. *Proc. 18th IEEE Conf. Decis. and Control*, 383-388.

[85] Goodman, I. R. and Boyer, R. P. (1974). Normal mixture approximation to prior densities in the linear regression model. *Proc. 5th Symp. Nonlinear Est.*, San Diego, 74-77.

[86] Goodman, I. R.(1983). A unified approach to modeling and combining of evidence through random set theory. *Proc. 6th MIT/ONR Workshop on C^3 Systems*, 42-47.

[87] Goodman, I. R., Wiener, H. L. and Willman, W. W.(1980). Naval Ocean Surveillance Correlation Handbook, 1979. NRL Report 8402, Sept. 17, 1980. Naval Res. Lab, Wash., D. C.

[88] Goodman, I. R. (1985). Identification of fuzzy sets with random sets. To appear in *Encyclopedia of Systems and Control* (M. Singh, Ed.), Pergamon Press, N. Y.

[89] Goodman, I. R.(1984). Some new results concerning random sets and fuzzy sets. *Inf. Sci.*, **34**, 93-113.

[90] Goodman, I. R. (1982). Fuzzy sets as equivalence classes of random sets. In *Recent Developments in Fuzzy Sets and Possibility Theory*. (R. Yager, Ed.), Pergamon Press, N. Y., 327-432.

[91] Goodman, I. R. (1982). Some fuzzy set operations which induce homomorphic random set operations. *Proc. 26th Conf. Gen., Syst. Res.*, 417-426.

[91'] Goodman, I. R. (1985). A critique of Lindley's paper on inadmissibility of uncertainty measures. (Submitted)

[91"] Goodman, I. R. (1984). Modeling natural language information for use in the combination of evidence problem. *Proc. 7th MIT/ONR Workshop on C^3 Systems*, 173-178.

[91'''] Goodman, I. R. (1984). An approach to the target data association problem using subjective and statistical information. *Proc. 1984 Am. Contr. Conf.*, 587-592.

[92] Goodman, I. R. and Nguyen, H. T. (1982). Uncertainty modeling and possibilistic approach to parameter estimation. Technical report NOSC, San Diego, Cal.

[93] Goodman, G. S. (1973-74). From multiple balayage to fuzzy sets. *Univ. Stud. Inst. Mate.*, Univ. of Firenze, **No. 40**.

[94] Gottwald, S. (1980). Fuzzy propositional logics. *Fuzzy Sets and Systems*, **3**, 181-192.

[95] Gottwald, S. (1978). Set theory for fuzzy sets of higher level. *Fuzzy Sets and Systems*, **2**, 125-151.

[96] Goguen, J. A. (1974). Concept representation in natural and artificial languages: axioms, extensions and applications for fuzzy sets. *Inter. J. Man-Machine Studies*, **6**, 531-561.

[97] Goguen, J. A. (1969). The logic of inexact concepts. *Synthese*, **19**, 325-373.

[97'] Grayson, R. J. (1979). Heyting-valued models for intuitionistic set theory. In *Lecture Notes in Math.*, **No. 753**: Applications of Sheaves, Springer-Verlag, N. Y. 402-414.

[98] Grenander, U. (1978). On Mathematical Semantics: A Pattern Theoretic View. Report in Pattern Analysis, No. 71, Brown Univ., R. I.

[98'] Gregg, L. W. (Ed.) (1974). *Knowledge and Cognition*. Wiley, N. Y.

[99] Guiasu, S. (1977). *Information Theory with Applications*. McGraw-Hill, N. Y.

[100] Haack, S. (1974). *Deviant Logic*. Cambridge Univ. Press.

[101] Haack, S. (1978). *Philosophy of Logics*. Cambridge Univ. Press.

[102] Haack, S. (1979). Do we need fuzzy logic? *Inter. J. Man-Machine Studies*, **11**, 437-445.

[102'] Hailperin, T. (1984). Probability logic. *Notre Dame J. Form. Logic*, **25**, **No. 3**, 198-212.

[103] Hajek, J. (1981). *Sampling From a Finite Population*. Marcel Dekker, N. Y.

[104] Halmos, P. (1960). *Naïve Set Theory*. Van Nostrand, N. Y.

[104'] Halmos, P. (1956). *Measure Theory*. Van Nostrand, N. Y.

[105] Hanrahan, D. J. (1981). Probability and Possibility: Random Variables and Fuzzy Variables. NRL technical memo 5707-281, Naval Res. Lab., Wash. D. C.

[106] Hanrahan, D. J. (1981). A Connection Between Fuzzy sets and Personal Probability. NRL technical memo 5707-341, Naval Res. Lab., Wash. D. C.

[107] Harris, Z. (1968). *Mathematical Structure of Language*. Interscience, N. Y.

[107'] Hayes-Roth, F., Waterman, D. A., and Lenat, D. B., (1983). *Building Expert Systems*. Addison-Wesley Co., Reading, Mass.

[108] Herdan, G. (1966). *The Advanced Theory of Language as Choice and Chance*. Springer-Verlag, N. Y.

[109] Hersh, H. M. and Caramazza, A. (1976). A fuzzy set approach to modifiers and vagueness in natural language. *J. Exp. Psych., Gen.*, **105, No. 3**, 254-276.

[110] Heyting, A. (1971). *Intuitionism: An Introduction*. (3rd ed.), Studies in Logical Foundations of Mathematics, North-Holland, Amsterdam.

[111] Hirota, K. (1981). Concepts of probabilistic sets. *Fuzzy Sets and Systems*, **5**, 31-46.

[112] Hisdal, E. (1981). The "If then else " statement and interval-valued fuzzy sets of higher type. *Inter. J. Man-Machine Studies*, **4**, 385-455.

[113] Hisdal, E. (1982). Possibilities and probabilities. *Proc. 2nd World Conf. Math. Serv. Man*. Las Palmas, Cana. Is., 341-345.

[114] Hisdal, E. (1980). Generalized fuzzy set systems and particularization. *Fuzzy Sets and Systems*, **4**, 275-291.

[115] Hisdal, E. (1978). Conditional possibilities, independence and noninteraction. *Fuzzy Sets and Systems*, **1**, 283-297.

[116] Höhle, U. (1981). A mathematical theory of uncertainty: fuzzy experiments and their realizations. In *Applied Syst. and Cybern., Vol. VI*, (G. Lasker, Ed.), Pergamon Press, N. Y., 2728-2733. Later expanded in *Recent Developments in Fuzzy Set and Possibility Theory* (R. R. Yager, Ed.), Pergamon Press, 344-355.

[117] Höhle, U. (1981). Representation theorems for L-fuzzy quantities. *Fuzzy sets and systems*, **5**, 83-107.

[118] Hooper, P. M. (1982). Sufficiency and invariance in confidence set estimation. *Ann. Statist*, **10, No. 2**, 549-555.

[119] Hooper, P. M. (1982). Invariant confidence sets with smallest expected measure. *Ann. Statist*, **10, No. 4**, 1283-1294.

[120] Ishizuka, M., Fu, K. S. and Yao, J. T. (1981). A Theoretical Treatment of Certainty Factor in Production Systems. School of Elec Eng, Purdue Univ., No. CE-STR-81-6.

[121] Ishizuka, M., Fu, K. S. and Yao, J. T. (1981). Inference Procedure with Uncertainty for Problem Reduction Method. School of Elec. Eng., Purdue Univ., No TR-EE-81-33.

[122] Jain, R. (1978). Comments on fuzzy set theory versus Bayesian statistics. *IEEE Trans. Sys. Man and Cybern*, **SMC-8, No. 4**, 332-333.

[123] Jaynes, E. T. (1957). Information theory and statistical mechanics. *Phys. Rev.*, **106**, 620-630; **108**, 171-182.

[124] Jaynes, E. T. (1968). Prior probabilities. *IEEE Trans. Sys. Sci. and Cybern.*, **SSC-4, No. 3**, 227-241.

[124'] Jardine, N. and Sibson, R. (1971). *Mathematical Taxonomy*. J. Wiley, N. Y.

[125] Joshi, V. M. (1969). Admissibility of the usual confidence sets for the mean of a univariate or bivariate normal population. *Ann. Math. Statist*, **40, No. 3**, 1042-1067.

[126] Johnson, R. W. and Shore, J. E. (1979). Solving Fuzzy Set Problems Using Probability Theory. NRL technical Memo 7503-211, Naval Res. Lab., Wash., D. C.

[127] Johnstone, P. T. (1977). *Topos Theory*. Academic Press, N. Y.

[128] Kahneman, D. and Tversky, A. (1972). Subjective probability: a judgment of representativeness. *Cognitive Psych.*, **3**, 430-454.

[129] Kandel, A. (1979). Reply to Tribus' comments. *Proc. IEEE*, 67, **No. 8**, 1168-1169.

[130] Kampé de Fériet, J. (1963). Théorie de l'information, principle du maximum de l'entropie et ses applications à la statistique et à la mecanique. *Publ. Lab. Calcul.*, Univ. Lille, France.

[131] Kampé de Fériet, J. (1982). Interpretation of membership functions of fuzzy sets in terms of plausibility and belief. In *Fuzzy Information and Decision Processes* (M. M.Gupta and E. Sanchez, Eds.), North-Holland, 93-98.

[132] Kampé de Fériet, J. and Forte, B. (1967). Information et probabilité. *C. R. Acad. Sci.* Paris, **A-265**, 110-114.

[133] Kampé de Fériet, J. and Nguyen, H. T. (1972). Temps d'entrée d'un processus stochastique et mesure de l'information. *C. R. Acad. Sci.* Paris, **A-275**, 721-725.

[134] Kampé de Fériet, J. and Nguyen, H. T. (1973). Mesure de l'information, temps d'entrée et dimension de Hausdorff. *C. R. Acad. Sci.* Paris, **A-276**, 807-811.

[135] Kampé de Fériet, J. (1969). Mesure de l'information fournie par un évènement. *Coll. Inter. C. N. R. S.*, **No. 186**, Paris, 191-221.

[136] Kampé de Fériet, J., Forte, B. and Benvenuti, P. (1969). Forme générale de l'opération de composition continue d'une information. *C. R. Acad. Sci* Paris, **A-269**, 529-534.

[136'] Kempton, W. (1984). Interview methods for eliciting fuzzy categories. *Fuzzy Sets and Systems*, **14**, 43-64.

[137] Kendall, D. G. (1974). Foundations of a theory of random sets. In *Stochastic Geometry* (E. F. Harding and D. G. Kendall, Eds.), J. Wiley, N. Y., 322-376.

[138] Kendall, D. G. and Moran, P. A. (1963). *Geometrical Probability*. Griffin, London.

[138'] Klaua, D. (1966). Grundbegriffe einen mehrwertigen Mengenlehre. *Monat. Deutsche Akad. Wiss. Berlin*, **Vol. 8, No. 11**, 782-802.

[139] Klaua, D. (1965). Über einem Ansatz zer mehrwertigen Mengenlehre. *Monatsber Deutcsh Akad. Wiss. Berlin*, **7, part 12**, 859-867.

[139'] Klement, E. P. (1980). Characterizations of finite fuzzy measures using Markoff-kernels. *J. Math. Anal. and Appl.*, **75, No. 2**, 330-339.

[140] Klement, E. P. (1981). Operations on fuzzy sets and fuzzy numbers related to triangular norms. *Proc. 11th Inter. Symp. Multi-Valued Logic*, 218-225.

[141] Klement, E. P., Schwyhla, W. and Lowen, R. (1981). Fuzzy probability measures. *Fuzzy Sets and Systems*, **5**, 21-30.

[142] Klement, E. P. and Schwyhla, W. (1982). Correspondence between fuzzy measures and classical measures. *Fuzzy Sets and Systems* , **7**, 57-70.

[143] Kloeden, P. E. (1980). Compact supported endographs and fuzzy sets. *Fuzzy Sets and Systems*, **4**, 193-201.

[144] Köchen, M. and Badre, A. N. (1974). On the precision of adjectives which denote fuzzy sets. *J. of Cybern*, **4, No. 1**, 49-59.

[145] Korner, S. (1957). Reference, vagueness and necessity. *Philos. Rev.*, **66**, 363-376.

[145'] Kullback, S. (1959). *Information Theory and Statistics*. J. Wiley, N. Y.

[146] Kruse, R. (1982). A note on λ-additive fuzzy measures. *Fuzzy Sets and Systems*, **8**, 219-222.

[146'] Kurtzberg, J. M. (1962). On approximation methods for the assignment problem. *J. Assoc. Computing Machinery*, **9**, 419-439.

[147] Kuzmin, V. B. (1981). A parametric approach to description of linguistic values of variables and hedges. *Fuzzy Sets and Systems*, **6**, 27-41.

[148] Kwakernaack, H. (1978). Fuzzy random variables I. *Inf. Sci.*, **15**, 1-29.

[149] Lake, J. (1976). Sets, fuzzy sets, multisets and functions. *J. London Math. Soc.*, **2**, **No. 12**, 323-326.

[150] Lakoff, G. (1973). Hedges: a study in meaning criteria and the logic of fuzzy concepts. *J. Philos. Logic*, **4**, **No. 1**, 458-508.

[150'] Lakoff, G. (1970). Linguistics and natural logic. *Synthese*, **22**, 151-271.

[151] Langrand, C. and Nguyen, H. T. (1972). Sur les mesures intérieures de l'information et les σ-précapacités. *C. R. Acad. Sci* Paris, **A-275**, 927-930.

[152] Lawvere, F. W. (1975). Continuously variable sets: algebraic geometry-geometric logic. *Logic Coll. '73* (H. Rose and J. C. Shepherdson, Eds.), North-Holland, N. Y., 135-156.

[153] Leech, G. (1974). *Semantics*. Penguin books, London.

[154] Lehmann, E. L. (1959). *Testing Statistical Hypotheses* . J. Wiley, N. Y.

[155] Lenneberg, E. H. (1967). *Biological Foundations of Language*. J.Wiley, N. Y.

[156] Lightstone, A. M. (1978). *Mathematical Logic, an Introduction to Model Theory* (Ed. by M. B. Enderton), Plenum Press, N. Y.

[157] Lindley, D. V., Tversky, A. and Brown, R. V. (1979). On the reconciliation of probability assesments. *J. Royal Statist. Soc.* Ser. A, **142, No. 2**, 146-180.

[158] Lindley, D. V. (1982). Scoring rules and the inevitability of probability. *Inter. Statist. Rev.*, **50,** 1-26.

[158'] Lindley, D. V. (1965). *Introduction to Probability and Statistics from a Bayesian Viewpoint. Vol. I, II*. Cambridge Univ. Press.

[159] Ling, C. H. (1965). Representation of associative functions. *Debrecen, Hung., Tud. Egy., Matem*, **12**, 189-212.

[160] Lowen, R. (1978). On fuzzy complements. *Inf. Sci*, **14**, 107-113.

[161] Lukacs, E. (1970). *Characteristic Functions* (2nd ed.). Griffin, London.

[162] Lyons, J. (1971). *Introduction to Theoretical Linguistics*. Cambridge Univ. Press.

[163] Lyons, J. (1979). *Semantics, Vol. I, II*. Cambridge Univ. Press.

[164] Lyons, J. (1981). *Language and Linguistics*. Cambridge Univ. Press.

[165] MacLane, S. (1971). *Categories for the Working Mathematician*. Springer-Verlag, N. Y.

[166] MacLane, S. (1975). Sets, topoi and internal logic in categories. In *Logic Coll. '73* (M. Rose and J. C. Shepherdson, Eds.), North-Holland, N. Y., 119-134.

[167] MacVicar-Whelan, P. J. (1978). Fuzzy sets,the concept of height and the hedge"very". *IEEE Trans. Syst. Man and Cybern*, **SMC-8, No 6**, 507-511.

[167'] Mandelbrot, B. B. (1983). *The Fractal Geometry of Nature*. Freedman and Co., San Francisco.

[168] Manes, E. G. (1981). Review of "Fuzzy switching and automata: theory and applications". *SIAM Rev.*, **23, No. 2**, 271-273.

[169] Manes, E. G. (1982). A class of fuzzy theories. *J. Math. Anal. and Appl.*, **85**, 409-451.

[170] Manes, E. G. (1982). Review of "Fuzzy sets and systems". *Bull. Am. Math. Soc.*, **7, No. 3**, 603-612.

[171] Matheron, G. (1975). *Random Sets and Integral Geometry* . J. Wiley, N. Y.

[172] Maydole, R. E. (1973). *Many-valued Logic as a Basis for Set Theory*. Ph.D. Dissertation, Boston Univ., Univ. microfilms No. 73-14, 162, Ann Harbor, Mich.

[172'] Maydole, R. E. (1975). Paradoxes and many-valued set theory. *J. Philo. Logic*, **4**, 269-291.

[173] McCawley, J. D. (1982). *Thirty Million Theories of Grammar*. Univ. of Chicago Press.

[173'] McDermott, D. (1982). A temporal logic for reasoning about processes and plans. *Cognitive Science*, **6**, 101-155.

[174] McShane, E. J. (1944). *Integration*. Princeton Univ. Press.

[175] Meyer, P. A. (1966). *Probabilité et potentiel*. Hermann, Paris.

[176] Michael, E. (1951). Topologies on spaces of subsets. *Trans. Am. Math. Soc.*, **71**, 152-182.

[177] Michalski, R. S. and Chilausky, R. L. (1980). Learning by being told and learning from examples. *Inter. J. Policy Anal. and Inf. Syst.*, **4, No. 2**, 125-161.

[178] Mirsky, L. (1963). Results and problems in the theory of doubly stochastic matices. *Z. Wahr*, **1**, 319-334.

[179] Mitchell, W. (1972). Boolean topoi and the theory of sets. *J. Pure and Applied Algebra*, **2**, 261-274.

[179'] Morrill, J. E. (1982). Set theory and the indicator function. *Am. Math. Monthly*, **89**, **No. 9**, 694-695

[179"] Miyakoshi M. and Shimbo, M. (1984). A strong law of large numbers for fuzzy random variables. *Fuzzy Sets and Systems*, **12**, 133-142.

[180] Nalimov, V. V. (1979). The probability distribution function as a method of defining fuzzy sets: meta-theoretic sketches (Discussion of the work of L. A. Zadeh.), *Soviet Auto. Control* (Trans. into English from USSR J. Automatika), **12, No 6**, 67-73.

[181] Nanlun, Z. (1982). A preliminary study of the theoretical basis of the fuzzy set. In *Advances in Fuzzy Set Theory and Application* (P. P. Wang, Ed.), Plenum Press, N. Y.

[181'] Natanson, I. P. (1961). *Theory of Functions of a Real Variable I*. Ungar Co., N. Y.

[182] Natvig, B. (1983). Possibility versus probability. *Fuzzy Sets and System*, **10**, 31-36.

[183] Nau, D. S. (1983). Expert computer systems. *IEEE Computer*, 63-85.

[184] Negoita, C. V. and Ralescu, D. A. (1975). Representation theorems for fuzzy concepts. *Kybernetes*, U.K., **4**, 169-174.

[184'] Neveu, J. (1965). *Mathematical Foundations of the Calculus of Probability*. Holden-Day, San Francisco.

[185] Nguyen, H. T. (1974). Sur les mesures d'information de type Inf. *Lecture Notes in Math* (Théories de l'information), **No. 398**, Springer-Verlag, 62-75.

[186] Nguyen, H. T. (1977). On fuzziness and linguistic probabilities. *J. Math. Anal. and Appl.*, **61**, **No. 3**, 658-671.

[187] Nguyen, H. T. (1978). On random sets and belief functions. *J. Math. Anal. and Appl.*, **65**, 531-542.

[188] Nguyen, H. T. (1978). On conditional possibility distributions. *Fuzzy Sets and Systems*, **1**, 299-309.

[189] Nguyen, H. T. (1979). Toward a calculus of the mathematical notion of possibility. In *Advances in Fuzzy Set Theory and Applications* (M. M. Gupta, R. K. Ragade and R. R. Yager, Eds.), North-Holland, N. Y.,235-246.

[190] Nguyen, H. T. (1979). Some mathematical tools for linguistic probabilities. *Fuzzy Sets and Systems*, **2**, 53-65.

[191] Nguyen, H. T. (1982). Possibility measures and related topics. In *Fuzzy Information and Decision Processes* (M. M. Gupta and E. Sanchez, Eds.), North-Holland, N. Y., 197-201.

[192] Nguyen, H. T. (1984). On modeling of linguistic information using random sets. *Inf. Sciences*, **34**, 265-274.

[193] Nguyen, H. T. (1984). On entropy of random sets and possibility distributions. To appear in *The Analysis of Fuzzy Information* (J. Bezdek, Ed.), CRC Press.

[194] Nickel, K. L. (Ed.) (1980). *Interval Mathematics 1980*. Academic Press.

[194'] Niedenthal, P. M. and Cantor, N. (1984). Making use of social prototypes: from fuzzy concepts to firm decisions. *Fuzzy Sets and Systems*, **14**, 5-27.

[194"] Norwich, A. R. and Turksen, I. B. (1984). A model for the measurement of membership and the consequences of its empirical implementation. *Fuzzy Sets and Systems*, **12**, 1-25.

[195] Novak, V. (1980). An attempt at Gödel-Bernays-like axiomatization of fuzzy sets. *Fuzzy Sets and Systems*, **3**, 323-325.

[195'] Nowakowski, M. (1977). Fuzzy concepts in social sciences. *Behav. Sci.*, **22**, 107-115.

[195"] Novak, V. (1984). Fuzzy Sets-the approximation of semisets. *Fuzzy Sets and Systems*, **14**, 259-272.

[196] Oden, G. C. (1983). On the use of semantic constraints in guiding syntactic analysis. *Inter. J. Man-Machine Studies*, **19**, 335-357.

[196'] Oden, G. C. (1984). Integration of fuzzy linguistic information in language comprehension. *Fuzzy Sets and Systems*, **14**, 29-41.

[196"] Oden, G. C. and Lopes, L. L. (1982). On the internal structure of fuzzy subjective categories. In *Recent Developments in Fuzzy Set and Possibility Theory* (R. Yager, Ed.) Pergamon Press, N. Y., 75-89.

[197] Orlov, A. I. (1978). Fuzzy and random sets. *Appl. Multi. Statist. Anal. J. Acad. Sci. USSR.*, Moscow (Central Econom-Math. Inst.) (in Russian), 262-280.

[198] Osgood, C. S., Suci, G. J. and Tannenbaum, P. M. (1971). *The Measurement of Meaning*. Univ. of Illinois Press, Urbana.

[198'] Osherson, D. N. and Smith, E. E. (1980). On the adequacy of prototype theory as a theory of concepts. *Cognition*, **9**, 35-58.

[199] Ovchinnikov, S. V. (1981). On Synonym, Antonym and Negations. Memo UCB/ERL M81/63, Univ. of Calif. Berkeley.

[200] Ovchinnikov, S. V.(1981). Involutions in fuzzy set theory. *Proc. 11th Inter. Symp. Multi. Logic*, 226-227.

[201] Paalman de Miranda, A. B.(1964). *Topological Semigroups*. Math. Centre Tracts, **11**, Math. Centrum, Amsterdam.

[202] Pareigis, B. (1970). *Categories and Functors*. Academic Press, N. Y.

[203] Pitts, A. M. (1982). Fuzzy sets do not form a topos. *Fuzzy Sets and Systems*, **8**, 101-104.

[204] Ponasse, D. (1983). Some remarks on the category Fuz(H) of M. Eytan. *Fuzzy Sets and Systems*, **9**, 199-204.

[205] Pratt, J. W. (1961). Length of confidence intervals. *J. Am. Statist. Assoc.*, **56**, 549-567.

[206] Puri, M. L. and Ralescu, D. A. (1982). A possibility measure is not a fuzzy measure. *Fuzzy Sets and Systems*, **7**, 311-313.

[207] Puri, M. L. and Ralescu, D. A. (1983). Strong law of large numbers for Banach space valued random sets. *Ann. Prob.*, **11**, 222-224.

[208] Quinlan, J. R. (1982). Inductive inference as a tool for the construction of efficient classification programs. To appear in *Machine Learning: An Artificial Intelligence Approach* (R. S. Michaski, J. Carbonell and T. Mitchell, Eds.), Tioga Publ.

[209] Radecki, T. (1977). Level fuzzy sets. *J. Cybern*, **7**, 189-198.

[210] Raiffa, H. and Schlaifer, R. (1972). *Applied Statistical Decision Theory*. MIT Press, Cambridge, Mass.

[211] Ralescu, D. A. (1979). A survey of the representation of fuzzy concepts and its applications. In *Advances in Fuzzy Set Theory and Applications* (M. M. Gupta, R. K. Ragade and R. R. Yager, Eds.), North-Holland, N. Y., 77-91.

[212] Rao, C. R. (1973). *Linear Statistical Inference and Its Applications* (2nd ed.), J. Wiley, N. Y.

[213] Reid, D. (1979). A multiple hypothesis filter for tracking targets in cluttered environment. *Proc. 17th IEEE Conf. Decis. and Control*, 1202-1211.

[214] Rescher, N. (1969). *Many-valued Logic*. McGraw-Hill, N. Y.

[215] Rescher, N. and Urquhart, A. (1971). *Temporal Logic*. Springer-Verlag, N. Y.

[216] Revesz, A. P. (1968). *The Laws of Large Numbers*. Academic Press N. Y.

[216'] Rich, E. (1983). *Artificial Intelligence*. McGraw-Hill, N. Y.

[217] Ripley, B. D. (1976). Locally finite random sets: foundations for point process theory. *Ann. Prob.*, **4**, 983-994.

[218] Ripley, B. D. (1981). *Spatial Statistics*. J. Wiley, N. Y.

[219] Robbins, H. E. (1944). On the measure of a random set. *Ann. Math. Statist.*, **15**, 70-74.

[220] Saaty, T. L. (1974). Measuring the fuzziness of sets. *J. of Cybern.*, **4**, 53-61.

[221] Savage, L. T. (1972). *The Foundations of Statistics* (2nd ed.). Dover, N. Y.

[221'] Savage, L. J. (1971). Elicitation of personal probabilities and expectations. *J. Am. Statist. Assoc.*, **66**, 783-801.

[222] Shackle, G. L. (1969). *Decision, Order and Time in Human Affairs*. Cambridge Univ. Press.

[223] Schank, R. C. (Ed., 1975). *Conceptual Information Processing*. North-Holland.

[224] Schefe, P. (1980). On foundations of reasoning with uncertain facts and vague concepts. *Inter. J. Man-Machine Studies*, **12**, 35-62.

[225] Schweppe, F. C. (1968). Recursive state estimation: unknown but bounded error and system inputs. *IEEE Trans. Auto. Control*, **AC-13**, **No. 1**, 22-28.

[226] Schweizer, B. and Sklar, A. (1983). *Probabilistic Metric Spaces*. North-Holland, N. Y.

[226'] Scott, D. S. (1979). Identity and existence in intuitionistic logic. In *Lecture Notes in Math: Applications of Sheaves*, 1977. **No. 753**, Springer-Verlag, 660-696.

[227] Searle, J. (1974). In *On Noam Chomsky: Critical Essays* (G. Harman, Ed.), Anchor Press/Doubleday, N. Y., 2-32.

[228] Shafer, G. (1976). *A Mathematical Theory of Evidence*. Princeton Univ. Press, N. J.

[229] Shafer, G. (1979). Allocations of probability. *Ann. Prob.*, **7, No. 5**, 827-839.

[230] Shafer, G. (1981). Constructive probability. *Synthese*, **48**, 1-60.

[231] Shafer, G. (1982). Lindley's paradox. *J. Am. Statist. Assoc.*, **77, No. 378**, 325-351.

[232] Shannon, C. E. and Weaver, W. (1949). *The Mathematical Theory of Communication*. Univ.of Illinois Press, Urbana.

[233] Sheppard, D. (1954). The adequacy of everyday quantitative expressions as measurements of qualities. *Brit. J. Psych., Gen. Sect.* **45**, 40-50.

[234] Shirai, T. (1937). On the pseudo-set. *Kyoto Univ. Coll. Sci. Memoir.*, Ser. A, Math., **20**, 153-156.

[234'] Shoesmith, D. J. and Smiley, T. J. (1978). *Multiple-Conclusion Logic*. Cambridge Univ. Press, London.

[235] Shore, J. E. and Johnson, R. W. (1978). Axiomatic Derivation of the Principle of Maximum Entropy and the Principle of Minimum Cross-Entropy. NRL Memo Report 3898, Naval Res.Lab., Wash., D. C.

[236] Shortliffe, E. H. and Buchanan, B. G. (1975). A model of inexact reasoning in medicine. *Math. Biosci.*, **23**, 351-379.

[237] Skala, H. J. (1978). On many-valued logics, fuzzy sets, fuzzy logics and their applications. *Fuzzy Sets and Systems*, **1**, 129-149.

[238] Sklar, A. (1973). Random variables, joint distributions and copulas. *Kybernetika* (Czech.), 449-453.

[239] Skolem, T. (1960). A set theory based on a certain 3-valued logic. *Math. Scand.*, **8**, 127-136.

[240] Smets, P. (1981). Medical diagnosis: fuzzy sets and degrees of belief. *Fuzzy Sets and Systems*, **5**, 259-265.

[241] Smets, P. (1978). Un Modèle Mathematico-Statistique Simulant le Processus du Diagnostic Medical. Doctoral Dis., Brussels Univ.

[242] Smets, P. (1981). The degree of belief in a fuzzy event. *Inf. Sci.*, **25**, 1-19.

[243] Smets, P. (1982). Subjective probability and fuzzy measures. In *Fuzzy Information and Decision Processes* (M. M. Gupta and E. Sanchez, Eds.), North-Holland, N. Y, 87-91.

[244] Smets, P. (1982). Probability of a fuzzy event: an axiomatic approach. *Fuzzy Sets and Systems*, **7**, 153-164.

[244'] Smith, G. R. (1980). Textured sets: An approach to aggregation problems with multiple concerns. *IEEE Trans. Syst. Man and Cybern.*, **SMC-10**, **No. 4**, 202-207.

[245] Snyder, D. P. (1971). *Modal Logic and Its Applications*. Van Nostrand, N. Y.

[246] Spiegelhalter, D. J. and Knill-Jones, R. P. (1984). Statistical and knowledge-based approaches to clinical decision-support systems with an application in gastroenterology. *J. Royal Statist. Soc.*, **A**, **147**, 37-77.

[247] Stallings, W. (1977). Fuzzy set theory versus Bayesian statistics. *IEEE Trans. Syst. Man and Cybern.*, **SMC-7**, 216-219.

[248] Stallings, W. (1978). Reply to Jain's comments. *IEEE Trans. Syst. Man and Cybern.*, **SMC-8**, **No. 4**, 333.

[248'] Sugeno, M. (1974). *Theory of fuzzy integrals and its applications*. Ph.D. Thesis, Tokyo Inst. of Tech., Tokyo, Japan.

[249] Suppes, P. (1961). *Axiomatic Set Theory*. Van Nostrand, N. Y.

[249'] Stout, L. N. (1984). Topoi and categories of fuzzy sets. *Fuzzy Sets and Systems*, **12**, 169-184.

[249"] Suppes, P. (1970). Probabilistic grammars for natural languages. *Synthese*, **22**, 95-116.

[250] Thöle, U., Zimmermann, H. J. and Zysno, P. (1979). On the suitability of minimum and product operators for the intersection of fuzzy sets. *Fuzzy Sets and Systems*, **2**, 167-180.

[251] Tong, R. M. and Efstathiou, J. (1982). A critical assessment of truth modification and its use in approximate reasoning. *Fuzzy Sets and Systems*, **7**, 103-108.

[252] Tribus, M. (1969). *Rational Descriptions, Decisions and Designs*. Pergamon Press, N. Y.

[253] Tribus, M. (1979). Comments on " fuzzy sets,fuzzy algebra and fuzzy statistics". *Proc. IEEE*, **67**, **No. 8**, 1168.

[254] Tribus, M. (1980). Fuzzy sets and Bayesian methods applied to the problem of literature search. *IEEE Trans. Syst, Man and Cybern.*, **SMC-10**, **No. 8**, 501-502.

[255] U.S. Government Printing Office (1968). *Principles and Applications of Underwater Sound*. Dept. of the Navy, pp. 179, 180, 193, 194.

[256] *The Official Warren Commission Report on the Assassination of President J. F. Kennedy*. (1964) Doubleday, Garden City, N. Y., 183-187.

[257] Von Neumann, J. (1967). An axiomatisation of set theory. In *From Frege to Godel: A Source Book in Mathematical Logic*. (J. Van Heijenoort, Ed.), Harvard Univ. Press.

[258] Vopenka, P. and Hajek, P. (1972). *Theory of Semisets*. North-Holland, N. Y.

[259] Walley, P. and Fine, T. L. (1982). Towards a frequentist theory of upper and lower probability. *Ann. Statist.*, **10**, **No. 3**, 741-761.

[260] Waltz, D. L. (1982). Artificial Intelligence. *Sci. Am.*, **247**, **No. 4**, Oct. 82, 118-133.

[261] Wang, P. Z. (1982). From fuzzy statistics to random subsets and a preliminary study of the theoretical basis of fuzzy sets. In *Advances in Fuzzy Set Theory and Applications* (P. P. Wang, Ed.), Plenum Press, N. Y.

[262] Wang, P. Z. and Sanchez, E. (1982). Treating a fuzzy subset as a projectable random subset. In *Fuzzy Information and Decision Processes* (M. M. Gupta and E. Sanchez, Eds.), North-Holland, N. Y., 213-220.

[263] Wang, P. Z. (1982). Fuzzy contactability and fuzzy variables. *Fuzzy Sets and Systems*, **8**, 81-92.

[264] Wang, P. Z. (1983). Random Sets and Fuzzy Sets. Dept. Math., Beijing Normal Univ., China.

[265] Wang, P. Z. (1983). σ-hyperfields and the Measurability of Multi-valued Mappings. Dept. Math., Beijing Normal Univ., China.

[266] Warren, R. H. (1981). Equivalent fuzzy sets. *Fuzzy Sets and Systems*, **6**, 309-312.

[267] Watanabe, S. (1978). A generalized fuzzy set theory. *IEEE Trans. Syst. Man and Cybern.*, **SMC-8**, **No. 10**, 756-760.

[268] Watanabe, S. (1959-60). Physical information theory. Lecture notes (unpublished), Yale Graduate School of Physics. Published and revised as: Modified concepts of logic, probability and information based on generalized continuous characteristic functions. *Inf. and Control.*, (1969), **15**, 1-21.

[269] Watson, S. R., Weiss, J. J. and Donnell, M. J. (1979). Fuzzy decision analysis. *IEEE Trans. Syst. Man and Cybern.*, **SMC-9**, **No. 1**, 1-9.

[270] Weidner, A. J. (1981). Fuzzy sets and Boolean-valued universes. *Fuzzy Sets and Systems*, 66 61-72.

[271] Whorf, B. L. (1956). *Language, Thought and Reality* (J. B. Carroll, ed.). J. Wiley, N. Y.

[272] Wiener, N. (1961). *Cybernetics* (2nd ed.). MIT Press, Cambridge, Mass.

[273] Wiener, H. L., Willman, W. W., Goodman, I. R. and Kullback, J. H. (1979). Naval Ocean Surveillance Correlation Handbook, 1978. NRL Report 8340, Oct. 31, 1979. Naval Res. Lab., Wash., D.C.

[274] Willmott, R. (1981). Mean measures of containment and equality between fuzzy sets. *Proc. 11th Inter. Symp. Multi. Logic*, 183-190.

[274'] Winograd, T. (1983). *Language as a Cognitive Process, Vol. I*. Addison-Wesley, Reading, Mass.

[275] Yager, R. R. (1979). A measurment-informational discussion of fuzzy union and intersection. *Inter. J. Man-Machine Studies*, **11**, 189-200.

[275'] Yager, R. R. (1980). On a general class of fuzzy connectives, *Fuzzy Sets and Systems*, **4**, 235-242.

[276] Yager, R. R. (1982). Fuzzy prediction based on regression models. *Inf. Sci.*, **26**, **No. 1**, 45-64.

[276'] Zadeh, L. A. (1965). Fuzzy sets. *Inf. and Control*, **8**, 338-353.

[277] Zadeh, L. A. (1971). Quantitative fuzzy semantics. *Inf. Sci.*, **3**, 159-176.

[278] Zadeh, L. A. (1971). Similarity relations and fuzzy orderings. *Inf. Sci.*, *3*, 177-200.

[279] Zadeh, L. A. (1975). The concept of a linguistic variable and its application to approximate reasoning. *Inf. Sci.*, **8**, 199-249; 301-357; **9**, 43-80.

[280] Zadeh, L. A. (1975). Fuzzy logic and approximate reasoning. *Synthese*, **30**, 407-428.

[281] Zadeh, L. A. (1978). Fuzzy sets as a basis for a theory of possibility. *Fuzzy Sets and Systems*, **1**, 3-28.

[282] Zadeh, L. A. (1979). On the Validity of Dempster's Rule of Combination of Evidence. Memo UCB/ERL M79/24. Univ. of Calif., Berkeley.

[283] Zadeh, L. A. (1978). PRUF-a meaning representation language for natural language. *Inter. J. Man-Machine Studies*, **10**, **No. 4**, 395-460.

[284] Zadeh, L. A. (1980). Fuzzy sets versus probability. *Proc. IEEE*, **68**, **No. 3**, 421.

[285] Zadeh, L. A. (1968). Probability measures of fuzzy events. *J. Math. Anal. and Appl.*, **23**, 421-427.

[286] Zadeh, L. A. (1981). Test-score semantic for natural languages and meaning representation via PRUF. In *Empirical Semantics* (B. B. Rieger, Ed.), Bochum, Brockmeyer, 281-349.

[287] Zadeh, L. A. (1983). A computational approach to fuzzy quantifiers in natural languages. *Comp. and Math. with Appl.*, **9**, **No. 1**, 149-184.

[288] Zadeh, L. A. (1983). A Fuzzy Set Theoretic Approach to the Computationality of Meaning: Propositions, Dispositions and Canonical Forms. Memo UCB/ERL M83/24. Univ. of Calif., Berkeley.

[289] Zadeh, L. A. (1983). The role of fuzzy logic in management of uncertainty in expert systems. *Fuzzy Sets and Systems*, **11**, 119-227.

[290] Zadeh, L. A. (1983). A Theory of Common-Sense Knowledge. Memo UCB/ERL M83/26. Univ. of Calif., Berkeley.

[290'] Zadeh, L. A. (1976). A fuzzy algorithmic approach to the definition of complex or imprecise concepts. *Inter. J. Man-Machine Studies*, **8**, 249-291.

[291] Zimmermann, H. J. (1978). Results of empirical studies in fuzzy set theory. In *Applied General Systems Research* (G. J. Klir, Ed.), Plenum Press, N. Y., 303-312.

[292] Zinov'ev, A. A. (1963). *Philosophical Problems of Many -Valued Logic*. (rev. ed.). D. Reidel, Dordrecht, Holland, especially, 75-78.

AUTHOR INDEX

(Name with main sections cited)

A

B

C

D

E

F

G

H

I

J

K

L

M

N

O

P

Q

R

S

T

U

V

W

Y

Z

SUBJECT INDEX

(Topic with basic cited sections)

A

B

C

D

I

J

K

L

M

Q

R

S

T

U

V

W

Y

Z

LIST OF SYMBOLS

The following list of symbols contains essentially only the most important ones.

Symbol	**Explanation**
ℓ	Formal language
ℓ_{syn}	Syntax part of ℓ .
Th(ℓ),$Th_K(\ell)$	Additional theory for ℓ .
Symb(ℓ)	Alphabet or collection of symbols.
$\vdash$, $\vdash_{\ell}$, $\vdash_{L}$	Formal deduction symbols.
Core(ℓ)	Category of types of things.
Ob(ℓ)	Collection of universes of discourse
Ar(ℓ),$Ar_{\alpha,\beta}(\ell)$	Collection of arrows between universes of discourse.
Rel(ℓ)	Collection of relations upon universes of discourse.
Cat(ℓ)	Collection of category theory function symbols.
DeCat(ℓ)	Collection of deduction category theory function symbols
Foun(ℓ)	Collection of function symbols representing set-theory concepts.
Ex	Existence map.
Loc(ℓ)	Collection of logical connectors
Quan(ℓ)	Collection of quantifiers.
$Th_{syn}(\ell)$	Theory of syntax.
De(Th(ℓ_{syn}))	Collection of deducts or theorems.
$\tilde{V}$ar(ℓ)	Collection of basic variables.
Wfv(ℓ)	Collection of individual variables.
Wft(ℓ)	Collection of individual terms.
Rel($\tilde{V}$ar(ℓ))	Collection of relation symbols.
Wfat(ℓ)	Collection of atomic well-formed formulas.
r[f]	Substitution of term f into relation r .
Wff(ℓ)	Collection of well-formed formulas.
Wfter(ℓ)	Collection of basic well-formed terms.
Wfex(ℓ)	Collection of well-formed expressions.
FuncSymb(ℓ) = Arr(ℓ)	Collection of function symbols of Core(ℓ) .
Typ(ℓ) = Obj(ℓ)	Collection of object classes of Core (ℓ) .
Sort(ℓ)	Collection of basic types or kinds of things.
$\times$, $\otimes$	(Cartesian) product map.
Ω , $\textcircled{\Omega}$	Exponentiation, subobject classifier.
Span(A;Q)	The span of A by operator(s) Q .
<f,g>	Function product.
σ	Signature map.
$\dagger$, $\textcircled{\dagger}$	(Cartesian) sum map.
$\asymp$	Equality map.

$\mathcal{G} \overset{\cdot}{\longrightarrow} \mathcal{H}$	Natural transform (between functors).
$\in$	Membership map.
$\mathcal{C}_n$	Class of all n-copulas.
co-$\mathcal{C}_n$	Class of all n-co-copulas.
Proj, proj, $proj_i(i\times i)$, p_G	Projection map.
$\circ$	Composition map.
T , T_H , 1_H	Truth (only) map.
$\perp$, $\perp_H$, F , 0_H	False (only) map.
not , nt , ~	Negation map.
&	Conjunction map.
or	Disjunction map.
$\Rightarrow$	Implication map.
Id, id.	Identity relation.
$Loc_n(\ell)$	Collection of n-ary logical connectors.
min , $\wedge$, $\wedge_H$	Minimum
max , $\vee$, $\vee_H$	Maximum
$\Leftrightarrow$	Double implication.
$Seq_{\mathcal{A}}(\ell)$, $Ser(\ell)$	Sequents class.
$Predsym(\ell)$	Collection of predicate symbols.
$Term(\ell)$	Collection of terms.
$Var(Ar(\ell))$	Collection of basic variables of $Ar(\ell)$.
$Ax(\ell)$	Collection of axioms.
$Rul(\ell)$	Collection of rules.
SET , Set	Category of ordinary sets.
$Cons(\ell)$	Collection of basic constants.
$Form(\ell)$	Collection of quantified formulas.
$Atom(\ell)$	Collection of atomic formulas.
$De(Th_K(\ell))$	Class of all deducts of $Th_K(\ell)$.
Mo , So	Most-, some-operators.
$\forall$, $\exists$	Universal, existential operators.
$Indterm(\ell)$	Collection of individual terms.
$Indvar(\ell)$	Collection of individual variables.
$Indconst(\ell)$	Collection of individual constants.
$Th_{I,syn}(\ell)$	First-level syntax theory of ℓ .
$Th_{II,syn}(\ell)$	Second-level syntax theory of ℓ .
$\mathcal{H}(\ell)$	Functor: $Var(\ell) \to$ Preord.
Preord , $Preord_{\leq}$	Category of preordered sets.
$Sent(\ell)$	Collection of formal sentences of ℓ .
TV	Total variable map.
FV	Free variable map.
BnV	Bound variable map.
$Open(\ell)$	Collection of open expressions of ℓ .
$(\mathcal{C}, \mathfrak{R})$	Deduction category
$\Vert\cdot\Vert$, $\Vert\cdot\Vert_\omega$	Semantic evaluation map.
S	Source (or domain) map.
B	Codomain map.
$R_{II,syn,3}$	3rd deduction rule for level II syntax.
ω	Individual variable assignment map.
$x^{(i)}$, $y^{(j)}_{i\times j}$	Individual variables.
$H^{\cdot}$	Exponential functor.

Sub	Subobject functor.
$\models\!\dashv$	Tautology equivalence.
$\models$, $(\Sigma \models_L \Psi)$	Logical (or material) implication.
Val($\mathcal{L}$, $\Vert\cdot\Vert$)	Sequents valid for $\Vert\cdot\Vert$.
$\{\cdot \mid \cdot\cdot\}$	Class abstraction map (generalizing standard set notation).
Mod(Th($\mathcal{L}$),L)	Set of models of Th($\mathcal{L}$) for logic L .
$Ł_n$, $Ł_{\aleph_1}$	Lukasiewicz logics.
$(\Psi \overset{n}{\Rightarrow} \theta)$	n-iterated implication.
B_n	Bochvarian logics.
G_n	Gödel-Intuitionistic logic.
δ , $\delta_x(X)$	Krönecker delta symbol.
PL	Probability logic.
LSL	Lebesgue-Stieltjes logic.
GC	Axiom of generalized comprehension.
Z7 , (Z7)	Set theory axiom # 7.
NST	Naive set theory
MH	Maydole-Hay set theory.
NGB	Von Neumann-Gödel-Bernays set theory.
ZF	Zermelo-Fraenkel set theory.
IZF	Intuitionistic-Zermelo-Fraenkel set theory.
Ch	Chapin's set theory
Wei	Weidner's set theory.
Nov	Novak's set theory
ϕ , p	Membership map/possibility functor.
ϕ_A	Membership function of attribute A .
ϕ_{nt}	Membership function of not (negation).
$\phi_{\&}$	Membership function of and (t-norm).
ϕ_{or}	Membership function of or (t-conorm).
$\phi_{\Rightarrow}$	Membership function of implication.
$\mathcal{O}(\underset{\sim}{\mathfrak{F}})$	Class of all ordinal sum systems over $\underset{\sim}{\mathfrak{F}}$.
$\phi_{or}(\varphi_{or}, \rho, K)$	t-conorm part of ordinal sum system generated by φ_{or} , ρ , K .
$\phi_{\&}(\varphi_{\&}, \rho, K)$	t-norm part of ordinal sum system generated by $\varphi_{\&}$, ρ , K .
$\mathfrak{F}(\underset{\sim}{\mathfrak{F}}, \rho, K)$	Ordinal sum system generated by $\mathfrak{F}$, ρ , K .
ϕ_{*}	Membership function of operation * .
ϕ_{wtdsum}	Membership function of weighted sum operator.
$\phi_{\&,(p)}$	p^{th} t-norm (Yager)
$\phi_{or,(p)}$	p^{th} t-conorm (Yager)
$\phi_{\&,s}$	s^{th} t-norm (Frank)
$\phi_{or,s}$	s^{th} t-conorm (Frank)
$\mathcal{Y}$	Yager's family of t-norms and t-conorms.

$\mathcal{G}_{(p)}$	$\mathcal{G}$ at the p-level.
L_γ	Affine operator ordinal sum.
$\mathfrak{D}$, $\mathfrak{D}e$	Class of all DeMorgan fuzzy set systems.
$\mathcal{S}$, $\mathcal{S}e$	Class of all semi-distributive t-norms, t-conorms.
$\mathcal{A}r$	Class of all Archimedean t-norms, t-conorms.
$\phi^{-1}(p)$, $\phi^{-1}(\mu)$	A_p, A_μ , the attributes corresponding to dispersions (or function) p , μ .
$1(q)$	The unity map 1 over $\mathbb{R}^q$.
$\mu_{f_1 \times_{\phi_\&} \cdots \times_{\phi_\&} f_n}$	Measure induced by applying (t-norm) $\phi_\&$ to marginal functions $f_1,..,f_n$.
$\underline{f}$, $\bar{f}$, $\bar{\bar{f}}$, $\hat{f}$, $\#(f)$, $\dagger\dagger(f)$	Extensions of f .
<x ∈ A>, (x ∈ A)	Wff "x is in A" or "x has attribute A"
$A \mathbin{\varDelta} B$	Incidence between A and B ($A \cap B \neq \emptyset$)
$A^{ⓝ}$	n-intensification of A .
$A^{\boxed{n}}$	n-stretching/extensification of A .
$\emptyset_A$	Initial object.
T_B	Terminal object.
Sh	Sheaves operator
$\mathcal{G}^{op}$	Opposite operator for $\mathcal{G}$ (category theory).
Zer_o , Zer	Weaker ZF set theory.
wpt	Well-pointed topoi theory.
wtt, wtr, wttr	Well-pointed/partial transitive theory.
$\leq_H$	Partial order on Heyting algebra H .
$\gamma \times_{g,f} \alpha$	Pull-back relative to γ and α through g and f .
$\mathcal{G}^*$, ${}^*\mathcal{G}$	Adjoints of $\mathcal{G}$.
P_a	Terminal arrow map.
$Bool_n(H)$, $\mathfrak{B}\mathcal{P}_n$	Collection of H-valued Boolean functions.
Higg(H), HIGG(H)	Higg's topos
Fuz(H) , $Fuz_{\asymp}$, Gog(H), GOG(H)	Categories representing fuzzy set theory.
$\mathcal{F}(X)$	Collection of fuzzy or generalized subsets of X .
$\mathcal{T}(X)$	Set of dispersions of X ; natural topology on $\{0,1\}^X$.
$\mathcal{P}(X)$, $\tilde{\mathcal{P}}(X)$	Power class of X = collection of all ordinary subsets of X .
$\mathfrak{f}(X)$	Collection of all finite subsets of X .
H , H_o	Heyting algebra (usually).
$\dagger\dagger$, #	Lifting operators.
$\mathbb{B}_q$	Borel σ-algebra of $\mathbb{R}^q$.
$L^q_{(m)}$	Equivalence classes of f such that $\|f\|^q$ is m-integrable.

$\mathfrak{BP}_n$, $Bool_n$	Class of Boolean polynomials (classical).
$\mathcal{LP}_n$	Fuzzy set exterior $\mathfrak{BP}_n$.
comb(·)	Combinatin operator.
C , ⊣ ,	Complementation symbols.
Pr, p	Probability operators.
BV	Bounded variation.
SBV	Strong bounded variation.
PM	Positive increment monotone.
ND	Non-decreasing.
g.d.f.	Generalized distribution function.

$\mathbb{S}_q$	Class of all step functions over $\mathbb{R}^q$
$\mathbb{F}_q$	____________ measurable functions ____________
$\mathbb{BV}_q$	____________ BV ____________
$\mathbb{SBV}_q$	____________ SBV ____________
$\mathbb{D}_q$	____________ c. d. f. ____________
$\mathbb{PM}_q$	____________ p. m. ____________
$\mathbb{SPM}_q$	____________ p. m. and SBV ____________
$\mathbb{BV}$	____________ BV functions.
$\mathbb{SBV}$	____________ SBV functions.
$\mathbb{C}_q$	____________ g. d. f. ____________
$\mathbb{C}_n$	____________ n $\phi_{\&}$-product of $\mathbb{SBV}_q$.
$\mathbb{Q}(V)$	____________ discrete probability functions over V.
$\mathbb{Q}_q$	____________ ordinary deficient p. f. over $\mathbb{R}^q$.
$\mathcal{P}r_q$	Class of all probability measures over $\mathbb{R}^q$.
μ , μ_f	Measure (signed, probabilistic, etc.)
$\mathfrak{Bv}_q$	Class of all measures corresponding to $\mathbb{BV}_q$.
$\mathcal{S}\mathfrak{Bv}_q$	________________________ $\mathbb{SBV}_q$.
$\widehat{\mathfrak{Bv}}$	Class of all elements of $\mathfrak{Bv}_q$ with values in [0,1].
$\mathcal{S}\widehat{\mathfrak{Bv}}_q$	____________ $\mathcal{S}\mathfrak{Bv}_q$ ____________
$C\mathfrak{Bv}_q$	$\{\mu + c \mid \mu \in \mathfrak{Bv}_q$, c constant$\}$.
$C\mathcal{S}\mathfrak{Bv}_q$	$\{\mu + c \mid \mu \in \mathcal{S}\mathfrak{Bv}_q$, c constant$\}$.
$\mathcal{C}_{(n)}$	Class of all measures corresponding to $\mathbb{C}_n$.
$(\mu_f)_C$	C-marginal measure of μ_f .
$DLSL_{\mathcal{F}}$	Class of all strings (wff's) generated by $\widehat{\mathfrak{Bv}}_q$. for fuzzy set system $\mathcal{F}$.
$LSL_{\mathcal{F}}$	A part of LSL : $DLSL_{\mathcal{F}}$ extended to Borel attributes.
J(x,y)	q-dimensional interval determined by x, y $\in \mathbb{R}^q$.
$\tilde{J}(x,y)$	$J(x \wedge y, x \vee y)$
Δ_q	q-difference.
$Vr(f,K,\mathcal{Q})$	Variation of f over K w.r.t. partition $\mathcal{Q}$.
Vr(f,K)	Total variation of f over K .

$\tau(f)$	Total variation of f .
$\mathcal{F}(\mu_f, \mathbb{R}^q)$	Class of al μ_f-measurable subsets of $\mathbb{R}^q$.
$\mathcal{F}(\mu_f, \mathbb{R}^q)$	__________ μ_f-measurable functions on $\mathbb{R}^q$.
$L(\mu_f, B)$	__________ μ_f-integrable functions over B .
$(\mathcal{F}(\mathcal{C},\mathfrak{R}),\mathrm{Sub})$	Benabou extension of $(\mathcal{C},\mathfrak{R})$.
Prodsum	Probability sum t-conorm.
Maxsum, maxbndsum	Maximum sum t-norm : max(0, x + y - 1)
bndsum, minbndsum, minsum	Bounded sum t-norm : min(1, x + y)
$\mathcal{F}r$	Frank's family of t-norms and t-conorms.
$\mathcal{F}_s$, $\mathcal{F}r_s$	$(1 - (\cdot), \phi_{\&,s}, \phi_{or,s})$.
Ent(S)	Entropy of random set S .
Poss, poss.	Possibility measure.
$\mathcal{C}_{\{x\}}$	Class of all subsets of space containing x .
$\mathcal{C}_{B,j}(X)$	Filter class on B restricted to sets of cardinality j .
$\emptyset$	Null set.
D(f), Diag(f)	Diagonal part of f .
$\mathcal{E}_\Psi$	Diagonal embedding operator.
rng(S)	Range of random set S .
Lev(A), Γ_A	Level map (α-cut map).
S(A)	A random set one point equivalent to A .
$S_U(A)$, $T(A)$, $S_\&(A)$, $S_{or}(A)$	Special random sets one point equivalent to A .
f_S	One point coverage function for S .
$\approx$	One point coverage relation between attributes and random sets.
$\mathcal{F}_{(m)}(f)$	Random sets m-point coverage equivalent to f .
$\dot{\cup}$	Disjoint union.
$\mathcal{F}_0$	Truth functional system (neg, min, max)
$\mathcal{F}_1$	Truth functional system (neg, prod, probsum)
$\mathcal{F}_\infty$	Truth functional system (neg, max sum, bndsum)
$\mathcal{F}'$	Truth functional system (neg, prod, bndsum)
$\stackrel{d}{=}$	is defined to be.
w.l.o.g.	without loss of generality.
w.r.t.	with respect to.
$\mathcal{O}_{\underset{\sim}{x},\underset{\sim}{a}}$	Collection of ordinary membership functions f with $f(x_j) = a_j \in \{0,1\}$, $j = 1,\ldots,n$, say.
$\mathcal{C}_B$	Filter class of sets over B .
$\mathcal{D}_B$	Containment class of sets over B .
$\mathcal{E}_B$, $\mathcal{F}^D$	Incidence classes.
Prod, prod.	Product t-norm.
e_Ψ	Intuitionistic Krönecker delta for Ψ .
$\frac{\Theta}{\Psi}$	Deduction of Ψ from Θ . (2.5)
Card.	Cardinality of
≈ 13	Approximate 13, etc.

∇_n , Δ_n , $\mu_G^{(2)}$	Choquet operators.
Pr^* , Pr_*	Upper (lower) probability.
g_λ	λ-fuzzy (or additive) measure.
$M(I,I')$	$\mathfrak{C}_I \cap \mathfrak{D}_{CI'}$.
ν_S , $\nu_{(S)}$	Measure corresponding to random set S .
$\mu_{(S)}(o)$, $\mu_{(S)}$	Filter class or subset coverage function induced by random set S .
$\mu_{(S)}(1)$	Containment class or superset coverage function induced by random set S .
$\mu_{(S)}(2)$	Incidence function induced by random set S .
S_μ	Random set corresponding to doubt measure μ .
Bel	Belief measure.
$\underset{\sim}{S}$	Joint collection of random sets.
$\underset{\sim}{V}$	Zero-one stochastic process.
B^{Tr}	Tranpose of matrix B .
vol_n, μ_n	n-dimensional Lebesgue measure.
$\underset{\sim}{A}_n$	Collection of generalized sets (using tilde).
w-hom	Weak-homomorphism.
L , U	Lower, upper probability bounds.
$\underset{\sim}{\mathfrak{T}}$	Manes theory ($\mathfrak{T}$,e,#) .
$L(x,\tau)$	Loss function (parameter x, decision τ).
CF(H,E)	Certainty factor for hypothesis H and evidence E.
$\phi(\underset{\sim}{\theta}\|\underset{\sim}{y})$	Conditional posterior posibility function for parameter(s) $\underset{\sim}{\theta}$ given data $\underset{\sim}{y}$.
ϕ_{univ} , ϕ_{Diag}	Special membership functions (Ch. 8).
$\overset{o}{Z}_k^{(j)}$, $Z_k^{(j)}$	Observed, theoretical data vectors corresponding to attribute A_k for track history j . (Ch. 9).
$P_k(\cdot\|\cdot\cdot)$	Error table for attribute A_k (Ch. 9).
R_t	t^{th} -inference rule (Ch. 9) .
M_k	Matching table (used in antecedent of inference rule) for A_k.
P_f	Lindley's transform for score function f .
s_j	Indicates a sentence.
pop , $\phi_{A(pop)}$	Population, membership for population.